MBS 6/02

The Person

AN INTEGRATED
INTRODUCTION TO
PERSONALITY
PSYCHOLOGY

THIRD EDITION

The Person

AN INTEGRATED
INTRODUCTION TO
PERSONALITY
PSYCHOLOGY

THIRD EDITION

DAN P. McADAMS
NORTHWESTERN UNIVERSITY

HARCOURT COLLEGE PUBLISHERS

Fort Worth   Philadelphia   San Diego   New York   Orlando   Austin   San Antonio
Toronto   Montreal   London   Sydney   Tokyo

PUBLISHER	Earl McPeek
ACQUISITIONS EDITOR	Brad Potthoff
MARKET STRATEGIST	Katie Matthews
DEVELOPMENTAL EDITOR	steve Norder
PROJECT EDITOR	Michele Tomiak
ART DIRECTOR	Linda Beaupré
PRODUCTION MANAGER	Christopher Wilkins

Cover, part-opening, chapter-opening photography: Copyright © 2000 Luminarist

ISBN: 0-15-508066-0
Library of Congress Catalog Card Number: 00-106326

Address for Domestic Orders
Harcourt College Publishers, 6277 Sea Harbor Drive, Orlando, FL 32887-6777
800-782-4479

Address for International Orders
International Customer Service
Harcourt, Inc., 6277 Sea Harbor Drive, Orlando, FL 32887-6777
407-345-3800
(fax) 407-345-4060
(e-mail) hbintl@harcourt.com

Address for Editorial Correspondence
Harcourt College Publishers, 301 Commerce Street, Suite 3700, Fort Worth, TX 76102

Web Site Address
http://www.harcourtcollege.com

Printed in the United States of America

0 1 2 3 4 5 6 7 8 9   039   9 8 7 6 5 4 3 2 1

Harcourt College Publishers

TO THE MEMORY OF MY TWO TEACHERS:

George W. Goethals

(1920–1995)

David C. McClelland

(1917–1998)

Preface

There is nothing more interesting to persons than persons. And there is nothing more important. Personality psychology is first and foremost the scientific study of the person. More than 60 years ago, both Gordon Allport and Henry Murray challenged psychologists to put the person at the center of their investigations—to take the individual human being as the scientific unit of analysis. Since then, personality psychology has developed in many directions and has extended through many phases. In the 1970s, when many questioned the scientific need for a study of the person, the discipline lost some of its early favor. But today, at the turn of a new century, personality psychology is more vital than ever. My goal in this book is to impart some of that vitality, to talk to you about the best and the brightest in theory and research that personality psychology has to offer.

The success of this text's first two editions was due largely to (1) an unswerving focus on the person as an integrative theme in personality psychology, (2) the innovative organization of classical and contemporary approaches to persons, and (3) what many have referred to as an engaging, literary style.

The positive reviews and reactions this text has received from many different quarters—from both professors and students at large universities and small colleges—continue to be a source of great satisfaction to me, for I consider this textbook to be far and away the most important intellectual project I have ever undertaken. Indeed, the only other thing I can think of that I have ever worked on so hard and felt so passionately about is my kids! It is because of my sense that this text is my "baby" and that I must nurture it toward its own unique identity, however, that I have reorganized and rewritten a great deal of this book for the third edition. The changes are partly reflected in the new title: *The Person: An Integrated Introduction to Personality Psychology*. The word I have added is "integrated."

All textbooks integrate in the sense of bringing together different topics and ideas under some general scheme. The two most common schemes employed in personality textbooks are (1) to organize the field according to the grand theories of personality (e.g., Freud, Jung, Maslow, Rogers, the behaviorists, and so on) and (2) to organize the field according to research topics (e.g., aggression, altruism, authoritarianism, and so on). Increasingly, authors have sought to blend these two approaches, organizing research topics within different theoretical traditions. My first two editions were a variation on this idea in that I organized research and theories into four different paradigms or approaches. I invited the reader to sample the different approaches, but I warned that it is difficult to blend ideas that come from different approaches because different approaches make different epistemological assumptions. I still think the warning makes sense, but I now believe that more integration across different viewpoints is possible than it might have been 15 years ago, when I began work on the first edition of *The Person*. Many researchers, theorists, and teachers have observed that the field of personality psychology has changed significantly during that time. I believe there is considerably more consensus in the field today than there was when I was a student. The time is right, I believe, for a strong integration—a synthesis of what we need to know to know persons in a scientific way. This book presents just such an integration and presents it in a way that college students can understand and appreciate.

The third edition of *The Person* presents a unifying vision of what personality psychology is and should be for the 21st century. It is a vision that reintegrates the classic theories with contemporary research and links it all to a central question that almost everybody is interested in. That question is "What do we know when we know a person?" This question is at the heart of personality psychology. It is also a question that most every student finds engaging, especially when we consider that the "person" whom we wish to "know" may be ourselves. To answer this question, we need first to say something about human nature and cultural context (Part I of this book). What do we all have in common as human beings and how do historical, cultural, social, and situational factors and contexts shape who we are? Once we understand something about human nature and cultural context, then we can begin to explore human individuality—what it is about individual persons that makes them characteristic individuals, individuals who are similar to and *different from* one another. Personality psychologists have traditionally studied individual differences in persons. The differences range from broad, dispositional traits (Part II of this book) to more specific and contextualized goals, strategies, values, and characteristic adaptations (Part III of this book). Especially in modern societies like ours, differences among people can also be seen in the ways in which they integrate their lives into unifying and purposeful identities. It is the belief of many scholars, both within personality psychology and outside the field, that modern people provide their lives with unity and purpose by fashioning their lives into stories. Our exploration of human individuality ends with a consideration of the different stories that people construct to make sense of their lives (Part IV of this book).

The integrative vision I present in this book reflects important developments in the field of personality psychology during the past 15 years. One of those developments is the strengthening of evolutionary approaches to personality (e.g., Buss, 1991a). It is clearer now than ever before that if one is to understand human nature from a scientific standpoint, one must have some understanding of how we have evolved as a species. Chapter 2 explores human nature from an evolutionary standpoint. A second development is a fuller appreciation of how human behavior is shaped by a *complex social context* (e.g., Mischel & Shoda, 1995). It makes little sense anymore to argue the question of whether or not persons or situations are the prime determinants of behavior. Behavior results from an interaction between the two. Chapter 4 examines how people learn to behave in social situations and how behavior is fundamentally contoured by the social ecology of everyday life. A third and rather dramatic development is the rapidly growing consensus that *personality traits* can be meaningfully organized into five or so clusters—the "Big Five" (McCrae & Costa, 1990). Traits provide a fundamental first level for understanding human individuality, as we will see in Chapters 5–7 (Part II). A fourth development is the proliferation of *cognitive-motivational* concepts in personality, such as goals, tasks, strategies, and other characteristic adaptations (Cantor & Zirkel, 1990). While traits give us a sense of the general outline of human individuality, characteristic adaptations such as goals and tasks fill in some of the details, as we see in Chapters 8–10 (Part III). A fifth development in the field of personality psychology—as well as in social, developmental, and clinical psychology—is the emergence of *narrative approaches* for understanding the person (McAdams, 1993). If traits sketch the outline and goals fill in the details, then a life story provides the overall meaning of a given person's life. Human individuality is layered as traits (Part II), adaptations (Part III), and stories (Part IV). In a sense, traits are the outline; adaptations are the substance; and stories are the meaning. And all three levels of human individuality must be understood with respect to human nature and cultural context (Part I).

What about the great theories? What about Freud? The behaviorists? They're still here, but I have reorganized theories and research to fit the integrated vision I have sketched above. This actually turns out to be very easy to do, for different theories address different aspects of human nature, cultural context, and human individuality. For instance, Bowlby's attachment theory comes out of an evolutionary understanding of human nature and fits comfortably into Chapter 2. Freud and the vast psychoanalytic tradition he launched have a great deal to say, as well, about human nature, and I have thus brought that all together into Chapter 3. The traditions of behaviorism and social learning theories are mainly about social context and how persons are shaped by their environments, as Chapter 4 makes clear. The trait theories of Allport, Eysenck, Cattell, and the proponents of the Big Five framework are the stuff of Chapters 5 and 6, while Chapter 7 examines traits across the lifespan and asks fundamental questions about the origins of traits, their remarkable stability over time, and the extent to which they can change over the life course.

Maslow, Rogers, and humanistic/existential theories provide a philosophical background for understanding the *motivational* adaptations that we explore in Chapter 8. This is where we also find the work of Murray, McClelland, and many contemporary researchers who show us how motives, goals, and strivings help fill in the details of human personality. George Kelly offered one of the first cognitive theories of personality, which is nicely integrated with more modern cognitive theories and research in Chapter 9, where we examine *social-cognitive* adaptations. The influential stage theories of self-development, such as Erikson and Loevinger, provide the backdrop for Chapter 10's examination of *developmental* adaptations. Finally, Chapters 11 and 12 consider some classic (e.g., Adler) and modern (e.g., Tomkins) approaches to personality that put scripts and stories at the center of human meaning. The scientific examination of life narratives represents an exciting new research agenda in personality psychology, but its roots are ancient. Psychologists are coming back to a very old idea—that certain kinds of truth about life and about people are best conveyed in stories (Bruner, 1990).

You can see that this new edition of *The Person* is more than just an update with a fancy new cover. Still, people who have used the first or second edition will surely recognize a great deal of what is contained herein. I hope I have kept all the good stuff. I have built on the distinctive strengths of the first two editions. As before, the person remains at the center. As before, I have incorporated many examples from classic and contemporary literature, mythology, biography, and the media to illustrate points and concepts. I have even drawn on a few personal anecdotes. As before, I have tried to bring in the most recent research findings so that the student can understand what is happening today in the scientific study of persons. I have also worked to streamline the presentation somewhat and to adopt a more conversational style. In my classes, I have the luxury of conversing with my students; they hear me, and I hear them. When I write the textbook, though, I do not have that luxury. But I try to make up for it by imagining what you, the reader, might be thinking and what you might say to me if we were lucky enough to be talking together about persons and personality psychology.

When you teach personality psychology for 20 years and you talk about it almost every day with colleagues, friends, and captive family members, you run up a pretty long list of people who manage to have an impact on how you understand your intellectual obsession. Consequently, I cannot begin to provide a complete and accurate list of the people I would like to thank for their direct and indirect input into this textbook. The undergraduate and graduate students who have worked with me and taken my courses have had a great and positive influence on this book, even when they didn't like the class. I would like to thank them and their parents for giving me the opportunity to teach them and for enabling me to participate, in a small way, in their own development. My colleagues at Northwestern University have also exerted a strong influence. In this regard, I would especially like to thank Phil Bowman, Sonny Cytrynbaum, Gunhild Hagestad, Bart Hirsch, Dan Lewis, Andrew Ortony, Penelope Peterson, Bill Pinsof, Peter Zeldow, and the regular members of our once-a-month personality lunch: Mike Bailey, Jack Bauer, Win Hill, Bill Revelle, and Rick Zinbarg. Some of my most treasured colleagues are members of the Society for Personology, and among those who have had the greatest positive impact on my thinking about personality are Jim Anderson, Irv Alexander, Bert Cohler, Gary Gregg, Ravenna Helson, Bert Hermans, Oliver John, Ruthellen Josselson, Jane Loevinger, Mac Runyan, Jefferson Singer, Brewster Smith, Abby Stewart, Avril Thorne, Paul Wink, and David Winter. With respect to this third edition, I owe a special and most sincere thank you to Ed de St. Aubin and Dan Mroczek, who read drafts of all the chapters and provided invaluable suggestions as well as support. Also sharing their insights for this third edition are James R. Averill (University of Massachusetts at Amherst), Richard J. Coelho (Lansing Community College), Robin S. Jacobvitz (University of New Mexico), Alfred D. Kornfeld (Eastern Connecticut State University), Alan J. Lipman (Georgetown University), Jerome R. Sehulster (University of Connecticut at Stamford), and Dennis Wanamaker (Bellevue College). I thank each of you.

Finally, let me thank my wife, Rebecca Pallmeyer. In that she is the core of who I am and in that this book is, for better or worse, an extension of me, Rebecca turns out to be the most important and the most positive force behind the making of this text.

—Dan P. McAdams

Contents

Special Contents

FEATURES

TABLES

FIGURES

Introduction

1 | Studying the Person

Personality psychology is the *scientific study of the whole person*. The ultimate goal of this science is to provide an account of an individual person's life. A good account of a person's life must situate that life in the biological, social, cultural, and historical contexts that give that life its meaning. Therefore, a personality psychologist must attempt to understand the individual person on many levels. More than other kinds of psychologists and more than other social scientists, personality psychologists focus on human *individuality*—on the reality and the experience of the human being as an individual. Individual persons are similar to and different from other individual persons in many ways. To paraphrase one of the most famous quotations in the history of personality psychology: Every individual is in certain respects

1. like all other persons
2. like some other persons
3. like no other person (Kluckhohn & Murray, 1953, p. 53).

When we say that every person is like *all* other persons, we are acknowledging that there are certain things that virtually all people have in common by virtue of being people. In the words of one personality psychologist (Buss, 1984), species-typical characteristics are those features of human persons that appear throughout humankind. In everyday conversation, we may speak of "human nature" as referring to those characteristics that human beings share with one another and that may differentiate human beings as a species from other living forms. Personality psychology has traditionally concerned itself with the big question: "What is human nature?" The great personality theories of the 20th century have had a major impact on how we think about this question. By contrast, when we say that every person is like *no* other person, we are suggesting that each person is, in some ways, unique. Even identical twins—who are genetically exactly alike—do not experience the world in the same manner. What is it that makes you unique? What differentiates you from every other person who has ever lived on this planet? Personality psychologists study both the universal and the unique in persons.

Between that which we all have in common and that which makes each of us unique is a large middle ground, corresponding to the idea that every person is like *some* other persons. Persons can be compared and contrasted. For example, your best friend and your mother may both be extremely domineering people who enjoy taking center stage in a large group. What they have in common, we might say, is a trait of dominance—a trait that makes the two of them similar to each other and different, say, from you. Yet nobody is going to claim that your best friend and your mother are the same people or that they are similar to each other on all possible dimensions of personality. Personality psychologists focus a great deal of their effort on distinguishing ways in which different people are similar to as well as different from other people—the ways in which any given person is like some other persons (but not like others). To put it differently, personality psychologists often study individual differences in persons. In sum, then, personality psychology concerns itself with (1) the species-typical characteristics that make up human nature, (2) those aspects of any given person's life that make him or her unique, and (3) individual differences among people that specify how any given person is like some persons in some ways and not like others.

How do personality psychologists accomplish these three goals? How do they endeavor to give a scientific account of an individual human life? In truth, it turns out that personality psychologists proceed in a manner that is similar to what we all do when we try to understand ourselves and one another. In that each of us expends a good deal of energy talking and thinking about particular persons, each of us is something of an amateur personality psychologist. Personality psychology formalizes and systematizes the general human effort to know persons. But knowing persons is something we all have a great deal of experience with already. What do we know when we know a person? And how do we talk about what we know?

WHAT DO WE KNOW WHEN WE KNOW A PERSON?

You are new on campus. You have transferred to the university after two years of attending a college in your home town. Or maybe you have come back to school after 10 years during which you worked in your parents' business. Or maybe you are a freshman. The point is that you are new, and you hardly know anybody in this new setting. You want to meet people, and you want to make some new friends. You are also eager to pursue some of your professional interests, which include writing and journalism. So you attend a planning meeting for the university student newspaper. You would like to work as a reporter for the paper. It is a good meeting. You learn a great deal about the newspaper and the staff. You listen to stories about how much fun it is to work on this paper and about how difficult it is sometimes to balance this work with the other things you need to do in college, such as attend classes. Afterward, one of the senior reporters asks you to join her and a few editors for coffee at her apartment. You say yes. You don't want to miss any opportunities to become more involved.

The evening goes very well. At the party, you have many opportunities to observe the woman who invited you in the first place. Let us call her Amanda. Amanda stands out in your mind, partly because she seems so different from the rest of this very friendly crowd. Everybody else is lounging around the apartment, freely talking, eating, drinking, and generally having a very good time. But at the beginning of the evening, Amanda seems tense. You would expect that since she invited you and these people to her apartment, Amanda would feel right at home, that she would be welcoming and comfortable. But instead she stays out of the boisterous conversations of the group; she never tells any stories, even after one of the editors asks her what she thinks about a professor they both know; she hardly smiles at all. Yet her friends do not seem to be bothered by this, as if she acts this way often. Nonetheless, you think it is strange, and stranger still when you spot her a little later, typing on her computer in the bedroom. It looks as if she is sending an e-mail message. Returning to the living room, you make a mild joke about Amanda's preferring the Internet to the company of real people. "No," the paper's sports editor maintains. "Amanda likes everybody. She is just a little moody and unpredictable. I wouldn't worry about her."

The rest of the evening proves him right, at least with respect to his claim that Amanda is unpredictable. When she returns from her computer, Amanda warms up appreciably. She is hardly the life of the party, but now she smiles more and seems much more attentive to what is going on. Later, she seeks you out and asks you about your past, your tastes in music, courses you might take, why you moved from sunny

California to this colder clime, whether or not you read your daily horoscope, whether or not you have met some of the more annoying people on campus—the usual sorts of things people talk about when they are just getting to know each other. She tells you about herself. Over the course of a half-hour conversation, you learn the following things about Amanda:

1. Amanda once shared this apartment with two roommates, but both moved out because they did not like Amanda's boyfriend, who visited frequently. Amanda doesn't like him anymore, either. They broke up last month.

2. Amanda stepped down from an editorial position on the paper last year in order to devote more time to her classes. Had she not, she might have been editor-in-chief this year, but she might have also flunked out of school. She is happier now that she is back to being a reporter, but she misses the power that came with her previous position.

3. The apartment is filled with books on psychology, philosophy, and religion. Amanda's major, however, is political science. She eventually wants to go to law school, that is, if her grades improve. She doesn't seem to know much about law or politics, however. She used to do yoga. She works out at the gym almost everyday.

4. Amanda loves junk food, and she eats a great deal of it over the course of the evening. She is tall and slim. She claims she has never dieted.

5. Despite all the books on religion, Amanda maintains she is an atheist. Her father, who died two years ago, was a Baptist minister. After squandering years of his youth on alcohol and drugs, her father experienced a religious conversion in young adulthood. He always said that the day he was "saved" was the happiest day of his life. Shortly after that experience, he married the woman who was to become Amanda's mother. But the two divorced three years before he died. "I loved him and I hated him," she says.

6. Amanda doesn't like the popular music that you like. She prefers jazz and bands popular in the 1970s.

Around 11:00 P.M., the party winds down, and people begin to leave. Amanda and you have agreed to get together tomorrow for lunch, to talk more about the newspaper and life on campus. You are struck by how much she seems to have changed over the course of the evening. Amanda was nervous and sullen at the beginning. Now she is kissing people goodbye! She seems to linger a bit longer than you expect with her goodbye to the sports editor. You hadn't noticed anything special between them before, but now you begin to wonder.

Sketching an Outline

How well do you know Amanda now? After an evening with her friends and coworkers and after spending some time talking with her alone, you have surely begun to form some impressions about this woman. How would you describe her to me?

One of the first things you might say about her is that Amanda is a little moody and unpredictable. Of course, you have seen her in only one setting. It is difficult to generalize with any confidence. But you were surprised by how sullen and tense she was at the beginning of the evening and how much more comfortable she seemed by the end. Throughout the evening, however, Amanda was kind and considerate toward everybody. The sports editor remarked that Amanda likes everybody, and it seemed to you that everybody likes Amanda as well. She was certainly friendly to you during the second half of the evening. She asked a lot of questions about your life; she listened very intently; she seemed genuinely interested in you; she invited you for lunch tomorrow. What does this all add up to? You might say that, in very general terms, Amanda seems to be moody but very warm and caring. There is a gentleness about her that comes out in her speech and her actions. She is not a domineering person.

In suggesting that Amanda is relatively moody, warm, and nondomineering, you have begun to sketch a personality portrait. You have begun to organize what you think you might now know about Amanda into some general statements concerning her characteristic patterns of behavior, thought, and feeling. Of course, you are doing this with skimpy behavioral evidence, not sufficient to give you complete confidence about your initial attributions. In other words, it may turn out that you do not know what you are talking about! You may be completely wrong about her. After all, you have observed her behavior on only one occasion. Maybe she is rarely moody; maybe she dominates many other social situations. You have talked to her for only half an hour. Maybe she is warm and friendly with strangers, like you, but as you get to know her better she becomes distant and cool. Maybe she was having an especially good day, or an especially bad one. You just don't know much yet. But you have to start somewhere. And where I think you are likely to start is with traits.

Personality **traits** are those *general, internal, and comparative dispositions* that we attribute to people in our initial efforts to sort individuals into meaningful behavioral categories and to *account for consistencies we perceive or expect in behavior from one situation to the next and over time.* You do not know Amanda well yet, but based on what you have observed you might begin to suppose that, in general, she tends to be relatively more moody, warm, and caring compared with many, if not most, other people, and relatively less domineering. These kinds of trait attributions might guide you in your future interactions with Amanda in that they might give you some clues about what to expect from her.

Personality psychologists make good use of the concept of trait in their efforts to sketch an overall outline of a person's individuality. Some of the most influential theories in the history of personality psychology, such as those proposed by Hans Eysenck (1952) and Raymond B. Cattell (1943), have been built around the concept of the personality trait. One of the singular contributions of personality psychology is the construction and validation of scientifically useful measures of individual differences in personality traits (Jackson & Paunonen, 1980; Wiggins, 1973). Good trait measures are useful in predicting behavior over time and across situations (Epstein, 1984). They have also been employed in efforts to discern the biological bases of human behavior (Zuckerman, 1995). Yet the concept of trait has proven to be one of the most contentious topics in the history of personality psychology (Mischel, 1968), and its use in personality studies raises some of the thorniest and most important questions that arise in the scientific study of persons, as we will see in Chapters 5–7.

Filling In the Details

In your evening with Amanda you learned a number of things and developed a number of hunches about her that do not fit neatly into the categories of personality traits.

For example, you learned that she likes junk food and jazz, that she works out at the gym regularly, that she wants to be a lawyer but doesn't know much about law, that she wanted to be editor-in-chief of the newspaper but dropped out of the running when her grades began to suffer, that she is very interested in popular psychology and mysticism, that she is an atheist, that she may be having a romantic relationship with the sports editor, that she recently broke off a romantic relationship with a member of the newspaper staff, that she once stole off to her bedroom to type an e-mail message while hosting a party (you saw her do it). All this material helps to fill in the details of Amanda's individuality. Over time, you will obtain many more details.

As you move beyond traits in your assessment of Amanda's individuality, you look for ways to organize the details. Personality psychologists offer a number of ways to do this. There is a vast domain in personality that contains concepts that provide ways to think about and talk about human individuality in the details. In Amanda's case, we might talk about her relatively strong *need* for power, as expressed in her desire to be editor-in-chief of the student newspaper, and the ways in which that need conflicts with other needs and demands in her life. We might consider her pattern of *interests* and *values*. We might suspect that she has substituted mysticism and New Age psychology for her childhood Baptist faith. Her spirituality focuses on her own inner development rather than on the external world. Self-improvement is important to her, as reflected in her reading interests and in her commitment to physical fitness. While she is a warm and caring person, she values the inner life over external and societal concerns, this despite the fact that she wants to be a lawyer and she enjoys wielding influence over others. Not surprising for a young, unmarried woman in contemporary American society, Amanda is very concerned about romantic relationships. She has experienced her fair share of disappointment in love. How does she view the prospects of love and intimacy? Because her parents divorced unexpectedly, does she worry that she will be unable to sustain a long-term romantic relationship?

Trait attributions are useful because they tell us about trends in behavior over time and across different situations, settings, and contexts. In talking about the details of Amanda's individuality, however, we have moved beyond general trait attributions to consider aspects of her personality that are *contextualized in time, place, and/or role.* The particulars of her personality include attributions that are situated in time: For example, *as a child* she was a Baptist, but *now* she is an atheist; *at this time* in her life, she is concerned about romantic relationships; she wants to be a lawyer *in the future.* In addition, some aspects of her personality are couched in terms of particular places or situations: For example, *at parties,* she is slow to warm up; *one-on-one,* she can be very intimate. Finally, we can identify aspects of her individuality that come out only within particular social roles: For example, *as a student,* she works very hard and virtually always succeeds when she has enough time; *as a citizen,* she is unaware of political happenings, doesn't vote, and has little knowledge of current events.

Borrowing a term from McCrae and Costa (1996), let us use the expression *characteristic adaptations* for these aspects of personality that are contextualized in time, place, and/or role. **Characteristic adaptations** are *contextualized facets of human individuality that speak to motivational, cognitive, and developmental concerns in personality.* As we will see in Chapters 8–10, characteristic adaptations address many of the most important questions in personality psychology: What do people want? How do people seek what they desire and avoid what they fear? How do people develop plans, goals, and programs for their lives? How do people think about and cope with the challenges of social life? What psychological and social tasks await people at particular stages or times in their lives? Historically, personality theorists have considered the vicissitudes of characteristic adaptations in their influential theories of *human motivation* (Deci & Ryan, 1991; Maslow, 1954; McClelland, 1985; Murray, 1938), *cognition and personality* (Cantor & Kihlstrom, 1987; Kelly, 1955), and *the development of self* (Erikson, 1963; Loevinger, 1976; Rogers, 1951). Furthermore, a great deal of scientific research in personality examines the characteristic ways in which people adapt to life vis-a-vis motivational, cognitive, and developmental concerns. As you move from traits to characteristic adaptations in the study of persons, you move from a focus on personality structure to one that emphasizes personality dynamics, process, and change (Cantor & Zirkel, 1990; Dweck, 1996; Pervin, 1989; Thorne, 1989). In examining the details, you begin to explore aspects of human individuality that may be more fluid and malleable than what you would typically see if you were to stick exclusively to the trait outline with which you began.

Constructing a Story

Now that you have begun to outline Amanda's individuality with dispositional traits and you have filled in some of the details by entertaining characteristic adaptations that speak to motivational, cognitive, and developmental concerns, what more is there to do? Is anything missing? What seems to be missing is any mention of what Amanda's life *means*. More specifically, what does her life *in the overall* mean *to her?* In what sense does Amanda organize her life into a unified and purposeful whole? Erik Erikson (1959) referred to these sorts of questions about persons as questions of *identity*. Identity is the problem of unity and purpose in life, a problem—or better, a challenge—that many persons, especially those living in modern societies, first encounter as they move from adolescence into young adulthood. Amanda is a young adult. What is her identity? What provides her life with an overall sense of unity, purpose, and meaning?

The question of identity points to a third way to think about human individuality. Beyond traits and adaptations, many people seek an integrative frame for their own lives that gives them a sense that the various pieces of who they are come together into some kind of sensible whole. Of particular interest is the desire on the part of many people to integrate their lives *in time*. Who am I today? How am I different from and similar to who I was in the past and who I may be in the future? What connects my past as I remember it, my present situation as I understand it to be now, and my future as I currently anticipate it? The challenge of modern identity is to come up with a way of understanding and talking about the self such that (1) despite the many different parts of me I am whole and coherent, and (2) despite the many changes that attend the passage of time, the self of my past led up to or set the stage for the self of the present, which in turn led up to or set the stage for the self of the future. According to a number of theorists, this kind of integration of the self into an identity is accomplished through the construction and revision of a "life story" (Bruner, 1990; Cohler, 1982; Hermans, Kempen, & van Loon, 1992; Howard, 1991; McAdams, 1985b, 1996a; Polkinghorne, 1988; Singer & Salovey, 1993). As we will see in Chapters 11–12, the third level of personality is the level of identity as a life story.

A **life story** is *an internalized and evolving narrative of the self that integrates the reconstructed past, perceived present, and anticipated future in order to provide a life with a sense of unity and purpose*. Beginning in late adolescence, many people in modern societies begin to think about their lives in terms of a unifying and purpose-giving story. Over time and across the adult years, they work on various aspects of the story, rewriting and revising as their views of their lives change with time and circumstances (McAdams, 1993, 1996b). The story is their identity, and thus as identity changes, so changes the story. Let us, then, entertain these further ideas about Amanda's individuality: Amanda's identity is an inner story, a narration of the self that she continues to author and revise over time to make sense, for herself and others, of her own life in time. It is a story, or perhaps a collection of stories, that Amanda continues to fashion to specify who she is and how she will eventually fit into the world of adults. Incorporating beginning, middle, and anticipated ending, Amanda's story tells how she came to be, where she has been and where she may be going, and who she will become. Amanda continues to revise the story across the adult years as she and her changing social world negotiate niches, places, opportunities, and positions within which she can live and live meaningfully.

What is Amanda's story about? You do not know Amanda very well yet, but perhaps you can take a few hints from your initial meeting. Amanda told you a kind of life story, implicit and indirect, about her father. Once upon a time, he was a drunken and dissolute youth. Then he found Christianity, which turned his life around. He married and became a Baptist minister. Eventually, his marriage ended in failure. Amanda told you that she both "loved and hated" her father. She told you she is an atheist. It is clear that she has rejected certain parts of her father's narrative—there are important ways in which her life story will depart from his, she seems to suggest. What have been the high points, the low points, and the turning points in her own life, as she sees it now? Who are her heroes? Who are the villains? What does she see as the future chapters of her life story? What does she make of her own history? How has the past given birth to the present? If you get to know her really well, you may learn the answers to these questions, and you may even participate with her, perhaps as a good friend, in the further construction of her own identity. Indeed, she could even have an impact on how *you* create a story in your own life. In the sharing of stories about themselves, people come to know one another in especially intimate terms. Similarly, the personality psychologist who seeks to know a person in his or her full individuality will eventually need to delve into the private mythology, the storehouse of narratives, characters, plots, settings, and images that a person invokes to make sense of who he or she is, was, and will be in the future.

Like dispositional traits and characteristic adaptations, self-defining life stories are important aspects of personality, of human individuality. As outlined in Table 1.1, a full account of an individual human life, therefore, needs to consider that life from at least three different standpoints. What do we know when we know a person? If we know that person well, we should have some sense of (1) where he or she stands on a series of dispositional traits that speak to general tendencies in behavior across situations and over time; (2) how he or she is confronting and adapting to motivational, cognitive, and developmental tasks and concerns that are contextualized in place, time, and/or role; and (3) what kind of identity he or she is articulating in life through the construction of stories about the self. Individuality is conveyed, therefore, through the patterning of traits, adaptations, and stories.

TABLE 1.1	*Three Levels of Personality*	
LEVEL	**DEFINITION**	**EXAMPLES**
Dispositional traits	Broad dimensions of personality that describe assumedly internal, global, and stable individual differences in behavior, thought, and feeling. Traits account for consistency in individual functioning across different situations and over time.	Friendliness Dominance Tendency toward depression Punctuality
Characteristic adaptations	More particular facets of personality that describe personal adaptations to motivational, cognitive, and developmental challenges and tasks. Characteristic adaptations are usually contextualized in time, place, situation, or social role.	Goals, motives, and life plans Religious values and beliefs Cognitive schemas Relational modes Psychosocial stages Developmental tasks
Life stories	Internalized and evolving narratives of the self that people construct to integrate the past, present, and future and provide life with some sense of unity, purpose, and meaning. Life stories address the problems of identity and integration in personality—problems especially characteristic of modern adulthood.	Earliest memory Reconstruction of childhood Perceptions of future self "Rags to riches" stories Imagery and theme in story

ONE PERSON'S LIFE: KAREN HORNEY, PSYCHIATRIST

To explore in more detail how a personality psychologist might approach an individual life, let us now move from the fictitious Amanda to a real person. The real person is Karen Horney (1885–1952), a famous psychiatrist who published numerous books on personality theory and clinical technique (e.g., Horney, 1939, 1945) and whose life has been the subject of a full-length literary biography written by Quinn (1988). As with Amanda, we will try to offer an account of Karen Horney's individuality by calling upon personality traits, characteristic adaptations, and life stories. But this time we will employ concepts and we will consider methods and issues that are prevalent in the field of personality psychology. We will consider Horney's life from the standpoint of personality psychology, introducing a few ideas that are frequently employed in the science of personality today.

A Biography

She was born Karen Danielson, the second child and only daughter of a ship captain and his wife who lived just outside Hamburg, Germany. From an early age, Karen surpassed her older brother in schoolwork and was prized as an intelligent and energetic girl. Growing up in Hamburg, she witnessed a good deal of social ferment in the 1890s, including a strong movement in support of women's rights. In the nascent women's movement, she may have found support for some of the highly unconventional goals she formulated for herself as an adolescent. In her teenage diaries she sketched out elaborate plans for studying at the Gymnasium (comparable to college) and ultimately becoming a physician. When Karen, against the strong wishes of her father, entered the medical school at the University of Freiburg in 1906, she was one of 58 women out of a total student population of 2,350 (Quinn, 1988, p. 100).

Karen's years as a student were among the happiest and most exhilarating in her life. She surrounded herself with a set of adoring friends, both men and women. She fell in and out of love a few times before committing herself to marry Oskar Hornveigh (Horney), a fellow student who was headed toward a career in business. Though she felt passionate attachments to a few other men, it was with Oskar that Karen was best able to share her dreams and plans. He was the man who seemed best able to understand "myself in every part" (Quinn, 1988, p. 106). After graduating from medical school, she moved with Oskar to Berlin, where he set up a lucrative business and she pursued the medical specialty of psychiatry. Karen was attracted to the relatively new approach to psychiatry and psychology offered by Sigmund Freud and called "psychoanalysis." She became an early devotee to psychoanalysis and an intellectual apostle of Freud.

During the years of World War I and after, Karen and Oskar brought up three daughters. Supported by Oskar's considerable income, the Horneys were able to hire maids and nannies to assist in household duties and childcare. Karen worked hard to juggle professional and family responsibilities. To the outside world, the Horneys seemed a remarkable family. Very few women of the day achieved the kind of professional status that Karen achieved, and few men, as well, seemed as tolerant and progressive about women's roles as was Oskar. But the marriage was not as harmonious as it appeared. Karen was subject to dark periods of depression and ennui. Oskar became more and more preoccupied with his work. The two had different friends and different political sympathies, and over time their lives became more and more separate. Karen became sexually involved with other men, and it is likely that Oskar became involved with other women as well. In 1923, an economic collapse in Germany ruined Oskar's business and added new strains to the relationship. Three years later, Karen and Oskar were divorced.

The years immediately following her breakup with Oskar were among the most productive in Karen's professional life. Taking issue with Freud's views on the psychological and sexual development of women, Horney began to articulate a radical counterargument that explained women's development more in terms of social and cultural forces as opposed to the biological and sexual factors emphasized by Freud. (We will explore Freud's views on this topic in Chapter 3.) Horney argued that Freud did not understand the psychology of women because he was oblivious to the experience of being a mother:

> "I, as a woman," Horney wrote in 1926, "ask in amazement, and what about motherhood? And the blissful consciousness of bearing a new life within oneself? And the ineffable happiness of the increasing expectation of the appearance of a new being? And the joy when it finally makes its appearance and one holds it for the first time in one's arms? And the deep pleasurable feeling of satisfaction in suckling it and the happiness of the whole period when the infant needs her care?" (Quinn, 1988, p. 171)

Horney eventually developed a full theory of personality functioning that deemphasized biological instincts and centered instead on the **basic anxiety** that all

Karen Horney

human beings—male and female alike—experience in significant interpersonal relationships. Basic anxiety is "the feeling a child has of being isolated and helpless in a potentially hostile world" (Horney, 1945, p. 41). The fear and jealousies of early childhood—which Freud linked to biological drives concerning sexuality and aggression—are instead manifestations of the basic anxiety that can be experienced throughout childhood whenever the security of the family is disrupted. The factors that may precipitate family insecurity and basic anxiety include too much or too little parental warmth, involvement, or dominance. An overabundance of basic anxiety in childhood may result in adult neurosis, generally expressed through maladaptive neurotic trends that *move* the person either (1) *toward* other people (excessive need for approval and affection), (2) *away* from other people (excessive need for self-sufficiency and independence), or (3) *against* other people (excessive need for power).

Horney left Berlin in 1932, and after a two-year stint in Chicago she settled in New York City. She became a member of the prestigious New York Psychoanalytic Society. But as Horney's theoretical views matured and she became more and more vociferous about her disagreements with the Freudian establishment, she became an increasingly controversial figure in the psychoanalytic world. Once a true believer in Freud, she was now seen as an apostate. In a pivotal event in her life, the New York Psychoanalytic Society voted in 1941 to demote Horney from her position as a trainer and supervisor of young analysts. Infuriated by the affront, Horney walked out of the meeting, accompanied by sympathetic colleagues. She never returned to the Society. Along with Erich Fromm, Harry Stack Sullivan, and a few other intellectual rebels, she tried, with limited success, to establish a rival psychoanalytic organization. Horney continued her writing and theorizing through the 1940s. In the two years before her death, she became interested in Zen Buddhism and hoped to incorporate ideas from Eastern philosophies into her evolving theory of human personality.

Level 1: Personality Traits

How might we identify the important personality traits displayed by Karen Horney? Personality psychologists have developed a number of methods for trait assessment, but the most well-established is probably the self-report questionnaire. An example of such a measure, designed to assess individual differences in the trait of **extraversion,** is reproduced in Table 1.2. As you can see, the instructions ask the person to answer "yes" or "no" to each of a series of simple questions. The questions are about such things as "enjoying yourself at a lively party," longing for "excitement," and tending to be "mostly quiet" when with other people. The questionnaire is set up such that high scores indicate relatively more extraversion and low scores indicate relatively more introversion. People can be readily compared through their scores. People with higher scores are predicted to be relatively more sociable, fun-loving, spontaneous, and talkative. People with lower scores are predicted to be relatively more withdrawn, reserved, inhibited, and quiet. Most people score toward the middle.

Where would Karen Horney score? We cannot give her the questionnaire now, but we might be able to guess what her ratings might be. This method of guessing is similar to what researchers sometimes do when they ask friends or acquaintances of a person to rate that person on trait scales—a method that is sometimes referred to as *peer ratings*. The biographical record suggests that Horney would score relatively high on the trait of extraversion. From childhood on, she was viewed by herself and by others as especially outgoing and energetic. She thrived in the company of many people. She was a socially dominant woman who loved to play to an audience, whether that audience was her friends and family or her fellow psychoanalysts. As we will see in Chapter 6, research suggests that people high in extraversion experience life with a great deal of positive emotion (Watson & Clark, 1997). Horney seemed always ready to have fun. Remarked a friend from Horney's later years: She was "like a child in front of a

---

TABLE 1.2	*Questionnaire Measuring Extraversion*

For each of the following 20 questions, answer either *yes* (if it is generally true for you) or *no* (if it is generally not true for you).

1. Do you often long for excitement?
2. Are you usually carefree?
3. Do you stop and think things over before doing anything?
4. Would you do almost anything for a dare?
5. Do you often do things on the spur of the moment?
6. Generally, do you prefer reading to meeting people?
7. Do you prefer to have few but special friends?
8. When people shout at you do you shout back?
9. Do other people think of you as very lively?
10. Are you mostly quiet when you are with people?
11. If there is something you want to know about, would you rather look it up in a book than talk to someone about it?
12. Do you like the kind of work that you need to pay close attention to?
13. Do you hate being with a crowd who play jokes on one another?
14. Do you like doing things in which you have to act quickly?
15. Are you slow and unhurried in the way you move?
16. Do you like talking to people so much that you never miss a chance of talking to a stranger?
17. Would you be unhappy if you could not see lots of people most of the time?
18. Do you find it hard to enjoy yourself at a lively party?
19. Would you say that you were fairly self-confident?
20. Do you like playing pranks on others?

To arrive at your score for extraversion, give one point for each of the following items answered *yes:* #1, 2, 4, 5, 8, 9, 14, 16, 17, 19, 20. Then, give yourself one point for each of the following items answered *no:* #3, 6, 7, 10, 11, 12, 13, 15, 18. Add up all the points to arrive at a total score. Your total score should be between 0 and 20 inclusive. The higher your score, the higher your extraversion (and, of course, the lower your introversion). Therefore, high scores suggest extraversion and low scores suggest introversion.

Source: Wilson (1978), p. 219. Properly standardized self-scoring scales may be found in Eysenck and Wilson (1976) and in Eysenck and Eysenck (1964).

Christmas tree, full of wonder, full of joy of the moment; I never knew anyone who could enjoy life so wholeheartedly" (Quinn, 1988, pp. 384–385). Her Japanese hosts on a trip to Asia described Horney as "cheerful and jubilant" (Quinn, 1988, p. 411).

The universe of possible personality traits is vast, but personality psychologists have had considerable success in mapping that universe into a small number of galaxies. As we will see in Chapter 6, one popular mapping suggests that there are five main trait group-ings, sometimes called "the Big Five" (Costa & McCrae, 1985; Goldberg, 1990; John, 1990; Wiggins, 1996; Wiggins & Trapnell, 1997). Table 1.3 presents one version of the Big Five. All versions of the Big Five view extraversion as one of the five broad trait clus-ters, incorporating such trait descriptors as sociable, outgoing, dominant, and impulsive. Certain other trait theories, such as the three-factor model proposed by Eysenck (1952), consider extraversion to be a superordinate trait as well. The extent to which a person is outgoing and sociable versus withdrawn and reserved represents a very common dimen-sion upon which we make initial judgments about people (Goldberg, 1981).

Beyond extraversion, another trait cluster in the Big Five that would appear to be especially salient in the life of Karen Horney is **openness to experience** (McCrae & Costa, 1997). Persons high in openness are described by themselves and others as es-pecially original, imaginative, creative, complex, daring, independent, analytical, non-traditional, artistic, liberal, and having broad interests. These adjectives describe Horney as well as any trait descriptors possibly can. From adolescence onward, Hor-ney defied society's conventions about women, work, and love. She rebelled against her father, her teachers, Freud, and eventually the entire psychoanalytic orthodoxy. She questioned and ultimately rejected traditional religious views as an adolescent and well-accepted psychological dogma in midlife. Her attraction to Zen Buddhism in her later years was the last installment of her lifelong quest to find a system of true ideas to which she could swear allegiance. She never found one. But she never quit searching. Horney's openness to new ideas and new experiences and her refusal to accept estab-lished conventions suggest a strong "independence of mind," which her biographer sees as the most consistent feature of Horney's personality:

> Karen Horney led a restless life, full of shifting passions and allegiances. But in one thing she was consistent: her independence of mind. She was simply incapable of accepting someone else's version of reality until she had measured it against her own experience, what she once called in an early diary, "the delicate vibrations of my soul." This was Horney's greatest strength, and sometimes her undoing as well. (Quinn, 1988, p. 15)

Level 2: Characteristic Adaptations

When we consider the characteristic adaptations that convey the individuality of Karen Horney, we might ask ourselves the following questions: What did she *want* in life and how did she *think* about what she wanted? What were her *goals* and *plans?* What did she *value?* What issues or ideas preoccupied her consciousness during par-ticular *periods* in her life, in particular *settings* and *situations*, and with respect to partic-ular social *roles?* For Horney's life, we could address each of these questions in many ways. For now, I will focus on only one. Let us consider the period of young adulthood in her life, when she found herself in the settings of college and medical school, and let us focus on her desires, goals, and plans concerning love and marriage. In young adult-hood, Horney confronted the **intimacy life task** (Cantor, Acker, & Cook-Flanagan,

TABLE 1.3	*The Big Five: Adjective Items That Describe Each of Five Basic Traits*

Extraversion *(E)*
  Sociable–Retiring
  Fun loving–Sober
  Affectionate–Reserved
  Friendly–Aloof
  Spontaneous–Inhibited
  Talkative–Quiet

Neuroticism *(N)*
  Worrying–Calm
  Nervous–At ease
  High-strung–Relaxed
  Insecure–Secure
  Self-pitying–Self-satisfied
  Vulnerable–Hardy

Openness to Experience *(O)*
  Original–Conventional
  Imaginative–Down to earth
  Creative–Uncreative
  Broad interests–Narrow interests
  Complex–Simple
  Curious–Incurious

Agreeableness *(A)*
  Good natured–Irritable
  Soft hearted–Ruthless
  Courteous–Rude
  Forgiving–Vengeful
  Sympathetic–Callous
  Agreeable–Disagreeable

Conscientiousness *(C)*
  Conscientious–Negligent
  Careful–Careless
  Reliable–Undependable
  Well-organized–Disorganized
  Self-disciplined–Weak-willed
  Persevering–Quitting

Source: Modified from McCrae and Costa (1987), p. 85.

1992). An important aspect of her individuality is captured in the characteristic manner in which she approached this task, how she thought about and acted upon it, what she wanted and valued in it, and how she experienced joy, misery, and conflict with respect to the intimacy life task.

As we will see in Chapter 10, Erik Erikson divides the human lifespan into eight psychosocial stages, each of which is centered on an issue or task that must be addressed. The sixth stage in Erikson's scheme—the stage associated with young adulthood—is organized around the issue of *intimacy versus isolation*. In the stage immediately preceding, argues Erikson (1963), the adolescent needs to make progress in establishing an initial identity in his or her life, sorting out what he or she believes in (ideology) and how he or she may work productively in the adult world (occupation). Once these identity questions of ideology and occupation have been addressed, the young adult is ready to join his or her life to others in bonds of long-term intimacy. Of special importance, of course, is the commitment to another in romantic union, typically marriage. By the time Karen Horney entered medical school, she was well into the intimacy versus isolation stage of psychosocial development. Her adolescent diaries reveal that she thought through fundamental religious and ideological questions in her teenage years and she made elaborate plans for her professional goal of becoming a doctor. By the time she reached medical school, then, she knew what she believed in, and she had a pretty clear sense of what she wanted to be professionally and how she might accomplish those professional goals. She was now preoccupied with friendship and romantic love, and she saw the next task in her life to be that of finding the right life partner.

As with many of her life challenges, Karen Horney approached romantic love with boldness, daring, and passion. Her central traits of extraversion and openness to experience are evident in the adventurous way in which she pursued romance. But knowing that Horney was highly extraverted and open to new experiences does not tell us much about what she *wanted* from her lovers and from a long-term love relationship. One begins to understand what she wanted, however, in reading the diaries she kept in young adulthood (McAdams, 1994a). Karen wrote that she had a strong desire *to be in control* when it comes to intimacy with men. If a woman does not control her passions and her impulses with a man, then she will lose her freedom and dignity, she maintained. At age 20, Karen wrote:

> To be free of sensuality means great power in a woman. Only in this way will she be independent of a man. Otherwise she will always long for him, and in the exaggerated yearning of her senses she will be able to drown out all feeling of her own value. She becomes the bitch, who begs even if she is beaten. (Horney, 1980, p. 104)

As a young woman, Karen feared that her impulses would get out of control—that love would destroy her freedom. To enhance control, she watched herself carefully. She cultivated what she called "an unremitting, ever more refined self-observation that never leaves me, even in any sort of intoxication" (Horney, 1980, p. 166). But Karen wanted love and wanted it desperately. She longed to escape from her controlling state, even as she feared the loss of freedom that such an escape would bring. She longed *to surrender* to the "brutal naturalism" (her words) of impulse and passion. According to her biographer, Karen "wanted to experience abandon, to be tossed about in the stormy seas of passion, under the sure lead of a man who would be skillful enough to awaken her" (Quinn, 1988, p. 84). At the same time, "she also wanted to be a captain, in control of her own destiny" (p. 84). With one of her lovers (Ernst), "I feel as woman only," swept away in sensual excitement, surrendering to the "elemental passion" and his power (Quinn, 1988, p. 80). But toward another lover (Rolf), Karen feels as if she is more of a "human being" (p. 80). Rolf loves her and she loves Rolf for the friendship and sharing they experience. Karen describes their relationship as "deeper and more valuable," in a sense, but it is bereft of the elemental passion she feels with Ernst. Neither relationship is fully satisfactory. At the end of this period, she settles for Oskar, who is rather more like Rolf than Ernst. She will have a marriage that enables her to retain a good deal of control over her passions and her life. Oskar is very accepting of her professional goals, so she does not lose control there. Further, with Oskar there is little chance that she will lose control of her sensual impulses. Karen loves him surely. But she will not lose herself in her affection for him. She will not do his bidding. She will retain her dignity and her independence of mind.

The conflict we have identified in Karen Horney's intimacy life task is that between control and surrender. It is a conflict that involves her desires (motivation) and her thoughts (cognition), and the conflict arises during a particular developmental stage in her life. Karen wants to, desires to, is motivated to be in control and to surrender to passion in her relationships with men in her young adult years. In a cognitive sense, she thinks about intimate relationships in terms of control and surrender. In the terms of George Kelly's cognitive theory of personality (Chapter 9), the young Karen Horney has established a **personal construct** around control versus surrender in romantic love as a young adult. According to Kelly (1955), a personal construct is a *bipolar category that a person uses to organize information*. Many people, for example, use the bipolar category of "liberal versus conservative" to organize information about political views. You may use the bipolar category of "gave me an A" versus "gave me a lower grade" in organizing information about professors you have had. Personal constructs are those bipolar categories that are most important in and characteristic of how a person understands the self and the world. Personal constructs are highly subjective. A person's system of characteristic personal constructs is a central feature of personality, according to Kelly, and a key source for understanding a person's individuality.

Karen Horney understood and apprehended love in terms of a troubling dialectic between control and surrender—a central personal construct in her system for making sense of the world and her personal experience. This particular personal construct presented her with an either/or choice in love: Either she could be in control (and retain her freedom) or she could surrender herself to a man (and lose her freedom). With Oskar, she chose the former. But as we know, the marriage was rocky and ended in divorce. Karen had several extramarital affairs, and she sought throughout her life to find relationships with men in which she could indeed surrender herself to passion, as she first did with Ernst. Returning to Erikson's developmental model, Karen Horney never seemed to resolve the difficult intimacy issues that first arose in young adulthood. She never seemed able to transcend the conflict between control and surrender. She could never develop a relationship with a man in which she could experience both. From a cognitive standpoint, her personal construct for love set up control and surrender as mutually exclusive opposites, like "hot" and "cold." She could not have both at once.

Level 3: Life Stories

What kind of story was Karen Horney working on in her life? How did she understand her overall life in narrative terms?

There are many features of stories and many ways to talk about what stories mean and how stories work. For now, we will focus on two aspects of stories: *imagery* and *characters*. As we will see in Chapter 11, imagery refers to the particular pictures, sounds, and metaphors that distinguish one story from another. We get a sense of the kind of imagery that Horney often used to portray her own life in a passage from her adolescent diary reproduced in Table 1.4. As you can see, the passage is striking for its romantic and idealistic flavor, but what I am most interested in for now is the imagery of *movement* and *light*. Notice how often she refers to movement and light in this segment of her diary. The life story that Karen began formulating in late adolescence and young adulthood may have drawn liberally upon the imagery of movement and light, along with a number of other images reflecting her relationship with her father (a ship captain) and other childhood themes—ships, seas, storms, and so on.

For Horney, rapid movement signified youth, vigor, passion, being in the flow of life, taking life on with no doubts and no fears. When things go badly, life bogs down, one feels sluggish, movement seems unnatural. On a hiking trip, she and her companions finally quit moving and decide to rest in the *sunlight*. "My only wish was to lie there for my whole life, staying in the sun" (Horney, 1980, p. 192). The imagery of

TABLE 1.4	*An Excerpt From Karen Horney's Adolescent Diaries*

Everything in me is storming and surging and pressing for light that will resolve the confusion. I seem to myself like a skipper who leaps from his safe ship into the sea, who clings to a timber and lets himself be driven by the sea's tumult, now here, now there. He doesn't know where he is going.

Homeless am I
With no sheltering abode I rove about.
Safe and quiet
I lived in the old masonry
stronghold that thousand of years
had built for me.
It was gloomy and close—
I longed for freedom.
A little light only, a little life.
Quietly, driven by an inner urge.
I began to dig.
Bloody my nails, weary my hands.
Mockery from others and bitter scorn
the end reward for the endless toiling.
The stone came loose—
one more powerful grip and
it fell at my feet.
A ray of light pressed through the opening
greeting me kindly, inviting and warming,
waked a shiver of delight in my breast.
But hardly had I drawn into myself
this first shimmer
when the rotting masonry broke to pieces
and buried me in its fall.
Long I lay
thinking nothing
feeling nothing.
Then my strength stirred, so freshly drunk-in
and I lifted the fragments with muscular arm.
All aglow with strength,
bloom of the storm,
delight flowing through me
I looked out far and wide.
I saw the world.
I breathed life.

The brightness of light
almost blinded me—
yet soon I was used to its brilliance.
I looked about.
The view was almost too wide,
my sight could roam to unlimited distances.
Oppressive almost
the New, the Beautiful invaded me.
At that an all powerful longing seized me,
almost bursting my breast,
and it drove me further to wander
in order to see, to enjoy
and to know the All.
And I wandered—
restlessly driven
I rove about,
released from the dungeon
I joyfully sing in jubilant tones
the old song of life,
to freedom, to light.
Only an anxious question often hems me in:
toward what goal am I striving?
A gentle longing, a mild lament:
When at last will you come to rest?
And I think I understand the answer
in the murmuring of the woods:
"Rest is only behind the prison walls,
life, however, does not know it."
Watchful searching
with no cowardly complaints,
restlessly striving
with no weary despair:
that is life—
dare to endure it.

Source: Horney (1980), pp. 55–57.

movement and light fascinated Horney throughout her life. As a child, she loved stories of the American "Wild West," starring the Native American hero Winnetou. Winnetou was "a noble savage, capable of swimming faster, creeping through woods more softly, and covering his tracks more deftly than any other mortal" (Quinn, 1988, p. 38). And in the personality theory she fashioned in her middle adult years, Horney imported the imagery of movement to convey how people cope with interpersonal conflict—*moving* toward, *moving* away from, and *moving* against other people. The narrative emphasis on movement (Level 3), furthermore, fits nicely with our characterization of Horney's traits of extraversion and openness to experience (Level 1) and seems consistent, furthermore, with the adventurous spirit that Horney showed as she moved into and out of relationships in an effort to resolve the intimacy life task (Level 2).

We might hypothesize, then, that Karen Horney developed a story for her own life in which movement and light were important and recurrent images. As she herself moved into middle adulthood, she settled into two major roles in her life that might be further personified as the two main characters of her story. These are *the doctor* and *the mother.* As a professional psychiatrist, she healed broken lives and psychic wounds. Even before she broke with Freud, she was an effective therapist who treated many of her clients in her own home, with nannies helping care for her children. In adolescence, she had dreamed of being a doctor, and as a young adult she realized the dream. She juggled the roles of doctor and mother about as well as any woman could do it in the 1920s. As a mother, Karen brought up three daughters—this much is obvious. She expended a great deal of energy and time and invested a great deal of herself in the project of rearing her children. The mother role, furthermore, appeared to generalize across many domains. Beyond her own daughters, many people described Karen Horney in maternal terms. "She was like a mother to me," remarked a young companion who accompanied her to Japan (Quinn, 1988, p. 406). "She was 100% maternal type," remarked a fellow psychoanalyst. Horney became something of a mother figure in the psychoanalytic establishment of the 1920s and 1930s. One of the few women of prominence in the movement, she nurtured and promoted the development of many young analysts in Chicago and New York.

But perhaps the most profound and intriguing way in which the protagonist of mother becomes a heroine in Horney's life story is that *by becoming a mother Horney helped to move mother to the center of psychoanalytic thinking.* Horney's first creative breaks from the psychoanalytic establishment involved her thoroughgoing critique of the Freudian view of motherhood, a critique that grew directly out of this doctor's experience as a mother. Her biographer noted:

> There is a wonderful irony here. Like most women pioneering in a male world, Karen Horney had devoted a great deal of energy trying to be one of the boys. And she *had* felt trapped, in the beginning, by the undeniably feminine position in which pregnancy placed her. And yet, as a result of the experience of birth, she felt compelled, for the first time in her professional life, to take an independent position. It was because the experience differed so strikingly from analytic theories that she was forced to propose an alternative theory. Birth was too remarkable to be only a substitute or a sublimation. In the end, because she was a truth seeker, she couldn't deny her femininity. And it was her femininity that led her to her first original, and important, conclusion. (Quinn, 1988, p. 172)

As Horney moved into middle adulthood, I would argue, her life story changed, and she began to merge her characters of "the doctor" and "the mother" into a larger and more integrative personification of herself, as a "teacher/visionary" (McAdams, 1994a). In her efforts to make a positive contribution to her profession and to future thinking about human personality, she took it upon herself to create a new vision for understanding personality and to teach that vision to others. In the late 1930s and 1940s, she presented her ideas in highly influential books that were written in a simple and elegant style that laypersons could understand. In her books and her lectures, Horney's first aim was to teach others about the human condition. Her biographer argues that "Horney's most important contribution to the history of psychoanalysis grew out of her teaching role" (Quinn, 1988, p. 200). Her gifts in this regard were legendary, including a down-to-earth and empathic style of presentation that made her students feel that she was speaking especially to them. Listeners sometimes came away from lectures given by leading male analysts feeling they had encountered a brilliant mind or a dazzling argument. But "they came away from Horney's lectures feeling they had encountered themselves" (Quinn, 1988, p. 300).

As she moved through her midlife years, Karen Horney seemed to refine her identity to capture in narrative the ever-widening influence she had on the world around her. As the contrasting characters of the doctor and the mother came together in midlife to form the teacher/visionary, Horney shifted her energies away from direct healing and caregiving to the formulation of new ideas that she could pass down to her students and the readers of her many influential books. Through teaching she created a legacy of scholarship and practice that survives with vigor, even today. Movement and light remained her strongest images as she moved deftly and creatively in midlife to enlighten others with the insights she had gained. The integration of the narrative characters of the doctor and the mother into the larger protagonist of the teacher/visionary marked a significant step toward wholeness and integration in Horney's life story. It signaled her growing ability to synthesize contrasting parts of herself. In that the teacher/visionary seeks to leave a legacy of the self for the next generation, furthermore, this midlife character in Horney's story signals her growing apprehension of a sense of an ending to life and of the new beginnings that may carry on in her children, her students, and her readers.

Table 1.5 provides a thumbnail sketch of our brief personality portrait of Karen Horney. The portrait is incomplete, but it begins to convey the individuality of this woman's life in terms that have proven useful to the science of personality psychology. At the first level of dispositional traits, we note that Karen Horney was an extravert who manifested a very strong trait of openness to experience. Evidence for the expression of these traits in a wide variety of situations and across time may be found throughout the biographical record. Moving to Level 2 of personality, we see that Horney represented romantic relationships with men in terms of a personal construct of control versus surrender. Beginning in the young adulthood stage of her life when she first confronted the intimacy life task, Horney understood her relationships with men in terms of two compelling but contradictory desires, and she was never able to resolve the conflict between the two. At the third level of personality, we see that Horney constructed an integrative story for her life that featured the recurrent imagery of light and movement—captured even in the language she used to describe her own personality theory—and that was populated by the two main characters of "the doctor"

TABLE 1.5	*A Thumbnail Sketch of Selected Aspects of Karen Horney's Personality, Organized in Three Different Levels*

Level 1: Dispositional Traits
High extraversion
High openness to experience

Level 2: Characteristic Adaptations
For the intimacy life task of young adulthood: Strong and conflicting needs for being in control and for surrender to passion in romantic relationships, represented cognitively as a central personal construct of control versus surrender.

Level 3: Life Stories
Recurrent imagery of movement and light. The preoccupation with movement is reflected in the central concepts of her personality theory: "moving toward," "moving against," and "moving away from" people.
Main characters of "the doctor" and "the mother," which merge in midlife to become "the teacher/visionary."

and "the mother." As she moved into midlife, Horney's story evolved in such a manner that she was able to integrate the two characters into a larger picture of herself as a teacher/visionary, leaving behind a powerful legacy for the next generation of psychoanalysts and others who were influenced by her teaching and writing. Although our portrait touches on only a few aspects of a rich and complex human life, we can see how it begins to sketch the outline of individuality via personality traits, fills in some of the details with contextualized characteristic adaptations, and attempts to consider how Horney might have understood the overall meaning of her life in terms of a self-defining and integrative life story.

SCIENCE AND THE PERSON

Personality psychology is best learned and appreciated through the lives of real, flesh-and-blood persons, which is why we have spent so much time on Karen Horney. Personality psychologists need not limit their studies to persons who are famous or whose lives seem strange and enigmatic. For instance, Robert White (1975) has shown that personality psychologists can find much to challenge and intrigue them in the careful case analysis of three very "normal" and "ordinary" American adults, whom he names Hartley Hale, Joseph Kidd, and Joyce Kingsley (see Feature 1.A). As we will see, most empirical research in personality psychology deals with everyday people, often college students like you.

Having introduced Karen Horney as a flesh-and-blood context for our discussion of persons, let us now shift gears. I stated at the outset of this chapter that personality psychology involves the *scientific* study of the whole person. It is time to examine the "science" part of this statement. What is science? How can we study persons scientifically?

In science, we try to make the confusion of everyday experience more understandable. Through science, we formulate statements about reality and then assess their truth value through rigorous and replicable tests. We do this in order to create an

FEATURE 1.A

Joseph Kidd: An Ordinary Guy

Karen Horney was an extraordinary person whose work and life are a matter of public record. Personality psychologists, however, do not limit their investigations to extraordinary and famous people. Personality theories are designed to illuminate the lives of the most ordinary among us, and most personality research conducted today takes as its subjects of study relatively normal and not-so-famous people, like college students, businessmen, nurses, store clerks, and homemakers.

A classic attempt to study in depth and over time the lives of three relatively normal, even ordinary, American adults is Robert White's (1952, 1966, 1975) *Lives in Progress*. White focused exclusively on the lives of two men and one woman in order to accomplish two goals: (1) "to understand them as fully as possible in light of existing ideas from biological research, psychology, psychoanalysis, and the social sciences" and (2) "to name some of the ideas that need to be added in order to account for natural growth" (1975, p. 3). Physician Hartley Hale, businessman Joseph Kidd, and social worker Joyce Kingsley (the names are pseudonyms) were each studied on several occasions, beginning in college and extending

(in two of the cases) past the subject's 50th birthday. The three were interviewed and administered a series of psychological measures, including questionnaires and open-ended tests of imagination at regular intervals. White's masterful case summaries illustrate the complexity of normal personality development while providing a great amount of interesting life data that can be interpreted in many different ways and on many different levels.

Raised as the second son in a close-knit Irish Catholic family, Joseph Kidd was a mentally precocious and physically beautiful child who enjoyed high levels of self-esteem until he was double-promoted from fourth to sixth grade in elementary school. As Kidd tells it, the double promotion marked the beginning of a difficult chapter in his life wherein he repeatedly behaved in a childish and silly manner in order to regain the praise and attention of his early years. Excessive masturbation in early adolescence exacerbated his painful self-consciousness and insecurity and left him with an image of himself as a "soft" and "sissylike" class clown. Kidd believed that he had reached the lowest point in his personality development a year or two before his first interview

orderly and predictable model of the universe and how it functions. Our motivations for doing this are many. They include the desire to control our environments in order to stave off threat and danger posed by the natural world (disease, natural catastrophe) or by other humans whom we fear (enemies in times of war, people we do not like). Our motivations for doing science also include the wish to improve our lives and the lives of generations to come, through understanding more about the world and by making things (telephones, x-ray machines, jet planes, computers) that promise to enhance our lives in the world. Most basic, however, is the simple desire to understand—the fundamental motive of curiosity. Science depends on the human desire to know for

for the study. After a series of setbacks, including learning that his first girlfriend, Mildred, had deceived him, the high school junior came to feel that he had "no personality." In terms of Erikson's psychosocial theory, we might restate Kidd's concern as a profound feeling of identity confusion: of not knowing who he is and how he fits into an adult world.

In subsequent years, Kidd appears to find an identity, though the process is by no means smooth. Indeed, a careful reading of the case may raise serious doubts about the extent to which Kidd ever attains "maturity." Nonetheless, a 4-year stint in the military, successes in the family business, a venture into local politics, marriage and the establishment of a family, and a number of other key events and transformations in Kidd's life bring with them a significant increase in self-confidence and a feeling of personal control over his own destiny: "It dawned on me after a while that I was knowing what I wanted. I was able to make up my mind" (White, 1975, p. 130). The course of the development, however, is uneven, full of fits and starts. In a rather dramatic turn of events, Mildred resurfaces 30 years after the conclusion of their high school romance, now unhappily married in her late 40s. For the next 8 months, Joseph and Mildred have the sexual affair they both wish they had followed through on in high school, "making up for the chastity we had sacrificed for in our six years of going together" (White, 1975, p. 204).

Now age 54 at the last interview White conducts, Kidd appears to be entering another extremely difficult period in his life. His political fortunes have ebbed, and he feels that he is unlikely to regain the prominence in public life he once enjoyed. Relationships with his wife and children are going fairly well despite occasional frustrations. But relationships with his brother and father have deteriorated badly, and he has not talked with either of them for 10 years, describing his relatives with such blunt words as "thief" and "drunk." Though his business continues to provide him with security and a decent income, new financial problems have emerged. At age 54, Kidd often feels discouraged and resentful, but he manages to cope moderately well with the many trials of everyday life as a middle-aged, middle-class American man. There is no return in Kidd's life to "the indiscriminate self-blame, conviction of inferiority, and disorganized behavior that were so conspicuous at eighteen" (p. 204). Concludes White (1975, p. 204), "the natural growth of personality does not necessarily go into reverse because conditions are hard. Sometimes it even works the other way."

the sake of knowing. Therefore, while the personality psychologist may study the person for a wide variety of reasons—to provide a diagnosis in the clinic, to help select a job candidate, to design an appropriate treatment strategy—the fundamental goal is to understand the person for the sake of understanding.

Science generally proceeds according to three steps: (1) unsystematic observation, (2) building theories, and (3) evaluating propositions. These three steps refer both to what the individual scientist does when exploring a new problem or issue and to what particular fields of science do or have done—fields such as organic chemistry, economics, botany, and personality psychology—as they evolve from "primitive" to more "mature" sciences. Because it is relatively new, personality psychology is still a fairly primitive science. Nonetheless, all three steps in the scientific process are clearly evident in what personality psychologists do today. Let us then examine each of these steps in some detail.

Step 1: Unsystematic Observation

The first step in developing a scientific understanding of anything is to look at, listen to, feel, smell, and/or taste the thing we want to understand. We may do this with the help of special instruments like telescopes and stethoscopes, or we may rely solely on our unassisted five senses (most often seeing and hearing). But however we do it, we must carefully *observe* the phenomenon of interest over a long period of time. Early observation is relatively unsystematic. We explore the phenomenon with few expectations about what we will see (or hear). We look for patterns, regularities in the phenomenon, so that we can arrive at a tentative first ordering or classification of what we are observing. The process requires a playful and almost naive approach to reality on the part of the scientist. The great physicist, Sir Isaac Newton (1642–1727), captured the attitude perfectly in this passage written shortly before his death:

> I do not know what I may appear to the world, but to myself I seem to have been only like a boy playing on the sea shore, and diverting myself in now and then finding a smoother pebble or a prettier shell than ordinary, whilst the great ocean of truth lay all undiscovered before me. (Judson, 1980, p. 114)

Let us not be fooled into thinking, however, that the scientist's curiosity is slaked by collecting innocent sense impressions about the world. The right image of the scientist in Step 1 of the scientific process is that of a *creative observer* who perceives order or pattern where it has not been perceived before. Discussing the physical sciences, Hanson (1972) states that the keen observer is "not the man who sees and reports what all normal observers see and report, but the man who sees in familiar objects what no one else has seen before" (p. 30). Thus, unsystematic observation is not a passive and casual sort of thing but rather an active attempt to *discern* and then *describe* organization, pattern, design, or structure in a phenomenon that initially seems to be unorganized and without design. This highly descriptive exploratory phase of the scientific enterprise is crucial, for it provides the scientist and the scientific community with a set of articulately described patterns in the concrete world that can be synthesized into a more general or abstract theory about how that world works.

It may be surprising to learn that science as described in Step 1 is an inherently *subjective* endeavor. We tend to believe science to be a rational, objective, and dispassionate sort of thing. Whereas this view has a good deal of merit with respect to certain aspects of science (especially Step 3, as described below), it is misleading when it comes to Step 1. The creative observer of reality who sees things in a way different than does anybody else is not necessarily "objective" in his or her point of view. Rather, the creative observer interacts in a highly subjective way with the phenomenon of study, in some cases altering the phenomenon by virtue of observing it (Hanson, 1972; Zukav, 1979). The scientist in Step 1, operating in the **context of discovery** (Reichenbach, 1938), seeks to discover new ways of seeing reality, formulating in a highly subjective manner new categories, new terminologies, and new distinctions to describe the careful observations that he or she undertakes. As the scientist begins to organize observations into categories, he or she moves from the *concrete* and *particular* events that are discerned to the more *abstract* and *general* representation of those events, a process that philosophers call **induction.** The ultimate result of induction is the creation of the abstract and general theory of Step 2, which is ultimately grounded in the subjective observations of Step 1 (Glaser & Strauss, 1967).

There are numerous examples in psychology of highly subjective observation of human behavior resulting in new insights and theories. The Swiss developmental psychologist, Jean Piaget (1952, 1965), based many aspects of his theory of cognitive development on the careful observations he made of his own three children in their first few years of life. Many of the most influential ideas in the personality theory of

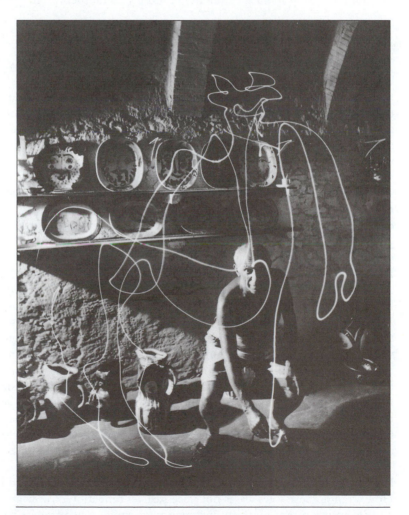

The creative observer, like Pablo Picasso, discovers new ways of looking at "reality."

Sigmund Freud (Chapter 3) are results of Freud's highly subjective observations of the dream reports, spontaneous utterances, and behavioral symptoms displayed by his neurotic patients, his colleagues, and (maybe most of all) himself. Both Piaget and Freud organized many of their initial observations within **case studies.** A case study is an in-depth investigation of a single individual, sometimes conducted over a substantial period of time. The case-study method gives the personality psychologist a good deal of information about one human being. Though case studies can be used in a number of different ways (Hersen & Barlow, 1981; Yin, 1984), personality psychologists have traditionally used them as ways to organize complex observations about a single person so as to build a theory about some (or all) persons in general (McAdams & West, 1997). In later chapters we will encounter examples of case studies in personality psychology that serve as bridges between the unsystematic observation of single individuals in Step 1 and the building of more general theories in Step 2.

Step 2: Building Theories

The second step of the scientific enterprise involves making a theory. Scientists organize the various observations collected in Step 1 into a more-or-less coherent system that explains the phenomenon of interest. Precisely how scientists do this, however, is one of the great mysteries of science. Though theories arise out of observations, they are not always arrived at in a completely logical or systematic manner. Some highly creative scientists stress the seemingly irrational and unconscious manner in which a theoretical insight may have come to them.

In a famous story, Friedrich Kekule, a German chemist of the 19th century, described how a series of discoveries concerning the structure of organic molecules came to him in hypnagogic reveries, or waking dreams. In Kekule's day, chemists had discerned a number of different chemical compounds containing carbon, hydrogen, oxygen, and a few other elements, but they had found it especially difficult to link these observations together via an abstract theory specifying the rules of their structure. Kekule had dwelt on the compounds' behavior so intensely that, on occasion, the atoms would appear to dance before him in hallucinations. One summer evening, he fell into a reverie and (he later wrote) "Lo! The atoms were gamboling before my eyes. . . . I saw how, frequently, two atoms united to form a pair; how a larger one embraced two smaller ones; how still larger ones kept hold of three or even four of the smaller; whilst the whole kept whirling in a giddy dance. I saw how the larger ones formed a chain" (Judson, 1980, p. 115). Another time, when Kekule was nodding in his chair before the fire, the atoms danced again, "all twining and twisting in snakelike motion. But look! What was that? One of the snakes had seized hold of its own tail, and the form whirled mockingly before my eyes" (Judson, 1980, p. 115). The chains and rings that Kekule imagined came to comprise the fundamental models or pictures of organic molecules that underlie basic theories of organic chemistry even today.

I do not want to suggest that scientific theories are always, or even often, formulated through dreams and reverie, but they are sometimes developed in strange ways. How strange these ways are is not necessarily a reflection of how good the theory is. This is an important point in personality psychology because (as we will see in the chapters to follow) the many theories of personality that have been offered have been created in a wide variety of ways, some stranger than others. There is no consensus in the scientific community about the *best* way of proceeding in Step 2 of the scientific process—the step in which the scientist builds a theory.

There is a lot of agreement, however, on what a theory is and what it should do. A **theory** is *a set of interrelated statements proposed to explain certain observations of reality.* A theory is always a tentative and somewhat speculative abstraction. A theory is generally accepted by a scientific community to the extent that it is consistent with observations of the phenomena it purports to explain. Theories are subject to change whenever new, inconsistent observations become available.

A theory provides at least four different tools that the scientist can use to increase understanding (Millon, 1973): (1) an abstract *model* or picture that serves as an easily envisioned representation for the structure of the theory, (2) a conceptual *terminology* or set of names for key ideas and major classes of observations in the theory, (3) a set of *correspondence rules* that describe the specific relationships to be expected between the various components, and (4) *hypotheses*, or testable predictions that are logically derived from the correspondence rules.

In other words, a theory provides a particular picture of reality, well-defined terms that name the major components of that picture, specified relationships among the components, and specific predictions about how those relationships can be tested in empirical research. The four aspects of theory are used by scientists to explain a set of observations in a clear and precise manner. Many psychologists in general and personality psychologists in particular lament that their theories do not explain as much as they would like. Nonetheless, virtually all agree that theories are at the heart of science. Furthermore, they agree that some theories are "better" than others, though they disagree wildly as to exactly *which* ones are better. What makes one theory better? What are the criteria of a good theory? Below are seven standards by which a scientific theory may be judged (from Epstein, 1973; Gergen, 1982).

1. *Comprehensiveness.* The wider the scope of a theory's explanatory abilities, the better. All other things being equal, a theory that explains more is preferred to one that explains less.

2. *Parsimony.* Science is a simplifying and economizing game. Theories attempt to explain the maximum number of observations with the minimum number of explanatory concepts. Thus, a simpler and more straightforward explanation is generally preferred to a more complex one.

3. *Coherence.* A theory should be logical and internally consistent. The various statements that make it up should hang together in a sensible manner.

4. *Testability.* From the theory, a scientist should be able to derive hypotheses that can be readily evaluated (tested) through empirical research.

5. *Empirical validity.* Empirical tests of hypotheses derived from the theory should support the theory's major claims. In other words, the results of hypothesis-testing research should be in accord with what the theory says.

6. *Usefulness.* Theories that are able, in some way, to solve humanly significant problems are generally preferred to those that seem less relevant, all other things being equal.

7. *Generativity.* A good theory should generate new research and new theorizing. It should give birth to a wide variety of creative activity on the part of scientists and laypersons alike. In the social sciences, a generative theory may serve "to challenge guiding assumptions of the culture, to raise fundamental questions regarding contemporary social life, to foster reconsideration of that which is 'taken for granted,' and thereby to generate fresh alternatives for social action" (Gergen, 1982, p. 109).

Step 3: Evaluating Propositions

Science distinguishes itself from all other modes of understanding the world by virtue of its insistence on evaluating propositions in an empirical fashion. The theories of Step 2 that derive from the observations of Step 1 must be empirically *tested* in Step 3 as the scientist moves from the context of discovery to the **context of justification** (Reichenbach, 1938). In Step 3, the scientist attempts to evaluate or "justify" the truth of a given statement proposed by a given theory. The scientist seeks to subject a portion of a theory to a rigorous and objective test. This is where the image of the scientist as a no-nonsense, hard-headed, cool, and dispassionate examiner of the real world has its origin and its validity. The context of justification is no place for flights of fancy and wild speculation; it is no place for exploring phenomena in an unsystematic and subjective manner. Rather, the scientist carefully determines the truth and utility of theoretical propositions that were formulated in the more freewheeling Steps 1 and 2 of the scientific process.

However, although Steps 1 and 2 are *more* freewheeling than Step 3, they are not so freewheeling that virtually anything goes. Indeed, the scientist's *anticipation* of Step 3— his or her knowledge that theories must ultimately be subjected to empirical test—influences the way in which the scientist explores the phenomenon of interest (Step 1) and the kinds of theories he or she eventually produces (Step 2). In other words, the anticipation of Step 3 in the scientific process feeds back to influence what the scientist does in Steps 1 and 2. Therefore, scientists who are making theories are urged by the logic of scientific inquiry to make theories that present *testable hypotheses.* In the words of the philosopher of science, Karl Popper (1959), a theory should be stated in such a way as to render its propositions **falsifiable.** The theory *should specify what observations it would take to disprove its major propositions*, or such observations should at least be deducible from the theory's propositions.

Popper's standard of falsifiability is a real bugaboo for the more speculative and philosophical among us because it puts fairly substantial constraints on the kinds of theoretical statements we can make. For instance, a personality theory that proposes that all human beings are basically good is not, in and of itself, falsifiable, because any instance of bad behavior can be dismissed as merely superficial behavior that masks the *fundamental* goodness of people. We can design no set of observations that would enable us to prove the statement false, to prove that people are *not* good. Therefore, as a scientific proposition, the statement that all people are good (or that all people are bad, or neutral, or even intelligent) flunks the basic test of falsifiability. There are many statements like this, and some are included as basic assumptions in certain personality theories existing today. Nonetheless, personality theories also contain a number of propositions that *are* falsifiable, such as Adler's claim (Chapters 7, 12) that firstborn children tend to be more conservative than other children, or Erikson's proposition (Chapter 10) that healthy psychosocial development involves the establishment of identity *before* one establishes intimacy with others. Statements such as these can be tested using standard personality research methods. Let us now consider in general terms how this is done. In later chapters, we will examine many specific examples of evaluating theoretical propositions through personality research.

Setting Up an Empirical Study Let us imagine that we wish to evaluate Alfred Adler's proposition, embedded within his more general personality theory (Chapter 12), that firstborn children tend to be more conservative than later-born children. How might we begin? Well, chances are that we have already begun! By stating a testable hypothesis derived from Adler's theory, we are showing that we have some familiarity with Adler's theory. *Scientific hypotheses should be grounded in theories.* Immersing oneself, therefore, in the theoretical and empirical literature that bears on a given proposition is an essential early task of hypothesis-testing research. Thus, our initial responsibility in carrying out this empirical study is to go back to Adler's writings to review exactly what his theory suggests. In doing this, we come to realize that we cannot possibly submit all of Adler's ideas to empirical test at once. Rather, we can test one hypothesis at a time. We would continue our background reading to include various other theories of birth order and theories about conservatism. We would eventually move to the empirical literature, much of it found in scientific journals, on both birth order and conservatism to see (1) how these ideas have been examined empirically by others (what methods scientists have employed) and (2) what empirical findings or results have been obtained. Our background reading would supply us with invaluable ideas concerning how to think about our present study and how to design it to test the hypothesis in a fair and precise way.

Having reviewed the literature on the relationship between birth order and conservatism, we should next choose an appropriate sample of persons to examine. All hypothesis-testing research in personality psychology must confront the problem of sampling. No sample is perfect. One researcher may choose to investigate Adler's hypothesis in a sample of 100 sophomores attending the University of Illinois in the summer of 1998. Another researcher may prefer to look at a sample of 60 girls attending a preschool in Alabama. Another more ambitious researcher may select a nationwide sample of middle-aged men and women, the data for which exist in a national archive that was established 30 years ago.

It is very easy to criticize another person's research in terms of the sample he or she employs, claiming, for instance, that the sample does not represent all people, that the sample is *biased* in some way. The problem is that *all* samples are biased in some way, though some certainly more so than others. In general, we should strive to obtain a sample for our study that is appropriate for the proposition to be evaluated. Therefore, if we are testing a hypothesis about, say, clinically depressed adults, a random sample of college students will not do. If we are testing a hypothesis about changes in normal personality development that occur around age 40, then we need a sample of midlife men and women who have little history of serious psychiatric disturbance. To confirm or disconfirm a given hypothesis, different researchers employing different kinds of samples should, over time, produce similar results. Thus, no single study, no matter how representative or how large the sample, establishes "truth" in science.

With the choice of an appropriate sample of participants within which to study our hypothesis, the next step is to operationalize the variables that we have chosen to investigate. A variable is *any quality that can assume two or more values.* In our example of testing Adler's hypothesis, both birth order and conservatism are variables because both can be given at least two different values or levels. For instance, a participant in our study can be a firstborn, a second-born, and so on. He or she can also be "extremely conservative," "mildly conservative," "not very conservative," and so on.

To operationalize a variable is *to decide how to measure it*—that is, to specify the "operation" through which it is to be assessed. In our example, birth order is relatively easy to measure. We would merely ask participants to indicate what their birth order is. Conservatism is a trickier variable. We might wish to administer an established paper-and-pencil test of political values to assess conservatism. Or we might wish to interview participants to determine the extent of their conservative orientation. Or we might wish to observe "conservative behavior" in a standard laboratory task. In light of our earlier discussion of Level 1 personality traits, we might consider conservatism to be one piece of the larger trait cluster of openness to experience. For example, Sulloway (1996) has reviewed historical records of famous scientists and politicians to argue that firstborns often show much lower levels of openness to experience compared with later-borns. According to Sulloway, later-borns are "born to rebel" against the conservative authority represented by their parents and their older siblings. Therefore, we might administer to the participants of our hypothetical study a standard questionnaire measuring openness to experience. But whatever measure we used, we would aim to translate our observations about conservatism, or openness to experience, into *numbers* in order to assess our hypothesis. In other words, the operationalization of most variables in personality research requires us to quantify the data. Personality psychologists have devised a number of different procedures for quantifying variables. We will have numerous opportunities to see these methods in action when we examine particular research efforts in subsequent chapters.

As they operationalize variables in order to evaluate theoretical propositions, personality psychologists tend to design studies according to one of two very simple, basic research designs, or combinations of the two. These two general formats for hypothesis-testing research are the *correlational* and the *experimental* design.

The Correlational Design   Empirical studies that assess the extent to which two different variables relate to each other are termed *correlational* ("co-related") studies. In a correlational study, the scientist asks a very simple question: When one variable changes in value, what happens to the other variable?

If an increase in the value of one variable tends to be associated with an increase in value of the other variable, the variables show a *positive correlation* to each other. An example of a positive correlation would be the relationship between the two variables of height and weight in a random sample of 200 American adults. In general, as height goes up, weight goes up, though of course there are exceptions. A positive correlation between height and weight in this sample says that taller people, on the average, tend to be heavier than shorter people. Thus, having information about one of the variables for a given subject gives you a reliable hint about the value of the other variable for that subject: If you know that John is tall, you might guess—with a fair chance of being correct—that he is relatively heavy (compared with a short person).

A *negative correlation* is indicated when an increase in one variable is generally associated with a *decrease* in the other variable. An example here might be the relationship between the variables of age and thumb sucking in a random sample of 500 American children between the ages 12 weeks and 12 years. In general, as age goes up, thumb sucking goes down: Older children suck their thumbs less frequently, on the average, than younger children.

When two variables are not related to each other in any systematic manner, we say that there is little or no correlation between them. An example of this third possibility might be the relationship between the variables of weight and intelligence in a random sample of 1,000 American adults. In general, heavier adults are neither consistently more intelligent nor consistently less intelligent than lighter adults. Therefore, weight and intelligence are uncorrelated with each other: Merely knowing an adult's weight will give you no reliable hint concerning his or her intelligence.

A numerical way of expressing the degree of correlation between two variables is the *correlation coefficient*. Readily calculated with a hand calculator or computer, correlation coefficients range from +1.0 (a perfect positive correlation) through 0.0 (no correlation between the two variables) to −1.0 (a perfect negative correlation). Figure 1.1 illustrates the distribution of scores on two variables that would produce five different values for correlation coefficients. In personality research, correlations generally fall within a "moderate" range. For instance, a moderately strong positive correlation between two personality variables might be +.50 ($r = +.50$); a moderately strong negative correlation between two personality variables might be −.50 ($r = −.50$).

Like most statistics used by personality psychologists, individual correlation coefficients are often evaluated in terms of their statistical significance. Statistical significance is a measure of the extent to which a given result can be attributed to chance. As a general convention, personality psychologists maintain that a given effect, relationship, or difference is statistically significant when the probability of obtaining that effect, relationship, or difference by chance is *less than 5%*. We say, in this case, that the finding is "significant at the .05 level," meaning that there is less than a 5% likelihood that the particular finding we have obtained is due to chance (or, saying it another way, there is more than a 95% likelihood that the finding is *not* due to chance). With respect to correlation coefficients, statistical significance is determined by the absolute value of the correlation coefficient and the number of participants from which the correlation was obtained. Thus a relatively strong negative correlation of −.57 would be statistically significant in a sample of 100 people, but the same −.57 would not be strong enough to reach statistical significance in a sample of only 10 people.

Although a correlational study shows which different variables naturally relate to each other, *correlation does not imply causation*. Just because variables A and B are correlated in a statistically significant manner, we cannot legitimately conclude that A causes B or that B causes A. Thus, a statistically significant correlation coefficient of +.45 between two variables—say, number of silk blouses owned and the size of one's office in a sample of 50 female business executives does not mean that owning silk blouses causes one to occupy large offices or that large offices cause one to own silk blouses. We might instead speculate that a third variable, such as executive status, is probably at work here, causally responsible for the other two variables. Female executives with higher statuses probably, because of their status, occupy larger offices and enjoy greater purchasing power (with which to buy silk blouses) than do low-status executives.

The Experimental Design It is generally believed that personality psychologists *can* determine cause-and-effect relationships between different variables *in an experiment*. In an experiment, a scientist *manipulates or alters one variable of interest in order to observe its impact on another variable of interest*. The first variable—the one that is manipulated or altered—is termed the *independent variable*. The second variable is the *dependent variable*. The dependent variable is understood as the individual's response to the

FIGURE 1.1 | *Scatter Diagrams Showing Various Degrees of Correlation Between Two Variables*

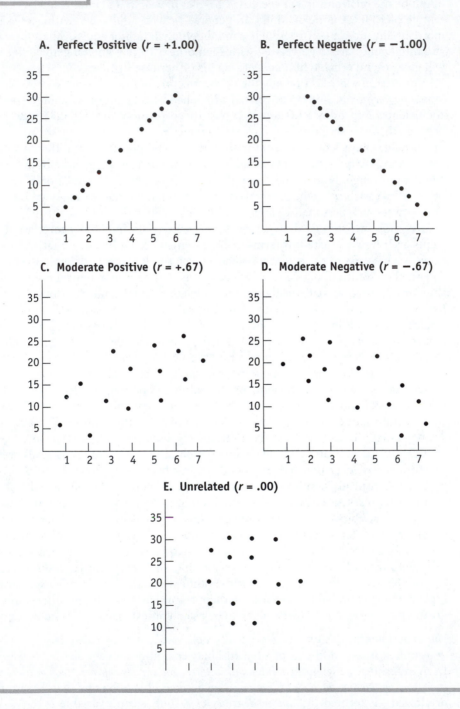

A. Perfect Positive (*r* = +1.00)

B. Perfect Negative (*r* = −1.00)

C. Moderate Positive (*r* = +.67)

D. Moderate Negative (*r* = −.67)

E. Unrelated (*r* = .00)

experimental alteration or manipulation of the independent variable. Thus, the dependent variable is a function of the independent variable: It is "dependent" on the independent variable. In cause-and-effect terms, experimentally controlled variations in the independent variable are seen as *causing* variations in the dependent variable.

If an experiment is to give valid information concerning cause and effect, the experimenter must be sure that the independent variable is the *only* variable that is systematically altered. Therefore, the experimenter designs the study to hold all variables constant except one—the independent variable—so that he or she can conclude that variations in the participant's responses (the dependent variable) are functions of variations in the independent variable, and *only* in the independent variable. Other extraneous variables threaten to confound the results; therefore, they must be controlled, to the greatest extent possible. This is why experiments are usually conducted in highly controlled environments, such as laboratory rooms. In these kinds of settings, the experimenter is able to control the kinds of stimuli to which the participants are exposed and to observe carefully the participants' responses.

Let us illustrate the basic principles of the experiment with a very simple example. Imagine that you wished to design an experiment testing the hypothesis that a person smiles more when interacting with another person who smiles than when interacting with a person who does not smile. You obtain a sample of 100 college students to participate in your study. Each person is asked to come to a laboratory room to engage in a one-on-one interview, which is to be videotaped. Participants are randomly assigned to one of two different groups: the experimental group and the control group. This means that 50 of your 100 participants are chosen by chance (such as by flipping a coin or pulling names out of a hat) to participate in each of the two *conditions*, or groups. For the experimental group, the interviewer talks with the participant for about 20 minutes, emitting smiles at regular intervals determined ahead of time by the experimenter. Participants in the control group experience the same interview except for one critical difference: The interviewer does not smile. *It is essential that the conditions of the experimental and control groups, therefore, be identical with the exception of one variable:* the interviewer's smiling. Thus, the independent variable in this experiment is whether or not the interviewer smiles. The dependent variable is the amount of smiling emitted by the person being interviewed, which could be assessed by observing the videotapes. The hypothesis would receive experimental support if the participants in the experimental group smile more than do participants in the control group, at a level reaching statistical significance. A statistically significant difference between the two groups in this experiment would suggest that variations in the experimentally manipulated independent variable were responsible for, or *caused*, variations in the dependent variable. In other words, the level of smiling of the interviewer was responsible for determining the level of smiling of the interviewee.

Because of the experiment's ability to tease out cause and effect through the careful manipulation and control of variables under standardized conditions, some psychologists consider the experiment superior to the correlational design as a basic method for doing hypothesis-testing research. For instance, one researcher terms the experiment "the basic method of science" (Mischel, 1986, p. 15), while others characterize it as the "preferred" (Byrne & Kelley, 1981) or the "most prestigious" (Singer, 1984) method. By contrast, other personality psychologists are highly critical of laboratory experimentation, arguing that experiments tend to be contrived, artificial, and trivial (Carlson, 1971,

1984; Gergen, 1982). Indeed, many empirical questions in personality psychology defy experimental investigation because the independent variables of concern cannot be systematically varied for individual participants—variables such as sex, age, ethnic origin, birth order, and body size. In some cases in which independent variables can be systematically varied, such an experimental manipulation is unfeasible or unethical. For instance, a scientist wishing to study the effects of child abuse on personality development in humans cannot legally or ethically subject half of the children in a sample to abuse (the experimental group) and half to nonabusive conditions (the control group) and then observe the effects of the manipulation. Rather, child abuse must be studied in the real world through some modification of a general correlational design.

The study of the person is a broad and rich enough endeavor to encompass *both* experimental and correlational approaches to hypothesis-testing research (Duke, 1986). Therefore, the chapters in this book contain numerous example of good personality research that is purely correlational in nature, some that are purely experimental, and some that are combinations of the two. Both correlational and experimental methods are alive and well, and both are extremely valuable in studying the person. When it comes to personality psychology, it is probably misleading to consider either of the two methods *the* basic method of science.

The three basic steps of scientific inquiry—unsystematic observation, building theories, and evaluating propositions—bring us full circle. We begin in Step 1 with observation; we move to abstractions in Step 2 in which our observations are organized within a theory; and then we move back to observation in Step 3—this time, a more systematic form of observation—as we attempt to test hypotheses empirically. The results of our experiments and correlational studies in Step 3 feed back to modify our theory. Therefore, the observations of Step 3 function in much the same way as their less systematic sisters of Step 1: They influence the making and remaking of theory. *Science progresses through a continuous dialogue between observation and theory.* Observations ultimately give rise to theories. Theories give rise to new observations designed to evaluate the theories' propositions. These new observations feed back to influence the theories from which they were derived, occasionally even giving birth to radically new theories. And so on. An underlying assumption of the whole procedure is that over the long course of observation followed by theory followed by observation, science formulates better and better ways of understanding the world, moving closer and closer, over a period of many years, to "truth."

PERSONALITY PSYCHOLOGY

The scientific focus on human individuality distinguishes personality psychology from all other branches of psychology and from the social sciences more generally. It takes a fair amount of hubris to place the individual human person at the center of all inquiry, to maintain that the person in his or her very individuality is important enough and cohesive enough to warrant special status as *the* main unit of analysis. Modern personality psychology is the heir to what psychological historian Daniel Robinson has called "Renaissance Humanism," the 16th-century worldview that celebrated "the dignity of man, the theme insisting that the world was made for man" (1981, p. 171).

Robinson points out that modern science, in its dispassionate objectivity and urge towards reductionism, has generally rejected Renaissance Humanism. But personality psychology has moved against the tide. For the personality psychologist, scientific investigation *is* made for man and for woman. In focusing unswervingly on the individual, personality psychology has come to occupy a unique and extraordinarily critical place in the world of science.

The Past and the Present

Personality psychology was born within psychology departments in American universities in the 1930s. Although personality theorists such as Freud, Jung, and Adler had been writing for over 30 years by then, it was during the 1930s that a number of separate lines of inquiry came together to generate a new academic discipline. The first issue of the journal *Character and Personality* (now the *Journal of Personality*) appeared in 1932. The journal aimed to join German studies of character with British and American studies of individual differences in persons, incorporating case studies, correlational surveys, experiments, and theoretical discussions. In 1937, Gordon Allport published the first major textbook in personality: *Personality: A Psychological Interpretation*. Although textbooks on mental hygiene, abnormal psychology, and character and personality had appeared in earlier years, Allport's was the first to articulate a grand vision for the field of personality and to place it within the context of historical and contemporary scholarship in the arts and sciences. Allport viewed personality psychology as the study of the individual person. He defined the personality as "the dynamic organization within the individual of those psychophysical systems that determine his unique adjustment to his environment" (Allport, 1937, p. 48).

From the beginning, personality psychology was a *dissident* field on the large scene of American psychology (Hall & Lindzey, 1957). In the 1930s, American psychology tended to focus minutely on such things as habits, reflexes, stimuli, and discrete responses—the basic molecular elements of organisms' behavior. By contrast, personality was holistic, taking the *whole person* as a primary unit of study, suggesting that unity, coherence, and wholeness are properties of human lives. In the 1930s, American psychology obsessed over the vicissitudes of animal learning, focusing on the relation between external stimuli and publicly observed responses in rats and pigeons. By contrast, personality concerned itself with the problems of human *motivation*, understood in terms of unobservable urges and promptings from within. This orientation is evident even in textbooks written before Allport. Writes Garnett (1928), "It is surely in the springs of human action, if anywhere, that the key to personality is to be found" (p. 14). In the 1930s, American psychology searched for universal laws applicable to all organisms. American psychology was a thoroughly **nomothetic** enterprise at this time, meaning that it aimed to discover and test general principles or laws of behavior. By contrast, personality emphasized how people were *different* from one another as well as how they were alike. Allport went so far as to suggest that the scientist should examine each individual personality as a unique entity. He argued for an **idiographic** approach to personality, which, in contrast to the nomothetic approach, would ignore general laws to discern the specific and individual patternings of particular lives. While Allport's insistence on the idiographic has always been controversial even within the field of personality psychology (e.g., Holt, 1962), personality psychologists have traditionally been much more interested than most other psychologists in the complexities of the single case.

The history of modern personality psychology can be divided into three periods (McAdams, 1997a). The first (approximately 1930–1950) was marked by the establishment of the field and the development of a number of general systems. In the 1930s and 1940s, personality psychologists proposed comprehensive conceptual systems for understanding the person. Some of these grand theories of personality are still very influential today and are discussed in subsequent pages of this text. Among the more influential personality theories proposed during this time were Allport's own (1937) psychology of the individual (see Feature 1.B), Murray's (1938) personological system (Chapters 8 and 12), the trait theories (Chapters 5–7) offered by Cattell (1946) and Eysenck (1952), Rogers's (1942) humanistic theory (Chapter 8), Kelly's (1955) cognitive theory of personal constructs (Chapter 9), Erikson's (1950) psychosocial theory of personality development (Chapter 10), and various derivatives of American behaviorism and social learning theory (Chapter 4).

By the 1930s, furthermore, Sigmund Freud (Chapter 3), Carl Jung (Chapter 3), and Alfred Adler (Chapter 12) had all developed comprehensive theories of personality derived from clinical observations and rooted in the European psychoanalytic tradition. These psychoanalytic theories became incorporated within personality psychology proper and began to have a significant influence on how personality psychologists thought about and empirically studied human individuality. Beginning with Hall and Lindzey (1957), personality textbooks organized the field according to these grand systems, variously dividing the systems into psychoanalytic and psychosocial theories (e.g., Freud, Jung, Adler, Horney, Fromm, Sullivan, Erikson), temperament and trait models (e.g., Sheldon, Cattell, Eysenck, Guilford, and sometimes Allport), approaches emphasizing needs and motives (e.g., McDougall, Lewin, Murray, McClelland), humanistic self theories (e.g., Rogers, Maslow, and sometimes Allport), organismic theories (e.g., Goldstein, Angyal, Murphy), cognitive theories (e.g., Kelly), learning theories (e.g., Hull, Skinner, Miller and Dollard), and cognitive/social-learning theories (e.g., Rotter, Bandura, Mischel). No other branch of psychology ever had more competing theories.

The years 1950–1970 mark a second historical phase. With the tremendous expansion of higher education after World War II, psychology departments grew and became more specialized, spawning professional specializations in such personality-related areas as clinical, counseling, and industrial-organizational psychology. In the United States, increased federal funding supported personality research in laboratories and field settings. Personality psychologists focused their research efforts on the examination and elaboration of particular personality *constructs*—such as extraversion (Eysenck, 1952), anxiety (Taylor, 1953), the need for achievement (McClelland, 1961), and a host of other traits, needs, motives, and so on that could be reliably and validly *measured* and whose impact on behavior could be directly *observed*. In the overall, personality psychology turned away from the grand theories of the 1930s and 1940s and came to focus instead on problems and controversies concerning personality measurement. What constitutes a valid measure of a personality construct (Cronbach & Meehl, 1955; Loevinger, 1957)? Are objective measurements of personality superior to clinical intuitions (Meehl, 1954; Sawyer, 1966)? Do personality scales measure what they say they measure, or do they simply assess a person's *style* of responding to tests (Block, 1965; Edwards, 1957; Jackson & Messick, 1958)?

In the late 1960s and early 1970s, psychologists delivered a series of devastating critiques of personality psychology that threw the field into a crisis. Carlson (1971) chastised personality psychologists for ignoring the grand theories of the early years and straying away from their implicit mandate to study real lives and whole persons in depth. Fiske (1974) wondered whether perhaps personality psychology had gone about as far as it could go, limited as it is by its reliance on imprecise verbal reports from people. Shweder (1975) questioned the need for any form of psychology based on individual differences. Most influential, however, was Mischel's (1968, 1973) critique, in which he argued against explanations of human behavior based on internal personality traits and in favor of explanations that focused on the situational and cognitive/social-learning determinants of behavior. As we will see in Chapter 5, Mischel's critique launched a protracted "debate" in the field of personality psychology over the efficacy of trait-based versus situation-based approaches to predicting and understanding social behavior. The "trait versus situation" debate preoccupied the field of personality psychology through the 1970s and into the early 1980s.

A third phase in the brief history of modern personality psychology, therefore, begins around 1970 and extends to the present day. The phase begins with critique and pervasive doubt concerning the legitimacy and worth of personality studies, but it evolves, by the mid-1980s, into a broad sense of renewal and revitalization (Buss & Cantor, 1989; Hogan, Johnson, & Briggs, 1997; Maddi, 1984; McAdams, 1990a, 1994b; Pervin, 1990; West, 1983). As the trait versus situation controversy has died down, contemporary research in personality has become more sensitive to the complex interaction of internal personality variables and external situational factors in the prediction of behavior (Kenrick & Funder, 1988). Trait models for personality have regained their strength and influence in psychology as a whole, especially with the emergence of the Big Five factor model for personality traits (McCrae & Costa, 1990; Wiggins, 1996). Having resolved or put aside a number of measurement controversies, personality psychologists have refined new research methodologies for the scientific study of persons (Craik, 1986). Recent years have also witnessed renewed interest in integrative personality theory (Mischel & Shoda, 1995; Tomkins, 1987; Westen, 1995) and a renewed commitment to studying whole persons in their full biographical complexity (Franz & Stewart, 1994; McAdams & Ochberg, 1988; Nasby & Read, 1997).

The contemporary renaissance in personality studies affirms what I have always felt deeply about this particular field of study: Personality psychology is the centerpiece of psychology as a whole. It is with reference to individual persons that many of the most important theories, findings, and applications in psychology as a whole must be oriented. Personality psychology addresses the most general and most fundamental questions in the field: What is human nature? What is a person? How do we understand persons? It is the most fundamental and the most fascinating field in psychology, in my view, because it reflects directly upon each of us, upon the self. While other branches of psychology offer many important insights into human behavior and experience, it is only personality psychology that focuses unswervingly on the individual person—on your particular individuality as a person. Indeed, I would go further, to suggest that personality psychology should be one centerpiece of any constellation of studies and programs promising to educate a person in the broadest sense. One of the goals of a liberal arts education is the conscientious examination of the self and its place in the world, the concerted reflection upon one's own life in culture, history, and the cosmos.

FEATURE 1.B

Gordon Allport and the Origins of Personality Psychology

Gordon W. Allport (1897–1967) may not have invented personality psychology, but more than anybody else he was responsible for establishing personality as a vigorous field of scientific inquiry in university settings. Allport's greatest contribution is probably the textbook he published in 1937: *Personality: A Psychological Interpretation*. In what is generally considered to be the first authoritative text in personality, Allport presented an integrated agenda for the field of personality psychology, and he foresaw many of the issues and controversies that have defined the field ever since.

Allport was born in 1897 in a small town in Indiana, one of four sons of a physician and his wife. He grew up in Cleveland, Ohio, attended Harvard University for his undergraduate and doctoral work, and studied extensively in Europe, through which he appears to have been influenced greatly by such German psychologists as William Stern and Edward Spranger. From 1930 to 1967, Allport taught at Harvard, where he helped establish the interdisciplinary Department of Social Relations. In his early years there, he articulated a vision for personality psychology that was to serve as a humanistic alternative to behaviorism and an optimistic antidote to Freud's unflattering view of the human condition. In his autobiography, Allport (1968) stated that he wished to create a field of study centered on an image of man "that would allow us to test in full whatever democratic and humane potential he might possess" (p. 394). In the middle of the Great Depression in Europe and the United States and on the eve of World War II, Allport wrote *Personality* in the spirit of social reform and the hope for a better world. Allport's text was cosmopolitan, erudite, and steeped in old-world European scholarship. But it was also profoundly American in its unabashed optimism and egalitarian tone.

In *Personality*, Allport presented an eclectic array of concepts and hypotheses, loosely tied to one dominant theme: The person is a unique whole. The person's wholeness is best captured in Allport's concept of the **proprium.** According to Allport (1955), "the proprium includes all aspects of personality that make for inward unity" (p. 40). Eight different aspects of the proprium can be identified, each arising at a particular period of development. The most basic element is (1) the sense of a *bodily self*, which develops in the first year of life as infants experience the regularities of interaction with the world. With the development of language in the second year and a maturing understanding of time and causality, a toddler's sense of self expands beyond the body to encompass (2) *self-identity*. Children come to understand that they are the same person over time, identified by a particular verbal name. In early childhood, children develop (3) *self-esteem* as they attain some mastery in play and social interaction. Around the age of 4 or 5, children experience (4) *self-extension* as they come to see their own likes and dislikes as integral parts of the self. Next develops (5) *self-image*, through which children distinguish their own good behavior (the good me) from bad behavior (the bad me). Because adolescents are able to engage in abstract thinking and systematic decision making, they may view the self as a (6) *rational coper* who is able to make important judgments in life. In adolescence, the sense of self expands to include (7) *propriate strivings* through which people sense ownership of and responsibility

Gordon Allport

for feelings, needs, and life-governing goals. The culmination of the proprium is (8) the unifying sense of the *self-as-knower*. Allport (1961) argued that the self-as-knower is the totality of the person as a process that is continually changing and becoming.

The uniqueness of individuals is expressed through personality traits. For Allport, the trait was the major structural unit of personality. He defined a trait as a "neuropsychic structure having the capacity to render many stimuli functionally equivalent and to initiate and guide equivalent (meaningfully consistent) forms of adaptive and expressive behavior" (Allport, 1961, p. 347). Allport held that traits are real, causal entities that correspond to as yet unknown neurophysiological structures.

They are not mere descriptive categories of functionally equivalent behaviors. Rejecting the distinction between motive and trait, Allport insisted that traits have motivational features, serving to energize, direct, and select behavior. While traits may account for consistency in behavior across situations and over time, Allport knew that human behavior is often inconsistent and strongly shaped by situational factors (Zuroff, 1986). A single person, furthermore, may be characterized by contradictory traits. Therefore, "the ever changing nature of traits and their close dependence upon the fluid conditions of the environment forbid a conception that is over-rigid or over-simple" (Allport, 1937, p. 312).

Allport's brand of trait psychology tended toward the literary in content and style. While he encouraged nomothetic research on common traits, he tended to distrust statistical analyses of group data because, he argued, they tend to blot out the uniqueness of the single person. While large-scale trait studies could be useful for deducing general laws of behavior, Allport believed that these should be supplemented by the idiographic, in-depth examination of the unique and common traits manifested in the single case. The best example of this approach is his *Letters from Jenny* (Allport, 1965), in which Allport analyzed a series of personal letters written by one woman over a long period of time in order to delineate the key traits in her personality. In *Letters from Jenny*, furthermore, Allport confronted the problems and possibilities of doing personality studies through the in-depth analysis of the single case. Allport championed idiographic case-study research throughout his career, as well as the use of personal documents such as letters, journals, and autobiographies in

continued on next page

FEATURE 1.B *continued*

personality research (Allport, 1942; Allport, Bruner, & Jandorf, 1941). It was only through the analysis of the single case, he believed, that a psychologist might convey the full individuality of the person. Allport's emphasis on single cases and the uniqueness of the individual, however, was always controversial, for many wonder how scientific explanation can proceed if every case is viewed to be completely unique (e.g., Holt, 1962). The use of case studies and psychological biography in personality research and theorizing is an extremely complex issue, as we will see in Chapter 12.

Beyond his seminal writings on personality, the self, traits, and case studies, Allport made major contributions in a wide range of areas, including the psychology of expressive movements (Allport & Vernon, 1933), the psychology of rumor (Allport & Postman, 1947), the psychology of religion (Allport, 1950), research on attitudes and values (Allport & Vernon, 1931), and the nature of prejudice (Allport, 1954). In his awesome breadth and his humanistic vision for a science of individuality, Gordon Allport personified the potential and the possibilities of personality psychology. His work and his career have inspired generations of psychologists who have chosen as their intellectual mission the scientific study of the whole person.

It is in personality psychology—if anywhere in psychology—that such an examination may begin, for personality psychology itself begins with just such an examination.

Personality psychology itself draws on fields as diverse as human physiology, evolutionary biology, sociology, cultural anthropology, mythology, biography, and even literary studies in the study of whole persons. As such, personality psychology lies at the crossroads of many disciplines. Within psychology proper, personality psychology shares some affinities with developmental, social, abnormal, and clinical/counseling psychology. Yet important differences may also be identified.

Although personality psychologists are concerned with the development of human beings from birth to death, they differ from most *developmental* psychologists in tending to focus their inquiries on the adult years. Further, whereas developmental psychology concerns itself with meaningful change and transition over time, personality psychologists tend to focus on those aspects of the person that show some degree of continuity or stability over time. Yet, these distinctions are fuzzy and matters of relative emphasis. For example, many personality psychologists are interested in personality change, so their inquiries sometimes overlap with those made by developmental psychologists.

Personality psychology has many ties to *social* psychology (Blass, 1984). Personality and social psychologists publish in some of the same journals; they belong to some of the same societies; and they tend to share many intellectual interests. Still, there is a fundamental difference between the cores of the two disciplines: *Social psychologists focus on human sociality, while personality psychologists focus on human individuality.* Having said this, I must blur the distinction, for human sociality must always take into consideration the role of human individuals, and human individuality must always be seen in social context. Therefore, in examining social behavior, social psychologists are quite likely to consider carefully the role of the self, as many contemporary textbooks in social psychology will show; similarly, in examining human individuality, personality psychologists must also consider social contexts, as we will see in this book. Still, the general fact remains that personality and social psychologists do show differences in matters of emphasis. To put things in simple behavioral terms, personality psychologists tend to be somewhat more interested in how different people react differently to the same situation, whereas social psychologists emphasize how people in general react differently to different situations. But you can always find exceptions to this tendency, as personality psychologists often examine the efficacy of situations as well and social psychologists are quite likely to consider individual differences, too.

There is a strong clinical tradition in personality psychology, going back to Freud and the origins of psychoanalysis at the turn of the 20th century. The fields of *abnormal* psychology and *clinical/counseling* psychology consider problems in human life that go under such names as psychopathology, mental illness, and behavioral dysfunctions. Many clinicians concern themselves with personality disorders of various kinds. Some theories of personality, furthermore, prescribe specific techniques for changing abnormal behavior and enhancing mental health (e.g., psychoanalytic therapy, Rogerian counseling). Nonetheless, personality psychology proper tends to focus more on relatively normal functioning and the wide varieties of individuality that may be expressed among more-or-less well-adjusted people. As the scientific study of the whole person, personality psychology is *not* centrally concerned with psychotherapy and other treatment aspects of clinical practice. However, there is no more important background for effective psychotherapy than a strong understanding of theory and research in personality psychology. As I hope you will also see, such an understanding can enhance your own life, as well.

Organization of This Book

After this opening chapter, *The Person* is organized into four parts. The first part (Chapters 2–4) considers the fundamental *contexts* of human individuality. Before we can examine the three levels of personality that I have identified in this chapter, we need to understand how human lives are situated in time and space. The ultimate context in this regard is human evolution. In Chapter 2, we will consider how human nature has been shaped by evolution. Recent years have witnessed an upsurge of interest in "evolutionary personality psychology." While some have argued for the emergence of new "sociobiological" and "evolutionary" theories of personality, I submit that *any* reasonable scientific effort to understand persons must consider the role of evolution as the macrocontext of human individuality. The conception of human evolution, as originally expressed by Charles Darwin (1859), is too important to be left out of any personality theory, in my view, but it is also too general to function as a personality theory itself. Human evolution is best viewed, then, as a fundamental context for human behavior and experience, and understanding human life from an evolutionary point of view is a necessary first step in studying the person, but only a first step.

Chapter 3 considers Freud's perspective on personality, now almost 100 years old, and some of the most important insights into human nature and human individuality that have come out of the psychoanalytic tradition. Included here are some relatively recent conceptualizations in psychoanalysis, such as object-relations theories and the self psychology developed by Heinz Kohut. Most textbooks in personality separate psychoanalytic theories from other personality theories (e.g., trait theories, cognitive theories), viewing them each as competing conceptualizations for understanding the person. I have chosen a different tack. Now that an entire century has passed since Freud (1900) published what is probably his greatest book, *The Interpretation of Dreams*, some of his central insights have been incorporated into our common Western understanding of human individuality (e.g., the idea of the unconscious, the working of defense mechanisms) while certain other ideas have been discarded as too vague or just plain wrong (e.g., the idea of the death instinct, the female Oedipal complex). I do not believe it is possible to be an educated person in Western society without some understanding of the tremendous influence Freud and his followers have had on Western thought. But I also do not believe that it makes as much sense as it once did to consider psychoanalysis as a single personality theory that is separated from all other theories (e.g., Hall & Lindzey, 1957). Instead, I see the psychoanalytic view of human nature as I see evolutionary theory—as a fundamental context for understanding human individuality. An integrative view of persons must bring into the picture evolutionary and psychoanalytic considerations.

A third fundamental context is culture. Chapter 4 brings together the many seminal ideas from behaviorism, social learning theory, theories of socialization, theories of human ecology and environments, and cross-cultural psychology that must be considered when examining the exquisite way in which human lives are socially and culturally contextualized. The theories of behaviorism that so dominated American psychology in the middle of the 20th century—theories offered by Clark Hull (1943) and B. F. Skinner (1938)—were never theories of personality. But their cornerstone ideas concerning learning and environments are fundamental for a scientific understanding of human individuality. Behaviorism was about how organisms learn by interacting with their environments. For human beings, those environments range from immediate physical and social situations to the larger contexts of family, neighborhood, class, and culture.

The remaining three parts of this book follow the tripartite scheme for conceptualizing persons that I have introduced in this chapter. The second part (Chapters 5–7) focuses on Level 1 in the study of persons—dispositional personality traits. Chapter 5 examines fundamental issues in trait psychology, including defining and measuring traits, the concepts of reliability and validity in trait assessment, and the interactions between traits and situations in the prediction of behavior. Chapter 6 focuses on particular traits that personality psychologists have studied, organized according to the Big Five classification scheme. We will look at how these traits are defined, what they mean, how they influence social behavior, and how they may be linked, in some cases, to psychophysiological underpinnings. Chapter 7 considers continuity and change in traits across the human lifespan and addresses these intriguing questions: To what extent are traits a product of genetics? Do traits have their origins in temperament differences apparent in infancy? Can traits change in adulthood?

The book's third part (Chapters 8–10) focuses on Level 2 in the study of persons—characteristic adaptations. Motivational adaptations are the subject of Chapter 8, as we will examine the most important ideas and research findings about human individuality as manifest in needs, goals, motives, strivings, and other expressions of human desire.

Here we find the seminal contributions of Henry Murray and David McClelland on psychogenic needs and social motives, humanistic theories of motivation (such as that offered by Carl Rogers), and more recent contributions such as self-determination theory and the study of personal strivings, tasks, and projects. Chapter 9 moves to cognitive adaptations, featuring George Kelly's personal construct psychology and the increasingly influential social-cognitive approaches to personality that address concepts such as social intelligence, cognitive schemas, and the cognitive regulation of behavior. Chapter 10 considers characteristic adaptations that are contextualized in time, as in developmental stages, phases, and seasons. The chapter is organized around two highly influential theories of self-development—Jane Loevinger's theory of ego development and Erik Erikson's theory of psychosocial stages. The former theory focuses on the *structure* of the self while the latter mainly considers the *content* of social life.

The book's fourth and final part (Chapters 11–12) focuses on Level 3 in the study of persons—life stories. Chapter 11 will examine theory and research concerning people's own self-defining life stories—internalized and evolving narratives of the self that provide a person's life with unity and purpose. Here I will describe some of my own research on identity as a life story and will consider the important theoretical contributions made in recent years by Tomkins, Hermans, and other narrative psychologists. Continuing the emphasis on stories, Chapter 12 takes up psychologists' efforts to construct their own narrative accounts to make sense of the lives of others, as in case studies and psychobiographies. Important theoretical contributions to this effort have been made by Henry Murray and what has been called the "personological tradition" in the study of lives and by Adler, Levinson, and theorists who focus on the human life course.

What do we know when we know a person? How can we understand the individual human life? I believe that such an understanding begins with (1) a solid grounding in the evolutionary, psychodynamic, and cultural contexts of human behavior and proceeds to a systematic consideration of (2) dispositional traits; (3) characteristic motivational, cognitive, and developmental adaptations; and (4) integrative life stories. I believe that this approach brings into a meaningful synthesis the best that personality psychology has to offer.

SUMMARY

1. Personality psychology is the scientific study of the whole person.

2. What do we know when we know a person? Observation of everyday social interaction shows that people tend to make at least three different kinds of attributions about persons in their efforts to know persons. They account for a person's individuality in terms of (1) dispositional traits, (2) characteristic adaptations, and (3) integrative life stories. These

three kinds of attributions about persons correspond to three levels of personality. A full understanding of the individual human life begins with a solid grounding in the evolutionary, psychodynamic, and cultural contexts of human behavior and experience, and it proceeds to a systematic consideration of traits, adaptations, and life stories.

3. At Level 1, personality traits are general, internal, and comparative dispositions that account for consistencies perceived or expected in behavior from one situation to the next and over time. Traits sketch an outline of human individuality. In the case example of the life of the psychiatrist and psychoanalytic theorist Karen Horney, two dominant traits were extraversion and openness to experience.

4. At Level 2, characteristic adaptations are contextualized facets of human individuality that speak to motivational, cognitive, and developmental concerns in personality. Contextualized in time, place, or social role, characteristic adaptations fill in the details of a human life. In Karen Horney's life, one especially important characteristic adaptation was the personal construct system she established for making sense of romantic relationships, a system that encoded the conflict between desires for control and surrender in the intimacy life task.

5. At Level 3, a life story is an internalized and evolving narrative of the self that integrates the reconstructed past, perceived present, and anticipated future in order to provide a life with a sense of unity and purpose. If traits sketch an outline and adaptations fill in the details of human individuality, life stories speak to what a human life means in the overall. In Horney's case, she constructed a life story featuring the recurrent imagery of movement and light and portraying the main characters of "the doctor," "the healer," and "the teacher/visionary."

6. As the scientific study of the whole person, personality psychology follows a three-step sequence of inquiry that is common to most sciences: (1) unsystematic observation, (2) building theories, and (3) evaluating propositions.

7. In the third step, scientists derive hypotheses from theories and test their adequacy in research. One general design of hypothesis-testing research is the correlational design, in which the psychologist determines the extent to which two or more variables covary. A second general design is the experiment, in which the psychologist manipulates the independent variable to assess its impact on the dependent variable.

8. Personality psychology was born in university psychology departments in the 1930s. The first authoritative text for the field was Gordon Allport's (1937), *Personality: A Psychological Interpretation*. Allport identified an important distinction in personality research between the nomothetic approach, which aims to discover and test general principles of behavior across many individuals, and the idiographic approach, which focuses on the specific and individual patterning of the single human life.

9. The history of modern personality psychology can be divided into three periods: (1) 1930–1950, the period of developing general systems and grand theories of personality; (2) 1950–1970, the period of refining measurement techniques and elaborating personality constructs; and (3) 1970–today, a period that began with a crisis concerning the legitimacy of personality studies and developed into the present sense of renewal and invigoration in the field of personality psychology.

10. Personality psychology is related to many other branches of psychology and sits at the crossroads of many different disciplines in the social sciences. It is distinguished from other fields, however, by its focus on human individuality, its tendency to examine relatively enduring rather than fleeting and momentary characteristics of persons, its interest in individual differences as manifest in adulthood, and its focus on relatively normal, healthy psychological functioning.

The Background
Human Nature and Cultural Context

I

Chapter 2
Human Evolution

Chapter 3
Freud and the
Psychoanalytic
Tradition

Chapter 4
Social Learning and
Culture

The goal of personality psychology is to provide a scientific account of human individuality. This account should ultimately enhance our understanding of the major features of personal adjustment and social life that distinguish a particular person from other persons. In order to recognize and understand a particular person, we must be able to pick him or her "out

45

of a crowd," in a sense. We must be able to identify and make sense of those aspects of his or her life that are particularly characteristic of that person. Among the most important aspects to consider are a person's dispositional traits, characteristic adaptations, and integrative life stories. But before we can talk about what makes any person different from others, we need to have a good understanding of what all persons have in common and what common challenges and opportunities persons face. An individual life must be viewed in context, and the context of any given life includes many things. In the next three chapters, we examine the major contexts of human individuality. In Chapter 2, we take up human evolution as the ultimate context and we consider how evolution has shaped and designed human nature in particular ways. While every person is unique and every human culture sets forth certain unique environments, human beings share a common evolutionary heritage. Any single human life must be viewed against the backdrop of this heritage. In Chapter 3, we examine Sigmund Freud's theory and the psychoanalytic tradition for what insights they may give on human nature. For the past 100 years, psychoanalytic theorists have proposed many controversial ideas about human individuality. While some of these ideas have led to scientific dead ends, certain others have profoundly shaped how we think about human nature—especially those ideas of psychic determinism, conflict and anxiety, and the unconscious. An integrative view of the person must bring into the picture a sense of the psychodynamics of everyday life. Chapter 4 turns our attention to culture and the interpersonal and social environments in which human individuality is situated. The traditions of behaviorism and social learning theory have provided personality psychology with tools and frameworks for understanding how persons learn to live in their immediate physical and social situations and within the larger contexts of family, neighborhood, class, and culture. In addition, factors such as social class, gender, and race/ethnicity contour human lives and serve as important contexts for human individuality. In sum, the next three chapters prepare us for our explorations of the individual human life by placing that life—any life—within the overarching and overlapping contexts of human nature and culture.

Human Evolution

William Golding painted a dark and frightening picture of human nature in his famous first novel, *Lord of the Flies* (Golding, 1962). In Golding's story, English schoolboys find themselves marooned on a deserted island after a plane crash during their evacuation from their homes in an atomic war. One of the older boys, Ralph, assembles all of the children and organizes a primitive society dedicated to securing their ultimate rescue. The boys establish rules and build a fire to signal passing ships and planes of their presence on the island. Ralph's society soon begins to fall apart, however, as many of the boys desert him to join Jack's rival group, dedicated to fun and feasting, to power and its ceremonies, to hunting pigs and sacrificing to the "beast," and to all of the pleasures and terrors of savagery. Jack rallies most of the children to his side, leading them on hunts in which they scream in unison, "Kill the pig! Bash his head! Run him in!" As the story progresses, the boys become increasingly intoxicated with aggression and cruelty. Killing pigs leads to killing each other, first in the spontaneous and unwitting slaughter of Simon, the kindest and gentlest of the boys, and then with ruthless premeditation in the murder of Piggy, a fat and rather intellectual boy who wears glasses. With the death of Piggy—the only boy who repeatedly insists that the children try to be "rational" and "civilized"—all vestiges of rational civilization disappear from the island. Ultimately, the children declare war on Ralph, who by now has become something of a beast himself as he realizes that "the desire to squeeze and hurt is overmastering" (p. 136). Under Jack's leadership, the children hunt Ralph down and set the island on fire. A nearby ship sights the smoke and fire and "rescues" the boys, whisking them back to England to face the reality of an adult war waged on a much grander scale.

Golding's innocent English schoolboys become frenzied murderers when transported to a natural setting and left to their own devices to survive. There is no beast stalking the island, concludes Simon, shortly before his death: *"It's only us"* (p. 103). The "beast" within each of the boys transforms him into a warmonger. Golding urges us to ask: Is there a "beast" within each of us? Many popular writings would suggest so. Books like *The Naked Ape* (Morris, 1967) and *The Social Contract* (Ardrey, 1970) made a large splash in the 1970s by arguing that human beings are explosive beasts by nature and that the psychological roots of human warfare lie within the aggressive souls of men. According to this still-popular view, aggression is the product of human evolution. We have evolved to be hunters, killers, and warmongers because these quintessential human traits enabled us to survive and reproduce over the long course of human evolution. The violence inflicted by our hunting and gathering evolutionary ancestors, therefore, may be the origin of modern warfare today. We are, by nature, selfish killers. We seek to promote our own interests first, and to do so we must oftentimes hurt others, and sometimes even kill them. We even fantasize about aggression and often live out our aggressive dreams.

That human beings are by nature aggressive and cruel is a common belief in many different societies and finds its way into a wide range of viewpoints concerning human nature—from the Judeo-Christian view of original sin to the Buddhist belief that human desires are fundamentally selfish and self-serving, leading to aggression, hatred, and suffering. For Jews, Christians, Buddhists, and members of many other faiths worldwide, human happiness, salvation, enlightenment, and fulfillment can happen only when human beings transcend their bestial nature. We must be *delivered from* our base instincts, our sinful nature, our selfish, hateful, and aggressive heritage. In *The Varieties of Religious Experience*, William James (1902–1958) observed that most all religious

Aggression: Is it part of human nature?

viewpoints the world over declare that there is something fundamentally wrong with human beings to begin with—human nature is flawed in some fundamental way, which is why people hurt one another and suffer so much—and that things can be made right only through some sort of belief, practice, or ritual that delivers people from a naturally bad state to a supernaturally good one. To be good, we must renounce the beast within.

To understand the individual person, the student of personality must begin with human nature. What is fundamentally true about all human beings? What are we all *really* like? Are we as bad, as evil, as egotistical and aggressive as Golding suggests? There are surely many different views of human nature. In contrast to the more pessimistic perspectives, we find viewpoints like that held by the French philosopher Jean-Jacques Rousseau (1712–1778), as well as many people today, who argued that human beings are born fundamentally pure and good. Left alone on a desert island, Ralph, Jack, and Piggy would not burn the island down, Rousseau might maintain, but would likely live in peace and build prosperous lives, assuming they had not been too tainted by civilization before they arrived. Rousseau believed that civilization corrupts people, that human nature can become spoiled by the social pressures and norms of complex societies. People who live in more primitive and natural conditions, Rousseau maintained, live noble and uncorrupted lives—"noble savages," as he put it—who act on instinct rather than social norms and who naturally develop the powers of reason over time and use these powers for good ends.

Yet another perspective on human nature has it that people are neither basically good nor bad; they are instead neutral. As we will see in Chapter 4, the British philosopher John Locke (1632–1704) contended that people are born as blank slates, without any particular quality of human nature to begin with. Over time, experience shapes people into forms that are consistent with what the environment dictates. This, too, is a common viewpoint: that we are what our environments make us to be, and only that. From this perspective, Golding's boys were beasts because they had been taught to be beasts. They lived in a violent society to begin with, one that was engaged in a nuclear war. They killed one another not because it is natural to do so, but because they had been taught no other way to live.

From a scientific standpoint, any discussion of human nature must consider how it is that human beings came naturally to be. If we are to understand what our basic nature is, then we must have some sense of our origins in the natural world. Where did we come from? How did we get where we are today? In 1859, Charles Darwin established a comprehensive scientific framework for addressing questions like these, when he introduced the theory of evolution in the landmark volume *On the Origins of the Species by Means of Natural Selection*. Evolutionary theory has changed significantly since Darwin's day, but it remains the indispensable paradigm for understanding how human nature has been shaped over the millions of years that humans and their evolutionary ancestors have inhabited the earth. While evolutionary theory itself does not mandate a particular view of human nature, it provides us with a set of conceptual tools for thinking clearly about what human nature might be (Buss, 1995; Pinker, 1997).

Since the 1970s, a growing number of psychologists has sought to apply principles of modern evolutionary theory to understanding human personality (e.g., Bowlby, 1969; Buss, 1984, 1997; Caporael & Brewer, 1995; Simpson, in press; Tooby & Cosmides, 1990, 1992). In a related vein, careful observations of chimpanzees and other primates with whom human beings share considerable evolutionary lineage provide provocative clues as to the nature of human nature (deWaal, 1996; Snowdon, 1983). Overall, these efforts suggest that Golding's picture of murderous schoolboys was only partly right, mostly wrong, and very incomplete as a depiction of human nature. What is emerging from contemporary scholarship in evolutionary psychology is a more complex portrait of human nature. While human beings are capable of unspeakable acts of aggression, we are also, *by our very nature*, an exquisitely caring and altruistic species whose adaptive successes owe as much to our powers of cooperation as to our tendencies toward aggression. Evolution has prepared us well to hate and to kill, to love and to care for others, to engage in many forms of cooperative social behavior, to deceive others and put ourselves first, and to express our sincerest emotions and put the welfare of certain others ahead of our own. Human nature is filled with *apparent* contradictions and paradoxes—but only apparent, for a closer consideration of human evolution and the many selective pressures that human beings have faced and challenges that human beings have met over the course of thousands of generations helps us to see that there may be a kind of awesome logic behind it all.

ON HUMAN NATURE: OUR EVOLUTIONARY HERITAGE

Principles of Evolution

A fundamental property of living things is that they replicate. All animals and plants produce copies of themselves, in one way or another, making for the continuity of life from one generation to the next. The origins of life on earth reside in the first instances of physical reproduction: Once upon a time, a physico-chemical phenomenon reproduced itself through some means, providing the jump start required for the evolution of life to begin. Steven Pinker (1997) tells us the story of how evolutionary scientists believe that life on earth began:

> In the beginning was a replicator. This molecule or crystal was a product not of natural selection but of the laws of physics and chemistry. . . . Replicators were wont to multiply, and a single one multiplying unchecked would fill the universe with its great, great- . . . -great grandcopies. But replicators use up materials to make their copies and energy to power the replication. The world is finite, so the replicators will compete for its resources. Because no copying process is one hundred percent perfect, errors will crop up, and not all of the daughters will be exact duplicates. Most of the copying errors will be changes for the worse, causing a less efficient uptake of energy and materials or a slower rate or lower probability of replication. But by dumb luck a few errors will be changes for the better, and the replicators bearing them will proliferate over the generations. Their descendants will accumulate any subsequent errors that are changes for the better, including ones that assemble protective covers and supports, manipulators, catalysts for chemical reactions, and other features of what we call bodies. The resulting replicator with its apparently well-engineered body is what we call an organism. (pp. 157–158)

Pinker's imagined scenario for the beginning of life on earth contains the essence of Darwin's insight about the evolution of life, updated with a contemporary understanding of genetics. Individual organisms are the product of a long chain of evolutionary events whereby replicating systems essentially compete for limited resources, with some systems proving more successful in the long run than others. The more "successful" systems are those that produce more viable copies of themselves for the next "generation." In order to do so, a system must meet the demands posed by the environment wherein it resides. The demands are many, including limited resources and challenges posed by other replicators (that is, other organisms). As time passes, the designs of organisms change, as some designs prove more promoting of replications in certain environments than do others. As environments change, designs of organisms change, not in direct response to environmental changes but simply because some designs of organisms will prove to be more successful in promoting replication than others. Over evolutionary time, as Tooby and Cosmides (1992) describe it, evolution "appears as a succession of designs, each a modification of the one preceding it. Generation by generation, step-by-step, the designs of all of the diverse organisms alive today—from the redwoods and manta rays to humans and yeast—were permuted out of the original, very simple, single-celled ancestor through an immensely long sequence of successive modifications" (p. 52). As Darwin argued, all existing living forms have evolved over time in response to their interactions with environments. Facing limited environmental resources for survival and replication, organisms compete with one another, and ultimately the "fittest" designs win out.

The key to evolution over time is **natural selection,** a process whereby nature gradually selects those characteristics of organisms that promote survival and reproductive success. Darwin observed that organisms within a species manifest wide variation in physical and behavioral characteristics. Certain characteristics may promote the survival of the organism within the environment. Those organisms possessing the advantageous characteristic should live longer and produce more offspring than those organisms not possessing the characteristic. The offspring of those possessing the advantageous characteristic likewise should be more likely to possess the same advantageous characteristic, enabling them in turn to live longer and produce more offspring similarly equipped. In this way, nature selects, and causes to persist, the most adaptive characteristics in a species.

Although Darwin did not understand the precise mechanism for biological transmission of characteristics from parent to offspring, he did recognize that such transmission occurs. Today, we know that *genes* are responsible for the inheritance of characteristics. Genes are segments of chromosomes found in every cell in the body and are composed of deoxyribonucleic acid (DNA), a long threadlike molecule that is particularly well suited for passing on hereditary information.

Because sexual reproduction involves a mixing of parents' genes, an individual organism receives half of his or her genes from the biological mother and half from the biological father, thus inheriting characteristics from both. Through sexual reproduction, then, genes are passed down from one generation to the next. But in the transmission of genes, strange things occasionally occur. Genes may be transformed, generally by accident. Most changes make little or no difference in the organism's life, and what difference they do make may render the organism less fit. Sometimes, however, genetic mutations can make for accidental advantages (what Pinker above called "dumb luck"), as when a transformation in the genes gives rise to a characteristic in the organism that promotes survival and success.

The movers and shakers in evolution are the genes, which ultimately produce the designs of the organisms that compete for resources in the environment. In a literal sense, it is the genes, not the organisms themselves, that are replicated. To take a simple example, my own biological children are not literal replications of me (fortunately, for the world), but rather my children contain the replications of my and my wife's (even more fortunately) genes. Through evolution, organisms have been designed to function such that the genes that lie behind those designs are replicated in subsequent generations. The evolutionary imperative, then, is to replicate the genes. Now, if a gene were a person, which of course it isn't (it is simply a DNA structure), then we could say that it is a very "selfish" person. In *The Selfish Gene*, Richard Dawkins (1976) made famous the idea that genes aim for one thing only—self-replication. Genes don't really "care" about anything else. They just "want" to be replicated. Of course, genes don't have the powers of "caring" for or "wanting" anything. It is persons who care for and want. Therefore, to say that the gene is selfish is not to say that persons, who (like all other living organisms) are designed by genes, are themselves selfish, or even that persons themselves want to replicate their own genes. The idea of a selfish gene is rather more metaphorical, and Dawkins's point is instead a more subtle and profound one: *Persons are designed to engage in behaviors that ultimately make for the replication of the genes that determine their design.* Pinker (1997) captures the point well:

> Many people think that the theory of the selfish gene says that "animals try to spread their genes." This misstates the facts and it misstates the theory. Animals, including most people, know nothing about genetics and care even less. People love their children not because they want to spread their genes (consciously or unconsciously) but because they can't help it. That love makes them try to keep their children warm, fed, and safe. What is selfish is not the real

motives of the person but the metaphorical motives of the genes that built the person. Genes "try" to spread *themselves* by wiring animals' brains so that animals love their kin and try to keep them warm, fed, and safe. (pp. 400–401)

There are at least two very different ways that persons can promote the likelihood of replicating in the next generation those genes that are responsible for their very design and, indeed, existence. The first and more obvious way is to generate and promote one's own biological offspring. A woman who bears and raises to maturity six children passes down twice as many of "her" genes to the next generation as a woman who bears and raises to maturity three children, all other things being equal. The second and less obvious way is to promote the reproduction and well being of those individuals *who share the same genes*. A woman who bears and raises no children but whose one biological sister bears and raises to maturity six children participates (perhaps unwittingly) in a scenario in which *more* of "her" genes are passed down to the next generation, through her biological sister's children, than is the case for a comparable woman who herself bears and raises to maturity two of her own children but whose one and only sister bears none. In that the first woman shares about half of her genes with her sister (as is the case with all biological siblings), six of her sister's children are genetically equivalent, in a simple quantitative sense, to three of her own. Speaking solely in the terms of evolution's cold calculus with respect to the selfish gene, more of the first woman's genes (the equivalent of three offspring) were replicated, even though she produced no offspring herself, compared with the second woman, who bore two of her own children but whose sister bore none. What this contrived example suggests to us is that organisms can participate in the business of replicating the genes that designed them in both direct (through one's offspring) and indirect (through the offspring of kin) ways. With respect to the indirect, anything that an organism does to enhance the reproductive success of those to whom it is biologically related promotes the likelihood that its "own" genes will be passed down to the next generation, in that many of its "own" genes exist "in" its kin.

Because the scientific community in Darwin's day had not yet discovered the role of genes in reproduction and inheritance, Darwin did not have a clear understanding of the different ways, direct and indirect, that organisms promote self-replication. Therefore, evolutionary understandings of behavior were hamstrung by the common appearance of altruism and self-sacrificial acts in the animal kingdom (Simpson, in press). Darwin could not provide a satisfactory answer to the question of why any organism would ever do anything that compromised its own survival, and even reproductive success, to assist another organism. It was not until William Hamilton (1964) elaborated the concept of **inclusive fitness** that a solution to the riddle began to appear. An organism's inclusive fitness is its overall (total, inclusive) ability to maximize the replication of the genes that designed it. Part of that total includes the results of the organism's own reproductive success, but part also includes the reproductive success of close relatives, with whom the organism shares genes. Not only, then, should some organisms be predisposed (by virtue of their genetic makeup) to assist their kin, but they might also be predisposed to sacrifice themselves, under certain circumstances, for the good of their kin. It makes good evolutionary sense that a parent might even give up his or her life if such an action appears necessary to assure the survival of his or her offspring, or even the offspring of kin. For human beings and many other social species, certain kinds of caring and altruistic tendencies should be selected by nature, for they may have functioned to enhance the inclusive fitness of those organisms that exhibited such tendencies.

The Environment of Evolutionary Adaptedness

Human evolution is a long saga of genetic recombination and alteration as individual organisms interact with their environments and struggle to survive. As E. O. Wilson (1978) puts it, "each living form can be viewed as an evolutionary experiment, a product of millions of years of interaction between genes and environment" (p. 17). One must, therefore, take "the long view" to understand the evolution of human beings. The long view tells us that for as much as 99% of our evolutionary history—indeed for at least 2 million years—we (our evolutionary ancestors) lived in small groups as hunters and gatherers (Kenrick, Montello, & McFarlane, 1985; Washburn & Lancaster, 1973). It has only been within the last 10,000 years that humans have taken up agriculture and within the last 4,000 years or so that they have built cities and become urbanites (Diamond, 1997). Some human societies remain hunting-and-gathering societies to this day. Thus, human beings have evolved as successfully adapted to a nomadic way of life, moving in small groups from one domicile to another, hunting prey and gathering food in the wild. This does not mean that we are unable to adapt to other kinds of environments: Obviously, we have created and have adapted quite marvelously to a wide variety of agrarian, industrial, urban, and technological kinds of environments. But human evolution has selected genes that directly or indirectly promote adaptation to a way of life quite different from what most of us experience today.

Current scientific estimates have it that life on earth emerged roughly 3.5 billion years ago. About 3 billion years later (500 million years ago), life evolved beyond simple cells, producing multicellular organisms. Mammals, of which we are one, emerged roughly 200 million years ago. Dinosaurs became extinct about 60 million years ago, and shortly thereafter (that is, 5 million years later) primates, of which we are also one, made their first appearance on the earth. Human beings finally entered the picture anywhere from 2–4 million years ago, emerging most probably in the heart of Africa as a particular kind of primate, which is a particular kind of mammal. Humans gradually migrated in all directions, eventually populating most ecozones on the planet. The period in which human beings emerged and evolved to their current form, therefore, spans at least the past 2 million years, most of which corresponds roughly with what geologists call the Pleistocene Epoch of earth history (running from 1.6 million years ago up to 10,000 years ago, marking the end of the last ice age). Human beings evolved to adapt to the challenges of life in the Pleistocene.

Borrowing a term from Bowlby (1969), let us call the Pleistocene world within which human beings lived and evolved the **environment of evolutionary adaptedness (EEA).** What was human life like in the EEA? The consensus among paleoanthropologists and others who study the evolutionary origins of human life is that our Pleistocene ancestors lived as foragers, gathering fruits and vegetables and hunting prey to supply their bodies with the calories and nutrients required for life. In the EEA, it was generally necessary to move from one hunting and gathering region to another, pursuing prey and seeking out the best geographic areas for gathering food. Humans lived in groups. Indeed, participation in the daily functioning of small cooperative groups may have been a principal survival strategy of early humans (Brewer & Caporael, 1990).

Group life brought with it numerous advantages in the EEA. Humans could better defend themselves against predators and other threats by living together in collectives, looking out for one another in times of danger and consolidating resources, skills, and strength to meet the many challenges they were likely to face, including threats from other groups of humans (deWaal, 1996). Human infants could be nurtured and children raised to maturity in the group, with parents relying on other group members to assist them in their efforts to care for, protect, and educate their own progeny, under the expectation, most likely, that those assisted now would in turn assist later. Hunters could work in groups, too, and once they accomplished the big kill, the meat could be shared and distributed widely in the group. This kind of cooperative activity would appear to benefit the group as a whole, but in addition it might also enhance the inclusive fitness of the individual hunter, for cooperating in the hunt should help to establish the kinds of social relationships and coalitions that benefit the individual's own survival and, ultimately, reproductive success. Pinker (1997) writes:

> The hunter with a dead animal larger than he can eat and about to become a putrefying mass is faced with a unique opportunity. Hunting is largely a matter of luck. In the absence of refrigeration, a good place to store meat for leaner times is in the bodies of other hunters who will return the favor when fortunes reverse. This eases the way for the male coalitions and extensive reciprocity that are ubiquitous in foraging societies. (p. 196)

Most of the human activities necessary for survival and reproductive success in the EEA were set within the parameters of the particular group or band of human beings into which an individual was born. Human beings are by nature social animals because social life proved to be the most propitious strategy for survival and reproductive success in the EEA. Humans have been designed by natural selection *to want to be* together in groups, to seek out one another in bonds of attachment, friendship, partnership, and various other alliances. Like most primates and certain other social species (e.g., dogs, elephants, and dolphins), humans deeply desire and enjoy the company of others. Those few individuals who do not seem to share this social sense (e.g., hermits, autistic children) stand out as oddities, often eliciting from others reactions of fear, pity, or bafflement. By virtue of the EEA, human nature was directed toward sociality; those individuals who did not possess this characteristic were less able to survive and reproduce, meaning they were relatively less successful than their more gregarious counterparts in spreading their own characteristics, via their genes, to subsequent generations, one of those characteristics being their preference for solitude. Darwin describes how it is that some animal species, like humans, have become especially sociable:

> It has often been assumed that animals were in the first place rendered social, and that they feel as a consequence uncomfortable when separated from each other, and comfortable whilst together, but it is a more probable view that these sensations first developed in order that those animals which could profit by living in society should be induced to live together . . . for with those animals which were benefitted by living in close association, the individuals which took the greatest pleasure in society would best escape various dangers; whilst those that cared least for their comrades and lived solitary would perish in greater numbers. (1871, p. 80)

Group life in the EEA was no picnic. While human beings evolved to be social animals, social life entailed competition and conflict as much as cooperation and care. As deWaal (1996) points out, the "greatest disadvantage [of group life] is that one is continuously surrounded by individuals searching for the same food and attracted to the same mates. Groups are breeding grounds for strife and competition, which ironically also pose the strongest threat to their existence" (p. 170). Certain forms of aggression often pay off handsomely in some group contexts, as the biggest, strongest, and most brutal sometimes get their way and capture the lion's share of the resources (e.g., food, shelter, mates) required for survival and reproductive success. Among human groups, dominance can also be established through cleverness, guile, and deceit. Human groups tend to be organized in hierarchical ways. Some individuals dominate others, and one's position in an elaborate dominance pecking order may be closely linked to the resources for survival and reproductive success to which one has access (Buss, 1995). In addition, groups would appear to compete, sometimes ferociously, with each other. Intertribe warfare is not a recent invention. The fossil record indicates that rival groups of humans fought each other often and with great brutality throughout the Pleistocene. As far as we can tell, there was no ancient time when all human beings lived together in peace.

Over evolutionary time, human beings adapted to the challenges of the EEA by honing a set of characteristics that, when taken together, set them apart from all other species on the planet. Humans stood upright, on two feet, freeing their fingers and opposable thumbs for a wide variety of complex and finely tuned motor tasks. They manufactured and depended upon a great many tools. They lived longer than other apes and bore helpless infants who required many years of care before reaching their

In the environment of evolutionary adaptedness, human beings were mainly hunters and gatherers

sexual maturity. Kin negotiated mating relations, such that groups would often exchange sexually mature daughters to build new families and to discourage intercourse between biological brothers and sisters. Sexual intercourse was not limited to particular times of the month for females (as it is in many mammals) but could occur at any time. Males tended to compete for the opportunity to engage in intercourse with females. Males tended to invest in their children, forming more-or-less stable pair bonds with their children's mother(s) and assisting in the defense and training of their young. They toted their children around, protected them against animals and other humans, gave them food. Females cooperated in the care of children and in gathering fruits and vegetables for the clan. Males cooperated in the defense of the group and in hunting, for meat was often a significant staple of the human diet. Humans transported food over long distances, cooked it with fire and processed it extensively, stored it, and shared it. They exchanged goods and favors over extended periods of time, building coalitions and partnerships, cementing friendships, establishing shared understandings and consensual expectations about reciprocity and fair play. They communicated with one another through language and used language, as well as other symbol systems, to disseminate information, pass on traditions, accumulate knowledge and adaptive wisdom, and create culture.

Different human groups developed different cultures. But the cultures may have shared many commonalities, reflecting shared adaptive challenges in the EEA. If indeed such commonalities existed, one might expect to see vestiges of them today in behavioral patterns and social customs that appear to be cross-culturally universal. Anthropological surveys have listed a large number of such universals. These include athletic sports, bodily adornment, cooperative labor, courtship, dancing, education systems, etiquette, family feasting, folklore, food taboos, funeral rites, games, gift giving, incest taboos, inheritance rites, law, marriage, medicine, penal sanctions, personal names, property rights, puberty customs, religious rituals, soul concepts, tool making, weaving, and attempts at weather control. E. O. Wilson (1978) argues that each of these universal patterns can be traced back to hunting-and-gathering societies, where they promoted individual survival and reproduction: "most and perhaps all of the . . . prevailing characteristics of modern societies can be identified as . . . modifications of the biologically meaningful institutions of hunter-gatherer bands and early tribal states" (1978, p. 92). Given that these patterns proved adaptive for thousands, perhaps millions, of years, each has become part of human nature, coded in human genes.

As just one example of a cross-cultural human universal, consider religion. Wilson (1978) states: "The predisposition to religious belief is the most complex and powerful force in the human mind and in all probability an ineradicable part of human nature" (p. 169). The power of religion today lies in the tremendous advantage it bestowed upon our evolutionary ancestors. Religion played a vital role in enabling hunters and gatherers to live together in bands and tribes. The shared beliefs and feelings of kinship engendered by religion helped persuade individuals to subordinate their immediate self-interests to the interests of the group. Such subordination promoted cooperative behavior in the acquisition of resources and defense against dangers, which increased the inclusive fitness of tribe members, as they were better able to reproduce and care for their kin. In addition, religion has always provided human beings with transcendent assurances in the face of the chaos of everyday life, and this, too, may enhance fitness. Wilson writes:

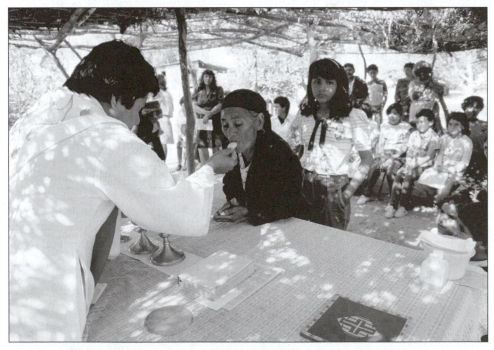

Religious rituals can be found in all cultures, suggesting that human beings have been designed by natural selection to engage in religious practices.

The highest forms of religious practice, when examined more closely, can be seen to confer biological advantage. Above all they congeal identity. In the midst of the chaotic and potentially disorienting experiences each person undergoes daily, religion classifies him, provides him with unquestioned membership in a group claiming great powers, and by this means gives him a driving purpose in life compatible with his self-interest. His strength is the strength of the group, his guide the sacred covenant. (1978, p. 188)

The Adapted Mind

When we think about evolution, we find it easier to consider the gross ways in which physical bodies might gradually change over time in response to selective pressures from the environment. If, for example, having a long neck helps an organism survive and ultimately reproduce more efficiently because it enables that organism, say a giraffe, to obtain food that is elevated above the ground, then subsequent generations may eventually and overall have longer necks. The reason is that those individuals who, by dumb luck, had longer necks to begin with would be more successful in reproduction, on the average, and would thus pass on that adaptive characteristic to subsequent generations. Eventually the characteristic would become a universal feature of the organism's design, as we see with giraffes, because it proved to be so beneficial to inclusive fitness. In the case of human beings, we can see an analogous process producing a retooling of the human skeleton and posture over evolutionary time such that human beings were ultimately able to walk efficiently on two feet and to engage in the kinds of fine motor tasks that helped them develop tools. The refinement of the human skeleton is surely no small evolutionary feat. But the grander legacy of human evolution is surely the way in which the human *brain* has evolved, producing complex behavioral patterns and mental programs that have no parallel in the animal kingdom. Let us think of the human *mind* as what the brain mainly *does*—our thinking, planning, wanting, feeling, and so on (Pinker, 1997). The evolution of the human mind may be more subtle and more difficult to discern than the evolution of the giraffe's neck, but it is far and away more spectacular, and it is first and foremost what makes human beings distinctively human.

Human beings survived and reproduced with felicity in the EEA not because they were bigger, stronger, more brutal, or more caring than their competitors, but because they were smarter. All animals must play with the cards they are dealt by evolution, and for humans the strongest suit has always been the human mind. By outwitting the competition, by teaming up to defend the group, by dividing labor among group members, by developing rational strategies for attack and defense, by refining these strategies through learning and feedback, by communicating these refinements to others and to the next generation via language, by imagining scenarios that have never happened but might and then developing plans to bring those scenarios into reality—through all of this mental activity and much more, human beings have carved out for themselves what Pinker (1997) calls a **cognitive niche** in the evolutionary landscape. Our primary mode of adapting to the challenges of the EEA was and continues to be the use of the human mind's extraordinary cognitive powers. Over evolutionary time, humans eventually

entered the *cognitive niche*. By learning which manipulations achieve which goals, humans have mastered the art of the surprise attack. They use novel, goal-oriented courses of action to overcome the Maginot Line defense of other organisms, which can respond only over evolutionary time. The manipulations can be novel because human knowledge is not just couched in concrete instructions like "how to catch a rabbit." Humans analyze the world using intuitive theories of objects, forces, paths, places, manners, states, substances, hidden biochemical essences, and, for other animals and people, beliefs and desires. People compose new knowledge and plans by mentally playing out combinatorial interactions among these laws in their mind's eye. . . . Living by their wits, human groups develop sophisticated technologies and bodies of folk science. All human cultures ever documented have words for the elements of space, time, motion, speed, mental states, tools, flora, fauna, weather, and logical connectives (not, and, same, opposite, part–whole, and general–particular). They combine words into grammatical sentences and use the underlying propositions to reason about invisible entities like diseases, meteorological forces, and absent animals. (Pinker, 1997, p. 188)

The human mind evolved to adapt to many different threats, challenges, and opportunities. Although the overall goal of adaptation is reproductive success, the EEA presented human beings with a dizzying array of more particular tasks that had to be accomplished if the overall goal was to be achieved. As a result, the adaptive mind may be organized into many different functional modules, each with a specialized design that makes it an expert in one arena of interaction with the world (Kenrick, Keefe, Bryan, Barr, & Brown, 1995; Pinker, 1997; Tooby & Cosmides, 1992). Rather than viewing the mind, therefore, as a general-purpose information-processing machine, contemporary evolutionary psychologists follow the philosophical writings of Fodor (1983) and others who have argued that the mind is more like a collection of rather more specialized subsystems or modules, each designed to address a particular adaptive task that humans faced in the EEA. The many different modules' working in coordination gives the mind its flexibility and adaptive power. To convey this idea, Buss (1997) analogizes the human mind to a carpenter's tool kit:

A carpenter's flexibility comes not from having a single, domain-general, "all-purpose tool" that is used to cut, screw, twist, wrench, plane, balance, and hammer, but rather from having many, more specialized tools, each designed to perform a particular function. It is the numerousness and specificity of the tools in the entire tool kit that give the carpenter greater flexibility, not a highly "plastic" single tool. (p. 325)

Therefore, the human mind contains evolved cognitive, emotional, and motivational mechanisms that are specially targeted to solve those problems in adaptation that have confronted human beings since the time of the Pleistocene. Over 100 years ago, William James (1890) suggested something very similar when he proposed, contrary to many people's intuition, that human beings are endowed *not* with *fewer* biological instincts than the animals, but rather with many *more*. By virtue of human evolution, we come to the world biologically prepared to see, think, feel, want, interpret, and interact in particular ways—ways that have proved, on the average, conducive to inclusive fitness in the evolutionary past and that have, as a result, become part of human nature, encoded in our genes. This is not to suggest that all behavior is determined by blind, evolutionary forces, but rather the contrary: The human mind's flexibility and capacity for creating complex culture and for being shaped by the culture that it creates are all the direct result of the human mind's very nature as a complex collection of domain-specific programs and modules. It is because we come into the world so exquisitely prepared to meet a wide range of particular challenges first posed in the EEA that we are so able to learn from and become products of our environments and so capable of exhibiting the kind of learning, flexibility, and cultural sensitivity that are the hallmarks of adaptive human behavior.

In sum, then, human behavior is not driven by one or two primary instincts or basic needs. Instead, human beings have evolved to solve many different problems, resulting in a panoply of highly evolved and specially designed subsystems, plans, desires, and so on, loosely organized into a complex arrangement we call the human mind. The many different demands of human living call upon us to be specialists rather than generalists. In the EEA, those demands might be grouped into two general classes: those of individual survival and reproduction. Darwin (1859) identified many of the survival problems under the heading of "hostile forces of nature." These include food shortages, harsh climate, disease, parasites, predators, and natural hazards. Reproductive problems are typically more social in quality and, therefore, more centrally implicated in personality. Buss (1991a) lists eight classes of reproductive problems:

1. *Successful intrasexual competition:* The individual must win out over competitors in gaining access to desirable members of the opposite sex so that sexual reproduction can occur.

2. *Mate selection:* The individual must select those mates who have the greatest reproductive value to maximize the opportunity for passing his/her genes down to the next generation.

3. *Successful conception:* The individual must engage in the necessary social and sexual behaviors to fertilize a mate or become fertilized by the mate.

4. *Mate retention:* The individual must retain the mate, preventing the encroachment of intrasexual competitors as well as preventing the mate's defection or desertion. This problem is more acute among species and individuals who pursue "long-term mating strategies" and does not apply to what Buss (1991a, p. 465) calls "brief, opportunistic copulation."

5. *Reciprocal dyadic alliance formation:* The individual must develop a relationship with the mate characterized by a certain degree of cooperation and reciprocity.

6. *Coalition building and maintenance:* The individual must cooperate with others whose interests are aligned with his/her own, building coalitions that compete successfully with rival groups.

7. *Parental care and socialization:* The individual must engage in actions that ensure the survival and reproductive success of his or her own offspring.

8. *Extraparental kin investment:* The individual must sacrifice his or her own self-interests to promote the survival and reproductive success of nondescendant genetic relatives. The reproductive success of genetic relatives is important because they share with the individual some of the same genes.

How do human beings deal with these problems? Drawing upon evolved internal mechanisms, we formulate goal-directed *tactics* and *strategies* that aim ultimately to assure our survival and reproductive success. We must remember, however, that the aims of survival and reproductive success are not typically conscious, or even unconscious, "goals" or "intentions" in human behavior and experience. In general terms, evolution has designed the human mind so that it will generate strategies and tactics to produce goal-directed behaviors that, on the average, tended to promote inclusive fitness in the EEA. To take the obvious example, sexual activity will, on the average, produce more babies than will no sexual activity. But people do not usually engage in sexual activity for the express purpose of conceiving children, although of course they sometimes do. Most typically, people are motivated to engage in sexual activity because sexual activity is so pleasurable. Evolution has shaped sexual activity to be extraordinarily pleasurable so that people will engage in it often, assuring that offspring will eventually be produced. It is a brilliant strategy! Rather than leaving it up to people to decide whether they want children or not, the selfish genes have conspired to assure that human beings, prior to the advent of modern contraception, will indeed produce children, whether they intend to or not, by offering them an activity that is so pleasurable and compelling as to be almost irresistible.

The *distal*, evolutionary reason for human sexual activity is to replicate the genes, but the *proximate*, individual motivation for engaging in sexual activity is that it feels good. The distinction between distal and proximate is crucial for understanding the significance of human evolution for personality psychology (Archer, 1988; Wright, 1994). To explain behavior in terms of proximate causes is to appeal to the immediate environmental, physiological, and cognitive mechanisms that determine a person's behavior. By contrast, distal explanations consider the significance of behavioral patterns in the ultimate terms of evolution and inclusive fitness. Some proximate causes may be derivatives of distal influences, but the influence of the distal on the proximate is typically very subtle and indirect, and it is typically best expressed in broad terms such as those applying to human nature in the overall rather than in the particular behaviors of any one individual person.

The distinction between proximate and distal is especially important in considering the different strategies and tactics that women and men may develop around sexual reproduction itself. In most ways, male and female humans faced pretty much the same selection pressures in the EEA. From an evolutionary standpoint, therefore, we would not expect to find strong sex differences in most areas of human behavior and experience. However, evolutionary theory would lead us to predict sex differences in any domain where women and men faced dramatically different selection pressures and adaptive challenges. The one area where that was surely true in the EEA is reproduction. The indisputable biological facts in this regard are that women, not men, become pregnant, that pregnancy requires a nine-month gestation period, and that at the end of that period women give birth to human infants and provide them with nourishment through breast-feeding. Seen in an evolutionary perspective, these facts suggest that men and women should, on the average, operate according to somewhat different strategies and express somewhat different goals when it comes to activities centered on sexual reproduction, such as the activity of human mating.

Mating

In terms of evolution, men and women mate for the prime reason of producing offspring, who will carry their genes into the next generation. The tactics and strategies whereby men and women seek to accomplish this end, however, differ markedly as a function of gender. For the male, it is to his "advantage" (technically, to the advantage of his genes) to impregnate as many females as possible, since this is the major way he can be assured of passing down his own genes. Theoretically, it is possible for a male to sire hundreds of offspring. (You may recall that, in a celebrated biography, the former professional basketball player Wilt Chamberlain claimed to have had sexual relations with 20,000 different women.) Hence, males may be biologically more inclined than females toward sexual promiscuity. The female, on the other hand, must invest a great deal of time and energy in each birth and can have only a very limited number of offspring. It is to her advantage (technically, to the advantage of her genes) to be "choosy" when it comes to sexual intercourse, securing a single mate for assistance in protecting and raising her offspring, thereby maximizing the likelihood of passing her own genes to the next generation.

My characterization of sex differences in mating as they apply to human evolution is exaggerated to make a point. But the point is actually rather subtle, and it needs to be qualified in a number of ways. First, an evolutionary explanation for sex differences in human mating strategies may not necessarily contradict or work against cultural and environmental explanations of the same phenomena, which tend to be couched in more proximate rather than distal terms. Proximate factors that discourage female promiscuity, for example, range from the cultural double standard with which most Americans are familiar (young women are supposed to be careful, while young men may "play around") to the oppressive laws and brutal practices (e.g., female circumcision in some African societies) that have been devised to keep women from seeking sexual gratification outside the marriage bond. Societal norms, values, laws, sanctions, and various other cultural practices shape sexuality in profound ways. Feature 2.A compares and contrasts evolutionary and cultural explanations for sex differences in mate selection preferences. Second, natural selection often operates on the emotional and motivational mechanisms behind behavior, rather than behavior per se. Behavioral strategies are manifestations of human *desire*. According to the evolutionary view, men typically *want* to engage in sexual relations with many partners, to a greater extent than women, on the average, typically want to engage in sexual relations with many partners; men can readily wrap their minds around the idea of having intercourse with a great many lovers over time and in many different situations; their *fantasies* go in the direction of promiscuity, even if their behavior often does not.

A third qualification is this: Evolutionary explanations for differences in mating strategies, just like cultural explanations, are not *moral* justifications or rationalizations for sex differences in sexual behavior. To seek a scientific explanation for any behavior pattern is *not* to seek a justification, ethical or legal, for that pattern. If the distal reason for male promiscuity is that such a strategy enhanced inclusive fitness of males in the EEA, we are still left to decide whether such a pattern of behavior today is good, is bad, should be promoted, should be sanctioned, or whatever. It is very dangerous, if not downright wrong, to look to the EEA for moral guidance in today's world.

Fourth, we should consider more carefully the evolutionary logic of sex differences in mating strategies. When it comes to reproduction, most mammals, including humans, show dramatic sex differences with respect to *speed*. Males are fast; females are slow (Bailey, Gaulin, Agyei, & Gladue, 1994). What this means is that any male's single reproductive venture is relatively short-lived, consisting simply of copulation. By contrast, any female's single reproductive venture must include, at minimum, copulation, gestation, and lactation. That all takes a long time. During that long period it

FEATURE 2.A

The Origins of Sex Differences: Evolution Versus Social Structure

That men and women tend to differ in their mating strategies is a point that few social scientists dispute. While significant variability across cultures and within any given human culture can be observed, human males in general would appear to be more desirous of sexual relations with a wider range of partners, whereas human females do in general appear to be more discriminating when it comes to sexual partners and more reluctant to engage in casual sexual activity. The controversy comes in when we try to explain why this is so. What are the ultimate origins of this general difference between the sexes?

Evolutionary psychologists such as David Buss argue that men and women tend to differ in mating strategies because they faced different mating challenges over the course of evolution. Because the minimal male contribution to paternity is the impregnation of a female, males can afford to invest little in any particular mate while increasing their chances of impregnating many mates through indiscriminate sexual activity. By contrast, because the female can give birth to no more than a small number of offspring and because she must invest heavily in any particular offspring if it is to survive and flourish, females are likely to be more selective in choosing sexual partners. Furthermore, males are likely to value youthful beauty in their choice of mates, for beauty may be a rough proxy for health and fertility, and the healthiest and most fertile women are most likely to bear offspring who will survive to maturity. By contrast, females may place more value on a mate's resources and status, for a man of means is more likely to provide the support needed to raise a child to maturity. As a result of different selection pressures that prevailed throughout the ancestral environment, males and females may have evolved different adaptive mechanisms for mating and mate selection, expressed as different patterns of desire and feeling.

The evolutionary-psychology explanation for differences in mating has not, however, gone unchallenged. Social psychologists Alice Eagly and Wendy Wood, for example, have offered a strong alternative explanation for these differences—an explanation that emphasizes social structures (Eagly & Wood, 1999). Eagly and Wood view sex differences in mating as just on example of a more general difference between the sexes in social dominance. Some men are able to engage in relatively indiscriminate sexual activity because they are accorded positions of status and power in society that enable them to behave in this manner with few negative consequences. "Men's adaptations to greater power and status produce dominant behavior," write Eagly and Wood (p. 412). By contrast, many women tend to occupy subordinate roles in many societies. "Subordinate behavior is more compliant to social influence, less overtly aggressive, and more cooperative and conciliatory" (p. 412). Futhermore, men and women generally seek to accomodate to sex-typical roles by developing sex-stereotypical skills, attitudes, and traits. Therefore, men learn skills that prepare them well for assuming male-dominated occupational roles, which produces patterns of assertive and independent behavior. By contrast, women learn domestic skills such as cooking that prepare them for assuming such female-dominated roles as homemaker and caregiver. Women's accomodation to the domestic roles and

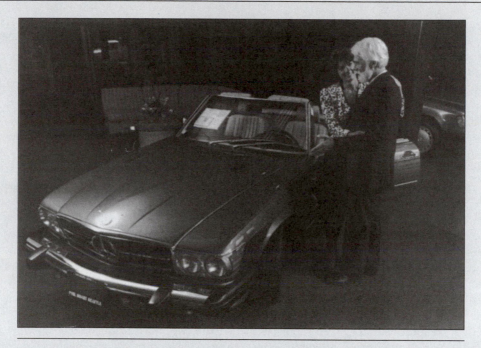

Popular ads reflect the sociobiology of human mate selection: a wealthy man and a beautiful woman.

female-dominated occupations produces a pattern of interpersonally facilitative and friendly behaviors. In particular, the assignment of the majority of child rearing to women encourages nurturant behaviors that facilitate care for children and dependent individuals.

To the extent, then, that men are more dominant and women are more communal in their social behaviors (including mating behaviors), these differences may originate in the contrasting social positions of men and women. In contemporary American society, as in many world societies, women have less power and status than men and control fewer resources. In addition, women perform more domestic work than men and spend fewer hours in paid employment (Shelton, 1992).

Although most women in the United States are employed in the paid wokforce, they tend to have lower wages than men, are concentrated in different occupations, and are thinly represented at the highest levels of organizational hierarchies. From the standpoint of social structures, therefore, sex differences in social behavior stem mainly from features of social organization—in particular from the gender hierarchy of power and status on the one hand and the sexual division of labor on the other.

Eagly and Wood concede that the factors of gender hierarchy and sexual division of labor themselves are influenced by biological

continued on next page

differences between men and women. Men's greater size and upper-body strength give them priority in traditional warfare and in occupations involving strenuous activity. The fact that women bear and raise children gives them priority in caring for the very young. But Eagly and Wood express considerable skepticism about the idea that men and women have evolved to develop innately different psychological perspectives on mating and reproduction. Instead, the differences that do exist are viewed to be by-products of social learning. Physical sex differences, such as men's greater strength and women's ability to bear children, therefore, interact with society's economic system and cultural beliefs to influence the roles held by men and women. When it comes to mating strategies, for example, it makes good sense from a social-structural perspective that women should seek out men with good earning potential, especially in societies in which men are the main wage earners. Both men and women seek to maximize their utilities with respect to mating choices, just as they do for other decisions. In many societies, then, men and women seek an equilibrium in marriage whereby a man's ability to provide earnings for his wife and family is exchanged for a woman's contributions in terms of household production and other attributes such as education and beauty (Becker, 1976). Every society finds a different equilibrium. Eagly and Wood have shown, for example, that in societies with relatively more egalitarian gender roles (e.g., societies in which women are relatively empowered with respect to political positions and occupational status), certain traditional sex differences in mating choice are reduced. In societies that empower women, women are somewhat less likely than they are in more patriarchal societies to choose mates based on their earning potential, and men are somewhat less likely to choose mates based on their domestic skills. These traditional sex differences in mate selection remain, but their strength is somewhat reduced when men and women assume roles that approach comparability in status and power.

Social-structural explanations for sex differences in social behavior are generally well-accepted in psychology, as we will see in Chapter 4. But there is considerable disagreement about how these kinds of explanations relate to those that emphasize biological factors and human evolution. Evolutionary psychologists tend to argue that social-structural determinants of behavior *are built on* biological differences that are the product of evolution. When it comes to differences in mating behavior and preferences, therefore, evolutionary psychologists argue that variables such as gender hierarchy and division of labor between the sexes may be *proximate* causes of some gender differences, but that these proximate causes stem ultimately from *distal* determinants rooted in human evolution. Because evolutionary and social-structural approaches to sex differences in human behavior can make many of the same predictions and explain many of the same findings concerning sex differences, it is difficult to disentangle the two approaches and to line them up against each other. At the present time, however, it would appear that more and more personality and social psychologists are becoming interested in evolutionary approaches. As this interest increases in the coming years, we will probably see more efforts to create a dialogue between those social scientists who emphasize evolutionary explanations for human nature and those who focus their energies on explaining human behavior in terms of culture and learning.

does her no good, in terms of inclusive fitness, to have intercourse with another man. She is already pregnant and must patiently wait as the slow process of bringing a viable offspring into the world (and then providing some care for it afterward) unfolds. Theoretically, her faster male counterpart can engage in numerous reproductive ventures (copulations) in the meantime, each offering the possibility of replicating his genes and thus enhancing his inclusive fitness. Of course, there is a limited supply of females to go around, there being roughly a 1:1 sex ratio. The male's reproductive efforts, therefore, are limited by the supply of available females and by the competitive efforts of his male peers to gain access to those females. Put another way, the fast sex (male) is constrained by the limited supply of reproductive opportunities afforded by the slow sex (female). Thus, the fast sex must compete for access to the slow sex, and the slow sex enjoys the relative luxury of picking and choosing among a host of eager mates. According to this logic, the fast sex should be predisposed toward maximizing quantity of offspring. In that sexual activity is the vehicle for accomplishing this, the fast sex should indeed be more promiscuous, *or at least desire to be so.*

That males, in fact, *are* more promiscuous has been documented repeatedly. In most societies, men in general have sexual relations with more partners than do women, a difference that is most striking when comparing homosexual men to lesbian women (Bailey et al., 1994; Cunningham, 1981). In addition, men appear to be much less discriminating in their choice of sexual partners. In one study, Kenrick (1989) asked college men to consider what personal qualities were required in a prospective sexual partner. Except on the dimension of physical attractiveness, women tended to be much choosier than men with respect to what attributes they insisted their partner should possess before they would consider sexual relations. In many cases, men reported that they were willing to have sexual relations with a woman who, by virtue of her low intelligence or obnoxious personality, they would not even consider dating! In other words, men held up stricter criteria for a casual date than they did for sex.

Cross-culturally, the widespread practice of polygyny—in which one man mates with more than one woman—also supports the evolutionary hypothesis concerning sex differences in mating strategies. In a polygynous arrangement, men are able to mate with many different women (increasing their fitness) while many different women are assured of a mate and (because the practice is culturally sanctioned) an attendant social system supportive of their offspring (increasing their fitness, as well). By contrast, the cultural arrangement of polyandry, whereby one woman mates with many different men, is extremely rare. Wilson (1978) describes the stark differences:

> [As a species, human beings are] moderately polygynous, with males initiating most of the changes in sexual partnership. About three-fourths of all human societies permit the taking of multiple wives, and most of them encourage the practice by law and custom. In contrast, marriage to multiple husbands is sanctioned in less than one percent of societies. The remaining monogamous societies usually fit that category in a legal sense only, with concubinage and other extramarital stratagems being added to allow *de facto* polygyny. (pp. 125–126)

If men and women have evolved to adopt markedly different reproductive tactics and strategies, then we might expect that these differences would create a good deal of conflict between the sexes, leading to anger and upset. From an evolutionary point of view, we might expect that men should become especially angry and upset about women's refusal to engage them in sexual relations (sexually withholding behaviors).

By contrast, women should experience anger and upset as a result of men's excessive insistence on sexual relations (sexually aggressive behaviors). Buss (1989b) presented college students and newlyweds with a long list of behaviors that are likely to evoke anger and upset and asked them to endorse those behaviors that their respective dating partners or spouses had committed during the previous year. The study's results support the evolutionary prediction about sexually withholding behaviors (men report that women do this more) but not the one about sexually aggressive behaviors (women do not report higher levels than do men). As is evident in Table 2.1, the respondents in the study endorsed a wide variety of partner behaviors eliciting anger and upset, most of which do not seem to be associated with sexual relations per se. Compared with men's reports, women tended to complain most about condescending, neglecting, and insulting behaviors on the part of their male partners. By contrast, men reported higher levels of moodiness and self-absorption on the part of their female partners.

Buss, Larsen, Westen, and Semmelroth (1992) asked undergraduate students how upset they would be if their romantic partners failed to be faithful to them in various ways. Which would bother you more? (a) Your partner develops a deep emotional attachment to another person, or (b) your partner engages in passionate sexual intercourse with another person. Among the male respondents, about 40% chose the first option and 60% chose the second. In other words, slightly more males said that they would be more bothered by their partner's sexual betrayal than they might be by their partner's emotional betrayal. By contrast, 82% of the female respondents chose option

| TABLE 2.1 | *Average Levels of Upset Elicitors in Male and Female Partners* |

	SEX OF TARGET OF COMPLAINT		
UPSET ELICITOR	MALE	FEMALE	P
Condescending	.14	.08	.000
Neglecting–Rejecting–Unreliable	.16	.11	.000
Inconsiderate	.23	.09	.000
Abuses Alcohol–Emotionally Constricted	.16	.13	.033
Insulting of Appearance	.04	.02	.021
Physically Self-absorbed	.07	.14	.000
Moody	.19	.30	.000
Sexually Withholding	.06	.14	.000
Possessive–Jealous–Dependent	.17	.19	ns
Abusive	.05	.06	ns
Unfaithful	.06	.07	ns
Sexualizes Others	.12	.15	ns
Disheveled	.07	.05	ns
Sexually Aggressive	.03	.02	ns
Self-centered	.21	.18	ns
Total	.12	.11	ns

Note: $N = 528$. "*Ns*" means the difference between males and females is *not* statistically significant.
From Buss (1989b), p. 740.

"a." In other words, approximately four-fifths of the women said they would be more upset by the emotional betrayal than by the sexual betrayal. In a second question, the researchers asked whether you would be more upset by your partner's "falling in love" with another person or by your partner's engaging in sexual activity with another person involving many "different sexual positions." For this one, the tendency for both men and women was to say that they would be more bothered by their partner's falling in love with another person. However, this response tendency was much stronger for women. Among men, 55% said they would be more bothered by their partner's falling in love, and 45% said they would be more bothered by their partner's engaging in various sexual activities with another. Among women, a whopping 88% said they would be more bothered by their partner's falling in love, and only 12% said that the sexual indiscretions would bother them more.

Beyond sex differences in evolved reproductive strategies, men and women also look for different qualities in a prospective sexual partner. Evolutionary theory suggests that the choosy female should prefer to mate with a male of high social status and significant material resources, since he is most likely to promote her inclusive fitness. By contrast, the male should prefer to mate with the most fertile young women available, since they are most likely to bear offspring to carry his genes. As a result, the argument goes, older men (who have more necessary resources) tend to marry younger women (who have many years of childbearing ahead of them) (Snowdon, 1983).

Consistent with these predictions are the data from a number of studies (e.g., Kenrick, Keefe, Bryan, Barr, & Brown, 1995; Sprecher, Sullivan, & Hatfield, 1994). For example, Buss and Barnes (1986) examined mate selection preferences among 92 married couples and 100 unmarried college students. They found that in choosing a sexual mate, men placed major emphasis on a woman's physical beauty (generally associated with youth) while women placed major emphasis on a man's earning potential. One might argue, however, that the inequality in earning potential for most men and women in contemporary American society renders mate selection one of the few viable means for securing adequate material resources for some women. Women's pragmatic approach to choosing a mate, therefore, may have as much to do with present cultural constraints and norms as it does with a biological mandate to maximize inclusive fitness. However, it is interesting to note that the differences Buss and Barnes found in the United States have also been found in a number of other cultures as well. In a study of 37 different cultures, Buss (1989a) found that men tend to prefer younger, physically attractive mates while women place greater value on slightly older mates possessing ambition, an industrious nature, and good financial prospects.

The sociobiology of human mate selection may even be evident in the way in which we judge the attractiveness of women's and men's faces (Cunningham, 1981; Cunningham, Barbee, & Pike, 1990). Both men and women prefer female faces with the childlike features of large eyes, small nose and small chin, the sexually mature features of high cheekbones and narrow cheeks, and the expressive features of a large smile and eyebrows set clearly above the eyes. A full, thick head of hair is also judged to be a significant female asset. Overall, the most attractive female face suggests youth, sexual maturity, good health, and friendliness. In our evolutionary past (long before people kept track of exactly how old they were—before indeed counting systems were invented), these features may have served as facial cues of fertility in females, suggests Buss (1989a). This is why we find them attractive today.

Surprisingly, attractive male faces share some of the same features. In three experiments, Cunningham, Barbee, and Pike (1990) demonstrated that American college women preferred faces of men who possessed large eyes, large cheekbones, and expressive smiles. In addition, prominent chins, thick eyebrows, and high-status clothing were judged to be especially attractive in men. The authors of the study argue that women judge men's faces with at least two implicit and somewhat contradictory criteria in mind. Women prefer men who are "cute" in an almost childlike way, as suggested by the big eyes and smiles. But in keeping with what evolutionary theory might predict, they also prefer men who exude maturity and social dominance, as indicated in the prominent chins, thick eyebrows, and high-status clothing. Women may see mature and socially dominant men as the best candidates for long-term relationships in that such men are best positioned in their society to provide the material resources that are required for the successful socialization of offspring.

A central tenet of Darwinian theory is that organisms compete with each other for limited reproductive resources. Darwin was intrigued by the existence in the animal kingdom of characteristics that seem to impair survival but nonetheless promote reproductive success by giving an organism a competitive edge. The elaborate plumage, heavy horns, and conspicuous displays of many species seem costly in the currency of survival. However, these characteristics increase success in mating and so evolve despite their cost. When it comes to humans, evolutionary theory predicts that men and women will compete for reproductive resources in contrasting ways. Given the evolutionary premium placed on feminine youth and beauty, women should strive to enhance their physical appearance in competing with one another to attract men. Given the evolutionary premium placed on masculine dominance and status, men should compete to attract women through displays of social dominance, employing tactics such as boasting of their accomplishments and future earning potential.

In order to test these hypotheses, Buss (1988) conducted a series of studies to identify the most common tactics of mate attraction employed by college men and women and by newlyweds. As predicted, women tended to use tactics aimed at enhancing their physical attractiveness, endorsing such behaviors as "wear makeup," "wear stylish clothes," "keep clean and groomed," and "wear jewelry." By contrast, men tended to use such tactics as "display resources" and "brag about resources." Men were more likely than women to display expensive possessions and to boast about accomplishments. However, the research is also noteworthy for the strong agreement that was found between men and women with respect to those behavioral tactics viewed to be most successful in obtaining reproductive resources. The acts frequently performed and considered most highly effective for *both sexes* involved displaying sympathy, kindness, good manners, helpfulness, and humor. In a related vein, Jensen-Campbell, Grabiano, and West (1995) found that women find men who exhibit "prosocial" tendencies (being kind, considerate, altruistic) to be especially attractive and desirable. Despite the sex differences obtained, therefore, men and women still show remarkable similarity in the tactics and strategies they employ to attract mates.

Of course the attraction of mates is only half of the story from the standpoint of inclusive fitness. Mating leads to reproduction. Here again marked sex differences are expected. The biology of sexual reproduction and child rearing dictates that the female "invest" more in any given offspring than the male (Trivers, 1971). Since the female expends much more time and energy than the male in bearing and raising the offspring, some have argued, she may be more inclined to form a closer emotional attachment to the offspring than is the male who happens to be the father. In addition, a male can rarely be 100% certain that he is in fact the father of any particular offspring, whereas maternity is never in doubt. Therefore, the bond between males and their offspring is likely to be tenuous and ambivalent. Furthermore, biological relatives of the mother (maternal grandparents, maternal uncles and aunts) should form closer attachment bonds to the offspring than should the biological relatives of the father, partly because of the uncertainty of the "true" father.

Littlefield and Rushton (1986) tested evolutionary hypotheses about differential investment in offspring in a study of parents whose children had recently died. A sample of 263 bereaved parents filled out a lengthy questionnaire assessing the degree of their own grieving after the death of the child, their judgments of the grieving process in other family members, and a number of other factors and issues concerning the death of the child. Supporting the authors' predictions, the findings showed that mothers grieved more intensely than fathers, mothers' siblings grieved more intensely than fathers' siblings, and maternal grandparents grieved more intensely than paternal grandparents. With respect to the last finding, the maternal grandmother showed the highest level of grieving, followed by the maternal grandfather and paternal grandmother, who were about even, followed finally by the paternal grandfather, who showed the lowest level of grieving.

As intriguing as the results from Littlefield and Rushton's study are, there may be a danger in equating, as the researchers do, the intensity of grief with the degree of attachment. The implication is that, because they grieve more intensely when their children die, mothers have a stronger emotional bond with their children than do fathers. Grief, however, is a very complicated human experience, and its relationship to love and attachment is not clearly understood (Archer, 1988; Freud, 1917/1957). In addition, the suggestion that the mother–infant bond is markedly stronger and more "natural" than the father–infant bond does not to date enjoy clear research support. As we shall see later in this chapter, psychologists have documented both important similarities and differences between mother–infant and father–infant attachments.

In conclusion, evolutionary theory suggests that overall sex differences should evolve only in those domains where men and women faced dramatically different selection pressures in the EEA. The one domain where such differential selection most likely occurred, therefore, is sexual reproduction. Men and women may have evolved different strategies and tactics for attracting and keeping sexual mates, differences that may be grounded in different patterns of desire. One writer has characterized these differences as resulting from an evolutionary arms race between the sexes (Wright, 1994). Men and women have built up two different arsenals in the age-old battle between the sexes. Both have at their disposal powerful weapons, accumulated and perfected over thousands of years of selection, for seducing, attracting, repelling, distracting, deceiving, maintaining, and exploiting their mates. Many popular songs tell it well: Romantic love is not for the faint of heart.

While selection pressures may have functioned as the distal origins of sex differences in human mating patterns, a wide variety of proximate causes for such differences can be observed in cultural norms and rules, religious and political values, and different patterns of socialization. Furthermore, while clear sex differences in mating strategies have been observed, research also indicates that men and women have much

FEATURE 2.B

Some Women (and Men) Are Choosier Than Others: Sociosexuality

Natural selection presents us with a stark question: How are we to maximize the possibility of passing our genes down to the next generation? The biology of sexual reproduction dictates two divergent answers: For men, it is best to impregnate as many females as possible, under the assumption that at least some of the resultant offspring will survive to maturity so that they, too, will reproduce and keep the genes moving down the line. For women, it is best to choose carefully, to select a mate who will provide reliable care and assistance and thus maximize the chance that the very limited number of offspring any particular woman can produce will indeed reach maturity and eventually reproduce themselves. The divergent challenges natural selection poses for men and women may help explain general sex differences in mating strategies, for women do indeed seem to be choosier than men. But we all realize that there is wide variation among both women and men with respect to sexual attitudes and behaviors. Why, for example, are some women choosier than others? And why aren't all men trying to seduce nearly every woman they meet?

In a series of provocative articles, Jeffry Simpson and Steven Gangestad argue that, in terms of inclusive fitness and human evolution, it is to some women's advantage to be especially *non*choosy. Similarly, some men may be naturally selected to adopt a more discriminating approach to sexual relations (Gangestad, 1989; Gangestad & Simpson, 1990; Gangestad, Simpson, DiGeronimo, & Biek, 1992; Simpson & Gangestad, 1991, 1992; Simpson, Gangestad, & Biek, 1993). Simpson and Gangestad attempt to provide an evolutionary explanation for differences in **sociosexuality.** On one end of the continuum, individuals exhibiting a *restricted* sociosexuality insist on commitment and closeness in a relationship prior to engaging in sex with a romantic partner. Like the prototypical choosy female, both men and women with restricted sociosexuality require emotional closeness before they feel comfortable with sexual relations. They have few sexual partners, but their sexual relationships tend to endure for a long time. On the other end of the spectrum, individuals exhibiting an *unrestricted* sociosexuality tend to feel relatively comfortable engaging in sex without commitment or closeness. Like the prototypical dominant male, both women and men with unrestricted sociosexuality have several different sexual partners, and each sexual relationship is likely to endure for a relatively short period of time.

To assess individual differences in sociosexuality, Simpson and Gangestad have developed a questionnaire that asks respondents (usually college students) to report frequency of sexual relations in the past six months, number of lifetime sexual partners, number of partners in the past year, number of partners desired, number of different partners foreseen for the next five years, number of "one night stands," frequency of sexual thoughts, and frequency of fantasies about having sex with people who are currently not their partners (Simpson & Gangestad, 1991). The research shows that college students scoring toward the unrestricted end of the scale tend (1) to engage in sex at an earlier point in their relationships, (2) to engage in sex with more than one partner during a given period in time, and (3) to be involved in relationships characterized by less investment, commitment, love, and dependency (Simpson & Gangestad, 1991). The results also show that sociosexuality is independent of sex drive. In other words, being unrestricted with respect to sociosexuality is not the same thing as, nor can it be explained by, having a strong sex drive. Within sexually active couples, for example, the woman's score on sociosexuality is uncorrelated with the frequency with which she engages in sexual intercourse with her partner.

In a study of romantic partner choice, Simpson and Gangestad (1992) found that individuals with unrestricted sociosexuality tend to prefer romantic partners who are especially physically attractive and have high social visibility. The authors presented college students with two hypothetical romantic partners, Person A and Person B:

> Person A is considered physically attractive and "sexy." He/she has a sort of charisma that attracts the attention of those around him/her. Although some might consider him/her arrogant, A possesses a kind of self-confidence that others admire. A is not known, however, for living a responsible life-style. In the past, he/she has had a series of relatively short-term relationships. Some have ended because of questionable faithfulness on the part of A.

> Person B is an average looking person, someone most people wouldn't consider "sexy." He/she is sufficiently socially skilled but does not possess the kind of magnetic personality that draws the attention of others. Rather B has a stable and responsible personality. In a relationship, B is caring, dependable, and faithful.

> He/she would like very much to have a family, likes children, and would probably be good with them. (Simpson & Gangestad, 1992, pp. 39–40)

After reading both vignettes, the participants in the study determined which of the two persons they were attracted to, which they would prefer as a romantic partner, and which was more similar to the person with whom they were currently involved. For both men and women, unrestricted individuals allotted a significantly larger number of their choices to the attractive and dominant Person A compared with restricted individuals. By contrast, restricted individuals tended to prefer the reliable and caring Person B. In a second study, the authors found that the actual partners of the respondents did indeed possess the qualities that the respondents tended to desire. For both men and women, the romantic partners of unrestricted individuals tended to score lower on measures of faithfulness/loyalty, kindness/understanding, and responsibility; higher on measures of social visibility; and were actually rated by observers as physically more attractive compared with romantic partners of respondents scoring toward the restricted end of the sociosexuality continuum.

So what does this have to do with evolution? Simpson and Gangestad argue that natural selection may have favored both restricted and unrestricted sociosexuality for both certain males and certain females. While it is easy to see the advantages of unrestricted sociosexuality for some dominant males, it is certainly true that every male cannot be a Don Juan. For one thing, there are not enough available women to go around, and in the starkly nonegalitarian world that Darwin

continued on next page

FEATURE 2.B *continued*

has described, dominant males will usually attract the most mates, leaving many nondominant males with fewer options. The competitive powers of such nondominant males may be enhanced, however, by exhibiting traits of reliability and willingness to invest in relationships. Therefore, "males in evolutionary history who invested heavily in a mate's offspring should have desired long-term partners who demonstrated sexual exclusivity to the relationship, as revealed by resolute faithfulness and commitment" (Simpson & Gangestad, 1992, p. 34). Restricted sociosexuality can prove adaptive for some men in making them especially appealing to certain women who are most strongly concerned about relational investment.

For many females, the advantage of restricted sociosexuality is very clear. The choosy female enhances her inclusive fitness by selecting the most reliable mate. She may indeed end up "settling down" with a mate whose sociosexual orientation is similarly restricted, as suggested in the above paragraph. But men have more to offer women than rela-

tional investment, Simpson and Gangestad point out. Men can also offer "good genes." For women, relatively unrestricted sociosexuality may have the advantage of enabling them to mate with the most attractive and most dominant men. (Recall that both college men and women with unrestricted sociosexuality show strong preferences for attractiveness and social visibility in their partners.) While some of these attractive men may not prove to be reliable mates in the long run, they still offer the prize of a genetic endowment tending toward dominance and attractiveness. If the distal, evolutionary goal is to pass one's own genes to succeeding generations, then the unrestricted female who mates with attractive and dominant men enjoys the potential advantage of seeing those traits of attractiveness and dominance replicated in her own offspring. Should these offspring survive to maturity, they themselves may be blessed with an advantage in the mating marketplace. This should be especially apparent in male offspring, or what Simpson and Gangestad refer to as "sexy sons." If a woman's son grows up

in common when it comes to mating. Both sexes, for example, value honesty, compassion, and sincerity in their mates, and both work hard to induce their mates to be faithful. Inclusive fitness, for both females and males, depends on the maturation of *viable* progeny. If a male sires 10 offspring and *none* survive (say, for lack of resources), then the evolutionary scoreboard records a big, fat zero for his inclusive fitness. Human males and females establish long-term pair bonds in all societies. Males and females have a common vested interest today, as they did even in the EEA, in assuring that the carriers of their genes—the next generation—survive, flourish, and ultimately reproduce themselves. Even in mating, then, we are all as much alike as we are different.

Getting Along and Getting Ahead

Robert Hogan has developed a broad theory of personality that incorporates an evolutionary understanding of the person while tying together strands from Freudian psychoanalysis (Chapter 3 in this book) and sociological role theory. Hogan calls his to be especially attractive and dominant, then he is relatively well positioned to mate with many different women, potentially passing his own (and his mother's) genes down to the next generation.

If the above reasoning is correct, then the woman exhibiting unrestricted sociosexuality should maximize her genetic fitness in the production of sons, for the "sexy son" may potentially sire a greater number of offspring than the most fertile (and attractive) daughter could ever produce. One would predict, therefore, that natural selection should have arranged things such that unrestricted women should give birth to more sons than should women with a restricted sociosexual orientation. Gangestad and Simpson provide some very limited but tantalizing support for this startling hypothesis, drawing upon data on sexual attitudes and behavior of Americans collected by Alfred Kinsey in the late 1940s and 50s (Gangestad, 1989; Gangestad & Simpson, 1990). Using reported number of premarital sexual partners as a rough index of sociosexuality in women, Simpson and Gangestad found a very modest but statistically significant correlation between number of premarital partners and the tendency to bear male children. Those women who scored in the top 5% of sociosexuality (greatest number of premarital sexual partners) had close to 60% boys, compared with 50% for those women at the bottom of the distribution (fewest number of premarital sexual partners).

Simpson and Gangestad conclude that "both unrestricted and restricted female strategies may, in our evolutionary past have been potentially viable: a restricted strategy enhancing parental investment; an unrestricted strategy enhancing the reproductive abilities of surviving male offspring" (Gangestad & Simpson, 1990, p. 81). Their work suggests that human nature allows for evolutionarily grounded individual differences in reproductive strategies. These differences may be associated with particular personality traits (such as dominance, nurturance, and reliability) that prove especially adaptive in certain kinds of environmental situations and under certain kinds of selection pressures.

approach **socioanalytic theory** (Hogan, 1982, 1987; Hogan, Jones, & Cheek, 1985; Jones, Couch, & Scott, 1997). Socioanalytic theory asserts that human beings are biologically predisposed to live in social groups that are variously organized into status hierarchies. Group living provided our evolutionary ancestors with advantages in cooperative ventures such as defense against predators. At the same time, having high status in one's group conferred decided advantages on the person who had it, providing first choice of food, romantic partners, living space, and whatever other desirable commodities and privileges the group afforded, ultimately promoting reproductive success. Therefore, human beings are genetically mandated to seek attention and status, to seek to be liked and to be powerful. As Hogan puts it, "getting along and getting ahead are the two great problems in life that each person must solve" (Hogan et al., 1985, p. 178).

These two great problems are always addressed and resolved, argues Hogan, in the context of ritualized social interaction. As sociologists such as George Herbert Mead (1934) and Erving Goffman (1959) have long maintained, social behavior is an elaborate game, governed by rules and conventions, scripted into roles and routines, and mastered by the most skillful game players among us. Hogan suggests that this was just as true in the EEA as it is today. This is also true of the most informal aspects of living (morning coffee) and the most formal (a presidential inauguration), of the most trivial social interactions (passing strangers in the hallway) and the most personally meaningful (proposing marriage). Like actors on a stage, persons must play roles and follow scripts so that their "performances" in society can be affirmed and rewarded by their "audiences," who are also fellow "actors and actresses." Those human beings who adapt most successfully in a given society—those who are highly popular and power-ful—know how and when to play the most effective roles and to engage in the most appropriate social rituals in the society. They are able to present themselves in ways that make positive and significant impressions on others. This is not to trivialize social behavior, nor to suggest that it is natural for people to be insincere. Rather, role play-ing and impression management are unconscious, central, genetic tendencies for all human beings. Hogan writes:

> Self-presentation and impression management are not trivial party games. They are funda-mental processes, rooted in our history as group-living animals. They are archaic, powerful, compulsive tendencies that are closely tied to our chances for survival and reproductive suc-cess. (Hogan et al., 1985, p. 181)

Furthermore, role playing and impression management are the major mechanisms through which we define who we are as social beings. The distal, evolutionary goal of life is to produce viable progeny so that the individual's genes can be passed down to the next generation. To achieve this goal, however, the person must first find a part to play, a social identity that specifies a recognized niche in the community. Once such an identity is found, the person must employ role playing and impression management to sustain that identity.

Hogan argues that the expected audience for a person's self-presentational behav-iors changes. In childhood, family members (especially parents) are the most impor-tant audience. Our ways of displaying the self to them come to comprise our **character structure.** In adulthood, the audience broadens to include colleagues, friends, peers, one's children, and even society at large. The characteristic ways in which we display ourselves to this larger audience become our **role structure.** But the earlier character structure does not go away. Rather, it lingers on in the unconscious, Hogan asserts. Identity conflicts in adulthood may turn on the discordance between unconscious character structure and conscious role structure, as when the blue-collar, working-class boy rises into the professional white-collar echelons of adult society. He may find it difficult to feel comfortable with an elite role structure that so contradicts the street-wise, tough-guy posture that carried him through his childhood years.

Some people are clearly better at adapting to society and mastering its roles and rit-uals than are others. Argues Hogan, these people are generally approved and accepted by others and attain high positions of influence. One personality variable that appears to have a significant effect on such adaptation is **shyness.** Jones, Briggs, and Smith (1986) define shyness as "discomfort and inhibition in the presence of others" (p. 629). As you might expect, shyness is quite common. One survey indicated that 73% of a large sample of American college students reported having experienced shyness and 42% claimed that they were chronically and characteristically shy (Zimbardo, 1977).

Although virtually anyone may feel shy in certain highly unusual or threatening situations, shyness also appears to be a relatively stable personality disposition, with some people regularly and consistently experiencing more of it than others. As a personality disposition, shyness is "the propensity to respond with heightened anxiety, self-consciousness, and reticence in a variety of social contexts; a person high in the trait of shyness will experience greater arousal than a person low in shyness independent of the level of interpersonal threat in the situation" (Jones et al., 1986, p. 630).

Table 2.2 lists some of the items included in questionnaires for measuring individual differences in shyness. Persistent shyness brings with it discomfort and personal anguish. People scoring high in shyness tend to report greater fearfulness and self-consciousness and lower self-esteem than people scoring low in shyness (Cheek & Buss, 1981; Jones & Russell, 1982). Shy people tend to describe themselves as especially inhibited, awkward, unfriendly, and incompetent (DePaulo, Kenny, Hoover, Webb, & Oliver, 1987). When interacting with a member of the opposite sex, shy people report relatively more negative thoughts about themselves and feelings of tenseness than do persons scoring low on measures of shyness (Bruch, Gorsky, Collins, & Berger, 1989; Hill, 1989). Shy persons report that they lack the confidence and skill necessary to perform effectively many of the roles and rituals necessary for social adaptation. (The popular radio humorist, Garrison Keillor, hits the mark squarely when he advertises "Powdermilk Biscuits"—the recipe that "gives shy people the strength to get up and do what needs to be done.") Other people tend to judge quite harshly the shy person's reticence and reluctance to interact. Shy persons are seen by others as untalented, unfriendly, aloof, snobbish, and lacking in leadership (Hogan et al., 1985). Objective ratings show that shy people actually do talk less, initiate fewer conversational sequences, avert their gaze more often, smile less, show less facial expressivity, and are more likely to engage in nervous self-touching, compared with nonshy people (Cheek & Buss, 1981; Mandel & Shrauger, 1980; Pilkonis, 1977). In Hogan's view, shyness is a common but highly unfortunate handicap in social interaction, and it renders the person less "fit." Shyness leads to personal distress, poor self-esteem, and a lower

TABLE 2.2	*Items From Questionnaires Measuring Shyness*

1. I am often uncomfortable at parties and other social gatherings.
2. I often think up excuses in order to avoid social engagements.
3. I tend to withdraw from people.
4. I get nervous when I speak to someone in a position of authority.
5. I am socially somewhat awkward.
6. I usually feel relaxed when I am with a group of people.
7. I often find myself taking charge in group situations.
8. I have little difficulty being assertive, especially when it is appropriate or I need to be.
9. I make new friends easily.
10. It does not take me a long time to overcome my shyness in new situations.

Note: For each of these items, the person answers "yes" or "no." Answers of "yes" to items 1–5 and of "no" to items 6–10 indicate shyness.
From Jones, Briggs, & Smith (1986), p. 636.

likelihood that the person will be able to attain the social approval and the status that all of us are biologically predisposed to want.

Caspi, Elder, and Bem (1988) followed the life course patterns of individuals born in the 1920s and who, as children, were described by their mothers as particularly shy and inhibited. Shy boys were more likely than their peers to delay entry into marriage, parenthood, and stable careers. They tended to attain less occupational achievement and stability. Those who were especially late in establishing stable careers were also likely to experience high levels of marital instability.

The costs of shyness among girls in this cohort, however, were much less pronounced. Shy girls were more likely than their peers to follow a conventional pattern of marriage, child rearing, and homemaking. Although most women in this cohort placed marriage and children well above occupational concerns, the women with a history of childhood shyness were even less likely to engage in paid work outside the home than their nonshy peers. Interestingly, shy women tended to marry men who had *higher* occupational status at midlife than the husbands of other women. The authors of the study suggest that shy women in the 1950s and 1960s may actually have aided their husbands' careers by fulfilling the traditional homemaker role. With respect to socioanalytic theory, the surprising finding suggests that under certain societal arrangements shyness may in fact enhance the adaptiveness of an individual by promoting the social standing of related others.

In conclusion, shyness is an example of a personality *trait* upon which people show marked individual differences. We will have much more to say about traits in Chapters 5–7 of this book. I have introduced shyness here in the context of Hogan's socioanalytic theory to elaborate on one personality factor that may have important implications with respect to an individual's ability to get along and get ahead in the social world that he or she inhabits. There is no reason to doubt that shyness has been around as a personality trait since the beginning of the EEA. There were doubtlessly many shy people and many very gregarious ones who lived in the countless bands of human foragers who roamed the globe in the Pleistocene epoch. Being shy may have occasionally exacted some cost with respect to an individual's ability to obtain the status and the acceptance necessary for promoting inclusive fitness in the EEA. But the costs were probably minimal, inconsistent, and highly dependent on the vicissitudes of group life. In some social contexts, furthermore, shyness may be an advantage, as we saw in the results of one study showing that shy American women in the 1950s and 1960s tended to marry more financially successful men. When we observe significant variability in a given trait (for example, shyness), we should be reminded that the EEA afforded many different and equally viable adaptational solutions to the many pressures and challenges that our evolutionary ancestors faced. Human nature allows for a tremendous amount of human variability. We are designed to be very different from one another, as well as similar, and to be open to the many proximate forces that ultimately render each life unique.

Hurting and Helping

Aggression   On October 24, 1997, *The New York Times* described the preparations that citizens of the African nation of Algeria were making for upcoming elections. At the time, Algerian society was locked in a power struggle between individuals loyal to the government party and supporters of a rival, religiously based political party dedicated to Islam. According to the vote count, the Islamic party had won the previous election but was prevented from assuming office by the military, who supported the party already in power. Claiming that the election had been stolen from them, Islamic bands killed many supporters of the regime and terrorized many other Algerian citizens. On the eve of the upcoming election, a band called the Armed Islamic Group issued this manifesto:

> As we fight the atheist regime, which we have stripped of all legitimacy, we fight their kin, their followers, all those who support them or work for them. It is therefore essential to track them down in the cities, towns, and villages, and in the deserts, to liquidate them, annihilate their homes, confiscate their wealth, and possess their women. We will do it with bombs, with repeated massacres, and [with] blood that will flow everywhere, until they shut their eyes only after their heads are separated from their bodies. (Ibrahim, 1997, p. A7)

The brutal sentiment expressed in this chilling passage is one that has burst forth from the human heart with alarming regularity since the beginning of recorded history, and surely before. Human warfare is about men (rarely women) killing other men in organized and savage campaigns, committing massacres, employing widespread torture, raping the women who get caught in the crossfire, plundering the opposition's home, stealing their land and making their territory and their resources our territory and our resources, and defending our territory against their murderous onslaughts, their wicked ways, and often in the name of virtue, or religion, or our righteous cause, or for the sake of revenge. It is no accident that the oldest and most famous epic poem in the history of Western literature, Homer's *The Iliad*, begins this way:

> Rage—Goddess, sing the rage of Peleus' son Achilles,
>
> murderous, doomed, that cost the Achaeans countless losses,
>
> hurling down to the House of Death so many sturdy souls,
>
> great fighters' souls, but made their bodies carrion,
>
> feasts for the dogs and birds,
>
> and the will of Zeus was moving toward its end.
>
> Begin, Muse, when the two first broke and clashed,
>
> Agamemnon lord of men and brilliant Achilles.
>
> What god drove them to fight with such a fury?
>
> (Fagles, transl., 1990, p. 77)

The oldest story bequeathed to us by the ancient Greeks—from the eighth century B.C.—is a war story that begins with the rage of Achilles. Homer wonders what drove the doomed protagonists to fight with such a fury. It was the gods, he concludes. But today we might speculate about the many proximal insults, the frustrations, and the deprivations that drive men to do battle in war. And we might speculate about the distal legacy of human evolution, the adaptive function of brutal aggressiveness in the EEA. Given the virtual universality of warfare across human cultures and over recorded time, and given the fossil evidence to suggest that organized group killings were probably a rather common social phenomenon in the EEA, it is difficult to avoid the conclusion that going to war is something that human beings, in particular male human beings, have been selected by nature to do, an outgrowth of human evolution. This is not to suggest that warfare is good or inevitable, only that human beings seem naturally inclined to engage in this sort of activity, with typically deadly results. In terms of evolutionary theory, Wilson (1978) has speculated that war has typically resulted from the rupture of the intricate and powerful fabric of the territorial taboos observed in social groups. An outgrowth of human sociality, territoriality is reinforced by the feeling of kinship and affinity that one has toward relatives, fellow citizens, and/or those with whom one shares ideological beliefs. A major force behind many warlike campaigns is ethnocentrism—the tendency of human beings to ally themselves with their own groups and to distrust deeply those groups that are not one's own. In warfare, states, tribes, and other social groups marshal forces and organize aggressive actions to defend or expand their respective geographic, cultural, ethnic, or ideological turfs.

Human warfare is the deadliest and most dramatic expression of human aggression. The myriad incidents of human violence and cruelty that you have read about, seen on television, and witnessed in your own life are all manifestations of aggression. We are, by nature, a *moderately aggressive* species, writes Wilson (1978). An instinctual predisposition to aggression, encoded indirectly in the human genome, has likely proven adaptive over the long course of human evolution, enabling the more aggressive to survive longer and reproduce with more success. However, human aggression is extremely flexible and malleable, Wilson maintains, and is subject to the limits and opportunities provided by society, learning, and context.

Table 2.3 shows how the term *aggression* can be used to designate a host of very different responses, from nagging one's roommate, to killing prey, to committing suicide. As you might imagine, defining the concept of aggression is a very difficult task. Psychologists have offered a number of formal definitions of aggression. Whereas some definitions focus on observable behavior patterns (such as hitting, biting, and killing), others underscore the *intent* of the behavior, suggesting that aggression is behavior *for the purpose of* hurting others (Parke & Slaby, 1983). Psychologists further distinguish between **instrumental aggression,** which involves hurting others in order to attain a nonaggressive aim, and **hostile aggression,** which has as its explicit aim or end hurting a victim (Hartup, 1974). Thus, a mugger who beats a middle-aged businessman in order to steal his wallet is displaying instrumental aggression—aggression as a means to another end. When the mugger, in a fit of rage, continues to beat and kick the businessman after he robs him, he is displaying hostile aggression—aggression as an end in itself, presumably motivated by a desire to hurt the other. Many aggressive actions appear to be combinations of both instrumental and hostile aggression.

Some scientists and popular writers have made much of the comparison of human aggression to aggression in other species, especially among nonhuman primates. For a time, writings on the topic suggested that human beings were the most murderous of all animals, virtually unique in their propensity for systematically killing their own kind. Indirectly supporting this view were ethological observations suggesting that, while many primates and other mammals engage in a great deal of aggressive behavior, much of this ostensibly "violent" action has a benign quality, especially when exhibited toward members of the same species. For example, certain carnivores will kill members of *other* species in order to eat them (instrumental aggression), but they will rarely kill each other (hostile aggression).

TABLE 2.3	*Some Examples of Aggression*

1. A boy swats at a hornet and gets stung.
2. A cat kills a mouse, parades around with it, and then discards it.
3. A wolf kills and devours a stray sheep.
4. A farmer beheads a chicken and prepares it for Sunday dinner.
5. A hunter kills an animal and mounts it as a trophy.
6. A dog snarls at the mailman but never bites him.
7. A tennis player smashes his racket after missing a volley.
8. A boxer gives an opponent a bloody nose.
9. A small boy daydreams of beating up the neighborhood bully.
10. A woman nags and criticizes her husband, and he ignores her in return.
11. A firing squad executes a prisoner.
12. A bombardier presses a button and hundreds below are killed.
13. A bank robber is shot in the back while attempting to escape.
14. A politician evades legislation that might help clear up a crime-ridden slum.
15. A man commits suicide.
16. An assassin misses his target.
17. A man dislikes all blacks, Jews, and long-haired college students.
18. Two friends get in a heated quarrel after drinking too much.
19. A man rapes a woman.
20. A secretary insults the boss.

Items 1–18 are from Johnson (1972), pp. 4–5.

Instead, much of intraspecies aggression may be ritualistic, involving only threats rather than real attacks. When fights do break out, the combatants often seem to be instinctively guided by inhibitory mechanisms that stop the fighting short of death and serious injury. For example, a dog who is the loser in a fight may present its unprotected neck to the mouth of the victorious dog or roll over on its back to expose its vulnerable underside (Lorenz, 1969). Such an appeasement gesture signals that the fight is over and that the victor emerges dominant. Some observers have argued that this kind of ritualistic fighting and mock aggression serves to establish stable dominance hierarchies in certain advanced animal societies. Dominance hierarchies, in turn, may promote the more efficient use of resources and space in a given group's habitat (Wynne-Edwards, 1963/1978). By establishing and affirming the status of dominant and submissive members of the group, instinctive ritualistic aggression may serve to decrease actual intraspecies violence.

While this view of benign aggression in the animal kingdom has some merit, more recent studies of hyenas, lions, monkeys, chimpanzees, and certain other species paint a much more menacing picture of intraspecies violence. Lethal fighting, cannibalism, and group warfare are observable in a number of nonhuman species. One of the most gruesome examples is *competitive infanticide*, documented in Indian monkeys known as Hanuman langurs (Konner, 1983). Langur social groups consist of a hierarchy of related females with their offspring and a small number of males attached to the group, often for a year or more. From time to time, new males appear on the scene, drive out the old males, and take over. Within a few days they may kill all infants under the age of 6 months and then reimpregnate the infants' mothers. One can explain such brutality in terms of inclusive fitness. By killing off the owners of competing genes (the children sired by their predecessors) and by producing new offspring to replace them, the new langur males are maximizing the chances of passing on their own genes.

Infanticide is by no means unknown to human societies (see Bakan, 1971), but one is hard pressed to find human examples as grotesque as the langur monkeys. Nonetheless, graphic examples of horrific human violence abound. Konner (1983) suggests that singling out the most violent of human societies—such as the Yanomamo culture of highland Venezuela, the Plains Indians of the United States, the Zulu of southern Africa, the Germans of the Third Reich—is the easy way out in proving the argument that human beings are innately aggressive. More instructive and interesting, he maintains, is to examine the *least violent* societies. A case example is the Semai of Malaysia, a very simple society described as a paragon of peacefulness and tranquility. Dentan (1968) reports that before the 1950s, the Semai knew virtually nothing of war, murder, or violence. Almost all forms of instrumental and hostile aggression were nonexistent in Semai society. This all changed for a time in the early 1950s, when the British recruited troops among the Semai to fight a communist insurgency in the region. Initially lured into the military by high wages and pretty clothes, gentle Semai men proved to be amazing fighters:

> Many people who knew the Semai insisted that such an unwarlike people could never make good soldiers. Interestingly enough, they were wrong. Communist terrorists had killed the kinsmen of some of the Semai counterinsurgency troops. Taken out of their nonviolent society and ordered to kill, they seem to have been swept up in a sort of insanity which they call "blood drunkenness." A typical veteran's story runs like this. "We killed, killed, killed. The Malays would stop and go through people's pockets and take their watches or money. We only thought of killing. Wah, truly we were drunk with blood." One man even told how he drank the blood of a man he had killed. (Konner, 1983, p. 205)

Though one case study cannot prove any generalization, the case of the Semai is provocative and capable of bolstering a number of divergent views of human nature. Those who see human nature through a glass darkly are likely to interpret the aggressive behavior of the Semai as a dramatic triumph of instinctual potential over environmental learning. Even this most peaceful group of men—trained from birth to eschew all violence—was capable of surprising acts of brutality in war. On the other hand, those who prefer to explain human aggression in the proximal terms of learning and cultural influences can argue that the inexperienced Semai were merely *conforming*, with shocking gusto, to the norms of warfare imposed upon them by an alien culture. That the Semai eventually returned to a peaceful way of life after the war, many seemingly baffled by their unorthodox behavior in battle, may be a tribute to the power of culture to control aggression. But it still leaves us wondering how a people so trained to live in peace could suddenly transform themselves into bloodthirsty warriors.

Altruism   If natural selection pulled human nature in the direction of aggression, how do we reconcile the many examples that we can summon forth in which humans exhibit compassion and care, engage in acts of stupendous altruism, and sometimes even sacrifice their own lives for the sake of others? One possible answer is that human aggression and human altruism are really two sides of the same evolutionary coin. Both spring from the fundamental feature of human life in the EEA: *We evolved to live in*

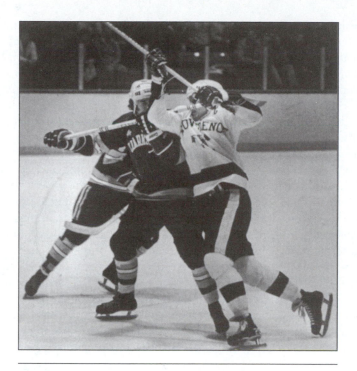

Human aggression is often on display in men's ice hockey, which is considered one of the most violent sports in the world today.

groups. Group life is all about competition and cooperation—getting ahead, but also getting along. Like many primate groups, human societies are structured in hierarchical ways (deWaal, 1996). Members of the group jockey for position and status, and those who fight their way to the top command considerable power over their less aggressive and less effective peers. DeWaal (1996) writes: "The desire to dictate the behavior of others is such a timeless and universal attribute of our species that it must rank with the sex drive, maternal instinct, and the will to survive in terms of the likelihood of its being part of our biological heritage" (p. 98). Aggression can be a powerful tool in the quest for social dominance, especially among males. But dominance hierarchies also create the kind of stability and order necessary for the establishment of cooperation, sharing, and social support in the group. "Without agreement on rank and a certain respect for authority there can be no great sensitivity to social rules," writes deWaal (1996, p. 92). "Despite its grounding in competition, the hierarchy is essentially a tool of cooperation and social integration" (deWaal, 1996, p. 123).

Human beings have evolved to be both aggressive and altruistic because both proved adaptive for group life in the EEA. Indeed, group life would be unthinkable without both, for to the extent that dominance hierarchies are established in and through the aggressive activities of competing individuals, a tendency toward aggression indirectly supports cooperation, caring, and altruistic behavior by ultimately working to establish the social stability and structure that communal human activities require. Of course, aggression can also rip society apart, so natural mechanisms must evolve and cultural norms must be established to keep antisocial aggression more-or-less under control. Because we are by nature an exquisitely social species, human beings have evolved to be "moral animals," writes Wright (1994). "Universally, human communities are moral communities; a morally neutral existence is as impossible for us as a completely solitary existence," writes deWaal (1996, p. 10).

The origins of human morality can be traced back to three conditions of group life in the Pleistocene (deWaal, 1996). First is the condition of *group value:* Individual human beings depended on the group for finding food and defense against enemies and predators. Second is *mutual aid:* Individuals cooperated with one another in group activities and engaged in reciprocal exchange within the group. Third is *internal conflict:* Individual members had disparate interests and competed with one another for resources, status, and so on. Given these three conditions, argues deWaal (1996), intra-group conflict needed to be resolved through a balancing of individual and collective interests. Such conflict resolution can be accomplished at the dyadic level and at higher levels of social structure. At the *dyadic level,* individuals engage in one-on-one interaction such as direct reciprocation of aid and reconciliation following fights. At *higher levels,* community concern and care about good relationships between individuals are expressed in mediated reconciliation, peaceful arbitration of disputes, appreciation of altruistic behavior in the group, and group encouragement of individual contributions to the quality of the social environment overall.

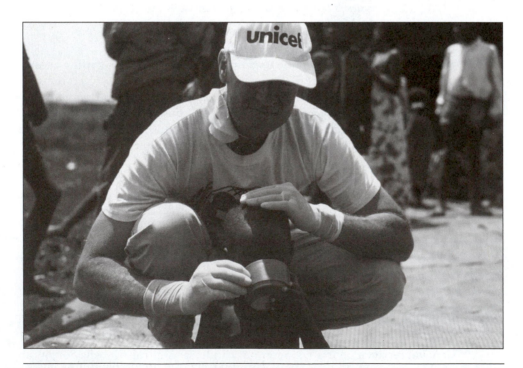

Altruism is as much a part of human nature as is aggression.

What features of human nature have enabled human beings to live effectively in groups and to establish the rudiments of human morality? DeWaal (1996) argues that it is hard to imagine human morality without positing the evolution of the following tendencies and capacities, each of which can also be found in some other primate species:

1. *Sympathy-related traits:*

   a. *Attachment, succorance, and emotional contagion.* Like many primate species, human beings are naturally inclined to bond with one another and share emotional experiences. We will examine the concept of attachment in depth later in this chapter.

   b. *Learned adjustment to and special treatment of the disabled and injured.* In many primate species, individuals take care of those who are helpless and disabled and provide them with special privileges and indulgences.

   c. *Cognitive empathy.* Humans are able to take the role of the other, to trade places mentally with the other and thereby imagine the other's individual experience. This capacity can also be observed in some primates, but human beings have taken it much farther and, through language and higher reasoning abilities, have incorporated it into religious belief systems, ethical frameworks, and legal codes.

2. *Norm-related characteristics:*

   a. *Prescriptive social rules.* Groups establish rules for appropriate conduct. The rules are often implicit and do not require a conscious understanding of their rationality or reasonability. Before the advent of language in the EEA, human beings lived according to implicit group rules, as we see in other primates, as well.

   b. *Internalization of rules and anticipation of punishments.* Humans take external rules and make them their own. They incorporate society's norms to establish conscience, mediated by such social emotions as guilt, shame, and fear. They imagine future scenarios in which bad consequences could follow rule violations, and they therefore seek to avoid those scenarios.

3. *Reciprocity:*

   a. *A concept of giving, trading, and revenge.* Implicit understandings of give and take, fair trade, and revenge are not confined to humans but can be observed in many social species. Many primates exhibit a strong, though by human standards primitive, sense of justice, and they behave according to expectations about reciprocal exchange and fair play. They also, like humans, may seek to exact revenge when expectations about reciprocity, justice, and honor are violated. DeWaal (1996, p. 160) writes: "A taste for revenge is the other side of the coin of reciprocity. To act negatively toward stingy individuals (along with direct and indirect retaliation) suggests a sense of justice and fairness."

   b. *Moralistic aggression against violators of reciprocity rules.* Humans and certain other primates have evolved sensitive cheating-detecting mechanisms. They are especially tuned in to violations of social norms and will experience powerful emotions, such as righteous indignation and rage, when they witness violations. Human beings will even kill in the name of principles, in the name of truth, God, the good, and so on. As Wright (1994) argues in his book *The Moral Animal*, human beings are designed by evolution to take their own values seriously and to believe sincerely that they are doing the right, the good, and the honorable thing. Such righteousness can fuel acts of tremendous kindness as well as acts of war.

4. *Getting along:*

a. *Peacemaking and avoidance of conflict.* Primate and human groups operate according to principles and practices that aim to minimize the kinds of conflicts that seriously disrupt group harmony. Social animals require stable group structures if they, the social animals themselves, are to survive and to pass their genes down to the next generation.

b. *Accommodation of conflicting interests through negotiation.* Competing individuals may ultimately engage in activities designed to achieve balance and reconciliation of conflicts. In human societies, certain individuals are chosen or trained to mediate disputes, such as negotiators, ambassadors, lawyers, and judges. Among other primates, you find some of the same kinds of behaviors exhibited by individuals who may regularly assume negotiating roles in the troop or clan.

c. *Community concern and maintenance of good relationships.* More than any other primates, humans have evolved the capacity to identify themselves with the good of the group as a whole and to develop strategies for living that promote the welfare of the group.

(partly based on deWaal, 1996, especially p. 211)

Set in juxtaposition with our inherent tendencies toward aggression and our strong desires to get ahead in social groups, human beings have evolved complex mechanisms for resolving conflicts in groups and getting along. In the EEA and today, group life is about getting ahead and getting along. Groups benefit from stable dominance hierarchies and effective strategies for peacemaking, caregiving, and building solidarity and community concern. However, it is important to realize that it is not groups that pass their genes down to the next generation, but rather individual organisms who do so. Inclusive fitness encompasses those characteristics that benefit the individual's efforts to move replications of his or her genes down the generational line. Therefore, tendencies toward sympathy, cooperation, and altruism must enhance inclusive fitness for the individual organism if such tendencies are to be selected through evolution to be aspects of human nature. Put another way, evolutionary theory challenges us to figure out how the "selfish genes" can predispose individual human beings to be "unselfish." On this point, contributions to evolutionary theory made in the past 30 years have highlighted the mechanisms of kin selection and reciprocal altruism to explain how many animals, including human beings, can engage in selfless, altruistic behaviors, even to the point of self-sacrifice, that promote inclusive fitness and the perpetuation of their own genes.

Because biologically related animals share some of the same genes, certain species are predisposed to engage in altruistic behavior *that benefits their relatives* (parents, children, siblings, and grandchildren, for the most part). Through **kin selection,** parents may sacrifice their own lives to save their children and thereby increase the likelihood of passing down their own genes, through their offspring, to subsequent generations. Siblings are inclined to help each other, even sacrifice themselves for each other, for to promote the survival and reproductive success of a sibling is to increase the chances of passing down the genes siblings have in common. In general, the closer the blood relationship, the greater the likelihood of altruism. Thus, we are biologically more strongly predisposed to help our children, brothers, or sisters than our cousins, uncles, or aunts. In general, altruism based on kin selection is most likely to occur (1) among closely related rather than distantly related individuals, (2) among individuals who live in close-knit and geographically limited societies wherein they are likely to share kinship ties, and (3) among species capable of recognizing relatives and distinguishing them from nonrelatives (Barash, 1977).

Even biologically unrelated members of the same species may be motivated to help each other if the helping is likely to result in selective advantages for both (Trivers, 1971). Individuals of certain species, therefore, may be instinctually predisposed to make implicit bargains with each other because such bargains ultimately increase their own reproductive success. For instance, rhesus monkeys, baboons, and anthropoid apes are known to form coalitions based on mutual assistance, while chimpanzees, gibbons, African wild dogs, and wolves beg for food from each other reciprocally (Wilson, 1975). Such **reciprocal altruism** is more likely to occur when the situation involves (1) low risk for the helper, (2) high benefit for the recipient, and (3) high likelihood that the situation will be reversed in the future (Barash, 1977).

From an evolutionary standpoint, therefore, altruistic behavior should occur either (1) among closely related individuals (kin selection) or (2) when the cost–benefit ratio for the helper is ultimately favorable (reciprocal altruism). Both forms exist among humans, Wilson argues, but the second is by far more important for the survival and success of human societies, because it is endlessly flexible and capable of producing strong emotional bonds between completely unrelated peoples. Human beings help each other in a variety of ways for many reasons, but behind much of the help, maintains Wilson, is the implicit expectation that the helper will, some day, be rewarded. This implicit expectation motivates us to surrender our own self-interests, on occasion, for the good of others. Writes Wilson (1978), "lives of the most towering heroism are paid out in the [conscious or unconscious] expectation of great reward, not the least of which is a belief in personal immortality" (p. 154).

In an article entitled "Is Altruism Part of Human Nature?" psychologist Martin Hoffman (1981) endorses Wilson's view that altruism has a biological base but takes issue with the image of the altruist as a cold calculator of ultimate "cost and benefit." Drawing from a wide range of psychological research, Hoffman argues for the existence of a general, biologically based human tendency to help others in distress. The basis for the tendency is **empathy,** which Hoffman defines as "a vicarious affective response to others: that is, an affective response appropriate to someone else's situation rather than one's own" (p. 128). To experience empathy is to feel what the other person feels. If I see a tattered old woman struggling to cross an icy city street as the wind and the traffic threaten to knock her to the ground, I may experience alarm and arousal, not for my sake but for hers. Clearly *she* is in distress, but *I* feel a corresponding emotion, and I may therefore try to help her. Argues Hoffman, my empathy is biologically rooted—developed out of a predisposition coded in the genes and mediated primarily, Hoffman speculates, by a primitive part of the human brain called the limbic system. My altruistic behavior is motivated, at least in part, by the experience of empathy.

Batson, Fultz, and Schoenrade (1987) distinguish feelings of personal distress from empathy—either or both of which may be experienced when we encounter a person in need. Personal distress (feeling alarmed, upset, worried, disturbed, troubled, and so on) seems to evoke *egoistic motivation* to reduce one's own arousal. Though we may help the person in need, we may do so in order to relieve our *own* distress. On the other hand, true empathy (feeling sympathetic, moved, compassionate, tender, warm, soft-hearted, and so on) evokes *altruistic motivation*, in which the ultimate goal is to reduce the other person's distress rather than one's own. Some psychologists, however, take issue with this distinction, suggesting that most helping is motivated by the attempt to reduce one's own personal distress, even if that distress is in the form of "sadness" about the plight of another (Cialdini, Schaller, Fultz, & Beaman, 1987). Nonetheless, an impressive array of findings seems to support the legitimacy of the altruism-empathy link. In five studies testing egoistic alternatives to the empathy hypothesis, Batson and his colleagues (Batson, Dyck, Brandt, Batson, Powell, McMaster, & Griffit, 1988) found consistent support for the proposition that people tend to offer assistance and help when moved to do so by feelings of empathy and concern for those in distress or need. In something of a compromise position, Smith, Keating, and Stotland (1989) provide evidence to suggest that altruism is motivated by both a general empathic concern for the victim's plight and a specific sensitivity to the prospect of vicarious joy at the resolution of the victim's needs.

In human development, the earliest forms of empathy may be traced all the way back to the newborn. There is evidence that 1- and 2-day-old infants will cry in response to the sound of another infant's crying (Sagi & Hoffman, 1976). Such crying is vigorous and intense and does not appear to be merely a response to an annoying physical stimulus, since infants do not cry as much in response to equally loud nonhuman sounds, including computer-simulated infant cries. The finding indicates that babies experience distress in response to cues of the distress of others, even though they are doubtlessly not conscious of the nature of the outside distress. With development, more mature empathic responses to the distress of others can be observed. Typically, such responses are measured as verbal reports, facial expressions, or physiological changes. Thus, most 4–8-year-old children give empathic verbal reports to slide sequences portraying other children in highly emotional situations (Feshbach & Feshbach, 1969; Levine & Hoffman, 1976). Adults spontaneously emit empathic facial expressions, such as frowns, when witnessing others in physically painful situations or failing at a task (Gaertner & Dovidio, 1977; Krebs, 1975).

Hoffman (1981) reviews a large number of studies supporting a connection between empathy and altruistic behavior. He argues that empathy provides a biologically rooted emotional base for many selfless and cooperative acts among humans. Of course, empathy is not the only ingredient in altruism. Helping behavior in humans is complexly determined by numerous environmental factors: family, peer, and cultural factors; characteristics of the recipient of help; characteristics of the helping situation; and the individual's levels of cognitive development, self-esteem, and even mood (Radke-Yarrow, Zahn-Waxler, & Chapman, 1983). Nonetheless, natural selection may have predisposed human beings to feel the distress of others, designating empathy as a biological undergirding for "an altruistic response system that is reliable and flexible" (Hoffman, 1981, p. 27). A comprehensive review of many different studies of empathy and helping behavior finds a moderate positive association between measures of empathy and various kinds of altruistic, cooperative, and prosocial behaviors (Eisenberg & Miller, 1987).

In recent years, some psychologists have suggested that a particular combination of traits constitutes the **altruistic personality** (Bierhoff, Klein, & Kramp, 1991; Carlo, Eisenberg, Troyer, Switzer, & Speer, 1991; Rushton, 1980). Included within the cluster of characteristics defining this personality type are sympathy, social responsibility, and mature perspective taking. Altruistic people tend to experience strong feelings for others in distress; they tend to assume a substantial level of responsibility to assist others and to make positive contributions to society; and they are able to see problems and situations from many different vantage points, rather than merely their own. While people scoring high on these personality dimensions are not necessarily more altruistic in every situation they encounter in life, they do tend on the average to engage in a greater number of altruistic behaviors than individuals scoring low on these characteristics.

A team of researchers in Germany examined the personality characteristics of men and women who volunteered to provide first-aid to help victims of traffic accidents (Bierhoff et al., 1991). Working with ambulance teams, the researchers solicited the participation of 43 adults who had witnessed traffic accidents and volunteered first-aid. The first-aiders completed a lengthy battery of personality questionnaires. Their questionnaire responses were compared with those of a group of 34 adults who had also witnessed traffic accidents but who had not volunteered to provide aid. Compared with the nonhelpers, the first-aiders scored significantly higher on measures of empathy and social responsibility. In addition, the first-aiders were much more inclined than the nonhelpers to believe in a "just world," endorsing the optimistic viewpoint that life is basically fair and that good people are eventually rewarded for their efforts. Finally, first-aiders expressed greater confidence than did the nonhelpers in their ability to produce positive outcomes and to control their own destinies.

Most of the research on altruism has focused on discrete altruistic acts, such as providing first-aid or helping a victim in distress. But many forms of altruism involve long-term commitments to programs and causes that entail a complicated sequence of thoughts, intentions, actions, and consequences (Colby & Damon, 1992). People who work regularly with the mentally disabled, who volunteer time to distribute provisions at food pantries and soup kitchens, who take on roles as "big brothers" or "big sisters" for disadvantaged youth, who participate in such programs as the Peace Corps, and so on—these people have made commitments to programs of altruistic action. Altruism is not so much what they do on occasion; it is rather, in a sense, who they are.

THE EVOLUTION OF LOVE: ATTACHMENT THEORY

It is universally true that human infants fall in love with their mothers and other caregivers in the first year of life. In all known human cultures, babies bond to their caregivers by the time they reach their first birthday. The extraordinarily rare exceptions to this rule may be seen in profoundly disabled children (e.g., severe brain damage) and sometimes in children who suffer from the rare psychological disorder of autism. That a bond of love should and will develop between the infant and the caregiver in the first year of human life is as notable a feature of human nature as is the tendency for human beings to be born with two eyes, or to walk on two legs as children, or to develop language, or to desire sexual experiences once they pass through puberty. As with human vision, upright posture, language, and sexual desire, the bond of love that ties children to their caregivers evolved to become part of human nature during the Pleistocene epoch and before, functioning to solve adaptational problems that faced

Mary D. S. Ainsworth

our group-living, hunting-and-gathering forebears. How does this bond work? How does it develop? And what problems does it solve?

One of the most influential theories in psychology today is *attachment theory*, developed by John Bowlby and Mary Ainsworth. In his classic three-volume set entitled *Attachment and Loss* (Bowlby, 1969, 1973, 1980) and in his last book entitled *A Secure Base* (Bowlby, 1988), John Bowlby articulated a grand theory of the dynamics of affectional bonds in human life. The theory couches the sublime experience of human love in the no-nonsense language of natural selection and shows how attachments between human beings have proven exquisitely adaptive over the long course of human evolution. Mary Ainsworth pioneered the assessment and understanding of individual differences in attachment bonds, showing how the quality of early caregiver–infant interaction may have long-term effects on personality (Ainsworth, 1967, 1969, 1989; Ainsworth, Blehar, Waters, & Wall, 1978; Ainsworth & Bowlby, 1991). In recent years, attachment theory has generated a great deal of developmental research focused on infancy and childhood. The theory has also been extended in creative ways into the arenas of adult attachment histories (Main, Kaplan, & Cassidy, 1985) and attachment styles in romantic love (Hazan & Shaver, 1987, 1990).

Bowlby believed that the bond of love formed between the infant and the caregiver in the first year of life is a general prototype of all subsequent love relationships. He argued that this bond is driven by instinctual demands of biology. Human infants are predisposed to form affectional bonds with others for the primary benefits those bonds obtain. In this passage, Bowlby underscores the evolutionary significance of deep affectional bonds:

> It is . . . more than likely that a human being's powerful propensity to make these deep and long-term relationships is the result of a strong gene-determined bias to do so, a bias that has been selected during the course of evolution. Within this frame of reference a child's strong propensity to attach himself to his mother and his father, or to whomever else may be caring for him, can be understood as having the function of reducing the risk of his coming to harm. For to stay in close proximity to, or in easy communication with, someone likely to protect you is the best of all possible insurance policies. Similarly a parent's concern to care for his or her offspring plainly has the function of contributing to the child's survival. That success in the maintenance of these long-term relationships should usually bring satisfaction and contentment, and that failure should bring frustration, anxiety, and sometimes despair are, on this reading, the prizes and penalties selected during evolution to guide us in our activities. (Bowlby, 1988, p. 81)

Attachment in Infancy

Virtually no other human experience feels so "natural" as the love we feel for our babies. The **attachment** bond between caregiver (mother, father, or other who cares for the baby) and infant develops through a number of well-defined stages in the first years of the child's life. It begins with the newborn's vague and nondiscriminant orientation to social stimuli, develops through a phase of heightened sociality in which 2–7-month-olds smile and show various attachment behaviors toward people, and ends as an affectional partnership between the child and a select few clearly discriminated and preferred caregivers (Ainsworth, Blehar, Waters, & Wall, 1978; Bowlby, 1969). Although many cultural differences can be observed, the caregiver–infant attachment bond appears to develop in approximately the same manner in virtually all known human societies (Bowlby, 1969; Konner, 1983). The attachment experience may feel so natural because it is indeed an integral part of human nature.

In behavioral terms, attachment refers to seeking and maintaining proximity to another individual. Caregivers and infants seek to be physically close to each other and to engage in tender physical contact. Ethologists have regularly observed attachment behavior in nonhuman primates such as apes and rhesus monkeys. These behavioral patterns are generally considered to have a strong instinctual base. For instance, newborn rhesus monkeys, in the first few weeks of life, are in constant contact with their mothers, spending virtually all daytime hours gripping mother with their hands, feet, and mouth, and being held by her at nighttime. As they get older, the monkeys begin to venture away from mother, making tentative initial forays of a few feet and then checking back with mother as if to see if all is still well. During most of the first year of life, the rhesus monkey uses its mother as a secure base from which to explore the world and as a source of comfort during times of fear and anxiety.

The mother rhesus monkey, in turn, appears to be instinctually predisposed to maintain almost constant contact with the infant during the first few weeks and then to encourage slowly thereafter the infant's independent exploration. Some ethologists have suggested that the mother's behavior in this regard is akin to a fixed-action pattern released by the natural sign stimulus of the baby's face (Eibl-Eibesfeldt, 1975). In many species including humans, babies have large heads (in proportion to their bodies), prominent foreheads, large eyes set below the midline of the face, and soft, protruding cheeks. These "cute" features may serve as natural releasers of instinctual caregiving behavior (Cunningham, 1985).

Some ethologists regard attachment in some species to be a form of **imprinting**. A few hours after birth, for instance, ducklings will learn to follow a large, moving stimulus and to prefer that stimulus to other stimuli for a long time afterwards. In a natural setting, this large stimulus is almost invariably the mother. Imprinting, therefore, is a form of rapid learning whereby the infant forms a lasting preference for a particular stimulus, usually the natural mother, during a *sensitive period* of development. The implication is that if the sensitive period is missed, imprinting may not occur or will occur in a less adaptive manner. In laboratory experiments and other artificial settings, ducks and geese have imprinted on, and thereby established strong and lasting preferences for, such objects as flashing lights, electric trains, moving milk bottles, and even a squatting and quacking human scientist when these objects were presented to the animals during the sensitive developmental period for imprinting.

Human attachment appears to be a much more complex and malleable phenomenon than imprinting or fixed-action patterns. Nonetheless, many psychologists believe that human attachment is an instinctually grounded behavioral system of profound evolutionary significance. Bowlby (1969, 1973, 1980) argues that the caregiver–infant attachment bond is a *complex, instinctually guided behavioral system that has functioned throughout human evolution to protect the infant from predators.* In the hunting-and-gathering way of life of our ancestors, attachment improved an organism's inclusive fitness by increasing the likelihood that his or her genes would survive and be passed down. By ensuring that mothers and infants would seek contact and physical closeness with each other, the attachment system made it easier for older and stronger caregivers to protect their dependent and defenseless human infants from threats to their survival and ultimate reproductive success.

Bowlby conceives of attachment as a goal-directed system designed to ensure the overall end of caregiver–infant proximity. The system comprises a number of subsystems, called **attachment behaviors,** including sucking, clinging, following, vocalizing, and smiling. Infants emit attachment behaviors that beckon caregivers to seek or maintain physical closeness or contact. Although each attachment behavior follows its own independent developmental course in the first few months of human life, attachment behaviors become organized and integrated during the second half of the first year. Thus, newborn infants will cry and cling, but they do not show true smiles in response to social stimuli until about 2 months of age, and they are not able to follow mother until they are able to crawl, months after the first smile. Crying, clinging, smiling, following, and other discrete attachment behaviors, however, begin to work together, after 6 or 7 months, to achieve mother–infant proximity. During this time, infants begin to show clear preferences for mothers, fathers, and other *attachment objects* in their

The attachment bond between caregiver and infant affirms human joy and provides the infant with security and trust.

environments, engaging in a variety of behavioral combinations to promote proximity with attachment objects. These behavioral combinations are subtle and flexible instinctual strategies for relating to others, markedly influenced by learning and experience but deeply ingrained in human biology.

With respect to emotional development, the attachment system organizes the earliest experiences of human love and fear (Bowlby, 1969, 1973; Sroufe & Waters, 1977). Toward the end of the first year of life, infants begin to experience *stranger anxiety and separation anxiety*, two benchmarks of normal psychological development. At this time, infants begin to express caution and fear in the face of novel events and objects and when confronted with strangers. Stranger fear makes evolutionary sense, Bowlby suggests, for unfamiliar objects and persons have been associated with threat and dangers throughout evolution. The presence of the attachment object, however, can go a long way to relieve the fear that infants experience when faced with strangers and novelty. The felt security experienced in the attachment bond makes new and strange things seem less threatening and dangerous, as indeed they usually are, and have usually been throughout our evolutionary past, when human infants are in the presence of their caregivers.

When separated from their main caregivers, even for a short period of time, 8-month and older infants may show considerable distress, manifested in extreme wariness or crying. Brief separations from the caregiver are relatively harmless inevitabilities of everyday life, but long separations may be problematic. Feelings of abandonment are the most emotionally painful experiences human beings can know, Bowlby suggests. The pain is deeply rooted in the evolutionary fact that parental abandonment of the infant usually means death. This is why parental threats of abandonment are especially frightening to children and, when issued repeatedly, especially detrimental to healthy personality development. This is also why the experience of prolonged separation from one's attachment object may initiate a process of "mourning," through which the infant or child adjusts, over the period of weeks and months, to the perceived loss of the caregiver. In mourning, the infant will move through stages of angry *protest*, *despair* and sadness, and finally *detachment* (Bowlby, 1973). Detachment marks a defensive severance of the attachment bond. As a tragic example of detachment, observations of infants who have been removed from their caregivers for long periods of time, as during times of war, show that many infants will appear not to recognize their caregivers when they are eventually reunited (Bowlby, 1973). In these cases, the attachment has been emotionally undone.

Over the normal course of the first 2–3 years of life, the child builds up a set of expectations about the nature of relationships with other people. The expectations come to comprise a **working model.** Writes Bowlby (1973), "in the working model of the world that anybody builds, a key feature is his notion of who his attachment figures are, where they may be found, and how they may be expected to respond" (p. 203). The working model serves as an internalized template of love (Shaver & Rubenstein, 1980). When the attachment bond is *secure*, the infant may experience a basic trust in its surroundings, which provides the self-confidence to explore the world with enthusiasm and aplomb (Erikson, 1963; Sroufe & Waters, 1977). In the best attachment relationships, the human infant, like the rhesus monkey discussed earlier, uses the attachment object as a *secure base* from which to explore the world. When the attachment bond is generally *insecure*, however, the infant may come to consider the world a threatening and dangerous place. Out of this early pessimism about life the child formulates a working model of the attachment object that underscores uncertainty and rejection. A working model of an inconsistent and rejecting attachment object may lead to subsequent deficits in self-esteem and a lasting vulnerability to loneliness (Bowlby, 1980; Shaver & Rubenstein, 1980).

Secure and Insecure Attachments

Virtually all babies become attached to a caregiver in the first year of life. Yet, there are significant individual differences in the *quality* of that attachment relationship, and these differences can be measured. By the time the infant is 1 year old, individual differences in attachment quality are apparent. The most popular laboratory method for assessing these individual differences in 1-year-olds is the **Strange Situation** method, developed by Ainsworth and her colleagues (Ainsworth et al., 1978). The Strange Situation involves a series of short laboratory episodes through which the infant, the caregiver (usually mother, sometimes father), and a "stranger" (usually a woman who is working with the experimenter) interact in a comfortable setting and the behaviors of the infant are observed (Table 2.4). The infant and caregiver arrive and get comfortable; the stranger enters; the caregiver leaves for a short period of time; the caregiver returns, and the stranger leaves; the caregiver exits again, leaving the infant

TABLE 2.4	*Episodes in the "Strange Situation" Procedure for Assessing Individual Differences in Attachment*	

EPISODE	WHO IS INVOLVED	WHAT HAPPENS
1	Caregiver, Infant	After being introduced to the room and the many toys it contains, the caregiver (mother or father) sits and looks at a magazine while the infant explores the room and its contents.
2	Stranger, Caregiver, Infant	A woman whom the infant has never seen before enters, greets caregiver and sits silently for 1 minute. Then the woman engages caregiver in a conversation. Finally she initiates interaction with the infant.
3	Stranger, Infant	Caregiver quietly leaves room. If infant becomes too distressed, the episode is terminated.
4	Caregiver, Infant	Caregiver returns and stranger leaves. This is the first "reunion episode." Caregiver seeks to interest the infant in the toys.
5	Infant	After the infant appears comfortable again, caregiver leaves.
6	Stranger, Infant	The stranger enters again. She initiates interaction with the infant. If the infant prefers to play alone, the stranger retreats to a chair and reads a magazine.
7	Caregiver, Infant	Caregiver returns and stranger leaves. This is the second "reunion episode."

Some notes on method: Each of the episodes is approximately 3 minutes in length. All of the proceedings are observed by researchers behind a one-way mirror. Usually, the episodes are videotaped as well and later analyzed in various ways.

alone; the stranger reenters; and the caregiver finally returns again. Researchers analyze the behavior of the infant in all of the episodes of the Strange Situation, paying special attention to the two "reunion episodes" in which the caregiver returns after a brief separation.

Behavioral observations in the Strange Situation yield three different general patterns of attachment: what have been termed **A-babies, B-babies,** and **C-babies.** Between one-half and two-thirds of mother–baby pairs show *secure attachment.* The infants in these pairs are termed B-babies. Like most of the babies studied, securely attached infants find the brief separation from the caregiver and the entrance of strangers to be at least mildly upsetting. These are normal manifestations of mistrust shown by virtually all infants, regardless of their attachment classification, after about 8 months of age or so, at which time separation anxiety and stranger anxiety naturally emerge. However, when the caregiver is present, B-babies explore their environments with great ease and comfort, using the caregiver as a secure base. When the caregiver leaves, they show much less exploration, but when she returns again in the reunion episodes, they greet the caregiver with great enthusiasm and resume their exploration of the environment.

A-babies and C-babies show patterns of *insecure attachment.* The pattern for A-babies is termed *avoidant.* A-babies are most noted for their tendency to avoid the caregiver when she returns in the reunion episodes, as if to say, "Hey! You abandoned me; I'll do the same to you for a while." The pattern of insecure attachment for C-babies is termed *resistant.* C-babies show a mixture of approach and avoidance behavior in the reunion episodes of the Strange Situation. When the caregiver returns after the brief separations, the C-baby may approach the caregiver in a friendly manner but then angrily resist being picked up. C-babies are noted for their angry reactions to the caregiver, though they occasionally show passive reactions as well, reminiscent of the standard patterns shown by A-babies.

Developmental psychologists have undertaken investigations to determine what factors produce patterns of secure and insecure attachment in the first years. The quality of the early interaction between caregivers and the infant may play an important role. In this regard, Main (1981) has shown that mothers of securely attached infants tend to hold their babies more carefully and tenderly and for longer periods of time during early infancy than do mothers of insecurely attached babies. Others have suggested that maternal sensitivity is also a consistent predictor of attachment (Ainsworth et al., 1978; Egeland & Farber, 1984; Sroufe, 1985). A mother who is especially sensitive to her baby is "alert to perceive her baby's signals, interprets them accurately, and responds appropriately and promptly" (Ainsworth et al., 1978, p. 142). Observations of mothers and babies at home and in the laboratory during the infant's first three months suggest that mothers of infants who are later classified as securely attached respond more frequently to crying, show more affection when holding the baby, are more likely to acknowledge the baby with a smile or conversation when entering the baby's room, and are better at feeding the baby because of their attention to the baby's signals, compared with mothers of babies later deemed insecurely attached. One study of mothers and 12-month-old infants observed twice at home for two hours by two researchers shows a strong relation between secure attachment and maternal sensitivity (Pederson, Moran, Sitko, Campbell, Ghesquire, & Acton, 1990). Mothers of more secure infants were more frequently characterized as noticing their babies' signals and using the signals to guide their behavior; they also were more knowledgeable about their infants and appeared to enjoy them more than mothers of less secure infants.

In a small laboratory study of American children, Blehar, Lieberman, and Ainsworth (1977) found that the quality of early mother–infant play positively predicted attachment patterns at age 1 year. In this study, infants were first observed between the ages of 6 and 15 weeks as they played with their mothers. It is generally agreed that at this early point in development (during the first half-year of life) infants are not yet attached to their caregivers, but that the attachment bond is starting to form. Later, when the infants were around 1 year of age, the now-stable patterns of mother–infant attachment were assessed in the Strange Situation. Infants later identified as securely attached were more responsive in face-to-face play, and their mothers were more enthusiastic and encouraging, compared with infants later identified as insecurely attached. In general, the mother–infant pairs that were later classified as securely attached showed a high degree of *synchrony*, or interactive play. Isabella, Belsky, and von Eye (1989) found similar results in an intensive study of a wide variety of infant and mother behaviors, assessed at infant ages of 1, 3, and 9 months. The authors defined *interactional synchrony* as "the extent to which interaction appeared to be reciprocal and mutually rewarding, so that its frequent occurrence would presumably foster development of the infant's working model of mother as available, responsive, and trustworthy" (p. 13). Infants classified as securely attached at 9 months tended to show especially synchronous patterns of interaction with mothers at ages 1 and 3 months, compared with infants classified as insecure.

The importance of early caregiver–infant synchrony in the development of personality and interpersonal relationships has been underscored by a number of theorists (Brazelton, Koslowski, & Main, 1974; Stern, 1985). According to Stern (1985), early play between babies and caregivers resembles a synchronous "dance," with both partners continually adjusting the rhythm and tuning the exchange through a rich variety of verbal and nonverbal signals and signs. In Stern's view, the fundaments of a basic sense of self and one's relation to the outside world are established in early patterns of caregiver–infant play.

A large body of research supports the general hypothesis that secure attachment in infancy leads to greater levels of mastery and competence in the preschool years and beyond. A representative study in this regard was conducted by Hazen and Durrett (1982). Children aged 30–34 months who had been assessed at 12 months for security of attachment were observed exploring with their mothers in a large laboratory playhouse. The researchers measured how much exploration the children showed according to the number of different movements the child made from one area of the playhouse to another, and they measured the extent to which the exploration was "active" (child leads mother) as opposed to "passive" (mother leads child). As Table 2.5 shows, children who 2 years before had been classified as securely attached (B-babies) explored more and engaged in a greater ratio of active to passive exploration compared with children who had been classified insecurely attached (A- and C-babies).

Other studies examining the relation between quality of attachment in the first year and indices of mastery and independence at ages 2 and 3 have found that secure attachment is positively associated with (1) higher quality of exploration (Main, 1983), (2) higher levels of pretend play (Slade, 1987), (3) greater competence in problem-solving tasks (Matas, Arend, & Sroufe, 1978), and (4) more rapid and smooth adjustments to

TABLE 2.5	Exploratory Behavior of 3-Year-Olds as a Function of Attachment at Age 1 Year		
	ATTACHMENT CLASSIFICATION		
EXPLORATION MEASURE	AVOIDANT (A-BABY)	SECURE (B-BABY)	AMBIVALENT (C-BABY)
Number of movements	31.2	35.7	31.7
Active movements (%)	73	88	65

Source: Hazen & Durrett (1982), p. 755.

strangers (Lutkenhaus, Grossmann, & Grossmann, 1995). Fagot (1997) found that securely attached 2-year-olds elicited more positive and fewer negative reactions from children in their play groups compared with insecurely attached children. Sroufe (1988) reports that preschool children with histories of secure attachment neither victimized nor were they victimized by assigned play partners. In sharp contrast, children with resistant histories were quite likely to victimize, and children with histories of avoidant attachment were often victimized in their interactions with peers. In a study of 4-year-olds during free play, insecure boys tended to show more aggression, disruptiveness, and attention seeking compared with secure boys. Insecure girls were more dependent and less assertive than secure girls (Turner, 1991). The author suggests that gender differences in social behavior are exaggerated among children with histories of insecure attachments. The stereotypes of the aggressive boy and passive girl are *not* supported among preschool children with secure attachment histories, but the stereotypes *do* seem to characterize quite well the subgroup of insecure children examined in this study.

Following children into elementary school, research has shown that 5-year-olds who were securely attached as infants show more persistence and resourcefulness in challenging tasks than children who in infancy were rated less securely attached (Arend, Gove, & Sroufe, 1979; Sroufe, 1983). LaFreniere and Sroufe (1985) related attachment history to a broad array of assessments of peer competence in the preschool classroom. In this study, the researchers observed 40 children aged 4 and 5 years as they interacted with one another in class. They obtained the following five measurements of competence: (1) teacher ratings of social competence, (2) peer ratings of popularity, (3) observations of the quality of children's social participation, (4) the amount of attention each child received from other children based on analysis of whom the children looked at while playing, and (5) ratings of social dominance. As Figure 2.1 shows, preschool children who were securely attached as infants scored higher on all five measures of social competence than their peers who as infants were classified as insecurely attached.

To date, few longitudinal studies on individual differences in attachment have followed children beyond elementary school. Therefore, we are unable to draw informed conclusions concerning the long-term effects of attachment on personality development in adolescence and beyond. The picture we have for the first 10 years of life, however, reveals impressive continuity in attachment and in the organization of attachment-related behavior (Grossmann & Grossmann, 1991; Main & Cassidy, 1988; Sroufe, 1988).

FIGURE 2.1   *Peer Competence and Attachment History*

Five-year-olds with a history of secure attachment show higher levels of peer competence in school compared with children who have a history of insecure attachment.

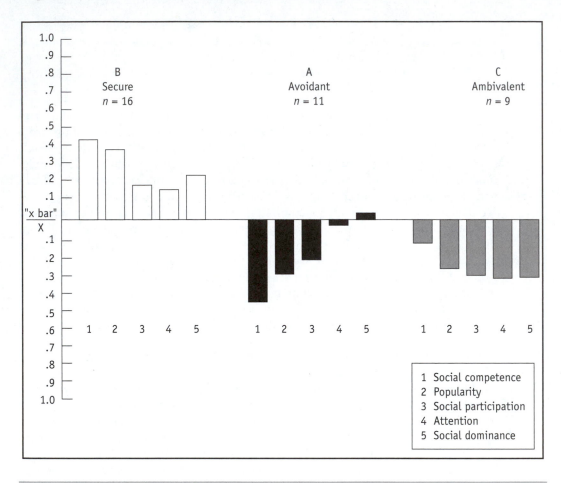

Source: LaFreniere & Sroufe (1985), p. 63.

A growing number of researchers are viewing attachment as a key organizational construct for social, emotional, and personality development. A growing number are coming to endorse what Bowlby (1973) termed the "strong case for believing that an unthinking confidence in the unfailing accessibility and support of attachment figures is the bedrock on which stable and self-reliant personality is built" (p. 322).

As the results of attachment research have become disseminated in the public arena, informed citizens and policymakers have posed hard questions about the effects of contemporary economic, political, social, and cultural arrangements on the development of secure and insecure attachments (Silverstein, 1991). Are certain types of parents at great risk for having children who will become insecurely attached? Are working mothers more likely to have insecurely attached children? What is the relationship between infant day care and attachment? Can fathers substitute for mothers? Are father–infant attachments the same as mother–infant attachments?

Each of these questions is embedded in a complex and evolving matrix of cultural values, historical trends, and economic realities. While psychological research can help inform the debate around such questions, it cannot itself provide definitive answers to any of them. To a certain extent, research findings themselves are cultural constructions, products of the values and beliefs held dear by the researchers themselves. This is not to say that psychological researchers are unduly biased in their inquiries. Rather, social scientists, like all other people, make inquiries in a particular social and cultural context. Their questions and their methods are influenced by the evolving social world within which they live. Take, for instance, the quote from John Bowlby above. He suggests that secure attachment is the "bedrock" upon which is built a "self-reliant" and "stable" personality. In contemporary Western society, "self-reliance" and "stability" are strongly valued as desirable characteristics in persons. But different historical eras and different cultures value different attributes in persons. In some cultures, "self-reliance" may be synonymous with selfishness, perceived as a threat to the community good. Keeping these caveats in mind, therefore, we are better positioned to evaluate the different possible meanings of contemporary attachment research.

Are certain types of parents at risk for having children with insecure attachments? As we have seen, research suggests that mothers who are especially sensitive, responsive, and encouraging are more likely to bring up children with secure attachments. But we should view these characteristics as relational attributes rather than personality traits per se. In other words, "responsiveness" and "sensitivity" refer to how a mother reacts to her infant and not necessarily to how she approaches the world overall. In general, research has not identified a set of global personality traits that predispose mothers to engage in interactions leading to a particular kind of attachment classification. There is one exception to this rule, however. Recent studies have suggested that mothers with chronic *negative affect*—such as chronically depressed mothers—tend to have infants who are less securely attached (Ainsworth & Eichberg, 1991; Spieker & Booth, 1988; Teti, Gelfand, Messinger, & Isabella, 1995). In these cases, the mother is unable to summon up the enthusiasm to engage her infant in joyous and reciprocal exchange. Interactions lack energy and synchrony, leading to the development on the part of the infant of a working model of a neglecting and lethargic caregiver.

Surprisingly, socioeconomic status per se does not appear to be significantly related to attachment classification (Spieker & Booth, 1988). Children from poor and working-class families are no less likely to establish secure attachments than middle-class and upper-class children, as long as cases of known abuse or neglect are eliminated from the samples. However, the stresses of poverty and unemployment may increase the likelihood of abuse and neglect, and therefore negative effects of disadvantaged social class may manifest themselves indirectly. Research suggests that children of abusive parents are indeed at risk for insecure attachment (Egeland & Sroufe, 1981). For example, Lyons-Ruth, Connell, Zoll, and Stahl (1987) found that maltreated infants were more avoidant of their mothers in the Strange Situation than nonmaltreated infants. Other studies suggest that chronic child abuse may promote the development of a "disorganized" attachment pattern—the **D-baby** (Carlson, Cicchetti, Barnett, & Braunwald, 1989). D-babies appear confused and disoriented in the presence of mother. Within this seriously disturbed pattern of attachment, the child appears to do little exploring in the mother's presence, and the mother appears unable to calm down the child during periods of distress. It is as if the infant perceives her to be as threatening as, or even more threatening than, the rest of the environment. In a recent review of research on attachment and behavioral problems in children, Lyons-Ruth (1996) found that infants with disorganized attachment patterns (D-babies) tend to show heightened levels of aggression when they reach grade school, compared with children whose attachment classifications in infancy were A, B, or C.

What about day care? In the 1990s, over half of American mothers of infants and approximately 75% of mothers with school-aged children participated in the paid workforce (Silverstein, 1991). As a result, paid child care has become an extremely important issue in contemporary American society. Unlike 75 other nations across the world, the United States has no comprehensive family policy that helps families cope with the competing demands of work and child care. Therefore, a growing number of families are dependent on the services of many different kinds of paid child-care providers.

A small number of studies have examined the development of attachment in infants who spend a considerable amount of time away from their mothers in day care. Data from the Netherlands, where government supports day-care programs, suggest that the day-care experience does not affect the quality of attachment in a negative manner (Goosens, 1987). Data from the United States, however, tend to show a slight tendency for infants in day care whose mothers work full time to manifest insecure attachment patterns (especially avoidant patterns of A-babies) in the Strange Situation, compared with infants cared for solely by their mothers at home. In a comprehensive review, Clarke-Stewart (1989) reports: "Of the infants of full-time working mothers, 36% have been classified as insecure; of the infants of nonemployed or part-time working mothers, only 29% have been so classified" (p. 266). The meaning of the finding is ambiguous, however. Different day-care providers vary significantly with respect to cost and quality. In addition, the Strange Situation may hold different experiences for day-care and home-care children. The procedure depends on the infant's experiencing separation from the caregiver as a mildly stressful event. But the Strange Situation may not be equally stressful for infants of working and nonworking mothers. Those with significant day-care experience may have adjusted well to brief separations from mother. Their occasionally avoidant responses in reunion episodes of the Strange Situation procedure may be more indicative of the rather routine nature of brief separations in their lives than of insecure attachment per se.

What about fathers? Studies suggest that infants may form intense attachment bonds with fathers, as well as other family members. Father–infant attachment resembles mother–infant attachment in many respects (Lamb, 1976, 1979). Infants may use fathers as secure bases for exploration; they may seek out fathers during periods of uncertainty or fear. Differences between mother–infant and father–infant attachments have been noted, too. Mothers spend more time with their infants and tend to be responsible for most of the caregiving. Fathers, in contrast, spend proportionally more of their interaction time in play. Moreover, fathers play in a more physical, idiosyncratic, and emotionally arousing way, whereas mothers tend to play in ways that are

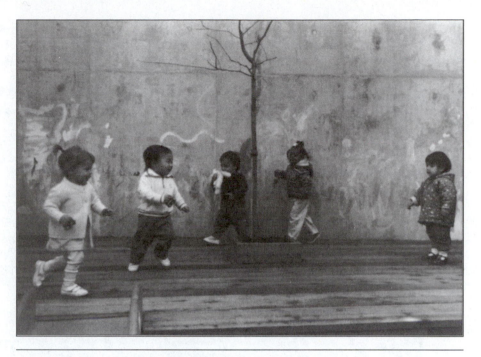

Attachment between mother and child may or may not be affected by sending the infant to day care. The current evidence is too ambiguous.

less arousing, more verbal, and more often involve toys and conventional games such as peek-a-boo. As a result, the father–infant relationship tends to be more concerned with affiliative needs (having fun) than attachment needs (felt security). The father as a socializer and playmate provides cognitive and social stimulation that is somewhat different from that provided by the mother (Bridges, Connell, & Belsky, 1988). It is not surprising to learn, therefore, that the level of security in an infant's attachment to mother may not be the same as that with father (Main & Weston, 1981). The two attachment relationships are relatively independent, though one study suggests a slight tendency for an infant's secure attachment with mother to be correlated with a corresponding secure attachment with father (Fox, Kimmerly, & Schafer, 1991). With respect to predictors of security in father–infant attachment, Belsky (1996) found that fathers of secure infants had friendlier and more outgoing personalities in general, tended to have more positive marriages, and were relatively more satisfied with the balance of work and family responsibilities in their lives, compared with fathers of insecure infants.

Finally, we should consider the intriguing possibility that, in some cases, insecure attachment may be just as adaptive, in an evolutionary sense, as secure attachment. In their "evolutionary theory of socialization," Jay Belsky, Laurence Steinberg, and Patricia Draper (1991) propose that evolution has provided for two divergent developmental pathways in the quest to pass one's genes to the next generation. For the securely attached infant growing up with adequate material resources and in the relative harmony of an intact, two-parent family, personality development is built on a working

Children's attachments with their fathers play an important role in early personality development.

model of trust and reliability in interpersonal relationships. The relative lack of stress in such families may slightly delay the onset of puberty, the authors claim, which is associated with later sexual activity and may become connected with more commitment to long-term intimate relationships in adulthood (e.g., stable marriage) and greater investment in parenting. This would appear to be the developmental model favored by middle-class American society. With respect to inclusive fitness, it works to maximize the *quality* of parent–child relationship to assure that the few progeny who are produced will survive and flourish, passing genes to subsequent generations.

A contrasting model emerges in unstable families, within which insecure attachment may be more likely. Children grow up in a stressful environment that is lacking in basic material and emotional resources. Their working models emphasize the unpredictability of interpersonal relationships, leading them to adopt an "opportunistic" rather than reciprocal orientation toward others. Boys may tend to be more aggressive; girls may become somewhat depressed or anxious. The childhood stress may accelerate the onset of puberty, as some studies have suggested, leading to earlier sexual maturity, earlier sexual activity, promiscuity, and eventually limited parental investment. The emphasis is on the *quantity* of offspring produced, assuring that the maximum number of opportunities for passing one's genes down to the next generation are fulfilled. The authors concede that such a developmental pattern *seems* to have little going for it:

To many readers it will no doubt seem counterintuitive to assert, as we and others do, that a developmental trajectory characterized by attachment insecurity, behavior problems, early maturation, precocious sexuality, unstable pair bonds, limited parental investment, and high total fertility makes "biological sense." In modern Western society, this reproductive strategy appears clearly dysfunctional and disadvantageous. Why, then, would it have evolved? (Belsky, Steinberg, & Draper, 1991, p. 653)

The authors argue that within certain unfavorable environments, characterized by poverty and familial instability, early sexual activity and higher fertility may prove especially adaptive in removing the young boy or girl from the family of origin early on and positioning him or her for greater reproductive success than might be possible for those whose sexual maturation is delayed (Figure 2.2). They write:

This strategy may be associated with higher offspring mortality, but from the point of view of fitness, individuals living in such adverse circumstances who *delay* reproducing may well be selected against (i.e., leave few or no offspring). In such an environment, a man who invests disproportionately in one woman and in children (who may not be his own) will leave relatively few of his own offspring behind. Likewise, a young woman who waits for the right man to help rear her children may lose valuable reproductive opportunities at a time when her health and physical capability are at their peak and when her mother and senior female kin are young enough to be effective surrogates. In such circumstances, nonbonded and relatively indiscriminate sexuality, as well as high fertility, can be positively selected. It is in this sense, then, that we assert that both of the reproductive strategies that we detailed make "biological sense," in that they are optimal given the contexts in which they develop—and for which they were selected. (Belsky, Steinberg, & Draper, 1991, pp. 653–654)

In this theory, the relative security of attachment is one barometer of the prevailing relational context within which the child will grow up. As such, it will work with other indicators to influence the timing of puberty and the development of an appropriate reproductive strategy. According to the authors, "evolution has primed humans to learn particular lessons during the first 5–7 years of life that will shape their subsequent pair bonding and child-rearing behavior" (Belsky, Steinberg, & Draper, 1991, p. 648). Just how this influence works out at the physiological level is a matter of some speculation, and its overall importance in shaping pair-bonding and child-rearing strategies is open to considerable dispute (Maccoby, 1991). Still, the theory proposed by Belsky, Steinberg, and Draper is noteworthy for its serious attempt to understand important individual differences in human personality from the standpoint of modern evolutionary theory. Like the work of Buss on mating strategies and Gangestad and Simpson on sociosexuality, the evolutionary theory of socialization provokes us to think about both human nature and individual differences in persons from an evolutionary perspective emphasizing human adaptation within a wide variety of environments and under divergent selection pressures.

Adult Attachments

Attachment theory describes an affectional relationship between two persons through which one person provides support, protection, and a secure base for the other. The most obvious example of attachment, therefore, is the bond of love between the mature caregiver and the relatively defenseless infant. However, the dynamics of attachment

FIGURE 2.2   *Two Development Pathways*

One evolutionary theory of socialization proposes that both secure and insecure attachments may be evolutionarily adaptive, depending on environmental conditions.

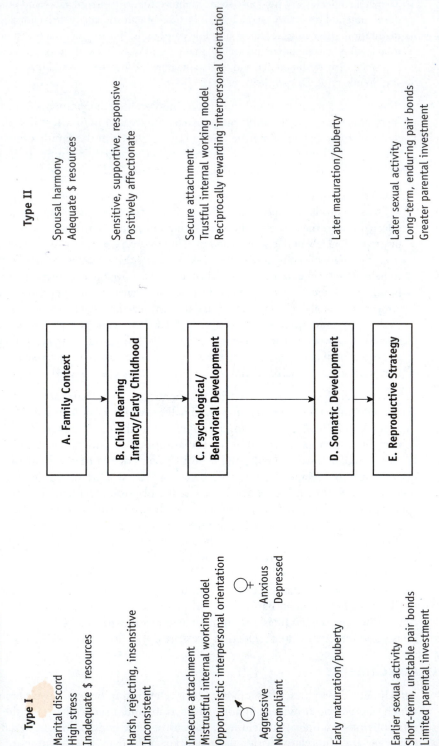

Source: Belsky, Steinberg, & Draper (1991), p. 651.

may be played out in many other relationships as well, throughout the human lifespan (Ainsworth, 1989; Bowlby, 1980). In recent years, psychologists have extended attachment theory into adulthood. To date their inquiries have focused on two ways in which attachments are influential in the adult years. First, they have examined adults' working models of their own childhood attachments, asking adults to tell the stories of their earliest relationships (Main, 1991). Second, they have entertained the possibility that romantic love in young adulthood and beyond may be understood in terms of secure and insecure attachment qualities (Hazan & Shaver, 1987).

Mary Main and her colleagues (George, Kaplan, & Main, 1985; Main, 1991; Main, Kaplan, & Cassidy, 1985) have developed an **Adult Attachment Interview** through which men and women respond to open-ended questions about their recollections of their own childhood attachment bonds with their parents or other caregivers. The adult is asked to choose five adjectives that best describe the relationship with each parent during childhood and then to provide an account of a particular episode from childhood illustrating each adjective. Later the adult is asked to describe what he or she did when upset as a child, to which parent he or she felt closer, whether he or she ever felt rejected as a child, why the parents may have acted the way they did, how the relationships with the parents have changed over time, and how the early experiences may have affected the adult's current functioning.

Based on the interview, Main classifies each adult into one of four categories: *secure/autonomous, dismissing* of attachments, *preoccupied* by past attachments, and *unresolved* with respect to traumatic attachment-related events. Her research suggests that mothers with secure/autonomous attachments from childhood tend to raise securely attached infants themselves. Dismissing parents tend to have avoidant children (A-babies); preoccupied parents tend to have resistant children (C-babies); and mothers with unresolved attachments from childhood stemming from traumatic events such as abuse tend to have children with disorganized attachments (D-babies). In a prospective study, researchers administered the Adult Attachment Interview to pregnant women expecting their first child and then conducted the Strange Situation with their babies at age 1 year (Fonagy, Steele, & Steele, 1991). In keeping with Main's results, adult attachments of pregnant women in the interviews tended to match the subsequent attachment classifications of their infants at age 1. (See Table 2.6.)

Main (1991) describes the Adult Attachment Interviews typically produced by secure/autonomous parents with securely attached children. Such parents "focused easily on the questions; showed few departures from usual forms of narrative or discourse; easily marked the principles or rationales behind their responses; and struck judges as

TABLE 2.6	*Corresponding Attachment Types From Adult Interviews and Observations of Infants*
ADULT ATTACHMENT INTERVIEW	**INFANT ATTACHMENT TYPE**
Secure/autonomous	Secure (B-baby)
Dismissing	Avoidant (A-baby)
Preoccupied	Resistant (C-baby)
Unresolved	Disorganized (D-baby)

both collaborative and truthful" (p. 142). An essential characteristic of their interviews appears to be the ease with which they are able to provide a *coherent* account of their childhood. Whether describing positive or negative experiences from childhood, secure/autonomous adults are able to fashion a story from childhood that is consistent and convincing.

By sharp contrast, dismissing and preoccupied parents tend to be "relatively incoherent in their interview transcripts, exhibiting logical and factual contradictions; inability to stay with the interview topic; contradictions between general descriptors of their relationships with their parents and actual autobiographical episodes offered; apparent inability to access early memories; anomalous changes in wording or intrusions into topics; slips of the tongue; metaphor or rhetoric inappropriate to the discourse context; and inability to focus upon the interviews" (Main, 1991, p. 143). In particular, dismissing parents of avoidant infants are usually distinguished for their insistence that they cannot remember much from their earlier years. Often they will idealize their parents in vague terms but be unable to provide behavioral proof for their claims. Preoccupied parents of resistant infants tend to provide lengthy but rambling responses about childhood that often contradict themselves.

Finally, unresolved parents of infants displaying disorganized attachment tend to provide moderately coherent narratives of childhood, but they slip into magical and bizarre thought patterns when considering attachment-related events such as loss. "In these statements, the adult may indicate beliefs in 'magical' causality surrounding a death or other trauma, or subtly indicate a belief that a deceased attachment figure is simultaneously dead and alive" (Main, 1991, p. 145). Overall, these accounts lack *plausibility*. Just beneath the surface of a seemingly sensible narrative lie primitive and irrational thought processes linked with unresolved trauma from childhood.

A recent research review examined 33 studies that employed the Adult Attachment Interview, sampling more than 2,000 adults, including mothers, fathers, and teenagers, from a number of different countries (vanIJzendoorn & Bakerman-Kranenburg, 1996). Each participant in each study was classified into one of Main's first three adult attachment types and then rated independently with respect to the extent to which he or she showed any characteristics of the fourth type (unresolved). The distribution for the first three types read as follows: 58% secure/autonomous, 24% dismissing, and 18% preoccupied. In addition, 19% of the participants showed some evidence of being unresolved with respect to loss or trauma in their lives. No significant sex differences in the distribution of scores were observed. Mothers from low socioeconomic status were more likely to show dismissing attachment representations and to express unresolved trauma or loss compared with mothers from higher social classes. Secure/autonomous women and secure/autonomous men were more often married to each other than would be expected by chance, as was also the case for those showing evidence of unresolved loss and trauma. In addition, those men and women who suffered from psychopathology and mental illness of various kinds were significantly more likely to be classified in the insecure categories (dismissing, preoccupied, and unresolved) compared with nonclinical adults.

Research employing the Adult Attachment Interview suggests that working models of attachment laid down in childhood may continue to influence adult behavior in the realm of caregiving. Cindy Hazan and Philip Shaver have extended this line of thought in a different direction by suggesting that working attachment models may also influ-

TABLE 2.7   *Attachment Styles*

Which of the following paragraphs best describes your feelings about being emotionally close to other people? Place a checkmark in front of the one paragraph that best describes you.

_____ I find it relatively easy to get close to others and am comfortable depending on them and having them depend on me. I don't often worry about being abandoned or about someone getting too close to me. *[Secure]*

_____ I am somewhat uncomfortable being close to others; I find it difficult to trust them completely, difficult to allow myself to depend on them. I am nervous when anyone gets too close, and often, love partners want me to be more intimate than I feel comfortable being. *[Avoidant]*

_____ I find that others are reluctant to get as close as I would like. I often worry that my partner doesn't really love me or won't want to stay with me. I want to merge completely with another person, and this desire sometimes scares people away. *[Ambivalent]*

Source: Hazan and Shaver (1987), p. 515.

ence the ways in which adults engage each other in romantic love (Hazan & Shaver, 1987, 1990). Borrowing Ainsworth's original division among B-babies, A-babies, and C-babies, Hazan and Shaver have identified three corresponding **attachment styles** in adult love. (See Table 2.7.) Adults with a secure attachment style say they find it relatively easy to get close to others and are comfortable depending on others and having others depend on them. They don't worry too much about others' getting too close. They describe their most important love experiences as happy, friendly, and trusting. They emphasize being able to accept and support their partners despite their partners' faults. Adults with avoidant attachment styles (akin to Ainsworth's A-babies) report that they are somewhat uncomfortable being close to others and find it difficult to trust others completely. They are characterized by a "fear of intimacy," by emotional highs and lows, and by excessive jealousy. Adults with anxious/ambivalent styles (akin to Ainsworth's resistant C-babies) say they want to merge with others but that this desire sometimes scares other people away. They worry that their partners do not love them and will eventually abandon them. They experience love as involving obsession, desire for reciprocation and union, emotional highs and lows, and extreme sexual attraction and jealousy.

Employing a set of simple self-report questions concerning a person's general view of romantic love, Hazan and Shaver (1987) report that approximately 60% of their adult respondents are classified as securely attached, with the remainder falling within avoidant or anxious/ambivalent (resistant) categories. The breakdown is roughly comparable to the ratios of secure and insecure attachments obtained in research on infants. In addition, recent studies suggest a person's overall attachment style is predictive of love-related behavior. For example, Simpson (1990) found that secure attachment style was associated with greater relationship interdependence, commitment, trust, and satisfaction among dating college students. Mikulincer and Nachson (1991) found that students with secure and ambivalent styles exhibit greater levels of self-disclosure than avoidant students. Kobak and Hazan (1991) found that spouses with secure working models—that is, expectations that partners are psychologically available and ready to be relied upon—deal with their emotional conflicts in more constructive ways and report better marital adjustment.

Simpson, Rholes, and Phillips (1996) videotaped dating couples as they tried to resolve a major problem in their relationship. They found that participants who were classified as ambivalent with respect to attachment style tended to perceive their dating partners in especially negative terms after discussing the major relational problem. Ambivalent men and women found the activity of discussing problems in their relationships to be especially stressful, and they reacted to the stress by lowering their estimation of their partners' worth. In a related study, Simpson, Rholes, and Neligan (1992) videotaped dating couples as they sat in a waiting room before participating in an activity known to provoke anxiety in most people. The researchers coded behaviors such as physical contact, supportive comments, and efforts to seek and give emotional support. They found that those men and women classified as avoidant in attachment tended to express significantly less helping and support behavior with their partners compared with those who had secure attachment styles. In times of anxiety, people with secure attachment styles are more active and effective in providing their romantic partners with a secure base of comfort, encouragement, and support, compared with people who have avoidant styles of attachment.

For both infants and adults, the provision of support is a key function of secure attachment. Securely attached infants experience more secure support in their environments, and adults with secure attachment styles should be especially effective in supporting others when they are in danger and in seeking and finding support for themselves in times of personal stress. Mikulincer, Florian, and Weller (1993) examined reactions to the stress of war by analyzing relations between attachment style and the ways in which Israeli citizens reacted to the Iraqi missile attack in the Persian Gulf War. A total of 140 Israeli students were interviewed two weeks after the war and classified according to their attachment styles (secure, avoidant, ambivalent) and residence area (dangerous versus less dangerous area). Among students living in dangerous areas during the war (areas directly threatened by missile attack), those with secure attachment styles tended to engage in more support-seeking behavior as a way of coping with trauma, compared with avoidant and ambivalent students. In addition, ambivalent students in high-danger zones reported the highest levels of distress following the war while avoidant students reported the highest levels of hostility and physical symptoms in response to the war.

Recent research suggests that attachment styles are predictive of the vicissitudes of everyday social behavior. Tidwell, Reis, and Shaver (1996) asked 125 college students to keep behavioral diaries for a week. In the diaries, the students recorded their social interactions with friends, teachers, family members, acquaintances, romantic partners, and so on. The findings indicated that compared with ambivalent and secure individuals, students with avoidant attachment styles reported lower levels of intimacy, enjoyment, and positive emotions and higher levels of negative emotions in daily interactions, especially interactions with the opposite sex. Avoidant persons tend to structure their interactions in ways that minimize emotional closeness. Compared with avoidant and secure individuals, students with ambivalent attachment styles tended to report a wider variety of emotional experiences in their daily social interactions, reporting many emotional highs and lows in their interactions with others. Overall, then, avoidant individuals experience low levels of joy and happiness in the presence of others and, perhaps as a result, tend to keep people at a distance. Ambivalent individuals experience a rich mixture of both positive and negative interpersonal events, perhaps contributing to their mixed or conflicted working model for attachment. Secure individuals report the highest levels of positive and lowest levels of negative interactions with other people in daily social life.

Outside the realm of interpersonal relationships, attachment styles appear to be implicated in the ways in which people understand themselves as individuals and how they make sense of their lives in the past, present, and anticipated future. Individuals with secure attachment styles tend to construct a more complex and coherent image of themselves compared with avoidant and ambivalent persons, and secure and avoidant people have generally more positive views of themselves and their lives compared with ambivalent individuals (Mikulincer, 1995). People with secure attachment styles describe themselves as more curious and exploratory, compared with avoidant and ambivalent individuals, and they hold more positive attitudes about being an open-minded and curious person (Mikulincer, 1997). Both ambivalent and avoidant attachment styles are associated with low levels of self-esteem and with higher levels of depression (Roberts, Gotlib, & Kassel, 1996).

A secure attachment style helps to fend off bad moods and chronic sadness. The link between secure attachment and positive feelings about the self is *not* due, however, to any immunity that securely attached people enjoy with respect to negative events in their lives. People with secure attachment styles have ready access to a wide variety of emotionally vivid experiences from their past, including negative experiences of sadness, anger, and anxiety. Individuals with secure attachment styles are able to process negative autobiographical information without getting overwhelmed by it. By contrast, avoidant individuals have a difficult time recalling negative events from their past, suggestive of a repressive approach to autobiographical recollections. Ambivalent individuals are often flooded by negative memories of the past. They cannot control their negative memories well, and they cannot integrate the negative events into a coherent story of the self (Mikulincer & Orbach, 1995).

The crucial link between caregiver–infant attachment and adult attachment styles is the concept of inner working models. Hazan and Shaver propose that adult styles are the legacies of internalized models of relating that are laid down in infancy. Modest support for this idea comes from a study by Feeney and Noller (1990) showing that college students with secure attachment styles report relatively positive perceptions of early family relationships. By contrast, avoidant students tend to report childhood separations from their mothers, and anxious/ambivalent students describe fathers who are especially nonsupportive. In another study, researchers found that young adults with a secure attachment style produced highly detailed and well-constructed representations of their parents, emphasizing parental kindness and care, whereas those with insecure attachment styles provided sketchier accounts that emphasized ways in which their parents were punitive and unavailable (Levy, Blatt, & Shaver, 1998). For the most part, however, the precise linkage between infant attachment and adult love remains a mystery. Indeed, there are certain ways in which romantic love is *not* like attachment. Ideally, lovers are relative equals who share themselves with each other in an intimate and egalitarian manner. By contrast, attachment suggests a relation of relative nonequals— the infant attached to the stronger, wiser, more mature attachment object (McAdams, 1992a). Still, there is little doubt that lovers often function as attachment objects for each other, providing secure bases for each other's explorations in the world. The relationship between infant attachment and adult love, therefore, remains an exciting realm for future research.

SUMMARY

1. The scientific study of the person begins with a consideration of human nature, which has been forged over millions of years through human evolution. Evolution is the ultimate context for understanding the person because it provides the most systematic and encompassing scientific framework to account for how the human organism was designed and what all human beings have in common. An evolutionary approach to personality helps to specify the distal and ultimate determinants of human behavior in the overall, which may be combined with an understanding of the more proximal and immediate determinants of any particular person's behavior in order to provide a full account of human individuality.

2. Over the course of evolution, organisms are designed through natural selection to engage in behaviors that ultimately make for the replication of the genes that determine their design. An organism's inclusive fitness refers to its overall or total ability to promote the replication of its own genes from one generation to the next. Inclusive fitness is enhanced through any mechanisms or systems that make it more likely than otherwise that the person's genes, or those genes that he or she shares with biological relatives, will be passed down successfully to the next generation through progeny.

3. Human beings have evolved over a 2–4 million year span as hunters and gatherers living in small, migratory groups. During the long period of time during which human beings inhabited this environment of evolutionary adaptedness (EEA), they came to occupy a cognitive niche in the general evolutionary landscape. The greatest adaptive advantages for humans came mainly from their powers of computation—that is, from the power of the human mind. Endowed with considerable cognitive advantages relative to other animals, human beings used tools, developed cooperative partnerships, and eventually created complex societies to adapt to the challenges of the EEA. The human mind evolved to adapt to many different evolutionary challenges, resulting in the mind's evolution toward a loose confederation of subsystems or modules, each designed to solve an evolutionarily significant problem.

4. Over the course of evolution, human beings have faced challenges relating to survival and reproduction. Reproductive challenges include finding and keeping a sexual mate and caring for the progeny that result from sexual reproduction. Evolutionary theory can be invoked to provide distal explanations for the significant sex differences that are typically observed in the realms of human mating and reproduction. In the overall, human males may have evolved to adopt mating strategies and goals that maximize the quantity of offspring they produce, pushing them in the direction of promiscuity. By contrast, human females may have evolved to adopt mating strategies and goals that maximize the quality of offspring, given that females must invest a great deal more energy and time in gestation, lactation, and eventually infant care in order to assure that the relatively few progeny they may produce will live long enough to reproduce themselves. As a result, evolutionary theory would predict that females should be relatively choosier when it comes to mating and less inclined toward multiple sexual partners. For the same evolutionary reasons, furthermore, males and females are likely to differ somewhat with respect to the qualities they seek in their mates, in reactions to possible betrayals in mating, and in their overall emotional investment in offspring.

5. As described in Hogan's socioanalytic theory of personality, human beings have evolved to live in groups wherein the prime social goals are getting along and getting ahead. Through role playing, impression management, and effective participation in the elaborate social rituals that define cultural life, human beings seek acceptance and status in groups. Heightened acceptance and status enhance inclusive fitness. One potential barrier to the attainment of social acceptance and status is the common personality trait of shyness.

6. Human beings are, by nature, a moderately aggressive species. Evolutionary theory provides distal explanations for the tendency of human beings to engage in many forms of instrumental and hostile aggression, including the deadliest and most organized form of aggression—human warfare. But evolutionary theory, like other explanations that invoke more proximate causes for aggression (e.g., culture, learning), cannot provide a justification for human aggressiveness; nor can it be used to articulate a moral perspective about aggression.

7. Human beings are also, by nature, an exquisitely altruistic species. Altruism and aggression are natural outgrowths of the basic feature of human life in the EEA: Humans evolved to live in groups. Human groups are hierarchical, and hierarchy is at least an indirect result of differential effectiveness in aggressive and dominant behaviors on the part of group members. Dominance hierarchies

provide the stability necessary for cooperative and altruistic behavior to occur. Human beings have evolved mental systems to develop emotional attachments, empathy, internalized social rules, concepts of giving and trading, peacemaking, negotiation, community concern, and other prosocial tendencies, most shared in one form or another with other primates but developed in more complex ways in the case of humans. These evolved adaptations aim to keep aggression in check and to undergird social cooperation, which itself enhances the inclusive fitness of those who cooperate. Undergirding altruistic behavior in human beings are the mechanisms of kin selection and reciprocal altruism, both of which enhance the individual's inclusive fitness.

8. One of the most notable features of human nature is caregiver–infant attachment. Attachment theory, articulated by John Bowlby and Mary Ainsworth, suggests that the bond of love that develops between caregiver and infant is a complex, instinctually grounded behavioral system that has functioned throughout human evolution to assure mother–infant proximity and thereby to protect the infant from predators and other dangers. As the attachment relationship develops in the first few years of life, the infant builds up a set of expectations concerning human relationships, which come to comprise an internalized working model.

9. Utilizing the Strange Situation procedure, researchers have identified four different types of attachment bonds in infants: secure (B-babies), avoidant (A-babies), resistant (C-babies), and disorganized (D-babies). Secure attachment is the most common form observed; the other three are variations on insecure attachment. The developmental antecedents of secure attachment include maternal sensitivity and synchrony in early mother–infant play. The consequences of secure attachment include positive indices of independence, mastery, and peer popularity in preschool and elementary school. While secure attachment appears to be connected to many positive outcomes in childhood, some theorists have made a provocative case for the evolutionarily adaptive nature of *in*secure attachments under certain especially stressful environmental conditions.

10. Attachments among adults have been studied in two ways. Through the Adult Attachment Interview, men and women recount stories of early attachment relationships with parents, which are subsequently analyzed to assess the kind of working models that adults may hold: secure/autonomous, dismissing, preoccupied, and unresolved. In a second research approach, psychologists have examined attachment styles in romantic love, identifying three different styles that roughly correspond to the secure, avoidant, and resistant categories obtained with infants. College students with secure attachment styles exhibit more commitment and self-disclosure in their romantic relationships, offer and obtain more social support during periods of stress, experience more positive affect in daily social interactions, and construct a sense of self that is especially positive, complex, and coherent.

Freud and the Psychoanalytic Tradition

The most influential psychologist of the 20th century was Sigmund Freud (1856–1939). One hundred years ago, Freud published his landmark volume, *The Interpretation of Dreams* (Freud, 1900/1953), wherein he described a way of making sense of human dreams and human lives that promised to shed light on the darkest recesses of the mind and expose the deepest secrets of the soul. For the next 40 years Freud taught us that the person is a mystery, even to the self. All that we do, all that we think, all that we feel, all that we love and hate is meaningful, and yet hardly anybody knows what it means. Our ignorance is so pervasive that, in most cases, we are completely in the dark about the meanings and causes of some of our simplest acts and experiences— our silly mistakes, for instance, and our seemingly senseless dreams. Were we to know the meanings, furthermore, we would shudder in disbelief, for even the most innocent comment or gesture may betray a shameful secret of the soul, a secret rooted in our unknown desires to kill, to love, to live, and even to die. In general, we are the anxious protagonists of a tragic drama we call human life. Our anxieties are the inevitable products of relentless conflict—conflict within the self and conflict between the self and the society within which the self resides.

Sigmund Freud was the prime inventor of a particular kind of psychology—usually called **psychoanalysis.** Drawing on extensive case studies of therapy patients seen in medical settings, Freud and his followers developed psychoanalysis outside the mainstream of scientific psychology. But psychoanalysis has had a substantial impact on personality psychology proper, to say nothing of its pervasive cultural influence in the 20th-century West. Anthropology, political science, literature, literary criticism, art, and the cinema all acknowledge certain Freudian underpinnings and influences. Psychoanalytic theories, valid or not, have even crept into our everyday parlance, as we speak knowingly of "inhibitions," "repressed memories," the "Oedipus complex," and "Freudian slips." Indeed, you cannot be a well-educated woman or man in Western society today without some understanding of Sigmund Freud and the psychoanalytic tradition.

The psychoanalytic tradition begins historically with Freud and can be traced through a number of subsequent contributions to our thinking about personality as expressed in the seminal writings of Carl Jung, Alfred Adler, Anna Freud, Heinz Hartmann, Melanie Klein, Karen Horney, Erich Fromm, Erik Erikson, Harry Stack Sullivan, Margaret Mahler, and Heinz Kohut, among others (see Table 3.1). If this were a book on the history of grand personality theories, each of these theorists might get his or her own chapter. But my goal in this one chapter is to provide a more general overview of psychoanalysis writ large, emphasizing some of the ways in which the different theoretical approaches that stem from Freud's original insights share common ground, even as they make provocative claims. From 1900 to the present day, the psychoanalytic tradition has offered a wide range of fascinating viewpoints concerning personality and psychopathology. Even within Freud's own writings, different theoretical perspectives can be observed. Not surprisingly, therefore, the many different psychoanalytic theories say many different things, and often one theory will contradict or take issue with another. Still, there are certain things that most psychoanalytically inspired theories have in common.

The most important thing that different psychoanalytic theories have in common is a set of assumptions about what it means to be a human being. In essence, all

TABLE 3.1	*Twelve Major Figures in the History of Psychoanalysis*

Sigmund Freud (1856–1939)
: The intellectual founder of the tradition and its most influential theorist. The main ideas of Freud's theory are described in this chapter.

Carl Jung (1875–1961)
: An early associate of Freud's, Jung broke with Freud after bitter disagreements concerning the role of sexuality in human life. Jung developed a rival theory, called *analytical psychology,* which emphasizes the collective unconscious and the role of myth and symbol in personality. The main ideas of Jung's theory are described in this chapter.

Alfred Adler (1870–1937)
: An early associate of Freud's, Adler also broke with Freud to establish a rival theory called *individual psychology*. Individual psychology identifies the striving for superiority as a main motive in life while tending to emphasize the rational and forward-looking aspects of human functioning. Because Adler is one of the first personality theorists to spell out the role of life stories, his theory is described in Chapter 12 of this book.

Anna Freud (1895–1982)
: Sigmund Freud's daughter, Anna Freud applied psychoanalytic principles to treatment of children and expanded the psychoanalytic understanding of defense mechanisms, as described in this chapter. Anna Freud is viewed as an early *ego psychologist* for her relative emphasis on the adaptive powers of the ego or self.

Heinz Hartmann (1894–1970)
: Called "the father of ego psychology," Hartmann led the movement in psychoanalysis away from Freud's original emphasis on instinctual drives and toward a strengthening of the ego as an adaptive and effective agent in the personality, as described in this chapter.

Melanie Klein (1882–1960)
: One of the first *object relations* theorists, Klein argued that infants experience strong feelings of love and hate toward others in their environment, which become the basis for the establishment of internalized "objects" or unconscious representations of important people in one's life. These emotionally charged objects reside within internal, unconscious fantasy but influence external, social behavior in profound ways.

Harry S. Sullivan (1892–1949)
: An American psychiatrist who did extensive clinical work with schizophrenics, Sullivan developed an *interpersonal theory* of personality that focused on how people cope with anxiety by developing a self-system in infancy and how they seek to overcome loneliness in later childhood through deep intimacy with friends.

Karen Horney (1885–1952)
: Introduced in Chapter 1 of this book, Horney began as an orthodox Freudian but broke with Freud over his interpretation of the female Oedipal complex. Like Sullivan, Horney focuses on the experience of basic anxiety in the early years as experienced within significant interpersonal relationships. Her theory of personality tends to emphasize social and cultural influences, rather than biological ones, in the formation of the self. She outlined three ways in which neurotic and normal people cope with challenges in their lives: by moving toward, moving against, and moving away from other people.

Erich Fromm (1900–1980)
: Like Horney, Fromm developed a neo-Freudian theory that emphasizes social and cultural forces in the formation of personality. Fromm blended insights about human nature gleaned from both Freud and Karl Marx to develop an integrative theory that attempts to link personal needs, character types, societal structures, and the movement of history. Fromm's psychocultural theory is discussed in Chapter 4 of this book.

Table 3.1 continued

TABLE 3.1	*Continued*
Erik Erikson (1902–1994)	Like Anna Freud and Heinz Hartmann, Erikson was an ego psychologist. His tremendously influential stage model of psychosocial development identifies eight successive life crises, running from "trust versus mistrust" in infancy to "integrity versus despair" in old age. Erikson introduced the concepts of "identity" and "generativity" into the personality lexicon. His ideas are described in Chapter 10 of this book.
Margaret Mahler (1897–1985)	A highly influential object relations theorist, Mahler outlined the process of separation/individuation in the first three years of life, as described in this chapter.
Heinz Kohut (1913–1981)	In the 1960s and 1970s, Kohut developed a branch of psychoanalytic theorizing that he called *self psychology*. The theory resembles object relations theories with its emphasis on the internalization of early interpersonal relationships, but it also focuses on the crucial problem of developing a cohesive sense of self early in life. Kohut's theory is further described in Feature 3.B in this chapter.

psychoanalytic theories *share a particular view of human nature*—a viewpoint that is extraordinarily compelling for many people. In a nutshell, their common view can be reduced to the four propositions, four statements about (1) determinism, (2) conflict, (3) the unconscious, and (4) psychoanalytic interpretation. First, all human behavior and experience is *determined* by forces over which we have little control. These powerful forces exist within us, for the most part, and can typically be traced back to basic and primitive issues rooted in childhood. Second, the many forces that determine all our behavior and experience are in perpetual *conflict* with one another, which causes us anxiety. There is no avoiding conflict and anxiety in life. We are destined to be, more or less, miserable. Third (and worse yet), we do not even know what those forces that determine our behavior and those conflicts that precipitate our anxiety are—in other words, the most important determinants of and conflicts in our lives are outside of our consciousness. They are *unconscious* to us. We are unconscious to them. We have virtually no control over our lives. We are conflicted and anxious. And we do not know why. The fourth proposition, however, offers a glimmer of hope, but only a glimmer. The psychoanalytic tradition tells us that it is indeed possible to gain some insight and help in our difficult lives by engaging in a peculiar kind of experiential exercise, what we will call psychoanalytic *interpretation*. Through a special kind of interpretation, as Freud (1900/1953) showed in the interpretation of dreams, we can come to some tentative understandings in our lives, which may help us cope with some of the many daunting challenges that we, as human beings, are destined to face.

In Chapter 1, I argued that personality psychology is the scientific study of human individuality and that human individuality can be conveyed in terms of each person's unique patterning of dispositional traits, characteristic adaptations, and self-defining life stories. Psychoanalysis provides us with a set of powerful ideas that can be used in creative ways to explain how it is that people develop the particular traits, adaptations, and narratives that characterize who they are. Therefore, many of the theoretical ideas and the research findings that psychoanalytic theories have inspired can be applied in extremely fruitful ways to the understanding of the individual life. Psychoanalytic theories provide necessary background for understanding lives. Furthermore, like evolutionary theory (Chapter 2), the psychoanalytic tradition addresses the fundamental problem of human nature. Indeed, it is what psychoanalysis has to say about *all* human beings—about our very nature as self-conscious, social beings, wrestling with the intractable conflicts that pervade our worlds and inhabit our minds—that qualifies as the greatest intellectual legacy of the psychoanalytic tradition.

In what follows, I will fill in some of the details of the psychoanalytic view of human nature. I will begin with Freud and his revolutionary ideas concerning the unconscious. We will see that while Freud's notions about unconscious processes and dynamics have always been controversial, several lines of contemporary research support part of his view and elaborate on the many ways in which much of what we know, feel, want, and even do occurs outside our conscious awareness. I will also consider the rather more expansive view of the unconscious offered by the theorist who began as Freud's disciple and ended up his archrival—Carl Jung. One of the more provocative ideas to come out of the psychoanalytic tradition is Jung's notion of the collective unconscious, which is at the heart of Jung's own theory of personality structure and personality growth. How does personality get formed? In the second large section of this chapter, I will consider the development of personality from a psychoanalytic point of view, discussing the impact of the earliest interpersonal relationships of infancy (what some theorists call "object relations"), the role of the Oedipus complex in the lives of little boys and little girls, the structure of the fully formed personality, and some of the ways in which the person adapts to and copes with the challenges of modern life through what psychoanalysts have called the ego's "mechanisms of defense." Finally, we will examine in some detail the peculiar methods of interpretation that psychoanalysts, beginning with Freud, have traditionally used to make sense of what seems to be senseless. Psychoanalytic interpretation begins with the interpretation of dreams, slips of the tongue, and clinical symptoms. But the general principles of psychoanalytic interpretation can be applied to all of life.

THE UNCONSCIOUS

In *Notes from Underground*, the Russian novelist Fyodor Dostoyevsky wrote:

> Every man has some reminiscences which he would not tell to everyone, but only to his friends. He has others which he would not reveal even to his friends, but only to himself, and that in secret. But finally there are others which a man is even afraid to tell himself, and every decent man has a considerable number of such things stored away. (1864/1960)

Those fearsome things that Dostoyevsky said were "stored away" by every "decent man" (or woman) constitute what Freud called the **unconscious**. A fundamental proposition of every psychoanalytic approach to personality is that much of what we know and feel is outside our conscious awareness. Our lives are driven by intrapsychic mysteries that transpire at an unconscious level, buried deep beneath the manifest surface of everyday waking consciousness. We do not, and typically cannot, know what the "real" reasons are for what we do because the prime determinants of human behavior are split off from what we typically can grasp in conscious everyday experience. Freud's earliest clinical cases convinced him that the neurotic symptoms from which his patients suffered stemmed from personal conflicts and fantasies, often sexual and aggressive in nature, that had been actively pushed out of consciousness (Breuer & Freud, 1895). For example, an intensely negative experience from the past may no longer be consciously remembered, but the event lives on in the unconscious and plays itself out in conscious experience through debilitating symptoms, anxiety, and dread. The patient is clueless about the causes of his or her suffering, for the original event can no longer be recalled. In Freud's view, conscious experience is but the tip of the iceberg in human life. Most of the iceberg is underwater—that is, most of what is really important in human life lies beneath the surface of consciousness.

The idea that much of who we are is outside of our awareness, residing in a shadowy unconscious realm, is not original with Freud. The notion that behavior is shaped by unconscious determinants was clearly in evidence some 100 years prior to Freud's theorizing (Ellenberger, 1970). For instance, the philosophies of Arthur Schopenhauer (1788–1860) and Friedrich Nietzsche (1844–1900) emphasized aspects of human functioning that are outside of consciousness, typically emotional and irrational urges that are antagonistic to conscious reason.

Nineteenth-century Romantics such as the poets William Wordsworth and John Keats generally placed the person's heroic and creative powers in an unconscious, though sometimes accessible, realm. Hypnotism was used to gain access to the unconscious mind as early as 1784, and one of Freud's teachers, Jean Martin Charcot, employed the method with legendary effectiveness. Baumeister (1986) and Gay (1986) argue that middle-class adults in 19th-century Europe accepted the general idea of an inner world unknowable to the conscious self. Baumeister even asserts that Victorian men and women were preoccupied with the involuntary revelation of this inner self to others. While you might not be able to attain conscious insight into the deep secrets of your own mind, the Victorians believed there was always the danger of inadvertently disclosing the nature of your own unconscious to others, who as objective outside observers might even come to know you better than you know yourself!

In his **topographical model** of human functioning, Freud distinguished among conscious, preconscious, and unconscious regions of the mind. The conscious region contains what a person is currently aware of. People typically can verbalize their conscious experience and can think about it in a logical way. The preconscious region contains material about which the person is not currently aware but which *could readily enter awareness* should the person decide to retrieve the material. Therefore, the preconscious region may be seen as corresponding to what most of us think of as ordinary memory. I may not currently be aware of the color of my daughter's bicycle but I can easily remember what the color is if I decide to move my thinking in that direction, thereby bringing up material from the preconscious to the conscious region. The preconscious contains a vast storehouse of important as well as trivial information that is reliably at our disposal.

By contrast, material residing in the unconscious region of the mind cannot be readily retrieved. Rather the unconscious contains elements of experience that have been actively *repressed*. In part, the unconscious is a repository for ideas, images, urges, and feelings that are associated with conflict, pain, fear, guilt, and so on. Therefore, unconscious material is unconscious *for a reason*. The mind is topographically organized such that material that is incompatible with the dominant self-protective mask of consciousness is cast into an unconscious abyss. We cannot bear to know certain things about ourselves. Therefore, we do not (consciously) know them. Yet what resides in the unconscious profoundly affects our behavior and experience, even though we do not know we are being affected. Repressed unconscious material is expressed in disguised or symbolic form, as in neurotic symptoms or when unconscious instinctual urges are indirectly satisfied in dreams, fantasy, play, art work, or virtually any other arena of meaningful human intercourse.

In the psychoanalytic view, **repression** is an inescapable fact of daily life. "The essence of repression lies simply in the function of rejecting and keeping something out of consciousness," Freud wrote (1915/1957, p. 105). Within the scientific community, psychoanalytic ideas concerning repression and the unconscious have traditionally been viewed with a great deal of skepticism, as rather fanciful notions that cannot be supported by empirical proof (e.g., Holmes, 1976; Mischel, 1986). But in recent years, a growing consensus has begun to emerge that, in some qualified ways, Freud was right all along. As we see next, there *is* an unconscious realm in human thought and feeling, and it appears to exert a significant influence in people's lives (Erdelyi, 1985; Kihlstrom, 1990; Shevrin & Dickman, 1980; Westen, 1990).

Unconscious Information Processing

Outside the psychoanalytic tradition, psychologists of many different persuasions have begun to show that a great deal of human information processing occurs outside of awareness. In an informative review, Hill and Lewicki (1991) claim that "cognitive psychologists have accepted the view that most of our thoughts are nonconscious; or, to put it in the more technical terms of cognitive psychologists, most information processing follows algorithms (i.e., rules of procedure for solving problems) that are not accessible to conscious awareness" (p. 212). A number of experiments have demonstrated that people acquire a great deal of complex knowledge about their social environments without ever knowing that they are acquiring it, or how they are acquiring it (Lewicki, 1986). What Lewicki (1986) calls "nonconscious social information processing" occurs automatically and without volitional control in daily life, as we spontaneously apply ingrained algorithms to make sense of social information. According to Hill and Lewicki (1991), such processing may trigger emotional reactions, such as automatic liking or disliking for certain events and stimuli. Furthermore, these emotional reactions may be at odds with our conscious picture of what we consider reasonable, justified, and desirable when it comes to judging events and people. Yet we may be unable to change the reactions.

As an illustration of these points, I ask you to imagine the following scene. You are briefly introduced to an older man at a party, and you strike up a friendly conversation. From the second you see him, you begin to process, in an automatic fashion, a vast array of social information, including the way he speaks, the clothes he wears, the way he seems to start a new sentence before finishing the old one, his enthusiasm about politics, and the smell of his cologne. Most all of this is being processed outside your awareness, as you concentrate on the conversation you are having at the time. Fifteen minutes later, he leaves, and you say to yourself, "He seems like a very nice and reasonable person. I *should* like him." But you don't like him. There is something about him that bothers you a lot, but you cannot put your finger on it. The psychological truth of the matter is that his voice reminds you of an uncle whom you detested as a

FEATURE 3.A

Sigmund Freud and the Birth of Psychoanalysis

Sigmund Freud came of age in a world very different from ours. It was a world of kings and queens and empires—a 19th-century European "old world" that was still highly aristocratic and, by our standards today, extremely oppressive. It was a world yet to experience a major global war or the threat of nuclear annihilation. It was a world that would have found unthinkable our contemporary belief that, for instance, women should be allowed to vote or that the child of a poor black mother might someday become a great leader, writer, or scientist. The first-born son in a struggling Jewish family, Freud dreamed of being a great scientist from the age of 5 onward. As Napoleon conquered lands and peoples, young Sigmund dreamed of conquering the mind, exploring new territories of knowledge and becoming their lord and master. Referring to his own childhood and his unalloyed love for his mother, Freud later wrote: "A man who has been the indisputable favorite of his mother keeps for life the feeling of a conqueror, the confidence of success that often induces real success" (in Jones, 1961, p. 6).

The heroes of Freud's youth were the great Romantics of the early 19th century, like Napoleon the conqueror and Goethe the German writer and philosopher. Flourishing between approximately 1790 and 1850, **Romanticism** was a European intellectual movement that rejected classical teachings emphasizing reason, order, and the common good and celebrated instead the vigorous and passionate life of the individual (Cantor, 1971; Russell, 1945). As an adult, Freud fashioned a revolutionary theory of the mind that reflected his Romantic heritage. From Romanticism he adopted the idea that the individual

person and society are destined to live in constant conflict. Romantics like Goethe and the poets William Blake and Lord Byron saw society as inherently oppressive in that it demands conformity to ensure social order. The Romantic self rebels against oppression to seek freedom and transcendence, often through the passionate pursuit of art or love. Romanticism taught Freud to focus on the uniqueness of the inner self and its development over time. For the Romantics, the development of the inner self was virtually a moral duty (Jay, 1984; Langbaum, 1982). In the famous Romantic drama, Goethe's Faust seeks self-fulfillment at all costs, going so far as to sell his soul to the devil to guarantee the full experiencing of his inner, unique being. Of psychoanalysis and the devil, one scholar writes that "to experience Freud is to partake a second time of the forbidden fruit" (Brown, 1959, pp. xi–xii). The Romantics glorified the emotional and irrational aspects of human nature. Freud, too, came to see human beings as irrational by nature, but, unlike his Romantic heroes, Freud was never able to celebrate that irrationality. Freud eventually taught that unconscious and irrational wishes concerning sexuality and aggression are the most basic motivators of the person's behavior, but that these wishes must be channeled into indirect and disguised expressions within an orderly society if the human being is to adapt to society and to survive. Despite his Romantic heritage, Freud was too much the rational scientist himself, and an upstanding member of conservative middle-class society, to endorse the free reign of sex and passion.

In 1873, Freud enrolled in the University of Vienna to study natural science. There he

Sigmund Freud and his daughter, Anna

as a psychic machine that uses energy. The energy is derived from biologically rooted instincts, such as sex and aggression. The system works according to the 19th-century laws of conservation of energy. The mind transforms a fixed amount of energy derived from instincts into useful work, Freud eventually argued, transforming a fixed amount of raw sensual and aggressive energy into various forms and expressions of human thought, feeling, desire, and behavior. From another teacher, Jean Martin Charcot, Freud learned that the mind's energy could work in strange ways. In 1885, Freud travelled to Paris to attend Charcot's lectures and demonstrations on hypnosis. Charcot investigated the symptoms and causes of **hysteria,** a common psychological disturbance of the 19th century in which patients suffered from bizarre bodily symptoms, such as paralysis of the limbs and visual disorders, which had no apparent *physical* cause. Charcot was fabulously successful in removing hysteric symptoms through hypnosis, suggesting to Freud that hysteria resulted from the patient's peculiar *ideas,* which themselves were manifestations of the mind's energy.

met the eminent physiologist Ernst Brücke. Working under Brücke's tutelage for three years, Freud learned that all natural phenomena must be explained in physical and chemical terms. From the standpoint of science, no spiritual or other-worldly forces could be invoked to account for the real world. Scientists of the day were fascinated with the power of machines and used machines as metaphors for their theories. A machine is a complex mechanical system that uses energy through work. The psychoanalytic theory that Freud would eventually bring forth viewed the mind

As a physician in Vienna, Freud worked with Joseph Breuer in the treatment of the hysterical symptoms exhibited by their neurotic patients, employing hypnosis and other psychological techniques. Breuer and Freud came to recognize that while hysterical symptoms may appear to be random and bizarre, they are in fact meaningfully organized according to an intricate emotional logic that

continued on next page

FEATURE 3.A *continued*

guides the neurotic's life. The symptoms symbolize an unresolved conflict or problem that may be traced back to intensely negative childhood experiences. Though no longer consciously remembered, an emotionally abrasive experience from childhood presses for release and goads the patient to find symptomatic expression of the discomfort within. In the famous case of Anna O., Breuer discovered that hysterical symptoms could be removed through a "talking cure," through which the patient talked through daytime hallucinations, fantasies, symptoms, and so on. The talking unstrangled the archaic emotions that were producing the neurotic symptoms, releasing the trapped emotional energy and temporarily freeing the patient from debilitating symptoms and distress.

The psychoanalytic tradition was launched when Breuer and Freud collaborated to investigate the psychological underpinnings of hysteria. Their work culminated in the publication of *Studies in Hysteria* (1893–1895/1955), wherein they write that "hysterics suffer mainly from reminiscences" (p. 7). In other words, the bodily symptoms of hysteria are caused by problems in the memory of emotionally charged events. Freud was almost 40 years old when he and Breuer published their discoveries. But the two physician/scientists had a major falling out over the interpretation of their clinical cases, with Breuer objecting to Freud's insistence that hysterical symptoms typically have sexual meanings. They parted, bitter enemies, and Freud entered a very difficult but ultimately productive period in his life, a time he later romanticized as that "glorious heroic age" of "splendid isolation" (Freud, 1914/1957, p. 22). During this time, Freud began a self-analysis wherein he subjected his own thoughts, fantasies, feelings, and dreams to an intensive scrutiny and from which, he later argued, he derived his greatest psychological insights. The next 10 years (between 1895 and 1905) were to witness the maturation of Freud's most important ideas concerning the interpretation of dreams, the psychopathology of everyday life, the role of the sexual instinct in human development, and the workings of the unconscious.

From about 1905 until his death in 1939, Freud established himself as the father of the psychoanalytic movement. A gifted writer who won the coveted Goethe Prize for literature in 1930, Freud filled 24 volumes on psychoanalysis, including wide-ranging essays and monographs on theory and clinical practice as well as special papers addressing religious, cultural, and artistic questions. Table 3.2 lists a few of his most important writings with capsule summaries of their contents. Attracting a large number of intellectual followers, Freud founded the Vienna Psychoanalytic Society. The group held regular meetings and published a journal. In 1909, American psychologist G. Stanley Hall invited Freud to Clark University, in Worcester, Massachusetts, where he delivered a famous series of lectures. Freud's writings were eventually translated into English and other languages as psychoanalysis became an international movement. By the time of his death, on the eve of World War II, Sigmund Freud was easily the most venerated psychologist in the world, but also the most maligned, for his ideas have always been viewed as extremely controversial.

TABLE 3.2	*Selected Writings of Sigmund Freud*

DATE	TITLE	THESIS
1895	*Studies in Hysteria (with J. Breuer)*	Neurotic symptoms are the result of "reminiscences" and can be relieved through a psychological talking cure. Neurotic disturbances are creative solutions to unconscious conflicts, usually concerning sexuality.
1900	*The Interpretation of Dreams*	Dreams are compromises in wish fulfillments and must be understood as creative products of unconscious processes such as condensation, displacement, and symbolism. All dreams can be interpreted by employing free association to trace the latent undercurrents of manifest content.
1901	*The Psychopathology of Everyday Life*	Like neurotic symptoms and dreams, many accidents and mistakes we make in daily life have important psychological meaning and can be traced back to unconscious conflicts and instinctual urges.
1905	*Three Essays on the Theory of Sexuality*	The sexual instinct develops through childhood stages designated as oral, anal, and phallic, before reaching maturity in adolescence. Children are overtly sexual beings whose pregenital manifestations of sex are similar to what polite society calls "perversions" in adults.
1913	*Totem and Taboo*	The Oedipus complex in children involves unconscious desires to make love to the parent of the opposite sex while killing the parent of the same sex. Freud speculates that social institutions such as government and religion have their historical origins in a prehistoric real-life enactment of the Oedipal complex, whereby the patriarch of a primal horde was overthrown by younger men and killed and eaten. The new younger leaders then prescribed laws and rules to inhibit sex and aggression and assuage their guilt.
1920	*Beyond the Pleasure Principle*	Two basic instinctual urges are the underlying motivators of all behavior and experience: life instincts, expressed directly in sexuality; and death instincts, expressed in aggression.
1923	*The Ego and the Id*	The human mind is structured into three compartments: the id, wherein reside unconscious impulses and thoughts; the ego, which serves the id by channeling the id's energy into realistic pursuits; and the superego, which is an internal representation of the parents, exerting a moral force. The id operates according to the pleasure principle, and the ego operates according to the reality principle.
1930	*Civilization and Its Discontents*	Human beings and societies are in constant conflict. Whereas the individual is motivated by unconscious sexual and aggressive impulses, society is built on the repression of sex and aggression. As a result, humans are generally anxious, miserable, and often neurotic.

Note: There is no substitute for reading Freud in the original. Indeed, part of his power as a theorist is the beauty of his writing, captured wonderfully in James Strachey's authoritative English translations of the original German. Unfortunately, many secondary sources on Freud are rather dry and technical compared with the rich original work. An exception is C. Monte's *Beneath the mask: An introduction to theories of personality* (Fort Worth, TX: Harcourt Brace, 1995), which has two long and splendid chapters on the evolution of Freud's thinking.

youth. Unconsciously, you immediately picked this information up, and it colored your subsequent perceptions, emotional reactions, and behaviors. Yet you were not aware of this happening at the time. And you still may not be aware of the processing algorithm you spontaneously employed. Write Hill and Lewicki (1991), "a person may find some of his or her 'automatic categorizations' of people or other stimuli unreasonable or even clearly wrong and still be unable to modify them or to stop their emotional consequences" (p. 218).

John Kihlstrom (1990) conceives of "the psychological unconscious" as a set of *implicit* systems. Within the unconscious realm, Kihlstrom identifies four related processes whose existence is well supported by empirical research. **Implicit memory** is revealed when a person's behavior is modified by the apprehension of a past event, though the event itself is not consciously recollected. Evidence for **implicit perception** may be seen when the performance of a task changes a current event, but the current event is not consciously perceived. **Implicit thought** is reflected in problem-solving activity that occurs outside of awareness. Finally, **implicit learning** is the acquisition of knowledge in the absence of any reflective awareness of the knowledge itself. Table 3.3 provides examples of each of the four. In Kihlstrom's view, consciousness is a quality of experience, that may be necessary for the voluntary control of certain cognitive functions and for communicating one's mental states to others. But many forms of complex psychological functioning operate in an implicit or unconscious way. In support of this claim is a great deal of research conducted by cognitive psychologists in the past 15 years (Bornstein & Masling, 1998; Roediger, 1990; Schacter, 1992; Westen, 1998).

TABLE 3.3   *Four Cognitive Aspects of the Psychological Unconscious*

	DEFINITION	EXAMPLE
Implicit memory	Unconscious recollection of past event that influences behavior	A grade-school boy avoids dogs because he was terrorized by a German shepherd at a very young age. He does not consciously remember the incident with the German shepherd.
Implicit perception	Current event that influences behavior without being consciously perceived	A young woman lingers over coffee for a longer time than usual because the background music at the restaurant is especially appealing. But she is not consciously attending to the music, rather focusing her concentration on her plans for the next day.
Implicit thought	Problem-solving activity that occurs outside of awareness	An executive dozes off at her desk and then awakens with an answer to a problem that has been bothering her for days.
Implicit learning	Acquisition of knowledge in the absence of any reflective awareness of the knowledge itself	After weeks of overhearing her roommate's instructional tape recordings for a French class, a college student realizes one day that she knows how to speak a number of French phrases, even though she never tried to learn them.

Much of everyday life is automatic; it could hardly be otherwise (Bargh, 1996). Take driving, for example. You get into the car, turn on the ignition, put the car in gear, press the accelerator, hit the brake when you need to slow down, maneuver through traffic on your way to your destination. Most of this is accomplished with little conscious thought and effort. As you are driving down the freeway, you may be thinking hard about that tough job interview you've got this afternoon, or about that new love interest in your life and your plans for seeing him or her tomorrow. But you are not likely to be thinking much about the driving unless something happens to focus your attention on it—bad weather, for example, or a reckless driver in the next lane. As you move along, your mind can focus consciously on a thousand different things because the critical business of driving the car and getting to your destination safely is happening simultaneously, monitored and controlled by generally offline, nonconscious processes. When you were first learning to drive, you needed to expend much more of your consciousness on the act of driving. But by now, driving is so overlearned and habitual that you can perform the necessary functions as easily as, say, walking or riding a bike. As Freud (1901/1965) wrote, "There is in fact a whole series of functions which we are accustomed to assume will be performed most exactly when done automatically—that is, with scarcely any conscious attention" (p. 173). We can afford to perceive, think, feel, want, and behave in automatic ways because we live in a world whose predictabilities we have come to know:

> Automaticity thus develops as a reflection of the regularities of the world. Eventually we come to recognize consistently occurring patterns with little mental effort. We do not see windows and doors and bricks but buildings, not glass and metal and rubber but automobiles; in short, we see the objects and events we interact with without having to consciously assemble them. This is known as preconscious processing. (Bargh, 1996, p. 177)

Social psychologist John Bargh (1996, 1997) has conducted a number of experiments showing that how we think and feel about people and social situations is strongly driven by nonconscious, automatic processes. We cannot help it: When we meet a person or encounter a situation we form immediate reactions and expectations, triggered by our implicit goals, fears, stereotypes, and so on. An attractive face may elicit our immediate interest; a person whose skin color is different from our own may trigger immediate caution or fear. Only by consciously overriding such initial impressions can we arrive at a fuller understanding of another person and a nuanced appreciation of a social situation. There would appear to be an initial phase of social information processing that is automatic, unintentional, uncontrollable, relatively smooth and efficient, and outside of conscious awareness. Such a first step has the virtue of enabling us to process a great deal of social information in a relatively effortless manner, freeing up our attention for other important tasks at hand. In the terms of Chapter 2, this kind of nonconscious information processing would seem to hold tremendous adaptive advantage for human organisms over the course of evolution, for it enables us to size up social situations quickly and efficiently, contributing to our efforts to get along and get ahead in social groups. The downside of such processing, however, is that it lays the cognitive groundwork for the kind of prejudice and negative stereotyping that so undermine human community and social understanding. Initial impressions can be overcome, but this often requires significant effort, conscious planning, and the imposition of more rational and fair-minded strategies for social cognition. Bargh (1996) writes: "These default [automatic, unconscious] processes can be adjusted or corrected in a second effortful processing stage—but again, only if the person has the time, attentional capacity, and interest in doing so" (p. 173).

In sum, cognitive and social psychologists often distinguish between two kinds of information processing in human beings. Many theories suggest that there is first an initial, automatic, involuntary, nonconscious, and relatively effortless kind of processing that human beings exhibit in a wide range of situations and, second, a more voluntary and conscious kind of thinking that appears to require more effort and would seem to be relatively more rational and guided by reason. This contemporary distinction vaguely resembles Freud's (1900/1953) older dichotomy between **primary process** and **secondary process** thinking. Exhibited best in dreams and fantasies, primary process thought is spontaneous and effortless thought that is very loose, irrational, and often driven by sexual and aggressive urges. Primary process thought is associated with the unconscious. By contrast, secondary process thought is rational and measured, linked to realistic perceptions rather than irrational fantasies, and generally assumed to be conscious and deliberate.

Having suggested that the contemporary social-cognitive distinction between automatic and voluntary thinking is reminiscent of Freud's older distinction between primary and secondary process thinking, I should emphasize that the two distinctions are not the same. The big difference is that the current view in social-cognitive theory does not link thinking to aggressive and sexual urges, as did Freud. Kihlstrom (1990) argues that what emerges from research on social cognition is "kinder, gentler, and more rational" than "the seething unconscious of Freud" (p. 460). Primary process thinking and the Freudian unconscious are closely tied to issues of aggression, survival, and sexuality. By contrast, quips one writer, you "can read a thousand pages of social-cognitive theory and never know that people have genitals" (Westen, 1990, p. 53). Therefore, contemporary research on nonconscious information processing does not support *all* of Freud's ideas about the unconscious. But the current research and theorizing *is* consistent with the general idea, that Freud and others have endorsed, that a great deal of human experience takes place unconsciously.

One contemporary theorist who sees many parallels between Freudian insights about the unconscious and primary process thought on the one hand and newer views of nonconscious information processing on the other is Seymour Epstein. In a paper entitled "Integration of the Cognitive and the Psychodynamic Unconscious," Epstein (1994) brings together many different lines of thought and research to suggest that human beings apprehend themselves and their worlds through two parallel and interacting mental systems, summarized in Table 3.4. What Epstein calls the **experiential system** operates according to "hot" emotions and the dynamics of pleasure and pain. The experiential system enables us to form rapid and holistic impressions that we encode through concrete images, metaphors, and stories. The workings of the experiential system feel spontaneous and involuntary. We are "seized by" our emotions; we experience certain nonrational "vibes" and "intuitions." The experiential system is not necessarily motivated by issues of sex and aggression, but like primary process thinking, Epstein argues, the experiential system operates in a largely unconscious and free-flowing manner, and it is closely tied to very personal issues and concerns over which we may have little conscious control.

| TABLE 3.4 | *Comparison of the Experiential and Rational Systems* |

EXPERIENTIAL SYSTEM	RATIONAL SYSTEM
Holistic	Analytic
Emotional: Pleasure–pain oriented	Logical: Reason oriented
Behavior mediated by "vibes" or intuitions from past experience	Behavior mediated by conscious appraisal of events
Understands reality in concrete images, metaphors, and narratives	Understands reality in abstract symbols, words, and numbers
More rapid processing: Oriented toward immediate action	Slower processing: Oriented toward delayed action
Slower to change: Changes with repetitive or intense experience	Changes more rapidly: Changes with the speed of thought
Makes broad generalizations; stereotypical impressions	Makes finer distinctions; precise and individuated portrayals
Experienced passively and preconsciously: We are seized by our emotions	Experienced actively and consciously: We are in control of our thoughts
Self-evidently valid: "Experience is believing"	Requires justification via logic and/or evidence

Source: Based on Epstein (1994), p. 711.

By contrast, what Epstein calls the **rational system** resembles closely Freud's notion of secondary process thinking and the social-cognitive idea of a second stage of effortful and conscious information processing. Guided by "cool" logic, the rational system appraises events in a realistic and relatively objective manner, enabling the individual to develop sensible strategies for effective social action. The rational system encodes reality in abstract symbols, words, and numbers. Its workings feel voluntary; we feel that we actively produce and are in control of our conscious thoughts. From Epstein's point of view, both the experiential and rational systems have strengths and weaknesses. An evolutionarily older system, the experiential mode is crude but efficient; it is largely responsible for human prejudice and superstition, but it can also be the wellspring of intuitive creativity and wisdom. Epstein argues that the rational system is a more recent evolutionary arrival. It is slow but precise; it produces high levels of abstraction that are ultimately responsible for the tremendous achievements human beings have enjoyed in science, technology, and other rational pursuits. But it can be "a very inefficient system for responding to everyday events," writes Epstein (1994, p. 715), and it is unable to apprehend fully the emotional aspects of human life, leaving us sometimes with a cold and mechanistic response to life's challenges.

Repression and Repressors

Freud believed that certain thoughts, feelings, desires, and memories are stored away in an inaccessible, unconscious realm. What makes these things unconscious, he

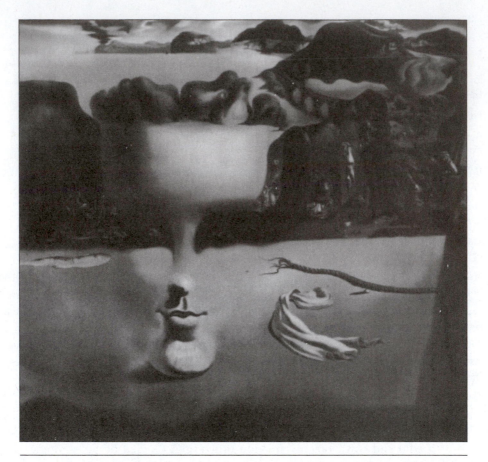

This painting, by Salvador Dali (1938), evokes images of primary process thought and the Freudian unconscious.

argued, is that they *threaten* the person's well-being. For Freud, repression is dynamic; it seeks to cast into the unconscious those aspects of life that bring anxiety and guilt; it works proactively to *protect* the individual from psychic harm. A long line of research on **perceptual defense** has evaluated this central psychoanalytic hypothesis (Erdelyi, 1974; Gur & Sackheim, 1979; Postman, Bruner, & McGinnies, 1948). Perceptual defense is *the unconscious monitoring of sensory perception by the censoring forces of repression* within the person. In a number of experiments conducted in the late 1940s and 1950s, researchers showed that it often takes a person longer to recognize presumably traumatic or anxiety-producing stimuli (such as obscene words, or stimuli previously associated with pain) than to recognize neutral stimuli (Bruner & Postman, 1947; Cowen & Beier, 1954; Lazarus & McClearey, 1951; McGinnies, 1949). For instance, McGinnies (1949) found that students who were exposed to quick flashes of words on a screen required longer exposures before they could recognize such stimulus words as *penis* and *kotex* compared with such neutral words as *apple* and *river.* McGinnies argued that repression functions to keep such stimuli out of awareness, at least for a time.

In recent years, studies have examined the possibility that some people are generally more "repressive" than others. Weinberger, Schwartz, and Davidson (1979) describe **repressors** as persons who experience little anxiety on a conscious level and who adopt a highly defensive approach to life. The researchers were able to classify certain individuals as exhibiting an especially repressive coping style by virtue of their scores on two self-report, paper-and-pencil questionnaires—one measuring anxiety (the Manifest Anxiety Scale; Taylor, 1953) and the other defensiveness, or "social desirability" (Crowne & Marlowe, 1964), which indicates the extent to which a person will describe the self in socially acceptable and overly "nice" ways. In an experiment in which people were exposed to verbal phrases containing sexual and aggressive content, repressors reported very low levels of subjective distress compared with "low-anxious" (low anxiety, low defensiveness) and "defensive-high-anxious" (high anxiety, high defensiveness) individuals. At the same time, however, physiological measures indicated that the repressors experienced significantly higher levels of internal arousal than did the low-anxious and defensive-high-anxious subjects. In other words, whereas the repressors claimed that the sexual and aggressive content did not make them anxious, their bodily processes suggested otherwise. From a psychoanalytic perspective, the repressors did not *consciously* perceive the drive-related stimuli as threatening. Their heightened physiological arousal, however, indicated that the threat may have instead been perceived at an *unconscious* level.

Penelope Davis has conducted a series of influential studies examining how repressors recall emotional experiences in their lives. In one study, female college students were asked to recall six kinds of personal experiences from childhood—general memories, experiences of happiness, sadness, anger, fear, and wonder (Davis & Schwartz, 1987). As Figure 3.1 shows, repressors (low anxiety, high defensiveness) recalled significantly fewer negative memories than did low-anxious (low anxiety, low defensiveness) and high-anxious (high anxiety, low defensiveness) individuals. The results are consistent with the psychoanalytic hypothesis that repression involves an inaccessibility to negative memories. However, the results also indicate, as can be seen in Figure 3.1, that repressors tended to report somewhat fewer *positive* memories as well, suggesting that repression may also involve a more general failure to retrieve emotional memories of various kinds.

In a second study, Davis (1987) found that repressors recalled fewer childhood experiences in which they felt happy, sad, angry, fearful, guilty, and self-conscious compared with other individuals. The inhibition was especially pronounced for fear and self-consciousness experiences. But she also showed that when recalling memories in which *someone else* felt happy, sad, angry, or fearful, repressors actually reported substantially *more* experiences. The findings suggest that repression is not simply a general memory deficit. Repressors actually report a greater number of memories involving emotional experiences of other people. But when it comes to recalling events in which the strong emotions experienced *are their own*, and especially when those emotions entail painful states of fear and self-consciousness, repressors seem to have difficulty summoning such memories into awareness. Fear and self-consciousness occur in situations in which attention is focused on the self in an evaluative and especially threatening way. What may make these kinds of experiences the most suitable grist for the repression mill is that they directly threaten the self with a negative evaluation, more so even than experiences of sadness, anger, and other negative emotions.

| FIGURE 3.1 | *Average Number of Memories Recalled* |

Repressors show significantly fewer memories of sadness, anger, and fear compared with high-anxious and low-anxious individuals.

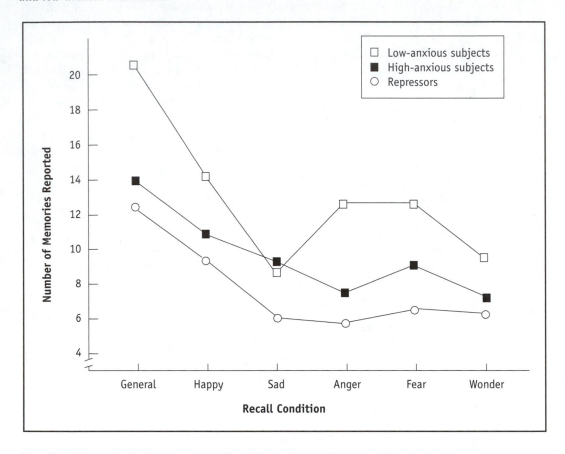

Source: Paris & Schwartz (1987), p. 158.

Repression may operate most powerfully in the domain of self-evaluation. We may be most prone to repress those experiences in which the self is judged in a negative manner.

Why is it that some people have such a difficult time recalling and articulating negative emotional memories? What makes repressors different from other people? Hansen and Hansen (1988) have explored what they call "the architecture of repression," described as the mechanisms whereby emotionally tagged memories, especially unpleasant memories, are left inaccessible. They argue that repressors have an "associative network" for negative emotional experiences that is substantially less complex and more discrete than that found for negative memories experienced by other people. For repressors, negative recollections have a characteristically simple structure, and these memories are split off from other memories, isolated outside the main network of interrelated autobiographical recollections. Repressors and nonrepressors organize their episodic memories in different ways. Repressors simplify negative memories to emphasize a single dominant feeling, as a way of keeping these memories from connecting in their minds to other autobiographical memories containing other feelings. By contrast, nonrepressors tend to describe their negative memories in more complex terms, emphasizing a number of different emotional states in the same memory and integrating the negative memory with the main lines of their autobiographical self.

Hansen and Hansen obtained evidence for their interpretation in a study of 433 undergraduate women and men, each of whom was assigned to recall, describe, and evaluate either an angering, embarrassing, sad, or fearful event from the past. For the particular event to be recalled, the participants were told to picture the situation in their minds and to remember as vividly as they could how it felt to be (angry, embarrassed, sad, or fearful) at that particular moment. After writing a description of the experience on a sheet of paper, the participants were asked to rate how they felt in the situation according to 10 different emotion dimensions—angry, embarrassed, sad, fearful, anxious, disgusted, ashamed, depressed, surprised, and happy. The results showed that each negative memory elicits a montage of different emotional reactions. For example, when subjects were asked to recall memories of sadness, they rated their feelings in these memories as very sad, but they also tended to rate highly feelings of depression, anger, and fear. By contrast, sad memories did not tend to elicit feelings of shame or embarrassment. For sad memories, then, the researchers determined that sadness was the dominant emotion but that other nondominant emotions of depression, anger, and fear could also be identified. Similarly, embarrassing memories showed the dominant emotion of embarrassment but were also tagged with the nondominant emotion of shame. Each category of emotional memory (angering, embarrassing, sad, and fearful), therefore, specified a corresponding dominant emotion and a set of nondominant emotions.

Differences between repressors and other individuals were revealed in the nondominant emotions, but not in the dominant ones. For any given negative event, repressors and nonrepressors reported comparable levels of dominant emotion intensity. For example, embarrassing memories were rated just as emotionally embarrassing by repressors as by nonrepressors. But repressors tended to rate the nondominant emotions associated with the given memory at less intense levels. Embarrassing memories, therefore, produced less shame for repressors than for nonrepressors. Sad memories produced less depression, anger, and fear for repressors than for nonrepressors. And so on. In purifying their particular memories to underscore a dominant emotional reaction rather than a host of related but nondominant emotions, repressors cordon off the negativity associated with any given memory, keeping it from spreading to other recollections of the past. Write Hansen and Hansen, "repression is fundamentally a phenomenon of the relatively impoverished structure of the repressor's memory linked to the less elaborate, more discrete emotional tags with which the repressor's memorial representations are associated" (p. 816). To protect the self from threat, repression works to keep negative memories from connecting to each other, rendering each a simple monad unto itself.

In another study, Myers and Brewin (1994) showed that while repressors report fewer negative memories from childhood, they nonetheless tend to recall their parents as being especially indifferent or neglecting. In other words, repressors may keep out of awareness especially negative emotional experiences, but negativity in general manages to seep into their accounts of their lives, couched in more general, abstract, and less threatening terms. Bonanno, Davis, Singer, and Schwartz (1991) showed that repressors are especially skilled at shifting their attention away from material that they wish to ignore. But the attentional shift may come with a price. Having a repressive coping style has also been associated with a variety of health problems, including asthma, cancer, hypertension, and suppressed immune function (Schwartz, 1990; Weinberger, 1990).

In sum, research on repressors has identified an important individual difference variable that appears to capture some of Freud's fundamental concept of repression. Some people do seem to employ repression as a coping strategy more so than do others, and this difference in people is associated with measurable outcomes with respect to everyday information processing, autobiographical memory, and even physical health. The research leaves open the question, however, as to just how common and important repression is for everybody. While Freud argued that repression is a universal fact of psychic life, research on repressors suggests that people differ rather substantially with respect to how extensively they employ repression as a way of dealing with anxiety.

A Collective Unconscious: Carl Jung

For Freud, the secrets of each person's soul are buried in the person's unconscious. Those secrets are likely tied to sexual and aggressive themes for all of us. But because my experiences in life have been different from yours, my unconscious and your unconscious are different from each other. The intrapsychic mysteries that define my life are different from the intrapsychic mysteries that define yours. By contrast, a strong line of thinking in the psychoanalytic tradition has tended to emphasize the ways in which we all share certain features of our unconscious lives. Carl Jung was an early follower of Freud who eventually established a rival theoretical perspective that differed from Freud's in many ways. With respect to the issue of human motivation, for example, Jung broke with Freud's exclusive focus on sexual and aggressive instincts and argued instead that human beings are motivated by a spectacular pantheon of unconscious forces and factors—internal urges and images about unity, death, androgyny, wisdom, innocence, and yes, sex and aggression, all of which are the result, Jung believed, of our common evolutionary heritage (Stevens, 1983). The wellspring for these many-splendored sources of our everyday behavior is what Jung called the **collective unconscious.** The collective unconscious is a storehouse of archaic remnants from humankind's evolutionary past. It is our inherited racial memory, what all of us know by virtue of our membership in the human race, in the deepest and most inaccessible layer of the psyche. The collective unconscious is what human nature really is, in Jung's view. A result of our evolution as a species, it is the richly textured unconscious that each of us is born with and that each of us takes with us as we move across the human life cycle:

> The archetypal endowment with which each of us is born presupposes the natural life cycle of our species—being mothered, exploring the environment, playing in the peer group,

adolescence, being initiated, establishing a place in the social hierarchy, courting, marrying, child-rearing, hunting, gathering, fighting, participating in religious rituals, assuming social responsibilities of advanced maturity, and preparation for death. (Stevens, 1983, p. 40)

The major structural components of the collective unconscious are **archetypes.** Archetypes are universal patterns or predispositions that structure how all humans consciously and unconsciously adapt to their world. As the major components of human nature, archetypes are inherited but somewhat flexible templates for human experience. They are not images or behaviors as such but rather are *predispositions* to develop universal images and to enact universal behavioral sequences (Jung, 1936/1969).

Table 3.5 describes some well-known Jungian archetypes, including the mother, the child, the wise old man, the trickster, and the hero.

Evidence for the existence of each of these, Jung argued, is pervasive in ancient myths, dreams, and universal symbols. For instance, the image of *mother* is a universal thought-form coded in stories, legends, art, ritual, customs, and fantasy around the world. Throughout history, mothers have behaved in certain instinctually bounded ways such that a template or pattern of who mothers are and what they do has come to exist as an archetype in the human collective unconscious. Thus, the human infant has within him or her an unconscious prototype of what mother is—a genetic predisposition to react to her and understand her in certain ways. The infant's perception of mother will, of course, be influenced by real-life experiences with her, but the internal and unconscious mother archetype will set limits on those experiences and help structure how they are understood. The mother archetype may be "released" and expressed in thought and image in response to one's real mother, mother-in-law, grandmother, stepmother, or any other person, place, or thing associated with maternity.

Three particularly prominent archetypes in the collective unconscious are the **anima, animus,** and **shadow.** Within all males exists an unconscious template of femininity, called the anima. Based on men's collective experiences with women throughout time, the anima resides deep within all men as a hidden feminine side of their personalities. Similarly, within all women exists an unconscious masculine aspect, called the animus. The anima and the animus constrain actual interactions between the sexes, each sex apprehending the nature of the other through an unconscious filter. The shadow archetype consists of a variety of unacceptable and socially reprehensible desires and impulses, inherited by virtue of our evolution from lower forms of life. The animalistic shadow is the "dark half" of our personality that most of us would prefer not to recognize. It is expressed in mythology via demons, devils, and evil ones, and it is partially responsible, argued Jung, for the Judeo-Christian belief in original sin.

We have seen that Freud's ideas on the unconscious have stimulated scientific research and have been compared with contemporary research-oriented views of nonconscious information processing. When it comes to the Jungian idea of the collective unconscious, however, linkages to scientific research are more difficult to discern. Research-oriented psychologists have tended to ignore Jung's view of the unconscious, regarding it as too mystical or hard to define for scientific scrutiny. It is difficult to figure out a way of scientifically evaluating archetypes, for example. The "evidence" for the existence of a collective unconscious comes from Jung's and others' observations that certain patterns of imagery in dreams, myths, and folklore are very widespread across different cultures, suggesting that they could be manifestations of a universal

TABLE 3.5	*Selected Jungian Archetypes*

ARCHETYPE	DESCRIPTION	PROJECTED SYMBOLS (ANCIENT AND MODERN)
Mother	The embodiment of caregiving and fertility, which may be elicited in response to real mothers, grandmothers, spouses, and other nurturant figures; incorporates positive (warm, supportive) and negative (rejecting, threatening) characteristics.	Earth Mother in ancient mythologies, Virgin Mary, Alma Mater, the Church, fairy godmothers, witches, dragons
Child-God	The embodiment of both innocence and future experience, representing "futurity" and potential for growth; often has divine or mystical powers.	Christ child, elves, dwarfs, the young Mozart, the child prodigy
Hero	The protagonist of the classic and universal hero myth: miraculous but humble birth followed by early proof of superhuman power, rapid rise to prominence, triumphant struggle with evil, fallibility to the "sin" of pride, and eventual fall through betrayal or heroic sacrifice.	Christ, Oedipus, King Arthur, Achilles, Abraham Lincoln, Martin Luther King, Jr.
Trickster	An early form of the hero archetype, fond of sly jokes, malicious pranks; possesses magical powers.	Hermes, Biblical demons, Harry Houdini
Wise Old Man	Embodiment of maturity and wisdom, able to foretell the future.	Oedipus in his later years, Tiresias, certain renditions of God-the-Father, prophets, Mahatma Gandhi
Anima	The hidden feminine side of man.	Various idealized images of women worshipped by men, such as Cleopatra, Helen of Troy, Virgin Mary, Mona Lisa; woman as temptress, mother, friend, mediator; woman as witch and bitch; cars, ships
Animus	The hidden masculine side of woman.	Various idealized images of men worshipped by women, such as Odysseus, Don Juan, Christ; man as seducer, hunter, statesman, mentor; man as pirate, rapist, outlaw
Shadow	The embodiment of unacceptable, animalistic desires and impulses; the "dark half" of personality.	Satan, devils, aliens, enemies, wild beasts, Hitler, Mussolini
Persona	The socially acceptable mask or front the person presents to the world. The persona is not a true archetypal form residing in the collective unconscious but rather an individual and highly conscious creation. Nonetheless, the individual's persona is built upon unconscious patterns concerning how a good "actor" presents an appropriate mask and plays an appropriate role for the world. The persona generally hides or disguises the true potential of the self.	Actors and actresses

human mentality (e.g., Campbell, 1949). This is not the kind of research evidence, however, that scientific psychologists usually gather. Nonetheless, Jung's conception of a collective unconscious remains an intriguing idea for many people. Many psychotherapists and counselors have been strongly influenced by Jung's ideas, and a large number of books have been written about how individuals might explore their own archetypes (e.g., Bolen, 1985; Feinstein & Krippner, 1988; Pearson, 1986).

To sum up, the idea of the unconscious, in its many different versions, is alive and well in psychology today. A great deal of mental life appears to take place outside of conscious awareness. The concept of the unconscious is a cornerstone of the psychoanalytic understanding of human nature. Freud wrote that "psychoanalysis aims at and achieves nothing more than the discovery of the unconscious in mental life" (1924, p. 397). For both Freud and Jung, the exploration of the unconscious is the key to personal insight. The psychoanalytic tradition has strongly influenced the ways in which psychologists and laypersons think about unconscious processes, though other traditions in psychology have also made significant contributions. As the scientific study of the whole person, personality psychology cannot ignore the person's unconscious mental life. A full account of human individuality must take into consideration the proposition that the unconscious is a fundamental feature of human nature.

A male archetype.

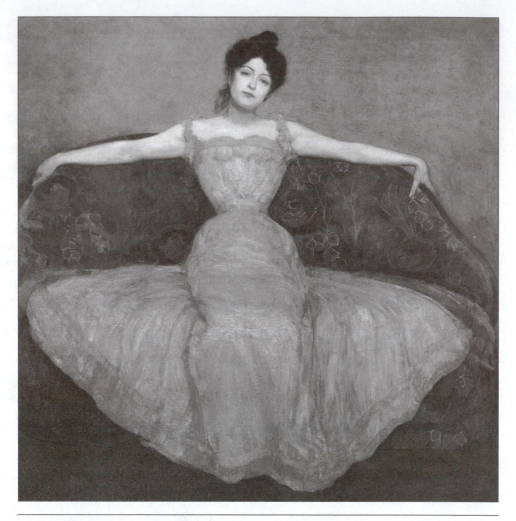

A female archetype.

THE FORMATION OF PERSONALITY

In 1905, Freud wrote *Three Essays on the Theory of Sexuality*, in which he spelled out the psychoanalytic tradition's first model of human development. It is a model that focuses on the sexuality of children. Sexuality is key for Freud, for sexuality carries the life energy of the human organism. Influenced by 19th-century models of energy mechanisms, Freud conceived of the human mind as a machine that uses energy, and he believed that this psychic energy was drawn from biological instincts. Freud eventually settled on the idea that there exist two sets of instincts: (1) sexuality and all other **life instincts** (this group of instincts sometimes goes under the name of "Eros") and

(2) aggression and all other **death instincts** (sometimes grouped under the name of "Thanatos") (Freud, 1920/1955). Life instincts serve the purpose of individual survival and reproduction. The form of the energy by which life instincts perform their work is called **libido;** sexual desires may be termed "libidinal urges." The person typically invests the libido in various "objects" (including persons and activities) that promise satisfaction of the instinct. Freud's first developmental model, therefore, was a model of libidinal investments, tracing changes over the course of childhood in how the organism invests its sexual energy.

Freud conceptualized sexuality in extremely broad and general terms. Working unconsciously to energize and direct many facets of our behavior and experience, the sexual instinct is a diffuse and deeply rooted desire for sensual, bodily pleasure (Freud, 1905/1953). The libido is not confined to seeking sexual intercourse between men and women but rather may express itself in a rich assortment of ways. Certain regions of the body, such as the mucous membranes of the mouth and anus, appear to be libidinally charged. In common sexual practices, such as kissing, petting, and oral/anal sexuality, the mouth and the anus "seem, as it were, to be claiming that they should themselves be regarded and treated as genitals" (Freud, 1905/1953, p. 153). Adds Freud, "the claim *is* justified by the history of the development of the sexual instinct" (p. 42). The mouth, anus, and genitals are all **erogenous zones,** functioning as favorite sites for the expression of the libido. To chart psychosexual development, therefore, is to follow the odyssey of the libido as it travels from one erogenous zone to another over the course of the person's life.

After Freud, theorists in the psychoanalytic tradition have tended to deemphasize the workings of the libido in psychological development and to focus instead on the vicissitudes of early interpersonal relationships (Erikson, 1950; Fairbairn, 1952; Guntrip, 1971; Kohut, 1971; Mahler, Pine, & Bergman, 1975; Winnicott, 1965). Following Freud's idea that the libido gets invested in various "objects" in the person's world, many psychoanalytic theorists speak of early **object relations** as important for the development of personality. Think of an "object" here as really a person; therefore, object relations are the many *gratifying involvements* we establish with other persons in our lives (Behrends & Blatt, 1985). Therefore, while Freud focused on changes in the expression of sexual energy over time, many psychoanalytic theorists who followed Freud shifted emphasis in the direction of the interpersonal relationships that resulted from the expression of sexual energy. Indeed, "object relations theorists" such as W. R. D. Fairbairn (1952) ignore the concept of the libido altogether and claim that personality develops solely as a function of changes in emotionally charged interpersonal relationships.

In what follows, I will sketch a general psychoanalytic view of human development that draws both from Freud and from the more interpersonally oriented theorists who followed Freud. Most psychoanalytic theorists have focused their attention on the early years of life, leaving relatively little to say about development in adulthood. Exceptions to this rule are Erik Erikson (whose stage theory of psychosocial development we will examine in Chapter 10) and Carl Jung. Jung viewed human development as a life-long process, and he identified especially important psychological changes that may occur at midlife. I will, therefore, conclude my discussion of psychoanalytic views of human development by considering Jung's understanding of personality growth during the middle adult years and beyond.

The Early Years

For Freud, psychosexual development begins with sucking:

> Sucking at the mother's breast is the starting-point of the whole of sexual life, the unmatched prototype of every later sexual satisfaction, to which phantasy often enough returns in times of need. This sucking involves making the mother's breast the first object of the sexual instinct. I can give you no idea of the important bearing of this first object upon the choice of every later object, of the profound effects it has in its transformations and substitutions in even the remotest regions of our sexual lives. (Freud, 1916/1961, p. 314)

We see in this marvelous quotation Freud's idealization of the mother–infant bond. In the first year of life, the baby obtains both nourishment and pleasure from sucking at the breast (or bottle). Sucking reduces the tension caused by the hunger drive, and the reduction of tension feels good. The mother is generally the source of these good feelings, the provider of food and pleasure. She becomes the infant's first human love object. From this oral expression of the libido develops a lasting image of an ideal sensual experience, a legacy of pleasure that we, as adults, are fortunate enough to reexperience only in the most rewarding of our intimate relationships.

The infant in the **oral stage** is completely dependent on caregivers for the satisfaction of basic bodily needs. When the tensions produced by needs are consistently and regularly satisfied (reduced), the infant comes to perceive the environment as a relatively

"Sucking at the mother's breast is the starting point of the whole sexual life."
—Freud

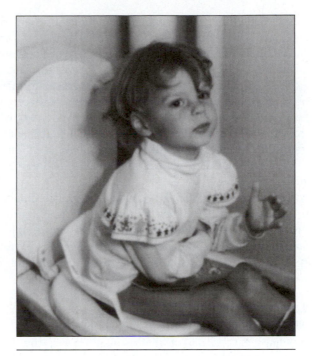

In the anal stage, toilet training is one of the toddler's first great accomplishments of self.

predictable and soothing milieu, laying the groundwork for healthy psychosexual development. Excessive indulgence or restriction, however, can make for **fixations** at the oral stage. In a fixation, certain problematic characteristics of a given stage remain central issues for the person long after he or she has moved to subsequent stages. A fixation at the oral stage might result from too much oral stimulation in the first year of life, or from too much frustration of oral activity—either of which results in the development of an **oral personality** in adulthood. Fixation at a relatively early point in the oral stage makes for the **oral-passive** personality type. The oral-passive type is blithely cheerful and overly dependent and expects the world to mother him or her. Fixation later in the oral stage, after the infant has begun to bite with teeth, makes for the **oral-sadistic** type. The oral-sadistic type is cynical, pessimistic, and "bitingly" sarcastic.

The next stop for the libido is the **anal stage.** During the second and third years of life, the toddler's sensual energy is expressed mainly in "holding in" and "letting go of" feces. Retention and elimination involve regular cycles of tension buildup and release, making again for the experience of bodily, sensual pleasure. As the child's sphincter muscles mature, he or she becomes better able to determine when and where the "letting go" will occur. Successful toilet training, therefore, signals a certain degree of mastery over the sexual instinct in that the libido comes under the control of socially prescribed schedules. Being able to control one's bowels is indeed one of the first great accomplishments of the self, suggesting a sense of autonomy and self-mastery that may be reexperienced in subsequent episodes of personal success.

The manner in which parents teach their children when and where to hold on and let go may have long-term effects for personality. Parents who shower praise upon their child's efforts at self-control foster a positive outlook concerning personal mastery and creativity. Parents who are excessively rigid and strict about toilet training, on the other hand, may be sowing the seeds of the **anal-retentive** personality, a fixation resulting in traits of stubbornness, stinginess, and an overly regulated scheduling of one's life. The anal-retentive adult lacks spontaneity and flexibility in his or her compulsive efforts to "hold on." Another form of anal fixation is the **anal-expulsive** type, who persists in "letting go" in the most impulsive ways and inappropriate circumstances. The anal-expulsive person is extremely disorganized and disorderly, often cruel, and wantonly destructive.

In contrast to Freud's emphasis on oral and anal libidinal strivings, psychoanalytic theorists who followed Freud have tended to view the first three years of life as a psychodynamic drama in which the protagonist—the infant/child—seeks *to establish the security and trust that are necessary for the establishment of a well-functioning and autonomous self.* Some theorists (e.g., Erikson, 1950) agree with Freud that the libido's oral and anal expressions are important, but these expressions indicate more than the mere manifestations of the sexual instinct. Sucking at the mother's breast helps to establish a *relationship*, many suggest the first (and perhaps most important) warm and caring object relationship in life. In line with our discussion in Chapter 2 about mother–infant attachment, many psychoanalytic theorists underscore the development of a bond of trust and security in the first year of life, with respect to which sucking at the breast may indeed play a part. (It is interesting to note that John Bowlby, the originator of attachment theory, was a psychoanalyst and that he viewed his theory as a blending of Freud, information-processing approaches, and evolutionary theory.) Similarly, Freud's anal stage may be reconceptualized as a time in the toddler's life in which he or she is seeking independence, autonomy, and the establishment of a competent self. Toilet training may be less important for what it says about the anal libido and more significant as an indication of self-mastery and independence. From Freud to the present day, furthermore, psychoanalysts have maintained that when good things happen in the first year of life, good things are more likely to happen thereafter. Therefore, the establishment of a trusting, secure, and predictable object relationship with a primary caregiver early on paves the way for the healthy emergence of an autonomous and individuated self in the second and third years of life.

The process through which early object relations establish the grounding for the development of an independent self is spelled out in Margaret Mahler's influential theory of early development. According to Mahler (1968; Mahler, Pine, & Bergman, 1975) the first three years of life are crucial for establishing lifelong, mature object relations. In the first month or two of life, the infant is in an initial stage of *normal autism*, in which its biological needs and rhythms outweigh most object-seeking efforts. Withdrawn behind a *stimulus barrier*, the newborn spends most of its time sleeping and eating as various physiological mechanisms work to achieve homeostasis. In the second month of life, the infant enters *normal symbiosis*, behaving now as though it and the mother were a dual unity within a common boundary. The infant develops a dim recognition of the mother as an object but is unable to distinguish her from the self. Thus, in symbiosis the infant and mother merge into unity, and boundaries between self and other are blurred.

At about the halfway point of the first year of life, the infant begins the critical process of **separation-individuation.** Emerging from the symbiotic bond of the early months, the infant enters the first subphase of separation-individuation, *differentiation of the body image* (5–9 months). Out of the unity of symbiosis, self and other become differentiated. As the infant moves and maneuvers, it may check back with the mother, making eye contact with her or exchanging sounds for assurance that, while she is no longer in perfect unity with the infant, she is still there. In the second subphase of *practicing* (10–14 months), the infant's expanded locomotor abilities enable it to explore the inanimate environment with much greater ease. The physical presence of the mother and other preferred caregivers promotes the infant's explorations, and when the mother is absent the infant may display low-keyed behavior, inhibiting exploration while focusing on an internal, imagined mother.

In the *rapprochement* subphase (14–24 months), the child develops an increased awareness of the separateness of the mother and may undergo a "crisis" wherein the conflict between the urge to reunite with her and the urge to separate completely becomes intense. The temporary result may be various forms of ambivalence and *approach–avoidance behavior,* as when the child follows the mother closely when she moves away but then darts away if she approaches. The resolution of the rapprochement crisis is reached in the last subphase, termed *consolidation of individuality* (2–3 years). At this time, the child establishes a stable sense of self and other and achieves emotional-object constancy, whereby he or she now accepts the fact that the mother and other caregivers remain loving and sustaining objects even when they are not present in a given situation. With the consolidation of individuality, the child has internalized a differentiated and complex image of the mother object and has integrated it successfully within the developing self.

We see, then, that whether you are considering Freud's initial views about libidinal stages or subsequent psychoanalytic theories emphasizing early object relations, the psychoanalytic tradition has generally viewed the first three years of life as a story about early dependency and love leading to independence, mastery, and the establishment of an autonomous self. Tremendous changes occur during this short period of time. The newborn is nearly oblivious to the outside world. Within two months, however, he or she is investing libido in many objects in the environment, relating to others in warm and reciprocal ways; by the age of 1 year the infant has consolidated a bond of basic trust with caregivers; and by age 3 the young child is moving around the world with remarkable confidence and aplomb, as a cohesive and individuated self relating to other selves in complex ways. Object relations theories contend that the first three years are the psychologically most important in all of life. But for Freud, things are just starting to heat up. Now that the child has established him- or herself as an autonomous agent in the world, it is time to enter the timeless battle over power and love. For Freud, the first three years are something of a warm-up act for the main event of childhood. That main event is the Oedipus complex.

The Oedipus Complex

Between the ages of 3 and 5, Freud argued, the child enters the third stage of psychosexual development, the **phallic stage.** At this time, the libido is centered in the genital region. Children become fascinated with their own sex organs and become overtly

FEATURE 3.B

Heinz Kohut's Self Psychology

One of the most influential developments in psychoanalytic theorizing in the past 20 years has been the rise of **self psychology,** championed by Heinz Kohut (1971, 1977, 1984). As a therapist, Kohut worked with patients whose central disturbance involved feelings of emptiness and depression. Many of the patients suffered from problems of *narcissism.* It was only through empathy, through careful listening to what his patients told him and understanding what they said in their own terms, that Kohut came to view the *self* as the central construct and problem in personality:

> In trying, again, and again, in analysis after analysis, to determine the genetic roots of the selves of my analysands [patients], I obtained the impression that during early psychic development a process takes place in which some archaic mental contents that had been experienced as belonging to the self become obliterated or are assigned to the area of the nonself while others are retained within the self or are added to it. As a result of this process a core self—the "nuclear self"—is established. This structure is the basis for our sense of being an independent center of initiative and perception, integrated with our most central ambitions and ideals and with our experience that our body and mind form a unit in space and a continuum in time. (Kohut, 1977, p.177)

At the center of personality is the **bipolar self.** Its two poles are (1) ambitions for power and success and (2) idealized goals and values. Linking the two poles in what Kohut describes as a "tension arc" are the person's basic talents and skills. In a sense, a person is driven by ambitions and guided by idealized goals and values in accord with talents and skills. The bipolar self is structured in the early years of life as the child interacts with important **self-objects** in the environment. Self-objects are people so central to our lives that we feel that they are, in some sense, parts of us. The bipolar self evolves through relationships with self-objects.

In most cases, the most salient self-object in the first year or two of life is the mother. With respect to the development of the self, one of the mother's main roles is to *mirror* the child's grandiosity. This means that she must confirm and admire the child's strength, health, greatness, and specialness. She must reflect and celebrate the child's budding agency and power. The mirroring relationship establishes, consolidates, and affirms the ambition pole of the bipolar self. Somewhat

curious about sexual practices among adults. During the phallic stage, children may begin masturbating. These manifest expressions of the libido's latest adventures are mirrored by a much more profound internal drama that plays itself out on an unconscious level. The drama is the ancient story of Oedipus, and its realization in the lives of young children is called the **Oedipus complex.**

One of the most famous tragic dramas in Western culture, Sophocles' *Oedipus Rex* was first performed in Athens between 430 and 426 B.C. The protagonist of the story is King Oedipus, a brilliant and courageous man in the prime of life who, at the outset of the play, has ruled the city of Thebes for many years. In the opening scene, a group later in development, the mother or the father may serve as the *idealizing* self-object. The child admires and identifies with idealizing self-objects as sources of strength, care, and calmness. The idealizing relationship establishes, consolidates, and affirms the second pole of the bipolar self, wherein are located idealized goals and values.

Healthy mirroring and idealizing pave the way for the development of an *autonomous self*, the ideal personality type in Kohut's scheme. Persons with an autonomous self enjoy high self-esteem and self-confidence. They are not overly dependent on others but are able to engage people in intimate and fulfilling relationships. As children, their parents generally supported their grandiose strivings, while serving as models of responsibility, steadfastness, and calm security. For healthy development to occur, the child must also experience some degree of frustration. "Occasional failures are not destructive; on the contrary, they may well turn into the episodes of 'optimal frustration' that stimulate the youngster to stretch his resources to the limit and himself take over some of the functions that had been performed by the self-object" (Wolf, 1982, p. 32).

By contrast, faulty mirroring and/or idealizing can result in various kinds of "injured" selves. In the *understimulated self*, the person loses vitality and feels chronically numb and empty, grasping for "aliveness" in drug or alcohol abuse, sexual adventurism, gambling, and other desperate life-styles. The roots of the understimulated self reside in the actions of self-objects who repeatedly failed to mirror and to provide ideals. Another result of insufficient mirroring and idealizing is the *fragmenting self*. In this case, the person suffers from low self-esteem and feels chronically vulnerable, unbalanced, out of kilter, or lacking in cohesion and harmony.

The *overstimulated self* develops in the child whose self-objects are overly indulgent, excessively and inappropriately responding to the child's mirroring and idealizing needs. As adults, these people are flooded by unrealistic fantasies of greatness that produce tension and anxiety. The fear and anxiety prompt them to shy away from situations in which they might be the center of attention. Finally, people suffering from the *overburdened self* experience the world as a hostile and dangerous place, and they are likely to respond to minor setbacks with fits of rage. They "are deficient in self-soothing capacity, due to early deprivation of opportunities for merger with calming self-objects" (Wolf, 1982, p. 38). In these cases, the childhood failure lies in the idealizing relationship, as parents were deficient in providing models of values and goals to be idealized.

of citizens, in despair over the recent famine and pestilence that have plagued Thebes, has gathered in front of the palace to ask the king for help. They have faith in the abilities of Oedipus to work wonders, for long ago he solved a great riddle and delivered the Thebans from the curse of the Sphinx. A monster with a woman's head and breasts and the body of a lion, the Sphinx had once sat on a rock outside Thebes and killed all travelers who could not answer her riddle: What animal walks on four feet in the morning, two at noon, and three at night? The clever Oedipus was the first to come up with the correct response: *man* (who crawls on fours when a child, walks erect in adulthood, and hobbles on a cane when he is old). Upon hearing the correct answer, the Sphinx killed herself. The Thebans, in gratitude, married the young Oedipus to their recently widowed queen, Jocasta, making him king of Thebes.

Oedipus learns that the city now faces a greater curse brought on by the evil deeds of one of its citizens. He pledges to find the villain and free Thebes a second time. A blind prophet, Tiresias, tells Oedipus the truth about the villain: that it is he, the king. But there is more. The nature of his villainy is an unspeakable horror: Oedipus has unknowingly killed his father (the former king of Thebes, Laius) and made love to his mother (the queen, his wife, Jocasta). Patricide and incest are his unforgivable and yet unwitting crimes, and for these Thebes now pays the price of the gods' curse. Incredulous and enraged, Oedipus listens as the blind Tiresias reveals the long-hidden truth that only he can see:

And I tell you again:

The man you have been looking for all this time,

The damned man, the murderer of Laios,

That man is in Thebes. To your mind he is foreign-born,

But it will soon show that he is a Theban,

A revelation that will fail to please.

A blind man,

Who has his eyes now; a penniless man, who is rich now;

And he will go tapping the strange earth with his staff

To the children with whom he lives now he will be

Brother and father—the very same; to her

Who bore him, son and husband—the very same

Who came to his father's bed, wet with his father's blood.

(O'Brien & Dukore, 1969, p. 21)

Oedipus, Jocasta, and all of Thebes eventually come to realize that Tiresias' vision is clear and true. Because of an oracle predicting that their son would kill his father and sleep with his mother, the king and queen of Thebes—Laius and Jocasta—long ago pierced the ankles of their newborn boy and left him to die on a lonely mountainside. A shepherd took pity on the boy, giving him to another shepherd, who gave him to the king and queen of another town, who named the boy "Oedipus" (meaning "swollen foot") and raised him as their own son, never telling him about his true origin. As a youth, Oedipus went to Delphi and learned of the oracle that he should grow up to murder his father and sleep with his mother. So that he could not fulfill what the gods had destined to be his fate, Oedipus fled, eventually happening upon the Sphinx, solving the riddle, and becoming the glorious king of Thebes. As an impetuous man of the sword, he killed his share of men along the way. One of these was Laius, slaughtered in a forgettable skirmish at the intersection of three roads.

The price of Oedipus' crime is enormous. When she finally realizes that her husband is in fact her son, Jocasta hangs herself. Oedipus rips the golden brooches from

In this production of **Oedipus Rex,** *Jocasta comforts Oedipus, who is both her lover and her son.*

his dead mother's gown and plunges them deep into his eyes. Blinded now like Tiresias, he finally sees the truth. At the end of the play, Oedipus banishes himself to a distant land. In later dramas (*Antigone, Oedipus at Colonnus*), he returns as something of a wise sage whose advice is greatly valued. In summary, then, *Oedipus Rex* is the story of a strong and clever young man who becomes an all-powerful king but eventually falls from glory and is maimed because of an unspeakable crime. The fall from power brings with it a kind of wisdom, in that Oedipus now knows "the truth" and eventually achieves a status, like that of Tiresias, of the blind sage. The crimes he commits are outside of Oedipus' own awareness. He kills his father and sleeps with his mother without knowing that he has done either—in other words, *unconsciously.*

So it goes with the young boy—and maybe the young girl. At an unconscious level, the young boy in the phallic stage of psychosexual development desires to have his mother as Oedipus had Jocasta. The desire to have the other in a powerful and sensual manner means investing the libido in that person—the process of object choice. In a vague, unspeakable, and mysterious way, claimed Freud, young boys seek to possess—to conquer in a powerful and an erotic manner—a primal feminine love object that exists in their fantasies and may correspond in reality to their own mothers. Equally vague and unspeakable is an unconsciously perceived threat—that from a powerful masculine force that stands in the way of the boy's conquests, represented by the father who threatens to castrate the boy. What Freud termed **castration anxiety** literally means the fear that one's penis will be cut off, but more profoundly it may symbolize the child's fear that he will, like Oedipus, lose his power (and his love object as well). Thus, the boy harbors an unconscious wish to kill the father, as Freud indeed discovered in the analysis of his own unconscious life.

The normal resolution of the Oedipus complex follows the ancient myth. The young boy eventually comes to identify with the aggressor of his fantasies, seeking to be like the father so to have the mother in a vicarious manner. The unconscious shift from object choice to identification marks both a major defeat and a victory for the boy. Like Oedipus, he can no longer be "king." On an unconscious level, the young boy at the close of the oedipal period understands that he is weaker, smaller, and more mortal than he (unconsciously) ever imagined. The loss of power is a kind of castration, symbolized in the Greek myth when Oedipus blinds himself. Omnipotence is replaced by a definite but painful sense of limitations. Yet, from the standpoint of healthy personality development, the oedipal defeat is ultimately a good thing. Like the blind Oedipus who knows the truth, the young boy who suffers the oedipal defeat eventually attains the rudiments of a certain kind of wisdom and maturity. Identification with the father (and to a lesser extent with the mother as well) at the end of the Oedipus complex leaves the boy with a basic moral attitude about life, encapsuled in what Freud termed the *superego*. Without the superego, the child would become a ruthless, though perhaps clever, tyrant—able to solve riddles, surely, but woefully deficient in the more challenging task of living in a moral society.

The little boy's resolution of the Oedipus complex is the prototype for the general tendency of all of civilized humankind to repress certain instinctual urges and establish in their place great institutions of social organization, such as government and religion. Freud's most powerful and controversial rendition of this argument is *Totem and Taboo* (1913/1958)—a wildly speculative account of human prehistory that can be interpreted in literal terms or as a Freudian allegory (Hogan, 1976). In *Totem and Taboo*, Freud followed Darwin in claiming that, long ago in the history of the human species, people lived in primal hordes, each ruled by an autocratic father. Acting on his unfettered instinctual urges, the patriarchal leader kept the women of the horde for his own sexual delight and prohibited the younger men (his sons) from sharing in the bounty. This form of social organization ended, speculated Freud, when young men rose up collectively to kill the ruthless father, subsequently devouring his flesh in a totem meal. The young men symbolically accomplished an identification with the father by eating him. Collectively assuming his authority, the new rulers established fraternal social clans with strict taboos on free sexual expression, especially incest. From this first socially organized restriction of the sexual instinct evolved more elaborate restricting structures, such as bodies of laws and norms designed to quell the wild instinctual impulses of men.

But what about women? Freud attempted to adapt his oedipal theorizing to the unconscious lives of girls and women, but even he was forced to admit that his efforts were far from satisfactory. The young girl's unconscious dilemma begins with a positive attraction toward the mother, a mixture of object choice and identification. However, the fantasized mother figure disappoints the girl when the daughter realizes that both she and the mother lack a penis, which may symbolize a lack of power. The little girl may blame the mother for the perceived deficiency, resulting in what Freud termed **penis envy.** As a result, the girl shifts some of her unconscious affections to a "stronger" father figure. The girl eventually resolves her Oedipus complex by repressing her attraction to the father and completing an identification with the mother.

Whereas the boy resolves the Oedipus complex by identifying with the father who threatens him with castration, the little girl is, in a sense, already "castrated," suggested Freud, in that she has no penis. Therefore, she cannot fear castration. Because she lacks the fear, the little girl may feel less urgency to resolve the complex via identification. For many girls, Freud suggested, the Oedipus complex may last a very long time, and for some it is only partially resolved (Freud, 1933/1964). In addition, because the superego is the heir to the Oedipus complex, many women develop superegos that are weaker and less independent than those developed by men. This may be interpreted to suggest that women have less moral sensibility than men. Another interpretation is to suggest that the woman's superego is less dogmatic and harsh, perhaps freeing her up to make moral decisions in a more flexible manner. It is probably fair to say, however, that Freud's inclinations—steeped as they were in the patriarchal world in which he lived—tended in the direction of the first interpretation.

Freud's views on the Oedipus complex in women were very controversial, even at the time of their publication. Many felt it unwise to apply a male-dominated model of sexuality to women, arguing that the little girl's oedipal attachment develops out of her intrinsic femininity undergoing its own maturation processes. Clara Thompson, an influential analyst writing around the time of Freud's death, took issue with the claim that women literally envy the male penis. Rather, women wish to be men's equals; if such a desire for the penis exists, it is in fact a symbolic desire for power and privilege, qualities typically bestowed upon men in male-dominated societies (Thompson, 1942). Other analysts, like Karen Horney (1939), argued that the Oedipus complex is a product of culture rather than instinct, and that its development for both men and women is strongly shaped by societal expectations, opportunities, and institutions.

I have presented a simplified rendition of the Oedipus complex in both sexes. Freud suggested complicated variations on the standard script. For instance, early object choice of both boys and girls may be directed toward *both* mother and father. Similarly, identifications that resolve the complex may incorporate both father and mother (Freud, 1923/1961). A given family's particular dynamics and constellation surely shape the oedipal scenario, but Freud also emphasized that the complex unfolds along certain biologically mandated lines. Exactly how it is played out in the unconscious, therefore, is a complex product of the interaction of biology and experience.

A Case of Oedipal Dynamics: The Death of Yukio Mishima

Freud's concept of the Oedipus complex is one of the richest sources of interpretation in the psychoanalytic tradition. While scholars have furiously debated the extent to which the Oedipus complex is a common phenomenon in human development (e.g., Malinowski, 1927), there is little doubt that dramatic instances of Oedipal dynamics can be observed in *some* people's lives. Let me give you one example. As a college student, I became fascinated with the writings and the life of Yukio Mishima, a Japanese novelist who committed suicide in 1970. I wanted to figure out why this tremendously successful man would, at age 46, plunge a dagger into his stomach. I believe Freud's theory of the Oedipus complex sheds some light on the mystery.

The Japanese novelist, Yukio Mishima, admires a sword of the type he eventually used to kill himself.

The morning he killed himself, Yukio Mishima rose early, shaved slowly and carefully, showered, and put on a fresh, white cotton loincloth and a military uniform. On a table in the hall, he left the final installment of his last novel. The envelope was addressed to his publishers, who were to send a representative for it later that day. At the front gate of his home, Mishima met with four students, and the five of them drove to a Tokyo army base. According to a plan rehearsed for weeks Mishima and the four fought off a group of army personnel with their swords, took hostage one General Mashita, and forced a temporary truce whereby a thousand men of the 32nd Infantry Regiment were to gather in front of the headquarters at noon to hear Mishima deliver a patriotic speech. Constant heckling cut the speech short. Mishima and the four then retreated to a back room and, as planned for weeks, performed the Japanese ceremonial rite of *seppuku*, in which he shouted a last salute to the Emperor of Japan and then plunged a samurai dagger deep into his stomach, forcing the cutting edge across his abdomen from left to right. One of the four students then chopped off his head. For years, Mishima had rehearsed this gory suicide in numerous plays and stories he wrote, and in his private fantasies.

Yukio Mishima was in the prime of his life when, on November 25, 1970, he enacted the suicide. He was healthy, successful, famous, rich, and, according to most who knew him, relatively happy. With over 100 full-length books to his credit, he was considered by many the single greatest novelist of modern Japan. And he was much more than a novelist. He was a playwright, a sportsman, a film actor, the founder of a private army, a family man, and a world traveler. Indeed, one biographer characterized Mishima as the "Leonardo da Vinci of modern Japan" (Scott-Stokes, 1974).

From the many notable elements in Mishima's life history, let us look quickly at seven, drawn from Mishima's autobiographical writings (Mishima, 1958, 1970) and the English biographies written by Scott-Stokes (1974) and Nathan (1974).

1. On Mishima's 50th day of life (in 1925), his paternal grandmother took the infant away from his mother and moved him, crib and all, into her dark sickroom downstairs, where Mishima lived until he was 12. In the first few years, Mishima's mother was able to see her son only during times of feeding. Later in childhood, Mishima would meet her on an occasional secret rendezvous. For the most part Mishima's grandmother strictly controlled the environment of his early years. Because of her neuralgia, she could tolerate little noise. Mishima was allowed to play quietly with three carefully chosen cousins, all girls. As a young boy, Mishima spent many of his waking hours nursing his sick grandmother, sponging her brow, massaging her back and hip, bringing her medicine, and leading her to the toilet.

2. From the age of 4, Mishima was obsessed with bizarre fantasies of heroism that presaged his eventual suicide—fantasies "tormenting and frightening me all my life" (Mishima, 1958, p. 8). One of these fantasies was formed in response to seeing a handsome young laborer bearing buckets of animal excrement. The 4-year-old Mishima was fascinated with the figure of the "night-soil man," experiencing a confusing mixture of excitement, longing, and sadness in his presence. The night-soil man became, in Mishima's fantasy life, a model for the tragic hero whose body is in constant communion with death. As decaying matter, the feces symbolize death.

3. Mishima's fantasies of heroism were suffused with homosexual longing. His feelings for the night-soil man were replayed again and again in subsequent fantasies in which he felt a powerful sexual attraction to muscular young men. One of the students who accompanied Mishima on the day of his death is thought to have been his homosexual lover.

4. Though little solid information is available, Mishima's marriage of 13 years to Yoko Sugiyama appeared to most people to have been a happy one. In their many public appearances, Mishima and Yoko seemed to enjoy each other. Mishima often brought Yoko into his conversations with others, soliciting her opinions and apparently valuing her responses to a degree that was unusual for other male Japanese writers. The couple raised two children.

5. In the late 1950s, Mishima began to express dissatisfaction with the process of writing fiction. Despite the critical acclaim of his work, he began to see writing as a cowardly escape from reality. He began to contrast the *word* and the *act*, arguing that words were "corrosive" and that heroism in life could be attained only by the pure action of a strong and beautiful body.

6.   In order to make his own body strong and beautiful, Mishima began, at the age of 30, a rigorous weight-lifting program that he followed religiously to the week he died. A frail and sickly boy and youth, Mishima transformed himself in his 30s into the muscle-bound hero of his fantasies. In strange ways, weight lifting was connected, in Mishima's mind, to death. Attacking the barbell involved "ceaseless motion, ceaseless violent deaths, ceaseless escape from cold objectivity—by now, I could no longer live without such mysteries" (Mishima, 1970, p. 76). The "ceaseless violent deaths" of weight training prepared him for the glorious final death that would make him a tragic hero:

> I cherished a romantic impulse toward death, yet at the same time I required a strictly classical body as its vehicle. . . . A powerful, tragic frame and sculpturesque muscles are indispensible in a romantically noble death. Any confrontation between weak, flabby flesh and death seemed to me absurdly inappropriate. (Mishima, 1970, pp. 27–28)

7.   In the 1960s, Mishima created a private army, called the Shield Society. The army was dedicated to the revival of patriotism in modern Japan and to the ultimate defense of the Japanese emperor. Mishima said he wished to save Japan from both communism and Western capitalism. The army was composed of college students, for the most part, including the four who witnessed the *seppuku* on that November day in 1970.

What was the psychological meaning of Mishima's suicide? I believe that part of the meaning derives from a fundamental and fatal confusion in Mishima's life between "having" and "being" (McAdams, 1985a). In Freud's terms, it is an Oedipal confusion between **object choice** and **identification**. According to Freud, the person tends, on an unconscious level, to relate to important other people in his or her life in one or both of two very primitive ways. The person seeks either to *have the other in a powerful/sensual way* (object choice) or to *be the other* (identification). In object choice, the person unconsciously desires the other as an object of affection. He or she feels, unconsciously, a strong need to "own" the other person, to hold on to the other as the exclusive object of his or her sensual longings. This is, argued Freud, the basic unconscious way that preschool boys relate to their mothers (and/or mother figures in their environment) and preschool girls to their father (and/or father figures) in the Oedipus complex. Identification, on the other hand, involves the desire to be like the other, to take in all of the other's qualities and, quite literally at the unconscious level, to become the other. The desire to be the other is sometimes commingled with a strong fear of or hatred for the same other, as in the case of what psychoanalysts have termed *identification with the aggressor*. Identification is, argued Freud, the basic unconscious way that preschool boys relate to their fathers (and/or father figures) and preschool girls to their mothers (and/or mother figures) in the Oedipus complex.

Object choice and identification appear to be related to each other in an extremely interesting way. Freud suggests that, in some sense, *object choice is generally preferred at the unconscious level* and that *identification arises often when object choice is thwarted*, as is the case most commonly in the Oedipus complex. In other words, we seek first to *have* the other, but when we cannot have the other we seek to *be* the other. This is why, said Freud (1917/1957), people often take on the personal characteristics of loved ones after those loved ones have died. With the death of the other, object choice is no longer a possibility, and the person thus comes to identify with the lost object. A symbol for the identification with the other in dreams, fantasy, and mythology is *eating* the other—the literal "taking in" of the lost object.

Because of a complex host of factors, including his 12-year stay in his grandmother's sickroom, Mishima was never able to sort out, on the unconscious level, object choice and identification. Rather than developing a typical sensual orientation to his mother and coming to identify with a father figure in the Oedipus complex, Mishima came to project both object choice and identification onto the same alternative object: the tragic hero initially identified as the night-soil man. Mishima's life story can thus be understood in terms of transformations over time in the tragic hero, whom he longed both *to have* and *to be*. In *Confessions of a Mask*, Mishima (1958) traces how the tragic hero was transformed in his childhood and adolescent fantasies from the night-soil man to a picture of Joan of Arc, then to the figure of the Christian martyr Saint Sebastian, and finally to his first real-life love object—a strapping teenaged boy named Omi.

At the age of 14, Mishima fell in love with a boy whom he also wished to become. Omi was the real-life personification of the tragic oedipal hero that Mishima had first identified as the night-soil man. In addition, Omi was everything that, in reality, Mishima was not. Whereas the teenaged Mishima was weak and sickly, Omi was strong and robust—the adored best athlete in class. Whereas Mishima was constantly absorbed in thought and fantasy, Omi seemed to be an unselfconscious youth devoted to the pure action of the body. Whereas Mishima was sheltered and naive, Omi seemed, in Mishima's perception, to exude real-world confidence, maturity, and an intimate acquaintance with sex, death, and heroism.

Mishima's homosexual love for Omi, however, came to a grinding halt one day on the playground when he felt pangs of jealousy while observing Omi's flawless performance on the parallel bars. In this moment, Mishima realized that he wished to be like Omi as much as he wished to have Omi in a sensual way. The fact that he was too weak and sickly to be like his lover infuriated Mishima, forcing him to abandon his object choice and, as Freud would have it, to accelerate his mission to *become* Omi, the tragic hero. Remember that eating the object may symbolize, in fantasy, identification with the object. The loss of Omi and subsequent identification with him are symbolized in a startling dream that Mishima had shortly after the playground scene in which he literally ate a naked young boy served to him on a platter.

In adulthood, Mishima struggled to become Omi through his rigorous weight-training program. By changing weak and flabby flesh into muscle, Mishima fashioned himself into the tragic hero that he had loved from the age of 4. No longer was his oedipal love object confined to internal fantasy or the external world. By becoming Omi and the night-soil man, *he came unconsciously to be his own lover.* Therefore, if he was to become Omi (identification), he *must have himself* (object choice). One result of this unconscious dynamic may have been the intensified narcissism of his later years: His egotistical manner suggested that he had quite literally fallen in love with himself. Another result I would argue, was his suicide.

For Mishima, the Japanese rite of *seppuku* had always had a profoundly sexual significance. Since the age of 4, Mishima had romanticized death, and his novels and stories are filled with erotic images of death and killing. *Seppuku* was, for Mishima, a macabre sexual union with himself. It enabled him to consummate symbolically both his desire to be and to have Omi. In thrusting the dagger into his own stomach, Mishima became both the lover and the beloved—symbolically, both the male phallus and the female vagina. At the moment of death, he was able, therefore, to become the tragic hero of his oedipal dreams and to have that same tragic hero simultaneously, in a deadly sexual union.

A Reinterpretation of the Oedipus Complex: Chodorow's Theory of Gender

No idea in the psychoanalytic tradition has stirred up more interest and dispute than the idea of the Oedipus complex. Within the psychoanalytic tradition, theorists and clinicians disagree strongly about whether to adopt a literal (e.g., a penis is a penis) or figurative (e.g., a penis stands for male authority, power, societal oppression, etc.) interpretation of the complex. They disagree, too, over the extent to which the Oedipus complex is an *important* phenomenon in human development (even if it happens, what influence does it have on the rest of life?), whether a great many people even experience an Oedipus complex, whether men and women have similar oedipal experiences, and so on. Within scientific psychology, researchers have not been very successful in operationalizing the Oedipus complex. How does one measure unconscious incestual wishes in 4-year-olds? How does one know when the complex has been "resolved"? Because of these measurement problems, there exists today only sparse and uneven empirical evidence for the existence of the Oedipus complex (e.g., Silverman & Fishel, 1981). This does not mean that the Oedipus complex is merely a myth—only that mainstream behavioral scientists have not found good and direct ways to demonstrate the Oedipus complex as a general phenomenon of human development. Outside psychology, many scholars have offered reinterpretations of the Oedipus complex, suggesting, for example, that Oedipus was a misogynist bigot (he kills the female sphinx and is responsible for the death of his mother/wife); that the real villains in the story are Laius and Jocasta, who sent the baby Oedipus off to die (a "Laius complex" is the father's wish to kill his offspring); that the Oedipus complex is an allegory for the oppression of the authoritarian state; and on and on (Boxer, 1997).

It can be argued, however, that provocative ideas like the Oedipus complex are very valuable in science because they stimulate a great deal of creative work. As I suggested in Chapter 1, an important criterion of a good theory or theoretical construct is its ability to generate new insights and unforeseen conceptualizations. One of the most interesting conceptualizations to be generated by the controversy over the Oedipus complex is Nancy Chodorow's theory linking psychoanalysis and the sociology of gender.

In her landmark book, *The Reproduction of Mothering*, Chodorow (1978) reinterprets the Oedipus complex in order to explain gender differences in personality and the role of mothering in contemporary Western societies. Chodorow begins her argument with a stark, cross-cultural fact: *Women mother.* Biologically speaking, women bear children; sociologically speaking, women, in virtually all human societies, "take primary responsibility for infant care, spend more time with infants and children than do men, and sustain primary emotional ties with infants" (p. 3). Although the percentage of adult women employed in paid work outside the home has increased dramatically over the course of the 20th century in the United States and western Europe, mothering is still the province of women. Indeed, most babysitters, nannies, daycare workers, and nursery school teachers are women, and most boys and girls spend most of their early childhood in the company of women. Even in those two-career households in which fathers endeavor to engage in greater levels of childcare than the traditional masculine role has typically allowed, mothers still tend to do the lion's share of caregiving, especially with very young children, as empirical research has decisively shown (e.g., Biernat & Wortman, 1991).

Chodorow focuses on the different experiences of little girls and boys as they grow up in "a male dominant but father-absent family where women mother" (p. 40). She argues that by age 3 or 4, children have developed a basic sense of themselves as either female or male as a result, in part, of the different ways in which mothers relate to girls and boys. Even before the onset of the Oedipus complex, mothers tend to relate to girls with a greater sense of "openness and continuity" (p. 109). They identify more with their daughters than they do with their sons. Mothers and daughters experience greater levels of intimacy, merger, and a sense of oneness with each other. The relationship between mother and daughter becomes emotionally richer and more complex over time, a relationship of dependence, attachment, and symbiosis. By contrast, "mothers experience their sons as a male opposite" (p. 110). Sons are viewed as differentiated from their mothers, and maternal behavior is geared toward enabling sons to attain independence and autonomy. While mothers may cherish their sons and love them intensely, their attitude toward sons will always be one of opposition: He is male; he is not like me; he will grow up to be different, separate.

Over the course of his career, Freud became increasingly aware of the different experiences of girls and boys in the preoedipal period. Freud observed that the girl's preoedipal attachment to her mother tends to last longer than the boy's attachment to mother and that the relationship between mother and daughter can be much more dramatically intense and ambivalent than that between mother and son. Nevertheless Freud felt compelled to describe the female Oedipus complex in terms that were parallel to the experience of boys. According to the orthodox Freudian position, the oedipal girl shifts her affection from mother to father when she realizes that father possesses the coveted penis. Chodorow concedes that the little girl may become disappointed in her mother, or see her as a rival, and the little girl may indeed form a new attachment to her father. But the relationship between father and daughter is rarely strong enough to erase the enduring mother/daughter bond:

> For a girl . . . there is no single oedipal mode or quick oedipal resolution, and there is no absolute "change of object." Psychoanalytic accounts make clear that a girl's libidinal turning to her father is not at the expense of, or a substitute for, her attachment to her mother. Nor does a girl give up the internal relationship to her mother which is a product of her earlier development. Instead, a girl develops important oedipal attachments to her mother *as well as* to her father. These attachments, and the way they are internalized, are built upon, and do not replace, her intense and exclusive preoedipal attachment to her mother. . . . (p. 127)

A girl's oedipal situation, therefore, is multilayered and complex, and it affords no simple resolution. As a result, the girl's basic gender identity is developed in the context of an ongoing and richly nuanced relationship with mother. The feminine self is defined *in relation*. For little boys, however, gender identity is a greater puzzle, a mysterious problem to be solved. Even though the boy may identify with the father, he is not likely to acquire the intimate familiarity with the father's traditional roles—as the man who works outside the house in order to bring home money and support the family—that little girls naturally develop with their mothers. In a sense, the boy must figure out how to be a man on his own, *through opposition*. According to Chodorow, the little boy experiences his own masculinity in opposition to the world of women. He knows that men are different from women, but he doesn't know exactly how. The little boy identifies with a disembodied "position" in the world—he renders a guess about what the position of men might be, and then he patterns himself after the guess. The masculine self is defined through separation and guesswork. By contrast, the feminine self develops from the connectedness of human relations.

What are the results of these two very different experiences of the oedipal period? Chodorow suggests that girls emerge from early childhood "with a stronger basis for experiencing another's needs and feelings as one's own." Girls come to experience themselves as "less differentiated than boys, as more continuous with and related to" other people (p. 167). Consciously and unconsciously, the girl experiences herself as continuous with her environment, connected in a web of intimacy (Gilligan, 1982). The boy, by contrast, must work to separate himself from the web, to identify the essential nature of maleness through separation, opposition, and individuation.

In addition, their differential experiences in the family prepare girls and boys for society's gender roles. Out of the mother/daughter bond emerge daughters with mothering capacities and the desire to mother, making for what Chodorow calls "the reproduction of mothering" from one generation to the next. By contrast, mothers (and fathers as nonmothers) produce sons whose nurturant capacities and needs are systematically curtailed and repressed, preparing the way for men's primary participation in the impersonal, nonfamily world of work and public life.

The Structure of Adult Personality

Following our extended exploration of the Oedipus complex, we now return to the psychoanalytic story of the development of personality from infancy to adulthood. With the resolution of the Oedipus complex in middle childhood, Freud argued, the libido is now ready for an extended holiday. The child now enters **latency.** During latency, the libido is rarely expressed in an overt manner. Rather, children channel instinctual energy into play, schoolwork, and peer relations. The elementary school years, therefore, are a time of expanding socialization as children come to internalize further the values, norms, rules, skills, and so forth offered by their society. With the exception of Erik Erikson (Chapter 10 in this book), however, psychoanalytic theorists have tended to ignore the many different changes that occur during the latency period. During this time of intensive socialization, children develop skills and values in many different contexts—at school, on the playground, at church, in the family, with peers, with older adults. Nonetheless, the libido itself seems relatively quiet during this time, which is why Freud had little to say about the latency period in the child's life.

The onset of puberty, however, marks the libido's return to center stage and its final mature expression. In adolescence, the individual enters Freud's **genital stage** of psychosexual development. Biologically capable now of full-fledged sexual intercourse, the young man or woman is finally at the point of attaining psychosexual maturity. He or she must now meet the challenges of expressing the libido in ways that benefit both self and society. This is very difficult. It involves channeling instinctual energy into genital *love* and productive *work* while simultaneously keeping at bay the anxiety that results from inevitable conflicts. Just how troublesome these conflicts can be in adulthood is best depicted in Freud's theory of how the adult mind is finally structured.

In one of his last theoretical innovations, Freud (1923/1961) proposed an integrative model of how the mind is organized. Figure 3.2 presents a picture of the model. Freud concluded that the mind can be broken down into three independent structures: id, ego, and superego. Each of the three exists for a different purpose. The major conflicts that produce anxiety in adults' lives are often the result of disagreements among

FIGURE 3.2   *Freud's Model of the Psyche*

The id, ego, and superego are the three main regions in Freud's model of the human mind.

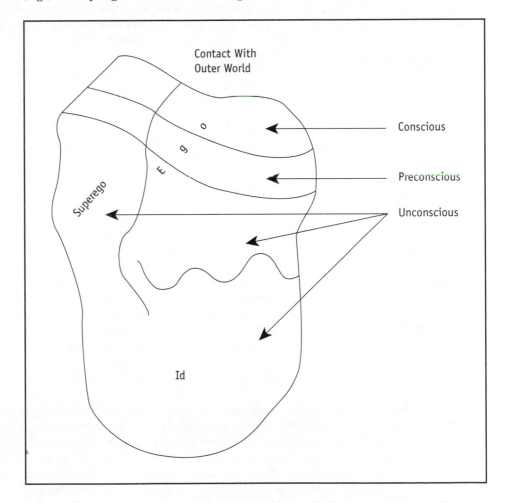

these three different agents of the mind. Resolving conflicts, therefore, involves forging creative agreements that enable the three to coexist with one another and with the outside world in relative, if short-lived, tranquility.

The most primitive structure is the **id** (German: *das Es*, or "the it"). Completely submerged in the unconscious, the id is the home of the instinctual impulses of sex and aggression and their derivative wishes, fantasies, and inclinations. The id is a chaotic, seething cauldron that provides all the instinctual energy for mental life. The id knows no inhibitions; it obeys no logical or moral constraints; it is completely out of touch with the outside world of reality, and will remain so always. The activity of the id is dictated solely by the **pleasure principle:** Pleasure derives from the reduction of tension in the immediate gratification of impulses.

If the mind remained "all id," the human being would quickly encounter very serious trouble. Though the id finds satisfaction in hallucinatory wish fulfillment, the organism cannot function for long on wish and fantasy alone. Beginning in infancy, therefore, a second structure of the mind emerges out of the id. This is the **ego** (German: *das Ich*, or "the I"). Borrowing its energy from the id instincts, the ego exists as the "handmaiden" to the id, working tirelessly to mediate between the blind demands of its master and the constraints imposed by logic and the external world. The ego thus helps ensure the safety and self-preservation of the organism by adopting the **reality principle** in conducting its affairs and by relying on the power of rational thought. The reality principle enables the individual to suspend immediate instinctual gratification until either an appropriate object or environmental condition arises that will satisfy the instinct. The ego is able to weigh the demands of the outside world and balance them with the needs and impulses expressed by the id, so to produce behaviors and modes of experience that best use the id's raw energy.

While the id is completely submerged within the unconscious, the ego manifests itself partly in certain conscious ways. When a person functions as a rational and self-reflective decision maker in the face of life's many challenges, he or she is displaying the ego's conscious powers. But significant aspects of the ego are unconscious, as well. A good deal of coping with the inevitable conflicts that arise in daily life is carried out unconsciously, by the ego through **defense mechanisms.** A defense mechanism is *an unconscious strategy of the ego that distorts reality in order to lessen anxiety.* In the defense mechanism of *projection*, for instance, the person unconsciously attributes to other people certain of his or her own characteristics whose existence within the self provokes unacceptable levels of anxiety. Therefore, a man who harbors strong unconscious uncertainties about his own masculinity may be more likely than most people to accuse other men of being homosexual. This is not a conscious deceit but rather a subtle and unconscious strategy of the ego to ward off anxiety by distorting, to a certain extent, objective reality. Table 3.6 describes some other defense mechanisms commonly employed by the ego.

As we have already noted, the **superego** emerges at the end of the Oedipus complex. The superego (German: *das Überich*, or "the over-I") is a primitive internalized representation of the norms and values of society as acquired through identification with the parents. As such, the superego is akin to an internalized authority that repeatedly tells the person what he or she should and should not be doing, as if the parents had quite literally been eaten and become now personified inside the self. The superego is typically a strict and inflexible agent who insists on the renunciation or

| TABLE 3.6 | *Some Defense Mechanisms of the Ego* | |

MECHANISM	DEFINITION	SIMPLE EXAMPLE
Repression	A dangerous impulse is actively and totally excluded from consciousness.	An aging father fails to recognize his own feelings of hostility toward his strong, athletic son.
Projection	Attributing one's own unacceptable and disturbing thoughts and impulses to someone else.	A man preoccupied with doubts about his own heterosexuality frequently accuses others of being homosexual.
Reaction formation	Warding off an unacceptable impulse by overemphasizing its opposite in thought and behavior.	A man threatened by his desire to dominate others and to be aggressive thinks of himself as a passive and retiring sort of person and acts accordingly.
Rationalization	Devising an extremely "reasonable" explanation or excuse for an event or behavior that threatens the person's esteem.	A wife explains her husband's repeated infidelity as a product of his unfortunate upbringing or an overly seductive environment.
Regression	Retreating to an earlier and more primitive stage or mode of behavior in order to avoid pain, threat, or anxiety.	A mother lapses into diversionary "baby talk" with her daughter whenever she confronts a tough decision or threatening situation.
Displacement	Shifting an impulse from a threatening to a nonthreatening object.	Angry at his boss because of a demotion, the businessman goes home and argues with his wife.
Sublimation	Channeling socially unacceptable impulses into acceptable, even admirable, behavior.	The surgeon channels aggressive energy into constructive medical work; the artist employs the libido to produce a masterpiece.

repression of the id's instinctual demands. Whereas the id yells out, "Yes! Go for it—now!" the superego sternly replies, "No! Not in a million years!" Despite the opposing points of view, however, the id and superego share a number of characteristics. Both, for instance, are demanding and inflexible—both are blind to the constraints and demands of the outside world. Only the ego operates according to the reality principle.

With the establishment of the superego, the ego now faces a third taskmaster and powerful source of conflict. The first, the reality of the outside world, poses objective dangers that produce realistic anxiety; the second, the id, threatens the ego with neurotic anxiety about the ever-present possibility of an uncontrollable release of instinctual energy; now the third source of conflict, the superego, adds the problem of moral anxiety, which may take the form of feelings of guilt over moral transgressions or regret in failing to live up to perfect ideals. The ego is a lonely agent of reasonableness amidst a host of uncompromising and relentless forces and factors. Dependent on the id for its energy, beholden to the superego as the lowly child to an omnipotent parent, and faced with almost impossible demands from the real world, the ego is perennially beleaguered, and occasionally it may even break down, resulting in neurotic symptoms. No wonder that Freud was pessimistic about the possibilities of human happiness.

But the **ego psychologists** who followed Freud—beginning with Anna Freud (1936) and including Heinz Hartmann (1939), Erik Erikson (1950), and Robert White (1959, 1963)—were much more optimistic about the potential of the ego. According to these theorists, the ego promotes healthy adaptation to life through the ego functions of learning, memory, perception, and synthesis. More than a hapless defender, the ego is a master integrator. It organizes experience so that the organism can become an effective and competent member of society. Furthermore, in its efforts to cope with anxiety the ego has at its disposal a formidable arsenal of weapons, including a wide range of defense mechanisms (Cramer, 1991; A. Freud, 1936; Haan, 1977; Schafer, 1968; Vaillant, 1977). The working of defense mechanisms is a topic that has attracted a considerable body of empirical research in personality (Paulhus, Fridhandler, & Hayes, 1997) and social (Baumeister, Dale, & Sommer, 1998) psychology. The research suggests that people do consistently employ effective defensive strategies in dealing with anxiety and stress.

There is considerable consensus among psychoanalysts that some defense mechanisms are relatively primitive and immature (such as denial) while others are more complex and mature (such as sublimation) (Anthony, 1970; A. Freud, 1946). The most significant empirical research on the development of defense mechanisms has been conducted by Phebe Cramer (1991). Cramer has tested the hypothesis that immature defense mechanisms should arise early in life and then taper off, while mature mechanisms should develop somewhat later. She has focused on three defense mechanisms. The most primitive of the three is **denial,** in which the person baldly refuses to acknowledge an anxiety-provoking event. For instance, a young child visiting the doctor may insist that he is not afraid of a shot, or a recently widowed woman may claim she feels no grief. Denial may be employed by people of all ages, argue psychoanalysts, but it tends to be most common among the very young. Adults tend to use denial only in the most upsetting and threatening situations. More mature than denial is **projection,** in which the person attributes unacceptable internal states and qualities to external others. For instance, an adolescent girl who doubts her own religious values may accuse others of being "sinful," or a businessman insecure about his own marriage may suspect that many of his colleagues are having extramarital affairs. Projection requires that standards of "good" and "bad" be internalized such that the "bad" can be projected outward. Therefore, the use of projection should await the development of conscience (Freud's superego) in middle childhood. The most mature defense mechanism studied by Cramer is **identification,** whereby the person forms an enduring mental representation of significant others, that is, he or she replicates the behavioral traits of others as a way of coping. Requiring the clear differentiation of self and others and a complex understanding of differences among various people, identification becomes an effective defense in adolescence and should remain so throughout life (Blos, 1979).

In one study Cramer studied the creative stories told or written by 320 children representing four age groups: young children (ages 4–7), intermediate (ages 8–11), early adolescent (ninth and tenth grades), and late adolescent (eleventh and twelfth grades). Each child was asked to look at two specially chosen pictures and make up an imaginative story about each. The stories were analyzed for examples of defense mechanisms according to the scoring categories shown in Table 3.7. As Figure 3.3 shows, the stories told by the youngest children contained a preponderance of denial themes, whereas those written or told by the children in the older three groups showed little denial. Projection and identification, on the other hand, were relatively low among the young children and increased markedly thereafter. The findings support the psychoanalytic hypothesis that these three defense mechanisms differ in relative maturity, with denial most prominent in the youngest children and projection and identification more evident in older children and adolescents.

The power of defense mechanisms is most apparent during times of great stress. Dollinger and Cramer (1990) describe an unusual study of the use of ego defenses

TABLE 3.7	*Scoring Categories for Three Defense Mechanisms as Expressed in Imaginative Stories Written About Pictures*

DENIAL

1. State of negation: A character in the story "does not . . . " an action, wish, or intention that, if acknowledged, would cause displeasure.
2. Denial of reality: The storyteller says that the story or situation is not "real," or characters do something that enables them to escape from something in reality that is unpleasant.
3. Reversal: A character takes on qualities that he or she had previously lacked.
4. Misperception: The storyteller perceives something in the picture in a distorted way or perceives a figure as being of the opposite sex from that usually perceived.
5. Omission of major characters or objects in the picture.
6. Overly maximizing the positive or minimizing the negative.
7. Unexpected goodness, optimism, positiveness, or gentleness.

PROJECTION

1. Attribution of hostile feelings: The storyteller attributes aggressive or hostile feelings or intentions to a character in the story.
2. Ominous additions: The storyteller adds people, objects, animals, ghosts, and so on that are threatening.
3. Protection against threat: The storyteller expresses a need for protection against threat or assault, as in the use of disguises and the creation of protective barriers, suspiciousness, spying, anticipation of kidnap, and so on.
4. Themes of pursuit entrapment, and escape.
5. Fear of death, injury, and attack.
6. The use of magic.
7. Bizarre or very unusual story or theme.

IDENTIFICATION

1. Emulation of skills: A character takes on the skill or talents of another.
2. Emulation of characteristics: A character takes on the attitudes or traits of another.
3. Regulation of motives or behavior: A character's behaviors or motives are controlled by external prohibitions, social demands, or self-criticism and self-reflection.
4. Self-esteem through affiliation: A character experiences satisfaction by associating with other people.
5. Work or delay of gratification.
6. Role differentiation: Characters assume specific adult roles, like teacher, lawyer, homemaker.
7. Moralism: The storyteller couches the story in moral terms—good versus bad, justice, fairness, and so on.

Source: Adapted from Cramer (1987), pp. 610–612.

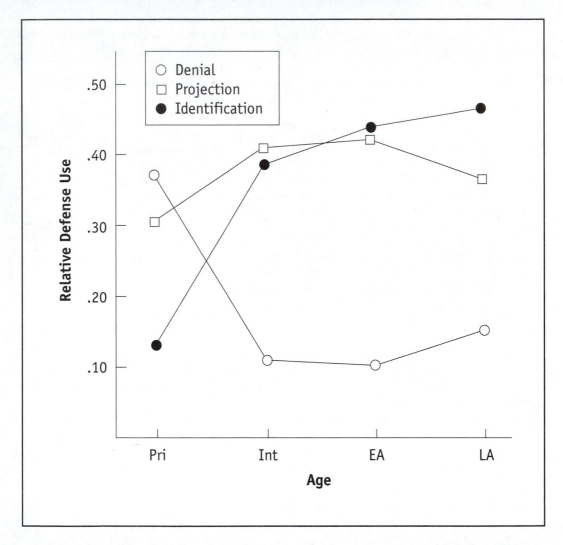

Source: Cramer (1987), p. 607.

among children who witnessed a traumatic event. Preadolescent boys from two rural Illinois towns were playing a league soccer game when a thunderstorm necessitated a delay in the action. The children retreated to their parents' cars to wait out the storm. Shortly after the game resumed, a lightning bolt struck the field and knocked down all participants and most of the children and adults on the sidelines. One boy was hit directly by the bolt. Never regaining consciousness, he died one week after the incident.

Clinical psychologists and counselors met regularly with the children who witnessed the tragedy and with their families. As part of their counseling efforts, the professionals took a number of measures of psychological variables during the course of the treatment. An especially useful index was an *upset rating* made by psychologists to gauge the overall level of emotional distress experienced by each child. The upset rating proved to be strongly related to parents' reports of children's sleep disturbances and somatic complaints after the event and to children's reports of fears (e.g., fears of storms, of dying, of bodily penetration, and of separation anxiety). In addition, children who scored high on emotional upset tended to avoid soccer in the subsequent two-year interval.

Children's imaginative stories told in response to pictures were also obtained. The pictures depicted scenes with lightning present. Examining the stories written by 27 10-to-13-year-old boys, Dollinger and Cramer found that denial was used as a defense at significantly higher levels in this sample than is typical in children of this age, probably because of the severity of the trauma. Psychoanalytic theory suggests that primitive defenses are more likely to appear during the most stressful points of a person's life. In addition, younger boys used significantly more denial than older boys, in keeping with previous research. Most interesting, however, was the relation between defense mechanisms and emotional upset. The stories written by those boys who showed the lowest levels of emotional upset tended to display the highest levels of *projection*. The authors point out that in boys of this age, projection is the most age-appropriate defense; denial is somewhat too primitive and identification too mature. It would appear that projection served these preadolescent boys quite well in their attempts to cope with the anxiety, fear, and sadness they experienced in the wake of the lightning incident. Those boys who showed low levels of projection exhibited high levels of emotional upset. For the most part, denial and identification were not effective defenses for coping with the upset. Only projection was negatively associated with upset. It would be expected, however, that denial would have been most effective among children at much younger ages than those in this sample and that identification would have proven most effective for adults. The lightning study underscores the psychoanalytic-developmental hypothesis that age-appropriate defense mechanisms may be most effective in warding off anxiety and helping people cope.

Like children, adults differ markedly with respect to the kinds of defense mechanisms they regularly employ. While some adults, like children, consistently use relatively immature mechanisms such as denial, others regularly adopt the more mature and complex strategies for dealing with anxiety and stress, such as identification, sublimation, and humor. George Vaillant (1971, 1977) has investigated the relationship between these characteristic defensive styles and overall adult adjustment. In a small sample of well-educated men studied over a 25-year period, Vaillant found that men's consistent use of mature defenses was positively associated with an overall index of adjustment, including physical health, career advancement, and marital enjoyment. Similarly, Vaillant and Drake (1985) found that the use of mature defenses predicted greater levels of interpersonal intimacy and meaningful and productive work in a large sample of working-class men.

In sum, empirical research suggests that defense mechanisms exist and are regularly used by children and adults to ward off anxiety and cope with stress. In keeping with

FEATURE 3.C

Adjusting to Life Changes: Stewart's Revision of Freud's Stages

In Freud's theory of psychosexual development, the libido moves through four successive stages: oral (infancy), anal (toddlerhood), Oedipal (preschool, sometimes called the "phallic" stage), and genital (adolescence and after). Personality psychologist Abigail Stewart sees in Freud's four-stage sequence a general pattern of adapting to life change. According to Stewart (1982; Stewart & Healy, 1985; Stewart, Sokol, Healy, & Chester, 1986; Stewart, Sokol, Healy, Chester, & Weinstock-Savoy, 1982), each of us develops through the four stages *many times over the course of life*, continually circling back through the four-stage sequence with each major life turning point. Freud's four stages, therefore, are not merely psychosexual epochs through which we pass, once and for all, in childhood and adolescence. Rather, the oral, anal, phallic, and genital stages present a sequence of socioemotional *stances* that we assume in response to many kinds of significant life changes. With each major change in life, we reassume various stances.

Stewart's method of measuring the four stages involves careful content analysis of imaginative stories told or written in response to ambiguous pictures. This method—called the Thematic Apperception Test (TAT)—is the same one used by Cramer (1987) in her study of defense mechanisms earlier in this chapter. Stewart developed her system by drawing on the orthodox Freudian descriptions of the four stages of the libido. She identified 24 college men whose behavior explicitly exemplified a preoccupation with one of Freud's four stages—six students for each of the four stages—and then she scrutinized the stories they wrote to detect Freudian themes.

To fit into one of the four types, a student had to meet all the criteria for that one type and none of the criteria from any of the other types. The six oral men reported unusually frequent and regular eating and smoking, suggesting an oral preoccupation. The six anal men reported highly ritualized and compulsive behaviors, an emphasis on cleanliness and order, and an excessively regulated lifestyle, in keeping with Freud's description of the anal-retentive type. The six phallic men reported high levels of sexual activity and a principal interest in sex and self-image, considered by Freudians to be phallic concerns. Finally, the six genital men personified Freud's formula for psychosexual maturity: They were preoccupied with issues related to love and work (*Lieben und Arbeiten*), involved in an intimate relationship with a woman while strongly committed to college studies.

One could argue that Stewart's behavioral criteria for psychosexual types are absurdly concrete. The results from her analysis of the imaginative stories written by these young men, however, strongly support the approach she uses. Oral men tended to write stories in which passive characters experiencing loss or confusion seek immediate gratification of their wishes in their relationships with others. The characters tend to regard powerful authorities, such as parents and teachers, as relatively kind and benevolent. In keeping with Freud's descriptions of the oral stage and the oral personality, therefore, Stewart's oral men wrote stories that were generally *receptive* (taking in, getting, incorporating) in tone and content. Paralleling Freud's descriptions of the other three stages, anal men wrote stories about *autonomy* (holding on, maintaining, hanging on);

phallic men emphasized *assertiveness* (expanding, reaching out, intruding); and genital men wrote stories underscoring *integration* (relating, committing, connecting).

According to Stewart, a person adapts to change by cycling through the receptive—autonomous—assertive—integrative sequence of adaptive stances. For instance, in adjusting to marriage, divorce, a new job, or entering college, a person would be expected to adopt first a relatively receptive stance toward the environment (as does the dependent oral infant), gradually becoming more autonomous and then assertive (like the anal and phallic child), and finally taking on a mature integrative perspective (similar to Freud's genital stage) that signals mastery of the challenge and full adaptation.

Support for Stewart's view comes from a small number of studies employing her scoring system to analyze imaginative stories written by people who have gone through life transitions. New college students should be at a lower stage in adapting to college than more experienced students and should, therefore, show earlier adaptive stances; that is, they should show more receptive and autonomous orientations, and fewer assertive and integrative orientations, to the college environment. Supporting this prediction, Stewart (1982) found that freshmen scored at significantly lower stages than seniors in three different colleges.

Entering elementary school is certainly a major life transition for most children, and thus we would expect younger students to be at earlier adaptive stances than older ones. In a study of elementary school children who made up stories in response to pictures, kindergarten children tended to score in the receptive range, first graders scored autonomous, and second graders scored assertive (Stewart et al., 1982).

The transition from elementary school to junior high school is also significant. Stewart and her colleagues (1982) found that, among middle-class students, those who had recently gone through this transition scored at lower stages than both those who had not yet gone through it and those who had gone through the transition longer ago. (Working-class students, however, did not show the predicted pattern of scores.) Looking at the transition of marriage, recently married women scored significantly lower than those not yet married but engaged. Also, new mothers scored lower than women who were expecting babies but who had not yet given birth.

Further support for Stewart's method and theory come from longitudinal studies that followed five groups of people over time: children beginning school, new junior and senior high school students, beginning college students, newlyweds, and new parents (Stewart et al., 1986). Each participant told or wrote an imaginative story in response to a picture at two different times: once immediately after the given transition (such as entering school or getting married) and again 1–2 years later. The results showed that, in all of the groups except new parents, scores increased over time. In other words, the participants made up stories indicative of lower or earlier adaptive themes immediately after the life transition, but showing higher or later adaptive themes a year or two later.

In sum, Freud's psychosexual scheme may be viewed as a general model for adaptation to life changes. Stewart's research suggests that when faced with major life transitions, persons tend to cycle through a sequence of socioemotional stances—from passive, to autonomous, assertive, and integrated—that bears thematic similarity to the psychosexual sequence of oral, anal, phallic, and genital stages.

hypotheses derived from Freud and the ego psychologists, defense mechanisms may be arranged in a developmental hierarchy, ranging from primitive defenses employed by young children to mature mechanisms shown by adults. Older children use more mature defenses than younger children, and defenses that are especially age-appropriate may be the most effective in dealing with stress. Among adults, the use of mature defense mechanisms has been associated with greater social adjustment and occupational achievement. With respect to the last finding, we do not know whether defense mechanisms help promote adjustment or whether adjustment helps promote the use of mature defense mechanisms. Most likely, both possibilities are true, as mature defenses and psychosocial adaptation work to reinforce each other.

Development in the Adult Years: Jung's View

When you combine Freud with the ego psychologists and the object relations theorists who followed him, you can discern a general psychoanalytic story of the development of personality from infancy into early adulthood. As we have seen, the story begins with the earliest stage of interpersonal dependency, what Freud viewed as the oral stage, and moves to stages of increasing independence and autonomy as the self builds strength and expands. The high point of early development is the unconscious drama of the Oedipus complex, the resolution of which marks the most significant socialization experience in the life cycle. The child who has passed through the oedipal drama now has an unconscious sense of his or her own limitations as well as the moral sensibility that one needs for effective and cooperative social life. The later childhood years bring with them many important socialization experiences before full-fledged sexuality erupts in adolescence and ushers in the genital stage. The well-functioning personality of adolescence and adulthood is able to employ the ego's powers of defense and adaptation to cope with anxiety and resolve the conflicts that may arise when id, superego, and real-world forces inevitably collide. The mature adult copes more-or-less effectively with the anxiety of everyday life and manages to love others and to work productively in society.

For some readers, this story of development may be fine as far as it goes, but it may not go far enough. What about personality development in the adult years? Are there interesting changes and growth opportunities awaiting us after we move into the genital stage? Most psychoanalytic theorists have ignored this possibility, assuming that the most important determinants of personality are set down in the childhood years. But Carl Jung took a very different view. In the same way that Jung expanded Freud's notion of the unconscious to encompass a collective unconscious filled with archetypes, so did Jung expand the general psychoanalytic view of personality development to chart significant changes in the adult years. In sharp contrast to Freud, Jung viewed personality development as a lifelong enterprise. Whereas a person's unique constellation of characteristics is established early in childhood for Freud, Jung saw possibilities for dramatic personality transformation across the human lifespan. During childhood, Jung argued, various components of the personality become established as separate entities. Psychic energy is expended on learning how to walk, talk, and other skills necessary for survival. Sexuality is not a prominent theme in the early years but becomes a significant force with the arrival of puberty and adolescence. In young adulthood, the person directs psychic energy toward learning a vocation, getting married, raising children, and becoming integrated into community life. Ideally, the young adult should be energetic, outgoing, and passionate in his or her active engagement of social reality.

Around the age of 40, however, a profound shift may be experienced, as the individual begins to move away from a passionate engagement of the world to an inner and more philosophical exploration of the self. Jung viewed midlife as the most important developmental period in the lifespan. Midlife is highlighted by a shift from materialism, sexuality, and propagation to more spiritual and cultural values. In addition, the adult may experience significant shifts in values, ideals, and interpersonal relationships at this time. Religion may become especially salient in the second half of the human life cycle, as the adult strives to find spiritual harmony, balance, and the full expression of the self. The goal of human development is the full development and flowering of the self, Jung argued. Jung used the term **individuation** to refer to the process of self-development. Individuation is a dynamic, complex, and lifelong balancing act whereby the person seeks to synthesize the various opposites in personality to become whole. Individuation, therefore, involves the full development of all aspects of the personality, both conscious and unconscious, and their ultimate integration within a grand unity.

Much of what may appeal to us in Jung stems from his characterization of human individuation. The development of the self is a romantic odyssey that each of us can and should undertake, a heroic adventure in self-discovery of truly mythic proportions. Like the Greek Odysseus exploring unknown lands, battling ferocious beasts, and communicating daily with the gods, each of us is challenged to do battle with and to explore all that hides and rages in the distant lands within us. In the later years of one's life, individuation brings wholeness and completion. The mature self reconciles all opposites within a psychological circle of unity. The ancient symbol of this unity is the **mandala.** (*Mandala* is a Sanskrit word meaning "circle.") In various mythologies, religious rituals, and dreams and fantasies, Jung observed an array of mandalalike figures. According to Jung, the mandala is the perfect symbol of the self's unity and integrity achieved through the lifelong adventure of individuation.

Jung also suggested that the way in which a person strives for individuation in personality development is partly dependent on his or her *personality type*. Types are determined by the intersection of **attitudes** and **functions.** Jung distinguished between two major attitudes about or orientations toward the environment: *extraversion* and *introversion* (discussed as central personality traits in Chapter 6). The extraverted attitude orients the person toward the external, objective world; the introverted attitude orients the person toward the internal, subjective world. Both attitudes are present in the personality, but for any given person one of the two is generally dominant and conscious while the other is subordinate and unconscious.

The four fundamental functions are used to understand events in life. Through *thinking*, a person analyzes an event in a rational and intellectual manner. Through *feeling*, a person experiences an event emotionally, through pleasure or pain, anger, fear, sorrow, joy, or love. *Sensing* yields concrete facts about an event, such as what it looks like and how it sounds. *Intuiting* goes beyond the facts, feelings, and ideas to apprehend the hidden or unconscious essence of an event. Usually, for a particular person, one of the four functions is most developed, dominant, and conscious, while one is least developed, subordinate, and most deeply buried in the unconscious. Therefore, the person whose superior function is thinking and whose inferior function is feeling may live a highly rational and dispassionate daily existence when the superior function holds sway. But when thinking gives way to the inferior function at night, he may dream as a "feeler" who apprehends the world primarily through emotion.

Crossing the two attitudes with the four functions yields eight possible personality types. For instance, the extravert–thinking type is the person who is primarily oriented toward the objective, outside world and who tends to understand that world as a thinker. The extravert–thinking type places a conscious premium on logical ideas about the world. His or her preoccupation with the intellect and the objective world may even appear cold and rigid. In contrast, the introvert–intuiting type is primarily oriented toward the subjective, internal world and tends to understand that world in terms of intuition. The introvert–intuiting type places a premium on mystical impressions about inner reality. The intuitive introvert may tend to be aloof and unconcerned with people and the outside world. Others may see this type as a peculiar artist, slightly mad genius, or wayward dreamer.

The various attitudes, functions, and archetypes in personality are organized around the *self*. As the midpoint of personality, the self holds these systems together and provides the person with unity, equilibrium, and stability. Over the course of individuation, different attitudes and functions may hold sway while others recede into the background. Therefore, the extravert–thinking type of young adulthood may move in the direction of introversion at midlife and may begin to cultivate the powers of feeling and intuition. Midlife often marks dramatic shifts in attitudes and functions, as the self strives to balance opposites and express the many different potentials that any given person holds within. We can see, therefore, that Jung's view of development in the second half of life goes well beyond the traditional psychoanalytic emphasis on successful coping with conflict, anxiety reduction, and efficacy in the realms of love and work. Individuation presents us with an intrapsychic adventure, a deep exploration of the collective and personal unconscious, and the full realization of the many different facets of the self. In many ways, Jung's views on human development presage those of the humanistic psychologists, such as Carl Rogers and Abraham Maslow (Chapter 8 in this book). For these theorists, like Jung, a main developmental theme in human life is the *full actualization of the self*.

THE INTERPRETATION OF LIVES

Among the most significant legacies of the work of Sigmund Freud is the particular method he devised for interpreting the meaning of people's lives. Illustrated mainly in the clinical case studies he published (see Table 3.8), Freud developed a psychoanalytic mode of investigation and interpretation that relies on decoding hidden and disguised meanings. From a psychoanalytic standpoint, interpretation is always a matter of going beneath the surface, beyond the obvious, to explore a mysterious realm of private imagery, symbol, and myth. While different theories within the psychoanalytic tradition emphasize different aspects of personality, most psychoanalytic interpretations seek to uncover secrets, solve mysteries, and decode disguised messages. The interpretive motto within the psychoanalytic tradition is this: Don't trust what you see; the surface is deceptive; the real truth lies between the lines and beyond the obvious. Let

TABLE 3.8	*Four Famous Case Studies in the History of Psychoanalysis*
1. Anna O.	From 1880 to 1882, Josef Breuer treated this young hysteric, whose symptoms included paralysis of limbs, disturbed vision, and dual personality. The symptoms worsened with the death of her father in 1881. Breuer and Anna O. discovered the "talking cure," through which Anna O. experienced relief from the symptoms by talking about her daytime hallucinations and fantasies associated with the symptoms. The talking "unstrangled" the emotions that were producing neurotic symptoms. The therapy ended badly, however, after Anna O. experienced "phantom pregnancy" and "hysterical childbirth," unconsciously believing that Breuer had fathered a child within her.
2. Frau Emmy von N.	In 1889, Freud began treating Frau Emmy von N., employing the cathartic "talking cure" pioneered by Breuer. The patient suffered from facial ticks and speech disturbances. Freud attempted to trace each of her symptoms to its root by asking her under hypnosis to explain its meaning. Though the method met with some success early on, the patient's problems eventually escalated to include the refusal to eat. Freud came to realize that each of her symptoms was highly overdetermined: Each overt symptom represented many emotional threads woven into a single pattern. For example, refusing to eat was the manifest culmination of many latent associations centered on the arousal of disgust for the act of eating, disgust over cold meat and fat, fear of contracting a disease by eating with shared implements, and revulsion at the act of spitting into a spittoon at dinner.
3. Little Hans	Little Hans was a 5-year-old boy who suffered from an intense fear of horses. Though Freud saw the boy only once, he was able to offer a psychoanalytic interpretation of his symptoms based largely on letters written to him by the father of Little Hans. Freud suggested that Little Hans was experiencing an especially severe Oedipus complex. Little Hans was fascinated with his own penis, calling it his "widdler." He liked to touch his penis and desired that his mother touch it, too. She warned him not to do this and even threatened to have it cut off. Little Hans's fear of horses was a manifestation of castration anxiety. Horses, with their large "widdlers," represented his father, whom Little Hans both loved and feared as the source of castration.
4. The Rat Man	This 29-year-old man suffered from severe obsession neurosis. He was tormented in his mind by a fantasy of rats nibbling at the backside of his girlfriend. He also had similar thoughts of rats feeding on his father's anus. Early childhood experiences relating to toilet training and erotic feelings were partial sources of the rat image. As a child, the patient had seen a rat near his father's grave and fantasized that it had been nibbling at the corpse. The neurosis was precipitated shortly after the man's army captain told him about an Asiatic punishment involving live burial of a prisoner who was then attacked from behind by rats. Freud was able to show that the symptoms provided a temporary escape from conflict by preventing him from finishing his education, marrying a socially acceptable woman, and thereby ending his current relationship with his beloved mistress.

Sources: Breuer & Freud (1893–1895); Freud (1909/1955; 1909/1963).

us examine Freud's method of making sense of human lives by looking closely at one of his most famous case studies.

The Case of Dora

On October 14, 1900, Freud announced to his good friend, Wilhelm Fliess, that he was working on a case worth recording for history. "It has been a lively time," he wrote, "and I have a new patient, a girl of eighteen: the case has opened smoothly to my collection of picklocks" (Freud, 1954, p. 325). Three months later, the case was over. The "girl of eighteen" broke off therapy, putting an abrupt end to Freud's attempt to unlock the coffered treasures of her mind. Before the vaults were shut, however, Freud managed to escape with a few precious jewels. In January of the following year, Freud wrote the account of his short but exhilarating expedition: "Fragment of an Analysis of a Case of Hysteria" (1905/1963). He gave to the girl of 18 the name *Dora.*

Attractive, intelligent, articulate, and economically well-off, Dora was rarely happy with her life. She suffered from a number of symptoms that, Freud believed, were manifestations of the psychological disturbance termed *hysteria.* These included periodic difficulties in breathing, recurrent headaches; fainting spells, and violent attacks of nervous coughing often accompanied by a loss of voice. Though these symptoms took a physical form, they did not appear to have a physical cause. In addition, Dora was frequently depressed and irritable, argued incessantly with both her mother and her father, and had, on one recent occasion, hinted at suicide, leaving a note that said she could no longer endure life. Alarmed by her deteriorating condition, Dora's father insisted that she see his friend, Dr. Sigmund Freud, for therapy. Dora had seen many doctors during her troubled adolescent years, and she was very skeptical about Freud's ability to help her. During her regular visits with Freud over the next three months of therapy, Dora repeatedly disputed his interpretations and recommendations. At times the willful patient and her equally stubborn analyst seemed to spar like gladiators in a deadly game. When Freud felt he was on the brink of understanding more clearly the source of her problems, Dora suddenly quit therapy and deprived him of the interpretive victory he sought. Freud was shocked and hurt: "Her breaking off unexpectedly, just when my hopes of a successful termination of the treatment were at their highest and her thus bringing those hopes to nothing—this was an unmistakable act of vengeance on her part" (p. 131).

Dora had good reason to take vengeance on the older generation, of which Freud was certainly a part. She had unwittingly become entangled in a web of deceit and infidelity that involved her father, mother, and a married couple who were their contemporaries—Herr and Frau K. Dora's father was a wealthy industrialist who had carried on a sexual affair with Frau K for many years. There is good reason to believe that Herr K knew of the affair and considered his friend's daughter—the teenaged Dora—to be a fair exchange for his wife, tacitly "handed over" to him as compensation for his tolerating the relationship between his wife and Dora's father. Herr K was extremely friendly to Dora, sending her frequent gifts and taking long walks with her. While Frau K nursed Dora's father back to health during his many illnesses, Dora worked as a babysitter for the K children and became a very good friend of her father's lover, discussing with Frau K a number of intimate topics, including sexuality. Unhappy in her marriage and repeatedly frustrated with her daughter, Dora's mother, on the other hand, spent most of her day cleaning house. All four adults attempted to conceal from Dora the truth about their tangled and pathetic lives. Dora, however, was well aware of the affair between her father and Frau K and suspected that her father, whom she claimed to love dearly, condoned Herr K's romantic interest in her. She may also have suspected that part of her father's reason for insisting on therapy was the hope that Freud would be able to convince Dora that no illicit affair was taking place. When he realized that Freud was more concerned about discerning the truth than lying to Dora, Dora's father lost interest in the therapy and apparently did not protest when his daughter terminated her sessions with Freud at the end of the year.

Two Traumatic Events   In her discussions with Freud, Dora revealed two incidents from her past in which Herr K had made sexual advances. Two years before, as they walked back to a vacation house from a visit to an Alpine lake, Herr K had proposed his love to Dora and, doubtlessly, intimated that the 16-year-old girl make love to him. Dora responded by slapping his face. Frightened and insulted, she told her mother of Herr K's proposition; her mother told her father, her father confronted Herr K about the report; and Herr K denied that any such event ever transpired and added that Dora was obsessed with sexual matters anyway—his wife had told him this—and doubtlessly fantasized the whole incident. Her father took Herr K's word over his daughter's. Two years before the incident, when Dora was 14, Herr K had suddenly embraced and kissed her at his place of business. Experiencing a "violent feeling of disgust" (p. 43), Dora broke loose from Herr K and ran into the street. Though neither of them ever mentioned this first incident (until Dora reported it to Freud in therapy), Dora continued to be friendly to Herr K afterward, meeting him for regular walks, accepting his gifts, and babysitting for the children. It was not until the scene at the lake, two years later, that she began to express extreme dislike for Herr K.

Freud saw these two incidents as the traumatic kernels around which Dora formed her hysterical symptoms. Freud believed that all neurotic symptoms have meaning. In content and form, *neurotic symptoms are symbolic manifestations of unconscious fears, desires, conflicts, and mysteries.* Trying to connect Dora's symptoms to the two incidents with Herr K, Freud asked Dora to engage in **free association** in response to her memories of the events. A standard procedure in psychoanalysis, free association involves the patient's letting his or her mind wander in response to a stimulus and reporting all thoughts (associations) aloud to the therapist as they occur. Freud believed that unconscious currents rise to the surface in free association and that the perceptive therapist can interpret the associations in order to make psychological sense of the case.

Based on Dora's associations to the two traumatic incidents, Freud arrived at a tentative and partial explanation for some of her symptoms, especially her troublesome bouts of coughing. Herr K was a handsome man toward whom the young Dora had obviously been attracted. Freud reasoned that the disgust Dora felt in response to Herr K's first kiss disguised her sexual interest. Her disgust took the place of excitement by the neurotic process of *reversal of affect*—a pleasurable emotion that is in some sense threatening (sexual excitement) is replaced by an unpleasurable one that is less threatening (disgust). In addition, Freud believed, disgust is a common, though neurotic, "means of affective expression in the sphere of sexual life" (p. 47), especially on the part of women in response to the male sexual organ because it supposedly serves as a reminder of urination (and, relatedly, defecation). Furthermore, *displacement of* sensation transferred the positive sensation of sexual arousal from the lower region of the body (Dora's genitals) to the upper region (her thorax and mouth). Since the incident, Dora had occasionally been troubled by a sensory hallucination in which she could feel the pressure of Herr K's embrace on the *upper* part of her body. Freud speculated that when Herr K embraced her on that first fateful day, he was highly sensually aroused and that Dora felt in the *lower* part of her body, through the layers of clothing they both wore, the pressure of his erect penis:

> In accordance with certain rules of symptom-formation which I have come to know, and at the same time taking into account certain other of the patient's peculiarities, which were otherwise inexplicable—such as her unwillingness to walk past any man whom she saw engaged in eager or affectionate conversation with a lady,—I have formed in my own mind the following reconstruction of the scene. I believe that during the man's passionate embrace she felt not merely his kiss upon her lips but also the pressure of his erect member against her body. The perception was revolting to her; it was dismissed from memory, repressed, and replaced by the innocent sensation of pressure upon her thorax, which in turn derived an excessive intensity from its repressed source. Once more, therefore, we find a displacement from the lower part of the body to the upper. On the other hand, the obsession which she exhibited in her behaviour was formed as though it were derived from the undistorted recollection of the scene. She did not like walking past any man who she thought was in a state of sexual excitement, because she wanted to avoid seeing for a second time the somatic sign which accompanies it. (pp. 45–46)

As we have already learned, Freud believed that the mouth was the first erogenous zone. For the infant, the libido is centered in the oral zone, and sucking at the mother's breast is therefore the "starting point of the whole of sexual life, the unmatched prototype of every later sexual satisfaction," to which fantasy recurs in times of need (Freud, 1916/1961, p. 341). For Dora, the mouth retained an extraordinary sensual significance as she grew older. Compared with most other people, Freud argued, Dora had probably experienced excessive oral stimulation in childhood. She had been a thumbsucker for many years, continuing to derive sensual pleasure from sucking as she developed through her early and middle child years. A key childhood memory for Dora involved her sitting contentedly on the floor, sucking her thumb as she tugged at her brother's ear. Overlying this oral sensitivity was Dora's unconscious and highly charged personal symbolism for sucking. Again based on Dora's associations, Freud speculated that she unconsciously fantasized sexual relations between her father and Frau K in oral terms. Indeed, Dora consciously believed that her father was frequently impotent and that he therefore often obtained sexual satisfaction and experienced orgasm with Frau K through oral stimulation. (She had read about such sexual practices while babysitting for the K children.) Dora's sexual fantasy about her father and Frau K, combined with other images and experiences centered on orality, produced an oral symptom of hysteria: her persistent cough. A short time after Dora "tacitly accepted" Freud's interpretation (p. 65), the cough disappeared.

The Dream of the Jewel-Case   During the course of therapy, Dora reported to Freud that she had again had a dream that she had dreamed in exactly the same way on a number of prior occasions. As one "royal road to the unconscious," a recurrent nighttime dream was a particularly rich piece of psychological data, in Freud's view, so he devoted a good deal of time and energy to interpreting it. Here is the dream as related by Dora:

> A house was on fire. My father was standing beside my bed and woke me up. I dressed myself quickly. Mother wanted to stop and save her jewel-case; but father said: "I refuse to let myself and my two children be burnt for the sake of your jewel-case." We hurried downstairs, and as soon as I was outside I woke up. (p. 81)

Dora reported that she had first had this dream two years ago, on the three successive nights at the lake immediately following Herr K's proposition. Now it had come back, in the wake of her recollection of the same incident. What was the meaning of the dream? To find out, Freud asked Dora to associate freely to each part of the dream, letting her mind wander in response to each element and symbol and reporting aloud the stream of thought and affect as it spontaneously flowed. Freud tied the rich web of her dream associations together with the facts and conjectures of the case, attempting to make sense of both the dream and Dora's symptoms as alternative expressions of the same unconscious dynamics (see Figure 3.4).

Dora's first association is to a recent argument between her father and mother. For some reason that she does not understand, the dream reminds her of a parental dispute about locking her brother's bedroom door. Recently, Dora's mother wanted to lock the door at night, but her father objected, claiming that "something might happen in the night so that it might be necessary to leave the room" (p. 82). Something like a *fire*, Freud conjectures, and Dora agrees. Dora then remembers that, two years ago at the lake, her father had worried about a fire. The family and the K's were staying during this time at a small wooden house that her father feared might easily burn down. This was precisely the time that the dream first occurred and, of course, the time of Herr K's proposition. The fire in the dream is a natural outgrowth of these events.

Dora remembers that she returned from a walk with Herr K to the wooden house at noon and decided to take a nap on a sofa in one of the bedrooms. Shortly after lying down, she awoke, startled, to see Herr K standing beside her (as her father had awakened her and stood at the foot of her bed in the dream). She protested sharply, but Herr K responded that he was "not going to be prevented from coming into his own bedroom when he wanted" (p. 84). Determined to stay clear of Herr K for the rest of their time on the lake, Dora secured a key for the bedroom, but Herr K subsequently stole the key! After that, she always *dressed quickly* in the bedroom, as she did in the dream, in fear that Herr K would break in on her at any time. On one level, then, the dream brings to resolution Dora's problem with Herr K. In the dream, her father *saved* her from the fire by whisking her through the unlocked door of her bedroom so that she could escape. In so doing, her father symbolically saved her from the "fiery" sexual advances of Herr K.

The significance of sexuality in the dream is best seen, argues Freud, in the image of the *jewel-case*. Dora's associations to this particular element in the dream bring to mind an argument between her father and mother about jewelry. Mother had wanted pearl *drop* earrings, but father insisted instead on buying her a bracelet. Dora is also reminded that Herr K had once bought her a jewel-case—one of his many gifts to her. Freud points out that the word "jewel-case" (*Schmuckkästchen* in German) is a common slang word for a virgin girl's *genitals*. Dora quickly retorts, "I knew you would say that" (p. 87), a response that Freud remarks is "a very common way of putting aside a piece of knowledge that emerges from the repressed" (p. 87).

FIGURE 3.4   *Some Associations From Dora's Dream of the Jewel-Case*

The many connections among these dream images, behavioral symptoms, and other elements in the Dora case are explained in the text and in Freud (1905/1963). Lines between boxes show associations; arrows show oppositions.

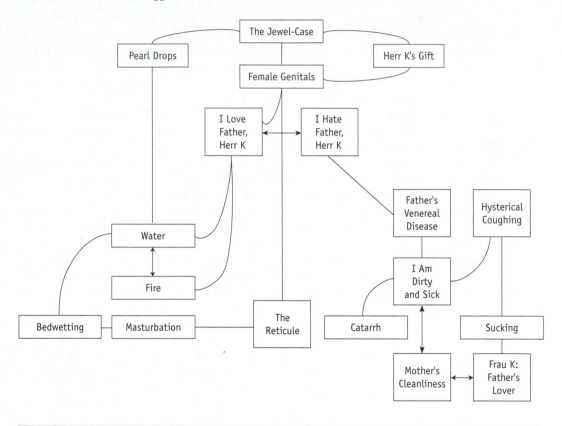

The dream concerns Herr K's attempt to make Dora's jewel-case his own—that is, to have sexual intercourse with her—and Dora's contradictory wishes (1) to escape his attempt and (2) to give in and thereby offer her jewel-case—her virginity, her genitals, her love—to him as a "gift." While her father functioned as a savior in the dream, he also represented, argues Freud, the object of Dora's own romantic/sexual longings, in accord with a young woman's Oedipus complex. The image of her father in the dream represents, argues Freud, both her father and Herr K—both of whom Dora loves, fears, and occasionally resents. The image of her mother represents both her mother and Frau K—both of whom she also resents and yet wishes, on some level, to be. Though her mother spurned her father's gifts, Dora would be happy to accept the bracelet from her father (symbolically accepting her father's love) and would be happy to return the favor with the gift of her jewel-case to him. *All of this is deeply unconscious.* On a conscious level, however, Dora knows that her mother offers her father no sexual satisfaction; similarly, Frau K offers none to her husband. Unconsciously, Dora believes that she would prove a better wife to either of these men.

At this point in the interpretation, Dora's dream appears to be a cleverly disguised rendition of the standard Oedipus complex in young women. It is complicated somewhat by actual events in her life involving Herr K, making two older men, rather than just one, the objects of her unconscious sexual longing. Things become much more complicated, however, with Freud's further interpretations of the dream, revealing a number of highly peculiar meanings that link the dream content to Dora's neurotic symptomatology. Dora's associations to *fire* run in the opposite direction to *water*, hinted at in her mother's pearl *drops*. Freud reminds Dora of an old folk belief that children who play with matches (fire) tend to wet their beds (water). (Dora claims she is not familiar with the belief.) The father's fear that "something might happen in the night so that it might be necessary to leave the room" (in Dora's first association to the dream) may suggest both fire and bedwetting. Dora reports that both her brother and she had problems with bedwetting well into childhood. In her case, the problem was most serious when she was age 7 and 8, so serious that her parents brought in a doctor. As in the dream, her father may have occasionally woken her up in the middle of the night to take her to the toilet, so that she would not wet her bed. The problem of bedwetting subsided shortly before Dora developed her first neurotic symptom: periodic difficulties in breathing, described as "nervous asthma" (p. 90).

Bedwetting is an important association in the dream because of Freud's belief that bedwetting is intimately associated with *masturbation*.[1] Freud is never able to extract a conscious confession of childhood masturbation from Dora, although he believes that he has incontrovertible unconscious evidence one day in therapy when, after discussing at length the topic of masturbation in their previous session, Dora shows up wearing at her waist a small *reticule* (a small, purselike bag) that "she kept playing with," "opening it, putting a finger into it shutting it again, and so on" (p. 94). This innocent behavior, argues Freud, in fact symbolizes masturbation, the reticule serving as a substitute for the female genitals.

Based on these circumstances, Freud surmises that Dora masturbated frequently as a child of age 7 and 8; that she was, at the same time, an inveterate bedwetter, and that she experienced a great deal of guilt about both behaviors. Dora came to see both of them as *dirty* actions associated with sexuality. Indeed, all sexuality acquired a dirty connotation after Dora learned, at an early age, that her father had contracted a *venereal disease* by leading a sexually loose life before his marriage. In Dora's mind, Freud conjectures, her mother's obsession with *cleanliness* is a reaction to being dirtied by her husband's venereal disease. Freud is surprised that Dora is consciously aware of her

---

[1]Modern medical science has documented no link between childhood masturbation and enuresis. In 1901, however, many members of the medical establishment still held to the notion that masturbation was at the root of a number of personal illnesses and problems. Freud appears to have adhered to this view (Sulloway, 1979) and apparently believed that chronic bedwetting problems extending well into the elementary-school years were often by-products of excessive masturbation in children.

father's disease, though Freud himself and many other people apparently were also aware of it. Dora's associations lead Freud to the conclusion that she blames her father for her illnesses in that, she believes, he has passed on his venereal disease to her. She unconsciously believes, asserts Freud, that she has a sexually transmitted disease simply by being born of a father afflicted with one. There was no medical evidence for Dora's hypothesis, Freud points out, but Dora nonetheless believes the infectious connection to be true and cites as evidence her recurrent *catarrh*—an infectious secretion, manifested in periodic vaginal discharges, about which Dora felt great shame and disgust. On an unconscious level, the catarrh is one of Dora's psychological "proofs" that her many problems in life are her father's fault. Not only had he "handed her over" to Herr K, but he had also given her a dirty disease. The disease is a sexual disease. All sexual phenomena are dirty and bring about feelings of disgust, in Dora's private system of meaning. This is why, in part, Dora felt disgust, not sexual excitement, when Herr K kissed her in his office when she was 14 years old.

Many of Dora's symptoms affirm her unconscious convictions that (1) she is her father's daughter, (2) she, like him, is sick and dirty, and (3) this is because of sex. Though she is still drawn to sexuality and wishes unconsciously to consummate her love for her father and Herr K in typical oedipal fashion, venereal disease becomes her unconscious symbolic embodiment of sexual relations, and her neurotic symptoms all take on a sexual meaning. We have already seen how, for Freud, the cough symbolized oral sexuality and Dora's incestuous wishes concerning her father. Her difficulties in breathing, according to Freud, also express a sexual dynamic. Dora's father suffered from periodic shortness of breath, and doctors warned him that he should not exert himself too much. Thus, Dora's analogous symptom is another way of proving that she is her father's daughter and that her problems are due to his transgressions, not hers. Further, Freud submits that the difficulties in breathing may have stemmed from Dora's having heard, as a child of perhaps 7 or 8, her parents' heavy breathing while engaged in sexual intercourse. Her first asthmatic attacks occurred during a trip with her father to the mountains. Subsequently, Dora experienced difficulties in breathing when her father left home on trips. Thus, according to Freud, Dora was able to identify with her lost lover—her father—by acting in a way reminiscent of him. The dynamics behind her sympathetic imitation of her father's illnesses were, of course, completely unconscious.

Even in 1901, Freud realized that his case of Dora was both a great success and a great failure. From the standpoint of psychotherapy, Freud was unable to effect a satisfactory solution or cure for Dora's deeply ingrained neurotic symptoms. This failure was due in part to Dora's resistance to Freud's interpretations. Just when Freud felt he was gaining insights into the nature of her neurosis, Dora broke off the therapy relationship. Furthermore, Freud admitted that certain key realizations about Dora came to him too late in the course of her therapy. For example, Freud seems to have underestimated the problems of **transference** and **countertransference** in the case (Muslin & Gill, 1978). Belatedly, Freud came to see that Dora was unconsciously transferring dynamics from her interactions with Herr K and her father onto the therapeutic relationship, unconsciously relating to Freud as father/lover/enemy. Moreover, Freud may have been unwittingly doing something very similar—countertransferring some of his own unconscious feelings about young neurotic women onto Dora.

Methods of Interpretation

Text and Treaty   In thinking about psychoanalytic interpretation, it is helpful to keep the metaphor of the *text* on the top of your mind. Human behavior is like a text, for Freud. The great texts in our literary traditions are rich enough in *text*ure to be interpreted on many different levels. A great poem or novel suggests a multitude of meanings, some of which may even be outside the awareness of the poet or novelist who produced the text. Thus, a masterpiece like Herman Melville's *Moby-Dick* or James Joyce's *Ulysses* captures many meanings, and indeed literary critics make it their livelihood to discover and critique these various "truths." You may have done the same thing yourself, perhaps in a class on English literature. When writing your analysis of, say, Nathaniel Hawthorne's *The Scarlet Letter,* you may have come to the realization that, while your particular interpretation may have been valid, no single interpretation could possibly be complete. And so it is with every aspect of human behavior and experience, suggests Freud. *There is no single complete interpretation* of anything, no single answer. Rather, human behavior has multiple meanings, and like a text it can be interpreted on multiple levels. In Dora's dream, the jewel-case does not simply signify the female genitals. This may be one meaning—perhaps a particularly important one, in Freud's view—but it is not the only one, nor is this meaning necessarily better than alternative meanings. In much of our behavior and experience, suggests Freud, we are each like the master novelist, unconsciously constructing literary masterpieces—such as our dreams, our symptoms, and our relationships with others—that can be interpreted on more than a single level. Psychoanalysts, therefore, should be skilled in the interpretation of multivalent texts (Bakan, 1958).

A second useful metaphor is that of the political *treaty.* A treaty is a compromise among conflicting forces. Two countries at war decide to end hostilities, and so they draw up a treaty that is designed to keep the peace. In a good treaty, all conflicting sides make peace by forging compromises. And so it is again with our behavior and experience, says Freud. Much of what we do, say, and experience is a product of compromise among internal conflicting forces. These internal forces assume an infinitude of forms—from deeply repressed wishes concerning sexuality and aggression to conscious interests and aversions. At any given moment, a thousand and one voices are clamoring within us—most of them unconscious—and making conflicting demands. *We behave and experience in such a way as to appease as many of these voices as we can,* and we do this, for the most part, unconsciously. Dora loved her father dearly, and yet she hated him for having made her sick and dirty. While overtly displacing her hatred for her father onto Herr K, she could continue to claim, consciously, that she loved her father while continuing to hate him through K. Of course, she had good reason to hate Herr K, too. Therefore, slapping Herr K and openly expressing her disgust with his behavior enabled Dora to kill many birds of the unconscious with the same behavioral stone, forging a tentative peace treaty among the wishes and desires at war within her.

Manifest and Latent   Psychoanalysts distinguish between the *manifest* level of behavior and experience, which is consciously known and seen, and the *latent* level, which is hidden in the unconscious and must be discovered. In reality, the latent comprises *many* levels, in that behavior is complexly determined, like a text. In the dream of the jewel-case, the manifest level is the actual dream as Dora remembered it and as Freud reproduced it for us in print The manifest level of any behavior and experience is relatively straightforward and concise. Dora's dream seems, on the surface, simple enough, a short, clear scenario about a fire and a jewel-case. The latent levels of the dream, however, consist of the hidden forces, conflicts, impulses, wishes, and other determinants that went into the making of the dream. These are the unconscious building blocks of the dream. Whereas the manifest content of the dream is a simple, five-sentence story, the latent content could fill a volume, Freud suggests. *There is always much more material in the latent arena than in the manifest*, and much of what is hidden as latent never comes to be known consciously. In Freud's terminology, the manifest content of the dream is **overdetermined** by the latent content. What Dora remembers as the manifest content of the dream is but the tip of a large, mostly submerged, iceberg.

Figure 3.5 illustrates the relationship between manifest and latent content in dreams. The process of moving from the manifest to the latent content is what Freud (1900/1953) termed *dream analysis*. The movement involves, as we saw in Dora's dream, the dreamer's associating freely to the various dream elements. The psychoanalyst listens carefully to the spontaneous associations in order to discern patterns and recurrent themes. Dora's first association to her dream was to a seemingly unrelated argument her parents had recently had about her brother's bedroom door. This association eventually led to a host of latent images and meanings, having to do with fire, water, masturbation, jewelry, and sexuality. In dream analysis, the dreamer and the therapist break the dream apart and attempt to discover its hidden mechanisms.

The reverse process, of moving from the latent to the manifest, is what the dreamer has already done by dreaming. This spontaneous and unconscious process of synthesizing, rather than analyzing, is what Freud termed **dream work.** Freud suggests that each dreamer draws upon the various determinants that reside in the latent arena and fashions a full-blown manifest dream out of them. We synthesize our dreams, unconsciously, out of the latent material at hand. Dreaming is, therefore, a highly creative act, and each dreamer is like a poet who makes artful verse from a vast storehouse of images, ideas, experiences, and words. Writes Ricoeur (1970), "dreams attest that we constantly mean something other than what we say, in dreams the manifest endlessly refers to hidden meaning; that is what makes every dreamer a poet" (p. 15).

Dream work operates by "cunning distortion" (Ricoeur, 1970). In its attempt to construct a satisfactory compromise among all the warring factions in the personality, dream work disguises, cajoles, and cuts deals, thereby transforming an unwieldy bulk of latent material into a tidy manifest story. The text is written; the treaty is forged; the dream is made—all unconsciously. What emerges as the manifest story, therefore, is a masterpiece of deceit, for the dream is indeed not what it seems to be. Dora's innocent dream about a fire masks an unconscious story about sexual love, bitter hatred, sickness and filth, betrayal, and childhood bedwetting. We need not accept Freud's particular interpretations of Dora's dream to appreciate the psychoanalytic assumption that dreams mean much more than we might initially think and that these meanings are disguised.

What methods does dream work employ to disguise the meanings of dreams? Freud suggests that there are many, but he describes in some detail four dream-work strategies that are frequently used. In **condensation,** the dreamer compresses various latent elements into a single manifest image or theme. In Dora's dream, the manifest father standing at her bedside is a condensation of her real father, Herr K, and, perhaps, a few

FIGURE 3.5 *Manifest and Latent Dream Content*

Dream analysis involves the movement from manifest to latent content in the dream. The reverse movement, from latent to manifest, is what the dreamer does when he or she dreams, a process called dream work.

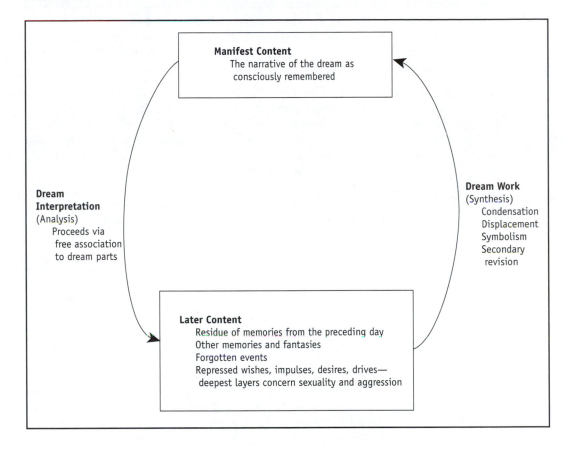

Manifest Content
The narrative of the dream as
consciously remembered

**Dream
Interpretation**
(Analysis)
Proceeds via
free association
to dream parts

Dream Work
(Synthesis)
Condensation
Displacement
Symbolism
Secondary
revision

Later Content
Residue of memories from the preceding day
Other memories and fantasies
Forgotten events
Repressed wishes, impulses, desires, drives—
deepest layers concern sexuality and aggression

other authority figures in her life whom she both loves and resents. It is largely through condensation that a dream can say so much with so little. **Displacement** involves a shift of emphasis in a dream from an important but potentially threatening source to a trivial but safer one, as when one displaces a powerful emotion from its intended object to a substitute. Thus, Dora displaces hatred for her diseased and dishonest father onto Herr K, experiencing overwhelming disgust and resentment in his presence rather than in the presence of her father.

Symbolism is the third method of dream work. Through symbolism, the dreamer conjures up concrete images and actions that convey hidden but common meanings.

According to Freud, hollow, boxlike objects into which things can be inserted—such as Dora's reticule and her mother's jewel-case—may symbolize, at the latent level, the female genitals. Though Freud tended to see symbolism as less important than condensation and displacement in the dream work (Freud, 1900/1953), psychoanalysts have catalogued many different kinds of Freudian symbols that can be discerned in dreams, myth, legends, and literature (Grinstein, 1983; Hall, 1953). Many, though not all, of these concern various aspects of human sexuality. Finally, through a fourth method of dream work termed **secondary revision,** the dreamer unconsciously smooths over the dream's rough spots, fills in gaps, clears up ambiguities, and edits the dream experience into a more-or-less coherent story with a setting, characters, and plot. It is this smooth narrative form that is recalled as the manifest content of the dream.

Symptoms and Everyday Life The interpretation of dreams is the model for all psychoanalytic intervention. Neurotic symptoms, artistic expressions, and certain everyday slips and mistakes are, like dreams, analogous to texts and treaties, with manifest and latent levels of meaning. To understand these phenomena, the psychoanalyst must piece together associations to manifest content as Freud pieced together Dora's associations to her dream. Similarly, symptom formation, artistic expression, and the "construction" of a mistake (a "Freudian slip") parallel dream work: All involve the creation of textlike and treatylike products through condensation, displacement, symbolism, and other unconscious methods that disguise the true meanings of the behaviors they create. Figure 3.6 shows how the psychoanalyst's interpretation of each of these phenomena (moving from manifest to latent) mirrors dream interpretation, while the person's construction of each phenomenon (moving from latent to manifest) mirrors dream work.

Dora's neurotic symptoms were ingenious products of complex unconscious dynamics, whereby internal conflicts were translated into physical infirmities. A good example is her hysterical coughing. Freud describes how Dora's most famous symptom was highly overdetermined and indicative of many different meanings at many different levels:

> We will now attempt to put together the various determinants that we have found for Dora's attacks of coughing and hoarseness. In the lowest stratum we must assume the presence of a real and organically determined irritation of the throat, which acted like the grain of sand around which an oyster forms its pearl. This irritation was susceptible to fixation, because it concerned a part of the body which in Dora had to a high degree retained its significance as an erotogenic zone. And the irritation was consequently well fitted to give expression to excited states of the libido. It was brought to fixation by what was probably its first psychological wrapping—her sympathetic imitation of her father—and by her subsequent self-reproaches on account of her "catarrh." The same group of symptoms, moreover, showed itself capable of representing her relations with Herr K; it could express her regret at his absence and her wish to make him a better wife. After a part of her libido had once more turned towards her father, the symptom obtained what was perhaps its last meaning; it came to represent sexual intercourse with her father by means of Dora's identifying herself with Frau K. I can guarantee that this series is by no means complete. (Freud, 1905/1963, pp. 101–102)

All neurotic symptoms—phobias, obsessions, compulsions, anxiety reactions, and so on—can be interpreted as overdetermined texts or treaties with disguised meanings at

FIGURE 3.6   *Symptoms and Everyday Mistakes*

Like dreams, Freud maintained that psychological symptoms and everyday mistakes can be understood in terms of manifest and latent content.

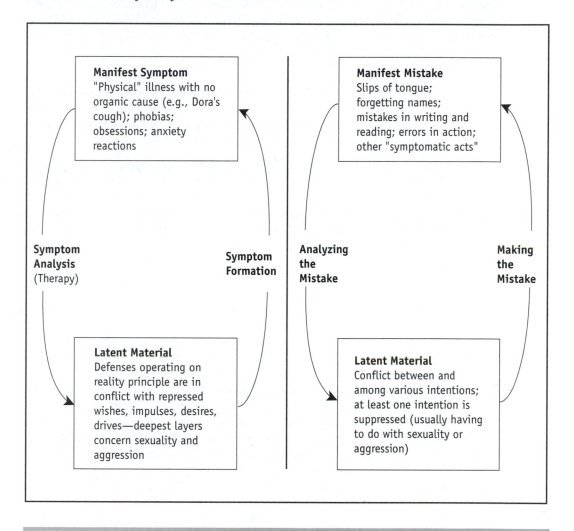

several levels. Neurotic patients like Dora, therefore, are creative masters of symptom formation, though the profound meanings of their masterpieces are generally outside their own awareness. But such creativity is not limited to neurotics. All of us do much the same thing, argues Freud, in much of our everyday behavior and experience. We continuously create texts and forge compromises, and we display these masterpieces of overdetermination in the most unexpected and seemingly trivial ways. In *The Psychopathology of Everyday Life* (1901/1960), Freud gives many examples of slips of the tongue, forgetting names, mistakes in reading and writing, and everyday errors in simple actions that, like dreams and symptoms, can be interpreted as indicators of unconscious conflicts. Some of Freud's best examples, such as his forgetting a famous artist's name during a conversation on a train, are from his own life. In the case of Dora, her "symptomatic act" with the reticule is likewise an overdetermined example of the psychopathology of everyday life. A surprising amount of common behavior can be interpreted from a psychoanalytic framework, argues Freud, as each of us unconsciously betrays the secrets of the mind:

> He that has eyes to see and ears to hear may convince himself that no mortal can keep a secret. If his lips are silent, he chatters with his finger-tips; betrayal oozes out of him at every pore. And thus the task of making conscious the most hidden recesses of the mind is one which it is quite possible to accomplish. (Freud, 1905/1963, p. 96)

In what other ways do we forge unconscious treaties and compose overdetermined texts? In countless ways, suggests Freud: in our jokes (Freud, 1905/1960), our art (Freud, 1910/1957), our religious beliefs (Freud, 1927/1961), and our relationships with others (Freud, 1921/1955), to name a few. The psychoanalytic vision of human life is a profoundly radical portrait of *creative deceit*. Virtually all of our behavior is meaningful, but we unconsciously deceive ourselves and others so that we and they do not know what the behavior means. Our deceptions are the complex treaties and texts that we unconsciously and ingeniously weave. Psychoanalytic interpretation attempts to unravel our deceits and expose the truths that lie behind the creative cover-ups of everyday life.

Myth and Symbol: Jungian Meanings   From its origins in Jung's break with Freud before the onset of World War I, Jungian psychology has shared with other strains in the psychoanalytic tradition a fascination with unconscious processes and the intrapsychic mysteries of the human soul. But in its emphasis on spirituality over sexuality and its portrayal of human development in terms of individuation across the life cycle, the Jungian alternative departs from Freud in a number of critical ways. Like Freud, Jung viewed dreams and symptoms as overdetermined manifest products replete with latent meanings. But whereas Freud viewed dreams as wish fulfillments originating in conflicts concerning sexual and aggressive urges, Jung portrayed dreams as *symbols* of the striving for *balance* in personality, as expressions of *universal myths*, and *anticipations* of life problems for the *future*.

What makes the human species so fascinating and so unique, according to Jung, is its use of symbols. A symbol is "a term, a name, or even a picture that may be familiar in daily life yet that possesses specific connotations in addition to its conventional and obvious meaning. It implies something vague, unknown, or hidden from us" (Jung, von Franz, Henderson, Jacobi, & Jaffe, 1964, p. 20). Symbols are especially useful in the apprehension of concepts and phenomena that we cannot fully define or comprehend. This is one reason that all religions employ symbolic language or images. Individuals produce symbols consciously and spontaneously, in the form of dreams. The psychologist who seeks to interpret the symbols of dreams should be careful not to get led astray by the dreamer's free associations. Whereas Freud distrusted the manifest content of dreams and sought to find meanings in the dreamer's far-flung associations, Jung argued that one should pay closer attention to the form and content of the manifest dream itself. Associations to the dream itself are also important, but the interpretation should repeatedly come back to the dream itself, Jung maintained, for it is in the dream proper that the symbols reside.

Whereas Freud argued that dreams fulfill hidden wishes, Jung saw dreams as seeking to restore balance and harmony in the self. For example, one of Jung's male patients reported a dream in which his gentle and attractive wife appeared as a drunken and disheveled hag. Jung's interpretation of the dream rejected the possibility that the man was in fact dreaming about his wife per se and entertained instead the hypothesis that the vulgar woman symbolized the feminine side of his own personality—the anima. Whereas he behaved in a gentlemanly fashion in public, the man's inner anima was harsh and repulsive. Interestingly, Jung concluded that the dream should *not* be seen as urging the man to "change" or "make better" this inner reality. Instead the dream urges the man simply to see, to acknowledge, and to integrate what already exists, so that the self may be apprehended in more balanced and holistic terms:

> In the Middle Ages, long before the physiologists demonstrated that by reason of our glandular structure there were both male and female elements in all of us, it was said that "every man carries a woman within himself." It is this female element in every male that I have called the "anima." [In this particular man's case] this "feminine" aspect is essentially a certain inferior kind of relatedness to the surroundings, and particularly to women, which is kept carefully concealed from others as well as from oneself. In other words, though an individual's visible personality may seem quite normal, he may well be concealing from others—or even from himself—the deplorable condition of "the woman within."
>
> That was the case with this particular patient: His female side was not nice. His dream was actually saying to him: "You are in some respects behaving like a degenerate female," and thus gave him an appropriate shock. (An example of this kind, of course, must not be taken as evidence that the unconscious is concerned with "moral" injunctions. The dream was not telling the patient to "behave better," but was simply trying to balance the lopsided nature of his conscious mind, which was maintaining the fiction that he was a perfect gentleman throughout.) (Jung et al., 1964, p. 31)

In the case of Dora, we see that Freud traced dream associations back to conflicts and issues rooted in Dora's adolescent and childhood past. The dream of the jewel-case connected to the masturbation and bedwetting of her early years and to her unconscious longings and fears about men, rooted in her early experiences with her father. By contrast, Jung's dream analyses sometimes focus on events yet to happen—on the future. Jung believed that "dreams may sometimes announce certain situations long before they actually happen" because they bring to consciousness a step-by-step movement toward danger of which the individual may not be previously aware (Jung et al., 1964, p. 50). For example, a man who had "developed almost a morbid passion for mountain climbing" (as a way of compensating, Jung argues, for his dissolute private life) began to dream of stepping off mountains into empty space (Jung et al., 1964, p. 50). The dream was a warning, in Jung's view, that the man was headed for disaster and that he should get his private life in order and cut back on his dangerous mountain ventures. The man did not heed the warning. Six months later he jumped off of a mountain and was killed.

The identification of archetypal themes and universal myths may be the most characteristic feature of Jungian dream analysis. This mode of interpretation is dramatically illustrated in Jung's interpretation of a series of dreams from the young daughter of a psychiatrist (Jung et al., 1964, pp. 69–82). At age 8, the girl recorded a series of her dreams in a notebook. Each dream account was fashioned like a fairy tale, beginning with the words, "Once upon a time. . . ." While the dreams were very childlike, they contained uncanny images that were totally incomprehensible to her father. Puzzled and troubled, he brought the notebook to Jung. Jung describes 12 of the dreams:

1. "The evil animal," a snakelike monster with many horns, kills and devours all other animals. But God comes from the four corners, being in fact four separate gods, and gives rebirth to all the dead animals.

2. An ascent into heaven, where pagan dances are being celebrated; and a descent into hell, where angels are doing good deeds.

3. A horde of small animals frightens the dreamer. The animals increase to a tremendous size, and one of them devours the little girl.

4. A small mouse is penetrated by worms, snakes, fishes, and human beings. Thus the mouse becomes human. This portrays the four stages of the origin of mankind.

5. A drop of water is seen, as it appears when looked at through a microscope. The girl sees the drop is full of tree branches. This portrays the origin of the world.

6. A bad boy has a clod of earth and throws bits of it at everyone who passes. In this way, all the passers-by become bad.

7. A drunken woman falls into the water and comes out renewed and sober.

8. The scene is in America, where many people are rolling on an ant heap, attacked by the ants. The dreamer, in a panic, falls into a river.

9. There is a desert on the moon where the dreamer sinks so deeply into the ground that she reaches hell.

10. In this dream the girl has a vision of a luminous ball. She touches it. Vapors emanate from it. A man comes and kills her.

11. The girl dreams she is dangerously ill. Suddenly birds come out of her skin and cover her completely.

12. Swarms of gnats obscure the sun, the moon, and all the stars, except one. That one star falls upon the dreamer. (Jung et al., 1964, p. 70)

The remarkable series of dream accounts contains startling similarities to certain classical myths and stories from ancient texts and other arcane sources with which the little girl could surely have had no familiarity. Some of the dreams play out motifs and images from sacred Jewish and Christian writings, Jung argued. For example, the first dream recalls the early Greek fathers of the Christian church who argued that at the end of time everything would be restored by a redeemer to its original and perfect state. Yet the little girl apparently had no religious instruction whatsoever, and her father was not familiar with the particular religious stories to which her dreams seemed to refer. Some of the other dreams seem to connect to primitive myths that predate Christianity, as in archetypal stories of creation, the flood, and the quest of the hero. The element of fourness—as in the four corners of the first dream—plays a great role in many

The Sun, *a sculpture by Robert Lippold, is a modern-day mandala, or Jungian symbol of the unity of self.*

religions and philosophies and was familiar to students of Hermetic philosophy in the 18th century. The horned serpent appears in 16th-century Latin alchemy as the *quadri-cornutus serpens* (four-horned serpent), a symbol of Mercury and an antagonist of the Christian trinity. Needless to say, this is an extraordinarily obscure reference.

Jung was familiar with many ancient and esoteric myths and writings, but the little girl simply could not have consciously known about these sources, he maintained. The dream images, he argued, arose from a *collective* unconscious, wherein are stored archaic images and symbols whose meanings have been elaborated by humankind since the dawn of human history. Rather than instinctual urges concerning sex and aggression, the girls dreams were driven and shaped by the same archetypal patterns that shaped ancient myth and folklore—symbols of creation, death, rebirth, and so on. But why should this particular girl dream these particular dreams? Why, for instance, should the dreams be so preoccupied with death and destruction? A year later the girl died of an infectious illness. Could her strange dreams have foreshadowed this turn of events? It may seem unlikely, but Jung entertains the possibility, in light of his belief that dreams may sometimes predict future happenings by projecting into the future from current unconscious trends. Although he comes to no firm conclusion on this is-sue for this particular case, Jung writes:

> These dreams open up a new and rather terrifying aspect of life and death. One would expect to find such images in an aging person who looks back upon life, rather than to be given them by a child who would normally be looking forward. Their atmosphere recalls the old Roman saying, "Life is a short dream," rather than the joy and exuberance of springtime. For this child's life was like a *ver sacrum vovendum* (vow of vernal sacrifice), as the Roman poet puts it. Experience shows that the unknown approach of death casts an *adumbratio* (an antic-ipatory shadow) over the life and dreams of the victim. Even the altar in Christian churches. represents, on the one hand, a tomb and, on the other, a place of resurrection—the transfor-mation of death into eternal life. (Jung et al., 1964, p. 75)

SUMMARY

1. Beginning with the monumental writ-ings of Sigmund Freud, the psychoanalytic tradition presents a provocative view of hu-man nature that has had a major impact on the scientific study of the whole person. In a nutshell, Freud proposed that all human be-havior and experience is determined by forces over which we have little control, that these forces invariably conflict with one an-other and cause us anxiety, that the most im-portant forces and conflicts that determine human life are buried in an unconscious realm, and that persons can gain insight into this realm only through a special method of interpretation that can be applied to dreams, symptoms, and everyday life. Concurrent with and following Freud, a large number of diverse theorists have made significant con-tributions to the psychoanalytic tradition, but the theorists hold in common a view of hu-man nature emphasizing determinism, con-flict, the unconscious, and the power of psychoanalytic interpretation.

2. A fundamental proposition of every psy-choanalytic theory is that much of what we

know and feel is outside of conscious aware-ness. Contemporary research and theorizing in cognitive and social psychology show that a great deal of human information process-ing—perceiving, thinking, remembering, and learning—occurs outside of awareness, in an implicit, nonconscious, and automatic man-ner. Nonconscious information processing is generally smooth and efficient, though it is subject to many errors, and it can be con-trasted to the slower and more rational mode of thought and reason typically associated with consciousness. Human nature appears to have equipped persons with both experi-ential and rational systems for processing in-formation about the world.

3. Freudian theory departs from contem-porary cognitive-social research in its linkage of the unconscious to sexual and aggressive instincts and its insistence that unconscious processes often work to repress threatening impulses, thoughts, and feelings that are as-sociated with these instincts. Scientific efforts to document repression in the laboratory have not been overwhelmingly successful, but recent research has shown that some people appear to use repression to a greater extent than do others. Repressors report little anxiety on a conscious level, but they adapt a highly defensive approach to life. Research suggests that repressors report fewer negative memories from their past and are able to keep emotionally negative scenes separated from one another in memory.

4. An early follower of Freud, Carl Jung eventually developed a rival psychoanalytic approach that underscored the significance of a collective unconscious. According to Jung, the collective unconscious is a storehouse of archaic remnants from humankind's evolutionary past. The collective unconscious is inhabited by archetypes, which are universal patterns of experience that structure how people approach life. Common Jungian archetypes include the anima (a man's unconscious femininity), the animus (a woman's unconscious masculinity), and the shadow (reprehensible, bestial tendencies in all humans). Despite its appeal, Jung's notion of the collective unconscious has proven very difficult to evaluate scientifically.

5. The first psychoanalytic model of the development of personality was Freud's theory of psychosexual stages. In the first three years of life, the sexual instinct, or libido, develops through an oral stage (infancy), in which the libido is expressed through sucking, and a subsequent anal stage (toddlerhood), in which the holding in and letting go of the feces attains a sensual significance. Psychoanalytic theorists following Freud have tended to underscore the development of interpersonal relationships in the first three years of life. They have either focused on how libidinal investments establish bonds of trust and love or they have rejected outright Freud's libido theory and substituted theories of object relations. Mahler's very influential object-relations theory describes a sequence of stages whereby the individual first establishes a symbiotic bond with the caregiver and then gradually develops in the direction of separation and individuation.

6. Beginning around age 4, Freud argued, children experience an unconscious drama concerning sexuality and power, called the Oedipus complex, after the ancient Greek myth. In the Oedipus complex, the child shifts from a libidinal object choice to identification with respect to the parents, paving the way for the establishment of the superego. The Oedipus complex is the great socializing event of childhood, Freud thought, for it curbs the child's power and consolidates the moral sensibility necessary for living in human groups. Although research evidence for the existence of the Oedipus complex is mixed at best, clinicians and biographers have found the Oedipus complex to be a powerful explanatory concept in some lives, as can be seen in the case of Yukio Mishima.

7. It has always been difficult to apply the concept of the Oedipus complex to little girls and women. Critics have taken issue with many of Freud's ideas in this regard, especially his explication of penis envy in girls. Nancy Chodorow has reinterpreted the Oedipus complex in terms of the sociology of gender. Her influential theory argues that during and after the oedipal period little girls establish identity in relation to and little boys in opposition to their mothers, producing divergent developmental pathways for women and men respectively, which are reproduced in subsequent generations by virtue of the fact that the prime caregivers for both girls and boys are almost always women.

8. With the resolution of the Oedipus complex, Freud argued, the personality attains its mature structural form, incorporating id, ego, and superego. The id obeys the pleasure principle; the ego operates according to the reality principle; and the superego works as a primitive moral voice, representing the internalized rules of authority. Caught among the impulsive id, harsh superego, and demanding outside world, the ego seeks to resolve conflicts and reduce anxiety. Defense mechanisms are unconscious strategies that the ego employs to reduce anxiety while distorting reality in the process. Considerable research on defense mechanisms supports the psychoanalytic view that defenses can be arranged on a developmental continuum, from least to most mature. Among children, age-appropriate defenses are associated with more effective coping; among adults, more mature defenses are associated with psychosocial adaptation. While the Freudian view of human development has little to say about significant changes that occur after adolescence, Jung provides an intriguing model of personality development in the adult years in terms of individuation, or the full actualization and expression of the self. Each adult approaches the challenges of individuation from the standpoint of his or her particular psychological type, which is determined by the intersection of two opposing attitudes (extraversion and introversion) and four psychological functions (thinking, feeling, sensing, and intuiting).

9. The psychoanalytic method of interpreting lives involves searching for hidden meanings in the manifest content of everyday life. Freud showed how dreams, slips of the tongue, symptoms, and indeed all aspects of human behavior and experience can be viewed as overdetermined treaties and texts. Like treaties, they exist as compromises among conflicting forces (for dreams: wish fulfillments); like texts, they must be interpreted on many different levels, with no ultimate and final meaning ever to be found. In the case of Dora, Freud illustrates the psychoanalytic interpretation of both symptoms (Dora's cough) and dreams (the dream of the jewel-case). Symptoms, dreams, and ultimately all of human experience are constructed according to the same principles—such as condensation and displacement—through which a multitude of unconscious forces, factors, and components are synthesized into a manifest expression whose ultimate identity is always disguised.

10. Variations on the psychoanalytic model of interpreting lives can be seen in many different theorists. Applied mainly to dreams and fantasies, Jung's method of interpretation emphasizes universal themes and the collective unconscious. Jung portrayed dreams as symbols of the striving for balance in personality, as expressions of universal myths, and as anticipations of life problems for the future. Consistent with Freud and the entire psychoanalytic tradition, nonetheless, Jung's method of interpreting dreams and lives searches for the deep meanings that lie beneath the surface and between the lines of everyday life.

Social Learning and Culture

4

In the climactic scene of B. F. Skinner's novel *Walden Two*, Frazier, the founder of a scientifically engineered utopia, gazes down on his creation from a hilltop, concludes that "it is good," and falls back onto the ground in a pose of crucifixion. His companion, a visiting college professor named Burris, fears that, in assuming this Christlike pose, Frazier now believes that he has become God. Hoping against hope that he will renounce any divine powers, Burris half-jokingly asks Frazier if he thinks he is God:

> "There's a curious similarity," he [Frazier] said. I [Burris] suffered a moment of panic.
> "Rather considerably less control in your case, I should imagine," I said, attempting to adopt a casual tone.
> "Not at all," he said, looking up. "At least, if we can believe the theologians. On the contrary, it's the other way around. You may remember that God's children are always disappointing Him."
> "While you are in complete command. Well, I congratulate you."
> "I don't say I'm never disappointed, but I imagine I'm rather less frequently so than God. After all, look at the world He made." (Skinner, 1948/1962, p. 296)

Frazier has made a different kind of world—a community of about 1,000 people who live in near-perfect peace and happiness. His world rarely disappoints him, for it is carefully engineered to provide its inhabitants with the Good Life—good health, a minimum of undesirable labor, the opportunity to exercise talents and abilities, intimate relationships with others, and a maximum of relaxation and rest. Most of the citizens of Frazier's community work no more than four hours a day, leaving a prodigious amount of time for leisure, art, music, and conversation. The citizens are generally happy and satisfied with life, highly productive and creative, and emotionally tied to one another in bonds of tender friendship. They appear to experience little jealousy, rage, depression, or guilt. They are prosperous and well educated. Divorce and family violence are rare. Crime is virtually nonexistent.

Following after Henry David Thoreau, the 19th-century author and visionary who created his own ideal world of solitude on Walden Pond, Frazier names his community "Walden Two." Like Thoreau's Walden, Walden Two provides refuge from the grasping materialism, petty frustrations, and ceaseless violence of modern life. Like Thoreau, the citizens of Walden Two learn how to simplify their lives and to get by with few personal possessions. Unlike Thoreau's isolated existence, however, Walden Two builds a life "in which people live *together* without quarreling, in a social climate of trust rather than suspicion, of love rather than jealousy, of cooperation rather than competition" (Skinner, 1979, p. 346). The Good Life is not the life of the isolated and self-sufficient hermit, according to Frazier. It is rather a thoroughly *communal* existence that, at the same time, provides ample opportunities for individual expression and personal fulfillment. We learn to be good and happy people in *social* situations, argues Frazier. The person is shaped by the social environment. The better and happier the environment, the better and happier the person.

Walden Two is designed according to scientific principles of "behavioral engineering." The principles are simple, but their potential application is vast. The basic principle is **positive reinforcement.** Essentially, this means that people act to obtain positive consequences, or rewards. When a positive consequence follows a behavior, the behavior is strengthened, or reinforced, and its subsequent occurrence is made more likely. Whether in "God's world" or Frazier's, the behavior of persons is shaped, influenced, indeed controlled by the reinforcement that societies provide. Walden Two, therefore, provides a social environment that, like all social environments, controls the behavior of its inhabitants. But the control is more consistent and effective than that exerted in the real world. And it is benevolently aimed to engender peace, happiness, and creativity for all.

From birth onward, the citizens of Walden Two are enrolled in an elaborate educational program that systematically reinforces positive behaviors. Infants and children are trained to restrain negative emotions, practice self-control, and care for themselves and for each other by eschewing jealousy, rivalry, fighting, and pride. The training is accomplished without punishment: by rewarding socially desirable behavior, rather than by punishing socially undesirable behavior, the educational system of Walden Two gently and gradually instills behaviors compatible with the Good Life in all citizens.

Walden Two's use of positive reinforcement to shape beneficial behaviors is a grand experiment in the shaping of social behavior. Frazier tells Burris:

> "I'll let you in on a secret," he [Frazier] continued, lowering his voice dramatically. "You have just described the *only* side of Walden Two that really interests me. To make men happy, yes. To make them productive in order to assure the continuation of that happiness, yes. But what else? Why, *to make possible a genuine science of human behavior!*
>
> "These things aren't for the laboratory, Burris. They're not 'academic questions.' What an apt expression! They concern our very lives! We can study them only in living culture, and yet a culture which is under experimental control. Nothing short of Walden Two will suffice. It must be a real world, this laboratory of ours, and no foundation can buy a slice of it." (pp. 291–292)

Has Frazier indeed organized an ideal world? Might a society based on systematic positive reinforcement truly make men and women happy? Like Burris in the early chapters of the novel, many readers of *Walden Two* are likely to be extremely skeptical, or to conclude, as did one reviewer, that Frazier's utopia is "alluring in a sinister way, and appalling, too." Like every utopia since Plato's *Republic*, somebody must make the key decisions and hold power over the many. In the case of *Walden Two*, the elected planners and managers of the community make momentous decisions about what behaviors are to be reinforced, and how. Furthermore, one wonders whether all people can be shaped to behave in accord with the public good, or even whether such behavior is always beneficial. Though Frazier can be very convincing, the reader may fear that blind conformity and ultimate oppression are the likely results of a social system explicitly designed to program people for good behavior. Frazier's utopia raises as many questions as it answers. Yet, at the end of the novel, Burris is won over. After leaving *Walden Two*, he turns back and makes the 3-day, 60-mile pilgrimage back to the little community on foot, ready to take his place in this brave new world of social engineering. Thirty years later, in one of Skinner's last writings, Burris is still there— serving as a "historian" for *Walden Two*, happy with his life at last (Skinner, 1987).

How did you become the person you are? What explains why you do what you do? In *Walden Two*, Skinner turns our attention to the environment. In Frazier's mythical world and in the real world where you and I live, Skinner suggests, we learn to be who we are in a social context. Human behavior and persons' lives are primarily the products of *social learning in culture*, Skinner maintained. Beginning with Skinner's behaviorist view, we turn our attention in this chapter to the role of social learning and culture in the making of persons. We will begin with the particular mechanisms of learning that are spelled out in the behaviorist tradition—principles of classical conditioning, operant learning, and observation. We will consider some of the more influential theories of social learning as they bear upon human personality. Next, we will consider the multilayered ecology of everyday human behavior, how it is that our actions, thoughts, and feelings are always situated in a multitude of complex contexts. Moving from the smallest to the most encompassing contexts, we will consider social situations, social class and gender, and finally culture and history as determinants of human behavior and shapers of persons' lives. Our central theme in this chapter is the environment. Our focus is on those factors and forces that we tend to see as outside our bodies, in the social worlds we inhabit, in the interpersonal and cultural landscape across which we move over time and situations. Our goal is to appreciate the tremendous power of the environment in determining who we are and the intricate ways in which virtually every aspect of our lives is *situated in social and cultural context.*

BEHAVIORISM AND SOCIAL-LEARNING THEORY

The Behaviorist Tradition

Shortly after World War II, psychologist B. F. Skinner wrote *Walden Two* to imagine a society built on the principles of **behaviorism.** Behaviorism is a brand of psychology that explores the ways in which observable behavior is learned and shaped by the environment. B. F. Skinner (1904–1990) was arguably behaviorism's most ardent enthusiast and eloquent spokesman. John B. Watson launched the behaviorist movement in the United States in 1913 with the publication of "Psychology as the Behaviorist Views It." Behaviorism was *the* dominant force in American academic psychology from about 1920 through the 1950s, and its principles are still influential today. Through the 1950s, a number of very different behaviorist theories were developed, such as Clark Hull's (1943) biological-drive theory and Edwin Tolman's (1948) cognitively oriented "purposive behaviorism." Despite the considerable diversity in behaviorist theories, virtually all approaches to behaviorism share three central tenets or themes that characterize behaviorism as a whole. These are the themes of *observation, environmentalism,* and *learning.*

Observation   Behaviorism has traditionally concerned itself with directly *observable* behavior. A person's private thoughts and feelings cannot be directly observed by others, and therefore thinking, feeling, mind, and consciousness are outside the realm of scientific psychology, according to the behaviorist view. While some behaviorists have almost gone so far as to suggest that subjective thinking and feeling do not even exist (Watson, 1924), most behaviorists acknowledge the existence of such phenomena but insist that internal states (1) cannot be directly observed and therefore cannot be studied scientifically and (2) do not need to be taken

B. F. Skinner

into consideration anyway because behavior can be predicted well enough through careful observation and measurement of public behavior and the environment in which it occurs.

More than any other approach to psychology, behaviorism has traditionally been reluctant to make inferences that go much beyond what can be observed. Therefore, behaviorists have had little need for such hypothetical constructs as "ego" (Freud), "trait" (Eysenck), "archetype" (Jung), or "internalized object" (Mahler). Nobody has ever seen an "ego" or a "trait," and therefore such constructs cannot be of much direct scientific use, argue the behaviorists. Behaviorists tend to invoke the minimum number of theoretical concepts to account for the maximum amount of behavior. In the terms of Chapter 1, they tend to distrust inductive approaches to science as well as elaborate theories containing many hypothetical constructs, while they favor careful experimentation under controlled conditions to test empirically precise hypotheses about how changes in a directly observable environment can produce changes in directly observable behavior. All behaviorist approaches, therefore, place a premium on objectivity in observation, experimental rigor, and precision of measurement.

Environmentalism   In 1690, the British philosopher John Locke penned these famous words:

> Let us then suppose the Mind to be, as we say, white Paper, void of all Characters, without any *Ideas;* How comes it to be furnished? Whence comes it by that vast store, which the busie and boundless Fancy of Man has painted on it, with an almost endless variety? Whence has it all the materials of Reason and Knowledge: To this I answer in one word, from *Experience:* In that all our Knowledge is founded; and from that it ultimately derives itself. (From *An essay concerning human understanding*, reprinted in Herrnstein & Boring, 1965, p. 584)

Locke is speaking here of his doctrine of the *tabula rasa*, or "blank slate." For the newborn, the mind is like a blank slate or white piece of paper. Nothing is written on the slate; it is completely clean and empty. Over time, "experience" "writes" upon the slate, giving the mind its characteristic content. Locke rejected the notion of innate ideas and argued instead that the *environment* shapes the person. If the human mind is originally a blank slate, then all humans are born psychologically equal. From this view, individual differences in personality are a function of different environmental exposures. Personality is made (by the environment), not inborn. As Skinner (1971) puts it, "a person does not act upon the world, the world acts upon him" (p. 211). Therefore, if the environment shapes the person, then a just and happy society should produce just and happy citizens.

All brands of behaviorism emphasize the environment as the key determinant of the person's behavior. To predict precisely what a person will do, behaviorists maintain, the psychologist is only wasting time looking "within" the person. Instead, the psychologist should scrutinize the person's external environment and analyze the subtle behavior–environment interactions shown over time. Environments are generally understood as providing *stimuli* that shape the person's behavior which is seen in terms of a *response* to the stimuli. Thus, behaviorists have traditionally deemphasized and, on occasion, even denied the validity of genetic and inborn differences between persons. The most dramatic statement to this effect was made by John B. Watson, who in this much-quoted passage sounds much like Skinner's Frazier in *Walden Two:*

> Give me a dozen healthy infants, well-formed, and my own specified world to bring them up in and I'll guarantee to take any one at random and train him to become any type of specialist I might select—doctor, lawyer, artist, merchant, chief and, yes, even beggerman and thief, regardless of his talents, penchants, tendencies, abilities, vocations, and race of his ancestors. There is no such thing as an inheritance of capacity, talent, temperament, mental constitution, and behavioral characteristics. (Watson, 1924, p. 104)

Learning   How does the environment shape behavior? Through learning, answer the behaviorists. Each of us is who we are because of what we have learned. According to the behaviorists, our environments teach us to be who we are; we are what we learn to be. But why do we learn to be anything at all? What *motivates* us to learn? The behaviorist answer is that we learn in order to obtain pleasure and avoid pain.

That the ultimate determinants of behavior reside in pleasure and pain is an idea at least as old as Aristotle, but it found its earliest flowering in the ancient school of thought called Epicureanism. Epicurus (341–270 B.C.) was a Greek philosopher who preached that freedom from pain and the pursuit of gentle pleasures and peace of mind were the hallmarks of the Good Life. Not only do optimal pleasure and minimal pain make men and women happy, they also serve as the foundations for ethical action, according to Epicurus. In an ethical or moral sense, the world is constructed so that, in general, what is good is what eventually brings pleasure and peace of mind; what is ethically or morally bad is what ultimately brings displeasure or pain. Through the ages, this doctrine has been adapted to play a central role in many different philosophical systems, including that of Locke.

In the 18th and 19th centuries, the philosophy of **utilitarianism** put forth the idea that the "good" society should make for the greatest happiness or pleasure for the greatest number of people. Utilitarians such as Jeremy Bentham (1748–1832) and John Stuart Mill (1806–1873) argued that this could be accomplished if societies were structured in a more egalitarian fashion. Thus, the utilitarians advocated equality for all, women's suffrage, the abolition of discrimination on the basis of religion and race, and redistribution of society's wealth (Russell, 1945). They tended to distrust the authority of king and church and to glorify democratic education as the answer to many of life's problems. In ethics, the utilitarians were pragmatic and nondogmatic, insisting that principles need to be flexible to accommodate changing ethical circumstances. Behaviorism, in all its forms, is steeped in a utilitarian ideology. Like its philosophical forerunner, behaviorism has always been egalitarian, pragmatic, and supremely optimistic about the possibility of changing the person's life for the better through education—that is, through learning or training in social contexts. Ultimately, learning is shaped by pleasure and pain. And learning should, in turn, make for the greatest amount of pleasure and the least amount of pain.

According to Mill and other utilitarians, a great deal of learning occurs through the *association* of actions with either positive (pleasurable) or negative (painful) events. The doctrine of **associationism** has it that various objects and ideas that are contiguous in time or space come to be connected, or associated, with each other into meaningful units. Simple forms of learning proceed by associations.

Classical conditioning represents one such form of simple learning. In Pavlov's well-known examples of classical conditioning, a hungry dog *learns* to salivate in response to a neutral stimulus (a tone) because that neutral stimulus has become

FIGURE 4.1   *Classical Conditioning*

A neutral stimulus becomes conditioned through its association with an unconditioned stimulus, and as a result the conditioned stimulus eventually produces the same kind of response produced by the unconditioned stimulus. In the case of Pavlov's dog, the tone elicits salivation because the tone is consistently paired with meat.

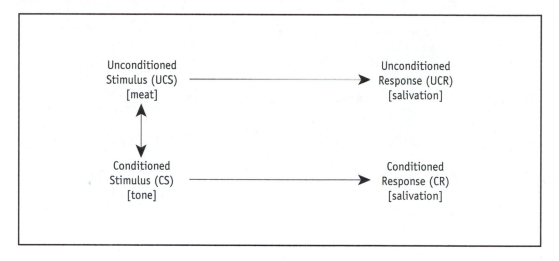

associated with a stimulus (meat) that typically elicits salivation naturally. In the terminology of classical conditioning, the meat is an *unconditioned stimulus* that naturally gives rise to salivation, which is the *unconditioned response*. When on a number of experimental trials, however, the dog hears the neutral stimulus of the tone immediately *preceding* the presentation of meat, the dog learns to salivate *(conditioned response)* to the tone, now called a *conditioned stimulus*, even when no meat is present. The tone (conditioned stimulus) and meat (unconditioned stimulus) therefore become associated with each other because of their contiguity in time. Figure 4.1 illustrates the process.

Watson believed that classical conditioning was a cornerstone of human learning. In the legendary case study of Little Albert, Watson and Rayner (1920) showed how an 11-month-old infant could be conditioned to fear white rats by being repeatedly exposed to a white rat (a presumably neutral conditioned stimulus) and a loud, frightening noise (unconditioned stimulus) at about the same time. The loud noise naturally gave rise to an unconditioned fear response (Albert would cry and avoid the stimulus), but the previously neutral stimulus of the rat also came to elicit fear (conditioned response) by virtue of its repeated association with the unconditioned stimulus. Although the results of this study are murky, there is some evidence that little Albert's fear of rats may have naturally expanded over time to include other white, furry objects, an example of what behaviorists have called **stimulus generalization.**

FIGURE 4.2   *Higher-Order Conditioning*

In this hypothetical example, a mother's perfume eventually comes to elicit anxiety.

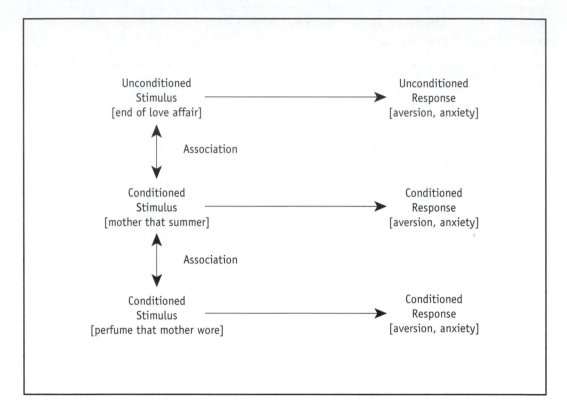

Classical conditioning may be implicated in the development of certain neurotic symptoms, especially phobias, and in the ontogeny of more complex attitudes and behavior systems. In some cases, such complex associations are achieved through **higher-order conditioning.** In higher-order conditioning, conditioned stimuli, which have obtained their eliciting power through associations with unconditioned stimuli, come to be associated with other neutral stimuli, which themselves become conditioned stimuli by virtue of the association (Figure 4.2). Therefore, a young man may develop an aversion to a particular brand of women's cologne because that was the cologne his mother wore the summer he broke up with his girlfriend. In other words, the aversion is a higher-order conditioned response to the conditioned stimulus of the previously neutral cologne, now associated with "mother that summer," which is itself a conditioned stimulus by virtue of its association with the aversive unconditioned stimulus of the end of a love affair. Higher-order conditioning could also produce emotionally positive associations, as might be the case if the young man's sister wore the cologne on the day he found out that he had been named his high school's outstanding student.

Traditionally, classical conditioning has been viewed as an extremely simple, low-level form of learning whereby two stimuli become associated because of their appearing together at the same time. Recent thinking about the phenomenon, however, suggests a more complicated and high-level process. Rescorla (1988) argues that contiguity in time and place is not what makes conditioning work. Instead, classical conditioning enables the organism to form an accurate representation of the world. In the standard Pavlovian example, the tone becomes associated with the bell not because the two arrive on the scene at about the same time but rather because one stimulus (the tone) *provides information* about another (the meat). Rescorla summarizes his cognitive interpretation of classical conditioning by saying:

> Pavlovian conditioning is not a stupid process by which the organism willy-nilly forms associations between any two stimuli that happen to co-occur. Rather, the organism is better seen as an information seeker using logical and perceptual relations among events, along with its own preconceptions, to form a sophisticated representation of the world. (1988, p. 154)

Since the time of Pavlov's dog, psychologists have garnered research support for the importance of classical conditioning in the development of some aspects of personality. For example, there is evidence that people acquire some particular feelings and attitudes about certain objects and groups of people through classical conditioning (Petty & Cacioppo, 1981; Zimbardo & Leippe, 1991). For example, one experiment indicated that when research participants were shown words supposedly representing names of groups of people they had not heard of before, they tended to express liking for those group names that were paired with positive words (e.g., "happy") and dislike for those group names paired with negative words (e.g., "dumb") (Lohr & Staats, 1973). Classical conditioning would also appear to be involved in the development of certain phobias, which are intense fear responses to particular stimuli (Comer, 1995). Behaviorally oriented therapists sometimes apply principles of classical conditioning to help phobic patients deal with their fears. If phobias are learned responses, the logic goes, they can be unlearned through the same kinds of processes that established them in the first place.

A second form of learning is **instrumental conditioning,** termed by Skinner **operant conditioning.** (The basic principles of operant conditioning are outlined in Table 4.1) In operant conditioning, behavior is modified by its consequences. Positive consequences for a behavior increase the likelihood of its recurrence, thus reinforcing the association between the behavior and the various stimuli in the environment present at the time the behavior occurred. Negative consequences decrease the likelihood the behavior will recur, thus weakening stimulus–response connections.

Skinner has conducted the best-known experiments in operant conditioning. In these laboratory studies, he employed the basic principles of reinforcement and punishment to teach animals, such as rats and pigeons, to perform complex behaviors. Typically, the animal is placed in a tightly controlled laboratory setting and allowed to do whatever it pleases. When, in its random activity, the animal happens to behave approximately as the experimenter wants it to, the animal is rewarded—often with a small amount of food. The experimenter thus selectively reinforces the desired behavior, and over time the animal emits the reinforced behavior with increasing frequency. The process of reinforcing closer and closer approximations to a desired behavior in an attempt to elicit that behavior is called *shaping*. Shaping was a central practice in the educational regimen of Frazier's *Walden Two*.

TABLE 4.1		*Key Concepts of Operant Conditioning*
CONCEPT	**DEFINITION**	**EXAMPLE**
Positive reinforcer	Any stimulus that, because of its *presentation* after a response, *strengthens* (increases the probability of) the response. In effect, the organism is rewarded for the response.	A first grade teacher's praise for a child's obedient behavior leads to increased obedience in the future.
Negative reinforcer	Any stimulus that, because of its *removal* after a response, *strengthens* (increases the probability of) the response. In effect, the organism experiences relief (a kind of reward) after the response.	Criticism from one's mother-in-law about smoking cigarettes ceases when the individual quits smoking. Removal of criticism is reinforcing, serving as a reward for giving up cigarettes.
Positive punishment	Any stimulus that, because of its *presentation* after a response, *weakens* (decreases the probability of) the response. Positive punishments are aversive or painful stimuli that reduce the behavior they follow.	A speeding motorist on his way to the Indianapolis 500 is pulled aside by a state patrolman and given a $100 citation. The traffic ticket serves as a punishment, which leads to less speeding by the motorist in the future.
Negative punishment	Any stimulus that, because of its *removal* after a response, *weakens* (decreases the probability of) the response. Negative punishments remove pleasurable stimuli.	A teenager who repeatedly breaks curfew is "grounded" by her parents for a week. A positive reinforcer (going out with her friends) is therefore removed. In subsequent weeks the teenager comes home at the correct time.
Extinction	A previously reinforced behavior is no longer reinforced; eventually the behavior decreases and drops to baseline levels.	A child no longer says "please" and "thank you" at the dinner table because the parents no longer reinforce the behavior with smiles and compliments.

Operant conditioning is more than merely a matter of increasing certain behaviors through reinforcement and decreasing others through punishment or lack of reinforcement. Organisms must also learn when and where to perform or refrain from certain behaviors. Quiet activity, therefore, may be reinforced in the classroom but not on the playground. The school child may learn to discriminate between these two environmental settings and to perform the appropriate behaviors for each. Thus, the classroom desks and the teacher may serve as *discriminant stimuli* for the child: when these stimuli are present in the environment, certain behaviors (reading, writing, being quiet) are likely to be reinforced, while others (running and playing ball) are likely not to be reinforced and may even be punished. Certain response patterns, however, may be reinforced in a great variety of environmental settings. In this case, *generalization* occurs. For example, the child may be rewarded for telling the truth at home, in school, *and* on the playground. Ideally, he or she would learn that such behavior is virtually always appropriate and that it should therefore be shown in the presence of a great variety of stimuli.

	TABLE 4.1	*Continued*	

CONCEPT	DEFINITION	EXAMPLE
Shaping	Getting the organism to emit a complex response by reinforcing successive approximations to the response. A complex, final response may be shaped by rewarding the organism for the simple component responses that make it up.	A Little League coach teaches a child to hit a ball by praising a number of simple behaviors that make up the complex behavior of batting. Early on, the child is reinforced for standing in the appropriate way, then for level swinging of the bat. Then the child is praised when bat actually strikes ball. Finally, praise is delivered only when the child shows the entire proper batting stance and swing and hits the ball solidly.
Continuous reinforcement	Delivering reinforcement after every instance of a particular response. Behavior submitted to a continuous reinforcement schedule is learned rapidly.	Every time a man tells his girlfriend he loves her, she kisses him.
Partial reinforcement	Not reinforcing every instance of the behavior, but rather delivering reinforcement intermittently according to a particular schedule. *Interval* reinforcement schedules administer reinforcement after a particular period of time. *Ratio* reinforcement schedules administer reinforcement after a particular number of responses. Behavior submitted to partial reinforcement schedules, either interval or ratio, is more resistant to extinction than behavior that is reinforced continually.	*Interval* schedule: A factory worker receives a paycheck once every two weeks. *Ratio* schedule: A vacuum cleaner salesman receives a bonus after he sells 25 vacuum cleaners.

Concepts of reinforcement and punishment are both intuitively obvious and paradoxical. Most people know that behavior can be shaped through the judicious use of rewards and punishments. Indeed, parents employ basic principles of operant conditioning routinely in daily child care and discipline. However, they employ them wrongly in many cases, Skinner would argue. For instance, many parents rely much too heavily on punishment. Because punishing a response merely alerts the person to what should *not* be done while providing no example of a constructive alternative, punishment is generally a rather weak form of behavioral control, Skinner maintains. Overt punishment played virtually no role in the educational program in *Walden Two*.

Parents also routinely *under*estimate the power of **partial reinforcement.** In partial reinforcement a particular response is reinforced intermittently, whereas in cor reinforcement the response is reinforced every time it occurs. When beh longer reinforced, *extinction* might eventually occur: The behavior decre quency and eventually dies out. However, behavior that has been partial' is much more difficult to extinguish than continuously reinforced behavi a parent who only occasionally rewards a child's temper tantrums may unwittingly be establishing a partial reinforcement schedule for the tantrums, making it difficult to eliminate this undesirable behavior. Particularly thorny problems can arise when the same undesirable behavior—such as a temper tantrum, physical aggression, or immature dependence—is occasionally reinforced, occasionally punished, and occasionally ignored.

Reinforcement comes in many different forms. Although experiments with animals routinely employ such basic reinforcers as food and drink, human beings are typically subject to a multitude of positive consequences that subtly shape behavior. Some of the most powerful reinforcers are called **conditioned generalized reinforcers**—reinforcers that acquire their power because of their association with a variety of other reinforcers. The best example of a conditioned generalized reinforcer is money, which enables one to purchase a great variety of other reinforcers. Many human reinforcers, moreover, are highly social in nature. Arnold Buss (1986) divides social reinforcers into two general classes: *stimulation rewards* and *affective rewards*. Stimulation rewards include receiving attention from others; affective rewards include receiving respect, praise, and affection. Affective rewards constitute an *emotional* response from others; stimulation rewards merely indicate that others are responding in some way to the self. Table 4.2 lists the basic social rewards in Buss's scheme and the consequences of receiving too much or too little of each of these fundamental reinforcers.

In sum, the behaviorist tradition emphasizes the ways in which organisms learn observable behavior through interaction with the environment. Through basic processes of classical and instrumental (operant) conditioning, people acquire behavioral repertoires that come to make up their personalities. Rather than explaining a person's behavior, then, in terms of drives, traits, motives, or other internal attributions, psychologists influenced by the behaviorist tradition turn their attention toward the environmental situations within which behavior is embedded. For any given person,

TABLE 4.2	*Types of Social Reward*	
STIMULATION REWARDS		
REWARD	**ABSENCE**	**EXCESS**
Presence of others	Isolation	Crowding
Attention from others	Shunning	Conspicuousness
Responsivity	Boredom	Overarousal
Initiation	No interaction	Intrusion
AFFECTIVE REWARDS		
REWARD	**OPPOSITE**	
Respect	Insolence	
Praise	Criticism	
Sympathy	Disdain	
Affection	Hostility	

Source: A. Buss (1986), pp. 14, 27.

those situations include not only the current situation that the person finds him- or herself in but also the *history* of those similar situations that the person has experienced in the past. Therefore, the determinants of any particular behavior can be found both in the current situation and in similar situations in the past in which the person has learned similar responses. In their formulation of a contemporary operant theory of personality, Parker, Bolling, and Kohlenberg (1998) write:

> To the behaviorist, similar behavior across differing situations does not indicate that a drive or trait is causing that particular style of behavior, no matter what the situation. Nor do we agree that the [current] situation is most important. Rather it is the current situation *in combination with* an individual's history that dictates the probability (but not the necessity) of behavior. A functional analysis of the different situations based on the individual's reinforcement history relative to those stimulus conditions will reveal contextual similarities that evoke the behavior. In other words, people are sensitive to different situations (contexts) based on their past experience with similar settings. (p. 164)

Although American psychology is no longer dominated by the behaviorist perspective, the radical science of behavior launched by Watson in 1913 and dramatized by Skinner in *Walden Two* has left a powerful legacy. Some of the strongest features of behaviorism have been incorporated into the mainstream of American psychology, such as its pragmatic and functional spirit and its emphasis on empirical rigor and quantification. Behaviorism has also had a major impact on clinical practice and has led to a wide variety of practical techniques for changing problematic behaviors, loosely grouped under the rubric of "behavior modification" or "behavior therapy." With respect to personality theory, behaviorism has spawned a number of influential approaches that fall under the name of **social-learning theories.** These theories retain some of behaviorism's emphasis on the observables, environmentalism, and learning, while adopting a broader view of human behavior that incorporates important *cognitive* variables that cannot be directly observed. Standing as an ambitious effort to link behaviorism to Freudian psychoanalysis, the first social-learning theory was developed by Neal Miller and John Dollard, around the time of World War II. Influential postwar theories were later articulated by Julian Rotter, Walter Mischel, and Albert Bandura.

The First Social-Learning Theory: Miller and Dollard

Miller and Dollard began with the problem of human aggression. Freud and the psychoanalysts tended to view aggression as the eruption of destructive instinctual urges. According to Freud, the establishment of the superego at the end of the Oedipus complex helps to rein in the aggressive instinct by unconsciously teaching the person that hurting other people is (usually) wrong. In addition, many of society's laws and institutions are designed, argued Freud, to repress the expression of unfettered aggressive urges. Miller and Dollard believed that Freud might be right about the inevitable conflict of aggressive urges and societal demands, but they sought to reframe the problem of aggression in more behavioral and social terms. As a consequence, they argued that aggression is a socially molded behavior aimed at injuring another person *as a consequence of frustration* (Dollard, Doob, Miller, Mowrer, & Sears, 1939). According to the **frustration-aggression hypothesis,** the greater the extent to which an organism's goals are blocked, the greater the frustration and, in turn, the greater the resultant aggression. Frustrations can mount over time, minor frustrations adding up to produce major aggressive reactions. The threat of punishment may inhibit aggressive responding, but as frustrations increase and aggression remains inhibited, the build-up is likely to lead to an *indirect* expression of the aggression: kicking a chair instead of one's frustrating boss; making sarcastic jokes instead of hitting one's father. Freud's notion of the displacement of the aggressive instinct, therefore, was explained as the inhibition of an aggressive response in the face of anticipated punishment and the substitution of a socially dictated "safer" response that serves to relieve pent-up frustration.

According to Miller and Dollard, all significant human behavior is *learned* in a particular social, cultural, and historical context. Learning involves four fundamental factors. First, learning is motivated by *drives*, a proposition that brings together Freud's idea of instincts and Hull's (1943) idea of a generalized drive. A drive is a strong internal stimulus that propels behavior. Examples include such primary or physiological drives as hunger and thirst and such secondary or learned drives as dependency and autonomy. Learned drives are social needs that derive ultimately from primary drives. Second, learning is given direction and guidance by *cues*, which are stimuli in the environment that provide information concerning what the organism should attend to and how it should respond. Third, learning involves a *response:* Propelled by drive and guided by cue, the organism *acts*. This response leads to a *reduction of drive*, which in itself is rewarding and thus constitutes *reinforcement*, the fourth and final component of learning. *There can be no reinforcement without some kind of drive reduction*, maintained Miller and Dollard. In sum, then, learning is generally a matter of "wanting something" (drive), "noticing something" (cue), "doing something" (response), and, as a result, "getting something" (reinforcement) (Miller & Dollard, 1941, p. 2).

Miller and Dollard translated a number of classic Freudian ideas into the more objective and operational language of drive, cue, response, and reinforcement. For instance, they substituted for Freud's "pleasure principle" the "principle of reinforcement," understood as the reduction of a primary or secondary drive. The psychoanalytic concept of "transference" was seen as a special case of "stimulus generalization." "Repression" became "inhibition." "Anxiety" was a learned, secondary drive, acquired through repeated experiences of pain (a primary drive itself) and threatened pain. Psychosexual development was explained according to basic principles of learning applied to the realms of feeding and weaning, cleanliness training, sex training, and the socialization of a child's anger (Dollard & Miller, 1950).

One of the most enduring contributions of Miller and Dollard is their theory of conflict. According to this view, conflicts are socially anchored goal-dilemmas that possess *approach* and *avoidance* characteristics. Laboratory studies with rats have shown that the tendency to approach a desired goal becomes stronger as the organism nears the goal (approach gradient), just as the tendency to avoid a negative or feared stimulus becomes stronger as the organism nears the stimulus (avoidance gradient). However, avoidance gradients are generally *steeper* than approach gradients (Figure 4.3). An increase in the drive behind either an approach or avoidance raises the general level of that gradient. When two response tendencies compete in any given situation, the conflict is resolved when the stronger tendency prevails over the weaker.

The dynamics of approach and avoidance produce four different kinds of conflict. In an *approach–approach* conflict, the individual finds him- or herself between two equally attractive goals. If some random activity points in the direction of one of the

| FIGURE 4.3 | *Approach and Avoidance Tendencies* |

In conflict situations, avoidance tendencies increase at a more rapid rate than do approach tendencies as the organism gets closer and closer to the feared goal.

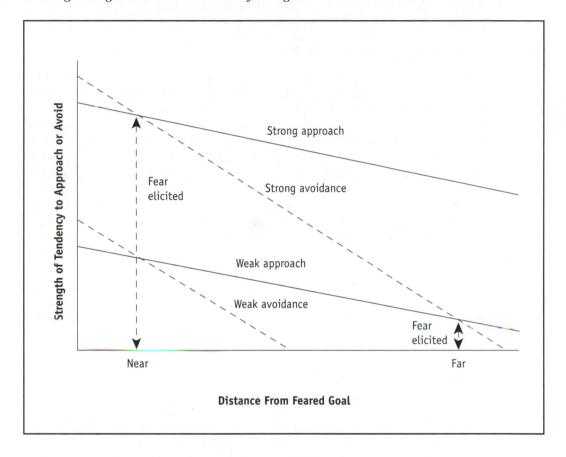

Source: Adapted from Dollard & Miller (1950), p. 361.

two goals, he or she is likely to resolve the conflict quite easily by proceeding toward that goal, given that the strength of the tendency to approach the goal has increased with closer proximity. In an *avoidance–avoidance* conflict, on the other hand, the individual is stuck between two equally unappealing or feared stimuli. Such a conflict is more difficult to resolve because movement in the direction of either stimulus is likely to increase the tendency to avoid or retreat from that same stimulus and to push the individual back to the middle between the two.

In an *approach–avoidance* conflict, the individual perceives the same goal as having both approach and avoidance characteristics—what Freud would term "ambivalence."

As the individual gets closer to the goal, both approach and avoidance tendencies increase, but avoidance tendencies increase at a faster rate. If the avoidance tendencies finally outstrip the approach tendencies, the individual retreats from the goal. Finally, many complex human dilemmas may take the form of *double approach–avoidance* conflicts, in which the individual is caught between two goals, both of which are both desired and feared. Double and even multiple approach–avoidance conflicts may be the experiential stuff of which human neuroses are made.

Rotter's View: Expectancies and Values

One of the first psychologists to introduce cognition into behaviorist accounts of human personality was Julian Rotter. While Miller and Dollard sought to integrate psychoanalytic theory with the principles of behaviorism, Rotter found little of value in Freud and sought instead to emphasize the nonobservable but readily inferred *thinking processes* that human beings often employ in the learning and performance of behavior in social situations. Rotter's eclectic viewpoint broadened the traditional boundaries of behaviorism to account for certain aspects of learning that appeared to be unique to human beings. Rotter (1954, 1972) views the person as actively constructing his or her own reality, rather than merely passively responding to it. In this sense, Rotter's approach bears striking resemblance to social-cognitive views of the person, discussed in Chapter 9. Most human learning, furthermore, occurs in a social context, as people learn to anticipate what others will do and then act on those anticipations.

A key concept in Rotter's theory is the **expectancy,** a subjectively held probability that a particular reinforcement will occur as the outcome of a specific behavior. Over time and across different situations, each of us learns to expect that we will probably be reinforced for certain behaviors in certain situations but not in others. For instance, a college student may expect that working hard in her psychology class will earn her a high grade. On the other hand, she may also expect that working hard at improving her relationship with her boyfriend is not likely to earn her much satisfaction. In this case, the woman holds very different subjective expectancies as to the probability that "hard work" will pay off in two very different situations. Over time, furthermore, people develop *generalized expectancies* about the nature of reinforcement in the world at large. In Chapter 9, we will examine some of the empirical research that has come out of Rotter's view of generalized expectancies, under the topic of "locus of control."

A second key concept is **reinforcement value.** Reinforcement value refers to the subjective attractiveness of a particular reinforcement. For the college student, the reinforcement value of improving her relationship may be much higher than the reinforcement value of obtaining a high grade in her psychology course. Therefore, she may work hard at mending the relationship anyway, and she may even neglect her psychology course, even though her expectancies dictate that she will be more "successful" if she acts in an opposite manner. To predict how a person will behave, the psychologist must take into account that person's particular combination of expectancy and reinforcement value for a particular goal-directed action in a given situation. In Rotter's terminology, behavioral potential *(BP)*, that is, the likelihood that a particular person will perform a given behavior, equals the combination of the expectancy *(E)* and the reinforcement value *(RV)* that the behavior holds for that person: $BP = E + RV$. People are most likely to act to obtain goals for which (1) they expect to be reinforced (high E) and (2) the expected reinforcements are highly valued (high RV). They are least likely to act to obtain goals for which (1) they do not expect to be reinforced (low E) and (2) the reinforcements they might obtain are not especially valued (low RV).

Mischel's Approach: Cognitive/Social-Learning/Person Variables

An influential spokesman for the social-learning view of personality has been Walter Mischel. An associate of Rotter's at Ohio State University in the 1950s, Mischel stunned the field of personality psychology in 1968 with his vigorous attack on trait psychology. As we will see in Chapter 5, Mischel argued for the supremacy of situational factors in the prediction of behavior over and against the use of personality-trait measures. In arguing that behavior is primarily a function of the situation rather than of internal personality traits, Mischel aligned himself philosophically with the behaviorist tradition of Watson and Skinner. Mischel (1973, 1979) has put forth a list of **cognitive/social learning/person variables** to suggest that people invest situations with particular *meanings*, which are directly implicated in producing behavior. These meanings can be seen as characteristic strategies or styles of approaching situations, and are thought to grow out of the individual's previous experiences with both situations and rewards. Like Rotter, therefore, Mischel has developed a brand of social-learning theory with a distinctively cognitive flavor.

Mischel delineates five basic cognitive/social learning/person variables. The first, *competencies*, refers to what a person knows and can do. Each person approaches a situation with his or her own set of skills or competencies. One person may be particularly adept at showing empathy for other people; another person is extremely skillful in analyzing social problems in a cool and dispassionate manner; and a third person has a gift for making small talk. Each skill is likely to influence what each person in fact does in a particular situation.

A second person variable, *encoding strategies*, deals with the manner in which people interpret information. Each person sees a particular situation from a different point of

Walter Mischel

view. Imagine, for a moment, that two weeks into the semester a professor explodes at his students, chastising them all in class for their poor performance on a written assignment. He tells them that he has been too easy on them for the first two weeks and that the class is now going to be a lot tougher. For one student, this professor's "no more Mr. Nice Guy" lecture is interpreted as a legitimate threat that may motivate the student to work harder (or perhaps to drop the course and find a more mild-mannered professor). Another student may interpret the outburst as a carefully orchestrated bluff designed to scare students: underneath it all, the professor didn't really mean what he said. A third student may conclude that the professor did mean it at the time, but that he was simply having a very bad day and that, therefore, there is no need to worry. People clearly behave according to their own characteristic ways of interpreting, or "encoding," information—a theme we return to in some detail in Chapter 9.

Following Rotter (1954), Mischel's third person variable is *expectancies*. Three different kinds of expectancies are identified: expectancies concerning (1) the outcome of behaviors in a particular situation; (2) the meaning of particular stimuli in a given situation; and (3) a person's confidence that he or she will be able to perform a specific behavior in a particular situation.

Again following Rotter, Mischel's fourth person variable is *subjective values*, which refers to what we like, dislike, and fear with respect to specific outcomes of behavior in certain situations. Subjective values are often closely tied to particular situations. Therefore, not only may two people differ radically from each other with respect to what they value within a given situation, but each person may hold different values across situations. John may revel in the fact that he is considered a leader in his small group of friends, but he has no interest in obtaining fame in the population at large. Roger, on the other hand, shuns a high profile with his close friends, preferring comfortable sharing and intimacy. In a larger setting, however, he values and strives for fame—so much so that Roger has recently decided to run for public office.

Mischel's fifth person variable is *self-regulatory systems and plans*. These refer to the ways we regulate and guide our own behavior through self-imposed goals and standards. Wanda's plans to attend law school and eventually work for a large law firm in New York City clearly influence the way she approaches situations. Such a plan dictates that she spend a good deal of her time studying to obtain high grades, that she take certain courses as an undergraduate that best prepare her for law school, and that she discuss with her fiancé, who thinks he might like to be a psychology professor, how the two of them hope ultimately to merge their careers and their lives. Plans provide our lives with guidelines and agendas. They specify how we might achieve important goals, and they help us determine what is worth doing and what is not worth doing at particular times and in particular situations.

Bandura's Theory: The Role of Observational Learning

The most wide-ranging and influential social-learning theorist today is probably Albert Bandura. As a graduate student at the University of Iowa, Bandura came under

Albert Bandura

the influence of the prominent behaviorist Kenneth Spence. He received training as a clinical psychologist at Wichita Guidance Center in Kansas and then assumed a faculty position at Stanford University, where he has remained to the present. Bandura provides an especially inclusive social-learning perspective, which greatly expands the domain of learning to encompass observational learning and cognitive processes and which pays close attention to the complex and recursive ways in which person variables, environmental variables, and behavior itself influence one another.

Observational Learning The social-learning approaches of Rotter and Mischel are mainly concerned with predicting what a person will do in a particular situation. This is to say, these theories concern themselves with *performance*. They tend not, on the other hand, to focus on the *acquisition* of behavior per se. Bandura's theory complements Rotter's and

Mischel's in that it emphasizes how people acquire or learn particular behaviors—behaviors that they may or may not perform (Phares, 1988). The distinction between acquisition (learning) and performance is a crucial one. Bandura has argued that some of the traditional principles of learning that derive from behaviorism—such as the laws of reinforcement and punishment—have more to do with performance than with acquisition or learning per se. Rewards and punishments directly shape what people will *do*, concedes Bandura, but they may not always be implicated in what people *learn*.

The behaviorist theories of Skinner, Hull, and Miller and Dollard cannot explain why people learn in the absence of reinforcement and/or the satisfaction of biological needs. Taking issue with the legacy of Epicurus, Bandura argues that certain learning occurs *outside* the bounds of pleasure and pain. We do not need to be rewarded in order to learn. Rather, argues Bandura, human beings learn a great deal simply by watching other people behave, reading about what other people do, and generally *observing* the world. This deceptively simple process is called **observational learning.** People routinely learn by observing, and they often perform (behave) by imitating what they see.

Figure 4.4 presents Bandura's (1971, 1977) conceptual scheme for observational learning and imitation. Bandura views the sequence as four sequential component steps through which a person observes another person's behavior (the model) and eventually imitates what the model does. Step 1 specifies the *attentional processes* involved in observing the model. Certain features of the model may increase the likelihood that the person will notice or pay attention to what the model is doing. For instance, a highly distinctive model, or one who is especially attractive, familiar, or even strange, may capture the observer's attention better than a less distinctive model. Conversely, attentional processes can also refer to characteristics of the observer. A person must have the capacity to observe the model. (A blind person cannot imitate what he or she cannot see, but can rely on other sensory modalities in observational learning.) A person must also be motivated to observe. It may not matter how distinctive or attractive a particular model is, for if the observer is too tired to notice the model, no observational learning will occur.

The second step in observational learning is *retention processes*. The person must be able to encode, remember, and make sense of what he or she observes if learning is to occur. However much you present addition and subtraction flashcards to a newborn infant, the infant will not learn basic arithmetic, because newborns cannot encode this kind of symbolic information.

Bandura's third step—*motor reproduction processes*—concerns the capabilities of performing what is observed and the availability of such performance in the observer's repertoire of behavior. My brother and I spent hours—years, in fact—of our youth carefully observing Ernie Banks hit baseballs for the Chicago Cubs. In his glorious career, Ernie hit 512 home runs, and I think we saw most of them on TV. My brother and I obsessively and repeatedly attended to the model (Bandura's Step 1), and both of us can remember Banks' beautiful swing with perfect clarity (Step 2). Yet between the two of us, we hit all of two home runs in our many years of playing Little League.

Finally, Step 4 in Bandura's scheme is *motivational processes*. An observer must *want* to imitate behavior if imitation is to occur. It is at this point in Bandura's scheme that rewards and punishments play their strongest roles. Assuming the person has attended to the model's behavior, has encoded the behavior, and is capable of reproducing the behavior, the person is now most likely to imitate the model if reinforced for doing so.

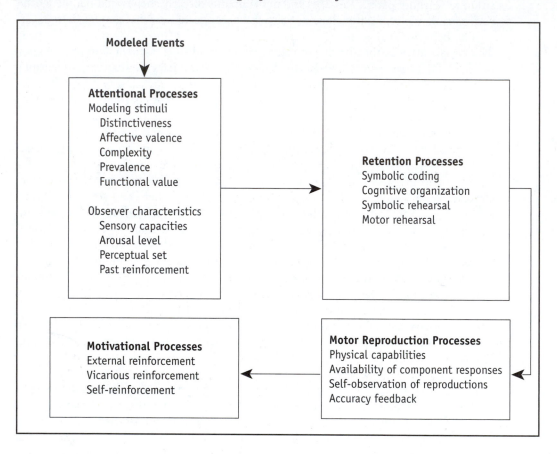

FIGURE 4.4   *Four Steps of Observational Learning*

The person must proceed through attentional, retention, motor reproduction, and motivational processes in order for observational learning to produce successful imitation.

Modeled Events

Attentional Processes
Modeling stimuli
    Distinctiveness
    Affective valence
    Complexity
    Prevalence
    Functional value

Observer characteristics
    Sensory capacities
    Arousal level
    Perceptual set
    Past reinforcement

Retention Processes
Symbolic coding
Cognitive organization
Symbolic rehearsal
Motor rehearsal

Motivational Processes
External reinforcement
Vicarious reinforcement
Self-reinforcement

Motor Reproduction Processes
Physical capabilities
Availability of component responses
Self-observation of reproductions
Accuracy feedback

Source: Bandura (1977), p. 23.

Reinforcement in this case might come directly from the external environment, from the individual observer him- or herself (what is called "self-reinforcement"), or by seeing or imagining someone else being reinforced for the behavior ("vicarious reinforcement").

Bandura's views on observational learning underscore the profoundly social quality of human learning and performance. Observational learning occurs within a particular interpersonal context. Observer and model are involved in a complex personal relationship, the nature of which can profoundly influence how learning occurs and the extent to which imitation will be shown. Empirical literature on imitation in children, for instance, shows that a number of characteristics of the model and of the relationship between the model and the child may promote or hinder imitation. In general, children are more likely to imitate models of their own sex (Bandura, Ross, & Ross, 1961), models who are perceived as powerful (Bandura, Ross, & Ross, 1963), and models whose behavior is observed to be reinforced by others (Bandura, 1965; Parke & Walters, 1967).

Self-Efficacy   A central concept in Bandura's social-learning theory is **self-efficacy.** Self-efficacy is a person's belief that he or she can successfully carry out "courses of action required to deal with prospective situations containing many ambiguous, unpredictable, and often stressful elements" (Bandura & Schunk, 1981, p. 587). In other words, self-efficacy is our belief in our own behavioral competence in a particular situation. High self-efficacy is reflected in a strong belief that I can perform a particular behavior; low self-efficacy is reflected in the belief that I cannot perform the behavior (Table 4.3).

Self-efficacy should be distinguished from outcome expectancies, which refer to a person's beliefs about what the outcome of a particular action is likely to be in a given situation. A positive outcome expectancy means that I believe that a behavior will produce a desired result; a negative outcome expectancy means that I suspect the behavior will not produce a desired result. It is theoretically possible, therefore, that I might have a high self-efficacy expectation in a given situation but a low outcome expectancy: For example, I might be certain that I can explain logically and forcefully to my good friend why I think that he should not divorce his wife (high self-efficacy), but I might also be sure that any explanation of this sort will nonetheless do very little good (low outcome expectancy).

Research has suggested that self-efficacy judgments help determine whether we undertake particular goal-directed activities, the amount of effort we put into them, and the length of time we persist in striving for goals in particular situations. A representative empirical study of the relation between self-efficacy judgments and behavior was conducted by Manning and Wright (1983). These researchers studied 52 pregnant women who were attending childbirth classes designed to teach them how to master the pain of labor and delivery without medication. The women completed self-efficacy

---

TABLE 4.3	*Four Sources of Self-Efficacy*

Performance Accomplishments. Past experiences of success and failure in attempts to accomplish goals are the most important regulators of self-efficacy.

Vicarious Experience. Witnessing other people's successes and failures provides one with a basis of comparison by which to estimate one's own personal competence in similar situations.

Verbal Persuasion. Being told by others that one can or cannot master a task may also increase or decrease self-efficacy, though the effect of such persuasion is usually weak.

Emotional Arousal. A person's feelings of self-efficacy are influenced by the degree and quality of emotional arousal he or she feels in a given performance situation. The degree of anxiety felt provides important information about the perceived degree of difficulty, stress, and persistence that a task represents. Very high levels of anxiety signal to the person that he or she is not feeling very masterful.

questionnaires before and during labor. The questionnaires asked them to assess how well they thought they would be able to handle the pain of childbirth without medication. Outcome expectancy was also assessed before and during labor through a questionnaire that asked the women to rate the extent to which they believed that the pain-control techniques they learned in their childbirth classes were generally effective in enabling a woman to go through labor and delivery without medication. After their babies were born, the women were interviewed to assess the timing and amount of medication used in labor and delivery. The results of the study showed that women who manifested high self-efficacy judgments were ultimately able to cope with pain better during labor and delivery and to resist the use of medication, compared with women scoring low in self-efficacy.

In recent writings, Bandura (1988, 1989) couches the concept of self–efficacy in the cognitive and humanistic language of human "agency" and "control." By believing in their capabilities to mobilize the motivation and cognitive resources needed to carry out a difficult task, people exercise control over given events. Whereas Skinner suggested that personal agency is an illusion in the face of strict environmental control of human behavior, Bandura tells us that, at minimum, a *belief* in one's agency may enable a person to exert significant control over the environment. Judgments of self-efficacy affect choice of activities and selection of environments. Thus, people tend to avoid activities and situations they believe exceed their coping capabilities, but they readily undertake activities and select environments they judge themselves capable of handling. As they move into activities and situations wherein they feel high levels of self-efficacy, they meet new people and develop new skills and interests that expand their domain of expertise and competence.

The development of self-efficacy is a key mechanism whereby people are able to exercise control over threatening events. Bandura conceives of "threat" as a "relational property concerning the match between perceived coping capabilities and potentially hurtful aspects of the environment" (Ozer & Bandura, 1990, p. 473). A person experiences a situation as threatening when he or she perceives that the personal resources at hand are not adequate to meet the strong demands of the environment. In these situations, the person feels highly anxious and is likely to experience a flood of negative thoughts about the extreme hazards of the situation and his or her personal inadequacies in dealing with the hazards. Heightened self-efficacy reduces anxiety and moves the person's thinking processes in the direction of effective interactions with the environment. In this way, self-efficacy exerts "empowering effects" (Ozer & Bandura, 1990).

Research on self-efficacy has highlighted its clinical applications and possible health benefits. Bandura and his colleagues have designed intervention strategies for promoting self-efficacy among people facing various kinds of environmental threats. For example, Ozer and Bandura (1990) documented increases in self-efficacy among women who participated in a program in which they mastered the physical skills to defend themselves successfully against unarmed sexual assaults. The "mastery modeling" program enhanced self-efficacy, decreased perceived vulnerability to assault, and reduced the incidence of intrusive negative thinking and anxiety arousal in encounters with men.

Another group of researchers focusing on self-efficacy implemented a program to reduce anxiety about snakes among 20 individuals whose snake phobias were so severe that they were unable to engage in camping, biking, gardening, swimming in lakes, or traveling to rustic areas (Wiedenfeld, O'Leary, Bandura, Brown, Levine, & Raska, 1990). In this study, increases in self-efficacy were associated with enhanced functioning of the body's immunological system, as measured by the concentration of lymphocytes and "helper" and "suppressor" T cells in the blood. When the subjects participated in the "guided mastery" program, which involved gradual mastery of progressively more threatening forms of interactions with snakes, they initially experienced a great deal of anxiety. But this stress activated in the process of gaining coping mastery, and thus increasing self-efficacy, proved to be immunoenhancing rather than immunosuppressing. In other words, whereas stress often weakens the body's powers to fight off illness and disease, stress experienced *in the process of building up mastery and self-efficacy* may actually strengthen the body's immune system. Put simply, heightened immune system functioning, and thus better health, is associated with high levels of self-efficacy, but the benefits of self-efficacy training begin to show up even before self-efficacy has had a chance to improve. The sometimes stressful process of *building up* one's self-efficacy in the face of threat may enhance the body's defenses. This kind of stress—stress in the service of promoting self-efficacy—is a good kind of stress to have.

Reciprocal Determinism As Bandura's social-learning theory has adopted a more cognitive flavor in recent years, it has also distanced itself somewhat from the standard behaviorist assumption of environmentalism. Though behaviorists have traditionally argued that behavior is largely determined by the environment, recent editions of Bandura's theory have acknowledged important determinants of behavior within the person as well. Bandura's (1978, 1983) concept of **reciprocal determinism** maintains that behavior is determined by multiple factors in the environment and within the person. According to Bandura, external determinants such as rewards and punishments and internal determinants such as beliefs and expectancies are all part of a complex system, and all parts of the system—external determinants in the environment, internal determinants within the person, and the person's behavior—interact in a complex and intricate manner (Figure 4.5). Change in one part of the system, therefore, potentially influences all other parts, and none is more important than any other.

A Research Example: The Case of Aggression

Social learning is everywhere in your life. Indeed, try to imagine some important aspect of the way you characteristically behave that has not in some way been influenced by observational learning, social reinforcement, and the like. It is difficult to do so. Therefore, it should come as no surprise that social-learning theories have been brought to bear to explain a wide range of psychological phenomena. For example, the power of social learning has been documented in studies of language development, impulse control, friendship, competition and cooperation, persuasion, altruism, and aggression, to name only a few of the psychologists' favorite topics. Let us take a look at one of those areas of research now—human aggression. A large body of research has investigated individual differences in aggression from a social-learning point of view. The take-home message from these studies is twofold: First, people can learn to act in an aggressive manner by imitating aggressive models; second, the more a person observes aggression, the greater the likelihood that he or she will become an especially aggressive person, displaying high levels of cruel and destructive behavior toward others. That children acquire aggressive responses through observational learning was

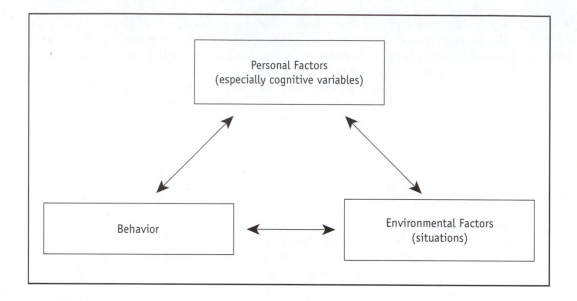

FIGURE 4.5 — *Bandura's Model of Reciprocal Determinism*

documented most memorably in Bandura's famous experiments with the bobo doll (Bandura, 1965; Bandura, Ross, & Ross, 1961, 1963). A bobo doll is a large, plastic, inflated doll that is weighted at the bottom. It is fun to punch a bobo doll because each time you hit it, it pops back into an upright position by virtue of its weighted bottom. Children (or adults) are not likely to punch the doll ferociously—unless they observe somebody else, especially a role model or authority figure, "punch out" the doll. Once such behavior is observed, it may be repeated with great enthusiasm, especially if the observer finds him- or herself frustrated in some way.

In Bandura's original study, 72 preschool children were randomly assigned to one of three experimental conditions. One group observed an adult repeatedly hit and kick the bobo doll and scream such things as "sock him in the nose, hit him down, boom, boom!" A second group observed an adult behave tranquilly and ignore the doll. A third (control) group did not see a doll. Following the observations, the children were taken to a room containing a bobo doll and a number of attractive toys, such as a fire engine, a colorful spinning top, and a doll set complete with wardrobe. They were told they could play with the toys. After two minutes, however, the experimenter returned to tell them that she had changed her mind and decided they could *not* play with these toys. The children expressed their disappointment in various ways. Those who had seen the adult pummel the bobo doll tended to aggress against the doll with fury, often mimicking the identical behaviors and uttering the same expressions they had observed in the adult model. The children in the nonaggressive condition and in the control condition, on the other hand, showed much lower levels of aggression (Bandura, Ross, & Ross, 1961).

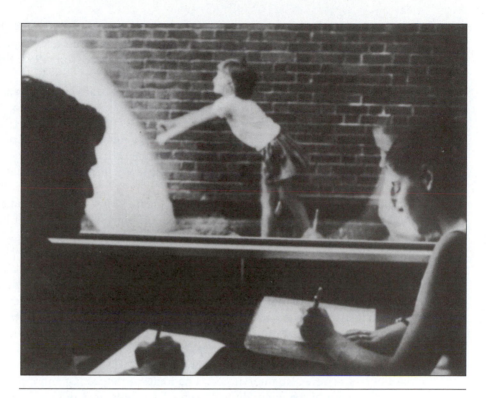

Researchers take notes as they watch a child hitting a bobo doll.

Research has identified a number of other factors that influence the extent to which children and adults will imitate the aggressive behavior they observe. For instance, children are more likely to imitate the aggressive behavior of a model who is *rewarded* for aggression than one who is punished. In a study of first and second graders, Slife and Rychlak (1982) found that children are most likely to imitate aggressive behaviors that they like to perform and that are performed with toys they like. College students are more likely to imitate the aggressive behavior of "teachers" in a learning experiment when the aggression is seen as leading to successful teaching (Lando & Donnerstein, 1978). Other studies have shown that aggression tends to be imitated when it appears to the observer that the aggression is justified (Berkowitz & Powers, 1979; Geen, 1981). Children are more likely to imitate the aggressive behavior of a superhero who hits or kills a bad guy for the good of society than the less justified aggression of a villain.

If people can learn aggressive responses by simply observing them in others, what might be the effect of the relentless drumbeat of violence and aggression on American television, in movies, and in the media? The question is quite alarming, in that it has been estimated that the average American 10-year-old watches over 40 hours of television per week and that by the time that child reaches college age he or she is likely to have observed some 18,000 murders on television, many of these on weekend cartoon and adventure programs produced especially for children (National Institute of Mental Health, 1982).

A great deal of empirical research in the past 25 years has examined this. The bulk of the findings strongly suggests a positive link between viewing television violence and engaging in aggressive behaviors, in both boys and girls (Eron, 1987; Friedrich-Cofer & Huston, 1986; Huesmann & Malamuth, 1986).

Laboratory studies have consistently documented short-term increases in aggressive behavior following the viewing of violent films and television shows (Geen & Thomas, 1986). After viewing segments of such violent shows as "The Untouchables," children were more willing to hurt others than after viewing a neutral program about a track race (Liebert & Baron, 1972). Similarly, after watching cartoon characters clobber one another for some time, children engaged in greater levels of aggressive behavior compared with their peers who viewed nonviolent cartoons (Steuer, Applefield, & Smith, 1971). Viewing erotic films laced with themes of aggression—such as sadomasochism and rape—is especially likely to stimulate aggression in males and to result in greater acceptance of sexual violence directed against females (Donnerstein, 1980; Malamuth & Briere, 1986). Viewing erotic films that do *not* portray violence, however, has not consistently been shown to have an effect on subsequent aggressive behavior.

The most impressive longitudinal study of aggression and television viewing has been in progress for more than 40 years now, originally conceived by Leonard D. Eron and his colleagues (Eron, 1987; Eron & Huesmann, 1984; Eron, Huesmann, Lefkowitz, & Walder, 1972). In the spring of 1960, the researchers began interviewing and testing 870 children between the ages of 7 and 9 years—the entire third-grade population of Columbia County, a semirural area in New York State. Most of these children's parents were also interviewed. The focus of the testing and interviews was aggressive behavior in schools and the presumed psychological and social antecedents and correlates of aggressive behavior. Individual differences in aggressiveness were determined by peer ratings. Third-grade children were asked to rate their classmates with respect to how aggressive they were: to what extent their classmates "were bullies," "hit other kids," and so on. Early results centered on parental behaviors associated with high levels of aggression in children. For instance, it was found that parents who were less nurturant and accepting of their children and (contrary to initial expectation) parents who physically punished their children severely for aggression at home were particularly likely to have aggressive children (Eron, Laulicht, Walder, Farber, & Spiegel, 1961).

In three follow-up assessments—at ages 8, 19, and 30 years—the amount of television violence regularly viewed was strongly and significantly related to aggressiveness. One of the best predictors of how aggressive a young man would be at age 19 was the violence of the television programs he preferred to watch when he was 8 years old. Television-viewing habits in third grade also predicted criminal activity at age 30 (Figure 4.6). Essentially, the more frequently children watched violent television at age 8, the more serious were the crimes for which they were convicted by age 30. The relationship between viewing violence on television and crime holds up for both men and women, though men show much higher levels of criminal activity overall.

Eron and his colleagues have conducted other longitudinal studies of aggression among elementary school children living in Finland, Poland, and Australia (Eron, 1982). The results are consistent with those found in the United States: In first, second, and third grade, viewing violent television and peer-nominated aggressiveness are strongly related. These studies have also implicated a number of other social and

FIGURE 4.6   *Criminal Acts and TV Viewing*

At age 30, adults who watched more violent television (when they were 8 years old) showed higher levels of criminal behavior. Note: Seriousness of crime refers to a score assigned to each crime by the New York State Criminal Justice Division in which each type of offense is assigned a specific seriousness score.

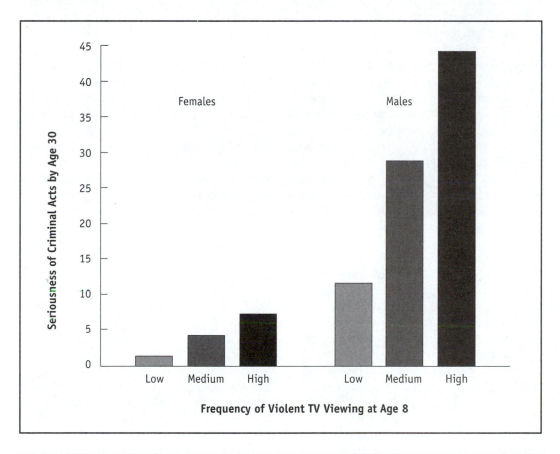

Source: Eron (1987), p. 440.

psychological factors that predict aggressiveness. Aggressive children are less popular with their peers, they score lower on tests of intellectual ability and achievement, and they are likely to engage in aggressive fantasy. In addition, the parents of aggressive children are likely to reject them and to use excessive physical punishment, and they are likely to endorse antisocial attitudes and values.

Many of these factors can coalesce in a tragic manner in the single life. Consider the case of Ronald, one of the third graders who participated in Eron's original study in New York. Here we see a number of factors converge into the making of a highly

How Should Parents Raise Their Children?

Because all of us have been children and many of us will have children, we tend to formulate our own pet theories about how parents should raise them—how to enforce rules and carry out discipline, how and when to show affection, how to deal with conflicts between children, and what mistakes not to make. As generally optimistic Americans in the great empiricist tradition of John Locke, we tend to hold highly environmentalistic views of child development: We sincerely believe that what we do to, and for, our children really matters, that patterns of child rearing actually make a difference in the child's ultimate adjustment to the world. Like the behaviorists and social-learning theorists, we believe that parents create environments for their children within which crucial learning takes place and personalities are formed. Therefore, we read with great interest the many child-training manuals written by child psychologists, pediatricians, and others whose expertise we consider to be even greater than our own.

Over the past 60 years, child psychologists and other researchers have amassed a huge literature on patterns of child rearing and their effects on personality development. It is impossible to summarize this body of study with any hope of being accurate, comprehensive, and detailed—even textbooks in developmental psychology only skim the surface. Nonetheless, there are three extremely general conclusions that we *can* draw from this body with some degree of assurance.

The first conclusion is that we really don't know much. Many of the rules, norms, tips, and guidelines offered by popular books on child training have virtually no basis in scientific research (Kagan, 1984). This does not

mean that these books and manuals are necessarily bad or useless. Rather, it means that many of the conclusions stated with such assurance by experts in child care are based on common sense, intuition, informed speculation, or ideology. In the absence of scientific knowledge, this is probably the best we can do—but readers should adopt an open-minded and critical approach to reading and evaluating child-rearing advice, perhaps comparing many different views and integrating what they read with what they feel and think, based on their own personal experience.

A second general conclusion is that most of the informed advice offered by experts in child rearing—whether or not such advice is based on scientific evidence—reflects a *cultural ideal* about what it means to be a good (healthy, happy) child and a good (healthy, happy) adult. This cultural ideal in the United States and in a number of other Western industrialized nations emphasizes individualism, freedom, and the autonomous self. To be healthy, happy, and well-adjusted, we believe, the child and the adult should be self-sufficient and able to cope with challenge on their own. Thus, we idealize such personality traits as "competence," "mastery," and "independence," and we seek to nurture such characteristics in our children.

Keeping in mind, therefore, our very limited scientific understanding of child rearing and our cultural bias toward individualism, we can draw a third general conclusion about child rearing and personality. A broad and coherent literature on family patterns points to four basic styles of parenting: the authoritative–reciprocal, authoritarian, indulgent–permissive, and neglecting styles. The four types can be

FIGURE 4.A.1   *A Two-Dimensional Classification of Parenting Patterns*

	Accepting (responsive, child-centered)	Rejecting (unresponsive, parent-centered)
Demanding (controlling)	Authoritative—reciprocal	Authoritarian
Undemanding (low in control attempts)	Indulgent—permissive	Neglecting

Source: Maccoby & Martin (1983), p. 39.

organized according to the two basic dimensions of "demanding/undemanding" and "accepting/rejecting" (Maccoby & Martin, 1983). Figure 4.A.1 illustrates the four types and the two dimensions. *A consistent body of research favors the authoritative–reciprocal pattern as the style most likely to promote competence and mastery in children.*

The *authoritative–reciprocal* pattern of child rearing is one in which "children are required to be responsible to parental demands, and parents accept a reciprocal responsibility to be as responsive as possible to their children's reasonable demands and points of view" (Maccoby & Martin, 1983, p. 46). In the authoritative–reciprocal pattern, parents establish clear standards for appropriate behavior in the family, but they are open to and accepting

of the points of views of the children. Thus, parents are both highly controlling and highly responsive in their relations with their children. A number of studies have shown that the authoritative–reciprocal pattern of child-rearing is positively associated, though at generally moderate statistical levels, with children's independence and autonomy in both cognitive and social realms, with ability to control aggression, with social responsibility, and with self-esteem (Maccoby & Martin, 1983; Steinberg, Darling, & Fletcher, 1995).

The *authoritarian* pattern of child rearing, on the other hand, is high on demands but low on responsiveness. Authoritarian parents may be autocratic and rigid. Strict rules are

continued on next page

FEATURE 4.A *continued*

enforced as if they were divine edicts; the reasons behind rules are rarely explained and virtually never discussed. These parents strongly value obedience and discourage spontaneous give-and-take between children and their elders. Research has shown that children of authoritarian parents tend to lack social competence with their peers; they are somewhat withdrawn and lacking in spontaneity; they tend to show relatively low levels of self-esteem. Some studies also suggest that authoritarian styles may retard the development of an internalized conscience in children. Children of authoritarian parents are more likely to make moral decisions based on what external authorities tell them to do; other children may rely more on internalized standards.

The *indulgent–permissive* parenting style is the opposite of the authoritarian. In this case, parents fail to set high standards for behavior but tend to be highly responsive to the demands of children. Indulgent parents take a tolerant and accepting attitude toward the child's impulses, including sexual and aggressive impulses. They use little punishment and

avoid, whenever possible, asserting authority or imposing control and restrictions, making few demands for mature behavior. Children raised in these highly egalitarian and free-wheeling families tend to be relatively impulsive, aggressive, and lacking in independence or the ability to take responsibility for their behaviors. While certain benefits of highly permissive parenting have also been identified, the indulgent–permissive pattern appears "on the whole to have more negative than positive effects" (Maccoby & Martin, 1983, pp. 45–46).

Finally, the most seriously flawed parenting style is the *neglecting* and uninvolved pattern shown by parents who are unresponsive to their children and who place few demands on them. The neglecting pattern comes in different forms, ranging from passive neglect and emotional indifference to active child abuse. Children growing up in these families may show a variety of negative characteristics—from low self-esteem to poor impulse control to high levels of aggression (Baumrind, 1971; Block, 1971; Egeland & Sroufe, 1981; Martin, 1981).

---

aggressive young man. Among these are overly punitive and rejecting parents, chronic academic problems, unruly behavior at an early age, low popularity among his peers, excessive viewing of violent television programs, and a belief that the violence depicted on the television screen accurately represents the real world:

> Ronald was first seen by me when he was eight years old and in the second grade. His teacher, who described him as "a likeable and happy-go-lucky child," had referred him because of immature behavior and poor work habits. He had repeated the first grade, but the teacher felt he was brighter than group tests indicated. Ronald was the youngest of three children. His brother, age 11, was out of the home at a special school for emotionally disturbed youngsters and his sister, age 12, was progressing normally in school. Ronald had been sickly since infancy, having suffered from severe attacks of asthma until the previous year. . . .
>
> Ronald was next seen by another psychologist when he was 12 years old and in the sixth grade. At this time he was failing in school, reading at a second-grade level, and a manage-

ment problem in class. He talked back to the teacher, provoked fights, and was constantly making noise. He was not allowed to go to the lavatory with his classmates because he would get into fights with them. . . . The parents did not seem to be concerned about the boy's behavior. . . .

By coincidence Ronald was a subject in the longitudinal study of aggression. It was possible to retrieve the parent interviews conducted when Ronald was nine years old and his own interview, when he was 19. In the third grade, Ronald was already seen by his peers as one of the most aggressive boys in his class, doing things that bothered others, starting a fight over nothing, saying mean things, not obeying the teacher, and pushing other children. At the same time the father and mother indicated that Ronald was disobedient at home, that he annoyed and pestered them, had a bad temper, and used foul language. They did not approve of a number of things that he did, giving many indications of a rejecting attitude toward Ronald and little indication that they understood him or were concerned about him. They related having had many arguments between themselves that did not settle anything; they moved around a lot, so Ronald continually had to find new friends. These behaviors and occurrences must have created a very frustrating situation at home that probably instigated Ronald to be aggressive both there and at school. The father related using many physical punishments when Ronald was aggressive, including spanking him severely and washing out his mouth with soap, thus adding to the youngster's frustration and providing a model of an aggressive adult. Other aggressive models were furnished on Ronald's favorite TV programs, "Maverick," "Have Gun Will Travel," and "The Three Stooges." The parents indicated that Ronald showed few signs of internalized standards of behavior, such as feeling sorry after he disobeyed, worrying about telling a fib or a lie, or confessing when he had done something naughty. Thus according to information furnished by his parents at that time, Ronald at age nine was experiencing many instigations to aggression at home, had a physically punitive father as well as other aggressive models, and showed little indication of having developed a conscience.

When Ronald was interviewed at age 19, he was on probation for three years for petty larceny. A few weeks after the interview, he was picked up by the police and charged with "criminal mischief in the third degree," and one week later with "criminal possession of drugs, fourth degree." During the interview it was revealed that he had dropped out of high school in the 10th grade, but he insisted that he expected to go to graduate school so that he could eventually do research in "brain biology." He admitted that he engaged in many aggressive behaviors. On the MMPI [a clinical test] he had high scores on a pattern of scales characteristic of recalcitrant delinquents (Scales 4, 8, and 9—psychopathic deviate, schizophrenia, and mania, respectively). He continued to prefer violent television programs and thought that "Mod Squad," "Mannix," and "Dragnet" were very realistic in showing what police work was really like.

Unfortunately, Ronald is no longer a subject in our 21-year longitudinal study. He was killed in a violent accident within a year of the second interview. (Eron, 1982, pp. 207–208)

Violent television shows provide *models* for observational learning. Children and adults observe the aggressive behavior of these models and then imitate them in their daily lives. Violent television also provides the viewer with aggressive *cues*. Berkowitz (1974) has argued that certain stimuli such as guns and blood, repeatedly paired with violence on television, may become conditioned stimuli that are likely to arouse aggressive behavior in some people. Repeated exposure to television violence may also serve a *disinhibiting* function. In this case, television violence sends to the viewer the implicit message that aggression is acceptable and that one need not inhibit violent responses. Finally, repeated exposure to violence on television may serve to *desensitize* the viewer. Whereas excessive violence may have at one time elicited feelings of disgust, horror, or revulsion, it may no longer have the power to stimulate strong emotional responses after, for instance, a child has witnessed 18,000 murders on TV. People get used to aggression and, in this subtle way, come to accept it and to condone its continued proliferation.

But does television viewing actually *cause* aggressive behavior? The results of empirical studies like Eron's, as well as the case of Ronald, suggest that a simple cause-and-effect interpretation *cannot* be justifiably made. A number of other factors appear to be involved as determinants and correlates of aggressive behavior. Furthermore, studies have suggested that, while viewing television violence may lead to higher levels of aggressiveness, higher levels of aggressiveness may also lead to increased viewing of television violence (Eron, 1982, 1987). Individuals who are more aggressive to begin with tend to watch more television violence, which in turn may increase their characteristic aggressiveness, and so on. In other words, violent television viewing and aggression appear to be related to each other in a reciprocal or circular manner. Each is the cause and the effect of the other.

THE ECOLOGY OF HUMAN BEHAVIOR

The behaviorists and social-learning theorists have traditionally accounted for human behavior in terms of the environment's influence upon the person. We learn to behave as we do though interaction with the world around us. The world "teaches" us to act in particular ways. Through classical conditioning, operant conditioning, and observational learning, we accumulate a repertoire of behaviors that more or less reflect the learning history we have each experienced. Whether we are learning to act in destructive and aggressive ways or in accord with society's most exalted standards of socialization, we are learning what to do, how to do it, when to do it, why we do it, and who we are according to the ways in which our environments are set up—according to the rewards and punishments we experience, the contingencies of reinforcement we encounter in different situations, the associations we form as a result of our perceptions of environmental stimuli, the models we imitate, the lessons we learn from our parents, teachers, peers, and so on. The behaviorists and the social-learning theorists underscore the extent to which each of us is a reflection of our environment—how our behavior and indeed our very lives sit within and are defined by the environment around us.

But what is the nature of that environment? What are those environmental contexts that influence our behavior and shape who we are? At first glance, these questions seem simple. We might say that at any given moment our "environment" is the situation that we find ourselves in. As I am writing this paragraph, I am sitting in my office at home, on the third floor of an old house in a suburb of Chicago. The air conditioning is on, but I am still hot. The temperature outside is about 95 degrees Fahrenheit. My older daughter is downstairs, and I can hear her practicing the oboe in her room. These things are all part of my current situation. As you read this chapter, you may be sitting in your dormitory room or in the library. You may be studying with a friend. It may be late at night, and you may be facing an examination in the morning. These factors may all be part of your current situation.

But as we think more about our respective situations—mine and yours—we soon realize that each of us is currently acting within and with respect to a number of different situations or contexts that define our respective environments. For me, it is July 20, 1998, and I have promised my publisher that I will finish revising the first half of this textbook by the end of the summer—that is, in about two months. Quite frankly, I don't think I am going to make it. I will need to finish this chapter and the next two by mid-September, which is when classes start up again at Northwestern University, where I teach. This is all part of my current situation, as is the fact that I am 44 years old, married with two children, a white male, was raised in the Baptist church, and went to college at Valparaiso University in the early 1970s. I don't know you, but I am sure that you can spell out similar information about your life—about what is going on in your life now, where you came from, and vital statistics depicting your own demographic profile. All of this is, in a sense, part of the context within which you are currently situated. All of this defines your environment.

When we study the "environment" in the biological sciences, we learn to think about the complex "ecology" of the natural world. Making up that ecology are a number of interrelated environmental systems that define the natural world at a given place and time. In a similar way, we can think about the environments that situate human behavior in terms of a **social ecology** (Bronfenbrenner, 1979; Moen, Elder, & Luscher, 1995). The social ecology consists of the many different environmental contexts that influence a person's behavior and shape his or her life. The social ecology includes those immediate and close-in contexts such as the particular social situation within which one finds oneself at a given point in time. Personality psychologists who have been strongly influenced by behaviorism and social-learning theories are especially interested in the immediate situational factors that shape behavior at a given time and in a given place. In Bandura's famous experiments, for example, the children learned how to act in an aggressive manner by observing adults punch out the bobo doll. That immediate social situation influenced their behavior at that time. Similarly, a child's exposure to hours and hours of television violence may constitute a string of immediate situations that shape his or her behavior, through observational learning and other mechanisms, toward more and more aggressive ends. Social situations make up the **microcontexts** of social ecology—the immediate environmental influences for behavior.

Beyond these immediate situations, however, are larger and more distal contexts for behavior such as our families, neighborhoods, schools, and churches. Take the family, for instance. A family can be a context for behavior in at least two different ways. For one, a person is likely to act in different ways when he or she is in the presence of his or her family than at other times. Psychologists who study family systems speak of how each member of the family regularly assumes a particular role in that family and displays behavior that is consistent for that role (e.g., Minuchin, 1974). In my family of origin, I am typically a kind of authority figure who is supposed to know all the answers and provide guidance for my brother, sister, and mother. (In other contexts, however, I am much less likely to assume this role.) In a second sense, a family is a context in that patterns of behavior and values learned in the family may sometimes generalize to other parts of a person's life. The fact that I am currently writing this chapter rather than spending the afternoon at the beach is perhaps partly due to how I learned to be a conscientious student and hard worker growing up in my family. As such, the legacy of my family is part of my current environment. You can develop similar ideas for your own life with respect to your family, the neighborhood you grew up in, and perhaps the schools and churches of which you have been a member in the past.

The most encompassing and distal contexts for behavior are what we will call **macrocontexts,** and these include social class, gender, race, culture, and the historical context within which we live. At any given time, a person's life is situated within a hierarchy of contexts, ranging from the microcontext of the immediate social situation to the macrocontexts of class, culture, and history. A full understanding of behavior and of the person who displays any given behavior requires our situating that behavior and that person's life in a number of overlapping contexts, ranging from the micro to the macro. It turns out, therefore, that defining the environment for our behavior is a very ambitious task, for that environment is many different things at many different levels, all operating at the same time. Let us, then, briefly consider some aspects of the social ecology of human behavior, beginning with immediate social "situations" and moving toward the macrocontexts of class, gender, culture, and history.

Microcontexts: The Social Situation

What is a situation? Rudolph Moos (1973, 1974, 1976) provides a useful starting point for considering this surprisingly difficult question. Moos formulated a six-part taxonomy of human environments, identifying the various features that can be taken into consideration in conceptualizing a particular situation. The six categories of human environments identified by Moos are (1) dimensions of the physical ecology, (2) behavior settings or episodes, (3) organizational structure, (4) characteristics of persons in the situation, (5) organizational climate, and (6) functional and reinforcement properties. Table 4.4 summarizes the scheme and provides examples.

Barbara Krahe (1992) offers an alternative outline that arranges situational characteristics into a nested hierarchy. At the lowest level of the hierarchy are the *situational*

TABLE 4.4	*Six General Categories of Human Environments*
CATEGORY	**EXAMPLES**
Ecological	Climate, geography, type of building one lives in, physical characteristics of the setting
Behavior settings	Church, football game, kitchen, classroom
Organizational structure	Population density in an organization, site of organization, degree of hierarchic structure, student–teacher ratio in a school
Characteristics of inhabitants	Age, sex, abilities, status, talents, and so on of people in the environment
Organizational climate	Social morale, nature and intensity of personal relations
Functional properties	Reinforcement consequences for particular behaviors in the situation, such as whether aggressive acts are rewarded or encouraged

Source: Moos (1973).

stimuli such as single objects or acts inherent in a situation that are meaningful in their own right. For example, in the situation "taking an examination at the end of the term," situational stimuli would include a specific array of tables and chairs, pens and paper, fellow students sitting in the room, and so on. At the next level, we may view *situational events* or episodes. In the examination example, these might be "being told to begin the exam" and "answering the essay questions at the end of the exam." At the third level, events combine into an overall picture, or *total situation*. What is characteristic of the total situation is its unique occurrence in time and space. The examination might be the first one a student takes in her college career, or, say, the only examination she has ever taken in a psychology course. At the next level up, situations are defined in generalized terms, such as "exams in general." While each exam may be unique, most may share certain features defining the essence of "examness." Finally, at the fifth and most encompassing level, we may talk about *life situations*. According to Krahe (1992) these are "the totality of social and physical factors which affect the person and are affected by his or her actions at a certain stage of development" (p. 196). The life situation pertaining to our example of the college examination might be defined as "being an undergraduate in her first year at college," involving all the particular circumstances associated with this point in life.

You might think that since situations are "out there" in the environment, we might easily classify them in terms of objective properties that are outside the self—properties such as air temperature, room size, and number of people present. When psychologists have asked people to classify social situations, however, they have found that people do not typically focus on these kinds of objective external qualities. Instead, people tend to perceive situations in terms of their own subjective criteria, classifying environments in terms of what those environments can make possible for them. People tend to perceive situations in *psychological* rather than physical terms (Krahe, 1992). As such, situations reside as much in the minds of the observers as in the external environment itself. Writes Ball (1972), "the definition of the situation may be conceived as the *sum of all recognized information, from the point of view of the actor, which is relevant to his locating himself and others, so that he can engage in self-determined lines of action and interaction*" (p. 63).

People often characterize particular situations in terms of their psychological *affordances*—what opportunities for behavior and experience the situations afford or offer for the participant (Dworkin & Goldfinger, 1985). For example, Magnusson (1971) asked persons to evaluate 36 heterogeneous situations and found that the key dimensions upon which the situations could be ordered included how rewarding the situation was, the extent to which the situation induced negative feelings, how passive a person might be in the situation, the amount of social interaction afforded in the situation, and level of activity. Forgas (1978) identified four dimensions that organize 15 different kinds of interpersonal environments: the amount of anxiety the situation elicits, the extent to which a person feels involved in the situation, overall goodness versus badness of the situation, and the extent to which the situation involves accomplishing tasks versus socioemotional interaction. Other studies have arrived at different schemes. There turn out to be a dauntingly large number of dimensions upon which immediate situations can be compared and contrasted and little agreement about which dimensions are the most important.

If situations are best defined in terms of people's subjective psychological affordances, then it becomes extremely difficult to separate what's "really" in the situation from what's "really" in the person. Furthermore, if a person's personality shapes his or her perceptions, then it would seem to be equally difficult to separate internal personality variables (such as traits) from external situations, for traits may determine how a person interprets the environment. In support of this idea, Forgas (1983) found that introverted people tended to organize information about situations in terms of a self-confidence dimension. Extraverts, by contrast, categorized situations in terms of how pleasant the situations were and how strongly they afforded interpersonal involvement. Put simply, introverts and extroverts are usually in different situations (in terms of their subjective perceptions), even when it appears from the outside that they are in the same.

Whether introvert or extravert, however, the average person appears to possess a "vast and varied expertise about situations" that can be tapped and translated into behavioral guidelines (Cantor, Mischel, & Schwarz, 1982, p. 70). According to one approach to the understanding of situations, people may routinely formulate elaborate personal taxonomies specifying **situational prototypes** (Cantor et al., 1982; Schutte, Kenrick, & Sadalla, 1985). A situational prototype is an abstract set of features about a given class of situations. It serves as a working model for the person, telling him or her what to expect and how to behave in situations of a particular type. A situational prototype may include information about the physical setting, the physical features of the people involved, and common behaviors exhibited by the people in the situation.

For example, the situation of "party" may suggest a large number of features typically associated with parties. Perhaps the prototypical party generally occurs in the evening and involves a large number of people congregating in a circumscribed space, informal dress, eating and drinking, lively conversation, laughing, music and dancing, and lots of noise. Of course, parties vary, and each party contains its own constellation of defining features. Nonetheless, we extract from our experience a core of "partyness" that represents for each of us the "best example" or "ideal case" for defining the situation we call "party." Subsequently, each party we encounter may be evaluated in terms of this implicit categorization. A large dance party at a sorority house may, therefore, appear to us to be a highly prototypical party, embodying many of the features that parties tend to have in common. On the other hand, a poetry-reading party at the home of a college English professor may seem less prototypical, farther away from what we typically think of when we think of the party situation.

Bem and Funder (1978) describe a similar way of classifying situations in their **template-matching** approach. In template matching, a person sorts 100 personality statements into nine piles, ranging from those characteristics deemed to be "most like" to those "least like" an "idealized 'type' of person expected to behave in a specified way in that setting" (Bem & Funder, 1978, p. 486). For example, the rater might sort items according to the idealized type of "person most likely to achieve success as an attorney in a small law firm." This distribution is the *template* (model, pattern, portrait) for the situation. Therefore, situations are classified according to the personality traits of the idealized person who "fits" the situation in a particular way. Two different situations would be functionally similar if they produce similar templates, that is, if similar types of people were deemed likely to behave in a certain way in each of the situations. Likewise, two situations that might seem similar to some observers would be functionally dissimilar if they produce markedly different templates.

A situational prototype: Grandmother's birthday.

Macrocontexts: Social Structure

There are no perfectly egalitarian human societies on earth. In all societies and in virtually all human groups, power and resources are unevenly distributed. We can debate why this is so and whether or not it has always been so, but it is surely true today that some people have more access to those resources most valued in society than do others. In American society, those resources include especially money and education, each of which can directly or indirectly confer prestige, status, and power. The unequal distribution of resources creates complex relationships among members of society and exerts pervasive influences on how people develop over time, what they strive for, and how they understand themselves and the world. The term **social structure,** therefore, refers to those conditions of society that differentiate people along the lines of power and resources. Social structure provides an encompassing macrocontext for human behavior (Pettigrew, 1997). The impact of this macrocontext on personality is evident when we look at the relation between personality and social class.

In a classic review of social stratification research in different countries, Inkeles (1960) found that people in higher socioeconomic classes (those with higher-paying, professional jobs and with higher levels of education) showed different patterns of attitudes and behavior than people from lower classes. For example, Inkeles found that individuals in higher classes tended to report higher job satisfaction compared with individuals in lower social classes. Social class was also associated with attitudes about one's job and about human nature. Individuals from higher social classes tended to express greater concern that their job be interesting and fulfilling rather than merely a source of steady income, and they tended to believe in the possibility of changing human nature for the better. By contrast, lower-class individuals valued security first and foremost in their work and tended to be much more fatalistic and pessimistic about human nature.

Over the past 30 years, Melvin Kohn and his colleagues have undertaken a series of influential studies examining social structure and personality (Kohn, 1969; Kohn, Naoi, Schoenbach, Schooler, & Slomczynski, 1990; Kohn & Schooler, 1969, 1973). Kohn argues that the impact of social class on personality can be seen both in the demands of the workplace and the dynamics of the family. Professional, higher-status occupations place significant cognitive demands upon workers. Teachers, doctors, lawyers, and other white-collar professionals are challenged to exercise initiative and independent judgment in their work to a greater extent than are blue-collar factory employees and other workers in lower-status jobs. Higher-status employees, therefore, enjoy and cultivate greater levels of *self-direction* at work. By contrast, lower-status employees find fewer cognitive challenges in their work, are given fewer opportunities to exercise initiative, and must typically instead obey the orders of their superiors. Consequently, lower-status employees are socialized to value *obedience to authority*. Kohn et al. (1990) found that American, Japanese, and Polish men from higher social classes all had a more self-directed orientation, encompassing higher internal control and higher trust, compared with men of lower social classes. Higher social class was also associated with lower conformity, lower anxiety, and greater intellectual flexibility.

What is especially fascinating about the distinction between higher-class self-direction and lower-class obedience to authority is that it tends to generalize to the family realm as well. Kohn (1969) showed that in both the United States and Italy, middle-class parents more often stressed intent and self-direction while lower- and working-class parents more often stressed obedience to authority in the family. Children whose parents enjoy professional, high-status jobs, therefore, tend to be socialized in such a way as to encourage self-direction, which itself becomes a valuable asset for those children when they grow up and pursue professional positions themselves. By contrast, children whose parents work in lower-status occupations tend to be socialized toward obedience to authority. While such a socialization pattern fits the demands of lower-class work and family life, it may not prepare these children well for their later efforts to move up into higher-status occupations. Developmental psychologist Jerome Kagan emphasizes how lower- and working-class families value security first and foremost and seek to instill in their children those qualities that have historically reinforced stability and stasis in the occupational world. Kagan (1984) writes:

> Parents who have not attended college, who see themselves and their children as part of the
> working class, and who live with chronic financial insecurity, often attribute their personal

angst to economic stress, which they view as being not completely under their control. These families award a high priority to job security; and a central goal in socializing their child is to ensure that he or she will develop the qualities that guarantee a secure job. Two key qualities are acceptance by peers and the ability to resist being exploited by those with more power. (p. 249)

In contrast, middle-class families are likely to be better educated and better off financially. The parents are likely to have professional positions, and the children are likely to be socialized within a much different macrosystem of values, beliefs, and world views:

> College-educated parents, especially those with professional vocations, regard freedom of choice, intellectual challenge, and the status of one's work as more important than job security. They believe that anxiety over peer rejection or disapproval obstructs the attainment of these goals, and they try to inoculate their youngsters against the anxiety that accompanies peer rejection, while emphasizing autonomous choice and competition. (Kagan, 1984, p. 249)

Studies carried out in the United States and in England have shown that middle-class adolescents and adults use more complex and less stereotyped language than do lower-class people, even when their intelligence test scores are similar (Hess & Shipman, 1965). Bernstein (1970) has argued that lower-class parents adopt a restricted linguistic code in communicating with their children, which means that they limit their verbal exchanges to direct expressions of concrete statements and commands. Middle-class parents, on the other hand, tend to use an elaborated linguistic code consisting of complex syntax, conditional statements, and the expression of abstract ideas. Critical of this characterization, Labov (1972) argues that middle-class psychologists are not sensitive to the nuance and range of meaning in lower-class speech. Both Bernstein and Labov would agree, however, that language reflects context, and that differences in verbal behavior between lower- and middle-class people reflect different systems for making meaning in the world and thus different contexts within which behavior can be understood.

Gender as a Macrocontext

If social structure refers to those conditions of society that differentiate people along the line of status and power, then one of the great structural divides in human life is *gender*. Gender encompasses all those social and personal characteristics, constructions, and roles typically associated with one or another of the two biological sexes in human life. As a product of social learning, we come to expect that women and men will differ from each other in a number of important ways. In the extreme, we may form *gender role stereotypes*, which are relatively inflexible ideas about how males and females do and should act. For example, we may expect that in the overall men should be relatively more assertive and aggressive than women, while women should be more nurturing, affectionate, and gentle (Spence, 1985). Social psychologists have documented the pervasiveness of gender role stereotypes in American society, as well as in other societies, and have shown how such stereotyping is at the root of sexism and prejudice.

Like social class, gender has profound implications for power and prestige. In many if not most societies (including contemporary American society), men generally have more access to social and economic power than do women. Men control more public resources, make more decisions about the society as a whole, and enjoy more freedom and autonomy. While moves toward equality have accelerated in the past 30 years, American men (especially white men) still occupy most of the highest positions of societal power and prestige. For example, they vastly outnumber women at the levels of top corporate executives and government leaders, and they still make considerably more money than do women, even when their professional positions are roughly comparable. Within the family, men typically occupy the most dominant roles; in many American families women and children are expected to defer to the man of the house when it comes to major life decisions, especially those involving how the money should be spent. On a more brutal and insidious level, men harass, rape, and kill women to a much greater extent than the other way around. While such behavior may spring as much from frustration and rage as it does from social dominance, physical aggression constitutes yet another mechanism through which males can exert power and control over females.

Gender role stereotypes typically reinforce the power differential between men and women. Stereotypically masculine attributions such as "dominant," "assertive," and "controlling" reinforce the idea that men have the power in society, whereas stereotypically feminine attributions of "submissive," "nurturant," and "gentle" suggest that women occupy subservient positions. From an early age, children learn that such characteristics are differentially applicable to human beings as a function of biological sex. Little girls may be rewarded for cooperative and friendly play, while little boys may receive reinforcement for their rambunctious outbursts (instrumental conditioning). Both little girls and boys see that women occupy the primary caregiving roles in society while men tend to be both the breadwinners and the action heroes (observational learning). Gender socialization is pervasive in contemporary American society—in ways both obvious and subtle, well-meaning and invidious. Through rewards, punishments, and observational learning, male and females become intimately familiar with society's expectations as to gender-appropriate behavior (Brody, 1999). Of course, not everybody follows the stereotypic path. But virtually everybody is aware of the expectations, even as those expectations continue to change and even as many people, both men and women, work hard to change them.

Alice Eagly and Wendy Wood (1991) argue that socialization into gender roles accounts for most of the general sex differences that are observed in human social behavior. Reviews of the empirical literature indicate, for example, that the sexes typically differ in a variety of social behaviors, including aggression, helping, nonverbal behavior, and interactions in groups (Eagly, 1987). From an early age onward, males tend to be more aggressive than females (Eagly & Steffen, 1986; Maccoby & Jacklin, 1974), a difference that becomes especially apparent by the teenage years, when boys exhibit markedly higher levels of antisocial activity, including violent crime. On the flip side of the coin, men also exhibit higher levels of altruistic, helping behavior in short-term interactions with strangers (e.g., when a stranger is in distress; Eagly & Crowley, 1986). Women, however, show considerably higher levels of daily helping behavior, as in acts of caring for and tending to the needs of others, primarily in close or long-term relationships. Compared with men, women tend to be more sensitive to nonverbal cues in social interaction. In social situations, women smile and laugh more than do men, use their faces and bodies more expressively, show more involvement with others' behavior, touch other people more, and approach them more closely (Hall, 1984;

Stier & Hall, 1984). Women also report greater empathy for others' emotional experiences (Eisenberg & Lennon, 1983). These sex differences are generally consistent with the widespread belief in our society that women are more socially skilled, emotionally sensitive, and expressive than men, as well as more concerned with personal relationships. In group discussions, women, more than men, act friendly and agree with other group members (Anderson & Blanchard, 1982). In contrast, men, more than women, contribute behaviors that are strictly oriented to accomplishing the task that the group was assigned. In leadership roles, women adopt a more democratic and participatory style than men; men tend to lead in a more authoritarian manner (Eagly & Johnson, 1990).

Although the sex differences that have been documented for social behavior are not always large in magnitude, they tend to be consistent with society's expectations about gender roles. On a most general level, these expectations can be summarized in terms of the constructs of **agency** and **communion** (Bakan, 1966). Agency refers to the tendency of an individual to assert the self in a powerful and expansive manner and is associated with such characteristics as being aggressive, independent, masterful, and instrumentally competent. Communion refers to the tendency of an individual to merge with other individuals and is associated with such characteristics as being friendly, unselfish, concerned with others, and emotionally expressive. In a nutshell, gender roles suggest that men should be slightly more agentic and women slightly more communal. Empirical research into social behavior provides modest support for these expectations. In other words, men and women do seem to behave in accord with gender role expectations, though the tendencies are moderate. Eagly and Wood (1991) maintain that sex differences in agentic and communal qualities are mainly the result of social learning over the life span. Socialization practices and cultural norms reflect the uneven distribution of women and men into different societal roles. Of particular importance in this regard is the traditional assignment of women to the roles of child rearing and domestic work as well as the tendency for men and women to carry out different types of paid employment in a largely sex-segregated economy.

Now, there are at least two very different ways to interpret the empirical literature on sex differences in social behavior and their relation to gender roles and gender socialization. The more upbeat and innocent interpretation is to say that gender roles reflect those differences between men and women that have arisen through a beneficent blending of nature and choice. One variation on this line of argument has it that because women are biologically fit to bear children and because men tend on the average to be somewhat larger and stronger than women, women and men have gravitated toward different but equally valuable (and valued) roles in society. Separate but equal, in a sense. A second, less sanguine interpretation emphasizes *hegemony,* or the expression of power by one group over another. According to this second line of thinking, gender roles are the result of unequal power between the sexes. In patriarchal societies, men have assumed the most dominant roles. In both conscious and unconscious ways and through both overt and covert means, men's power has worked to subjugate women into those roles that afford less status, impact, and freedom. Why, then, are women somewhat more communal than men? According to arguments that emphasize power and hegemony, women have assumed more communal orientations and developed interpersonal skills as *strategies for survival and success in subservient roles.* It is incumbent upon girls and women to hone their skills in interpersonal relations as a way of exerting

Aggression: Learning and culture shape how aggressive we are and how we express aggression.

what little power they are able to summon forth in a patriarchal society. By contrast, men do not need to be as interpersonally sensitive and communally oriented because they can generally achieve their ends through direct, agentic means.

Whatever interpretation you wish to make of why it is that men and women show differences in social behavior and how those differences relate to gender roles and gender role stereotypes, you are likely to conclude, as you should, that gender is a pervasive macrocontext for human behavior. One of the first things, if not *the* first thing, we learn about a person is whether that person is male or female. That knowledge shapes our expectations as to how that person should behave, who that person is, and how we should interact with that person. Gender roles inform our approaches to a vast array of social situations, everything from what we do on a first date to how we act as a leader of a group. Even when we act in defiance of gender roles, we are acknowledging our understanding that such roles exist, even as we hope to transcend them. Therefore, while gender roles may not control our lives and do not necessarily leave us powerless to engage in role-incongruent behavior, they are nonetheless formidable forces to confront across the human life span. Put another way, gender is a ubiquitous category for human experience. It is fair to say that personality is itself gendered. A human life is, to a certain extent, a gendered construction. And each of us lives in a gendered world.

Culture

The most encompassing and far-reaching macrocontext for human behavior is **culture.** Social scientists have formulated many different definitions of culture. We will begin with Robert LeVine's (1982) view that culture is a tradition of rules embraced by a particular society of people. According to LeVine, culture is

> an organized body of rules concerning the ways in which individuals in a population should communicate with one another, think about themselves and their environments, and behave toward one another and toward objects in their environments. The rules are not universally or constantly obeyed, but they are recognized by all and they ordinarily operate to limit the range of variation in patterns of communication, belief, value, and social behavior in the population. (LeVine, 1982, p. 4)

The "rules" of which a particular culture is made generate two fundamental features of that culture: (1) its maintenance system and (2) its projective system (Whiting & Child, 1953). A culture's **maintenance system** is its ecological, economic, and sociopolitical structure and the child-training or socialization practices accepted by the society as appropriate. The maintenance system exists to ensure the survival of the group in its relation to its external physical environment. Thus, external environments give birth to maintenance systems and their corresponding patterns of socialization. For example, harsh physical climates with relatively little rainfall, such as desert and arctic tundra, have traditionally called for cultural maintenance systems centered around hunting and fishing. Human societies living in such regions, such as the Eskimo, have traditionally moved from one place to another, across the terrain in search of food and temporary shelter. Within this nomadic lifestyle, the individual must rely on wits and expertise to survive, and therefore socialization practices in these societies tend to encourage the values of autonomy and self-reliance. In contrast, temperate climates have traditionally been associated with agricultural maintenance systems calling for large-scale accumulation of food and a more sedentary settlement pattern. In these societies, socialization practices tend to emphasize the values of obedience and social responsibility (Berry, 1976).

The **projective system** of a culture refers to a society's art, religion, folklore, and other expressive media. Whereas the maintenance system is seen as *shaping* the personality of the society's members, the projective system is generally considered to be *an expression of* personality. Anthropologists have documented fascinating connections between maintenance and projective systems within cultures. For instance, Whiting and Child (1953) used available ethnographic records to examine child-rearing methods (maintenance system) and beliefs about disease (projective system) in 75 preliterate societies. They found that societies that tended to punish children severely for aggressive behavior tended also to view disease as caused by hostile sorcerers who invaded the people's bodies. Societies in which mothers weaned their infants early tended to see disease as caused by consuming bad food or poison.

When we think of culture as an organized body of rules that binds people together in a society and expresses itself in corresponding maintenance and projective systems, we are emphasizing the extent to which culture exists outside the person as a coherent and encompassing whole. In the 1940s and 1950s, social scientists who examined the relations between culture and personality tended to exhibit just this emphasis. Their work was based on the assumption that people's lives corresponded in a coherent manner to the rules of their culture. Therefore, particular cultures might produce distinctive character types or "modal personalities." In recent years, however, anthropologists and other social scientists who examine the intersection of culture and individual lives have come to emphasize the inconsistencies and diversities in any given culture and the inevitable mismatches and incongruencies that follow from the relations between culture and individual lives. For example, Geertz (1973) argues that culture should not be seen as a tightly constructed, rule-governed system. Culture consists of many different elements, some in conflict with each other (Holland, 1997). Furthermore, people do not match up neatly to the cultures wherein they reside. Instead, each person makes use of the cultural resources that are available to him or her. Each culture provides "a tool kit of habits, skills, styles, perspectives, norms, roles, and values out of which each individual can construct a potentially unique strategy of action" (Triandis, 1997, p. 443). People act and think selectively and strategically within culture. "As constructors of experience, people are capable of selecting among various imperatives, claiming, elaborating, and personalizing some of the available collective resources so that they are both individually and jointly held, while ignoring, resisting, contesting, and rearranging others" (Markus, Kitayama, & Heiman, 1998, p. 859).

In a fundamental sense, culture is as much inside the person as it is in the world surrounding the person. Culture provides a way of knowing and construing the self, the world, and others (Bruner, 1990). Cushman (1990) writes that culture "is not indigenous clothing that covers the universal human; it infuses individuals, fundamentally shaping and forming them and how they conceive of themselves and the world, how they see others, and how they engage in structures of mutual obligation" (p. 31). The idea of culture as the *meanings that infuse human lives* is central to the conception of culture offered by Shweder and Sullivan (1993), who write that a culture is "that subset of possible or available meanings, which by virtue of enculturation—informal or formal, implicit or explicit, unintended or intended—has become so active in giving shape to the psychological processes of individuals in a society that those meanings have become, for those individuals, indistinguishable from experience itself" (p. 29). As a complex macrocontext for human behavior, culture offers up a rich mix of meanings, practices, and discourses that shape individual lives (Holland, 1997). But individuals do not passively submit to culture. Instead, each of us appropriates certain cultural meanings and ignores others, and each of us is likely to do battle with those aspects of culture that we find disagreeable or even repugnant. Culture infuses us with meanings, but as active agents in the world we each participate in culture and leave our mark on those meanings, making for a dynamic and evolving interplay between culture and self (Holland, 1997).

Individualism and Collectivism   A major theme in the literature on cross-cultural psychology is that while some cultures emphasize the autonomy of individual selves, other cultures provide meanings organized around the interdependence of selves within communities. On a cultural level, **individualism** is a meaning system that exalts the autonomy of the individual over and against the interdependence of the group. People in individualist cultural contexts typically give priority to their own personal goals, even when the goals are in conflict with the goals of family, work group, or country (Triandis, 1997). By contrast, cultural **collectivism** is a meaning system that gives priority to the in-group or collective over and against the individual. People in collectivist cultural contexts typically put the interests and values of their groups (e.g., family, community, nation) ahead of their own personal agendas (Triandis, 1997). On self-report scales designed to measure collectivism, people living in collectivist societies tend to endorse such items as these: "I stick with my group even through difficulties" and "I am prepared to do things for my group at any time, even though I have to sacrifice my own self-interests" (Kashima, Yumaguchi, Kim, Choi, Gelfand, & Yuki, 1995).

Among those societies that appear to express the most individualist cultural meanings are the United States, Canada, Australia, and the democracies of northern and western Europe (e.g., Great Britain, Germany). The emphasis on competition, autonomy, individualism, and the self is generally considered to be a hallmark of industrial and postindustrial Western culture. The emphasis is complexly determined and has historical roots in Western religion, philosophy, economy, and government (Bellah et al., 1985, 1991; Bloom, 1987). This pervasive ideological context for behavior suggests that we as Westerners tend to see people as potentially self-sufficient agents endowed with fundamental and even inalienable individual rights—such as the rights to "life, liberty, and the pursuit of happiness," the right of free speech, and the right of assembly. We view society as comprising autonomous agents who freely choose to behave as they do. This position contrasts starkly with the view of persons espoused in, say, a traditional Hindu village in India. Miller (1984) has shown that children in American society tend to explain everyday social events in terms of the personal dispositions of individual persons. Hindu children, on the other hand, tend to explain everyday events in terms of the pressures of the environment and the influences of society on persons.

The promise and the problems of American individualism are described in this passage from Bellah's critique of American society (Bellah et al., 1985):

> Clearly the meaning of one's life for most Americans is to become one's own person, almost to give birth to oneself. Much of this process, as we have seen, is negative. It involves breaking free from family, community, and inherited ideas. Our culture does not give us much guidance as to how to fill the contours of this autonomous, self-responsible self, but it does point to two important areas. One of these is work, the realm, par excellence, of utilitarian individualism. Traditionally, men, and today women as well, are supposed to show that in the occupational world they can stand on their own two feet and be self-supporting. The other is the lifestyle enclave, the realm, par excellence, of expressive individualism. We are supposed to be able to find a group of sympathetic people, or at least one such person, with whom we can spend our leisure time in an atmosphere of acceptance, happiness, and love. (p. 83)

The emphasis on collectivism is especially strong in many traditional societies and in Asia, the Pacific Islands, and Africa (Triandis, 1997). Collectivist values are at the heart of Eastern Asian religious and cultural traditions, as evidenced in Buddhism and Confucianism. The Buddha taught self-renunciation as a goal of human life, through which the person transcends the limits of the individual self and finds connection to others and the cosmos. Confucius codified a social doctrine of familial and community obligations. In the Confucian tradition, social order takes precedent over individual expression. A person needs to know his or her proper place in the hierarchical order of things. Special emphasis is placed on the vertical (across generations) relationships between parents and children. Sons and daughters are obligated to serve their parents and show them considerable deference (filial piety); the same obligations are to be expressed toward the authority of the state.

Markus, Kitayama, and Heiman (1998) write that the idea of assuming one's proper place within a social hierarchy is so pervasive in some Asian cultures that it shapes language. The earliest language learning by children in Western Samoa contains a set of important assumptions about authority—who can speak when and who can express certain ideas. Children are taught to look for the hidden meanings behind words so that they do not need to ask their parents and teachers the many questions that might ultimately lead them to challenge authority. In Japan, it is said that before asking a question, it is essential—Confucian style—to ask oneself, "Does this question need to be asked?" And if yes, "Am I the right person to ask it?" (from Markus, Kitayama, & Heiman, 1998, p. 876). In talking about personality and social life, the Japanese often invoke the concept of *amae* (Doi, 1962). Amae roughly translates as "depending on or presuming another's benevolence." While dependency may seem to be an immature, childhood characteristic from an individualist standpoint, the Japanese conceive of the entire life span in terms of *amae*. Not only children, but Japanese adults, too, view themselves as being linked to others in a social hierarchy through bonds of benevolent interdependency.

The distinction between individualism and collectivism should not be drawn too sharply but should instead be seen as a matter of degree. Any given culture is not completely individualist or collectivist as a whole. Instead, every culture has both individualist and collectivist meanings. For example, in American society people speak easily about the development of an autonomous self (individualism) as well as their obligations and commitments to families and other groups (collectivism) (Holland, 1997). Cultures tend to differ from one another, therefore, in terms of their *relative emphasis* on individualism and collectivism. These relative differences can be further spelled out in terms of four defining attributes of individualism and collectivism (Triandis & Gelfand, 1998).

The first attribute concerns goals. From an individualist standpoint, personal goals are more important than the goals of the in-group (e.g. family, community, state), whereas from a collectivist standpoint the in-group goals are more important. It is important to note in this regard that a collectivist perspective connects the person to a *particular* in-group rather than, say, to all humankind in general. From a collectivist standpoint, one is loyal to one's own group, and such loyalty may put one in strong opposition to other groups. A second attribute concerns relationships. From an individualist standpoint, rational exchange is the norm in relationships; separate and autonomous selves come together to "trade" resources (e.g., money, help, love), and social life resembles, in many ways, a marketplace. From a collectivist standpoint, people relate to one another more from the standpoint of communal obligations and bonds of loyalty. A third attribute concerns the determinants of social behavior. From an individualist standpoint, the person's own attitudes take precedent over group norms in motivating and guiding behavior. Individualist cultures emphasize the ideas of "standing up for what you think is right" and "being true to your own convictions." By contrast, the collectivist meaning system elevates social norms above the opinions or attitudes of individuals. People are encouraged to act in accord with the standards of the in-group. Finally, individualist and collectivist cultures suggest rather different construals of the self. The individualist self is defined over and against others as an autonomous and independent agent. The collectivist self, by contrast, is viewed as highly interdependent and embedded within the community.

The differences between construals of an *independent* self, so characteristic of individualist cultures, and the contrasting construals of an *interdependent* self, more common in collectivist cultures, have been described in detail by Markus and Kitayama (1991). As spelled out in Table 4.5, Markus and Kitayama propose that in Western, especially North American middle-class cultures, there is a strong belief in the independence of the self from others. The self is defined in terms of internal attributes such as motives, abilities, talents, or "personalities," and a major cultural task is to discover, actualize, or confirm these personal attributes of the self. The independent way of being is widely elaborated in a variety of cultural practices, such as conversational styles that emphasize individual choice and self-fulfillment over and against conformity to social norms, and in such cultural institutions as the merit pay system. By contrast, many non-Western, especially Asian, cultures (and to an important extent some non-European groups in the United States) do not value such a strict separation or independence of the self. These cultures, instead, believe in the fundamental connectedness or interdependence among those within an in-group. The self is made in reference to the relationships of which it is part. The major cultural task is to fit in, adjust to the relationship, while constraining, taming, or otherwise conditioning internal desires or wishes so as to facilitate the paramount goal of interpersonal harmony and unity. The interdependent way of being is elaborated in such cultural practices as conversational styles emphasizing sympathy and kindness to others and in cultural institutions such as the seniority system.

Markus and Kitayama's distinction between independent and interdependent self construals neatly parallels the distinction between individualist and collectivist cultures, and both distinctions share conceptual space with a contrast we considered

TABLE 4.5	*Key Differences Between Independent and Interdependent Construals of Self*	
FEATURE	**INDEPENDENT**	**INTERDEPENDENT**
Definition	Separate from social context	Connected with social context
Structure	Bounded, unitary, stable	Flexible, variable
Characteristics	Internal, private (abilities, thoughts, feelings)	External, public (statuses, roles, relationships)
Tasks	Be unique Express self Realize internal attributes Promote own goals Be direct: "Say what's on your mind"	Belong, fit in Occupy one's proper place Engage in appropriate action Promote others' goals Be indirect: "Read other's mind"
Role of others	Self-evaluation: others are important for social comparison, reflected appraisals	Self-definition: relationships with others in specific contexts define the self
Basis of self-esteem	Ability to express self, validate internal attributes	Ability to adjust, restrain self, maintain harmony with social context

Source: Markus & Kitayama (1991), p. 230.

FEATURE 4.B

Race and Personality in the United States

Ever since Europeans imported African men and women to the New World as slaves, race has served to divide Americans into different economic and cultural camps. Slavery was abolished in the United States more than 130 years ago, but African Americans and European Americans continue to inhabit somewhat separate cultural worlds. African Americans are still disproportionately represented in the lower economic classes. Therefore, race and class cannot be readily separated from each other. Nonetheless, many sociologists and other scholars insist that one's racial background, regardless of social class, exerts a marked influence on the person's development and relationships with others. In a provocative and rueful analysis of psychological research comparing African Americans and white Americans, Jones (1983) remarks:

> Over the past few decades, psychological analysis of race has identified an unending stream of dysfunctions, maladaptations, deficient social organization, poor intellectual performance, inadequate motivation, restricted ego domains, doubts, stresses, and fears. One wonders, on the basis of this extensive literature, how black Americans have managed to survive. The genetic versions of these negativistic analyses are based on the assumption that deficient genes explain the poor adaptation to American society; the environmental versions instead point the finger at poverty and racist oppression. While the environmentalists often accuse the geneticists of racism, black psychologists cannot help noticing that neither position recognizes a single attribute, capacity, or contribution of black people that could be considered positive, desirable, or worth preserving. An essential goal of black psychology, then, is to go beyond the reactive conception of black Americans' history to develop a cultural-evolutionary perspective that recognizes African origins, and more recent developments in the United States (and other countries), and the effects of prolonged oppression. The new perspective should include what is distinctively good and useful in the Afro- or African-American experience. (p. 142)

Jones indicts American social scientists for failing to understand the macrocontext of black culture. Cole (1976) identifies three principal components of black culture: (1) an "American mainstream" component shared with white Americans and espousing such values as individualism and materialism, (2) a "minority sense" component shared with other disadvantaged minorities in American society, reinforcing the sense that being black is likely to make one the subject of discrimination, and (3) a unique "blackness" component that incorporates certain African and African-American values, mannerisms, and styles. The blackness component includes what Cole terms "soul"— a sense of people facing hardship together as a spirited and vital community—and "style," which refers to characteristic ways of talking, walking, dressing, and thinking.

Many black scholars draw sharp contrasts between European-American philosophical orientations (which provide a foundation for the American white culture) and African philosophical orientations (which are more instrumental in the black culture) (e.g., Akbar, 1991; Dixon, 1976; White & Parham, 1990). The differences suggest that black heritage is highly social rather than individualistic, oriented toward the present rather than the future, and focused on subjective emotional experience over and against objective rationality. These are *cultural* rather than personal differences. They represent contrasts in the implicit philosophical contexts behind behavior rather than differences in behavior per se. Again, we see that different contexts imbue a person's behavior with different meanings.

Social psychologist Philip Bowman (1989, 1990) is one of a small but growing number of researchers who are working to understand the complex influences of racial macrocontexts on the development of personality. Bowman underscores both the *risks* and the *resiliency* inherent in African-American family life today. According to Bowman, African-American families exhibit at least four distinctive qualities that serve as *adaptive cultural resources.* First, compared to the European-American majority, African-American families tend to incorporate extended kin networks. The many aunts, uncles, grandparents, and other relatives living close to one another create a community of support that is especially significant for the rearing of children. Second, family roles are likely to be especially flexible in the African-American community. For example, black men and women tend to assume both agentic and communal roles in the family, rather than specializing along sex-stereotypic lines (Boyd-Franklin, 1989). Third is the powerful role of religion and spirituality

among African Americans. Blacks in the United States have traditionally attended church more often and reported more significant religious involvements than whites. The church has traditionally been an extraordinarily integrative and sustaining force in the black community, functioning as a source of spiritual guidance, agency for social service, and catalyst for societal change. Finally, black racial consciousness can be viewed as an adaptive cultural resource. To the extent that African-American children identify proudly with a distinctive cultural heritage, they can eventually draw on that heritage for shaping their own identities and leading productive and fulfilling lives.

Adopting the frameworks of cross-cultural psychology (e.g., Triandis, 1997), Bowman argues that different cultural groups often have a great deal in common. For example, blacks in the United States tend to want the same kinds of successes and fulfillments for themselves and their children that whites want. They tend to hold very similar values with respect to social and political issues. These commonalities comprise what anthropologists call *etic* dimensions across cultures, or ways in which different cultures share similar means and goals. Nonetheless, every culture also has its own *emic* dimensions, or those characteristics that serve to distinguish it from other cultures. A sensitive and productive approach to understanding the macrocontext of race in the United States must, therefore, focus both on those etic aspects of culture that most all Americans share and those emic features—especially adaptive cultural resources—that are unique to particular cultural groups.

earlier when we discussed gender—the distinction between *agency* and *communion* (Bakan, 1966). With respect to gender, we suggested that some of the sex differences in psychological processes that have been identified in the empirical literature paint a portrait of men as somewhat more agentic (power oriented, striving for autonomy) than women and women as somewhat more communal (intimacy oriented, striving for connection) than men. An important study by Kashima et al. (1995), however, warns against equating cultural and gender differences. The authors examined self-construals in five cultures—Australia, United States, Hawaii, Japan, and Korea. Their findings showed that differences among these cultures were indeed captured by measures of individualism and collectivism. But the same measures did not capture differences between men and women. Instead, gender differences showed up on measures of the extent to which people feel emotionally related to others (a concept that is not related to collectivism), with women scoring higher on these measures than men. Both men and women in individualist cultures (e.g., the United States, Australia), therefore, tended to view their actions and attitudes as expressing their own self-strivings, whereas both men and women in collectivist cultures (e.g., Hawaii, Japan, Korea) tended to view their actions and attitudes as expressing their connections to family and social group. With respect to gender, women in both individualist and collectivist cultures reported greater levels of empathy and emotional connection to other people than did men in both individualist and collectivist cultures. In simple terms, the data suggest that "women are not like Asians" (Kashima et al., 1995, p. 932), and men are not like Americans. The individualist/collectivist distinction applies more to cultural differences than gender differences. Put another way, saying that Asians espouse a more collectivist viewpoint than Americans, in the overall, does not mean that Asians are more emotionally connected to other people than are Americans. If Kashima's findings are valid, it would appear that emotional connection to others is more tied up with gender than it is with culture.

Modernity   Another cultural concept that is related to the distinction between individualism and collectivism is **modernity.** Modernity refers most generally to the economic, political, and cultural systems spawned in the 19th and 20th centuries by the Industrial Revolution, the expansion of capitalism and the proliferation of markets and trade, the increasing domination of science and technology, and the rising power of nationalist states, especially democracies, beginning in Western Europe and America and eventually spreading to parts of Asia (e.g., Japan) as well. Although there remain substantial cultural differences among those societies that have been impacted by modernity, modern societies still tend to share certain features and outlooks. For example, modernity is often perceived as encouraging a rationalistic and scientifically minded approach to the world (Gergen, 1992). Modernity is associated with growing skepticism toward religion and other traditional sources of authority (such as the monarchy) and the spreading belief that progress and human betterment reside in the advances of science, technology, and economic and political development (Harvey, 1990). The cultures that prevail in modern societies tend to value reason, objectivity, rational discourse, and developmental progress in accord with scientific laws and other consensually validated systems of knowledge and belief. As societies become more modern, values and attitudes of people change. In a study of six developing countries, Inkeles and Smith (1974) found that the move toward modern industrialization was accompanied by an increase in all of the following aspects of personality and social life: (1) openness to new experiences, (2) assertion of independence from traditional authorities, (3) belief in scientific efficacy rather than fatalism, (4) ambitious occupational and educational goals for one's self and children, (5) concern for punctuality and planning, (6) interest and participation in local politics, and (7) interest in national and international news.

Cultural modernity tends to promote individualism. The value systems that promote and are promoted by science, democracy, and free trade tend to celebrate the virtues of self-initiative, self-expression, and independence. But modernity and individualism are not the same concepts. For example, modern societies vary considerably with respect to their emphasis on individualism, with some modern societies, such as Japan and South Korea, tending toward collectivism rather than individualism. Still, it is probably fair to say that as traditionally collectivist societies become more modern they move somewhat in the direction of cultural individualism. Modernity appears to bring with it certain characteristic problems and opportunities in the development of the self (Baumeister, 1986; Giddens, 1991; Langbaum, 1982; McAdams, 1996a; Taylor, 1989). In modern societies, people tend to view the self as a *project* that they "work on," develop, improve, and strive to perfect. In contemporary American society, for example, there is no shortage of advice and instruction on how to improve the self—lessons can be gleaned from television talk shows, popular self-help books, therapists, counselors, advisors, and virtually anybody else who feels the need or qualifications to instruct another person on how to "make the most" of life, to "live up to one's potential," to reach self-fulfillment or self-actualization. Self-making is a veritable industry in many modern societies, and people invest a tremendous amount of psychic energy and real cash into their own projects of self-construction.

The modern view of the self tends to emphasize the extent to which the self is complex and multilayered. Even before Sigmund Freud proclaimed the power of the unconscious, 19th-century Europeans were keenly aware of and fascinated by the distinction between the public and private selves. The advent of industrialization in Europe moved men and some women off the family farm to factories—new public spaces where work was to be done. The public experience of modern work came to be separated from the private experience of family life. A person could develop a public self that was very different from the private self. Furthermore, each of the many selves that a person might develop would itself possess significant depth and complexity. Modernity ushered in the idea that there is a great deal about the self that is hidden, buried, or even disguised. The exploration of the deep, inner regions of the self has become an especially appealing psychological adventure in the modern world (Gay, 1984; Taylor, 1989). For many modern people, such an inner voyage promises to reveal some form of personal truth or moral conviction. Modernity teaches us that it is especially important to be "true to one's self."

From the modern perspective, not only does the self possess significant depth and complexity, but the self is also changing constantly over time. Modern men and women routinely use developmental ideas and metaphors to make sense of their lives (Bellah et al., 1985). As the advances of modern medicine have significantly lengthened the expected life span, modern men and women increasingly expect to live a long and full life, growing, changing, and moving through passages and stages on life's journey. Over time, therefore, modern people expect to "make progress," to move ahead, to develop to higher or better stages and levels. Yet amidst the constant change and growth, modern adults also seek to create some kind of coherence in the self. How can a deep and constantly changing self—a self that I work on day in and day out—come together to provide my life with a sense of unity, purpose, and coherence? This is perhaps the most challenging question for the making of the self in modern societies. It is a problem that we will return to in Chapters 11 and 12 of this book when we consider how modern adults work on their selves by formulating life stories in order to create an *identity*.

History

The role of macrocontexts in human behavior usually becomes apparent to us when we notice differences. For example, should we encounter a person from a culture very different from our own, we may begin to think about how our own culture's values and norms have shaped us to be the people we are. When we witness the great inequalities in economic resources that characterize modern societies today, we cannot help but be struck by the social-structural dimension of class and how it is that different people in the same nation grow up under radically different material circumstances. In noticing cultural and social-structural differences in a given society, we may begin to imagine how our own lives and our very personalities might be rather different if we had grown up in a different set of macrocontexts—if I were black instead of white, for example, rich instead of poor, male instead of female, and so on. But there is a different kind of macrocontext that infuses our lives but that we may rarely think about because we are rarely confronted with differences on it. This is the macrocontext of history. Given that everybody reading this book is alive and functioning at the very same historical moment, we are not likely to think about how all of our lives are profoundly shaped by the simple fact that we all live today—here and now at the beginning of the 21st century. Things would be very different, would they not, if this were the year 1901, 1776, or 200 B.C.?

The historical context for human behavior situates our lives in time. As people get older, they tend to have a greater sense of the role of history in the shaping of lives. Your grandparents may have told you stories about the good (or not-so-good) old days when they were children, how the world was very different then, before computers, before you had hundreds of television channels, when the Soviet Union was the great enemy of "the free world," when Americans fought the Japanese in a ferocious war. (My children still ask me what it was like to live during the Civil War.) It is perhaps in our interactions with people from other generations, as well as in our history classes, that we become most cognizant of how life was once very different than it is today, and how it is likely to be very different in the future. The sociologist Karl Mannheim (1928/1952) argued that different generations of people develop along different paths because of their different historical experiences. For Mannheim, a **generation** consists of those people who are born at the same point in historical time and thereby develop a shared understanding of the world, common beliefs and aims, and a shared generational style. Mannheim maintained that social and historical events occurring during a person's late adolescence and young adulthood are especially likely to shape his or her personality for the future.

Abigail Stewart and Joseph Healy (1989) have developed a theory to account for the ways in which history and social events are incorporated into personality. The theory is summarized in Table 4.6. Following Mannheim, Stewart and Healy argue that the influence of history is strongly contingent on a person's age or place in the life course. A major historical event, such as a world war, will have one kind of impact on a 10-year-old child and quite a different impact on a midlife adult. According to Stewart and Healy, historical events occurring during a person's *childhood* are likely to shape his or her fundamental expectations about how the world works. At a very basic level, for example, a child whose family suffers the poverty that comes from a severe economic downturn (e.g., the Great Depression of the late 1920s and early 1930s) may come to assume implicitly that scarcity is the norm in life and that the world is a place where there will never be enough for everybody. Historical events experienced in *late adolescence and early adulthood*, by contrast, may shape life opportunities and choices, especially in the area of occupational identity. One of the outgrowths of the Watergate scandals of the early 1970s, for example, was the rise in prestige of investigative journalism in the United States. The newspaper reporters who exposed the scandals surrounding President Richard Nixon at that time helped to glorify the profession of journalism, which enhanced the appeal of journalism as a vocation for adolescents and young adults like myself. Many college students in my generation were quite taken with the idea of becoming an investigative reporter.

In the *early middle-adult years*, Stewart and Healy argue, historical events are less likely to shape fundamental values and vocational identity since adults in their 30s and early 40s have likely consolidated a viewpoint of the world and their place in it. But events can still have a significant impact on what people actually do—that is, on behavior. The eruption of a major war may dramatically change the lifestyle of a 35-year-old homemaker, who may now seek paid employment because of the labor shortage that has resulted from young men being drafted into military service. In a fundamental sense, she may not be changing her values or her identity, but her daily actions are now very different than they were before the war. Finally, events occurring during a person's *later years* (midlife and beyond) may offer new opportunities and stimulate revisions in a person's identity. Adults whose children have now grown up and established their own families may feel freed up to explore new possibilities in lifestyle, occupation, and even personal ideology. Major historical events or social movements may, therefore, feed into this new readiness for change. The women's movement of the 1960s and 1970s afforded new opportunities for women across the life course (Duncan & Agronick, 1995). For mature women who had already brought

TABLE 4.6	*Links Between Individual Development and Social/Historical Events*
AGE WHEN EVENT IS EXPERIENCED	**FOCUS OF IMPACT OF EVENT**
Childhood and early adolescence	Fundamental values and expectations (e.g., family values, assumptive frameworks)
Late adolescence/early adulthood	Opportunities and life choices; identity (e.g., vocational identity)
Early middle-adulthood	Behavior (e.g., labor force participation)
Midlife and later	New opportunities and choices; revision of identity

Source: Adapted from Stewart and Healy (1989), p. 32, and from Duncan and Agronick (1995), p. 559.

FEATURE 4.C

History and Character Types: Erich Fromm's Theory

No personality theorist has taken more seriously the idea that the person is embedded in culture and history than has Erich Fromm. In Fromm's theory of **dialectical humanism,** the person's behavior is the complex and overdetermined product of internal needs manifesting themselves within the external social arrangements prescribed by a society at a particular moment in history. In Fromm's own life, the societal context that so influenced his view of persons was a heady European intelligentsia immersed in the writings of Freud and Marx. The decisive historical moment was World War I.

Fromm was born in Frankfurt, Germany, in 1900. A Jew raised among Christians, the 12-year-old Fromm was devastated by the suicide of an attractive young woman, an artist, who had been a close friend of the family (Fromm, 1962). This pivotal event from Fromm's childhood occurred shortly before the outbreak of World War I, during which the teenaged boy's abhorrence of and curiosity about human destructiveness and death grew to become a lifelong obsession. During the war, he asked himself a question that haunted many Europeans of his day: "How is it possible that millions of men continue to stay in the trenches, to kill innocent men of other nations, and to be killed and thus to cause the deepest pain to parents, wives, and friends?" (Fromm, 1962, p. 8). Fromm ultimately committed himself to exploring the question. The answers he formulated were strongly shaped by his reading of Freud and Marx. From Freud, Fromm learned that human beings are not conscious of the most significant determinants of their behavior. From Marx, he adopted the conviction that humans are not free and that they cannot be free as long as they accept uncritically external control exerted by social custom and institutions.

In Fromm's view, men and women living in contemporary Western societies are overwhelmed by *too much freedom* and thus seek to escape freedom by submitting and conforming to authority or through wanton destructiveness (Fromm, 1941). Freedom began to pose serious problems for Westerners, argues Fromm, with the decline of the medieval world, the onset of the Protestant Reformation, and the rise of capitalism. As European society became more economically and religiously diverse in the 16th and 17th centuries, Europeans came to experience what was both an exhilarating and an uncomfortable surfeit of choice and opportunity. Over time, European middle-class society came to place greater emphasis on independence from the once all-powerful Catholic Church, on individual decision making, on personal achievement, and on fashioning one's own identity (Erikson, 1958; Fromm, 1941; McClelland, 1961.). Industrialization, urbanization, and the rise of science and technology endowed Westerners with even greater freedom, but the freedom has bred greater separation from nature and alienation from other human beings.

Expressed against this cultural and historical background of freedom and isolation, six basic human needs motivate the person's behavior (Fromm, 1955, 1973). These are the needs for relatedness, transcendence, rootedness, identity, stimulation, and a frame of orientation. Personal needs find expression within the rules of culture. Through the categories of experience implied by a particular language, through social customs, prohibitions, and conventions, a society shapes how its members construe their life choices, subtly but powerfully molding the expression of needs. The interaction of personal needs and social context ultimately gives rise to specific character types, each of which represents a particular solution to the problem of adapting to social realities against a pervasive existential backdrop of freedom and aloneness. In contemporary capitalist societies, Fromm identifies five basic character types.

The **receptive** type fulfills personal needs by adopting a passive and dependent orientation, committed to the belief that all worthwhile comforts and values may be received from the outside. For the receptive type, the central task of life is to be loved, but not necessarily to love. Such an essentially unproductive individual may be described as submissive, unrealistic, cowardly, wishful, gullible, and sentimental. However, some basically receptive individuals show a more positive side of this character type, revealing an optimistic, idealistic, and accepting approach to life.

The **hoarding** type strives to accumulate possessions, power, and love, and to hold on to all that is accumulated. Objects, people, ideas, and most all of the world exist to be collected and stored away. The hoarding type is unimaginative, stingy, suspicious, obsessional, and possessive, reminiscent of Freud's description of the "anal retentive" personality type. The more positive version of the hoarding type may be practical, careful, reserved, methodical, and loyal.

The **exploitative** type is aggressive and self-centered. This type views the world as filled with objects, people, and ideas to be stolen, grabbed, or snatched away. This essentially Machiavellian and aggressive approach to life encourages a wanton individualism that masks a deep and troubling sense of isolation from humankind. In its less extreme versions, though, the exploitative type can appear self-confident, proud, and even captivating.

The **marketing** type is a peculiar product of modern industrial society. In the marketing orientation, one seeks to market oneself in the manner one might market a commodity to be sold. Such a person carefully manufactures him- or herself to attract "customers." Like a high-priced appliance, the well-marketed adult is very much in demand. The marketing type is described as opportunistic, aimless, tactless, and indifferent. In a more positive light, the marketing type has the potential to appear purposeful, curious, and open to change.

Although they each may show modestly positive characteristics, the receptive, hoarding, exploitative, and marketing types are essentially nonproductive solutions to the problem of finding a viable way to express human needs within contemporary Western societies. They, therefore, stand in marked contrast to the fifth character type: the **productive** type. This type fulfills his or her inner potential to become a creative worker and lover within a well-defined social identity. Such a person transcends superficial social roles to "use his powers and to realize the potentialities inherent in him" (Fromm, 1947, p. 91). The productive person is autonomous, spontaneous, loving, creative, and committed to the social good.

up their children, the women's movement provided them with new modes of expression and new ways to think about who they were.

Historical time is perhaps the most complex and subtle macrocontext for human behavior. It is clear that history has an impact on people's lives. But the impact depends, in part, on the particular timing of a life, as Stewart and Healy's theory shows. Therefore, historical time (history) and personal time (biography) interact in very complex ways (Elder, 1995; Mills, 1959). The impact of history, furthermore, is filtered through the macrocontexts of race, class, gender, and culture. For example, many African Americans who lived through the Great Depression of the late 1920s and 1930s report that the economic hardships they experienced were not much worse than what they were used to all along (Angelou, 1970). The economic downturn hit middle- and upper-class whites especially hard because they had much more to lose and were not used to the economic privations that most blacks had known from birth onward. To take another example, wars have traditionally affected men and women in very different ways: Men traditionally fight the wars; women work to keep the home front strong. Moreover, different cultural groups articulate different interpretations of the same historical events. The antiwar protests that rocked American college campuses in the late 1960s shaped the consciousness of many politically liberal and radical young people. The same movement, however, also galvanized politically conservative forces and set the stage for a shift toward political conservatism in the United States in the 1980s and 1990s.

Beyond all of these complications, it is also true that the impact of any historical event or movement is in large part mediated by a person's own, idiosyncratic interpretation of that event. For example, Duncan and Agronick (1995) found that the women's movement of the 1960s and early 1970s certainly had an impact on the lives of many women who were college-aged at the time. But the impact depended on just how "meaningful" a woman considered this historical movement to be. Those women who saw the women's movement to be especially meaningful and important for their own lives ultimately attained higher education levels, work status, and income levels; were employed in upwardly mobile careers by midlife; and reported significant increases in self-confidence and assertiveness in the years following college. For those women in the same generation who did *not* see the women's movement as especially meaningful, however, these trends did not occur.

We will return to the issue of historical time and the timing of lives in Chapter 7 when we consider the extent to which personality dispositions are either stable or changing over the human life course. Our take-home message at this point is that historical time is an especially complex and encompassing macrocontext for human behavior. Human lives are time-structured and historically contingent. Like social class, gender, race, and culture, historical time situates a human life within a set of complex and overlapping environments. The social ecology of human behavior incorporates those many contexts within which we learn to be who we are. From the microcontexts of social situations to the macrocontexts of culture and history, personality is always situated in context. You cannot take the person out of that context; you cannot talk meaningfully about "personality" without examining the context in which personality is embedded. Human individuality is a thoroughly contextualized phenomenon. Only when we understand the worlds in which we live, therefore, can we fully appreciate the ways in which each of us is a singular human being.

SUMMARY

1. B. F. Skinner's behaviorist novel, *Walden Two*, turns our attention to the environmental contexts of persons' lives and the roles of social learning and culture in the formation of personality. A dominant movement in American psychology in the first half of the 20th century, behaviorism focused on how environments shape the observable behavior of organisms. Although behaviorism's presence has faded considerably in recent decades, its fundamental emphases have lived on in social-learning theories of personality and in the widespread recognition that individual lives must be understood in terms of the environmental contexts within which they are situated.

2. According to the behaviorist view, behavior is learned in the environment. Two fundamental forms of learning are classical and instrumental (operant) conditioning. In classical conditioning, an organism forms associations between different stimuli that are contiguous in time. In instrumental conditioning, learning occurs through rewards and punishments, as behavior is shaped by its consequences. From an operant standpoint, personality characteristics are shaped primarily by reward-and-punishment learning that occurs in particular social situations over time. The determinants of any particular behavior, therefore, can be found both in the current situation and in similar situations in the past in which the person has learned similar responses.

3. Behaviorism spawned a number of different social-learning theories that have been and continue to be influential in the field of personality psychology. Social-learning theories share behaviorism's emphasis on observables, the environment, and learning, but they tend to adopt broader and more eclectic viewpoints that incorporate the cognitive dimensions of human functioning. Miller and Dollard formulated an early social-learning theory that sought to bring together the behaviorist views of Clark Hull with some of the psychoanalytic concepts found in Freud's writings. According to Miller and Dollard, significant human behavior is learned in a particular social, cultural, and historical context. Learning is motivated by biological drives and guided by environmental cues. Learning results in behavioral responses that work to reduce drive levels, resulting in reinforcement. Rotter's value-expectancy theory of social learning sought to predict what a person will do when confronted with choices for goal-directed behavior in a particular situation. Mischel's social-learning theory identified five cognitive social-learning person variables that need to be considered when attempting to predict what a person will do in a given situation: competencies, encoding strategies, expectancies, subjective values, and self-regulatory systems and plans.

4. Especially influential has been Albert Bandura's social-learning theory. Bandura emphasizes the roles of observational learning, self-efficacy, and reciprocal determinism in human behavior. While reinforcement and need satisfaction may be instrumental in behavioral performance, Bandura shows that learning does not necessarily require reinforcement and may proceed instead through simple observation and imitation. As people observe and learn new responses over time, and as they obtain experience in the performance of those responses, they develop beliefs about their abilities to carry out particular behaviors in particular situations, producing characteristic levels of self-efficacy. The development of self-efficacy is a key mechanism whereby people are able to exercise control over threatening events in the environment.

5. Social learning is a pervasive phenomenon in human life. Psychologists have documented the power of social learning in many different areas of human functioning. An especially provocative area in this regard is the study of aggression. Research documents the powerful role of observation in the formation and performance of aggressive responses. One especially important line of studies suggests that excessive viewing of television violence increases the likelihood of aggressive behavior in the viewer, which in turn increases the viewing of television violence, and so on.

6. People learn and perform behaviors within a social ecology. The social ecology consists of the many different environmental contexts that influence a person's behavior and shape his or her life. The social ecology ranges from the microcontexts of the immediate social situation, to larger contexts of family, neighborhood, and community. At the largest, most distal, and encompassing levels are the macrocontexts of social class, gender, race, culture, and history. At the level of microcontext, psychologists have sought to define the different kinds of situations that people encounter in daily life. Research suggests that situations are best characterized in terms of their subjective psychological affordances, or what people perceive as the opportunities for behavior and expression in a particular situation. People form situational prototypes or scripts for certain sorts of stock situations, such as prototypes for "party," "classroom," and "sporting event." The template-matching perspective on microcontexts classifies situations in terms of the internal personality characteristics of a hypothetical person deemed to fit the situation in a particular way. Situations appear to be as much in the minds and eyes of the person as they are in the objective environment in which the person's behavior occurs.

7. Social structure defines an important macrocontext for human behavior. Research documents significant relations between social class variables on the one hand and aspects of personality and social life on the other. Individuals in lower socioeconomic strata report lower job satisfaction, greater concerns for security and stability, and more fatalistic and pessimistic views of human nature, compared with individuals in the middle and upper classes. Professional, high-status occupations place significant cognitive demands on workers and encourage them to take initiative and cultivate self-direction at work. By contrast, lower-status employees find fewer cognitive challenges and opportunities for initiative in their work and are strongly urged to follow the demands of supervisors. Research has shown that in both work and family life, higher social class is associated with greater self-direction and internal control while lower social class is associated with an emphasis on obedience to authority and conformity.

8. Like social class, gender constitutes a powerful macrocontext, in part because it tends to differentiate individuals on the basis of social power and resources. In many if not most societies, men control more public resources, make more decisions about the society as a whole, and enjoy more freedom and autonomy than do women. Gender role stereotypes reinforce this power differential, as men are expected to be dominant and assertive while women are expected to be caring and nurturant. Socialization into gender roles may account for most of the sex differences that have been observed in human social behavior. Among the most well-established findings are that men tend to be more aggressive than women, to be somewhat more directive in leadership and group behavior, and to be more instrumental in public acts of helping; by contrast, women report higher levels of empathy and interpersonal intimacy, show better skills in encoding and decoding nonverbal interpersonal behavior, and express higher levels of friendliness and care in leadership and group roles. On the most general level, gender-congruent behaviors tend to fall along the dimensions of agency (masculine) and communion (feminine). Whatever the source of these differences between men and women, it is quite clear that social environments and social life for human beings are highly gendered.

9. The most encompassing and far-reaching context for human behavior is culture. Among other things, culture is a system of rules and norms that bind people together in a given society or group, providing a toolkit of habits, skills, styles, perspectives, roles, and values out of which the person can construct a life. Culture infuses human lives with meanings. Two major dimensions upon which different cultures can be organized are individualism and collectivism. Individualist cultures give priority to personal goals, individual attitudes and opinions, exchange relationships, and the efficacy of the autonomous and independent self. By contrast, collectivist cultures give priority to the goals and norms of the in-group or community, communal relationships, and the development of an interdependent construal of the self. While some societies tend to exhibit individualist cultures (e.g., North America) and others exhibit collectivist cultures (e.g., Asia), differences in individualism/collectivism are a matter of relative degree, with all societies having concepts and ideas that pertain to both individual agency and collective harmony. A related cultural concept is modernity, which refers to the economic, political, and cultural systems established by the advent of the Industrial Revolution and the proliferation of democracy and capitalism in the 19th and 20th centuries. Modern cultures tend to be individualist (though there are exceptions), and they tend to articulate a view of the self as a complex and evolving project that a person develops, expands, improves, and generally "works on" over time.

10. History situates lives in time. People from different generations have different historical experiences, which influence the development of personality. One theory links individual development with historical events by proposing that the timing of an event in terms of a person's life course partly determines the way in which that event will influence the person. Historical events (such as wars, economic downturns, social movements, and so on) experienced when a person is a child help to shape the person's basic values and assumptions about how the world works. Events that occur in late adolescence and young adulthood, by contrast, may impact one's developing vocational identity as well as important life choices. Events that occur in early- to mid-adulthood may not have a profound influence on values and identity but are still likely to affect what a person does—that is, behavior. Finally, historical events experienced at midlife and after hold the potential to offer new opportunities for identity change and the revision of one's sense of self. The impact of any historical event on a person's life is largely determined by how that person actively makes sense of the event.

Sketching the Outline: Basic Traits and the Prediction of Behavior

A human life must be understood in the twin contexts of human nature and culture. Now that we have examined these contexts and seen how complexly determined and situated any given life is likely to be, we are ready to begin our exploration of particular lives. The goal of personality psychology is to provide a full account of human individuality. We begin that account by examining the first level or domain of personality description—dispositional traits. A trait account begins to sketch the outlines of human individuality. Traits give us a sense of the general and relatively stable trends in behavior, thought, and feeling that we can expect to see in any given life. Individual differences in personality traits provide a dispositional signature for a life and begin to make clear how one person is different from and similar to other persons with respect to certain common dimensions. In Chapter 5, we explore the history of the trait concept, its various definitions, and the many issues that must be addressed in the measurement of traits. Personality psychologists have given considerable thought to the issue of the extent to which individual differences in traits versus differences in situations account for the lion's share of variance in behavior. Chapter 5 introduces this perennial controversy and lays out various responses to it. In Chapter 6 we examine the particular traits that personality psychologists have studied in most detail. There are likely to be hundreds of traits that could be invoked to account for human individuality, but in recent years many personality psychologists have come to believe that most of those traits can be found in one or more of five different groups or clusters. The names we will use for the "Big Five" trait clusters are extraversion–introversion (E), neuroticism (N), openness to experience (O), conscientiousness (C), and agreeableness (A). We will examine each of these trait domains and consider research on such topics as the impact of traits on social behavior, traits and psychological well-being, the role of personality in work and love, and possible psychophysiological underpinnings of traits. Chapter 7 adds the dimension of time to our understanding of traits. To what extent are individual differences in traits stable over the human life span? To what extent do people's traits change? And where do traits themselves come from? We will examine recent research and current thinking on genetic and environmental influences on traits and the possible beginnings of traits in infant temperament. By the end of Chapter 7, we will see that traits do a good job of sketching an outline for individuality. But we will also begin to appreciate that we need more than traits if we are to arrive at a full and rich accounting of the individual person's life.

Personality Traits: Basic Concepts and Issues

5

Trait talk. We do it all the time. Let me tell you about my wife's family. My brother-in-law, Dwight, is impulsive and very friendly. He strikes up conversations with strangers in the grocery line. His twin sister, Sara, is more serious, more deliberate, very conscientious. Her husband, Jack, is also very conscientious; more than most adults I know, the two of them are very concerned about doing the right things with their lives, about making a positive contribution to society. But Jack is also very competitive, as, I must confess, am I. He wins in anything that involves hand-eye coordination, but I can run faster. My wife's oldest brother, Tom, is very analytical and has a sharp sense of humor. My wife's oldest sister, Barb, is extremely well organized, is very sensitive and caring, and rarely judges others harshly. Her husband, Bill, is the great optimist in the family. He can put a positive spin on anything. When my kids complain about how rough life is for them, I tell them to be like Uncle Bill. Lois is the youngest sister. She has many of the traits of her siblings and relatives, but she seems to have them all in moderation. She is harder for me to characterize in a word or two. My wife, well, she is perfect. And she is the only one who will still be speaking to me after reading this paragraph.

Actually, I think they will all still speak to me. They probably won't be angry with my trait talk because (1) I have focused on mainly positive-to-neutral traits (I haven't said anything about who is neurotic, domineering, nerdy, or shallow) and (2) they all know, as do you, that people talk this way about other people, and about themselves, all the time, and that it is not necessarily a bad thing to do. They know, as do you, that the currency of everyday trait talk is generalizations. Personality generalizations may be true or useful in a relative sense, but they do not apply to every instance of a person's behavior. Therefore, you would not be surprised if I told you that while Bill is the supreme optimist, he does occasionally fall into a dark mood. You would not discount my trait portrayal if I told you that Barb's desk at work is messy sometimes, even though she is very well organized, or that I rarely compete with my wife, even though I am very competitive. You and I both know that trait attributions are relative, approximate, and very general. Imagine if they weren't! Imagine if people displayed their characteristic trait profiles every moment of every day. Imagine if Dwight talked to *everybody* in the grocery line—*every* time. Imagine if the most conscientious man you ever knew was perfectly dutiful, hard working, and righteous in every situation he ever encountered—at home, at work, on vacation, when talking with his mother, when arguing with his wife, when choosing a dessert at a restaurant, when surfing the Internet, in bed, at 5:00 P.M. on January 4, 1997, at 5:10 P.M. that same day, 20 years before that. Imagine how predictable people would be, how boring life would be.

It is difficult for you and me to imagine life like that because we know that that is not how people are. People are not robots who do the same thing over and over again. Nobody, no matter how strong a given trait, is perfectly consistent; no single trait can characterize any person; life offers too many different situations for people to do the same thing in each one. This is all so obvious that I am almost embarrassed to bring it to your attention at the outset of this chapter. But I feel compelled to do so in order to make clear that just because trait talk is relatively imprecise and general, there is no getting around it in everyday discourse. And there is no getting around it in personality psychology. Just as we find ourselves using trait attributions in conversations about people every day (knowing, as we do, that these attributions are not even close to perfect in their predictive power and in their truth value), so, too, do personality psychologists invoke traits to account for human individuality. In everyday talk and in the scientific study of human individuality, we use general descriptors to characterize individual differences among people. We say that somebody is relatively friendly, soft-spoken, spiteful, fastidious, thoughtful, slovenly, arrogant, humble, dominant, considerate, or honest. And so on. Trait talk is irresistible. Despite its important limitations, trait talk is an extraordinarily useful and natural way to account for human individuality.

Now, it is important to note at the outset of this chapter that trait talk, like many things, can be used for good or ill. Characterizing somebody in terms of a few well-chosen and carefully considered trait adjectives can provide a compact and efficient portrayal of that person in general terms, a portrayal that may be useful for describing the person to others, for remembering what the person is generally like, and for making better-than-chance predictions about how that person might behave in the future and what to expect from that person when you meet again. But trait talk is also fraught with dangers. Traits can become "labels" or "stereotypes" that objectify people—that is, labels that turn people into objects in the minds of others. A trait description can oversimplify and gloss over the many important details of a personality, to the detriment of that person being described. Trait talk can be the lazy way out—used by people who want to size up others quickly but have little interest or motivation to get to know a person better. Most odious of all is the use of trait attributions in the service of oppression and prejudice. Stereotyping of strangers and out-groups is one of those pervasive human tendencies that has contributed as much as any other to human suffering. One group may consider members of another group to be especially stupid, lazy, arrogant, sinful, barbaric, rapacious, deceitful, or virtually any negative trait you can name. In its mildest forms, we hear trait talk of this sort in ethnic jokes and other common forms of group stereotyping. But this sort of talk may be no joking matter. Trait talk that stereotypes out-groups and strangers can be used to fuel hatred and justify discrimination, warfare, slavery, and even genocide.

In this chapter and the two that follow, we will learn about how personality psychologists have sought to explore and refine trait talk in the service of behavioral science and human understanding. Over the past 60 years, personality psychologists have learned a great deal about personality traits. They have developed important conceptualizations of trait ideas. They have built and validated good measures of individual differences in traits. They have linked traits to trends in behavior and have examined the interactions of traits and situational variables in the prediction of behavior. They have studied the stability and change in personality traits over the life course. They have studied the extent to which traits are products of genetic differences among people and products of environmental effects. They have begun to explore the psychophysiology of traits. And they have considered in detail the many controversies surrounding trait talk—both as a form of everyday conversation and a manner of scientific discourse.

Just as trait talk is an unavoidable aspect of everyday conversation, so are traits indispensable units for understanding personality (A. Buss, 1989; Johnson, 1997). It is virtually impossible to account for human individuality without resorting to traits in some way or another. As I suggested in Chapter 1, traits provide an initial outline or sketch of a person's individuality. Good and accurate trait talk, of the sort developed by personality psychologists, provides a kind of dispositional signature for a person. From a good and accurate trait description, we get a sense of which general characteristics or dispositions differentiate that person from others. Trait talk, however, can take us only so far. Eventually, we will want to know things about a person that go beyond general characteristics. We will eventually want to fill in details that cannot be captured in trait talk. These other forms of discourse about human individuality will be the topic of Chapters 8–12 in this book. For now, though, we need to see just how far we can go with traits. It turns out to be pretty far indeed.

THE IDEA OF TRAIT

What Is a Trait?

The concept of a personality trait is rooted in common sense and everyday observation. As we watch, and try to make sense of, the behavior of other people, we notice consistencies within a given person and differences between different persons. For example, we notice that Rachel smiles at people and talks with them in a friendly manner in many different situations—in class, at the gym, eating lunch, studying in the library. Maria, on the other hand, seems rarely to smile or exchange friendly words with others. Whereas Rachel appears consistently warm and outgoing, Maria seems cool and detached. Of course, Rachel has her cool moments, and Maria may really warm up to people in certain situations, but Rachel seems *generally* friendlier than Maria.

Personality psychologists consider a number of aspects of personality traits such as "friendliness." First, they generally conceive of traits as *internal* dispositions that are relatively *stable* over time and across situations. If we are to conclude that my sister-in-law Sara has a strong trait of conscientiousness, we must find evidence that she is consistently conscientious in a variety of situations (such as in her work for the organization Habitat for Humanity, in her volunteer activities, and in her family life) and over time (such as an adolescent, a young adult, and at midlife).

Second, traits are typically conceived in *bipolar* terms. Friendliness can be understood as a continuum ranging from one extreme of "high friendliness" to the other extreme of "high unfriendliness" (synonymous with "low friendliness"). Traits, therefore, are often couched in the language of opposites: friendliness *versus* unfriendliness, extraversion *versus* introversion, dominance *versus* submissiveness. People are seen as situated along any particular trait continuum in a relatively normal distribution, with many people residing toward the middle of the continuum (such as "moderately friendly" or "moderately unfriendly") and fewer lying at the extremes.

Third, different traits are generally seen as *additive* and *independent.* My sister-in-law Barb is very high in agreeableness, is highly organized, is relatively nonjudgmental, and is low on a trait of tendency toward risk taking. The four traits thus combine as four independent "ingredients" in Barb's personality. Mix them together in the proper amounts and you have a recipe for predicting consistency in her behavior and for describing how she is different from other people who have different recipes, that is, different trait profiles.

Finally, personality traits usually refer to *broad* individual differences in *socioemotional* functioning. Writes Conley (1985a), "personality traits constitute very generalized behavior patterns in response to emotional tendencies" (p. 94). Personality traits, therefore, may be distinguished from other variables that appear to be less socioemotional and more cognitive in nature, such as values, attitudes, worldviews, and schemas (Conley, 1985a; McClelland, 1951). Indeed, the distinction between socioemotional personality traits on the one hand and cognitive variables on the other goes back at least as far as the philosopher Immanuel Kant (1724–1804), who distinguished between "temperament" (traits) and "character" (schemas) (Conley, 1985a). In a similar vein, concepts that fall directly under the umbrella of "intelligence" are not usually considered to be part of personality per se, though not all personality psychologists agree with that distinction (e.g., Revelle, 1995). For the purposes of this chapter and this book, we will consider the general trait of intelligence to be outside the personality domain, sticking with the common view that personality traits are concerned mainly with socioemotional functioning.

Overall, then, personality traits refer to individual differences among people in characteristic thoughts, feelings, and behaviors (McCrae & Costa, 1995). Psychologists use trait concepts to account for consistencies in behavior from one situation to the next—for example, Rachel is consistently friendly from one situation to the next (though, of course, not always friendly), and Maria is consistently less friendly. Traits are typically viewed to reside within the person in some sense, as relatively general, global, and stable dispositions. These dispositions are typically conceived in bipolar terms, suggesting that people are more-or-less normally distributed on any given linear trait continuum from one extreme end to the other. Most people, therefore, fall within the middle range of any given trait. People can be compared and contrasted with respect to their traits. Traits, therefore, are almost always viewed as comparative dimensions, and one's position on a trait continuum is always relative to the positions of others. From the standpoint of traits, each person may be characterized by his or her standing on a series of relatively independent dimensions, which add up to a trait profile. Personality traits, in contrast to traits of intelligence, typically refer to consistencies in thought, feeling, and behavior associated with social interaction and the socioemotional aspects of life.

The characterization of personality traits that I have provided for you is probably consistent with the general impressions you had about the term *(personality trait)* before you read this chapter, even if you have never given the topic much thought. It is perhaps surprising to learn, therefore, that psychologists have fought many long and nasty intellectual battles about just what the concept of trait means and just how useful it might be. At least four different positions have been staked out over the years. (These positions are summarized in Table 5.1.) The first position is that traits literally exist in the central nervous system as what Gordon Allport (1961) called "neuropsychic structures" (p. 347). These hypothesized patternings of psychophysiology—say, particular brain circuitry or neurotransmitter pathways—exert a causal influence on behavior, accounting for consistencies over time and across situations. The second position keeps its options open when it comes to psychophysiological substrata but maintains, nonetheless, that traits exist as dispositions that exert a significant impact on behavior. Therefore, both of these positions view traits as causal mechanisms in human functioning. Traits—be they neuropsychic structures or behavioral dispositions—are instrumental in causing behavior to occur and, therefore, in accounting for consistency in behavior across situations and over time.

By contrast, the third and fourth positions argue that traits do not really cause behavior but exist instead as convenient categories for describing the behaviors that

	TABLE 5.1	*Four Positions on the Nature of Traits*	

TRAITS ARE	DESCRIPTION	THEORISTS
Neurophysiological substrates	Traits are biological patternings in the central nervous system that cause behavior to occur and account for the consistencies in socioemotional functioning from one situation to the next and over time.	Allport (1937) Eysenck (1967) Gray (1982) Cloninger (1987) Zuckerman (1991)
Behavioral dispositions	Traits are tendencies to act, think, or feel in consistent ways that interact with external influences, such as cultural norms and situational variables, to influence a person's functioning. Trait attributions can be used both to describe behavior summaries and to suggest causal or generative mechanisms for behavior.	Cattell (1957) Wiggins (1973) Goldberg (1981) Hogan (1986) McCrae & Costa (1990)
Act frequencies	Traits are descriptive summary categories for behavioral acts. Acts that have the same functional properties may be grouped together into families, with some acts being more prototypical or representative of the general family features than others.	Buss & Craik (1983)
Linguistic categories	Traits are convenient fictions devised by people to categorize and make sense of the diversity of human behavior and experience. Traits do not exist outside the mind of the observer, and therefore they can have no causal influence. Through social interaction and discourse, people construct meanings for trait terms.	Mischel (1968) Shweder (1975) Hampson (1988) Harre & Gillett (1994)

people show. The third position was staked out by Buss and Craik (1983, 1984) in their **act-frequency** approach to personality. According to this view, traits are merely language categories for the organization of discrete behavioral acts. As such, traits do not influence behavior per se. Rather, traits *are the behaviors*. The trait of extraversion, for example, consists of the acts that make it up—such acts as "I danced in front of a crowd" and "I entered a conversation with a group I didn't know." Acts may be grouped together into trait families, with some acts more prototypical or representative of a given category than others.

Finally, a fourth position has it that traits do not exist in any objective sense, even in the sense of act categories. Instead, traits are merely convenient fictions that people (and personality psychologists) invent in their efforts to understand social life (Shweder, 1975). You and I use trait terms like "friendly" and "conscientious" to simplify and organize reality, but these terms are just words. They have no meaning beyond our shared social construction. Therefore, it makes no sense, from this fourth position, to explain behavior in terms of traits. To say, for example, that Rachel smiles a lot because she is a relatively friendly person is akin to saying that Rachel is friendly because she is friendly. The label explains nothing. Furthermore, the causes of Rachel's smiling are not likely to be found within the person but rather in the environment in which the person resides. Psychologists who dismiss traits as convenient fictions usually look to the environmental situation for the causes of behavioral consistencies (e.g., Mischel, 1968).

Strong arguments can be made for all four positions on traits. Each position highlights an important aspect of the idea of trait. The first position suggests that traits have a biological reality; the second points to the dispositional nature of traits; the third suggests that traits connect to functionally similar behaviors; and the fourth points out that trait labels are useful in everyday social cognition. At the same time, the four positions contradict one another in many ways. The contradiction is sharpest between the first and fourth positions: Logic tells us that traits cannot be neuropsychic structures that cause the behavior of actors (first position) if, at the same time, they are merely convenient fictions in the minds of observers (fourth position). We cannot resolve the inconsistencies among the different views. As we will see later in this chapter, different understandings of what traits are or should be have been at the heart of important controversies in the field of personality psychology.

Nonetheless, when it comes to the nature of traits, many personality psychologists today seem to have adopted a fuzzy but reasonable compromise view that is probably closest to the second position I have outlined above. Most contemporary personality psychologists seem to view traits as dispositions (second position) that have some causal influence on behaviors, though the influences are complex and in interaction with situational factors. They tend to see traits as more than mere descriptive summaries of act categories, but they acknowledge that traits line up with certain predictable behavioral acts (third position). Further, personality psychologists are generally open to the possibility that dispositional traits may have neurophysiological concomitants (first position), but they are also cognizant of the fact that dispositions are language categories with socially determined meanings (consistent with the fourth position). The meaning of a trait is partially determined by its cultural context. Friendliness, therefore, may express itself somewhat differently and be understood somewhat differently from one culture to another. Different cultures may have different rules or conventions for being friendly. A certain kind of smile or a certain way of touching another might be considered friendly behavior in one cultural setting and rude or boorish in another.

A History of Traits

Characterizations of personality traits can be found even in ancient texts (Winter, 1996). In the book of Genesis, Rebekah gives birth to twins whose contrasting natures seem apparent even as they struggle in the womb. Esau, the "hairy" one, grows to be an active and adventurous man who is skilled at the hunt. His brother Jacob is "smooth" in appearance, and he prefers the quiet domestic life, spending more time in the tents. His mother's favorite, Jacob eventually proves more cunning than Esau as he swindles away his brother's birthright and tricks his father, Isaac, into giving him a blessing that Isaac meant to confer upon Esau. In the ancient story, the traits of guile and shrewdness win out over brute strength.

In the fourth century B.C., Theophrastus generated one of the first trait taxonomies in Western civilization. A botanist by trade and a pupil of Aristotle, Theophrastus devised a series of semihumorous character sketches depicting different types of people that one might encounter in Athenian social life. Each sketch personifies a trait (Anderson, 1970), producing a recognizable but exaggerated caricature. In each sketch, the hypothetical character possesses one and only one trait in his life, influencing virtually everything he does. Here is how Theophrastus described a type of person that is still with us today, "The Penurious Man":

> Penuriousness is economy carried beyond all measure. A Penurious Man is one who goes to a debtor to ask for his half-obol of interest before the end of the month. At a dinner where expenses are shared, he counts the number of cups each person drinks, and he makes a smaller libation to Artemis than anyone. When his servant breaks a pot or a plate, he deducts the value from his food. If his wife drops a copper, he moves furniture, beds, chests and hunts in the curtains. If he has something to sell he puts such a price on it that the buyer has no profit. He forbids anyone to pick a fig in his garden, to walk on his land, to pick up an olive or a date. Every day he goes to see that the boundary marks of his property have not been moved. . . . He forbids his wife to lend anything—neither salt nor lamp-wick nor cinnamon nor marjoram nor meal nor garlands nor cakes for sacrifices. "All these trifles," he says, "mount up in a year." (from Allport, 1961, p. 43)

The most famous ancient system for personality traits is attributed to the Greek physician Galen (A.D. 130–200). Galen developed the theory of the four humors, a "humor" being a bodily fluid associated with a particular behavioral trait. The four key bodily fluids were blood, black bile, yellow bile, and phlegm. Blood was associated with the *sanguine* personality. A person whose blood was the dominant bodily humor was bold, confident, and robust in temperament. Black bile connected to the *melancholic* type. Too much black bile in the system produced a depressed and anxious person, pessimistic and brooding. Yellow bile corresponded to the *choleric* person, who was restless, irritable, and wont to explode in anger. Finally, the *phlegmatic* person, unfortunate enough to be housed in a body with too much phlegm, was aloof, apathetic, cold, and sluggish, and probably no more fun to be around than the melancholic type. Although the sanguine trait seems the best, Galen maintained that a balanced and ideal temperament resulted from a harmonious mixture of the four humors. The optimal mix of traits produced a person who

> in his soul . . . is in the middle of boldness and timidity, of negligence and impertinence, of compassion and envy. He is cheerful, affectionate, charitable, and prudent. (Stelmack & Stalikas, 1991, p. 259)

By the time of the Middle Ages, scholars dismissed the idea that bodily fluids were directly implicated in personality traits. But the behavioral descriptions associated with the four humors lived on and have survived even to today. In the 18th century, Immanuel Kant recast the four temperament types along the dimensions of activity and feelings: cholerics had strong activity and phlegmatics weak activity; sanguines had strong feelings and melancholics weak feelings. In the late 19th century, Wilhelm Wundt argued that the four temperaments sprang from emotional strength and emotional variability. And in the mid-20th century, Hans Eysenck recast the four types along the lines of two superordinate traits: extraversion and neuroticism, as we will shortly see. Eysenck also argued for the biological bases of these traits, though he looked to brain structures and functioning, rather than bodily humors, to find the deep origins of individual differences in dispositional traits.

The ancient belief that bodily forms and differences are associated with personality traits was most famously revived by Ernst Kretschmer (1921) and William Sheldon (1940) who developed a theory of *constitutional psychology*. Few social scientists ascribe to constitutional psychology today (many of its assumptions have been discredited), but in the early part of the 20th century Kretschmer and Sheldon attracted considerable interest. The body's constitution was associated with particular personality characteristics, Kretschmer and Sheldon argued. Sheldon conducted many studies in which he correlated men's body types, rated from photos of nude men, with personality ratings of these men made by observers who studied the men's behavior. His findings clustered into three body types and three corresponding trait profiles. The person whose body is round and soft, with an overdevelopment of fat and underdevelopment of muscle and bone, is an *endomorph*. According to Sheldon, endomorphs tend to be easygoing, affable, very desiring of social approval, and oriented toward relaxation and comfort. The person whose body is thin and bony, with an underdevelopment of fat and muscle, is an *ectomorph*. The ectomorph body type is associated with the traits of restraint, privacy, introversion, and self-consciousness. Finally, the *mesomorph* is relatively muscular, exhibiting a physique that is neither round nor skinny and suggestive of physical vigor and stamina. Personality descriptors that correspond to mesomorphy are aggressive, dominant, adventurous, courageous, and sometimes callous toward the feelings of others. Note that each of these body types and corresponding trait profiles refers solely to men. Constitutional psychology never focused much attention on women (Hall & Lindzey, 1957).

The first scientific studies of traits were conducted in the late 19th century. Francis Galton (1884) was one of the first scientifically minded psychologists to focus empirical attention on individual differences. Galton also proposed that important individual differences in personality could be gleaned from language. All languages are full of adjectives for describing differences among people, Galton reasoned, and an examination of these words might provide clues to the nature of traits. Researchers began to collect data on personality traits based on people's ratings of their own characteristics (self-ratings) and ratings made by observers (peer ratings). Advances in statistics, including the invention of the correlation coefficient and the development of factor analysis, paved the way for quantitative studies of personality traits in large groups of people. By the time World War II began, the stage was set for the development of a number of modern trait theories, each articulating a particular research agenda.

Gordon Allport   In his groundbreaking book, *Personality: A Psychological Interpretation*, Gordon Allport (1937) both established personality psychology as a legitimate intellectual discipline (as I described in Chapter 1) and introduced one of the first modern trait theories. "In everyday life, no one, not even a psychologist, doubts that underlying the conduct of a mature person there are characteristic dispositions or traits," Allport (1937, p. 339) proclaimed. Traits account for the consistency and coherence of human behavior, and as such traits are the major structural units of personality. Allport defined a trait as "a neuropsychic structure having the capacity to render many stimuli functionally equivalent and to initiate and guide equivalent (meaningfully consistent) forms of adaptive and expressive behavior" (Allport, 1961, p. 347). You should note two important things about this definition. First, Allport insisted that trait labels were more than mere semantic conveniences. Traits really exist—they exist as unobservable neuropsychic structures. As real physiological entities, traits are among the more important causal factors in human behavior. We, therefore, may infer the existence of traits from observing behavior. Second, by rendering different stimuli "functionally equivalent," traits account for consistency in human behavior. Behavior is more-or-less lawful and predictable because of the action of traits. The existence of a particular trait in a person's life may be ascertained from at least three kinds of evidence: frequency, range of situations, and intensity. A particularly strong trait of "stubbornness," for instance, might be revealed in the person who is frequently stubborn over time and in many situations and who, when behaving stubbornly, does so with prodigious intensity.

Allport was especially interested in characterizing persons' traits such that the individual's uniqueness could come through. To this end, he distinguished between two senses of the term *trait*. The more typical sense, and the one I have employed in this chapter, is what Allport called a **common trait.** Common traits are dimensions of human functioning upon which many different people are likely to differ. Therefore, we can compare many different people on such common traits as friendliness and conscientiousness. A second sense of trait, however, comes across in Allport's conceptualization of the **personal disposition.** A personal disposition is a trait that is especially characteristic of a given individual and is, therefore, instrumental for depicting that individual person's uniqueness. The distinction is a little confusing because the same trait—say, friendliness—can be viewed either as a common trait or as a personal disposition, depending on the point of reference. If the point of reference is a research study comparing many different people with one another (what Allport called a nomothetic inquiry; see Chapter 1), then the researcher can compare and contrast different people's corresponding scores on a scale measuring the common trait of friendliness. But in the intensive study of a single individual (Allport's idiographic approach; see Chapter 1), the trait of friendliness—or any trait, for that matter—might be especially important or salient for characterizing that particular person's characteristic approach to the world. In such a case, the trait may be viewed as a personal disposition for that person—one of a handful of traits that must be invoked when considering that particular individual.

Personal dispositions themselves can be broken down into different varieties. A *cardinal disposition* is a very general and pervasive trait for a given person, so general and pervasive that it seems directly or indirectly involved in a wide range of the person's activities. Many people may have no cardinal dispositions at all; at most, a person would have one or two cardinal dispositions. For example, we might say that "generosity" is a cardinal trait in the life of the late Mother Teresa, because this trait seemed to be so powerfully salient in her life. A cardinal disposition serves as a defining feature of a person's personality profile. More common are *central dispositions*, which refer to a wide range of dispositions that may be characteristic for a given person and called into play on a relatively regular basis. People typically have between 5 and 10 central dispositions, Allport suggested. In a famous case study, Allport (1965) analyzed the letters written to her son by a woman named Jenny to derive a set of personality descriptors for the letter writer. Allport concluded that Jenny's personality could be well described by invoking eight central dispositions, including "quarrelsome-suspicious," "aesthetic-artistic," and "self-centered." Finally, *secondary dispositions* are more limited in scope and less critical to the description of overall personality. A person is likely to have a great many secondary dispositions. Each secondary disposition is exhibited under a relatively limited set of conditions. Thus, secondary dispositions differ from central (and cardinal) dispositions in that they are narrower, more contingent on particular situational cues, and less central to defining the overall character of a person's individuality.

Allport anticipated most of the controversies that were to surround trait psychology in subsequent years. For example, Allport discussed, but ultimately rejected, the idea that traits are merely semantic categories in the minds of observers, as opposed to causal agents in the behavior of the actor. Allport discussed the problem of cross-situational consistency in traits. He acknowledged that people's behavior is highly variable from one situation to the next and that traits must be understood against the backdrop of this variability. One can still observe relative consistencies in responding indicative of traits, Allport maintained, if one examines a person's trait-related behavior in a wide variety of situations and over time. Finally, Allport recognized the limitations in descriptive and explanatory power provided by common trait profiles. Comparing people's scores on common traits is useful, Allport maintained, but unless one examines personal dispositions, one will never get a sense of what makes a particular person especially unique. Allport's insistence that personality psychologists examine the uniqueness of the individual case rendered him forever ambivalent about the idea of common, comparative traits of personality. He preferred to talk about unique personal dispositions. But most trait research and all other trait theories that followed Allport focused almost exclusively on common traits, examining dispositional dimensions upon which many different people can be said to differ in consistent and important ways.

Raymond B. Cattell   Beginning in the 1940s, Raymond B. Cattell advocated a brand of trait psychology that emphasized rigorous quantification and statistical analysis in research with the ultimate goal of improving scientists' ability to predict behavior. For Cattell, personality itself was defined in terms of behavioral prediction. He defined personality as "that which permits a prediction of what a person will do in a given situation" (1950, p. 2). Among the many variables that might be employed to predict behavior, Cattell considered traits to be especially important. While Cattell acknowledged the existence of traits that might be unique to certain individuals (what Allport called personal dispositions and what Cattell simply labeled as *unique traits*), he focused his research attention on what Allport called common traits—traits that express individual differences among many different people.

How might a researcher obtain information on people's traits? Cattell distinguished among three different sources for data on traits as shown in Table 5.2. **L-data** (life-data) consist primarily of information pertaining to a person's real-life behavior. Included in L-data might be public records such as college transcripts and letters of recommendation, personal accounts such as diaries or journals, and trait ratings of a person made by others. **Q-data** (questionnaire data) include self-ratings on personality traits and self-report scores

Raymond B. Cattell

TABLE 5.2	Cattell's Three-Part Classification of Personality Data	
TYPE OF DATA	**DESCRIPTION**	**EXAMPLES**
L-data	Information derived from observers' ratings and evaluation of individuals leading more or less natural lives	Teacher ratings of children in nursery school; parent ratings of children's temperament; peer ratings of personality; psychologists' ratings of family interaction in natural settings
Q-data	Information derived from self-observations and evaluation of one's own behavior, feelings, and personality characteristics	Various self-report scales and standard personality inventories; the Adjective Check List, the MMPI, trait measures of extraversion, neuroticism, and openness to experience
T-data	Information derived from observations of behavior under structured and controlled conditions, as in the laboratory	Experiments in which observations are made of aggressive, altruistic, or conforming behavior under a variety of controlled conditions

on various personality questionnaires of the kinds I will describe later in this chapter. **T-data** (test data) involve observations of an individual in a well-controlled assessment situation, as in behavioral records from laboratory experiments. These different sources of data—public ratings, self-reports, and test behavior—provide very different readings on a person's dispositions. By combining data from all three sources, the researcher can get a more accurate reading on personality traits and enhance behavioral prediction.

In an extraordinarily ambitious program of research that Cattell followed for almost 50 years, he employed the statistical approach of **factor analysis** to derive a complex classification scheme for traits. In factor analysis, the researcher examines the ways in which responses to different questions and measures cluster together. Factor analysis enables the researcher to reduce a large number of items or variables to a smaller set of underlying dimensions, called "factors." Cattell's studies produced a large number of what he called **surface traits,** which were related elements of behavior that, when empirically measured and intercorrelated, tended to cluster together. As their name suggests, surface traits are readily observable in behavior. Further factor analysis, however, indicated that the many surface traits that might be observed could be reduced to a smaller number of underlying **source traits.** Therefore, three or four readily observable surface traits—say, friendliness, outgoingness, spontaneity, and cheerfulness—might ultimately stem from the workings of a single, underlying source trait—say, sociability. By subsuming many surface traits under a smaller number of source traits, Cattell formulated one of the first hierarchical models for trait organization. Traits could be further subdivided into three functional categories: *dynamic traits*, which set the individual into action to accomplish a goal; *ability traits*, which concern the effectiveness with which the individual reaches a goal; and *temperament traits*, which concern such stylistic aspects of response as speed, energy, and emotional reactivity.

Cattell's analyses convinced him that human individuality could be well described in terms of 16 source traits, one of which was intelligence. Individual differences on these source traits can be measured on Cattell's **Sixteen Personality Factor Questionnaire,** or **16PF** for short. The 16PF presents the respondent with 187 questions, each of which asks for a choice among alternatives. For example, one question asks whether in a typical social occasion you would rather "come forward" or "stay quietly in the background." The responses are tallied into 16 separate scores, one for each of the source traits. Cattell gave some of his source traits unusual names to limit their associations with common language. For example, the source trait of "affectia-sizia" measures such characteristics as being warmhearted and outgoing. Table 5.3 on page 262 lists by letter rather than name 15 of the 16 factors on the 16PF, excluding intelligence. For each source trait, you can find in the table simple descriptions of high and low scorers and examples of famous people from history who might have scored in one direction or another on the trait.

For Cattell, the proof of a trait measure's value was its ability to predict behavior. To enhance behavioral prediction, Cattell combined scores on different traits into a **specification equation,** which differentially weighted each trait according to its relevance for a given behavioral situation. For example, Cattell (1990) contended that he could predict well a salesperson's annual earnings from the following source trait equation: Earnings = .21 outgoingness + .10 emotional stability + .10 dominance + .21 easygoingness + .10 conscientiousness − .10 suspiciousness − .31 imaginativeness + .21 shrewdness. To increase predictive power for some behavioral outcomes in some situations, the specification equation could also include nontrait variables pertaining to transient *states* (such as fatigue and temporary moods) and particular *roles* demanded by the situation. Therefore, to predict behavior with any degree of precision, Cattell believed, the personality psychologist should obtain precise measures on a host of internal and external variables: personality traits, temporary states and roles, and situational factors.

Hans J. Eysenck

Hans Eysenck   A contemporary of Cattell's, Hans Eysenck was another pioneer in the history of traits whose voluminous writings and influential conceptualizations have had a major impact on personality psychology. Like Cattell, Eysenck employed the statistical procedure of factor analysis to reduce the many possible traits that could be measured in questionnaires to a reasonable number of basic dimensions. Eysenck and Cattell parted company, however, over a rather esoteric but ultimately consequential controversy in the world of statistics—that is, the question of how to "rotate" factors in a factor analysis. To put it very simply, Eysenck believed, along with another contemporary stalwart in trait psychology named J. P. Guilford (1959), that the resultant trait factors obtained from factor analysis should be

TABLE 5.3	The Fifteen Source Traits of Personality Assessed by the 16PF

	TRAIT DESCRIPTIONS		FAMOUS INDIVIDUALS	
TRAIT	HIGH	LOW	HIGH	LOW
A	Outgoing Warmhearted	Reserved Detached	Falstaff	Greta Garbo
C	Unemotional Calm	Emotional Changeable	Washington	Hamlet
E	Assertive Dominant	Humble Cooperative	Genghis Khan	Jesus
F	Cheerful Lively	Sober Taciturn	Groucho Marx	Clint Eastwood
G	Conscientious Persistent	Expedient Undisciplined	Mother Teresa	Casanova
H	Venturesome Socially bold	Shy Retiring	Columbus	Sylvia Plath
I	Tough-minded Self-reliant	Tender-minded Sensitive	James Bond	Robert Burns
L	Suspicious Skeptical	Trusting Accepting	De Gaulle	Pollyanna
M	Imaginative Bohemian	Practical Conventional	Van Gogh	Henry Ford
N	Shrewd Discreet	Forthright Straightforward	Machiavelli	Joan of Arc
O	Guilt-prone Worrying	Resilient Self-assured	Dostoevsky	Stalin
Q_1	Radical Experimental	Conservative Traditional	Karl Marx	Queen Victoria
Q_2	Self-sufficient Resourceful	Group-dependent Affiliative	Copernicus	Marilyn Monroe
Q_3	Controlled Compulsive	Undisciplined Lax	Margaret Thatcher	Mick Jagger
Q_4	Tense Driven	Relaxed Tranquil	Macbeth	Buddha

Note: Dimension B (Intelligence) is omitted.
Source: Adapted from Matthews and Deary (1998), p. 22.

statistically independent of one another—that is, the factors should be arranged (rotated) so that they are uncorrelated or *orthogonal* (at right angles) to one another. Cattell insisted that this was not necessary, preferring statistical solutions that resulted in correlated factors, or what is called *oblique* factors. Because of this difference as well as disagreements over the preferred level of generality for basic traits, Eysenck and Cattell differed dramatically with respect to the number of basic traits they believed to exist. For Cattell, it was 16 source traits; for Eysenck, it all boiled down to 3.

Eysenck's big three supertraits (sometimes called types) are extraversion–introversion, neuroticism, and psychoticism. The first two factors deal with personality characteristics within a relatively normal range of functioning, whereas psychoticism taps

FIGURE 5.1

The Four Ancient Personality Types

The ancient types may be recast as combinations on the traits for extraversion, introversion, neuroticism, and stability.

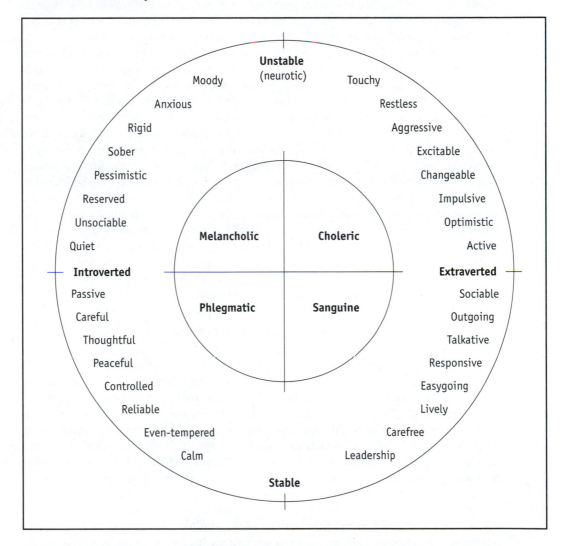

Source: Eysenck (1973), p. 18.

into dimensions of functioning that are typically associated with psychotic and psychopathic behavior, such as delusional thinking, excessive cruelty, and antisocial behavior. Eysenck's first two factors, extraversion–introversion and neuroticism, recapture the ancient typology of humors, as shown in Figure 5.1. As we can see, persons may be classified in a two-dimensional space created by the intersection of these two traits in a way reminiscent of the ancient types. The extraverted and highly neurotic (emotionally unstable) person is outgoing, easily irritated, restless, and excitable—the choleric type. The extraverted and emotionally stable (low neuroticism) person is outgoing, stable, and cheerful, like the sanguine type. The melancholic type is introverted and highly neurotic, resulting in characteristics of moodiness, depression, and anxiety. Finally, the phlegmatic person is introverted and low in neuroticism (emotionally stable), producing such descriptors as quiet, steady, and stoic.

As we will see later, Eysenck's first two dimensions of extraversion–introversion and neuroticism have received a tremendous amount of research attention. Studies provide impressive evidence that individual differences in these two large traits are significantly associated with many behaviors that theory predicts they should be associated with. In addition, longitudinal studies show that individual differences in extraversion–introversion and neuroticism are highly stable over long periods of time, especially in adulthood. Studies with twins suggest that individual differences in these two traits are at least moderately (if not substantially) determined by genetic differences among people. The last fact suggests that extraversion–introversion and neuroticism may be linked to identifiable biological substrates, in particular patternings in the central nervous system. Eysenck (1967) proposed just such a linkage. He theorized that individual differences in extraversion–introversion are linked to the activity of the brain's reticular activating system, which itself is implicated in the modulation of arousal. He proposed further that individual differences in neuroticism might arise from differences in the workings of the brain's limbic system, which has been hypothesized to be implicated in emotionality. Eysenck's bold hypotheses linking brains and traits have generated 30 years of provocative research on these questions, as we will see in Chapter 6.

The Big Five   How many traits are there? Over 2,000 years ago, Theophrastus described more than 20 different character types, while Galen's ancient typology listed four. In modern times, Cattell's factor analytic procedures convinced him that 16 source traits account for much of human individuality, while Eysenck, using similar procedures, arrived at a set of three. In the 19th century, Francis Galton suggested that researchers might look to language to determine what the basic dimensions of individual differences might be. All languages contain many descriptors for traitlike terms. Take English, for example—words like affable, belligerent, callous, dutiful, energetic, friendly, gregarious, hospitable, irritable, jolly, knowledgeable, lazy, magnanimous, neurotic, obnoxious, playful, quarrelsome, righteous, sorrowful, tenacious, unctuous, vivacious, wacky, xenophobic, yielding, and zealous.

I just pulled those adjectives off the top of my head, with some help from the dictionary for the letters *k* and *y*. But, in 1936, Gordon Allport decided to be much more systematic. Following Galton's suggestion and earlier work done in Germany by Klages (1926) and Baumgarten (1933), Allport and Odbert (1936) plowed through an unabridged English dictionary, containing 550,000 entries, to compile a list of all English words referring to individual differences in psychological functioning. They came up with about 18,000 words referring to psychological states, traits, and evaluations. Of these, about 4,500 reflected, in their judgment, relatively stable and enduring personality traits.

Raymond B. Cattell picked up where Allport left off. Cattell (1943) reduced Allport's list of 4,500 to 171 by grouping similar descriptors and eliminating rare and

Lewis Goldberg

metaphorical usages. He then asked people to rate other people on these 171 traitlike terms. On the basis of correlations among these ratings, Cattell developed a set of 35–40 clusters of related terms and used them for the construction of self-report and peer-report rating scales. At a time when factor analysis was just being invented and long before computers made such a complicated statistical procedure relatively simple to do, Cattell and his colleagues embarked upon the herculean task of factor analyzing by hand data from hundreds of ratings of the personality terms. What emerged eventually was Cattell's well-known list of 16 source traits. But other people who factor-analyzed data based on Cattell's clusters came up with different results. The first of these was Donald Fiske (1949), who worked with 22 of Cattell's rating scales and, after a year of calculating, concluded that *five basic traits* accounted for most of the intercorrelations. Similar studies yielding very similar results were done in later years, most notably by Tupes and Christal (1961) and Norman (1963).

By the mid-1960s, therefore, a handful of well-designed and painstakingly analyzed studies suggested that ratings of personality traits could be grouped into approximately five basic categories. Yet not until the 1980s did the significance of this finding begin to be realized more widely. During the 1980s and 1990s, a growing number of researchers began to reach a consensus about what has come to be called the **Five-Factor Model** of personality traits or, more simply, the **Big Five** (Angleitner & Ostendorf, 1994; Digman, 1996; Goldberg, 1993; John, 1990; McCrae & Costa, 1995). Among the most important contributors to this development have been John Digman (1990; Digman & Takemoto-Chock, 1981), Lewis Goldberg (1981, 1990), Robert McCrae and Paul Costa (Costa & McCrae, 1985, 1988; McCrae & Costa, 1987, 1990, 1995), and Jerry Wiggins (1996). Different researchers have suggested different names and slightly different conceptualizations for the five factors, but most agree that two of the factors are quite similar to what Eysenck called (1) extraversion–introversion and (2) neuroticism. Adopting Costa and McCrae's well-known labels, the other three factors of the Big Five may be called agreeableness, conscientiousness, and openness to experience. In Chapter 6, we will examine each of these five trait clusters in detail.

MEASURING TRAITS

Trait Judgments

The measurement of traits relies on words used to account for observations. When we make a trait attribution or judgment about a person's behavior, we take our observations of that person and translate them into words. We hope the words we choose convey the meanings we intend. But words are slippery. You may implicitly define "friendliness" in a different way than I do. To you, a person who smiles a lot and talks with most anybody she meets deserves the label of "friendly." For me, though, this person seems "pushy," rather than friendly. You and I may use the term *friendly* in different ways. Furthermore, it may be difficult to make trait judgments for some characteristics, even if we could agree on the definitions, because trait-relevant behavior may be hard to observe. How, for example, are you to determine whether your psychology professor is "neurotic" or not based solely on observing her in class? She may seem as normal as the day is long when you see her give lectures, but she may spend much of the rest of her time being depressed or anxious. How would you know? Similarly, I may notice that one of my students seems listless and lethargic in class, but it may turn out that he is a ball of energy as soon as he walks out the door and finds himself in a less boring situation. How would I know? We get incomplete and imperfect information about other people, to the extent that we get information at all. Therefore, how is it that we can ever make accurate and reliable trait judgments?

For many years in psychology it has been fashionable to believe that people do not do a very good job in making trait judgments. Personality psychologist David Funder (1989, 1993, 1995) has traced more than 20 years of research, much of it coming out of cognitive-social psychology, that documents the many shortcomings of human judgment (e.g., Nisbett & Ross, 1980). People make many mistakes when they evaluate other people. They often generalize from insufficient information. They fail to take into consideration social norms and expectations. They are readily swayed by unusual occurrences that suggest something "strange" about another person. They use different standards for judging others than they use for evaluating their own behavior. All of this research has resulted in what Funder calls an *error paradigm* in the study of social perception. According to Funder, however, the error paradigm tells only half the story. "The avoidance of error is not quite the same thing as the achievement of accuracy," he writes, "and explanations of how errors arise shed relatively little light on how correct judgments are ever made" (Funder, 1995, p. 652). What many psychologists have failed to realize, Funder contends, is that amidst all the uncertainty, imprecision, and error in human judgment, people are nonetheless often surprisingly accurate when it comes to evaluating others (and even themselves). The *accuracy paradigm* suggests that when it comes to personality traits, people turn out to be pretty astute observers and good judges of both themselves and others. This is a critical point for the study of traits because most trait measurements involve a person's rating his or her own behavior or rating the behavior of others.

Evidence for accuracy in trait judgments comes from many sources. First, a considerable body of research shows that people tend to offer similar independent ratings of the same people. For example, the trait ratings of college students made by parents tend to be similar to the ratings of those same students made by the students' friends (Funder, 1995). Second, agreements between self-ratings and peer ratings are typically found in personality research. Reviewing some of this research, Johnson (1997) concludes that "self-ratings of traits correlate substantially (*r*s in the .40 to .60 range) with ratings of the same traits made by others" (p. 79). The "*r*s" refer to correlation coefficients (Chapter 1 in this book), assessing the degree of agreement between the self-ratings and peer ratings of the same people on the same traits. Correlations in the range between .40 and .60 are considered fairly substantial for this sort of thing. To put it in the simplest terms, findings like these suggest that when a person tends to rate himself as, say, "especially high" on a particular trait, people who know him or are judging his behavior are likely to rate him in the high range as well. If he sees himself as low, they are likely to see him in the low range, too. And so on. Of course, the agreement between self-ratings and peer ratings is far from perfect. But the positive correlations between the ratings are often substantial. Finally, evidence for the accuracy of trait judgments comes from many studies indicating that various kinds of trait ratings are successful in predicting what a person may eventually do (Funder, 1995; Hogan, Hogan, & Roberts, 1996; Johnson, 1997). The extent to which trait ratings are indeed successful in predicting behavior is a fundamental topic to which we will return later in this chapter and the next.

How is it that people manage to be accurate? Block (1993) offers the explanation of "the duck test." In judging traits, people (and psychologists) take into account evidence from many sources. All of the evidence is incomplete and faulty, but the evidence nonetheless tends to converge and result in a more-or-less reasonable attribution about a person. Something, then, that looks like a duck, sounds like a duck, and acts like a duck is probably a duck, but of course, it may not be. You make an educated guess—in this case, you guess "duck." Traits are like that, too. Therefore, if you see Mary on five different occasions and each time she seems friendly and outgoing, if you hear other people describe Mary as especially friendly and outgoing, and if on the sixth time you see Mary she seems rather cold and aloof and then remarks to you later that she is rarely like that, then you might begin to think that Mary is indeed a relatively friendly person. Of course, you could be wrong. But more often than not we tend to be relatively accurate, especially as we get to know people better over time and in different situations. Funder (1995) extends this logic to what psychologists do when they put together different information on people's traits:

> When a person reports that he or she is sociable, is described by several acquaintances as sociable, is quick to initiate conversation with a stranger in a laboratory situation, and spends most of his or her spare time in social situations, then he or she is very probably sociable, no matter how elusive such a determination may be as a matter of ultimate philosophical truth. So when someone describes this person as sociable, it is reasonable to regard this judgment as accurate. And when someone describes this person as nonsociable, it is reasonable to regard this judgment as wrong. (p. 657)

Funder concedes that in an ultimate sense we may never really know whether a personality rating is accurate or "wrong." Trait labels, after all, are social constructions—words with imprecise meanings used subjectively and in a cultural context to make sense of inherently ambiguous activity (Kruglanski, 1989). Nonetheless, for practical purposes we can talk about the extent to which a judgment is *probably* accurate or *probably* wrong (Cook & Campbell, 1979; Rorer, 1991). "Truth" in trait attribution may indeed exist in some sense, but there is no sure pathway to it. There is only a wide variety of alternative pathways, each of which is extremely unsure. In other words, we do the best we can under ambiguous circumstances when it comes to making judgments, and we usually, though not always, do so with reasonable effectiveness and utility. Indeed, if would make evolutionary sense (in the terms of Chapter 2 in this book) that humans should be relatively effective and accurate in their judgments of personality traits in that such judgments should have an important impact on the success with which we get along and get ahead as social animals. Reasonable accuracy in social perception would appear to be something for which human beings have been selected over evolutionary time, serving to promote adaptation in the environment of evolutionary adaptedness.

TABLE 5.4		*Four Influences on the Accuracy of Trait Judgments*
ASPECT	**EXPLANATION**	**EXAMPLES**
Good judge	Quality of the rater	Perceptiveness of rater Rater's judgment ability (Non)defensiveness of rater
Good target	The ease with which the person being rated can be judged	Sincerity of the target Consistency of the target's behavior Willingness of the target to be rated Ability of target to display trait-relevant behavior
Good trait	The extent to which the trait is easy to rate	Visibility of trait-relevant behavior Frequency of trait-relevant behavior Social desirability of the trait How clearly defined the trait is
Good information	The extent to which good data on the trait can be obtained	Quantity of data (more is usually better) Quality of data (e.g., how objective is it?)

Source: Based on Funder (1995), p. 660.

In our efforts to make good (accurate, valid) judgments about traits, four classes of variables may have an impact, as shown in Table 5.4. First, there are characteristics of what Funder calls the *good judge:* Some raters are more astute, less defensive, more perceptive, and so on, sometimes making them more accurate in trait judgment compared with other raters. Second, there are characteristics of the *good target:* Some people are easier to judge than others, are more consistent, transparent, or disclosing in their behavior compared with other people. Third, there is the *good trait:* Some traits are easier to judge than others, perhaps because they are associated with public and readily observable behavior (e.g., "friendly") rather than private thoughts and feelings (e.g., "ruminative"). Funder and Dobroth (1987) showed, for example, that agreement between self-ratings and peer ratings was higher for more visible traits such as talkativeness compared with less visible traits such as styles of thinking. Finally, there is *good information:* A rater who has lots of high-quality information about the person's trait is in a better position to be accurate than a rater whose information is scanty or low in quality. People tend to get more (and usually better) information as they get to know a person better. Consequently, research has shown that personality judgments by close acquaintances agree with each other more highly than do personality judgments made by strangers (Funder & Colvin, 1988). Accuracy in trait assessment should be maximized, then, when perceptive or well-trained raters (good judges) employ a large quantity of relevant data (good information) to determine the relative salience of a well-defined variable that is readily linked with behaviors (good trait) in people who characteristically express themselves in authentic and consistent ways (good targets). To the extent that these four conditions are not met in personality research, the quality of trait measurements should decrease.

Constructing a Trait Measure

Most personality psychologists who study traits assume that people are able to make trait judgments with some degree of accuracy. The methods used to assess traits, therefore, tend to be relatively straightforward and simple (Burisch, 1984). The most popular methods are self-report questionnaires and rating scales. These objective measures of personality ask the person to report directly on his or her own behavior, typically by answering a series of questions with "yes" or "no" answers or by making a rating—for instance, on a 1–7 scale—concerning the extent to which the person "agrees with" or "disagrees with" a particular item.

Although a paper-and-pencil test designed to measure a personality trait may appear simple and straightforward from the standpoint of the person filling out the scale, constructing a reliable and valid trait measure is not easy. Psychologists have developed and evaluated a number of approaches to test construction (Burisch, 1984; Hase & Goldberg, 1967; Wiggins, 1973), but there is no single approach that everybody agrees is the best for all testing situations. Nevertheless, most personality psychologists generally endorse a **construct approach** to test construction (Jackson, 1971; Jackson & Paunonen, 1980; Loevinger, 1957; Wiggins, 1973).

The construct approach begins with a clear conceptual definition of the trait of interest, usually embedded in a larger personality theory. Take, for instance, the trait of "conscientiousness." If we were to design a personality questionnaire to assess individual differences in conscientiousness, we might begin with the definition of and theory for this trait provided by Cattell (1965). One of Cattell's 16 basic "source traits" in human personality, conscientiousness is defined as a general disposition "governing conscientious, perserving, unselfish behavior and impelling the individual to duty as conceived by his [or her] culture" (p. 374). A highly conscientious person is "honest; knows what is right and generally does it, even if no one is watching him [her]; does not tell lies or attempt to deceive others; respects others' property." A highly unconscientious person is "somewhat unscrupulous; not too careful about standards of right and wrong where personal desires are concerned; tells lies and is given to little deceits; does not respect others' property" (p. 63). Most people fall somewhere between the two extremes. Cattell emphasizes that conscientiousness is "not just a rational politeness or conformity but a somewhat fierce 'categorical imperative' (to use Kant's description) of the kind exemplified by the biblical saints" (p. 94).

After defining our trait, we would begin writing *items*, which are the test questions or statements. Here are three items that Cattell wrote for his scale for conscientiousness (1965, p. 94):

Do you usually keep emotions under control?

Are you a person who is scrupulously correct in manners and social obligations and likes others to be the same?

Are you cautious and considerate that you do not hurt people's feelings by unconsidered conversational remarks?

For each of these items, the respondent would answer "yes" or "no." In the case of these three items, "yes" answers indicate conscientiousness and "no" answers suggest unconscientiousness. Each item relates to the others in an additive way. Thus, a subject might receive one point for each "yes" answer on the scale. Adding up all the points would produce the total trait score for conscientiousness. Because some people, however, may answer "yes" to virtually any question ("yea-sayers") and others "no" to almost any question ("nay-sayers") regardless of content, we would do well to include items for which a "no" answer suggests conscientiousness and a "yes" answer suggests unconscientiousness (Jackson, 1971). Therefore, we might add such "reversed" items as these:

I frequently find that I must "cut corners" and "bend the rules" in order to achieve my goals.

Other people would *not* describe me as a dutiful and highly responsible person.

In writing test items, our goal would be to generate an item pool that completely covers the content domain of conscientiousness. Therefore, we should aim to include a large number of items initially, so that we might tap into the various manifestations of conscientiousness that our theory suggests might exist. In fact, it is a good idea, argue some test theorists, to include items that are hypothesized *not* to tap into the trait of interest—in other words, items that seem to have nothing to do with the trait of conscientiousness, such as these:

Other people regard me as a dominant person.

I enjoy parties and other opportunities to get together with large groups of people.

In covering a content domain that is larger than that envisioned for our trait, we decrease the chances of excluding unexpectedly relevant items while increasing the chances of learning precisely where the boundaries of our trait lie—that is, finding what content the particular trait does and does not include (Loevinger, 1957; Wiggins, 1973).

In the next step of test construction, we would administer the item pool to a large number of individuals and examine the results to determine which items should be retained in the final version. There are many statistical procedures available for examining the empirical results at this stage. For instance, we would probably perform an **item analysis,** through which we would determine the contribution that each item makes to the scale by correlating the scores on each item with the total score. Those items that make a negligible contribution (that is, those that produce low correlations) to the total would then be dropped. Presumably a number of the conceptually irrelevant items that we included by design would be dropped at this stage, though those correlating highly with the overall score would be retained. Further, a number of items that we initially thought were tapping the trait well might be deleted for lack of correlation with the total.

We might also perform a factor analysis on the data, through which each item is correlated with every other item to determine empirical clusterings. Let us imagine that our final scale has 30 items. We might administer the scale to 500 persons and then perform a factor analysis to determine which items "hang together" in clusters. The factor analysis might yield two relatively independent clusters of items—*factors*—that appear to tap into two somewhat different facets of conscientiousness. Perhaps 10 of our items appearing to tap into moral concerns hang together as a first factor, and another 12 items having more to do with conscientiousness in work hang together to form a second, independent factor. We might conclude that the overall scale in fact assesses two separate, though related, ideas—two facets of the trait "conscientiousness": "moral conscientiousness" and "task conscientiousness." Alternatively, we might decide that the two facets are in fact two separate traits, each having little to do with the other.

In the final step of test construction, we would examine the extent to which the trait measure predicts behavior. For instance, we might design a study in which people who fill out our conscientiousness measure participate in a laboratory experiment in which they are given various opportunities to choose between either responsible, conscientious behavior or competing, nonconscientious behavior. Or we might examine the relationship between conscientiousness scores on our test and behaviors thought to be conscientious in daily life, such as church attendance, contributions to charities, and community involvement. Or we might correlate people's scores on our measure of conscientiousness and ratings of the same people made by their friends and acquaintances, our prediction being that those individuals scoring high on our measure would be rated by their friends and acquaintances as significantly more responsible and dutiful than low-scoring individuals.

As a trait measure develops, researchers learn not only what the particular scale measures but also what it does *not* measure. Therefore, we would expect scores on our measure of conscientiousness would correlate positively with scores on *other* measures of conscientiousness. Evidence for positive associations between different measures of the same trait constitute **convergent validity:** the two measures are said to "converge" on the same trait (Campbell & Fiske, 1959). Further, scores on our measure of conscientiousness should not correlate with scores on measures of apparently unrelated traits. For instance, our theory of conscientiousness suggests that this trait should have little to do with such traits as "dominance," "extraversion," "intelligence," "friendliness," and so on. In other words, highly conscientious people should not be consistently high (or low) on dominance or on any other independent trait. If conscientiousness scores *were* highly positively (or negatively) correlated with dominance scores, we should suspect that our measure is in fact assessing something different from, or in addition to, "pure" conscientiousness. Evidence, therefore, that our trait measure does not correlate with measures of other, conceptually distinct traits would support the **discriminant validity** of our measure (Campbell & Fiske, 1959).

Criteria of a Good Measure

The construct approach to devising a personality trait measure follows logically from a crucial idea in personality psychology as a whole—the idea of **construct validity.** Construct validity is the process of simultaneously validating a test and the construct that the test is measuring. Cronbach and Meehl (1955) introduced the concept of construct validity in order to address a common and vexing problem in personality psychology: How do you know whether a measure designed to assess something that you cannot observe directly is a good measure? Although we may be able to observe friendly behavior, we cannot directly observe "friendliness" per se. The trait of friendliness is an abstraction that cannot be directly seen, heard, touched, smelled, or tasted. The same could be said for all personality traits and, indeed, many other concepts in psychology overall—such as intelligence, prejudice, religious values, the superego. These ineffable abstractions are termed *constructs.* Trait scales measure such constructs.

The process of construct validity begins with the construct itself, which is typically embedded in a larger theory of personality functioning. With an eye toward the

FEATURE 5.A

Narcissism: The Trait of Excessive Self-Love

In the ancient Greek legend, the beautiful boy Narcissus falls so completely in love with the reflection of himself in a pool that he plunges into the pool and drowns. If we are to believe a number of contemporary journalists, psychologists, and social critics, something very much like the fate of Narcissus is happening all around us today. Contemporary American society is a "culture of narcissism," wrote Christopher Lasch (1979). The ethic of the "me generation" encouraged us all to love ourselves first and foremost, to seek, develop, perfect, and master *the self*. As a result, many of us are incapable of mature love for and commitment to others and are unwilling to devote ourselves to pursuits that transcend our own selfish concerns, to social institutions and communities that have traditionally integrated individuals within society (Bellah, Madsen, Sullivan, Swidler, & Tipton, 1985). In the eyes of the popular press, the narcissistic young person or middle-aged American adult today is obsessed with perfecting his body at the health club, desperately trying to "be all that she can be," "born to buy" and to accumulate both high-priced possessions and exotic personal experiences.

A number of prominent psychoanalysts consider **narcissism** to be the prototypical pathology of our time, rendering the "narcissistic personality disorder" one of the most popular and talked-about clinical syndromes of the 1980s and 1990s. But narcissism may also be viewed as a personality trait upon which relatively normal people who do not suffer from a clinical syndrome nonetheless differ. Raskin and Hall (1979, 1981) constructed a self-report questionnaire designed to measure the trait of narcissism. The Narcissistic Personality Inventory (NPI) includes 54 pairs of items. For each pair, the subject chooses the one item that he or she agrees with more. Here are some examples of items that score for narcissism:

> I really like to be the center of attention.
> I have a natural talent for influencing people.
> I like to look at my body.
> I think I am a special person.
> Everybody likes to hear my stories.
> I insist on the respect that is due to me.
> I will never be satisfied until I get all that I deserve.

The NPI taps four dimensions of narcissism: exploitiveness/entitlement, superiority, leadership, and self-absorption. It is the first of these four factors—exploitiveness/entitlement—that is believed to be associated with

theoretical meaning of the construct, the psychologist carefully designs a measure of the construct and then observes the extent to which the measure itself produces empirical results—observable behaviors—that conform to the theory. For instance, I might conduct a study to test my prediction that persons scoring high on my new measure of "friendliness" will spend more time smiling in a friendly laboratory interview than persons scoring low on the measure, under the theoretical assumption that smiling is generally an index of friendly sentiment. Should my prediction be confirmed in my study, I will have obtained some small evidence for the construct validity of the psychological maladjustment. Exploitiveness/entitlement is associated with anxiety, depression, and lack of empathy for others (Emmons, 1984; Watson, Grisham, Trotter, & Biderman, 1984). In general, males score significantly higher on all four dimensions of narcissism than do females.

Raskin and Shaw (1988) found that students scoring high on narcissism tended to use significantly more first-person singular pronouns (*I, me, my*) in spontaneous speech. Emmons (1984) found that narcissism is positively associated with other measures of dominance, exhibitionism, and self-esteem, and negatively associated with deference toward others. Some research suggests that college students scoring high in narcissism express more hostility and are more likely to behave aggressively when they are insulted compared with students lower in narcissism (Bushman & Baumeister, 1998; Rhodewalt & Morf, 1995, 1998). Narcissism has also been linked to extreme mood swings and intensity of emotional experience in daily life (Emmons, 1987). With respect to this last finding, it is believed that the narcissist's superficial smugness masks a deeper insecurity and narcissistic vulnerability (Kernberg, 1980). Narcissists may be more sensitive to both success and failure experiences than are most other people, experiencing intense joy when the self is uplifted with success but devastating depression and anger in the wake of even minor setbacks.

Wink (1991, 1992a, 1992b) has distinguished among three types of narcissism observable in *women* studied over time. The *hypersensitive* narcissists display a "covert" quality of narcissism that is linked to feelings of vulnerability, hostility, and depression. In Wink's longitudinal study, women who had high scores on hypersensitivity at age 43 were characterized by a downward spiral in their fortunes and resources during their 20s and 30s and by a lack of success either in a career or as a homemaker. The *willful* narcissists, by contrast, exhibit an "overt" quality of narcissism. From college days through midlife, they were consistently described as self-assured, grandiose, and exhibitionistic. Finally, the *autonomous* narcissists express a healthy form of narcissism. They were described at age 43 as creative, empathic, achievement-oriented, and individualistic. Following conflict in their 20s, the autonomous women experienced substantial personality growth into midlife. Hypersensitivity and willfulness, but not autonomy, were associated with evidence of troubled childhood relations with parents, particularly with mothers. In addition, willfulness was associated with early identification with a willful father.

new measure of friendliness. Should my prediction not be supported by the data, I might begin to question the adequacy of my measure, the adequacy of my construct "friendliness," or perhaps the adequacy of the particular study I conducted to test the hypothesis linking friendliness to smiling.

Each new empirical finding with a particular personality test contributes to the **nomological network** for the construct that the test measures. The nomological network is the interlocking system of propositions that constitute the theory of a given construct. The propositions specify how test performance should be related to particular nontest behaviors that can be directly assessed. Results from studies employing a particular trait measure may even feed back to change the nomological network, making for new propositions about the particular trait, thus redefining it and ultimately changing the theory in which it is embedded. There are numerous examples of this sort of thing in personality research—cases in which a particular trait assessed in a particular way starts out with one definition and theory, but over time (typically many years), and with extensive study, new empirical results change the trait's meaning and theory. For instance, early definitions of the "achievement motive" (Chapter 8) characterized it as a general desire to succeed, but subsequent research employing a particular measure of the need for achievement provided new evidence to suggest that its meaning was more closely tied to the "need to be efficient" and the "need to succeed at tasks of moderate challenge" (McClelland, 1985).

Construct validity, therefore, refers to the extent to which empirical support has been gathered for the propositions contained in the construct's nomological network. Constructs and their measures that have generated a large amount of empirical support for a rich variety of propositions in the nomological network can be said to have the greatest degree of construct validity. However, construct validity is never carved in stone: Each new study employing a particular construct and its measure ultimately ties into the nomological network and thus contributes some kind of evidence—supportive or nonsupportive—for construct validity. A number of other forms of validity fall in the general category of construct validity (Table 5.5).

In addition to construct (and other forms of) validity, **reliability** is a cardinal criterion of a trait measure's worth. Reliability refers to the consistency of a particular

TABLE 5.5	*Forms of Validity in Personality Testing*
Construct	The extent to which a test measures the construct that it is theoretically intended to measure. Construct validity increases as empirical support is garnered for the various propositions contained in the construct's nomological net. Construct validity is the most basic and encompassing form of validity, and other forms of validity can be seen as derivatives from it.
Content	The degree to which the items of a test cover the entire content domain of a construct and are not confounded with other content.
Convergent	The extent to which different measures of the same construct relate to one another.
Criterion	The extent to which a test is associated with external behaviors that it is designed to predict. When a test seeks to predict criterion behaviors that will occur in the future, we speak of "predictive validity." When the criterion behaviors are obtained at the current time, we speak of "concurrent validity."
Discriminant	The extent to which different measures of different constructs do *not* relate to one another.
Face	The extent to which test items seem, in the eyes of the respondent, to measure what they are supposed to measure. Face validity refers to the degree to which a respondent views the test as fair and appropriate under the given conditions of administration (Jackson & Paunonen, 1980).

personality measure. For self-report trait tests, two forms of reliability are especially important. In **test–retest reliability,** psychologists assess a test's *consistency over time*. Persons who score high on a particular trait on first taking the test should score high again on the same test a second time, say, a few months later. Similarly, those who score low at Time 1 should score low again at Time 2. Test–retest reliability is usually calculated by correlating the subjects' scores on a measure at Time 1 with their corresponding scores at Time 2. The most reliable trait measures exhibit test–retest correlation coefficients of +.85 and higher over relatively short periods of time (such as a few months). In **split-half reliability,** a test's *internal consistency* is assessed by correlating subjects' scores on one half of a particular test with their corresponding scores on the other half. If a test is internally consistent, each part of the test yields comparable results; indeed, each test item can be seen as contributing to a homogenous pool of information about a given trait.

Beyond validity and reliability, personality psychologists have identified a number of other criteria of a test's worth. *Utility* is a criterion frequently raised—a test that provides practical information that can be used for specific purposes is preferred over one that cannot. Burisch (1984) suggests that *economy* and *communicability* should routinely be considered—all other things being equal, a short test is better than a long one (economy), and a test whose results are easily interpreted and communicated to others should be preferred to one whose results are more ambiguous. In addition, a number of personality psychologists argue that trait measures should be as free as possible of **social desirability** bias (Edwards, 1957; Jackson & Messick, 1958). This means that a good trait measure should not be influenced greatly by a person's desire to present a favorable or socially desirable facade. One common method of determining the extent to which social desirability plays into a particular trait measure is to correlate scores on the given measure with scores on a standardized social desirability scale. Low, nonsignificant correlations between this and another trait measure suggest that the latter is relatively free of social desirability bias.

Trait Inventories

It is often useful in personality research and in clinical work to assess many different traits at once. To do so, psychologists sometimes call upon omnibus **personality inventories,** which contain numerous trait scales, each scale comprising a subset of items contained in the large item pool for the inventory.

The **Minnesota Multiphasic Personality Inventory (MMPI)** has been the most widely used and thoroughly researched personality measure in the past 60 years. Developed by a psychologist, Starke Hathaway, and a psychiatrist, J. C. McKinley, in the 1930s, the MMPI condenses questions that might be asked in a lengthy psychiatric interview into an efficient paper-and-pencil form. The original test contains 550 statements such as "I have nightmares every few nights," "At times I feel like smashing things," "I would like to be a florist," and "I am sure I am being talked about." For each item, the respondent simply answers "true" or "false." The items are grouped into 10 different scales, named hypochondriasis, depression, hysteria, psychopathic-deviancy, masculinity–femininity, paranoia, psychasthenia, schizophrenia, hypomania, and social introversion. The inventory also contains scales designed to assess the extent to which the subject is lying, faking, or responding in a careless fashion.

The MMPI was originally designed to be a *clinical* diagnostic instrument. Scores on the various scales were designed to assist the psychologist or psychiatrist in distinguishing various psychopathologies. Indeed, the MMPI was constructed by administering various items to different diagnostic groups—such as schizophrenics, manic-depressives, anxiety neurotics—and determining which items they repeatedly endorsed. This general method of construction, called the **criterion-key method,** assumes that a valid scale for, say, the "trait" of "depression" will consist of items that people whom clinicians have diagnosed as "depressives" frequently endorse, regardless of the content of those items and regardless of the theory of depression with which one is working. Therefore, if known depressives repeatedly answer "true" to the item "I am a Boston Red Sox fan," then this item becomes part of the scale for diagnosing depression, even though one is hard-pressed to come up with a cogent theoretical reason for its inclusion. The criterion-key method contrasts markedly with the theory-oriented construct method of test construction outlined earlier in this chapter.

Despite the fact that the MMPI scales were designed to assess *abnormality*, the test has been used to assess individual differences among normals as well, though with limited success (Kunce & Anderson, 1984). Even as a tool for clinical diagnosis, the MMPI has been resoundingly criticized for weak reliability and validity with respect to many of the scales, and for the fact that many of the test items seem out of date (Anastasi, 1976). In response to some of these critiques, psychologists developed a revised and updated version of the test, the MMPI-2. Containing 567 items, the MMPI-2 is widely used today in clinical assessment.

The **California Psychological Inventory (CPI)** was designed to assess a broad range of traits applicable to normal populations. Developed by Harrison Gough in the 1950s, the CPI was originally administered to thousands of normal individuals, resulting in a pool of 462 true/false items. The items are grouped into 20 scales, measuring such traits as dominance, sense of acceptance, self-control, and achievement via independence (Table 5.6). Compared with the MMPI, the individual scales on the CPI show relatively high reliabilities. Evidence for validity comes from many sources, including correlations between subjects' trait scores and ratings of the subjects made by

friends and acquaintances. One major criticism of the CPI, however, is that the different scales tend to overlap, showing correlations with each other of .50 and higher. Apparently, each scale does not assess an independent and unique trait (Thorndike, 1959). Nonetheless, most experts agree that the CPI is one of the best personality inventories in use today (Anastasi, 1976; Kleinmutz, 1982).

Gough argues that the CPI's scales tap into common **folk concepts** of personality. Folk concepts are categories of personality that arise naturally out of human interactions in most, if not all, societies. For example, most all cultures signify a concept of social responsibility—a tendency to act in accord with the good of the group rather than out of pure self-interest. Within each culture, individuals vary widely in the extent to which they and their behavior implicitly endorse this folk concept. The two CPI scales of "socialization" and "responsibility" aim to assess this important individual

Harrison G. Gough

| TABLE 5.6 | *Scales on the California Psychological Inventory* |

SCALE	BRIEF DESCRIPTION OF A HIGH SCORER
1. Dominance	Confident, assertive, dominant, task-oriented
2. Capacity for status	Ambitious, wants to be a success, independent
3. Sociability	Sociable, likes to be with people, friendly
4. Social presence	Self-assured, spontaneous; a good talker; not easily embarrassed
5. Self-acceptance	Has good opinion of self, sees self as talented and as personally attractive
6. Independence	Self-sufficient, resourceful, detached
7. Empathy	Comfortable with self and well-accepted by others; understands the feelings of others
8. Responsibility	Responsible, reasonable, takes duties seriously
9. Socialization	Comfortably accepts ordinary rules and regulations; finds it easy to conform
10. Self-control	Tries to control emotions and temper; takes pride in being self-disciplined
11. Good impression	Wants to make a good impression; tries to do what will please others
12. Communality	Fits in easily; sees self as a quite average person
13. Well-being	Feels in good physical and emotional health; optimistic about the future
14. Tolerance	Is tolerant of others' beliefs and values, even when different from or counter to own beliefs
15. Achievement via conformance	Has strong drive to do well; likes to work in settings where tasks and expectations are clearly defined
16. Achievement via independence	Has strong drive to do well; likes to work in settings that encourage freedom and individual initiative
17. Intellectual efficiency	Efficient in use of intellectual abilities; can keep on at a task where others might get bored or discouraged
18. Psychological mindedness	More interested in why people do what they do than in what they do; good judge of how people feel and what they think about things
19. Flexibility	Flexible; likes change and variety; easily bored by routine life and everyday experience; may be impatient, and even erratic
20. Femininity/Masculinity	On this scale, a person scoring in the Femininity direction is seen as sympathetic, helpful, sensitive to criticism, and tending to interpret events from a personal point of view. A person scoring in the Masculinity direction is seen as decisive, action-oriented, not easily subdued, and rather unsentimental.

Source: Adapted from Gough (1987), pp. 6–7.

difference. A substantial body of research supports the construct validity of these scales. For example, Gough and Bradley (1992) administered the CPI to hundreds of delinquent and criminal men and women as well as a comparable group of control subjects. Delinquent and criminal adults scored significantly lower than control subjects

on a number of different CPI scales (such as empathy and achievement via conformance) but the two scales that showed the strongest difference were socialization and
responsibility.

Recent work with the CPI has revealed three *vectors* or general dimensions that underlie the more specific folk-concept scales. Vector 1 pertains to an interpersonal orientation, which ranges from an involved, participatory approach to life on one end to
a detached, privacy-seeking orientation on the other. Vector 2 pertains to norms and
values, ranging from a norm-accepting to a norm-rejecting pole. Vector 3 pertains to
what Gough calls "ego integration," which extends from self-defeating and interpersonally unacceptable behavior on one end to self-realization and superior ego functioning on the other.

The first two vectors may be crossed to produce four distinct lifestyles, or ways of
living. *Alphas* are high on Vectors 1 and 2; they are interpersonally involved and rule
respecting. *Betas* are more detached and internalized (low on Vector 1) but still rule accepting. *Gammas* tend to enter into the interpersonal arena but remain dubious about
its norms and conventions. They are interpersonally engaged but rebellious or dismis-
sive of rules and regulations. Finally, *deltas* seek escape from the interpersonal world
and reject its norms and values. Research in career assessment suggests that alphas do
best in leadership and managerial roles, betas function well in subordinate support positions, gammas look for and are adept at creating change, and deltas work best alone,
in fields such as art, literature, and (depending on their abilities) mathematics (Gough,
1995). Ego integration from Vector 3 may be seen as modifying all four types. For example, alphas who are high in ego integration may show impressive leadership skill but
those low in ego integration may prove to be authoritarian and invasive. Deltas who
are high in ego integration may be visionary and prescient in very personal ways, as in
artistic or musical accomplishment. Deltas with low ego integration, however, may experience disintegrative conflict and may react with explosive violence or with disabling
psychological disorders.

Another well-regarded trait inventory is the **Personality Research Form (PRF),**
developed by Douglas Jackson in the 1960s. This instrument incorporates a number of
sophisticated advances in test construction and format that
were not available to the authors of the MMPI and CPI. In
constructing and validating the PRF, Jackson closely followed
the construct approach outlined earlier in this chapter. The
resulting test contains 320 true/false items, making up 20 independent scales. Each of the scales purports to measure a basic personality "need," taken from a list delineated by Murray
(1938). This list, described in Chapter 8 of this book, includes
the needs for dominance, affiliation, achievement, aggression,
and nurturance. The different PRF scales show much less
overlap than occurs in the CPI, and a substantial body of research supports the validity of many of the scales in predicting attitudes, values, and behavior. In addition, Paunonen,
Jackson, and Keinonen (1990) have developed a nonverbal,
pictorial version of the PRF in which each item is represented
by a line drawing of a figure performing a need-relevant behavior. (See Figure 5.2.) For each item, the subject is asked to

Paul T. Costa Jr.

FIGURE 5.2 | *Two Nonverbal Trait Items*

On the Nonverbal Personality Questionnaire, Item A depicts aggressive behavior while Item B shows thrill seeking.

A.

B.

Source: Paunonen, Jackson, & Keinonen (1990), p. 485.

indicate the likelihood that he or she might engage in the behavior represented in the drawing. The nonverbal PRF looks to be a promising research tool for cross-cultural personality research and for use with populations who are not linguistically adept.

Paul Costa and Robert McCrae (1985, 1992) have developed self-report inventories to assess the Big Five traits. The **NEO-PI-R** (Neuroticism-Extraversion-Openness Personality Inventory Revised) consists of 240 items assessing the Big Five traits of neuroticism, extraversion–introversion, openness to experience, agreeableness, and conscientiousness. For each item, the respondent indicates the extent to which he or she agrees or disagrees on a five-point rating scale. Costa and McCrae have divided each of the Big Five traits into six subtraits, called *facets*. For example, the six facets making up extraversion–introversion are *activity level, assertiveness, excitement seeking, positive emotions, gregariousness,* and *warmth*. Each item is keyed to a particular facet. Items such as "When I do things, I do them vigorously" and "My life is fast-paced" contribute to the activity level facet of extraversion. Therefore, each person receives a score on each of six facets for each of five traits, resulting in an individual profile of 30 scores.

Robert R. McCrae

FEATURE 5.B

Cubness: The Most Dreaded Trait

Whenever I try to trace back my occasional dark moods and deep-seated doubts about the world, I find myself reflecting on my father and an incident that occurred when I was in the second grade. I had just started collecting baseball cards and was gradually becoming interested in the game when I made the mistake of turning on the television to watch the Chicago White Sox play a few innings. My father came home, saw what I was doing, and quickly shut the television off. With great fervor and seriousness, he told me: "You don't watch the ————— White Sox; you're a Cubs fan." I did not know who the Cubs were, for I had not as yet obtained a baseball card portraying a Cubs player. But I figured that this was a pretty big deal, so I endeavored to learn about the Cubs and what it meant to be a fan.

My current membership card in the Chicago Cubs Die Hard Fan Club (# 0-275-99) is embossed with the date 1962—designating the year of my conversion and the beginning of the curse. As most baseball fans know, the Cubs are the perennial losers of the National League. Though virtually all fans of other teams claim that they have suffered great misery, Chicago fans who root for the Cubs have the saddest stories to tell. This can be documented. The last time the Cubs made it to the World Series was 1945—no other current team has a longer Seriesless streak. The last time the Cubs *won* the World Series was *1908:* William Taft was president and Sigmund Freud was still 12 years away from developing his idea of a "death instinct" (an idea to which Cubs fans have always resonated). Yet Cubs fans are the most devoted in sports. (This can also be documented.) And every year the Cubs break their hearts.

A Chicago writer has recently discovered that the Cubs manage to make nonCubs fans miserable, too, through an insidious personality trait called *Cubness.* Ron Berler did extensive research on the composition of World Series teams since 1946. He discovered a simple and frightening truth: When a team has at least three players who *used* to be Cubs, it loses. Since 1946, a dozen teams with three or more ex-Cubs have been in the World Series. Many of these teams were extremely good. But only one of these 12 teams was able to win. Chicago *Tribune* columnist Mike Royko (1986) describes recent evidence:

The trait and facet scales of the NEO-PI-R show good test-retest and split-half reliability. Significant correlations with other measures of the Big Five traits contribute to the construct validity for this measure and for the Big Five taxonomy in general. Costa and McCrae have also developed peer-report versions of the NEO-PI-R. In several studies, they have compared self-reports on Big Five traits with the ratings made by spouses and other peers. McCrae and Costa (1990) report substantial agreement of self-ratings with peer and spouse ratings on all five factors. Agreement between self and spouse tends to be higher than between self and other peers, probably because spouses tend to know each other better than do other peers.

We've seen the Cubs factor at work in recent years. In 1984, when the hated [San Diego] Padres beat out our Cubs [in the National League Playoff], the laugh turned out to be on them. They had three ex-Cubs, the fools, while the Tigers [their opponents in the World Series] had only one and, of course, the Tigers won.

The year before it was the same story. The Phillies had three ex-Cubs. The winning Orioles prudently had kept their roster free of Cubs.

It is Berler's theory that having been a Cub infects a player with something called "Cubness," which seems to spread to other members of their new team.

As Jim Brosnan, a former Cubs pitcher, once said: "You have to have a certain dullness of mind and spirit to play here. I went through psychoanalysis and that helped me deal with my Cubness."

Royko has devised a corollary to Berler's theory. You don't really need three ex-Cubs to lose the World Series, he maintains. All you need is to have more ex-Cubs than the other team has. For the 1986 World Series, Royko bet on the Mets (who had no ex-Cubs) over the Red Sox (who had one—Bill Buckner). Red Sox fans are still plagued with nightmares about the 1986 World Series—how the Red Sox lost it in seven exciting games and how

Bill Buckner played a pivotal last-inning role in the defeat.

It is interesting to speculate on the nature of this trait. It clearly seems to be due to environment over heredity. A person is not born with Cubness. But if he is unfortunate enough ever to don a Cubs uniform, he seems to be cursed for life with the trait. Yet the trait manifests itself only in certain critical situations. An ex-Cub can have a distinguished career with another team, showing few behavioral signs of the inner flaw. But, if that team gets into the World Series. . . .

Is Cubness a component of one of the Big Five traits—like neuroticism? Is Cubness a linear and continuous trait? Or is it an "all-or-none" sort of thing? Are there degrees of Cubness? Does the length of time a player spends with the Cubs increase the trait's severity? Does the trait manifest itself in other realms? Do ex-Cubs have smaller checking accounts? More traffic accidents? Should a woman marry an ex-Cub? Or even date him?

Perhaps future research will provide the answers.

Note: In response to a few letters I received about previous editions of this textbook, Feature 5.B should not be taken seriously and is not meant to show any disrespect for the concept of a trait.

THE CONTROVERSY OVER TRAITS

Even as he constructed the entire field of personality psychology around the central concept of the trait, Gordon Allport (1937) was aware of the controversy over traits. The behaviorists who dominated American psychology in the 1930s saw no reason to acknowledge the importance, even the existence, of traits. After all, traits were hypothesized to exist within the person rather than in the observable public sphere. Unlike behavior, traits could not be directly observed. The behaviorists' commitment to environmentalism made them skeptical, furthermore, about the idea that individual-difference variables within the organism—rather than differences in the environment—might account for individual differences in behavior. And why would anybody want to study individual differences between persons anyway? Research psychologists of the 1930s focused their energies on basic processes, such as perception and learning—processes that were assumed to play themselves out in similar ways from one organism to the next. The differences between organisms that might be detected represented unimportant and doubtlessly random variability. This variability should be of no interest to serious research psychologists.

While trait advocates like Allport, Cattell, and Eysenck pressed on, skepticism about the utility of trait concepts persisted over the decades. In the 1950s, researchers became especially concerned about test-taking styles in trait assessment (Christie & Lindauer, 1963; Edwards, 1957; Jackson & Messick, 1958). Do trait scales really measure the traits they claim to measure, or do they instead merely assess a person's general style of responding to personality scales? Some people try to make themselves look good; a few try to make themselves look bad; some people will say "yes" or "agree" to almost anything; others will persistently say "no." It doesn't matter what particular trait the scale is designed to measure, some skeptics argued, for what the score on the test gives you is a measure of response style rather than the trait itself. The controversy eventually led to refinements in test construction to minimize the bias of response sets, as well as the realization that some response styles are themselves important aspects of personality.

A favorite criticism of traits is that they are labels designed to stereotype and even discriminate against people. Influenced by labeling theory in sociology and social psychology, some writers in the 1960s argued against the use of diagnostic categories such as "schizophrenic" and "obsessive-compulsive disorder" in the assessment of psychological functioning. Such labels were seen to be discriminatory against those unfortunate people whose problems in living were deemed "mental illness" by an oppressive society. Labels served to control people, to keep them in their place (Goffman, 1961). While personality traits are not psychiatric labels, trait theories suffered by guilt through association. Saying that somebody is relatively "low on the trait of agreeableness" is also a label which reifies, or makes overly concrete, what some people consider to be a dubious way of talking about people. Traits are sugar-coated stereotypes. Rather than celebrating human diversity, traits simply lump people into groups. While very strong arguments against these positions have been repeatedly spelled out (e.g., Block, 1981; Hogan, DeSoto, & Solano, 1977; Johnson, 1997; McCrae & Costa, 1995; Wiggins, 1973), this kind of criticism of personality traits can still be heard, especially outside the field of psychology.

The most significant critique ever levied against traits, however, came from a book with the innocuous title *Personality and Assessment*, written in 1968 by the personality psychologist Walter Mischel. Mischel revived a problem in trait assessment that was identified by Allport back in 1937. It is what Allport called the problem of "generality versus specificity." Ideally, traits refer to relatively general tendencies in behavior. A critical assumption of trait theories is that people do indeed show some general consistency in their behavior across situations and over time. If, by contrast, behavior is more specific to the situation, rather than cross-situationally general, then the entire concept of trait comes into question. Mischel (1968, 1973, 1977) called trait concepts into serious question. Because behavior is more situationally specific than cross-situationally general, Mischel maintained, personality trait measures are not particularly useful in the prediction of behavior. And if they can't predict behavior, then what good are they?

Mischel's Critique

The concept of trait implies that behavior is, to a certain extent, cross-situationally consistent: An extraverted person, for instance, is supposed to act in an extraverted, outgoing manner in many different settings, as a general trend across various situations. Mischel argued instead that human behavior is much more situationally specific than the concept of trait would suggest. In the traditions of behaviorism and modern social-learning theory (Chapter 4), Mischel maintained that behavior is shaped largely by the exigencies of a given situation. That people act in consistent ways across different situations, reflecting an underlying consistency of personality traits, is a myth.

Mischel's argument was not new. Behaviorists had made many of the same points, though usually in a different context, since the early days of John Watson (1924). Mischel's thesis, however, was extremely powerful because of the wealth of empirical data he presented. Reviewing scientific literature on such personality variables as honesty, dependency, aggression, rigidity, and attitudes toward authority, Mischel showed that the correlations between (1) personality-trait scores, as determined by personality tests and rating procedures and (2) actual behavior in a particular situation were generally low, rarely exceeding the modest level of +.30. Furthermore, the correlation between indices of the same kind of behavior (such as "honest behavior," "friendly behavior," or "aggressive behavior") emitted by the same persons across different situations was also low.

For example, a classic study of moral behavior in over 8,000 school children (Hartshorne & May, 1928) found that copying from the answer key on one classroom test showed only the modest correlation of +.29 with another form of cheating whereby students inflated their own scores on a different test. The major lesson from this study, argued Mischel, is that individual differences in moral behavior are not consistent across different situations: Children who cheat on one particular test don't necessarily cheat on another. If one wishes to predict the extent to which different children will actually cheat in a particular situation, it makes little sense to invoke a general trait of "honesty" upon which children can be said to differ. As Skinner might have put it in *Walden Two*, there is no such thing as an "honest" or a "dishonest" child, only honest or dishonest behavior displayed in a given situation.

Mischel (1968, 1973) suggested the disturbing possibility that personality traits exist nowhere but in the mind of the observer. The same argument has been forcefully made by social psychologists such as Jones and Nisbett (1972) and Ross (1977), who speak of the **fundamental attribution error**—a general tendency for people to overemphasize traits and underemphasize situations when explaining the causes for *other* people's behaviors. According to this view, when people are asked to explain why another person does what he or she does, they are likely to invoke a general *personality* trait: "Randy punched another basketball player because Randy is an aggressive person" or "Martha got 100% on the mathematics exam because she is brilliant." When asked to explain their own behavior, on the other hand, people are more likely to invoke the specific *situation*: "I punched another basketball player because I was provoked to do so" or "I scored 100% on the mathematics exam because I studied hard." The implication here is that trait psychologists, in attempting to predict and explain the behavior of other people, repeatedly commit the same fundamental attribution error. Personality traits, therefore, are no more than convenient but misleading labels about other people. They exist in the mind of the observing psychologist, not in the personality of the person being observed.

If personality traits exist in the minds of observers rather than in the behavior of those they observe, then traits may tell us more about how people think about other people's behavior than they tell us about behavior itself. In one of the more acerbic critiques of trait conceptualizations, Shweder (1975; Shweder & D'Andrade, 1979) insisted that when trait researchers do indeed demonstrate empirical correlations among different traits (e.g., between, say, "dominance" and "aggressiveness"), their findings simply reflect the semantic similarity of the constructs involved. For example, Passini and Norman (1966) asked students to rate people *whom they had never met* on a number of personality scales. The raters were instructed to base these ratings on what they imagined these people might be like. Factor analysis of the ratings yielded a structure of correlations among the different scales that was almost identical to those structures obtained in other studies employing the same scales—studies in which the raters *were* acquainted with the subjects they were to rate or in which they directly observed subjects' behavior.

Shweder interpreted results like these to suggest that our ratings of personality traits are probably based more on our knowledge of how words (trait descriptors) go together than on our observation of real behavioral associations. If the traits of dominance and aggressiveness, for instance, seem to be similar in meaning, then we assume that behavioral manifestations of these traits are similarly correlated. In this view, people develop a set of assumptions about how certain trait words go together and then they apply these assumptions uncritically in judging the behavior of others. Each person, therefore, develops his or her own **implicit personality theory** (Bruner & Tagiuri, 1954)—the set of associations in the person's mind. Some have suggested that once people have formed an initial impression about where another person stands on a given trait continuum, then they use their implicit personality theories to infer the person's relative standing on other traits as well (Berman & Kenny, 1976). Thus, traits are convenient categories for our perceptions rather than real characteristics of the persons we perceive.

Mischel's critique of personality traits and other highly critical reviews of personality psychology as a whole (for example, Fiske, 1974) launched what has been termed the *person–situation debate* in personality psychology. Defenders of traits (such as Alker, 1972; Block, 1977; Hogan, DeSoto, & Solano, 1977) argued that Mischel had (1) misrepresented many trait theories and trait theorists, (2) selectively reviewed the empirical literature in an unfair way, and (3) overlooked many methodologically sophisticated studies that supported cross-situational consistency of behavior and the inner coherence of personality. Supporters of the Mischel position (such as Argyle & Little, 1972; Mischel, 1977; Shweder, 1975) marshalled more data to buttress their "situationist" claims, often invoking findings from social psychology documenting the influence of situations on behavior.

Throughout the 1970s, a doctrine of **situationism** seemed to threaten the viability of the trait concept in particular and, according to some views, the very enterprise of personality psychology *in toto*. The doctrine may be summarized in four points:

1. Behavior is highly situation-specific, not cross-situationally consistent.

2. Individual differences within a situation are attributed primarily to measurement error rather than broad internal dispositions.

3. Observed response patterns can be causally linked to the stimuli present in the situation.

4. The experiment is the most appropriate method for discovering such stimulus-response links. (Krahe, 1992, p. 29)

In other words, situations rather than traits drive and shape human behavior, a fact that is clearest to see under well-controlled conditions of the laboratory experiment. Observed behavioral differences among persons in the same situation are small, unimportant, or the result of errors or biases on the part of observers and/or methods of measurement. With its conceptual emphasis on the external environment (situation) and methodological preference for controlled laboratory experimentation, situationism came to be associated with certain aspects of the behaviorist legacy—that is, with social-learning theories such as Bandura's and Mischel's (Chapter 4) and with the kind of research conducted by experimental social psychologists.

The person–situation debate seemed to die down in the mid 1980s (Krahe, 1992; Maddi, 1984; West, 1983) as most advocates appeared to settle on something they claimed they were advocating all along: a compromise position of **interactionism.** As the eminent psychologist Kurt Lewin said over 60 years ago, behavior is a function of the person (and his or her traits) in interaction with the environment (Lewin, 1935). Yet this seemingly simple, even obvious, statement is more complex than might first appear, and there still exists considerable controversy as to how it is to be interpreted. There are many ways to conceive of and study the interaction of the person and the environment in the prediction of human behavior. Mischel's critique and the subsequent person–situation debate stimulated considerable thought and research in the field of personality psychology and shaped the thinking of a generation of personality psychologists.

Predicting Some of the People Some of the Time

The heart of Mischel's critique was that people are not consistent in their behavior across different situations. Is it possible, however, that this conclusion is true for only some people? Are some people relatively consistent in their behavior across different situations while certain other people are highly inconsistent? If this is true, then lumping the two types of people together may fool us into concluding that *everybody* is inconsistent.

This intuitively appealing response to the Mischel critique was offered by Daryl Bem (Bem & Allen, 1974) in an influential article, "On Predicting Some of the People Some of the Time." In traditional trait research, argued Bem, the investigator assumes that the trait scored for each subject is equally relevant to all subjects. In other words, while some people may score high and some low on a measure of the trait "friendliness," we generally assume that all people in the study recognize friendliness to be a trait that is germane to their lives. Bem suggested that this assumption may be wrong. For some people (regardless of how they score), friendliness may not be a relevant dimension and may, therefore, not be linked in a consistent fashion to friendly behavior.

Significant correlations between behavior and traits are likely only among people for whom a trait is especially relevant: these people are the "some of the people" whose behavior we can predict "some of the time." The other people are less predictable.

Some studies support Bem's position (Bem & Allen, 1974; Cheek, 1982; Kenrick & Stringfield, 1980; Underwood & Moore, 1981). In investigations of this kind, the researchers typically administer a conventional measure of personality traits and a second measure asking respondents to judge how consistent their behavior is with respect to each of the traits assessed. Those who report that their behavior is consistent with a particular trait (regardless of their score on the trait) are identified as the people for whom the trait is especially relevant. It is for these people only that the actual trait score is assumed to be a good predictor of behavior. Employing this strategy, Bem and Allen (1974) found that consistency between self-reports and peer ratings on the traits of "friendliness" and "conscientiousness" was much higher for individuals who reported consistent behavior compared with individuals who reported low consistency. Kenrick and Stringfield (1980) obtained similar results employing Cattell's 16 source traits. For this study, Table 5.7 shows the intercorrelations of the subjects' personality ratings made by the subjects themselves, by their parents, and by peers for those traits deemed by the subjects to be "most consistent" and "least consistent" in their lives. The correlations between self-ratings and the parent/peer ratings on traits deemed by the subject to be especially consistent are generally quite high, around +.61. For traits considered by the subjects to be inconsistent, on the other hand, the correlations are much lower.

Research that fits under the heading of "predicting some of the people some of the time" makes use of what psychologists call **moderator variables** (Ghiselli, 1956). In a nutshell, studies employing moderator variables are based on the idea that a relation between two variables is moderated or influenced by a third. For example, the relation, between Variable A (a self-report measure of friendliness) and Variable B (friendly behavior observed by others) is moderated by Variable C (the "relevance" of the trait friendliness for the individual's life, as judged by the individual). Variable C is the moderator. In the simplest case, we might divide subjects on the Variable C distribution into two groups: those for whom the trait friendliness is relevant (say, above the median or middle score in the distribution of scores on self-reported trait relevance) and those for whom the trait friendliness is irrelevant (below the median). For the first

TABLE 5.7	*Intercorrelations of Personality Ratings*[a]	
	TRAIT[b]	
RATERS	MOST CONSISTENT	LEAST CONSISTENT
1. Self × Parent	.62 (75)	.16 (76)
2. Self × Peer	.61 (77)	.12 (70)
3. Parent × Peer	.61 (64)	.39 (62)

[a]Ratings made by self, parents, and peers for self-chosen most- and least-consistent traits.
[b]Numbers in parentheses are numbers of subjects.
Source: Modified from Kenrick & Stringfield (1980), p. 95.

group (relatively high relevance on friendliness), the relation between Variable A and Variable B may be strong: One can predict accurately friendly behavior (Variable B) from the level of friendliness trait (Variable A). For the second group (relatively low relevance on friendliness), the relation between Variable A and Variable B may be weak: One cannot predict accurately friendly behavior (Variable B) from scores on friendliness trait (Variable A). In this way, then, the score on Variable C determines the extent to which the behavior is predictable from the trait score.

The same logic can be used in a study in which Variable A is a self-rating on friendliness (or any other personality trait) and Variable B is a peer rating on friendliness (or any other corresponding personality trait). Again, Variable C (trait relevance) may moderate the relation between A and B, such that self-ratings and peer ratings on friendliness are highly correlated among those individuals for whom the trait is relevant (Variable C) and only weakly correlated or noncorrelated among those individuals for whom the trait is not relevant, as we saw in the study by Kenrick and Stringfield (1980). The same logic can also be used with other kinds of moderator variables, that is, other kinds of Variable C. For example, Wymer and Penner (1985) have shown that the consistency between self-ratings (Variable A) and peer ratings (Variable B) of traits is significantly moderated by the variable of *communication skill* (Variable C, the moderator variable). People with good communication skills rate themselves on traits (Variable A) in ways similar to the way they are rated by others (Variable B). Wymer and Penner have also shown that *inner-directedness* can be an important moderator variable. People who value their own beliefs and attitudes, thus showing more inner-directedness than other-directedness—behave in ways that are highly consistent with their trait scores. They are more predictable (Variable A is highly correlated with Variable B) than subjects who are other-directed. Wymer and Penner conclude that inner-directed people are generally "unwilling, unable, or both to change their behavior in response to situational demands" (1985, p. 1002).

A key distinction in research with moderator variables is that between *person-specific* and *trait-specific* moderators (Chaplin, 1991; Koestner, Bernieri, & Zuckerman, 1989). Person-specific moderators are assumed to influence the relation between Variable A and Variable B *for all traits* in a given person. The logic is that some people (those "high" on Variable C) are more predictable overall than are other people (those "low" on Variable C). Moderator variables such as "communication skills" and "inner-directedness" are examples of person-specific moderators. By contrast, trait-specific moderators are based on the logic that some people are more predictable than other people *for some traits*. For example, John may be especially predictable (his trait score predicts his corresponding behavior) for the trait of friendliness, but he may not be especially predictable for the trait of conscientiousness (his trait score does not predict well his behavior). Biesanz, West, and Graziano (1998) have shown that individuals who show stability in their behavioral response patterns over time have higher self–other agreement on trait ratings for conscientiousness and extraversion.

Roy Baumeister and Dianne Tice have coined the term **metatraits** to refer to trait-specific moderators (Baumeister & Tice, 1988; Tice, 1989). A metatrait is "the trait of having vs. not having a particular trait" (Baumeister & Tice, 1988, p. 573). People who are *traited* "have" the trait in question, and thus their behavior should be predictable from their trait score. People who are *untraited* "do not have" the trait in question, and thus their behavior should not be predictable from their trait score. Baumeister and

Tice suggest that one index of traitedness is the degree of variability that a person exhibits in responding to individual items on a particular trait scale. As an example, imagine two people—Jennifer and Rebecca—who both score "moderately high" (say, about a 7 on a scale ranging from 1 to 10) on the trait conscientiousness. In Jennifer's case, her responses to the individual items on the measure are consistently in the moderately high range, around a 7 throughout. By contrast, Rebecca arrives at the total score of 7 by giving some extremely high responses on some items (scores of 9 and 10) and some relatively low-to-medium responses on some other items (scores of 4 and 5). Rebecca's total score averages out to be the same as Jennifer's, but Rebecca shows much more variability in her responding on the trait test. According to Baumeister and Tice, Rebecca's high variability suggests that she is relatively untraited on conscientiousness: She does not "have" this trait to the extent that Jennifer does. By virtue of her consistent responding from one item to the next, Jennifer is "traited" on conscientiousness. Therefore, even though Rebecca and Jennifer have the same conscientiousness scores (they both score 7 on the average), Jennifer's conscientious behavior should be more predictable from her trait score than should Rebecca's conscientious behavior. For the traited Jennifer, the link between the trait and behavior is closer, suggesting greater consistency in the domain of conscientiousness. For the untraited Rebecca, the link is not so close; she shows less consistency in this domain. However, it is entirely possible that for a different trait—say, extraversion—Rebecca is traited and Jennifer untraited.

Personality psychologists have proposed a number of trait-specific moderator variables. They include the aforementioned concept of "trait relevance" (How relevant is the trait in your life? Amelang & Borkenau, 1986) and the similar idea of self-reported "trait consistency" (How consistent are you on this trait? Bem & Allen, 1974), as well as "uniqueness" (How similar to other people are you on this trait? Zuckerman, Miyake, Koestner, Baldwin, & Osborne, 1991), and "observability" (How observable are the manifestations of this trait for you? Kenrick Stringfield, 1980; Zuckerman, Bernieri, Koestner, & Rosenthal, 1989). Some research supports the notion that persons for whom the trait is especially relevant and observable and who see themselves as relatively consistent and unique with respect to the trait do indeed show more correspondence between their self-report trait scores and other indices of the trait (e.g., peer ratings, behavior).

Despite the success that some researchers have reported with trait-specific moderator variables, some reviews of the empirical literature have tempered the early enthusiasm about the moderator approach (Chaplin, 1991; Chaplin & Goldberg, 1984). In general, research has shown that moderator effects are usually quite small, though often statistically significant. For example, Chaplin (1991) concludes that moderator effects in personality are rarely larger than the equivalent of a +.10 correlation. While even small moderator effects can be important and interesting, "moderator variables generally will not serve to transform weak relations among personality variables into strong ones," Chaplin (1991) concludes (p. 143). Other researchers, by contrast, see more promise in the moderator approach (Zuckerman et al., 1989). In the overall, nonetheless, the concept of moderator variables suggests that behavior is more complexly determined than the Mischel critique might lead us initially to believe. Taking some of this complexity into consideration can improve, though perhaps only modestly, the ability of personality psychologists to predict behavior from traits.

Aggregating Behaviors

According to Mischel, traits do not work well in the prediction of behavior because behavior itself is not very consistent from one situation to the next. The lack of such cross-situational consistency in behavior poses a formidable problem for trait theories. However, personality psychologist Seymour Epstein suggested a solution to the problem that is quite old and familiar, making that perennial observation that "sometimes the obvious escapes us." For Epstein and a number of personality psychologists, the answer to the problem of cross-situational consistency in human behavior is quite simple and has been around for a long time. The answer is **aggregation** (Epstein, 1979, 1984, 1986).

To understand Epstein's argument, we have to recall how a psychologist might construct a questionnaire designed to measure a particular personality trait. That procedure involves generating a large pool of "items," which is then reduced through a number of different methods to an economical scale with maximum reliability and validity. Each item on the test is seen as contributing something to the test as a whole: Each item "zeroes in on" the trait from a slightly different angle. Such "zeroing in" is necessary because a trait is a complex construct that might be manifested in a large number of ways, and no single item can successfully capture all the complexity. Therefore, psychologists get as close as they can to a "pure" measure of a trait, minimizing measurement error by constructing tests with multiple items—that is by aggregating test items. Even the simplest trait test, therefore, requires more than 1 or 2 items if it is to be considered reliable. Within reason and all other things being equal, the more items a test has, the more reliable it will be.

With this in mind, then, consider a typical personality study in which an investigator administers a questionnaire containing many items designed to assess a particular trait and correlates scores on that measure with a single instance of behavior, perhaps emitted under laboratory conditions, shown by the respondent. While the trait measure itself may be highly reliable by virtue of aggregation of test items, the single measure of behavior is likely to be highly unreliable, unrepresentative, and saturated with error. It is no wonder, stated Epstein, that Mischel's review of the personality literature found so much inconsistency between trait measures and behavior. According to Epstein, Mischel clearly identified a problem, but he misinterpreted its primary cause. *Overall, the trait measures are sound; it is the single measures of behavior that are at fault.* Substantial consistency between trait scores and behavior across different situations should appear, Epstein maintained, when single instances of behavior are aggregated across many different situations. Trait scores, therefore, should predict consistent trends in behavior across different situations and over time.

A growing body of research suggests that Epstein was right. Figure 5.3 presents data from Epstein (1979) that show that the reliability of a number of different measures—ranging from headaches and stomachaches to social behavior—increases as the number of occasions upon which the measures are taken increases. Therefore, if we wish to obtain a reliable estimate of a person's blood pressure, positive

Seymour Epstein

FIGURE 5.3 *Reliability and Aggregation*

For a number of different measures, reliability (measured as correlations between scores on even days and odd days) increases as the researchers collect and aggregate more data over longer periods of time. (The correlations were obtained by correlating the mean of odd days with the mean of an equal number of even days. The values plotted are the means of the correlations for the variables in a category.)

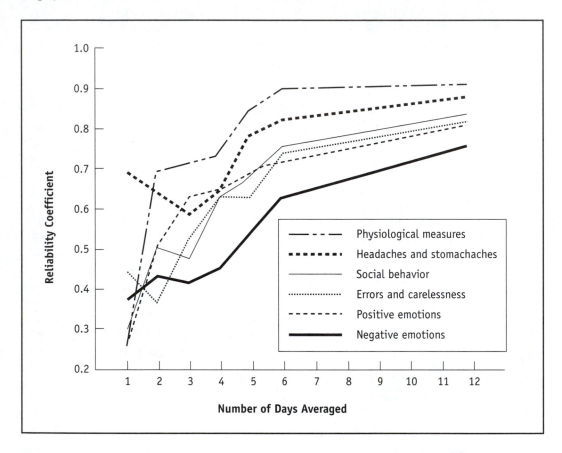

Source: Epstein (1979).

mood, verbal eloquence, food consumption, smile frequency, or whatever, we will do better to sample the phenomenon in question on numerous occasions. As Figure 5.3 shows, the greater the degree of aggregation over time, the higher the reliability of the measure and the closer we get to a pure, stable, and representative estimate of behavior. Table 5.8 presents similar findings from a study by Moskowitz (1982).

In an impressive review, Rushton, Brainerd, and Presley (1983) illustrated the usefulness of aggregation in 12 different areas of psychological research. Especially

TABLE 5.8	Coefficients of Generalizability Dominance and Dependency Behaviors of Preschool Children	
	NUMBER OF WEEKS	
BROAD CONSTRUCT AND REFERENTS	**1**	**8**
Dominance	.34	.76***
Displace	.23	.70***
Command	.24	.71***
Suggest	.08	.40**
Direct	.10	.47***
Threat	.00	.00
Dependency	.07	.38*
Proximity	.16	.60***
Touch	.14	.23
Seek help	.07	.36*
Seek recognition	.06	.36*
Seek supervision	.02	.14

$N = 47$ children (9 children omitted because they were absent for 1 complete week); $*p < .05$;
$**p < .01$; $***p < .001$.
Source: Moskowitz (1982), p. 759.

interesting was their discussion of the famous Hartshorne and May (1928) study of moral behavior—a study that Mischel (1968) cited forcefully as an example of failure to find cross-situational consistency in behavior. Suggesting that the findings in this study have perennially been misinterpreted, Rushton argued that children's moral behavior manifested considerable consistency when appropriate behaviors were aggregated across different tests and situations. Although any single behavioral test of "honesty" correlated, on the average, only .20 with any other single test of honesty, much higher relationships were found when the measures were aggregated into meaningful groups and correlated with other combined behavioral measures, with teachers' ratings of the children, or with children's moral-knowledge scores. Often these correlations were on the order of .50 or .60. For example, a battery of tests measuring cheating by copying correlated +.52 with another battery of tests measuring other types of classroom cheating. Contrary to Mischel's conclusion, aggregation reveals that the children in the Hartshorne and May (1928) study showed consistent individual differences in cheating behavior. Thus, some children may indeed be consistently more honest than others.

Like any good research procedure, aggregation can be used wisely or foolishly (Epstein, 1986). For instance, merely lumping together different instances of behavior will not necessarily increase reliability in measurement. Aggregated items must "hang together" conceptually and/or empirically. In determining how to aggregate data, the psychologist must keep clearly in mind what he or she wishes to learn from a particular study. Therefore, if a child's aggressive behavior toward her sister is a topic of interest, the researcher should not aggregate aggression across different targets (such as aggression toward father, mother, brother, or pets) but should nevertheless aggregate across occasions with the sister. Similarly, if a researcher wishes to know how three different situations differentially influence altruistic behavior in college students, it would be useless to aggregate data across the different situations. In this case, the data should be aggregated across students—the researcher would seek to cancel out individual differences in students in order to see more clearly situational effects for all students in general.

Critics of aggregation argue that it bypasses rather than resolves the problem of cross-situational consistency in behavior (Mischel & Peake, 1982). When researchers aggregate behaviors across many different situations, they fail to show how a particular trait score predicts particular behavior in a particular situation. In settling for predicting general trends across a wide variety of situations, they sacrifice a great deal of precision with respect to any particular situation—precision that may come from a careful analysis of the exigencies in the situation itself. Recent research, however, has examined more precisely the extent to which different kinds of situations and different traits can be successfully examined through aggregation. The results of these studies suggest that aggregation works better across certain kinds of situations than across others.

For example, Moskowitz (1990) examined behavioral manifestations of dominance and friendliness in six different laboratory situations—two involving a same-sex friend, two involving a male stranger, and two involving a female stranger. Friendly and dominant behaviors were rated by observers and by the subjects themselves. As in other studies of aggregation, behavioral self- and observer ratings pooled across the six situations were more strongly correlated with each other than were ratings made within any particular situation itself. But cross-situational consistency was stronger across certain situations than across others. In particular, the greatest degree of convergence between self-ratings and observer ratings on dominance and friendliness occurred *in the two situations with friends.* Less consistency was revealed across the four situations with strangers. Moskowitz concludes that "validity varies as a function of the situation" (p. 1105). Aggregating across different situations in which one is interacting with close friends reveals especially strong levels of cross-situational consistency in behavior. Aggregating across different situations in which one is interacting with strangers reveals less consistency. In the former case, behavior appears to be more strongly shaped by traits. In the latter, situational influences appear to be stronger.

Modern Interactionism

In the aftermath of Mischel's critique of traits and the subsequent person–situation debate, many personality psychologists today endorse some variation of what Krahe (1992) calls the doctrine of *modern interactionism.* The core of the modern interactionist approach is captured in four basic postulates:

1. Actual behavior is a function of a continuous process of multidirectional interaction or feedback between the individual and the situation he or she encounters.

2. The individual is an intentional, active agent in this interactional process.

3. On the person side of the interaction, cognitive and motivational factors are essential determinants of behavior.

4. On the situation side, the psychological meaning of situations for the individual is the important determining factor. (pp. 70–71)

Persons Versus Situations Versus Interactions   There are many different ways of thinking about interactionism (Ozer, 1986). One approach, termed **mechanistic**

interactionism (Endler, 1981), derives from the concept of an interaction effect as it appears in certain statistical procedures. In mechanistic interactionism, a person's trait constitutes one independent predictor, the situation constitutes a second independent predictor, and the interaction between trait and situation constitutes a third predictor. The dependent variable, or outcome to be predicted, is some form of measurable behavior. In such a study, a significant effect for the trait–situation interaction indicates (1) that there exists a statistical tendency for the trait to be associated with the behavior *when a particular level of the situation* is involved, or, similarly, (2) that there exists a tendency for the situation to be associated with the behavior *when a particular level of the trait* is involved.

Many studies in personality and social psychology draw implicitly upon a mechanistic model of interactionism (Blass, 1984). A good example of this approach is a study of altruism by Romer, Gruder, and Lizzadro (1986). The researchers administered questionnaires designed to identify two types of college students, enrolled in a psychology class, likely to show helping behavior. One type, scoring high on the need for nurturance (need to care for others) but low on the need for succorance (need to be cared for by others), was called "altruist." The other type, scoring high on both needs for nurturance and succorance, was called "receptive–giving." Helping behavior was operationalized as the student's volunteering to help a distressed experimenter complete a research project by participating in a psychological experiment. The experimenter appealed for the student's help over the phone. In one scenario (the "no-compensation" situation), the student was told that his or her help was desperately needed but that the experimenter could not offer any course credit for the help. The "compensation situation" involved the same plea but in this situation the student was promised that course credit would be received as compensation.

The researchers believed that helping behavior was likely to be a function of the interaction of personality and situation. Specifically, they predicted that altruists would show high levels of helping behavior in situations in which they were *not likely to be compensated* given that their need for succorance was low. Receptive–giving persons, on the other hand, should show high levels of helping behavior in situations in which they *were likely to be compensated*, since their need for succorance was high. As Figure 5.4 shows, the percentage of students agreeing to help is well predicted as an interaction of person and environment supporting the interactional hypothesis. Altruists helped more in the no-compensation condition than they did in the compensation condition. Receptive–giving students showed the reverse pattern, exhibiting higher levels of helping when compensated.

Reciprocal Interactionism   While mechanistic interactionism partitions the variance in behavior into that accounted for by persons, situations, and their interactions, **reciprocal interactionism** conceives of a more fluid and complex pattern in which person, situation, and behavior continually and reciprocally influence one another (Endler, 1981). This general way of seeing interactions is similar to Bandura's notion of "reciprocal determinism" (Chapter 4) and bears resemblance, as well, to systems theory. Person, situation, and behavior are parts of an interdependent system of causes and effects. Another way of understanding reciprocal interactionism is in terms of two multidimensional systems—the person and the environment—repeatedly "coming to terms" with each other via mutual and dynamic transactions (Brunswik, 1957):

Personality, Compensation, and Helping Behavior

The percentage of individuals who helped is a function of 1) personality type (altruistic vs. receptive–giving) and 2) the situational condition (compensation vs. no compensation).

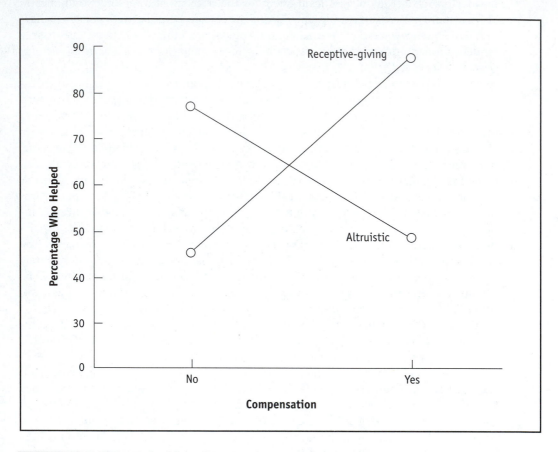

Source: Romer, Gruder, & Lizzadro (1986), p. 1006.

Both organism and environment will have to be seen as systems, each with properties of its own, yet both hewn from the same block. Each has surface and depth, or overt and covert regions . . . the interrelationship between the two systems has the essential characteristic of a "coming-to-terms." And this coming-to-terms is not merely a matter of the mutual boundary or surface areas. It concerns equally as much, or perhaps even more, the rapport between the central, covert layers of the two systems. It follows that, much as psychology must be concerned with the texture of the organism or of its nervous processes and must investigate them in depth, it also must be concerned with the texture of the environment as it extends in depth away from the common boundary. (p. 5)

It is probably some form of reciprocal interactionism that is regularly implied by most personality psychologists when they say that behavior is a function of the interaction of person and environment. It has, however, proven extremely difficult to design studies that can measure dynamic, reciprocal interactions in a meaningful way (Ozer, 1986). One successful effort however, is the work of Emmons, Diener, and Larsen (1986) and Emmons and Diener (1986b), who have offered two alternative models of reciprocal interactionism. The "choice of situations" model suggests that people select situations and avoid others on the basis of certain personality traits and needs. The "affect congruence" model suggests that people experience greater positive affect and less negative affect in situations congruent with their personality characteristics. Research in support of congruence can be found in many places (Ickes, Snyder, & Garcia, 1997). There are several lines of evidence for the proposition that people chose to enter and spend time in situations that promote the expression of their own trait-relevant behavior, and that they often enjoy doing so. A long tradition of research in career psychology shows that people flourish in their work environment when there is a good fit between their personality traits and the characteristics of the environment (Holland, 1996). Lack of congruence between traits and work situations, by contrast, leads to dissatisfaction, unstable career paths, and lowered performance levels.

Traits as Conditional Statements   Throughout the years of the person–situation debate and up to the present time, Walter Mischel has continued to offer astute observations and critiques of trait psychology. His recent theorizing appears to leave more room for the working of broad dispositional traits than was the case when he offered his first important critique in 1968. Nonetheless, he has continued to underscore the issue of variability in responding across situations (Mischel & Shoda, 1995, 1998; Shoda, Mischel, & Wright, 1994). How do we put together the fact that people act in very different ways from one situation to the next with the fact that broad personality traits appear to account for trends in behavior across situations? As Mischel and Shoda (1998, p. 229) put it, how do we "reconcile dynamics and dispositions"?

Like many personality psychologists today, Mischel ascribes to an interactionist approach for understanding human behavior. But Mischel has articulated the nature of the interaction in more detail than is usually the case. While conceding that aggregation studies support the general idea that traits predict a modicum of behavioral consistency across different situations, Mischel has turned his attention to a second kind of consistency—consistency in variation. People change their behaviors from one situation to the next in consistent ways, Mischel asserts. And people differ from one another in their characteristic ways of doing so. Let us take a simple example. Matthew and Julie are both relatively easygoing people, but both of them can become very irritated in certain situations. When a teacher or parent offers advice to Matthew, he tends to be gracious and accepting, but he becomes very irritated when his friends or siblings tell him what to do. By contrast, Julie finds extremely annoying her mother's and her teacher's suggestions for how she should improve her life, but she is quite willing to take the same kind of advice from her friends. In an overall sense, Matthew and Julie don't seem to differ in their level of irritability, but each of them becomes irritable in a different situation. For Matthew, *if* peers give him advice, *then* he becomes irritated, but *if* authority figures offer advice, *then* he is gracious. For Julie, *if* authority figures give her advice, *then* she becomes irritated, but *if* peers offer advice, *then* she is gracious. Matthew and Julie each show a different consistency in *if . . . then* relations.

An *if . . . then* relation is a *conditional statement. If* certain conditions are satisfied, *then* a particular result will occur. In the cases of Matthew and Julie, *if* a particular situation occurs (*if* peer offers advice, *if* authority offers advice), *then* a particular behavioral response is expressed (*then* person is irritated, *then* person is gracious). Mischel and his colleagues have conducted studies to document consistencies in *if . . . then* relations, arguing that this kind of conditional and interactional consistency is an extremely important and underrated aspect of personality functioning. In one study, the researchers collected behavioral observations of 84 children (whose average age was 10 years old) attending a 6-week summer camp. The children's behavior was painstakingly documented. Specifically, within each hour of camp activity, observers recorded the frequency with which five different types of situations occurred: (1) peer teased, provoked or threatened the child; (2) adult warned the child; (3) adult punished the child by giving him or her "time out"; (4) peer initiated positive social contact; and (5) adult praised the child verbally. Within each situation, the observers recorded the frequency of five different kinds of behavior on the part of the child: (1) verbal aggression, (2) physical aggression, (3) whined or displayed babyish behavior, (4) complied or gave in, and (5) talked prosocially. Crossing the five situations by the five behavioral responses results in 25 different conditional patterns. For example, one pattern would be *if* adult warned the child, *then* the child whined. Another would be *if* a peer initiated positive social contact, *then* the child engaged in verbal aggression. And so on. The design of this study enabled the researchers, therefore, to examine in detail 25 different kinds of interactions, each conceived as an *if . . . then* relation.

The most interesting results from the camp study were the *intraindividual profiles* that the observers obtained. For each individual child, the researchers were able to calculate a number of different profiles exhibiting consistency in behavioral variability. Figure 5.5 gives examples from four different children. The solid line for each profile charts the relative occurrence of the behavior verbal aggression in each of five different situations during one time period (Time 1) in the study. The broken line charts the relative occurrence of the same kind of behavior across the same five situations at a second time period (Time 2). As you can see, for three of the four children, the profile at Time 1 matches closely the profile at Time 2. For example, in both time periods, Child 17 shows low levels of verbal aggression in situations of peer approach and peer teasing, moderate levels in situations of adult praise and adult warn, and very high levels of verbal aggression in the situation of adult punishment. By contrast, at both Time 1 and Time 2, Child 9 shows high levels of verbal aggression in the peer approach situation and generally moderate levels in the other four. The two lines for Child 17 match more closely than do the two corresponding lines for Child 9, indicating somewhat greater stability or consistency in behavioral variability for Child 17. The one child who shows low consistency in variability is Child 48, whose verbal aggression appears to be moderate across all five situations at Time 1 but high in situations of peer tease and adult praise at Time 2.

In the camp study, the researchers documented considerable consistency in *if . . . then* relations for most of the children. Combining the results of all 84 children, they also found that intraindividual profiles were, on the average, highest for the behaviors of verbal aggression and compliance and lowest for prosocial talk. This means that

| FIGURE 5.5 | *Profiles of Behavioral Variability* |

Variability in verbal aggression across five different conditions differs for four different children. Note: The two lines indicate the profiles based on two different samples of occasions in which each child encountered each type of psychological situation, shown as Time 1 (solid) and Time 2 (broken).

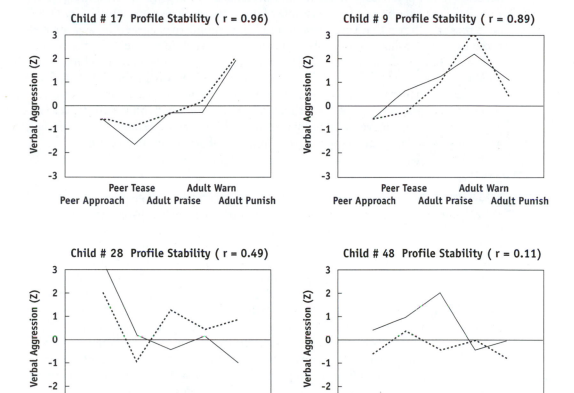

Source: Shoda, Mischel, & Wright (1994), p. 678.

children tended to be most consistent from Time 1 to Time 2 in the patterning of their verbal aggression and compliance behaviors across the five different situations, while they tended to be somewhat less consistent from Time 1 to Time 2 in the patterning of their prosocial talk across the five situations. Yet even for prosocial talk, the intraindividual profiles showed significantly more than a chance amount of consistency in behavioral variability.

The camp study is one of the best examples anywhere of research inspired by an interactionist view of personality. Mischel and his colleagues have reconceptualized

individual differences dimensions in such a way as to reconcile dispositions and dynamics. The "traits" that these researchers focus on are consistent individual differences in the variability that people show across different situations for the same kind
of behavior. Individual differences in behavioral variability offer a new way to think
about traits and about the ways in which people differ from one another in consistent
ways. Mischel's work, furthermore, reflects growing interest in personality, social, and
developmental psychology in lawful and predictable variability in responding across
situations and over time. As one example of this interest, Brown and Moskowitz (1998)
have recently shown that variations in dominant, submissive, agreeable, and quarrelsome behaviors follow predictable cycles from one week to the next. In the overall,
these four classes of behavior tend to rise over the course of the week, reaching a peak
on Wednesday or Thursday, and then drop rather precipitously by the weekend. Some
individuals, furthermore, show predictable daily cycles in behavioral fluctuation,
Brown and Moskowitz reveal. In particular, highly extraverted individuals tend to engage in increasingly more social behaviors as the day wears on, exhibiting an especially
wide range of social activities with a large number of people in the evening.

Conclusion

Mischel's (1968) critique of traits launched a 20-year "debate" in personality psychology about the extent to which differences in internal personality dispositions versus external situational variables should be taken into consideration in the prediction of
behavior. Initially, Mischel (1968) mounted a forceful attack against traits and strongly
urged personality psychologists to refocus their attention on external situational variables. This argument spawned the position of situationism, which seemed to hold sway
for most of the 1970s. The proponents of trait approaches launched a series of intellectual counterattacks in the late 1970s and 1980s (e.g., Funder & Ozer, 1983). Some
of their best ammunition came from aggregation studies, which showed that individual differences in well-measured personality traits were indeed predictive of general
behavioral trends when those trends were observed across many different situations
and over time. Still, when it comes to predicting behavior in any particular situation, a
single personality trait is likely to account for only a modest amount of variance. After
all, any particular piece of behavior is strongly *overdetermined* by many different internal and external factors, as Freud (Chapter 3) first taught. Focusing research attention
on each of several different kinds of situations, Mischel and his colleagues have recently documented strikingly consistent individual differences in response variability.
Thirty years after his original critique of traits, Mischel has come around to an interesting kind of trait idea—the idea that major, traitlike, individual differences in people's behavior can be observed at the level of *if . . . then* relations.

   The person–situation debate helped to refine psychologists' thinking about traits and
situations (Funder & Colvin, 1991; Kenrick & Funder, 1988). Personality research today would appear to be much more interactional in spirit and design than it was 30 years
ago. Psychologists appear to have a much better appreciation of the extent to which personality dispositions and situational exigencies interact in the making of behavior. At the
same time, the general concept of a personality trait has emerged from the controversy
stronger than ever before. As we will see in the next two chapters, personality psychologists have utilized trait measures and trait theories in new and powerful ways in the past

20 years. As studies employing moderator variables and aggregation designs made a stronger case for the predictive efficacy of personality traits, psychologists in the 1980s were also examining the longitudinal stability of traits over the life course, the origins of traits in genetic differences and environmental effects, the psychobiological underpinnings of traits, and the extent to which a viable taxonomy of traits could be developed. It is to these issues that we will turn in the next two chapters.

SUMMARY

1. Personality traits are broad individual differences among people in characteristic thoughts, feelings, and behaviors. Psychologists typically conceive of traits as bipolar linear dimensions that capture general, global, and stable dispositions of personality. People can be compared and contrasted with respect to their traits. Psychologists have traditionally disagreed about the technical nature of traits, with opinions ranging from those who argue that traits are neuropsychic structures that exert a causal influence on an actor's behavior to those who suggest that traits are mere cognitive categories used by observers to make sense of social life.

2. Characterizations of personality traits can be found in ancient texts. A pupil of Aristotle, Theophrastus generated one of the earliest known trait lists through his semihumorous character sketches. Later, the Greek physician Galen codified the humoral theory of traits, delineating four basic personality types that were each linked to characteristic bodily fluids. The sanguine, phlegmatic, melancholic, and choleric types were later depicted by the philosopher Kant and have been recaptured in Eysenck's modern theory of personality traits. Scientific research on traits began in the late 19th century and was greatly promoted by advances in statistics, such as the invention of the correlation coefficient and factor analysis.

3. Two highly influential trait theorists of the 20th century were Gordon Allport and Raymond B. Cattell. Allport centered the entire discipline of personality psychology on the concept of trait, which he defined as a neuropsychic structure responsible for consistencies in behavior over time and across situations. Allport distinguished between common traits, upon which many people could be compared, and personal dispositions, which were characteristics that were unique to a given person. While Allport's approach to traits tended toward the literary, Cattell developed a rigorously quantitative program for trait research. Combining life record (L) data, questionnaire (Q) data, and laboratory test (T) data, Cattell distinguished between surface and source traits. Through extensive factor analysis, he derived 16 basic source traits (measured on Cattell's 16PF inventory) that, he believed, accounted for the lion's share of variance in personality. In Cattell's characteristic approach to research, scores on source traits, states, social roles, and situational factors were combined into a weighted specification equation to predict a person's behavior.

4. Another pioneer in trait psychology, Hans Eysenck used factor analysis to develop a highly influential theory that accounted for human individuality through three basic traits—extraversion–introversion, neuroticism, and psychoticism. Eysenck argued that each of the three traits is linked to individual differences in neurophysiology. Building on the work of Allport and Cattell and employing some of Eysenck's concepts as well, many personality psychologists today believe that the entire universe of trait concepts can be divided into five general trait domains or clusters, called the Big Five. According to one widely cited description, the five basic factors of personality traits can be labeled extraversion, neuroticism, openness to experience, agreeableness, and conscientiousness.

5. The measurement of traits typically relies on ratings or judgments. An influential tradition of psychological research suggests that people are prone to make characteristic errors in judging their own behavior and the behavior of others. Nonetheless, recent studies of trait judgments show that despite errors, people are surprisingly accurate in overall trait judgments and that agreement between ratings of a person's behavior by different observers and between self-ratings and peer ratings tend to be relatively high. Characteristics of the observer, the person observed, the particular trait being considered, and the information used to make the trait rating have strong effects on the extent to which trait ratings are accurate and valid.

6. Most personality traits can be measured through self-report scales. The construction of self-report trait measures typically follows a systematic approach of item generation, item analysis, evaluation of the item pool, and efforts to predict external behavior from the items that make up the final scale. A trait scale should show high test-retest reliability and internal consistency (split-half reliability). Ultimately, a scale's worth is understood in terms of construct validity. Construct validation is the process of simultaneously validating a scale and the construct it is designed to measure, and it involves the gradual articulation of a nomological network of research findings. Beyond reliability and construct validity, other indices of the worth of a trait scale include utility, economy, and communicability.

7. Personality psychologists have developed a number of omnibus personality inventories that measure individual differences in many traits at the same time. The oldest of these is the clinically oriented Minnesota Multiphasic Personality Inventory (MMPI). Popular and well-designed inventories used in contemporary trait research include the California Psychological Inventory (CPI), the Personality Research Form (PRF), and the NEO-PI-R (the Neuroticism-Extraversion-Openness Personality Inventory Revised). The NEO-PI-R measures individual differences in each of the Big Five traits and provides for each trait six individual facet scores.

8. Since the time of Allport, the concept of a personality trait has been controversial. The most important critique of the concept was levied by Walter Mischel in the late 1960s. While the concept of trait assumes some degree of cross-situational consistency in behavior, Mischel argued that behavior is much more situationally specific than cross-situationally consistent. He also suggested that trait labels exist more in the minds of observers than in the actual personality of the person being observed. Mischel's review of the literature suggested that trait scores fail to predict what a person will do in particular situations. Mischel's critique launched the person–situation debate in personality psychology, which ran through the 1970s and 1980s and eventually shaped a good deal of thinking in personality psychology today.

9. In response to the Mischel critique, researchers began to use moderator variables to enhance the predictive power of trait scores. The logic of this approach was that introducing certain variables that moderated the relation between a trait and trait-related behavior would enhance the psychologist's success in predicting some of the people some of the time. Researchers also began to employ the method of aggregation in trait research. By pooling or aggregating behavioral scores across many different situations and over time, researchers obtained more reliable assessments of the behavior to be predicted by trait scores. Aggregation studies have shown that trait scores often account for substantial variance in behavioral trends across situations and over time.

10. Many psychologists have endeavored to tease apart the interaction of traits and situations in the prediction of behavior. Mechanistic interactionism divides up the variance in dependent behaviors into that accounted for by the trait, that accounted for by the situation, and that accounted for by the interaction of trait and situation. Reciprocal interactionism conceives of a more fluid and complex pattern in which person, situation, and behavior continually and reciprocally influence one another. A third approach to interactionism focuses on individual differences in behavioral variability across situations. According to this approach, each person shows a relatively consistent pattern of changing behavior from one situation to the next. Individual differences in these patterns of behavioral change may be understood as characteristic differences in *if . . . then* relations. As the person–situation debate has died down and researchers have come to endorse different forms of interactionism, psychologists have developed a clearer understanding of the relations between traits and situations in the prediction of behavior. In addition, the concept of the personality trait itself would seem to have emerged from the debate as a more powerful and useful concept than perhaps it has ever been before.

6

The Big Five

In order to keep up with what is happening in personality psychology, I have to read the journals. I say "have to" because I must admit that even though personality psychology is, in my view, the most fascinating topic in the world, not everything that is written in the field of personality psychology—or in any scientific field, for that matter—is interesting and fun to read. Still, there is no way to get around it. Important findings and ideas in any scientific field are communicated through that field's professional journals, as well as in some scholarly books and through conferences where scientists get together to show one another what they have been doing. Certain journals are especially prestigious and influential; certain books attract considerable attention; and certain conferences have the reputation of consistently stimulating scientific discourse. Increasingly, scientific findings are also communicated through the Internet. In addition, the popular press will pick up what it considers to be really important scientific findings or those likely to be of interest to a wide readership. High-quality newspapers and magazines, therefore, can sometimes serve as good secondary sources for scientific information. Furthermore, scientists may go so far these days as to call a news conference to announce an especially significant breakthrough.

It is quite ironic, therefore, that what has turned out to be one of the more important scientific studies ever done on the topic of personality traits was communicated as an obscure technical report put out by the United States Air Force. Ernest Tupes and Raymond Christal worked at the Lackland Air Force Base in the mid-1950s. As research psychologists, Tupes and Christal were given the job of developing personality assessment procedures for Air Force Academy cadets. Borrowing rating scales developed by Raymond B. Cattell, the researchers administered a series of questionnaires to cadets and eventually factor-analyzed the results. They also re-analyzed studies of trait ratings done by Cattell (1947) and Fiske (1949). Their analyses led them to conclude that the many different traits that might account for the richness of human individuality can be boiled down to five basic dimensions. Borrowing labels that had been in the personality literature for some time, Tupes and Christal (1958, 1961) called the five factors "surgency/extraversion," "emotional stability," "culture," "agreeableness," and "conscientiousness." Factor scores on these traits (especially emotional stability, culture, and conscientiousness), furthermore, were shown to predict objective assessments of the cadets' leadership abilities and superiors' ratings of their potential to be Air Force officers (Tupes & Kaplan, 1961). "In many ways it seems remarkable," commented Tupes and Christal (1961), that such stability and coherence in the structure of personality traits "should be found in an area which to date has granted anything but consistent results" (p. 12). These big five trait dimensions have "always been there," they concluded, but the consistency "has been hidden by inconsistency in factorial techniques and philosophies, the lack of replication using identical variables, and disagreement among analysts as to factor titles" (p. 12).

Tupes and Christal communicated their findings without fanfare and celebration. No newspapers picked up the story. No more than a handful of people read the original report. Nonetheless, their investigation of the factorial structure of trait ratings eventually had a big impact (Digman, 1996; Wiggins & Trapnell, 1997). The study done by Tupes and Christal provided considerable empirical support for a five-factor model of personality traits—a model suggested by Donald Fiske's (1949) findings a decade before and hinted at even in early studies done by Webb (1915), Garnett (1919), Thurstone (1934), and Guilford and Guilford (1939). One of the few who apparently did read Tupes and Christal's paper was Warren Norman (1963), who conducted his own factor-analytic study of trait ratings and arrived at a very similar five-factor solution. Norman suggested that the five factors might represent "an adequate taxonomy of personality attributes" (p. 582). Similar factor solutions were derived in trait rating studies done by Borgatta (1964) and Smith (1967). Among the small group of psychologists in the 1960s and 1970s who read about and discussed these findings, however, skepticism abounded (Digman, 1996). Five factors are too few and too simplistic, some argued. Cattell, for example, set forth 16 basic source traits. Even Norman (1967) came to agree that there have to be more traits than five, and he went back to the dictionary to generate a new list of 18,125 trait terms in the English language. On the other end of the spectrum, Hans Eysenck was convinced that three basic, biologically rooted traits are all that is needed.

Throughout the 1960s and 1970s, a small group of researchers explored in detail the proposition that personality traits can be grouped into five basic clusters. Lewis Goldberg and his colleagues worked with the set of dictionary words listed by Norman. Following an idea that Sir Francis Galton (1882) entertained long ago, Goldberg reasoned that the structure of personality traits may be revealed in language. If traits specify important individual differences that people are likely to notice in everyday life, then the language people use to talk about human behavior and experience should reflect or encode those differences. If the extent to which a person is outgoing and sociable is an important dimension of human conduct, for example, then there should be a set of words in the language people use to depict this individual difference in personality. Goldberg (1981, 1990; Saucier & Goldberg, 1996) articulated what has come to be called the **lexical hypothesis** in personality psychology. The lexical hypothesis holds that "the most important individual differences in human transactions will come to be encoded as single terms in some or all of the world's languages" (Goldberg, 1990, p. 1216). In addition, "the degree of representation of an attribute in language has some correspondence with the general importance of the attribute" (Saucier & Goldberg, 1996, p. 26). To put this second point differently, the most important individual differences should be encoded through the greatest number of words, especially adjectives. Through painstaking studies of adjectival ratings, Goldberg eventually concluded that a five-factor structure best accounts for the interrelations among trait ratings, whether those ratings are ratings of the self or ratings of others. Other researchers working with the lexical hypothesis eventually came to similar conclusions (Angleitner, Ostendorf, & John, 1990; DeRaad, Mulder, Loosterman, & Hofstee, 1988; Digman & Takemoto-Chock, 1981; Sneed, McCrae, & Funder, 1997).

Goldberg worked with the English language. Other researchers, however, have employed the lexical hypothesis to examine the structure of trait terms in a number of other languages. Results of these many cross-cultural studies are not uniform, but the pattern of results tends to support the idea that approximately five basic trait clusters can be discerned. Comparable five-factor schemes have been proposed by German and Dutch psychologists (John, 1990). Early studies identified the five factors in trait inventories written in Japanese, Chinese, Tagalog (Filipino), and modern Hebrew (e.g., Church & Katigbak, 1989). Recent factor-analytic studies have examined languages in India (Narayanan, Mensa, & Levine, 1995), Hungary (DeRaad & Szrimak, 1994), and Estonia (Allik & Realo, 1997), among others. Again, the results are not all perfectly consistent but generally support models approaching the five-factor scheme. For example, researchers factor-analyzed trait ratings made by Filipino high-school and college students and found dimensions that strongly paralleled four of the five basic dimensions found in English. However, the fifth dimension in English (referring to emotional stability, or neuroticism) did not find a clear match in the students' native language (Church, Reyes, Katigbak, & Grimm, 1997). Psychologists have also translated self-report personality scales directly from English into other languages and then factor-analyzed the responses to those tests. Data from translations of the NEO-PI-R into German, Portuguese, Hebrew, Chinese, Korean, and Japanese generally support the five-factor structure of traits originally delineated in the English lexicon (McCrae & Costa, 1997b).

It took about 25 years from the publication of Tupes and Christal's obscure report for the Big Five model of personality traits to re-emerge as a strong intellectual force in personality psychology. In the 1980s and 1990s, advocates of the Big Five approach conducted a large number of studies to support the legitimacy of the five-factor model. Among the most prolific researchers continue to be Paul Costa and Robert McCrae, who designed the most widely used self-report inventory for measuring the Big Five— the NEO-PI-R. Costa and McCrae have also shown that some comprehensive trait measures developed without awareness of the Big Five model can be factor-analyzed to reveal a five-factor trait structure. For example, Costa and McCrae (1988) factor-analyzed responses on Jackson's 20-scale PRF and obtained the predicted five-factor solution, and Paunonen, Jackson, Trzebinski, and Forsterling (1992) did the same with the pictorial, nonverbal form of the PRF, employing the measure in four countries (Canada, Finland, Poland, and Germany).

I do not wish to overstate the degree of consensus about the five-factor model for personality traits. Some critics have questioned the fundamental logic of applying factor analysis to derive basic dimensions (Block, 1995), and others have cautioned against seeing the five-factor model as encompassing *all* of personality itself (McAdams, 1992b). There is more to personality than traits. Others have objected that the five basic trait dimensions may be too general for predicting precise behavioral outcomes (Briggs, 1989; Paunonen, 1998). Some researchers believe that a six- or seven-factor solution is better for personality traits, and those strongly influenced by Eysenck contend that two or three factors are what is needed. Within the growing community of researchers who employ the five-factor framework, there is still considerable disagreement on what the factors should be called and how each should be defined. One of the factors, for example, has been variously labeled as "culture" (Norman, 1963), "intellectance" (Hogan, 1986), and "openness to experience" (McCrae & Costa, 1985b).

Despite the diversity of views, there appears to be a general consensus in the field today that the thousands of traits that might be imagined for human personality can be reduced to a very manageable set of five or so basic groups, clusters, or dimensions. To label those dimensions, I will borrow Costa and McCrae's influential and easy-to-remember framework. I will refer in this chapter to the five factors of extraversion *(E)*, neuroticism *(N)*, openness to experience *(O)*, agreeableness *(A)*, and conscientiousness *(C)*. The first letters of the five can be combined to yield the word OCEAN. The vast ocean of personality traits, therefore, can be divided into five areas. Furthermore, each of the areas can be further subdivided. Costa and McCrae suggest that each of the Big Five dimensions is made up of six *facets*, or subordinate traits. The six facets of

TABLE 6.1	*The Big Five Traits and Their Facets as Measured on the NEO-PI-R*

E: Extraversion	*A:* Agreeableness
Warmth	Trust
Gregariousness	Straightforwardness
Assertiveness	Altruism
Activity	Compliance
Excitement seeking	Modesty
Positive emotions	Tender-mindedness
N: Neuroticism	*C:* Conscientiousness
Anxiety	Competence
Angry hostility	Order
Depression	Dutifulness
Self-consciousness	Achievement striving
Impulsiveness	Self-discipline
Vulnerability	Deliberation
O: Openness to Experience	
Fantasy	
Aesthetics	
Feelings	
Actions	
Ideas	
Values	

neuroticism, for example, are anxiety, angry hostility, depression, self-consciousness, impulsiveness, and vulnerability. While not all researchers accept Costa and McCrae's view of facets, I will refer to them again and again in this chapter, because I think the facets help to convey the many meanings and possible components of each of the factors. In this chapter, we will examine each of the Big Five trait domains. Table 6.1 lists Costa and McCrae's version of the Big Five factors with the corresponding labels for facets.

E: EXTRAVERSION

When I began teaching at Northwestern University, my office was located in a building that also housed the graduate school of business and management. Offices and seminar rooms for my department were on one side of the building, and the business school occupied the other side. The business school ran a small cafeteria that also served as a study lounge, and I would occasionally walk over there to grab lunch or a mid-afternoon snack. The place was a beehive of activity—students talking, laughing, working in groups, everything very busy and upbeat. Every time I went there, I was struck by how different this place was from comparable settings I had come to know as a graduate student myself and as a faculty member. The students looked and acted differently. For starters, they wore beautiful and presumably expensive clothes. The women wore nicely tailored suits; the men often sported ties. I virtually never saw blue jeans or T-shirts in this place. Second, the students were so much more lively and outgoing than those I have typically known. I am not suggesting that most graduate students in psychology and related fields are depressive people who do not know how to have fun. But these business and management students seemed different, still. So much talk and laughter, so much earnest activity, always in groups. And so much smiling! I thought if I smiled that much my face would hurt. I found the place very refreshing and energizing at first, but after a while I began to feel as if I were drowning in a sea of extraversion. Eventually, I quit going. I have to admit I like the library better.

My little anecdote proves nothing, is completely unscientific, and can be interpreted in many different ways. My impression was that the graduate students in business and management were much more outgoing, lively, and sociable than most other graduate students I have known. But I have to concede that I have never observed a setting of graduate students exactly comparable to the study lounge I described. Maybe if you put 100 psychology graduate students into a study lounge situation exactly like this one, they would show the same patterns of outgoing behavior, group activity, lively discussion, and seemingly incessant smiling and laughter. I think not, but I could be wrong. Surely, this kind of social setting pulls for and encourages the kind of behavior I repeatedly observed. As we saw in Chapter 4 and in the context of the person–situation debate of the 1970s and 1980s, a strong case must be made for the idea that behavior patterns are always a function of situational opportunities and constraints. We must understand behavior in its social context. Contexts that encourage and support extraverted behavior are likely to produce extraverted behavior.

For the sake of argument, however, let us say that I am right at a behavioral level in surmising that those business students I encountered behaved in more outgoing and lively ways than a comparable group of psychology graduate students might behave, even in the same social setting. The reasons for such a difference, should it exist, could be couched in terms of the socialization of graduate students. Northwestern's business school emphasizes the methods of case analysis and group projects. Business school students are taught to work on case problems together in "teams" or groups. This is part of their socialization as graduate students. By contrast, graduate training in psychology is somewhat more individualistic. Students do work in groups, but a great deal of study involves working alone, as in reading texts and articles and writing papers. There is more emphasis on a student's developing a unique perspective of his or her own, typically expressed most fully in the student's Ph.D. dissertation. On the topic of clothing, this line of reasoning seems especially valid. The business students were better dressed because the norms of the business world typically require this. They "looked the part" of young managers and business professionals. In addition, they probably had more money than psychology graduate students I have known, which they could use to purchase fine clothing. (Indeed, some of the business students had come back to school after enjoying some financial success in the business world.)

The behavioral differences I observed can be accounted for by considering the environmental, contextual, and socialization differences between the business and the psychology graduate students I encountered. But such an accounting cannot rule out another very simple and plausible possibility—a possibility that is not inconsistent with these other explanations but that instead can complement them. Put simply, maybe their traits are a little different. Maybe business students are a bit more extraverted than other graduate students I have known. On the average, maybe business graduate students score slightly more in the direction of the extraversion pole on a general trait continuum and psychology graduate students score slightly more in the direction of the introversion pole. It would not need to be a big difference—just a tendency, a slight difference in the mean or average tendencies of each of the two groups. This possibility fits many people's intuitive sense that individuals who are drawn to the worlds of business, management, and marketing are and need to be rather outgoing in their behavior and very comfortable in working with other people. By contrast, people expect that research scientists and academics, the professions to which many psychology graduate students were headed, are likely to be somewhat more introverted. These intuitions, of course, could be wrong, and if they are taken too seriously or interpreted too rigidly, they can lead to stereotypic thinking. But research in career psychology provides some support for the hunch, suggesting that extraversion is associated with participation and success in the business world (Eysenck, 1973; Holland, 1996). People who are especially outgoing, lively, energetic, enthusiastic, warm, gregarious, and sociable may gravitate toward activities and roles that capitalize on these characteristics.

As a mildly introverted kind of a person myself, I ended up avoiding the study lounge and seeking out settings that were quieter and more conducive to individual reading and study, as the research suggests I should (Eysenck, 1973). Sure, I enjoy being with people; I have a good time at parties (usually). But I do not think I would enjoy a job that required the high levels of teamwork and intense social interaction that many people enjoy as business managers and in other more "people-oriented" professions. I just can't summon up the necessary extraversion.

The Evolution of *E*

Carl Jung introduced the dimension of **extraversion** into psychology in 1913. As you may recall from Chapter 3, Jung was originally a disciple of Freud's, but he eventually broke from Freud because of disagreements concerning the role of sexuality in human life. Jung established his own psychodynamically based theory—analytical theory—which emphasized the workings of a collective unconscious and the individuation of the self. Shortly before the break with Freud, however, Jung (1913/1971) proposed that a person's libido, or sexual energy, can flow in one of two very different directions—either outward toward the world or inward toward the self. After the break with Freud, Jung substituted concepts such as "psychic energy" and "motivation" for libido, but he retained the idea that this energy, whatever it may be, tends to flow in a particular direction for a given person (Jung, 1923/1971). For the extravert, the energy flows toward objects and people in the world; for the introvert, it flows toward the subjective world that lies within. According to Jung, therefore, extraversion and introversion are psychological *types*—you are either one or the other, either an extravert or an introvert, depending on the orientation of psychic energy. To complicate matters a bit more, Jung surmised that if a person's conscious and public life suggests the extraversion type or attitude, then his or her hidden, unconscious life plays itself out in introverted terms, and vice versa. Put simply, people who are extraverted in their behavior may be introverted in their dreams and unconscious life; people who are introverted in their behavior may be extraverted in their dreams and unconscious life. This contrast illustrates a kind of psychic compensation and balance in human personality—a theme that runs throughout Jung's thought.

Jung's own descriptions of extraversion and introversion make clear the contrast he had in mind:

> Extraversion is characterized by . . . a ready acceptance of external happenings, a desire to influence and be influenced by events, a need to join in and get "with it," the capacity to endure bustle and noise of every kind, and actually find them enjoyable . . . the cultivation of friends and acquaintances, none too carefully selected, and finally by the great importance attached to the figure one cuts, and hence a strong tendency to make a show of oneself. . . .
>
> The introvert holds aloof from external happenings, does not join in, has a distinct dislike of society, as soon as he finds himself among too many people. In a large gathering, he feels lonely and lost. . . . He is not in the least "with it," and has no love of enthusiastic get-togethers. . . . His own world is a safe harbour, a carefully tended and walled-in garden, closed to the public and hidden from prying eyes. . . . His best work is done with his own resources, on his own initiative, and in his own way. Crowds, majority views . . . popular enthusiasm never convince him of anything, but merely make him creep still deeper into his shell. (Jung, 1936/1971, pp. 549–551)

Jung was especially interested in how one's overall attitude toward the world—that is, extraversion or introversion—played itself out in intellectual work. For example, he believed that Freud was very much an extravert and that his theory contained extravert themes. Freud was interested in the investment of psychosexual energy in the outside world of people and objects, as manifested in psychological symptoms, slips of the tongue, and social behavior more generally. Jung saw himself as an introvert, more focused on the private, inner world. In Jung's theory, the most dramatic dynamics and transformations take place deep within and may entail no visible external effects. It is clear that Jung saw his own life in the same introverted terms. In his remarkable auto-biography, *Memories, Dreams, Reflections*, Jung (1961) pays very little attention to the changes and developments that occurred in the external world during his life. We hear very little, even, about his own behavior, what he did and when he did it. Instead, the book focuses on Jung's fantasies and dreams and the ways in which his ideas about human personality developed over time. In typically introverted fashion, Jung garnered his ideas about extraversion and introversion from his own readings and ruminations. He did not collect systematic data about these constructs; he did not do any systematic scientific work to test hypotheses about this dimension of human personality.

Beginning his work in the 1940s, Hans Eysenck adopted a very different approach. Conducting careful experiments, large-scale surveys, and factor-analysis of responses to objective questionnaires, Eysenck (1952, 1967) found extraversion–introversion to be a primary dimension of individual differences in personality. He developed valid and reliable measures of extraversion–introversion, speculated as to biological bases of the trait, and conducted numerous studies showing that individual differences in the trait are associated with predicted behavioral outcomes. Although Eysenck (1973) expressed considerable disdain for Jung's armchair approach to psychological types, the concepts he derived were rather similar to Jung's in some ways. First, both Jung and Eysenck viewed extraversion–introversion to constitute broad "types" in personality. Second, both defined the concepts by making reference to the direction of a person's approach to life. The extravert is directed toward the outside world while the introvert directs his attention inward. Eysenck described the extravert as outgoing, sociable, and enthusiastic, but also somewhat impulsive and heedless. The introvert, by contrast, is more quiet and withdrawn, but the introvert is also more contemplative, deliberative, and less likely to take bad risks. The extravert may have many more friends, but the introvert has deeper friendships with a few people. Jung would seem to agree.

In other ways, though, Eysenck's concepts are quite different. While both theorists spoke of extraversion and introversion as types, Jung made a sharp demarcation between the two, suggesting that people can be neatly classified as either extraverted or introverted, whereas Eysenck proposed a more continuous conception. For Eysenck, many people fall into a middle range on the typology—these are "ambiverts," combining qualities of both the extraverted and introverted poles. In measuring extraversion and introversion on trait scales, the researcher typically observes a bell-shaped, normal distribution of scores, with extreme scores on either end of the continuum constituting purer types for extraversion and introversion and the many middle scores suggesting a blending in the ambiversion range. Eysenck, furthermore, rejected Jung's idea that conscious extraversion is connected to unconscious introversion, and vice versa. It should be noted that virtually no scientific research has ever supported Jung's odd claim in this regard, though perhaps it is difficult to know how to measure extraversion and introversion as trends in the unconscious. Unlike Jung, Eysenck linked extraversion and introversion to different patternings of brain function. Finally, Eysenck highlighted certain facets of the extraversion concept that do not seem to be apparent in Jung's view. For Jung, the key distinction between extraversion and introversion was the *direction* of psychic energy. Extraverts are directed outward, and introverts are directed inward. But Eysenck's conception seems to go farther in suggesting that there may be differences in some sense of energy itself. Not only are extraverts more outgoing, sociable, and impulsive, Eysenck argued, but they show higher activity levels. They move with great enthusiasm to an upbeat tempo. They seem to have more energy.

The concept of extraversion–introversion *(E)* has gradually evolved over time. The aspect of energy and enthusiasm has gradually moved toward the center of the construct. Indeed, some investigators label the *E* dimension "surgency," which connotes surgent energy and some degree of *social dominance* (Goldberg, 1981; Tupes & Christal, 1961). By contrast, the idea of "impulsivity" has gradually moved away from the center of the construct, though theorists differ on where they believe impulsivity belongs. In their original formulations, Jung and Eysenck described the extravert as spontaneous, daring, impulsive, and even a little reckless. The introvert arguably had more impulse control. However, some theorists now view impulsivity to be separate from extraversion, and some argue that it is a component of neuroticism or (on the negative end) conscientiousness instead. Finally, the concept of extraversion has come to take on a more evaluative meaning than Jung and Eysenck ever intended. As we will see, many investigators believe that a tendency toward positive emotional experiences is a component of extraversion itself (e.g., Costa & McCrae, 1992), and some argue that positive emotionality is itself the core of extraversion (Watson & Clark, 1997). According to the latter view, extraversion may be first and foremost a tendency to experience positive affect.

As the concept of *E* has evolved over time, research has continued to accumulate to support the construct validity of self-report measures of extraversion–introversion. A large body of research shows that differences in *E* as assessed on questionnaires are meaningfully related to corresponding differences in social behavior. For instance, extraverts talk more and sooner when they meet someone than do introverts (Carment,

Miles, & Cervin, 1965) and engage in more eye contact when interacting with another (Rutter, Morely, & Graham, 1972). Among college students, extraverts study in places that afford opportunities for social interaction (like the business school study lounge I described) whereas introverts seek out more secluded spots (Campbell & Hawley, 1982). Introverts are somewhat more likely to live alone (Diener, Sandvik, Pavot, & Fujita, 1992). Extraverts do more gambling (Wilson, 1978). Extraverts also tend to be more sexually active than introverts (Giese & Schmidt, 1968). Wilson and Nias (1975) have shown that extraverts are more permissive in their sexual attitudes than introverts, confess to higher levels of sex drive, and are less prone to nervousness and inhibition in sexual relations. In the occupational realm, extraverts are drawn to and excel in occupations that involve dealing directly with other people, such as sales, marketing, personnel work, and teaching (Diener et al., 1992; Wilson, 1978). By contrast, introverts tend to prefer more solitary pursuits, sharing many interests with artists, research scientists, mathematicians, and engineers (Bendig, 1963).

Laboratory research has also examined relations between *E* and various forms of cognitive performance. It appears that extraverts and introverts show different cognitive strengths and weaknesses with respect to certain tasks and under certain conditions. For example, extraverts tend to show superior performance to introverts on tasks requiring divided attention, resistance to distraction, and resistance to interference (Eysenck, 1982). Relative to introverts, extraverted locomotive drivers show better detection of railway signal stimuli (Singh, 1989), extraverted post office trainees tend to perform better on a demanding speeded mail-coding task (Matthews, Jones, & Chamberlain, 1992), and extraverted TV viewers show better short-term recall of television news broadcasts (Gunter & Furnham, 1986).

Conversely, introverts tend to perform better on tasks requiring vigilance and careful attention to details (Harkins & Geen, 1975). Some evidence suggests that introverts show better long-term memory for words (Howarth & Eysenck, 1968) and superior performance under conditions of very low arousal, as when deprived of sleep for long periods of time (Matthews, 1992). To the extent differences are found in learning styles, extraverts tend to show a preference for speed over accuracy, whereas introverts focus more on accuracy over speed. Accordingly, Brebner and Cooper (1985) characterize extraverts as "geared to respond" and introverts as "geared to inspect."

Feeling Good

A significant body of research has found that *E* is positively associated with reports of feeling good about life. In other words, extraverts report greater levels of *positive affect* in everyday life than do introverts. Costa and McCrae (1980a, 1984) have conducted a number of studies in which they administered self-report measures of *E* and subjective well-being to large samples of adults. Measures of subjective well-being tap into two independent features: positive affect (reports of good feelings) and negative affect (reports of bad feelings). Costa and McCrae have consistently found that, for both men and women, *E* is positively associated with reports of good feelings but unrelated to reports of bad feelings. In other words, extraverts report more positive affect than introverts, but they do not necessarily report less negative affect. Similar results have been obtained by other researchers (e.g., Watson, Clark, McIntyre, & Hamaker, 1992).

Eysenck originally argued that E is made up of at least two related components: sociability and impulsivity. To test the extent to which these two components are related to well-being, Emmons and Diener (1986a) administered an extraversion scale from the Eysenck Personality Inventory (Eysenck & Eysenck, 1964) to two samples of college undergraduates who each completed mood reports daily for 6–8 consecutive weeks. Each night before they went to bed, students filled out a form that asked them to rate their current mood on nine seven-point adjective scales. The nine mood adjectives were broken down into four positive terms—"happy," "joyful," "pleased," and "enjoyment/ fun"—and five negative ones—"unhappy," "depressed," "frustrated," "worried/anxious," and "angry/hostile." A student's total positive affect score on a given day, therefore, was the sum of his or her ratings on the four positive mood adjectives; the total negative affect score was the sum across the five negative mood items.

Table 6.2 shows correlations between E and its components "impulsivity" and "sociability" on the one hand, and positive and negative affect scores summed over the 6–8 week period on the other, for both samples in Emmons and Diener's study. While total positive affect was significantly correlated with total E, it was even more strongly associated with "sociability" and completely uncorrelated with "impulsivity." In other words, it is the sociability component of E—that having to do with friendliness, cheerfulness, warmth, and openness to people—that significantly predicts positive moods. The impulsivity component—having more to do with thrill seeking, risk taking, and seeking social stimulation in crowds—was unrelated to positive affect and even showed a positive, though weak, association with negative mood.

Why do extraverts report more positive feelings than introverts? One explanation is that extraverts may be less responsive to punishment than introverts. Introverts appear to dwell on the negative and punitive features of certain social situations (Graziano, Feldesman, & Rahe, 1985). Researchers report that introverts recall less positive information and rate others less positively in social situations (Lishman, 1972), report interpersonal disagreements as being more aversive (Norman & Watson, 1976), and anticipate more disagreements between themselves and others than do extraverts (Cooper & Scalise, 1974).

| TABLE 6.2 | *Correlations Between Dimensions of Extraversion and Reports of Positive and Negative Affect* | | | |

	POSITIVE AFFECT		NEGATIVE AFFECT	
TRAIT	SAMPLE 1[a]	SAMPLE 2[b]	SAMPLE 1	SAMPLE 2
Impulsivity	.08	.04	.30**	.25**
Sociability	.49**	.44**	−.10	.11
Extraversion total	.32**	.34**	.01	.24*

Note: Impulsivity and Sociability are subscales of Extraversion total.
[a]$N = 68$
[b]$N = 72$
*$p < .05$
**$p < .01$
Source: Emmons and Diener (1986a), p. 1213.

Extraverts are more likely than introverts to continue responding in the face of punishment and frustration. Pearce-McCall and Newman (1986) exposed each of 50 introverted and 50 extraverted college men to one of two "pretreatment conditions" in a problem-solving experiment: either a "reward condition" in which the student received $2.50 for good performance or a "punishment condition" in which the student was told that his earnings had dwindled from $5.00 to $2.50 because of poor performance. (In reality, the students had been randomly assigned to the groups, and actual performance thus had nothing to do with whether they received rewards or punishments.) After the pretreatment, the students made bets on how well they might perform on a subsequent problem-solving task. In comparison with those introverts who had received pretreatment punishment, extraverts who had been punished placed larger wagers on their ability to succeed, reported higher levels of expecting to succeed, and expressed greater confidence that they could "control" the situation in the future. As Figure 6.1 shows, extraverts and introverts did *not* differ in their betting behavior following the reward pretreatment but *did* differ markedly following punishment, with extraverts making significantly higher wagers.

In another problem-solving experiment, Patterson, Kosson, and Newman (1987) showed that extraverts typically fail to pause following punishment, pushing ahead to the next trial before they can learn from their mistakes. Impulsively seeking out rewards, extraverts may actually be motivated by punishment to work even faster and more impulsively, failing to reflect on the reasons for punishment. In some situations, therefore, extraverts may show an overly impulsive approach to problem solving, continuing to produce errors even after they are punished for doing so (Nichols & Newman, 1986).

Research suggests yet other explanations for the relationship between *E* and positive affect. Barrett (1997) asked 56 students to complete a self-report measure of *E* and then report on their emotional states three times a day—in the morning, afternoon, and evening—for 90 consecutive days. As in prior research, he found that *E* was positively associated with the momentary reports of positive moods. However, at the end of the 90 days, Barrett also asked the students to rate what their mood states *had been* over the course of the 90 days. Barrett found that the retrospective ratings of what moods the students remembered experiencing did not match exactly the reports of the mood states made at the time they were experienced. But the mismatches were not random. When thinking back over the 90 days, extraverts tended to recall even more positive moods than they in fact reported during the 90-day period. In other words, extraversion is associated both with reporting greater positive affect and remembering even greater positive affect later than what was reported at the time. In a similar vein, Mayo (1990) found that extraversion was associated with the tendency to remember a greater number of happy scenes from the past. The tendency to recall the past in more positive terms than it was experienced at the time may contribute to the generally positive and upbeat emotional life that extraverts tend to experience.

To what extent is the positive association between extraversion and positive affect a function of the greater levels of participation in social activities that extraverts show? Brandstatter (1994) argues that extraverts are more assertive in social situations, which gives them more social competence and effectiveness. Their positive emotional states may be a direct function of this kind of social skill. Argyle and Lu (1990) tested a

---

| FIGURE 6.1 | *Betting Behavior and Introversion/Extraversion* |

Introverts and extraverts bet the same amount of money after receiving a reward, but following a punishment, extraverts show higher levels of betting and introverts show lower levels.

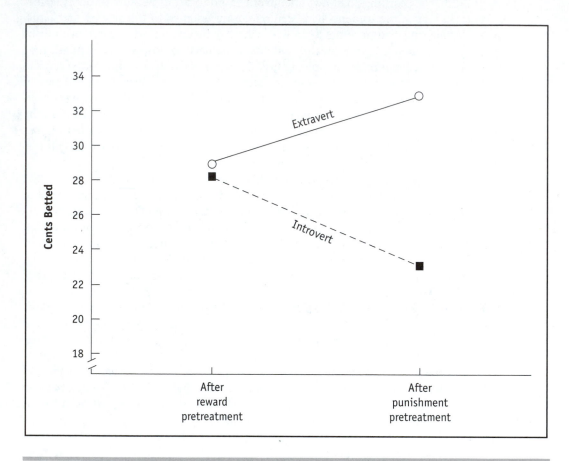

Source: Pearce-McCall & Newman (1986), p. 442.

similar idea by conducting what is called a *path analysis* with different psychological measures. A path analysis enables the researcher to sort out both direct and indirect effects of variables on one another. As Figure 6.2 illustrates, Argyle and Lu found a positive and significant association between extraversion and social competence (path coefficient = .49) and then a positive and significant association between social competence and happiness (path coefficient = .36). This means that there is a significant direct effect of extraversion on social competence and significant and direct effect of social competence on happiness. Extraversion, therefore, exerts an indirect effect on happiness by virtue of the path that runs through social competence. When you statistically remove that pathway, however, you are still left with a positive direct association

| FIGURE 6.2 | *Extraversion's Effect on Happiness* |

In this path model, the findings show that the positive effect of extraversion on happiness is due partly to a direct correlation between two variables and partly to extraversion's positive association with social competence, which itself predicts happiness.

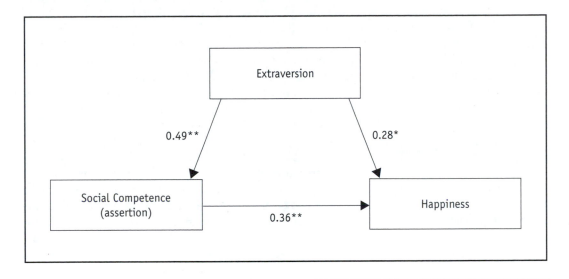

*p < .05
**p < .01
Source: Argyle & Lu (1990).

between extraversion and happiness (path coefficient = .28). Putting this in simple English, Figure 6.2 tells you that the association between extraversion and happiness in this study happens in two different ways. First, highly extraverted people tend to have more social skills and competence, which tends to produce or lead to more happiness. Second, even after you account for this first relationship, there is still some leftover direct effect of extraversion on happiness itself. Social skills explain some of the story, but not all of it.

Just how strong and consistent is the relation between E and positive emotions? Psychologists differ on this issue. One camp argues that the relation between E and positive emotions is so consistent that E itself should be renamed "Positive Emotionality" or "Positive Affectivity" (Tellegen, 1985; Watson & Tellegen, 1985). According to this view, positive affect constitutes the affective core of what has traditionally been called extraversion (Watson & Clark, 1997). Independent measures of E and positive affects correlate in the range of +.20 to +.50 across different studies, and the two sets of measures tend to predict some of the same sorts of things. For example, measures of positive affectivity predict high levels of social activity, such as frequency of dating and attending parties and socializing over dinner or drinks (Watson & Clark, 1997).

Other researchers interpret the literature on extraversion and affect as suggesting that while positive affect and extraversion are indeed correlated, they are by no means the same thing. Accordingly, Costa and McCrae (1992) view positive emotions as but one of six facets of *E*. Yet other researchers are more skeptical about the association between the trait of extraversion and positive emotion states (Matthews & Deary, 1998). Some studies show rather low correlations (in the range of +.20) between *E* and measures of positive affectivity. Furthermore, high *E* can be associated with lower positive affect in some situations. As an example of the latter point, Brandstatter (1994) found that *E* was associated with positive affect when mood ratings were collected in social situations, but extraverts reported significantly lower levels of positive emotion, compared with introverts, when they were alone. Brandstatter's findings remind us that traits must be viewed in interactional terms. While *E* may generally be associated with positive emotions across time and over different settings, there are certainly situations in life in which extraversion makes you feel worse rather than better.

The Theory of Arousal

From the beginning of his research program in the 1940s, Eysenck argued that the roots of *E* lie in underlying biological processes. Eysenck borrowed concepts from the great Russian physiologist Ivan Pavlov, whose seminal work on classical conditioning was reviewed in Chapter 4 of this book. In some of his studies with dogs, Pavlov measured the relationship between increases in stimulation and increases in response. Beginning at low levels of stimulation, as Pavlov increased stimulation the dogs exhibited increases in the associated responses. But eventually a point would be reached in which further increases in stimulation would lead to what might seem to be paradoxical *decreases* in responding, as if the dog's body were beginning to shut down in response to stimulation levels that were perceived to be too high. This point at which the dog began to inhibit responses to increased stimulation was called the *threshold of transmarginal inhibition*. Pavlov noticed that different dogs differed with respect to how quickly they reached the threshold of transmarginal inhibition. Those dogs with what Pavlov called a *strong nervous system* were able to reach higher levels of stimulation before they began to inhibit their responses, whereas those with what he called a *weak nervous system* reached the threshold more quickly. Put simply, it was as if the dogs with the strong nervous systems could "take more" stimulation before they eventually found it too aversive, leading to inhibition. By contrast, the dogs with the weak nervous systems could take less, and they began to inhibit their responding sooner and at lower levels of external stimulation.

Eysenck analogized extraverts to dogs with strong nervous systems and introverts to dogs with weak nervous systems. Stimulation from the environment leads to arousal, Eysenck reasoned. As individuals experience greater levels of stimulation, they become more aroused in a general sense. Each individual prefers an optimal level of arousal—a point at which arousal leads to maximal pleasure and optimal responding. This level is analogous to the threshold of transmarginal inhibition in dogs. When arousal goes beyond the optimal level, the individual begins to withdraw from the stimulus situation. It takes more stimulation to get an extravert to an optimal level of arousal, Eysenck proposed. It is as if extraverts start out at especially low levels of arousal to begin with and therefore are "hungry" for greater and greater levels of stimulation in order to kick their arousal levels up to the optimal point. By contrast, introverts at low levels of stimulation are rather highly aroused to begin with. It does not take much more stimulation to push them beyond the point of transmarginal inhibition.

As he refined his ideas about arousal, Eysenck (1967) came to propose that the brain's *reticular activating system (RAS)* is responsible for individual differences in arousal and arousability, and therefore individual differences in *E*. The RAS is a network of nerve fibers ascending from the spinal chord to the thalamus of the brain. The RAS is considered to be a relatively primitive part of the brain, uninvolved with thinking and other higher cortical functions. Rather, it is responsible for general arousal, regulating patterns of wakefulness and attention. Essentially, Eysenck argues that the RAS is "tuned" differently in introverts and extraverts. Given standard conditions of external stimulation, introverts are generally more highly aroused than extraverts: The RAS is set at a higher level. Both introverts and extraverts seek an optimal arousal in daily life, but because introverts are more aroused to begin with they can tolerate less increase in arousal than can extraverts. The introvert's cortex, therefore, must exercise more inhibition or control over the primitive lower brain centers. Consequently, the introvert exhibits more restrained and inhibited behavior than does the extravert. The introvert tends to avoid increases in arousal, whereas the extravert tends to seek them out.

If introverts are chronically more aroused than extraverts, we would expect it to be more difficult to calm down an introvert. Some support for this proposition comes from studies with drugs. Employing depressant drugs ("downers") to reduce levels of arousal, psychopharmacologists have found that introverts are somewhat more difficult to sedate than extraverts, requiring a higher dosage of a drug such as sodium amatyl (Wilson, 1978). Sedation threshold—which may be measured by changes in electrical patterns in the brain, slurring of speech, or loss of facility on cognitive tasks such as adding numbers—is significantly higher in "dysthymics" (introverted neurotics) than hysterics (extraverted neurotics). There is also some evidence that depressant drugs (which decrease arousal) cause introverts to behave more like extraverts on certain laboratory tasks whereas stimulant drugs ("uppers," which increase arousal) may cause extraverts to act more like introverts (Wilson, 1978).

If introverts are chronically more aroused than extraverts, we would also expect them to be more sensitive to stimuli at all levels of intensity. Eysenck (1990) has reported a number of studies indicating that, in general, introverts have greater sensitivity to barely detectable stimuli as well as lower pain thresholds, compared with extraverts. A rather amazing example of individual differences in stimulus sensitivity in introverts and extraverts is the lemon-drop test. Four drops of lemon juice are placed on an individual's tongue for 20 seconds. The person scores according to the amount of salivation produced under lemon-juice stimulating conditions as compared with the amount produced under neutral conditions (that is, when no lemon juice is present). Extreme extraverts show little or no salivation increase in response to the lemon juice, whereas extreme introverts show an increment of almost one gram of saliva. In other words, introverts respond vigorously to the lemon-juice stimulus, suggesting that they are more sensitive to stimulation. In a sample of 50 male and 50 female students, Eysenck (1973) obtained an extremely high correlation of +.71 between salivation increase on the lemon-drop test and introversion assessed on a questionnaire. In a review of nine subsequent studies on lemon drops and saliva, Deary, Ramsay, Wilson, and

Raid (1988) find that Eysenck's original results are generally well replicated, especially when studies are done in the morning, during which time cortical arousal differences among introverts and extraverts seem to be at their peak. They write:

> The negative correlation between extraversion and acid-stimulation salivation holds: for both male and female Ss with different saliva collection procedures; whether fresh or synthetic lemon juice or citric acid is used as a stimulus (although fresh lemon juice appears to be the most reliable); whether the stimulation is dropped or swabbed on to the tongue and whether the saliva is collected for 10 sec. or 10 min. There is, however, some evidence that the correlation is more robust when testing is performed in the morning when arousal differences are at their greatest. Swallowing the stimulus also appears to reduce the correlation. (p. 906)

Similar results have been obtained in other laboratory situations. Weisen (1965) found that extraverts would expend considerable effort to obtain a reward of loud jazz music and bright lights whereas introverts would work hard to avoid these same stimuli. Geen (1984) found that extraverts chose higher levels of noise stimulation in a learning task than introverts and performed better in the presence of intense noise, whereas introverts performed better at lower levels of noise. Holmes (1967) looked at the pupillary response. When a person is exposed to bright lights, the pupils of his or her eyes automatically contract to ward off the sudden increase in stimulation. This is a natural, unlearned response. The rate at which such pupil contraction occurs, however, is a function of E, Holmes's study suggests. When a bright light was shone onto the eyes of an introvert, pupil contraction occurred significantly more quickly than when the light was shone onto the eyes of an extravert. Conversely, extraverts showed faster pupil dilation (opening up the pupils to let light in) when they were exposed to dark conditions, compared with introverts. In other words, even at the level of autonomic responding of the eye's pupil, introverts exhibit an avoidance of high levels of stimulation whereas extraverts manifest a kind of stimulus hunger.

The hunger for increasing levels of stimulation is directly assessed on Zuckerman's (1978) Sensation Seeking Scale. **Sensation seeking** is the "need for varied, novel, and complex sensations and experiences and the willingness to take physical and social risks for the sake of such experiences" (Zuckerman, 1979, p. 10). Sensation seeking appears to incorporate four related factors: (1) thrill and adventure seeking (interest in activities involving physical risk), (2) experience seeking (desire for new experiences through music, art, travel, meeting unusual people, mood-altering drugs), (3) disinhibition (pursuit of pleasure through parties, social drinking, sex with various partners, gambling), and (4) boredom susceptibility (restlessness in unchanging environments and dislike for dull people). Although sensation seeking is *not* the same thing as E, it shares certain similarities and correlates positively, though modestly, with measures of extraversion. A substantial body of empirical literature supports the construct validity of Zuckerman's sensation-seeking trait. Some important findings are summarized in Table 6.3.

Looking over the many studies that have been conducted on arousal and E, there appears to be reasonable empirical support for the general idea that extraverts and introverts differ with respect to their preferred levels of stimulation. Extraverts seek out greater levels of stimulation, presumably seeking some sort of optimal arousal that is experienced in a positive way. Introverts seem to prefer somewhat lower levels of stimulation, which are assumedly creating optimal levels of arousal for them. Although the

TABLE 6.3	*Some Behavioral Correlates of Sensation Seeking*

Greater variety of sexual activities and greater number of sexual partners for both heterosexual and homosexual adults, males and females.

Greater use of recreational drugs, such as marijuana and amphetamines.

Smoke cigarettes.

Prefer spicy, sour, and crunchy foods.

More gambling and higher betting.

Engage in physically risky activities such as parachuting, motorcycling, scuba diving, and fire fighting.

Volunteer for unusual types of experiments such as sensory deprivation, hypnosis, and drug studies.

Volunteer for unusual types of activities such as encounter groups, alpha training, and transcendental meditation.

In leaderless, task-oriented groups, tend to begin conversations, speak more, and be selected by others as leaders of the group; tend to score high on measures of dominance.

Prefer complex artistic forms to simple ones.

Like the color blue.

With respect to the general trait of extraversion, are more likely to manifest characteristics of impulsivity rather than sociability.

Among delinquents, engage in more impulsive behavior such as fighting and defiance of rules.

Among psychiatric patients, score higher on scales reflecting elevated mood and sociopathy rather than schizophrenia.

Among heterosexual couples, tend to be romantically attracted to and marry people who are also high in sensation seeking, particularly on the subscales of experience seeking, disinhibition, and boredom susceptibility. (Lesnik-Oberstein & Cohn, 1984)

Note: These findings are reviewed in Zuckerman (1978) and Zuckerman (1998).

results are not perfectly consistent by any means, there is some research support for the idea that extraverts and introverts differ in their arousability (Matthews & Deary, 1998; Stelmach, 1990). At low-to-moderate levels of stimulation, introverts appear to be more physiologically reactive to sensory input, compared with extraverts. Some studies using brain wave patterns (electroencephalogram, or EEG, patterns) show that when introverts are presented with low levels of stimulation they respond with EEG patterns indicative of strong attention and arousal.

The aspect of Eysenck's proposals that has received the least support, however, is arguably his most fundamental proposition—that *E* is associated with characteristic arousal levels as mediated by the RAS. More than 1,000 studies have been conducted to test Eysenck's propositions about arousal and *E* (Geen, 1997). Arousal has been indexed by EEG responses, electrodermal activity (e.g., how much the skin sweats), heart rate, and functional brain scanning techniques (Matthews & Deary, 1998). Across the many studies and methods, it has proven extraordinarily difficult to show consistently that introverts in general operate at higher levels of arousal than do extraverts. Some researchers provide data to suggest that if differences in characteristic arousal levels are to be found, they are more likely to be associated with the trait of impulsivity rather than E. Anderson and Revelle (1994) have documented subtle relations among impulsivity, time of day, caffeine consumption, and rate of change in arousal levels. Other researchers reject the concept of general arousal in its entirety (Geen, 1997; Zuckerman, 1998). The core argument against the concept comes from many studies which suggest that the various indices of what might be general arousal— brain wave activity, heart rate, skin conductance, and so on—are themselves not highly correlated. There would appear to be many different kinds of arousal and different indices of these different kinds. Furthermore, when one part of the brain appears aroused and active, other parts may be inhibited and quiet. Eysenck viewed the RAS as a general arousal system that would turn neural stimulation on and off as if it were a faucet. After years of research on the matter, this idea would appear to be wrong, or at best oversimplified.

In sum, Eysenck's theory of arousal has stimulated a wave of empirical research over the past 35 years. The results of these many studies are inconsistent, but some general themes can be discerned. First, on a behavioral level there would appear to be substantial evidence for the idea that extraverts prefer higher levels of stimulation than do introverts. Extraverts seek out various kinds of stimulation, especially stimulation that is social in nature. Second, there would appear to be modest support for the idea that under certain conditions and generally at low levels of stimulation, introverts are somewhat more sensitive to increases in stimulation than are extraverts. These differences, however, are mediated by many different factors, including time of day. Third, the research yields conflicting and inconclusive results with respect to the basic Eysenckian idea that E is linked to stable, traitlike differences in general levels of arousal. It does not appear to be true that introverts are generally more aroused than extraverts. Indeed, the whole concept of general arousal has been called into question. Relatedly, the idea that the brain's reticular activating system (RAS) is the location for individual differences in E has pretty much been rejected. The brain is more complex than Eysenck's original proposals suggested. Nonetheless, these proposals have stimulated some of the most creative research in personality psychology for more than 35 years, and it is likely that they will continue to do so.

The Behavioral Approach System

We have seen that as the construct of extraversion–introversion has evolved over time, psychologists have become increasingly interested in (a) understanding its relation to positive emotional states and (b) discovering its psychobiological bases. Both of these themes are reflected in the work of Jeffrey Gray (1982, 1987). Gray coined the term **behavioral approach system,** or **BAS,** to refer to an hypothesized system in the brain that is responsible for motivating behavior aimed at achieving goals and obtaining positive emotional rewards. Gray proposes that the BAS is made up of various pathways and structures in the brain that are implicated in the release of the neurotransmitter *dopamine* and involved in the working of certain regions that make up the brain's *limbic system.* Studies with rats have indicated that reward in the brain is associated with the release of dopamine in the mesolimbic system running through the medial forebrain bundle to centers in the brain's frontal lobes (Zuckerman, 1995). On the human level, individual differences in mesolimbic dopaminergic pathways and related structures are hypothesized to underlie differences that people show in reward-seeking behaviors. While some people characteristically approach positive incentives and reap the rewards of good feelings when their goals are achieved, other people are less eager to approach, more cautious, and thereby less likely to experience the positive emotional rewards that may come from successful goal achievement.

From Gray's perspective, the BAS links up with the trait of *impulsivity*. Impulsive behavior is uninhibited and forward looking; the impulsive person moves rapidly and sometimes thoughtlessly toward potentially rewarding stimuli. In Eysenck's original formulation, extraverts were thought to be impulsive, as well. Some conceptions of extraversion have suggested that impulsivity is a component of *E*. For example, Sutton and Davidson (1997) write that "individuals with a relatively strong BAS (more sensitive and responsive to incentives) are more likely to be extraverted and impulsive" (p. 204). Zuckerman (1995) writes that the BAS "probably subsumes several basic traits, including extraversion, impulsivity, and sensation seeking" (p. 329). In a similar line of thinking, Tellegen (1985) has proposed that *E* be renamed "positive affectivity" and that behavior related to this trait is likely to be directed by the working of the BAS. According to Tellegen, extraversion (positive affectivity) represents individual differences in sensitivity to pleasurable, reward-producing incentives. Different theorists have proposed, therefore, that *E* may be linked to the activity of an hypothesized brain system called the BAS. The link between *E* and the BAS, then, comes by virtue of its association with impulsivity (Gray), with positive affect states (Tellegen), or with both.

Scientists have not yet put together a clear story about how *E* may be related to the BAS at the level of brain functioning. But two lines of recent research are suggestive. In the first line of research, investigators have tried to find direct links between dopaminergic activity and *E* in humans. Depue, Luciana, Arbisi, Collins, and Leon (1994) selected individuals who scored high and low on self-report measures of *E* and gave each of them a substance that induces dopamine activity in the brain. They found that the substance stimulated higher levels of dopaminergic activity among extraverts compared with introverts. In other words, extraverts and introverts differed with respect to the reactivity of the mesolimbic dopaminergic system. The results are generally consistent with the idea that the characteristic good cheer and approach behavior in the face of incentives seen in extraverts may be linked to enhanced activity of the neurotransmitter dopamine in certain parts of the brain. But much more research is needed to clarify the specifics of such a relationship.

The second line of research involves the brain's electrical activity. Studies employing EEG measurements show that positive affect, as expressed by smiling, is associated with activation of the left-frontal and anterior portions of the brain (Davidson, 1992). In laboratory studies, researchers have induced positive emotions and approach behavior by showing film clips (Davidson, Ekman, Saron, Senulis, & Friesen, 1990) and providing monetary rewards (Sobotka, Davidson, & Senulis, 1992) to adults, and by providing human infants with pleasant-tasting foods (Fox & Davidson, 1986), as they monitored the brain's electrical activity from multiple scalp sites. These manipulations systematically influenced the asymmetry of electrical activity in anterior (front) but not posterior (back) regions of the brain. Pleasant film clips, pleasant tastes, and monetary incentives all increased left-sided anterior activity, whereas unpleasant film clips, unpleasant tastes, and threat of monetary loss increased brain activity in the anterior right regions. Clinical and laboratory observations, furthermore, suggest that the left prefrontal cortex may be a biological substrate of approach behavior and positive affect. Clinical reports have shown that patients with damage to portions of the brain located in or near the left prefrontal cortex are more likely than patients with damage to other brain regions to exhibit depressive symptomatology. Lesions of these brain regions may result in a deficit of approach behavior, which when combined with negative life events, culminates in depression (Davidson, 1993).

In sum, a small but growing body of research suggests that individual differences in E and related traits (e.g., sensation seeking) may be linked to an hypothesized behavioral approach system (BAS) in the brain. Scientists have not pinned down just what this system is made up of and how it works. Some studies suggest that dopaminergic pathways in the brain are implicated in the BAS. Others point to the electrical activity of the left anterior regions of the cortex. The story is likely to become increasingly complex as more research is conducted. For example, a recent study challenges the idea that left anterior activity is exclusively associated with positive affect. Harmon-Jones and Allen (1998) provide data showing that individuals predisposed toward *anger* exhibit the same kind of EEG asymmetries associated with the BAS. Harmon-Jones and Allen suggest that anger motivates approach behavior in the face of incentives, even though it is a negatively valenced emotion. From their perspective, the BAS is more about active approach in human behavior rather than positive affect per se. Other investigators suggest that systems and factors beyond dopaminergic activity and EEG asymmetry are likely to be implicated in the BAS (Zuckerman, 1998). Included in these other factors may be hormones such as testosterone and cortisol and enzymes such as monoamine oxidase (MAO). Remarking on the complexity of all of this, Zuckerman (1995) writes:

> We do not inherit personality traits or even behavior mechanisms as such. What is inherited are chemical templates that produce and regulate proteins involved in building the structure of nervous systems and the neurotransmitters, enzymes, and hormones that regulate them. We are not born as extraverts, neurotics, impulsive sensation seekers, or antisocial personalities, but we are born with differences in reactivities of brain structures and levels of regulators like MAO. How do these differences in biological traits shape our choices in life from the manifold possibilities provided by environments? (pp. 331–332)

We do not know the answer to Zuckerman's last question. But researchers have begun to collect some intriguing clues.

N: NEUROTICISM

You are hard-pressed to find a character who is not neurotic in Fyodor Dostoyevsky's greatest novel, *The Brothers Karamazov*. Dostoyevsky (1881/1933) fills his story with all manner of zealots and buffoons, hysterical women and raving men whose fears, obsessions, and insecurities torment them from the first page to the last. Neuroticism can be the stuff of great fiction, as we see especially in the character of Dmitri, the oldest son of Fyodor Karamazov. His mother dead and his father drunk, the 3-year-old Dmitri is raised by the faithful family servant, Grigory. Grigory is selflessly devoted to the boy, but Dmitri grows to be an unruly young man with violent passions. He drops out of the Russian equivalent of high school, enlists in the military, does a tour of duty in the Caucasus mountains, is promoted but then demoted after he fights a duel, leads a wild life, and gets into debt. Upon his return to civilian life, Dmitri becomes obsessed with obtaining from his dissolute father the extensive property and fortune that he, mistakenly it turns out, believes his father owes him. When his father is murdered, Dmitri becomes the prime suspect.

By his own admission, Dmitri suffers from the curse of the Karamazovs. Psychologically speaking, the curse manifests itself as a proclivity for obsessing over the tiniest trifles, as well as the big contradictions, in human life and the complete inability to control one's emotions in response to those trifles and conflicts. Emotional life is a roller coaster careening out of control. At five o'clock Dmitri leaps for joy, but by 5:05 he has fallen into the pit of despair. He is tormented by these emotional contradictions and by a sense that humankind is fated to suffer incessantly and to wallow in that suffering. "Everything in the world is a riddle," Dmitri laments. "But I cannot solve the riddle. I will never be able to solve it:

> Never! For I'm a Karamazov. For when I do leap into the abyss I pitch in head foremost and heels up, and am positively pleased to be falling in that degrading attitude, and pride myself upon it. And in the very depths of that degradation I suddenly begin a hymn. Let me be accursed. Let me be vile and base, but let me, too, kiss the hem of the garment in which my God is clothed. Though I may be following the devil, I am Thy son, O Lord, and I love Thee, and I feel the joy without which the world cannot exist and have its being. . . . What a terrible lot of mysteries there are! Too many riddles weigh men down on earth. We must solve them as best we can, and try to keep a dry skin in the water. Beauty! I can't endure the thought that a man of lofty mind and heart begins with the ideal of the Madonna and ends with the ideal of Sodom. What's still more dreadful is that a man with the ideal of Sodom in his soul does not renounce the ideal of the Madonna, and his heart is on fire with that ideal, genuinely on fire, just as in the days of his youth and innocence. Yes, man is broad, too broad, indeed. I'd have him narrower. (pp. 79–80)

Dmitri wishes that human beings were drawn more narrowly. He wishes that they did not experience such a broad and confusing range of emotional states. He wishes they did not harbor such contradictory passions of the soul. As a devout Christian who finds his own sensual lust to be overwhelming, Dmitri cannot understand why God would design man to desire both "Sodom" and "the Madonna." In other words, how can a man or a woman want desperately to be evil and good at the same time? (Dmitri might have done well to read Freud, though of course it was Freud who read Dostoyevsky.) Human beings are contradictions—they want opposite things. While many people seem to know this at some level and seem more-or-less able to cope with it, as we might say today, Dostoyevsky's characters do not cope very well. For all their passion and their wholehearted engagement of the world, people like Dmitri spend a great deal of time in life being miserable. And not just people like Dmitri. Neuroticism casts a wide net in literature and life. There are many, many ways to be miserable—many styles of human unhappiness. But almost by definition, they all have in common the experience of negative emotions such as fear, anxiety, sadness, shame, guilt, and despair. The problem of neuroticism is the problem of negative emotionality. How bad do we feel? And how able are we to regulate, modulate, control, and cope with the bad feelings that will inevitably befall us?

The Many Ways to Feel Bad

The second of the Big Five trait clusters is known by many names, but the most common label is **neuroticism.** Measures of chronic anxiety, depression, excessive emotionality, nervousness, moodiness, hostility, vulnerability, self-consciousness, and hypochondriasis all converge in this general factor, which is most generally described as a continuum from emotional instability to emotional stability. Watson and Clark (1984) point out that this general personality dimension is concerned with individual differences among people in their experience of negative emotions, such as sadness, anger, fear, anxiety, guilt, and the like. Consequently, they label the dimension "negative affectivity" (Watson & Tellegen, 1985). People who score high on this general trait have a tendency to be distressed and upset in many realms of their lives. They are chronically worried, nervous, and insecure, and they hold a low opinion of themselves. People who score low on N, on the other hand, are generally calm, relaxed, hardy, secure, self-satisfied, and rather unemotional.

A considerable body of research suggests that individual differences in neuroticism are linked to differences in the experience of negative emotional states. In these studies, researchers typically employ self-report measures of N containing items like those presented in Table 6.4. N is consistently associated with reports of unpleasant moods, higher tension levels, and a preponderance of negative emotional experiences (Emmons & Diener, 1986a; Matthews, Jones, & Chamberlain, 1989; Thayer, 1989; Watson & Clark, 1992). People high in neuroticism are lonelier (Stokes, 1985) and less satisfied with interpersonal relationships in their lives (Atkinson & Violato, 1994; Russell & Wells, 1994) than are people low in neuroticism. Clinical patients suffering from affective disorders such as depression and generalized anxiety show elevated levels of N (Eysenck & Eysenck, 1985) and of similar traits related to negative affect (Clark, Watson, & Mineka, 1994). College students high in N report more stress symptoms and higher levels of homesickness (Matthews & Deary, 1998). These results concerning N contrast with those from research on extraversion, suggesting that E is associated with positive affect states. As we have already seen, extraverts tend to report greater levels of good feeling about themselves than do introverts. But extraverts and introverts do *not* differ with respect to bad feelings. Persons scoring high on N, by contrast, report more bad feelings than do persons scoring low on N, but they do not necessarily report fewer good feelings. Rather than being opposites, good feelings and bad feelings seem to be rather independent. Thus, to oversimplify somewhat: Extraverts report high levels of good feelings, introverts report low levels of good feelings, persons high in neuroticism report high levels of bad feelings, and persons low in neuroticism report low levels of bad feelings (Costa & McCrae, 1980a, 1984; Emmons & Diener, 1985; Meyer & Shack, 1989; Watson & Clark, 1984).

Individual differences in N have been shown to predict a number of important behavioral and attitudinal trends. For example, N has been associated with complaints about poor health among men (Costa & McCrae, 1980b). In a study following the daily life of 43 undergraduate students over the course of a semester, Larsen and Kasimatis (1991) found that students high in N tended to report a greater number of illnesses. Ormel and Wohlfarth (1991) found that high levels of N were a significantly stronger predictor of psychological distress than were environmental factors such as negative changes in one's life situation. Individuals high in N are likely to see the problems of

TABLE 6.4	*Questionnaire Items Assessing Neuroticism* **(N)**

1. Do you sometimes feel happy, sometimes depressed, without any apparent reason?
2. Does your mind often wander while you are trying to concentrate?
3. Are you inclined to be moody?
4. Are you frequently "lost in thought" even when you are supposed to be taking part in a conversation?
5. Are you sometimes bubbling over with energy and sometimes very sluggish?
6. Are your feelings rather easily hurt?
7. Do you get attacks of shaking or trembling?
8. Are you an irritable person?
9. Are you troubled with feelings of inferiority?
10. Do you suffer from sleeplessness?

Source: Eysenck (1973), pp. 33, 43–45.

middle age as a "crisis" according to Costa and McCrae (1978). In a 50-year longitudinal study of 300 married couples, neuroticism scores of both husbands and wives were a major predictor of divorce (Kelly & Conley, 1987).

Why is *N* so strongly associated with so many bad things? Bolger and Schilling (1991) conducted a study of daily stressors that provides insight into this question. The researchers recruited 339 adults who provided daily reports of minor stressful events and mood for 42 consecutive days. Each day the respondents indicated how strongly they had felt each of 18 emotions over the previous 24 hours. Emotion items included indices of anxiety, depression, and hostility, such as "nervous," "tense," "irritable," "worthless," and "angry." In addition, each respondent indicated whether or not he or she experienced any of nine different kinds of stressors during the day, including "overload at work," "argument with spouse," "argument with child," and "transportation problem." Scores on *N* were determined from an 11-item neuroticism scale that was administered before the daily reporting began.

The results indicated that on average, high-*N* adults were more distressed than low-*N* adults over the six-week period, as indexed by the daily mood reports. The sources of their distress were three. First, high-*N* adults tended to report a greater number of daily stressors than did low-*N* adults. Now one could argue that this is because high-*N* individuals complain more; perhaps they are overly sensitive and tend to report minor events that most other people would overlook. The results show, however, that the difference was *not* due to oversensitivity on the part of high-*N* adults, for reports from their spouses tended to support the accuracy of their own accounts of stressful events. In essence, then, high neuroticism appears to *expose* individuals to a greater number of stressful daily events. Especially significant in this regard were stressful events having to do with interpersonal conflict. Of the nine stressor categories, "argument with spouse" and "argument with other" were the two areas that showed the largest distinction between high-*N* and low-*N* adults.

A second source of distress was the respondents' *reactivity* to stressful events. Not only did the high-*N* subjects report a greater number of stressful events, but their negative emotional reactions to stressful events were significantly stronger than the negative emotional reactions to stressful events shown by low-*N* respondents. In fact, reactivity to stressful events was *twice as important* as exposure to stressful events as an explanation for the link between *N* and distress. The authors argue that this reactivity in high-*N* adults is a result of ineffective coping strategies such as self-blame and wishful thinking. Rather than taking constructive steps to deal with stressful situations, high-*N* individuals rely on self-defeating strategies that do not relieve their anxiety, depression, and hostility in the face of daily setbacks.

A third source of distress among high-*N* individuals was *unrelated to stressful events*. The authors show that as much as 60% of the relationship between neuroticism and

---

FIGURE 6.3 | *Intimacy and Neuroticism*

Under low intimacy conditions, individuals high and low on neuroticism show equivalent levels of intimate behavior, but when the conditions call for higher levels of intimacy, individuals with low neuroticism show higher (and appropriate) levels compared with individuals high in neuroticism.

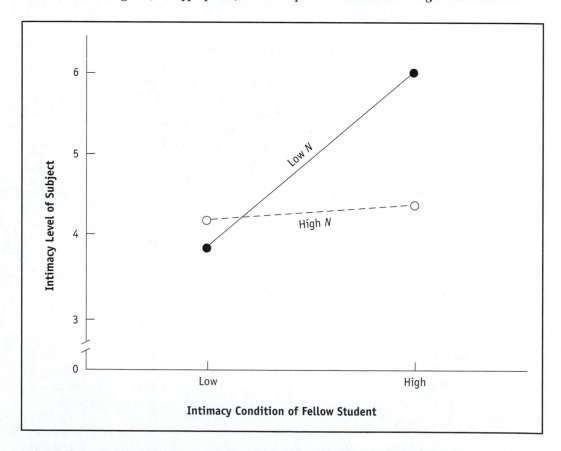

Source: Adapted from Chaikin, Derlega, Bayma, & Shaw (1975), p. 16.

distress had nothing to do with either the bad things that happened to the high-*N* individuals or their overly negative reactions to these bad things. It appears that on top of a greater exposure to stressful situations and a greater negative reaction to such stressors when they occur is a general negativity about life among high-*N* adults that cannot be explained by what happens on a daily basis. Even when bad things aren't happening, neuroticism brings with it bad feelings.

Other studies suggest that *N* is associated with inappropriate and awkward behavior in a number of different social situations. In one experiment, college men scoring either high or low on *N* were randomly assigned to one of two experimental conditions: a "low-intimacy" or a "high-intimacy" condition (Chaikin, Derlega, Bayma, & Shaw, 1975). In the low-intimacy condition, the participant spoke over the phone with a stranger who was a fellow student and who had been previously trained to talk about topics that were superficial and nonintimate, such as his house or apartment, how his family got together, and so on. In the high-intimacy condition, the person spoke over the phone with a fellow student who had been previously trained to talk about topics that were highly intimate, such as the birth-control methods he would prefer to use in marriage, the number of times he had cried as an adult, the frequency of his sexual behavior, and how he had felt when he saw his father hit his mother. The subjects were each given a list of topics to discuss over the phone. The topics varied with respect to their intimacy level, and thus the study's dependent variable was the amount of intimacy content that the participant introduced into the conversation.

Figure 6.3 presents the major finding of the study—subjects scoring low in *N* adjusted their level of intimacy to correspond to the level introduced by the experimental condition. In other words, when the fellow student disclosed intimate information (the high-intimacy condition) the participant reciprocated, offering intimate information about himself. Similarly, when the fellow student kept the conversation light and nonintimate, the participant reciprocated with less intimate information about himself. Men high in *N*, on the other hand, did *not* adjust their intimacy disclosure to the condition, disclosing at moderate levels of intimacy regardless of what the fellow student said. The results suggest that persons high in *N* find it difficult to adjust their social behavior to meet situational demands. Neurotic individuals appear to be oblivious to social cues, perhaps too self-preoccupied to note what their environments are saying to them.

Stress and Coping

N is the trait that is most strongly and consistently related to stress symptoms of various kinds. We have already seen that *N* is linked to negative emotional states and problems in interpersonal relationships. High levels of *N* are also associated with self-reports of illnesses and various somatic symptoms, though *N* does not itself appear to be a risk factor for serious diseases (Wiebe & Smith, 1997). The relation between *N* and stress-proneness is evident in other aspects of everyday functioning as well. For example, individuals high in *N* report that they are more prone to carelessness and everyday errors in thinking (Matthews, Coyle, & Craig, 1990). Automobile drivers high in *N* are more prone to stress in the form of anger, irritation, anxiety, and lack of confidence (Matthews, Dorn, & Glendon, 1991). Another correlate of *N* is self-reported sexual problems such as nervousness, guilt, and inhibition (Eysenck, 1976). Neuroticism tends to be high in certain types of criminals, such as those who feel that

FEATURE 6.A

Feeling Really Good and Really Bad: Affect Intensity

A central message of the research on E and N is that positive affect and negative affect are relatively independent. Compared with introverts, extraverts tend to experience life with a greater degree of positive affect (joy, excitement, happiness) but no less negative affect. Compared with stable (low N) individuals, neurotic people tend to experience life with a greater degree of negative affect (anxiety, fear, sadness) but no less positive affect.

There may be one sense, however, in which positive and negative affect are strongly related. Personality psychologists Randy Larsen and Ed Diener (1987) have conducted extensive research on the dimension of *affect intensity*, which refers to how strongly a person tends to experience both positive and negative emotions. Their studies support the commonly held notion that people who tend to experience strong emotional highs are the same people who also feel the intense lows. In four separate studies of daily mood involving

204 participants, the correlations between positive affect intensity and negative affect intensity ranged from +.70 to +.77. These results strongly suggest that, over time, people who experience intense positive affect will also experience intense negative affect. That is, intensity of emotional response appears to be a characteristic that generalizes to both positive and negative emotion domains (Diener, Colvin, Pavot, & Allman, 1991).

Larsen and Diener view affect intensity as a stable individual difference variable in behavioral style. This traitlike characteristic may have its origins in early infant temperament. Indeed, studies of infants show that emotional intensity is a readily observable dimension upon which newborns differ markedly from one another. Like the traits of E and N, individual differences in affect intensity appear to be quite stable over time. The relative stability of individual differences masks a general tendency, however, for affect intensity to

---

they are socially inadequate (Eysenck, Rust, & Eysenck, 1977), and in alcoholics and drug abusers (Furnham, 1992).

These correlational results, however, do not directly answer a fundamental question: Does neuroticism *cause* stress, or does stress cause neuroticism? Both possibilities seem reasonable. It is possible that being high on N to begin with predisposes a person to stress experiences. But the reverse possibility also seems plausible: High levels of stress may make us more neurotic. Researchers who have tried to tease out these causal relations have obtained evidence for both possibilities, but it would seem that the first of the two has recently garnered more support. For example, Ormel and Wohlfarth (1991) report a longitudinal study of 296 Dutch adults who were given measures of N at the beginning of the study (Time 0) and then asked about stressful life events and psychological distress 6 (Time 1) and 7 (Time 2) years later. Stressful events were broken down into endogenous and exogenous events. Endogenous events are those that are strongly influenced by the person's own behavior, such as serious marital discord, whereas exogenous events are those that are more likely to originate in outside decrease with age. As people move from young adulthood into middle adulthood, they tend to report less intense emotional reactions, both positive and negative. Why this occurs is not known. One possibility is that age differences reflect biological changes. Another is that life activities vary markedly by age. Young persons may be exposed to more positively stimulating as well as stressful experiences than their older counterparts. Yet another possibility is that as people grow older they become habituated to various emotional experiences. Ecstatic moments of youth may give way to more peaceful positive experiences in the middle-adult years and beyond. Intense angst and despair may shade gradually into melancholy as people grow older.

Research also suggests that overall, women experience more intense positive as well as negative affects compared with men. This sex difference in affect intensity helps explain the common finding in survey research that whereas women report greater levels of depression than do men, there is no general difference between the sexes in overall life satisfaction. Fujita, Diener, and Sandvik (1991) reason that women's greater depression is a direct result of greater affect intensity but that their greater affect intensity also produces higher levels of positive affect, which counterbalance the negative and provide them with life satisfaction and happiness scores that are comparable with those of men.

Still, there appear to be some negative ramifications of high levels of affect intensity. For example, strong affect intensity is predictive of tendencies to develop cyclothymia, a mild form of bipolar affective disorder (manic-depressive disorder). In addition, affect intensity is positively associated with such somatic symptoms as headaches, nervousness, nausea, and heart-pounding. Certainly the regular experience of strong emotion exacts a price to be paid in terms of wear and tear on the body. But it seems to be a price that some people are willing to pay. For some, life lacks vividness, vitality, and taste when they are not fully emotionally engaged. The crying and the laughing are all of a piece—you can't have one without the other.

sources, such as accidents and illnesses. The researchers found that both endogenous and exogenous events at Time 1 had an impact on psychological distress at Time 1 and Time 2. In other words, high reports of stresses such as illness and marital problems were associated with high levels of overall distress at that time (6 years after the beginning of the study: Time 1) and one year later (Time 2). However, a much stronger predictor of distress at Times 1 and 2 was the person's score on *N* at Time 0. Neuroticism scores strongly predicted levels of psychological distress 6 and 7 years later. *N* also predicted endogenous life events. Individuals high in neuroticism at Time 0 experienced more self-generated stressful events 6 years later, which, in turn, predicted psychological distress. The relations among these different variables across the 3 time periods in this study are illustrated in Figure 6.4.

Magnus, Diener, Fujita, and Pavot (1993) conducted a similar study, administering measures on two occasions 4 years apart. They found that high levels of *N* predisposed a person to experience a greater number of stressful events in the next 4 years. However, the number of stressful events experienced during the 4-year period did not

Neuroticism, Negative Events, and Distress Over Time

Negative events predict psychological distress over time, but original levels of neuroticism are even stronger predictors of distress in the long run. Note: The numbers are path coefficients. The higher the number, the stronger the direct link between the two boxes connected by the path. Direct links go from one box to another; indirect links go from one box, through a second box, and to a third one. Therefore, neuroticism at Time 0 is directly predictive of psychological distress at Time 1 (0.56) and indirectly predictive of psychological distress at Time 1 by virtue of its direct effect on endogenous negative life events at Time 1 (0.44) and the direct effect of endogenous negative events on psychological distress at Time 1 (0.25). In general, the results show that while negative events do have some impact on psychological distress, N itself is a stronger predictor of distress.

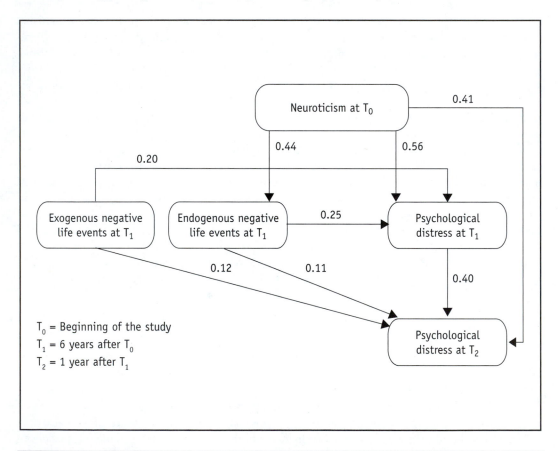

predict the neuroticism score at the end of the period, after statistically accounting for the original N score. In simple terms, the data suggest that N tends to cause stressful events, not the reverse. The researchers offer two reasons for this association. They argue that people high in N tend to react to a wider variety of events in negative ways.

The very same event—say, finding yourself stuck for a semester with an obnoxious roommate—might represent a minor hassle for a person low in *N* but a major stressor for a person high in *N*. Second, they suggest that people high in *N* "bring it on themselves" sometimes. Their difficulties in social interaction may actually initiate negative events in their lives such as job loss, divorce, and other setbacks and failures.

Longitudinal studies have examined the causal relations between the trait of *N* and clinical depression. Here the research provides equivocal results, in part because a tendency toward depression is one aspect of *N* itself. Some reviews have suggested that heightened *N* may be seen as a symptom or result of clinical depression (Barnett & Gotlib, 1988). An acute bout of depression can leave lasting emotional scars, and among those scars may be the heightened levels of anxiety and distress associated with *N*. However, recent studies also suggest that being high on *N* to begin with may predispose some people to major depressive episodes (Bagby, Joffe, Parker, Kalemba, & Harkness, 1995). In a 12-year longitudinal study of depression, Surtees and Wainwright (1996) showed that, out of many clinical, demographic, and social measures taken at the beginning of the study, one of the strongest predictors of poor outcome in treatment for depression was the trait of neuroticism.

When stressful events do occur, how do people high in neuroticism cope with them? The simple answer is "not very well." Research suggests that individuals high in *N* go into a stressful situation with a negative view of things to begin with. They tend to appraise what is already a negative situation in even more negative terms. They tend to see themselves as having relatively few resources and relatively weak support systems to help them cope with the problem (Stokes & McKirnan, 1989). Rather than adopting an action plan for coping with the stressful situation, individuals high in *N* may adopt "emotion-focused" or avoidant coping strategies (Endler & Parker, 1990). Instead of tackling the problem that is causing the stress, they may focus their efforts on soothing their fears and calming their nervousness, or they may simply seek to escape the whole problem through drinking, drug use, or even just staying in bed.

Bolger (1990) studied how medical students coped with the stress of the Medical College Admission Test (MCAT), a grueling day-long ordeal that weighs heavily in medical school admission decisions. Bolger followed 50 pre-medical students during the three-week period before they took the MCAT. Students high in *N* tended to cope with the stress of the impending exam by daydreaming, engaging in fantasies of escape, or wallowing in self-blame for not studying more. As a result, over the course of the three-week period their levels of anxiety continued to increase. By contrast, students low in *N* either tried to prepare for the exam, sought support from friends, or simply reassured themselves that the whole situation was not as bad as it initially seemed. Consequently, their anxiety levels did not increase as much over the three-week period. We see, then, that different levels of *N* are associated with different strategies for coping with stress. Some coping strategies, furthermore, are more effective in dampening stress than are others. The low-*N* students managed their stress better than did high-*N* students. But, you may ask, how did the students perform on the exam? Here you may be surprised. The results of the MCAT exams showed that the two groups did *not* differ. Neuroticism itself was not associated with performance levels on the MCAT. While the students high in *N* suffered more stress and coped badly with the stress over the three-week period, they did just as well on the exam as did their low-*N* counterparts. (Perhaps you find this reassuring, as do I.)

The Behavioral Inhibition System

As he did for the trait of extraversion, Hans Eysenck (1967) proposed a biologically based theory for individual differences in neuroticism. Whereas Eysenck proposed that differences in E were linked to the activity of the brain's reticular activating system, he linked N to the working of the hypothalamus and the limbic system—two areas in the brain that regulate the involuntary or autonomic nervous system and that have been implicated in the experience of some emotional states. People whose hypothalamus and limbic system are set at a low threshold for activation, Eysenck reasoned, are likely to be easily aroused emotionally. Events that would likely have little effect on many people may arouse in these persons a vigorous affective response. Such individuals are emotionally "labile" and thus likely to exhibit neurotic tendencies. Persons whose hypothalamus and limbic system are set at a relatively high threshold, by contrast, are less likely to experience intense and chronic emotional upheaval and thus are less likely to exhibit characteristics associated with high levels of N. Emotional stability and instability, therefore, are largely a function of biological differences beyond the individual's control, Eysenck contended. Though experience and learning surely influence the extent to which a person manifests neurotic tendencies, Eysenck insisted that inborn differences in functioning of the brain predispose some people to develop in the direction of neuroticism and others in the direction of emotional stability. More than 30 years of research, however, have not been kind to Eysenck's biological hypotheses about N. Psychophysiological studies have not produced consistent results linking the hypothalamus and limbic system to N (Geen, 1997), and in one of Eysenck's later works he conceded that little of substance can yet be concluded concerning the biological underpinnings of neuroticism (Eysenck, 1990).

One of the problems with Eysenck's original hypothesis concerned the brain's limbic system. At the time that Eysenck proposed a biological explanation for N, brain researchers believed that the phylogenetically primitive regions of the amygdala, septum, hippocampus, and prefrontal cortex in the brain could be grouped together into an integrated unit called the limbic system (MacLean, 1949). The limbic system was thought to be involved in the production and modulation of emotionality. In that emotional responses of fear, sadness, and joy were believed to have roots in the distant evolutionary past, it made sense to propose that these response systems should be linked to relatively older parts of the brain. In that all emotional responses seemed to share certain common features (which distinguished them from the "higher" mental processes of thinking and reasoning), it made sense to group them together and link them to a single integrated brain system. Therefore, the limbic system was proposed to be the biological seat of human emotions. Recent research, however, suggests that different emotional responses link up with different parts of the brain, and no single emotion center, such as the limbic system, can be reliably identified (LeDoux, 1996). Each of the basic human emotions would appear to have evolved to address a particular set of adaptational challenges. Similarly, different emotional systems would appear to be linked to different regions and functional patterns in the brain. Nonetheless, one region that was originally viewed to be a part of the limbic system does appear to be implicated in the experience and regulation of one particular emotional response. That region is the tiny **amygdala,** and the emotion with which it seems to be associated is *fear.*

In Latin, the word *amygdala* means almond. Early anatomists named a small, almond-shaped region in the forebrain the amygdala. Brain researchers now believe that certain parts of the amygdala activate behavioral, autonomic, and endocrine responses to the presence or perception of *danger* (LeDoux, 1996). When the amygdala receives a stimulus indicating that the organism senses (or even imagines) a dangerous threat, this almond-shaped agent mobilizes a number of different systems designed to defend the organism against whatever may be threatening it. The amygdala may set into motion systems that ultimately stimulate stress hormones and heightened blood pressure and may invoke startle responses and sudden freezing in the presence of a threat. The amygdala is centrally involved in the conditioning of fear. LeDoux (1996) writes that "research by several laboratories has shown that lesions of the central nucleus [of the amygdala] interfere with essentially every measure of conditioned fear, including freezing behavior, autonomic responses, suppression of pain, stress hormone release, and reflex potentiation" (p. 158). Animals and humans who suffer damage to certain parts of the amygdala may be unable to experience normal fear responses and may consequently be unable to learn what to fear in the world.

Several psychologists have proposed that the amygdala is part of a **behavioral inhibition system (BIS)** in humans and related animals (e.g., Davis, 1986; LeDoux, 1996). The behavioral inhibition system mediates responses to threat and signs of danger, punishment, and extreme novelty. Once activated, the BIS may stimulate intense vigilance and attention in the wake of threat, and it may ultimately help to produce responses that lead to defensive withdrawal from a threatening situation. The behavioral inhibition system (BIS), therefore, stands in sharp conceptual contrast to the behavioral approach system (BAS). While the BAS arouses a person to move toward desired incentives that promise positive emotional reward, the BIS causes a person to draw back from goals in the anticipation of a negative emotional punishment. My BAS may motivate me to walk confidently into a room of good friends to enjoy the night's party, but my BIS may keep me standing on the perimeter should I find myself in a very different sort of gathering in which, say, I know very few people, and they all look intimidating. In the first situation, I act spontaneously and on *impulse;* I am comfortable and ready for fun. In the second situation, I feel *anxious* and vigilant; I scan the room warily; I look for opportunities to escape.

The emotional quality of BIS-induced responding, therefore, is likely to be fear and anxiety. Gray (1987) proposes that while individual differences in impulsivity may be linked to variations in the BAS, individual differences in the trait of anxiety correspond to variations in the BIS. Under all conceptions of the terms, anxiety is viewed to be a major component of neuroticism, which itself is sometimes called "negative affectivity" (Watson & Tellegen, 1985). Consequently, some researchers argue that the biological bases for individual differences in *N* reside in the behavioral inhibition system. Put in simple terms, people high in neuroticism have developed, for whatever reasons, a dominant and readily activated BIS, compared with individuals low in neuroticism. Like the BAS, the BIS is an hypothesized functional system, rather than a clearly defined location in the brain. The amygdala may play an important role in the BIS, but it is one role among many different roles played by many different neuronal and hormonal agents and networks. Table 6.5 summarizes hypothesized connections between the BAS and BIS on the one hand and personality traits on the other.

TABLE 6.5	Hypothesized Linkages Between Personality Traits and Brain Systems	
	EXTRAVERSION	**NEUROTICISM**
Alternative trait name (Tellegen)	Positive affectivity	Negative affectivity
Gray's trait dimension*	Impulsivity	Anxiety
Eysenck's proposed biological substrate	Reticular activating system	Limbic system
Associated functional brain system	Behavioral approach system (BAS)	Behavioral inhibition system (BIS)
Purpose of brain system	Response to incentives, positive approach, positive emotions	Response to punishments, withdrawal or vigilance in the face of threat or novelty, negative emotions (especially fear)
Associated brain pathways and structures	Dopaminergic pathways	Amygdala
Associated EEG activity	Left anterior cortex	Right anterior cortex

*Jeffrey Gray's (1982, 1987) theory of personality traits positions the dimensions of impulsivity and anxiety within a two-dimensional coordinate space that is tilted 45 degrees from the dimensions of E and N. Thus, in Gray's terms the extravert is high on impulsivity and low on anxiety, the introvert is low on impulsivity and high on anxiety, the highly neurotic individual is high on impulsivity and high on anxiety, and the emotionally stable (low neuroticism) individual is low in impulsivity and low on anxiety.

You may recall that recent research employing EEG patterns suggests that the behavioral approach system may be indexed by activation of the left anterior regions of the cortex. In a parallel fashion, researchers have suggested that the BIS may be linked to activation of the *right* anterior regions of the cortex. Sutton and Davidson (1997) administered self-report measures of behaviors likely to be associated with BAS and BIS activity among 46 students, employing a questionnaire procedure developed by Carver and White (1994). BAS-linked behaviors included responses that are typically associated with extraversion and positive affectivity, while BIS-linked behaviors included those that are associated with neuroticism and negative affectivity. The researchers calculated a simple BIS/BAS index by subtracting the BIS score from the BAS score. This index, then, assessed the relative strength of BIS-linked versus BAS-linked behaviors. They then took various EEG readings of all of the students on two different occasions. The results of their study showed that prefrontal EEG asymmetry was strongly associated with the BIS/BAS behavioral score. Those students who showed relatively more EEG activity in the right anterior region, compared with the left, tended to score toward the BIS end of the BIS/BAS scale, whereas those who showed relatively more left anterior activity scored toward the BAS end of the behavioral scale. EEG measures from other parts of the cortex were unrelated to the behavioral scores.

Recent research supports the idea that individual differences in N or in traits related to N may be linked to individual differences in a behavioral inhibition system. The BIS is as yet a loosely configured construct, but it would appear to implicate the functioning of parts of the brain's amygdala and be indexed by heightened activity in the right anterior regions of the brain. Future research promises to give us a clearer and more articulated picture of the biological underpinnings of the human tendency to experience anxiety, fear, and other negative emotional states.

O: OPENNESS TO EXPERIENCE

The third of the Big Five traits is something of a curiosity. In his original formulation of 16 basic source traits, Cattell (1943) included a dimension of "intelligence." On the "intelligence" scale of the 16PF trait inventory, a person responds to a series of self-report items that essentially ask him or her to rate the extent of his or her own intelligence. These self-ratings, however, are only modestly correlated with intelligence scores obtained on IQ tests. To nobody's surprise, including Cattell's, how intelligent a person rates him- or herself is not the same thing as how intelligent a person turns out to be as measured on a test of intellectual *ability*. Nonetheless, while many personality psychologists may view intelligence, as measured on cognitive tests, to lie somewhat outside the central domain of personality per se, the extent to which a person thinks that he or she is intelligent would appear to be an interesting self-ascribed personality trait. Early factor-analytic studies of English-language traits showed that self-ratings of intelligence tended to cluster with ratings on other trait dimensions, such as measures of reflectiveness, imagination, tender-mindedness, aesthetic sensitivity, and preference for complexity in life. In an early five-factor model, Norman (1963) identified a dimension of "culture" as including traits having to do with how reflective, imaginative, artistic, and refined a person is. High scorers were thought to be intellectually rounded, broad and insightful; low scorers were narrow, unimaginative, and even crude and boorish. Reflecting its association with intelligence and intellectual interests, other researchers have labeled this trait domain "inquiring intellect" (Fiske, 1949) and "intellectance" (Digman, 1990). In this chapter we will use the label popularized by Costa and McCrae: **openness to experience** (or simply, *O*).

Whether we call it culture, intellectance, or openness to experience, this trait would seem, on first blush, to be a very good thing. Many classical models of personality development and growth describe the mature individual as being reflective and imaginative, as having insight and a broad perspective on life (e.g., Erikson, 1963; Fromm, 1973; Loevinger, 1976; Rogers, 1951; Vaillant, 1977; White, 1975). In Chapter 1, I identified *O* as a strong personality trait in the life of Karen Horney, the renowned psychoanalytic theorist. From adolescence onward, Horney described herself and was described by others as especially imaginative, original, broad-minded, creative, intellectually daring, independent, nontraditional, and complex. Her inquiring intellect and restless curiosity led her to reject the authoritarian values of her childhood and to establish a strong "independence of mind," which her biographer (Quinn, 1988) identified as a cardinal disposition in her personality structure.

Pioneers in the sciences, arts, and religion are often highly imaginative and innovative people whose insights can have a dramatic impact on their respective fields. For example, Gardner (1993) focuses on the development of creative genius in the lives of Freud, Picasso, Einstein, Gandhi, Martha Graham (dance), Igor Stravinsky (music), and T. S. Eliot (literature). Not only are all seven of Gardner's protagonists readily described as high in *O*, but a great deal of their development as creators and as people can be viewed as a progressive enrichment, over time, of their experiential openness. A similar conclusion can be drawn from biographies of political revolutionaries and some individuals who dedicate their lives to social change (Andrews, 1991; Colby & Damon, 1992). For example, Colby and Damon trace the intellectual and political development of Andrei Sakharov, a physicist and political activist in the former Soviet Union. Sakharov headed the Soviet efforts in the 1940s and 1950s to develop the hydrogen bomb. But over time, Sakharov became increasingly disenchanted with life in the Soviet Union. Furthermore, he began to question the wisdom of developing weapons that were ultimately aimed at destroying human civilization on earth. Sakharov was a bold and innovative scientist whose intellectual daring began in early adulthood to generalize to the domains of political and social life. As he read and learned more and interacted with a progressively wider array of colleagues and associates, Sakharov began to carve out for himself the role of social critic and dissident in an authoritarian society. As he matured through middle age, Sakharov became more and more open to new experiences, expressing what Colby and Damon (1992) describe as a "striking openness to moral change" and an "active receptiveness" to important social influences in his world (p. 13). Sakharov gained more and more confidence in his radical ideals and expanded his revolutionary vision for a freer and more just society. Eventually, he became the most prominent dissident in the entire Soviet Union. A tireless advocate for democracy and human rights, Sakharov came to symbolize the revolutionary intellectual whose transformative vision for a better society inspired not only Russians but people from around the globe. In the case of Sakharov, openness to experience helped to catalyze a heroic struggle against authoritarian oppression.

But Sakharov's life story does not inspire everybody. The leaders of the former Soviet Union, for example, and the many Russian citizens who were deeply committed to the communist regime saw Sakharov as a dangerous threat and a malcontent rather than a hero. In a less comfortable example that is closer to home, Fidel Castro led a revolution in Cuba in the 1950s. As he began to translate his radical ideas into the reality of a socialist state, Castro was vilified in the United States and cast in the role of enemy. Described as daring, imaginative, nonconventional, and intellectually insightful as a young man, Castro has never been a hero for most Americans. While we may be able to come up with good reasons to distinguish Castro from, say, Sakharov or Karen Horney, my example illustrates a basic curiosity about *O*. Put simply, *O* invokes a great deal of ambivalence for many people. What seems on first blush to be a trait that is linked to such good things as creativity and psychological maturity may also invoke more negative associations.

Our ambivalence about *O* is especially evident in the realm of politics. One of the most popular U.S. presidents in recent memory was Ronald Reagan. Yet even President Reagan's greatest admirers would *not* describe him as high in openness to experience. Indeed, it was partly Reagan's unquestioning embrace of a small number of simple principles in life and politics that made him so admirable to many Americans. Yet President Reagan's detractors viewed the same characteristics in decidedly negative terms, describing him as rigid, simple-minded, and out of touch with the complexities of life. By contrast, President Bill Clinton was generally viewed, even by his detractors, as creative, imaginative, complex, curious, and having very broad interests. But his high openness to experience seemed to come with a cost, according to many of his critics. From his time as governor of Arkansas through his two-term presidency, Clinton was repeatedly criticized for being too "slick" and lacking a moral and political center of conviction. In politics and in life more generally, one person's "intellectual daring" is another person's "intellectual recklessness;" one person's "broad-mindedness" is another person's "lack of conviction;" one person's "independence of mind" is another person's "disregard for the viewpoints of others." Unlike *N*, it is hard to decide whether *O* is really a good or a bad thing. Your evaluation of the concept may indeed partly depend on where you stand on this personality dimension.

Correlates of *O*

McCrae and Costa (1997a) describe *O* as fundamentally "a matter of inner experience and mental phenomena related to the scope of [a person's] awareness and the intensity of [his or her] consciousness" (p. 835). Openness to experience is manifested in the depth, breadth, and permeability of a person's conscious experience and in the desire or drive to expand that experience to encompass a richer array of sensations, perceptions, thoughts, and feelings. Openness may be expressed in many different domains. On the NEO-PI-R, McCrae and Costa identify six different facets of openness: fantasy, aesthetics, feelings, actions, ideas, and values. Therefore, the person high in *O* may reveal a rich and elaborate fantasy life, may be especially sensitive to the aesthetic dimensions of life, may experience a greater range of personal feelings, may seek out a wider range of activities in life, may hold many different and even contradictory ideas, and may express a complex and highly differentiated value system. In the overall, persons high in *O* are described by themselves and by others who know them as especially original, imaginative, creative, complex, curious, daring, independent, analytical, untraditional, artistic, liberal, and having broad interests. Persons low in *O* are described as conventional, down-to-earth, uncreative, simple, incurious, nonadventurous, conforming, nonanalytical, unartistic, traditional, conservative, and having narrow interests. Sample items from a self-report measure of *O* are presented in Table 6.6.

In one of the earliest investigations of *O*, McCrae and Costa (1980) administered a number of trait scales and a sentence-completion exercise to 240 adults between the ages of 35 and 80 years. On the sentence-completion exercise, the participants were

---

TABLE 6.6	*Questionnaire Items Assessing Openness to Experience* (O)

1. I enjoy concentrating on a fantasy or daydream and exploring all its possibilities, letting it grow and develop.
2. I am sometimes completely absorbed in music I am listening to.
3. Without strong emotions, life would be uninteresting.
4. I enjoy trying new and foreign foods.
5. I find philosophical arguments boring. (reversed)
6. The different ideas of right and wrong that people in other societies have may be valid for them.

Source: McCrae & Costa (1985b). These items come from the NEO Openness Scales.

presented with sentence fragments such as "A good father/" and "Rules are/" and were asked to complete the sentences in any way they wished. Table 6.7 provides examples of how persons high and low on O responded to this task. Persons scoring high on O on the trait scales provided richer and more complex responses on the sentence-completion test, compared with persons scoring low in O. Their responses reveal a more differentiated fantasy life, more psychological insight, and a greater variety of experience. Whereas persons low in O held to rather rigid and traditional views of authority and society (Rules are/ "there to obey"), persons high in O tended to reject, or at least question, these stereotypical attitudes, revealing more flexible and personalized understandings of rules, authority, the family, and sex roles (Rules are/ "necessary, but civil disobedience is one way to change them for 'progress'"). The study suggests that openness to experience is associated with a more complex, nonconforming, and individualized understanding of the world.

Persons high in O are thought to have broad intellectual and aesthetic interests. This does not mean, however, that these people are necessarily highly intelligent. McCrae and Costa (1985a) argue that intelligence and O are very different constructs. To support this claim of the discriminant validity of trait scales assessing O, McCrae and Costa report a correlation of +.32 between vocabulary score on a standard adult intelligence (IQ) test and openness to experience in a sample of 253 men. Remember that, to show

TABLE 6.7	*Sentence-Completion Responses of Men Scoring High and Low on Openness to Experience* (O)

LOW	
SENTENCE STEM	**RESPONSE**
Rules are	there to obey.
	laws to be governed by for the best interests of all concerned.
My main problem	is financial.
When they avoided me	I wondered why.
If my mother	gave a command, it was done.
A husband has a right to	come home and find his wife looking nice.

HIGH	
SENTENCE STEM	**RESPONSE**
Rules are	things that should be flexible enough to fit the real world.
	necessary, but civil disobedience is one way to change them for "progress."
My main problem	is I am too emotional or sensitive sometimes.
When I am criticized	I try to remain open-minded and not get defensive. It doesn't always work, however.
A good father	remembers the anxieties of childhood.
The worst thing about being a man	is the false image built for us by society.

Source: McCrae & Costa (1980), p. 1186.

discriminant validity, one must prove that a particular trait scale does *not* measure the same thing that scales of *other* traits measure. In this case, the correlation of +.32 suggests a statistically significant but rather modest relationship between intelligence and O, meaning that the two measures—intelligence (via vocabulary) and openness to experience—seem to be measuring somewhat different dimensions of human functioning. Education level is also positively associated with O. In a nationwide sample of nearly 10,000 adults over the age of 35, researchers found a positive correlation between number of years of education and scores on a short scale measuring openness to experience (McCrae & Costa, 1997a). The label of "culture" for this personality dimension suggests that such an association is not surprising. The Western tradition of a liberal arts education aims to expose the student to a wide range of intellectual experiences and to encourage a critical attitude toward accepted values and assumptions. There is, therefore, reason to believe that a strong liberal arts education should promote openness to experience. At the same time, it may be true that people with high levels of openness to experience to begin with might be more likely to obtain such an education or more likely to find such an educational experience to be especially broadening.

People high in O appear to welcome challenge and change. For example, in one study of career changes in adults under the age of 55, 64% of the men and 71% of the women who changed jobs over a particular time period scored above the midpoint on O (McCrae & Costa, 1985b). Whitbourne (1986) interviewed 34 women and 23 men (average age 41 years) about anticipated work and family changes. Such changes might include seeking different work, finding employment outside the house, adding another child to the family, or retiring. Openness to experience, assessed via a questionnaire, was positively associated with anticipated change in life, as was age. In other words, older adults and adults scoring high in O anticipated more changes in their lives in the future. (In a 12-month follow-up of the same adults, however, O was not significantly associated with the number of *actual* changes that had occurred.)

Within the general domain of O resides an interesting trait that goes by the name of **absorption.** Absorption is formally defined as a predisposition to "experience emotional and cognitive alterations across a variety of situations" (Roche & McConkey, 1990, p. 92). The concept of absorption has its origins in Auke Tellegen's research into why some people seem especially susceptible to hypnotism and some do not. Tellegen and Atkinson (1974) found that hypnotizable individuals were more open to and more likely to have subjective experiences in which their attention was fully engaged by some object or event, resulting in an altered sense of reality. To assess individual differences in a predisposition to show such experience, they designed the Tellegen Absorption Scale (TAS), which later became part of Tellegen's (1982) Multidimensional Personality Questionnaire (MPQ).

Absorption is associated with an intense and vivid fantasy life. Persons who score high on absorption may become so immersed in their imaginative experiences that they lose all track of time, place, and identity (Pekala, Wenger, & Levine, 1985). Research shows that absorption is positively related to reports of parapsychological phenomena, such as out-of-body experiences, as well as reports of naturally occurring altered states of consciousness. According to a recent factor-analytic study, absorption connects closely to those aspects of O that invoke aesthetic sensitivity, unusual perceptions and associations, fantasy and dreams, unconventional views of reality, and awareness of inner feelings. It is perhaps due to the presence of the trait of absorption within the broader trait domain of O that researchers have found O to be positively associated with mild forms of magical and bizarre thinking (West, Widiger, & Costa, 1993). Individuals high in O are also more likely to believe in "esoteric and dubious phenomena, such as astrology and the existence of ghosts" (Epstein & Meier, 1989, p. 351).

Dollinger and Clancy (1993) conducted an interesting study examining how personality traits relate to artistic self-expression. Each of the 201 college students completed questionnaire measures of O and other traits and was then instructed to obtain photographs that express his or her individual identity. The researchers provided these instructions:

> We want you to describe how you see yourself. To do this, we would like you to take or have someone take 12 photographs that tell who you are. These photographs can be of anything just as long as they tell something about who you are. You should not be interested in your skill as a photographer. Keep in mind that the photographs should describe who you are as you see yourself. When you finish you will have a book about yourself that is made up of only 12 photographs. (Dollinger & Clancy, 1993, p. 1066)

The researchers collected all the photograph books and proceeded to rate the students' work on a number of different artistic and psychological dimensions. People high in O tended to receive significantly higher ratings on the artistic *richness* of their photographic essays. Richness referred to the extent to which the photographic arrangement expressed abstract, self-reflective, and aesthetically compelling qualities. Students high in O produced work that showed a creative and imaginative interpretation of the photography task, evidence of an aesthetic or artistic sensibility, and illumination of a wide range of self-expressive themes. By contrast, the photographic essays produced by students low in O tended to be rated as especially concrete, commonplace, prosaic, unimaginative, and dull. With respect to other traits, the researchers found that low E and high N among *women* also predicted richness. In other words, introverted and relatively anxious (neurotic) women tended to construct photographic essays that were more imaginative and self-expressive compared with extraverted and emotionally stable women. These relationships between E and N on the one hand and richness on the other were not found, however, among men. Finally, the researchers also found that extraverted students (men and women) were more likely than introverted students to illustrate interpersonal themes in their photographs.

Folk beliefs suggest that a vivid imagination and high levels of creativity may come with a price. The ancient Greeks spoke of the "divine madness" of creative genius, and in modern times many accounts have been written suggesting that especially creative people may be plagued by self-doubts and suffer from periods of severe depression. At least one study has examined the relation between depression and openness to experience. Wolfenstein and Trull (1997) administered self-report measures of O and depression to 143 college students. The students were chosen to comprise three groups—those who were currently suffering from depression, those who reported severe bouts of depression in the past, and those who reported that they had never experienced a bout of severe depression. The researchers found that those students who were currently depressed and/or who reported high levels of depressive symptoms on the self-report measures tended to score high on two of the facets of O: aesthetics and feelings. In other words, those students who showed a strong appreciation for art and beauty (aesthetics facet of O) and especially vivid and intense emotions (feelings facet of O) were more likely to be depressed than those students who scored low on the O facets of aesthetics and feelings. Although the results from only one study do not establish a well-documented finding, the study nonetheless reinforces the more general view that being high in O may bring with it both positive and negative characteristics and outcomes.

How do people differing on O cope with the inevitable stresses and the setbacks of everyday life? McCrae and Costa (1997a) report that O is positively associated with using intellectualization as a defense mechanism and negatively associated with using denial. People high in O are more likely to try to explain away their problems and to translate deeply personal issues into more abstract and depersonalized rationalizations. By contrast, people low in O are more likely to deny the existence of the problems in the first place or to distract themselves from paying concerted attention to the sources of stress.

McCrae and Costa (1986) examined the relations between the traits of O, E, and N on the one hand and coping with stress on the other in two large adult samples. Men and women who had reported a recent stressful life event participated in the study. Stressful events included losses (such as a death of a parent), threats (such as an illness in the family), and challenges (such as marriage). The participants completed a questionnaire that asked them to recall the particular stressful event and to indicate which of a series of 27 coping strategies they had ever used in dealing with it.

Table 6.8 shows that E, N, and O were significantly associated with use of particular coping strategies. Neuroticism, for example, was correlated with the coping strategies of hostile reaction, escapist fantasy, self-blame, sedation, withdrawal, wishful thinking, passivity, and indecisiveness. Virtually all of these coping strategies were rated by the participants as extremely *in*effective in dealing with stress. Extraversion and openness to experience, on the other hand, were associated with a number of effective coping strategies. E was correlated with rational action, positive thinking, substitution, and restraint. Adults high in O were more likely to use humor in dealing with stress; those low in O relied heavily on faith. McCrae and Costa argue that basic personality traits manifest themselves in times of stress by predisposing people to adopt certain corresponding coping strategies. While the choice of a coping strategy is likely partly determined by the nature of the stressful event and other situational factors, stable and internal personality traits like E, N, and O also play an important determining role.

The Authoritarian Personality

Among the Big Five traits, O appears to be the one that relates directly to certain political beliefs and attitudes. Within Western societies, high levels of O tend to be associated with moderate-to-liberal political viewpoints while low levels of O tend to be associated with moderate-to-conservative points of view (McCrae & Costa, 1987, 1997a). To the extent that political liberalism may challenge traditional authority and argue for significant social change, its appeal to people high in openness might be expected. Similarly, conservative positions in many contemporary Western democracies tend to underscore traditional social conventions and authoritative systems, which are likely to appeal to people low in O. Among Chinese high school students in Hong Kong, high levels of O are associated with the desire to adopt the political norms of Western democracy whereas low scores on O are associated with skepticism about

TABLE 6.8	*Coping Strategies Associated With* E, N, *and* O

EXTRAVERSION *(E)*	
Positive thinking:	thought about the good side, the positive aspects of the situation.
Rational action:	took some direct action to change the circumstances that were giving you a problem.
Restraint:	resisted making snap judgments or hasty decisions.
Substitution:	found satisfaction somewhere else in life.
NEUROTICISM *(N)*	
Escapist fantasy:	spent time daydreaming to forget your troubles.
Hostile reaction:	became irritable and took it out on others.
Indecisiveness:	thought about the problem over and over without really reaching a decision.
Passivity:	procrastinated and delayed while others were waiting for you.
Sedation:	used tranquilizers, alcohol, meditation, or relaxation exercises to calm yourself down.
Self-blame:	blamed yourself, felt guilty, or became apologetic.
Wishful thinking:	just wished that the problem would be gone or that help would come.
Withdrawal:	withdrew from others and attempted to cope with the problem by yourself.
OPENNESS TO EXPERIENCE *(O)*	
Faith *(negatively correlated with O):*	just put your faith in God, or other people, or institutions.
Humor:	saw humor in the situation.

Source: McCrae & Costa (1986), pp. 393, 404–405.

social change and a preference for traditional Chinese ways (Yik & Bond, 1993). The way in which *O* relates to political views, therefore, is a function of the sociopolitical context and the traditions of the society within which the person lives. What might be viewed as "conservative" in one setting can be seen as "liberal" in another. Nonetheless, it would appear that high levels of *O* tend to correlate with political and social beliefs that underscore progressive change, skepticism toward traditional authority, and tolerance for competing viewpoints. By contrast, low levels of *O* tend to fit more congenially with political and social beliefs that emphasize stability over change, obedience toward traditional authority, and preference for a uniform or unifying point of view.

When it comes to the relation between personality traits and political viewpoints, what is arguably the most influential idea ever developed in personality psychology is the concept of the **authoritarian personality.** Deeply troubled by the rise of Nazi fascism in Germany during the 1930s and 1940s, the psychoanalyst and social critic Erich Fromm (1941) identified an authoritarian character type prevalent among Western Europeans of the day, especially among the lower-middle classes in Germany. Authoritarian men and women sought desperately to *escape from the freedom* that modern capitalist societies afforded them, by striving to idealize authority and by yearning to pledge unqualified allegiance to those in power above *and* to receive the same allegiance from those below. Fromm believed that the authoritarian character structure was partly responsible for Hitler's fateful domination of German politics. Historical and economic conditions had conspired to create in the minds of the German people a readiness and a willingness to be dominated by powerful authority. This partly explains, argued Fromm, how an otherwise intelligent and sensible German populace could rally around such a ruthless tyrant and passively acquiesce to the Nazi programs of persecution, enslavement, and genocide.

Following up on some of Fromm's ideas, a group of eminent social scientists launched an ambitious study of authoritarianism among Americans, resulting in the publication of a landmark book, *The Authoritarian Personality* (Adorno, Frenkel-Brunswik, Levinson, & Sanford, 1950). Conducting extensive interviews of groups of American adults who indicated that they were highly prejudiced against Jews and other ethnic and religious minorities, the researchers developed a questionnaire, the California F [for "Fascism"] Scale, to measure authoritarianism. Authoritarianism was identified as a cluster of nine attitudes and traits, each tapped by certain items on the F Scale. The nine characteristics made up a coherent personality syndrome or type:

1. *Conventionalism:* Rigid adherence to conventional, middle-class values.
2. *Authoritarian submission:* Uncritical attitude toward authority.
3. *Authoritarian aggression:* Tendency to be on the lookout for and to condemn or punish people who violate conventional values.
4. *Anti-intraception:* Opposition to imaginative and subjective aspects of life, to such things as art, literature, and psychology.
5. *Superstition and stereotypy:* The belief in mystical determinants of the individual's fate, and the tendency to think in rigid categories.
6. *Power and toughness:* Preoccupation with dominance and strength.
7. *Destructiveness and cynicism:* Generalized hostility toward people.
8. *Projectivity:* The disposition to believe that wild and dangerous things go on in the world; the projection outward of unconscious emotional impulses.
9. *Sex:* Exaggerated concern with sexual "goings on."

Heavily influenced by psychoanalytic theory, the authors of *The Authoritarian Personality* argued that authoritarianism had its roots in a complex web of family dynamics. In essence, a highly repressive family environment sows the seeds for the development of authoritarianism. The child represses strong biological impulses because of an overly punitive environment, ultimately projecting those impulses onto others in a defensive way. Parents who are emotionally distant and highly punitive fail to provide appropriate models for healthy identification, stunting ego development in the child and keeping the superego from being fully integrated into the personality. A pervasive sense of personal weakness and dependency on others, and perhaps a latent homosexuality in men, may further underlie the authoritarian syndrome.

Hundreds of empirical studies have been done on the authoritarian personality, employing the original F-test and subsequent scales that have incorporated many improvements in psychometric design (Altemeyer, 1981, 1988; Dillehay, 1978; Winter, 1996). A substantial body of research suggests positive relations between authoritarianism and a number of attitudinal variables such as extremely conservative political values, anti-Semitism, distrust of outsiders, and highly punitive attitudes toward those deemed to be "deviant" in a society. Duncan, Peterson, and Winter (1994) found that authoritarian women and men espouse traditional sex-role attitudes and are hostile toward feminism and the women's movement. Peterson, Doty, and Winter (1993) found that authoritarians hold hostile and punitive attitudes toward people with AIDS, drug users, and the homeless. Among Dutch students, authoritarianism strongly predicted ethnocentric prejudice, as evidenced in strong support among authoritarians for a Dutch political party that advocated the expulsion of immigrant workers (Meloen, Hagendoorn, Raaijmakers, & Visser, 1988). Authoritarianism is associated with support for the caste system among citizens of India (Hassan & Sarkar, 1975) and with nostalgia for the old Soviet regime and distrust of democratic reforms among citizens of Russia (McFarland, Ageyev, & Abalakina-Paap, 1992).

Authoritarians tend to cherish the traditions of their own group but are highly distrustful of the traditions of other groups. Among American college students, authoritarianism is associated with support for pro-Christian religious instruction in the public schools (Altemeyer, 1993). The same study, however, shows that authoritarian American students are *opposed* to pro-Muslim religious instruction in public schools of Muslim countries! Authoritarians tend to be highly respectful of traditional authority in their own society, and they find the questioning of authority to be highly distasteful. They have relatively little tolerance for those who disobey authority or whose lifestyle and viewpoints contradict or call into question the legitimacy of traditional authority. Authoritarians will advocate a strong defense of traditional authority, especially when they perceive that authority is being threatened (Doty, Peterson, & Winter, 1991; Sales, 1973). It is perhaps no surprise, therefore, that authoritarianism among American citizens was positively associated with strong support for U.S. involvement in the Vietnam war in the 1960s and 1970s (Izzett, 1971) and in the Persian Gulf war in 1990–91 (Winter, 1996). Shortly before the onset of the Persian Gulf war, American students high in authoritarianism advocated stronger U.S. responses, including even the use of nuclear weapons. After the war was over, these students took greater pride in the American victory and were less likely to express any regrets about the loss of Iraqi lives caused by the war.

The authoritarian personality is one manifestation of the low end of the trait continuum for openness to experience. For sure, not all people who score low on O would be classified as authoritarian. But authoritarianism tends to be highly negatively associated with O, meaning that there is a strong tendency for low scores on O to be associated with high scores on measures of authoritarianism. Trapnell (1994) reported a correlation of −.57 between O and Altemeyer's (1981) measure of right-wing authoritarianism in a sample of 722 individuals. This is a fairly robust correlation in a sample so large. While low O and authoritarianism are by no means the same thing, they would appear to covary and to share many similarities. Like authoritarians, people low in O are expected to value conventional norms and rules and to be suspicious of complex, imaginative, and nonconforming expressions of the human spirit—expressions that may threaten the security of the status quo. At the heart of the overlap between low O and authoritarianism, moreover, may be an intolerance of ambiguity. Winter (1996) suggests that "the key component of authoritarianism is actually a cognitive style—intolerance of ambiguity or rigidity" (p. 218). The person low in O prefers simple solutions and clear answers to life's problems. Too much abstraction, too much complexity, too many different points of view get in the way of *the truth*.

The authoritarian personality, therefore, would appear to share some basic features with low levels of the trait openness to experience. Not only do empirical findings show a strong association between low *O* and authoritarianism, but the two constructs are defined in somewhat similar ways. Perhaps the most important commonality between the two is an intolerance for ambiguity. At the same time, there would seem to be features of authoritarianism that have little to do with *O*. For example, the classic definition of the authoritarian personality includes such characteristics as "authoritarian aggression," "power and toughness," and "destructiveness and cynicism" (Adorno et al., 1950). These characteristics seem to relate to other trait domains in the Big Five taxonomy. Authoritarianism may be something of a blend—combining low levels of *O* with trait constructs that are found in one or more of the other four trait clusters. The obvious candidate for inclusion in this regard is the Big Five trait domain of agreeableness *(A)*. The low pole of *A* includes such descriptors as "aggressive," "cruel," and "tough-minded." At minimum, the authoritarian personality may represent a trait combination of low *O* and low *A*.

C AND *A*: CONSCIENTIOUSNESS AND AGREEABLENESS

The great 19th-century British novelist, Charles Dickens, was something of a literary trait psychologist. One of Dickens's favorite devices was to craft a character around a central defining feature or trait. The particular character, then, might display the defining feature in many different scenes, making him or her instantly recognizable to the reader. Dickens went so far as to have some characters affect the same mannerisms or utter the same signature lines again and again across different scenes in the story. Dickens's novels, such as *David Copperfield* and *Oliver Twist*, were very long, and they contained many different characters. Furthermore, the novels were typically published in installments, a chapter or two at a time. Therefore, it could be difficult for the reader to remember who was who in the story. Dickens's method of infusing many of his characters with a distinctive and immediately recognizable feature helped the reader to remember the characters from one chapter to the next. It also made for delightful reading in many cases, for Dickens was a master at identifying amusing features of human personality.

In *Bleak House*, Dickens (1853/1956) tells the story of a lawsuit that goes on for generations—the case of Jarndyce vs. Jarndyce—and the impact it has, direct and indirect, on a cast of memorable characters. Many of the characters personify a particular personality trait or social quality. You have Lady Dedlock, a party to the lawsuit, who is forever the model of the phlegmatic personality. In virtually every scene, she affects a standoffish and aloof manner; she is bored, sophisticated, and jaded. You have the comical Mrs. Jellyby who "devotes herself entirely to the public" (p. 26) and, therefore, never feeds her children or cleans her house. She is the self-righteous do-gooder who supports esoteric causes in faraway lands and who can usually be found writing earnest letters to the African country of Borrioboola-Gha (there never was such a place). You have Mr. Bagnet, a former military officer, whose admiration for his wife—whom he affectionately calls "the old girl"—is expressed in every scene in which he appears. The novel's protagonist, Esther Summerson, has no signature line or behavior. But she is, nonetheless, a study in personality consistency as well. From her humble beginnings as an orphan to the happy ending that Dickens provides for her as a young adult, Esther is dutiful, hard-working, responsible, gentle, compassionate, and loyal. She never wavers in these traits. She is a personification of conscientiousness and agreeableness.

Her birth is a scandal. The product of an illicit love affair between a lady of nobility and a military officer, Esther is removed from her biological mother at birth (her mother is told that the baby was born dead) and raised in a rough, working-class family. From an early age onward, she is told that her very existence is a disgrace to polite society. Yet, Esther prospers. Her sweet temperament and her hard-working ways win her many friends and admirers. As an adolescent, she is taken in by an older man—Mr. Jarndyce (a descendant of the original disputants in the long-standing legal case)—and employed as a housekeeper and, eventually, the manager of his estate. Esther is selflessly devoted to the well-being of Mr. Jarndyce, whom she calls her "guardian," and to the welfare of two other people whom her guardian has also taken in. The two are the beautiful Ada and the dashing but headstrong Richard. Richard and Ada fall in love, and Esther works tirelessly to comfort Ada when Richard lets her down and to shepherd the ill-fated couple through very difficult times. Esther is not beautiful, but at least three different men are so enamored with her kindness and her strength of character that they eventually propose marriage to her. Her looks are further compromised by a disfiguring illness she contracts when she is ministering to the sick. She suffers many indignities and setbacks in the book, and the illness almost kills her. But Esther perseveres and ultimately flourishes. The case of Jarndyce vs. Jarndyce corrupts the lives of many, but Esther is never corrupted. Her conscientiousness and her agreeableness prove to be ennobling qualities that enable her to transcend the disgrace of her birth and build an exemplary life centered on mature love and generative work.

Esther portrays the positive poles of the traits conscientiousness and agreeableness. To comprehend the full spectrum for these two traits, however, you have to look at the negative poles as well. Dickens is very accommodating in this regard, for he portrays two of the more unconscientious and disagreeable people one might ever meet. In *Bleak House*, Mr. Harold Skimpole personifies the negative pole of conscientiousness. When Esther first meets Skimpole she finds him to be oddly charming in his childlike repudiation of all adult responsibilities. Skimpole is a refreshing contrast to the hard-driven, money-grubbing lawyers who work on Jarndyce vs. Jarndyce. Skimpole has no concerns about wealth or status. He feels no need to work. He delights in music and the arts, good food, pleasant conversation, and an occasional glass of fine wine. Upon first meeting, Esther learns that Skimpole was trained as a physician, but he lost that job when he found it too bothersome to make house calls on sick people. He would rather lie in bed and read the paper. After his failure in medicine, Skimpole's friends repeatedly loaned him money and helped him along in life, enabling him eventually to marry and to have three daughters. But no matter how much charity he received from others, Skimpole never seemed able to organize his life into any sort of coherent pattern. This was because he was afflicted with

> two of the oldest infirmities in the world: one was, that he had no idea of time; the other, that he had no idea of money. In consequence of which he never kept an appointment, never

could transact any business, and never knew the value of anything! Well! So he had got on in life, and here he was! He was very fond of reading the papers, very fond of making fancy-sketches with a pencil, very fond of nature, very fond of art. All he asked of society was, to let him live. *That* wasn't much. His wants were few. Give him the papers, conversation, music, mutton, coffee, landscape, fruit in the season, a few sheets of Bristol-board, and a little claret, and he asked no more. He was a mere child in the world, but he didn't cry for the moon. He said to the world, "Go your several ways in peace! Wear red coats, blue coats, lawn sleeves, put pens behind your ears, wear aprons; go after glory, holiness, commerce, trade, any object you prefer; only let Harold Skimpole live!" (p. 53)

Harold Skimpole's welcome soon wears a little thin with Esther. Though she remains conscientious and agreeable throughout, Esther gradually comes to see that Skimpole is a selfish lout. It may be fine for a child to be irresponsible, but Skimpole is not a child and he does not live in a child's world. Skimpole never pays his bills. He never provides for his family. By seeming so innocent and childlike, Skimpole swindles charity from almost everybody he meets. In the adult world where people work and love, Skimpole does no work and seems to love little beyond himself. Sure, he claims to love his three daughters, but he does nothing to provide for their well-being. Instead, his daughters wait on him. They bring him wine. They fetch the newspaper, like dogs. Despite his charm, Skimpole proves to be completely irresponsible, undependable, disorganized, lazy, and weak-willed. Eventually, he betrays Esther's guardian for money—this from a man who claims he cares nothing for money. After he dies, Skimpole's family digs up his letters and diaries, and these are published to some public acclaim. Many readers are charmed by Skimpole's portrayal of himself as an innocent child living in a tough adult world. But the conscientious Esther sees little of merit in what he writes.

The Big Five trait domain of **conscientiousness (C)** encompasses a great many characteristics of personality that center on how hard-working, self-disciplined, responsible, reliable, dutiful, well-organized, and persevering a person is. At the high end of the *C* continuum, people may be described as well-organized, efficient, and dependable (Goldberg, 1990). They approach tasks in a systematic and orderly fashion. They analyze problems logically. They provide concise answers to questions and perform according to exacting standards in their work and their play. You can depend on conscientious people. Self-disciplined and duty-bound, they are reliable and responsible in their dealings with other people. They are rarely late for meetings; they don't miss class. Conscientious people plan their lives carefully, according to principles and goals. While they may seem overly cautious at times, they are, nonetheless, able to make hard decisions and stick by them when things get rough. They are persistent, steady, predictable, conventional, and thrifty. At the other end of the continuum, people low on the *C* dimension tend to be disorganized, haphazard, inefficient, careless, negligent, and undependable. It is difficult to predict what they will do from one situation to the next, so erratic and inconsistent is their behavior. Life lacks plan and purpose. Low-*C* people may be lazy and slothful, indecisive and wishy-washy, extravagant and impractical. Unconscientious people have little regard for serious standards of work or morality. While their spontaneity may seem like a breath of fresh air in the face of stale social conventions, their irresponsibility and utter inability to stand *by others* or stand *for anything* in the long run make them very poor risks in friendship and in love.

If Harold Skimpole is Esther's opposite on the trait of conscientiousness, Grandfather Smallweed is Dickens's best candidate in *Bleak House* for Esther's opposite on the trait of agreeableness. Smallweed is a comical character. In body, he is little more than a bag of bones. One of his signature behaviors is slamming couch cushions against the head of his poor wife. Whenever she expresses any sentiment that is not in accord with his own, Smallweed beats the poor woman with a cushion. In the process of hitting her, Smallweed always manages to slump farther and farther down in his seat. At that point, he must be "shaken up" by his granddaughter, Judy. She shakes his body violently, as if to pound some new life into it, and pulls him to an upright and seated condition. Replenished, he can now proceed to his next act, which typically involves arguing with some person or another. Smallweed cannot walk, so he must be carried from one argument to the next. This most disagreeable man has disagreements with many different characters in the book, and most of these disagreements are about money. Smallweed is a wealthy man, but he continues to extort money from others and to concoct elaborate schemes to enrich himself further. The comic nature of Smallweed's character cannot hide his avarice and his cruelty. He shows no mercy to any character in the book, even the helpless. Despite his frail appearance, Smallweed is arguably the most aggressive person in the entire novel. Not only does he bully people with verbal threats, but he is one of only two people in the entire book who commits an unabashedly violent act. In an argument with the eminent and fearsome attorney, Mr. Tulkinghorne, Smallweed grabs the man by the throat and tries to choke him. Grandfather Smallweed is not a nice man.

People high in **agreeableness (A)** are nice men and women. But they are more than nice. Agreeableness incorporates the expressive qualities of love and empathy, friendliness, cooperation, and care. Indeed, the term *agreeableness* may be a bit too meek for the *A* domain in traits, a domain that includes such concepts as altruism, affection, and many of the most admirably humane aspects of human personality (Digman, 1990; John 1990). Individuals at the high end of the *A* continuum are described as interpersonally warm, cooperative, accommodating, helpful, patient, cordial, empathic, kind, understanding, courteous, natural, and sincere (Goldberg, 1990). They are also described as especially honest, ethical, and selfless—peace-loving humanists, committed to their friends and their family, and to the social good. Their counterparts on the other end of the *A* continuum, however, get some of the worst press in the entire Big Five dictionary. Like Smallweed, they are antagonistic, belligerent, harsh, unsympathetic, manipulative, disingenuous, scornful, crude, and cruel. While the low-*C*s may be unreliable, the low-*A*s are untrustworthy and malicious. They operate with wanton disregard of other's feelings. They get in fights. They hurt people.

It has been claimed that when Sigmund Freud was once asked what makes for a psychologically healthy and mature adult he answered simply, in German: *Lieben und Arbeiten*. To love and to work. The Big Five trait domains of *C* and *A* are thematically connected to the worlds of work and love, respectively. It is no coincidence that Esther Summerson distinguished herself in both of these areas. Nor is it a coincidence that Mr. Skimpole never worked and Grandfather Smallweed never loved.

Work

The trait domain of *C* would appear to have extensive relevance for the world of work. Hogan and Ones (1997) identify the three central themes of *C* as control, orderliness, and hard work. McCrae and Costa (1997b) divide the C domain into the six facets of competence, order, dutifulness, achievement striving, self-discipline, and deliberation. People who score high on measures of C are described as hard-working, responsible, well-organized, and productive. These would appear to be characteristics of personality that would promote success in the world of work. Of course, there are many factors, both within the person and in the environment, that can predict occupational success. But one is hard pressed to imagine a work situation in which being high in C would *not* be an asset.

Results from applied research in work settings underscore the importance of conscientiousness (Hogan, Hogan, & Roberts, 1996; Hogan & Ones, 1997). Barrick and Mount (1991) reviewed a large number of studies examining how the various trait scales that can be subsumed within the Big Five framework have been used to predict occupational success in a wide range of work settings. Of the Big Five traits, C was the one that consistently predicted success across different organizations, jobs, and situations. Examining professional positions, police work, business managers, salespersons, and skilled and semiskilled jobs, Barrick and Mount found that employees scoring high on measures subsumed under C were rated more highly by supervisors on such dimensions as job proficiency and training proficiency. The correlations between C and job ratings are typically in the $+.25$ range. While these are not extremely robust correlations, they are typically statistically significant, and they indicate that measures of C have practical utility in predicting important occupational outcomes. Furthermore, C proves to be an even stronger predictor as the level of occupational autonomy increases. Barrick and Mount (1993) showed that as the level of autonomy and responsibility for a given job goes up, individual differences in conscientiousness become even more powerful predictors of job performance. Longitudinal studies indicate that high levels of C predict job success many years in the future. In a study of graduates of an elite women's college, Roberts (1994) found that measures of C-related traits taken in college predicted successful participation in the paid labor force 20 years later.

Why is C so consistently related to job performance? There are probably many reasons. First, people high in C work very hard to begin with. They may put in longer hours and put forth greater effort to achieve the goals of their job. Second, they may be better organized and efficient. Among the many different features of conscientiousness is the tendency to exert an organizing control over one's environment, to be able to prioritize tasks and schedule events in ways that maximize productivity. Third, people high in C tend to play by the rules. They believe in and behave in accord with the norms, values, and standards set forth by society in general and by various socializing institutions in particular—institutions such as one's school, church, or company. They see themselves as being dutiful, principled, and honest. Hogan and Ones (1997) identify conformity and impulse control to be important ingredients in the mix of traits that make up C. Industrial-organizational psychology has developed a number of *integrity tests* to assess these important qualities in employees. Integrity tests are typically filled with items that fit under the Big Five domains of conscientiousness and (low) neuroticism. Reviewing the research in this area, one study estimates the average correlation between integrity tests and ratings of job performance in a variety of settings to be $+.41$, suggesting a very robust relationship between the two (Ones, Viswesvaran, & Schmidt, 1993).

The fact that people high in C tend to be relatively more rule-abiding than those scoring low in C has been documented in many ways. One of the most useful measures of C is the Socialization scale of the California Psychological Inventory (CPI: see Chapter 5), which was originally developed to distinguish between delinquents and nondelinquents. In developing the Socialization scale, Gough (1960) proposed that people are normally distributed along a continuum of socialization from those who are unusually scrupulous and conscientious on one end to those who are hostile to society's rules and conventions on the other. In the middle of the continuum are most citizens, who are generally compliant and tend to obey many, if not most, of society's rules. Decades of research on the CPI scale for Socialization show that it is a very valuable predictor of behaviors that are relevant to rule compliance. Relatedly, scales that measure personal *reliability* (another component of C) are negatively associated with irresponsible behaviors in the workplace. People who score *low* on these scales tend to miss work more often, tend to be recommended for counseling because of problems on the job, and tend to be fired more often from jobs. By contrast, those scoring high on personal reliability receive more commendations from their supervisors (Hogan & Ones, 1997). Low scores on personal reliability are also positively associated with blood alcohol levels of persons arrested for drunk driving (Hogan & Ones, 1997). In a study of almost 500 young adults, Arthur and Graziano (1996) found that overall levels of C were negatively associated with automobile accidents. In other words, drivers who described themselves as self-disciplined, responsible, reliable, and dependable were less likely to be involved in car accidents than those drivers who rated themselves lower on these characteristics of C.

Even before we learn to drive, it appears that conscientiousness can confer important benefits. The best predictor of educational achievement may be a person's overall intellectual aptitude, as assessed on intelligence tests and other aptitude measures. Beyond these, however, C may play an important role. Renaming C the "will to achieve," Digman (1989) reviews many studies to suggest that this dimension of personality can account for a good deal of the variance in achievement left unexplained by aptitude measures. In other words, intelligence is not the only thing that matters when it comes to predicting school grades. Conscientiousness is also very important. In a similar vein, Graziano and Ward (1992) examined adjustment to junior high school in a sample of 91 adolescents. Classroom teacher ratings of how well the students had adjusted to the challenges of school were positively associated with students' self-ratings of C.

Beyond conscientiousness, other personality traits have been shown to predict occupational success for particular occupations or under particular conditions. As I described a few pages back, extraversion has been linked to success in certain arenas of business, such as sales and management. Agreeableness is also a good predictor of job success in some situations. Along with low levels of N, high levels of A are strongly associated with positive ratings of employees working in customer service jobs (Hogan, Hogan, & Roberts, 1996). When exchanging merchandise or making inquiries about products, customers prefer to deal with emotionally stable and friendly service providers. Employees high in A also appear to work very well in teams (Barrick & Mount, 1993). They cooperate well with other employees and they work hard to reach group consensus. By contrast, however, high A is negatively associated with ratings of creativity and autonomy among managers. Agreeableness can sometimes get in the way of innovation. Individuals who are especially kind, considerate, and cooperative may have a somewhat more difficult time formulating bold initiatives and carrying out independent courses of action. For these efforts it may sometimes help to be at least moderately disagreeable.

Personality traits are associated with work performance. For example, retail customers generally prefer to do business with friendly salespersons who are high on the trait of agreeableness and relatively low in neuroticism.

Love

Agreeable people are easier to love than disagreeable people. They may also be better lovers, or at least better friends, collegial colleagues, caring caregivers. Part of their value in the realm of love is their sincere commitment to other people and their willingness to conform to the norms of interpersonal communion. Like people high in *C*, they play by the rules, but in this case it is the rules of intimacy, love, and personal commitment. You can trust them. They will not betray you. Nor will they go out of their way to disagree with you. Digman and Takemoto-Chock (1981) suggest the label "friendly compliance" (versus "hostile noncompliance") for this trait domain. Hogan (1982) calls it "social likability." McCrae and Costa (1997b) list trust, straightforwardness, altruism, compliance, modesty, and tender mindedness as the six facets of *A*. As we saw in Chapter 2, human beings evolved to live in small groups in which interpersonal cooperation likely proved crucial for individual and group survival. Agreeableness, then, would appear to have profound evolutionary significance:

> If we recognize that 99% of human evolution occurred when humans lived in hunting/gathering bands consisting of approximately 30 individuals and if we recognize that cooperation is seen as an essential attribute in such groups, then it is plausible that an individual's agreeableness might be a dimension receiving special attention. It is not implausible that dispositional disagreeableness and selfishness could lead to exclusion from social groups. (Graziano & Eisenberg, 1997, p. 798)

A number of personality scales tap into dimensions of *A*. The California Psychological Inventory (Chapter 5), for example, presents scales assessing sociability, empathy, and tolerance. Scales on the Personality Research Form (Chapter 5) assess the needs for affiliation, nurturance, and succorance—all of which are assumed to tap into the interpersonal warmth and caring believed to lie at the heart of *A*. Dimensions coming out of other non-trait theories described in later chapters of this book also cover some of the same conceptual ground—constructs such as McAdams's measure of intimacy motivation (Chapter 8) and Adler's concept of social interest (Chapter 12).

An important component of *A* is what Graziano and Eisenberg (1997) call "prosocial tendencies." Prosocial behavior is typically defined as voluntary behavior intended to benefit others. People who engage in high levels of prosocial behavior are typically described with trait words that fit well into the *A* domain, such as sympathetic, generous, kind, helpful, and considerate. A considerable body of research in developmental psychology examines the family conditions and learning experiences under which prosocial behavior is nurtured and encouraged. Cross-cultural research shows that children who are routinely expected to assist in caring for other family members are more prosocial than children from cultures in which such expectations are not stressed (Whiting & Whiting, 1975). Moreover, children are more likely to engage in prosocial actions when they have been exposed to altruistic models or when they have been instructed in the virtues of putting others' welfare on a par with their own. As we saw in Chapter 2, an important body of research has sought to articulate the main features and determinants of the "altruistic personality" in adulthood. Strong predictors of altruistic behavior among adults are measures of sympathy, social responsibility, mature perspective taking, and high moral standards (Bierhoff, Klein, & Kramp, 1991; Carlo, Eisenberg, Troyer, Switzer, & Speer, 1991; Oliner & Oliner, 1988).

In the realm of direct caregiving, we would expect that mothers and fathers who are dispositionally high in *A* might be more effective in their parenting roles than parents low in *A*. Belsky, Crnic, and Woodworth (1995) administered trait measures to mothers and fathers when their children were 10 months of age and then observed the parents as they interacted with their children in their own homes when the children were 15 and 21 months old. They also obtained measures of transient mood states and daily hassles reported by the parents just before the 15-month and 21-month assessments. Their results indicated that being an agreeable parent (high *A*) contributes to high levels of positive mood and thereby to high levels of cognitive stimulation and low levels of neglect and detachment in interactions with children. *A* was an especially strong predictor of quality of parenting in mothers. The trait of neuroticism was also implicated. High levels of *N* contributed to negative moods and to experiencing daily hassles, which were associated with insensitivity in interactions with children. The researchers concluded that "from a child's perspective, it would appear that one is better off—in terms of the pleasure of everyday interactions with mother—having a parent who is agreeable and not neurotic" (p. 926).

In the realm of love, Shaver and Brennan (1992) examined the relations between Big Five trait ratings and adult attachment styles. As we saw in Chapter 2, Bowlby and Ainsworth's theory of caregiver–infant attachment has been expanded to incorporate individual differences in adult attachment styles. Adults with a secure attachment style find it relatively easy to get close to others. They seem especially comfortable with intimacy, friendship, and love. Adults with an anxious-ambivalent style, by contrast, desire closeness but either draw back from others or feel that they drive others away when they attempt to establish intimate relationships. Adults with an "avoidant" attachment style feel that they cannot trust other people and therefore withdraw from close relationships.

Shaver and Brennan administered a measure of attachment styles and standard questionnaire for assessing the Big Five Traits to 242 college students. Table 6.9 shows the mean trait scores for the three groups of attachment styles. Students showing the secure attachment style scored significantly higher on agreeableness compared with those with the avoidant styles. Anxious-ambivalent students scored in between—not significantly higher nor lower than the other two groups. Extraversion and neuroticism also showed significant differences. Students with secure attachment scored significantly higher on *E* and lower on *N* than avoidant and anxious-ambivalent students. Conscientiousness and openness were unrelated to attachment. The results suggest that a secure attachment style in early adulthood is linked with traits denoting energy and positive affect *(E)*, interpersonal warmth *(A)*, and low levels of negative affectivity or neuroticism *(N)*. Correlational studies such as this one cannot tell us about the causal relations between traits and attachment styles—whether, that is, trait levels precede or lead to certain attachment styles, attachment styles lead to traits, or the two are caused by some third factor, such as early caregiving experiences or genetic effects. But the research is still instructive as to how traits and relational styles line up with each other. And it is further noteworthy for its attempt to bring together two lines of personality theory and research—atttachment and traits—that are usually thought to be quite separate.

A recent study by Asendorpf and Wilpers (1998) was designed to examine the causal effects of personality traits on the quality of social relationships. The researchers tracked the social relationships of 132 German students over the course of 18 months, beginning when the students entered the university as freshmen. On six different occasions over the 18-month period, the students completed extensive questionnaires describing the status of the most important relationships in their lives. The questionnaires examined romantic relationships, friendships, and family relationships. Among the most important features of these relationships assessed on the questionnaires were amount of contact spent with other people, amount of available social support, conflict

TABLE 6.9	*Mean Scores on the Big Five Traits as a Function of Adult Attachment Style*		
	ATTACHMENT STYLE TYPES		
TRAIT	SECURE	ANXIOUS	AVOIDANT
Neuroticism	2.84[a]	3.28[b]	3.15[b]
Extraversion	3.58[a]	3.41[b]	3.37[b]
Openness	3.48	3.48	3.46
Agreeableness	3.63[a]	3.51[ab]	3.39[b]
Conscientiousness	3.57	3.47	3.43

Note: Items were answered on a 1–5 continuum with higher scores indicating higher ratings on the given trait dimension. Means with different superscripts differ significantly from each other at the .05 level. A total of 226 subjects participated in the study.
Source: Shaver & Brennan (1992), p. 539.

in relationships, and falling in love. In addition, the students participated in a 21-day intensive diary exercise. During the 21-day period, they recorded all social interactions they participated in by filling out a set of standard forms at the end of each day. To assess individual differences in traits, self-report measures of the Big Five factors were administered to the students every six months.

Because they obtained multiple measures of traits and social relationships over an extended period of time, Asendorpf and Wilpers were able to determine the extent to which traits predict relationships and relationships predict traits. The results showed that whereas students traits remained relatively stable over time, their relationships changed in many significant ways. In general, individual differences in personality traits influenced social relationships, but not vice versa. The traits of extraversion, conscientiousness, and agreeableness influenced the number and quality of the students' social relationships, whereas strong changes in these relationships had no effect on any of the Big Five personality scales. Being high in extraversion led to developing relatively large social networks, spending more time in social interactions, and feeling that one has more social support from friends. In addition, extraverts were more likely to fall in love over the 18-month period than were introverts. Conscientiousness predicted higher levels of contact with family members. The authors speculated that the more conscientious students may have felt stronger bonds and more obligations to their home families than students low in *C*. Agreeableness predicted levels of conflict. Students high in *A* were less likely than those low in *A* to experience conflict in their relationships with members of the opposite sex. Like Esther in *Bleak House*, agreeable people are predisposed to turn the other cheek in times of interpersonal stress and avoid serious conflicts with those they love. They do not antagonize their lovers, and they are not readily antagonized. In the tumultuous world of love, people high in agreeableness are able to maintain relative harmony and peace.

Life

The benefits of conscientiousness and agreeableness may go beyond the worlds of work and love. Recent research suggests that high levels of *C* and *A* may enhance overall quality of life and even promote longevity. McCrae and Costa (1991) showed that self-report measures of *C* and *A* are positively correlated with psychological well-being. In a sample of 429 adults, both conscientiousness and agreeableness were positively related to reports of positive affect, negatively related to reports of negative affect, and positively related to total well-being. McCrae and Costa suggest that high levels of conscientiousness and agreeableness create life conditions that promote well-being. They write:

> Although personality traits may directly affect the tendencies to experience positive or negative emotions, they may also have indirect effects on well-being: Certain traits may be instrumental in creating conditions that promote happiness or unhappiness. In particular, the dimensions of *A* and *C* might be hypothesized to have instrumental effects on well-being. Agreeable individuals are warm, generous, and loving; conscientious people are efficient, competent, and hard-working. The interpersonal bonds that *A* fosters and the achievements and accomplishments that *C* promotes may contribute to greater quality of life and higher life satisfaction. This is perhaps what Freud meant when he suggested that *Liebe und Arbeit*, love and work, were the keys to psychological health and happiness. (McCrae and Costa, 1991, p. 228)

The role of personality traits in determining how long a person may actually live has been examined in an impressive longitudinal study of intellectually gifted men and women. In 1921, Lewis Terman and his associates launched what has become the most famous longitudinal study in the history of psychology. Terman chose over 1,500 children living in California (mean age 11 years) who all scored at very high levels on standard tests of intellectual aptitude. These extremely bright boys and girls—later dubbed the "Termites"—were administered various psychological measures and followed up at 5- to 10-year intervals for the rest of their lives. Indeed, the survivors are still being followed. Many of the Termites grew up to be very successful people. Included in the sample are many businesspeople, physicians, lawyers, teachers, writers, and scientists. Nonetheless, a wide range of lifestyles and occupational groups are represented.

By the year 1986, about two-thirds of the participants in the original Terman sample were still alive. All of the survivors were at least 70 years old by this time. A group of researchers culled through the massive data sets available for the Termites to obtain measures of childhood personality traits, family stresses, parental divorce during childhood, adult adjustment, and health behaviors (Friedman, Tucker, Schwartz, Tomlinson-Keasy, Martin, Wingard, & Criqui, 1995; Friedman, Tucker, Tomlinson-Keasy, Schwartz, Wingard, & Criqui, 1993). Their goal was to use psychological and social factors present in childhood and adulthood to predict longevity. In one analysis, the authors compared data from those Termites who had died before the age of 70 and those who lived beyond 70. In another procedure commonly used in epidemiological studies, they employed what is called a statistical *survival analysis.* A survival analysis estimates the effects of a series of predictors on the probability of people living to advanced ages.

One of the strongest predictors of longevity in human beings is gender. As has been documented time and again, the researchers found that women tend to live longer than men. In the Terman sample, a history of family stresses was also significantly associated with longevity—the greater the stress, the lower the longevity. Among the strongest predictors, however, was childhood personality. In particular, childhood ratings of personality traits subsumed under the general umbrella of conscientiousness predicted how long the men and women in the Terman study were likely to live. Conscientious and socially responsible children in the Terman study are statistically more likely to live into old age than their less conscientious peers. The results of the survival analysis for *C* are shown in Figure 6.5. The four curves show the survival probability for high-*C* females, low-*C* females, high-*C* males, and low-*C* males as a function of age. Consider females first. Terman women who in childhood scored high on conscientiousness traits have about an 82% probability of living to be at least 70 years of age while women who in childhood scored low in conscientiousness show about a 77% probability of living to be age 70. Among the Terman men, the probabilities of living to at least age 70 for high-*C* versus low-*C* groups are approximately 73% and 67%, respectively. While these may not sound like large differences, they are rather striking for studies of this sort. The authors point out that the effects of childhood *C* on longevity are about as statistically strong as the biological risk factors of high blood pressure and serum cholesterol. In other words, the negative effect of high blood pressure on longevity is about as strong as the negative effect of low conscientiousness on longevity. Other childhood personality traits measured in this study—sociability (an aspect of *E*), self-esteem, emotional stability *(N)*, and energy level—did not predict longevity.

FIGURE 6.5 | *Survival and Conscientiousness*

*The probability of a 20-year-old's surviving to advanced ages is a function of gender (females live longer) and the trait of conscientiousness (high conscientiousness is associated with greater longevity). Note: High = scoring in the top 25 percent of the distribution on **C** in childhood. Low = scoring in the bottom 25 percent of the distribution on **C** in childhood.*

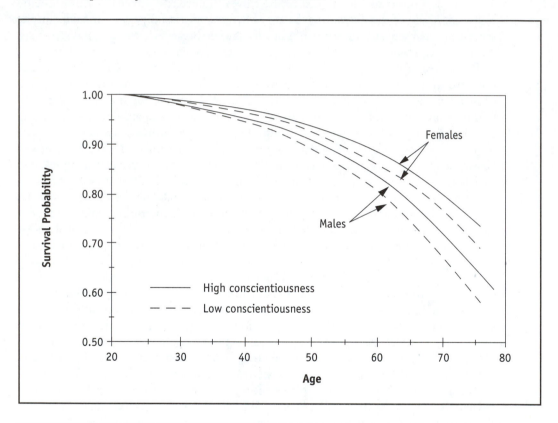

We do not know why children who are highly conscientious grow up to live longer than children who are low on conscientiousness. Are high-*C* children more likely to adopt a healthful lifestyle when they grow up? Are they more careful and less likely to take risks? Do they live longer because they develop successful careers and avocations that keep them busy and satisfied with life? The authors of the Terman study point out that tracing the mechanisms that link *C* to longevity is a very difficult task. They also remind us that these results, as provocative as they are, come from only one study, and like any study, it has limitations. All of the participants in the study were white and intellectually gifted. Most grew up to be members of the middle and upper-middle classes, and they all lived in American society during the middle of the 20th century. The contours of their lives were doubtlessly shaped by a myriad of cultural, historical, and personal factors. The Terman study is the first to document a significant link between childhood personality traits and longevity across seven decades of life. The results suggest that the Big Five domain of conscientiousness may have important implications not only for the quality of life but for how long people actually live. More research is needed, however, to tease apart this relationship and to examine, in more detail, the ways in which personality traits may impact the long course of adult life.

VARIATIONS ON A THEME: ALTERNATIVE TAXONOMIES

Over the past 15 years, many personality psychologists have come to view the Big Five as a reasonably adequate framework for organizing the many personality traits that can be invoked in accounting for human individuality. The consensus on the Big Five, however, is by no means uniform. First, different adherents to the Big Five model have developed different labels and slightly different conceptualizations of each of the five factors. As we saw in the case of O, some view this dimension to be openness to experience, some see it as culture, and some speak of intellectance. Each of these three labels brings with it different denotative and connotative implications for defining the O trait domain. Second, many alternative taxonomies that were developed before the reemergence of the Big Five in the 1980s continue to draw supporters and prove useful for personality research. Eysenck's 3-factor scheme and Gray's 2-factor model of impulsivity and anxiety remain very influential. Some researchers find Cattell's model of 16 source traits to be more adequate than the Big Five. In Chapter 5, I introduced the California Psychological Inventory (CPI), which is based on the assumption that a full accounting of traits requires readings on 20 different folk concepts, such as "achievement via conformance," "socialization," and "flexibility." The 20 concepts can be further reduced to three basic dimensions or vectors which can be described as interpersonal orientation, orientation toward social norms, and ego integration. Another very fruitful line of personality research, conducted by Jack Block (1971) and his associates, employs a sorting methodology for 100 personality descriptors (the California Q-Sort), yielding two broad traitlike dimensions of human functioning—ego resiliency and ego control. We will examine Block's approach to personality dimensions in Chapter 7.

Beyond the traditional taxonomies that preceded the popularization of the Big Five frameworks, psychologists have also recently proposed some new alternatives to the five-factor taxonomy described in this chapter. Based on factor analysis of personality scales and questionnaire items, Marvin Zuckerman (1994) has proposed an "Alternative Five." According to Zuckerman, the five basic trait dimensions for personality are best characterized as *sociability*, *neuroticism-anxiety*, *impulsive sensation-seeking*, *aggression-hostility*, and *activity*. Sociability and neuroticism-anxiety line up roughly with the Big Five dimensions of E and N; impulsive sensation seeking bears some relation to the negative pole of C; and aggression-hostility looks to

Marvin Zuckerman

FEATURE 6.B

Eysenck's Psychoticism: Low A, Low C, and Some Other Bad Things

Hans Eysenck proposed that the entire gamut of personality characteristics can be divided neatly into three super traits: extraversion–introversion, neuroticism, and psychoticism. The first two of Eysenck's Big Three correspond well to the dimensions of E and N in the Big Five framework. But what about psychoticism? Eysenck (1952) proposed that a susceptibility to psychosis represented an important dimension of personality. Even in the 19th century, the founders of modern psychiatry observed that the biological relatives of schizophrenics and other psychotics often showed signs of abnormality themselves, such as bizarre ideas. Might there not be an underlying susceptibility to psychosis that, in mild form, is present in the general population? Eysenck believed there was, and he developed questionnaires to assess individual differences among people in the extent to which they expressed characteristics that, in stronger forms, are typically associated with the severe mental illnesses that are grouped under the label of psychosis.

Questionnaire measures of psychoticism ask questions about such things as liking practical jokes that harm others, indifference to the suffering of animals and children, experiencing bizarre thoughts and feelings,

preferring unusual or antisocial activities, and a host of other behavioral and attitudinal characteristics. People who score high on psychoticism are described as highly impulsive, aloof, nonconforming, aggressive, inhumane, and lacking in responsibility. They have disregard for the law, for danger, and for the feelings of others. They have a taste for the bizarre and even the macabre. They tend to hold dogmatic and extreme attitudes about social issues—standing on the extreme right or left wing of political issues. By contrast, people low in psychoticism are described as cooperative, empathic, tender-minded, and conventional. Consistent with these generalizations, research has shown that people high on psychoticism tend to have unsatisfactory marriages, poor work records and low levels of occupational satisfaction, higher incidence of infidelity, a greater willingness to engage in high-risk behaviors of many kinds, and favorable attitudes about the use of violence (Corr, 2000). A strong antisocial theme runs through the psychoticism literature, suggesting that this dimension may tap into tendencies toward both psychosis and psychopathy.

The susceptibility to psychosis-psychopathy is evident from an early age (Corr, 2000).

be similar to low A. Activity, however, does not fit neatly into the Big Five scheme I have presented in this chapter, though aspects of it can probably be found in E. Zuckerman leaves out trait descriptors that refer mainly to the cognitive dimensions of personality, such as those that may be part of the Big Five O domain. Zuckerman (1995, 1998) has also endeavored to link the traits that make up his Alternative Five to biological substrates incorporating brain structures, neurotransmitters and hormones.

Coming out of biological psychiatry, Robert Cloninger (1987, 1991) proposes a taxonomy of seven basic traits. The first four may be viewed as fundamental dimensions

Children who score high on the child version of Eysenck's psychoticism scale are more prone to learning and behavioral difficulties and antisocial behaviors. They also tend to be disliked by teachers, who see their behavior as spiteful and disruptive. Experimental research indicates that people high in psychoticism may have deficits in stimulus processing, as seen in their inability to inhibit unimportant and irrelevant stimuli. The same problem of stimulus inhibition is characteristic of some schizophrenics, such as those who report recurrent hallucinations. In addition, defective stimulus processing may result in impaired learning of society's rules, which may account for the poor socialization that is so characteristic of psychoticism. This inability to inhibit irrelevant input, however, can also have a positive side to it. Some individuals high in psychoticism produce especially rich and fluid cognitive associations, which may actually enhance their creativity.

Where does psychoticism fit into the Big Five scheme? A great deal of the content in Eysenck's conceptualization of psychoticism can be found on the low poles of agreeableness and conscientiousness. Like people who score low on both C and A, individuals high in psychoticism are irresponsible, nonconforming, cruel, and aggressive. Those scoring low in psychoticism, by contrast would appear to be relatively agreeable and conscientious. Beyond A and C, there would appear to be some other elements in Eysenck's conception. The strong impulsivity component can be found in some characterizations of extraversion and neuroticism. The rigid and extreme ideological beliefs may reflect low openness to experience. The most bizarre and psychotic-like traces of psychoticism, however, are difficult to place within the Big Five space. Personality and clinical psychologists have not reached a consensus on the extent to which the Big Five dimensions can capture the vicissitudes of abnormal psychology. Some argue that the characteristics of different psychopathologies are qualitatively different from those that define the realm of normal personality. Others argue that psychopathologies are not different in kind but simply amount, that the behavioral patterns we associate with psychopathological types are the product of extreme scores on the same dimensions of personality that can be used to assess individual differences in the "normal" range of human functioning. This controversy is not going to be resolved in the near future. As for the trait of psychoticism, however, it makes good sense to say that what Eysenck saw as a susceptibility to psychosis and psychopathy looks a lot like very low A and very low C, with a few other very bad things thrown in.

of human temperament, Cloninger argues. These are *novelty seeking, harm avoidance, reward dependence*, and *persistence*. Cloninger suggests that individual differences in these four dimensions can be seen in very young children and are likely to have a very strong biological base. Indeed, Cloninger proposes that three of these four temperament traits can be linked to specific biochemical pathways in the brain, each governed by a particular neurotransmitter. According to Cloninger, novelty seeking is modulated by the brain's dopamine pathways; harm avoidance links to serotonin pathways; and reward-dependence is dependent on the operation of the norepinephrine pathways. As the person matures into adulthood, new traits begin to manifest themselves. Important individual differences in adults' self-concepts can be seen with respect to the traits of *self-determination, cooperativeness,* and *spirituality* (sometimes called *self-transcendence*). Self-determination refers to the extent to which a person sees the self as an autonomous individual. Cooperativeness refers to one's connection to the rest of humanity. Spirituality taps into one's connection to the universe as a whole. You can see that Cloninger's traits expand outward from a temperament core to self-evaluations of one's sense of integral wholeness (self-determination), one's sense of being an integral part of humanity (cooperativeness), and one's sense of being an integral part of something even larger than humankind (spirituality).

One of the criticisms of the Big Five taxonomy is that it does not specify how particular traits that reside within each of the five domains relate to one another. What is the relation, for example, of the different facets of *E* to one another? And how do particular facets of *E,* say, relate to particular facets of *A?* One approach to mapping the interrelations of many different traits to each other is to arrange descriptors into a circle. Going back to the 1950s and the work of Leary (1957), many psychologists have found this approach especially useful in efforts to map the domain of *interpersonal* characteristics. Interpersonally oriented traits and behaviors can be arranged into what has been called an interpersonal circumplex. As Gurtman (1992) describes it, "the interpersonal circumplex is a comprehensive model of interpersonal tendencies (e.g., motives, needs, orientations, problems, and traits) depicting an interpersonal space as a circular array of variables organized around the two principal axes of Dominance and Love" (p. 105). Figure 6.6 shows a version of the circumplex from Gurtman (1991). Characteristics are arranged on the circle such that those at 180 degrees from each other (on the opposite sides of the circle) are opposite in meaning (e.g., dominant vs. submissive, friendly vs. hostile, exhibitionistic vs. inhibited, trusting vs. mistrusting), whereas those at 90 degrees from each other are conceptually unrelated (e.g., dominant vs. friendly, hostile vs. submissive, inhibited vs. trusting, exhibitionistic vs. mistrusting). A considerable body of research in psychology and social relations supports the power of the circumplex for organizing and making sense of interpersonal phenomena (Kiesler, 1982; Wiggins, 1982).

Jerry Wiggins (1979; Wiggins & Broughton, 1985; Wiggins & Trapnell, 1996) has analyzed self-report data from a large number of personality measures and found a good deal of statistical evidence to support the utility of organizing interpersonally oriented traits in a circular manner. In his **circumplex model of traits,** Wiggins bisects the circular space with the independent axes of *agency* and *communion,* which roughly correspond to dominance/power and love/warmth, respectively. Following Bakan (1966), Wiggins argues that primacy of these two dimensions goes beyond their statistical salience on the circumplex. Throughout folklore, myth, and history, these two general themes—agency and communion—are the principal organizers of human interpersonal behavior. Indeed, many theories of personality outside the trait tradition present interpersonal dichotomies that capture the basic distinction between agency and communion. Examples in this book include Hogan's (Chapter 2) distinction between getting ahead and getting along in the context of human evolution, Freud's (Chapter 3) motivational distinction between the aggressive death instincts (agency) and the erotic life instincts (communion), Adler's (Chapter 12) distinction between striving for superiority and social interest, and McAdams's (Chapter 11) distinction

FIGURE 6.6   *The Interpersonal Circumplex*

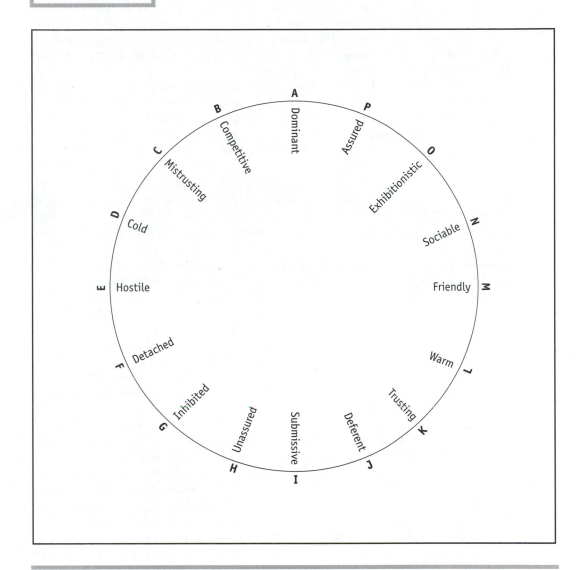

Source: Gurtman (1991), p. 670.

between the thematic lines of agency/power and communion/intimacy in life narratives. In addition, the agency/communion distinction appears in many sociological and anthropological theories and is reflected in the cross-cultural distinction, which we examined in Chapter 4 of this book, between individualist and collectivist cultures.

On first blush, the circumplex model of traits would appear to be a competing alternative to the Big Five scheme. However, Wiggins and others have suggested that the interpersonal circumplex gives definition and articulation to the intersection of *E* and *A* (McCrae & Costa, 1989; Trapnell & Wiggins, 1990; Wiggins, 1992). It is indeed easy to see how the agreeableness domain *(A)* corresponds neatly to Bakan's notion of communion, incorporating dimensions of love, care, warmth, and so on. The match between extraversion and dominance is a bit more problematic, but it would appear that the general *E* domain, with its emphasis on energy and surgency, may overlap considerably with the notion of dominance.

Wiggins and Trapnell (1996) argue that the dimensions of extraversion/surgency/dominance *(E)* and agreeableness/nurturance *(A)* should have some conceptual priority in the Big Five scheme because they map dimensions of human functioning that have such wide relevance. Agency and communion are fundamentally implicated in everything from interpersonal behavior to the structures of societies. In that human beings are by nature exquisitely social animals, the trait domains that are most centrally related to social functioning would seem to hold special importance in understanding human individuality. If *E* and *A*, then, can be conceptualized in terms of the circumplex language of agency and communion, what is to be done with *N*, *O*, and *C?* Wiggins and Trapnell suggest that agency and communion may be cross-cutting themes that have relevance for these three trait domains as well. Within each of the three domains of neuroticism, openness, and conscientiousness, there may exist both agentic and communal facets. Put another way, the traits of *N*, *O*, and *C* may each contain within them agentic and communal elements. While one individual's highly neurotic tendencies may apply mainly to issues having to do with caring and nurturance in interpersonal relationships, another person's neuroticism may be channeled in the direction of agency, self-determination, and problems in autonomy. Examining the trait domain of *C*, Wiggins and Trapnell (1996) argue that there appear about an equal number of *C* descriptors that code for agentic qualities as communal qualities. Agentic conscientiousness comes across in such adjectives as "efficient" and "disciplined" while communal conscientiousness is expressed through terms like "dutiful" and "dependable."

Finally, John Digman (1997) offers a different take on the relation between agency and communion on the one hand and the Big Five on the other. Digman factor-analyzed correlations from 14 studies supporting a Big Five model for personality description—5 studies based on children and adolescents and 9 studies on adults. Two especially general factors were clearly evident in all the studies. The first encompassed mainly the Big Five dimensions of *A*, *C*, and *N*. Digman describes this first super factor as a very general principle of *socialization*. Agreeableness, conscientiousness, and neuroticism all refer in one way or another to the extent to which a person is well socialized in the culture wherein he or she lives. Highly agreeable, conscientious, and emotionally stable individuals are able to fit well into society as adults. They are able to love and work and meet the many challenges and cope with the many stresses of social life. They can function well in human communities. They are, in this sense, very communal. Problems in *A*, *C*, and *N*, furthermore, are likely to be problems in communion. The disagreeable, unreliable, and emotionally unstable person is likely to be especially compromised and to suffer greatly in the realm of human communion—that is, in love, friendship, family life, interpersonal cooperation, social integration, and the sense of belonging to a defining human community.

By contrast, Digman found that *E* and *O* comprised a second super factor, which appears to be more concerned with *the growth of the self.* Highly extraverted and open individuals are energetic experience seekers. Self-confident, optimistic, and open to new experiences, they are models for self-fulfillment, for expanding the self and getting as much out of life that it is possible to get. In this sense, they are especially agentic. Problems in *E* and *O*, furthermore, are likely to manifest themselves in the realm of human agency. Digman argues that the excessively introverted and rigid person is unable to experience the full potential of human agency. He or she is restricted and cut off from many potentially enriching experiences. Low *E* and low *O*, therefore, may stunt the psychological growth of the self.

Digman's very general "Big Two" recapture ideas that can be found in many different theories of personality development. In sketching a model of the mature and well-adjusted individual, theorists have often tried to balance the agentic tendencies toward self-fulfillment with the communal tendencies toward socialization. If an adult is to be able to love and to work in a given human society, and if he or she is to operate in such ways as to be able both to get along and get ahead in the interpersonal world he or she inhabits, then the individual must find some compelling way to live out the potentialities that reside within the agentic self while, at the same time, internalizing the standards of his or her self-defining group so that cooperative and meaningful social life is possible. It is likely that all five of the Big Five traits contribute in one way or another to these two meta-goals in life. But Digman raises the intriguing possibility that extraversion/introversion *(E)* and openness to experience *(O)* may shade more in the direction of that first goal—the goal of fulfilling one's personal agency—while agreeableness *(A)*, conscientiousness *(C)*, and neuroticism *(N)* may be somewhat more centrally implicated in that second, communal goal of living together with others in a viable human community.

SUMMARY

1. How might you ever organize the many different personality traits that could be invoked to account for human individuality? In the 1980s, an answer to this question began to emerge as the result of decades of research employing statistical analysis of responses to trait questionnaires and rating scales. A growing number of personality psychologists today believe that traits can be organized into five basic trait clusters—called the Big Five. While considerable disagreement still exists with respect to the exact meanings of each of the Big Five traits, one well-established taxonomy labels the five: extraversion–introversion *(E)*, neuroticism *(N)*, openness to experience *(O)*, conscientiousness *(C)*, and agreeableness *(A)*. Cross-cultural studies of trait ratings suggest that factors resembling most, if not all, of these five dimensions can be found in many different languages and cultures.

2. Introduced to modern psychology by Carl Jung and Hans Eysenck, extraversion–introversion *(E)* encompasses such qualities of human personality as gregariousness, assertiveness, excitement seeking, and positive affectivity. Highly extraverted people are described as generally outgoing, sociable, and energetic; highly introverted people (low in *E*) are seen as generally withdrawn, quiet, and introspective. Arguably the most well-researched trait in all of personality psychology, extraversion has been empirically linked to individual differences in social behavior, occupational choice, learning, and emotional life. Recent studies on E show that highly extraverted people tend to experience more positive emotional events in their lives and report higher levels of happiness and life satisfaction compared with introverted people. Possible reasons for this relationship include enhanced social skills, confidence and assertiveness in social relations, and a tendency to ignore or gloss over social punishments on the part of extraverts. Empirical support for the connection between E and positive emotions is so consistent that some psychologists have argued that E should be renamed "positive affectivity."

3. Eysenck argued that individual differences in E were the product of innate differences in the organization of the central nervous system. More specifically, he suggested that by virtue of differences in the functioning of the brain's reticular activating system, people differ with respect to characteristic levels of arousal and arousability. Extraverts operate at a generally lower level of arousal, he reasoned, and therefore seek out more stimulation to raise arousal to an optimal level. By contrast, introverts operate at a generally higher level of arousal, and therefore they reach an optimal level more quickly, after which they are likely to withdraw from social stimulation. Empirical support for Eysenck's biologically based ideas has been mixed, in part because psychologists today question the validity of the concept of general cortical arousal. A newer line of research has suggested, however, that individual differences in E, or positive affectivity, may be linked to a behavioral approach system (BAS) in the brain. The BAS is hypothesized to govern positive approach behaviors in response to incentives. Important components of the BAS may be dopamine pathways and electrical activity in the left anterior portion of the brain.

4. Eysenck also pioneered theory and research on the second of the Big Five traits:

neuroticism (N). Measures of chronic anxiety, depression, excessive emotionality, nervousness, moodiness, hostility, vulnerability, self-consciousness, and hypochondriasis all converge in this general factor, which is most generally described as a continuum from emotional instability (high N) to emotional stability (low N). Individual differences in N have been linked to a wide range of behavioral outcomes, from interpersonal communication patterns to reports of health problems. Research shows that individuals high in N experience more negative emotional events, compared with individuals low in N. The connections between N and negative affect are so consistent that some psychologists argue that N should be renamed "negative affectivity." People high in N experience more stress in their lives, and they tend to employ relatively ineffective and nonproductive coping strategies for dealing with the stress.

5. While Eysenck believed that individual differences in N were biologically rooted in differences in the brain's limbic system, more recent approaches have implicated what has been called a behavioral inhibition system (BIS). The BIS is hypothesized to mediate responses to threat and signs of danger, punishment, and extreme novelty. One key component in the BIS may be a tiny, almond-shaped region in the forebrain called the amygdala, which appears to be implicated in the production and control of fear. In addition, electrical activity in the right anterior regions of the brain have also been linked to experiences of negative affectivity.

6. Variously called "culture," "intellectance," and "inquiring intellect," the trait cluster of openness to experience (O) encompasses many dimensions of personality that relate to cognitive functioning. While intelligence itself is generally not viewed to be part of O per se, people high in O have many intellectual interests; they are also described as imaginative, curious, broad-minded, creative, intellectually daring, nontraditional, and complex. By contrast, those scoring low in O are usually viewed to be unimaginative, pragmatic, down-to-earth, having narrow interests, and relatively simple. O is positively associated with level of education. While O has been empirically linked to such things as having a rich and complex emotional life and displaying flexibility in response to life challenges, it has also been linked to less positive outcomes such as beliefs in esoteric and dubious phenomena and to mild forms of magical and bizarre thinking. The only Big Five trait to be directly associated with political attitudes, people high in O tend to be somewhat more liberal in their sociopolitical outlooks (underscoring progressive change, skepticism toward traditional authority, and tolerance for competing viewpoints) while people low in O tend to be more conservative (underscoring stability over change, obedience toward authority, and preference for a uniform or unifying point of view).

7. One interesting personality constellation that is associated with extremely *low* scores on O is the authoritarian personality. Authoritarianism combines rigid adherence to conventional values, uncritical attitudes toward authority, opposition to the imaginative and subjective aspects of life, power and toughness, cynicism, and a tendency to condemn those who do not fit into the traditional frameworks of society and religion. Research has shown that authoritarians tend to express higher levels of overt prejudice toward outgroups and stronger support for aggressive actions in response to threat. Although low O and authoritarianism are not the same thing, they have much in common. At the heart of their commonality is an intolerance for ambiguity.

8. Conscientiousness (C) encompasses a great many trait terms that center on how hard-working, self-disciplined, responsible, reliable, dutiful, well-organized, and persevering a person is. Individual differences in C are consistent predictors of instrumental effectiveness in work. Across many different types of occupational groups, employees who are high in C are rated by their supervisors and co-workers as more competent and proficient. Low C, by contrast, is associated with job absenteeism and being fired from jobs. In general, people high in C are more rule-abiding than those low in C, a finding that is reflected in the fact that low C is correlated with alcohol abuse, criminality, and even poor driving. A seven-decade longitudinal study of intellectually gifted women and men shows that ratings of conscientiousness-related traits in childhood are predictive of longevity. Adults who were rated as high in conscientiousness as children were statistically more likely to live to an older age compared with adults who were rated as children to be low in C.

9. Variously labeled "friendly compliance" and "social likability," agreeableness *(A)* incorporates the expressive qualities of love and empathy, friendliness, cooperation, care, altruism, and affection. The negative pole of A denotes qualities of antagonism and aggressiveness. Research has shown that highly agreeable mothers provide their infants with more warmth and cognitive stimulation, compared with mothers scoring low on A. Research has also connected A to attachment styles and the quality of romantic love. College students high in A tend to have fewer disagreements and conflicts with members of the opposite sex.

10. While the Big Five framework is proving to be a useful taxonomy for personality traits, personality psychologists still employ a number of competing frameworks that were developed before the emergence of the Big Five, and in recent years they have also proposed some new alternative taxonomies. Zuckerman has proposed an "Alternative Five," and Cloninger has enumerated seven basic traits, three of which are hypothesized to be directly linked to specific neurotransmitters in the brain. The circumplex model of personality traits organizes interpersonally oriented descriptors in a two-dimensional space bisected by the independent constructs of agency (dominance, self-expansion) and communion (nurturance, connection to others). Wiggins has argued that the first of these dimensions, agency, corresponds roughly to E and the second, communion, to A. In addition, the traits of N, O, and C each have agentic and communal facets, Wiggins maintains. Finally, one psychologist has recently suggested that the dimensions of agency and communion can serve as higher-order factors for the Big Five. According to this new view of the "Big Two," the dimensions of E and O compose a higher-order factor that might be called agency or self-growth while the dimensions of N, C, and A compose a higher-order factor of communion or socialization within a community.

Traits Across the Lifespan: Continuity and Change

7

You may not be old enough to have gone to your first high school reunion. I have only been to one. In 1982 I went back to Gary, Indiana, for my 10th-year reunion (class of '72, Gary Lew Wallace High School). As I remember it, probably 200 people showed up for the reunion, out of a graduating class of almost 500. So many things change in your life between your 18th and 28th birthdays, especially if you move away from home after graduation. Returning to the scene of so much adolescent anxiety, I was now a young adult, married, employed, well-educated, and more confident in life than I had been 10 years before. I felt I had changed, and I am sure that many of my former classmates in the crowd felt that they had changed significantly, too. After all, we had all grown up now; many of us had gone on to get college degrees; some had been through the military; many had travelled; most of us were now working; many had started families; a few were embarking on a second (or even third) marriage. For sure, our life circumstances had changed.

But had *we* changed? Were we really different, as people, than we were before? For some of us, the answer surely seemed to be yes. Take, for example, Mary Anne Cromwell (I've changed the names). I hardly recognized her. I remembered Mary Anne Cromwell as a shy and painfully thin adolescent girl, poorly dressed, not very popular. I know she was the butt of jokes. I am ashamed to admit that as a junior I spread rumors that an ex-friend of mine was in love with Mary Anne; I wanted to get back at him for some insult he had hurled my way (I don't remember what it was). Mary Anne sat next to me in junior-year trigonometry, and I don't believe we ever exchanged words. Well, the 10th-year reunion could be labelled "Mary Anne's revenge." Mary Anne had grown up to be a beautiful woman, attracting a crowd of men at the reunion who seemed not even to know that she existed 10 years before. Mary Anne had gone on to get an M.B.A., and she had already enjoyed considerable success in business. What struck me most, though, was her increased poise and her assertiveness. Gone was the timidity and the awkwardness I remembered. Now, you may say that I just didn't know her very well in high school, and that certainly is true. Maybe she always had this poise, and I never saw it. But not too many other people saw it either, it seemed, for everybody I spoke with at the reunion seemed astounded by how much Mary Anne Cromwell had changed.

But now, let's look at a counter-example—Robert Amundson. Robert is the guy about whom I spread the rumors concerning Mary Anne Cromwell back in our junior year. After my prank, Robert had the good sense to dump me as a friend and move on to more exalted social circles. Actually, Robert was always a social climber, which was one of the reasons our friendship was stormy and short-lived. In high school, I remember him as socially dominant, outgoing, spontaneous, and not especially conscientious. His social dominance was clearly in evidence the night of the reunion. Just like old times, Robert was the center of attention. It seemed to me that he boasted just as much as he always had. He dominated conversations, as he always had. People seemed to accord his opinions an especially high status, just as they always had. The only difference I could see with respect to Robert Amundson was his newfound eagerness to talk with Mary Anne Cromwell.

While Mary Anne Cromwell seemed to have changed significantly, my overall impression from the high school reunion was that Robert Amundson was more the norm. This is to say that the evidence for continuity in personality seemed very powerful to me that night. I could not help but be struck by how most people seemed so much the same as they had always been. Ten years had passed and yet almost everybody was so recognizable in their characteristic social mannerisms, their modes of relating to others, the way they spoke, even the things they spoke about. Michael still had the best sense of humor. Roberta was still nonconventional and rebellious. Kevin was still obsessed with sports. Barbara still danced in a provocative way. Keith still seemed depressed.

Now, I must admit that my nonscientific conclusions about personality continuity over time were based on very limited "data"—a few hours of interacting with many people after 10 years had passed. The stability in personality I seemed to perceive that night may have been largely due to the fact that all of these people were back together in the *same kind of situation* we had all been in before—that is, the situation of being together in school. Maybe the ways people had changed could be seen more clearly outside this reunion setting. And maybe my observations were even more deeply biased than that. Maybe I was *looking for continuity* more than change to begin with, eager to assimilate new information to old stereotypes I had formed of these people long ago. I remember hearing that an especially well-liked person in our class (let's call him David) had suffered what a classmate of mine called "a nervous breakdown." At first, this information seemed to contradict my memory of David as a socially competent and popular boy. But I found myself explaining the discontinuity away: "He always seemed a little strange to me," I remember telling myself. In this way, I managed to transform in my head what might be a case of dramatic personality change into an example of personality continuity over time. David was always a little brittle, I thought. He must have encountered some major stress, which made him crack.

My observations about Mary Anne's "poise," Robert's "social dominance," and David's "brittleness" were really attributions about the personality traits these people seemed to display, as seen in high school and 10 years later. We have taken a close look at personality traits in the previous two chapters of this book. In Chapter 5, we learned that traits are broad individual differences among people in characteristic thoughts, feelings, and behaviors. Well-designed paper-and-pencil measures of personality traits do a reasonably good job of predicting important trends in people's behavior summed across different situations. In any given situation, however, behavior is a function of the interaction between internal traits and external environmental variables. In Chapter 6, we examined the five basic trait categories of extraversion, neuroticism, conscientiousness, agreeableness, and openness to experience. Each of the five has generated a large and growing body of research speaking to behavioral correlates and possible physiological underpinnings of traits. We have seen that while the concept of personality traits has always sparked some controversy, trait attributions provide an indispensable first language for describing human individuality. It is virtually impossible to talk about differences among people without invoking trait concepts. It should come as no surprise, then, that the science of personality psychology has invested considerable effort in delineating trait concepts, developing valid measures for traits, and showing the far-reaching implications that individual differences in personality traits can have for human behavior and experience.

In this chapter, we extend our consideration of traits to encompass the dimension of *time*. Are traits stable over time? How much do traits change over time? Can we expect that Robert Amundson will still be socially dominant when I see him, God willing, at my 30th high-school reunion? Will Mary Anne Cromwell go through new changes over time? Will I make the same kinds of attributions that I made at the 10th reunion about Roberta, Michael, and Barbara? What can we expect from David 30 years after graduating from high school? The issue of time leads naturally to a related question: Where do personality traits come from, anyway? They don't just emerge out of thin air. Traits must develop, in some sense, over time. Is their development driven by our genes? By our environments? These are surely some of the most interesting questions in all of personality psychology. Some of the answers that are beginning to emerge from personality research may fit your expectations. But some, I bet, will surprise you.

THE CONTINUITY OF TRAITS

In everyday talk, attributing a trait to a person presupposes a certain degree of continuity over time. If I tell you, for example, that my nephew is a very "agreeable" person, I am implying that his high level of agreeableness has some staying power over time. Despite momentary fluctuations, I am suggesting that he *tends to be* agreeable. Just how long-term that staying power might be, however, is not clear from my attribution. Do I mean that he is likely still to be an agreeable person a week from now? Yes, I do mean to suggest that. What about next year? Probably. Twenty years from now? I don't know. Am I suggesting that he will continue to be a relatively agreeable person for the rest of his life? No, I am not necessarily saying that.

When people use trait terms in everyday talk, they seem to be operating from an implicit assumption that certain features of human individuality are more-or-less stable "for a while." My nephew is a highly agreeable person, and I expect that he will remain highly agreeable for a while. It is not clear how long that "for a while" is. But it is long enough in time to allow me to make the attribution of a trait. For this reason, psychologists expect personality trait scales to show high test–retest reliability in the short run (Chapter 5). Traits are not supposed to change dramatically from, say, one day to the next. If they did, then they wouldn't be "traits." Therefore, a trait scale that gives wildly different scores for a given individual from one day or week to the next is thought to lack test–retest reliability, and such a scale is likely to be rejected by the scientific community. But what about a given trait for a given person over the long haul? Beyond the "for a while," how much continuity can we expect in traits from one year to the next? From young adulthood to middle adulthood? From childhood through old age?

Different Meanings of Continuity

Before we can begin to answer these questions, we need to make some important distinctions among different meanings of continuity in personality traits. As you can see in Table 7.1, we can distinguish among four very different meanings of continuity, each of which can raise different issues and provide different kinds of answers to our general questions.

The first meaning is **absolute continuity.** Caspi (1998) defines absolute continuity as "constancy in the quantity or amount of an attribute over time" (p. 346). In absolute terms, "how much" social dominance did Robert Amundson have in 1972 and in 1982? Let us say that we administered a well-validated scale of this trait to Robert in 1972, and at that time he scored "27." On the exact same scale in 1982, he again scored

TABLE 7.1		*Four Types of Continuity*
TYPE	**DEFINITION**	**HYPOTHETICAL EXAMPLE**[a]
Absolute	Constancy in the quantity or amount of a characteristic over time, typically calculated in terms of group means or averages	The group average score on the trait "punctuality" remains stable over time: The mean score on punctuality for college students at age 20 is not significantly different from the mean score on the same group of individuals obtained 5 years later as young adults.
Differential	Consistency of individual differences in a sample of persons over time	Individual differences in intelligence test scores remain stable over time: The correlation between IQ scores obtained from a group of individuals at age 35 and again at age 40 is high, showing that people who tended to score relatively high on IQ the first time, also tended to score relatively high the second time, the lows tended to stay low, and so on.
Ipsative	Intraindividual continuity with respect to a pattern of variables over time	A person's rank ordering of a set of goals, from "my most important" to "my least important" goal, remains stable between the ages of 50 and 60 years.
Coherence	Conceptual or theoretical continuity displayed when one set of variables leads to a second set of variables over time in accordance with theoretical predictions	A pattern of behaviors at Time 1 leads to a different but theoretically predictable pattern of behaviors at Time 2: Experiencing highly punitive parenting and being a bully as a child is associated with criminal behavior in adulthood.

[a]*Note:* These examples are purely hypothetical and do not necessarily represent real research findings.

"27." In this case, we could say that Robert showed absolute continuity on the trait of social dominance over a 10-year span. But the concept of absolute continuity is virtually never applied to the single individual. Instead, absolute continuity is usually understood in terms of group averages on a given trait (Caspi, 1998). As an example, we might compare the average social dominance score for the graduates of Gary Lew Wallace High School obtained in 1972, when they were 18 years of age, with the average score obtained from the same group of people 10 years later, when they were 28. Such a study would help us answer this question: How much absolute continuity do we observe on social dominance across a 10-year period in the lifespan? If the average scores for age 18 and 28 are highly similar, then we might conclude that the *group*, as a whole, exhibited continuity on this trait. People were no more or less socially dominant, on the average, at age 28 compared with age 18.

The issue of absolute continuity comes into important play when personality psychologists consider certain hypotheses and expectations about human *development*. For example, some developmental theories suggest that adolescence is a time of confusion and anxiety for many people, but that things settle down a bit as individuals move into adulthood (e.g., Blos, 1979). With respect to my reunion experience, then, we might expect that the group average scores on measures of "anxiety" or "insecurity" or even "rebelliousness" might have been higher among my peers in 1972, when we were high

Individual differences in personality traits tend to show substantial differential continuity over time. In the same way that this woman is recognizable from her appearance at three different points in her life, so, too, may certain characteristic aspects of a person's personality be recognizable over time.

school students, than in 1982, when we were young adults. Our expectations would suggest that absolute continuity would *not* occur across this developmental time period, that people in general would change, and that these changes would be captured in changing average scores over time. I did not have the foresight to administer personality tests to my classmates in 1972 and 1982. But my overall gut impressions suggested to me that while there may have been absolute continuity on many traits, a few things did seem to have changed *for the group as a whole.* My nonscientific sense was that as 28-year-olds we were generally more comfortable with our lives and our identities in the overall than we had been in high school. Had someone done the study, I would have expected a slight drop in social anxiety from age 18 to age 28 for the group as a whole, and perhaps a slight increase in friendliness, too. But we will, of course, never know.

Differential continuity refers to "the consistency of individual differences within a sample of individuals over time, to the retention of an individual's relative placement in a group" (Caspi, 1998, p. 345). When I suggest that Robert Amundson seemed to be as socially dominant at age 28 as he was at age 18, I am making a statement about differential continuity. I am suggesting that, *relative to his peers,* Robert tends to be pretty high on the social dominance dimension. Differential continuity is always a matter of individuals' relative standing to one another on a given dimension. In the case of Robert's social dominance, I might suggest that in a random sample of, say, 100 of my classmates from Gary Lew Wallace, Robert was probably about the second or third most socially dominant person in 1972. My observations 10 years later suggested to me that he remained toward the top on this dimension, compared again with his peers. But the extent to which the trait social dominance shows differential continuity in my example is a product of not only Robert's placement on the social dominance dimension, but everybody else's placement, too. For there to be high levels of differential continuity for this trait, not only would Robert need to continue to score toward the top of the distribution over time, but other people would also need to hold their relative positions on this trait over time. In other words, if social dominance shows high differential continuity over a 10-year span, then Robert would need to continue to score very high (let's say a "10" on a 10-point scale), Barbara (who, let us say, scored an "8" in 1972) would need to continue to score moderately high, I would need to continue to score in the medium range (let's figure I was around a "5"), and Keith (who scored "2" in 1972) would need to continue to score in the low range. In simple terms, Robert, Barbara, Dan, and Keith would "stay the same" over the 10-year period relative to one another on this trait. They would each continue to hold their positions in the distribution.

The extent to which individuals continue to hold their relative positions on a trait dimension over time is typically calculated with a correlation coefficient (Chapter 1). The correlation is calculated between the same individuals' scores on the same trait at Time 1 (in this case, 1972, at age 18) and Time 2 (1982, age 28). High correlation coefficients (those approaching the value of +1.0) suggest high differential continuity. If, for example, we actually had obtained social dominance scores from 100 of my classmates in 1972 and again (the same 100 classmates) in 1982, then we could calculate the correlation between those two sets of scores. Had we done so and had we obtained, let us say, a correlation value of +.80, we would have evidence for very strong differential continuity on this trait. The high value of the correlation coefficient (+.80) would tell us that people tended to hold their relative positions on the given trait over the 10-year span. Thus, a person's score on the trait in 1972 would be a good predictor of the same person's score on the same trait assessed 10 years later. By contrast, had we obtained, let us say, the modest correlation value of +.10 in this study, then we would have to conclude that social dominance, as measured by our scale, does not show strong differential continuity. Low differential continuity means that people's relative positions on the given dimension change unpredictably over time. Thus, if there were low differential continuity on the trait, it would be very difficult to predict a person's social dominance score at age 28 from his or her score at age 18, because individuals' relative positions to one another on this trait would appear to vary markedly over time. In the case of low differential continuity, Keith may have been "low" in social dominance at age 18, but there's no telling where he might score 10 years later. Low differential continuity suggests that people change relative to one another over time on a given dimension. Low differential continuity does not, however, tell us in what direction people change. It simply says that their scores are likely to fluctuate unpredictably.

It is important to note that absolute continuity and differential continuity are completely unrelated to each other. Absolute continuity typically refers to the consistency of the average score on a given trait over time while differential continuity refers to the stability of individual differences in scores. Because these two metrics are independent of each other, information about one of these forms of continuity tells you little, if anything, about the other. Therefore, just because you have high absolute continuity on a given trait does not mean that you necessarily have high differential continuity. Let me take you, then, through four simple hypotheticals.

In the first hypothetical, we have *high* absolute continuity and *high* differential continuity. Let us imagine that this was the case for social dominance in my reunion example. We would say that the group average score on social dominance at age 18 was very similar to the group average score at age 28 (high absolute continuity), and the relative positions of individuals on the dimension of social dominance did not change much from age 18 to age 28 (high differential continuity). For the second hypothetical, let us consider *low* absolute continuity but *high* differential continuity. Let us imagine that this were the case for the dimension of social anxiety in the reunion example. As a group, the social anxiety average decreased significantly, let us say, from age 18 to age 28, but individuals' relative positions vis-a-vis one another were stable. In this example, the entire group became less anxious over time, perhaps suggesting greater maturity and social poise. But the people who were the most anxious at age 18 still tended to be the most anxious at age 28, even though their absolute scores went down. Keith scored a "10" in 1972 on social anxiety, but his score "improved" dramatically to a "7" in 1982. Given that almost everybody's scores improved (decreased), however, Keith is still toward the high social anxiety end. In the case, then, of low absolute continuity combined with high differential continuity, the entire distribution of scores may shift in one direction or another, but individuals' relative positions in the distribution might not change much. As we will see, this pattern is pretty common for some traits.

In the third hypothetical, *high* absolute continuity is combined with *low* differential continuity. This is a bit harder to imagine, but it is still quite possible in principle. What you would have is a trait or feature whose group average is stable over time but for which the distribution of individual differences is unstable. Let us imagine this scenario for the idea of "warm feelings for my parents." Let us imagine that in 1972 and again in 1982 we asked my classmates to report on a 1–10 scale how warm their feelings were for their parents. The class averages in 1972 and 1982 were highly similar— let us say, around 7.0. In both years, furthermore, people showed a broad distribution of scores. Some people felt very warm feelings for their parents, and some reported feeling cold and angry toward them. But the people who had the warmest feelings toward parents in 1972 were *not necessarily the same people* who had the warmest feelings toward their parents in 1982. Robert identified strongly with his parents in 1972, but since they divorced in the interim his feelings toward both of them have cooled markedly. By contrast, Barbara felt a medium level of warmth in 1972, but over time she has warmed up considerably. Keith felt low levels of warmth in both years. Mary Anne felt very warm in 1972 but now reports less warmth for her parents. David was medium in 1972 and high-medium in 1982. And so on. In simple terms, you cannot predict the individual scores on this dimension in 1982 based on the individual scores in 1972. The overall group mean hasn't changed much, but people's individual positions in the distribution have changed rather randomly.

Our fourth hypothetical is one in which *both* absolute and differential continuity are *low*. For this example, I need to move out of the personality realm and consider the variable of "personal income." As a group, the 28-year-olds were making considerably more money in 1982 than they were as 18-year-olds in 1972. Thus, absolute continuity on personal income would be very low. But differential continuity might also be low. The people who were making the most money at age 18 (let us say through part-time and summer jobs) were not necessarily the same ones making the most money at age 28, after people had moved differentially into careers. Mary Anne was never employed in high school, so her personal income was zero. But at age 28, she was making considerably more money than most of the other people in the class, by virtue of her successful business. Keith had a lucrative summer job, so his annual personal income was toward the top of the distribution in 1972. But he dropped out of college and has held a series of low-paying jobs ever since, so in 1982 he was making considerably less than Mary Anne and most other people in the class. An examination of other individual cases in my hypothetical example might show that personal income at age 18 was a poor predictor of personal income at age 28. Thus, while the entire distribution of scores shifted markedly to the higher end of the income spectrum from 1972 to 1982 (low absolute continuity), individuals did not hold onto their initial relative positions in the distribution (low differential continuity).

Both absolute and differential continuity typically refer to characteristics of groups of individuals, and each is calculated through some form of a group statistic. By contrast, a third form of continuity, called **ipsative continuity,** focuses exclusively on the patterning of traits for a given individual. Ipsative continuity is "continuity in the configuration of variables within an individual over time" (Caspi, 1998, p. 349). In a sense, ipsative continuity is the reverse of differential continuity. Whereas differential continuity looks at the relative standing of persons across variables, an ipsative approach looks at the relative standing of variables within a person. Let us consider again Robert Amundson. Let us imagine that in both 1972 and 1982 we asked Robert to give himself scores on each of 10 trait variables. His task was to rank order the variables from highest (most like me; it gets a score of "10") to lowest (least like me; it gets a score of "1"). He must rank order *all* the variables he is given. In other words, he is forced to make a choice for each variable and to assign it a particular rank with respect to how much the variable applies to him. For example, if Robert believes the two variables "honest" and "compassionate" are equally "most like me," he still must decide which of the two gets a higher rank. Let us say, then, that in 1972, Robert rank orders the 10 variables he is given in the following way:

10: outgoing and sociable person

9: self-confident, sure of oneself

8: emotionally stable

7: enjoys intellectual tasks

6: socially responsible, concerned about others' welfare

5: highly religious

4: well-organized, structured lifestyle

3: dependent, wants to merge with other people

2: impulsive, risk-taking

1: emotionally volatile, explosive personality

The question of ipsative continuity concerns the extent to which Robert will rank order the same variables in the same way 10 years later. In other words, to what extent is the pattern of these 10 variables continuous over time for Robert? If, say, Robert gives pretty much the same rank ordering in 1982 (let us say that he ranks "emotionally stable" one position higher and "self-confident, sure of oneself" one rank lower, but otherwise his distribution stays the same), then we can say that we have demonstrated substantial ipsative continuity with respect to Robert and the patterning of these 10 variables. If, however, his rank orderings change markedly (many of his previous low ranks now attain a higher status, and so on), then we would have to conclude that there is little ipsative continuity with respect to Robert and these variables over the 10-year span.

While personality researchers have shown great interest in absolute and differential continuity, few studies have directly examined ipsative continuity over time. Ipsative studies are difficult to do, and their interpretation as they apply to groups of individuals is considered by some to be controversial. For example, some researchers wonder how you can compare, say, Robert's rankings with Mary Anne's, since each individual's scores on an ipsative scale are based solely on how the variables rank for that particular person. Nonetheless, ipsative approaches have value in that they focus directly on continuity as experienced by the individual person (Mroczek & Spiro, in press). In other words, ipsative approaches look directly at *intra*individual (within a person) continuity and change across the life course, whereas most research that follows individuals over time examines *inter*individual (between persons) continuity and change. We will examine one especially important demonstration of ipsative continuity later in this chapter when we consider the research of Jack Block and his colleagues on the topics of ego resiliency, ego control, and personality typologies.

Some researchers have argued that continuity in personality can sometimes be demonstrated in ways that go beyond the stability of particular variables or patterns of variables. This fourth form of continuity is sometimes called **coherence** (Caspi, 1998). A good example of this idea is the research that we reviewed in Chapter 2 concerning caregiver–infant attachment. Research with infants and children has shown that secure attachment patterns at age 1 lead to greater levels of autonomy and interpersonal competence in the preschool years (Sroufe, 1988). Attachment at age 1 and interpersonal competence at age 4 are very different constructs, but developmental theory suggests that they are *conceptually* linked. Secure attachment provides the infant with the trusting base of experience that paves the way for higher levels of autonomy, mastery, and interpersonal competence. Research that shows how attachment leads to autonomy and competence demonstrates a certain kind of personality continuity over time. What is continuous, however, is not a particular behavior or trait per se but rather an underlying phenomenon or structure that coherently links together things that appear on the surface to be different.

Continuity via coherence is an especially important issue in studies that attempt to link childhood personality to adult personality. The same kinds of behaviors can mean very different things in children as opposed to adults. For example, the behavior of crying when frustrated may be viewed as a relatively normal behavior for a 6-year old but a sign of emotional immaturity at midlife. Researchers are not likely to attempt to document differential continuity in crying behavior across the lifespan because the behavior itself means different things at different points in development. However, researchers might propose a theoretical model in which excessive crying at one particular age indicates a developing underlying syndrome or pattern that may manifest itself in a very different way later in life. Developmental coherence might be shown, then, if one set of variables at Time 1 predicts a different set of variables at Time 2 in a way that is consistent with a particular developmental theory. We will see many examples of research that is guided by this general idea of developmental coherence in Chapter 10 of this book.

Differential Continuity in the Adult Years

By far, the one form of continuity that has attracted the most research attention among psychologists and the greatest interest among the public is differential continuity.

People are especially interested in knowing whether individual differences in various psychological qualities are consistent over time. The most informative research on this topic has examined differential continuity in personality traits in the adult years. Psychologists have conducted a number of longitudinal studies to examine this issue. In a longitudinal study, the researchers follow the same group of individuals over time to chart continuity and change in psychological variables. Differential continuity in personality traits is typically assessed by correlating trait scores at Time 1 with trait scores obtained later at Time 2 (and again at subsequent followups). By their very nature, longitudinal studies require a great deal of time to complete. Studies begun decades ago finally began to yield important results on differential continuity of traits in the 1980s and 1990s (e.g., Conley, 1985a, 1985b; Costa, McCrae, & Arenberg, 1980; Finn, 1986; Nelson & Moane, 1987; McCrae & Costa, 1990; Schuerger, Zarrella, & Hotz, 1989). To date, results have been collected from studies that examine intervals of as much as 30 years over the adult life course. What do these studies show?

Longitudinal studies show *remarkable differential continuity in personality traits over the adult lifespan*. For example, Conley (1985b) analyzed data from a 50-year longitudinal study of several hundred adults. All newlyweds at the beginning of the study, the participants rated themselves and were rated by their spouses on a series of personality trait dimensions in 1935–1938, 1954–1955, and 1980–1981. Supporting the inter-rater reliability of trait dimensions, Conley found that spouse ratings tended to agree with self-ratings on many personality traits. For example, a husband who saw himself as highly conscientious was likely to be viewed as highly conscientious by his wife as well. With respect to differential continuity, both self-ratings and spouse-ratings showed considerable consistency over time. Ratings that make up the Big Five dimensions of extraversion and neuroticism showed particularly strong longitudinal consistency. Further support for differential continuity was evidenced by the fact that self-ratings on a given trait at Time 1 tended to predict spouse-ratings of a given trait at Time 2, and so on. In other words, differential continuity in trait ratings was displayed when examining (1) self-ratings over time, (2) spouse ratings over time, and (3) the ability of one kind of rating to predict another kind of rating of the same trait over time.

Costa, McCrae, and Arenberg (1980) assessed a number of different traits at two different times for 460 male volunteers in the Baltimore Longitudinal Study of Aging. At the time of the first testing, the participants ranged in age from 17 to 85 years. Correlations between extraversion scores at Time 1 and Time 2, separated by a 6- to 12-year period, were generally above +.70, indicating substantial differential continuity. The researchers likewise found high stability coefficients for ratings making up the trait of neuroticism. Results from longitudinal studies have also examined the Big Five traits of openness to experience, agreeableness, and conscientiousness. Table 7.2 displays results from some of these studies. In general, substantial differential continuity has been shown for all five of these large trait clusters across intervals of time ranging from 3 to 30 years. Correlations between Time 1 and Time 2 assessments are different for different studies, different time intervals, and different measures. Looking across the studies, however, the observer notices that many correlation coefficients are around +.65. This is a very high correlation, especially when you consider the fact that personality trait scales are not perfectly reliable measures anyway. Because a scale is not likely to give exactly the same score for a person from one day to the next (test-retest reliabilities are typically around +.85 or so), documenting longitudinal consistency over many years at the magnitude of a +.65 correlation coefficient is especially

TABLE 7.2   *Stability Coefficients for Selected Trait Scales in Adult Samples*

FACTOR/SCALE	SOURCE	TIME INTERVAL	r
Neuroticism			
NEO-PI	Costa & McCrae, 1988a	6 years	.83
16PF: Tense	Costa & McCrae, 1978	10 years	.67
ACL: Adaptability	Helson & Moane, 1987	16 years	.66
Neuroticism	Conley, 1985b	18 years	.46
MMPI factor	Finn, 1986	30 years	.56
Extraversion			
NEO-PI	Costa & McCrae, 1988a	6 years	.82
ACL: Self-confidence	Helson & Moane, 1987	16 years	.60
Social extraversion	Conley, 1985b	18 years	.57
Sociability	Costa & McCrae, 1992	24 years	.68
MMPI factor	Finn, 1986	30 years	.56
Openness to Experience			
NEO-PI	Costa & McCrae, 1988a	6 years	.83
16PF: Tender minded	Costa & McCrae, 1978	10 years	.54
Thoughtfulness	Costa & McCrae, 1992	24 years	.66
Intellectual interests	Finn, 1986	30 years	.62
Agreeableness			
NEO-PI	Costa & McCrae, 1988a	3 years	.63
Agreeableness	Conley, 1985b	18 years	.46
Friendliness	Costa & McCrae, 1992	24 years	.65
Low cynicism	Finn, 1986	30 years	.65
Conscientiousness			
NEO-PI	Costa & McCrae, 1988a	3 years	.79
16PF: Conscientiousness	Costa & McCrae, 1978	10 years	.48
ACL: Endurance	Helson & Moane, 1987	16 years	.67
Impulse control	Conley, 1985b	18 years	.46

Scale names: NEO-PI is the Neuroticism-Extraversion-Openness Personality Inventory
16PF is the Sixteen Personality Factor Scale
ACL is the Adjective Checklist
MMPI is the Minnesota Multiphasic Personality Inventory

Source: Costa & McCrae (1994), p. 32.

impressive. Costa and McCrae (1994) point out that if such scales were perfectly reliable, then the correlations over long periods of time would be even higher.

Is the evidence for differential continuity in personality traits so strong as to suggest that personality traits are set in stone by the time we reach our adult years? The general answer is no. Despite the evidence for impressive stability over time, trait scores are not perfectly stable. As we have already suggested, one reason for instability is the error of the measures themselves. But going beyond error, there still appears to be some room for change and fluctuation in traits. Differential continuity is substantial but not all-powerful. The wide range of longitudinal stability coefficients displayed in Table 7.2 suggests that there is still change that occurs over time. People's positions in the distribution can and do change from one assessment to another. Robert Amundson will not necessarily score at the top of the pack on social dominance 20 years from

| FIGURE 7.1 | *Trait Continuity With Increasing Time Intervals* |

As the time between trait assessments increases, the test–retest correlations on the trait decreases, suggesting less differential consistency over time. Nonetheless, at 198 months (an interval of 16.5 years) differential continuity for traits overall is rather high (between +.55 and +.60).

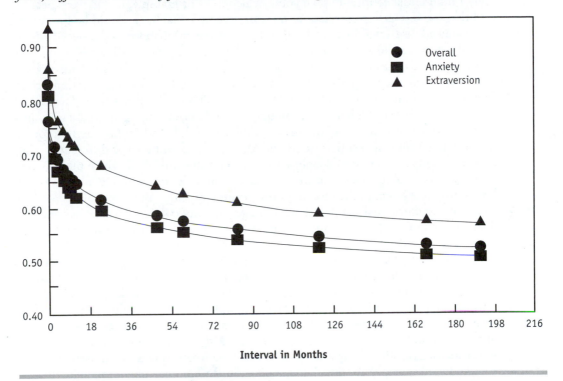

Interval in Months

Source: Adapted from Schuerger, Zarrelia, & Hotz (1989), p. 781.

now, though of course he may, and it is highly unlikely (though not impossible) that he would score toward the bottom. Personality trait scores at Time 1 in adulthood are good but not perfect predictors of scores on those same traits at Time 2.

One of the factors that influences the strength of differential continuity is the length of the time interval between testing. The longer the time interval, the lower the differential continuity. This makes intuitive sense. We would expect that people would show less stability in trait scores over a 20-year period as compared with a 5-year period. One group of researchers (Schuerger, Zarrella & Hotz, 1989) reviewed 89 longitudinal studies of personality traits, focusing especially on the Big Five dimensions of extraversion and neuroticism (anxiety). They found that test-retest correlations on traits tended to decline as the time interval increased. Figure 7.1 summarizes their results. As you can see, differential continuity tends to be higher (around +.70) for short time intervals (e.g., 1 year), and it tends to decrease gradually as the time interval lengthens, reaching a level of about +.50 for very long time intervals (e.g., more than

10 years). The researchers also found that extraversion tends to show slightly higher differential continuity than the trait of neuroticism (anxiety) and higher continuity than the overall average of other traits as well.

Another factor that influences differential continuity is the age of the participants in the study. A common belief is that as people age they change less and less, relative to one another. Given comparable time intervals, are older people more likely to show higher differential continuity than younger people? For example, would we expect to find that the test–retest correlations on traits over a 5-year span would be lower for, say, young adults (tested first at age 20 and then at age 25) than for middle-aged adults (tested first at age 40 and then at age 45)? Roberts and Friend-DelVecchio (in press) investigated this question in a comprehensive review of studies reporting data on longitudinal consistency of personality traits. In keeping with general expectations, they found that stability coefficients were lowest in studies of children's traits (averaging around +.41), rose to higher levels among young adults (averaging around +.55), and then reached a plateau for adults between the ages of 50 and 70 (averaging around +.70). The results suggest that we should expect greater and greater differential continuity in personality traits as people age up through late mid-life. Early in the lifespan, there is considerable movement in the distribution of scores, and individuals do not hold onto their places in the distribution as firmly over time. But as people move into adulthood and eventually into late middle-age, stability coefficients increase and the distributions of trait scores show less internal fluctuation and more interindividual continuity.

The study by Robert and Friend-DelVecchio raises the issue of personality traits *in children*. The results of their review suggest that trait ratings in children show less differential continuity than do trait ratings in adulthood. Because children seem to be developing at a more rapid pace and in a more fluid manner than adults, however, many psychologists have historically been reluctant to view children's traits in the same kinds of terms for understanding adult traits. Indeed, most research on personality traits per se has focused on adults. But what is the relation between aspects of children's personality and adult personality traits? Do adult traits develop out of comparable, though perhaps less stable, dimensions in children? To address these questions we must consider the phenomenon of *temperament* as it is observed and measured in the early years of life, even back in infancy.

Childhood Precursors: From Temperament to Traits

I had a professor once who remarked that all parents are environmentalists until they have their second child. Before the second child, the parents may believe that the development of their firstborn is mainly a product of the kinds of environments they provide for their child—say, the warmth of the family environment, the quality of daycare, and so on. It is not until parents see just how different the second one is, compared with the first, and indeed how different the second one is *from the very beginning*, from the first weeks of life onward, that parents may begin to appreciate the power of inborn differences among children. My professor was being facetious, but not completely. The point he was making is that the possibility of inborn differences in personality functioning becomes rather apparent when we observe how different children seem to be from one another, even at birth. Differences in basic behavioral style, often observed early in life and presumed to be under significant and rather direct bi-ological control, are often viewed as indications of **temperament** (Caspi, 1998; Kagan, 2000). According to Gordon Allport (1961):

> Temperament refers to the characteristic phenomena of an individual's nature, including his susceptibility to emotional stimulation, his customary strength and speed of response, the quality of his prevailing mood, and all the peculiarities of fluctuation and intensity of mood, these being phenomena regarded as dependent on constitutional make-up, and therefore largely hereditary in origin. (p. 34)

Developmental psychologists have devised a number of methods for measuring temperament and a number of conceptual schemes for understanding what they measure. The simplest and best-known scheme was delineated by Thomas, Chess, and Birch (1970), based on their interviews of mothers of babies. They distinguished among three different types of temperament patterns. **Easy** babies show consistently positive mood, low-to-moderate intensity of emotional reactions, and regular sleeping and eating cycles. **Difficult** babies show consistently negative moods, intense emotional reactions, and irregular sleeping and eating cycles. **Slow-to-warm-up** babies reveal a combination of the previous two forms, with relatively negative moods, low intensity of emotional reactions, and the tendency to withdraw from new events at first but then approach them later. Other researchers have adopted more fine-grained schemes for categorizing temperament. For instance, Rothbart (1986) enumerates six temperament dimensions reliably observed in infants in the first year of life: activity level, smiling and laughter, fearfulness, distress to limitations, "soothability," and vocal activity.

One temperament dimension that has received a great deal of attention is what Jerome Kagan (1989) calls *behavioral inhibition*. Extremely inhibited young children show great timidity in the face of new events and people. Kagan has shown that about 15% of Caucasian children in the second year of life are consistently shy and emotionally subdued in unfamiliar situations ("inhibited children") whereas another 15% are consistently sociable and affectively spontaneous ("uninhibited children"). As 2-year-olds, inhibited children may be especially reluctant to play with an unfamiliar toy. In kindergarten they may shy away from new activities and people, showing a kind of stagefright in new situations. Compared with uninhibited children, inhibited children show intense physiological responses, such as more dilated pupils and higher heart rates, when confronted with mildly stressful social situations. In addition, inhibited children show higher levels of morning cortisol in the blood (indicating heightened arousal) compared with uninhibited children, a difference that is also apparent when comparing shy, inhibited rhesus monkeys with their more sociable peers. Kagan argues that extremely shy and extremely sociable children constitute two separable genetic types whose striking behavioral differences are partly a function of different thresholds of reactivity in the brain's limbic system. Inhibited children have a lower threshold of reactivity. They are more easily aroused in social situations and respond by withdrawing.

Kagan's physiological portrait of temperamental inhibition is reminiscent of Eysenck's (Chapter 6) account of the trait introversion. Eysenck argued that introverts are overly aroused in general and that their withdrawal behavior is an effort to decrease arousal levels. In addition, recent research suggests that behaviorally inhibited children are more likely to show neural activation of the right frontal lobe while uninhibited children are more likely to show activation of the brain's left frontal lobe (Kagan, 1994). As we saw in Chapter 6, right frontal activity is associated with negative affectivity (including emotions of fear and depression) and the behavioral inhibition system whereas left frontal activity has been linked to positive affectivity (including emotions of joy and happiness) and the behavioral approach system. Will Kagan's excessively inhibited children grow up to be introverted and anxious adults? Will uninhibited children become extraverted adults? Research has not provided clear answers, but Kagan believes that the link between inhibition and some combination of introversion and neuroticism in adulthood will eventually be shown. Out of every 100 Caucasian newborns, Kagan maintains, approximately 20% will show extreme irritability and excitability shortly after birth. By the age of 2 years, 75% of these (say, 15 or so) will be very shy, timid, and fearful when they meet unfamiliar people, are put in unfamiliar rooms, or encounter unfamiliar objects. By adolescence, 10 will still be very shy, and by adulthood you are likely to find that 6 or 7 of the original 20 are extremely introverted in their behavior. The two-thirds who lost their excessive shyness by adulthood may have been strongly influenced by environmental experiences encouraging them to be more outgoing. Indeed, American society tends to favor outgoing and sociable people. Like the 6 or 7 resultant introverts, however, the former inhibited children who grew up to be somewhat less introverted than we might have originally expected retain what Kagan believes to be a "shyness physiology." Further research is needed to assess the validity of Kagan's interpretation.

Personality psychologists Arnold Buss and Robert Plomin (1975, 1984) believe that enduring personality traits develop out of temperament endowments. In their *temperament theory of personality*, they argue for the existence of four basic temperament dimensions upon which people may differ from birth onward: emotionality, activity, sociability, and impulsivity. In the view of Buss and Plomin, all four of these dimensions are (1) inherited, (2) stable during development, (3) present across the lifespan, (4) generally adaptive, and (5) present as meaningful behavioral dimensions in animals biologically similar to humans. People are born with predispositions to develop these four temperaments to different levels. The social environment reacts to these dispositions, modifying and shaping them in certain ways, but only within the limits established by heredity. Table 7.3 displays items from the EASI Temperament Survey, used to assess these four dimensions in children.

To date, few longitudinal studies have examined the relationship between early childhood temperament variables on the one hand and adult personality traits on the other. Furthermore, the methods and conceptual systems used by researchers studying infant and child temperament on the one hand and adult personality on the other have historically been very different. For example, many temperament scales rely on maternal reports or behavioral observations of infants and children. By contrast, research on personality traits has tended to favor self-report rating scales. Temperament theorists have proposed a number of different taxonomies for organizing such temperament dimensions as irritability, positive affect, activity level, rhythmicity, adaptability, sensory threshold, soothability, intensity of mood, and a host of other dimensions that seem especially applicable to children (Caspi, 1998; Rowe, 1997). Trait researchers have also proposed many different systems, as we saw in Chapter 5, but in recent years the Big Five taxonomy has won considerable support as a comprehensive framework for adult

| TABLE 7.3 | *The EASI Temperament Survey* |

EMOTIONALITY

Child gets upset easily.
Child tends to cry easily.
Child is easily frightened.
Child is easygoing or happy-go-lucky. (reverse)
Child has a quick temper.

ACTIVITY

Child is always on the go.
Child likes to be off and running immediately on awakening.
Child cannot sit still long.
Child prefers quiet games such as block play or coloring to more active games. (reverse)
Child fidgets at meals and similar occasions.

SOCIABILITY

Child likes to be with others.
Child makes friends easily.
Child tends to be shy. (reverse)
Child tends to be independent. (reverse)
Child prefers to play by himself rather than with others. (reverse)

IMPULSIVITY

Child tends to be impulsive.
Child has difficulty learning self-control.
Child gets bored easily.
Child learns to resist temptation easily. (reverse)
Child goes from toy to toy quickly.

Source: Adapted from Buss & Plomin (1975).

personality traits. Some researchers have recently argued that the Big Five framework could be used to classify dimensions of childhood functioning, too, including variables that have traditionally been viewed as part of temperament (Kohnstamm, Halverson, Mervielde, & Havill, 1998). But others are skeptical that such an easy conceptual match can be found (Kagan, 2000).

What is the difference between a temperament dimension and a personality trait? Rutter (1987) writes that individual differences in temperament refer to basic stylistic differences between people "that appear early in life, show substantial stability over time, represent predictable modes of response, and possibly have fairly direct neurobiological correlates" (p. 447). Kagan (2000) describes temperament as a psychobiological profile that combines aspects of behavior, emotion, and physiology. Temperament dimensions are viewed as part of a person's basic native endowment, closely tied to fundamental psychobiological differences among people. By contrast, personality traits appear to be more cognitively and socially elaborated, more complex and multifaceted, and perhaps less directly tied to basic endowment (Rutter, 1987). Temperament dimensions may provide a psychobiological substratum out of which personality traits may develop. To this end, Caspi (1998) has proposed that at least five well-studied temperament dimensions—activity level, positive affect, behavioral inhibition, negative affect, and persistence in children—may provide the basic psychobiological profiles out of which the Big Five personality traits develop.

Figure 7.2 displays Caspi's proposed model for links between temperament dimensions in early childhood and adult personality traits. The first of Caspi's temperaments—*activity level*—consists of rapid tempo and physical vigor in children. Caspi proposes that this dimension may be an early childhood precursor to adult extraversion *(E)*, which includes such surgent characteristics as being active, dominant, outgoing, and energetic. Because, however, high activity level has been linked in children with certain externalizing (acting-out) behavioral problems, Caspi proposes that it may also be negatively associated with adult conscientiousness *(C)* and agreeableness *(A)*. The temperament dimension of *positive affect* encompasses reward-seeking activities that are expressed in pleasure, enthusiasm, and contentment. This dimension may be most closely linked to adult extraversion *E* and agreeableness *(A)*. We have already discussed behavioral *inhibition* as the tendency in some children to be fearful of and to withdraw from novelty. In accord with the views of Kagan (1994), Caspi links behavioral inhibition with low levels of adult *E* and high neuroticism *(N)*. *Negative affect* in children is expressed as irritability, fussing, anger, and lack of control. Caspi proposes that negative affect should predict high levels of adult *N* and low levels of *A*. Finally,

---

| FIGURE 7.2 | *Childhood Temperament and the Big Five* |

These are hypothesized relationships between major temperament dimensions observed in children and the Big Five traits assessed in adulthood. Note: Solid lines represent hypothesized positive associations; dashed lines represent hypothesized negative associations.

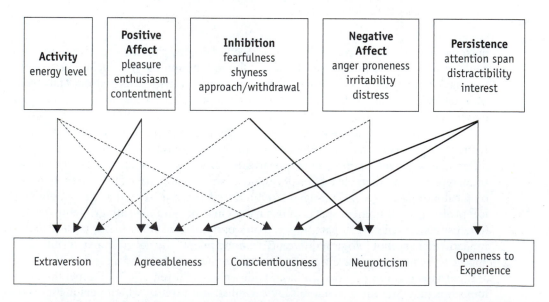

Source: Caspi (1998), p. 336.

persistence refers to individual differences in children's attentional capacities—attention span, distractibility, task orientation, and interest. Caspi hypothesizes that high levels of persistence may make a temperamental contribution to high levels of *A, C,* and openness to experience *(O)* in adulthood.

What are the ways by which basic temperament dimensions expressed in early childhood might eventually develop into fully formed personality traits in adulthood? Caspi (1998) views temperament as the psychobiological core around which personality is structured. Through a process of **developmental elaboration,** temperament dimensions gradually develop into more fully articulated personality traits. According to Caspi (1998), developmental elaboration "refers to the mechanisms by which those temperamental attributes that are part of each individual's genetic heritage accumulate response strength through their repeated reinforcement and become elaborated into cognitive structures strongly primed for accessibility" (pp. 339–340). Caspi enumerates six mechanisms through which developmental elaboration works. The six are summarized in Table 7.4.

The first mechanism is what Caspi calls *learning processes.* From infancy onward, temperamental differences may have a strong impact on such basic learning processes as reinforcement, extinction, and discrimination learning (Chapter 4). A highly distractible child may have a more difficult time than a more focused and persistent child in learning the appropriate connections between prosocial behaviors and positive rewards. Over time, distractibility may expand into low conscientiousness and an inability to

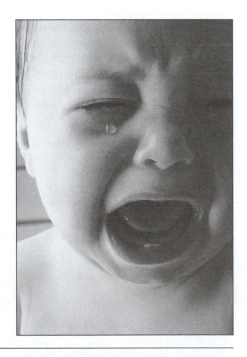

Temperament refers to basic differences in behavioral style that are assumed to be part of a person's genetic endowment. While some babies tend to smile a lot, others may show a more difficult temperament.

TABLE 7.4	Six Mechanisms of Developmental Elaboration: How Temperament Dimensions Develop Into Personality Traits
Learning processes	Temperamental differences impact what children learn and how they learn it, which contributes to the formation of personality traits.
Environmental elicitation	Temperamental differences elicit different reactions from the environment, which may reinforce the initial differences.
Environmental construal	Temperamental differences influence how children understand and process information about their environments, shaping their experiences of the environments.
Social and temporal comparisons	Temperamental differences impact how children compare themselves with others and with themselves over time, which shapes their developing self-concepts.
Environmental selection	Temperamental differences influence how children choose environments, which in turn influences the development of personality traits. Children may choose environments that are consistent with their temperaments to begin with, reinforcing dispositions that are already present.
Environmental manipulation	Once children's self-concepts are firmly established, they will alter, modify, or manipulate their environments to match, confirm, or elaborate the temperamental dispositions they already have.

assume a socially responsible attitude in life. By contrast, the child endowed with a longer attention span may find it easier to learn that positive rewards redound from kind and conscientious behaviors. Social responsibility is easier to learn in his case because his temperamental dispositions have paved the way for this kind of operant conditioning. In this simple example, then, we can imagine how temperament influences learning, which in turn influences the development of personality traits.

A second mechanism of developmental elaboration is what Caspi calls *environmental elicitation*. Temperament differences elicit different reactions from the environment. Individual differences in temperament influence how adults react to children over the course of development, beginning already in the first few months of life. Thus, infants who are temperamentally more inclined toward smiling elicit more positive responses from their environment than, all other things being equal, more irritable and fussy infants. These environmental responses may, in turn, gradually influence the behavior of the infant over time. Research has shown that adults draw inferences from children's temperament differences concerning the kinds of adults those children grow to be, and those inferences have an impact on how the adults react to children. For example, Graziano, Jensen-Campbell, and Sullivan-Logan (1998) found that preschool teachers anticipated developmental consequences for the temperamental dimensions they observed. In this study, the teachers expected that children who were not shy and who had high-quality interactions with their classmates would grow up to be extraverted adults. They expected that the children who were well-liked by their peers and who were especially adept at handling interpersonal conflict would grow up to show high levels of agreeableness. These kinds of expectations, then, likely influence how socializing agents such as parents, teachers, ministers, counselors, and so on relate to children, serving to reinforce tendencies that the children already show.

Third on Caspi's list is *environmental construal*. Temperament differences may influence how children make sense of their environments, thus shaping their personal experiences in profound ways. An irritable and negativistic child may construe reality in especially negative ways, while a child with a sunnier disposition may see the same "reality" in much more positive terms. It is the old question of whether the glass is half empty or half full—the answer depends, perhaps, on one's temperamental inclinations. As children become increasingly verbal and socially observant, their temperamental dispositions may come to color their own conceptions of self. This is where Caspi's fourth mechanism of developmental elaboration comes in—*social and temporal comparisons*. As children become more cognitively sophisticated, they begin to compare themselves with other people, and they begin to compare themselves in the present with what they were like in the past. These comparisons play into their developing self-concepts. It is likely that temperament influences the comparison process in many ways. For example, a child predisposed to negative affect may accentuate the ways in which he does not live up to the high standards set by his peers. His social comparisons repeatedly show that he is second-best, which further imbue his self-concept with expectations of sadness and frustration. A highly persistent child may take special notice of how her present situation compares with her remembered past and anticipated future. Because she is able to focus her attention on matters of the long-term, she works hard and persistently to improve her performance in areas that are especially important to her. Her temperamental dispositions contribute to the articulation of the conscientiousness trait and to the development of a self-concept as one who works hard and improves over time.

Through Caspi's fifth process of *environmental selection*, temperament influences how children choose the environments that will, in turn, influence them. As children mature to assume more responsibility for their own lives, they make choices and display preferences concerning with whom they wish to be friends, what activities they wish to pursue, and so on. These choices and preference are partly a function of their temperament dispositions. Research has shown that people select and create environments that serve to reinforce the dispositions that they already have. Highly active children, for example, may seek out environments that enable them to exercise their high activity levels, which, in turn, reinforce their tendencies toward high levels of activity and operate to build that temperament inclination into a more-or-less stable feature of personality. Relatedly, temperament impacts *environmental manipulation*, which is Caspi's sixth mechanism. Once children's self-concepts have been firmly established, Caspi argues, they are more likely to alter, modify, and manipulate the environments they find themselves in to match, confirm, and elaborate the dispositions they already have. By choosing environments that match their temperaments and by manipulating environments in ways that are consistent with their temperaments, children engage in experiences that enable them to express their temperamental dispositions further. Over time, temperaments become associated with a wide range of experiences that further strengthen and articulate them, eventually resulting, Caspi argues, in the consolidation of personality traits.

In sum, temperament dispositions such as positive affect, behavioral inhibition, and persistence in childhood may be the psychobiological dimensions around which personality traits such as extraversion and conscientiousness are eventually formed. Through the process of developmental elaboration, initial dispositions appearing even in infancy may gradually gain strength and scope and become more cognitively and socially articulated over time. Although research has yet to document clear connections between early temperament on the one hand and adult personality traits on the other, it seems sensible to suppose that some sorts of connections will eventually be shown. Those connections are likely to be due to the complex interplay between people's genetic endowments and the influences of environments.

THE ORIGINS OF TRAITS: GENES AND ENVIRONMENTS

It is a common observation that genetically identical twins—that is, *monozygotic* (MZ) twins—tend to be remarkably similar. Not only do they look very much alike, but it seems that their interests, tastes, styles, and behavior patterns are often strikingly concordant. By contrast, *dizygotic* (DZ), or fraternal twins, tend to look no more similar to each other than any other set of biological siblings, and their behaviors often seem to be equally discordant as well. In that they developed out of the same zygote, monozygotic twins have the same genetic makeup; dizygotic twins have only about half of their genes in common. In the 1980s, a group of researchers at the University of Minnesota undertook a large study of about 350 sets of MZ and DZ twins, a number of whom, from infancy onward, *had been raised apart* (Bouchard, Lykken, McGue, Segal, & Tellegen, 1990). In most of these cases, the twins had been given up for adoption, and each of the two members of the twin pair was adopted by a different family. Thus, each grew up not knowing his or her twin. Bringing the twin pairs back together for the study, the researchers were struck by some of the amazing similarities in personality revealed in the MZA (monozygotic, raised apart) twin pairs:

> While videotaping an interview with one [MZA] twin, we discovered he was an accomplished raconteur with a fund of amusing anecdotes, so, while interviewing the co-twin, we asked him if he knew any funny stories. "Why sure," he said, leaning back with a practiced air. "I'll tell you a story" and proceeded to demonstrate his concordance. A pair of British MZAs, who had met for the first time as adults just a month previously, both firmly refused in their separate interviews to express opinions on controversial topics; since long before they discovered each other's existence, each had resolutely avoided controversy. Another pair were both habitual gigglers, although each had been raised by adoptive parents whom they described as undemonstrative and dour, and neither had known anyone who laughed as freely as she did until finally she met her twin. Both members of another pair independently reported that they refrained from voting in political elections on the principle that they did not feel themselves well enough informed to make wise choices. A pair of male MZAs, at their first adult reunion, discovered that they both use Vadmecum toothpaste, Canoe shaving lotion, Vitalis hair tonic, and Lucky Strike cigarettes. After that meeting, they exchanged birthday presents in the mail that proved to be identical choices, made independently in separate cities.
>
> There were two "dog people," among the MZA individuals; one showed her dogs, and the other taught obedience classes—they were an MZA pair. Only two of the more than 200 individual twins reared apart were afraid to enter the acoustically shielded chamber used in our psychophysiology laboratory, but both separately agreed to continue if the door was wired open—they were a pair of MZA twins. When at the beach, both women had always insisted on entering the water backwards and then only up to their knees; they were thus concordant,

not only in their phobic tendencies, but also in the specific manifestations of their timidity. There were two gunsmith hobbyists among the group of twins; two women who habitually wore seven rings; two men who offered a (correct) diagnosis of a faulty wheel bearing on Bouchard's [one of the researcher's] car; two who obsessively counted things; two who had been married five times; two captains of volunteer fire departments; two fashion designers; two who left little love notes around the house for their wives . . . in each case, an MZA pair. (Lykken, McGue, Tellegen, Bouchard, 1992, pp. 1565–1566)

Are these examples just coincidences? The authors of the account concede that a few of the many incredible similarities they observed among MZA pairs could have been flukes, due to chance. But the sheer number and detail of the similarities observed suggest that there is more than just coincidence going on here. How can it be that MZ siblings who have never lived a day in the same household, who have been raised in different families and grown up in different neighborhoods, who have attended different schools and made different sets of friends, who have indeed never even met each other—how can it be that they should turn out to be so much alike? We should, perhaps, not be surprised that they would look alike. Most of us accept the idea that our appearance is strongly driven by our genetic endowment. But personality traits seem different.

Up to this point in this chapter, we have learned that individual differences in personality traits are fairly stable over the adult lifespan, showing substantial differential continuity from early adulthood onward. We have learned that temperamental differences in infancy and childhood, assumed to reflect a psychobiological substrate for human individuality, are often striking and readily recognized by parents, teachers, and other socializing agents. We have speculated that temperament dimensions in early childhood may eventually become elaborated through a long and complex series of person X environment interactions into full-fledged personality traits in the adult years. Implicit in our discussion has been the idea that personality traits develop out of some combination of genetic and environmental effects. But we have not been specific about this. The anecdotal examples from the University of Minnesota study of identical twins raised apart strongly hint that a person's genetic makeup is a major factor in determining his or her standing on personality trait dimensions. Should we believe the anecdotes? Is "nature" stronger than "nurture" when it comes to determining personality traits? How can we separate genetic from environmental effects on personality traits? Where do personality traits *ultimately* come from?

The Logic of Twin and Adoption Studies

Let us begin with a simple truth: You cannot have personality, you cannot have behavior, you cannot have life without *both* genes and environments. In a fundamental sense, your personality traits and mine are products of the interaction of our genes and our environments, for indeed genes cannot have any impact on behavior if there is no environment within which the person can act, and environments can have no impact on behavior if there are no genes out of which to make the person in the first place. In that genes fundamentally depend on environments and environments fundamentally depend on genes in the making of a person, nature and nurture are tightly intertwined in a given human life. Each of us is a complex and evolving product of the interaction between nature and nurture.

Having said that, we must now encounter a second, less simple truth: It does make scientific sense to examine the relative influences of genetic differences and environmental differences on the variability we perceive in a given sample or population of organisms. Let me give an example. Full-grown (adult) human beings differ noticeably with respect to height. Some people are taller than other people. Does it make sense to try to understand the reasons for these differences among people by appealing to genes and environments? You bet it does. We can sensibly ask what the relative contributions are of genetic and environmental variance in determining differences between people in height. Note how I have framed this statement. I am not talking here about why any particular individual is tall or short. I am instead talking about variability in height *in a group of individuals*—why it is that people differ on height. Research suggests that in the United States about 90% of the variability in height is associated with genetic differences among people, while only about 10% is associated with such environmental differences as nutritional levels and social class (Rowe, 1999). People who tend to have genetic endowments that produce relative tallness (people who are most likely tall themselves) tend to have taller children than people whose genetic endowments code for shortness. Nutritional differences among people account for a tiny part of the difference—the main factor is the genes. Americans can eat and eat and eat; they can do stretching exercises; they can try to improve their posture—but all of this will probably not make them much taller than they would have been anyway had they not gone to these extreme measures.

Now you need to realize two very important implications of the scientific finding concerning height. The first implication is that our figure of 90% refers to differences in the group; it does not apply to any particular person. It would be silly to say that 90% of a person's height comes from his genes and 10% of his height comes from his environment. For a 6-foot-tall man, that would mean that 7.2 inches of his height came from his environment. This kind of statement makes no sense. Instead, we have to remember that we are accounting here for differences or variability among people, not for any particular person's height. In accounting for the wide range of variability in height among Americans, we can say that 90% of the variability is due to genetic variability: People have different genes, and different genes produce different heights. The second implication of our statement about height is that the percentages of "variability accounted for" that we identified (90% for genetic differences, 10% for environmental differences) depend dramatically on characteristics of the population to begin with. It is definitely true that severe malnutrition *can* dramatically stunt people's growth, proving that a certain kind of environment can have a major impact. But the incidence of severe malnutrition and starvation is thankfully very low in most modern societies, so few people in the group are faced with these circumstances. But in a society where many people were on the brink of starvation while many others had plenty to eat, environmental differences could certainly play a larger role in determining height. In such a context, we would expect the relative contribution of genetic differences to be lower than 90% and the relative contribution of environmental differences to be higher than 10% in determining differences among people in height. These sorts of group estimates depend critically on the characteristics of the population from which the group is drawn.

With my example of height, I am introducing you to one of the most misunderstood concepts in all of psychology—the idea of the **heritability quotient.** A *heritability quotient estimates the proportion of variability in a given characteristic that can be attributed to genetic differences between people.* In the case of height among American adults, the heritability quotient is estimated to be 90%. This group statistic tells us how much of the observed variation in height is associated with genetic variation among people in the group. The example of height is noncontroversial, since most of us realize that height seems to "run in families." The example is also noncontroversial for another reason. While scientists have never found a particular gene that codes exclusively for height, we do not have a hard time believing that genes strongly influence height. Genes are merely segments of DNA. In these segments, biochemically active molecules are arranged in a sequence analogous to letters in a word. These "letters"— which essentially comprise the four biochemical bases of tymine, adenine, cytosine, and guanine—make up the genetic code, with different combinations of three letters in sequence coding for each of the 22 amino acids that make up the building blocks of proteins. Genes are directly implicated, then, in the making of proteins and other basic biochemical events. A phenomenon as complex as people's height is determined by the working of many different genes.

We move now from the relatively noncontroversial topic of heritability in height to heritability as it applies to personality traits. We have already acknowledged that an individual's particular personality traits are a complex product of genes interacting with environments. But as we did with height, we can consider the extent to which genetic differences and environmental differences account for variability in traits across many people. As with height, we must remember that heritability refers not to the individual but to accounting for variance in groups. We must remember that variance in groups is due to many factors within a group. We must remember that genetic influences on traits, should we find them, are indirect and complex. Just as there is no single gene that determines a person's height, so, too, is there no single gene that matches cleanly to a particular personality trait. Finally, we must understand that discussion of genetic difference among people must always be understood against a backdrop of tremendous genetic similarity across our species. Humans are highly similar to one another genetically. Many human genes—about 90% of them—are identical from one individual to another. In discussing heritability we are focusing exclusively on the 10% of the human genome that does vary.

The two main methods through which behavioral scientists have sought to make heritability estimates for personality traits are studies of twins and studies of adopted children. In the case of twin studies, the usual design is to obtain a sample of monozygotic (MZ) twins and a sample of dizygotic (DZ) twins, to administer measures of traits or other variables to the participants, to compute correlations between the trait scores for respective members of twin pairs, and finally to compare the magnitude of the correlations obtained for the MZ twins and the DZ twins. Let us make up an example. Say that we administered a measure of the trait "punctuality" to a sample of 50 MZ twin pairs and 50 DZ twin pairs—200 participants in all. In the DZ subsample, we obtained a correlation coefficient of +.30 between punctuality scores of respective twins. This means that there was a modest positive association between punctuality scores of the twins—when one member of the twin pair scored high on punctuality, there was a slight tendency for the other member of the twin pair to score high, and so on. Among the MZ twins, we obtained a correlation coefficient of +.50, indicating a much stronger positive association. While DZ twins seem to be moderately similar to each other on this trait, MZ twins appear to be rather more similar to each other, as indicated by the stronger magnitude of the correlation coefficient. Why should that be? MZ twins and DZ twins share environments, but while MZ twins also share all their genes, DZ twins share only half their genes on the average. In simple terms, the big difference between the MZ and DZ pairs is in genetic similarity. If the MZs are more similar to each other on punctuality than the DZs, then the difference must be due to their greater genetic similarity. Punctuality would appear to be heritable.

How heritable might punctuality be in our hypothetical example? Researchers have developed a simple formula for estimating heritability in twin studies. The formula makes certain assumptions that are not necessarily true in all studies, but for our purposes here the formula works well to illustrate the concept. To provide a rough estimate of heritability in twin studies, one may simply subtract the DZ correlation from the MZ correlation and then multiply by 2. In other words:

$$h^2 = 2(r_{mz} - r_{dz})$$

where h^2 is the heritability quotient, r_{mz} is the correlation between respective trait scores for MZ twins, and r_{dz} is the correlation between respective trait scores for DZ twins. Plugging in our numbers for the punctuality example, we find that

$$h^2 = 2(.50 - .30)$$

Our rough estimate for heritability is .40. According to the logic of this make-believe study, approximately 40% of the variability in the trait of punctuality in this population can be attributed to genetic differences among people. Approximately 60% of the variance in punctuality, therefore, remains at this point unexplained.

Adoption studies follow a similar logic. In this case, researchers typically examine the extent to which adoptive children share similar traits with members of their adoptive families, typically with siblings. Like DZ twins, biologically related siblings share about 50% of common genetic endowment. By contrast, adopted children are biologically unrelated to the members of their adoptive family, and therefore have 0% common genetic endowment. As in twin studies, researchers may wish to compare correlations between trait scores of two different groups: pairs of biological siblings (50% common genetic endowment) and pairs of nonbiologically related (e.g., adoptive) siblings (0% common genetic endowment). Evidence for heritability can be obtained when correlations between trait scores of biologically related siblings significantly exceed correlations between trait scores of nonbiologically related (e.g., adoptive) siblings.

Adoption studies shed light on nature and nurture in other ways, too. Say, for example, that a researcher is able to locate the biologically related parents or siblings of adoptive children and administer trait measures to them. In this case, any significant positive correlations that a researcher would obtain between trait scores of adoptive children and biologically related relatives would have to be due to genetic effects, since these individuals did not share environments. In a similar way, any significant positive correlations obtained between trait scores of adoptive children and their (nonbiologically related) siblings would have to indicate common environmental effects. Remember that adoptive siblings share no common genetic endowment with their siblings in the adoptive family. Consequently, if we were to find a significant positive correlation between punctuality scores of adoptive siblings, then we would have to conclude that growing up in the same family had some effect in making these siblings somewhat similar to each other on this trait.

Twin and adoption studies are natural experiments through which researchers are able to estimate the relative power of genetic and environmental differences in accounting for trait variation within a sample of people. The logic of twin and adoption studies undergirds research in the growing field of **behavior genetics.** Behavior genetics is a scientific discipline, with roots in psychology, genetics, biology, and related fields, that explores the empirical evidence concerning the relative influences of genetic and environmental factors in accounting for variability in human behavior (Rowe, 1997, 1999). Increasingly in recent years, research in behavioral genetics has employed complex statistical modeling procedures in which data from different family constellations and types are combined to test hypotheses about nature and nurture. Still, twin and adoption studies form the basis for many of the field's central findings about heritability of personality traits. Now that we have covered the basics, we must ask: What does the research show?

Heritability Estimates of Traits

The research shows that *virtually all personality traits that can be reliably measured are at least moderately heritable.* The evidence is especially compelling from twin studies. A huge study of 13,000 adult twins in Sweden obtained heritability estimates of slightly more than 50% for both extraversion and neuroticism traits (Floderus-Myrhed, Pedersen, & Rasmuson, 1980). Other twin studies have yielded moderately high heritability quotients (between .30 and .60) for a range of personality traits measured on a number of scales and personality inventories (Loehlin & Nichols, 1976; Rushton, Fulker, Neale, Nias, & Eysenck, 1986). In the University of Minnesota study, broad heritabilities (over 40%) were obtained for the traits of leadership/mastery, traditionalism (tendency to follow rules and respect authority), stress reaction (similar to neuroticism), absorption (the tendency to become engrossed in sensory experiences), alienation, well-being, avoidance of harm, and aggressiveness (Tellegen, Lykken, Bouchard, Wilcox, Segal, & Rich, 1988).

In an authoritative review of behavioral genetic studies in personality, Robert Plomin and colleagues (1990) conclude that

> genetic influence on self-report measures of personality is nearly ubiquitous. Much of this evidence relies on comparisons between correlations for identical, or monozygotic (MZ), and fraternal, or dizygotic (DZ), twins. On average, across diverse personality dimensions, MZ correlations are about .50 and DZ correlations are about .30. These twin correlations suggest that genetic influence on personality is not only significant but substantial. Doubling the difference between the two correlations results in an estimate that heritability, the proportion of phenotypic variance explained by genetic variance, is 40%. (Plomin, Chipuer, & Loehlin, 1990. p. 226)

Studies conducted in the 1990s examining directly the Big Five traits add further support for the conclusions of this review. Table 7.5 shows intraclass correlations on self-report measures of the Big Five traits for a sample of 123 MZ and 127 DZ twin pairs (Jang, Livesley, & Vernon, 1996). As you can see, the correlations for MZ pairs range from +.37 for conscientiousness to +.58 for openness to experience while the

Identical twins at age 18
Source: Rebecca R. Pallmeyer

correlations for DZ pairs range from +.18 for neuroticism to +.27 for conscientiousness. For the traits of neuroticism, extraversion, and openness, the MZ correlations are more than twice as large in magnitude as the DZ correlations. Based on these correlations and other statistical procedures, the authors of the study concluded that heritabilities for the Big Five traits were mainly in the 40%–50% range, with the strongest heritability in this study shown for openness to experience.

Other studies have shown similar heritability estimates for self-report measures of the Big Five traits. Loehlin, McCrae, and Costa (1998) used sophisticated statistical procedures that attempt to fit data to various theoretical models in a re-analysis of self-report trait ratings made by 490 MZ and 317 DZ twin pairs in 1962, when all the participants were high school students. The authors obtained heritability estimates ranging from 51% to 58% for the Big Five traits. They concluded that the Big Five trait dimensions are substantially and about equally heritable. Jang, McCrae, Angleitner, Riemann, and Livesley (1998) analyzed twin data from Canada and Germany and found that not only do the Big Five dimensions show substantial heritability but that many of the smaller traits or facets that make up each of the Big Five summary dimensions also appear to be substantially heritable.

Riemann, Angleitner, and Strelau (1997) examined both self-report and peer-report measures of the Big Five traits. In their study, the researchers asked 660 MZ and 304 DZ twin pairs, ranging in age from 14 to 80 years, to complete a standard measure of extraversion, neuroticism, openness, agreeableness, and conscientiousness. In addition, each twin was asked to identify two friends, relatives, or acquaintances who would be

TABLE 7.5	Twin Correlations for the Big Five Traits	
	MZ TWINS	**DZ TWINS**
Neuroticism	.41	.18
Extraversion	.55	.23
Openness	.58	.21
Agreeableness	.41	.26
Conscientiousness	.37	.27

Source: Adapted from Jang, Livesley, & Vernon (1996), p. 584.

willing to complete the same questionnaire *as it applied to the twin.* Therefore, the researchers collected three different measures of Big Five traits on each twin—one self-report measure and two peer-report measures from friends, relatives, or acquaintances. The researchers found that heritability for self-report measures of the Big Five traits appeared to be around 50%, as has been shown in other twin studies. However, the heritability estimates based on peer reports were even higher, ranging from 57% for agreeableness to an astonishing 81% for openness to experience. In general, there is no consensus as to whether a self-report or a peer-report measure of a personality trait is the more accurate. For sure, self-report measures are more commonly used. As we saw in Chapter 5, self- and peer-report measures are typically strongly correlated with each other, but of course, they are not the same. This study suggests that when Big Five traits are assessed by peer ratings, the evidence for substantial influence of genetic differences on trait variability is even stronger than when the traits are assessed directly through self-report.

Conservatively speaking, then, twin studies consistently suggest that personality traits are at least moderately heritable and in some cases substantially so. Heritability estimates are typically in the 40%–50% range, though some studies show even higher values. This simple story, however, gets a bit more complicated when you consider two puzzling findings that continue to emerge. The first is that some studies show MZ correlations that are *more than twice as high as* DZ correlations. Indeed, the data in Table 7.5 reveal this to be true for openness, extraversion, and neuroticism. As another example, in four large twin studies of extraversion and neuroticism totalling over 23,000 pairs of twins, the weighted average MZ and DZ correlations were about .51 and .18 respectively. For neuroticism, the corresponding MZ and DZ correlations were .48 and .20, respectively (Loehlin, 1989). The conventional wisdom on twin studies is that, because MZ twins share 100% common genes and DZ twins share 50% common genes, MZ twins should be no more than twice as similar to one another as DZ twins. In other words, genetic variance should be *additive.* A second puzzling finding is that studies of adoption yield *significantly lower heritability estimates.* If heredity is a major factor in determining traits, then we would expect that biological siblings (50% common genes) should be significantly more similar to each other than adoptive siblings (0% common genes). But this does not seem to be the case. A number of adoption studies suggest surprisingly small differences between correlations, yielding heritability estimates around 20% (Loehlin, Willerman, & Horn, 1987; Scarr, Webber, Weinberg, & Wittig, 1981).

Let us put these two puzzling findings in the simplest possible language: First, for some traits (like extraversion) *identical twins seem to be even more similar to each other* (over twice as similar to each other as fraternal twins) than expected. Second, adoption studies suggest that *biological siblings are less similar to each other* (only barely more similar to each other than are adoptive siblings) than expected. Your relative standing on personality traits bears only modest similarity to that of your biological siblings (including fraternal twins), your parents, your cousins, or anybody else to whom you are biologically related, unless, of course, you have an identical twin, in which case the two of you are likely to be remarkably similar (Dunn & Plomin, 1990). When it comes to personality traits measured on self-report questionnaires, why are you likely to be so remarkably similar to an identical twin and so remarkably dissimilar to anybody else with whom you share common genes?

One possible explanation is **nonadditive genetic variance.** Genes may not influence traits in a linear, additive way, but rather combine and interact in a "configural" pattern in which all components are essential and "the absence of, or a change in any one (i.e., any gene) can produce qualitative or a large quantitative change in the result" (Lykken et al., 1992). Thus, if two individuals (DZ twins or any biological siblings) share only 50% common genes, they may be *less than half* as similar to each other as are two individuals (MZ twins) who share 100% common genes: Because genes influence traits in a nonadditive fashion, 100% is, in a sense, *more than twice* as large as 50%. I am not likely to be concordant with my brother (we are not MZ twins) on, say, extraversion because the nonadditive genetic configurations that may be required to give us a similar extraversion makeup cannot occur (unless we share 100% of our genes). There is a threshold in trait genetics. Either your genotype is the same as another person's (MZ twins) or it isn't (everybody else). If it is the first, then your trait ratings are likely to be very similar to those of your MZ twin, the data suggest. If it is the second, you are probably not especially similar (in traits) to anybody in your family, although there is likely to be some modest similarity. Merely sharing 50% common genes with another (a sibling) does not make much of a bang in making the two of you all that similar. In this sense, 50% *is not much more than* 0%. Thus, biological siblings (non-MZs) are not very much more similar to each other than are adoptive siblings. This may be one of the answers, write Dunn and Plomin (1990), to the question of "why siblings are so different."

The possibility of nonadditive genetic effects on personality traits is an example of what some psychologists call **emergenesis.** Emergenesis is "an emergent property of a configuration of genes or perhaps a configuration of more basic traits that are themselves genetic in origin" (Lykken et al., 1992, p. 1569). What this means is that certain patterns of genes may give rise to particular behavioral tendencies that would not themselves be produced, even in a weaker or more attenuated form, by the pieces that make up the pattern. The behavioral tendency is an emergent property of the pattern. A simple analogy for this comes from playing poker. Think of your biological mother and father as each holding a hand of six cards, which represent their genes. The cards all come from the same deck, so your mother's and father's cards are different from each other—that is, they are genetically dissimilar. Your mother has an ace, two kings, a seven, a five, and a four. Your father has a king, a jack, a ten, a seven, and two sixes. To make you, they each randomly contribute (copies of) three cards (half their genes) to make a new hand. You (the new hand) get both of your mother's kings, her seven, your father's king, his seven, and his four. What do you have? You have a "full house"—three kings and two sevens (and a four). A full house is a pretty good poker hand, and (more importantly) it is very different from the hands your parents have. They each have "two of a kind." The point I am making (besides showing that you have beaten your parents in poker) is that the value of your poker hand is determined by its unique configuration of cards. The cards came from two other hands that did not have this unique configuration. The full house is an emergent property of the new configuration. So, too, may certain behavioral tendencies be emergent properties that come from particular configurations of genes. Genotypes are like poker hands with millions and millions of cards. The cards combine in complex ways to produce a wondrous variety of patterns. With the exception of MZ twins, every person is dealt a unique hand.

Shared Environment

What about the environment? If heritabilities for personality traits are in the 40%–50% range, that still leaves over 50% of the variance in trait scores unaccounted for. That must mean half or more of the variance in personality traits can be explained by environmental effects, such as child-rearing styles, family patterns, schools, neighborhoods, and the like. Right? Not exactly. The issue of environmental effects on traits turns out to be much more complicated than you might expect and, for many people, quite surprising.

Let us begin with data from the University of Minnesota study that examined twins reared together and apart (Tellegen et al., 1988). Table 7.6 provides intraclass correlations for a number of self-report personality trait scales for MZ twins only. In the first column you find correlations for 217 MZ twin pairs who each grew up in the same family. In the second column, you find correlations for 44 MZ twin pairs reared apart. Each of these 44 cases involves adoption. One member of the MZ pair, therefore, grew up in one particular family and the other member of the MZ twin pair grew up in another family. In most cases, the twins had no contact with each other in childhood and were reunited (in some cases for the first time) by the University of Minnesota study. Therefore, the first group of MZ twins were reared together, sharing a common childhood environment. The second group was reared apart.

What do you make of the correlations in Table 7.6? First, we see that the correlational values for the MZ twins reared together on such traits as "social potency" and "stress reaction" are in line with what we have come to expect in studies that have examined other and similar traits. The correlations range from +.41 to +.65 for the 11 traits listed, with an average value of +.52. This is old news; these correlations are very similar, for example, to those displayed for MZ twins in Table 7.5 for the Big Five traits. The second thing we should note in Table 7.6, however, is that the correlational values for the twins reared apart are, in many cases, almost identical to those of the MZ twins reared together. The average value is +.49. What does this mean? It essentially means that MZ twins reared apart are just about as similar to each other as MZ twins reared together. But shouldn't the common environments experienced by the MZ twins reared together be worth something? Given the substantial heritability of

TABLE 7.6	Twin Correlations for Monozygotic Twins Reared Together and Apart	
TRAIT	**MZ TOGETHER**	**MZ APART**
Well-being	.58	.48
Social potency	.65	.56
Achievement	.51	.36
Social closeness	.57	.29
Stress reaction	.52	.61
Alienation	.55	.48
Aggression	.43	.46
Control	.41	.50
Harm avoidance	.55	.49
Traditionalism	.50	.53
Absorption	.49	.61
Mean correlation	.52	.49

Source: Adapted from Tellegen et al. (1988), p. 1035.

personality traits, we should not be surprised that MZ twins reared apart would have similar traits. But shouldn't MZ twins *reared together* be even *more* similar to each other? Looking over Table 7.6, the only trait that seems to show an expectable pattern like this is social closeness, for which the MZ-together correlation (+ .57) is markedly larger than the MZ-apart correlation (+ .29). Otherwise, the evidence for the effects of common environment is sparse.

In general, twin studies and adoption studies have shown that *growing up in the same family seems to have little, if any, impact on personality traits.* There are a few exceptions to this rule. For example, there is some evidence that certain traits having to do with intimacy and love for others, such as the "social closeness" trait tapped in the Minnesota study, may show family environment effects (Plomin, Chipuer, & Loehlin, 1990; Waller & Shaver, 1994). Juvenile delinquency, furthermore, appears to show considerable influence of family environment, although adult criminality does not (Miles & Carey, 1997). Another exception involves severe maltreatment. Child abuse and extraordinary neglect do appear to have deleterious effects on psychological development, which show up clearly in personality traits. But these sometimes tragic situations are still relatively rare, at least in modern societies. The vast majority of children grow up in families that, while imperfect, offer expectable rudimentary care (Scarr, 1997). It is, therefore, within this broad spectrum of average expectable environments that research has repeatedly failed to show measurable effects of family environments on personality traits.

For example, it appears that most of the modest positive association (correlation) found between siblings (including DZ twins) on personality traits is a function of the fact that siblings share about half of their genes in common. Once you take into consideration the trait similarity that is due to genetic similarity, there is virtually no trait similarity left over to attribute to the fact that the siblings grew up in the same environments. Adoption studies offer even clearer evidence. Typically, adoptive children show virtually no predictable similarity on traits to the members of the families who adopt them, even after they have lived in the family for many years. Eaves, Eysenck, and Martin (1989), for example, found that the correlation between adopted children and their *biological* mothers (whom they had never met) on extraversion was +.21, while the correlation between these same children and their adoptive mothers (who raised them) was essentially zero (−.02).

If you find nothing counterintuitive in these results, then you are not reading carefully enough. These studies are saying that the kind of family environment people experience growing up has little or no effect on their personality traits. How caring and loving your parents were, the level of conflict in your family, the quality of the schools you attended, the kind of neighborhood you lived in, the church your family went to, how much your parents emphasized discipline and hard work growing up, the degree of wealth or poverty you experienced—none of this mattered. Nor will it matter with respect to your own children's traits, the research suggests. In teaching personality psychology for almost 20 years, my experience has been that students (and many colleagues) simply do not believe these results. How can it be that family doesn't matter? Such a claim flies in the face of some of our most cherished beliefs.

There is no easy way to get around these findings. The data are clear: Approximately half of the variance in personality traits can be attributed to genetics; with a few exceptions, virtually none of the variance can be attributed to family environment. This still leaves, however, about half of the variance in personality traits. What accounts for the large amount of variation that cannot be accounted for by genetic and family effects? There are two answers. First, trait measures contain error, which adds unexplainable variation. Even the most reliable index of extraversion does not give you exactly the same score for the same person from one day to the next. Test–retest reliabilities of good trait measures may be between +.80 and +.90—really good, but not perfect. These scales are not as accurate and reliable as thermometers. Therefore, it is likely that some of that unexplained variance in traits is simply a function of error in the measures. Psychologists have estimated that as much as 10%–20% of the variance in scores for trait measures in any given sample is simply due to the inherent imperfections in the measurement devices used. Nonetheless, this still leaves a lot of variance unexplained.

The second answer involves making a key distinction between two different kinds of environmental effects. Up until now, when I have been talking about environmental effects on traits, I have been implicitly referring to what behavior geneticists call **shared environment** effects. Shared environment effects are those *environmental influences that operate to make family members alike*. These would include various kinds of conditions and experiences that different members of a family might share and that might, therefore, work to increase similarity among family members. Most of what we think of when we think of family environments fits into the concept of shared environment—such things as amount of family conflict, warmth, discipline, and so on. Also included would be social class, parents' education, and other social structural variables that impact the family as a whole. As we have already noted, shared family environment effects on personality traits appear to be very small. By contrast, **nonshared environment** effects are *environmental influences that operate to make family members unalike*. Many researchers now believe that nonshared environmental effects must account for the rest of the variance in personality traits. But what is a nonshared environment, and how would these effects work?

Nonshared Environment

If you talked to my wife and her brother, you would never think that the two grew up in the same family. While my wife recalls many happy family scenes and lively interactions among her siblings, her brother remembers a lot more tension and conflict. Their accounts of what are supposedly the very same scenes from the past—a family vacation in the Canadian Rockies, for example—have virtually nothing in common. It makes you wonder about social reality—does it even exist or is it all in the minds of the beholders? Their discordant accounts also, however, begin to make clear the concept of nonshared environments. Just because people grow up in the same family, it does not follow that they experience the family in the same way. Indeed, there are many factors within family environments that vary significantly across family members. A good example is birth order. Firstborn and laterborn children occupy very different positions in the family system. A major part of the firstborn's nonshared environment may be the exalted status of being the oldest, biggest, strongest, and smartest. The second-born may need to scramble to find a comfortable niche in the family system, making for a very different experience of family life. As you will see in Feature 7.A, psychologists and laypersons alike have expressed considerable interest in the issue of birth order effects as one kind of nonshared environmental influence on personality traits.

Rowe (1999) lists six categories of nonshared family effects. *Perinatal trauma* are injuries or damage sustained by the fetus before birth. Trauma of this sort differentiate the child from all other family members from the beginning. *Accidental events* run the gamut from physical injuries to winning the raffle prize at the state fair. Chance happenings and lucky breaks may have an impact on personality, serving to differentiate a child further from other family members. *Family constellation* is Rowe's third category, and it includes birth order and birth spacing between siblings. A fourth category is *sibling mutual interaction*. Children in a family interact with one another in complex ways over time, forming alliances of various sorts, competing and cooperating, adopting a wide range of social roles. The third daughter in a family of five children may develop an especially close relationship with the youngest daughter, who goes to her for help and counsel. The second daughter is left out of this relationship and establishes a closer bond instead with the oldest child in the family, who is the only son. It is possible that such nonshared family patterns might have some differential impact on the development of personality traits. Fifth is *unequal parental treatment*—a favorite in many families. Mom always liked you the most! Dad played sports with the sons but ignored the daughters. And so on. Finally, there are *influences outside the family*, such as teachers and peers. Though we lived in the same home and went to the same school, my brother and I had very different friends and different teachers. Such differential experience may have some impact on the development of personality.

The nonshared influence of peer groups has been highlighted by Judith Harris (1995) in her **group socialization theory of development.** Harris notes that shared environments appear to have little influence on personality traits. She questions the almost sacred assumption in American society that what parents do in the family really matters with respect to how children eventually "turn out." The main impact of parents on children, Harris avers, is biological. Parents pass on their genes, but that is about it. She writes:

Group socialization theory explains the shaping of adult personality characteristics in terms of the child's experiences outside the parental home. It is important to note that this theory does not imply that children can get along without parents. Children are emotionally attached to their parents (and vice versa), are dependent on them for protection and care, and learn skills within the home that may prove useful outside of it; these facts are not questioned. What [group socialization] theory implies is that children would develop into the same sorts of adults if we left them in their homes, their schools, their neighborhoods, and their cultural and subcultural groups, but switched all the parents around. (Harris, 1995, p. 461)

Harris's claim is provocative. Substituting for the impact of parents, she maintains, are various socialization experiences that children have outside the home. For the most part, these experiences would serve to make children somewhat different from other members of their family, since each child is likely to be involved in a different set of group experiences. Children learn separately how to behave at home and how to behave outside the home, Harris argues. As children get older, the outside-the-family behavior system takes precedence and eventually becomes incorporated into adult personality traits. A main group that children identify with when they are outside the home is the peer group—a group of others who share socially relevant characteristics such as age, gender, ethnicity, and (in adolescence) abilities and interests. Children's peer groups create culture and pass it on; over time, children move through a series of child-created cultures. As children identify more strongly with their own peer groups (in-group favoritism), they distance themselves from other groups (out-group hostility), which serves to enhance their similarity to in-group members and accentuate their dissimilarity to members of other groups. These group socialization processes are assumed to have a major impact on the shaping of personality characteristics in childhood and adolescence, and to eventually find their way into adult personality traits.

To date, ideas are many but data are few when it comes to understanding the workings of nonshared environment effects. While proposals about such nonshared influences as differential parental treatment (within the family) and group socialization processes (outside the family) seem reasonable, there is not yet much research to support the claims directly. The entire arena of nonshared environment influences on personality traits remains wide open for future research.

As portrayed in Figure 7.3 (on page 404), Dunn and Plomin (1990) estimate that nonshared environment effects account for as much as 35% of the variance in personality traits. They attribute 40% to genetic effects, 20% to measurement error, and only 5% to the effects of shared environments. Given what we know to date, their estimates make good sense. However, it is important to note that the 35% figure for nonshared environments comes by way of a process of elimination. The logic is this: We have strong evidence for heritabilities of at least 40% for almost all personality traits; we have little evidence to support a figure any higher than about 5% for shared environment effects, and it may indeed be even lower; we have good reason to believe that error accounts for at least 10%–20% of the variance, so we'll round up. That leaves us with 35% unexplained variance. The 35% must be attributable to nonshared environment effects *because there is nothing left to attribute it to!* Therefore, while it makes good sense to contend that personality traits may be influenced by nonshared environments, we do not as yet know exactly what those environments are or how they work.

FEATURE 7.A

Birth Order: A Nonshared Environmental Effect

In his popular book, *Born to Rebel: Birth Order, Family Dynamics, and Creative Lives*, Frank Sulloway (1996) makes a very strong case for the power of birth order as a nonshared environmental influence in personality. Adopting a Darwinian perspective on family dynamics, Sulloway argues that children compete for parental investment in any family setting. Blessed with a natural advantage by virtue of being first on the scene, oldest children are likely to identify strongly with the parents and to adopt the traditional viewpoints of authority writ large. By contrast, later-borns must define themselves over and against the dominant firstborns so that they can carve out a niche that will bring them parental resources. Consequently, later-borns are more likely to adopt a rebellious and contrarian attitude toward authority. One interesting result of this development is that later-borns should be more open to innovation and change. In simple trait terms, firstborns should be more dominant (an aspect of extraversion in the Big Five) and perhaps conscientious while later-borns should be more open to experience.

Sulloway finds rather extraordinary support for his hypotheses by examining historical records. In one of his studies, he surveyed the published responses of 19th-century scientists to the introduction of Darwin's theory of evolution. Darwin (himself a later-born) launched a scientific revolution that defied the authority of the church as well as many accepted scientific canons of the day. Following the publication of his landmark *Origin of the Species* in 1859, the historical record shows that later-born scientists were 4.4 times more likely to support Darwin's revolutionary views than were firstborn scientists. During the hundred years or so before the publication of Darwin's theory but during which time evolutionary ideas were being debated in the scientific community, later-born scientists were 9.1 times more likely to support evolutionary perspectives than were firstborns. Sulloway finds similar results for initial reactions of scientists to the discoveries of Copernicus, Newton, and Freud. Eager to embrace perspectives that challenge the status quo, later-borns are more open to innovation and more willing to accept radical theoretical change, Sulloway

How Genes Shape Environments

When we attempt to account for variation in personality traits by appealing to genetic and environmental effects, we typically assume that genes and environments are two different things. In a literal sense, this is true. Genes are segments of DNA; environments are things like families, neighborhoods, and social classes. But, in another sense, the separation between the two is misleading, for the effects of genes and environments often get mixed up in the making of behavior. Rather than exerting independent effects on behavior, genes and environments seem to work together. However, this collaboration between the two is not fully reciprocal. Environments cannot readily influence a person's genes. No matter how many soothing experiences a temperamentally contends. More conservative and invested in the norms of authority, firstborns resist these innovations at first, though if the innovation begins to bear fruit, firstborns will eventually catch on. Once they do catch on, firstborns will strive to attain dominant positions in the new status quo.

Sulloway's predictions are not new. The same kinds of hypotheses were put forth by the psychoanalytic theorist Alfred Adler (Chapter 12 in this book) in the early years of the 20th century. Adler predicted that firstborns should be relatively conservative and power-oriented while second-borns should be rebellious, competitive, and skeptical of authority. Despite Adler's theorizing and Sulloway's compelling historical examples, empirical research on personality traits and birth order has not produced many clear-cut findings (Falbo, 1997; Forer, 1977; Sampson, 1962; Schooler, 1972). Among the few consistencies in the literature is a tendency for firstborns to be somewhat more achievement-oriented than later-born siblings. First-borns also tend to score higher on intelligence tests (Zajonc, 1976), though the differences are small.

Birth order may exert a small effect on personality, but the effect is mediated by such demographic factors as sex, social class, and ethnicity, and by a host of other variables that are more difficult to assess. Without intensive study of each family, it is difficult to know what a particular ordinal position means in a particular family constellation. A firstborn son in a large intact Catholic family living in a working-class section of Boston is likely to have a very different experience of family life than a firstborn daughter of a small but wealthy Florida family where the parents are divorced and in which neither parent claims a religious affiliation, both parents travel extensively, and the daughter spends the weekdays with Mom and the weekends with Dad.

Nonetheless, Sulloway's historical presentation has rekindled interest among psychologists in birth order, and new research may be in the offing. Many laypersons are convinced that their own ordinal position in the family profoundly shaped who they are. Parents often explain differences in their children in terms of birth order. Indeed, I have found myself doing it. By the age of 10, my older daughter seemed to have "bought the system," as a friend of mine says. My younger one—she was born to rebel.

irritable infant enjoys, the genes that are (partially) responsible for that irritable temperament will not be altered. The behavior may change; the infant may even become a much less irritable person; but the genes, they stay the same. By contrast, genes themselves do seem to influence environments. Genes alter and shape how people experience their environments, and genes shape what environments people will choose to experience.

As a striking indication of just how mixed up genes can be in the determination of environments, recent studies in behavior genetics suggest that *environments themselves are heritable*. For example, MZ twins reared together report their environments to be more highly similar than do DZ twins reared together. Plomin and Bergmann (1991) reviewed many different measures of socialization environments and concluded that

FIGURE 7.3   *Components of Variance in Personality Traits*

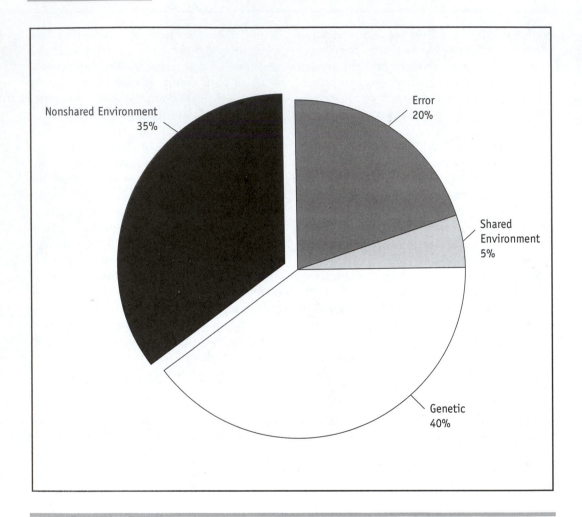

Source: Dunn & Plomin (1990), p. 50.

these measures are likely to be confounded with genetic variation. We typically see the environments as "out there," independent of the observer. And, of course, environments themselves literally have no DNA. But researchers typically measure "out there" environments through the reports of people who are experiencing them. To find out how warm and responsive an adolescent's parents are, a researcher may ask the adolescent. The adolescent's report of her environment, however, is influenced by her own genotype. People may be predisposed to see their environments in a certain way. "What appear to be stable and enduring features of the environment," writes Caspi

(1998, p. 352), "may be a reflection of stable, enduring, and partially heritable individual differences" in personality traits.

Researchers have found that the influence of genetic differences on perceptions of environments seems to increase with age. Elkins, McGue, and Iacono (1997) examined how MZ and DZ twins in two different age groups—11-year-old boys and 17-year-old boys—described their family environments. All of the twins in this study were males. MZ twins were more similar than DZ twins in their reports of parent–son conflict, parental involvement, and overall support from parents. This finding suggests that these dimensions of the family environment, as measured through the perceptions of the male adolescents in this study, are partially heritable. In addition, the 17-year-olds showed significantly higher heritabilities on family dimensions than did the 11-year-olds, especially in the realm of the father–son relationship. The researchers argued that as adolescents get older, their own partially heritable personality tendencies take on more and more power in shaping their perceptions of their environments. In addition, older adolescents may have more control over their respective environments, shaping their worlds to fit more closely their own genotypes. As children grow up and assume greater responsibility for their own lives, their environments may come under greater and greater genetic control.

But the influence of genes on environments can be traced back even to the first few months of life. Genetic influences manifest themselves through the creation of environments. By virtue of their genetic endowments, infants shape their environments in subtle ways, and those environments, in turn, shape the development of personality, which further shapes environments in an endless cycle of mutual influence. Scarr and McCartney (1983) distinguish among three different ways in which one's genetic endowment, or genotype, may shape the environments that ultimately shape the development of personality traits.

The first way is *evocative influence:* people respond to a child according to its genotype. Easy babies may evoke different patterns of caregiving than difficult babies. Smiling and active babies are likely to receive more attention, at least in many middle-class American families, than somber and irritable ones. Even at the level of infant temperament, therefore, the genotype subtly influences the social environment, which in turn influences the development of the baby.

The second form of genotype-environment influence is *passive influence.* The child's biological parents provide an environment for the child that is compatible with *their own* genotypes, which are similar to the genotypes of their biological children. For example, parents who are genetically inclined to read well and enjoy reading are likely to buy more books for their children and to read to them. Their children are likely, then, to enjoy books and to read well. Twin studies of cognitive abilities suggest that reading ability and interest in reading are influenced by heredity. Thus, by virtue of sharing genetic similarities with the biological parents, a child is likely to be exposed to environments that are relatively consonant with its own genotype, since it is the parental genotypes that partially determine those environments.

Finally, *active influence* manifests itself in the direct selection of and search for environments that fit one's genotype. Active niche choosing and niche creating are well documented in research and everyday experience. A gregarious boy will seek out friends in his neighborhood and thereby partially create the environments that will have an influence on his development. An athletic girl will join the softball team. To the extent that gregariousness and athletic ability are determined by one's genotype, these examples suggest how genotypes may exert an impetus in niche choosing. While evocative and passive influences are likely to predominate in childhood and early adolescence, Scarr and McCartney suggest that the process of active influence of genotype on environment may intensify as the person moves into and through adulthood.

CHANGE AND COMPLEXITY

The very concept of a personality "trait" is biased in favor of continuity over change and simplicity over complexity. Traits are by definition more-or-less stable over time, at least stable enough to warrant the label of "trait" rather than the more fleeting notions of "state," "mood," "momentary feeling," and so on. We have reviewed evidence in this chapter suggestive of substantial differential continuity in trait scores across the adult years. The evidence for heritability of traits, furthermore, implicitly supports a continuity view. We know our genes don't change; therefore, if personality traits are partially determined by genes, then it should not be surprising that over long durations traits do not change very much either. Ideally, traits are simple. By "simple," I mean that they convey clear, straightforward, and nonconditional behavioral tendencies in people. What determines any given behavior in any given situation is likely to be a complex blend of many factors, including many different traits. But in trait psychology, we can single out one discrete personality dimension and examine its manifestations across a range of situations. Over many different situations and over time, highly extraverted people *tend to* engage in more conversations, meet more people, and attend more social events than do highly introverted people. Straightforward and simple. (And generally true.)

If traits were *not* relatively stable over time and if traits did *not* predict simple and broad behavioral tendencies across situations and over time, then it would be very difficult, I would submit, to build a credible science of personality psychology. Our common understanding of human nature has it that people differ from one another in recognizable ways, that at least some of these differences can be communicated in simple words and ideas, and that these differences have some staying power over time. Personality research supports all these claims. But there is more to it. In what remains of this chapter, I seek to emphasize the countervailing notions of change and complexity as they apply to personality traits. I will make three general points:

1. Despite the strong evidence for differential continuity, personality traits can be shown to change over time.

2. Traits are organized in different patterns, and different patterns change in different ways over time.

3. Those aspects of human individuality that appear *most* likely to change dramatically over time are *not* traits at all. There is more to personality than traits.

Different Meanings of Change

We have already seen that the idea of "continuity" in personality traits has many different meanings. So, too, does the idea of change. Some of these meanings parallel the meanings I have already identified for continuity. Recall that *absolute* continuity in traits is typically measured via group averages. If the average score on the trait "exhibitionism" in a group of college seniors is close to the average score this same group showed three years earlier as freshmen, then we can say that exhibitionism in this sample shows absolute continuity over a three-year span. But if the seniors score significantly lower (or higher) as a group than they did as freshmen, then we have evidence for personality change. As a group, these students have moved in a particular direction with respect to this particular trait. This is a common way to think about personality change. By contrast, recall that *differential* continuity refers to the stability of individual differences in trait scores. We have seen that evidence for differential continuity of traits in adulthood is impressive. If a trait, however, did not show high levels of differential continuity, then that would indicate a kind of personality change. But it is difficult to characterize this kind of change, for there is no obvious direction or plan to it. Lack of differential continuity simply means that you cannot readily predict people's scores on a given trait from Time 1 to Time 2. People have changed relative to each other between Time 1 and Time 2. But this absence of differential continuity does not spell out how they have changed.

The idea of personality change conjures up other associations as well. Although change can be for the better or for the worse, people typically strive to change for the better over time. Psychotherapists and counselors are in the business of promoting personality change under the banners of "adjustment," "adaptation," "increased mental health," "better coping," "recovery," and so on. These meanings of change suggest processes of healing and solving life problems. Change becomes the cure or solution. A set of related ideas comes from our understandings of personality *development*, and such associated notions as "maturation," "fulfillment," and "self-actualization." Here we are talking about change in a particular direction and toward something that is usually seen as bigger, better, higher, further along, or more "age appropriate." Change as growth. Ever optimistic about the possibilities of personality growth, Gordon Allport (1961) argued that personality development should ideally move in the direction of five criteria for maturity:

1. emotional security and the regulation of behavior by social rules designed to reduce interpersonal friction and obtain social rewards;

2. the capacity for investing the self in significant life projects and endeavors rather than being preoccupied with immediate needs;

3. the capacity for compassionate and intimate relations with others;

4. a realistic appraisal of self and others; and

5. the establishment of a personally derived philosophy of life.

As we will see in Chapter 10, other developmental theorists have offered their own visions of what personality change *should* look like as people move across the lifespan. Lifespan personality change has been studied by many different researchers, including sociologists and anthropologists. Researchers have tended to adopt variations on two basic research designs. In **cross-sectional studies,** researchers typically compare data from individuals in two or more discrete age groups. For example, a cross-sectional study might compare mean (average) scores on the trait openness to experience among 20-year-old, 30-year-old, and 40-year-old American adults, all sampled in the year

2000. In **longitudinal studies,** by contrast, researchers typically follow a single sample of individuals over time, comparing scores at different age points. Thus, a longitudinal study begun in the year 2000 might obtain openness to experience scores from a sample of 20-year-old American adults and then obtain scores again from the same sample when they turned 30 (2010) and 40 (2020) years of age.

Cross-sectional and longitudinal studies have different strengths and weaknesses. For our purposes, it is worth noting one important limitation of cross-sectional studies. Because cross-sectional studies examine differences among age groups at a given point in time, they do not really examine change and development directly. In our example above, if 40-year-olds score lower in openness to experience than 20-year-olds, we cannot conclude for sure that this is a developmental change. It may instead be an example of a **cohort effect.** In the cross-sectional study, the 20-year-olds and the 40-year-olds are from different birth cohorts. The 20-year-olds were born in 1980; the 40-year-olds in 1960. The two groups are different in age, for sure, but as cohorts they also experienced different historical events and represent different historical generations. Should we find that the 40-year-olds are lower on openness, we would have to entertain the possibility that the difference between the two groups might be due to different historical experiences of the two cohorts, rather than to developmental change per se. It may not be the case that as you get older, you become less open. Instead, perhaps the advent of the Internet in the 1990s profoundly shaped the young minds of the now 20-year-old cohort, making them more open to innovation and change than they would have been had they all grown up in the 1970s. This is not to suggest that cross-sectional studies are not useful in determining personality change. But findings from cross-sectional studies typically need to be supplemented by findings from longitudinal studies before researchers can come to clear conclusions about lifespan change in personality.

Trait Change in the Adult Years

In general, cross-sectional and longitudinal studies do *not* show *dramatic* shifts in personality over the course of the adult lifespan. But evidence for *gradual* and systematic changes in all of the Big Five trait domains *can* nonetheless be found. Overall, studies suggest that traits related to extraversion *(E)*, neuroticism *(N)*, and openness to experience *(O)* may decline gradually from early through middle adulthood while traits related to agreeableness *(A)* and conscientiousness *(C)* may rise gradually during that period. For example, college students typically score higher on measures of *E*, *N*, and *O* than do middle-aged adults, while their scores on *A* and *C* tend to be lower (Costa & McCrae, 1994). A large cross-sectional study conducted among German, Portuguese, Italian, Croatian, and South Korean adults showed a similar pattern: higher levels of *E*, *N*, and *O* and lower levels of *A* and *C* among college-aged adults compared with middle-aged adults (McCrae, Costa, de Lima, Simoes, Ostendorf, Angleitner, Marusic, Bratko, Caprara, Barbaranelli, Chae, & Piedmont, in press). Figure 7.4 shows the data for conscientiousness and openness to experience. As you can see, mean levels for *C* tend gradually to increase and for *O* to decrease as you move from the age 18–21 group through ages 22–29, 30–49, and 50+.

Longitudinal studies show age changes that parallel these cross-sectional findings. In longitudinal followups of college students, Watson and Walker (1996) reported declines in negative affect (related to *N*), and Mortimer, Finch, and Kumka (1982)

FIGURE 7.4 | *Conscientiousness and Openness to Experience Related to Age in Five Nations*

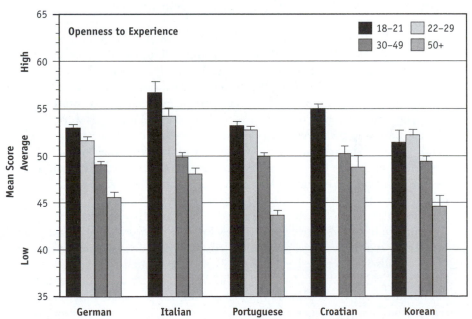

Source: Adapted from McCrae et al. (in press), pp. 28 (top) and 26 (bottom).

reported declines in sociability (related to E) as the participants in their study moved toward middle adulthood. Jessor (1983) found longitudinal increases in achievement (related to C). McGue, Bacon, and Lykken (1993) followed 127 pairs of twins over a 10-year span. The average age of the twins at the beginning of the study was about 20 years old. Although the researchers did not find the expected decrease in extraversion scores over that 10-year period, they did report declines in stress reaction (related to N), absorption (related to O), and aggression (indicating an increase in A), and they found increases in achievement and control (both related to C). Helson and Klohnen (1998) found decreases in negative emotionality (N) and increases in constraint (C) in a sample of 80 women traced from age 27 to 43. Helson and Klohnen also found increases in positive affect. Reviewing research findings like these, Aldwin and Levensen (1994) conclude that "there appears to be a decrease in levels of neuroticism and increases in those personality traits [e.g., aspects of C and A] reflecting competence from early adulthood to midlife" (p. 194).

The development toward greater levels of competence, autonomy, and responsibility with increasing maturity in adulthood is a common theme in longitudinal studies of adult development conducted in the United States (Cartwright & Wink, 1994; Stewart & Vandewater, 1993; Vaillant, 1977). Two especially influential studies in this regard are the AT&T Study (Howard & Bray, 1988) and the Mills College Longitudinal Study (Helson, 1967; Helson & Wink, 1992).

The AT&T Study followed a sample of 266 male managerial candidates at AT&T over 20 years, from the late 1950s, when the men were in their 20s, to the late 1970s, when they were in their 40s. The men were studied in assessment centers, where they were put through behavioral simulations, interviewed, and administered a variety of cognitive, personality, attitudinal, and biographical measures. A major focus of the study was to explore career and personal development among managers in corporate America. One interesting finding in the study was a strong drop in measures of ambition over the 20-year span. At the beginnings of their managerial careers, the young men showed strong levels of ambition and somewhat unrealistic expectations of how far they might climb in the company structure. After only 8 years in the company, however, their ambition scores dropped sharply and they expressed more realistic views of the possibilities of promotion. Still, the managers maintained strong interest in their jobs and strong motivation to do their jobs well. Substantial increases were noted over the 20-year period in measures of autonomy. The men showed increasing levels of independence and focus on productive work as they moved from their mid-20s to their mid-40s. Increasing autonomy, however, may have exacted something of an interpersonal cost for this cohort of men. Over time, the men showed decreases in measures of friendliness and empathy for others. The authors of the study suggest that a move away from brash ambition and toward productive autonomy may characterize many men as they mature from their early years in the work world toward their middle years, during which they typically assume greater and greater levels of responsibility.

The Mills Longitudinal Study began with 140 women who graduated in 1958 or 1960 from Mills College, a small and elite West Coast college for women. As college seniors, the women completed a number of standard personality measures. They were recontacted by mail at ages 27, 43, and 52. The Mills cohort is an especially interesting one because of the significant historical events these women experienced in young and middle adulthood. At the time of their college graduation, American society

Ravenna Helson

generally expected these women to forego careers in favor of marriage and family life. But the Women's Movement of the 1960s and early 1970s galvanized the ambitions of many of these women and strongly impacted how they thought about the relationship between work and family life. A significant number of the women went on to achieve considerable success in their careers, in some cases breaking into male-dominated professions. Researchers have traced both personality change and continuity in the Mills cohort, and they have supplemented their findings on the women with measures of personality obtained from a subset of the women's husbands as well (Helson & Stewart, 1994).

Examining the period from college graduation to age 43, Helson and Moane (1987) documented increases in overall scores on responsibility, self-control, and responsiveness to others among the Mills women. Between the ages of 43 and 52, furthermore, significant changes were noted on a number of other traits. As they moved through their 40s and into their early 50s, the women became increasingly *less* dependent and self-critical and increasingly *more* confident and decisive. Over this time period, significant increases were also noted on the variables of coping through intellectuality, logical analysis, and tolerance for ambiguity. Evidence from this study indicated that the women became increasingly more comfortable with their self-conceptions over time and came to believe more strongly that their accomplishments and commitments reflected well their basic needs and aspirations (Helson & Wink, 1992).

Some theorists have suggested that men and women show different developmental trajectories with respect to personality traits in young adulthood and midlife. For example, Gutmann (1987) has proposed that young parents (say, in their 20s) are likely to show traditional sex-role patterns, with men scoring higher than women on agentic dimensions such as dominance and competence, and women higher on communal dimensions such as nurturance. But once men and women move out of the direct parenting roles (say, in their late 40s), women may become increasingly agentic and men increasingly communal. The Mills Study provides some data to support part of Gutmann's claim. Wink and Helson (1993) compared the Mills women and their husbands in the early parental (age 27) and postparental (age 52) periods of life. Figure 7.5 shows the results for a cluster of self-report adjectives indicative of instrumental "competence." High scorers on competence described themselves as goal-oriented, organized, thorough, practical, efficient, clear-thinking, realistic, precise, and confident. As you can see in the figure, women at age 27 scored lower than their husbands on this dimension, but at age 52 they scored about the same. Figure 7.5 also shows the mean scores for a subsample of the *parents* of the women, contacted in 1961 (shortly after the women had graduated from Mills). As you can see, the women's then-midlife fathers scored much higher on competence than did their wives (the women's mothers). The findings point to the effect of changing gender roles and historical events on personality traits. At age 27, the Mills women looked much like their mothers with respect to competence scores. But by age 52, they looked much more like their fathers had looked when they were of comparable age. The increased societal acceptance of

FIGURE 7.5	*Competence Ratings and Adult Development*

The average scores on competence, measured via the Adjective Check List, increase from early parental to postparental years for wives, more so than for husbands. The figure also shows competence scores for wives' parents in their postparental period, suggesting that as wives age their competence levels come to match their fathers' (relatively high) competence levels, rather than their mothers' (relatively low) levels.

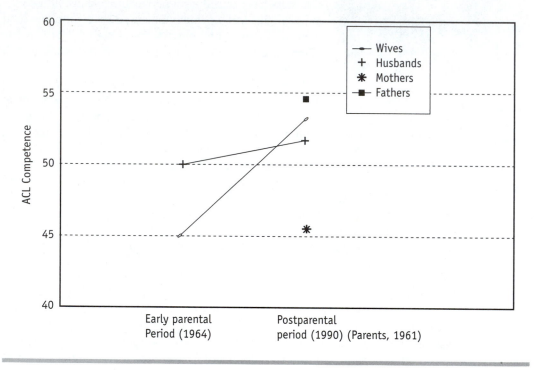

Source: Adapted from Helson & Stewart (1994), p. 214.

women's agency and the movement out of direct parental roles may have combined to bolster the self-confidence of these women in midlife and pull them in the direction of a more agentic and goal-oriented approach to life.

Overall, longitudinal studies of adult development support a case for significant change in personality traits, at least through midlife. (Studies of traits in later adulthood, however, are scarce.) The available data suggest that against the backdrop of considerable stability in individual differences in traits over the adult life course, developmental trends in overall levels can still be observed. As men and women move from early to middle adulthood, they tend to become gradually more comfortable with themselves, showing decreasing levels of self-criticism, negative affect, and other indices of neuroticism. Indices of positive affect appear to rise, even when extraversion scores tend gradually to drop. At the same time, adults appear to increase in responsibility, self-confidence, autonomy, and certain other indices of conscientiousness.

Increases in self-confidence are especially apparent in well-educated women. Though the data are not completely consistent, there is some evidence of a "warming up" in personality from early to middle-adulthood, as people may become somewhat more agreeable and nurturant over time. People tend to feel somewhat better about themselves as they grow older, at least into middle age, and somewhat better about other people, too.

Patterns of Traits Over Time

Many years ago, Jack Block (1971, 1981, 1993) and his colleagues devised a procedure for personality research that has shed considerable light on the issue of personality continuity and change over the human lifespan. While most trait research employs self-report scales that assess individual traits, Block has advocated the use of expert observers who evaluate overall patterns of traits in people's lives. Block pioneered the use of the **California Q-sort** in personality assessment. The Q-sort consists of 100 statements about personality (such as "Is a genuinely dependable and responsible person," "Has a wide range of interests," "Is skeptical, not easily impressed") that a rater sorts into nine different piles, ranging from those statements deemed by the rater to be most characteristic of the individual being rated to those being least characteristic.

In one study, Block trained 36 psychologists to compose Q-sorts for 70 men and 76 women at four different points in the participants' lives. For the four different points in time, Block assembled four separate files, one each for information obtained about the participant when he or she was in early adolescence (age 13–14), late adolescence (15–17), his or her 30s, and his or her 40s. For each of the files, then, a trained psychologist composed a Q-sort for each participant, arranging the 100 personality descriptors into nine groups based on the wide variety of information on the person contained in the file.

One reason the Q-sort is an appealing method is that each of the 100 items is grouped into one of the nine stacks with other items that are relatively equally characteristic of the same individual. Such a procedure enables the researcher to examine *patterns* of personality traits within the person. Furthermore, comparing Q-sorts of the

Jack Block

same individual over time allows the researcher to examine the longitudinal coherence of these patterns. In his study, Block (1981) also identified clusters of individuals manifesting similar patterns of traits over time, some of which are listed in Table 7.7 (page 416). Each cluster represents a personality type, specified in terms of individuals displaying a particular pattern of personality traits that evolves in a particular fashion over time. For example, men who are "belated adjusters" appear rebellious and belligerent in adolescence, but they develop in the direction of conscientiousness and prosocial behavior as adults. As another example, women categorized as "cognitive copers" start out as overly sensitive and insecure in their junior-high years, but they mature over time to emerge as warm, introspective, and independent adults. Block's typology portrays patterns of both continuity and change in personality characteristics over time.

FEATURE 7.B

Happiness Over the Human Lifespan

For many of us, happiness is the bottom line in life. We try to do things that make us happy and avoid things that make us unhappy. When we evaluate how our lives are going, one of the first things we may ask ourselves is this: Am I really happy? Most people report that they are at least moderately happy with their lives. But who are the happiest people? Who are the most unhappy? What causes happiness? And does happiness change over time?

Happiness proves to be an interesting window through which to view continuity and change in personality. Psychologists often use the term "well-being" to refer to what most laypeople mean when they talk of happiness. Well-being is made up of different components, but three main parts of it appear to be positive affect, negative affect, and life satisfaction (Diener, 1984; Myers & Diener, 1995). Although well-being itself may not qualify as a personality trait (there is debate about that idea), some of the conclusions we have drawn in this chapter about traits can be loosely applied to the area of well-being. As with traits, for example, there is evidence for both continuity and change in well-being over the human lifespan.

Virtually everybody knows that well-being can fluctuate from one moment to the next. When you receive that unexpected high grade on a tough assignment, you are likely to feel good, and your well-being shoots way up. A person you are in love with tells you that he or she never wants to see you again, and you find your well-being plummeting to the ocean floor. Some psychologists argue that well-being fluctuates around a *set point* for every individual. Different people have different set points; some people may be predisposed to be happier than others, this argument goes.

Evidence for the set point idea comes from studies showing that despite fluctuations, individual differences in well-being show considerable differential continuity over time (Costa, McCrae, & Zonderman, 1987; Watson & Walker, 1996). There is also surprising evidence to suggest that well-being itself may be heritable. In a study of more than 2,000 twins, Lykken and Tellegen (1996) report that MZ pairs were substantially more similar to each other on a self-report measure of well-being than were DZ pairs. Retesting their participants over a 10-year span, the authors tried to estimate a set point value for each participant, which they determined to be "the stable component of subjective well-being" (p. 186). They concluded that the heritability of this stable component could be as high as 80%.

If individual differences in well-being are strongly driven by genetic differences, do environmental effects have much influence on how happy we are? The answer appears to be that they do in the short run, but perhaps their influence in the long run is less. Day-to-day changes in well-being parallel shifting successes and failures in our lives, but each of us tends eventually to return to our own set point, research suggests. Macrosocial variables such as race, sex, and social class have surprisingly little impact on overall well-being (Myers & Diener, 1995). In the United States, men and women, blacks and whites, show comparable mean levels of well-being. Income and education are only mildly and positively associated with happiness, accounting for less than 2% of the variance in well-being in Lykken and Tellegen's study (1996). Other predictors of well-being include being married and having strong religious convictions, but again these variables show surprisingly small associations with how happy people are. Lykken and Tellegen (1996) offer the disquieting conclusion that happiness is mainly the luck of the draw, a matter of heritability and chance external events:

> If the transitory variations of well-being are largely due to fortune's favors, whereas the midpoint of these variations is determined by the great genetic lottery that occurs at conception, then we are led to conclude that individual differences in human happiness—how one feels at the moment and also how happy one feels on average over time—are primarily a matter of chance. (p. 189)

Do overall levels of happiness change over the lifespan? We have seen that while individual differences in traits can be highly stable, changes in overall levels of trait scores can still be observed over the lifespan. For the variable of subjective well-being, different theories of adult development propose different variations on this same theme. One view has it that since people encounter greater physical limitations and health problems as they get older and because they must endure an increasing number of losses, older adults should show lower levels of well-being than younger adults. By contrast, some theories argue that older adults are better able than the young to regulate their emotional lives by exerting selective control over their interpersonal worlds, which may lead to increases in well-being with age (Baltes & Baltes, 1990; Carstensen, 1995). Findings from different studies provide something of a mixed picture on this question. In a unique cross-sectional examination, for example, Ingelhart (1990) compared single-item self-report happiness ratings made by young, midlife, and elderly adults in 16 countries. He found that some nations showed decreases in happiness among their oldest cohorts (e.g., France, Japan), some showed increases (e.g., Britain, Ireland), some showed a dip in happiness in midlife (e.g., The Netherlands, Canada), and others showed no difference across the age cohorts (e.g., the United States, Greece).

Mroczek and Kolarz (1998) completed an especially comprehensive study of positive and negative affect in 2,727 Americans ranging in age from 25–74 years. Controlling for a host of sociodemographic, personality, and contextual factors, the authors documented systematic relations between age and well-being. Overall, Mroczek and Kolarz found that positive affect tends to go up and negative affect tends to go down across the age span they studied. However, a more detailed analysis revealed different variations on this general pattern for men and women. With respect to positive affect, both men and women showed an increase with age, but men who also scored *high on the trait of extraversion* reported high levels of positive affect *at all ages*. With respect to negative affect, scores went down for men over the lifespan, but women did not show an age-related decrease. Furthermore, among the men marital status had a moderating effect. It was mainly for *married men* that an inverse relation between age and negative affect was found. Older married men showed especially low levels of negative affect. Marriage may increasingly help men, as they get older, to regulate their own emotional states and select the kinds of social and instrumental experiences that minimize feelings of sadness, anger, and despair.

The full answer to the question of how much happiness changes and remains the same over the human lifespan has not yet been spelled out. But Mroczek and Kolarz's careful study shows that the ultimate answer, if one ever arises, will be a complicated one and dependent on many factors.

TABLE 7.7	*Eight Personality Types for Men and Women*

MEN

Ego resilients	Men who showed long-standing characterological integrity and resourceful-ness. In junior high school, they were seen as dependable, productive, ambi-tious, bright, likable, philosophically inclined, and satisfied with self. In their 40s, they continued to exhibit many of these characteristics. As adults, they valued independence and objectivity, and they evaluated situations in motivational terms. On the California Psychological Inventory (CPI), they scored high on dominance, self-acceptance, intellectual efficiency, and psy-chological mindedness.
Unsettled undercontrollers	Men who showed a pervasive impulsivity and changeableness. In junior high school they were seen as rebellious, talkative, hostile, unconventional, ver-bally fluent, irritable, and self-dramatizing. In their 40s, they continued to exhibit undercontrol and were rated especially rebellious, hostile, deceitful, and unpredictable. On the CPI, they scored high on dominance and social presence and scored low on socialization, self-control, achievement via con-formance, and femininity. Over a 10-year span, they changed jobs more than other men.
Vulnerable overcontrollers	Men who showed consistently excessive restriction. In junior high they were seen as aloof, thin-skinned, ruminative, distrustful, submissive, and intro-spective. In their 40s, they were withdrawn, self-pitying, fearful, bothered by demands, and despondent. On the CPI, they scored high on overcontrol and good impression; they scored low on social presence and sense of well-being. They remained bachelors.
Belated adjusters	Men who showed a delayed but impressive adjustment. In junior high they were generally belligerent and negativistic. By contrast, however, as adults they were seen as dependable and sympathetic, though lower in achieve-ment orientation than other men. These men often came from lower socio-economic classes and showed improvement in their socioeconomic standing in adulthood.

Underlying the personality types identified by Block are two central dimensions of personality that organize many different aspects of human functioning. The first is what Block calls **ego control** (Block & Block, 1980). Ego control is the extent to which a person typically modifies the expression of impulses. At one extreme of the ego control continuum are undercontrolled people who cannot inhibit their desires and impulses, cannot delay gratification for longer-term rewards. Such people may be-come enthusiastic about many different things in their lives, but their involvements are fleeting and frustrating. They are distractible and exploratory and seem to live a rela-tively impromptu rather than planned life. At the other extreme are overcontrolled people who are especially conforming and restrained. Their lives may be well scripted, but their inhibitions sometimes keep them from spontaneous joy and creativity. In

WOMEN	
Female prototypes	Women who personified many of the qualities and values prescribed by American society as ideal for women in the 1940s and 1950s. In junior high they were poised, likable, gregarious, cheerful, dependable, warm, productive, giving, sympathetic, and socially perceptive. In their 40s, they continued to show many of these qualities. On the CPI, they scored high on dominance, sociability, social presence, responsibility, and achievement via conformance. They had more children than other women.
Vulnerable undercontrollers	Women who were "homogeneous in their unmodulated impulsivity of action and reaction coupled with a plaintive submissiveness that leaves them open to exploitation by others" (Block, 1981, p. 39). In junior high they were seen as undercontrolled, self-indulgent, changeable, limit-testing, irritable, hostile, brittle, and affected. In their 40s, they were undercontrolled, self-defeating, self-indulgent, socially obtuse, unconventional, and lacking in fastidiousness. On the CPI, they scored low on responsibility, socialization, femininity, and ego control. They married early, more often, and less satisfactorily compared with other women. They smoked too much and were somewhat overweight.
Hyperfeminine repressives	Women who showed a repressive and emotionally fitful adaptation and an ambivalent expression of sexuality. In junior high they were seen as feminine, repressive, submissive, dependable, dependent, and concerned with physical appearance. In their 40s, they continued to be highly concerned with their bodies and physical well-being; they were withdrawing, fearful, brittle, distrustful, self-pitying, moralistic, negativistic, and overcontrolled. On the CPI, they scored high on psychoneurosis and neurotic overcontrol; lower on dominance, social presence, tolerance, flexibility, and achievement via independence. They had significantly more menopausal surgery.
Cognitive copers	Women who showed gradual improvement in adjustment over the years. In junior high they were seen as thin-skinned, uncomfortable with uncertainty, and ruminative. In adulthood, by contrast, they were viewed as introspective, aesthetically sensitive, warm, talkative, straightforward, and valuing independence. These women pursued intellectual interests.

Source: Block (1971, 1981).

general, it would seem that a rating somewhere in the middle of the ego control continuum is one that best fits contemporary American views concerning appropriate adaptation to life and mental health.

The second major dimension underlying Block's types is **ego resiliency.** This is the capacity to *modify* one's typical level of ego control—in either direction—to adapt to the demands of a given situation. In contrast to ego control, ego resiliency would appear to be a characteristic for which "more is better." People who are high on ego resiliency are resourceful and flexible and able to adapt to a wide range of life challenges. In a recent study of the extent to which adolescents are able to delay immediate gratification to obtain longer-term benefits, Funder and Block (1989) found that ego resiliency, ego control, and intelligence all contributed to the significant prediction of delay behavior. Teenagers who scored high on Q-sort ratings suggestive of high ego resiliency and strong (less impulsive) ego control, as well as those who scored high on measures of IQ, tended to reveal the highest levels of adaptive delay behavior.

Taking a somewhat different tack, Norma Haan (1981) has analyzed longitudinal data obtained from 136 adults, some of whom were included in Block's (1981) analysis, for developmental trends in six basic personality factors: *cognitively invested* (verbally fluent, intellectual, philosophically inclined, achievement-oriented), *emotionally under/overcontrolled* (highly volatile and dramatic *versus* calm and restricted), *open/closed self* (self-aware and insightful *versus* conventional and repressive), *nurturant/hostile* (warm and responsive *versus* cold and suspicious), *under/overcontrolled heterosexual* (uninhibited *versus* inhibited in the realm of sexual expression), and *self-confident*. Haan's statistical analyses showed that Q-sort scores on these six dimensions were relatively stable for both men and women over time but more stable for women. Men were more likely than women to show significant change on these dimensions, especially between late adolescence and adulthood. Over time, both men and women, furthermore, appeared to become more cognitively invested, more open to self, more nurturant, and more self-confident. Sexual expressiveness, on the other hand, appeared to reach high levels in late adolescence, drop to lower levels when the subjects were in their 30s, and then rise again to surprisingly strong levels when the participants reached their 40s.

Integrating the work of Block and Haan with a number of other approaches to personality structure, including the Big Five personality traits, York and John (1992) developed a new typology of women's personality at midlife—what they call "the four faces of Eve." York and John argue that personality types should be defined as prototypes rather than discrete categories of traits. As such, types lack clear boundaries but rather shade into each other. While some persons exemplify the central features of a given type, other people appear to reside on the fuzzy boundaries between types, as mixtures or blends that are especially difficult to characterize in a clear-cut fashion.

York and John analyzed longitudinal data on 103 graduates (from the years 1958 and 1960) of Mills College. Included in the data were followup questionnaires administered in 1981, when the women were in their early-to-mid-40s. York and John employed a statistical procedure called "inverse factor analysis," whereby individuals rather than variables are intercorrelated across a wide range of personality characteristics. In the current study, the procedure provided a numerical estimate of the extent to which each of the 103 women was well represented on each of four "person factors": *Individuated*, *Traditional*, *Conflicted*, and *Assured*. In this person-centered rather than variable-centered approach, therefore, each woman in the study could be viewed in terms of "how much" of her personality was well captured by each of the four factors. Some women proved to be "exemplars" of particular factors—"pure" Individuated, Traditional, Conflicted, or Assured types. Other women, by contrast, expressed characteristics that were spread across a number of factors. For example, one woman might appear on the border between Individuated and Traditional; another might show equal elements of three types.

Table 7.8 lists the items from the California Q-set that were most and least characteristic of each of the four person factors. The "factor scores" indicate how strongly a descriptor is associated with the type. A high positive number suggests a strong positive association; a "high" (in terms of absolute value) negative number suggests a strong negative association. Exemplars of the Individuated type combined strong

TABLE 7.8	*Factor Scores of the California Q-Set Items Most and Least Characteristic of Each of Four Person Factors*

ITEM NUMBER/FACTOR	FACTOR SCORE	ITEM NUMBER/FACTOR	FACTOR SCORE
FACTOR 1: INDIVIDUATED		**FACTOR 2: TRADITIONAL**	
Characteristic		**Characteristic**	
71. Has high aspirations	2.2	11. Is protective	2.2
96. Values independence	2.1	2. Is dependable	2.1
16. Is introspective	1.8	5. Is giving	2.1
8. Has high intellectual capacity	1.7	25. Overcontrols needs	2.0
52. Behaves assertively	1.5	7. Has conservative values	1.9
35. Has warmth	1.5	17. Is sympathetic	1.7
3. Has wide interests	1.5	93. Has a feminine style	1.7
66. Has aesthetic sensitivity	1.3	47. Is guilt prone	1.6
Uncharacteristic		**Uncharacteristic**	
30. Gives up, withdraws	−2.3	62. Is nonconforming	−2.5
14. Is genuinely submissive	−2.1	65. Pushes limits	−2.3
97. Is affectively bland	−2.0	53. Undercontrols needs	−2.2
42. Avoids action	−2.0	99. Is histrionic	−2.2
7. Has conservative values	−1.9	94. Expresses hostility directly	−1.9
55. Is self-defeating	−1.6	37. Is guileful, deceitful	−1.9
78. Is self-pitying	−1.6	67. Is self-indulgent	−1,8
37. Is guileful, deceitful	−1.6	50. Is unpredictable	−1.7
FACTOR 3: CONFLICTED		**FACTOR 4: ASSURED**	
Characteristic		**Characteristic**	
72. Questions self-adequacy	2.6	24. Is rational, objective	2.2
68. Is basically anxious	2.3	52. Behaves assertively	2.2
38. Is hostile	2.0	74. Is satisfied with self	2.0
74. Is satisfied with self	2.0	48. Is distant, aloof	2.0
48. Is distant, aloof	2.0	91. Is power oriented	2.0
12. Is defensive	1.8	1. Is critical, skeptical	1.7
40. Is generally fearful	1.8	26. Is productive	1.6
22. Lacks personal meaning	1.4	96. Values independence	1.5
Uncharacteristic		**Uncharacteristic**	
75. Has clear-cut personality	−2.4	90. Is philosophical	−2.3
54. Is gregarious	−2.1	47. Is guilt prone	−1.8
74. Is satisfied with self	−2.1	16. Is introspective	−1.8
84. Is cheerful	−1.8	21. Arouses nurturance	−1.5
33. Is calm, relaxed	−1.8	46. Daydreams, fantasizes	−1.5
50. Is unpredictable	−1.7	40. Is generally fearful	−1.4
77. Is straightforward	−1.5	45. Has a brittle ego	−1.4
29. Gives advice, reassurance	−1.4	19. Seek reassurance	−1.3
83. Is insightful	−1.4		

Source: York & John (1992), p. 499.

ambitions in life with interpersonal warmth and sensitivity. They tended to manifest the highest levels of ego resiliency of all four types and relatively low levels of ego control, suggesting that they were spontaneous and uninhibited in their expression of impulses but that they knew well when to hold themselves back and when to let go. Of all the types, they were the most flexible and adaptive in the expression of their feelings, needs, and desires. With respect to the Big Five traits, they tended to score high on measures of extraversion *(E)*, agreeableness *(A)*, and openness to experience *(O)*. By contrast, the women who exemplified best the Traditional person factor expressed characteristics indicative of high levels of ego control, as well as high scores on the Big Five trait conscientiousness *(C)*. Like the Individuated women, the Traditionals were rated as especially agreeable *(A)*, but unlike the Individuated women they expressed very conservative values about the proper role of women in contemporary society. While they were described as especially giving and sympathetic, the Traditionals were also more prone to feelings of guilt than were women exemplifying the other types.

Exemplars of the Conflicted person factor consistently showed the lowest levels of ego resiliency and highest levels of neuroticism *(N)*. They appeared less satisfied with themselves than the other types; they were described as anxious, hostile, and aloof. Finally, the Assured women appeared to be the most emotionally stable of the four groups, though their stability hinted at narcissism and an interpersonally detached approach to life. They were the most confident, rational, productive, and skeptical women in the group. They showed relatively high levels of ego resiliency and conscientiousness *(C)* and the lowest levels of neuroticism *(N)*. They were the least likely to suffer from guilt and doubt. But they were also the least likely of all the types to engage in fantasy and introspection.

In sum, personality typologies organize groups of trait dimensions into patterns that show both continuity and change over time. Typologies are popular with some personality psychologists because, it is sometimes argued, they provide a more holistic, person-centered understanding of human behavior and experience than is possible through the examination of single, independent traits (Mumford, Stokes & Owens, 1990; Ozer & Gjerde, 1989; Wink, 1996; Zeldow & Bennett, 1997). Furthermore, the kind of typological research inspired by Jack Block's work underscores complexity and change in personality over time, while also providing strong support for the continuity and coherence of adult personality.

What Else Might Change?

It has always been easier to document continuity in personality traits than meaningful and systematic change (Heatherton & Weinberger, 1994). In this chapter, we have seen that evidence for differential continuity in traits, at least across much of the adult lifespan, is very impressive. Of course, the continuity is not perfect, and over many decades of time the retest correlations on personality traits drop somewhat. Still, individual differences in traits show remarkable longitudinal stability. The stability is surely due in part to the significant heritabilities of traits and to the ways in which genotypes contribute to the selection of environments that are consistent with those genotypes themselves. We have also seen that changes in trait levels do indeed occur, as documented in longitudinal studies of individual traits themselves and of constellations or patterns of traits. For example, neuroticism scores seem to drop slowly and conscientiousness scores to increase gradually over the adult lifespan. Developmental movements toward greater levels of autonomy, warmth, and social responsibility have been documented in studies following young adults into their midlife years.

Nonetheless, many adults feel that they have changed in many *other* ways over time (Levinson, 1977; McAdams, 1993; Roberts & Newton, 1987). People often report dramatic turning points in their lives, episodes of quantum change (Miller & C'deBaca, 1994) through which they feel personally transformed. People speak of religious conversions, life-changing events, personal awakenings, recovery and revitalization, changing priorities and goals, identity crises, and the like. People often feel that they have developed through "stages," embarked on personal journeys, and undertaken personal projects designed to fulfill, improve, or even remake the self. Furthermore, psychotherapists and counselors devote themselves to helping people change their lives for the better. An entire industry of self-help guides—from 12-step programs to spiritual advisors—has grown up in America and other modern societies over the past 40 years, premised on the deeply held belief that people can and do change. Given the widespread belief in personality change and the sustained efforts of so many mental health professionals to promote change in personality over time, might we not expect to see *more* and perhaps more dramatic evidence for personality change than we have seen in this chapter?

One response to my question is this: No, we should not expect to see more change, once we realize just how hard it is to change. The massive scientific literature on the effects of psychotherapy and psychoeducational efforts to induce change is littered with hundreds of failed efforts to change people's lives and thousands of studies showing that even when change occurs, it is hard-won and halting. People may feel that significant events in their lives have major impacts on changing their personalities, but these beliefs may be mistaken, argue some experts. Caspi and Moffitt (1993) argue that, if anything, major life changes sometimes accentuate or consolidate the trait tendencies that people have to begin with. Facing a new challenge or encountering a major life transition, an extravert may end up coping with the life change by displaying the same outgoing and sociable tendencies that he or she has been predisposed to display all along, maybe even more so. Consistent individual differences among people sometimes appear most glaring in times of transition, Caspi and Moffitt argue. Events that might be thought to change people may have the paradoxical effect of affirming who they were and how they behaved in the first place.

A second answer to my question goes like this: Sure, people change, but not so much their traits. Significant personality change may occur, but that change may not be captured in a person's trait scores (McAdams, 1994c). As I suggested earlier in this chapter, the concept of the trait is better designed to express the way in which personality is continuous over time rather than the way in which personality changes. The assumption of some degree of longitudinal consistency is built into the very definition of a trait. Dispositional trait measures speak to a level of personality functioning where we expect to see considerable stability and continuity over time. But there may be other levels, other manifestations of human individuality that more readily express how it is that people believe they change over time—and indeed how it is that they really *do* change over time, if not with respect to their traits. Psychotherapists and counselors do not usually aim their interventions directly at personality traits. More often, they tackle specific problems, some of which may have implications for traits. Similarly, when people think of significant personality changes in their own lives, they do not always couch those changes in terms of basic dispositional traits. Their language may suggest instead something more particular than a trait, something that must be understood in the full context of their own lives.

Beyond traits, what other aspects of personality might change over time? A short list might include characteristic desires and wants, goals and motives, life plans and projects, values and beliefs, coping strategies and defense mechanisms, patterns of interests, developmental concerns, conscious preoccupations, hopes, wishes, fears, aversions, expectations for intimate relationships, confidence in one's identity, vision for the future, understanding of the past. All of these things are features of a person's unique adaptation to the world at any given point in time. All of these features go into the making of human individuality, and yet none of them is well expressed as a trait. Personality psychology seeks to give a scientific account of human individuality. Dispositional traits such as extraversion and conscientiousness provide indispensable information about human individuality. It is hard to imagine a science of personality *without* traits. But there is more to personality than traits.

Traits and Beyond

It is time to wrap up our discussion of personality traits and move on to other levels of personality functioning. Chapters 5–7 in this book have focused exclusively on the concept of the personality trait. As you may remember from Chapter 5, there was a time in personality psychology when the trait concept was under strong attack, and many doubted the concept was even necessary for a science of persons. In the late 1960s and 1970s, Walter Mischel and other critics raised important questions about the very legitimacy of the trait idea. Among other things, they argued that traits are sometimes no better than linguistic conveniences that people use to label other people's behavior. Traits don't predict behavior very well. Instead, behavior is strongly driven by the requirements of the situation. At the beginning of the 21st century, however, the trait concept appears to be stronger than ever in personality psychology. As the last three chapters have shown, personality psychologists have made considerable progress in accounting for human individuality in terms of basic dispositional traits. Looking over the past 25 years of research on traits, we can see at least four reasons that the concept of the personality trait has become such an indispensable part of the science of personality psychology:

1. *Traits are more than mere linguistic conveniences.* Standard situationist rhetoric of the 1970s had it that traits are in the minds of observers rather than in the behavior of the people they observe. Social psychologists such as Richard Nisbett argued that when people (and trait psychologists) observe the behavior of others, they make simplistic attributions about cross-situational consistency—fundamental attributional errors—that are, in fact, not supported by empirical evidence (Nisbett & Ross, 1980). Similarly, Richard Shweder and others (Bourne, 1974; Shweder, 1975; Shweder & D'Andrade, 1979) argued that trait ratings simply reflect observers' biases about how different words in language "go together." A significant body of research, however, shows that these critiques were probably more clever than true (Block, Weiss, & Thorne, 1979; Funder & Colvin, 1991; Kenrick & Funder, 1988; Moskowitz, 1990). While there is no doubt that trait ratings reflect in part the subjective cognitive processes of the raters themselves, research shows rather conclusively that when raters are given sufficient opportunity to observe the behavior of those persons whom they are to rate, their ratings are generally both reliable and valid. In other words, trait attributions made by subjective raters are *not* illusions—residing merely in the eyes of the beholder. Rather they reflect real differences in behavior and personality of the people being rated (Funder, 1995).

2. *Many traits show remarkable longitudinal consistency.* There are at least two simple ways to think about the consistency of individual differences in personality traits—consistency *across situations* and consistency *over time*. Mischel's (1968) critique of traits mostly concerned the first way. He argued that behavior was not consistent enough from one situation to the next to warrant the use of the trait concept. Mischel said much less, however, about the extent to which individual differences in traits were consistent over time. But at the time of Mischel's critique there was relatively little empirical data collected to support longitudinal consistency (or "stability") in traits. Since then, things have changed dramatically. Longitudinal studies of the 1980s and 1990s demonstrate that individual differences in many traits, such as extraversion and neuroticism, are quite stable over long periods of time (Conley, 1985b; McCrae & Costa, 1990). Stability has been demonstrated when trait scores come from self-ratings, spouse ratings, or peer ratings. Findings such as these tend to increase psychologists' faith in the concept of trait. You can easily see why. If, for example, Bill's high school teachers rate him as "highly extraverted" relative to other teenagers in 1940, his wife rates him "highly extraverted" on their 20th wedding anniversary in 1965, and his coworkers rate him as "highly extraverted" in 1990 when he retires from his company, and if Bill rates himself as "highly extraverted" compared with most other people he knows at ages 18, 43, and 68, then we might start to think that Bill really *is* highly extraverted! It makes sense to use the trait concept here, we might conclude.

3. *Aggregation shows that traits often predict behavior fairly well.* As we saw in Chapter 5, personality psychologists have sought to increase the predictive power of trait scores by employing moderator variables and aggregation strategies in their research. Aggregation has proven to be an especially powerful tool. Beginning with Epstein (1979), studies consistently show that individual differences in personality traits are often strongly correlated with individual differences in theoretically related behavior when behavior is aggregated or summed across situations. Individual differences in traits can often account for a substantial amount of variance in aggregated behaviors (Kenrick & Funder, 1988). In addition, situational effects are often no stronger than trait effects. The person-situation debate of the 1970s centered on the question of what accounts for the greatest degree of variance in behavior: Is it traits? Or is it situations? According to the situationist view if traits are weak predictors, then situations must be strong predictors. Mischel and others tried to show that traits were weak predictors. But they neglected to demonstrate that situational variables were especially strong predictors. Funder and Ozer (1983) reexamined some of the most well known laboratory studies of the 1960s and 1970s demonstrating significant effects for *situational variables* in predicting behavior. They found that the statistical effects obtained in these studies were typically no higher than those obtained in many studies employing personality traits. Funder and Ozer argued that while trait scores may sometimes account for only modest amounts of variance in behavior, it appears that carefully measured situational variables often account for no more.

4. *Trait psychologists have rallied around the Big Five.* The most important development in trait psychology of the 1980s and 1990s was the emergence of the Big Five model. As we saw in Chapter 6, findings from many recent studies converge on a five-factor model of personality traits. The five broad factors have been labeled extraversion *(E)*, neuroticism *(N)*, openness to experience *(O)*, conscientiousness *(C)*, and agreeableness *(A)*. Once upon a time, many personality psychologists seemed to be despairing over the possibility that traits might not exist. Today, there appears to be little doubt about the existence of traits. And there is growing consensus about how all the many different kinds of traits that might be invoked can be organized into a five-factor scheme. The emergence of a sensible and empirically grounded taxonomy for personality traits represents a tremendous boost for the trait concept. As we saw in Chapter 1, an important first step in science is an adequately comprehensive *description* of a phenomenon. The Big Five scheme appears to be the first truly comprehensive and consensual description of the trait domain to appear in the history of personality psychology. This is not to say that the Big Five is the last word on traits (Block, 1995; Briggs, 1989; McAdams, 1992b). But the model is an impressive achievement, and it has substantially enhanced the position of trait psychology in the eyes of the scientific community.

This said, the ascent of the Big Five model of traits has begun to reveal some important limitations of trait psychology. Some of the limitations have to do with the model itself. For example, the five factors of *E, N, O, A,* and *C* operate at such a general and abstract level of analysis that they may not always be useful in the prediction of specific behaviors. More narrowly defined traits sometimes show stronger predictive power, especially when the behavior to be predicted is narrowly defined (Briggs, 1989; A. Buss, 1989). In addition, the Big Five model tells us very little about (1) personality development and (2) personality organization. How do traits develop and change? How are they linked to particular stages of the life cycle? How are they organized within the individual? How do they make for personality coherence and wholeness? It does not appear that the Big Five model of traits is conceptually well positioned to answer questions like these (McAdams, 1992b).

Other limitations point to problems with the concept of trait itself—problems that have still not been resolved, even as the concept has regained prominence in recent years. To what extent are traits able to *explain* behavior? With the possible exception of such biologically grounded trait theories as Eysenck's and Gray's, trait approaches to personality have never offered especially compelling explanations for why people do what they do. To say that a person engages in warm and friendly behavior because he or she has a strong trait of agreeableness may represent a first step in explanation, but only a first step. We want to know precisely how this trait of agreeableness makes for the behavior. We want to know what the *causal mechanisms* are, the linkages between the trait label we invoke and the behavior we observe.

Beyond the problem of explanation is the problem of *context*. In their search for trait universals, proponents of the five-factor model of personality traits have disregarded the roles of situational, cultural, and historical contexts. McCrae and Costa (1984) claim that the Big Five model is "transcontextual." Life conditions and contexts may change over time, but traits remain the same. McCrae and Costa (1984) write: "The life course, then, can profitably be studied as the interplay of enduring dispositions and changing contexts" (p. 178). According to this view, extraversion is extraversion is extraversion. The meaning of the trait is the same, whether we're talking about extraversion in childhood or among adults, whether extraversion is measured among African-American men or German women, in 19th-century London or among Australian aborigines last week. Yet many psychologists argue that personality needs to be seen in contextual terms. Context appears to be necessary for accurate prediction, detailed description, and comprehensive understanding. But the concept of trait has not traditionally encompassed context.

In one way or another, the Big Five traits point to a good deal of information one might expect to gather in order to describe an individual's personality. Indeed, the five factors are ultimately derived from and appear to be ingrained within the common language we use to describe persons. As such the five factors cover the fundamental questions we seek to answer about persons. Goldberg (1981) writes:

> They [the five factors] suggest that those who have contributed to the English lexicon as it has evolved over time wished to know the answers to at least five types of questions about a stranger they were soon to meet: (1) Is X *active and dominant* [E] or passive and submissive (Can I bully X or will X bully me)? (2) Is X *agreeable* [A] (warm and pleasant) or disagreeable (cold and distant)? (3) Can I count on X [C] (Is X *responsible and conscientious* or undependable and negligent)? (4) Is X crazy [N] (unpredictable) or sane (stable)? (5) Is X *smart* [O] or dumb (How easy will it be for me to teach X)?
>
> Are these universal questions? (p. 161)

Notice the language in this revealing passage. Goldberg suggests that the Big Five traits apply to fundamental questions about personality that we would be likely to ask *when meeting a stranger*. In an initial encounter with a person, we are likely to want to obtain information about *E, N, O, C*, and *A*. Such information provides us with a "first read" of another person. It provides us with important guidelines concerning how we should interact with this person in the future. But as we get to know the person better, as we learn more about a person's *life*, we tend to move beyond the dimensional realm of the Big Five and develop conclusions about the person that are more nuanced and contextualized. We see the person in many different situations, noting both cross-situational consistencies (traits) and interesting situational variations on general behavioral trends. We begin to see the person in terms of the person's developmental past and life goals for the future. We begin to appreciate the texture of the person's life in a way that goes well beyond the Big Five traits, indeed goes well beyond traits in general. It would appear that the Big Five scheme represents a comprehensive *psychology of the stranger*. The five factors encapsule those most general and encompassing attributions that we might wish to make *when we know virtually nothing else about a person*.

As we saw in Chapter 5, personality psychologists employ the trait concept to refer to linear dimensions of behavioral functioning upon which individuals can be observed to differ. Traits are inherently comparative. If I score "high" on agreeableness, it means that I score high *relative* to other people. As I rate myself on items making up a scale measuring agreeableness, I am implicitly comparing myself with others, to provide the psychologist with a first and very general read on just how "warm and friendly" (agreeable) I am relative to other people. When other people rate me on trait items, they, too, are implicitly comparing me with others. As we saw in Chapter 5, if such ratings are to be reliable and valid, the items to be rated must be simple, clear, and straight-forward. Such is the nature—the necessary nature, it would seem—of trait ratings and trait psychology. The greatest strength of the trait concept is also its greatest limitation. Traits provide us with simple and noncontextualized generalizations about how people differ from one another.

If behavior is to be viewed in contextual terms, however, then information on a person's traits must be supplemented by information on the person's situations, including how a *person's life* is currently situated, how it has been situated in the past, how it might be situated in the future. In and of themselves, dispositional traits are *noncondi-tional* constructs. For example, a "high" trait score on extraversion suggests that a person would show relatively high levels of outgoing and impulsive behavior over time and across situations, but it does not specify *under what conditions* such behavior would appear. By contrast, *conditional* constructs are more interactional than traits in that they provide information about how a person would behave under particular conditions. Thorne (1989) describes the distinction:

> By nonconditional attributes, I mean traits such as dominance and extraversion, moods such as happiness, and behaviors such as talking and smiling. These kinds of concepts can be con-trasted with explicitly conditional categories such as: My dominance shows when my com-petence is threatened; I fall apart when people try to comfort me; I talk the most when I am nervous. (p. 149)

Trait scores provide us with nonconditional information about a person. From scores on the dimension of agreeableness, we learn about the extent to which a person would show warm and friendly behavior over time and across situations. We are given no information, however, about the conditions under which we are likely to see espe-cially high levels or low levels of warm and friendly behavior. We are told only about trends. Conditional statements, by contrast, provide information about the conditions under which particular kinds of behavior might occur. As we get to know a person bet-ter, we are likely to become better informed about the conditions under which partic-ular patterns of behavior should occur in the person's life. We should be able to move beyond nonconditional trait statements—the initial read on personality—to more con-ditional personality attributions made in context. We should be able to move beyond traits to explore the goals, tasks, challenges, conflicts, and situational and develop-mental demands that characterize a person's life. Think about a person whom you know very well. What is it that you know about him or her that you don't know about other people? Is it traits? Probably not. It is likely that you know a person well by virtue of knowing what the person's *life* is like, what it has been like in the past, and what it may be like in the future. As part of this knowledge, you may have access to the person's desires, needs, wishes, wants, goals, challenges, conflicts, values, and the unique way in which the person him- or herself puts this all together, puts it together into a narrative pattern to make sense of who he or she is. This kind of knowledge about a person is exquisitely conditional and contextualized.

Conditional and contextualized aspects of human individuality reside in the second and third levels of personality functioning, which I introduced in Chapter 1. These are the levels of characteristic adaptations and integrative life stories. It is at these two lev-els of personality that we are likely to see some of the best examples of personality change over the life course. As the field of personality psychology has celebrated the re-emergence of the trait concept for more than 20 years, many personality psychologists have also redoubled their efforts to explore those aspects of human individuality that are more contextualized, more conditional, and more subject to environmental impact and developmental change than personality traits. To move beyond a psychology of the stranger, we must now move beyond traits.

SUMMARY

1. Over the human lifespan, to what extent do our personality traits change and to what extent do they remain the same? There are many different meanings of personality continuity and change. With respect to continuity, four different meanings can be distinguished: absolute continuity, or consistency in the amount of trait shown, typically assessed by examining group averages at different points in time; differential continuity, or stability in individual differences in trait scores over time; ipsative continuity, or stability in a particular person's pattern of different characteristics over time; and coherence, or continuity shown when one set of variables leads in a theoretically predictable way to a second, different set of variables over time.

2. Longitudinal studies show remarkable differential continuity in personality traits over much of the adult lifespan. Even for periods of 30 years, individual differences in personality traits show considerable stability, especially with respect to the Big Five dimensions of extraversion, neuroticism, and openness to experience. Stability appears to increase with age, such that differential continuity over, say, a 5-year period among middle-aged adults is higher than differential continuity over a 5-year period for adolescents and younger adults.

3. Although few studies have examined directly the longitudinal relation between childhood and adult personality characteristics, many psychologists believe that childhood temperament dimensions may provide a core around which adult traits eventually develop. Temperament refers to differences in basic behavioral style, observed early in life and presumed to be under significant and rather direct biological control. Aspects of temperament that have received the greatest research attention include behavioral inhibition, intensity of mood, soothability, irritability, activity level, positive affect, and persistence.

4. Caspi has proposed that through a process of developmental elaboration, temperament dimensions in childhood gradually develop into more fully articulated personality traits in adulthood. He has identified six mechanisms that make this process work: learning processes, environmental elicitation, environmental construal, social and temporal comparisons, environmental selection, and environmental manipulation.

5. In a fundamental sense, personality traits are a product of a complex interaction between people's genetic endowments and their environmental opportunities and constraints. But genetic and environmental effects on variance in trait scores of groups of individuals can be separated out and estimated from studies of twins—MZ (identical) and DZ (fraternal) pairs—and from adoption studies in which children are brought up in families with whom they do not share a genetic lineage. Twin and adoption studies show that the impressive differential continuity exhibited for personality traits may be partly due to heritability. The research provides strong evidence that at least 40%–50% of the variance in personality trait scores in a given group can be accounted for by genetic differences among people in the group. Moderate to substantial heritabilities have been shown for virtually all personality traits measured, including all of the Big Five factors.

6. While genetic influences appear to account for around half the variance in trait scores, the influence of shared environments—such as child-rearing styles, social class, and other common experiences that siblings share—is surprisingly small, bordering on zero in many studies. Researchers in behavior genetics now believe that, along with genetic differences, *non*shared environmental effects may account for a significant portion of variance in personality traits. Whereas shared environment effects are environmental influences that operate to make family members alike, nonshared environmental effects are environmental influences that operate to make family members different. Nonshared environmental influences might include perinatal trauma, accidental events, family constellation patterns (e.g., birth order), patterns of interaction among siblings, differential parental treatment, and influences outside the family such as peer groups and teachers.

7. Although studies can separate the relative effects of genetics and environments in accounting for trait variability, genetic differences may themselves influence environments. Recent studies in behavior genetics suggest that self-reports of environments themselves are heritable. Genetic differences may shape how people experience their environments and what environments they choose to experience. Genotypes can shape environments in at least three ways: through evocative influence, whereby a person's genetically driven tendencies evoke responses from the environment that reinforce those tendencies; through passive influence, whereby a person grows up in environments that are created by individuals (e.g., biological parents) who have similar genotypes, such that the environments one experiences from the beginning are likely to have some correspondence to one's own genotype; and active influence, through which a person's genotype influences how an individual acts upon, manipulates, and transforms the environments that he or she chooses to experience. Whereas evocative and passive influences may predominate in childhood, active genotype-environment influences are more likely to characterize adult behavior.

8. Against the backdrop of substantial differential continuity in traits, research has also documented gradual and systematic changes in absolute values of personality dimensions. Both cross-sectional and longitudinal studies suggest that from adolescence and early adulthood through late middle-adulthood, traits related to the Big Five factors of extraversion, neuroticism, and openness to experience may decline somewhat, and traits related to agreeableness and conscientiousness may increase. A handful of longitudinal studies document movements toward increasing responsibility, autonomy, and self-confidence as people move from early to middle adulthood, especially among well-educated women. People tend to feel somewhat better about themselves as they grow older, at least into middle age, and somewhat better about other people, too.

9. Patterns of both continuity and change over time have been documented in the longitudinal studies conducted by Jack Block and his colleagues, employing the ipsative measure called the California Q-Sort. Block's research has generated a taxonomy of personality types, each of which exists as a constellation of different traits developing over time. Underlying these constellations are the personality dimensions of ego control and ego resiliency. Recent studies employing the Q-Sort with women have generated four different personality types: individuated, traditional, conflicted, and assured.

10. The concept of a personality trait is somewhat better suited for displaying continuity in personality over time, rather than change. Significant change in personality may occur outside the realm of personality traits, as in changing patterns of life goals, tasks, projects, values, coping strategies, interest patterns, visions for the future, and reconstructions of the past. Personality traits provide an indispensable starting point for the understanding of human individuality. But a full and detailed account requires a consideration of personality features that are not necessarily well expressed as traits. We may view dispositional traits as occupying the first level of personality. In the chapters that follow, we will move to the second and third levels—characteristic adaptations and integrative life stories.

Filling in the Details: Characteristic Adaptations to Life Tasks

III

Personality traits such as extraversion and neuroticism begin to sketch an outline of human individuality by estimating where an individual person may be placed along a series of dispositional dimensions. But to get to the details beyond the outline, the personality psychologist must examine aspects of individuality that are more personalized and contextualized in

431

time, place, and social role. If traits, then, comprise the first level of personality description, characteristic adaptations such as motives, goals, personal constructs, and developmental tasks fill in a second, more contextualized level. In Chapter 8, we consider those characteristic adaptations that speak directly to human motivation. Motives and goals energize and direct human behavior by guiding organisms in the direction of desired states and away from those states that are undesired. We will consider the humanistic motivational theories proposed by Carl Rogers and Abraham Maslow, contemporary self-determination theory, and theory and research on three important social motives that are assessed through content analysis of imaginative stories—achievement, power, and intimacy motivation. Motives are often expressed through more personalized goals, such as personal strivings and projects, which provide greater detail, specificity, and context for understanding a person's motivational life. Chapter 9 considers those characteristic adaptations that are more social and cognitive in nature, such as personal constructs, cognitive styles, beliefs, expectancies, scripts, attributions, and self-conceptions. Social-cognitive approaches to personality psychology focus on the mental representations that people form to process information about the self and social behavior. After examining George Kelly's theory of personal constructs and the tradition of studying such cognitive styles as field independence-dependence, we will explore the wide-ranging research on self-schemas, possible selves, explanatory styles, and other social-cognitive aspects of individuality that together constitute social intelligence and help to govern and guide behavior in many different social situations. Chapter 10 examines characteristic adaptations that are specifically linked to developmental stages and tasks, such as the concepts of young-adult identity and midlife generativity, and stages of ego development. We will examine in detail two rich theoretical traditions in personality development—Erik Erikson's theory of psychosocial development and Jane Loevinger's theory of the development of "ego" or "the I." While Erikson's eight-stage model proposes a series of developmental tasks that a person must address in life, Loevinger's scheme specifies the characteristic framework of meaning that a person uses to make sense of experience at a given stage in life.

Motives and Goals

8

When my younger daughter was around 5 years old, she asked me what my job was. I told her I was a professor of psychology.

"What is that?" Amanda asked.

"Well, I teach students about psychology," I replied.

"What is psychology?" she wanted to know.

"It's about human behavior," I explained. "I study why people do what they do."

"Oh." She rolled her eyes. "Well, why *do they* do what they do?"

"I really don't know, sweetheart. I guess that's why I study it."

"I know why people do what they do."

"Oh?"

Looking at me with a mixture of pity and disgust, Amanda proclaimed: "Because *they want to,* that's why."

She marched out of the room, no doubt wondering how her father could be so stupid. It is a basic fact of life: People do what they want to do. Even at age 5, Amanda knew something very important about human behavior. With no graduate training in psychology, she had developed her own implicit theory of human **motivation.** People have inside of them "wants," desires, aims, intentions. People act upon these wants, producing behavior. At its root, the word motivation refers to "movement." What gets people moving? What *energizes* and *directs* human behavior? Like Amanda, theorists of human motivation going back more than 2,000 years have suggested that people want things, that they are motivated to get what they want (and to avoid what they don't want), that they develop goals to obtain those things they want, and that they act upon those goals. Furthermore, many have suggested that what we want is often derived directly from what we *need* (Lewin, 1935; Murray, 1938). Motivational psychologist Eric Klinger (1987) expands Amanda's theory of human motivation and gives it a Darwinian spin so that it even applies to animals:

> We animals have our drastic differences, but almost all of us—from amoebas to humans—have at least one behavioral imperative in common: We almost all have to go out and get the things we need in order to survive and procreate. We have to identify them, reach out or ambulate toward them, and bring them to those of our organs that can make use of them. Our morphology, our physiology, and our behavioral organization are all arranged so as to satisfy this imperative. This means that, from the beginning, animals have necessarily been constructed to pursue necessary goals, which means in turn that they have been shaped by the requirements of goal pursuit. Goal-striving, and therefore motivation in the larger sense, are integral facets of life as an animal. (Klinger, 1987, p. 337)

What do you want in life? What are your goals? What kinds of projects and tasks are you working on these days? What are you striving to accomplish? These are all motivational questions, and they speak to a very important aspect of what makes you you, of what makes you similar to and different from other people around you. If personality psychology seeks to provide a full scientific account of human individuality, then a central aspect of that account must concern an individual's motives and goals. Indeed, motivation has been a central concern for personality psychologists ever since the field of personality psychology began (Emmons, 1997; Little, 1999; McAdams, 1997a; Winter & Barenbaum, 1999). Most of the grand theories of personality developed in the 20th century made sweeping statements about fundamental human motivations, about basic needs and goal-seeking tendencies that define what it means to be a human being. As we have already seen, Freud (Chapter 3) built psychoanalysis around the idea that behavior is motivated by unconscious needs and drives. The behaviorists (Chapter 4) focused on how rewards, punishments, and other contingencies in the environment shape human needs to produce behavior. Evolutionary psychologists (Chapter 2) argue for species-typical tendencies that energize and direct human behavior in order to assure survival and procreation. Even trait theorists, such as Eysenck and Gray (Chapters 5 and 6), speak of motivational processes. For example, it has been proposed that the trait of extraversion is derived, in some psychophysiological sense, from a reward-seeking system in the brain (called the behavioral activation system), motivating approach behavior in pursuit of incentives. It is virtually impossible to talk about personality without talking about motivation.

With its focus on motives and goals, the current chapter takes us beyond the important individual differences in behavior typically associated with personality traits to a second level or domain in personality functioning. I have already suggested that personality traits such as the Big Five help to provide an initial sketch of human individuality. It is now time, however, to fill in some of the details in that sketch. To begin filling in the details, we need to move beyond traits and consider the various kinds of characteristic adaptations that define a particular human life. Motives and goals are one class of characteristic adaptations. They are those aspects of personality that speak directly to what Amanda considers to be the basic fact of human behavior—that people *want* things and they *act* upon those wants.

But what do people want? We begin by reviewing four different motivational traditions that address the question of what people want. We then consider a number of contemporary theories of human motivation, including those that derive from the humanistic theorists Carl Rogers and Abraham Maslow. We then turn our attention to the taxonomy of motives and needs developed by Henry Murray and David McClelland and to empirical research on three basic social motivations—the needs for achievement, power, and intimacy. Finally, we discuss how general needs get translated into daily goals and strivings, how people develop and pursue what they want through their own projects and programs of activity in daily life, and how the kinds of goals we have and the ways in which we pursue them have important implications for our own well-being and the quality of our lives.

THEORIES OF HUMAN MOTIVATION

What Do People Want? Four Views

Western scholars have traditionally answered the question of what people want in at least four different ways. Each of the four reflects a particular view of human nature and of the extent to which human beings are capable of living good lives versus bad lives, experiencing happiness versus misery, and obeying the dictates of reason versus irrationality. As outlined in Table 8.1, I will call these the traditions of (1) optimism, (2) pessimism, (3) neutrality, and (4) diversity.

The optimistic tradition says that people are (basically) good, reasonable, and more-or-less able to lead happy lives. People want to be good; they consciously strive to realize goals that are positive for themselves and for others; they pursue rational

TABLE 8.1	Four Traditions in the Study of Human Motivation	
TRADITION	**MAIN IDEA**	**SPOKESPERSONS AND MODERN THEORIES**
Optimism	People are (basically) good and capable of rational thought; reason guides behavior; people act in accord with conscious goals, which makes them happy.	Plato (4th century B.C.) Enlightenment philosophers (1700s) Carl Rogers (1951) Abraham Maslow (1954) Self-determination theory George Kelly (1955) (Chapter 9) Cognitive theories (Chapter 9)
Pessimism	People are (mainly) bad and often miserable (because they want bad things); behavior is motivated by irrational and/or bodily instincts and goals; human reason is overrated.	Old Testament idea of original sin Freud (1900) (Chapter 3) Evolutionary psychology (Chapter 2)
Neutrality	People are (at birth) blank, unformed; the environment shapes goals and motives through rewards, punishments, and so on; beneficent environments make for good and happy people.	John Locke and the doctrine of *tabula rasa* Behaviorism (Chapter 4) B. F. Skinner (1971) (Chapter 4)
Diversity	People are many things; different people want different things, have different goals.	Galen's ancient typology (Chapter 5) William James (1892) William McDougall (1908) Henry Murray (1938) David McClelland (1951) Contemporary goal theories

solutions to the problems they face; they try to make good decisions; they generally know what they are doing and why. More than 2,000 years ago, Plato (427?–347? B.C.) recognized the human being's privileged status in the world as the one being capable of reason. In *The Republic*, Plato argued that human behavior is energized and directed by bodily appetites, courage and fortitude, and reason. Reason is the highest motive, and it impels human beings to strive for "the Good." By contemplating the nature of reality in an abstract and purely rational manner, some human beings (especially those designated to be the leaders, or "philosopher kings," in a utopian republic) may come to understand what is true, good, and harmonious. Centuries after Plato, European poets and philosophers of the Enlightenment, such as Alexander Pope (1688–1744) and Jean-Jacques Rousseau (1712–1778), celebrated the rational and prosocial aspects of human nature. In Pope's view, human behavior is driven by self-love but guided by reason. Therefore, although selfish wants may energize us to act, rational thought tempers our selfishness and provides good direction for behavior. According to Rousseau, human beings are born into a state of natural goodness and perfection. Society, however, is capable of perverting human goodness and substituting destructive motives for benevolent and reasonable ones. Rousseau believed that only by ignoring societal trappings and returning to nature could human beings fully realize their own goodness.

As we see later in this chapter and in the next, the optimistic tradition represented in the Platonic and Enlightenment views of human motivation finds its modern

Jean-Jacques Rousseau believed that human beings were born into a state of natural goodness.

equivalents in theories that emphasize cognitive processes and the power of human thought (Chapter 9 in this book) and those that underscore humankind's proactive and self-determining tendencies (the current chapter). Most representative of the optimistic view are **humanistic** theories of personality and motivation, especially those offered by Carl Rogers and Abraham Maslow. According to the tradition of humanistic/phenomenological psychology, the supreme motivator for human behavior and experience is the *striving to actualize and perfect the self.* An especially influential variation on this viewpoint can be found in Ed Deci's and Richard Ryan's self-determination theory, which we will examine later in this chapter.

In sharp contrast to the optimistic tradition is the view that people are (mostly) bad (or at best, "not good") and (often) miserable (because they are bad). People want bad things, and this gets them into trouble. The idea that men and women are inherently flawed, conflicted, and even evil—that we are all "sinners" at heart, or at best "polymorphously perverse," as Freud put it—is deeply ingrained in Judeo-Christian thought. The Old Testament tells the story of the original sin of Adam and Eve and of many other instances in which the people created in God's image murdered, raped, destroyed, and disobeyed. Although Freud (Chapter 3) had little use for religion (Freud, 1927/1961), his view of human nature was not all that different from the generally pessimistic portrayal of the Old Testament. Rather than sin, human beings are motivated by dark, unconscious forces linked to sexuality and aggression, and these forces almost invariably bring us anxiety and pain. Neurosis may not be as bad as eternal damnation, but it is bad enough, and human reason is simply not powerful enough to overcome the insatiable needs of the id, the inflexible demands of the superego, and the stifling conventions of the real world. Like Freud and the psychoanalysts, evolutionary theorists (Chapter 2) tend to de-emphasize the power of reason and rational thought and underscore instead instinctually grounded motivational tendencies that ultimately serve "the selfish gene." Evolution sets forth a motivational agenda for the species. The various tactics, strategies, and goals that make up that agenda (Buss, 1991a) may be refined by rational thought and planning, but evolutionarily adaptive behavior does not *require* the assistance of reason, or even consciousness, in order to be effective. Indeed, it may be assumed that long before the advent of reason—before the human brain evolved to the point where it was capable of Plato's rational and abstract thought—our ancestors were motivated to engage in behaviors that met the evolutionary challenges facing them (Wright, 1994). That motivational agenda is still with us.

A third tradition in human motivation asserts that human beings are neither good nor bad, neither inherently happy nor inherently miserable, neither rational nor irrational. Fundamentally, human beings are blank, empty, unformed—at least at the beginning (infancy). In the famous words of the Enlightenment philosopher John Locke (1632–1704), the human mind at birth is a *tabula rasa*, or "blank slate." Over time and with experience in the world, the person comes to receive the particular contents of human life, essentially learning from society what he or she should and should not want. A person's motives and goals are shaped by the environment. Good environments make for happy people; bad environments ruin our lives. As we saw in Chapter 4, this position of neutrality in the study of human motivation characterizes, in albeit simple terms, the classic behaviorist view of why people do what they do. The most influential spokesperson for this view was probably B. F. Skinner (1971). Skinner's brand of operant behaviorism looks for the motivators of human behavior in the environment rather than within the person. According to this view, psychologists (and by extension, Amanda) would do well *not* to make inferences about the internal wants, needs, desires, and goals of the person, because these internal phenomena cannot be directly observed and precisely measured. Rather, the psychologist should examine carefully the particular environments within which behavior is displayed in order to understand how the environments reward or reinforce certain behaviors and punish or fail to reinforce others. Goal-directed human behavior is virtually as malleable as are the environments in which it is exhibited.

The traditions of optimism, pessimism, and neutrality tend to emphasize how people's basic motivations are similar. Humanistic psychologists suggest that *all* people are potentially self-actualizing; Freud argued that *all* people are motivated by unconscious drives for sexuality and aggression; Skinner maintained that *all* behaviors are subject to the vagaries of reward and punishment. A fourth tradition in the study of human motivation takes the view that everybody is different. Some people are motivated by certain classes of goals and incentives; other people are motivated by other goals and incentives. The tradition of diversity basically asserts that people are not good, not bad, not even neutral; rather, different people have different motives and goals. John may be strongly motivated by achievement needs; Sara has devoted her life to helping others; Brian wants to get into graduate school in anthropology; Maria is strongly driven by contrasting motives for intimacy and power, and the conflict makes her anxious; Maria's brother, Miguel, has never known this conflict, for his main drive in life is to make money.

Different people's lives are governed by different basic wants and desires. In this vein, early 20th-century psychologists such as William James (1892/1963), William McDougall (1908), and Henry Murray (1938) set forth classification systems for fundamental human motives. Murray's list of about 20 "psychogenic needs" has been especially influential, and we will focus on it later in this chapter. As we will also see, other psychologists have sought to generate taxonomies of motivational domains by asking people to list their most important goals, tasks, commitments, strivings, projects, and so on. For example, Novacek and Lazarus (1990) statistically analyzed people's reports of their personal commitments and concluded that most of the commitments fall into one of six groups: affiliation, power/achievement, personal growth, altruism, avoiding stress, and sensation seeking. Drawing upon a number of studies, Pervin (1996) came up with a slightly different list. He argues that five psychological goal categories can be consistently identified in people's descriptions of what they want in life: relaxation/fun, aggression/power, self-esteem, affection/support, and anxiety reduction.

In sum, ancient and modern theories of human motivation can be roughly grouped into the four traditions of optimism, pessimism, neutrality, and diversity. Cutting across all four traditions is the dialectic of body versus mind. According to motivational psychologist Bernard Weiner (1992), contemporary research into human motivation tends to proceed according to two different classes of metaphors. The first class emphasizes the biological or bodily aspects of human existence, conceives of motivation as "pushing" the organism along, and implicitly compares human beings with various kinds of machines. Such mechanistic metaphors, most notable in the pessimistic and neutrality tradition of human motivation, provide conceptual space for an understanding of the person as an intricate biological mechanism that obeys the laws of physics and physiology. Like other members of the animal kingdom, we must meet the incessant demands of thirst and hunger, and we are completely beholden to the vagaries of pain, sickness, disease, and bodily breakdown. By contrast, a second set of metaphors tends to underscore the fact that, relative to all other organisms, the human being is blessed with incomparable powers of the mind. These powers enable one to reflect on the biological condition, to ponder one's own mortality and imagine alternatives to it, to be conscious of one's own predicament, and to think about virtually anything at all. Rather than a mere machine, the human being is almost like a god (Weiner, 1992). Connected mainly with the optimistic and the diversity positions on motivation, this second class of metaphors, then, emphasizes the cognitive or mindful aspects of human existence, conceives of motivation as "pulling" the organism along, and implicitly compares human beings with the kinds of all-knowing and supremely rational idealizations that Western culture has traditionally associated with deities. Weiner concludes that a comprehensive approach to the question of what people really want requires a consideration of both body and mind.

In this chapter, we focus mainly on the approaches to human motivation that stem from the optimistic and diversity positions and tend to emphasize the mindful aspects of goal-directed behavior over the physiological underpinnings. One reason for this emphasis here is that we have already discussed in some detail the evolutionary (Chapter 2), psychoanalytic (Chapter 3), and behavioristic (Chapter 4) approaches, with their implications for the pessimistic and neutrality positions on human motivation. In addition, while research into the biological bases of human motivation has continued to flourish in psychology, approaches emphasizing potentially conscious and rational aspects of the mind—values, expectancies, cognitions, conscious thought, planning, and so on—have become increasingly influential in personality and social psychology in the past few decades (Cantor & Zirkel, 1990; Emmons, 1997; Little, 1999; Pervin, 1996). These approaches tend to underscore the planful nature of goal-directed activity, the role of cognition and consciousness in motivation, and the ways in which different social needs and motives are translated into behavior through daily goals, tasks, and strivings. Consequently, we begin our review with the classic humanistic theories of motivation offered by Carl Rogers and Abraham Maslow. Both Rogers and Maslow provide highly optimistic views of human potential, underscoring the power of consciousness and the ability of well-functioning people to pursue goals that promote growth and self-actualization. We then consider what is arguably the most well-developed and empirically supported motivational theory in the optimistic tradition—self-determination theory. Next, we move to Henry Murray's diversity position and examine the wealth of research that his viewpoint has generated. In the chapter's last section, we focus more intensively on daily goals and plans and their relation to the more general motivational tendencies identified by Rogers, Maslow, Murray, and others.

Carl Rogers's Theory

Carl Rogers was one of the most influential psychologists of the 20th century. Born in Oak Park, Illinois, in 1902, Carl Rogers grew up in a deeply religious and financially secure family. After receiving a degree in history and attending the Union Theological Seminary in New York, Rogers moved to clinical psychology and earned a Ph.D. in 1931. He worked as a staff psychologist in a child-guidance center before moving to Ohio State University and then the University of Chicago, where he directed the Counselling Center. It was at Chicago in the 1950s that his point of view became a major force in psychological theory and practice, following the publication of his major work, *Client-Centered Therapy: Its Current Practice, Implications, and Theory* (Rogers, 1951). Rogers's developing humanistic perspective contrasted markedly with the prevalent psychoanalytic approaches to therapy and with popular behavioral approaches, such as behavior modification. Many of the hallmarks of *Rogers's* **client-centered therapy**—his emphasis on the therapist's warmth and sincerity, empathy, acceptance, role playing, and the dignity of the client—have become mainstays of a wide variety of therapeutic and educational approaches employed by clinicians, social workers, teachers, child-care workers, and other helping professionals today. It is difficult to overestimate Rogers's profound influence on clinical practice and in education.

Carl Rogers

Rogers offers a simple and elegant theory of personality and motivation. In Rogers's view, the person must be understood from the perspective of his or her **phenomenal field.** The phenomenal field is the entire panorama of a person's experience, the person's subjective apprehension of reality. It is the individual's overall frame of reference—the most encompassing interpretive structure for the person, which can be fully known only to the person him- or herself. To learn about another person's phenomenal field, the psychologist must listen carefully to the person's subjective report of experience, thereby achieving empathy with the other. The roots of behavior are in the phenomenal field, says Rogers. Unconscious conflicts, biological needs, environmental influences, and all other forces impinging on the experiencing person are rendered meaningful or irrelevant through and only through the phenomenal field.

Human behavior and experience are guided by one basic striving in life. Writes Rogers, "The organism has one basic tendency and striving—to actualize, maintain, and enhance the experiencing organism" (1951, p. 487). There is "an inherent tendency of the organism to develop all its capacities in ways which serve to maintain or enhance the person" (1959, p. 196). While Freud viewed human motivation in terms of two classes of instinctual demands (death and life instincts) and Murray identified some 20 basic psychogenic needs, Rogers insists on a simple, monistic theory of human motivation. All urges, desires, wants, goals, values, and motives may be subsumed under the general umbrella of *organismic enhancement.* Each person's fundamental mandate in life is to become all that he or she can become, to fulfill one's inner potential. In so doing, the person advances toward greater differentiation, independence, and social responsibility over the lifespan. People change through conscious, goal-directed choices. Choices must be clearly perceived if the person is to continue *becoming*, to continue moving toward full actualization of inner potential.

The person who is able to fulfill his or her potential is described as the **fully functioning person.** For the fully functioning person, the self has expanded to encompass the lion's share of the phenomenal field. The person is, therefore, consciously aware of the many different facets of his or her life, is able to integrate seemingly inconsistent aspects of experience into a coherent whole. Such a person leads a life that is rich in emotional experience and self-discovery. He or she is reflective, spontaneous, flexible, adaptable, confident, trusting, creative, and self-reliant. The fully functioning person operates according to the **organismic valuing process.** This means that those experiences in accord with the basic organismic-actualizing tendency are viewed as satisfying and therefore are approached and maintained. Those that are contrary to actualization—those experiences that do not promote growth and fulfillment—are avoided or minimized. Unlike many theorists, Rogers does not delineate a series of developmental stages as stepping stones to full functioning. But he does identify important environmental conditions that promote the fulfillment of the organism. All people experience a need for *positive regard*, or the desire to be loved and accepted by others. The fully functioning person is likely to have experienced a great deal of **unconditional positive regard.** This means that he or she has been loved and accepted by others in an uncritical and noncontingent manner. People need to be loved for their very existence as persons, through the kind of unconditional love that the ancient Greeks and the Christian church have called *agape*. Regard from others promotes basic *self-regard*. Every person needs to be regarded positively both by others and by him- or herself.

But love and acceptance are often conditional: We are praised, rewarded, liked, admired, and blessed for particular things that we do, say, think, and feel. Such conditional positive regard from others leads to the apprehension of **conditions of worth.** We come to believe that certain aspects of our experience are worthy and others are not worthy. A young boy who is repeatedly praised for good school performance may introject this condition of worth and make it a positive part of the self-structure. The person builds a self-image commensurate with what other important people, who provide the person with positive regard, urge him or her to adopt.

Those aspects of self that are viewed by others as not worthy may ultimately be denied or distorted, for they engender no positive regard and may, instead, be the harbingers of punishment. For instance, a young girl who enjoys vigorous sports may be criticized by her parents or peers for playing basketball with the boys. Their regard for her becomes conditional: dependent on her adherence to appropriate feminine roles. As a result, she may revise her self-image to deny that she enjoys playing vigorous sports. Her conscious denial hides an inner truth, which results in inner conflict and distress.

Like Freud, Rogers believes that people suffer from important conflicts, many of which involve unconscious issues in their lives. But the conflicts derive from conflicts between the self and apprehended conditions of worth rather than between instinctual forces and superego demands. Rogers is much more optimistic than Freud about the possibility of living without conflict, of transcending conditions of worth to accept the self unconditionally. If we attain the fully functioning status, Rogers argues, we no longer impose conditions of worth on our experience but accept our entire organismic experience as good and fulfilling.

The road to full functioning, however, is not a smooth one. Along the way, the person is sure to experience disappointment and anxiety. Anxiety results when a person unconsciously perceives—"subceives"—an experience as incompatible with the self-structure and the introjected conditions of worth. **Subception** is the detection of an experience before it enters awareness. When faced with an event that threatens the self, the person quickly and unconsciously recognizes the threatening nature of the event and endeavors to protect the self from harm, typically by distorting or denying the event's reality. In this case, the event is unconsciously evaluated with regard to internal conditions of worth rather than with regard to the organism's general tendency toward growth and actualization. We see here that the directional tendencies of the self may come into conflict with the organism's general actualizing tendency. A person may consciously desire one thing to enhance the conscious self but unconsciously desires another thing to fulfill the spontaneous and growth-promoting tendencies of the entire organism.

But for the fully functioning person, no denial or distortion need take place, for he or she need not evaluate experience according to conditions of worth. The fully functioning person is keenly aware of those subtle feelings and impressions in life signalling opportunities for growth and enhancement. Therefore, the fully functioning person has less anxiety in life. Free from conditions of worth and willing to risk the conscious self in order to fulfill deeper yearnings, the fully functioning person embraces unconditionally the entire panoply of subjective experience. In a very real sense, the fully functioning person feels unconditional positive regard for all aspects of his or her subjective human experience.

Abraham Maslow's Psychology of Being

Abraham Maslow was born in Brooklyn, New York, in 1908, the son of Jewish parents who had emigrated from Russia. In contrast to Rogers, Maslow grew up isolated and very unhappy in a socially and economically deprived family. He earned his Ph.D. in psychology from the University of Wisconsin in 1934 under the tutelage of Harry Harlow, completing a dissertation on the sexual behavior of monkeys. At first an ardent behaviorist, Maslow's firsthand experience with his own children convinced him that this mechanistic approach to the person was not for him. Sometime around the beginning of World War II, Maslow experienced a profound personal conversion that eventually led to his formulation of a humanistic alternative in psychology. According to his own reports, he witnessed a pathetic and beggarly civilian parade designed to drum up support for the war, shortly after the bombing of Pearl Harbor. In Maslow's eyes, the parade only underscored the futility and tragic waste of war. With tears streaming down his face, he made a firm vow: to prove that human beings were capable of achievements grander than hate and destructiveness, and to do so by studying the people in the world who seemed to be the psychologically *healthiest* (Hall, 1968). In 1951, Maslow became a professor at Brandeis University where he gained international fame as the foremost spokesman for humanistic personality theory.

Maslow shares Rogers's view that human beings strive to actualize their inner potential. His term for this fundamental human striving is **self-actualization.** But Maslow (1954, 1968) suggests that the need for self-actualization is undergirded by at least four other kinds of needs, forming a **need hierarchy** (Figure 8.1). At the base of the hierarchy are *physiological* needs, such as the needs for food, water, and sleep. Above them are *safety* needs: the needs for structure, security, order, avoidance of pain, and protection. *Belongingness and love* needs are the third level. People desire to be accepted and loved by others and to form affiliative, loving, and intimate unions. Next are the *esteem* needs, which refer to needs for self-respect and esteem from others, the desire to be seen by others and by the self as a competent and effective organism. Finally, there are the needs for *self-actualization*, which motivate the person to fulfill his or her own potential above and beyond the lower needs.

The key notion in Maslow's need hierarchy is that higher needs cannot generally be addressed until the lower needs are satisfied. For instance, a starving man will not act in accord with his needs for belongingness until he has secured food (physiological needs) and a safe position in life (security needs). A lonely woman will not be able to fulfill her needs for esteem until she finds belongingness and love. Self-actualization sits at the pinnacle of the hierarchy. We cannot expect people to fulfill their innate potential, says Maslow, until they have taken care of business at the lower and more basic levels of the hierarchy.

While many theories of personality derive from clinicians' work with neurotics and other people suffering psychological pain, Maslow is especially refreshing for his opposite point of view. Though he was a clinician, Maslow's theory of motivation is most heavily influenced by his understanding of the healthiest subjects, the most mature and actualized people

Abraham Maslow

FIGURE 8.1   *Maslow's Need Hierarchy*

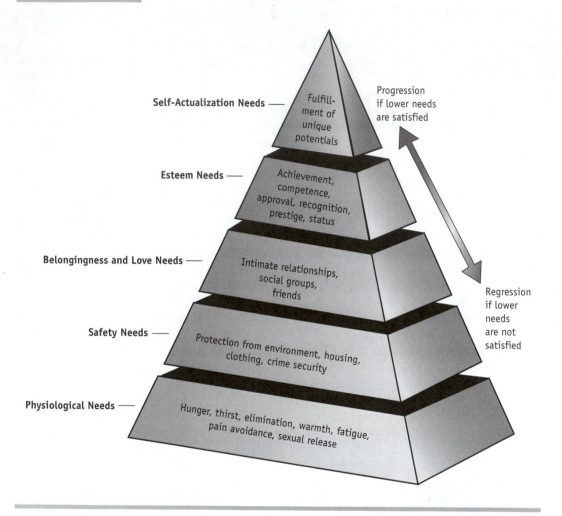

Self-Actualization Needs — Fulfillment of unique potentials

Esteem Needs — Achievement, competence, approval, recognition, prestige, status

Belongingness and Love Needs — Intimate relationships, social groups, friends

Safety Needs — Protection from environment, housing, clothing, crime security

Physiological Needs — Hunger, thirst, elimination, warmth, fatigue, pain avoidance, sexual release

Progression if lower needs are satisfied

Regression if lower needs are not satisfied

among us. From interviewing friends and clients, reading biographies, and conducting structured research, Maslow sketched a personological portrait of the "self-actualizing" person, or "self-actualizer" (SA). Table 8.2 lists some of the characteristics Maslow identified as common in SAs.

The SA is motivated primarily by **being values (B-values).** Some of Maslow's B-values are listed in Table 8.3. B-values encourage growth and the enrichment of experience. The person who structures his or her life in accord with the B-values has transcended the **deficiency motives,** which exist in lower parts of the need hierarchy. Deficiency motives are based on lacks, absences, and tensions: eating out of hunger is motivated by a lack of food; exploitative sexual behavior may be motivated by a build-up of libidinal tension or by sadistic aggressive urges. Behavior dominated by deficiency

TABLE 8.2	*Some Characteristics of Self-Actualizing Persons*

Superior perception of reality
Increased acceptance of self, of others, and of nature
Increased spontaneity
Increased detachment and desire for privacy
Greater freshness of appreciation and richness of emotional reaction
Increased autonomy and resistance to conformity
Higher frequency of peak experiences
Increased identification with the human species
Improved interpersonal relationships
More democratic character structure
High levels of creativity

Source: Modified after Maslow (1968), p. 26.

motives operates to return the organism to a steady state of equilibrium—to fill the lack or reduce the tension. Thus, people quit eating when they are full. Behavior motivated by B-values, on the other hand, grows and becomes richer over time. The woman who acts out of an appreciation for "beauty," for instance, does not quit once she has experienced something beautiful but seeks yet other beautiful experiences.

Another important characteristic of the SA is his or her proclivity for **peak experiences.** Peak experiences are just what they sound like: wonderful moments of happiness, ecstasy, transcendence. Put simply, SAs have more of these than do the rest of humankind. Yet virtually anyone can have a peak experience. Maslow sampled peak experiences among his friends and some of his college students by asking them to respond to this request:

> I would like you to think of the most wonderful experience or experiences in your life; happiest moments, ecstatic moments, moments of rapture, perhaps from being in love, or from listening to music or suddenly "being hit" by a book or a painting, or from some great creative moment. First list these. And then try to tell me how you feel in such acute moments, how you feel *differently* from the way you feel at other times, how you are at the moment a different person in some ways. (Maslow, 1968, p. 71)

TABLE 8.3	*The B-Values*

Wholeness	Richness	Effortlessness
Perfection	Simplicity	Playfulness
Completion	Beauty	Truth
Justice	Goodness	Self-sufficiency
Aliveness	Uniqueness	

Source: Adapted from Maslow (1968), p. 83.

Maslow's admittedly impressionistic analysis of the responses to his request suggested that in peak experiences people perceive and understand their world from the standpoint of **being cognition (B-cognition).** In B-cognition, the "experience or the object tends to be seen as a whole, as a complete unit, detached from relations from possible usefulness, from expediency and from purpose" (Maslow, 1968, p. 74). The "percept is exclusively and fully attended to" (p. 74), and "perception can be relatively ego-transcending, self-forgetful, egoless" (p. 79). There may even be a "disorientation in time and space" (p. 80), through which the person loses the subjective sense of time passing or of existing in a particular place. Most of all, though, B-cognition makes for a *unity* of consciousness:

> In some reports, particularly of the mystic experience or the religious experience or philosophical experience, the whole of the world is seen as unity, as a single rich live entity. In other of the peak experiences, most particularly the love experience and the aesthetic experience, one small part of the world is perceived as if it were for the moment all of the world. In both cases the perception is of unity. Probably the fact that the B-cognition of a painting or a person or a theory retains all the attributes of the whole of Being, i.e., the B-values, derives from this fact of perceiving it as if it were all that existed at the moment. (Maslow, 1968, p. 88)

Humanistic Research on Human Motivation

The humanistic approaches of Rogers and Maslow have had their greatest influence in the realms of clinical treatment, counseling, and education. Researchers, too, have drawn extensively from Rogers's theory in studies of psychotherapy process and outcome and in applied research in clinical and educational settings. Rogers's theory has also been a prime stimulus for research on the self (Chapter 9). Beyond these important contributions, motivation researchers have found two humanistic concepts especially worthy of empirical scrutiny: self-actualization and peak experiences.

Starting from Maslow's theory, Shostrom (1965, 1966) developed the **Personal Orientation Inventory (POI),** a 150-item questionnaire designed to assess various dimensions of self-actualization. The test yields two summary scores for "inner-directedness" and "time competence." In addition, 10 subscales provide scores on such characteristics of SAs as "spontaneity," "capacity for intimate contact," and "self-acceptance." The POI appears to have adequate reliability, and validity studies are generally positive (Maddi, 1980). Studies have shown that scores on all of the POI scales are negatively correlated with Eysenck's trait of neuroticism (Chapter 6) and positively correlated with self-report tests of autonomy and creativity. POI scales correlate negatively with alcoholism, felony, and hospitalization for psychopathological symptoms, and they correlate positively with teaching and therapist effectiveness (Maddi, 1980).

Jones and Crandall (1986) developed a short index of self-actualization. Their 15-item scale is reproduced in Table 8.4. In a study of over 500 college students, Jones and Crandall found that scores on this short scale correlated highly with the overall self-actualization scores from the much-longer POI ($r = +.67$). The scale shows good reliability and in general does not seem to be susceptible to "social desirability" response sets (see Chapter 5). Self-actualization on the scale was positively associated with measures of self-esteem and "rational behavior and beliefs" and was negatively associated with neuroticism.

TABLE 8.4	*A Short Scale Measuring Self-Actualization*

I do not feel ashamed of any of my emotions.

I feel I must do what others expect me to do. (N)

I believe that people are essentially good and can be trusted.

I feel free to be angry to those I love.

It is always necessary that others approve of what I do. (N)

I don't accept my own weaknesses. (N)

I can like people without having to approve of them.

I fear failure. (N)

I avoid attempts to analyze and simplify complex domains. (N)

It is better to be yourself than to be popular.

I have no mission in life to which I feel especially dedicated. (N)

I can express my feelings even when they may result in undesirable consequences.

I do not feel responsible to help anybody. (N)

I am bothered by fears of being inadequate. (N)

I am loved because I give love.

Note: Respondents answer each item on a 4-point scale: "agree," "somewhat agree," "somewhat disagree," "disagree." Items followed by an "N" are coded in the negative direction, meaning that *dis*agreement with them suggests greater self-actualization.
Source: Jones & Crandall (1986), p. 67.

A few empirical studies have supported Maslow's claim that people who are self-actualized should report a greater number of peak experiences (Klavetter & Mogar, 1967; Rizzo & Vinacke, 1975). Other studies have examined qualitative differences among peak experiences (Hallaq, 1977). For example, McAdams (1982b) found that college students scoring high in intimacy motivation (described later in this chapter) described peak experiences laden with themes of love and friendship, reciprocal communication and sharing, helping others and being helped, and tender interpersonal touch. Students high in power motivation, on the other hand, underscored themes of perceived strength, powerful inspiration, having impact, vigorous activity, and increased fame or recognition. Underlying personality dispositions, such as intimacy and power motivation, may shape and be shaped by the quality of a person's peak experiences. Interestingly, McAdams found no relation between (1) power and intimacy motivation on the one hand and (2) corresponding themes of power and intimacy on the other in students' descriptions of "nonpeak" experiences, such as everyday neutral experiences. The finding suggests that the content of peak experiences is an especially revealing piece of personological data, much more informative of a person's fundamental strivings and orientations than a random slice of subjective experience.

Exploring people's strong motivation to engage in activities of deep personal satisfaction, Mihalyi Csikszentmihalyi (1977, 1990) has argued for a psychology of *optimal experience*. Taking a lead from Maslow, Rogers, and other humanistic approaches, Csikszentmihalyi has explored the phenomenology of artists, athletes, creative professionals, and other active people when they are involved in the life activities they enjoy most. Csikszentmihalyi terms these **autotelic** activities—behaviors deeply enjoyable in and of themselves, functioning as their own ("auto") ends ("telos"). The subjective experience that a person feels when engaged in an autotelic activity is best described as **flow.** Rock climbers describe the flow experience:

> When I start on a climb, it's as if my memory input had been cut off. All I can remember is the last thirty seconds, and all I can think ahead is the next five minutes. . . . With tremendous concentration the normal world is forgotten.

> You're moving in harmony with something else, you're part of it. It's one of the few sorts of activities in which you don't feel you have all sorts of different kinds of conflicting demands on you.

> It's the Zen feeling, like meditation or concentration. One thing you're after is the one-pointedness of mind. You can get your ego mixed up with climbing in all sorts of ways and it isn't necessarily enlightening. But when things become automatic, it's like an egoless thing, in a way. Somehow the right thing is done without you ever thinking about it or doing anything at all. . . . It just happens. And yet you're more concentrated. (Csikszentmihalyi, 1977, pp. 81, 87)

Dancers report flow experiences in dance; surgeons report flow when operating on patients; chess players report flow in the middle of an especially intense match. All flow experiences are not the same, but they do appear to share a common structural dimension, suggests Csikszentmihalyi. First, flow involves a *focused and ordered state of consciousness,* described by one of the rock climbers as the "one-pointedness of mind."

FIGURE 8.2   *The Flow State*

Flow happens when skills match challenges.

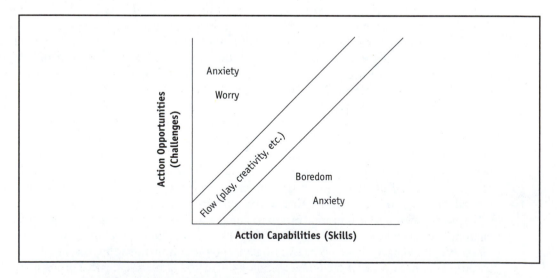

Source: Csikszentmihalyi (1977), p. 17.

The person focuses complete attention on the event or activity. Consciousness is highly structured and organized as the information that the mind deals with appears at an optimal level for comprehension. Second, flow involves an *equivalent ratio of skills to challenges*. If the challenge vastly exceeds the person's skill (for example, if the mountain is too rough), the person may experience worry or anxiety and a fragmentation of consciousness. If, on the other hand, the person's skill vastly exceeds the task challenge (if the mountain is extremely easy to climb), the person may subside into boredom. Figure 8.2 shows how flow goes beyond (or is it between?) boredom and anxiety.

Flow may be experienced in all sorts of activities and situations. Although intense forms of play and recreation (such as rock climbing and dancing) often yield flow experiences, many people also report flow when they are optimally engaged in their work, as Table 8.5 shows. In a study of 82 adult workers, 87% reported that they had had flow experiences. Of these, 30% reported that they experienced flow less than once a week, 40% reported that they experienced it about once a week, and 30% said they experienced flow daily. Those adults who reported more flow experiences also spent more time on the job actually working and less time "goofing off." They also reported many fewer instances in daily life in which they "wished they were doing something else" (Csikszentmihalyi, 1982).

Csikszentmihalyi's description of flow resembles Maslow's peak experiences. Privette and Landsman (1983) identify yet a third form of optimal functioning, which they call **peak performance.** In peak performance, a person performs above and beyond expectations, as in breaking an athletic record or putting on a truly exceptional performance in the arts.

Peak experience, flow, and peak performance all share certain basic features. Yet they have different emphases. Peak experience nearly always involves intense joy

| TABLE 8.5 | *Frequency of Activities Mentioned as Producing Flow Experiences* |

	PERCENTAGE OF SUBJECTS MENTIONING
Social Activities (Vacationing with family; being with children, wife, or lover; parties; traveling)	16
Passive Attending Activities (Watching TV; going to the theatre; listening to music; reading)	13
Work Activities (Working; electrical work; challenging problems at work)	31
Hobbies and Home Activities (Cooking, sewing; photography; singing; etc.)	22
Sports and Outdoor Activities (Bowling; golf; dancing; swimming; etc.)	18
	___
	100

Note: For each subject ($N = 71$), the one activity mentioned most often in response to the three quotes was selected.
Source: Csikszentmihalyi (1982), p. 24.

FIGURE 8.3   *Peak Experience, Peak Performance, and Flow*

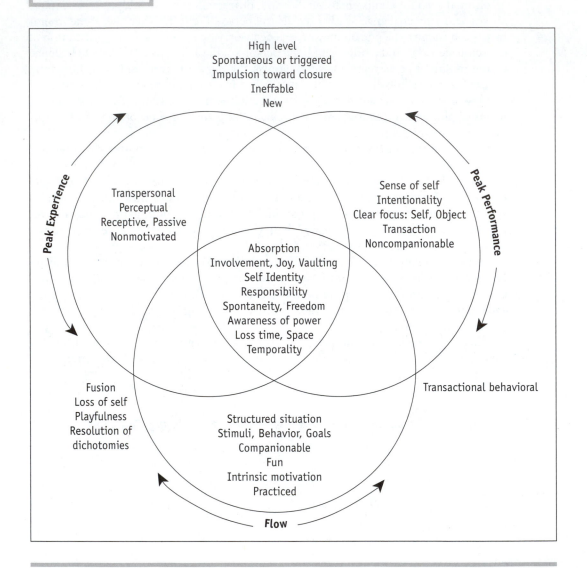

Source: Privette (1983), p. 1366.

whereas peak performance always involves superior functioning. Flow may involve either joy or superior functioning, but it is more centrally defined as an intrinsically rewarding experience. Privette (1983) has examined the similarities and differences among the three forms of optimal functioning. Her interesting characterization of the three, shown in Figure 8.3, is an attempt to discern the phenomenology of three different ways in which human beings engage their worlds in authentic ways suggestive of full functioning and self-actualization.

Intrinsic Motivation and Self-Determination Theory

We value peak experiences and moments of flow in our lives for the intensely positive feelings they provide and for their ability to involve us so fully in the best that life has to offer. These kinds of experiences are so good that they almost render the question of motivation meaningless. What I mean is that you don't typically have to explain to people *why* you would like to feel ecstasy, excitement, vitality, or any of the B-values that Maslow suggests may accompany the most wonderful moments in our lives. It is patently obvious that virtually anybody would want to feel these things. I, for one, can't think of anybody I've ever met who would say that he or she is not interested in feeling utter joy. In other words, peak experiences and moments of flow seem to be *self-reinforcing* experiences. We are likely to value them in and of themselves—not because they lead to any other goal but because the good feelings that accompany them are themselves the "goal." Put differently, especially positive experiences in our lives may be *intrinsically motivating*. No outside motivation or incentive is needed. Indeed, providing a reward might have the paradoxical effect, some would say, of robbing the experience of its value and worth.

Research on **intrinsic motivation** suggests that providing rewards and incentives for intrinsically enjoyable behaviors may work not to reinforce but rather to undermine these behaviors. Research on intrinsic motivation began in the early 1970s with the observation that in certain situations material rewards produce surprising *decreases* in human performance (Deci, 1972; Lepper & Greene, 1978). While traditional theories of reinforcement, like Skinner's behaviorism (Chapter 4), tell us that people learn and perform best when they are rewarded for what they do, numerous studies show that receiving an extrinsic reward has its *costs* in certain situations. Extrinsic rewards may undermine the intrinsic value of certain behaviors and reduce the person's perceived freedom to do what he or she wants to do.

Consider these simple experiments conducted by Deci (1971). College students were typically asked to solve a series of interesting mechanical puzzles. In the experimental condition, the students were told that they would be paid $1 for each puzzle solved during a specified period of time. In the control condition, the students were given no information about monetary rewards. After the time period had elapsed, the students were given an opportunity to choose from a number of different activities available to them. Their behavior during this free-choice period was observed through a one-way mirror. Deci found that those students who had been promised payment for their puzzle performance (the experimental group) spent significantly less time playing with the puzzle during the free-choice period than did the students who were not promised payment (control group). Furthermore, the students who were paid for their performance reported that they enjoyed the puzzle task less and found it less interesting than did the students who were not paid.

What do these differences mean? Deci concluded that the students who received an extrinsic reward for their performance experienced a decrease in intrinsic motivation. The reward undermined their interest in the puzzles. Now that they were no longer being paid for their performance, they saw little reason to continue playing with the puzzles. Similar studies have produced parallel results. For instance, Lepper, Greene, and Nisbett (1973) found a decrease in children's intrinsic motivation when they were rewarded for their artwork. Children who had received rewards for using certain highly desirable materials in their artwork were less motivated to use those same art materials days later than were those children whose use of the materials had not been rewarded before. College students working on interesting word games became less intrinsically motivated when external deadlines were imposed on their finishing than when none was applied (Amabile, DeJong, & Lepper, 1976). The external contingency of a deadline, like an external reward, shifts the person's perceived reason for undertaking a task from the intrinsic qualities of the task itself to extrinsic factors. The person loses interest in the task when he or she comes to see the motivation for doing the task as prompted from the outside.

Rewards, however, do not always undermine intrinsic motivation (Eisenberger & Cameron, 1996). First, a task must be intrinsically interesting if the costs of reward are to be seen. In boring routine tasks, the introduction of a reward may increase a person's interest in the task and improve performance (Calder & Staw, 1975). Second, not all rewards in all situations are equal. While money, grades, and other more or less material rewards that are clearly contingent on performance may undermine intrinsic motivation in certain situations, such social reinforcers as verbal praise and encouragement are likely to increase intrinsic motivation. Furthermore, it depends on exactly what aspect of behavior is being rewarded. Rewards for *effort* (trying hard) are perceived differently from rewards for *ability* (doing well).

A study by Koestner, Zuckerman, and Koestner (1987) illustrates the complexity of intrinsic motivation. In this laboratory study, the experimenters used verbal praise to reinforce college students' performance on an interesting hidden-figures puzzle. In one condition, the students were told that their performance was a test of creative intelligence, inducing an "ego-involvement" attitude. In another condition, the task was introduced as a neutral game, inducing a "task-involvement" attitude. After working with the puzzles, the students received either (1) ability praise ("That's very good; I see you really have a knack for these"), (2) effort praise ("That's very good; I can see you've really applied yourself on these"), or (3) no praise. Then, the students were left alone in a free-choice period during which they were secretly observed in order to determine how much time they spent playing with the hidden-figures puzzles—the behavioral measure of intrinsic motivation. Finally, they were given questionnaires measuring their interest in and enjoyment of the puzzle task.

Table 8.6 shows some of the results from this experiment. First, task-involved students showed more intrinsic motivation (measured as the amount of time spent playing with the puzzles during the free-choice period) than did students in the ego-involved group. In other words, when the students were told that their performance measured creative intelligence, they showed less intrinsic interest in the puzzles later on. The ego-involving instructions diverted their attention away from the intrinsic enjoyment of the task. Second, students who were praised for their ability showed greater intrinsic motivation than those praised for effort and those who were not praised. Providing positive feedback about how well they were doing increased the students' interest in the task.

A third important finding, not apparent in Table 8.6, is that ability praise was relatively more effective in promoting intrinsic motivation in the ego-involving condition, whereas effort praise worked especially well in the task-involving condition. In other words, if you are performing a task that you enjoy mainly for the sake of enjoyment,

TABLE 8.6	Free-Choice Time (in Seconds) for Type of Involvement and Style of Praise			

	STYLE OF PRAISE			
TYPE OF INVOLVEMENT	ABILITY	EFFORT	CONTROL	M
Ego	270	52	120	147
Task	295	229	120	215
M	283	141	120	181

Note: M = "mean" or "average" score
Source: Koestner, Zuckerman, & Koestner (1987), p. 386.

then being praised for your effort is likely to increase your intrinsic motivation more than being praised for your ability. But when you perform the task in a context that tests your ability (in this case, a test of "creative intelligence"), receiving praise for your ability is likely to be especially reinforcing and to promote intrinsic motivation.

In an important theoretical development, Edward Deci and Richard Ryan have integrated research on intrinsic motivation into the broader framework of what they call **self-determination theory** (Deci & Ryan, 1980, 1985, 1991; Ryan, 1991, 1995). According to their view, intrinsic motivation is "the energizing basis for natural organismic activity" (Deci & Ryan, 1991, p. 244). Human beings are endowed with a natural tendency to encounter new challenges that will promote their self-development. Intrinsically motivated behaviors are experienced with "a full sense of choice, with the experience of doing what one wants, and without the feeling of coercion or compulsion" (Deci & Ryan, 1991, p. 253), such that the person spontaneously engages in activity that appears inherently interesting and enjoyable. Such activity "emanates from oneself, and is thus *self*-determined" (p. 253).

Intrinsically motivated behavior, therefore, is self-determined. By contrast, behavior that is not self-determined may be perceived by the actor as *controlled* or *amotivated*. Controlled behavior occurs when a person acts to meet the demands of some internal or external force; even though controlled behaviors may be "intentional," they feel as if they are things that the person does not truly want to do. Amotivated behaviors are unintentional and often disorganized because the person cannot regulate his or her own actions. For example, under the stress of an imminent writing deadline, a newspaper reporter may wander around her office in a daze. She cannot bring herself to do what she wants to do. She feels that she cannot possibly complete her project in the short time period allotted, so her behavior becomes random and amotivated.

Self-determination begins at birth. Deci and Ryan write:

According to our perspective, a central feature of human nature is an active agency and a synthetic tendency that we ascribe to the self. From the time of birth, human beings are oriented toward the active exercise of their capacities and interests. They seek out optimal challenges, and they attempt to master and integrate new experiences. In other words, they are engaged in a developmental process that is intrinsic to their nature and is characterized by the tendency toward a more elaborate and extensive organization. (1991, pp. 238–239)

The infant is endowed with a nascent self—a vital core of personality that contains the potential for tremendous expansion. As Deci and Ryan (1991) put it, "the nature of life is to overtake itself" (p. 239). The self seeks to overtake its initial boundaries and limitations, to grow, to master its surroundings, to appropriate things, people, ideas, and environments, to make that which is nonself part of the self. As the infant masters and synthesizes new experiences, the self becomes more encompassing (it takes in more things) and more integrated (it organizes its contents into meaningful systems). Over time, self-determined behavior enhances the development of self, and as the self develops, more and more of the person's behavior may become self-determined. An expanded self makes for a greater degree of *self-involvement* in behavior. The person's experience of life becomes akin to that of the "author" or "owner" of his or her own behavior. Behavior becomes less controlled and amotivated. Action becomes incorporated within and guided by the self.

Deci and Ryan argue that self-determined behavior stems from three basic psychological needs. First, the need for *competence* encompasses the person's strivings to control the outcomes of events and to experience a sense of mastery and effectiveness in dealing with the environment. Second, the need for *autonomy* involves the desire to feel that one is independent of external pressures and able to relate to the world as an origin rather than a pawn. Third, the need for *relatedness* encompasses a person's strivings to care for others, to feel that others are relating to the self in authentic and mutually supportive ways, and to feel a satisfying and coherent involvement with the social world more generally. The three needs generate self-determined behavior, and self-determined behavior promotes development, or what Deci and Ryan call *organismic integration*. Organismic integration has two facets—unity of the self and integration into the social order. Over time, self-determined behavior helps the person experience his or her inner life in a more cohesive and unified manner, and it helps involve the person in coherent and meaningful interactions with other people.

Sheldon and Kasser (1995) distinguish between the self-determination theory concept of organismic integration on the one hand and the more common notion of personality congruence on the other. Personality congruence refers to the extent to which a person's goals are consistent with one another and, therefore, work well together. For example, a successful entrepreneur's goals of (1) becoming rich and (2) traveling around the world may be consistent with each other in that his success in making money will enable him to pay for expensive vacations. These two goals suggest some personality congruence. However, these goals do not make a strong case for organismic integration. Organismic integration concerns the extent to which a person's goals are self-determined and consistent with organismic needs. In the case of the entrepreneur, getting rich is viewed as an extrinsic rather than intrinsic goal. Extrinsic goals include such things as financial success, social recognition, and physical attractiveness. When goals are linked to needs for autonomy, competence, or interpersonal relatedness, organismic integration is enhanced. In two research studies, Sheldon and Kasser show that students scoring high on measures of organismic integration tend to report more positive daily moods, heightened vitality, and engagement in meaningful daily activities. Other studies have shown that as people make significant progress in the attainment of goals that contribute to the needs for autonomy, competence, and interpersonal relatedness, they experience higher levels of mental health and adjustment, self-actualization, and psychological well-being (Sheldon & Elliot, 1999; Sheldon & Kasser, 1998).

Not only should developing goals that meet organismic needs be associated with positive feelings and behaviors, but self-determination theory suggests that pursuing extrinsic goals that do not promote organismic integration should be associated with lower levels of psychological well-being. Kasser and Ryan (1996) argue that the classic "American dream" is a story of financial success and material well-being. Yet, these extrinsic goals may do little to promote feelings of autonomy, competence, and interpersonal relatedness. In samples of both college students and adults, Kasser and Ryan found that the relative importance and efficacy of extrinsic aspirations for financial success, an appealing appearance, and social recognition were associated with lower vitality and self-actualization and more physical symptoms. Conversely, the relative importance and efficacy of intrinsic aspirations for self-acceptance, affiliation, community feeling, and physical health were associated with higher well-being and less distress. According to Kasser and Ryan, there is a dark side to the classic American dream. American society's obsession with material wealth may undermine the pursuit of intrinsic goals that promote organismic integration. As they get richer and live yet more comfortable lives, Americans may be losing sight of the goals in life most able to give them a sense of deep happiness and meaning.

The development of the self is a product of an intricate dialectic between the person and the social world. Deci and Ryan view the social world in terms of the opportunities and constraints it may provide for self-determined behavior. Three social dimensions are particularly important. First, the social environment may offer *autonomy support*. In other words, it may be encouraging of choice and innovation in behavior. Environments that discourage choice function to control a person's behavior. Second, the social environment may provide *structure* for behavior. Highly structured environments provide clear guidelines about what kinds of behaviors lead to what kinds of outcomes, and they give the actor explicit feedback concerning how "well" he or she is doing in the environment. Third, the social environment may offer interpersonal *involvement*. Involvement describes the degree to which significant others (e.g., parents, teachers, friends, spouse) are interested in and devote time and energy to a relationship. All in all, social contexts that provide high levels of autonomy support, *moderate* structure, and that contain involved others are optimal for encouraging self-determined behavior and organismic integration.

In sum, intrinsically motivated behavior is inherently interesting and enjoyable, involves optimally challenging tasks and activities, and is often performed in the absence of external rewards. Such behavior is self-determined. Self-determined behavior serves the basic needs of competence, autonomy, and relatedness. Self-determined behavior flourishes in environments that support autonomy, provide moderate structure, and involve people who care about the person and are invested in the person's life. Self-determined behavior makes for organismic integration, by promoting unity of one's inner life and integration into a social order. Deci and Ryan argue that self-determination ultimately enables the person to experience the "true self," so that he or she may lead an "authentic" life:

> Authenticity, we suggest, is a descriptor for behavior that is an expression of the true self and for which one accepts full responsibility. When an action is endorsed by its "author," the experience is that of integrity and cohesion—the experience is one of being true to one's *self*. Authenticity is thus self-determination. (1991, p. 277)

FEATURE 8.A

Daily Reversals in Motivation: Telic and Paratelic

Different theories of motivation agree that much of human behavior is goal directed and purposeful. Needs, motives, and goals pull behavior along, give it energy and direction. But sometimes behavior appears to have no goal at all, no end-state to which it is oriented. According to Michael Apter's (1982, 1989) **reversal theory,** daily experience is organized according to contrasting pairs of *metamotivational modes*. In the **telic mode,** consciousness is centered on achieving an end state, a "telos" of some kind. In the **paratelic mode,** activity is an end in itself, and no end state serves to give activity its purpose and meaning. Apter writes that in the telic mode "pleasure comes primarily from the feeling of movement towards the goal, of progress and improvement, as well as from the attainment of the goal itself" (1989, p. 33). But "in the paratelic mode, pleasures comes primarily from the activity—from the immediate sensual gratification, from the satisfaction of skilled performance and kinesthetic sensation which go with it, from the continuing interest in seeing what will happen next" (1989, p. 33). While the telic mode is oriented toward the future, the paratelic mode focuses on the here and now.

The sharp distinction between telic and paratelic modes can be well illustrated when considering the psychological phenomenon of *arousal*. By arousal, Apter simply means "the degree to which one feels oneself to be 'worked up' or emotionally intense about what one is doing" (1989, p. 9). Four arousal-related emotions with which everybody is familiar are relaxation, boredom, excitement, and anxiety. When arousal is low, a person may feel relaxation or boredom. Relaxation feels good; it is hedonically positive. Boredom feels bad; it is hedonically negative. Similarly, under conditions of high arousal, one may feel excitement (hedonically positive) or anxiety (negative). The key point here is that a given level of arousal may be experienced as either positive or negative. I may experience a calm autumn day as relaxing or boring. I may find that a lively party brings me excitement or anxiety.

Part of what determines the hedonic tone of my experience at a given level of arousal is my momentary metamotivational mode. In essence, the telic is an *arousal-avoidance* mode; the paratelic is an *arousal-seeking* mode. Therefore, when my consciousness is focused on goals to be achieved in the future, anything that makes those goals more difficult to achieve, such as obstacles or challenges of some sort, is likely to increase my arousal and lead to the negative experience of anxiety. But when I make progress toward the goal and when I eventually achieve the goal, then arousal tapers off and I experience the pleasant emotions of relaxation and gentle enjoyment—that good feeling of a job well done, progress made, goals achieved or soon to be achieved. When I am in the paratelic mode, by contrast, I adopt a more activity-oriented, rather than goal-oriented, approach to existence. I move from work to play. In the paratelic mode, I may find high levels of arousal to be especially exciting, and I may therefore seek them out. At high levels of arousal, I may experience passion, fascination, thrill, exhilaration, elation, euphoria, and so on. But low levels of arousal may be viewed as understimulating. I become bored in the absence of emotional involvement. There seems to be nothing to do; no activity seems involving enough to provide my conscious experience with the stimulation jolt I need to feel good.

According to reversal theory, daily experience frequently reverses itself, sometimes from one moment to the next. John may start the day out in the telic mode, moving in a goal-directed fashion through his shower, shave, breakfast, and first class—focusing more on getting things done, accomplishing the goals of the day, rather than on the activities themselves. He may switch into the paratelic mode at lunch, as he sits with his good friends and talks about last night's basketball game. Switching to the telic mode for his class in personality psychology, he may find himself drifting into the paratelic as the professor drones on and on about self-determination theory. His doodling on a sketch pad evolves into an opportunity to draw humorous caricatures of the teaching assistant. The activity becomes fun in and of itself; the goal of obtaining information from the lecture no longer takes center stage in consciousness. John loses track of time, is startled when class is suddenly dismissed. The bell jolts him out of the paratelic into the telic. He's got to get to the gym for soccer practice. Dinner that evening represents a failed attempt in the paratelic. He cannot keep his mind on the conversation with his friends; he does not even taste his food. He keeps thinking about all of the homework he has. In the grip of the telic mode, he goes up to his room and works hard to prepare for tomorrow's examination in his history class. But one of the books for the course proves more interesting than he expected. He finds himself immersed in a chapter that wasn't even assigned by the professor. As the paratelic takes hold, he comes to enjoy the material for its own sake, forgets about the test for a few minutes. He calls his girlfriend; excitement mounts as the two of them engage in a witty conversation about people they know and about their own soaring relationship. But excitement shifts quickly to anxiety as he remembers the examination again, reversing modes suddenly from paratelic to telic. As he works through the material for the history exam, he begins to feel better, more relaxed. It looks as if it is going to be a pretty easy examination. He is well prepared. Savoring the low arousal of a telic mode, he decides it's time to go to sleep.

For a given individual, metamotivational modes shift frequently over the course of a day. But people differ significantly with respect to how dominant one or the other mode is in daily consciousness. Some people appear to be telic-dominant, some are paratelic-dominant, and some fall in the middle between the two modes. Apter assesses individual differences in mode dominance through a self-report **Telic Dominance Scale.** The scale incorporates three aspects of telic-dominance: seriousmindedness, planning-orientation, and arousalavoidance.

Research employing the Telic Dominance Scale has identified telic and paratelic "lifestyles." Telic-dominant individuals carry out more carefully planned activities, continually monitor themselves while doing so, and appear to spend more of their lives accomplishing tasks or moving toward long-term goals. When asked to talk about themselves, they tend to describe their lives in detailed and objective terms, sometimes providing specific names, dates, and times for important experiences in their past. Paratelic-dominant individuals (those scoring low on the Telic Dominance Scale) appear to indulge in a greater variety of activities, to have a more exciting time, and to be less well organized and more spontaneous than telic-dominant people. Their life stories are more impressionistic, dramatic, and sometimes exaggerated.

THREE SOCIAL MOTIVES

Henry Murray's Theory of Needs

The most well-known representative of the diversity tradition in the study of human motivation is Henry Murray's theory of needs. Murray was a monumental figure in the history of personality psychology whose contributions to the biographical study of lives will be examined in Chapter 12 of this textbook. For now, what is important is Murray's (1938) conception of needs. Murray argued that human lives must always be understood in the context of time. People live both in response to the past and in anticipation of the future. As we move through our daily lives, we bind together our remembrances of things past and our expectations about what is to come:

> What he [the human being] does is related not only to the settled past but also to shadowy preconceptions of what lies ahead. Years in advance he makes preparations to observe an eclipse of the sun from a distant island in the South Pacific and, lo, when the moment comes, he is there to record the event. With the same confidence another man prepares to meet his god. Man lives in an inner world of expected press (pessimistic or optimistic), and the psychologist must take cognizance of them if he wishes to understand his conduct or his moods, his buoyancies, disappointments, resignations. Time-binding makes for continuity of purpose. (Murray, 1938, p. 49)

The directedness of human lives becomes apparent over time. A given momentary behavior may seem meaningless in light of the current situation in which it is displayed. But with respect to the person's life over time, the behavior may be seen as part of a purposeful sequence of actions. Time-binding provides lives with their characteristic direction and purpose. But what forces direct and select the ways in which human beings organize their lives and bind their time? Such forces, according to Murray, reside both within the organism and in the organism's environment. Within the organism are located the basic physiological and psychological **needs.** In the environment are located the various situational constraints and opportunities for need expression, or what Murray called **press** (plural = press). When a particular need repeatedly interacts with a particular press over an extended period of time, you have what Murray called a **thema.** Therefore, human motivation must be understood in terms of the interaction of needs and press to produce themas.

Murray defined a need as a

> construct (convenient fiction or hypothetical concept) which stands for a force (the physico-chemical nature of which is unknown) in the brain region, a force which organizes perception, apperception, [interpreting perceptions], intellection [thinking], conation [striving], and action in such a way as to transform in a certain direction an existing unsatisfying situation. (Murray, 1938, pp. 123–124)

Therefore, a need is the representation of a brain force that energizes, directs, selects, and organizes human perceiving, thinking, feeling, and striving. It operates to transform an unsatisfying situation into a more satisfying one. In this last regard, Murray's view of needs is similar to Freud's in that both held to the doctrine of *tension-reduction.* The tension for a particular need builds up over time and then is released through need-satisfying thought or behavior. However, Murray departed from Freud dramatically with respect to the kinds of human needs he identified. *Viscerogenic* needs are physiological wants and desires such as the need for air, water, and sentience (sleep). More relevant for personality, however, are the *psychogenic* needs, such as the needs for autonomy, achievement, affiliation, dominance, play, order, and so on. Murray proposed 20 basic psychogenic needs, each of which exerts important effects on human behavior. Table 8.7 defines selected psychogenic needs from Murray's influential taxonomy.

At any given point in time, human behavior may be organized by a number of different viscerogenic and psychogenic needs operating simultaneously. But some needs are likely to be stronger or "prepotent" relative to others at a given time. Stronger or more urgent needs sometimes override weaker ones, as when a person's strong craving for dominance moves him to act in Machiavellian ways that violate his need for affiliation. In other instances, different needs may fuse, thereby working together to attain the same behavioral end. Playing softball with one's friends may, for example, satisfy the needs for affiliation, dominance, and play. Another important kind of relation among needs is *subsidiation*. A subsidiary need is one that operates in service of another. For example, a person may act in an aggressive way (revealing a strong aggressive need) in order to avoid pain (the need for harm avoidance). In this instance, the aggressive need serves the more encompassing need to avoid pain. The only reason the person desires to be aggressive is in order to remain safe.

Needs also interact with traits (Chapter 5). In general, the way in which a person achieves a goal may be partly determined by traits, such as extraversion–introversion. But the nature of the goal itself is more likely determined by needs. Traits and needs, therefore, fulfill different functions in the personality: needs establish goals; traits describe behavioral means whereby goals are met (McClelland, 1981). In a sense, needs tell us *why* a person does what he does; traits tell us *how*.

Just as the concept of "need" represents the significant determinants of behavior within the person so the concept of "press" represents the effective or significant determinants of behavior in the environmental situation. A press is a tendency in the environment to facilitate or obstruct the expression of a need. Wrote Murray, "the *press* of an object is what it can *do to the subject or for the subject*—the power that it has to affect the well-being of the subject in one way or another" (1938, p. 121). Such an "object" may indeed be a person or some feature of an interpersonal situation. Murray distinguished between *alpha* and *beta* press. An alpha press is made up of characteristics in the environment as they exist in reality or as objective inquiry discloses them. By contrast, a beta press is the person's subjective impression of those characteristics in the environment. Beta press, therefore, is always a matter of interpretation.

The full dynamics of human behavior are revealed in the interaction of needs and press, producing a thema. Imagine this example. A college student's strong need for order cannot be well expressed in her ceramics class, in which she is forced to work with materials that are sloppy and difficult to control. A thema develops whereby her inability to act in an orderly fashion initially produces a great deal of anxiety, which quickly gives way to an attitude of "don't worry about it, you don't have to be neat." The thema is the entire pattern of need/press interaction. In these kinds of unruly experiences (press), she experiences anxiety because her need for order cannot be expressed. But the anxiety eventually gives way to relaxation. Indeed, the relaxation response may be a function of the arousal of her need for play. Themas sometimes involve multiple needs and press.

TABLE 8.7	*Selected Psychogenic Needs From Murray (1938)*
NEED	**BRIEF DEFINITION**
n Achievement	To accomplish something difficult. To master, manipulate, or organize physical objects, human beings, or ideas. To do this as rapidly and as independently as possible. To overcome obstacles and attain a high standard. To excel oneself. To rival and surpass others. To increase self-regard by the successful exercise of talent.
n Affiliation	To draw near and enjoyably cooperate or reciprocate with an allied other (an other who resembles the subject or who likes the subject). To please and win affection of a cathected object. To adhere and remain loyal to a friend.
n Aggression	To overcome opposition forcefully. To fight. To revenge an injury. To attack, injure, or kill another. To oppose forcefully or punish another.
n Autonomy	To get free, shake off restraint, break out of confinement. To resist coercion and restriction. To avoid or quit activities prescribed by domineering authorities. To be independent and free to act according to impulse. To be unattached, irresponsible. To defy convention.
n Dominance	To control one's human environment. To influence or direct the behavior of others by suggestion, seduction, persuasion, or command. To dissuade, restrain, or prohibit.
n Exhibition	To make an impression. To be seen and heard. To excite, amaze, fascinate, entertain, shock, intrigue, amuse, or entice others.
n Harm avoidance	To avoid pain, physical injury, illness, and death. To escape from a dangerous situation. To take precautionary measures.
n Nurturance	To give sympathy to and gratify the needs of a helpless object: an infant or any object that is weak, disabled, tired, inexperienced, infirm, defeated, humiliated, lonely, dejected, sick, mentally confused. To assist an object in danger. To feed, help, support, console, protect, comfort, nurse, heal.
n Order	To put things in order. To achieve cleanliness, arrangement, balance, neatness, tidiness, and precision.
n Play	To act for "fun" without further purpose. To like to laugh and make jokes. To seek enjoyable relaxation of stress. To participate in games, sports, dancing, drinking parties, cards.
n Sentience	To seek and enjoy sensuous impressions.
n Sex	To form and further an erotic relationship. To have sexual intercourse.
n Succorance	To have one's needs gratified by the sympathetic aid of an allied object. To be nursed, supported, sustained, surrounded, protected, loved, advised, guided, indulged, forgiven, consoled. To remain close to a devoted protector. To always have a supporter.
n Understanding	To ask or answer general questions. To be interested in theory. To speculate, formulate, analyze, and generalize.

Source: Adapted from Murray (1938), pp. 152–226.

The Thematic Apperception Test

Murray (1938) developed many methods for the study of personality, but the most popular and influential has probably been the Thematic Apperception, or TAT (Morgan & Murray, 1935; Murray, 1943). In the TAT, a person is presented with a series of ambiguous picture cues and is asked to compose, either verbally or in writing, a story in response to each. The TAT is considered a "projective test," in that the person assumedly projects his or her own needs, wishes, conflicts, and so forth onto the ambiguous picture cue. The ambiguous picture cue is merely a stimulus designed to put into motion the process of constructing an imaginative narrative response (Lindzey, 1959). In Murray's view, such narrative responding reveals partially hidden themes of the personality, especially those concerning basic needs, conflicts, and complexes.

Murray (1943) provided rough guidelines for interpreting the stories told in response to TAT pictures. He believed that the psychologist should first identify the *hero* in the story—usually the main character or the character who most resembles the storywriter. Second, the psychologist should consider the hero's *motives, trends, and feelings*. Careful attention should be paid to story content that indicates psychogenic needs: a story in which the main character is trying to succeed in a difficult task would indicate a strong *n* Achievement; another story in which the character seeks friendship with others would suggest the affiliation motive. Third, the psychologist should note the *forces in the hero's environment* that impinge upon or provide opportunities for need-expression. Murray believed that a TAT story may reveal as much about how a person perceives the world as it does about internal needs. Fourth, the *outcomes* of stories may indicate the extent to which the storyteller believes that his or her own needs can be fulfilled in daily life. In this regard, Murray suggested that the psychologist keep track of the ratio of happy to unhappy story endings. Fifth, the psychologist should document the recurrent combinations of particular needs and particular environmental situations (what Murray termed *press*) across the stories. A need/press combination constitutes a simple *thema*. Sixth, *interests and sentiments* may appear in the story content. The psychologist may be able to obtain information on the storyteller's feelings about particular kinds of people (for example, authority figures, older women, children) or about particular aspects of the environment (such as politics, religion, the natural world). Regardless of how the psychologist interprets the TAT, Murray emphasized that "the conclusions that are reached by an analysis of TAT stories must be regarded as good 'leads' or working hypotheses to be verified by other methods, rather than as proved facts" (1943, p. 14).

Because there are so many ways of using and interpreting the TAT, it is virtually impossible to pass judgment on the measure's overall reliability and validity. While many clinicians express a great deal of faith in the TAT's clinical usefulness, some reviews of the test have provided mixed results (Eron, 1950; Holt, 1978; Rosenwald, 1968). Lindzey (1952) has cast doubt on some of the interpretive assumptions first laid out by Murray, such as the belief that the person projects needs onto a single hero in the story. Zubin, Eron, and Schumer (1965) suggest that TAT responses are more subject to conscious control than many clinicians suspect. As do most other investigators, these investigators caution against relying too heavily on the TAT for individual clinical diagnosis. On the other hand, they suggest that the measure is a useful indicator of general interests, motives, and areas of emotional disturbance, and can be used quite profitably in personality research.

The most profitable use of the TAT is to view it as an indicator of psychogenic needs, or **motives.** Three such motives have been studied in great detail: achievement, power, and intimacy. In considering each of these three motives, we will focus on the research tradition fathered by personality psychologist David C. McClelland. Reconceptualizing Murray's notion of "need," McClelland defines a motive as a recurrent preference or readiness for a particular quality of experience, which energizes, directs, and selects behavior in certain situations. The achievement motive, therefore, refers to the quality of human experience entailed in *doing better;* the power motive refers to *having impact;* and the intimacy motive denotes *feeling close.* McClelland (1980) argues that motives lie outside a person's conscious awareness and cannot, therefore, be accurately assessed through conscious self-report. By sampling the everyday stream of imaginative thought, the TAT enables the researcher to find central themes that may indicate unconscious motives.

Achievement Motivation

My best friend, a research chemist who was my roommate in college, has a high **achievement motive.** He is strongly motivated to perform better—better in relation to other people and better in relation to personal standards of excellence—in all aspects of life. He strives with great persistence to be the best in his professional field. He is a fierce competitor on the basketball court. He even plays board games with a vengeance. More important, my friend's estimation of his own well-being depends strongly on the extent to which he is successful in different life realms. Although, like virtually all people, his mind covers diverse topics in a normal day, my friend spends more time than most thinking about achievement, often comprehending new events and environments as either opportunities for or obstacles to successful personal performance. A person whose achievement motivation is significantly lower than my friend's, on the other hand, is likely to be less preoccupied with achievement concerns. His or her conscious thought may run in different thematic directions, perhaps more in the direction of power, intimacy, or some other motive or goal.

Measuring the Achievement Motive David McClelland and John Atkinson pioneered the use of the TAT to assess individual differences in achievement motivation (Atkinson, 1958; Atkinson & Birch, 1978; McClelland, Atkinson, Clark, & Lowell, 1953). The most important innovation of their approach was the derivation and validation of an objective, reliable, and quantitative system to score TAT stories for achievement motivation. In their original derivation studies, McClelland and Atkinson asked college students to write short TAT stories under various laboratory conditions. In one condition, the students were first administered a series of cognitive tasks (such as unscrambling words) and then told that their performance on the tasks would be an indication of their general intelligence and leadership ability. It was assumed that such instructions would temporarily *arouse*

David McClelland

TABLE 8.8	Selected TAT Scoring Categories for Achievement Motivation	
CATEGORY	**DESCRIPTION**	**EXAMPLES**
Achievement imagery	A character in the story wants to perform better either by (1) out-performing someone else, (2) meeting an internal standard of excellence, (3) doing something unique, or (4) being involved in a long-term achievement project.	"Mary decided she would win first prize in the gymnastics competition." "Robert had spent 8 years practicing for tonight's performance."
Anticipating success	Someone in the story thinks about or anticipates reaching the achievement goal.	"They feel certain they will be able to pull off the theft and become great thieves."
World block	An obstacle in the environment blocks achievement.	"They will never be successful because they do not have the right equipment."
Negative feelings	The person is discouraged when the achievement goal is not reached.	"Cindy failed the examination, and now she is very depressed."

Sources: McClelland et al. (1953) and McClelland & Steele (1972). These are 4 out of 11 categories in the achievement-motive scoring system. For each category, the scorer determines "presence" (score 1 point) or absence (0 points) in each story.

achievement thoughts and feelings in these subjects, and that these thoughts and feelings would be projected onto the stories written on the TAT, administered immediately following the task. In another (neutral) condition, students were administered the same tasks but were told that the tasks were newly developed and not likely to be valid measures of much of anything. It was assumed that these subjects would be less aroused with respect to achievement strivings than the subjects in the first group.

McClelland and his colleagues detected a number of consistent content differences between the groups. Students in the arousal group tended to write more stories involving characters striving to do better, compared with students in the neutral group. Subsequent comparisons from different studies and various refinements produced a content scoring system for the TAT. The system is made up of the particular content themes that consistently differentiated between stories written under achievement arousal and under neutral conditions. The themes involve the story characters' behaviors, attitudes, and feelings about task performance (Table 8.8).

Although the achievement-motive scoring system was derived by examining group differences in narrative content, the system has proven extremely sensitive and valuable as an index of *individual differences* within groups. In a typical individual-differences study, a large number of people are administered the TAT under standardized *neutral* conditions. The subjects' TAT stories are then scored by trained coders according to the system referred to in Table 8.8. The results typically reveal a normal distribution in the sample, with achievement-motive scores ranging from high to low. It is assumed that each person's "natural" level of achievement motivation will be expressed in TAT stories written under such neutral, nonarousing conditions.

A substantial empirical literature suggests that people who score high on TAT achievement motivation behave in different ways than people who score low, supporting the construct validity (Chapter 5) of the TAT measure. For instance, people high in achievement motivation tend to prefer and show high performance in tasks of moderate challenge that provide immediate feedback concerning success and failure; they tend to be persistent and highly efficient in many kinds of performance, sometimes cutting corners or cheating in order to maximize productivity; they tend to exhibit high self-control and a future time perspective; and they tend to be restless, innovative, and drawn toward change and movement (Atkinson, 1957: Atkinson & Raynor, 1978; Crockett, 1962; Feather, 1961; Heckhausen, 1967; McClelland, 1961, 1985; Mischel, 1961; Mischel & Gilligan, 1964; Spangler, 1992; Winter & Carlson, 1988). Some of the best-established findings in this regard are summarized in Table 8.9.

Careers in Business   Young adults who are high in achievement motivation tend to be drawn to careers in business. In one study, college men with a high need for achievement manifested patterns of personal interests and values very similar to those expressed by stockbrokers, real estate agents, advertisers, merchandise buyers, and factory managers (McClelland, 1961). In another study, men with high achievement motivation in college tended to become employed in small businesses years later (McClelland, 1965). McClelland argued that business is a good match for the achievement motive, because business requires that people take moderate risks, assume personal responsibility for their own performance, pay close attention to feedback in terms of costs and profits, and find innovative ways to make products or provide services. These hallmarks of **entrepreneurship** precisely characterize the behavior and attitudes of people high in achievement motivation (McClelland, 1985).

TABLE 8.9   *Selected Correlates of High Achievement Motivation*

High aspirations but moderate risk taking
Preference for situations where personal responsibility can affect results
Tendency to take personal credit for success but blame others or the situation for failures
Cheating and/or bending the rules in order to reach a desired goal in an efficient and expeditious manner
Penchant for travel
Self-control, inhibition, and delay of gratification
Preference for somber colors and formal fashion
Extended future time perspective
Upward social mobility and higher educational attainment
Entrepreneurial activity and innovation
Success in business
Being reared in a family in which parents set high standards for performance
Scheduled feeding during infancy and relatively stringent toilet training

Note: Much of the research on achievement motivation has focused exclusively on men. While the relatively few studies investigating correlates of achievement motivation in women are generally consistent with results for men, there are some areas (such as entrepreneurship and risk taking) in which virtually no data on women have been obtained (Stewart & Chester, 1982).
Sources: McClelland (1985), Winter & Carlson (1988).

Among men, then, high achievement motivation is associated with a number of indexes of business success and productivity. Scoring high in the achievement motive, however, does *not* guarantee that one will reach the highest echelons of all large businesses and corporations. Andrews (1967) followed the careers of executives in a large company over 3 years and found that those with high achievement motivation received a larger number of promotions than those scoring low in achievement motivation. However, this was true only at an "achievement-oriented" firm, in which "doing well" was the major criterion of advancement. In another firm run by an authoritarian owner, achievement motivation was unrelated to promotions. McClelland and Boyatzis (1982) found that achievement motivation in managers at the time of their entry into the American Telephone and Telegraph (AT&T) Company was associated with promotion up to Level 3 in the company after 16 years, but not above that point. The managerial positions at Level 4 and above may have required skills and motives less associated with "doing better" and having more to do with "influencing people." McClelland has argued that, in large hierarchical organizations, high achievement motivation is likely to be instrumental in career advancement only up to a certain point. At the highest levels of prestige and influence, strong *power* motivation may prove more valuable.

Only a few studies have examined achievement motivation and career advancement in women (Stewart & Chester, 1982). Baruch (1967) and Stewart (1975) found that college women scoring high in achievement motivation tend to pursue challenging career patterns. Bloom (1971) showed that adolescent girls aiming to combine career and family are higher in achievement motivation than girls who do not plan to pursue a career. In a 14-year longitudinal study, Jenkins (1987) found that women with high achievement motivation in college tend to pursue careers in teaching, including college teaching. In Jenkins's study, professors and businesswomen showed larger increases in TAT achievement motivation over 14 years—the span from college through the mid-30s—than did women otherwise employed. A longitudinal study of both women and men showed that high achievement motivation at age 31 was associated with a relatively high income 10 years later (McClelland & Franz, 1992).

The Achieving Society   One of the more intriguing and controversial applications of McClelland's approach to achievement motivation is the analysis of *societal and historical differences*. McClelland (1961) has argued that entire societies and historical epochs differ in overall achievement motivation. While some societies actively promote achievement values and entrepreneurship, others appear less motivated to do so; in addition, a particular society's preoccupation with achievement may wax and wane over time. Such societal and historical differences should correspond to economic growth and ultimately to the rise and decline of entire states, regions, or peoples.

How might a personality psychologist measure societal differences in achievement motivation? McClelland answers that the procedure is virtually identical to that used with individuals: imaginative stories should be coded for achievement themes. Selected passages from a society's representative folktales, myths, textbooks, or even its popular literature can be coded as if they were discrete TAT stories in order to provide a rough estimate of overall achievement motivation in a society at a particular time in history. McClelland assumes that these narrative expressions reflect pervasive cultural assumptions and values.

In his best-known book, *The Achieving Society*, McClelland (1961) reports a study in which he collected second- and fourth-grade readers (elementary school textbooks) published from 1920 to 1929 from 23 different countries and scored selected passages for achievement themes. McClelland found that achievement motive themes in children's readers in the 1920s were positively correlated with his index of economic growth, even when other societal factors, such as differences in natural resources, were taken into consideration. In other words, economic growth between 1929 and 1950 was much more pronounced in those countries showing a strong emphasis on achievement in children's readers in the 1920s (such as Turkey, Israel, and India) than in countries whose children's readers showed relatively few achievement themes (such as Italy, Belgium, and Algeria). The explanation for the linkage is presented in Figure 8.4. A society's books for children mirror prevalent cultural values that are inculcated in children through various socialization processes, such as schooling and child training. Socialization for achievement encourages children to be masterful and independent, to plan for the future, to take moderate risks, and to value efficiency and gradual improvement or growth. Such training likely increases the achievement motivation of young boys and girls, who eventually develop a preference and proclivity for entrepreneurship as adults, which ultimately makes for greater economic growth.

Another index of a society's economic vitality is the proliferation of inventions and innovations. Figure 8.5 (page 468) presents the rather striking findings from a study of the relationship between achievement motivation expressed in children's readers and the number of patents per capita issued to inventors over a period of 140 years in the United States (de Charms & Moeller, 1962). The rise and decline in the number of U.S. patents issued between the years 1810 and 1950 neatly parallels the rise and decline of achievement imagery in American children's readers. A similar relationship was discovered between achievement imagery in English popular literature and the amount of coal imported by England during the years 1550 to 1800. Again, changes in collective achievement motivation predict economic growth. A positive relation between achievement motivation and economic growth can be seen in non-Western, preliterate societies, as well. Among 39 preliterate tribes, 75% of those with high achievement content in their folktales were characterized as having at least some full-time entrepreneurs, as contrasted with only 38% of the tribes with less amounts of achievement imagery in their folktales.

McClelland's impressive findings on collective achievement motivation are not without their detractors. Some sociologists and historians object to McClelland's attempts to "reduce" complex societal phenomena to the workings of a single personality variable. Other critics have claimed that while McClelland's results are worthy of attention, they are not as statistically robust as his rather grand interpretations would suggest. In this regard, McClelland's more recent (1975, 1985) attempts to predict and explain social reform, civil unrest, and even war in terms of collective levels of achievement, power, and intimacy/affiliation motivation strike some readers as unconvincing. Finally, some critics have pointed to the mixed success that other researchers have had in replicating McClelland's findings, especially for more recent historical periods. While some studies support McClelland's claim for a strong positive linkage between collective achievement motivation and economic growth in nations since 1950 (Tekiner, 1980), others do not (Beit-Hallahmi, 1980).

| FIGURE 8.4 | *Maternal Values and Societal Achievement* |

According to McClelland's theory, maternal values associated with industrialism lead to independence training, which promotes the development of achievement motivation in children. This eventually leads to entrepreneurship and higher productivity in society when those children grow up.

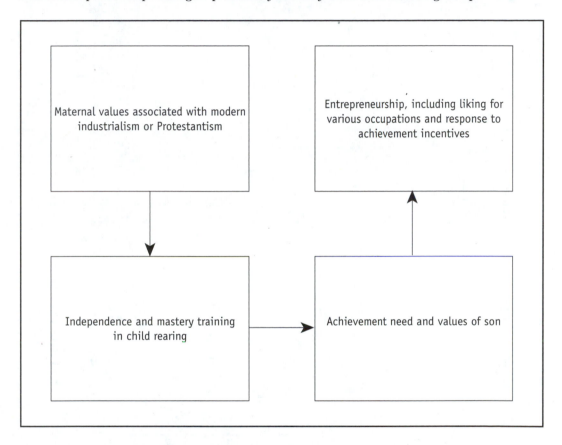

Source: Adapted from McClelland (1961), p. 58.

Power Motivation

The **power motive** is a recurrent preference for having an impact on other people. People high in power motivation strive to wield power and to feel stronger, more masterful, more influential than others. Like the achievement motive, this recurrent desire for power energizes, selects, and directs human behavior in predictable ways. Also like achievement motivation, individual differences in the power motive are assessed through objective content analysis of TAT stories.

FIGURE 8.5	*Achievement Imagery in Children's Readers and Societal Productivity*

As achievement imagery in children's school reading books increases over time, the number of patents issued in the United States also increases; as the achievement imagery decreases, patent numbers follow suit. The data are from the United States between the years 1810 and 1950.

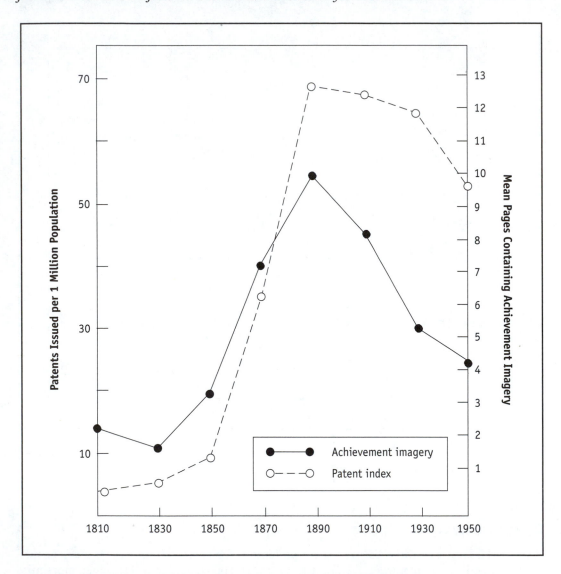

Source: de Charms & Moeller (1962), p. 139.

Veroff (1957) and Uleman (1966) designed early TAT scoring systems for the need for power, but the most popular system in recent research is the one developed and validated by David G. Winter (1973). Like McClelland and Atkinson on achievement, Winter derived the coding system for power motivation through comparing stories written by people under power-arousal and neutral conditions. Among the power-arousal conditions employed to derive the power-motive scoring system, Winter sampled TAT stories written by (1) candidates for student government office awaiting the results of voting, (2) subjects about to enact the powerful role of "psychological experimenter," (3) students who had seen a film of President John F. Kennedy's inauguration, and (4) students who had witnessed a multimedia presentation of inspirational speeches, such as Winston Churchill's speech on the evacuation of Dunkirk in World War II and excerpts from Shakespeare's *Henry V.* For "neutral" conditions, subjects wrote TAT stories in standard classroom settings. Table 8.10 describes a few thematic categories in Winter's (1973) scoring system for power motivation. Table 8.11 lists a few ways in which people high in power motivation differ from those scoring low on the motive.

Leadership   Because people high in power motivation desire to have an impact on others, a number of researchers have explored the ways in which such impact is accomplished. Fodor and Smith (1982) investigated how students high in power motivation direct the behaviors of others in group decision making. Forty groups containing five students each met to discuss a business case study that concerned whether a company should market a new microwave oven. In each group, a leader was appointed. Based on a prior administration of the TAT, half the leaders scored extremely high on

TABLE 8.10	*Selected TAT Scoring Categories for Power Motivation*	
CATEGORY	**DESCRIPTION**	**EXAMPLES**
Power imagery	A character in the story desires to have impact or to make an impression on others. This may be accomplished through strong, forceful actions (aggression), giving unsolicited help, or trying to control, persuade, or impress. Alternatively, a character may elicit strong emotions in others, or express concern about personal reputation.	"Barbara pushed the intruder aside and rescued the baby." "Bob tried to persuade the audience that he was right." "He is worried that his son will disgrace him."
Increased prestige	The setting of the story or a character is described in ways that increase prestige or position.	"Ed was elected senator for the state of Maine."
Lower prestige	The setting of the story or a character is described in ways that decrease prestige or position.	"He was a two-bit conman whom even the inmates scorned."
Effect	A power action produces a major, striking effect.	"The world was shocked by her bold words and brazen acts."

Source: McClelland & Steele (1972), Winter (1973).

| TABLE 8.11 | *Selected Correlates of High Power Motivation* |

Holding elected offices

Liking for careers in which one directs the behavior of individuals in accordance with preconceived plans and with the use of positive and negative sanctions (careers such as executive, teacher, and psychologist)

Career success among women in power-related occupations but not in careers emphasizing interpersonal relationships

Active, forceful, and influential in small groups

Effective organizational leader

Accumulation of prestige possessions, such as luxury cars and major credit cards

Taking large risks in order to gain visibility

Agentic, assertive style of friendship that emphasizes self-display and helping the other

Getting into arguments

Writing letters to the newspaper

Somewhat negative self-image

Prone to impulsive and aggressive behavior (men only)

Precocious and exploitative sexual activity (men only)

Instability in romantic relationships (men only)

Being reared in a family in which parents were relatively permissive concerning sexual behavior and aggression

Sources: Jenkins (1994), McAdams (1985b), McClelland (1985), Stewart & Chester (1982), Winter (1973), Winter & Carlson (1988).

the power motive and half scored extremely low. In addition, half the groups were given the opportunity to win a group reward for superior performance (in order to build "high group cohesiveness") and half were offered no reward ("low group cohesiveness"). Each group member was given a fact sheet containing information that could be shared with the group during discussion.

Three major dependent variables were assessed in Fodor and Smith's study: (1) the number of *facts* from the sheet that each person shared with the group during discussion, (2) the number of alternative *proposals* for marketing the microwave considered by the group, and (3) the level of *moral concern* evidenced by the group, which was determined by a rating of the extent to which the group discussed such issues as the possible harmful effects of microwave radiation on people's health and the ethical propriety of various marketing strategies. Those groups in which the leader was high in power motivation tended to offer fewer facts and proposals and to show less moral concern, compared with groups headed by a low-power leader (Table 8.12). The level of group cohesiveness, on the other hand, did not influence the results. The authors interpreted these findings to mean that leaders high in power motivation encourage what Janis (1972) calls *group-think*—a form of hasty decision making characterized by diffusion of responsibility, failure to consider long-term ramifications, and the domination by a single strong leader whose opinion generally goes unchallenged.

TABLE 8.12	*Average Number of Facts and Proposals and Mean Moral Concern Ratings of Discussion Groups*

LEVEL OF GROUP COHESIVENESS

LEVEL OF *n* POWER IN PRESIDENT	LOW			HIGH		
	FACTS	PROPOSALS	MORAL CONCERN	FACTS	PROPOSALS	MORAL CONCERN
Low	17.5	4.8	1.7	16.3	1.4	1.4
High	14.2	4.0	0.9	14.8	3.2	1.1

Source: Fodor & Smith (1982), p. 183.

A large number of studies have shown that people who perennially adopt strong leadership roles and/or rise to positions of high influence tend to score relatively high in power motivation (McAdams, Rothman, & Lichter 1982; McClelland & Boyatzis, 1982; McClelland & Burnham, 1976; Winter, 1973). The most intriguing line of research in this regard is probably Winter's (1987; Donley & Winter, 1970) studies of American presidents. Winter has analyzed the published inaugural addresses of virtually all the American presidents, going back to George Washington, for achievement, power, and intimacy motivation. Winter has argued that, despite the help of speech-writers and the influences of various sociohistorical forces and events, the motivational imagery contained in these major speeches partially reflects the president's own personality.

Table 8.13 presents the standardized scores for the three motives for each inaugural address coded in Winter (1987) and Winter (1996). Presidents scoring particularly high in power motivation include Franklin D. Roosevelt (1933), Harry Truman (1949), John Kennedy (1961), and Ronald Reagan (1981). Especially low in power motivation are Warren Harding (1921) and Calvin Coolidge (1925). Richard Nixon (1969) and Jimmy Carter (1977) both score very high on achievement motivation. Winter (1987) correlated motive scores with various ratings of the presidents made by historians and political scientists. Power motivation was positively associated with ratings of "presidential greatness" ($r = +.40$) and number of historically significant decisions made ($r = +.51$). In other words, those presidents who have been rated as especially forceful and influential by political scholars tend to be the same ones whose inaugural addresses indicated especially high levels of power motivation. In addition, presidents high in power motivation were also more likely to lead the United States into war ($r = +.52$).

Love and Health   What about the personal lives of people high in power motivation? Some research suggests that *men* high in the need for power experience numerous difficulties in romantic relationships with women. Stewart and Rubin (1976) conducted a longitudinal study of 63 dating couples living in the Boston area. At the time of the initial testing, high power motivation in males was significantly associated with greater expressed dissatisfaction with the relationship on the part of both members of the couple and greater anticipation of future serious problems among the men. Two years later, 50% of the couples in which the man was high in power motivation had broken up, and only 9% had married. In those couples in which the male was low in power

| TABLE 8.13 | *Motive Imagery Scores of American Presidents' Inaugural Addresses, 1789–1993* | | | |

| | | STANDARDIZED MOTIVE SCORES | | |
PRESIDENT	DATE	ACH	INT/AFF[a]	POW
Washington, George	1789	39	54	41
Adams, John	1797	39	49	42
Jefferson, Thomas	1801	49	51	51
Madison, James	1809	55	51	57
Monroe, James	1817	57	46	51
Adams, John Quincy	1825	48	51	37
Jackson, Andrew	1829	43	47	45
Van Buren, Martin	1837	42	48	40
Harrison, William Henry	1841	32	41	40
Polk, James	1845	33	41	50
Taylor, Zachary	1849	53	53	41
Pierce, Franklin	1853	49	44	50
Buchanan, James	1857	46	47	42
Lincoln, Abraham	1861	36	45	53
Grant, Ulysses	1869	56	47	36
Hayes, Rutherford	1877	51	48	48
Garfield, James	1881	46	35	49
Cleveland, Grover	1885	53	46	63
Harrison, Benjamin	1889	37	45	45
McKinley, William	1897	47	41	46
Roosevelt, Theodore	1905	62	38	38
Taft, William Howard	1909	44	38	58
Wilson, Woodrow	1913	66	49	53
Harding, Warren	1921	48	57	42
Coolidge, Calvin	1925	44	46	45
Hoover, Herbert	1929	68	45	48
Roosevelt, Franklin	1933	53	44	61
Truman, Harry	1949	56	65	78
Eisenhower, Dwight	1953	43	57	49
Kennedy, John	1961	50	85	77
Johnson, Lyndon	1965	55	59	49
Nixon, Richard	1969	66	76	53
Carter. Jimmy	1977	75	59	59
Reagan, Ronald	1981	60	51	63
Bush, George	1989	57	83	54
Clinton, Bill	1993	71	60	65

[a] "Int/Aff" refers to intimacy/affiliation motivation. Although intimacy and affiliation are two separate motives with separate TAT scoring systems, they do overlap somewhat in that both refer to warm relationships. Intimacy motivation is the desire to share what is innermost with another in a warm and communicative relationship (McAdams, 1980); affiliation motivation is the desire to establish, maintain, or restore positive-affect relations (Atkinson, Heyns, & Veroff, 1954). In this particular study, Winter combined the two systems to assess motivational imagery concerning "warm relationships" in presidential speeches.
Source: Winter (1987), p. 198, and Winter (1996), p. 163.

David Winter

motivation, only 15% had broken up, and 52% had married over the 2-year span. Additionally, males high in power motivation were more likely to report that during the 2 years immediately preceding the start of this dating relationship, they had been seriously involved in a romantic relationship that eventually terminated. Stewart and Rubin concluded that men high in power motivation showed marked instability in romantic relationships, moving from one serious involvement to another in relatively rapid succession. Bolstering their claims are the findings of Winter (1973) in which power motivation among men was positively associated with the number of sexual partners and frequency of intercourse.

Well-educated *women* high in power motivation tend to marry successful men (Winter, McClelland, & Stewart, 1981). Further, Veroff (1982) reports that power motivation in women is positively associated with marital *satisfaction*. While high-power women tend to report happy marriages, men high in power motivation show a higher divorce rate (McClelland, Davis, Kalin, & Wanner, 1972) and greater degree of marital *dissatisfaction* (Veroff & Feld, 1970). At the root of the high-power man's apparent dissatisfaction with and instability in romantic heterosexual relations may be a latent fear of women and the control they may exert. Slavin (1972) has shown that men high in power motivation express more themes of "feminine evil" in their fantasies than do men lower on the motive. These themes include females harming men through physical contact, females exploiting men, females rejecting men, females proving unfaithful in relationships, and females triumphing over men. In this regard, Winter and Stewart (1978) report that men high in power motivation, when asked to draw pictures of women, produce sometimes frightening and bizarre sketches with exaggerated sexual characteristics.

In the area of health, studies by McClelland and his colleagues suggest a possible association between power motivation and susceptibility to disease (McClelland, 1979; McClelland, Alexander, & Marks, 1982; McClelland, Davidson, Floor, & Saron, 1980; McClelland & Jemmott, 1980; McClelland, Ross, & Patel, 1985). However, the association seems fairly complex. McClelland (1979) has argued that a strong need for power increases a person's vulnerability to illnesses of various sorts *if* the person's need for power is inhibited, challenged, or blocked. Especially vulnerable are individuals who show *all* of the following characteristics: (1) high power motivation, (2) low intimacy motivation, (3) high self-control (sometimes called "activity inhibition" and suggesting a tendency to "block" or "inhibit" one's own expression of power), and (4) high levels of power-related stresses (Jemmott, 1987).

Some evidence suggests that people high in power motivation are predisposed to show heightened activation of the sympathetic nervous system when faced with obstacles to or frustrations in the experience of having impact and feeling strong (Fodor, 1984, 1985). If power motivation is associated with heightened sympathetic activity, then one might expect it also to be associated with elevated blood pressure. In three different samples of German and American men, McClelland (1979) documented just such an association. In one sample followed longitudinally, 61% of the men scoring above average on a TAT index of power + self-control (taken when they were in their

FEATURE 8.B

A Movie Is Like a TAT: The Case of Alfred Hitchcock

If presidential speeches (Winter, 1987) and children's readers (McClelland, 1961) can be coded for motivational themes as if they were TAT stories, then other works of the imagination explicitly crafted as creative narratives should prove to be even richer and more illuminating sources for personological scrutiny. In his brilliant analysis of the life of film director Alfred Hitchcock, biographer Donald Spoto (1983) treats each of Hitchcock's movies as if it were a kind of projective test, through which the director plays out some of his most troubling conflicts in desire. Just as any person in a TAT research study is assumed to project certain dominant needs and issues into his or her imaginative stories, so Hitchcock revealed himself through the plots, characterizations, settings, themes, scenes, and techniques of such popular film classics as *North by Northwest* (1958), *Rear Window* (1954), and *Psycho* (1960).

Alfred Hitchcock

One of Spoto's many insights into Hitchcock's troubled life and complex personality is the idea that the film director was obsessed, from early adulthood onward, with what seemed to be two very different sides of his own genius. On the one hand, he was the consummate perfectionist in the conception and realization of a film. A craftsman who was both bold and meticulous, Hitchcock made movies that were emotionally riveting while being revolutionary with respect to filmmaking technique. In this guise, Hitchcock was a brilliant, innovative, fastidious, suave, and sophisticated artist—a man of prodigious creative and financial means. On the other hand, he was a bumbling "fat boy" from a working-class neighborhood, a 300-pound glutton who was a physical slob and an emotional cripple. A cruel and alienated man who could not remember having a single playmate as a child, Hitchcock withdrew from interpersonal relationships to a world of macabre fantasy. He was incapable of experiencing intimacy with friends, acquaintances, and even his family. He behaved in grossly inappropriate ways in numerous social settings, threatening to slit his own throat at dinner parties and playing grotesque practical jokes on actors and actresses while they were on the set. And he lived "with inner demons of lust and possessiveness, of romantic, dark fantasies

North by Northwest

about killing, and of unfulfilled sexual day-dreams" (Spoto, 1983, p. 275).

The two sides of Hitchcock are revealed in the many instances in his films in which he sets up antagonistic *doubles*. Frequently, double characters and double scenes reflect opposite aspects of Hitchcock himself. The duality played itself out in Hitchcock's ambivalent treatment of women. His beautiful leading ladies, like Grace Kelly and Kim Novak, played roles as flawless paragons of feminine elegance and grace, worshiped and idealized by glamorous men. On the other hand,

women were savagely raped, mutilated, and debased as we see in the famous shower scene in *Psycho*, in the last attack of Tippi Hedren in *The Birds*, and in numerous strangulations and slashings. Writes Spoto:

> Hitchcock's conflicting feelings about women were perhaps the single most dramatic and painful realization of a divided personality. On the one hand, Woman was an abstraction, almost a remote goddess in her purity and coolness. But—"in the back of a taxi," as he liked to say—what such a woman might do was really what he *wished* she would do. (p. 432)

Spoto argues that Hitchcock's dual nature was also projected onto his two favorite leading men—Cary Grant and Jimmy Stewart. Grant represented what Hitchcock wished to be: the suave and sophisticated man of the world who always got the girl. Stewart, on the other hand, was closer to what Hitchcock saw as his own reality. Stewart was the theorist of murder in *Rope*, the chair-bound voyeur in *Rear Window*, and the obsessed and guilt-ridden pursuer of romance in *Vertigo*. While Grant personified the fastidious perfectionist who made his way in the world with style and grace, Stewart hinted at the darker underside of the brooding, inept fat boy. As Hitchcock got older, the fat boy became more dominant in both daily life and cinematic fantasy, exploding onto center stage one climactic February afternoon in 1964 when the aging director made an overt sexual proposition to his leading lady. Hitchcock's personal life appeared to deteriorate completely from this point onward, and the films he made in his last few years deteriorated, too, into virtual pornography.

30s) showed elevated diastolic blood pressure 20 years later, compared with only 23% of the men scoring below average on this index.

There is empirical evidence, albeit scattered, to suggest that high power motivation may be modestly associated with small deficits in the body's immune system. If this is true, one might expect high power motivation to be implicated indirectly in the breakdown of the body's defenses to sickness and disease. McClelland and Jemmot (1980) administered the TAT to 95 students and obtained self-report measures of health problems and life stresses. They classified each life stress identified by a subject as either a power/achievement event, an affiliation/intimacy event, or "other." Examples of power/achievement events included troubles with an employer, a substantial academic disappointment, and participating in a major sports event. The results of the study indicated that the students with (1) relatively high power motivation, (2) relatively high activity inhibition (self-control), and (3) an above-average number of power/achievement stresses over the past year reported more physical illnesses in the previous 6 months than did other students. In addition, the illnesses they reported were more severe. Thus, the highly controlled and highly power-oriented person may "bottle-up" his or her frustrations in such a way as to tax an internal physiological equilibrium. The result may be a greater number of colds, bouts of flu, and other maladies, especially during times of excessive power stress.

Intimacy Motivation

While our desires for achievement and power may motivate us to assert ourselves in effective and influential ways and to control, even master, our environments, our longings for close and warm relationships with other human beings pull us in a different direction, to the private life of intimate interpersonal communion (Bakan, 1966). Indeed, for some of us, the desire for intimacy is even grander and more compelling than our wishes for success, fame, and transcendence. As the novelist E. M. Forster wrote, "It is the private life that holds out the mirror to infinity; personal intercourse, and that alone, that ever hints at a personality beyond our daily vision" (1910, p. 78).

The desire for intimacy is a desire to share what is innermost with others. Ideally, the sharing is mutual; each person in an intimate encounter gives as well as receives. The intimate moment is intense and emotionally engaging; each person focuses unswervingly on the other, as if to suggest that during an intimate exchange virtually nothing else is important to the participants outside the process of relating to each other. The philosopher Martin Buber referred to this intense quality of interpersonal give-and-take as the *I–Thou* experience. He wrote:

> When I confront a human being as my Thou and speak the basic word I–Thou to him, then he is no thing among things nor does he consist of things. He is no longer He or She, a dot in the world grid of space and time, nor a condition to be experienced and described, a loose bundle of named qualities. Neighborless and seamless, he is Thou and fills the firmament. Not as if there were nothing but Thou; but everything else lives in his light (1970, p. 59)

My own contribution to the scientific literature on human motivation concerns this quality of intimate experience described so lyrically by Martin Buber (McAdams, 1980, 1982a). While all people doubtlessly desire to engage in close, warm, and communicative interaction with other people, some seem consistently more preoccupied with such intimate experience than others. **Intimacy motivation** is a recurrent preference for experiences of warm, close, and communicative interaction with others. Like the achievement and power motives, individual differences in intimacy motivation are assessed through content analysis of TAT stories. A few of the scoring categories for the intimacy motive are described in Table 8.14. These categories were derived and cross-validated in four different arousal experiments, wherein the stories written by people engaged in various kinds of intimate and friendly experiences were contrasted to stories written under neutral conditions (McAdams, 1980).

Research supports the construct validity of the intimacy motive as assessed on the TAT. People high in intimacy motivation spend more time, over the course of a normal day, thinking about relationships with others than do people scoring lower in intimacy motivation (McAdams & Constantian, 1983). People high in intimacy motivation partake in a greater number of friendly conversations over the course of a normal day, and they laugh, smile, and make more eye contact when conversing, compared with people low in intimacy motivation (McAdams & Constantian, 1983; McAdams, Jackson, & Kirshnit, 1984). On the other hand, the person high in intimacy motivation may not be the "life of the party"; intimacy motivation is unrelated to extraversion–introversion. Instead, the high-intimacy person is likely to value close, one-on-one exchanges over boisterous group activities. When confronted with a large group, he or she is likely to promote group harmony and cohesiveness, viewing group activities as opportunities for everybody to get involved rather than for one or two people to dominate the action (McAdams & Powers, 1981). Partly for this reason, people high in intimacy motivation

TABLE 8.14	*Selected TAT Scoring Categories for Intimacy Motivation*	
CATEGORY	**DESCRIPTION**	**EXAMPLES**
Positive affect	A relationship among characters promotes positive feelings, such as joy, excitement, love, liking, and happiness.	"She believes that she is in love with this strange man." "Sam and the boys are having a good time."
Dialogue	Characters in the story communicate with each other in a reciprocal and noninstrumental fashion.	"They talked all afternoon—about classes, music, the state of the world, and their feeling about each other."
Commitment or concern	A character commits him- or herself to another or expresses humanitarian concern. The result is often a helping or self-sacrificial act.	"Dan had pity on the old woman and spent the next hour trying to cheer her up."
Surrender of control	Characters in the story find themselves in a relationship that they cannot control; they give up any attempt to control and let events transpire spontaneously.	"She could not help herself; the sympathy she felt for the scoundrel made her stay and talk to him."

Source: McAdams (1984b).

are rated by their friends and acquaintances as especially "sincere," "natural," "loving," "not dominant," and "not self-centered" (McAdams, 1980).

McAdams, Healy, and Krause (1984) investigated the relation between intimacy and power motivation on the one hand and patterns of friendship on the other. In this study, 105 college students wrote TAT stories, subsequently scored for intimacy and power motivation, and then described in some detail 10 friendship episodes that had occurred in their lives in the previous 2 weeks. A friendship episode was defined as any interaction with a friend that lasted at least 15–20 minutes. For each episode, the student provided information on how many friends were involved in the episode, what activity was undertaken, what the friends talked about, what role the person played in the episode, and what emotions were experienced.

Table 8.15 shows the main results of the study. Students high in intimacy motivation tended to report friendship episodes involving one-on-one interaction with a single other friend ("dyads") rather than "large-group" interactions (friendship episodes involving 5 or more people) and to describe conversations in which the participants in the episode disclosed personal information about themselves ("self-disclosure"). Therefore, when they got together with their friends, high-intimacy students were more likely than low-intimacy students to talk about, and listen to their friends talk about, their own fears, hopes, feelings, fantasies, and other highly intimate topics. Power motivation, on the other hand, was associated with large-group interactions and assertive friendship activities like making plans, initiating conversations, and helping others. In general, intimacy motivation is associated with a *communal* friendship style that places prime importance on *being* together and *sharing* secrets with others, while power motivation is associated with an *agentic* friendship style that emphasizes *doing* things and *helping* others (McAdams, 1984a, 1988a).

In another study, students high in intimacy motivation engaged in a greater number of dyadic interactions over a one-week period of time, reported higher levels of self-disclosure with close friends, and experienced more positive emotion in their relationships, compared with students low in intimacy motivation (Craig, Koestner, &

TABLE 8.15   *Correlations Between Motives and Friendship Patterns in College Students*

	MOTIVE	
FRIENDSHIP MEASURE[a]	INTIMACY	POWER
Dyads (2 friends)	.20*	−.23*
Large groups (5 or more)	−.10	.21*
Listening role	.43***	−.15
Assertive role	−.04	.43***
Self-disclosure	.49***	−.16

Note: Total number of subjects was 105 (70 female and 35 male).
[a]These measures were based on students' descriptions of 10 friendship episodes that occurred in their lives in the previous 2 weeks.

*p < .05
***p < .001

Source: Adapted from McAdams, Healy, & Krause (1984), p. 834.

Zuroff, 1994). High intimacy motivation appears to sensitize people to opportunities for caring and empathic behavior. Not surprisingly, therefore, people who express callousness and contempt for others tend to score extremely low on intimacy motivation (Smith, 1985).

Because so many psychologists, novelists, and poets have told us that loving relationships with others are the key to happiness and well-being, we are certainly justified in asking whether high intimacy motivation leads to health, happiness, and overall life satisfaction. A few studies have examined the question directly. In one, McAdams and Vaillant (1982) found that high intimacy motivation at age 30 among male graduates of Harvard College significantly predicted overall psychosocial adjustment 17 years later, when the men were in their mid-40s. Men high in intimacy motivation in early adulthood reported greater marital satisfaction, job satisfaction, and even a marginally higher income at midlife compared with men scoring low in intimacy motivation.

In a second study, McAdams and Bryant (1987) drew upon a nationwide sample of more than 1,200 U.S. adults who were administered the TAT and a structured interview (Veroff, Douvan, & Kulka, 1981). The researchers found that, though intimacy motivation appears to bring certain benefits for both men and women, the benefits do not seem to be exactly the same for both sexes. High-intimacy women are relatively happy and satisfied, compared with low-intimacy women. On the other hand, high-intimacy men are *not* necessarily happier and more satisfied than low-intimacy men, but they do report less strain in life and less uncertainty.

Zeldow, Daugherty, and McAdams (1988) examined the relation between social motives assessed on the TAT and students' adjustment to medical school. Students high in intimacy motivation and low in power motivation showed the highest levels of well-being. However, those high in intimacy motivation and *high* in power motivation were more depressed, neurotic, fatalistic, and self-doubting in their first years of medical school, a relationship that was significant for both males and females. The authors suggested that the rigors of medical school make it extremely difficult for students with strong needs to feel close to others *and* to feel powerful and agentic to find satisfaction for their competing desires. By the time the students had finished their first two years and entered their clerkships, however, the negative effects of the high-intimacy/high-power pattern were no longer evident. A later study of this same cohort showed that those medical students high in intimacy motivation were more likely to choose pediatrics as a medical specialty than were students scoring low in intimacy motivation (Zeldow & Daugherty, 1991).

One other major sex difference has been found in research on intimacy motivation. Analysis of thousands of TAT stories, written mostly by college undergraduates in the United States, suggests that women tend to score higher than men on intimacy motivation (McAdams, Lester, Brand, McNamara, & Lensky, 1988; Smith, 1985). The difference is small but relatively consistent, and it is in keeping with the generally accepted view in American society that women tend to be more concerned with interpersonal relationships than are men (Bakan, 1966; Gilligan, 1982; Lewis, 1985). Even among fourth and sixth graders, girls score higher on intimacy motivation than boys (McAdams & Losoff, 1984). Interestingly, consistent sex differences in overall levels of achievement and power motivation have *not* been observed (Stewart & Chester, 1982).

A motive that bears resemblance to intimacy motivation and that is also assessed via the TAT is the **affiliation motive** (Atkinson, Heyns, & Veroff, 1954; Boyatzis, 1973).

Drawn from Murray's (1938) original list of psychogenic needs, affiliation motivation is the desire to establish, maintain, or restore positive-affect relations with others. TAT stories in which characters actively strive to improve or restore their relationships with others tend to score high on affiliation themes. McClelland (1975) has combined affiliation-motive scores with scores on achievement and power to yield interesting motivational profiles linked to behavior and attitudes. In general, however, the evidence for the construct validity of the affiliation motive is rather weak (Boyatzis, 1973), with many empirical studies yielding insignificant or contradictory results. Affiliation motivation tends to be positively correlated with intimacy motivation. To the extent that the two motive systems differ, the intimacy motive appears to emphasize the qualities of *being* in a warm and close relationship, whereas the affiliation motive emphasizes *doing*, or striving to achieve relationships.

Implicit and Self-Attributed Motives

The research employing the TAT to assess individual differences in motives of achievement, power, and intimacy rests on one crucial assumption, an assumption that Murray and McClelland share with Freud: People are not consciously aware of their motives. If motives were directly accessible to consciousness, psychologists would not need to use a projective measure like the TAT to tap motivational themes in narrative. Instead, people could simply report the strength of their motives on self-report questionnaires, like those used to assess personality traits (Chapter 5). Indeed, numerous self-report questionnaires have been developed to assess such constructs as achievement motivation (for example, Jackson, 1974). But these self-report questionnaires provide scores that rarely correlate significantly with TAT scores of purportedly the same motive. For example, questionnaire measures of achievement motivation are typically uncorrelated with McClelland's TAT measure of achievement motivation (Entwisle, 1972; Klinger, 1966; Niitamo, 1999). A similar lack of convergence has been demonstrated for power and intimacy motivation (King, 1995; McClelland, 1985). But how can this be? If the two measures are assessing the same thing—say, two measures of achievement motivation—shouldn't they be highly correlated?

McClelland and his colleagues argue that the two measures are *not* assessing the same thing (Koestner, Weinberger, & McClelland, 1991; McClelland, 1980; McClelland, Koestner, & Weinberger, 1989; Schultheiss & Brunstein, 1999). Achievement motivation measured via a self-report questionnaire is different from achievement motivation measured via the TAT. Questionnaire measures of achievement tendencies are *respondent* measures in which the subject is limited in what kinds of responses he or she can make. For example, on a self-report assessment, the subject is asked to mark "true" or "false" for each item, or to rate an item on a Likert-type scale. By contrast, the TAT is what McClelland called an *operant* measure. In an operant measure, the subject is able to generate his or her own unique response. The ambiguous picture cues for the TAT provide stimuli for virtually any kind of open-ended, narrative-like response the subject wishes to reveal. With respect to measurement, McClelland (1980) has argued that respondents predict respondents and operants predict operants. But respondents do not predict operants. The kinds of responses that people make under forced-choice respondent conditions are very different from the kinds of spontaneous responses they show when provided with an open-ended operant task.

Consequently, respondent questionnaire measures tap into people's conscious evaluations of their own achievement tendencies, or what McClelland called *self-attributed motives*. By contrast, the operant TAT measure samples people's spontaneous narrative thought, revealing less-than-conscious *implicit motives*. The distinction between self-attributed and implicit motives parallels distinctions that I introduced in Chapter 3 of this book when discussing recent research on the cognitive unconscious. Cognitive psychologists have suggested that perception, learning, and memory can occur both in explicit and implicit ways (Kihlstrom, 1990; Schachter, 1992). Explicit learning, for example, takes place in a conscious and rational manner whereas implicit learning is the acquisition of knowledge in the absence of any conscious awareness. The two kinds of learning are very different, and contemporary research shows they involve very different processes in the brain. In the case of motivation, then, self-attributed motives assessed via respondent self-report questionnaires are similar to explicit forms of cognition whereas implicit motives assessed via the operant TAT are parallel to implicit forms of cognition.

Explicit, self-attributed motives are very much like personality traits. Assessed via respondent questionnaires, a person's conscious evaluation of the overall extent to which he or she values, say, achievement goals is functionally an aspect of what the Big Five theorists describe as conscientiousness (*C:* Chapter 6 in this book). Similarly, self-report measures of intimacy tendencies are likely to be aspects of Big Five agreeableness *(A)*. Like other traits, these measures are expected to predict general trends in behavior. But McClelland and his colleagues have argued that the trends they predict are rather different from those associated with individual differences in implicit motives. Because respondent measures of self-attributed motives tap into a person's conscious image of him- or herself, these self-report questionnaires should predict what people do in situations that explicitly demand behavior that is in accord with the motive. For example, people high in self-attributed achievement should perform well in highly structured social situations in which they are expected to perform well, behaving in accord with a conscious, cognitively elaborated self-image of a high-achieving person. By contrast, operant measure of implicit motives tap into naturally occurring trends in spontaneous thought, which themselves indicate people's deeper and less-consciously elaborated longings. Therefore, people high in TAT-based achievement motivation are likely to show long-term trends of spontaneous achievement activity. Put simply, people high on self-attributed achievement motivation seek out the *social* incentives of being seen (by others) as an achievement-oriented person whereas people high on implicit (TAT-based) achievement motivation seek out *activity* incentives because they enjoy achievement (that is, doing well) for achievement's sake. Put yet another way, self-attributed motives connect to extrinsic rewards ("I value achievement because I am reinforced by others for doing so") whereas implicit motives are intrinsically motivating ("I value achievement because of the enjoyment of achievement itself") (Koestner & McClelland, 1990). Table 8.16 reviews these distinctions.

Recent reviews of research provide some support for McClelland's distinction between self-attributed and implicit motives (Spangler, 1992; Winter, John, Stewart, Klohnen, & Duncan, 1998). For example, Spangler (1992) reviewed 105 research articles on achievement motivation. He found that across all the studies, TAT-based (implicit) achievement motivation was, at best, a modest predictor of achievement

TABLE 8.16	*Self-Attributed Motives Versus Implicit Motives*	
	SELF-ATTRIBUTED MOTIVES	**IMPLICIT MOTIVES**
Definition	Conscious, cognitively elaborated image of self as oriented toward particular goal states.	Recurrent, nonconscious desires for particular goal states.
Measures	Respondent: questionnaires, rating scales, and other measures in which the participant responds in a forced-choice format to a circumscribed stimulus situation.	Operant: TAT and other methods in which the participant provides a spontaneous response to an open-ended, ambiguous stimulus, such as a TAT picture.
Incentives	Social: The motive is related to behavior that is in keeping with social norms and expectations of a given situation.	Activity: The motive is related to naturally occurring behavior that is valued for its own sake.
Personality level	Level 1: Self-attributed motives are similar to dispositional traits, such as those comprising the Big Five cluster (Chapters 5–7 in this book).	Level 2: Implicit motives are less like traits and more like the characteristic adaptations in personality, more contextualized, contingent, and less stable over time than traits (Chapters 8–10 in this book).

behaviors. However, when Spangler divided up the studies into those assessing situations containing social incentives and those assessing situations with activity incentives, Mc-Clelland's predictions were born out. In studies in which the dependent variable was achievement behavior in social situations that put pressure on the subject to do well, the TAT-based achievement motivation was not a strong predictor of performance, whereas self-attributed achievement motivation was. By contrast, in studies in which the dependent variable was naturally occurring achievement behavior (under conditions with few social incentives but strong activity incentives), TAT-based achievement motivation proved to be a very strong and significant predictor of performance, whereas self-attributed achievement motivation was not.

A related controversy concerning TAT-based measures of implicit motives concerns the reliability of the TAT itself. In Chapter 5, we considered the issues of test–retest reliability and internal consistency in the measurement of traits. The same kinds of psychometric standards have been applied to TAT-based measures, though defenders of the TAT have sometimes argued that the application is not altogether appropriate (Atkinson, Bongort, & Price, 1977; Reuman, Alwin, & Veroff, 1984). Critics of the TAT maintain that the test shows low test–retest reliability and internal consistency. Although the details of these controversies are beyond the scope of this book, there are two important points to make about the limitations of TAT assessments of human motives. First, despite its potential for revealing rich narrative data for personality, the TAT is a somewhat less reliable measure than a typical well-constructed personality questionnaire, all other things being equal. Under the best conditions, test–retest correlations for TAT motives are still lower (around $r = +.55$) than those for the best-established self-report traits (around $r = +.80$) (Lundy, 1985; Winter & Stewart, 1977). Ironically, this limitation stems directly from a cardinal TAT strength—the measure's exceptional *sensitivity*. Because the TAT is more sensitive to factors and influences in the person and in the situation than are most questionnaires assessing personality traits, a TAT assessment of motivation will naturally "reflect" a lot of extraneous and irrelevant material, like the subject's mood at the time of testing. There is no way to rid the TAT of this problem without undermining its essential sensitivity.

Second, the motives of achievement, power, and intimacy assessed on the TAT are probably less stable over time than are personality traits, such as extraversion and neuroticism, which are generally assessed on questionnaires. As we saw in Chapter 7, certain basic personality traits show marked longitudinal consistency. For instance, a highly extraverted person at age 16 is likely to be relatively extraverted at age 60. Part of the reason for this stability in certain traits over time may reside in their presumed biological or genetic basis, as in the case of extraversion. Although comparable TAT data do not exist, motives do not appear to be as stable over time as certain basic traits. Further, there is no evidence at present to suggest a genetic basis for motives.

The possibility that motives may change over time to a greater extent than basic traits reflects a fundamental distinction between motives and traits: Motives deal with goals and desires; traits refer to basic behavioral style. Whereas it seems plausible to assume that a basic personality style is established early in life, perhaps partly as a function of biological temperament, and carried forward into adulthood as a stable set of personality traits, it appears equally reasonable to suggest that desires and goals may change markedly over the human life course. Motive scores indicate the major goal areas with which a person is concerned at a particular time in his or her life. For example, a person may experience high needs for intimacy and achievement in college, but these needs may subside somewhat in later years—in his or her 30s or 40s—to be "replaced" by high levels of power motivation. Less stable than traits but more enduring than temporary moods and states, motives appear to reflect major thematic goals, desires, and preoccupations during *a given period* of a particular person's life.

PERSONALIZED GOALS

Going back to the time of Gordon Allport (1937), personality psychologists have distinguished between traits and motives as fundamental concepts for understanding human individuality (Winter et al., 1998). As we saw in Chapters 5–7, trait concepts emphasize the cross-situational consistency of behavior, the dispositional nature of what people do. Traits are most useful in predicting *what* people will do, aggregating across situations and time. While constructs such as achievement and intimacy motivation also speak to consistencies in what people do, these concepts are typically employed to provide explanations for the dynamics behind human action, *why* people do what they do. As Allport (1937) realized, this distinction is not clean, in that people do things for many different reasons, including reasons having to do with social situations and even with their traits. Nonetheless, motivational constructs directly address the wants, desires, goals, and ends *for the sake of which* people often act. As such, motivational constructs have a different emphasis than do trait concepts. In the terminology of this textbook, motivational constructs such as achievement, power, and intimacy motivation are closer to characteristic adaptations of personality (Level 2) than they are to dispositional traits (Level 1). As characteristic adaptations, motives are more contextualized than traits, and they speak more specifically to the contingent nature of human behavior.

What does it mean to say that motives are more contextualized than traits? To say that something is contextualized is to say that its meaning comes partly out of a context, out of that with respect to which it is grounded. Traits are generally *non*contextualized because they refer to broad tendencies in behavior that may be observed across many different contexts—that is across different situations, in different roles, and over time. Although motives for achievement, power, and intimacy are also broad, they have a built-in context by virtue of their very status as motivational concepts. All motivational concepts are contextualized *in time*. Put simply, motives are defined in terms of desired or anticipated goal states, and these goal states exist *in the future*. If we say that you are high in power motivation, we are saying that you recurrently desire to have impact on your world, that you want power, that you will articulate more specific goals for the future through which you hope to be able to experience power. By matter of contrast, if we say that you are high on the trait of extraversion, we have said nothing about what you recurrently desire, what you want, or what your goals for the future are. Extraversion is not in and of itself a motivational concept. You do not need to talk about goals and future time to understand the meaning of extraversion. I am not saying that power motivation is a more important concept than extraversion; I am simply saying that it is different—different in kind. Both concepts are equally important in understanding personality. But they are important for different reasons. Traits provide an indispensable first read on individuality; they sketch out the broad outline of human individuality, which is what Level 1 of personality is all about. In focusing on the goal-directed nature of human behavior *in time*, motives move us to Level 2 in personality, the level of characteristic adaptations.

Having identified implicit motives for achievement, power, and intimacy as examples of characteristic adaptations in personality, let me now suggest that motivational psychologists have recently proposed a range of new motivational constructs that are themselves more contextualized than implicit motives, more specific, situated, and personalized. Motives for achievement, power, and intimacy go beyond dispositional traits to fill in some of the details of human individuality, but even more detail and specificity can be observed when psychologists examine the personalized goals that people formulate and pursue in daily life and the ways in which those goals translate into behavior. Like motives, personalized goals speak to what people want in life. But personalized goals are more specific. Maria may want power in general, showing a high level of implicit power motivation. But her power motivation is likely to be expressed through some goals and not others. Among her current goals in life are (1) to be accepted into law school and (2) to win the election for senior class president. By contrast, she sets forth no goals concerning the experience of power in, say, her personal relationships or in the area of sports. If we know Maria has high power motivation, we certainly know something very important about her. But to know more of the details, we need to explore the various concerns, strivings, projects, and tasks she is currently working on—the personalized goals that speak to why Maria does what she does.

Concerns, Strivings, Projects, and Tasks

One of the first personality psychologists to focus on personalized goal concepts was Eric Klinger (1977). Klinger argues that human experience is organized around the pursuit of incentives. Daily life is filled with all kinds of possible incentives, from making money to finding true love to experiencing the beauty of a sunset. In any given person's life, the incentives that are most important or pressing at a given point in time are represented as **current concerns.** A current concern is the *motivational state* of a person between his or her initial commitment to a goal and either the attainment or abandonment of that goal. Until she either gets into law school or decides to abandon the goal, Maria is in a motivational state of being concerned about getting into law school. While she may not be thinking about this goal every minute of the day, it is nonetheless one of a handful of current concerns toward which she is strongly oriented. Research suggests that current concerns influence thoughts and feelings. For example, Klinger, Barta, and Maxeiner (1981) found that the degree to which current concerns are valued or threatened predicts the frequency with which people think about the incentives associated with the concern. Therefore, the more strongly Maria is committed to her goal (e.g., it's the most important thing in her life) and the greater the obstacles to achieving it (her LSAT scores were low the first time she took the test), the more she will think about getting into law school. Laboratory studies have shown that people rate words closely related to their current concerns (for Maria: attorney, jury, U.S. Constitution, grades) as more arousing than words unrelated, and that they even show higher levels of physiological reactivity (e.g., palm sweating) in response to words associated with their current concerns (Nikula, Klinger, & Larson-Gutman, 1993). Current concerns are often a window into problems that people are experiencing in daily life. Klinger has developed motivational counseling programs that aim to assess and change people's current concerns and has applied the programs to the treatment of alcoholism (Cox & Klinger, 1988), depression (Ruehlman & Wolchik, 1988) and problems in work satisfaction (Roberson, 1989).

Robert Emmons (1986, 1989, 1992, 1999) launched a very successful research program on the meaning and function of **personal strivings.** Personal strivings are "characteristic, recurring goals that a person is trying to accomplish" (Emmons, 1992, p. 292). Whereas Klinger focuses on the "motivational state" that a person is "in" between the time he or she commits to a goal and the time he or she attains or abandons the goal, Emmons looks more closely at the goal itself, and he is especially interested in how different goals relate to one another and how some goals may be grouped together whereas others may conflict. For example, a young man's goal to obtain the grade of "A" in his biology class and his goal to read classic literature during summer break may both center on his more general striving to transform himself into a well-rounded scholar. His goal to become a better athlete may, however, conflict with these other two goals, for they take away from his practice time on the football field. People's personal strivings come in many different and overlapping forms. People are trying to do many different things at any given period in their lives. Some strivings, furthermore, may reflect more general motivational tendencies. For example, Emmons and McAdams (1991) found that TAT-based power and intimacy motivation were positively associated with corresponding power and intimacy strivings. Therefore, a

woman with a strong power motive may report that the most important personal strivings in her life are "getting to the top of my company," "persuading my daughter that
she should stay away from drugs," "becoming president of the local school council,"
and "freeing myself from my abusive husband." Each of these four strivings displays a
strong concern for having an impact on others, a strong need for power. However, the
strivings tell us much more as well. They specify the particular ways in which this
woman's motives are enacted and understood in the context of her own life. They provide as much information about the situation as they do about the person herself. Personal strivings provide a good deal of idiographic description—concrete details about
the person's life in context.

Emmons (1999) reports that fewer than half of the personal strivings typically reported in his research fit neatly into the big three motive categories of achievement,
power, and intimacy/affiliation. Accordingly, Emmons has developed content coding
systems for categorizing strivings in many different ways. Most recently, he describes
12 different categories for coding the content of personal strivings:

1. Avoidance goals ("To avoid letting anything upset me");
2. Achievement ("To do well in school");
3. Affiliation ("To meet new people");
4. Intimacy ("To be a caring person to my girlfriend");
5. Power ("To take control of the organization I'm in");
6. Personal growth and health ("Not to eat between meals, to lose weight");
7. Self-presentation ("To appear intelligent to other people");
8. Independence ("To be myself and not do what other people want me to do");
9. Self-defeating ("To do things that annoy other people");
10. Emotionality ("To be honest with myself about how I truly feel");
11. Generativity ("To make a lasting contribution to society");
12. Spirituality ("To deepen my relationship with God").

Emmons (1999) reports that intimacy strivings and generativity strivings are associated
with independent ratings of psychological well-being. In other words, people who describe a greater number of strivings having to do with warm and close relationships
(intimacy) and with making positive contributions to society and the future (generativity) are happier and more satisfied with their lives, compared with individuals who
have fewer intimacy and generativity strivings. By contrast, power strivings and avoidance strivings tend to be associated with lower levels of psychological well-being and
greater levels of anxiety. Spiritual strivings tend to be associated with low levels of conflict among life goals and what Emmons terms the overall integration of the personality. Emmons maintains that spiritual strivings are especially powerful carriers of life
meaning for many people.

Like personal strivings, **personal projects** also provide a rich picture of the psychosocial ecology of everyday life. Brian Little (1989, 1998, 1999) conceives of the
personal project as a series of activities coordinated to achieve a specific personal goal.
The concept is very similar to Emmons's personal striving. Like Emmons, Little emphasizes the wide range of projects that people propose, from trivial pursuits to

magnificent obsessions. Table 8.17 lists some examples of personal projects from one of Little's studies. Little's research, however, focuses more explicitly on the steps that a person goes through in attempting to put a project into action. He identifies four steps. In the *inception* phase, the person imagines the goal and initially defines it; in the *planning* phase, the person organizes a series of actions that is designed to achieve the goal; in the *action* phase, the person carries out the plan, though he or she must often change the plan as things work out in unexpected ways; in the *termination* phase the person concludes the project pursuit, perhaps because the goal has been attained, perhaps because he or she has lost interest in attaining the goal, or perhaps for other reasons. Personality traits may have an impact on project pursuits. Research has shown that people high on the trait of openness to experience (*O:* Chapter 6) tend to propose a wider diversity of projects, compared with those scoring low on *O* (Little, Lecci, & Watkinson, 1992). High levels of neuroticism (*N:* Chapter 6), furthermore, are associated with experiencing high levels of stress in the pursuit of projects (Little, 1999). Neuroticism is also associated with pursuing projects and goals that involve avoidance (Elliot, Sheldon, & Church, 1997). In other words, people high in *N* are more likely than those scoring low in *N* to pursue such projects as "avoiding dealing with my mother," "staying away from obnoxious men," and "escaping stress." Rather than pursuing positive end states, they seek to avoid negative ones.

Nancy Cantor and her colleagues (Cantor & Zirkel, 1990) have proposed the cognitive-motivational construct of **life task.** A life task is a problem that an individual is motivated to solve, to which he or she devotes considerable energy and time, and

---

TABLE 8.17	*Examples of Personal Projects from Seven Different People*

1. Become more extraverted and approachable.
   Come to terms with my stance on religion and its relevance in my life.
   Not to be intimidated by others older than myself.

2. Wishing my brother would solve his problems with his sickening girlfriend.
   Overcome the habit of saying the wrong thing at the wrong time.

3. Maintaining repair of the family vehicle.
   Change oil in girlfriend's car.

4. Help husband tolerate Christmas.
   Increase harmony at home—especially between children.

5. Read all of Victor Frankl's books.
   Help my roommate overcome his lack of organization.

6. Scoring 20 goals [hockey] by Christmas.
   Achieve at least 40 points [hockey: "points" = goals + assists] by Christmas.
   Get drafted into the NHL [National Hockey League].
   Clean up my room.

7. Continue to "grow" as a person and find contentment in everyday life.
   Help a good friend who is going through a bad time.
   Let my fingernails grow.

Source: Adapted from Little (1998), p. 197.

that he or she sees as organizing daily activity during a particular life period or life transition. Life tasks often arise from developmental demands—challenges and opportunities we face at particular developmental periods in our lives. For example, a recent college graduate may see her life task as that of "becoming established in a line of work" or "beginning a family," whereas a college freshman may be most concerned with the tasks of "adjusting to leaving home" and "finding an academic major." Cantor and her colleagues have been especially interested in what they call the *intimacy life task of early adulthood* (Cantor, Acker, & Cook-Flannagan, 1992; Sanderson & Cantor, 1997). The pursuit of intimacy, especially through dating and marriage, becomes an increasingly salient concern for many Western men and women as they move into and through their 20s and early 30s. Yet each young adult appears to meet the social and developmental demands of this task in a different way, expressing and experiencing a unique set of satisfactions, difficulties, and conflicts in the areas of intimate relationships. Of critical import in the intimacy life task are the cognitive strategies that young adults develop and utilize to deal with the stress and meet the challenges involved in intimacy. As we will see in Chapter 9, Cantor's research on life tasks brings to the fore a wide range of cognitive adaptations, such as cognitive schemas and styles, that people routinely employ to make sense of the challenges they face in life.

Although differences among these four concepts can be discerned, current concerns, personal strivings, personal projects, and life tasks have a great deal in common. Each is a different way of talking about the personalized goals that people develop and pursue in daily life. More specific and idiographic than the motives of achievement, power, and intimacy, these goal concepts address directly what people are trying to do during particular periods of their lives, with respect to particular social roles, and in particular life situations. Given the similarities among these concepts, Little has proposed that they be grouped together under the label of **personal action units (PACs).** PACs are the characteristic concerns, strivings, projects, and tasks that organize the motivational life of a particular person at a particular time in his or her life. PACs are "not fixed features of personality but dynamic and potentially tractable aspects of agentic conduct" (Little, 1999, p. 503). PACs are among the most important characteristic adaptations going into Level 2 in personality.

Purposive Behavior and the Quality of Life

When you think about how well or badly your life is going or how happy or unhappy you are with the present state of your life, you are likely to make some kind of explicit or implicit assessment of the status of your goals. Are you satisfied with the goals you have set? Are you making progress toward achieving important goals? Do your goals conflict with one another? Psychologists who study PACs have focused a great deal of attention on the relationships between goals and psychological well-being. They have found that goal-directed, purposive behavior is intimately tied up with the overall assessments people make of the quality of their lives. For example, considerable research suggests that when people feel they are making substantial progress in meeting the most important goals in their lives, they report higher levels of life satisfaction and emotional well-being (Pervin, 1989, 1996). As another example, Palys and Little (1983) found that individuals who reported involvement in enjoyable and moderately difficult projects oriented toward short-term goals tended to be happier and more satisfied with their lives. Adults with less enjoyable and highly difficult projects oriented to the long term tended to score low on happiness and life satisfaction. In addition, relatively happy participants reported that they shared involvement in their goals with a supportive network of friends, family, and acquaintances.

In examining the relations between personal projects and well-being, Little routinely asks research participants to evaluate each of their personal projects on five dimensions: (1) *meaningfulness* (how worthwhile the project is, how enjoyable I find the project to be, how much the project contributes to my sense of identity), (2) *manageability* (how easy the project is, how much control I have over the project, how much time I have to do the project well), (3) *support* (to what extent other people support the project, how visible my project is for other people), (4) *efficacy* (how well my project is progressing, how capable I am of achieving the project), and (5) *stress* (how anxious or depressed the project makes me, how much I worry about the project). In constructing and living out our personal projects, Little finds, we need to strike a balance between "meaning" and "manageability." In some cases such long-term and abstract projects as "making myself into a better human being" may prove highly meaningful but too hard to manage effectively. On the other hand, short-term and concrete projects such as "cooking delicious dinners for my spouse" may be fairly manageable but may not provide a satisfactory level of meaning in one's life. The challenge is to organize one's purposive behavior according to personal projects that are grand enough and humble enough to be both meaningful and manageable. The organization of purposive behavior is always accomplished in an interpersonal context. Personal projects are constantly negotiated and renegotiated with important people in one's life and within the opportunities and constraints offered by one's family, community, profession, and society at large. Within a complex social context, it is essential that people find effective ways to *communicate* their personal projects to others. Other people need to know clearly what goals you have in mind for your life if they are to facilitate the accomplishment of those goals and find creative ways to integrate their goals with yours.

Robert Emmons has examined what happens when different strivings conflict with one another. For instance, your striving to "improve my relationship with my mother" may conflict with your striving to "gain independence." Emmons (1986) administered various personal strivings measures to 40 undergraduate students who then reported their daily moods and thoughts for three weeks. Positive emotional experiences during that period were positively associated with reports of strivings that were highly valued and for which the person had experienced success in the past. Negative emotional experiences were associated with striving ambivalence and with greater levels of conflict between different strivings. In a similar study, Emmons and King (1988) found that conflict and ambivalence in strivings were associated with higher levels of negative affect, depression, neuroticism, and psychosomatic complaints, and with a greater number of illnesses and visits to the campus health center. In examining the connections between strivings and behavior, the researchers also found that when people reported conflicting strivings they often were unable to act upon those strivings but instead spent an inordinate amount of time thinking about the conflict itself. To sum up, high levels of conflict among strivings lead to poor health, low levels of happiness, high levels of depression and anxiety, and a tendency to ponder obsessively about conflictual strivings rather than acting upon them.

TABLE 8.18	*Examples of High-Level and Low-Level Strivings*

HIGH-LEVEL STRIVING ("GHANDI")	LOW-LEVEL STRIVING ("COFFEE BEAN")
Treat others with dignity	Look well-groomed and clean cut
Increase my understanding of the Bible	Stand out when engaging in physical/recreational activities
Deepen my relationship with God	Be funny and make others laugh
Be totally honest	Speak clearly and straightforward to strangers
Express my feelings to close friends and family openly and honestly	Look physically conditioned and physically fit
Be humble	Act physically aggressive around those folks I dislike
Discern and follow God's will for my life	Keep good posture/walk straight
Expose my faith to others without offending them or pushing it on them	Look attentive and not bored in class
Keep positive thoughts in my mind	Avoid being stereotyped
Make new friends	Use proper language and manners around adults and attractive girls
Be a fun person to be around	Make myself noticeable
Make others feel good about themselves	Work hard (or at least make it look like it)
Express to people that I love them	Keep quiet and not go talking about myself freely with others
Compete against myself rather than others	Be organized and neat, always have a clean room and a made bed
Increase my knowledge of the world	

Source: Emmons (1992), p. 295.

Strivings also differ from each other with respect to their level of abstractness. Consider these two strivings: (1) "going to church more often" and (2) "getting closer to God." Both strivings concern a person's religion, but the first one is framed in concrete behavioral terms whereas the second is more abstract or general. People differ on how abstract versus concrete their strivings are. Those who frame their goals in primarily broad, abstract, expansive, introspective, and self-reflective ways may be termed *high-level strivers*. Those who frame their goals in more concrete, specific, and superficial terms are *low-level strivers*. Table 8.18 provides strivings from two different people—code names "Gandhi" and "Coffee Bean." "Gandhi" is a high-level striver, and Coffee Bean is a low-level striver.

Gandhi and Coffee Bean were two participants in a study by Emmons (1992) that examined the relation between abstractness of strivings on the one hand and physical and mental health on the other. Emmons administered strivings measures and various assessments of mood, well-being, and symptomatology to two samples of college students and a sample of young married couples. He found that high-level strivers tended to be more depressed and *psychologically* distressed than low-level strivers. However, low-level strivers reported more *physical* illness. In Emmons's words, the results illustrate a "depression vs. sickness tradeoff." Basing his interpretation on the work of Pennebaker (1989b), Semmer and Frese (1985), and others, Emmons suggests that high-level strivers are more likely to confront directly the stresses and disappointments in their lives and experience negative affect as a result. In addition, the highly abstract nature of their strivings makes it difficult for them to obtain satisfying feedback from their environment concerning progress toward their goals. For example, it is much more difficult to tell at the end of the week if you are "closer to God" (abstract striving) than you were at the beginning of the week, but it is quite easy to determine whether or not you "attended church" (concrete striving).

Psychological distress, therefore, may be a function of the complexity and ambiguity of high-level goals. In sharp contrast, the low-level strivers may be more susceptible to physical illness as a result of failing to confront stress directly. In focusing on excessively concrete goals, low-level strivers may avoid the psychological distress that accompanies a more introspective and probing attitude toward the self. They may manifest a *repressive personality style* (Chapter 3), characterized by a denial of distress but a correspondingly more highly aroused sympathetic nervous system, making them more vulnerable to psychosomatic illness. Keeping their goals simple and concrete enables low-level strivers to avoid a direct confrontation with difficult and more abstract problems in life, but such a strategy may exact the cost of poorer physical health.

Finally, a recent research study by Brunstein, Schultheiss, and Grassmann (1998) returns us to the more general motives assessed on the TAT and relates the motives to personal goals and psychological well-being. In an initial testing session, the researchers administered the TAT to a group of German college students and then asked them to list two agentic (achievement- or power-oriented) goals and two communal (intimacy- or affiliation-related) goals. For each goal, the students also evaluated how much progress they had recently made in accomplishing the goal. Over the following two weeks, the students each completed a series of mood checklists at regular intervals, to assess overall psychological well-being. The researchers scored the TAT stories for the standard motives developed by McClelland and his associates, classifying achievement and power motivation as "agentic" (self-oriented) motives and intimacy and affiliation motivation as "communal" (other-oriented) motives. To arrive at a single agency-communion motivational score, they simply subtracted the TAT communion score (intimacy + affiliation motives) from the TAT agency score (achievement + power motives). Consequently, the higher the overall score, the more agentic (achievement and power oriented) was a person's overall motivational stance, whereas the lower the score the more communal (intimacy and affiliation oriented).

The results of the study showed an interaction between motivational scores and goal progress in the prediction of well-being. In a nutshell, students with highly agentic motivational profiles (high power and achievement motivation relative to affiliation and intimacy motivation on the TAT) reported greater levels of psychological well-being (as determined by the mood checklists) *when they were making progress on agentic goals*, relative to other students. Similarly, students with communal motivational profiles (high affiliation and intimacy motivation relative to power and achievement motivation on the TAT) reported greater levels of well-being *when they were making progress on communal goals*. The key thing to know here is that well-being is a function of progress and success in the pursuit of *motive-congruent goals*. When you are making good progress and receiving good support on daily goals that are congruent with your more general motivational tendencies, you are likely to be experiencing positive emotions and satisfaction. In general, making progress toward goals is a good thing for everybody. But some goals are more important for well-being than others. Of most importance are those most valued goals that encapsule experiences that are congruent with what an individual most deeply wants out of life.

In conclusion, many personality psychologists and laypeople find personal goals to be such an important aspect of human individuality because of both their links to psychological well-being and the general belief that goals, unlike perhaps traits and more general tendencies in personality, may be relatively easy to change or work on. Recall that Little described PACs as characteristic personal goals that are "not fixed features of personality but dynamic and potentially tractable aspects of agentic conduct" (1999, p. 503). By claiming that personal goals are "tractable," Little is saying that goals are subject to change, modification, growth, and the influence of the environment. Psychotherapists and counselors of many different persuasions often spend a great deal of time working on people's goals, helping their clients to refashion goals into more realistic terms, helping people find ways to get support from their environment for their goals, moving people in the direction of new goals that are both meaningful and manageable, helping people make their goals more congruent with their general motivational tendencies, their personality traits, and the constraints and opportunities they face in the environment. And when people work on their own lives, when they try to make changes for the better, they often begin by re-evaluating their own personal goals.

SUMMARY

1. If dispositional traits make up a first level of personality, motives and goals are important characteristic adaptations at the second level. Motivational concepts concern the internal forces and factors that energize and direct human behavior, including those most important and recurrent human wants, needs, and desires. The Western understanding of human motivation can be divided into four different traditions. Going back to Plato's *Republic*, the optimistic tradition celebrates human potential and rational thought and may be identified today with humanistic and cognitive approaches to motivation. The pessimistic tradition encompasses the Christian doctrine of original sin as well as the Freudian emphasis on irrational, unconscious, and uncontrollable motives. Behaviorism epitomized the third, neutral position in human motivation, suggesting that all human motives are learned from the environment. Finally, the diversity tradition suggests that human beings are motivated by many

different needs and goals. This chapter focuses on theories and research derived from the optimistic and diversity traditions.

2. Carl Rogers developed a highly influential theory of personality and psychotherapy that posited one, all-encompassing motivational force—the motive to actualize or fulfill the self. Rogers's approach urges the psychologist to explore the person's phenomenal field of conscious experience through empathy and, ideally, unconditional positive regard. In Rogers's view, the fully functioning person operates according to the organismic valuing process, which enables him or her to fulfill the self's potential and to expand the self to encompass the lion's share of the phenomenal field.

3. Like Rogers, Abraham Maslow developed a humanistic theory of personality that underscored the motive for self-actualization. Maslow argued that self-actualizing tendencies are built on more basic needs for physiological equilibrium, safety and security, belonging and love, and self-esteem. Motives may also be divided into those promoting growth and those stemming from deficiencies. Highly self-actualized individuals espouse humanistic virtues and have a greater number of peak experiences in life. Humanistic theories have stimulated research on the qualities of peak experience and on related issues such as experiences of peak performance and flow.

4. Intrinsically motivated behavior is valued for its own sake rather than for the rewards that may follow it. Research on intrinsic motivation suggests that material rewards can sometimes undermine people's interest in the activities for which they are rewarded. Growing out of research on intrinsic motivation, Deci and Ryan's self-determination theory proposes that human beings are endowed with a natural motivation to encounter new challenges that will promote organismic integration. Self-determined, intrinsically-motivated behavior often meets basic human needs for autonomy, competence, and interpersonal relatedness. Self-determination theory has stimulated research on how self-determined behaviors that stem from needs for autonomy, competence, and interpersonal relatedness enhance growth and well-being whereas behaviors in the service of material wealth, seeking prestige, and other extrinsic rewards tend to undermine morale and stifle organismic growth.

5. Henry Murray's influential motivational theory proposes a taxonomy of approximately 20 psychogenic needs that energize and direct behavior in concert with environmental forces or press. As one assessment device for the measurement of individual differences in psychogenic needs or motives, Murray developed the Thematic Apperception Test (TAT). On the TAT, participants tell or write imaginative stories in response to picture cues. The stories are coded for various content themes indicative of implicit

(unconscious) motivational tendencies. Motivational research with the TAT has focused on the needs for achievement, power, and intimacy.

6. The achievement motive is a recurrent preference or readiness for experiences of doing well and being successful. People high on TAT-measured achievement motivation tend to be highly efficient in their goal-directed activity, show high achievement aspirations but moderate risk taking, show high levels of self-control and delay of gratification, and show a range of behaviors and attitudes that promote successful entrepreneurship. The extent to which a society encourages achievement motivation can be estimated by scoring folk tales, children's readers, and popular literature for achievement themes, as if these documents were TAT stories. David McClelland has shown that a society's achievement motivation is associated with economic growth.

7. The power motive is a recurrent preference or readiness for experiences of having an impact and feeling strong. People high on TAT-measured power motivation show a mixture of characteristics associated with both aggression and leadership. They tend to be active and forceful in small groups, to accumulate prestige possessions, and to be drawn to public office and professions that involve directing the behavior of others. Among men, power motivation is associated with instability in romantic relationships. With respect to physical health, some research suggests that individuals with strong but inhibited power motivation may be susceptible to disease, especially when they experience high levels of power stress.

8. The intimacy motive is a recurrent preference for experiences of warm, close, and communicative interaction with others. People high on TAT-based intimacy motivation tend to be seen by others as especially loving and sensitive, exhibit more eye contact and smiling in friendly interactions, are more self-disclosing and intimate with their friends, and engage in a wide range of behaviors suggestive of an especially communal approach to life. Intimacy motivation is also positively associated with psychological well-being. Whereas consistent gender differences have not been shown for achievement and power motivation, women score consistently and significantly higher than men on the intimacy motive.

9. Whereas research on implicit motives for achievement, power, and intimacy examines general goal states, another line of recent research has focused on more specific goals themselves—personal goals as expressed in current concerns, personal strivings, personal projects, and the pursuit of life tasks. These goal concepts have been called personal action units (PACs), and they include such mundane strivings as "Trying to improve my grammar" and "Being less competitive with my brother-in-law" to such abstract and encompassing projects as "Trying to figure out the meaning of my life." Among the most important characteristic adaptations in personality, PACs provide detail, specificity, and context for understanding a person's motivational life.

10. Research on PACs suggests that personal goals are intimately involved in people's psychological well-being. People are happiest when they are making progress in pursuing their personal goals, especially when those goals are consistent with more general motivational trends in their personality. Goals for intimacy and for making positive contributions to other people tend to be associated with positive emotion whereas goals concerning avoidance and personal power are associated with negative emotions. Goal conflict and ambivalence may undermine life satisfaction. Goal-directed activity often involves a meaning/manageability tradeoff. Sometimes the most meaningful and involving goals are the most difficult to attain, so the challenge is to organize purposive behavior according to goals that are grand enough and yet humble enough to be both meaningful and manageable.

Social-Cognitive Adaptations: Construing the Self and Social Behavior

9

Once upon a time, American psychologists refused to study the human mind. From the 1920s through the 1950s, behaviorism dominated American psychology and set the standards for what constituted appropriate psychological research. If they were to be true scientists, psychological researchers were to restrict their studies to those phenomena that could be objectively observed and measured. Of most importance were the observable *stimuli* in the organism's immediate environment and the observable behavioral *responses* the organism emitted in the presence of those stimuli. As we saw in Chapter 4, behaviorists such as Clark Hull and B. F. Skinner argued persuasively for a stimulus-response approach to psychology. Between the environmental input (the stimulus) and the behavioral response lay, of course, the organism—the individual entity, be it a white rat or a human being, whose response to the stimulus was being observed. What was going on inside that organism? What was going on "inside the head" of the person emitting a response? What thoughts and feelings accompanied the person's behavior? Behaviorists ruled out the mind as a focus of study because those thoughts, feelings, and other purported processes going on inside the head of the organism could not be directly and precisely observed. While only the most radical behaviorist might deny the presence of a human mind altogether, behaviorism essentially ignored the mind and tried instead to account for the vicissitudes of behavior solely in terms of stimulus-response connections, patterns of reward and punishment, and (for some behaviorists, such as Clark Hull) biologically based drives (e.g., drives of hunger, thirst, sex). As outlandish as this effort may seem to us today, the behaviorists were surprisingly successful, and many of the methodological standards and conceptual insights they set forth have been incorporated into the mainstream of psychology today.

Nonetheless, all (good or bad) things eventually come to an end. Behaviorism's dominance began to wane as psychologists became increasingly impatient with the restrictions imposed by behaviorist doctrine and began, hesitantly at first, to make forays into the processes of mind. In the second half of the 20th century, psychology became increasingly oriented toward **cognition.** An extremely broad term, the word *cognition* includes a wide range of mental processes having to do with "the activity of knowing: the acquisition, organization, and use of knowledge" (Neisser, 1976, p. 1). Cognitive processes include attention, perception, thinking, abstraction, problem solving, learning, memory, language, and other aspects of knowing that we typically associate with the activity of the mind. What is arguably the most significant conceptual development in psychology in the past half century has been the rise of *cognitive psychology* as the systematic study of "perception, memory, attention, pattern recognition, problem solving, the psychology of language, cognitive development, and a host of other problems that had lain dormant for half a century" (Neisser, 1976, p. 5). Although psychologists had examined these problems in numerous ways before the 1950s, their various investigations were quite limited and unintegrated, and they were not generally viewed as part of a common enterprise focused on human cognition.

The historical roots of cognitive psychology lie in the study of verbal learning, human engineering, communications, computer science, linguistics, and the rigorous experimental methods of laboratory science (Lachman, Lachman, & Butterfield, 1979). But the single most important reason for the emergence of cognitive psychology as a viable scientific area is probably the development of the computer. The computer provides a new and powerful *metaphor* for human cognition. Like computers, human beings appear to accept information from the environment, manipulate symbols, store events in "memory," retrieve memories, classify inputs, recognize patterns, and engage in a number of other cognitive operations by which they organize and utilize information:

> Computers take symbolic input, recode it, make decisions about the recoded input, make new expressions of it, store some or all of the input, and give back symbolic output. By analogy, that is most of what cognitive psychology is about. It is about how people take in information, how they recode and remember it, how they make decisions, how they transform their internal knowledge states, and how they translate these states into behavioral outputs. (Lachman et al., 1979, p. 99)

It is probably fair to say that cognitive psychology has come to replace behaviorism as the dominant intellectual force in psychology in recent years. Methods and ideas from cognitive psychology have had a major impact on many, if not most, branches of psychology. Much of psychology today has a strong cognitive flavor. For example, developmental psychologists in America became enamoured of the writings of Jean Piaget (1954) on cognitive development at about the same time that cognitive psychology was beginning to replace behaviorism—that is, in the 1960s and 1970s. While Piaget's theory of cognitive development has lost some of its favor since then, the development of cognitive processes remains at the top of the agenda for developmental research today. Social psychologists, too, began to adopt cognitively based theories for social behavior in the 1950s and 1960s, such as Festinger's (1957) theory of cognitive dissonance. Since then, the field has become increasingly oriented toward cognitive processes, with a great deal of research today focused on social cognition, or the ways in which people think about social situations and how those thoughts may influence social behavior. In the clinical realm, behaviorist therapies of the 1960s and 1970s have become increasingly "cognitive-behavioral," and psychodynamic and client-centered therapeutic approaches have also borrowed liberally from cognitive approaches. What used to be called "physiological psychology" is now "cognitive neuroscience" in many university departments. Indeed, cognitive approaches have helped to integrate certain subfields of psychology with other intellectual fields, such as linguistics, anthropology, neurology, biological psychiatry, and engineering.

The turn to cognition has had a significant impact, as well, within personality psychology. Kihlstrom and Hastie (1997) write: "Cognitive approaches to personality, social, and clinical psychology share the assumption that behavior is cognitively mediated—guided by our perceptions of the current situation, memories of similar situations encountered in the past, impressions of ourselves and other people in the current environment, attributions concerning their (and our own) experiences and actions, and other sorts of judgments and inferences that go beyond the information given in the stimulus situation" (p. 712). Among the first personality psychologists to move in the cognitive direction were the social learning theorists of the 1950s and 1960s. As we saw in Chapter 4, Julian Rotter, Albert Bandura, and Walter Mischel formulated theories that began with behaviorist principles but ended up emphasizing such cognitive phenomena as expectancies, values, schemas, and plans. These theories, furthermore, have come to place more and more emphasis on the concept of "self"— a concept that had no respectable place in orthodox behaviorism. Bandura (1999) and Mischel (1999) continue to be prominent spokesmen for the social-cognitive agenda in personality psychology (Cervone & Shoda, 1999a, 1999b). It is this agenda that we consider in the current chapter.

Social-cognitive adaptations in personality concern how people make and use *mental representations* of themselves and their social worlds and how those representations are implicated in behavior. People actively seek information in the world. They "take in" or encode that information, store it in memory, and then summon forth the stored representations in preparation for and in the process of subsequent action. People formulate images, concepts, beliefs, values, plans, and scripts that govern what they do, and what they do comes to influence the nature of these mental representations. Put simply, cognition influences social behavior, and social behavior influences cognition. Of special significance are the characteristic ways in which people construe themselves, construe others, and construe the social situations within which their interactions with others occur. People differ from one another with respect to the kinds of self-representations and social construals they characteristically formulate and act upon. Consequently, an essential domain of human individuality is the characteristic social-cognitive representations that people create. Furthermore, like motives and goals (Chapter 8), social-cognitive adaptations take us beyond dispositional personality traits to consider the contextualized and contingent nature of human lives (Cervone & Shoda, 1999a). If traits provide an initial sketch of human individuality, then the characteristic mental representations of self and social behavior that people construct—their characteristic self-conceptions, expectancies, beliefs, scripts, and so on— help to fill in the details.

In considering, then, the social-cognitive aspects of human personality we will begin this chapter with George Kelly's (1955) psychology of personal constructs— arguably the first thoroughly cognitive theory of personality ever formulated. We will move from Kelly to the study of cognitive styles in personality, which speak to individual differences in the ways in which people characteristically process information in the world. Finally, we will consider in some detail contemporary social-cognitive ideas such as social intelligence, self-representations, explanatory style, and the cognitive regulation of social behavior as they speak to understanding human individuality. We will see that along with motives and goals, social-cognitive adaptations constitute much of what we implicitly consider to be at the heart of who we are as people and of what gives each of us a characteristic sense of self. Like motives and goals, social-cognitive adaptations reflect who we are in the social ecologies of our everyday lives (Cervone & Shoda, 1999b). More than do the dispositional traits we studied in Chapters 5–7, social-cognitive adaptations situate us in time, space, and social role. In that they are so intimately tied to social context, we might expect that social-cognitive adaptations should change markedly over time and across social situations.

THE PSYCHOLOGY OF PERSONAL CONSTRUCTS

One of the most idiosyncratic figures in the history of personality psychology is George A. Kelly (1905–1966). Kelly labored in relative obscurity as a school teacher, aeronautical engineer, and clinical psychologist until he wrote and published his two-volume *The Psychology of Personal Constructs* in 1955. The book took the field of personality psychology by storm. It presented a boldly original theory of the person that seemed to bear little if any resemblance to the classic theories of the day, such as those proposed by Freud, Jung, Murray, Allport, Eysenck, Cattel, and the behaviorists. The unusual terms Kelly proposed became part of the standard lexicon of personality psychology—terms such as *personal construct, range of convenience, fixed-role therapy,* and *Rep Test.* Indeed, Kelly became something of an overnight celebrity in the field. Unfortunately, Kelly's one major book is the only comprehensive statement of the theory he ever produced. An early death prevented his developing and refining the theory further, though selected papers from his last years were edited into a valuable collection (Maher, 1969). Since Kelly's death, his theory has remained popular and influential. Yet it is difficult to classify for, like Kelly himself, the theory stubbornly refuses to fit into the mainstream. Because it rejects such time-honored personality concepts as "motivation," "the unconscious," "needs," "instincts," "traits," "reinforcement," and "developmental stages," Kelly's theory seems an oddity in the field of personality psychology. Yet linkages and relations between Kelly's theory and other approaches can be discerned. For instance, Kelly's focus on subjective conscious experience aligns him with humanistic psychologists such as Rogers and Maslow (Chapter 8), but unlike these theorists Kelly did not view human beings to be self-actualizing organisms. Two of the most important social learning theorists—Julian Rotter and Walter Mischel (Chapter 4)—worked closely with Kelly at Ohio State University, and Kelly's influence can be seen in their overall approaches. Yet Kelly's theory is rarely put in the same category as social learning theories. The field of cognitive psychology developed independently of (and mainly after) Kelly's theory of personal constructs. Kelly employed no computer metaphors in conceptualizing human lives. He did not speak of such things as input, output, storage, retrieval, and the processing of information—ideas that are central to cognitive perspectives today. Nonetheless, Kelly's theory reinforces a cognitive image of the person—as a hypothesis-testing classifier of subjective experience, seeking to understand and predict the social world. At the dawn of the cognitive revolution in psychology writ large, George Kelly articulated a theory of personality whose main emphases are highly consistent with the main themes of cognitive psychology as it came to be articulated in the years that followed.

George Kelly's Theory

George A. Kelly

As we saw in Chapter 8, many personality theories have traditionally assigned a central role to human motivation. Why do people do what they do? What gets behavior going? What internal motives, needs, drives, desires, and so on energize and select human action? In a striking departure from common practice in personality psychology, Kelly (1955) asserts that the "problem" of human motivation is not a problem at all. The search for underlying principles to explain *why* people do what they do is futile, he asserts. We need not posit life and death instincts (Freud), unconscious archetypes (Jung), drives (Miller & Dollard), principles of reinforcement (behaviorists), traits (Eysenck, Cattell, Allport), needs and motives (Murray, McClelland), affects, goals, strivings, or the urge toward self-actualization (Rogers, Maslow) to explain what motivates people to act. People are alive. They act by virtue of being alive. It's really quite simple.

Well, not that simple. Kelly's radical dismissal of the concept of motivation is really only partial, for his theory implies a fundamental principle of motivation itself (Hogan, 1976; Shotter, 1970): *A person is motivated to predict or anticipate what will happen to him or her.* What moves people to act is their desire to know what the world has in store for them. Fundamentally, the person is like a scientist, seeking to predict and control events:

> Mankind, whose progress in search of prediction and control of surrounding events stands out so clearly in light of the centuries, comprises the men we see around us every day. The aspirations of the scientist are essentially the aspirations of all men. (Kelly, 1955, p. 43)

Table 9.1 summarizes the main points of Kelly's theory in terms of the postulates and corollaries he presented in *The Psychology of Personal Constructs*. Kelly's model for human life is a commonsense brand of science. As we saw in Chapter 1, the first step of scientific inquiry is the classification of experience. Science begins when the observer seeks to make initial sense of the world by imposing some kind of organization upon it. What William James called the "blooming, buzzing confusion" of subjective

---

TABLE 9.1	*Kelly's Fundamental Postulate and Eleven Corollaries*

Fundamental Postulate: A person's processes are psychologically channelized by the ways in which he or she anticipates events.

Construction Corollary: A person anticipates events by construing their replications.

Individuality Corollary: Persons differ from one another in their construction of events.

Organization Corollary: Each person characteristically evolves, for his or her convenience in anticipating events, a construction system embracing ordinal relationships between constructs.

Dichotomy Corollary: A person's construction system is composed of a finite number of dichotomous constructs.

Choice Corollary: A person chooses for himself or herself that alternative in a dichotomized construct through which he or she anticipates the greater possibility for extension and definition of his or her system.

Range Corollary: A construct is convenient for the anticipation of a finite range of events only.

Experience Corollary: A person's construction system varies as he or she successively construes the replications of events.

Modulation Corollary: The variation in a person's construction system is limited by the permeability of the constructs within whose range of convenience the variants lie.

Fragmentation Corollary: A person may successively employ a variety of construction subsystems which are inferentially incompatible with each other.

Communality Corollary: To the extent that one person employs a construction of experience which is similar to that employed by another, his or her psychological processes are similar to those of the other person.

Sociality Corollary: To the extent that one person construes the construction process of another, he or she plays a role in a social process involving the other person.

Source: Modified from Kelly (1955).

human experience must be ordered, classified, and divided into categories if the scientist is to know anything at all. From these initial classifications are built synthesizing theories, from which are subsequently deduced discrete hypotheses to be tested through experimentation and other systematic procedures.

According to Kelly, each of us classifies his or her world by developing **personal constructs,** which are characteristic ways of construing how some things are alike and some things are different from one another. Every construct is *bipolar* (the "dichotomy corollary"), specifying how two things are similar to each other (lying on the same pole) and different from a third thing (lying at the opposite pole). For example, I may routinely classify my friends in terms of the personal construct "serious/funny." Grant and Jack are relatively serious; Dean differs from them both in that he is relatively "funny." All three friends are, in fact, similar to and different from one another in a great many ways. Despite the blooming, buzzing complexity of my experiences with these friends, I nevertheless anticipate my interactions with them, in part, by virtue of the construct "serious/funny." The construct helps me predict and control my interpersonal world. I know from past experiences with these friends (the "experience corollary") that when I am with Jack or Grant we will usually talk seriously about professional issues or current events; getting Dean to talk seriously about anything at all, on the other hand, requires a lot of extra effort.

People are best understood in terms of their own construct systems. Each person develops his or her own construct system that contains a number of constructs organized into a hierarchy ("organization corollary"). This means that within any construct system certain constructs are *superordinal* (encompassing many other constructs) and others are *subordinal* (being encompassed by larger constructs). Thus, the subordinal construct of "helpful/unhelpful" may be encompassed by the more general superordinal construct of "friendly/unfriendly." Every person's construct system is unique ("individuality corollary"), which means that everybody divides up subjective experience in a slightly different way. To know another person's construct system is to see the world through his or her eyes ("sociality corollary").

Within a given person's construct system, particular constructs differ from one another with respect to their **range of convenience** ("range corollary"). Thus, the construct "friendly/unfriendly" may have a wide range of convenience: It is likely to guide the person's anticipations of events in a large number of situations. By contrast, the construct "liberal/conservative" is likely to have a narrower range of convenience for most people. For most people, "friendly/unfriendly" is a more salient and determining dimension in their interactions with other people than is "liberal/conservative." Of course, there are marked individual differences across persons with respect to range. For instance, a politically astute woman who is especially sensitive to political issues may utilize the construct "liberal/conservative" in a wide range of situations. She may be tuned in to information in her environment suggestive of political meaning. Therefore, one of the first dimensions upon which she judges people may be their perceived political persuasion. At a cocktail party, she is introduced to a middle-aged man who looks like a banker, dressed in a three-piece suit. His hair is impeccably groomed; his wristwatch, expensive. She immediately says to herself, "I think this guy is a political conservative; I bet he usually votes Republican." Of course, she may be wrong. She may learn that he is an activist lawyer for the American Civil Liberties Union and that he always votes for liberal candidates. The woman need not be wedded to her initial hunch; constructs are more like hypotheses to be tested than like assumed facts. But the hunch provides her with an important starting point in her interaction, a way of anticipating what may or may not happen next. Anticipations guide behavior and experience. In the words of Kelly's "fundamental postulate," "a person's processes are psychologically channelized by the ways in which he [or she] anticipates events" (Kelly, 1955, p. 46).

Constructs differ in other ways, too. Some constructs are highly *permeable* whereas others are not ("modulation corollary"). A permeable construct is open to modification and the introduction of new elements. A person with an especially permeable construct system is likely to be seen by others as very open-minded. By contrast, a person who is unable to modify his or her constructs in light of new information and expanding experiences is likely to be viewed by others as relatively rigid and inflexible. Complete permeability, however, is not altogether good. If a construct is so permeable that it changes with virtually every relevant happening, it does not function well as an aid in anticipating events. Another problem can arise when different constructs within a person contradict each other. When a person's constructs are mutually incompatible and contradictory ("fragmented"), then he or she is likely to have a difficult time making consistent sense of the world and anticipating events in an adaptive way ("fragmentation corollary").

Kelly's personal-construct theory provides an interesting perspective from which to view a number of traditional concepts in personality psychology. Take, for instance, the concept of "the unconscious." Kelly sees no need to posit a mysterious unconscious domain to which have been consigned repressed wishes and conflicts. In Kelly's cognitive view, "the unconscious" is merely those constructs that are nonverbal, submerged, or suspended. For certain constructs, we are unable to assign a verbal name; thus, we may not be aware of them. Other constructs are submerged beneath other constructs or suspended from the construct system because they do not seem to fit. A highly fragmented construct system, therefore, is likely to contain submerged or suspended constructs of which the person is not aware. Yet these unconscious constructs continue to "channelize" behavior and experience.

Kelly views "anxiety" as "the recognition that the events with which one is confronted lie outside the range of convenience of one's construct system" (Kelly, 1955, p. 482). In other words, when we confront inexplicable events in the world for which our construct system does not seem to be prepared, we experience anxiety. Ultimately, then, anxiety is a fear of the unknown—the fear that the blooming, buzzing confusion cannot be understood. "Guilt" is a "perception of one's apparent dislodgment from his core role structure" (Kelly, 1955, p. 502). "Core role structure" is the construction a person has of who he or she is in relation to significant people, like parents. It is embedded within the person's general construct system. In essence, then, guilt follows the perception that one is no longer living according to an especially valued aspect of one's personal-construct system.

Exploring Personal Constructs: The Rep Test

Despite the formal postulates and corollaries, Kelly's theory of personal constructs has an appealing commonsense quality that fits well with most people's daily experience. One of the best ways to get a feel for Kelly's approach is to participate in the **Role**

TABLE 9.2	*Role Title List*

1. Your mother or the person who has played the part of mother in your life.   _____

2. Your father or the person who has played the part of father in your life.   _____

3. Your brother nearest your age. If you have no brother, the person who is most like one.   _____

4. Your sister nearest your age. If you have no sister, the person who is most like one.   _____

5. A teacher you liked or the teacher of a subject you liked.   _____

6. A teacher you disliked or the teacher of a subject you disliked.   _____

7. Your closest girl (boy) friend immediately before you started going with your wife (husband) or present closest girl (boy) friend [Ex-Flame].   _____

8. Your wife (husband) or closest present girl (boy) friend.   _____

9. An employer, supervisor, or officer under whom you served during a period of great stress [Boss].   _____

10. A person with whom you have been closely associated who, for some unexplainable reason, appears to dislike you [Rejecting Person].   _____

11. The person whom you have met within the past six months whom you would most like to know better [Sought Person].   _____

12. The person whom you would most like to be of help to, or the one whom you feel most sorry for [Pitied Person].   _____

13. The most intelligent person whom you know personally.   _____

14. The most successful person whom you know personally.   _____

15. The most interesting person whom you know personally.   _____

Construct Repertory Test (Rep Test), a personality assessment procedure designed by Kelly to explore personal constructs in people's lives. The Rep Test is a very flexible procedure that can be used in clinical work and in research. It is also easy to administer to yourself, and it is fun to take.

One version of the Rep Test asks you to make a series of comparisons among those people who play important roles in your life. Kelly defined a role as an understanding or expectation of what particular people in a person's life do. The role of "mother," therefore, consists of a person's understanding of how mothers behave in various situations. The first step in the Rep Test is to compile a Role Title List. Let us consider 15 different roles in your life. For each of the 15 roles listed in Table 9.2, write the name of the person who fits the description presented. Do not repeat names. If any role title appears to call for a duplicate name, substitute the name of another person whom the second role suggests to you.

When you have listed 15 people who play important roles in your life, compare and contrast them in a way to discern some of the important personal constructs you employ to make sense of your interactions with these people. Table 9.3 lists 15 sets of numbers. Each set contains three numbers, referring to the role titles you have listed above. Thus, the number "14" refers to "the most successful person whom you know personally." For each set of three numbers, think of how the people corresponding to the *first two* numbers are *similar* to each other and at the same time *different from* the person corresponding to the *third* number. Write a word or phrase in the blank under "Similar" to denote how the two are similar and then a contrasting word under "Contrast" to denote how the two people differ from the third. For example, the first set presents the numbers "9, 11, 14" (corresponding to "Boss," "Sought Person," and "Successful Person," respectively). Imagine that the Boss you have in mind is similar to your Sought Person in that they are both "easygoing" and that they both differ from the Successful Person who seems, by contrast, "hard-driving." You would write "easygoing" in the "Similar" blank and "hard-driving" under "Contrast."

Each of the 15 pairings of "Similar" and "Contrast" represents a single construct. At this point, the analysis of your responses can take many different paths. You may wish to look carefully at the ways in which you characterize certain critical contrasts in your life, such as those between Ex-Flame and current Boy (Girl) Friend. Or you may

TABLE 9.3	*Personal Constructs, Represented by "Similar" and "Contrast" Pairings*	
	SIMILAR	CONTRAST
1. 9, 11, 14	_____	_____
2. 10, 12, 13	_____	_____
3. 2, 5, 12	_____	_____
4. 1, 4, 8	_____	_____
5. 7, 8, 12	_____	_____
6. 3, 13, 6	_____	_____
7. 1, 2, 9	_____	_____
8. 3, 4, 10	_____	_____
9. 6, 7, 10	_____	_____
10. 5, 11, 14	_____	_____
11. 1, 7, 8	_____	_____
12. 2, 7, 8	_____	_____
13. 3, 6, 9	_____	_____
14. 4, 5, 10	_____	_____
15. 11, 13, 14	_____	_____

Source: Kelly (1955).

wish to look at the overall pattern of constructs you have delineated. How do the various constructs relate to one another? Are some constructs subordinal or superordinal to other constructs? Do you use many different constructs? Do you tend to use certain constructs again and again? If you tend to view many of the similar–contrast characterizations in terms of, say, the construct "honest/dishonest," or some variation on this idea, then you may conclude that this is an especially robust and meaningful construct in your life.

Procedures have been developed for quantifying results from the Rep Test for personality research. One line of research has examined individual differences in *cognitive complexity* as revealed by the Rep Test (Crockett, 1965). People who use many different kinds of constructs are said to manifest higher levels of cognitive complexity. They tend to view the world in a highly differentiated manner. People who use few different kinds of constructs are viewed as having a simpler, more global construct system.

Another line of research has examined *construct similarity* among friends and acquaintances (Duck, 1973, 1979). Researchers have administered various forms of the Rep Test to college students and then examined their patterns of peer interaction and friendship formation. In general, those students who have similar construct systems tend to become close friends and to remain friends for longer periods of time. For example, Duck and Spencer (1972) obtained personal-construct measures for female college freshmen at the beginning of the school year. The women in the study had all been assigned to the same residence hall. Though they were unacquainted at the beginning of the study, those women who shared similar constructs were most likely to become friends over the course of the school year. In another study, similarity of constructs was a more significant predictor of friendship formation than was similarity on self-report measures of traits (Duck & Craig, 1978). In other words, friends may be drawn together not so much by a perception that they behave in the same kinds of ways (that they are both extraverted or achievement-oriented, for instance) but rather by the perception that they see the world in the same way. People look to match their subjective experience with that of others. People look for affirmation of their own conscious meanings in the meanings of others. In relating to fellow men and women, *sharing meanings* may be more important than *doing* the same thing.

COGNITIVE STYLES AND PERSONALITY

Kelly viewed the person to be like a scientist, continually categorizing experience and testing out hypotheses as he or she anticipates and reacts to events in the world. In more contemporary terms, people are constantly processing information about the world in order to anticipate and adapt to the challenges of social life. Kelly's individuality corollary stressed that people differ from one another in the manner in which they construe events. Indeed, individual differences in styles of processing information have been recognized for centuries. Suedfeld (2000) writes that the recognition that people think differently from one another goes back to the myths of antiquity—for example, Homer's epic tales show how the subtle and occasionally convoluted thought patterns of Odysseus contrast markedly with the straightforward, simple cognitions of Achilles. **Cognitive styles** are people's "characteristic and typically preferred modes of processing information" (Sternberg & Grigorenko, 1997, p. 700). In principle, cognitive styles are not the same thing as cognitive *abilities*, like verbal, numeric, and spatial abilities measured on intelligence tests. While cognitive abilities assess *how well* a person performs on cognitive tasks, cognitive styles tap instead into a person's characteristic *way* or *manner* of processing information. As such, cognitive styles exist on the borderline between what has traditionally been associated with personality and what has traditionally been associated with intelligence and cognition.

Psychologists have studied many different kinds of cognitive styles, and they have studied them for many different reasons. In recent years, educational psychologists have been especially interested in identifying different styles of learning among students in order to improve teaching in the schools (Sternberg & Grigorenko, 1997). Within personality psychology, one of the first theorists to identify cognitive styles was Carl Jung (Chapter 3), who distinguished among different psychological types. For example, "sensing" types of persons tend to rely on empirical data from their senses as they process information in a detailed and precise manner while "intuiting" types tend to intuit overall meanings as they process information in a more holistic manner. Cognitive style is also captured in the Big Five trait taxonomy, via the trait cluster of openness to experience (*O:* Chapter 6). People high in *O* tend to process information in a more nuanced, differentiated, and abstract manner, research suggests, while those low in *O* see fewer distinctions and adhere to concrete and clearly defined categories. Indeed, many personality constructs relate to information processing in one way or another, and psychologists have been very interested in studying the relations between individual differences in, for example, traits and motives on the one hand and ways of perceiving and thinking on the other. Still, certain constructs stand out for their explicit focus on characteristic styles of information processing and for the systematic research that psychologists have conducted on them. In what follows, we will consider two dimensions of cognitive style that have received a great deal of attention from personality psychologists. They are (1) field independence–dependence and (2) integrative complexity.

Field Independence–Dependence

In the 1940s, Solomon Asch and Herman A. Witkin began studying how people decide whether an object is perpendicular to the ground or tilted to some degree. They asked people sitting in tilted chairs placed in custom-built tilted rooms to adjust their chairs until they felt that they were in an upright position—objectively perpendicular to the ground (Witkin, 1946). The task is tricky because the tilted room provides visual information that conflicts with the body's inner cues concerning what is upright. Some people tilt their chairs to become perpendicular to the (tilted) room; others ignore the tilt of the room and adjust their chairs according to inner cues. The people who use the room as the reference for their adjustment exhibit a **field-dependent** style for solving the problem. Their perception and judgment of perpendicularity depend on the "field," or environment. The people who bypass the field and make their perception and judgment according to inner cues show a **field-independent** style.

For more than 50 years Witkin and his colleagues have come to understand field independence–dependence as a broad and pervasive cognitive style that underlies many important personality differences (Bertini, Pizzamiglio, & Wapner, 1986; Goodenough,

1978; Lewis, 1985; Witkin, Goodenough, & Oltmann, 1979). The dimension has two poles. At one extreme, highly field-independent people process information in an especially analytical and differentiated style. They rely on internal frames of reference that enable them to act upon information in a highly autonomous fashion. At the other extreme, highly field-dependent people employ external frames of reference available in the field. They tend to base their perceptions on the external context within which they occur. Each pole has certain benefits and liabilities, depending on specific conditions. Therefore, neither end of the continuum is "better" than the other. Most people fall somewhere in the middle of the field independence–dependence continuum.

Field independence–dependence is one of the most thoroughly researched personality dimensions in the world. It ranks with extraversion (Chapter 6) in terms of its perennial popularity with researchers, having generated more than 3,000 experimental studies. A few of the many research findings employing the construct are summarized in Table 9.4.

| **TABLE 9.4** | *Selected Research Findings on Field Independence–Dependence* |

Correlates of Field Independence

Greater accuracy in estimating what confused or distorted images "should" look like.

Better problem solving in tasks requiring unconventional use of common objects and tools.

Hypothesis-testing approach to complex problems.

Experiences of guilt rather than shame.

Tendency to describe other people in negative terms.

Preference for solitary games in childhood.

Careers in mathematics and science, such as physics, architecture, and engineering; in health professions such as medicine and dentistry; and in certain practical occupations such as carpentry, farming, and mechanics.

Socialization patterns emphasizing independence and autonomy.

Predominant in hunting societies.

Unrelated to overall academic achievement.

Correlates of Field Dependence

Tendency to rely on other people for guidance.

Greater sensitivity to nuances of interpersonal relationships.

Higher levels of eye contact.

Better memory for names and faces.

Knowing more people and being known by more people.

Greater levels of self-disclosure with other people.

Experiences of shame rather than guilt.

Tendency to describe other people in relatively positive terms.

Preference for social play in childhood.

Careers in helping humanitarian occupations such as social worker, minister, and rehabilitation counselor; in certain teaching areas such as elementary school and social sciences; and in certain business occupations such as selling, advertising, and personnel.

Socialization patterns emphasizing conformity and dependence on authority.

Predominant in agricultural societies.

Sources: Goodenough (1978), Singer (1984), Witkin et al. (1979).

FIGURE 9.1   *An Embedded Square*

Find the square shown in A camouflaged in the coffeepot shown in B. (The solution is shaded in C.)

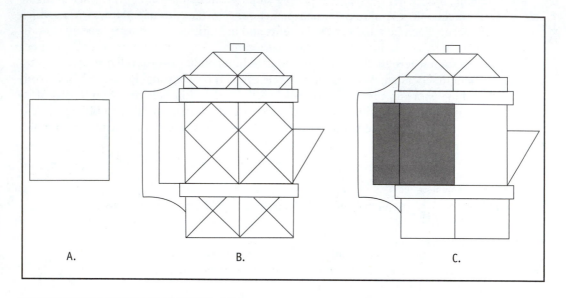

A.   B.   C.

Source: Goodenough (1978), p. 175.

Field-independent people are adept at pulling information out of an embedding context. A good example of this is identifying camouflaged figures, as assessed on the **Embedded Figures Test** (Witkin, 1950). In Figure 9.1, the problem is to locate a square, like the one shown in A, that is hidden in the picture of the coffeepot shown in B. (The solution is shaded in C.) As you may discover for yourself, the several parts of the square in B are difficult to imagine as belonging to the same (square) figure. Instead, the right half of the square is immediately seen as part of the coffeepot while the left is seen as part of the background. To find the camouflaged square, it is necessary to *restructure the perceptual field*. People who are field-independent restructure the perceptual field so that they perform quite well in camouflage tasks.

In general, field independence is associated with greater levels of perceptual and cognitive restructuring. Field-independent people tend to reshape information from the environment according to internalized plans, rules, and goals to a greater extent than do people who are field dependent. They tend to view information in the nonsocial world in a highly differentiated manner. In one study, 32 field-dependent and 32 field-independent college women solved a series of anagrams (scrambled words) under various conditions (Frank & Noble, 1985). The results showed that field-independent students solved the anagrams more quickly and found the task easier than did field-dependent students. The field-independent students found it easier to provide a disorganized field with organization.

Field-dependence may be adaptive in predominately agrarian societies, such as in China, with environmental clues playing a larger role than perceptual clues.

Like Kelly's model of the scientist, the field-independent person approaches the world as a hypothesis-tester, systematically differentiating causes and effects and analyzing the world in terms of its separate parts. Not surprisingly, people who are field-independent are drawn to careers that require cognitive restructuring and objective analysis of information, such as careers in science, mathematics, management, and mechanics. By contrast, field-dependent people are more global and intuitive in processing information about the world. They tend to engage in less cognitive restructuring, accepting information from the environment in its own contextual terms, rather than employing internal plans and guidelines for information processing. Interestingly, field-dependent people tend to be more interested in humanitarian and social-welfare professions, such as careers in the ministry, social work, teaching young children, the social sciences, and selling and advertising (Goodenough, 1978).

Cognitive style appears to have significant influences on interpersonal functioning. Numerous studies suggest that the field-dependent person is more sensitive to social context than the field-independent person. Field-dependent people pay closer attention to interpersonal cues and social information. They tend to spend more time looking at people than at inanimate objects and to make more sustained eye contact when talking with others. Field-dependent people prefer being physically closer to others than do field-independent persons. In one study, for example, participants were required to give prepared talks on several topics to the experimenter, and the physical distance between the speaker and the experimenter was measured during the presentations (Justice, 1969). Field-dependent speakers chose to stand closer to their listeners than did field-independent speakers. In another study of interpersonal distance, field-dependent people showed more speech disturbances when seated 5 feet away from their conversational partners than when seated only 2 feet away. In contrast, the interpersonal distance had less of an effect on field-independent speakers (Greene, 1973).

Helen Block Lewis (1971, 1985) has revealed interesting emotional differences between field-dependent and field-independent people. Field dependence is associated with experiences of *shame* whereas field independence is associated with experiences of *guilt*. The experience of shame or humiliation requires a social context within which the emotion is experienced. The field-dependent person is especially sensitive to social context and is likely, therefore, to be susceptible to real or imagined mockery, derision, or contempt expressed by other people. In contrast, people usually feel guilt when they sense that they have violated some internal standard of their own. Guilt does not require an explicit social context. Field-independent people are less likely to feel humiliated in the presence of others, since they are not especially sensitive to other people's opinions. But they *are* susceptible to condemnation from within as they evaluate their own actions according to internalized standards that are independent of the particular interpersonal field within which their behavior is displayed. The result is that they are more likely to experience guilt than shame.

In general, women score toward the field-dependent end of the continuum whereas men score toward the field-independent end. This gender difference is not huge, but it is relatively consistent. From childhood to adulthood, people develop in the direction of field independence. Thus, children are generally more field dependent than adults. Nonetheless, individual differences in elementary school are predictive of adult differences. Thus, a boy who is relatively field independent compared with his male peers at age 10 is likely to remain somewhat more field independent than his peers 20 years later. Certain socialization practices have been associated with differences in cognitive style. In general, evidence supports the commonsense conclusion that development proceeds toward greater field independence when socialization encourages separation from parental control. A more tightly organized and controlling milieu, on the other hand, is likely to encourage field dependence. In general, field-independent people report that their parents were relatively permissive, whereas field-dependent persons often report an emphasis on parental authority in their families.

Some of the most interesting findings on field independence–dependence come from cross-cultural studies. Witkin and Berry (1975) provide evidence that migratory hunting-and-gathering tribes tend to be field independent, whereas societies organized around subsistence-level agriculture tend to be more field dependent. Hunting-and-gathering societies are constantly on the move from one geographical setting to the next. Field-independence would appear to be an adaptive cognitive style for this migratory and predatory lifestyle. Witkin and Berry (1975) write:

> The ecological demands placed upon persons pursuing a hunting and gathering subsistence economic life style require the ability to extract key information from the surrounding context for the location of game and the ability to integrate these bits of information into a continuously fluctuating awareness of the hunter's location in space for the eventual safe return home. (p. 16)

On the other hand, agrarian societies are much more sedentary. Because agrarian societies stay put for long periods of time, their members build up elaborate systems of social interaction. Adherence to group norms may become more valuable to group survival than autonomous individual functioning.

Integrative Complexity

Witkin maintains that individual differences in field independence–dependence are differences in *style*, and that neither style is generally better than the other. Some researchers dispute this claim, arguing that field independence is a *skill* reflecting a particular cognitive ability (McKenna, 1984). According to this view, field-dependent people are deficient in a general cognitive skill associated with organizing and differentiating information. Nonetheless, the major thrust of the research on cognitive style is that neither style is better in all situations. Cognitive restructuring may be useful in certain nonsocial, task-oriented situations, whereas the field-dependent person's sensitivity to context may promote certain forms of interpersonal functioning. The same nonevaluative position cannot be taken, however, in the area of **integrative complexity.** Here, complexity is superior to simplicity. The person who is integratively complex sees the world in more sophisticated terms, making more distinctions between various things and ideas (differentiation) and seeing more connections (integration):

> Increasing levels of complexity are marked by clearer recognition that more than one point of view or evaluation on an issue can exist and may be legitimate; the identification of larger numbers of relevant dimensions and points along these dimensions; the acceptance and eventual integration of conflicting positions; and the combinatorial use of ideas, attitudes, and approaches in the development of plans to reach some generally desired goal. (Porter & Suedfeld, 1981, p. 325)

Individual differences in integrative complexity are assessed through content analysis of written material (Schroder, Driver, & Streufert, 1967). For example, a person's account of a particular experience, a speech or diary entry, an essay, an argument, or a letter written to a friend can all be scored for integrative complexity. The researcher rates particular passages in the text with respect to the degree of differentiation and integration shown. Passages that rely on simplistic explanations and isolated single judgments receive relatively low scores. Those that bring in many different perspectives and that balance different explanations and considerations receive relatively high scores for integrative complexity. While people differ with respect to their characteristic levels of integrative complexity, the same person may also show many different levels depending on the situation. For example, when a college student writes a love letter to her boyfriend, she may show a rather low level of integrative complexity. But in composing a history essay to explain economic changes in Europe during the 1800s, her expressed integrative complexity may be higher.

Some of the most creative research on integrative complexity has been conducted by Philip Tetlock on political reasoning, and Peter Suedfeld on literary correspondence. In one especially provocative study, Tetlock (1981a) analyzed selected speeches of 20th-century American presidents before and after their elections to office. He found that integrative complexity was generally low while the man was campaigning for the presidency but rose markedly after he was elected. Tetlock interpreted the finding to mean that presidential candidates tend to present issues in simplistic black-and-white terms in order to get elected but, once elected, adopt more complex reasoning patterns. Interestingly, when incumbent presidents begin campaigning for a second term, the integrative complexity levels of their rhetoric drop again, as they again seek to sway the voters by simplifying the issues.

Coding Supreme Court decisions (Tetlock, Bernzweig, & Gallant, 1985) and the political rhetoric of American senators (Tetlock, 1981b; Tetlock, Hannum, & Micheletti, 1984) and of members of the British House of Commons (Tetlock, 1984), Tetlock has made a compelling case for a connection between political ideology and integrative complexity. Politicians with relatively liberal voting records (for the most part, liberal Democrats in the United States Senate and moderate socialists in the British House of Commons) tend to exhibit higher levels of integrative complexity in their speeches than do those with relatively conservative voting records. Also low in integrative complexity are politicians with extremely liberal (such as extreme socialists in the Britain) or extremely conservative views. The data for the British House of Commons are displayed in Figure 9.2.

Tetlock explains his controversial findings in terms of *value plurality*. Adopting Rokeach's two-factor view of political values, Tetlock argues that *freedom* and *equality* are the two fundamental dimensions upon which political rhetoric can be evaluated. Conservatives tend to value freedom over equality. Extreme liberals (extreme socialists, communists) value equality over freedom. Moderate liberals, however, value both. Therefore, a moderate liberal is likely to fashion a more complex political ideology in order to accommodate his or her allegiance to both freedom and equality—two values that often conflict. While a traditionally conservative politician in Great Britain or the United States is likely to oppose increases in taxes for welfare spending because of the belief that citizens should be free to spend their hard-earned money on what they want, the liberal may find the issue more difficult in that he or she places a premium on equality, as well as freedom. According to the value of equality, tax dollars should support those who are less well-off. Yet, freedom dictates low taxes and laissez faire capitalism. As a result, the liberal is likely to bring in more considerations and find more shades of grey in political rhetoric about such issues as taxation and social programs. In Tetlock's view, the liberal is more complex and conflicted. From the

FIGURE 9.2   *Integrative Complexity and Political Affiliation*

In the British House of Commons, politicians with moderate to moderately liberal affiliations tend to show the highest levels of integrative complexity as determined from political speeches.

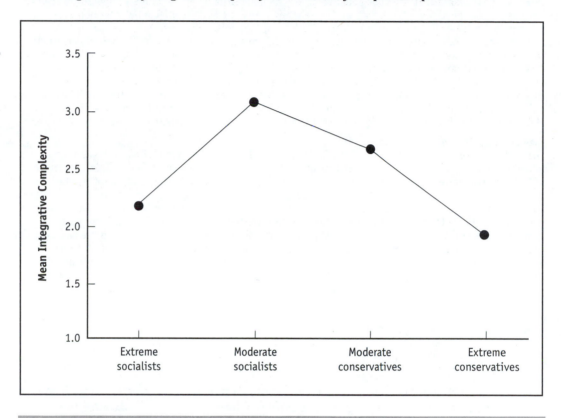

Source: Tetlock (1984), p. 370.

standpoint of the conservative, on the other hand, the liberal may seem "wishy-washy" or "afraid to take a stand."

A very different approach to integrative complexity is apparent in the research of Suedfeld on the relation between social events and literary correspondence (Porter & Suedfeld, 1981; Suedfeld, 1985). Porter and Suedfeld (1981) analyzed the personal correspondence of five eminent British novelists of the 19th and 20th centuries: Charles Dickens, George Eliot, George Meredith, Arnold Bennett, and Virginia Woolf. Each novelist's life was divided into 5-year periods and the investigators randomly sampled between 10 and 20 paragraphs from the novelist's personal correspondence for each period. Each paragraph was scored on a 7-point scale, ranging from very low to very high integrative complexity. Table 9.5 provides an example of a verbatim paragraph scoring relatively low and another scoring relatively high in integrative complexity.

TABLE 9.5	*Verbatim Passages From the Correspondence of Eminent Novelists Scored for Integrative Complexity*

Low on integrative complexity (score = 2)

Tonight I finished *First Principles*. I suppose that I can never have again the same thrills of admiration as this book has given me. If any book could be called the greatest book in the world, I suppose this can. I have never read anything a tenth part so comprehensive. And it makes its effects by sheer honest argumentative force. There are no ornaments of brilliance, wit, ingenuity, or even eloquence. Yet the closing pages of Part I, and the closing pages of Part II, are equally overwhelming in their effect. Faults there, of course, are in it but it is surely the greatest achievement of any human mind. This I do think. And Spencer has not yet come into his own, in England. As a *philosopher,* in the real sense—not as a discoverer, or a man of science—but as a philosopher, he is supreme in the history of intelligence. I say this, not because I have read all the other great ones, but because I cannot imagine the possibility of anyone having produced anything else as great as *First Principles*. [Note that in this passage the author elaborates on an absolute rule or declaration. There is little by way of alternative perspectives discussed.]

High on integrative complexity (score = 6)

The professor says you do not consort with Germans at all. I am grieved at this. I am sure you do not altogether underrate the fine qualities of German youth; but perhaps your immediate sympathies, and a somewhat exaggerated sensitiveness, stand in your way. It will be a pity, if this is so, and for more reasons than one. If you do not cultivate the people you are living amongst in your youth, you will fail in having pleasant places to look back at—landmarks of your young days. And besides, the Germans are your hosts, and you owe them at least a guest's thankfulness. I esteem them deeply for their fine moral qualities. Just now they are abusing us roundly, but that will pass away. I know they have the capacity for friendship, and that as a rule English friendships are not so lasting. Look around you, and try to be accessible to your German associates. Consider whether you are not yielding to luxurious pre-dispositions in your marked preference for English ones. You will see enough of the latter when you return here. [This passage shows simultaneous operation of alternatives and consideration of the functional relations between them.]

Source: Porter and Suedfeld (1981), pp. 325–326.

Porter and Suedfeld correlated integrative complexity scores with various historical events and personal changes in the novelists' lives. They found that integrative complexity scores *decreased* during times of war but *increased* during periods of civil unrest. War appeared to exert a simplifying effect on literary correspondence. During periods in which their countries were involved in international combat, the novelists tended to present issues in relatively undifferentiated terms, failing to take into consideration multiple and complex points of view. Porter and Suedfeld speculate that war has the general effect of restricting the "information flow" in the environment. By contrast, civil unrest (such as major political changes) appeared to evoke a more flexible and integrative outlook, perhaps by stimulating new ideas and possibilities in the environment's information flow.

With respect to personal changes, Porter and Suedfeld found that integrative complexity decreased during times of illness, was unrelated to other stressful events, increased with age, and decreased shortly before death. The last finding is especially intriguing in that research on life-span developmental psychology has suggested that just before people die they experience a marked decrease in cognitive functioning, called a *terminal drop*. In another study, Suedfeld and Piedrahita (1984) examined the correspondence of 18 eminent individuals during the last 10 years of their lives.

Supporting the hypothesis of terminal drop, they found that integrative complexity scores fell markedly in the last 5 years before death for those who died of a protracted illness and during the year immediately prior to death for those who died suddenly.

In general, research suggests that high levels of integrative complexity are associated with making more informed and well-balanced decisions, with open-mindedness and tolerance for ambiguity in confronting complex issues, and with cognitive self-direction. Nonetheless, high integrative complexity can sometimes come with a cost. High scorers sometimes find it difficult to make a clear-cut decision based on firm moral principles. For example, during the debate on slavery before the American Civil War, moderate leaders and politicians who sought compromise on this issue tended to score high on integrative complexity, based on coding of their public speeches. By contrast, the abolitionists—who argued strongly that slavery should be abolished—tended to score low, as did the leaders and politicians who defended slavery. We see here that what virtually everybody today would view as the morally right choice—to abolish slavery—was most strongly pushed and clearly articulated by leaders whose speeches scored relatively *low* for integrative complexity. (Interestingly, their arch-opponents—leaders arguing in favor of keeping the slavery system in place—also scored low.) By contrast, those leaders adopting more complex and integrative arguments took intermediate, and morally compromised, positions in the debate—for example, they argued that slavery might still be tolerated in the South but prevented from spreading to the new territories of the United States. In this interesting and troubling historical case, high levels of integrative complexity seem to have clouded people's moral vision (Tetlock, Armor, & Peterson, 1994).

In another study suggesting costs for high integrative complexity, researchers studied interactions among graduate business management students (Tetlock, Peterson, & Berry, 1993). The students showing high levels of integrative complexity were rated by their peers as more creative, as might be expected, but also as more disagreeable, narcissistic, and lacking in conscientiousness. The students low in integrative complexity were viewed as simple, acquiescent, and conforming, but they were also seen as being warm, giving, and more self-controlled, compared with the students high in integrative complexity. In some situations, then, there would appear to be an interpersonal downside for high integrative complexity.

In conclusion, it is worth noting similarities and differences between the two cognitive styles we have identified—integrative complexity and field independence–dependence. Both refer to individual differences in how people process information. For both, people on one end of the spectrum seem to process information in a more analytical and differentiated manner, making finer distinctions and differentiating complex phenomena into component parts (field independence and high integrative complexity). People on the other end seem to process information in a more global and holistic manner, making fewer distinctions and failing to disembed components from their defining context (field dependence and low integrative complexity). These individual differences appear to relate to a wide spectrum of important outcomes, ranging from political viewpoints to social relationships. Nonetheless, the two concepts are also very different from each other. Whereas field independence–dependence assesses a style of *perceiving*, integrative complexity refers instead to a style of *reasoning*. Furthermore, the two differ in breadth and consistency. Field independence–dependence is a broad cognitive style that is assumed to be more-or-less consistent across situations and over time. In this sense, it is a rather "traitlike" cognitive style. By contrast, integrative complexity is thought to rise and fall as a function of age, circumstances, situational demands, and a host of other external factors, making it less "traitlike" and somewhat more contingent and contextualized. Nonetheless, people also appear to show overall mean-level differences on integrative complexity, which appear to relate positively to both intelligence and openness to experience. Thus, Person A may score higher in general than Person B on measures of integrative complexity, but both A and B show a great deal of range and variability in their scores as a function of the different contexts under which their reasoning might be assessed.

SOCIAL-COGNITIVE THEORY AND THE PERSON

Contemporary social-cognitive approaches in personality psychology view the person as a more-or-less rational and planful knower who actively seeks information in the social world and draws upon a rich storehouse of social knowledge in order to regulate his or her own behavior and enact plans and goals in a wide range of social environments (Cantor & Kihlstrom, 1989; Cantor & Zirkel, 1990; Cervone & Shoda, 1999b; Higgins, 1999; Kihlstrom & Hastie, 1997; Markus & Wurf, 1987; Shoda, 1999). Like Kelly, these approaches suggest that people are especially adept at construing and anticipating social situations in ways that enhance their ability to predict and control the social world. Within the rich storehouse of social information upon which people routinely draw are their most salient personal constructs for categorizing social experience. In their emphasis on human agency and their portrait of an active and self-organizing knower, social-cognitive theories also underscore themes that are at the heart of some humanistic approaches to personality, including especially Deci and Ryan's (Chapter 8) self-determination theory. These theories provide an optimistic take on human nature: As human beings, we are potentially rational and effective; we are intelligent and planful in our social interactions; we are flexible in the strategies we employ to obtain our goals; our behavior is responsive to situational demands, but it is also coherent and self-organized.

Contemporary social-cognitive approaches, furthermore, share with social learning theories (Chapter 4) a focus on how people craft particular kinds of behaviors for particular kinds of situations and domains (Bandura, 1999; Cervone & Shoda, 1999a; Mischel, 1999). According to this view, the coherence of personality is shown not so much by the cross-situationally consistent behavior associated with broad traits such as extraversion (Chapter 5) but rather through the intricate patterning of different social-cognitive mechanisms that a person uses to address different situations. In other words, the fact that a highly extraverted person tends to be outgoing and sociable across a wide range of situations may be evidence for a modicum of *consistency* in responding, but it says little about how that person's individuality is organized and integrated. From the social-cognitive perspective, personality organization emerges out of the beliefs, expectancies, constructs, competencies, values, schemas, scripts, and the like that comprise a person's store of social information and which a person uses, more-or-less effectively, to meet the demands of many different social situations. Cervone and Shoda (1999a) summarize this view:

The social-cognitivist strives to understand how multiple mechanisms operate, in concert, as coherent psychological systems. Personality coherence is viewed as an emergent property of interactions among multiple psychological processes, including the processes that enable people to interpret the environment, develop knowledge and skills, reflect upon their capabilities, and plan and self-regulate courses of action. Personality is an integrated self-system, through which people contribute to coherent patterns of consistency and variability in response. (p. 31)

By interpreting their social environments, developing social knowledge and skills, reflecting upon their social capabilities, making plans for particular social contexts, and regulating their social behavior in accord with those plans, people can behave in socially intelligent ways. Social-cognitive adaptations, then, speak directly to a person's social intelligence.

Social Intelligence

Nancy Cantor and John Kihlstrom argue that the key to understanding personality coherence is **social intelligence** (Cantor & Kihlstrom, 1985, 1987, 1989). Each person brings a set of skills, abilities, and knowledge to every social situation. Such "lawful intraindividual variability, especially across situations, is precisely the characteristic we ascribe to intelligence" (Cantor & Kihlstrom, 1985, p. 16). They write, "intelligent action, as contrasted with the instinctual or the reflexive, is flexible rather than rigidly stereotyped, discriminative rather than indiscriminate, and optional rather than obligatory" (p. 16). The implication is that people differ in social intelligence. Some people appear to have more than others. More important, however, people use their social intelligence in different ways to interpret and solve current tasks and problems in life.

In Cantor and Kihlstrom's view, social interaction involves problem solving. The social world confronts each of us with a series of mundane and momentous problems that call for socially intelligent behavior. We must interpret each problem we encounter and devise a strategy for mastering it, or at least for coping with it. For each social situation, the person asks such questions as "What do I want here?" "What are the likely consequences of my actions?" "How can I get what I want?" In working

through the various facets of a social problem (situation), the person draws extensively on a repertoire of social intelligence, which "is stored in memory as organized knowledge" and which "forms the structural basis for personality" (p. 18).

As shown in Table 9.6, social intelligence consists of three different kinds of organized knowledge: *concepts*, *episodes*, and *rules*. Concepts and episodes may be grouped together as aspects of *declarative* knowledge. Think of them as "things" that are contained in the information storehouse. Concepts are the abstract and categorical things contained in the storehouse, such as concepts of who you are and what you typically expect to happen in social life. Concepts are aspects of what Cantor and Kihlstrom call **declarative-semantic knowledge.** Episodes are more concrete and particular kinds of things contained in the storehouse, such as memories of particular scenes in your life. These make up **declarative-episodic**

Nancy Cantor

knowledge. The distinction between the two forms of declarative knowledge—concepts (declarative-semantic knowledge) and episodes (declarative-episodic knowledge)—is a fundamental distinction in cognitive psychology. Many cognitive psychologists believe that the brain processes these two kinds of declarative knowledge very differently. Consequently, your conception of yourself as, say, "an honest person" (declarative-semantic) involves different brain processes and is itself a very different piece of knowledge compared with your memory of one particular episode in your life (declarative-episodic) in which you acted in an especially honest fashion. In contrast to both concepts and episodes, rules are aspects of what Cantor and Kihlstrom identify as **procedural knowledge.** Whereas concepts and episodes are like things contained in the mind's storehouse, rules are not things but rather procedures or processes that determine how things are used.

Among the most important concepts that make up declarative-semantic knowledge are your concepts of self, others, and social interaction—all of which you have accumulated over the many social experiences that make up your life. Every person has accumulated a very large store of concepts about who he or she is, what other people are like, and what a person should expect to happen in social interaction. Concepts of *self* are perhaps the most salient components of declarative-semantic knowledge, and we will have much more to say about them later in this chapter when we consider the topics of self-schemata, possible selves, self-guides, and self-with-other units in personality. Among the different concepts of *other* people contained in declarative-semantic knowledge are what Mark Baldwin (1992) calls **relational schemas.** Relational schemas are mental representations of especially important interpersonal relationships that a person has experienced. Baldwin's idea is very similar to what you may recall from Chapter 2 as the notion of "working models" of attachment relationships. Over the course of social life, we each come to expect certain kinds of interactions with certain people. Therefore, your relational schema (working model) of your relationship with your mother may involve her tending to reprimand you when you are not especially conscientious whereas your relational schema for your interactions with your best friend may involve having lots of fun and staying up late at night talking about your problems. Our relational schemas guide and shape our expectations and reactions in social relationships, and as social relationships unfold they may also come to influence

---

TABLE 9.6	*Aspects of Social Intelligence*

DECLARATIVE-SEMANTIC KNOWLEDGE (CONCEPTS)	DECLARATIVE-EPISODIC KNOWLEDGE (EPISODES)	PROCEDURAL KNOWLEDGE (RULES)
Conceptions of self	Person memories	Attributional styles
Self-schemata	Autobiographical memories	Judgmental heuristics
Possible selves		Hypothesis-testing styles
Self guides		
Self-with-other units		
Relational schemata		
Scripts		
Implicit personality theories		

our relational schemas. As important aspects of declarative-semantic knowledge and, more generally, social intelligence, relational schemas serve as "cognitive maps in navigating the social world" (Fehr, Baldwin, Collins, Patterson, & Benditt, 1999, p. 301).

Yet another important kind of concept contained in declarative-semantic social knowledge is **scripts** (Abelson, 1981; Schank & Abelson, 1977). Scripts are knowledge about how certain kinds of stereotypical social events typically unfold (Abelson, 1981; Schank & Abelson, 1977). Many people have scripts for "going to church," "attending a football game," "exiting the building when the fire alarm goes off," and many other common social events. Perhaps the best example of a script is eating at a restaurant. When we enter a restaurant, we expect to involve ourselves in a certain behavioral routine. We walk in and wait to be seated. Once seated, we expect to meet a waiter or waitress, to have our water glass filled, to receive and read the menu, to order what we want to eat, to spend a certain amount of time eating the food, to enjoy the conversation while eating, to receive the bill at the end of the meal, and so on. When we enter a restaurant, therefore, we activate a restaurant script, which then guides our behavior and our experience in the situation. We expect other people to do the same thing. The script provides general guidelines within which a good deal of behavioral flexibility may be manifest. Thus, I may order anything on the menu; I may discuss the upcoming presidential election over dessert; I may choose to pay with a credit card or cash. But I am not likely to stand on the table and juggle the plates. Violations of the script may be seen as odd and even troubling, for they undermine our well-established assumptions about how the world is supposed to work.

In Chapter 5 we encountered the concept of *implicit personality theories* (Rosenberg, 1976). Every person develops a "theory" of human functioning, made up of intuitive knowledge concerning the causes of human behavior, norms for various attributes of personality, and the relation of various personality attributes to one another. For example, my mother's implicit personality theory holds that, for the most part, smart people are morally good. In other words, she tends to believe that intelligence and morality are highly correlated. Another relative of mine seems to hold the opposite view. According to her implicit personality theory, highly intelligent people tend to be crafty and devious, and for the most part they should not be trusted. Like scripts, implicit personality theories are embedded in a person's repertoire of declarative-semantic knowledge.

Implicit personality theories may also encode our expectations about the extent to which certain human attributes may or may not change over time. Take, for example, the attributes of "intelligence" and "honesty." Rachel may take it for granted that these attributes are more-or-less fixed for any given person. In other words, Rachel believes that the "amount" of intelligence or honesty that a person "has" does not (and cannot) change much over time. A smart person will remain smart; a person who is not very smart is not likely to get much smarter over time. By contrast, Katie believes that these attributes develop over time. People can become smarter over time, with experience and training. People who are not very honest may become more honest over time with the right kind of social experiences, she believes. Rachel and Katie show contrasting implicit theories about the nature of human attributes. According to Carol Dweck (1996; Dweck, Chiu, & Hong, 1995), Rachel holds implicitly to an *entity* theory of human attributes—attributes are fixed entities that do not change over time. By contrast, Katie appears to believe in an *incremental* theory—attributes are malleable and can

John Kihlstrom

change incrementally over time. Dweck's research shows that people who hold entity-based theories tend to interpret their own and other people's actions in terms of fixed traits ("I failed the test because I am dumb"; "He stole the bread because he is dishonest") whereas those holding incremental theories focus less on broad traits and more on the situational and temporary forces that influence action ("I failed the test because I used the wrong strategy in studying for it"; "He stole the bread because he was desperate"). Dweck maintains that entity-based theories can undermine a person's efforts, especially when he or she faces failure. People with entity-based implicit theories tend to feel helpless when they meet failures, because they believe that they cannot change the fixed traits that are responsible for their failures. By contrast, incrementalists, like Katie, respond in a more proactive manner to setbacks and are more likely to work hard to master the challenges they face. Their motivation to do so is grounded in an implicit belief that people (including themselves) *can* change, develop, and grow.

Moving from declarative-semantic to declarative-episodic knowledge, Cantor and Kihlstrom argue that people encode and store a great many particular events in their lives in concrete and episodic form, and they draw upon these memories to engage in socially intelligent behavior. For example, I have very clear memories of my first day in kindergarten (in 1959), the moment I heard that President John F. Kennedy had been assassinated (November 22, 1963), a fight with Charlie Waytovich in my back yard (sometime around fifth grade), the junior prom in high school, running out of gas while driving on a Chicago expressway, meeting good friends on a train while traveling in Spain, and a host of other scenes or episodes from my life that stand out in my memory. These are all aspects of declarative-episodic knowledge. Cantor and Kihlstrom make a rough distinction between episodes that primarily involve the self and those that primarily involve other people. Self-based episodes, like those I have listed above, are examples of *autobiographical memory* (Kihlstrom, 1981; Robinson, 1976). Episodes that center on other people are aspects of *person memory* (Hastie, Park, & Weber, 1984). An example of person memory might be my recollection of an episode from my father's life—for example, his story of how he once took an unauthorized leave from the U.S. Navy to meet up with a woman he loved, and the trouble he got into after that. Cantor and Kihlstrom (1989) write: "Personal recollections tend to be hot and wet rather than cold and dry: They often involve vivid images and feelings that are lacking in the raw factual material drawn up from semantic memory" (p. 25). Because declarative-episodic knowledge is encapsuled in recollections of concrete events, it provides a richness of texture and pattern to social intelligence that more abstract knowledge (declarative-semantic knowledge) can rarely provide. In addition, "there seems to be a sense of narrative integrity to autobiographical memory, with people able to reflect on the beginning, middle, and potential end of their life stories," write Cantor and Kihlstrom (1989, p. 26). In Chapter 11, we discuss how autobiographical memory may indeed be organized in terms of a life narrative that integrates past, present, and anticipated future to provide life with unity and purpose.

After declarative-semantic and declarative-episodic knowledge, the third domain of social intelligence is procedural knowledge. Procedural knowledge consists of various competencies, strategies, and rules "that enable us to form impressions of others, make causal attributions, encode and retrieve social memories, and predict social behaviors" (Cantor & Kihlstrom, 1985, p. 20). People operate according to a great many rules and strategies when engaging in socially intelligent behavior, and many of these rules are outside conscious awareness. Included here are various *judgmental heuristics* people use, or rules of thumb about how to make social judgments. Another aspect of procedural knowledge is *hypothesis-testing styles.* People differ from one another with respect to the characteristic ways in which they try to predict social behavior. Of special interest are **causal attributions,** the perceived causes of events. A huge body of research in social psychology has examined how people understand causation in social events (Jones, Kanouse, Kelley, Nisbett, Valins, & Weiner, 1971; Kelley & Michela, 1980). In Chapter 5, we briefly discussed the "fundamental attribution error," whereby people tend to view their own behavior as caused by situational factors and the behavior of others as caused by internal traits. The general principle is that people tend to make different causal interpretations for events in which they're personally involved (as actors) than they do for events that they witness or hear about (as observers). Observers tend to say that the behavior of other people is caused by intentions or dispositions residing within the other people. By contrast, the actors themselves tend to say that their behavior is caused by various factors in the situation. Actors offer a more contextualized account of their own behavior. Their intimate knowledge of their own role as a participant in a behavior sequence provides important information for their causal attributions. In that observers may not be privy to the same kind of information about the actors, observers tend to attribute cause in a rather noncontextual manner, by making global attributions about the actor's traits, motives, intentions, and so on.

Bernard Weiner (1979, 1990) offers another well-known scheme for understanding causal attributions, especially as they apply to outcomes of success and failure. To explain why a person succeeded or failed in a given task, we often resort to one or more of four basic attributions: ability, effort, task difficulty, and luck. Why, for example, did Maria receive a low grade on her term paper for American Literature 101? Her failure to do well on this assignment might be explained in terms of ability: Maria is simply not a very good writer. Or it may be explained in terms of effort: Maria did not put much time into the paper; she didn't try hard enough. Both ability and effort are *internal* attributions. They suggest that the cause of Maria's failure is in factors within Maria—her poor ability or her weak effort. By contrast, we may explain Maria's failure in terms of task difficulty: The assignment was too hard, too ambiguous; perhaps, the professor expected too much or failed to give the students enough time to write a good paper. Or we may say that Maria was just plain unlucky on this assignment. During the same week that her paper was due, Maria's boyfriend broke up with her and her mother called to say that she did not have enough money to pay the recent tuition bill. Because of her bad luck, Maria was distracted and failed to write the kind of paper she would normally write. Task difficulty and luck are *external* attributions: The causes of her failure are in the environment, not in Maria herself. The four attributions may also be organized along the lines of *stability*. Ability and task difficulty refer to stable factors; effort and luck are unstable. Maria's luck may change or she may try harder next time.

In general, people tend to make internal and stable attributions when accounting for successes in their lives. Had Maria received an "A" on the assignment, she might attribute her good fortune to her strong writing ability. By contrast, people tend to make unstable attributions when accounting for failure—not trying hard enough, or bad luck. In the wake of a failure, an unstable attribution has the advantage of suggesting that things are likely to change in the future. It would seem, therefore, that explaining failure in terms of momentary causes such as effort or luck helps protect one's self-esteem. Things will be better next time. I'm still okay. Nonetheless, people differ markedly in their characteristic attributional patterns. As we will see later in this chapter, some empirical evidence suggests that chronically depressed people tend to make causal sense of their successes and failures in ways that go against the norms. They may tend to explain their own successes in terms of unstable factors (e.g., "I got lucky") but their failures in terms of causes that are internal and stable (e.g., "I failed because I'm stupid.").

Summing up the concept of social intelligence, Cantor and Kihlstrom argue that people employ concepts (declarative-semantic knowledge such as scripts and implicit personality theories), episodes (declarative-episodic knowledge such as autobiographical recollections), and rules (procedural knowledge such as attributional patterns) to solve social problems they encounter in everyday life. Problem solving is most effective when people are able to act in flexible and discriminating ways, when they can enact creative solutions to the social problems they confront, enabling them to move forward in life with efficacy and aplomb. Especially significant for personality are those social problems that take the form of *life tasks*. As we learned in Chapter 8, life tasks are "self-articulated problems that individuals are motivated to try to solve, to which they devote energy and time, and that they see as organizing their daily life activity" *during a particular life period or life transition* (Cantor & Zirkel, 1990, p. 150). Therefore, life tasks may arise from developmental demands—challenges and opportunities that we confront by virtue of the particular period or stage in the life cycle in which we are currently placed. For instance, a recent college graduate may see her main life task as that of "becoming established in a line of work" or "beginning a family" or "making new friendships." College freshmen may be most concerned with "adjusting to leaving home," "getting good grades in school," and "finding an academic area in which to major."

Cantor, Norem, Niedenthal, Langston, and Brower (1987) conducted a longitudinal study of life tasks and cognitive strategies among honors students in college. As freshmen, the students completed a life-tasks questionnaire. They were asked to list life tasks on which they were currently working and to categorize each task (if possible) into one of six groups: three achievement categories (doing well academically, establishing future goals, managing time) and three interpersonal categories (making friends, being on one's own, establishing an identity). The researchers detected two very different cognitive strategies for dealing effectively with the relatively stressful academic life tasks confronting the students. One group of students exhibited consistent *optimism* in their approach to academic life tasks. They viewed academic tasks as challenging but not especially overwhelming, and they tended to accurately predict their own academic performance, as evidenced by later grades in classes. A second group of students showed *defensive pessimism* (Norem & Cantor, 1986). The defensive pessimists rated their academic tasks (such as "getting good grades") in much more negative terms than did the optimists, though they did not differ from the optimists in their ratings of interpersonal tasks (such as "making friends"). Defensive pessimists did not accurately predict the grades they eventually received. They tended instead to underestimate their own performance, setting defensively low expectations in spite of good past performance. Interestingly, these students were not debilitated by their pessimistic outlooks. In fact, the reverse seemed to be true. For pessimists, the higher the anxiety surrounding academic tasks, the higher their first semester GPA! Overall, the optimists and the defensive pessimists achieved comparable grades in their first semester of college.

Self-Schemata

A central concept in cognitive approaches to personality is the **schema.** A schema (plural: *schemata*) is any abstract knowledge structure. Fiske and Taylor (1984) write that a schema is a "cognitive structure that represents one's general knowledge about a given concept or concept domain" (p. 13). There are many ways to think about schemata. You may view them as "filters" or "templates" that we use to perceive, organize, and understand information, much like Kelly's concept of a "personal construct." Neisser (1976) writes that a schema is like a "format" in a computer-programming language. Formats specify that information must be of a certain sort if it is to be interpreted coherently. The format allows the program to deal effectively with a particular kind of information while ignoring or downplaying the rest. A person's schemata go beyond the information given by (1) simplifying information when there is too much for the person to handle efficiently and (2) filling in gaps when information is missing.

Every person employs a vast and complex set of schemata to make sense of the world. Social-cognitive approaches to personality contend that human adaptation is accomplished through the schematic processing of social information. Furthermore, schemata are applied to the self. Each person builds up a view of the self, a **self-schema** or series of self-schemata that structure the processing of self-relevant information and guide behavior. A self-schema is like all other schemata in that it simplifies incoming information and fills in gaps when information is missing. For example, if an important part of a young man's self-schema is the idea that he is especially attractive to women, he is likely to pick up information from the social environment that confirms his view and ignore or fail to process information that seems irrelevant. Seeing the puzzled facial expression of a woman sitting next to him in class, he may assume that she is thinking of him and wondering if he might ask her out. But self-schemata differ from other schemata, too. Self-schemata are generally (1) larger and more complex than other schemata, (2) richer in their network of associations and relationships among components, (3) more frequently activated in daily information processing, and (4) loaded with emotion (Markus & Sentis, 1982). One's own self-schema contains a vast and complex array of emotionally laden information. For each of us, it is probably our most popular, most frequently used schema.

The self-schema does not contain all information about the person. Rather, it emphasizes personally significant information about the self. We tend to place at the center of the self-schema those self-defining properties such as our name, representative aspects of physical appearance, significant personal relationships, and perceived traits, motives, values, and goals that we view as most representative of who we are. Figure 9.3 illustrates a small portion of a hypothetical person's self-schema. Many concepts may

FIGURE 9.3 *Portion of a Hypothetical Self-Schema*

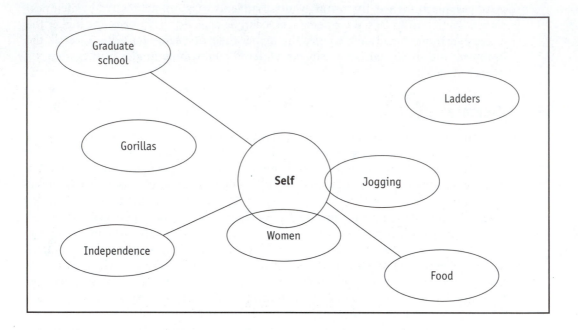

Source: Markus & Smith (1981), p. 244.

be linked with the self-schema, because we experience most things with reference to the self. In Figure 9.3, the self is linked to food and graduate school. Other concepts in memory that are not self-relevant, such as "ladders" and "gorillas," are not shown as connected to the self. Repeated associations of the self with other concepts and structures will lead to stronger and more certain links. Eventually, there may be some overlap between the self and another concept, as when a person takes up jogging and comes to see himself or herself as possessing many of the characteristics of other joggers.

A major finding in research on self-schemata is that people process information that is especially relevant to their self-schemata in highly efficient ways (Lewicki, 1984; Markus, 1977, 1983; Markus & Smith, 1981). In a classic study, Hazel Markus (1977) investigated the dimension of "independence–dependence" in self-schemata. Depending on how college students presented themselves in an initial phase of her research, Markus classified each as having a strong independence schema, a strong dependence schema, or as aschematic (having neither). Three to four weeks later, the students participated in an experiment in which adjectives were presented on a screen one at a time. The adjectives were either *schema-relevant* (related to independence or dependence) or *schema-irrelevant* a set of adjectives related to the dimension of "creativity"). The student's task was to press one of two buttons, labeled either ME or NOT ME, to indicate whether the adjective described him or her.

Those students whose self-schemata underscored dependence showed faster reaction times in response to dependent adjectives than they did to schema-inconsistent (independent) adjectives and schema-irrelevant adjectives. Markus concluded that the dependent schematics were accustomed to thinking of themselves as "conforming," "obliging," and so on and could, therefore, make these judgments more quickly. The independent schematics showed a similar pattern of results, with faster reaction times to independent adjectives. The aschematics, on the other hand, did not differ at all in their processing times for dependent and independent words. Aschematics appeared not to have defined themselves with respect to independence and to be equally at ease labelling their behavior in these terms. They apparently did not have a structure for independence–dependence to guide their information processing about the self.

Studies similar to Markus's have shown that people with self-schemata emphasizing particular areas are readily able to (1) evaluate new information with respect to its relevance for the particular area, (2) make judgments and decisions in the domain with relative ease and certainty, (3) retrieve episodes and other behavioral evidence from their past that illustrates the particular area, (4) predict future behavior in the area, and (5) resist information that is counter to the prevailing schema (Markus & Smith, 1981).

Markus (1983) hypothesizes that a self-schema emerges as a person begins to experience feelings of personal responsibility in a particular domain of behavior. "Acquiring a self-schema becomes equivalent to staking out a personal claim in a given behavioral arena," writes Markus (1993, p. 561). "It is as if one is saying 'I have control over my actions here' (or 'I would like to have control over my actions here' or 'I am both the cause and the consequence of actions in this domain')." As a self-schema develops, the person becomes more concerned with his or her own behavior in the particular domain and seeks to exert control over the causes and consequences of that behavior.

Take for example a dominant self-schema from my own life—one that has sadly passed into oblivion to be replaced by others. I began to develop a self-schema related to baseball and athletics in the second grade. Before this time, I knew virtually nothing about baseball and had no interest in learning. If someone had told me in first grade that I was a poor baseball player, I would have reacted as I might now should someone tell me that I'm a poor mechanic: "Who cares?!" However, in the second grade, I started watching the Chicago Cubs on television (as related previously in Feature 5.B) and began to entertain the idea of playing the game. As I cautiously joined in the neighborhood sandlot baseball games, I began to see myself as a pretty good hitter and a very good fielder and pitcher. I worked hard to improve my performance. I fantasized about playing in the big leagues as an adult, going so far as to calculate my statistics for an envisioned 20-year career as a star pitcher for the Chicago Cubs, even down to my lifetime earned-run average and number of batters I would strike out. By the time I was in fifth grade, I was especially sensitive to compliments and criticisms about my baseball playing. My "good baseball player" self-schema expanded and became probably the largest part of my self-understanding in grade school. It served to organize information about myself and it functioned to regulate my behavior—I spent countless hours in the sun throwing, hitting, and catching balls.

Individuals develop very different self-schemata. Differences in the *content* of self-schemata—the self-relevant material contained within a schema—are virtually infinite in that no two people see themselves in identical ways. Differences in the *structure* of

FEATURE 9.A

Gender, Sex, and Schema

With the strong impact of the women's movement in the United States in the 1970s, many American psychologists conducted research on the extent to which men and women identify with sex-role stereotypes. According to common social lore, men are supposed to be strong, assertive, independent, and instrumental—that is, masculine. And women are supposed to be gentle, caring, dependent, and expressive—in other words, feminine. Psychologists developed a number of self-report measures of *sex-role orientation* to assess the extent to which people saw themselves as relatively masculine or relatively feminine. Arguing that masculinity and femininity were not opposite but rather independent dimensions, many researchers showed that scoring high on both of these dimensions—that is, showing **psychological androgyny**—might be a preferred orientation in contemporary American society (Bem, 1975; Heilbrun, 1981). In recent years, individual differences in self-ascribed masculine and feminine traits have been reconceptualized in social-cognitive terms. In her **gender schema theory**, Sandra Bem (1981, 1987) suggests that people differ in the extent to which they understand their lives and contexts in gender-related terms. Some people repeatedly process social information along the lines of gender, showing strong gender schemata. Other people are relatively "aschematic" with respect to gender, less inclined to interpret social life in terms of masculinity and femininity.

Bem argues that individual differences in sex-role orientations are best understood in terms of different gender schemata. A man who scores high on masculinity or a woman who scores high on femininity exhibits a strong gender schema, or generalized tendency to process information on the basis of sex-linked associations. These people should be especially sensitive to gender differences in daily information processing. Androgynous and undifferentiated men and women show weaker gender schemata. They are less likely to see and interpret the world in terms of gender.

In a famous experiment that has been repeated many times, Bem (1981) administered a sex-role inventory (the BSRI) to college students and then engaged the students in a memory task. She first presented a list of 61 words in random order consisting of proper names (such as *Henry*, *Deborah*), animal names, (*gorilla*, *butterfly*), verbs (*hurling*, *blushing*), and articles of clothing (*trousers*, *bikini*). Within each of the four categories, some of the words were masculine oriented (*Henry*, *gorilla*, *hurling*, *trousers*) and some were feminine oriented (*Deborah*, *butterfly*, *blushing*, *bikini*).

After the words were presented, the students were given 8 minutes to write down as many of the words that they could remember in any order. The important finding in the study concerns the *order* in which words were remembered. College students with strong gender schemata (masculine men and feminine women) tended to show higher levels of *clustering* in their recall of words. This means that they tended to string together words of the same gender designation. For instance, if the first word they remembered and wrote down was *Henry* (a masculine word), their second word remembered was likely to be masculine as well (for example, *hurling*). Thus, sex-typed men and women (those with strong gender schemata) tended to group together masculine and feminine words in recall. In Bem's words, they "spontaneously imposed a gender-based classification system on the stimulus array" (1987, p. 267). Non-sex-typed men and women—those with presumably weaker gender schemata—showed lower levels of clustering. These students tended not to use gender as an organizing principle for recalling the words.

MacKenzie-Mohr and Zanna (1990) examined the role of men's gender schemata and their tendency to treat women as sexual objects in a nonsexual or professional setting. Gender-schematic (high on masculinity, low on femininity) and gender-aschematic college males watched either a pornographic or neutral video and were then interviewed by a female research assistant. The researchers reasoned that viewing a pornographic video would likely "prime" or make salient thoughts about heterosexual relations among the men. As a result, gender-schematic men would be more likely than gender-aschematic men to adopt a "heterosexuality schema" in subsequent interaction with a woman in a professional setting, thinking and acting in a relatively sexist manner. The results of the experiment supported the researchers' prediction. Even though she did not know anything about the men she interviewed, the female research assistant experienced her interaction with the gender-schematic men who had viewed the pornographic video as more

sexually provocative than interaction with subjects in the other three conditions (schematic/neutral, aschematic/pornography, aschematic/neutral). For example, she reported that gender-schematic men who had viewed the pornographic video were more likely than the other men to look at her body while she was interviewing them. In addition, these men tended to sit closer to her than men in the other conditions. Finally, all the men were asked to describe their interaction with the female assistant immediately after the interview. In the first minute of this free-recall task, 72% of the information recalled by the gender-schematic men who had viewed the pornographic video centered on the interviewer's physical characteristics, compared with 49% of the information recalled by men in the other three conditions. Summing up their results, the authors write:

> For gender-schematic males, exposure to nonviolent pornography seems to influence the way they view and act toward a woman in a task-oriented (or "professional") situation. These males were seen by the female experimenter as more sexually motivated, they positioned themselves closer to her, and they had faster reaction times and greater recall for information about her physical appearance. Importantly, these males also recalled less about the survey the female experimenter was conducting. These variables all triangulate on the conclusion that this group of males treated our female experimenter, who was interacting with them in a professional setting, in a manner that was both cognitively and behaviorally sexist. (MacKenzie-Mohr & Zanna, 1990, p. 305)

self-schemata can also be observed. For instance, some people present highly articulated and complex self-schemata, whereas other people see themselves in simpler terms (Linville, 1987). Some people have many different self-aspects, which are kept relatively separate from one another. Each aspect of their self-schema may be connected to a particular role they play in life, but the different roles may be relatively unconnected. Therefore, should they experience failure or trouble with respect to one area in their self-schema, other areas may remain relatively unscathed. In a sense, these people with high levels of *self-complexity* manage to compartmentalize the many different aspects of the self-schema, such that what happens in one aspect has little effect on the others. By contrast, people low in self-complexity present a less differentiated self-schema. For people low in self-complexity, feelings associated with a bad event in one aspect of life tend to spill over into other aspects as well. In the wake of failure in one domain, misery may spread quickly across the entire self-schema (Dixon & Baumeister, 1991; Linville, 1987).

Differences in the complexity of self-schemata have also been linked to differences in the focus of one's consciousness. Whereas some people tend to focus their attention on the outside, public world, others are more taken with their own inner lives, their private world of thought, feeling, and fantasy. Research by Nasby (1985) and others suggests that people who score high on scales measuring **private self-consciousness**—a tendency to introspect about the self (Fenigstein, Scheier, & Buss, 1975)—develop more elaborate and extensive self-schemata than do people who score low on self-consciousness. Not surprisingly, people who dwell on and ponder over the meanings of their own behaviors tend to develop self-schemata that are rich in detail and nuance.

A Confederacy of Selves

Declarative-semantic knowledge about the self comes in many different forms and qualities. For example, you may have some general attributions about yourself that seem to hold in most situations and contexts—say, you see yourself as a generally kind and considerate person who is modestly outgoing and generally not very neurotic. But you also have images and conceptions of yourself in particular situations that do not fit that general trait portrait. When you are with a younger sister, for example, you may not be able to help but be obnoxious and inconsiderate. When you are in the role of student, you are hard-driving and achievement-oriented, but when you are with your friends on weekends, you completely forget about your studies. It is not that you are a completely different person in each different context, but different parts or aspects of the self seem to be expressed in different situations. Capturing this complexity in selfhood, many recent theories of the self emphasize the *multiplicity* of selfhood—you are many different selves. Included in the mix may be selves you want to be but cannot be, selves you ought to be, selves you might be, selves you can be but only under certain conditions, and so on. To borrow a felicitous phrase from Daniel Hart (1988), there may exist a "confederacy of self-concepts" in a single individual. Let us briefly consider three different theoretical views of this confederacy—possible selves, self-discrepancy theory, and the role of self-with-other units in personality.

Possible Selves A significant portion of our behavior may be guided as much by who we *might* be as by who we are. A young man trains for years to be an Olympic swimmer. A struggling author labors over what she hopes will become "the great American novel." A married couple save all their extra money so that they will never sink into poverty. In each of these cases, the person strives to become something, or to avoid becoming something, that he or she is (currently) not. In these and countless other instances, people behave according to what Markus and Nurius (1986) call **possible selves.** Possible selves "represent individuals' ideas of what they might become, what they would like to become, and what they are afraid of becoming." They are "the cognitive components of hopes, fears, goals, and threats and they give the specific self-relevant form, meaning, organization, and direction to these dynamics" (Markus & Nurius, 1986, p. 954).

In the view of Markus and Nurius, the self-schema contains multiple generalizations about the current and past self as well as prominent possible selves that link the self to the future. The possible selves that we wish to become in the future might be "the successful self, the creative self, the rich self, the thin self, or the loved and admired self." On the other hand, "the dreaded possible selves could be the alone self, the depressed self, the incompetent self, alcoholic self, the unemployed self, or the bag lady self " (Markus & Nurius, 1986, p. 954).

Each possible self is a *personalized* construction that has been articulated in rich detail. Therefore, if one of my dreaded possible selves is "the unemployed self," then I am likely to have developed a painfully clear picture of what this self would be like. I might imagine myself losing confidence in my ability to support my family, having to mortgage the house, struggling to get by on food stamps, living in an overpriced and undersized apartment in a "bad section" of the city, spending long hours with nothing to do, applying for menial jobs for which I feel overqualified, being humiliated in the presence of my parents, resenting my peers who have profitable jobs, gradually sinking into despair and hopelessness. Although many people may fear unemployment, my unemployed self is personally crafted to be unique to my personality. If this is an important possible self within my general self-concept, then I am likely to go to great lengths to avoid its realization.

Markus and Nurius view possible selves as the crucial link between motivation and cognition in self-understanding. Markus and Nurius contend that people are motivated by strong internal needs, desires, and inclinations. But these motivational dynamics are not activated in personality functioning until they are transformed into self-relevant form. Therefore, my fear of being unemployed may be a personalized translation of a strong "power motive" (Chapter 8) combined with certain fears rooted in my past history. Motives, fears, desires, hopes, and dreams are given expression through possible selves. In this sense, then, possible selves function first as *incentives* for future behavior—they are selves to be approached or avoided.

A second function of possible selves is *self-evaluation*. Possible selves provide frameworks by which the person can evaluate how well or poorly his or her life is going. Possible selves are therefore powerful structures for determining the meaning of personal events. For example, a junior in college who desires to become a physician will evaluate her current standing with regard to that possible self in very negative terms should she be carrying an extremely low grade-point average. Her boyfriend, whose most cherished possible self involves his future career as a professional athlete, will feel good about his prospects after being drafted for a professional team. His equally low grade-point average has less impact on his self-evaluation in that it is not linked to a dominant possible self.

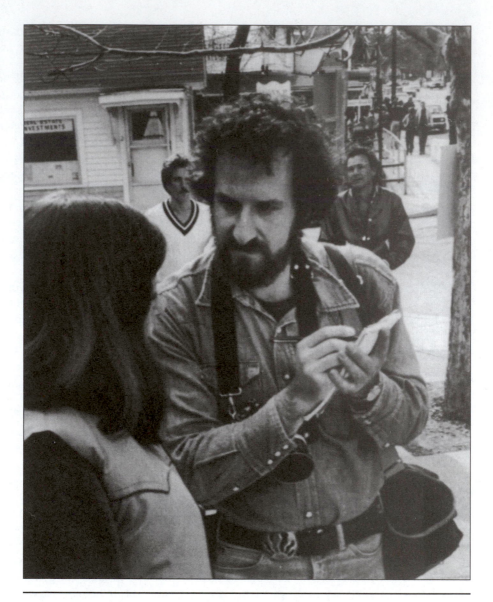

A man living out one of his "multiple selves" as a journalist . . .

In sum, the concept of possible selves leads to two interesting implications. First, the self may be viewed as a complex schema or knowledge structure within which is contained a finite number of personified characters. Each possible self personifies specific and highly personal information connected to the person's basic needs, wants, and fears. Second, an important aspect of the self is information about who the person *might be* in the future. Markus and Nurius view the self-schema as encompassing not only what "is me" now but also what "might be me" in the future, whether I like it or not.

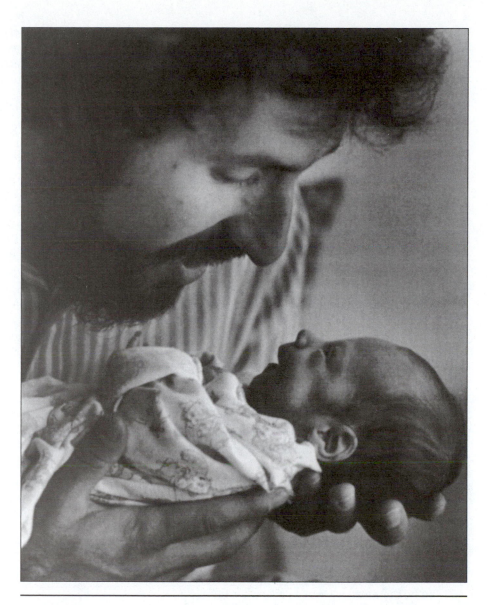

. . . as father

Discrepancies Among Selves E. Tory Higgins (1987) suggests that self-knowledge encompasses three major domains: the *actual self*, the *ideal self*, and the *ought self*. The actual self consists of your representation of the attributes that someone (yourself or another) believes you actually possess. The ideal self consists of your representation of the attributes that someone (yourself or another) would like you, ideally, to possess— that is, a representation of hopes, aspirations, or wishes. The ought self consists of your representation of the attributes that someone (yourself or another) believes you should or ought to possess—that is, a representation of duties, obligations, or responsibilities.

Each of the three domains, furthermore, may be seen from either the person's *own* standpoint or the standpoint of a significant *other* in the person's life, such as a parent, spouse, or friend. Therefore, the "actual/own self" consists of the characteristics that the person believes he or she actually possesses. The "actual/other self" consists of the characteristics that the person believes that a significant other believes he or she (the person) actually possesses. Similarly, Higgins distinguishes between "ideal/own self" and "ideal/other self" and between "ought/own self" and "ought/other self."

According to Higgins's (1987) **self-discrepancy theory,** problems occur when various selves in different domains or from different standpoints are inconsistent, or discrepant, with one another. Two kinds of discrepancies are especially salient, and each leads to a corresponding emotional reaction. Discrepancies between the *actual/own* self and *ideal* (either own or other) selves leads to the experience of *dejection-related emotions*, such as sadness, disappointment, and shame. In these cases, the person believes that he or she has been unable to attain hopes, dreams, or aspirations that either the person him- or herself or a significant other has set for him or her. When my own baseball performance failed to live up to my father's (and my own) hopes and dreams, I felt dejected and downcast. A huge discrepancy between actual and ideal was revealed. On the other hand, discrepancies between the *actual/own* self and *ought* (either own or other) self leads to the experience of *agitation-related emotions*, such as fear, anxiety, guilt. In these cases, the person believes he or she has failed to live up to standards (established by self or other) for good, dutiful, or responsible behavior. The agitated emotions stem from the experience of feeling that one is being punished (by self or other) for not doing what one ought to do.

A number of research studies support Higgins's characterization of the linkages between self-discrepancies and negative emotional experiences (Higgins, 1987). In most of these studies, college students list traits or attributes that describe the various selves that Higgins has identified. The researchers code matches and mismatches in traits across the various self domains. For instance, a person might describe his actual/own self as "ambitious," "honest," "sincere," "friendly," and "hot-tempered" and his ought/own self as "honest," "friendly," "easygoing," "forgiving," and "helpful." In this example, we can identify two clear matches—both lists contain "honest" and "friendly"—and one clear mismatch—"hot-tempered" and "easygoing" seem to be discrepant. The greater the number of mismatches, the greater the discrepancy and corresponding negative emotional reaction. The link between discrepancy and negative emotion is strongest, Higgins maintains, for self domains that the person judges to be the most relevant in his or her life.

In one study, Higgins administered these kinds of self-description measures and (1 month later) various assessments of *depression* (involving dejection-related emotions) and *anxiety* (involving agitation-related emotions) to undergraduate students. Figure 9.4 displays the results. As predicted, actual/ought discrepancies predicted anxiety (but not depression) whereas actual/ideal discrepancies predicted depression (but not anxiety). Students who felt that they were not living up to their ideal selves reported high levels of sadness and depression. Those who felt they were not living up to their ought selves reported high levels of fear and anxiety.

Ideal selves and ought selves may be called **self-guides** in that they offer standards and goals to which a person may aspire and against which a person may compare his or her current life situation. Recently, Higgins (1997) has argued that these two self-guides represent two very different motivational foci in social behavior. A *promotion* focus is associated with strong ideal self-guides, sensitivity toward positive outcomes, and approach strategies in social behavior. A *prevention* focus is associated with strong ought self-guides, a sensitivity toward negative outcomes, and avoidance strategies in social behavior. Higgins's distinction between promotion and prevention focus is highly reminiscent of the distinction between the behavioral approach system (BAS) and the behavioral inhibition system (BIS) for personality traits, as we saw in Chapter 6, and parallels distinctions between approach and avoidance goals that have been made by motivational and learning psychologists for many years (e.g., Lewin, 1935; Maslow, 1954; Miller & Dollard, 1941).

Research conducted by Daniel Ogilvie (1987) has examined a different kind of discrepancy in self-conceptions. Whereas Higgins focuses on the extent to which the actual self *differs* from other positive selves (ideal and ought), Ogilvie turns things around to discern the extent to which the actual self is *similar* to *undesired* selves. Undesired selves contain attributes that the person fears, dreads, hates, and actively seeks to exclude from experience. Ogilvie suggests that we may be in closer touch with our undesired selves

---

FIGURE 9.4   *Self-Guides and Negative Emotion*

Discrepancies between actual and ought self-guides are associated with anxiety while discrepancies between actual and ideal self-guides are associated with depression. (The numbers on the arrows are akin to correlation coefficients: the higher their values, the stronger the association. *p < .01.)

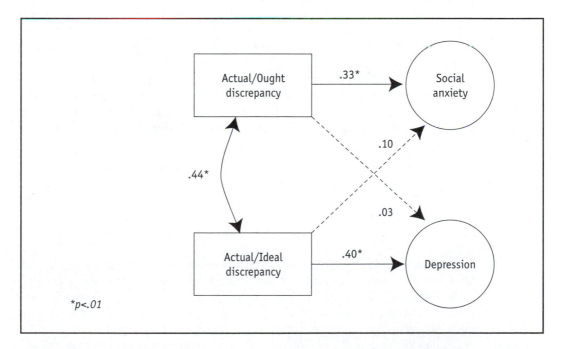

than with our ideal and ought selves. Our undesired selves are likely to be rooted in concrete past experiences in which we felt humiliation, despair, fear, anger, and so on. Our ideal and ought selves, on the other hand, are more hypothetical. They are abstractions toward which we strive but which we rarely attain.

Ogilvie (1987) obtained students' characterizations of their actual, ideal, and undesired selves and measured the "distance" between each student's selves through a complicated statistical procedure that positions selves in a hypothetical space. Questionnaire measures of life satisfaction were also obtained. The results showed that the distance between a person's ideal and actual selves was negatively associated with life satisfaction. In other words, the greater the discrepancy between ideal and actual, the lower the life satisfaction. The distance between a person's undesired and actual self was positively associated with life satisfaction. People whose actual selves were "far away from" their undesired selves were happier with their lives. Most important, however, the second result was much stronger than the first. This is to say that the distance between undesired and actual selves was a much stronger predictor of life satisfaction than was the distance between ideal and actual selves. The implication of Ogilvie's findings is straightforward and intriguing: If we want to be happy, we will do better to avoid being the way we dread being rather than striving to be the way we wish to be. Future research should examine the validity of this claim.

Self-With-Other   Ogilvie and Ashmore (1991; Ashmore & Ogilvie, 1992; Ogilvie, Fleming, & Pennell, 1998) examine the self's multiplicity from the standpoint of what they call **self-with-other** representations. Ogilvie and Ashmore give special scrutiny to the person's cognitive representations of interactions with specific people. As we interact with a particular person again and again, we begin to form an *impression of ourselves in interaction with that particular person.* For example, I may come to realize that when I am with my best friend, I feel relaxed, extraverted, and creative. By contrast, when I am with my sister, I perceive myself to be tense, domineering, serious, and responsible. Each of these two self-perceptions is a representation of self-with-other. The self is different with different people. From the perspective of Ogilvie and Ashmore, an important aspect of self-knowledge consists of the many different self-with-other units that we might identify in the most important relationships in our lives. Ogilvie and Ashmore summarize their conception of self-with-other in seven points:

1. The self-concept comprises multiple components.

2. One particularly important constituent is the social or interpersonal self.

3. A crucial, yet to date neglected, unit of analysis in investigating the social self is "self-with-other." The "self-with-other" variable is a hypothetical construct. It is provisionally defined as a mental representation that includes the set of personal qualities (traits, feelings, and the like) that an individual believes characterizes his or her self when with a particular other person.

4. Although each self-with-important-other internal representation is unique, the individual develops groupings of similar self-with-other representations. As an individual experiences self similarly in relationships with multiple specific others, a self-with-other family or constellation develops; for example, a preschool boy experiences himself as competent and comfortable with Mom, with Judy (a teenage babysitter), and with Grandpa.

5. Constellations of self-with-others are, in turn, mentally organized into an overall self-with-others structure. The exact nature of this structure is impossible to specify at this time,

and it is likely to vary considerably from person to person. At the same time, however, it is useful as a starting point to construe self-with-other groupings to be hierarchically arranged. This assumption is congruent with most current models of long-term memory and allows for the identification of self-with-others that vary in specificity versus generality.

6. Individually, and as an overall structure, the mental representations of self-with-others are assumed to serve a variety of important functions for the individual. These include (a) summarizing past experience; (b) guiding present actions, especially interpersonal behavior; and (c) interpreting own and others' (especially interaction partners') behavior.

7. Although self-with-other representations are dynamic rather than static, they are, for most adults most of the time, sufficiently stable to allow for reliable measurement. (Ogilvie & Ashmore, 1991, pp. 290–291)

Ogilvie and Ashmore have developed a sophisticated method of measuring self-with-other representations. In the first step of the method, a person is asked to list 25 important people (called "targets") in his or her life (e.g., parents, friends, children, lovers, bosses, coworkers, teachers, and so on) and to generate a lengthy set of adjectives (called "features") that describe how the person feels when he or she is with each of these various people. The researchers then reduce the lengthy list of features to a manageable set of descriptors. In a second session, the person is asked to envision a specific and representative scene in which he or she interacted with each of the 25 targets listed in the previous session. For example, if one of the targets is "my sister," I might think of a recent argument I had with my sister about her children's behavior at Christmas dinner. Then, the person rates each of the features, derived from the first session, as they apply to how he or she felt in the particular scene with the target person. In my example, therefore, I would think about how I perceived myself in the recent argument with my sister and I might rate highly the descriptors of "argumentative" and "angry," and I might rate as low the descriptors "easygoing" and "intellectual." Remember that these are ratings of me—how I perceive myself with this particular target person.

The person responds to the target/feature matrix by pushing keys on a computer. In addition, the person is asked to rate such items as "How I usually am," "Me at my best," and "Me at my worst" for each of the features. Also, targets may be split into two. For example, I might have one target that represents "my mother before she got divorced." A second target would be "my mother after she got divorced." The splitting may be necessary because I see myself as having behaved very differently with the earlier version of my mother compared to the later one. When all of the ratings have been made, a computer program generates a self-with-other portrait for that person. Each configuration is unique, reflecting the unique structure of a person's self-with-other representations. Figure 9.5 displays a self-with-other configuration for a subject named Sarah. The top half of the figure contains targets (written in capital letters). The bottom half of the figure contains features (in lowercase letters).

Notice the second row of the figure. This contains three clusters of targets: Cluster A (current boyfriend, past boyfriend, and so on), Cluster B (past boyfriend, past female high school enemy), and Cluster C (mother, me as I usually am, and so on). These three clusters are linked to corresponding feature lists (in the next row down). Cluster A targets link up with Cluster 1 features—peaceful, adventurous, courageous, and enthusiastic. This means that Sarah tends to see herself as being highly peaceful, adventurous, courageous, and enthusiastic when she is with the various people who make up

FIGURE 9.5   *Sarah's Self-With-Other Representations*

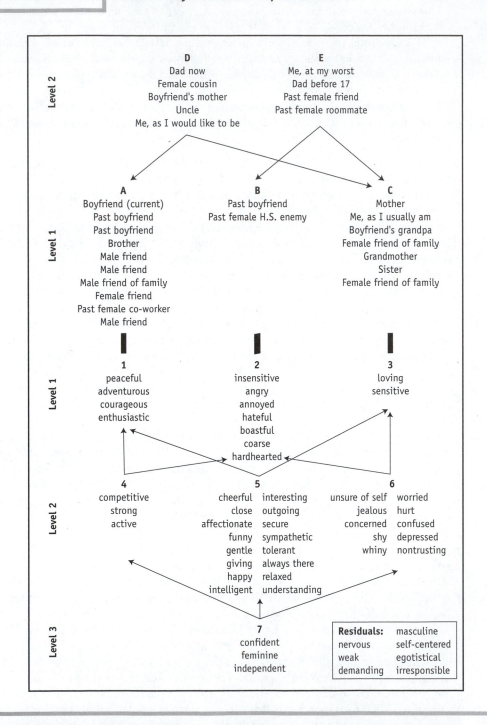

Cluster A. Almost all of the people in this cluster are in her age cohort. By contrast, she feels insensitive, angry, annoyed, and so on (Cluster 2) when she is with one particular past boyfriend and with a particular female high school enemy. She feels loving and sensitive with mother and other members of Cluster C, most of whom are considerably older than Sarah.

The complexity of Sarah's configuration becomes apparent as you move away from the middle and toward the top and the bottom of Figure 9.5. Looking at the top row ("Level 2" of Targets), you see that Cluster E (which contains me at my worst, dad before I was age 17, past female friend, and past female roommate) connects to the negative images she has in Cluster B and the mostly positive ones she has in Cluster C. The targets in Cluster E refer to people who elicit in Sarah highly contradictory or ambivalent feelings and self-perceptions. In reflecting on her relationship with her father before she was 17 years of age, she reports feeling both loving and hateful, both sensitive and insensitive. Clusters 4, 5, and 6—which make up "Level 2" of Features—group descriptors according to their relations with one another. Following the arrows, you see that "competitive" (Cluster 4) links to Clusters 1 and 2, which themselves link directly to Clusters A and B, respectively. This means that Sarah feels herself to be competitive when she is with people who are in Cluster A and Cluster B. The descriptor "competitive," therefore, distinguishes between her self-with-other representations for brother (Cluster A) and past female high school enemy (Cluster B) on the one hand and mother (Cluster C) on the other. In simple terms, Sarah feels herself to be competitive when she is with her brother and with her past enemy from high school, but *not* when she is with her mother.

Finally, the bottom row ("Level 3" of Features) of Figure 9.5 refers to characteristics of Sarah's self-with-other configuration that apply either universally or not at all. Cluster 7 is made up of the features confident, feminine, and independent. This cluster connects to all other clusters in the configuration. This means that no matter whom she is with, Sarah consistently perceives herself to be confident, feminine, and independent. You might view these as cardinal or core traits of her social self-concept. By contrast, the box called "residuals" refers to descriptors that Sarah rarely, if ever, uses to describe herself when she is with other people. Regardless of which particular other she finds herself with, Sarah tends not to perceive herself as nervous, weak, demanding, masculine, self-centered, egotistical, or irresponsible.

One appealing virtue of the self-with-other approach to research is that it provides a detailed and precise idiographic account of self-knowledge. In addition, different configurations from different persons may be compared and contrasted in terms of such dimensions as the overall complexity of the self-with-other structure, enabling researchers to launch nomothetic investigations. Recent research in this regard hints at an interesting gender difference in self-with-other structures. Ashmore and Ogilvie (1992) report a tendency for men to isolate their negative self-with-other representations, separating them neatly from their positive clusters. By contrast, women tend to produce patterns with greater connections between negative and positive self-with-other representations. In other words, men more than women may tend to cordon off the negative elements of the self to keep the negative safely distanced from the positive aspects of the self. For women, there appears to be a greater degree of fluidity in the self-with-other configuration. Negative elements may shade into positive ones. A woman may report that she feels a mixture of happiness and dread when she is with her boss or her sister. By contrast, a man may be more likely to report one or the other of these conflicting emotions, but not both for the relations with the same person. He may feel energetic with his sister, father, best friend from college, and next-door neighbor, but feel nervous with his older brother. The self-with-older-brother representation may be split off from all of the others, tucked away in a lonesome corner of the self-with-other configuration. Further research, however, is needed to determine whether this possible gender difference really exists and, if it does exist, what it might mean.

Schemata, Attributions, and Explanatory Style: The Case of Depression

Social-cognitive approaches to personality have proven especially valuable in recent years in efforts to understand the phenomenon of depression. In the past 25 years, there has been a veritable explosion of scientific research on the ways in which people who are chronically depressed process information in daily life. Scores of books and hundreds of scientific articles have addressed the topic. A number of major theories have been developed. While these theories differ from one another in important ways and while scientific research does not consistently support all of their tenets, a general theme cuts across all cognitive approaches to human depression: *Depressed people perceive, understand, and interpret their worlds and themselves in a peculiar and dysfunctional way.* Cognitive theories of depression do not deny that other noncognitive factors may be implicated in the experience of depression, especially biological factors that may predispose some people to chronic depression. But they do assert that at the center of the depressive experience are depressive cognitions—depressive thoughts, beliefs, values, attributions, schemata. Some theories suggest that these cognitions *cause* the emotional feelings of sadness and despair; others suggest that the depressive cognitions are a *result* of depression.

Psychotherapist Aaron Beck was one of the first to offer a cognitive theory of depression (Beck, 1967, 1976). Beck observed that depressed people typically hold a negative view of themselves, are pessimistic about the future, and have a tendency to interpret ongoing experience in a negative manner. These negative interpretations lead to feelings of sadness and despair. During an episode of depression, the depressed person is caught in a downward spiral, as bad thoughts lead to bad feelings, which lead to more bad thoughts and more bad feelings. Therefore, depressed people tend to see the world through **depressive schemata.** Depressive schemata *distort* reality by casting information in a negative light. For instance, depressives tend to recall more negative and unpleasant adjectives (such as *bleak, dismal, helpless*) in memory tasks than do nondepressed people (Derry & Kuiper, 1981; McDowall, 1984). They tend to have a difficult time recalling positive themes from stories (Breslow, Kocis, & Belkin, 1981). Depressives tend to recall unpleasant memories more rapidly than pleasant ones (Lloyd & Lishman, 1975). They tend to remember failures and forget successes (Johnson, Petzel, Hartney, & Morgan, 1983). In describing various positive and negative autobiographical memories, depressed college students tend to recall more *different kinds* of negative episodes from their pasts and fewer different kinds of positive episodes than do nondepressed students (McAdams, Lensky, Daple, & Allen, 1988).

Inspired by Beck's schema theory, a good deal of the cognitive research on depression has assumed that depressives *negatively distort* reality. Some studies suggest, however, that "distortion" is, in fact, more characteristic of nondepressives than

The emotional experience of depression is associated with particularly negative thought patterns, such as depressive schemata and an explanatory style that attributes negative events to internal, stable, and global causes.

depressives. Rather than assuming that depressives process information in an overly negative fashion, we may wish to consider the possibility that "normal" or nonde-pressed people process information in an overly positive manner! The staving-off of depression may be a function of seeing the world through rose-colored glasses. Like Freud's defense mechanisms (Chapter 3), these glasses distort our view but keep us happy. While the idea that distorted perceptions and judgments promote health and happiness is controversial, some evidence has been obtained to suggest that *mildly* depressed people tend to be especially accurate and nonbiased in processing various kinds of social information, while nondepressed people tend to be less accurate because of a positivistic bias (Ruehlman, West, & Pasahow, 1985). *Severely* depressed people, on the other hand, show the negativistic bias in information processing that Beck first identified.

Ingram (1984) has argued that depressed people have a difficult time summoning up positive self-schemata, even in the wake of positive events in their lives. In one laboratory experiment, depressed and nondepressed college students were provided with either positive ("success" condition) or negative ("failure" condition) feedback concerning their performance on a multiple-choice test (Ingram, Smith, & Brehm, 1983).

(The bogus feedback was not related to their actual performance on the test, though the students thought that it was at the time.) The students then listened to a prerecorded set of 48 adjectives. After each adjective was presented, the student answered either "yes" or "no" to one of four different questions about the adjective:

1. Was the adjective read by a male? (structural question)
2. Does the adjective rhyme with _____? (phonemic)
3. Does the adjective mean the same as _____? (semantic)
4. Does the word describe you? (self-referent)

According to Ingram, the four different questions call for four different levels of information processing. At the "deepest" level of processing is the self-referent question, for it asks the student to make a very personal judgment about the applicability of the adjective to his or her personality. At the most superficial levels are the structural and phonemic questions, which simply ask the student to make a judgment about the acoustical sound of the adjective as it was heard on the tape.

Following the tape and associated questions, each student was asked to recall as many of the adjectives as possible. The results are shown in Table 9.7. Nondepressed students tended to recall more positive self-references in the success condition (5.13) than in the failure condition (3.06). Depressed students, on the other hand, recalled about the same number of positive self-referents in both conditions (3.04 vs. 3.33). The authors argued that the success feedback preceding the recall task activated a positive self-schema for the nondepressed students sensitizing them to positive adjectives about themselves. Therefore, they recalled a large number of positive adjectives about themselves in the success condition. By contrast, the success feedback was *not* effective in activating a positive self-schema in the minds of the depressed students, who remembered about the same low number of positive self-referent adjectives in both conditions.

Another influential cognitive approach to depression is Seligman and Abramson's **reformulated learned-helplessness theory.** In his early research with animals, Martin Seligman (1975; Seligman & Maier, 1967) discovered that dogs subjected to uncontrollable aversive stimulation, like random electric shocks, eventually become helpless and do not act to avoid the shocks even when they have a clear opportunity to do so. Analogously, Seligman reasoned, human beings subjected to uncontrollable negative events in life will eventually learn to be helpless and will become chronically depressed. In their reformulated interpretation of learned helplessness, Seligman and Abramson (Abramson, Seligman, & Teasdale, 1978; Peterson & Seligman, 1984) link

TABLE 9.7	*Self-Reference Scores for Recalled Words*	
	SUCCESS	**FAILURE**
Depressed	3.04	3.33
Nondepressed	5.13	3.06

Source: Ingram, Smith, & Brehm (1983), p. 417.

helplessness and depression to cognitive attributions, or what they have most recently called an **explanatory style.** They argue that depressed people experience the world in a helpless fashion by virtue of their characteristic patterns of assigning causality and explaining events.

According to the reformulated learned-helplessness model, depressives tend to explain *negative* events in their lives as stemming from *internal, global,* and *stable* causes. For example, they may attribute their low grade on an examination to their own general "stupidity"—"I am generally stupid" (stupidity is *internal* to the person, rather than a feature of the external situation); "I am stupid in many things" *(global);* and "I will always be stupid" *(stable).* On the other hand, depressives tend to explain *positive* events in their lives as stemming from *external, specific,* and *unstable* causes. Therefore, they may view a high grade on an examination as a lucky break. The high grade might be due to an easy test *(external)* in a particular area *(specific)* that is not likely to occur again in the future *(unstable).* In essence, the depressive person's explanatory style accentuates the importance of negative events by suggesting that they are due to broad and uncontrollable forces. At the same time, it minimizes the importance of positive events by suggesting that they are specific flukes that are not likely to recur.

Seligman's attributional approach to learned helplessness has stimulated much empirical research. Overall, the findings provide modest but inconsistent support for the model (Coyne & Gotlib, 1983; Peterson & Seligman, 1984; Peterson, Villanova, & Raps, 1985; Robins, 1988). A number of studies have shown that depressed people tend to attribute failures to internal, global, and stable factors, though the obtained relationships between these attributional patterns and depression are sometimes weak (Robins, 1988). Further, other sorts of nonattributional dimensions of information processing, such as the person's expectations about the extent to which particular negative events are "intended" or "likely to happen again," appear to be associated with depression, too (Gong-Guy & Hammen, 1980; Hammen & Cochran, 1981). In addition, many researchers appear to be skeptical about Seligman's claim that attributional patterns precede or cause depression. Teasing out such a causal relation requires a longitudinal study in which cognitions and depressive symptomology are monitored over time. Data from an intensive longitudinal case study collected by Peterson, Luborsky, and Seligman (1983) offer interesting support for the causal role of attributions. Other studies, however, are less supportive. For instance, Cochran and Hammen (1995) undertook a 2-month longitudinal study of college students and depressed outpatients and concluded that "in terms of the direction of causality, the data were more consistent in indicating that depression causes cognitions than in indicating the reverse" (p. 1562).

A person's characteristic explanatory style is a very important feature of the procedural knowledge that composes an individual's social intelligence. It should not be surprising, therefore, to learn that explanatory style is associated with a range of behavioral outcomes that go well beyond the phenomenon of depression. Researchers have examined the role of explanatory style in school achievement, job performance, success in sports, physical health, and longevity.

Nolen-Hoeksema, Girgus, and Seligman (1986) assessed explanatory style among school children. The children showed wide variation in characteristic styles, with some children exhibiting the kind of pessimistic style characteristic of depression. The children showing a pessimistic explanatory style (internal, stable, and global explanations for bad outcomes) were rated by teachers as showing more helpless behaviors and

---

FEATURE 9.B

What or Who Controls My Behavior? Research on Locus of Control

Among the intellectual forerunners to social-cognitive approaches in personality psychology are George Kelly's personal construct theory and the social learning theories developed by Rotter and Bandura in the 1950s and 1960s. A key concept in Rotter's theory (Chapter 4) is *expectancy*, which he defined as the subjectively held probability that a particular reinforcement will occur as the outcome of specific behavior. **Locus of control** refers to individual differences in expectancy. People with an *internal* locus of control expect reinforcements (rewards) to follow their own actions. In other words, they believe that their own behavior controls the consequences that subsequently follow—subsequent reinforcing events are contingent on the person's behavior. The person with an *external* locus of control expects that his or her behavior will not lead to predictable reinforcement. Rather, reinforcements are dispensed by external sources of control, such as powerful others, chance, luck, and so forth. Reinforcing events do not appear to be contingent on his or her behavior.

You may notice that locus of control bears some resemblance to explanatory style. For both concepts, the focus is on what a person believes to be the ultimate cause of social behavior. But locus of control is a more general concept than explanatory style and it is more oriented toward the reinforcing consequences that may follow a person's behavior. In research on explanatory style, people are asked to attribute cause in specific social scenarios. For example, I may be confronted with a particular bad event in my life and asked what the causes were of that event. For locus of control, by contrast, people are asked more general questions about their overall beliefs concerning personal agency and the power of the external environment. For example, I might be asked which of the following two statements I most agree with: "What happens to me is my own doing" or "Sometimes I feel that I don't have enough control over the direction my life is taking" (Rotter, 1966). The first option suggests an internal locus of control whereas the second suggests an external locus of control.

---

fewer mastery behaviors in school. They also scored lower in standardized achievement tests and, as has been shown with adults, and scored higher on measures of depressive symptoms.

Seligman and Schulman (1986) studied life insurance sales agents over the course of one year. At the beginning of the year, the researchers measured the agents' explanatory style. Agents showing the pessimistic explanatory style at the beginning of the year sold less insurance during the year than did the agents with an optimistic style. The agents with the pessimistic style were also more likely to quit the company. Seligman, Nolen-Hoeksema, Thornton, and Thornton (1990) used a similar methodology to study women's and men's college swimming teams. They found that pessimistic explanatory style measured at the beginning of the season predicted relatively poor swimming performance during the season.

Many self-report scales have been developed to measure locus of control (Phares, 1978). The most well-known measure is the **I-E Scale** (Rotter, 1966), which contains 29 forced-choice items like the example I have given above. Rotter's scale assumes that locus of control is a broad, generalized factor that cuts across many different domains in which expectancies might reveal themselves. In the past 20 years, however, psychologists have developed a number of specialized scales designed to assess beliefs about control in specific domains. These include scales to assess locus of control as it pertains to one's understanding of marriage (Miller, Lefcourt, Holmes, Ware, & Saleh, 1986), affiliation situations (Lefcourt, Martin, Fick, & Saleh, 1985), intellectual functioning (Lachman, 1986), and health (Wallston & Wallston, 1981).

The I-E Scale has been used in literally thousands of research studies, and the massive literature suggests that locus of control is an extremely important social-cognitive variable in personality. The research suggests that, in general, *internal* locus of control is associated with many positive outcomes in life, from better academic achievement to better interpersonal relationships. For example, people with an internal locus of control tend to show less compliance and conformity, greater perceived competence and independence, greater efforts to acquire information from the environment, greater knowledge about their own health and sicknesses, more positive attitudes about physical exercise, lower levels of cigarette smoking, lessened susceptibility to hypertension and heart attack, and greater levels of overall psychological adjustment, compared with people who have an external locus of control (Lachman, 1986; Phares, 1978, 1988). People with an internal locus of control tend to be healthy and independent information seekers who adapt well to many of life's challenges. However, internal locus of control is not always an asset. In *nonresponsive* environments, wherein efforts to exert personal control are repeatedly thwarted, the person with an internal locus of control may encounter many difficulties and report lower levels of satisfaction, compared with people who have an external locus of control (Janoff-Bulman & Brickman, 1980; Rotter, 1975). Believing that reinforcements will come from your own efforts can work against you when you find yourself in an environment that does not value personal agency and individual effort.

Peterson, Seligman, and Vaillant (1988) reported results from a 50-year longitudinal study of men who graduated from Harvard College in 1938 and 1940. In 1946, when they were in their late 20s, 99 of the men who had served in World War II responded to open-ended questions about their difficult war experiences. The researchers scored these narrative accounts for explanatory style and then related the scores to the men's subsequent physical health as assessed in periodic medical checkups. Explanatory style was a significant predictor of health over a 40-year span. Those men whose essays (written in their late 20s) showed an optimistic explanatory style exhibited significantly better health in their medical checkups in their 40s, 50s, and 60s, compared with the men whose essays showed a pessimistic explanatory style.

Another longitudinal investigation suggests that explanatory style may even predict how long people live! Peterson, Seligman, Yurko, Martin, and Friedman (1998) coded open-ended questionnaires written in 1936 and 1940 by participants in the Terman longitudinal study of the intellectually gifted (Chapter 6) for explanatory style. The open-ended questions asked the participants to account for disappointments, failures, and negative relationships they had experienced in their lives and to describe their most serious personal flaws. The globality aspect of explanatory style—attributing negative events to global causes—predicted mortality as of 1991. In other words, those individuals who tended to explain negative events in terms of global causes in their early to middle adult years tended to die earlier than individuals who used a more optimistic explanatory style. Explanatory style was especially predictive of untimely death among men, and it predicted especially well accidental and violent deaths. According to the authors of the study, attributing global causes to negative events is a form of cognitive *catastrophizing*. Globality taps a pervasive style of catastrophizing about bad events, expecting them to occur across diverse situations and thereby magnifying even small misfortunes into potential catastrophes. This kind of explanatory style is hazardous, they maintain, because it tends to be associated with poor problem solving, social estrangement, and risky decision making. If you believe that every bad event is indicative of a potential catastrophe, you may come to see the world as a frighteningly untrustworthy place—a place wherein it does not pay to be prudent and rational because all your good efforts may be swept away in a moment by large and uncontrollable forces. If you hold the belief that catastrophes will inevitably occur, you may even adopt a "who cares" or "what the hell" attitude about life. "It doesn't matter what I do."

The Regulation of Social Behavior

The ultimate purpose of social intelligence is to guide social behavior. The concepts, episodes, and rules that people draw on to process information about the self and social life prove their worth in the crucible of everyday interpersonal action. Social-cognitive perspectives in personality psychology portray people as planful and more-or-less effective actors who move across a wide range of demanding social situations virtually every day. Therefore, the social-cognitive adaptations we have sampled in this chapter—personal constructs, cognitive styles, self-schemata, possible selves, explanatory styles, and the like—all contribute to the implementation of intelligent social behavior—that is, behavior aimed at solving the many problems in social living that individuals face.

As we saw in Chapter 8, such behavior is typically goal directed in some manner, motivated by the anticipation of accomplishing particular goals or ends in social life. Social-cognitive theories of personality view human beings as purposive social actors, processing social information in ways that promote the accomplishment of personal goals, strivings, projects, tasks, and the like (Bandura, 1999; Cantor & Kihlstrom, 1989; Dweck, 1996; Cervone & Shoda, 1999b; Markus & Nurius, 1986). Social-cognitive adaptations *regulate* social behavior in the service of personal goals. These goals may be nested in a *hierarchy* such that concrete and simple goals are contained within more abstract and complex goals (Carver & Scheier, 1988; Hyland, 1988; Vallacher & Wegner, 1987). According to some social-cognitive perspectives, there exists for every person a hierarchy of levels of behavioral control, with various levels of standards or goals arranged from the most concrete and narrow to the most abstract and broad organizing principles. The lower levels indicate how the action is to be carried out, whereas the higher levels provide information on the purposes or implications of the action. Goals or standards can be characterized at different levels within this hierarchy, and people may be said to differ as to the level at which they characterize their goals within the hierarchy.

Charles Carver and Michael Scheier have developed a representative hierarchical model of how cognition regulates purposive behavior (Carver & Scheier, 1981, 1988, 1992; Scheier & Carver, 1981). The model draws heavily on the concept of **feedback.** In a feedback loop, a system regulates itself around a set point, as in a thermostat. Deviations from the set point stimulate adjustment activities, which are terminated when the set point is once again achieved. In the case of a thermostat, the set point might be 65° Fahrenheit. When the temperature in the room dips below 65°, the thermostat turns on the furnace, which will shut off when the air temperature reaches or exceeds the set point. In the case of human behavior, the set point might be any goal, standard, or reference value against which behavior is compared. These comparison points for behavior, however, come in almost an infinitude of forms, and include such things as values, self-schemata, situational expectancies, and conscious intentions.

Figure 9.6 illustrates the feedback relation between comparison points and behavior. According to the model, a person is constantly monitoring his or her own behavior and

FIGURE 9.6   *A Simple Self-Regulation System*

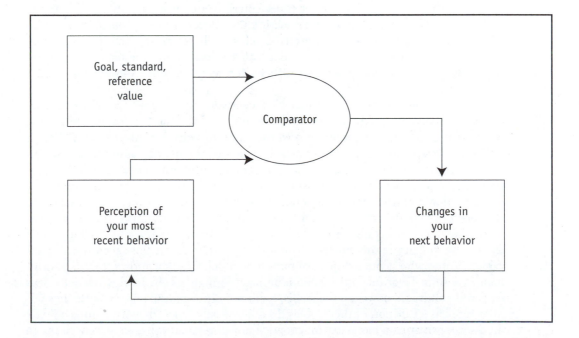

Source: Carver & Scheier (1988), p. 476.

the behavior of others. Sometimes people literally watch what they are doing (as in weight-lifting rooms with mirrored walls), but, more often, "monitoring your behavior is a matter of sensing in a vague, general way the qualities you've been displaying in your actions" (Carver & Scheier, 1988, p. 476). When the perception of your behavior matches well the goal or standard to which you are comparing the perception, then you do not alter your behavior. This is analogous to the thermostat's sensing that the air temperature is still above 65°—the furnace is not switched on. However, when the person perceives a *discrepancy* between the current behavior and some goal, standard, or value to which the behavior is compared, he or she changes behaviors in order to move closer to the comparison point. Therefore, if in the middle of a conversation in which you desire to be friendly, you feel that you are beginning to offend the person to whom you are speaking, you will probably change your behavior in some way. You may begin to compliment the person, or you may change the topic to something lighter and friendlier in order to move the interaction toward the goal. Once the goal is achieved, you may change goals and alter your behavior accordingly. According to Carver and Scheier (1988), "behavior is inherently purposive (even if the purposes underlying some acts are pretty trivial)." As they put it, "human life is viewed as a continual process of establishing goals and intentions, and adjusting current patterns of behavior so as to match them more closely, using informational feedback as a guide to progress" (Carver & Scheier, 1988, p. 476).

The goals and intentions that regulate human behavior are dynamic; they shift from one situation to the next and over time. Thus, the process of self-regulation is continuous and neverending. Every change in output (behavior) creates a change in the perceived present condition. This new input, then, must be checked against the reference value, which itself will change over time. There is a continuous interplay between making adjustments to action and evaluating the effects of those adjustments. Better regulation, furthermore, is accomplished by closer self-scrutiny. Therefore, any environmental condition that promotes a person's self-examination is likely to promote the smooth and effective regulation of behavior, as numerous experimental studies have shown.

In these studies, a person's self-focus is accentuated in some way, as when the person must observe his or her own behavior in a mirror (Wicklund & Duvall, 1971). The result of the self-focus is increased goal matching in behavior. In one study, Carver (1975) chose students who either opposed or favored the use of punishment in teaching. Several weeks after the students' attitudes on punishment were assessed, they participated in a laboratory task in which they administered punishments for errors committed by a person they thought (erroneously) was another subject in the study. In the self-focus condition, the students observed their own administration of punishments in a mirror. In the control condition, no mirror was present. As Figure 9.7 shows, the students in the self-focus condition tended to act in close accord with their values. Those who said they opposed punishment delivered only low levels of punishment; those in favor of punishment administered high levels. In the low self-focus (control) condition, however, the students did not differ on the punishments they administered as a function of their values. In other words, when they were not explicitly monitoring their own behavior, they tended not to regulate what they were doing in accord with their stated beliefs about punishment.

| FIGURE 9.7 | *Self-Focus and the Link Between Behavior and Values* |

Individuals who are in a self-focus condition tend to deliver punishments that are in accord with their personal views on punishment whereas individuals not focused on the self show behavior less clearly connected to their values.

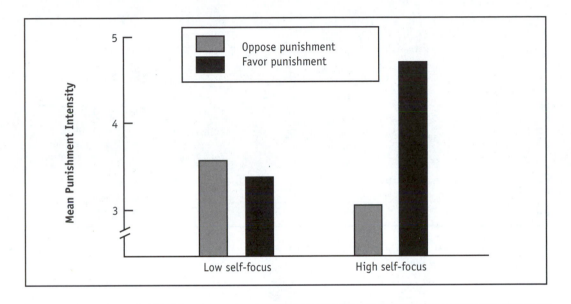

Source: Carver & Scheier (1988), p. 480.

The feedback loops that regulate human behavior are much more complex than the simple illustration portrayed in Figure 9.6. To deal with this complexity, Carver and Scheier propose a **feedback hierarchy** made up of subordinate and superordinate goals. According to this view, illustrated in Figure 9.8, the output of one feedback loop becomes the reference value for the feedback loop subordinate to it (Powers, 1973). Higher-order or superordinate levels in the hierarchy provide reference values for lower levels. There are many possible levels, but the three highest ones in the hierarchy are *program, principles,* and *system concept.*

At the program level, behavior is guided by scripts (Abelson, 1981) and other general guidelines for courses of action. Many of our daily intentions operate at the program level, from taking out the garbage to preparing for an examination. At the principles level, behavior is regulated by overriding qualities that might be realized through various scripts or programs. For example, a woman may see herself as a generally "friendly" person. This self-ascription serves as a principle for behavior, providing the reference value of "being as friendly as I can be" for various scripts or programs she may enact. Finally, her principle of friendliness may itself be regulated and organized

FIGURE 9.8   *A Three-Tiered Hierarchy of Feedback Systems*

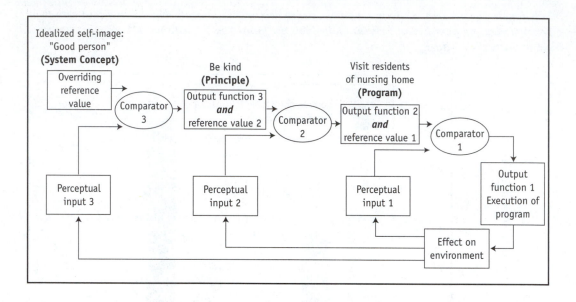

Source: Carver & Scheier (1988), p. 482.

by the highest level in the hierarchy, the level of system concept. Here reside the highest abstractions for behavioral analysis, such as the "generalized sense of self that people try to maintain over time and place" (Carver & Scheier, 1988, p. 483). One's general sense of self, sometimes called *identity*, is an overarching regulator for behavior. It provides reference values for the principles level in the hierarchy, which in turn provides reference values for the program level, and so on.

A similar point of view is expressed in Vallacher and Wegner's (1987) *action identification theory*. According to Vallacher and Wegner, an action can be identified in a wide variety of ways, ranging from the most concrete to the most abstract. For example, the same behavior can be identified as "moving wooden pieces on a board," "playing a game of chess," or "improving my mind through intellectual stimulation." Lower-order identifications frame action in simple behavioral terms: Writing a term paper is reduced to "making marks on a sheet of paper." Higher-order identifications frame action in broad conceptual terms: Writing a term paper may be elevated to "striving for excellence in academics." Research on action identifications suggests that when both a low-level and high-level identification are available, people tend to adopt the higher one, as long as they can do so comfortably. In other words, people tend to view (and regulate) their activities *in as abstract a way as they can without difficulty.* When faced with difficulty, however, they will retreat from higher-order to lower-order identifications. Such a move may make it easier to master the challenges of a given act. Once the problem is resolved, movement toward a higher-level identification may ensue.

A fascinating application of this point of view may be found in Roy Baumeister's (1990) theory of suicide as an "escape from self." Baumeister suggests that suicide may result from a relentless cognitive movement from higher-order to lower-order identifications in response to tremendous pain and suffering. According to this view, a person first experiences a series of painful setbacks in a number of different life domains, such as romantic involvements and work life. These failures are attributed to the self. The person may come to believe that he is at fault for the bad things that have happened, or he may believe that he is a helpless victim of forces he cannot control. In either case, what results is a painful state of self-awareness.

To escape this excruciating self-awareness, the person launches into a process that Baumeister calls *cognitive deconstruction*. Cognitive deconstruction involves a dramatic slide from relatively adaptive, higher-order thinking into a narrowly focused and concrete frame of mind that blocks out emotion and erases concerns for meaning. The person comes to adopt a narrower and narrower time perspective, as concerns for the future give way to an obsessive focus on the here-and-now. The person comes to focus on progressively more concrete events, as well. For example, eating a meal may be cognitively reduced to moving the food from plate to mouth. The person obsessively focuses on the molecular action of moving the knife and fork in order to blot out any awareness of the larger contexts for action, for those larger contexts are painful. To think of the act as "eating" might lead to thoughts about "having meals," which might remind the person of the people with whom he has shared meals in the past, who indeed may be the sources of his current pain. Better, then, to focus consciousness on the fork.

As life becomes reduced in time and space, the person abandons higher-level meanings (as in "What is my life about?") for the relatively meaningless minutiae of simple acts (as in "Will I move the food to my mouth again?"). This intense focus on only the most immediate, concrete, and meaningless things works to divest life of its characteristic emotional tone. Operating at the lowest possible level of action identification, the person has retreated from time, thought, feeling, and significance. The retreat has not enabled him, however, to master the challenges of a simpler order of life. There is still too much pain and suffering awaiting him, should he seek to reverse the tide of deconstruction. Thus, the suicide act may follow as a final retreat from the complexity of life to the simplicity of death, a tragic result of a progressively more nihilistic narrowing of one's cognitive focus, the ultimate escape from self.

In conclusion, Baumeister's conception illustrates that even a human action as portentous as suicide can be understood in terms of social-cognitive processes—the mental representations that a person forms to construe the self and social behavior. Social-cognitive processes are involved in virtually every behavior we exhibit in daily life. In that persons differ from one another with respect to their characteristic personal constructs, self-schemata, explanatory styles, and other social-cognitive adaptations, social-cognitive processes constitute an essential aspect of human individuality. Like motives and goals (Chapter 8), social-cognitive adaptations specify many of the particulars of human personality. More contextualized and contingent than the dispositional traits we examined in Chapters 5–7, social-cognitive adaptations provide us with details concerning how the person construes the self, other people, and social behavior. Social-cognitive adaptations tell us how people understand and interpret the social world. It is indeed impossible to understand people if we do not have some sense of how they understand who they are and what constitutes the world in which they live.

SUMMARY

1. Social-cognitive approaches to personality psychology focus on the mental representations that people form to process information about the self and social behavior. Social-cognitive adaptations are the characteristic personal constructs, cognitive styles, beliefs, expectancies, scripts, attributions, self-conceptions, and the like that people draw upon in their efforts to meet the many demands of social life. Along with personal goals, social-cognitive adaptations help to regulate social behavior. Like motives and goals, furthermore, social-cognitive adaptations go beyond general personality traits to specify some of the contingent and contextualized details of human individuality.

2. Developed in the 1950s, George Kelly's theory of personal constructs foreshadowed many of the central themes of contemporary social-cognitive theory. Kelly viewed the person as akin to a scientist, seeking to categorize and make sense of his or her environment in order to predict and control it. According to Kelly, people develop personal constructs based on their perceptions of social events, and these constructs help to guide subsequent social behavior. A personal construct is a characteristic way of construing how some things are alike and some things are different from one another. Constructs differ from one another in terms of such dimensions as permeability and range of convenience. People differ from one another with respect to the content and organization of their construct systems.

3. Cognitive styles refer to individual differences in people's characteristic and typically preferred modes of processing information. One of the most well-researched cognitive styles is field independence–dependence. Highly field-independent people process perceptual information in an especially analytical and differentiated style, whereas highly field-dependent people process perceptual information in a more global and contextual style. Individual differences in field independence–dependence have been linked to a wide range of cognitive, social, and behavioral outcomes.

4. A second well-researched cognitive style is integrative complexity. Whereas field independence–dependence concerns differences in perception of stimuli, integrative complexity refers to styles of reasoning. Integratively complex individuals reason about issues in a highly differentiated manner, construing many distinctions and nuances and taking into consideration multiple points of view. By contrast, integratively less complex or simple individuals see fewer distinctions and nuances and tend to rely instead on a handful of broad principles or categories. Integrative complexity appears to wax and wane as a function of age and situations. Nonetheless, individual differences in overall integrative complexity can be assessed. People high in integrative complexity tend to make more well-informed and well-balanced evaluations of complex issues, are more open-minded and tolerant, and show considerable cognitive self-direction, but they also may sometimes encounter more difficulty in making clear-cut decisions based on moral principles, compared with individuals low in integrative complexity.

5. Social-cognitive perspectives on personality view the person as a planful and more-or-less effective agent in the social world who is able to respond in flexible ways to a wide range of social situations. The person's social effectiveness is largely determined by what Cantor and Kihlstrom call social intelligence. Social intelligence consists of the characteristic concepts, episodes, and rules that a person draws on to solve social problems in everyday life. Concepts constitute declarative-semantic knowledge, and they include conceptions of self, conceptions of others (as in relational schemata), and social scripts. Scripts provide the behavioral outlines of stereotypical event sequences often encountered in the social world. Episodes constitute declarative-episodic knowledge, which may be broken down into autobiographical memory and person memory. Rules constitute procedural knowledge, and they include such things as attributions and heuristics.

6. Perhaps the most salient components of declarative-semantic social knowledge are self-schemata, or knowledge structures about the self. Each person builds up conceptions of the self—self-schemata—that structure the processing of self-relevant information and guide behavior. People process information that is relevant to their self-schemata in highly efficient ways. Contemporary social-cognitive views tend to emphasize the multiplicity of self-schemata. People may have many different images of themselves, including possible selves. Possible selves represent an individual's ideas of what he or she might become or what he or she fears becoming. Possible selves are cognitive vehicles for carrying a person's most important motives, desires, hopes, dreams, and fears.

7. Self-knowledge can be further broken down into actual, ideal, and ought selves. Ideal selves incorporate attributes that a person strongly desires to possess whereas ought selves contain attributes that a person believes he or she should possess. Ideal selves connect to a promotion focus in life, sensitivity toward positive outcomes, and approach strategies in social interaction. Ought selves connect to a prevention focus, sensitivity toward negative outcomes, and avoidance strategies in social behavior. People often experience discrepancies between different selves. Large discrepancies between actual and ideal selves have been associated with depression whereas large discrepancies between a person's actual and ought selves have been linked to anxiety.

8. The multiplicity of self-knowledge is further evident in self-with-other representations.

A self-with-other representation refers to how a person views him- or herself when interacting with a particular other person. People differ from one another with respect to the content of their self-with-other representations and the overall organization and complexity of their self-with-other representational system.

9. Social-cognitive theories have proven especially useful in understanding depression. While some approaches have focused on depressive schemata, others have examined the attributional or explanatory style that depressed people employ to make sense of good and bad events in life. Research suggests that depression is associated with a pessimistic explanatory style, through which people attribute the causes of negative events to internal, stable, and global factors. This style of explaining negative social events may lead to self-blame and feelings of hopelessness and helplessness. Pessimistic explanatory styles are also associated with poor school performance, poor work performance, poor performance in athletics, poor health, and even untimely death.

10. The ultimate purpose of social intelligence is to guide social behavior. Social-cognitive adaptations such as personal constructs, cognitive styles, self-schemata, possible selves, and explanatory styles help to regulate social behavior in the service of personal goals. Self-regulatory goals and standards may be nested in a hierarchy from simple and concrete action goals to more complex and abstract organizing principles. Intelligent social behavior, therefore, may be regulated by informational feedback systems, organized hierarchically, whereby such things as personal constructs and self-schemata serve as reference points against which current behavior is compared. Deviations from the reference point stimulate change in behavior, as the system seeks to accomplish social goals that are consistent with a person's mental representations of the self and the social world.

10

Developmental Adaptations: Erikson and Loevinger

Martin Luther was a Catholic monk in his early 20s when he suddenly fell raving to the ground one day and began roaring like a bull. According to three of Luther's contemporaries who witnessed the event, young Martin began screaming like one possessed by a demon after reading a passage in the New Testament about Christ's cure of a man who could not speak (Mark 9:17–27). In the midst of his fit, Martin was heard to exclaim *"Ich bin nit! Ich bin nit!"* ("I am not! I am not!"). Occurring during a period of profound religious doubt in Luther's life, his exclamation was a desperate cry of negation: "I am *not* this; I am *nothing*; I do *not* know who I am!"

Luther's emotional outburst took place some time around the year 1507 in the monastery choir, located in the German town of Erfurt. In psychological terms, the basic problem in young Luther's life at this time was that of *ego identity* (Erikson, 1958, 1959; McAdams, 1985b). In essence, young Luther was unable to formulate a coherent and convincing answer to the two fundamental questions of identity: "Who am I?" and "How do I fit into the adult world?" However, Luther soon made substantial headway in resolving his identity problem. By 1512, he had worked out an ideological solution. By 1517, he was translating the solution into radical public action. And by 1522, he had achieved the status of a religious and political celebrity destined to become one of the most influential men in the history of Western civilization. How did Luther do this? And what does his struggle tell us about personality today?

MARTIN LUTHER'S IDENTITY CRISIS

Martin Luther (1483–1546) is credited with starting the massive religious and cultural movement termed the Protestant Reformation, through which many Europeans severed their ties with the Roman Catholic Church and ultimately formed the various Protestant denominations of Christianity, such as the Lutherans, Methodists, Presbyterians, and Baptists. He is also credited with bringing the sacred writings of Christianity to the common people by providing the first authoritative translation of the Bible into German. He was a voluminous writer and a great preacher, and he wrote some of the most inspiring hymns in the Christian musical tradition. Outside the immediate domain of the church, Luther has been viewed as a monumental *political* figure in German history—one of the fathers of German nationalism and a hero for some revolutionaries. Of course, all of this would have been impossible to predict that day in the choir when young Martin fell raving to the ground. In 1507, Martin Luther was living out a rather conventional life story of the "good monk"—devoted to the Catholic Church and properly respectful of the authority of the Roman pope. The story changed radically, however, as Luther came to fashion a new kind of identity that provided his life with a sense of purpose.

One of the most provocative applications of personality theory to the life course of a single adult is Erik Erikson's (1959) psychobiographical analysis of Luther's identity formation, entitled *Young Man Luther*. Erikson begins his analysis with the "fit in the choir." In this critical life event, Luther expresses the utter terror and confusion of a young man who has come to deny the very assumptions upon which he has built his own sense of who he is and how he fits into the adult world. The fit in the choir symbolizes the low point of Luther's identity struggle—the point in his own life where he felt cut off from all that had previously provided his life with meaning. In Luther's biography, this incident is sandwiched between two other key events.

The first event took place in the summer of 1505. At this point, Luther was following the career path sketched out for him by his father, a middle-class copper miner and early capitalist named Hans Luder. Hans wanted his son to be a lawyer. Entering the University of Erfurt in 1501, Martin appeared destined to fulfill his father's mandate. On one fateful summer evening, however, Martin was returning to the university by foot in a fierce thunderstorm when a bolt of lightning struck the ground near him, hurling him to the earth and sending him into what some biographers have claimed was a convulsion. Before he knew what was happening, the 18-year-old Martin screamed out, "Help me St. Anne . . . I want to be a monk!" On his safe return to Erfurt, he entered the monastery, telling his friends and eventually his father that his experience in the thunderstorm affirmed a commitment to the Catholic church.

This would-be-lawyer-turned-monk was no ordinary religious novice. He prayed more than the other monks. He tortured his body and his mind by denying himself even the simplest earthly comforts and ruminating obsessively, day and night, over the meaning of the tiniest nuances of scripture. Erikson suggests that Martin's initial love affair with the Catholic church and with the idea of being the most devout monk the church had ever seen was too intense, too passionate, and it provided a thin disguise for a deeper doubt and ambivalence:

> It makes psychiatric sense that under such conditions a young man with Martin's smoldering problems, but also with an honest desire to avoid rebellion against an environment which took care of so many of his needs, would subdue his rebellious nature by gradually developing compulsive-obsessive states characterized by high ambivalence. His self-doubt thus would take the form of intensified self-observation in exaggerated obedience to the demands of the order; his doubt of authority would take the form of an intellectualized scrutiny of the authoritative books. This activity would, for a while longer, keep the devil in his place. (Erikson, 1958, p. 137)

But who was the Devil? And where was his "place"? As 21st-century readers, it is difficult for most of us, regardless of our religious persuasion, to understand how literal a force Luther believed the Devil to be in his life. In the monastery at Erfurt, Luther struggled daily with the Devil, seeing him, fleeing him, fighting him, debating him, hating him, fearing him as a real person with superhuman power. Though many people of Luther's day believed, like Luther, that the Devil could be seen and tangibly experienced in daily life as if he were a flesh-and-blood person, few were as completely obsessed with the Devil's doings as was the troubled monk. In Luther's words, the Devil was "the old evil foe." In every human's raging war with the Devil, faith in God served as "the mighty fortress" and "sword and shield victorious." The battle cry was set to music in Luther's most famous hymn:

A mighty fortress is our God,

A sword and shield victorious;

He breaks the cruel oppressor's rod

And wins salvation glorious.

The old satanic foe

Has sworn to work us woe!

With craft and dreadful might

He arms himself to fight.

On earth he has no equal.

More significant from a psychological standpoint, however, was Luther's *projection* of the Devil onto others. Throughout his life, Luther cast his enemies in the guise of the Devil, responding to them in the same way he daily responded to the old evil foe. The best example is the Catholic pope (and the church establishment he represented) who became for Luther and his life story the prototype of the Devil incarnate.

The seeds of Luther's discontent with the pope and the church were sown in the Erfurt monastery as he witnessed the enactment of corrupt church policies. Chief among these was the practice of selling "indulgences," through which a Christian could pay money to the church to purchase salvation for his or her dead relatives. The selling of indulgences was to become a rallying point for the entire Protestant Reformation as it came to represent both corruption in the church and the Catholic view of salvation as a commodity to be bought and sold.

By the time of his fit in the choir, then, Luther was renouncing his old identity as an obedient monk, identifying the Roman church as the enemy rather than the savior, and groping furiously for an alternative image of self with which to build a new identity. According to Luther's own account, his spiritual questioning and reformulation culminated in 1512 in a revelation of truth that took place, believe it or not, when visiting the monks' toilet in the Wittenberg tower. There, Luther was struck with a new insight into the meaning of the last sentence of Romans 1:17: "The just shall live by faith."

In the tower, Luther envisioned a new image of God more directly accessible to the common person than the distant God of the Catholic orthodoxy. According to Luther's radically new reading of this old passage, salvation was to be achieved by faith, not through good works or the sale of indulgences. God was not to be viewed as a distant force who waits for the day of judgment to decide if each man's and woman's earthly deeds merit entrance into the kingdom of heaven. Rather, men and women encounter God in the here and now—personally, rather than through the institutions of the church—through God's son Jesus; men and women need only accept Jesus—have faith that Jesus is the son of God—in order to be redeemed.

The course Luther's life followed after the revelation in the tower of Wittenberg is summarized in Table 10.1. These public events and developments marked the rise of Luther as a religious leader in Europe and the spread of his influence in the Protestant Reformation. Over the course of his adult years, Luther continued to "work on" his identity. He continued to change and develop with respect to his understanding of who he was and how he fit into the world. But many of the key incidents that spoke to his identity concerns occurred in his late adolescent and early adult years. It is during this critical period in the human lifespan, Erikson argued, that many of us *first* confront the problem of identity. By contrast, children in grade school are not generally worried about who they are and how they fit into the adult world. And people in their 60s and 70s may not typically be as concerned about identity, either. Erikson's concept of identity is, therefore, a characteristic *developmental* adaptation. It is an aspect of personality that becomes especially salient during a particular developmental stage or epoch.

Some of the most illuminating features of human individuality cannot be understood outside of a developmental context. Erikson's concept of identity is one of those features. In accounting for Martin Luther's individuality, we might talk about his inordinately high conscientiousness, his moderately high neuroticism, and the anal-compulsive traits that Erikson assigned to him in *Young Man Luther.* At the level of dispositional traits (Chapters 5–7), Martin Luther was consistently hard-working and strong-willed, he was subject to intense emotional mood swings, he could be stubborn

TABLE 10.1	*Major Events in the Life of Martin Luther*
1483	Born into a strict and pious mining family in Eisleben in eastern Germany.
1501	Became a student at Erfurt, then the best university in Germany.
1505	January: graduated from Erfurt. May: to please father, Luther took up law. July: the thunderstorm incident, in which he vowed to St. Anne to become a monk. He entered the Augustinian cloister at Erfurt without telling his family.
1507	Became a priest and celebrated his first mass at age of 23. Then fell into severe doubts, which may have precipitated the "fit in the choir."
1512	Became doctor of theology at age 28 and gave his first lectures on the Psalms at the University of Wittenberg, where he experienced the revelation "in the tower." Formulated the essential Protestant doctrine that human beings are saved by faith, not by good works. Despite having developed a revolutionary viewpoint, Luther still considered himself orthodox at this point.
1517	Emerged as a practical reformer by preaching against the system of indulgences. On October 31st, he nailed to the door of Wittenberg Castle Church his 95 theses "For Elucidation of the Virtues of Indulgences." This event has traditionally been seen as the starting point of the Protestant Reformation.
1518	Luther was accused by many of heresy. He wrote to the pope in defense of his views.
1520	The pope publicly condemned Luther and his followers and gave him 60 days to retract his heretical views. Luther publicly burned the document of condemnation. Wrote major treatises on church reform.
1521	The pope moved to have Luther excommunicated (expelled) from the church. Luther went into hiding.
1522	Due to growing public support. Luther came out of hiding and resumed activity at Wittenberg. Published German translation of the New Testament and continued controversial writing. Composed hymns, including "A Mighty Fortress Is Our God." Luther's activities began to motivate radical evangelists and political movements in Germany.
1525	After expressing initial sympathy for the peasants' demands that serfdom be abolished, Luther sided instead with the lords and princes and called for the extermination of the "murdering hordes" of peasants. Luther married an ex-nun.
1526	First son, Hans, born. Hans was followed by two more sons and two daughters.
1526–1546	In these years, Luther was always active. He composed hymns, translated the Old Testament, issued many pamphlets, engaged in controversies with other reformers, and travelled extensively. He became the authoritarian father of the movement he had started.
1546	Died in Eisleben.

Source: Osborne (1961).

and obsessive, and he seemed to oscillate between the two poles of openness to experience—that is, at times he was open-minded and advocated change while at other times he was authoritarian and wedded to the orthodoxy. At the level of motives (Chapter 8), Martin Luther seemed to move from high achievement motivation in his youth and early adulthood to high power motivation in midlife. In terms of social-cognitive adaptations, he had a relatively simple construct system (Kelly) that was dominated by the bipolarity of God versus the Devil. Indeed, the Devil may have represented one of Luther's possible selves (Chapter 9), though the most undesired one. His explanatory style emphasized *external*, stable, and global forces: He believed that God and the Devil were the ultimate causes of earthly events. There is indeed much that can be learned about Martin Luther by invoking the concepts of personality that we have examined in the previous chapters of this book. But what Erikson believed to be the most important part of Luther's personality portrait—Luther's struggle to construct an identity—is left out until we begin to see his life in its full developmental context.

This chapter presents what I believe to be the two most integrative and influential theories of personality *development* ever put forth. Erik Erikson's theory of psychosocial development lays out eight stages of life through which individuals progress, from birth to death. Each stage sets forth an agenda for human individuality by specifying the central psychosocial concerns an individual faces during that period in his or her life. Especially significant for students of personality psychology are the early-adult stage of identity, as illustrated in Martin Luther's case, and the two stages following it—intimacy and generativity. These three stages comprise the bulk of the human lifespan—from early adulthood up to old age. The ways in which people meet the challenges of identity, intimacy, and generativity are among the most interesting and socially significant aspects of human individuality to be found. Jane Loevinger offers a very different developmental model—a theory of the development of the "ego." For Loevinger, the ego is a person's characteristic manner of making sense of experience. While Erikson focuses more on the emotional and social aspects of the developing person, Loevinger's theory emphasizes cognition and knowing. Like the perspectives on personality covered in Chapter 9, Loevinger examines how people make sense of themselves and the world in which they live. But unlike the approaches in Chapter 9, Loevinger spells out the development of this sense making, from infancy into adulthood.

Human lives are set in time. At any given time point, certain developmental issues and developmentally anchored ways of knowing the world can take center stage in a person's life, as identity did when Martin Luther was a young man. Erikson and Loevinger provide us with two powerful frameworks for identifying these developmental adaptations. Along with motives and goals (Chapter 8) and social-cognitive adaptations (Chapter 9), developmentally anchored features of personality go beyond dispositional traits to fill in the details of human individuality.

ERIK ERIKSON'S THEORY OF PSYCHOSOCIAL DEVELOPMENT

Erik Homburger Erikson was born of Danish parents, in 1902, in Frankfurt, Germany. His father, a Protestant, abandoned the family prior to Erik's birth, and his Jewish

Erik Erikson

mother subsequently married Dr. Theodor Homburger, a Jewish pediatrician. Growing up as Erik Homburger, the boy was a tall, fair-haired, and blue-eyed Jew of Scandinavian descent. To his Jewish peers, he did not look like a Jew. But he was not fully accepted by his non-Jewish peers, either. Thus, from an early age, Erikson cultivated an image of self as *outsider*, forced to define clearly how he was different from as well as similar to others in his environment (Friedman, 1999).

An unexceptional student, Erik Homburger never earned a university degree of any kind. Dashing his adoptive father's hopes that he become a physician, he wandered around Europe in his early 20s, studying briefly at art schools and painting children's portraits. "I was an artist then," he later wrote, "which can be a European euphemism for a young man with some talent, but nowhere to go" (Erikson, 1964, p. 20). During this very difficult period, Homburger experienced a crisis in identity that brought with it excessive anxiety and even occasional panic. A major problem was the young artist's inability to work with discipline and regularity (Erikson, 1975). In 1927, he moved to Vienna and accepted a teaching position at a small school established for children of Freud's patients and friends. He was received warmly by a group of psychoanalysts who included Dorothy Burlingham and Anna Freud, and he eventually undertook training in psychoanalysis with and was psychoanalyzed by Anna Freud. In 1933, Homburger emigrated to the United States and settled in Boston, where he worked as a psychoanalyst for children and associated temporarily with Henry Murray at the Harvard Psychological Clinic. In 1939, he became a naturalized American citizen and officially adopted the surname of "Erikson," a highly symbolic event that marked the maturation of his own identity.

Erikson and the Psychoanalytic Tradition

One cannot deny Erikson's debt to Freud. Like Freud, Erikson delved into the intrapsychic mysteries of persons' lives, engaging in dream interpretation and utilizing free association to unearth the latent meanings of manifest behavior and thought (Chapter 3). Like Freud, he couched early personality development in terms of stages that are linked to the libido. Because of his emphasis on the adaptive features of the human ego, furthermore, Erikson is often grouped as one of the preeminent ego psychologists, like Anna Freud herself (Chapter 3), whose main intellectual heritage is classical psychoanalysis.

Nonetheless, there are profound differences in content and style between Erikson and much of the rest of the psychoanalytic tradition. One of the most important differences is that Erikson is generally *optimistic* about the human condition, whereas Freud and much of the psychoanalytic tradition appear far more pessimistic. The difference shows up clearly in three basic tenets or assumptions of psychoanalysis, outlined in Chapter 3.

Recall that the first tenet of classic psychoanalytic theory is *determinism*, Freud's belief that all human behavior is determined by forces over which the individual has little control. Erikson's perspective on determinism is a bit different. Erikson agreed wholeheartedly with Freud that all kinds of behavior and experience—especially such potentially rich manifestations as dreams, art, and play—can be interpreted as expressions of unconscious internal determinants rooted in childhood. To quote an oft-used expression, Erikson endorsed Freud's view that "the child is father to the man." But, he also endorsed the quintessentially anti-Freudian view that the "man can be father to the child." In other words, while early (childhood) events may determine later personality structure, *later personality structure can also feed back to determine past childhood events!* While Freud believed that the "early" (childhood) forever determines the "late" (adulthood), Erikson endorsed the opposite view, that the late can determine the early. We are not simply what our childhoods have made us. Erikson firmly maintained: Our childhoods are also what we, as adults, make them. This intriguing idea will become clearer when we look more closely at Erikson's concept of identity.

The second psychoanalytic tenet is *conflict:* Human beings are in perpetual conflict, both with society and with themselves. Freud's tragic, romantic view of human nature dictated that the demands of society and the instinctual urges of the individual would forever clash, with society generally winning out. Further, Freud discerned conflict even at the core of the human instincts themselves, for all people are ultimately motivated by opposing life and death instincts. Because of conflict, people suffer anxiety; there is no way to escape conflict, and therefore anxiety is inevitable, even in the best of lives. According to the third tenet of psychoanalysis, the sources of anxiety are generally *unconscious* to the individual. We do not know why we are miserable, so buried are the unconscious springs of human experience and action.

Erikson shared Freud's romanticism, but not his sense of inevitable tragedy. And while he would not deny the importance of the unconscious, Erikson also emphasized such conscious shapers of personality as interpersonal relationships, social opportunities, and ideology. As Erikson viewed it, conflict may be a nemesis in many if not all lives, but there exist domains of living in which conflict is at a minimum, such as certain forms of play and art. More important, the individual need not be the pitiful loser in an unavoidable conflict with oppressive society. As active participants in—rather than helpless victims of—human societies, individuals can sometimes have as much impact on society as society has on them, as we see in the case of Luther. Further, many societies provide niches and opportunities for the expression of individuality— natural resources for the construction of identity. These resources include such abstractions as an economic order, specifications about adult roles, and value systems from which the individual can forge a personal ideology, as well as the more personal resources of role models, teachers, guides, and mentors. This is not to say that all societies at all times are equally beneficent. Erikson was keenly aware of the ways in which certain societies may pervert human development and ruin lives. Yet his view of social influence was much more charitable than Freud's, affirming a subtle and intricate dialectic between society and the individual.

The key to understanding the person, argued Erikson, is **triple bookkeeping** (Erikson, 1963). The person's life must be comprehended on three complementary levels: (1) the level of the *body* and all of the constitutional givens with which the individual is endowed, including sexual or libidinal dynamics; (2) the level of the *ego*, which refers to the person's unique ways of synthesizing experience to make sense of the world and cope with anxiety and conflict; and (3) the level of *family and society*, which refers both to the individual's developmental history within the family and the particular societal, cultural, and historical ethos that shapes and, in the cases of such extraordinary individuals as Luther, is shaped by the individual person. Erikson wrote, "being unable to arrive at any simple sequence and causal chain with a clear location and a circumscribed beginning, only triple bookkeeping (or, if you wish, a systematic going around in circles) can gradually clarify the relevances and relatives of all the known data" (1963, p. 46). Each stage of the human life cycle integrates body, ego, and society.

Developmental Stages in Childhood

Erikson (1959, 1963, 1964, 1968, 1982) identified eight stages of human development. Like Freud, Erikson argued that early stages are linked to basic psychosexual issues. As you recall from Chapter 3, Freud delineated the oral, anal, Oedipal, latency, and genital stages of the libido. Erikson's first five stages parallel Freud's in certain respects. But unlike Freud, Erikson underscored the interpersonal-social-cultural-historical context within which each stage is given its essential meaning. Thus, while Freud's are typically designated "psychosexual" stages, Erikson provided a model of "psychosocial" stages of development. For Freud, each stage is defined by a transformation in the libido (the sexual energy). By contrast, Erikson defined each stage in his scheme in terms of a central interpersonal/social issue that confronts the individual and the society within which the individual's life is embedded.

Freud's stage model ends in adolescence, when the individual attains full-fledged genital maturity. At that point in the individual's life, the libido has now reached its final form of expression. Erikson's stage model, by contrast, extends through the entire lifespan. Erikson proposed a full lifespan conception of development with eight psychosocial stages, extending from birth to old age and death. At each of Erikson's eight stages, changes within the individual and within the individual's social world combine to create a central conflict that defines the stage. The conflict must be addressed, though not necessarily resolved, within the given stage, says Erikson, before the individual may move to the next stage. In a sense, the individual's experiences give rise to a unique question at each stage, which is typically "asked" and eventually "answered" through the individual's behavior. Though this question may not be consciously posed by the individual, the overall pattern of the individual's behavior within a given stage is structured as if the individual were asking a particular question. The stages, their corresponding questions, and other associated features are briefly outlined in Table 10.2.

We should begin by thinking of the eight stages summarized in Table 10.2 as eight chapters in a generic interpersonal story that people live out in one way or another as they develop from infancy through adulthood. Each chapter is defined by a central psychosocial challenge, such as "trust *versus* mistrust" for the first chapter. The challenge can also be posed as a fundamental experiential question in life, which for the first chapter is, "How can I be secure?" Much of personality development in the first chapter, therefore, can be understood in terms of how the infant negotiates with the environment to answer the basic question of how to be secure.

However, other things are also happening: Other issues and topics are playing themselves out, though in minor and peripheral ways as secondary "subtexts" in the chapter. Thus, while the first chapter of the life cycle is dominated by the question

TABLE 10.2		Erikson's Eight Stages of Life		
AGE	PSYCHOSOSEXUAL STAGE (FREUD)	PSYCHOSOCIAL ISSUE	CENTRAL QUESTION	ASSOCIATED VIRTUE
1. Infancy	Oral	Trust vs. mistrust	How can I be secure?	Hope
2. Early childhood	Anal	Autonomy vs. shame and doubt	How can I be independent?	Will
3. Childhood (play age)	Oedipal	Initiative vs. guilt	How can I be powerful?	Purpose
4. Childhood (school age)	Latency	Industry vs. inferiority	How can I be good?	Competence
5. Adolescence and young adulthood	Genital	Identity vs. role confusion	Who am I? How do I fit into the adult world?	Fidelity
6. Young adulthood		Intimacy vs. isolation	How can I love?	Love
7. Mature adulthood		Generativity vs. stagnation (or self-absorption)	How can I fashion a "gift"?	Care
8. Old age		Ego integrity vs. despair	How can I receive a "gift"? (the "gift of life")	Wisdom

"How can I be secure?" other questions are being set up, other lines of development are getting started, other life motifs are taking form at the same time. These other issues will emerge later in the lifespan to dominate their own chapters: "autonomy *versus* shame and doubt" will dominate the second chapter of life, "initiative *versus* guilt" will dominate the third, and so on. As the life unfolds, the concerns of early chapters fade into the subtexts of subsequent chapters. Therefore, the issue of "trust *versus* mistrust" never truly disappears in the later chapters. Instead, it fades from being of primary importance early on to secondary importance as new issues arise in the lifespan. Psychosocial development, therefore, is the ebbing and flowing of particular life motifs in a storied sequence over the lifespan.

Erikson's first chapter parallels Freud's first stage of libidinal development termed the oral stage. Erikson agreed with Freud that for the first year or so of life the libido is centered in the oral zone as sucking at the mother's breast or bottle becomes the starting point of sexual life. However, the expression of the libido through oral activity is only a part of a larger, multidimensional development of a series of interpersonal relationships in the first year of life. These relationships determine the extent to which the infant will experience basic **trust** or security on the one hand and basic **mistrust** or insecurity on the other. Most important, sucking forms a bond of love between the mother and the infant. More than anything else, this bond of love has the potential to provide the infant with a sense of trust and security in the first year, a feeling or understanding that the world is safe, the environment is predictable, and life is trustworthy. Experiences of mistrust or insecurity will inevitably arise in the first year of life. The infant must and will experience both trust and mistrust: Healthy development is a function of the balance between the two.

Erikson's second stage of development—that concerned with the issue of **autonomy** *versus* **shame and doubt**—parallels Freud's second psychosexual stage, the anal stage. Again, Erikson agreed with Freud that, as far as psychosexuality in the toddler is concerned, the libido expresses itself through anal activity, as in the holding in and letting go of feces. For Erikson, however, the centerpiece of the 2- or 3-year-old's psychosocial experience is the struggle to attain a certain degree of autonomy, freedom, independence, and mastery of the self, and to avoid humiliation, shame, doubt, and other experiences in which the child's budding sense of self-sufficiency is threatened. Therefore, toilet training is important not so much as an expression of the libido but as an achievement of self-mastery and control. Major advances in locomotion, language, and exploratory play in the second and third years of life provide unprecedented opportunities for attaining a certain degree of independence in the world. The child's environment must support his or her fledgling efforts to master the self and obtain a modicum of independence. As Erikson put it, the "environment must back him [the child] up in his wish to 'stand on his own feet' lest he be overcome by that sense of having exposed himself prematurely and foolishly which we call shame, or that secondary mistrust, that looking back which we call doubt" (1963, p. 85). The overlapping psychosocial themes of the second chapter of life, therefore, are independence, self-mastery, self-control, and the avoidance of humiliation.

Simply being autonomous and independent, however, is not enough for the average 4-year-old. Unconsciously preoccupied with Freud's Oedipus complex, and confronting numerous challenges to efforts to move forward and to expand influence in the world, the naturally egocentric child in Erikson's third stage of the life cycle is preoccupied with questions of *power*. **Initiative** *versus* **guilt** is the basic psychosocial issue for the Oedipal boy or girl. At this time in the life cycle, children begin to take initiative in their daily lives—striving to master, divide, and conquer their worlds. They experience guilt when their aggressive attempts to make the world their own run afoul and as they, often unwittingly, threaten to hurt or damage others and their environment.

In keeping with Freud's view of the Oedipus complex, Erikson observed major sex differences in this third developmental chapter in the ways children carry out initiative and seek power. Boys tend to adopt a more **intrusive mode** of operation, which includes "the intrusion into other bodies by physical attack; the intrusion into other people's ears and minds by aggressive talking; the intrusion into space by vigorous locomotion; the intrusion into the unknown by consuming curiosity" (Erikson, 1963, p. 87). Girls tend to adopt a more **inclusive mode** of operation that can be "teasing, demanding, and grasping" (p. 88). Both boys and girls, however, are "on the make," to use Erikson's felicitous term. Though their styles may differ, both boys and girls at this stage in development strongly desire to make the world their own—to be king or queen, all-powerful and all-important, the center of everything.

Freud had little to say about the fourth stage. The latency period following the resolution of the Oedipus complex and the establishment of the superego (Chapter 3 in this book) was viewed as a relatively peaceful and uneventful period in life wherein the libido simmers on a back burner. For Erikson, however, the elementary school child has begun a very important phase in which he or she will repeatedly face the challenges of **industry *versus* inferiority.** While internal changes such as the resolution of the Oedipus complex may help usher in this period, society overtly marks the transition with the virtually universal custom of beginning systematic instruction—schooling—of children at this time in their lives.

Beginning around age 6 or 7, children in most cultures undergo some form of systematic instruction outside the family. This schooling is designed to render the young boy or girl proficient in using the *tools* and assuming the *roles* of adulthood (Erikson, 1963). Tools include the basic implements of daily life in the society, ranging from bows and arrows to computers, which extend the powers of the human body and mind to promote the economic, technological, political, educational, and religious systems. Roles include those particular structured activities that adults perform with more or less skill as working members of society, such as the roles of teacher, parent, hunter, priest, and healer. Though children have been exposed to these tools and roles in previous stages, it is now time to learn them and learn about them in a systematic and societally scripted way.

The protagonist of the fourth chapter in Erikson's scheme, therefore, is the industrious schoolchild immersed in the "reading-'riting-'rithmetic" of his or her culture. The child learns the rudimentary skills required to become a productive member of society, as well as the proper modes and manners of conduct expected outside the workplace. Erikson (1963) writes, "It is at this point that wider society becomes significant in its ways of admitting the child to an understanding of meaningful roles in its technology and economy" (p. 260). The elementary school child is learning how to be a good worker, a good citizen, and a good member of society.

Because this learning applies to matters that are both material and moral, economic and ethical, we may characterize the central psychosocial question of this stage as "How can I be good?" It is during this highly formative developmental period that churches and schools deliver their most influential lessons on how to be a good boy or girl. And though we may be able to distinguish from an early age the subtle differences between being "good" by getting an "A" on a spelling test and being "good" by telling the truth (Nucci, 1981), both involve *being good* and thus converge on the central theme of experience for the schoolchild living Erikson's fourth chapter. In Erikson's essentially Freudian perspective on this particular point, the question of "How can I be good?" must await the resolution of the Oedipus complex, the establishment of a superego or internalized standard for goodness and badness, and the child's unconscious realization that the power he or she desired in the third chapter of life cannot yet be attained.

The Problem of Identity

The early stages are but a prelude to the main act of late adolescence and young adulthood. As we saw in the life of Luther, it is at this time in the life course that the person seriously addresses the question of *identity:* Who am I? The four stages of childhood leave the person with a unique pool of resources and handicaps, strengths and weaknesses that will be called upon in the making of an identity. In this sense, the past (the early) partly determines the future (the late). But to a certain extent, the reverse is true, too. The adolescent or young adult looks back upon childhood now and comes to *de-*

cide what childhood meant. In that this decision is made after childhood actually happened, there is a sense in which the late (that which follows childhood) partly determines the early (childhood itself). We cannot literally change what has happened already, but we can change its meaning. This new meaning thus becomes another part of and influence upon the making of identity. In addressing the issue of identity, we look back to the past in order to arrive at a plausible explanation that tells us how we came to be and where we may be going in the future. In *Young Man Luther*, Erikson wrote:

> To be adult means among other things to see one's own life in continuous perspective, both in retrospect and prospect. By accepting some definition as to who he is, usually on the basis of a function in an economy, a place in the sequence of generations, and a status in the structure of society, the adult is able to selectively reconstruct his past in such a way that, step for step, it seems to have planned him, or better he seems to have planned it. In this sense, psychologically we *do* choose our parents, our family history, and the history of our kings, heroes, and gods. By making them our own, we maneuver ourselves into the inner position of proprietors, of creators. (Erikson, 1958, pp. 111–112)

Adolescence and Young Adulthood   In Freud's theory of psychosexual development, puberty marks the beginning of the libido's last stage—the genital stage—and the end of development. The physiological changes of puberty—such as the enlargement of the penis and testicles for boys, menstruation and the development of breasts for girls,

In modern societies, adolescence begins a period of identity exploration.

changes in the distribution of body hair, changes in voice, the adolescent growth spurt—and the associated awakening of overt sexual longing in the teenage years signal the end of the libido's transformations. Erikson, too, viewed puberty as an ending and a transformation. It marks the end of childhood, thus closing the chapters of trust, autonomy, initiative, and industry. And it denotes the movement to a new stage/chapter that has momentous psychosocial consequences. For Erikson, physiological puberty combined with a number of other developments in the teenage years to usher in the psychosocial stage of **identity *versus* role confusion.**

Why do we confront the identity issue first in adolescence? There are many answers to this question, but they can be generally grouped into three categories: body, cognition, and society. First, as adolescents we find ourselves the unwitting inhabitants of new adultlike bodies—both wonderful and frightening—that seem qualitatively different from what we have known before. As you probably remember from your own experience, attaining physiological puberty is not simply a matter of getting bigger, as was the bodily transition from, say, age 6 to age 7. The emergence of primary and secondary sexual characteristics and the eruption of overt sexual longings at puberty tell us that, with respect to our bodies and our biologies, we are now truly different from what we used to be. Puberty, thus, may mark a turning point in the adolescent's perceived developmental course, as childhood comes to represent, in the adolescent's mind, a bygone era. In other words, the physical changes of puberty may help jog us into this sort of realization: "Hey, I'm not what I used to be: I'm not a kid anymore; I'm different from what I was before, but I am not sure what I am now."

Second, cognitive development may play a major role in launching the identity chapter of Erikson's generic life story. The developmental psychologist Jean Piaget (Inhelder & Piaget, 1958) argued that in adolescence many people enter the cognitive stage of **formal operations.** According to Piaget, at this time in the life cycle we are first able to think about the world and about ourselves in highly abstract terms. In formal operations, one is able to reason about what is and what might be in terms of verbally stated and logically deduced hypotheses. Before adolescence, argues Piaget, we simply cannot do this. Therefore, the 10-year-old skillfully classifies and categorizes the world with wonderful accuracy and aplomb but is cognitively bound to the concrete world of *what is* rather than the abstract world of *what might be*. Ask a smart American 10-year-old to recite the capitals of the 50 states of the United States and you should not be surprised if he or she rattles them off with 100% precision. However, if you ask that same prodigy to speculate as to what the capitals of the United States might be if there were only 10 states, he or she is likely to have more trouble. First, the child may argue that the proposition is inherently ridiculous because the United States *is* in fact made up of 50 states. Second, he or she may find it extremely difficult to devise a systematic plan for determining what the criteria of a capital should be in this hypothetical scenario. The 10-year-old is a slave to concrete facts: Reality is everything. For the adolescent or adult blessed with formal operations, on the other hand, reality is understood as a *subset* of what might be. The real is one manifestation of the hypothetical, and viable and internally consistent alternative realities can also be imagined.

The serious questioning of the self—asking "Who am I?" and "How do I fit into the adult world?"—is catalyzed by the cognitive emergence of formal operations. The adolescent may look at the realities of the present and the past and contrast them with hypothetical possibilities concerning what might have been (in the past) and what might be (in the present and in the future). This introspective and abstract orientation to self and world may result in the formulation of hypothetical ideals: the ideal family, religion, society, life (Elkind, 1981). Adolescents begin to take seriously the possibilities of alternative lives and systems of living, motivating them in some cases to explore new and previously unthinkable ways of experiencing the world and to question those things learned in childhood that now seem "old." Furthermore, the adolescent may observe his or her own behavior and thought and come to question what the basic links are among the various different and conflicting ways in which he or she approaches the world: "Is there a real *me* behind all the different roles I play?" Such a cognitive problem is not likely to occur in the mind of the 10-year-old:

> During the early years, the child has different selves and is not bothered by inconsistencies between them, by his lack of unity or wholeness. He may be one person with his parents, another with his friends, and still another in his dreams. The limitations of [childhood thinking] permit such shifting about and contradictions. . . . The idea of a unitary or whole self in which past memories of who one was, present experiences of who one is, and future

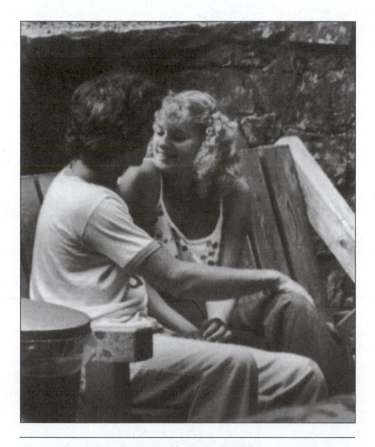

The conflict between intimacy and isolation is a central psycho-social issue faced by young adults.

expectations of who one will be, is the sort of abstraction that the child simply does not think about. . . . With the emergence of formal operations in adolescence, wholeness, unity, and integration become introspectively real problems. Central to the idealism of adolescence is concern with an ideal self. Holden Caulfield's preoccupation with phoniness is a striking example of this concern. [Holden Caulfield is the teenaged hero of J. D. Salinger's well-known novel *The Catcher in the Rye.*] He, and many young people like him, become critical of those who only play at roles, who are one moment this and another moment that. This critical stance is taken toward themselves as well. Wholeness is, thus, an *ideal* conceived in late adolescence; a goal which may be pursued thereafter. (Breger, 1974, pp. 330–331)

But the physiological and cognitive changes of adolescence do not tell the whole story of identity's emergence at this time as the central psychosocial issue in the individual's life. A third factor is society. Paralleling the changes taking place within the individual are shifts in society's expectations about what the individual, who was a child but who is now almost an adult, should be doing, thinking, and feeling. Erikson (1959) wrote, "It is of great relevance to the young individual's identity formation that he be responded to, and be given function and status as a person whose gradual growth and transformation make sense to those who begin to make sense to him" (p. 111). In general, Western societies "expect" their adolescents and young adults to examine the occupational, ideological, and interpersonal opportunities around them and to begin to make some decisions about what their lives as adults are to be about. This is to say that both society and the young person are ready for the young person's identity experiments and explorations by the time that he or she has, in fact, become a young person. As Erikson described it:

> The period can be viewed as a psychosocial moratorium during which the individual through free role experimentation may find a niche in some section of his society, a niche which is firmly defined and yet seems to be uniquely made for him. In finding it the young adult gains an assured sense of inner continuity and social sameness which will bridge what he was as a child and what he is about to become, and will reconcile his conception of himself and his community's recognition of him. (1959 p. 111)

There is, however, a tension in all of this. It is the tension between the "niche" carved out by society and the individual's desire to carve out his or her own niche. In constructing an identity that "fits" into society's roles and expectations, the young person should not blindly conform to what the family in particular or society in general wants him or her to do. In a sense, this is what Luther first did, in his initial decision to become a monk. But as we saw later, Luther eventually went beyond the niche carved out for him in the monastery to create a new and unique identity within his expanding and evolving world. Yet Luther did not—indeed could not—separate completely from society and its expectations. Even in the most revolutionary lives, Erikson maintains, *the individual and society create identity together.* The adolescent or adult should be neither victim nor master of his or her sociohistorical environment. Rather, the relationship between the self and society in the development of healthy identity is best characterized as one of dynamic tension.

Identity Statuses   One way to view identity is to focus on the *process* of formulating answers to the questions "Who am I?" and "How do I fit into the adult world?" during adolescence and young adulthood. According to this approach, the formation of identity in the adolescent and early adult years involves two related steps. In the first step, the young person breaks away from childhood beliefs and views, questions assumptions about the self and the world, and begins to investigate alternatives. During this first step of exploration, the person may challenge many of the viewpoints presented by parents, schools, churches, and other figures and institutions of authority. He or she may also come to question the past, wondering what might have been had things occurred differently in the earlier chapters of life—how life might be different now, for instance, if the person had been born into a different family, a different social class, a different ethnic group, a different society, a different period in history. Moving from what was and is to what might have been and what might be, the formal-operational thinker may begin to sample alternative beliefs, values, ideologies, behaviors, and lifestyles, searching for that overall approach to life that seems to "fit." The exploration ends in the second step of identity formation in which the young person makes commitments to various roles and outlooks that define how the young person sees him- or herself fitting into the adult world. In the second step, the questions and doubts of the exploration phase are resolved, and identity ceases to be a pressing psychosocial concern.

James Marcia (1966, 1980; Marcia, Waterman, Matteson, Archer, & Orlofsky, 1993) employs a semistructured interview to ask questions about exploration and commitment as they apply to the two areas of life that Erikson repeatedly suggested were at the heart of identity: (1) *occupation*, or what work role in society the person will occupy; and (2) *ideology*, or what the person's fundamental beliefs and values are, especially in the areas of religion and politics. Based on the responses to the interview, psychologists are able to classify young persons into one of four different **identity statuses,** displayed in Table 10.3. Each status may be viewed as a particular developmental position with respect to identity that the person holds at the current period in his or her life. Over time, people may move from one status to another, as identity is negotiated and reworked in different ways (Bourne, 1978; Waterman, 1982). Marcia's methodology and classification scheme have stimulated a large body of research over the past 30 years. Most of these studies have been done with college students, who as late adolescents and young adults are likely to be dealing, in one form or another, with the issue of "identity *versus* role confusion."

In terms of Erikson's theory, the most developmentally advanced of the four identity statuses is **identity achievement.** Identity achievers have gone through a period

TABLE 10.3	*Four Identity Statuses*

STATUS	PROCESS	
	EXPLORATION, CRISIS, QUESTIONING	COMMITMENT, RESOLUTION
Identity achievement	Yes	Yes
Moratorium	Yes	No
Foreclosure	No	Yes
Identity diffusion	No	No

of exploration and have come out of it having made commitments to well-articulated occupational and ideological goals and positions. They have successfully met the challenge of Erikson's fifth psychosocial stage and are now ready to begin the sixth. Identity achievers strive for internalized goals and rely on their own skills and capacities in meeting daily challenges. Less concerned with winning their parents' love than are young persons in some of the other identity statuses, identity achievers may perceive their parents in balanced though somewhat ambivalent terms (Jordan, 1971; Josselson, 1973).

Several studies indicate that identity achievers are more academically inclined than persons in the other statuses. Cross and Allen (1970) showed that identity achievers received higher grades in college courses. Marcia and Friedman (1970) found that, among women, identity achievers chose more difficult college majors. Orlofsky (1978) found that identity achievers scored very high on the TAT measure of achievement motivation (Chapter 8). Other studies suggest that identity achievers make decisions, especially moral decisions, in an autonomous and principled fashion. They tend not to conform to peer pressure and social norms (Adams, Ryan, Hoffman, Dobson, & Nielson, 1984; Toder & Marcia, 1973). And they tend to base their moral decisions on abstract principles of justice and social contract rather than the conventional laws of societies and the egocentric needs of individuals (Podd, 1972).

The second identity status identified by Marcia is **moratorium.** People in moratorium are currently exploring identity issues but have not yet made commitments. You might say that these people do not know yet who they are and they know that they do not know. Uncertainty about the present and future may launch, as we saw with Luther in the monastery, a full-blown "identity crisis." But the moratoriums of the present should become the identity achievers of the near future as they pass from the sometimes anxiety-provoking period of exploration to stable commitment. Consequently, like identity achievers, moratoriums in college are usually viewed as relatively "mature" in Marcia's scheme, and many of the empirical findings for identity achievers also apply to individuals classified as moratorium. For example, both identity achievers and moratoriums create richer and more individualistic conceptions of themselves, compared with individuals in other identity statuses (Dollinger & Dollinger, 1997).

Marked *ambivalence* is probably the best term to describe the characteristic relationship between the young person in moratorium and his or her parents. In moratorium, the individual may seek greater psychological distance from the family, rejecting old identifications and ingrained values and beliefs and setting up the parents or other authority figures as temporary **negative identities** (Erikson, 1959). These negative identities come to represent everything the young person does *not* want to be. Therefore, parents may be cast into the unenviable role of "the enemy" in the adolescent's battle to discover what to believe and how to live as an adult. It is not surprising, then, that adolescents and young adults in moratorium often report stormy and contradictory feelings about their parents (Josselson, 1973; Marcia, 1980) as well as relatively high levels of general anxiety (Marcia, 1967; Oshman & Manosevitz, 1974). On the other hand, young adults in moratorium are often described as extremely friendly, likable, sensitive, and insightful (Josselson, 1973; Marcia, 1980).

In Erikson's terms, the person in the third status of **foreclosure** has failed to meet the identity challenge. In foreclosure, the young person fails to explore, but makes commitments to unquestioned positions taken from childhood. Rather than risk the uncertainty that might accompany a serious questioning of the past and of authority, the young person in foreclosure has opted for the security of childhood roles, beliefs, and expectations. With respect to occupation, the foreclosed individual "chooses" to do exactly what important authority persons have suggested, or perhaps insisted, he or she do. With respect to ideology, beliefs and values from childhood are transported into early adulthood intact and unsullied—rarely questioned and never reformulated. Not surprisingly, foreclosures report that they are very close to their parents, especially sons to fathers. They tend to describe their homes as loving and affectionate (Donovan, 1975).

Foreclosures appear the "best behaved" of the statuses (Marcia, 1980). College students in this status tend to study diligently, keep regular hours, and appear happy. The good behavior may be grounded in relatively traditional and conventional values adopted wholesale from authorities such as parents and the church. Indeed, a number of studies suggest that foreclosures adopt a more *authoritarian* outlook on the world than people in the other statuses (Marcia, 1966, 1967; Marcia & Friedman, 1970; Schenkel & Marcia, 1972). As we saw in Chapter 6, authoritarianism is a constellation of traits and attitudes centered on submission to and reverence for strong authority, conventional societal values, and rigid standards of right and wrong. Foreclosures tend to show rigid, authoritarian responses to moral dilemmas and tend to obey the dictates of powerful authority, even when the authority asks them to do things that seem wrong (Podd, 1972). With respect to other personality variables, foreclosures score extremely low on autonomy and anxiety, and they tend to show unrealistically high levels of aspiration (Marcia, 1966, 1967; Orlofsky, Marcia, & Lesser, 1973).

Marcia's fourth identity status, **identity diffusion,** is the most enigmatic. Like foreclosures, individuals in the diffusion status have yet to enter exploration, but, unlike foreclosures, they have yet to make commitments. With few strong allegiances to the past and few explicit commitments to a particular future, these young men and women appear to be afloat in a sea of ambiguity. The few studies that have obtained clear findings on diffusions suggest that they may be best characterized by the word *withdrawal*. Donovan (1975) found that diffusions tended to feel out of place and socially isolated. They saw their parents as distant and misunderstanding, and they approached new relationships with extreme caution. Josselson (1973) points to fantasy and withdrawal as favorite coping strategies for women of diffusion status. Summarizing the little available evidence, Marcia (1980) concludes that diffusions "seemed to sense little past to integrate, little future for which to plan; they were only what they felt in the present" (p. 176).

Ruthellen Josselson (1996) conducted an intensive longitudinal study of 30 women who were categorized as college seniors into Marcia's identity statuses based on interviews conducted in 1972. Josselson found evidence for both continuity and change in identity from the college years into midlife. Describing them as *pathmakers*, Josselson (1996) shows that the women who were identity achievers in college moved ahead into their 30s and 40s with "a sense of conviction in the basic meaningfulness of their lives and choices" (p. 101). For pathmakers, "self-doubt was present but not disabling—they were aware that they might have made other choices, that some of their choices had led to pain or dead ends, but these women had the capacity to rally themselves and choose again, hoping to do so with better understanding and insight" (p. 101). The women who held the moratorium status in college continued to act as *searchers* in their

30s and 40s. Compared with pathmakers, they experienced more self-doubt and self-criticism and reported more vivid emotions and strong spirituality. Nonetheless, most of the searchers did, sooner or later, "find themselves," as Josselson puts it, and made the kinds of occupational, ideological, and interpersonal commitments so characteristic of pathmakers.

Significant growth and development were also apparent among college foreclosures (Josselson's *guardians*) and those classified as identity diffuse in college (*drifters*). Though they remained more rigid and moralistic than other groups, guardians used their firm principles as a foundation upon which to build new and interesting self-conceptions. By midlife, many of the guardians had discovered "inner aspects [of themselves] they had long ago buried. What was silenced was given voice as they learned to live on their own authority" (p. 70). Finally, the college drifters showed life paths that were "checkered and complex" (p. 168), but most of them had made considerable progress by midlife in organizing their lives around commitments and goals. Drifters reported the greatest number of regrets about their past, perhaps because of missed opportunities to seize the identity issue when it first appeared to them in their college years. Nonetheless, the drifters were actively exploring their options and revising their lives into their 30s and 40s. Josselson concludes that the central theme of their lives was "growing into greater consciousness and control" (p. 168). Making up for lost time, the women who drifted through identity diffusion as college students were now facing head-on the challenges of identity formation in their midlife years.

Identity and Intimacy   Erikson's stage model suggests that once an adult has arrived at some tentative answers to the question of Who am I? he or she is then psychosocially ready to begin the sixth chapter of life, **intimacy** *versus* **isolation.** The relationship between these two stages, however, can be very complex. Many people seem to define themselves (identity) through intimate relationships with others. The proper sequence for the stages may indeed be reversed in many lives. Intimacy issues may arise before identity issues in many cases. Some have suggested that women's lives in American society have traditionally exemplified a merging of intimacy and identity issues, such that a woman's identity is intricately connected to her intimate relationships. The establishment of the adult self and the development of intimate relationships may be difficult to separate from each other. Nonetheless, Erikson favored an idealized sequential scheme, suggesting that a person may be unable to be "truly" intimate with others until he or she has first made considerable progress in addressing the identity issue.

The closest thing to a definition that Erikson provided for intimacy is the following passage:

> Thus, the young adult, emerging from the search for and the insistence on identity, is eager and willing to fuse his identity with that of others. He is ready for intimacy, that is, the capacity to commit himself to concrete affiliations and partnerships and to develop the ethical strength to abide by such commitments, even though they may call for significant sacrifices and compromises. Body and ego must now be masters of the organ modes and of the nuclear conflicts, in order to be able to face the fear of ego loss in situations which call for self-abandon: in the solidarity of close affiliations, in orgasms, and sexual unions, in close friendships and in physical combat, in experiences of inspiration by teachers and of intuition from the recesses of the self. The avoidance of such experiences because of a fear of ego loss may

lead to a deep sense of isolation and consequent fear of self-absorption. (Erikson, 1963, pp. 263–264)

This difficult excerpt from *Childhood and Society* shows that Erikson held to an extremely general and inclusive conceptualization of intimacy. Intimacy appears to involve a willingness to fuse one's identity with another, which results in love and strong commitment. It suggests a courageous willingness to lose the self in another—through close friendships, sexual unions, learning from teachers, and even (curiously) "physical combat." To be intimate is to be open and receptive to that "other" that is outside the ego, even remarkably when the "other" is "inside," that is, when the other is an internal part of one's own unconscious: "intuition from the recesses of the self." Exploring the recesses of the unconscious self—as in psychoanalysis—is a kind of intimacy, for Erikson, in that the individual is opening up to that which is alien, foreign, outside the ego (even though inside the psyche).

Most of the personality research that has addressed intimacy from an explicitly Eriksonian perspective has examined the relation between the resolution of identity and the quality of intimacy. Following Marcia's concept of identity status, Orlofsky, Marcia, and Lesser (1973) developed the parallel idea of **intimacy status.** These researchers devised a semistructured interview designed to determine the quality of intimacy in a person's life. Based on the respondent's answers to questions about dating,

TABLE 10.4	*Four Intimacy Statuses in Studies of College Students*
Intimate	The person works at developing mutual personal relationships and has several close friends with whom he or she discusses personal matters. He or she is involved in a committed love relationship with a member of the opposite sex. This sexual relationship is mutually satisfactory, usually involving intercourse. The person is able to express both angry and affectionate feelings in the relationship. The person is generally interested in others.
Preintimate	The person has dated members of the opposite sex but is not involved in a committed love relationship. He or she is aware of the possibilities of relating intimately with a member of the opposite sex. The person has close friendships. The person has respect for the integrity of others, openness, responsibility, and mutuality. He or she feels conflicted about commitment, and love relationships may tend to be ambivalent.
Stereotyped	The person ranges from the moderately constricted and immature type of individual who has yet to go beyond superficial dating relationships to the playboy/playgirl type. Generally he or she has several friends; however, these relationships lack significant depth. He or she may date regularly but generally does not get involved.
Isolate	The isolated person lacks enduring personal relationships. Though he or she may have a few peer acquaintances seen infrequently, he or she rarely initiates social contact and rarely dates members of the opposite sex. The anxiety accompanying close personal contact forces the person to withdraw into isolation. The person tends to be anxious and immature and generally lacking in assertiveness and social skills. The isolated individual may present him- or herself as bitter and mistrustful or smug and self-satisfied.

Source: Orlofsky, Marcia, & Lesser (1973).

friendships, and interpersonal commitments, he or she may be classified as showing one of four intimacy statuses. Ranging from most intimate to least intimate, these are "intimate," "preintimate," "stereotyped relationships," and "isolate" (Table 10.4).

The small body of research employing identity and intimacy status constructs shows a modest but significantly positive correlation between the two measures. Orlofsky, Marcia, and Lesser (1973) found that male college students who showed the relatively mature identity statuses of identity achievement and moratorium tended also to exhibit the more mature intimacy statuses of intimate and preintimate. Tesch and Whitbourne (1982) examined the relation between identity and intimacy in 48 men and 44 women in their mid-20s. The subjects were administered the standard identity-status and intimacy-status interviews. The authors added a fifth intimacy status, termed "merger," which designated relationships in which one partner dominated the other. Some of the results of the study are displayed in Table 10.5. Men and women who had successfully resolved identity questions (identity achievement) tended to show relatively high levels of intimacy (intimate status). Those showing the lowest levels of identity resolution (identity diffusion) tended also to score at low levels of intimacy (preintimate, stereotyped, isolate).

Kahn, Zimmerman, Csikszentmihalyi, and Getzels (1985) examined the relation between the extent to which a young adult resolves identity problems on the one hand, and the quality of married life—assessed 18 years later—on the other. They found that the degree of identity resolution in young adulthood predicted the establishment (for men) and the stability (for women) of marital relationships at midlife. Young men with high levels of identity resolution were more likely to marry, whereas those with low levels of identity tended to remain bachelors. Young women with high levels of identity were less likely to experience divorce and separation in their subsequent marriages compared with young women scoring low on identity.

TABLE 10.5   *Relationship Between Identity Status and Intimacy Status in a Study of Young Adults*

| | IDENTITY | | | |
INTIMACY	ACHIEVEMENT	FORECLOSURE	MORATORIUM	DIFFUSION
	MALES			
Intimate	8	2	0	2
Merger	2	3	0	0
Preintimate	4	1	0	4
Stereotyped	0	2	0	1
Isolate	0	0	0	3
	FEMALES			
Intimate	7	4	0	1
Merger	0	2	0	1
Preintimate	3	1	3	1
Stereotyped	1	0	0	3
Isolate	0	0	0	0

Note: Numbers represent number of subjects (frequencies).
Source: Tesch & Whitbourne (1982), p. 1049.

FEATURE 10.A

Spiritual Beliefs and Personal Ideology

"The adolescent mind is an ideological mind," wrote Erik Erikson. "It is the ideological outlook of a society that speaks most clearly to the adolescent who is eager to be affirmed by his peers, and is ready to be confirmed by rituals, creeds, and programs which at the same time define what is evil, uncanny, and inimical" (1963, p. 263). Many young people want dearly to believe in something beyond the self. They may search for ultimate life meanings in political activity, community service, and/or religious and spiritual endeavors. As we saw in the case of Martin Luther, one's religious perspective on life can be at the center of ego identity. Erikson wrote: "We will call what young people in their teens and early 20s look for in religion and in other dogmatic systems *ideology*. At the most, it is a militant system with uniformed members and uniform goals; at the least, it is a 'way of life,' or what the Germans call a *Weltanschaung*, a worldview which is consonant with existing theory, available knowledge, and common sense, and yet is significantly more: an utopian outlook, a cosmic mood, or a doctrinal logic, all shared as self-evident beyond any need for demonstration" (1958, p. 41).

In Erikson's view, adolescence and young adulthood are prime time for developing a personal ideology in life. A person's fundamental beliefs and values about right and wrong, good and bad, the nature of God, and the ultimate meaning of life are at the center of a person's identity. Personality psychologist Ed de St. Aubin (1996, 2000) has developed a conception of *personal ideology*, which captures the breadth and richness of Erikson's view. According to de St. Aubin, personal ideology is "an individual's unique philosophy of how life should be lived and of what forces influence human living" (1996, p. 152). According to de St. Aubin, personal ideology includes, among other things, a person's political orientation, religious and spiritual beliefs, value systems, and assumptions concerning human nature. While other psychologists have studied one or two of these domains in isolation, de St. Aubin contends that the particular way in which ideology infuses human identity can be understood only when the psychologist uses a wide-angle lens to take in the person's encompassing worldview.

There are many ways to characterize individual differences in personal ideology. For example, psychologists studying moral development (Kohlberg, 1981) and stages of religious faith (Fowler, 1981) have focused on the *structure* of ideology, tending to differentiate between primitive and cognitively simple ideological structures (low stages) on the one hand and more developmentally advanced and cognitively differentiated belief systems (high stages) on the other. Other researchers have examined the *content* of belief and value systems. For example, Allport and Vernon (1931) distinguished among six value types—theoretical, economic, social, religious, political, and artistic. People of the theoretical type tend to value truth and rationality; the artistic person values beauty; the political type values power and influence. Rokeach (1973) delineated 36 basic human values. Half of them are *instrumental* values, referring to means and modes of human conduct (e.g., "ambitious," "clean," "courageous," "honest," "obedient"). Half are *terminal* values, referring to desired end states (e.g., "a world

FEATURE 10.A *continued*

at peace," "equality," "freedom"). On the Rokeach Value Survey, a person rank-orders each of the 18 instrumental and 18 terminal values from "most important to me" to "least important to me." Rokeach's approach has generated a considerable body of research examining, for example, national differences in value preferences and linking individual differences in value rankings to other dimensions of personality (Feather, 1984; Rokeach, 1973).

Like Rokeach, de St. Aubin tends to focus on the *content* of ideological beliefs. Drawing on the writings of Silvan Tomkins (Chapter 11 in this book), de St. Aubin identifies two broad content dimensions that cut across many different ideological domains. These are *normativism* and *humanism*. The normative ideological orientation maintains that "reality exists prior to and independent of humankind, and that human beings must struggle toward this (unattainable) potential through conformity to norms and set rules" (de St. Aubin, 1996, p. 153). De St. Aubin's research shows that people with a highly normative ideological orientation are likely to believe that humankind is inherently bad, that love should be given contingent on good be-

havior and accomplishment, and that God is a rule-based force that exists outside the realm of humanity. Normativists also tend to be politically conservative. By contrast, the humanistic ideological orientation "views humankind as an end in itself, an active, creative, thinking, desiring, and loving force" (p. 153). People with a highly humanistic ideological orientation tend to believe that reality exists to the extent that human beings perceive and construct it, tend to endorse unconditional regard for others (rather than conditional love), and see God as existing within people (rather than in the external world). Humanists tend to be politically liberal. It is also possible to score high on *both* normativism and humanism, which would suggest a mixed ideological orientation, or to score low on both dimensions, which would suggest an undifferentiated personal ideology.

A person's ideological orientation is more than beliefs and values, however. Personal ideology is grounded in *emotion*, de St. Aubin maintains. Normativists and humanists *feel differently* about the world and about life; their beliefs and values are intimately linked to different emotional states. For example, de St. Aubin (1996) provides data supporting

Generativity and Adult Development

The last two stages in Erikson's eight-stage model of psychosocial development correspond roughly to middle and later adulthood. Middle adulthood focuses on caring for and leaving a legacy to benefit the next generation. In later adulthood, the person is concerned with looking back upon his or her own life and coming to accept life as something that has been good.

Generativity *versus* stagnation is the seventh stage in Erikson's scheme, generally identified with that long period in the life course that follows early adulthood but comes before "old age." The prototype for generativity is raising children. By

Tomkins's contention that while normativists are more likely to report negative emotional experiences of *anger*, humanists are more likely to feel the negative emotions of *distress* and *fear*. It is in the area of religious beliefs and values, one might argue, that emotions are most deeply invoked. With a few notable exceptions (e.g., Allport, 1950), personality psychologists have not historically focused their research on religion and spirituality. However, recent years signal a shift. Among others, Robert Emmons (1999) has recently urged psychologists to examine the role of spirituality and ultimate concerns in human personality. Already, survey studies suggest that, among Americans, involvement in religious and/or spiritual endeavors is positively associated with self-reports of psychological well-being (Emmons, 1999; Koenig, 2000). The finding might not have surprised William James, considered by many the founder of American psychology. About 100 years ago, James wrote this:

> Happiness! Happiness! Religion is one of the ways in which men gain that gift. Easily, permanently, and successfully, it often transforms the most intolerable misery into the profoundest and most enduring happiness. (James, 1902/1958, p. 146)

Erikson did not assert that religion would make people happy. But he did recognize that religious and spiritual longings beckon many young people and that developing a personally satisfying perspective on issues of ultimate concern can be an important aspect of the young person's identity struggle. In this regard, Erikson's view is consistent with the personality psychologist Gordon Allport (1950), who argued that religion helps some individuals develop a unifying philosophy of life, which itself is a hallmark, Allport asserted, of the mature self. But neither Erikson nor Allport believed that religion was "the only way," or even the best. For some young people, religious beliefs and values are indeed central to personal ideology. For others, religious issues may be secondary or even absent, and they may place more importance on political and social involvements. What *is* important is that the young person develop a personal ideology that integrates him or her into society in a personally satisfying, productive, ethical, and prosocial manner.

being good and caring parents, Erikson argued, many adults fulfill their basic "need to be needed" (Erikson, 1963) and directly promote the next generation. Yet there are many other ways to be generative, especially in one's occupational life, in creative activity, and through community involvements such as Girl Scouts, Little League, charitable contribution, church activities, and the like. In all of these endeavors, the generative adult acts on "the desire to invest one's substance in forms of life and work that will *outlive the self*" (Kotre, 1984, p. 10). The generative adult commits him or herself to some activity that is larger than his or her own life, investing significant time and creative energy into an endeavor that will "live on." Kotre (1984) identifies four different ways in which adults may be generative: through biological,

TABLE 10.6	*Four Types of Generativity*

TYPE	DESCRIPTION
Biological	Begetting, bearing, and nursing offspring *Generative object:* the infant
Parental	Nurturing and disciplining offspring, initiating them into a family's traditions *Generative object:* the child
Technical	Teaching skills—the "body" of a culture—to successors, implicitly passing on the symbol system in which the skills are embedded *Generative objects:* the apprentice, the skill
Cultural	Creating, renovating, and conserving a symbol system—the "mind" of a culture—explicitly passing it on to successor *Generative objects:* the disciple, the culture

Source: Kotre (1984), p. 12.

parental, technical, and cultural generativity (Table 10.6). Connecting all four are *acts of caring*. In his psychobiographical study of the life of Mahatma Gandhi, Erikson (1969) wrote:

> A mature man of middle age has not only made up his mind as to what, in the various compartments of his life, he does and does not *care for*; he is also firm in his vision of what he *will* and *can* take *care of*. He takes as his baseline what he irreducibly is and reaches out for what only he can, and therefore, must *do*. (p. 255)

A Model of Generativity   Beyond Erikson, a number of theorists have written about the role of generativity in the adult life course (e.g., Browning, 1975; Cohler, Hostetler, & Boxer, 1998; Gutmann, 1987; Kotre, 1984, 1999; Neugarten, 1968; Peterson & Stewart, 1990; Snarey, 1993; Stewart & Vandewater, 1998; Vaillant & Milofsky, 1980). Generativity has been variously described as a biological drive to reproduce oneself, an instinctual need to care for and be needed by others, a philosophical urge for transcendence and symbolic immortality, a developmental sign of maturity and mental health in adulthood, and a social demand to create a productive niche in society. It has been identified with behavior (such as raising children), with motives and values (concern for preserving what is good and making other things better), and with a general attitude about the world (having a broad perspective and understanding one's place in the sequence of generations).

In order to create an integrative framework to guide research on generativity, my colleagues and I developed a model of generativity that brings together some of the best ideas on the concept and suggests specific ways to measure different dimensions of generativity (McAdams, 1993; McAdams & de St. Aubin, 1992; McAdams, Hart, & Maruna, 1998). The model suggests that generativity is a *configuration of seven psychosocial features*, all of which center on the personal and societal goal of *providing for the next*

FIGURE 10.1

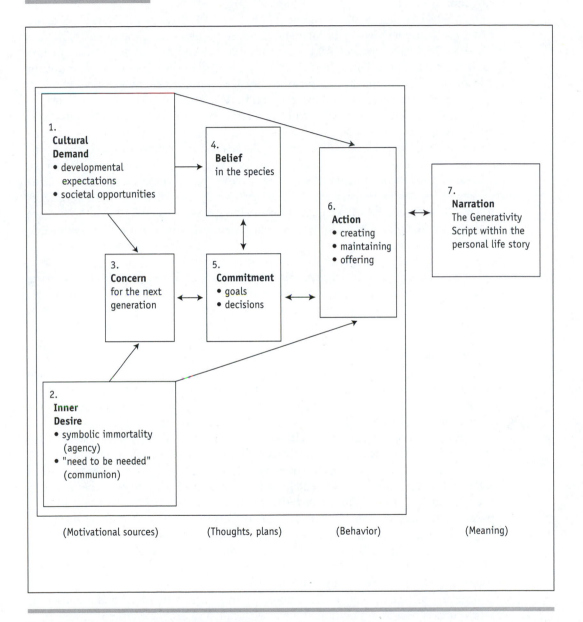

FIGURE 10.1   *Seven Features of Generativity*

Source: McAdams & de St. Aubin (1992), p. 1005.

generation. To understand this model, you should think of generativity as something that exists both within the person and in the person's world. It is as much a quality of environments as it is a quality of people. In that generativity links the person and the social world, generativity can "happen" only in a psychosocial context, when certain variables within the person and in the person's world come together to provide for the next generation.

The model of generativity is presented in Figure 10.1. Starting on the far left, Boxes 1 and 2 in the model identify ultimate motivational sources for generativity. The first of these is (1) *cultural demand*. All human cultures demand that adults provide for the next generation. These demands are implicitly encoded in the societal expectations for age-appropriate behavior. In American society, we do not expect 10-year-old children to provide primary care for the next generation. We generally do not expect them to be thinking about the legacy they will leave after they die. But as people move into young- and middle-adulthood, we come to expect an increasing awareness of and commitment to their roles as providers. One of the reasons generativity emerges as a psychosocial issue in the adult years is that society comes to demand that adults take responsibility for the next generation, in their roles as parents, teachers, mentors, leaders, organizers, "creative ritualizers" (Browning, 1975), and "keepers of the meaning" (Vaillant & Milofsky, 1980). As adults move through their 30s and 40s, those who are unable or unwilling to contribute to and assume responsibility for the next generation, usually through family or work, are considered "off time" and at odds with the expected "social clock" (Neugarten & Hagestad, 1976).

But generativity doesn't happen only because society wants it to. Many theorists suggest that generativity springs as much from deeply rooted (2) *inner desire* as it does from cultural demand. Two sharply contrasting desires have typically been identified. The first is a desire for symbolic immortality. As Kotre (1984) and Becker (1973) suggest, adults desire to defy death in symbolic ways by constructing legacies that live on. In generativity, the adult creates, promotes, nurtures, or generates something or someone in "one's own image"—as an extension of the self. One's generative legacy can be as humble as a wise piece of advice offered to a coworker. It can be as grand as raising a large family, building a business, composing a song, painting a picture, leading a community, making a discovery, or even building a nation. Ideally, the product of one's generative efforts outlives the self, such that mature adults ultimately come to define themselves in terms of what they leave behind. In middle adulthood and beyond, writes Erikson, "I am what survives me" (1968, p. 141). The second desire is what Erikson terms the "need to be needed," the desire to nurture others, to be of use to those who are in need. While the desire for immortality suggests power and self-expansion, the need to be needed reveals generativity's soft and loving side. One of the most fascinating aspects of generativity is its conflictual essence—it celebrates the infinite expansion of the self and the surrender of the self at the same time. To be especially generative is to want to live forever and to want to give oneself up completely for the good of others, at the same paradoxical time.

Cultural demand and inner desire combine to promote in adulthood a conscious (3) *concern* for the next generation. Thus, developmental expectations about making a contribution to the next generation and inner desires for agential immortality and communal nurturance come together in adulthood to promote the extent to which the person cares for and about the development of the next generation. Along with concern, an adult may develop what Erikson (1963, p. 267) calls a (4) *"belief in the species"* (Van de Water & McAdams, 1989). This is a basic and general belief in the fundamental goodness and worthwhileness of human life specifically as envisioned for the future. To believe in the (human) species is to place hope in the advancement and betterment of human life in succeeding generations, even in the face of strong evidence of human destructiveness and deprivation. A strong belief in the species can help an adult translate his or her concern for the next generation into (5) generative *commitment*, taking responsibility for the next generation and making decisions to establish goals and strivings for generative behavior. When such a belief is lacking, however, the adult may find it difficult to make a strong generative commitment, because it may appear that a generative effort may not be very useful, anyway. Why commit yourself to promoting the next generation, some might say, if you think that the world is headed for disaster anyway and there is little you can do about it?

Guided by commitment, which itself is a product of demand, desire, concern, and belief, a person may act, may actually do something to provide for the next generation. Generative (6) *action* may be expressed in any of three loosely related guises: (a) creating, (b) maintaining, or (c) offering. First, generative action may involve giving birth to people, things, and outcomes, making, creating, generating, formulating, or discovering that which may be seen as "good." Second, generative action may involve passing on good things, preserving, conserving, maintaining, fostering, cultivating, nurturing that which is deemed worthy of such behavior, as in raising children, preserving good traditions, protecting the environment, and enacting rituals (in the school, home, or church) that link generations and assure continuity over time (Browning, 1975; Erikson, 1982). Third, generative action may involve the seemingly selfless offering up of that which has been created or maintained, passing something or someone on to the next generation as a gift, granting the gift its own autonomy and freedom (Becker, 1973; McAdams, 1985b). For example, the truly generative father is both a self-aggrandizing creator and a self-sacrificing giver. Biologically and socially, he creates a child in his own image, working hard and long to promote the development of the child and to nurture all that is good and desirable in the child. But he must eventually grant the child his or her own autonomy, letting go when the time is right, letting the child develop his or her own identity, make his or her own decisions and commitments, and ultimately create those offerings of generativity that will distinguish that child as someone who was "given birth to" in order to "give birth to."

Recent research has examined the relations among generative action, commitment, and concern and their relative salience at different points in the adult life course. In order to assess individual differences in an adult's conscious *concern* for the next generation, McAdams and de St. Aubin (1992) developed and validated the Loyola Generativity Scale (LGS), a 20-item self-report questionnaire. To assess *action*, they employed a behavior checklist that asks a person to endorse the number of times in the preceding two months that he or she had engaged in a number of different behavioral acts, many of which suggest generativity. Examples of possible generative acts are "taught somebody a skill," "served as a role model for a young person," and "performed a community service." Generative *commitments* were assessed by asking persons to describe 10 "personal strivings" (Emmons, 1986; Chapter 8 in this book) or current goals that they were involved in, and then coding the responses for themes of generativity (McAdams, de St. Aubin, & Logan, 1993). Studies show that generative concern and generative actions are significantly positively correlated. In other words, people who express a greater concern for the next generation on the LGS also tend to report a greater number of generative behaviors over the preceding two months. Concern and action are also positively associated with number of generative commitments.

McAdams, de St. Aubin, and Logan (1993) administered measures of generativity to a community sample of 152 adults, divided into 3 age groups: young adults (ages 22–27), midlife adults (ages 37–42), and older adults (ages 67–72). Controlling for educational and income differences among the 3 groups, the researchers found a significant effect of age/cohort on generativity. Overall, midlife adults tended to score higher than younger and older adults, as can be seen in Table 10.7. In keeping with Erikson's idea that generativity is an especially salient issue of middle adulthood, the researchers found that generative concern and action were higher among adults between the ages of 37 and 42 than they were among younger adults in their mid 20s and older adults around the age of 70. Of course, these differences could be due to cohorts. Because this was a cross-sectional study, we cannot determine whether the differences observed are due to development per se or to possible historical differences between different generations of men and women growing up during different eras. In this study, the young adults were all born in the mid 1960s; the midlife adults were "baby-boomers" born in the early 1950s; and the older adults were from a generation who came of age during World War II.

Not all measures of generativity show the same age-related patterns. For example, older adults tended to score just as high as midlife adults on generative *commitments*. By contrast, young adults showed remarkably low scores on generative commitments. Adults between the ages of 22 and 27 years rarely reported that the things they were trying to do everyday (their personal strivings) involved such generative goals as becoming involved with younger people, caring for others, or making creative contributions to others. By way of illustration, consider the daily commitments reported by three women in the study—ages 26, 40, and 68 years, respectively. The young woman reports she is typically trying to "make my job more interesting than it really is," "be more open to others," "figure out what I want to do with my life," "be a good person," "enjoy life," "avoid uncomfortable situations," "keep up with current events," "be well-liked," "make my life more interesting and exciting," and "make others believe I am

TABLE 10.7	*Mean Scores on Three Features of Generativity by Age/Cohort*		
	AGES 22–27	AGES 37–42	AGES 67–72
Generative concern	40.14 (7.28)	41.82 (6.95)	38.26 (9.59)
Generative commitments	1.62 (1.43)	3.28 (1.78)	3.39 (2.19)
Generative action	26.63 (8.64)	31.55 (10.25)	28.16 (11.74)

Note: Numbers in parentheses are standard deviations.
Source: McAdams, de St. Aubin, & Logan (1993), p. 225.

Based on Erikson's seventh stage of generativity vs. stagnation, a retired person can impart his or her life—in a small way—to a younger generation by becoming involved with children, such as volunteering to tell stories to preschoolers.

completely confident and secure." Her strivings appear to revolve around social acceptance and the maintenance of daily well-being. There is no generative content, though she wishes to "be a good person." By contrast, the midlife woman describes 4 of her 10 strivings in generative terms. She is trying to "be a positive role model for young people," "explain teenage experiences to my son and help him work through difficult situations," "provide for my mother to the best of my ability," and "be helpful to those who are in need of help." Similarly, the 68-year-old woman writes that she is trying to "counsel another who was recently let go from job due to cutbacks," "help another daughter with her sick child," "help as a volunteer at a nonprofit organization," "assist a candidate running for election," and "offer financial aid to someone close (friend or relative) if needed."

The final feature of the model of generativity is (7) generative *narration*. Adults make sense of cultural demand, inner desire, concern for the next generation, belief in the species, generative commitment, and their own actions of creating, maintaining, and offering up in terms of their own narrative understanding of their life, evolving over time. Adults, therefore, consciously and unconsciously narrate for themselves and others a *generativity script.* This is an inner story of the adult's own awareness of where efforts to be generative fit into his or her own personal history, into contemporary society and the social world he or she inhabits, and, in some extraordinary cases, into society's own encompassing history. In the context of a person's self-defining life story (a concept that we will explore in greater detail in Chapter 11), the generativity script provides the adult with an envisioned ending. As adults envision how their own life stories will end, they give birth to new people (children), new ideas, and new creations that ultimately "outlive the self." Although generativity is likely to be a major concern from early adulthood onward, it may assume special prominence at midlife as the social clock suggests that the person begin the process of constructing endings, of figuring out how the story will eventually end. Of course, the literal end to life is a long way off for most midlife adults. But their apprehension that they are now at the midway point orients them to endings, motivating them to make sense again of the past and present in terms of an envisioned future ending.

Stories of Generativity   The various ways in which adults construct their life stories to accommodate their generative concerns are poignantly portrayed in Kotre's (1984) book, *Outlining the Self.* Over a series of lengthy interviews, Kotre asked adults to tell in detail the stories of their own lives. For each case, Kotre created a dramatic narrative encapsulating what he believed to be the heart of the story and then analyzed the story in terms of two or three key themes of generativity. A major theme in a few of the stories concerns the ways in which our efforts to create legacies of the self and then offer them to others may encounter insurmountable and even tragic obstacles. Some people who desperately want to bear children cannot. Some people who seek to be generative in artistic, political, scientific, literary, or social ways find their efforts stymied and their generated products rejected. Some people, by design or unwittingly, damage their own creations.

One of Kotre's most moving examples is the case of Dorothy Woodson, an African-American woman. Dorothy's account of her childhood and her adult years is pervaded by the issue of beauty *versus* ugliness. Growing up in a poor and abusive family, Dorothy believed that she was the ugliest girl in the world. "My mother was very beautiful, and I think she reacted to my ugliness." At 18, Dorothy married, and for a short time she felt that she had rid her life of ugliness. But then her first son was born:

> When my first son was born, he was very dark, and he was oh, so homely. He was just so little, you know, so withered. He was just three pounds, and he wasn't fully developed. I used to go up to the hospital every day to see him, and I'd think, "Why couldn't my first baby be more beautiful? He's ugly just like me. Why couldn't he have taken after his dad?" And sometimes I wonder, well, is that the reason he died? Did he sense that I didn't really accept him because he wasn't a beautiful baby? Didn't he have the will to live because he sensed that? I used to think that way. I try not to entertain those thoughts anymore. (Kotre, 1984, p. 42)

Though the baby gained weight and Dorothy eventually took him home, her son died shortly thereafter, from complications associated with his premature birth. Dorothy's second child, Diana, was born about one year later. She was the beautiful child for whom Dorothy had longed. The baby thrived at home for a number of months. During this time, Dorothy's husband was working extremely long hours, and she was able to spend virtually no time with him. One evening she decided to meet him for dinner. She left Diana with a babysitter, who was 13 years old. Tragically, the baby suffered third-degree burns in a mysterious mishap at home and died. Her ugly blistered and swollen body is an image that haunts Dorothy to this day.

Life has been somewhat kinder in the years since the death of Diana. Dorothy has raised a healthy son, now an adolescent, with whom she seems to enjoy a positive relationship. Though she divorced her husband, she has become closer to her family of origin. She has been relatively successful in a number of different jobs. She has become heavily involved in a church, through which she is able to be generative. She has experienced a good deal of generativity, as well, through ballet, as she believes her beautiful dancing is a gift that she can offer others. Dorothy believes that the purpose of her life is to "undo" the damage she has unwittingly inflicted on her generative creations. She seeks to erase the ugliness of the past, to replace it with the beauty of her third child, her ballet, and her religious vision of being reunited someday with a restored and beautified Diana. Kotre elaborates on the theme of "generative damage" and Dorothy's attempt to "undo":

> Recognizing that creations are flawed, knowing that one has in some way "slaughtered the innocents" under one's care can be devastating. Mirrorlike, progeny and works reflect their creator, misshapen ones saying that the creator's essence is deformed, for it grew and gave birth to this. From the subtle accusation lying in the product flows the urge to shatter or disown it, or, more commonly, to dim the recognition of damage. In the narratives I recorded, reactions to the recognition of damage varied from mild regret to extreme guilt, one of the most powerful emotions I encountered. Some realized that the destruction was a part of life, that one had both received it and dealt it out, and in neither case could it be undone. Some were silent about the harm they had done, while others alleviated their guilt by denying that harm existed, by blaming their victims, or by attributing their behavior to an uncontrollable disease that had afflicted them. A few rightly saw that their hand had been forced by external circumstances, and they were embittered; while they grieved, they retained their anger. The responsibility that Dorothy Woodson feels is almost beyond guilt, grief, or anger. No twisted defense mechanisms hide from her the fact of what happened. Her knowledge is tempered only by a belief in a resurrected life in which Diana will be "just as I saw her, but whole, not blistered." In this intuition of the future, the damage is emotionally undone. (pp. 60–61)

As in the account of Dorothy Woodson, stories of generativity often feature a theme of human *redemption* (McAdams & Bowman, in press). Protagonists struggle through difficult situations in order to create positive outcomes in the end. Parenting and other forms of generativity are usually hard work, and things do not always go according to plan. In order to keep the faith in the species that Erikson sees as central to generative strivings, adults must hold out hope that the sacrifices they make and the suffering they endure will, in some sense, "pay off" in the end. Bad things will give way to good things. People will grow and prosper. Difficulties and setbacks will be "redeemed," and life will get better in the future. As we will see in Chapter 11, highly generative adults are especially adept at crafting self-defining life stories that underscore the power of redemption. More than less-generative adults, they construct life stories that affirm human progress and growth. The differences in the stories people tell alert us to the fact that generativity expresses itself in many different ways in different people's lives. Furthermore, some people seem to be more generative at particular times in their lives than are other people. What do we know about individual differences in generativity?

Individual Differences in Generativity   In the 1990s, a number of researchers sought to measure individual differences in various aspects of generativity and to relate these differences to a range of behaviors and outcomes. As I have already mentioned, my colleagues and I developed a series of paper-and-pencil measures for assessing generative concerns, commitments, and actions. Examples of items from the Loyola Generativity Scale and the Generative Behavior Checklist appear in Table 10.8. Other researchers have used clinical ratings of case data (Snarey, 1993; Vaillant & Milofsky, 1980), classifications of semistructured interview responses (Bradley & Marcia, 1998), self-ratings of generative attributes (Ochse & Plug, 1986; Ryff & Heincke, 1983; Whitbourne, Zuschlag, Elliot, & Waterman, 1992), Q-sort personality profiles (Himsel, Hart, Diamond, & McAdams, 1997; Peterson & Klohnen, 1995), content analysis of TAT stories (Peterson & Stewart, 1996), ratings of life goals (McAdams, Ruetzel, & Foley, 1986), and content analysis of diaries and other autobiographical texts (Epsin, Stewart, & Gomez, 1990; Peterson & Stewart, 1990). The research employing these measures suggests that individual differences in generativity are significantly implicated in parenting behavior, social involvements, and psychological well-being.

An adult does not need to be a parent to be highly generative (Erikson, 1963, 1969). But highly generative adults exhibit different approaches to parenting compared with less-generative adults. Peterson and Klohnen (1995) found that highly generative women who were also mothers invested considerably more energy and commitment in parenting and showed an "expanded radius of care" (p. 20) compared with less-generative mothers. In two other studies, researchers have found that generativity in adults is associated with an *authoritative* approach to parenting (Peterson, Smirles, & Wentworth, 1997; Pratt, Danso, Arnold, & Norris, in press). As you may recall from Chapter 4 in this book, authoritative parenting combines an emphasis on high standards and discipline with a child-centered and caring approach to raising children. Authoritative parents provide their children with a good deal of structure and guidance, but they also give their children a strong voice in making family decisions. In studies done primarily in the United States, authoritative patterns of parenting have been consistently associated with a number of positive outcomes in children, including higher levels of moral development and greater self-esteem.

In a large-scale study of children enrolled in public and private elementary schools, Nakagawa (1991) found that parents scoring high on the Loyola Generativity Scale tended to help their children with their homework more, show higher levels of attendance at school functions, and evidence greater knowledge about what their children were learning in school, compared with parents scoring lower in generativity. In a sample of both African-American and white parents, another team of researchers

TABLE 10.8	*Selected Items From Generativity Measures*

The Loyola Generativity Scale: Generative Concern

For each item, mark "0" if the statement *never* applies to you, "1," if the statement *sometimes* applies to you, "2" if the statement *often* applies to you, or "3" if the statement *always* applies to you.

1. I try to pass along knowledge I have gained through my experiences.
2. I have made and created things that have had an impact on other people.
3. I have important skills that I try to teach others.
4. If I were unable to have children of my own, I would like to adopt children.
5. I have a responsibility to improve the neighborhood in which I live.
6. I feel as though my contributions will exist after I die.

The Generative Behavior Checklist: Generative Acts

Consider how often you have performed each of the behaviors listed below *during the past two months*. For each item, mark a "0" if you have not performed the behavior, mark a "1" if you have performed the behavior one time, or mark a "2" if you have performed the behavior more than once during the two-month period.

1. Read a story to a child.
2. Taught somebody a skill.
3. Donated blood.
4. Attended a neighborhood or community meeting.
5. Produced a piece of art or craft.
6. Gave money to a charity.
7. Assumed a leadership position in a group.

Source: McAdams & de St. Aubin (1992).

found that high levels of generativity were associated with valuing trust and communication with one's children and viewing parenting as an opportunity to pass on values and wisdom to the next generation (Hart, McAdams, & Hirsch, in press).

If parenting within the family is seen as the most private and local realm of generative expression, social involvements among one's peers, in churches, in the community, and through political action offer opportunities for a more public expression of generativity. It would be expected, therefore, that highly generative adults should show especially strong involvements in civic and/or religious affairs. In their study of African-American and white adults ranging in age from 35 to 65 years, Hart et al. (in press) found that high levels of generativity were associated with more extensive networks of friends and social support in the community and greater levels of satisfaction with social relationships. In addition, generativity was positively associated with church attendance and with involvement in church activities. Furthermore, adults scoring high in generativity were more likely than those scoring lower to have voted in the last U.S. presidential election, to have worked for a political party or campaigned for a candidate, and to have called or written to a public official about a social concern or problem. Cole and Stewart (1996) found that generative concern among both African-American and white women in midlife correlated highly with measures of sense of community and political efficacy, suggesting that adults with strong generative concerns also tend to express strong feelings of attachment and belongingness in their communities and tend to view themselves as effective agents in the political process. Peterson et al. (1997) showed that generativity is positively associated with interest in political issues. And Peterson and Klohnen (1995) found that highly generative women showed more prosocial personality characteristics.

Erikson believed that generativity was good for society and for the individual, too. The benefits of generativity should be seen in the strengthening of social institutions and the linking of individuals to both benevolent cultural traditions and progressive social change. At the same time, generativity should benefit the generative adult him- or herself. Erikson viewed generativity to be a sign of both psychosocial maturity and psychological health in the adult years. But what do the data show?

The data show that Erikson was probably right. Longitudinal investigations by Vaillant (1977) and Snarey (1993) have shown that ratings of generativity are positively associated with the use of mature coping strategies during times of stress and with clinically derived overall ratings of psychosocial adaptation. Studies employing the Loyola Generativity Scale and the Generative Behavior Checklist have consistently shown that these measures correlate moderately positively with self-reports of life satisfaction, happiness, self-esteem, and sense of coherence in life and negatively with depression (de St. Aubin & McAdams, 1995; McAdams et al., 1998). Similarly, Ackerman, Zuroff, and Moscowitz (in press) showed that generativity was positively associated with positive emotions, satisfaction with life, and work satisfaction among midlife adults. Among younger adults, generativity was associated with positive feelings about home life. Among midlife adults, self-report generative concern is negatively correlated with the Big Five trait of neuroticism (de St. Aubin & McAdams, 1995; Peterson et al., 1997). In a longitudinal study of women graduates from Radcliffe College and the University of Michigan, Stewart and Ostrove (1998) reported that, among a host of variables, quality of midlife roles and generativity were the only significant predictors of later midlife well-being.

Finally, in a nationwide study of over 2,000 American adults, Keyes and Ryff (1998) provided the most extensive documentation of generativity's relation to psychological well-being. The researchers found that nearly all their measures of generativity significantly predicted a composite measure of psychological and social well-being. Providing emotional support to younger people, feeling more obligated to society, having more concern for the next generation, seeing oneself as a generative resource, and possessing more generative personal qualities were all associated with higher levels of psychological and social well-being. As the authors conclude, "generative behavior, generative social obligations, and generative self-definitions are key ingredients in the recipe for psychological wellness" in adulthood (Keyes & Ryff, 1998, p. 249).

Integrity   The last stage of the life cycle, according to Erikson, is centered on the psychosocial issue of **ego integrity** *versus* **despair.** In old age, says Erikson, generativity fades as a major concern, and the adult becomes preoccupied with looking back and either accepting or rejecting one's own life as it was. In order to have integrity, the person must accept graciously his or her own life story as something that, for all its faults and foibles, "had to be and that, by necessity, permitted no substitutions" (Erikson, 1963, p. 268).

Erikson described integrity as a postnarcissistic approach to life through which a person looks back, reviews, and critiques the one life story that has been produced. Butler (1975) agrees, suggesting that many elderly people undertake a **life review,** through which they reflect upon the past in order to "settle accounts." Ego integrity seems to involve attaining a certain distance on one's own life. The elderly person who looks for integrity in life steps out of the life he or she has been making and remaking since adolescence—steps away from identity, in a postnarcissistic fashion. Now it is time to look back at the life as it was—not as something to be revised yet again, but as something to accept, enjoy, even savor (McAdams, 1993). With this acceptance comes a new wisdom, writes Erikson, which exists as the final virtue of the human life cycle. On the other hand, when the person is unable to accept his or her life as a gift, he or she experiences bitter despair.

Ego integrity and despair are probably the least examined of all of Erikson's ideas, the two most shrouded in conceptual mystery. One of the great mysteries concerns exactly *when* people encounter this final challenge of the lifespan. "Old age" is a very imprecise term. Many Americans who have been employed retire around the age of 65 or 70. The years of retirement may be seen as a postgenerative period in some, if not many, lives. Though many adults in their 70s and 80s continue to be generative by being grandparents and making other contributions to the next generation, others (finances and health willing) disengage themselves from virtually all generative pursuits and devote themselves to relaxation, fun, and golf. Does the concept of ego integrity aptly capture what is going on at this time? How do we make psychological sense of this kind of postgenerative period of the lifespan? Should it be seen as a kind of return to childhood? A reward for hard work? An escape? How does the older person make sense of this chapter in his or her life story in terms of those preceding it?

These are difficult questions that have generally not been addressed in personality theory and research. The healthy, postgenerative years that some American adults enjoy probably function in accord with a great many psychosocial demands that we do not yet clearly understand. To the extent that these years have anything to do with the urge to find ego integrity, they may be viewed as a movement away from seeing one's own life as a narrative in time. For some older adults, the "on-time" transition may, ironically, be a *transcendence* of time and the making sense of their life in time. In other words, the postgenerative years of healthy retirement may be the right time for loosening time's grip on the self. Certain Eastern religions and mystical traditions speak of the "eternal moment" that people experience when they have attained true wisdom and enlightenment. The enlightened person no longer struggles to make sense of beginnings, middles, and endings—time's great demarcations—in terms of unifying conceptions of the self and the world. The person simply exists in the moment, embracing all time in the present twinkling of an eye. Perhaps this is part of Erikson's message on ego integrity and why its attainment in the human life cycle must necessarily await the end.

JANE LOEVINGER'S THEORY OF EGO DEVELOPMENT

The highly influential theory of ego development proposed by Jane Loevinger (1976) is a neat complement to Erikson's theory of psychosocial development. Like Erikson, Loevinger proposes a broad theory that has implications for understanding the entire lifespan (Westenberg, Blasi, & Cohn, 1998). Like Erikson, Loevinger utilizes concepts that can be found in the psychoanalytic tradition. For example, Erikson is often viewed to be an "ego psychologist," and one of his central concepts is "ego identity." Similarly, Loevinger focuses on the development of "ego." The two theories differ with respect to what aspects of human experience they seek to explain. By specifying a series of developmental tasks that confront all people as they move from birth to death, Erikson's model set forth an agenda for the *content* of human life. Erikson focused on *what* we do at certain stages in the lifespan—for example, in infancy we "do" trust versus mistrust; in late adolescence we begin to do identity. By contrast, Loevinger's theory focuses mainly on *structure* as opposed to content. Structure refers to *how* something is organized or designed. Loevinger is interested in how we make sense of and synthesize our experience as we move across the human lifespan. In simple terms, Erikson tells us what life contains, and Loevinger tells us how we organize (in our mind) those contents.

The "I" and the "Me"

The word *ego* refers to "self." To understand what Loevinger is up to, we should begin by reading the opening quote from the most famous chapter ever written on the nature of "the self":

> The Me and the I—Whatever I may be thinking of, I am always at the same time more or less aware of *myself*, of my *personal existence*. At the same time it is *I* who am aware; so that the total self of me, being as it were duplex, partly known and partly knower, partly object and partly subject, must have two aspects discriminated in it, of which for shortness we may call one the *Me* and the other the *I*. I call these "discriminated aspects" and not separate things, because the identity of *I* with *me*, even in the very act of their discrimination, is perhaps the most ineradicable dictum of commonsense, and must not be undermined by our terminology here at the outset, whatever we may come to think of its validity at our inquiry's end. (James, 1892/1963, p. 166)

The quote is from the first comprehensive textbook ever written in psychology, published before the turn of the 20th century. Its author is William James

(1842–1910). James begins with a distinction that, on the surface at least, seems simple enough. The **self as I** and the **self as Me.** The self, according to James, is "duplex." Within its apparent unity are two discriminable aspects. First, there is the self as *subject:* the I who knows, feels, and acts. Second, there is the self as *object:* the Me who is known, felt, and observed in action. The I and the Me are fundamentally the same in that they both refer to the self. And yet they are fundamentally different, too. The difference is both subtle and profound, and it stems from a basic phenomenological characteristic of human experience: The person may be both the *subject and the object of consciousness at the same time. I* observe, know, and experience *myself.* The self is both knower and known.

It is easier to talk about the Me—the self as known. James suggests that the Me consists of all that a person considers to be his or her own. Not surprisingly, your body, your feelings,

William James

your values and beliefs are all aspects of your Me. In addition, however, your clothing, your boyfriend or girlfriend, your parents, the posters on your dormitory walls, your favorite sports team, and a host of other "possessions" may also be, more or less, subsumed within the Me, to the extent that they are experienced as belonging to you. Indeed, some of these external aspects of the Me may be more important components of the self than certain internal ones. For example, a very important part of my sense of self—my Me—is my books, papers, and notes collected in my office. Beyond their value to me in my everyday work, these things symbolize and affirm my sense of self as a professor of psychology who has spent much of the past 20 years studying personality. Now compare these external things to the little toe on my left foot. The toe is clearly (literally) part of me. I suppose I cherish my toe as much as most people. But what if I ran over my toe with a lawnmower? The loss of my toe would affect my life in important ways (my basketball playing would probably be compromised; I'd be embarrassed about going to the beach), but I honestly think that such a loss would be less of a jolt to my sense of self than the permanent loss of the contents of my office—losing the toe would have less effect on my understanding of who I am. Of course, I might feel different about this if I were, say, a professional athlete or a model, a person for whom the perfection of one's body is a more salient self-concern. Therefore, every person's total Me is unique. The intricate arrangement of its constituents differentiates the self from all other selves.

According to James, the Me can be roughly divided into three regions. The *material Me* is made up of one's body, clothing, certain possessions, and family members. The *social Me* consists of the recognition a person gets from other people. In fact, each person has many social Me's. In an influential passage, James writes, "a man has as many social selves as there are individuals who recognize him and carry an image of him in their minds" (p. 169). The many different self aspects we surveyed in Chapter 9—possible selves, ideal selves, ought selves, self-with-other aspects, and so on—may be seen as the confederacy of components that make up James's social Me. Aspects of the social Me can be arranged in a hierarchy. Paramount is an ultimate and ideal social Me, reflected in a person's apprehension of God or "fate" or some ultimate force, being, or power. Most human beings desire to fashion an ideal social self to be recognized by an ultimate "spectator" or ideal social "tribunal." Writes James, "all progress in the social Self is the substitution of higher tribunals for lower; this ideal tribunal is the highest; and most men, either continually or occasionally, carry a reference to it in their breast" (p. 179). The third aspect of the self-as-object is the *spiritual Me*, described by James as "the entire collection of my states of consciousness, my psychic faculties and dispositions taken concretely" (p. 170). The spiritual Me consists of our own understandings of ourselves as persons who think, feel, act, and experience life. Here are located most of the psychological attributions we make about the self—our understandings of our own traits, motives, values, beliefs, desires, fears, and so on.

As you can see by now, James's view of the Me is very broad. This contrasts starkly with his view of the I. The I is the knower at a given moment of knowing. James saw no need to posit a continuous and stable knower—a broad and pervasive I that remains the same over time. Rather, the knower changes from one moment to the next. The I is "that which at any given moment is conscious, whereas the Me is only one of the things which it is conscious *of*" (p. 182). Put simply, *the I is a moment in consciousness.* Moments follow moments in a stream of consciousness, each successive moment incorporating information from the moments preceding. Usually we experience the stream as a continuous flow, suggesting a continuity, even a permanence, of the I. Theologians have deemed this underlying, ineffable self the "soul." Some philosophers have called it the "transcendental ego." But scientific psychologists, James maintains, need not make such an assumption. To sum up:

> The consciousness of Self involves a stream of thought, each part of which as "I" can remember those which went before, know the things they knew, and care paramountly for certain ones among them as "*Me*," and *appropriate to these* the rest. This Me is an empirical aggregate of things objectively known. The *I* which knows them cannot itself be an aggregate; neither for psychological purposes need it be an unchanging metaphysical entity like the Soul, or a principle like the transcendental Ego, viewed as "out of time." It is a *thought*, at each moment different from that of the last moment, but *appropriative* of the latter, together with all that the latter called its own. All the experiential facts find their place in this description, unencumbered with any hypothesis save that of the existence of passing thoughts or states of mind. (p. 197)

Loevinger's theory focuses on the I. In the original German, Freud's concept of "the ego" is written as "das Ich." The literal translation of *das Ich*, however, is "the I." For Loevinger, the ego is the I; the ego is the individual's subjective sense of self. Therefore, the ego should not be confused with the self-as-object—that is, the various aspects of the self-concept that James identified as parts of the Me. For example, the fact that I am a professor of psychology, that I live in a white house, that I view myself as mildly introverted and generally conscientious, that I am a Cubs fan, that my model for my ought self is my wife, that I like barbecued ribs—all of this is part of my Me, my self-as-object. By contrast, the I is the perspective from which I make these self-attributions and the process by which I make them (Harre, 1998).

Developmental psychologist Augusto Blasi (1988) provides a full explanation of Loevinger's view of the I. Blasi begins by taking issue somewhat with William James. The I is more than a momentary state of consciousness, he maintains. Instead, a durable and pervasive sense of the I can be experienced and even known, albeit indirectly and not through thinking or introspection. According to Blasi, the I is tacitly and immediately grasped in and through *intentional action*. Writes Blasi, "in every intentional action that we perform, in fact in every experience that we undergo, we experience ourselves, *in the process of acting and experiencing*, as related to our actions and experiences" (1988, p. 228). In the heat of intentional action, we experience ourselves as distinct, whole agents and possessors of our own actions. Within this experience, we may isolate four dimensions of the I: agency, identity with oneself, unity, and otherness.

Agency refers to "the degree to which an action is unreflectively grasped as one's own and oneself is grasped as its source" (Blasi, 1988, p. 229). When I pick up my 2-year-old niece and give her a kiss, I never doubt the fact that I am the person who is kissing her. My sense that I am the sole agent of this action—that the kiss is mine and originates with me—is immediately and unreflectively grasped. In an intentional act, a person experiences an *identity with oneself*. In kissing my niece, I immediately understand that the person kissing her is the same person who is aware of himself kissing her. Such an identity is the foundation for self-reflection. The third dimension of the I is the experience of *unity* among the various components of an intentional action. I know that the entire sequence of picking up and kissing my niece is accomplished by the same person—that I am performing the complete sequence. It never occurs to me to suppose that the I who picked her up is different from the I who kissed her. Finally, the I is experienced in complete *otherness*. I am I; others are others. I do not confuse myself with the niece I am kissing, nor with other uncles who have kissed their nieces in identical situations.

In Blasi's view, the I is a *stance* with respect to which the person regards an object. He writes, "the subject's stance—his believing, desiring, controlling, or hoping—is not one component among others, but permeates every aspect of the action and gives unity to it" (p. 232). Similarly, a number of self theorists view the I as a *process* and the Me as a *product* of the process. The I is the *process of knowing, thinking, synthesizing, adapting, unifying, willing*, and so on. The I is understood as a grand function responsible for human intentionality and wholeness. For example, Hart (1988) writes that the self-as-subject functions to provide the person with a sense of (1) self-continuity, (2) distinctness from others, and (3) volition. The I functions to ensure that the person feels that he or she is a continuous entity across time and space, that he or she is essentially distinct from others, and that he or she is the agent of action that is willed or intended. If I feel that I am literally not the same person from one moment to the next, if I feel that I am somebody else or somebody else is me, or if I feel that my actions are not my own, then I am suffering from disorientations and disturbances of the subjective self. Such disturbances are commonly reported in schizophrenic episodes and in certain drug-induced states of consciousness.

Stages of the I

In Loevinger's view, the ego is the *master synthesizing I* that adapts to the world and makes sense of it. "The striving to master, to integrate, to makes sense of experience is not just another thing the ego does, it is what the ego is" (Loevinger, 1976, p. 5). If we see the I, then, as the general process by which each of us synthesizes or puts together our experience as our own, then we can imagine that this fundamental process changes in significant ways over the course of human life. Loevinger's model of ego development charts those changes over time.

Jane Loevinger

Loevinger's model is theoretically grounded in what she terms the *cognitive developmental paradigm* in personality psychology (Loevinger, 1987). Epitomized in the monumental work of Jean Piaget on cognitive development, this broad approach to psychology views the individual as an active knower who structures experience in ever more adequate and complex ways. Development is viewed as progression through hierarchical stages. Earlier stages must be mastered before subsequent stages can be approached. Each stage builds on its predecessor and ultimately encompasses all that comes before it. Movement from one stage to the next is a complex product of both internal maturation and external forces, which are in constant reciprocal interaction. Higher stages of development are "better" than lower ones, providing interpretive structures for the world that are more differentiated, integrated, and adequate. These and other basic tenets of cognitive developmentalism are spelled out in great detail in the huge corpus of Piaget's work (for example, Piaget, 1952, 1965, 1970; Inhelder & Piaget, 1958); in the influential writings of Kohlberg (1969, 1981) on moral development; in Perry (1970) on intellectual and ethical development; in Selman (1980) on interpersonal understanding; and in Baldwin (1897), Werner (1957), and many college textbooks in developmental psychology.

Loevinger's stages of ego development are summarized in Table 10.9. Each stage is designated by a name (for example, the "impulsive" stage) and an "I" label (for example, "I-2"). Each stage provides an overall framework of meaning that the person employs to make sense of the world. The framework of meaning can be understood in many specific areas. Table 10.9 specifies three areas: impulse control, interpersonal mode, and conscious preoccupations. In general, as one moves from lower to higher stages, the I becomes less the slave of immediate impulses and more a flexible agent that operates according to internalized standards of conduct. Interpersonally, the person moves from egocentrism through conformity to relative autonomy and mutual interdependence. With increased maturity, the issues that preoccupy the person's consciousness become less concerned with body and appearance and more centered on the internal life of feelings and fantasies as well as internalized goals and plans. With

---

TABLE 10.9   *Loevinger's Stages of Ego Development*

| STAGE | | TYPICAL MANIFESTATIONS | | |
LABEL	NAME	IMPULSE CONTROL	INTERPERSONAL MODE	CONSCIOUS PREOCCUPATIONS
I-2	Impulsive	Impulsive	Egocentric, dependent	Bodily feelings
Delta	Self-protective	Opportunistic	Manipulative, wary	"Trouble," control
I-3	Conformist	Respect for rules	Cooperative, loyal	Appearances, behavior
I-3/4	Conscientious-Conformist	Exceptions allowable	Helpful, self-aware	Feelings, problems, adjustment
I-4	Conscientious	Self-evaluated standards, self-critical	Intense, responsible	Motives, traits, achievements
I-4/5	Individualistic	Tolerant	Mutual	Individuality, development, roles
I-5	Autonomous	Coping with conflict	Interdependent	Self-fulfillment, psychological causation
I-6	Integrated		Cherishing individuality	Identity

Note: The first stage (I-1) is hypothesized to be nonverbal and therefore not readily measurable.
Source: Loevinger (1987), p. 226.

development, the person becomes more cognitively complex, adopting more sophisticated frames of reference for understanding the world. Simplistic black-and-white thinking gives way to more subtle analyses and, ultimately, to a tolerance for ambiguity and paradox.

Loevinger's model of the I is a developmental typology. While people are expected to progress through the stages in the order in which they appear, people differ with respect to their terminal level of development. In other words, people reach a particular stage and then quit moving upward, and different people quit at different stages. Individual differences in a given group are understood in terms of stages. An adult who is at the "conformist" stage of ego development (I-3) is a different "type" of person than an adult who is at the higher "autonomous" stage (I-5). Given that ego development seems to taper off after early adulthood (Lee & Snarey, 1988), it is not likely that the conformist adult will ever "catch up" with peers scoring at the autonomous level. This is a different understanding of "stage" than we see in Erikson, who assumed that normal human development involves the movement through *all* stages of psychosocial development.

The Infant I

As we will see later, Loevinger measures a person's ego development through a sentence-completion test. Because this test requires verbal ability, infants and very young children cannot take it. Consequently, Loevinger's method of assessment does not enable her to measure the development of the I in the earliest years. The first stage of ego development is a preverbal stage, Loevinger maintains, but her theory does not explicitly address what this stage is all about. A number of other theorists, however, have focused their attention on the first few years of human life, and some of their ideas help to put Loevinger's stage scheme into context.

Most theories of self assume that an infant is born without a sense of self-as-subject—without a sense of the I. For example, Allport (1955) suggested that an early sense of self develops out of basic bodily experiences in the first year of life. In his interpersonal theory of psychiatry, Harry Stack Sullivan (1953) argued that a basic self-system emerges in the first few years of life to cope with the anxiety experienced in the presence of caregivers. In Freud's view (Chapter 3), the ego emerges out of the id in order to meet the demands of the outside world. In addition, the infant comes to understand its separateness from mother with the realization that mother does not meet its every need. According to Mahler (Chapter 3), the self emerges out of interpersonal relationships via a gradual process of separation-individuation. In general, various theories affirm the view of developmental psychologist Susan Harter (1983), who writes:

> The infant's first task is the development of a sense of self as subject. Thus, the infant must come to appreciate that he or she exists as an active causal agent, a source and controller of actions, separate from other persons and objects in the world. Once this "existential" self . . . has been differentiated from others, the infant must learn to recognize those particular features, characteristics, and categories that define the self as object. A representation of self that the infant can identify must be developed. (p. 279)

The precise sequence whereby the infant first develops a sense of the I as an active causal agent and then begins to formulate a vision of the Me has been outlined by

Self-recognition: Research suggests that children begin to recognize themselves in mirrors and to develop a basic concept of self in the second year of life.

developmental researchers such as Michael Lewis and Jeanne Brooks-Gunn in their studies of visual **self-recognition** (Amsterdam, 1972; Bertenthal & Fischer, 1978; Lewis, 1990; Lewis & Brooks-Gunn, 1979). In these studies, infants are observed as they behave in front of mirrors or as they watch themselves on videotape or in photographs. Lewis and Brooks-Gunn (1979) studied infants between the ages of 5 and 24 months, employing a wide variety of measures such as attention, emotional displays, play, use of the mirror to locate objects, pointing at the self, and labelling the self. The overall results of their studies and the implications of these results for the developing I and Me are summarized in Table 10.10.

Between 5 and 8 months, infants show a wide variety of self-directed behaviors in front of mirrors. For example, they smile at their images and watch their bodies intently. However, they do not recognize distinctive features of their own bodies, and they do not appear to differentiate themselves from others. There is no evidence that they understand that what they see in the mirror is a reflection of themselves. Between 9 and 12 months, infants begin to understand the reflecting quality of mirrors. They will use mirrors to reach for actual objects attached to their bodies. Between 12 and 15 months, infants consolidate an initial sense of self as an independent causal agent. They will now use the mirror to locate other people and objects in space. When a person or object is spotted in the mirror, the infants will reach toward the actual person or object rather than toward the mirror. On videotape, infants are able to distinguish between their own movements and the movements of others.

| TABLE 10.10 | *Emergence of Self as Subject and Object, Based on Studies of Visual Recognition* |

BEHAVIORS	AGE IN MONTHS	INTERPRETATION
Self as Subject		
Interest in mirror image; regards, approaches, touches, smiles, vocalizes. Does not differentially respond to self *vs.* other in mirror, videotape, or pictorial representation.	5–8	No evidence that self is perceived as a causal agent, independent of others. No featural differentiation between self and other.
Understands nature of reflective surface: contingency play, imitation, rhythmic movements, bouncing, waving; can locate objects in space, attached to body.	9–12	Active agent in space emerges, awareness of cause–effect relationship between own body movements and moving visual image.
Uses mirror to locate people/objects in space. Reaches toward person, not image, and reaches toward object not attached to body. Distinguishes between self-movement and movement of others on videotape.	12–15	Self–other differentiation with regard to agency. Appreciates self as an active, independent, agent separate from others, who can also cause own movements in space.
Self as Object		
In mirror and videotape, demonstrates mark-directed behavior, sees image and touches rouge on nose. Points to self. Distinguishes between self and other in pictorial representation and videotape.	15–18	Featural recognition of self; internal schema for own face that can be compared to external visual image.
Verbal labeling: Infant can state name, attach appropriate personal pronoun to own image in mirror. Can distinguish self from same-gender infant in pictures and can label self.	18–24	Appreciation that one has unique featural attributes that can be verbally labeled as the self.

Source: Harter (1983), p. 283.

Now that the basic sense of I is established, an infant is ready to build an initial conception of the Me. This can be seen in mirror studies using infants between the ages of 15 and 18 months. In one version of this research, the mother applies rouge to the nose of her baby, leaving a large red spot that the baby can readily see when placed in front of the mirror. Infants younger than about 15 months of age will see the spots but not recognize them as alterations of their own faces. They may point at the spots in the mirror, but they are not likely to point directly at their own noses. After 15–18 months of age, most infants will touch their own noses when they see the rouge, showing that they have internalized an image of what their own faces should look like, that they recognize the image in the mirror as their own, and that they understand that the mark on the nose observed in the mirror signals that their own faces have been altered. As Table 10.10 shows, the Me continues to develop with the advent of language and the infant's increasingly sophisticated self-recognition behavior between the ages of 18 and 24 months.

Research and theory agree that by 2 years of age, the relatively normal and healthy infant has consolidated a basic sense of the I as an active agent clearly differentiated from the environment and others (Lewis & Brooks-Gunn, 1979; Mahler et al., 1975; Sander, 1975: Stern, 1985). The beginnings of what James called the material Me are also clearly evidenced. The four cardinal aspects of the self-as-subject—agency, identity with self, unity, and otherness (Blasi, 1988)—seem already to be manifesting themselves in the toddler's intentional acts.

The Child I

A major theme in many theories about the childhood self is the progressive movement from egocentric *impulsivity* to sociocentric *conventionality*. The synthesizing framework of meaning whereby the younger child makes sense of the world is generally viewed to be simple, concrete, one-dimensional, and rather "selfish." By the time the child has reached the age of 9 or 10 years, however, the I has become a more sophisticated and socialized structure for interpreting the world.

Loevinger (1976) argues that the self of early childhood is locked in an *impulsive* (I-2) stage. The child acts on impulse as a way of expressing the self. In general, the orientation of the impulsive stage is egocentric. The world is seen as a concrete setting for the satisfaction of personal wants and needs. The child is demanding and dependent in interpersonal relationships. Morality is primitive—what Kohlberg (1969) viewed as "preconventional morality," wherein the child understands good behavior to be that simply and only which is rewarded and bad to be that which is punished.

The impulsive stage as a general frame of reference is structurally quite simple. The child's classification of people into general categories of good *versus* bad is a global value judgment rather than an articulated moral judgment per se. Good and bad may be confounded with "nice to me" and "mean to me" or with "clean" and "dirty." Though emotional experiences may be intense during this time, the child's verbal descriptions of these experiences are relatively crude and global. The impulsive individual's orientation is primarily toward the present rather than toward the past or future. Loevinger states that the child who remains too long at this stage may be seen by others as "uncontrollable" or "incorrigible" (1976, p. 16).

Gradually the impulsive stage gives way to what Loevinger calls the *self-protective (delta)* stage of ego development. In Loevinger's view, self-protective individuals have "an appreciation of the world's rules, however wide their world may be, and know that it is to their advantage to play by the rules most of the time, (1987, p. 227). The self is a short-term hedonist at this stage, striving for the fulfillment of needs. The good life is the easy, happy life. Friendships may be viewed as nice things, to be collected, much like money: An older child or adult who stagnates at this stage may become opportunistic and deceptive in relations with others. As Loevinger (1976) puts it, "for such a person, life is a zero-sum game; what one person gains, someone else has to lose" (p. 17).

In late childhood and early adolescence, many people move from an egocentric frame of reference to an identification of one's own welfare with that of a group. This marks the developmental leap into what Loevinger calls the *conformist* (I-3) stage. Morality becomes what Kohlberg (1969) termed "conventional," defined strictly by the rules and norms of social groups or even society as a whole. People, as well, are essentially defined according to their group allegiances. The conformist values cooperation, niceness, and loyalty to the group.

According to Sullivan (1953), the conformist child or early adolescent is pressed by the emerging need for interpersonal intimacy to move beyond the safe maneuvers of the self-system and connect with others in collaborative and intimate ways. Interpersonal harmony, closeness, sharing, and identification with the other become the self's most cherished goals. The person seeks to find a special friend, or chum, who is as much like the self as possible. The welfare of the chum becomes a prime consideration, as important as one's own welfare. Through intimacy experienced with the chum, the self is able to affirm its fundamental *sameness* with another human being.

The Adolescent I

If the self of late childhood and early adolescence develops in the direction of conformity and celebrates its sameness with other selves, the self's movement through adolescence and into young adulthood is generally believed to be in the opposite direction. Many theories of self and identity suggest that the teenage years are marked by a search for individuality and uniqueness (Blos, 1979; Erikson, 1968). In Loevinger's model, conformity gives way to higher stages that emphasize how the person is no longer bound to social convention. From many different perspectives, adolescence in Western societies is often viewed as an extended *rite of passage* through which the person transforms him- or herself into an individuated adult (Conger & Petersen, 1984; Lapsley & Rice, 1988). In seeking individuality, the adolescent strives to integrate the various aspects of the self. Damon and Hart (1982) write:

> Virtually all researchers have found that, with development, adolescent self-understanding shows an increasing use of psychological and social relational concepts for describing the "Me," more prominent belief in the "I's" agency and volitional power, and a tendency toward integration of the disparate aspects of the self into an internally consistent construct system. (p. 855)

As we have already seen, "the integration of the disparate aspects of the self" is Erikson's concept of identity. In formulating an identity, the adolescent and young adult must fashion satisfying answers to the questions "Who am I?" and "How do I fit into the adult world?" The search for identity is the search for unity and purpose in life. To experience unity and purpose, a person must construct a new image of self—a

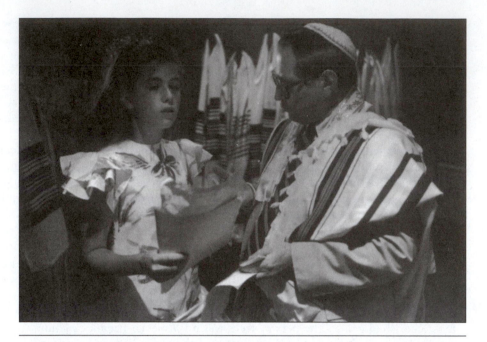

Many societies mark a person's passage from child to young adult with a ceremony, such as the Jewish Bas Mitzvah for a girl.

new Me—that incorporates the self into the world of work and love while providing opportunities for expressing unique talents, dispositions, and inclinations. The I of adolescence and early adulthood, therefore, is an ever-discerning identity maker.

According to Loevinger's theory, adolescence may usher in the transitional *conscientious/conformist* (I-3/4) stage, as the young person realizes that it is impossible to live up to all of the standards of his or her self-defining group. The break with the group and conventional thinking begins slowly with an increasing self-awareness and an appreciation for a situation's multiple possibilities. The person becomes increasingly aware of his or her inner life. In the subsequent *conscientious* (I-4) stage of ego development, the adolescent or adult has moved considerably away from conventional standards and has substituted internalized personal standards. The major elements of adult conscience are now present: long-term, self-evaluated goals and ideals, differentiated self-criticism, and a sense of responsibility. Human behavior is understood in terms of internal determinants such as traits and motives. The person experiences a rich and differentiated inner life.

The Adult I

In realizing its full potential, the adult I can become a prodigiously complex and sophisticated framework for making sense of the world. Loevinger's highest stages of ego development celebrate the synthesizing power of the adult I. Nonetheless, Loevinger maintains that most adults fall well short of the I's highest levels. Research employing

Loevinger's model of ego development suggests that most American adults score around the conscientious/conformist transition stage. Very few reach the highest echelons of her ego hierarchy. Writings on the adult self from Jung (Chapter 3) to Maslow (Chapter 8) consistently reveal that many people are unable, due to a host of internal and external circumstances, to realize the full potential of selfhood. Somewhere along the line, the knower stagnates, and the process of synthesizing experience—the self-as-subject—settles into a routine that may be adequate for daily functioning but that is less than inspiring for further growth.

Let us, however, follow the ideal and unencumbered scenario as set forth in Loevinger's scheme. At the *individualistic* (I-4/5) stage of ego development, the I develops a greater tolerance for the individuality of others and a greater awareness of the conflict between heightened individuality and increased emotional dependence. Though the realization that conflict is an inherent part of the human condition has not yet emerged, the person at the individualistic stage manifests an increased ability to tolerate paradox and contradiction—a sign of greater cognitive complexity. Distinctions are made between inner reality and outward appearances; between psychological and physiological responses; between process and outcome. Psychological causality and psychological development, "which are notions that do not occur spontaneously below the Conscientious Stage, are natural modes of thought" to people at the individualistic level (Loevinger, 1976, p. 23).

The *autonomous* (I-5) stage of ego development emerges with the capacity to cope adequately with the conflicts of the individualistic level. The individual at this level reveals tolerance for ambiguity and high cognitive complexity. He or she has acquired a respect for the autonomy of others while realizing that emotional interdependence is inevitable. Self-fulfillment partly replaces personal achievement as a central preoccupation in consciousness. The person at this stage expresses feelings vividly and convincingly, including sensual experiences, poignant sorrows, and existential humor intrinsic to the paradoxes of life. He or she formulates broad and abstract social ideals and makes decisions accordingly (Kohlberg's "post-conventional" morality). This developmental position is rare among adolescents and adults.

Rarer still is the fully *integrated* (I-6) individual. This is the most difficult stage to achieve. In general, most of what is true for the autonomous stage is also true at this level with the added elements of "cherishing individuality" and the full "consolidation of identity" (Loevinger, 1976, p. 26). At the two highest stages of ego development, the person transcends the polarities of earlier stages, seeing reality as complex and multifaceted. Opposites, from the vantage points of earlier stages, may be reconciled at the highest levels of ego development. Some of Maslow's "self-actualized" individuals (Chapter 8) may be examples of people who have attained the integrated stage of ego development.

Most Western formulations of the self's maturation in adulthood may be critiqued for their overemphasis on themes of independence, autonomy, and self-sufficiency (Broughton & Zahaykevich, 1988; Josselson, 1988). Yet themes of inclusion, connection, and interdependence can be seen in Loevinger's and many other recent formulations of self-development, as well as in Erikson's conceptions of intimacy, generativity, and integrity in adulthood. Harter (1983) suggests that the highest level of the adult self may involve "the coordination of one's own identities over a lifetime, with those of others and with cultural values, so as to form a meaningful whole" (p. 317).

In a somewhat similar vein, certain Eastern conceptions as well as humanistic theories like those of Maslow (Chapter 8) suggest that ultimate selfhood entails *transcendence* of the individual I and a *unity* with the cosmos. Such an "egoless" state is characterized by a total loss of self-consciousness and self-observation. Certain forms of Buddhism urge the adult to destroy the "illusion" of a separate I or ego. Enlightenment awaits the renunciation of self and the realization that one is subsumed by a larger whole. The same idea is expressed in other religious traditions. For example, the Christian concept of *grace* flies in the face of Western notions of the I as an active and intentional agent. According to this theological view, Christian salvation cannot be willed. Instead, the person must surrender the self to the power of Christ's gift of love and redemption.

Measuring Ego Development

Loevinger's model of ego development has been especially influential in personality psychology because the ego stages can be measured via a standardized sentence-completion test, the **Washington University Sentence Completion Test for Ego Development (WUSCTED)** (Loevinger & Wessler, 1970). The WUSCTED is composed of a series of sentence stems, such as "The thing I like about myself is . . . " and "At times she worried about. . . . " For each stem, the person writes an ending to the sentence. Each response is classified into one of Loevinger's stages, ranging from impulsive (I-2) to integrated (I-6), according to carefully designed scoring manuals (Hy & Loevinger, 1996; Loevinger, Wessler, & Redmore, 1970; Redmore, Loevinger, & Tamashiro, 1978). The scores are then tabulated and a final ego-stage score is derived according to a numerical formula. The WUSCTED is an especially useful instrument for examining individual difference in ego development among adolescents or adults. Because the test relies solely on verbal expression, all subjects must be able to read and write.

Table 10.11 presents sample responses scored for ego development to the especially self-relevant sentence stem of "I am. . . . " Loevinger's measure of ego development tends to be moderately, correlated with intelligence test scores, with correlations ranging from +.10 to +.50 (Hauser, 1976; Loevinger, 1979). But Loevinger maintains that ego development is not synonymous with intellectual ability. The WUSCTED appears to have adequate test-retest reliability and internal consistency (Redmore & Waldman, 1975). Scorers trained with Loevinger's extensive scoring manuals show very high reliability in their scoring of sentence stems.

A growing body of research attests to the construct validity (Chapter 5) of Loevinger's model of ego development and its measurement via the WUSCTED (Hauser, 1976; Lee & Snarey, 1988; Loevinger, 1979, 1983, 1984, 1987). Cross-sectional studies of people from different age groups show that, in general, adults score slightly higher than adolescents and that older adolescents score higher than younger adolescents, supporting the developmental assumptions of Loevinger's measure (Loevinger, 1984). In junior high and high school, girls tend to score slightly higher than boys, but boys may catch up in college (Loevinger, Cohn, Bonneville, Redmore, Streich, & Sargent, 1985). In adulthood, men and women show comparable overall levels of ego development (Cohn, 1991). Overall, the most common (modal)

TABLE 10.11	*Sample Responses of Women to the Sentence Stem "I am . . . "*
STAGE	**SAMPLE RESPONSES**
(I-2) Impulsive	a good girl. always good and respectful. a very pretty child when I want to be; I am *(age deleted)* and have been told to be good, so I try.
(Delta) Self-protective	easily hurt, ugly, nosy and not very tactful. crazy and in love. completely frustrated with selfish people.
(I-3) Conformist	a student. lucky to have such a wonderful husband. happy, and in a good mood, so please forgive my foolishness.
(I-3/4) Conscientious/Conformist	content most of the time. worried about my love affair. hoping for a successful future.
(I-4) Conscientious	lucky, because I love life. no better than anybody else. sorry for causing mother to worry about me.
(I-4/5) Individualistic	a rather complex person—as we all are, I think. a woman, a wife, a student, an individual person. hopeful that the state of man will become universally better.
(I-5) Autonomous	an introvert, shy, with a desire to be friendly and outgoing. too much in love with everything, and, I imagine, too unrealistic! woman living and creating life.
(I-6) Integrated	aware of human frailty and weakness, yet I believe that man can, through his own efforts, improve his own lot.

Source: Excerpted from Loevinger, Wessler, & Redmore (1970), pp. 275–286.

stage score for American youth between the ages of 16 and 26 is I-3/4, the conscientious/conformist transition stage (Holt, 1980).

Ego development is positively associated with moral development as assessed according to Kohlberg's stage model (Lee & Snarey, 1988). With respect to personality traits, McCrae and Costa (1980) found no relationship between ego level and objective measures of extraversion and neuroticism. However, openness to experience (Chapter 6) was strongly associated with ego development. People at higher (post-conformist) stages of ego development tend to score relatively high on openness to experience, reflecting an openness toward and tolerance for alternative points of view and strong aesthetic and intellectual interests. In another study pertaining to the Big Five traits, ego development among *women* was most strongly associated with openness to experience, but among *men* the strongest relation was between ego development and conscientiousness (Einstein & Lanning, 1998). Rootes, Moras, and Gordon (1980) investigated sociometrically evaluated maturity in 60 college women. After completing the WUSCTED, each woman evaluated all the others with respect to their potential for mature functioning in four adult social roles: career, marriage, parenthood, and community involvement. Ego development was positively related to peer ratings of maturity in careers and community involvement. However, it was unrelated to maturity in the two more interpersonally oriented social roles—marriage and parenthood.

Ego development is negatively associated with indices of deviance on the MMPI among adolescents (Gold, 1980) and measures of delinquency among inner-city girls (Frank & Quinlain, 1976). In general, however, ego development is *not* consistently associated with mental health and well-being. People at high stages are generally no more nor less likely to suffer from mental illness compared with people at lower stages. But mental illness may take different forms at different stages. For example, Noam (1998) has suggested that higher-stage individuals may suffer more *internalizing* forms of mental illness (e.g., depression) whereas lower-stage individuals may express mental illness in *externalizing* ways (e.g., antisocial behavior).

As one might expect, social conformity tends to peak at the middle conformist and conscientious/conformist levels of ego development and to decrease thereafter (Hoppe, 1972). Rosznafszky (1981) looked at ego development and individual differences in personality traits theoretically associated with particular ego stages. Employing the Q-sort personality ratings (Chapter 7) of 91 hospitalized male veterans made by nurses, therapists, and the patients. Rosznafszky found strong connections between stages and ratings. Impulsive (I-2) veterans manifested significantly higher levels of confused thinking, poor socialization, and limited self-awareness. Conformist (I-3) and conscientious/conformist (I-3/4) veterans placed great value on rules, accepted social conventions, material possessions, and physical appearance, and they appeared highly stable. Veterans at higher levels (I-4 and I-4/5) revealed greater insight into their own personality traits and motivations behind behavior, and expressed concern over interpersonal communication.

Oliver John and his colleagues at the University of California, Berkeley, have recently argued that Loevinger's stages of ego development map nicely onto a tripartite typology of personality characteristics (John, Pals, & Westenberg, 1998; Pals & John, 1998). In Chapter 7, we examined personality typologies, such as those developed by Jack Block (1971), which attempt to account for human individuality in terms of coherent *patterns* of traits. York and John (1992) used Q-sort ratings and inverse factor analysis to derive four different personality types among the midlife women they studied. Three of those types are the *Conflicted*, *Traditional*, and *Individuated* types. In terms of traits, Conflicted types showed high levels of neuroticism and low levels of ego resiliency, described by raters as generally anxious, hostile, and aloof. Traditional women were high in conscientiousness and ego control, tended to hold very traditional values, and suffered from relatively high levels of guilt. The Individuated women were rated as especially high in ego resilience and openness to experience, and they showed strong levels of individual ambition and personal warmth. John et al. (1998) argue that personality characteristics of Conflicted types map onto those associated with relatively low levels of ego development, Traditional types map onto middle levels, and In-

| TABLE 10.12 | *Description of the Three Personality Prototypes and Their Hypothesized Relations With Regions of Ego Development (ED)* |

PROTOTYPE	BASIC DESCRIPTION	HYPOTHESIZED RELATION WITH REGION OF ED
Individuated	Open-minded, introspective, achievement-oriented, resilient under stress, both autonomous and connected in relationships.	The Individuated prototype should be the most prevalent in the high region of ED—the Individualistic, Autonomous, and Integrated stages.
Traditional	Adopts conventional cultural norms (e.g., gender roles), and emphasizes the fulfillment of responsibilities and duties at the cost of self-expression.	The Traditional prototype should be the most prevalent in the middle region of ED—the Conformist, Self-aware, and Conscientious stages.
Conflicted	Experiences various forms of intra- and interpersonal problems, such as hostility, defensiveness, ambivalence towards commitments, anxiety, and dissatisfaction with self.	The Conflicted prototype should be the most prevalent in the low region of ED—the Impulsive and Self-protective stages.

Source: John, Pals, & Westenberg (1998), p. 1095.

dividuated types share characteristics with high levels of ego development. Table 10.12 lays out the proposed relations between types and ego development.

John et al. (1998) tested their hypothesis in a sample of women who graduated from Mills College in 1958 and 1960, the same sample used in York and John's (1992) study and in a number of longitudinal reports described in Chapter 7 of this book. When the women were 43 years of age, the researchers classified each into one of the personality types outlined by York and John, based on a wide set of personality descriptors. In addition, each woman at age 43 completed the Washington University Sentence Completion Test, which was scored for stages of ego development. In this highly educated sample, the ego scores tended to be higher than those commonly found among American adults. Nonetheless, scores from across the ego range—from impulsive (I-2) to integrated (I-6)—were found. The researchers grouped the ego scores into three "regions." The low region consisted of impulsive (I-2) and self-protective (delta) scores; the middle region consisted of conformist (I-3), conscientious/conformist, and conscientious (I-4) scores; the high region included individualistic (I-4/5), autonomous (I-5), and Integrated (I-6) stages. The researchers predicted that Conflicted women would score in the low region for ego development, Traditional women in the middle region, and Individuated women in the high region.

Figure 10.2 shows the results of the study. As you can see, the findings support the researchers' hypothesis. For example, all of the women scoring in the impulsive (I-2) and self-protective stages of ego development were classified as Conflicted based on independent personality ratings. The middle region contains women of all three types, but the Traditionals predominate. Indeed, all of the women in the conformist (I-3) stage

---

FIGURE 10.2   *Personality Prototypes and Ego Development*

The chart shows the distribution of three different personality prototypes—conflicted, traditional, and individuated—at each of six different levels of ego development. Conflicted types are overrepresented in the lowest stage, traditionals in the middle stages, and individuated at the highest stages.

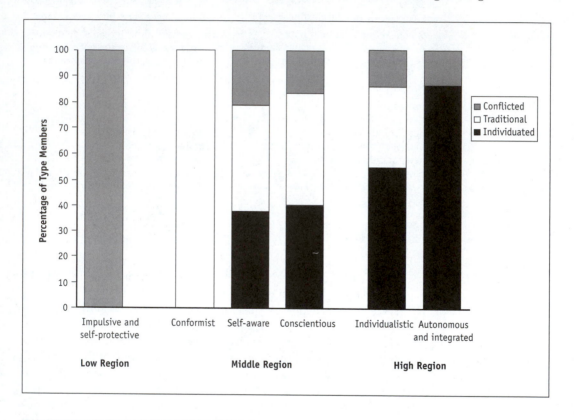

Source: John, Pals, & Westenberg (1998), p. 1102.

were rated as Traditional. The highest region of ego development has the highest percentages of Individuated women, although a few Conflicted women score at even the highest stages. In conclusion, the study by John et al. (1998) documents interesting linkages between ego development stages and independent ratings of personality characteristics comprising typologies. Women scoring at the highest levels of ego development tend to be classified by psychologists as Individuated and thereby rated as highly open-minded, introspective, and resilient under stress. Women in the middle regions of ego development tend to adopt conventional cultural norms and are seen as generally Traditional and dutiful. At the lowest levels of ego development, women are viewed as Conflicted, showing defensiveness, ambivalence, and high levels of dissatisfaction with self.

FEATURE 10.B

The I on Stage: Self-Monitoring

The famous sociologist Erving Goffman (1922–1982) took literally William Shakespeare's words that "all the world's a stage" and all the men and women are merely players on it. We are the roles we play, Goffman argued, and nothing more. From Goffman's (1959) radical *dramaturgical* perspective, the I is a position from which each of us enacts the many socially scripted roles we play, each of us performing for a particular social audience. The ultimate goal in play-acting is *impression management*. Each person must convey an appropriate impression to an audience in a given social situation. While most psychologists are uncomfortable with the idea that there may be nothing more to the self than mere play-acting, many would agree nonetheless that some people are especially adept at impression management. This individual difference has been explored by personality psychologist Mark Snyder (1974, 1983) in studies of **self-monitoring.**

Snyder assesses self-monitoring via a simple questionnaire, reproduced in Table 10.B.1. The items on the scale concern the extent to which a person monitors his or her own behavior in various situations. People who score high on self-monitoring strive to display the specific kind of behavior ideal for the situation in which they are operating at a given time. People scoring low on self-monitoring are less concerned with enacting the "correct" performance in a given situation. They are less vigilant in monitoring their own and others' behavior. Their social behavior tends to be guided by consistent internal standards rather than by the contingencies of the situation.

The self-monitoring scale has been used in a large number of research studies. Overall, the results show that people high in self-monitoring approach social situations in a highly observant and pragmatic fashion. They are quick to assess the demands of the situation and to respond accordingly. They prefer relatively structured social encounters in which roles are well understood. In terms of Chapter 5's controversy over whether behavior is determined by traits or situations, people high in self-monitoring appear to be guided by situations, more so than people low in self-monitoring, whose behavior appears to

Conclusion

From Loevinger's perspective, the I or ego may be understood as a subjective stance, process, or framework for synthesizing human experience. It is what William James called the self-as-knower, the subjective sense of self as an intentional agent in the world who is able to act upon and make sense of reality. For the most part, we take our "I-ness" for granted. We rarely question the nature of our subjective stance in the world. For most of us most of the time, therefore, the I is not a psychological problem. Instead, we seem to follow along blithely after Descartes, the French philosopher who asserted, "I think; therefore, I am." The fact that each of us comprehends the world from his or her own cognitive point of view, the fact that we experience ourselves as

FEATURE 10.B *continued*

TABLE 10.B.1	*A Scale to Measure Self-Monitoring*

1. I find it hard to imitate the behavior of other people.
2. At parties and social gatherings, I do not attempt to do or say things that others will like.
3. I can only argue for ideas which I already believe.
4. I can make impromptu speeches even on topics about which I have almost no information.
5. I guess I put on a show to impress or entertain others.
6. I would probably make a good actor.
7. In a group of people I am rarely the center of attention.
8. In different situations and with different people, I often act like very different people.
9. I am not particularly good at making other people like me.
10. I'm not always the person I appear to be.
11. I would not change my opinions (or the way I do things) in order to please someone or win their favor.
12. I have considered being an entertainer.
13. I have never been good at games like charades or improvisational acting.
14. I have trouble changing my behavior to suit different people and different situations.
15. At a party I let others keep the jokes and stories going.
16. I feel a bit awkward in public and do not show up quite as well as I should.
17. I can look anyone in the eye and tell a lie with a straight face (if for a right end).
18. I may deceive people by being friendly when I really dislike them.

Note: Score 1 point each for "Yes" answers to items #4, 5, 6, 8, 10, 12, 17, and 18. Score 1 point each for "No" answers to items #1, 2, 3, 7, 9, 11, 13, 14, 15, and 16. Add up the points. Higher scores mean higher self-monitoring.
Source: Snyder & Gangestad (1986), p. 137.

thinkers and knowers in the world and that we almost always take for granted that our thoughts are indeed *our own* thoughts gives us a deep confidence that we exist as selves—that the I *is*.

But even though the I is, the I does not remain the same I over the course of the lifespan. Rather the I appears to develop through a series of well-documented stages. The subjective stance from which the 4-year-old makes sense of the world is a very different I than what we see among adolescents and adults. Early and developmentally immature manifestations of the I are variously described as egocentric, preconventional, and impulsive. As the child grows up, the I takes on the perspectives of the social world; the I becomes conventional or conformist. This is an important and positive step in the development of the self, for it marks the person's emergence as a socialized being, a working member of the social context, able to take on the values, norms, and standards of the context, able to defer immediate gratification for long-term, socially sanctioned rewards, able to see reality from the collective point of view.

be guided more by internal dispositions (Snyder, 1983). Therefore, high self-monitors tend to show minimal consistency between their trait scores on standard personality measures and their display of trait-related behavior. For instance, an extravert who is high in self-monitoring will be outgoing and sociable *only* in situations that call for such a performance. If the situation suggests that an introverted display is more in order, he or she will readily alter the behavioral display. Not only will people high in self-monitoring astutely judge what the actor should do in a situation, but they are also likely to be better actors. For instance, they are especially adept at expressing emotions through facial movements, at deceiving others, and at reading others' facial expressions (Snyder, 1979).

By contrast, people scoring low in self-monitoring tend to be less sensitive to the nuances of situations and less likely to mod-

ify their behavior according to situational demands. More introspective than people high in self-monitoring, they show marked consistency between their personality-trait scores and the behavior they display in various situations. Of course, nobody is completely oblivious to situational information. But the extravert low in self-monitoring is more likely than his or her counterpart scoring high on Snyder's scale to behave in an outgoing and sociable fashion in many *different* situations, even when such behavior is not exactly what the situation demands. People low in self-monitoring tend to have fewer friends than those high in self-monitoring, but they engage in more different kinds of behavior with any or all of them. Less concerned with keeping roles clear and structured, they encourage social contact among their friends, even when the friends are very different from each other.

But conformity is not the end, suggests Loevinger. The most mature manifestations of the I move beyond social conventions and appeal to higher, post-conventional truths. If the person is to reach the highest stages of ego development, the I must come to synthesize experience in increasingly complex ways, adopting multiple perspectives, cultivating a rich inner life, and fashioning a personal code of conduct—a working conscience—that transcends the conventional do's and don'ts offered by parents, peers, religion, government, and even society at large (Loevinger, 1992). Ironically, as the I moves away from society's norms to adopt higher perspectives that are more complex and personalized, becoming more independent of social norms, it becomes more cognizant of the fact that no person is indeed fully independent and autonomous. Instead, I's are linked in bonds of interdependence. By maturing beyond the dictates of society, the I seems to move closer to people, both in the particular and in the abstract. At the highest level of ego development, people sometimes report a perceived kinship with their fellow human beings. And they may experience ever-more meaningful and fully reciprocal relationships with the most important particular people—

spouse, lover, children, parents, friends—in their own lives. As the I comes to cherish its own individuality, therefore, it becomes better able to cherish the individuality of others.

The two theories of personality development that we have examined in this chapter provide different but complementary views of how human individuality evolves across the human lifespan. As we have just seen, Jane Loevinger's model of ego development charts the evolving sense of subjective selfhood—the I—as it develops from a primitive and egocentric stance in childhood through stages of social conformity in the middle regions of ego development to the higher stages of autonomy and integration. Loevinger's theory focuses on systematic change over time in *how* people make sense of their subjective experience, the *structure of* their meaning-making efforts. Erik Erikson's theory of psychosocial development focuses less on the how and more on the *what*—that is, what kinds of psychosocial tasks and challenges a person faces as he or she moves across the lifespan, from birth to death. Each of Erikson's stages is defined by the *content* of a psychosocial dilemma, couched as a contrast between, for example, trust versus mistrust (infancy) or generativity versus stagnation (middle adulthood). If a person lives into old age, Erikson maintains, he or she will move through all eight of the psychosocial stages. By contrast, Loevinger's model suggests that most people will not reach the highest stages of ego development. Like Maslow's hierarchy of needs (Chapter 8), Loevinger's model is hierarchical; the highest stages are built upon the lower ones, and most of us are unable to climb all the way to the top. Erikson's stages build on one another only in a very loose sense, in that successes in early stages can help promote development through later ones. But the later stages are not really "higher" in a hierarchical sense; they are simply "later" in time. You don't "climb up" Erikson's stage model; instead, you move across it, over time.

Both Loevinger and Erikson alert us to the fact that critical aspects of human individuality are contextualized in developmental time. If we are to understand a person fully, we must tap into those constructs of individuality that are anchored in development. Concepts such as "generativity" and "the conformist stage of ego development" cannot be understood outside the context of developmental time. Unlike personality traits (Chapters 5–7), these kinds of concepts require a developmental framework to flesh out their meaning. Among other things, developmental adaptations suggest that people at different stages of development are to be understood with respect to different theoretical concepts. For example, a personality portrait of a 45-year-old woman would be very incomplete if it did not address the characteristic ways in which she has met the challenges of generativity versus stagnation. A personality portrait of a 21-year-old man, by comparison, may leave blank the concept of generativity but will instead focus on issues of identity and, perhaps, intimacy. In this sense, developmental constructs are contingent and contextualized. In sharp contrast, it makes perfect sense to speak of personality traits, such as extraversion and neuroticism, as they apply to both the 45-year-old woman and the 21-year-old man. Less contingent and contextualized than characteristic adaptations, personality traits offer generalizations about behavior that may be applicable across many different life contexts. A full account of human individuality, therefore, requires both kinds of perspectives. Traits (Chapters 5–7) provide an initial sketch of human individuality; characteristic adaptations such as motives and goals (Chapter 8), cognitive representations of self and other (Chapter 9), and developmental tasks and stages (Chapter 10) help to fill in the details.

SUMMARY

1. Erik Erikson's psychobiography of Martin Luther, the 16th-century church reformer, sets the stage for a consideration of developmental adaptations in the study of human individuality. Erikson documents the protracted identity crisis that Luther experienced as a young adult, beginning in 1505 when he decided to become a monk and culminating in 1517 when he nailed to the castle door in Wittenberg the 95 theses that instigated the Protestant Reformation in Europe. Erikson's concept of "identity" is a classic developmental adaptation, in that it specifies a particular psychosocial issue that lies at the heart of human individuality during a particular period in the lifespan. Like motives and goals (Chapter 8) and like social-cognitive adaptations (Chapter 9), developmental tasks and stages go beyond dispositional personality traits (Chapters 5–7) to flesh out the details of human individuality.

2. Erikson articulated a highly influential theory of psychosocial development. The theory sets forth eight stages of development, each defined by a critical psychosocial dilemma. Erikson's stages build on Freud's model of psychosexual development, but they go well beyond Freud in emphasizing social context and interpersonal relations and in extending developmental change across the entire human lifespan, from birth to death. Erikson argued that at each stage a person's life must be understood on three different but interrelated levels—body, ego, and family and culture.

3. The first four stages in Erikson's scheme mark the childhood years. In the first stage of trust versus mistrust, the infant forms attachment bonds with caregivers and establishes a sense of security in the world. In autonomy versus shame and doubt, the toddler begins to develop a sense of an autonomous self. The stage of initiative versus guilt parallels Freud's Oedipal stage, within which the young child struggles with the dynamics of power and sexuality. Children in the third stage are "on the make," as Erikson puts it, as they vigorously seek to make the world conform to their own, sometimes egocentric, wants and viewpoints. The fourth stage of industry versus inferiority follows the resolution of Freud's Oedipus complex and marks the child's movement into a broader world of socialization, as represented in schooling. Of central significance during this fourth stage are the developing use of tools and the emergence of important social roles.

4. Adolescence ushers in Erikson's fifth stage—identity versus role confusion. With the emergence of genital sexuality, advent of formal operational thinking, and rising cultural expectations concerning this period in the lifespan, adolescents first confront the psychosocial questions of "Who am I?" and "How do I fit into the adult world?" The problem of identity is the problem of finding unity and purpose amidst the diversity and contradictions of modern adult life. In order to consolidate an identity, a young person must develop an occupational niche and formulate a personal ideology. Research on identity has identified four different identity statuses among young people: identity achievement (the person has explored identity options and subsequently made identity commitments), moratorium (the person is currently exploring identity options but has not yet made commitments), foreclosure (the person did not explore options but made commitments to childhood or conventional modes of being), and diffusion (the person has not explored options and has not yet made commitments).

5. In Erikson's model, the person is best able to confront the sixth stage of intimacy

versus isolation after successfully consolidating an identity at Stage 5. In intimacy versus isolation, the young adult seeks to form long-term bonds with others, epitomized in marriage or long-term romantic commitments. With the resolution of intimacy, the person is then psychosocially ready to address the issue of generativity versus stagnation (the seventh stage). To be generative is to generate a legacy of the self for the good of future generations. The prototype of generativity is giving birth to and raising children, but generativity can also be experienced and expressed in mentoring, teaching, volunteer work, community involvements, and a wide range of other behaviors.

6. Recent theoretical and empirical work on generativity has distinguished among many different features of the concept. According to one model, generativity begins with desires for both symbolic immortality (agency) and nurturance (communion) which are reinforced and augmented by cultural demands and expectations concerning how men and women should behave as they move into and through midlife. Desire and demand give rise to a concern for the next generation, which may lead to generative commitments and goals designed to translate concern into action. Generative actions may take the form of creating or giving birth to new things (and people), maintaining that which is deemed to be of good use for the future generation, and offering up those things that have been created or maintained to others. What Erikson identified as a belief in the species, or a faith in the worthwhileness of the human enterprise, helps to enhance and vitalize generative efforts. Recent research has focused on individual differences in generativity, with studies showing that adults who score high on paper-and-pencil measures of generativity tend to combine warmth and discipline in effective ways as parents, tend to be highly involved in community and religious activities, and tend to show higher levels of psycholog-

ical well-being. Following generativity versus stagnation, the last stage in Erikson's scheme is ego integrity versus despair, associated with old age and the challenge to accept graciously the life that one has been given.

7. While Erikson's theory focuses on the content of developmental tasks, Jane Loevinger's theory of ego development focuses on the structure of the self, or ego, as it develops over time. Stemming from William James's distinction between the self-as-I and the self-as-Me, Loevinger focuses on the "I"—the subjective sense of selfhood, or process of knowing and appropriating experience as one's own. The ego is the master synthesizing I that adapts to the world and makes sense of it. The ego develops through stages, moving from primitive and egocentric ways of knowing to more complex, differentiated, and integrated perspectives.

8. Although the newborn may not have a sense of subjective self, the I emerges in development during the first two years of life. Studies of self-recognition behavior show that human infants develop a sense of self-as-subject—an active, causal I—by the time they are about 18 months of age. During this time, the ego is in a preverbal stage. Loevinger's stage model begins once this initial stage has been consolidated. Thus, the first measurable stage of ego development in her scheme is the impulsive (I-2) stage.

9. Through childhood, adolescence, and adulthood, the sense of self moves through the impulsive stage to more socialized stages of conformity and conventionality. In the conformist (I-3) stage of ego development, the self interprets the world from the standpoint of "fitting in" to groups, seeking social acceptance and approval. The self begins to emancipate itself from convention in the conscientious/conformist and conscientious (I-4) stages of ego development, wherein self-evaluated standards replace concrete rules and group norms as guides for behavior.

At the higher stages of ego development—the autonomous (I-5) and integrated (I-6) stages—the subjective self becomes highly differentiated and nuanced in its interpretation of experience. Higher stages are marked by concerns for self-fulfillment and actualization and the resolution of conflicts that emerge when individuality collides with interdependence.

10. Individual differences in stages of ego development are assessed through a sentence-completion test, developed by Loevinger and her colleagues. The test has generated a considerable amount of research. Studies show, for example, that while females score higher than males on ego development in adolescence, gender differences disappear by adulthood. The modal or most common level of ego development among American adults is between I-3 and I-4, or the conformist/conscientious stage. People at higher stages of ego development tend to score high on the trait of openness to experience.

Integrating a Life: The Stories People Live By

Personality traits and characteristic adaptations sketch an outline and fill in some of the details in accounting for human individuality. But what is still missing is the overall meaning of a person's life. At the third level of personality—the level of integrative life stories—the psychologist is able to discover and construct the narrative patterns that make human lives make sense. Many scholars argue that human lives are storied constructions, complete with beginnings, middles, and endings, and with the key story features of settings, scenes, characters, plots, and themes. People give their own lives meaning and purpose by constructing internalized and evolving life stories (first-person accounts), and psychologists sometimes attempt to understand the overall meaning of the single life by constructing a theoretically informed interpretive story (third-person account). In Chapter 11, we will examine theory and research concerning people's own, first-person, self-defining life stories. Tomkins's script theory highlights the organization of emotionally charged life scenes into self-defining scripts. McAdams's life-story model of identity contends that beginning in late adolescence, people living in modern societies construe their lives in narrative terms, creating life stories with self-defining life episodes and personified self-characters that can be reliably and systematically analyzed in terms of such themes as agency, communion, redemption, and contamination. Hermans offers a related narrative theory that underscores the dialogical nature of selfhood and multiple positions from which life stories are articulated. In Chapter 12, we will consider psychologists' efforts to construct third-person narrative accounts of the life course, as in case studies and psychobiographies. An important figure in this regard is Henry Murray, who launched the personological tradition in the 1930s. The personological tradition has typically emphasized biography, myth, narrative, and the intensive exploration of the single case. Like Murray, Alfred Adler developed an approach to personality that underscored the ways in which the human life course is structured like a story, beginning with the earliest memory or origin myth and projecting into the future and the story's ending through what Adler called a fictional finalism. We end by contrasting life-stage and life-course perspectives on life stories, illustrating how psychologists have conceived of adult life in terms of socially constructed chapters and turning points. The life-course perspective emphasizes the role of human agency and individuality in life stories, which brings us full circle and reminds us of the prime goal of personality psychology, which is to formulate a scientifically credible account of human individuality.

Life Scripts, Life Stories

11

A year or two before he was assassinated, the Reverend Martin Luther King, Jr., came to a small city in the midwestern part of the United States to speak to civic and religious leaders and to rally citizens, black and white, for civil rights. Jerome Johnson was assigned to be King's bodyguard. Johnson was a black policeman in his early 30s, an ambitious man who had been a football star in high school and who completed a tour of duty with the U.S. Air Force. Johnson dreamed of becoming a police chief. But he was frustrated. No black man had ever even been promoted to sergeant in that city, let alone been seriously considered for chief. Johnson's fellow officers counseled against taking the promotional exam. His friends told him that he should be satisfied with what he had. Johnson was beginning to lose hope in his dream. He was seriously considering quitting the force.

And then Martin Luther King, Jr., came to town, and this event turned Jerome Johnson's life around. In a life-story interview conducted over 30 years later, Johnson describes what happened:

> [The turning point in my life] was back during the time I had mentioned earlier [in the interview] about my thoughts and feelings about not taking the promotional exam the department had. Even thinking about leaving the police force because I felt it was a hopeless thing that a black could ever be a police chief. I mentioned before about quitting the basketball team [in college] and I have to say I had given strong thoughts to leaving the police force because of what I saw was happening to minorities there, you know, about [bad] assignments and all that stuff that happened. And then it was at the time I was assigned to be the bodyguard for Dr. Martin Luther King. And he was here, I think maybe two, three days. And so I spent some time with him. . . . [On the last day] he was getting ready to leave, and he was standing in front of the hotel and waiting for transportation to take him to the airport. And we started talking, and I told him how frustrated I was about the fact that no black had ever been promoted. Maybe it's time to move on [I told him] because I didn't see there was anything that was gonna change at all. And he just said a couple of things, just very briefly he said, you know, he said, "Never give up." And that was basically the end of the conversation, and I thought about that before, but when he said it to me, and the way he said, "Keep the faith," you know, and "Never give up," you know, and "Never stop dreaming the dream," you know. And I held on to that, and I went on, and things changed. . . . He turned me around from walkin' out the door. (McAdams & Bowman, in press, p. 1)

Jerome Johnson eventually took the exam and was promoted to sergeant. In the years following, he continued to rise through the ranks in the police department. He eventually realized his dream and became the first African-American police chief in that Midwestern town. After serving as chief, he took an early retirement. Today, Johnson spends more time with his wife and adult children. He plans to write a book about his experiences on the force. He hopes to be a grandfather soon. He invests a great deal of energy in volunteer community work with black youth.

Notice the structure of Jerome Johnson's turning point scene. The scene begins in hopelessness, but the situation is transformed rather dramatically by a fortuitous meeting with Martin Luther King, Jr. In simple terms, there is a movement in the scene from a negative situation to a positive outcome. Johnson's life story, as he tells it in retirement, is filled with these kinds of redemptive scenes, through which bad events turn good. He begins the account of his life in this way. He was born during the Great Depression of the 1930s: "I was a Depression baby," Johnson begins, "so we went through some very difficult times, when there was, you know, no food and there was no money available. I do remember the struggles and things we had to overcome, and I really remember the hungry stomach and I remember the Christmases when there was nothing under the tree" (McAdams & Bowman, in press, p. 4). But these difficult times eventually get better, and amidst the suffering Johnson recalls scenes of tremendous kindness and care. People were hungry, yes. But people helped each other out:

> I think about how growing up that things were like a real community. I mean, even though we were young and we were struggling and people all around you were all struggling, we all, people contributed to each other, you know. If we didn't have enough food, someone would bring us something. Vice versa, my dad would bring something in, and we'd be able to share that with somebody else, and just kind of a community of responsibility that was there and I think has always made an impact upon me, that people reached out and helped each other then. (McAdams & Bowman, in press, pp. 4–5)

Jerome Johnson was an above-average student in school and a first-rate athlete. In a large and overwhelmingly white high school in the early 1950s, he excelled in football and basketball. In his senior year, he was voted captain of the football team. Johnson made many friends among the white students. He remembers fondly the many good teachers he had, and the football coach who worked hard to bring more black students onto the team. But like all his black peers, he was also victimized by racial prejudice. In one scene, his mother runs home in tears after attending a basketball game in which the opposing team taunts Jerome by calling him a "nigger." In another scene, school administrators refuse to permit Johnson, as football captain, to walk out on stage with the homecoming queen to lead the traditional homecoming pep rally before the school's biggest game of the year. He is black, and the homecoming queen is white. The image of a beautiful white woman and a strong black man standing together on stage and jointly whipping the crowd into a frenzy was just too jarring for some white teachers, students, and parents to take in this small American city in the early 1950s. Forty years later, Johnson says that he still feels pain when he recalls the homecoming scene.

But Johnson persevered, and prospered. Repeatedly, bad events turn into good outcomes. The high school "environment was very difficult to deal with," he concedes, but "I think the things I faced there helped me to be stronger in my lifetime" (McAdams & Bowman, in press, p. 6). Through college and the Air Force, Johnson suffers his fair share of disappointments and setbacks, but he continues to grow in confidence and hope. Returning home after his military service, Johnson takes on a series of jobs but makes no progress until he joins the police force. Now in his mid 20s, he begins to make long-term plans for his life. He will marry and have a family. He will rise through the ranks, eventually to become police chief. He will do volunteer work in his community. He will build up a reputation as a good family man, solid citizen, and upstanding representative of the black middle class. He will be a leader. When asked to describe the high point in his life story, Johnson gives a detailed account of how he planned assiduously and worked so hard to become police chief, the strategic relationships he cultivated along the path, the vision he articulated for the future of the force. Throughout Johnson's story, he is the ever-hopeful protagonist who works hard to overcome obstacles and accomplish his goals. In his spare time, Johnson reads books about slave life and the history of blacks, "What they went through and overcame." "I guess I'm kind of one-dimensional on this," Johnson admits (McAdams & Bowman, in press, p. 8). His favorite stories from childhood were his grandfather's tales of overcoming adversity.

What might we say about Jerome Johnson's personality? Given the proper research instruments, we could certainly evaluate his dispositional traits. Indeed, the questionnaires Johnson completed suggested that he scored high in conscientiousness and agreeableness, in the moderate range on openness to experience and extraversion/introversion, and low in neuroticism. As we saw in Chapters 5–7, trait attributions like these provide an invaluable outline of a person's dispositional signature. To fill in some of the details, we might move to a second level of personality description, to specify the characteristic adaptations in Jerome Johnson's life (Chapters 8–10). He would appear to be a man with strong achievement motivation and clear goals to be a grandfather and to continue his work as a community volunteer in the future (Chapter 8). In terms of Kelly's cognitive theory, Johnson has developed strong personal constructs around the polarity of "hard work versus laziness" and "helping others versus self-indulgence;" his self-schemata likely capture these important social-cognitive distinctions that he repeatedly makes (Chapter 9). With respect to developmental adaptations, Johnson appears to be in Erikson's seventh stage of "generativity versus stagnation"—indeed he appears to be a highly generative man—and his sentence-completion responses place him roughly in the Conscientious/Conformist stage (I-3/4) in Loevinger's developmental scheme (Chapter 10).

Dispositional traits and characteristic adaptations do a good job of outlining and fleshing out some of the most important features of Jerome Johnson's individuality. But when we hear Johnson describe his encounter with Martin Luther King, Jr., and his account of growing up poor in the Depression and rising in society to become a chief of police, we may feel that the trait attributions and the analysis of motivational, social-cognitive, and developmental adaptations leave something out. We may feel that while we have a good understanding of behavioral consistencies in Johnson's life (via traits) and a good understanding of what his central motives and goals are, how he characteristically construes self and social behavior, and what developmental tasks he currently faces, we may nonetheless feel that something is missing from the picture. That something is *what Jerome Johnson's life means in the overall to Jerome Johnson*. In modern society, many men and women expect that their own lives and the lives of others should be endowed with some central meaning, some overall unity and purpose. As we saw in Chapter 4, cultural modernity has raised people's awareness of the extent to which they are responsible for constructing a self or identity that provides their own lives with some sense of overall meaning. While traits, motives, values, stages, and so on may hint at important meanings that people develop in their lives, none of the constructs that personality psychologists study at what I have identified in this book as Levels 1 and 2 have the breadth and scope to provide a full account of overall meaning and purpose in life. None of these concepts is integrative enough; none is able to put together the many different aspects of a human life into some kind of meaningful whole.

In the modern world, what gives human lives meaning and purpose? Many scholars have recently argued that modern lives are meaningful to the extent that they conform to or express culturally meaningful *stories* (Bruner, 1990; Cohler, 1982; Josselson, 1995; MacIntyre, 1984; McAdams, 1985, 1990b; Polkinghorne, 1988). In the modern world, writes Anthony Giddens (1991), "a person's identity is not to be found in behavior, nor—important though this is—in the reactions of others, but in the capacity *to keep a particular narrative going*" (p. 54). Jerome Johnson tells a life story in which negative events are repeatedly redeemed by positive outcomes. Beginning in the Great Depression and running into the late 1990s, it is a story of steady progress in the face of many obstacles, especially those obstacles related to race and class. The key event in the story is a transformative encounter with a famous historical person. Jerome Johnson's life story is unique to Jerome Johnson, but like most any life story constructed by an American adult, it is filled with some of the classic features of Western narrative: a setting, main characters (including heroes and villains), plots and subplots (stimulated by problems or conflicts), key scenes (high points, low points, turning points), and an envisioned ending (imagined for the future). Like you and me, Jerome Johnson "has" and is "working on" a life story. In order to provide a detailed account of Jerome Johnson's individuality, we must have some understanding of that story.

In this chapter, we will focus on people's life stories. We will see that a life story is not simply an objective account of "what really happened" in the past. Though life stories are (and should be) grounded in reality, they are nonetheless imaginative and creative productions that each of us constructs and reconstructs as we move through our adult years. A person's internalized and evolving life story is just as much a part of his or her personality as is his or her dispositional traits and characteristic adaptations (McAdams, 1995, 1996a). While life stories are no less or more important for understanding a person than are traits and adaptations, they do provide a different kind of information about human individuality. Put simply, traits (Level 1) provide a dispositional outline concerning cross-situational trends in behavior; characteristic adaptations (Level 2) fill in the details by specifying motivational, social-cognitive, and developmental issues and concerns; life stories (Level 3) tell us how a person sees his or her life in the overall and over time and what the overall meaning and purpose of that life might be. All three levels of personality are important. In order to obtain as full an account as possible of human individuality, the personality psychologist needs to examine the person's patterning of dispositional traits, characteristic adaptations, and integrative life stories.

THE MEANING OF STORIES

The Narrating Mind

Human beings are storytellers by nature. In its many guises as folk tale, legend, myth, epic, history, pantomime, motion pictures, and even the evening news, that form of expression we call "the story" appears in every known human culture (Howard, 1991; Mink, 1978; Sarbin, 1986). The story is a natural package for organizing many different kinds of information. Storytelling appears to be a fundamental way of expressing ourselves and our worlds to others (Coles, 1989; Howard, 1989; Linde, 1990; Vitz, 1990). Think of the last time you tried to explain something really important about yourself to another person. The chances are good that you accomplished this task by telling a story. Or think of an especially intimate conversation from your past. I suspect that what made the conversation good was the kind of stories that were told and the manner in which the stories were received. Indeed, much of what passes for everyday conversation between people is storytelling of one form or another. We are born to tell stories, some scholars suggest. This is part of what makes us so different from both the beasts and the computers.

Imagine our ancient ancestors, at day's end, in that ambiguous interlude between the victories and defeats of the daylight and the deep sleep of the dark. Home from the hunt, or resting at the end of a day's foraging for food, providing for the young, or defending the tribe, our primordial forebears sit down together and take stock. Before night falls, they tell stories of the day. They pass the time by making sense of past time. They tell of their experiences to entertain and enlighten each other, and perhaps, on occasion, just to stay awake. E. M. Forster (1954), the novelist and essayist, once wrote: [Primordial] "man listened to stories, if one may judge by the shape of his skull. The primitive audience was an audience of shock-heads, gaping round the campfire, fatigued with contending against the mammoth or the whooly rhinoceros, and only kept awake by suspense. What would happen next?"

The stories told at day's end created a shared history of people, linking them in time and event, as actors, tellers, and audience in an unfolding drama of life that was made more in the telling than in the actual events to be told. Stories are not like the secretary's minutes of the last meeting, written to report exactly what transpired at the meeting and at what time. Stories do not work to replay a videotaped past that can be

A !Kung bushman enthralls his audience with a story. Oral storytelling serves many functions in societies today just as it has throughout human history.

objectively known and reviewed. Stories are less about facts and more about meanings. In the subjective and embellished telling of the past, the past is constructed—history is made. The history is judged to be true or false not solely with respect to its adherence to empirical fact. Rather hi*story* is judged with respect to such narrative criteria as "believability" and "coherence." There is a *narrative truth* in life that seems quite removed from logic, science, and empirical demonstration (Spence, 1982). It is the truth of a "good story." In the words of one writer, this is a form of truth with which our ancient ancestors were intimately familiar:

> No one in the world knew what truth was till someone had told a story. It was not there in the moment of lightning or the cry of the beast, but in the story of those things afterwards, making them part of human life. Our distant savage ancestor gloried as he told—or acted out or danced—the story of the great kill in the dark forest, and that story entered the life of the tribe and by it the tribe came to know itself. On such a day against the beast we fought and won, and here we live to tell the tale. A tale much embellished but truthful even so, for truth is not simply what happened but how we felt about it when it was happening, and how we feel about it now. (Rouse, 1978, p. 99)

Jerome Bruner (1986, 1990) argues that human beings understand the world in two very different ways. The first is what he terms the **paradigmatic mode** of thought. In the paradigmatic mode, we seek to comprehend our experience in terms of tightly reasoned analyses, logical proof, and empirical observation. We seek to order our world in terms of logical theories that explain events and help us predict and control reality. In the paradigmatic mode, we look for cause-and-effect relationships. When we understand how our car's engine works or how a water molecule is formed from the joining of two hydrogen atoms and one oxygen atom, then we are employing successfully our gifts of logical, causal reasoning. Much of our educational training reinforces the paradigmatic mode. Good logicians and scientists are especially well-trained in this general way of thinking.

By contrast, the **narrative mode** of thought concerns itself with stories, which themselves are about "the vicissitudes of human intention" organized in time (Bruner, 1986). In stories, events are not explained in terms of physical or logical causes. The narrative mode does not generally operate in the realm of automobile engines or molecular chemistry. Instead, it deals with human wants, needs, and goals. In the narrative mode, events are explained in terms of *human actors striving to do things over time*. If I am to tell a good story about anything, then I must present a believable narrative concerning the motivated actions and meaningful ends of human behavior, rendered in time, with beginning, middle, and end. Therefore, I may wish to explain a friend's unusual behavior this weekend in terms of my understanding of what the friend wants in life and why he has never been able to get it, going back in my account to frustrations he experienced three years ago with his wife. To understand him and his behavior, I say, you must know the story I am to tell. Similarly, to understand what drives Jerome Johnson to defy the demographic odds and become the first African-American police chief in his city, you must understand *his* story as he understands it, from the Depression years to his meeting with Martin Luther King, Jr., to his current vision for his retirement years. We must comprehend his storied account of his intentions organized in time.

Good novelists and poets are masters of the narrative mode. These storywriters are especially effective when they, in Bruner's words, "mean more than they can say" (Cordes, 1986). In other words, a good story will generate many different meanings, functioning to trigger presuppositions in the reader. We have all had the experience of comparing what we "got out" of a good story—say, a movie, play, or novel—to the view of a friend, only to learn that the two of us have read or understood the same story in very different ways. This is part of the reason that stories are fun and valuable, for they give us many different ideas and opinions around which we can have friendly, and sometimes not-so-friendly, conversations and arguments. Good stories seem to *give birth* to many different meanings, generating "children" of meaning in their own image.

By contrast, masters of the paradigmatic mode try to "say no more than they mean" (Bruner, in Cordes, 1986). A good scientist or logician works for clarity and precision. Scientific and logical explanations are constructed in such a way as to block the triggering of presuppositions. These explanations do not create other explanations in their own image. They do not encourage differences of opinion. If they did, they would be accused of being vague or ambiguous, of generating too many different and competing interpretations for what demands a single objective truth. For all its power and precision, the paradigmatic mode is a strangely humbler form of thought than story making. While it seeks to untangle cause and effect and to explain the workings of the world in the clearest and most rational manner possible, it is not generally able to make much sense of human desire, goal, and social conduct. Moreover, unlike the story, it does not give birth.

What Is a Story?

My 6-year-old niece knows what a story is. Of course, she cannot give me a formal definition that would pass muster in a literary journal. But she knows a story when she hears one. And she can tell the difference between a story and something else.

I might try this experiment with my niece. Imagine that I were to read to her two different written passages, each about five minutes long. Let us say that she has never heard either passage before. The first is a Portuguese folk tale about a young boy who tries to find a special fruit that gives off magical powers. The second is a set of instructions from a brand new game involving Barbie dolls. Both accounts are written to be interesting and entertaining for children. After reading both, I ask my niece which one is "a story." She will probably think the question odd, but I guarantee that if I press her to answer, she will say that the first one is a "story," even though she hasn't heard it before, and that the second is "something else" or "not as much a story." Like most 6-year-olds, my niece knows what to expect in stories. She knows, for instance, that stories are about people, or peoplelike characters (Mickey Mouse, the three little pigs) trying to do things over time, that stories have beginnings, middles, and endings, that you need to know "how it's going to turn out" in a story. A set of instructions is different, no matter how well written or how beautiful the Barbie doll. There is no narrative tension in the instructions. We are not likely to await in eager anticipation the eventual victory or defeat of the protagonist, the resolution of the dramatic conflict, or the "happily ever after" ending. My niece has an inner understanding of **story grammar** (Applebee, 1978; Mandler, 1984; Trabasso, Secco, & Van Den Broek, 1984).

Like you and me, she knows a story when she hears one because she knows the implicit rules of story.

Here is what you, and I, and my 6-year-old niece expect in a story. We first expect that a story will have a *setting* of some kind, and that we will learn what the setting is very early on. "'Twas the night before Christmas when all through the house. . . . " "Once upon a time in a faraway place. . . . " We need to know where and when the action of the story is situated. The story of Dasher, Prancer, and Vixen makes no sense if we fail to realize at the beginning that it's all happening on Christmas Eve. Even fairy tales require a setting: It is important to know that they happened long ago in faraway places, not yesterday in Rock Island, Illinois. Of course, not all stories are equal in the extent to which they develop a setting. Whereas some evoke vivid associations of particular times and places, others move briskly through the where's and when's to get to the action, leaving the setting as a taken-for-granted backdrop for the plot. In the rare instance in which a setting is unknown or highly ambiguous, a story may seem confusing and disconcerting, as we see in some absurdist fiction and drama. For example, Samuel Beckett's *Waiting for Godot* is both jarring and effective because, in part, we are provided with no setting, beyond a barren and bleak landscape that seems to be anytime and anyplace, or more likely no time and no place. But Beckett's play is rather unusual in providing virtually no context within which to place the events. It violates some of our assumptions about the structure of stories, experimenting with strange new story forms that my 6-year-old niece (and I suspect many of us) may not expect nor fully appreciate.

Second, we expect a story to have human or humanlike characters. At the beginning of the story, a character exists in a kind of neutral equilibrium. Nothing has happened

A Native-American storyteller.

yet. Indeed, before anything happens, we may learn certain basic things about the character, such as what he or she looks like, how old he or she is, and so on. This information functions as a kind of "setting" for the character—a taken-for-granted background for the rest of the story. Eventually, however, something must happen. There must be an *initiating event*. The mother sends Little Red Riding Hood off to take cakes to her grandmother, and thus the action of the story begins. The initiating event motivates the character to make *the attempt*. The attempt is the character's effort to attain a certain goal. The character intends to reach the goal smoothly, but it is likely that a big, bad wolf, or its equivalent, will be waiting along the path. Tension builds when Little Red Riding Hood meets the wolf. "The plot thickens." In terms of story grammar, we see that the attempt leads in a narrative fashion to *the consequence*. The wolf is the consequence of Little Red Riding Hood's attempt to carry the cakes to her grandmother. Little Red Riding Hood reacts to the wolf. She divulges the location of the grandmother's cottage. We see, then, that *the reaction* complicates the plot further, for now her grandmother is also in danger and the story extends forward to future episodes in which the two main characters will face a showdown. Little Red Riding Hood intends to carry the cakes, but the wolf intends to eat her. Stories are about the vicissitudes of human intention, or in this case the intentions of humanlike wolves.

Each episode of a story may be seen as a sequence of the elements I have just described. You start with an initiating event that leads to the attempt. The consequence gives rise to the reaction. One episode follows another, each containing the same structural sequence (Mandler, 1984). Episodes mount and the story takes form. A great number of literary devices and conventions may enhance the buildup of tension in the story and enrich the ways in which different episodes relate to each other. The author may use flashbacks as when we learn half-way through the story that our middle-aged hero was abandoned by his parents shortly after birth. The author may shift perspectives, relating the same events from the competing points of view of different protagonists or observers. Trivial early events may foreshadow momentous later ones.

The buildup of tension within and across the many episodes of a story demands an eventual resolution. Aristotle proposed that the tension builds to a climax, a high point or turning point in the drama. What follows is the final unravelling or solution of the plot, what is called the *denouement*. Finally, the story reaches a conclusion. In Little Red Riding Hood, the tension builds as we move through the woods to grandmother's house, wherein awaits the wolf in granny's nightgown. The first-time listener feels *suspense* and *curiosity*—two indispensable emotions in a good story (Brewer & Lichtenstein, 1982). "What big teeth you have!" our heroine exclaims. "The better to eat you with," comes the falsetto reply. The wolf eats her, and then falls asleep. But the woodsman arrives. In the climactic scene, he chops open the wolf's stomach to rescue the little girl and her grandmother, neither one the worse for digestive wear. From here on, it's all denouement. Amazingly, the wolf is still sleeping. The woodsman fills his empty gut with boulders. When he awakes, the wolf falls down dead from the weight. Little Red Riding Hood returns home, and with her return the story ends. The story has taken us on a journey and then returned us to where we started, at home with Little Red Riding Hood. Things come around full circle. With the ending, we return to the beginning again, but we (and Little Red Riding Hood) have changed.

If you pay close attention to the kinds of things you hear and say in a normal day, you may be surprised to learn how much of your experience involves stories. When we

Stories are almost everywhere: A scene from the popular television show "Friends."

watch television, for instance, we observe an endless series of stories presented in a multitude of forms. Situation comedies from "I Love Lucy" to "Friends" are structured as relatively simple stories, with well-defined settings, initiating events, attempts, consequences, and reactions. As comic tension builds, the observer becomes curious to see how it is all going to turn out. Climaxes are followed by rapid denouement. After a commercial break, a brief, upbeat conclusion brings the story "home" again. We are now prepared to watch another, or move to something else.

Game shows follow a similar structure as we watch each episode to see who, in the end, will win. Serials, like "All My Children" and "The Practice," consist of a series of overlapping and intersecting stories, each developing at its own pace. The writers of these shows do not want to resolve everything in one afternoon or evening. They keep you curious and in suspense from one week to the next by building tension that cannot be resolved until future shows. Even the nightly news is structured, to a certain extent, like a story (Bird & Dardenne, 1988). Many news items are presented as mini-stories in their own right, each with a setting, characters, and goal-directed plot. Less obviously, the entire newscast itself seems to exemplify certain storylike qualities. The anchor men and women, the sportscaster, the weather expert take us on a narrative journey and then return us home, as safe and sound as Little Red Riding Hood, ending their newscasts with those upbeat human-interest stories or lighthearted commentaries and quips that, they hope, leave us smiling, resolved, and more likely than we were before to return to the set tomorrow night, same time and channel.

FEATURE 11.A

Time and Story in Bali

The philosopher Paul Ricoeur (1984) writes that "time becomes human time to the extent it is organized after the manner of narrative; narrative in turn is meaningful to the extent it portrays the features of temporal existence" (p. 3). What Ricoeur means is that human beings tend to comprehend time in terms of story. Therefore, stories work well when they make good sense of time. When we comprehend our actions over time, we see what we do in terms of story. We see actions leading to reactions, goals attained, obstacles confronted, intentions realized and frustrated over time, tension building to climax, climax giving way to denouement, tension building again as we continue to move and change, moving forward from yesterday to today to tomorrow.

Imagine a society, however, in which human conduct is *not* situated in time as we understand it. The anthropologist Clifford Geertz (1973) describes just such a society among the people of Bali. Bali is an Indonesian island just east of Java. Its native inhabitants live within a culture that is radically different from ours in a great many ways. Three intriguing differences stand out in

Geertz's account. These are differences in time, conduct, and identity.

First, Balinese life follows a complex and irregular calendar that seems neither to move forward nor in regular cycles. Time is classified by holidays. In Bali, today's "date" refers to how much time has elapsed since the last holiday and how much is left until the next one. Holidays fall irregularly on dates determined by overlapping cycles. As Geertz puts it, "the cycles and supercycles are endless, unanchored, unaccountable, and, as their internal order has no significance, without climax. They do not accumulate, they do not build, and they are not consumed. They don't tell you what time it is; they tell you what kind of time it is" (p. 393). For the Balinese, time is "punctual" rather than "durational." To know today's date is not to know time as we think of it; rather it is simply to know what kind of day today is. This is like calling today "Heavenday" and tomorrow "Baseball." In exactly a "week" from today (a "week" by our standards; the Balinese do not speak of weeks), we may have the day "Marshmallow." We do not know when the day "Heavenday" or "Marshmallow" will happen again, though of course

Healing and Integration

We are drawn to stories for many reasons. Stories entertain us, making us laugh and cry, keeping us in suspense until we learn how it is all going to turn out. Stories instruct. We learn how to act and live through stories; we learn about different people, settings, and ideas (Coles, 1989). Stories may teach us moral lessons, too. Aesop's fables and the parables of Jesus suggest lessons—some simple and some profound—about good and bad behavior, moral and immoral ways of conducting our lives, dilemmas concerning what is right and what is wrong. Beyond entertaining and edifying us, stories may also function to bring things together and to heal that which is sick or broken. Some scholars and scientists have suggested that *integration* and *healing* are each *will* happen again, some time. In this system, each day is punctuated like a discrete moment. It is not related to other days in a sequence of time.

Second, human conduct itself also seems to be punctual rather than durational. It is as if, Geertz maintains, the Balinese act and interact with one another in ways that themselves are outside of time. Each moment is discrete. Actions do not seem to build to climax and resolution the way we might expect they should. "Absence of climax," Geertz writes, is a remarkable quality of Balinese social behavior:

> It amounts to the fact that social activities do not build, or are not permitted to build, toward definitive consummations. Quarrels appear and disappear, on occasion they even persist, but they hardly ever come to a head. Issues are not sharpened for decision, they are blunted and softened in the hope that the mere evolution of circumstances will resolve them, or better yet, that they will simply evaporate. Daily life consists of self-contained, monadic encounters in which something either happens or does not, intention is realized or it is not, a task is accomplished or not. (p. 403)

Geertz is suggesting that, in Bali, social life does not seem to be construed in storied terms. Each moment is a discrete performance, standing alone outside of time, rather than a connected episode in a time-organized plot. Social activities follow one another, but they do not march to some destination, gather toward some denouement. Both time and life are punctual, unstoried.

Third, as it goes for time and conduct in Bali, so it goes for a person's identity. Geertz observes that the Balinese go to great lengths to "depersonalize" each other so that everybody may be seen as a "stereotyped contemporary." This can be seen even in the giving of names. An adult in Bali does not have a distinct name that differentiates him or her from everybody else. Instead, he or she is named according to offspring. Thus, I might be called "Father of Ruth." Were Ruth to grow up and have a child named Paul, she would no longer be called "Ruth" but rather "Mother of Paul." At that time, my name would become "Grandfather of Paul" (which might also be the name of "Ruth's" father-in-law). And so on. The naming pulls one to the present moment and out of any kind of meaningful time duration. Ruth and I are now linked in identity by virtue of our joint cooperation in the

continued on next page

two primary psychological functions of stories and storytelling. Stories may bring our lives together when we feel shattered, mend us when we are broken, heal us when we are sick, help us cope in times of stress, and even move us toward psychological fulfillment and maturity.

The psychoanalyst Bruno Bettelheim (1977) wrote eloquently about the psychological power of children's fairy stories. Bettelheim believed that such tales as "Jack and the Beanstalk" and "Cinderella" help children work through internal conflicts and crises. When a 4-year-old listens to the story of Cinderella, Bettelheim suggests, she may unconsciously identify with the heroine and vicariously experience Cinderella's frustration and sadness and her eventual triumph. Similarly, children may identify with such male heroes as Jack, who faces the menacing giant but eventually outwits him and

FEATURE 11.A *continued*

production of Paul. Paul is like the present moment; in a sense, he is all that matters, and he defines who I and my daughter are. The implicit aim, says Geertz, is to create a society that collapses time to the discrete present and blurs distinctions between people.

We are all more or less the same in Bali. Even though things change, reality remains the same. No climaxes. No resolution of tension. No denouement. Balinese life does not conform to the kinds of stories we, as Westerners, know and tell. Indeed, it seems to defy our sense of what story is all about. Geertz's fascinating account should remind us that ours is not the only way to see time and story. In its sharp contrast, however, Geertz's portrait also brings into bold relief the extent to which most of us think about time as story, and story in terms of time. I suspect that few

of us wish to exchange permanent places with one of the Balinese. Coming from a culture that stresses individual identity and the linear nature of time, we are not likely to feel comfortable in a society that seems to lie outside of time and personal identity. We may concede that their culture "works" for the Balinese, that perhaps it works so well as to make them quite happy and fulfilled. Geertz does not compare them to us on these points. But the reasons the Balinese seem so strange to us is that we, unlike them, appear to live according to narrative assumptions about time and lives. Similarly, we, unlike them, appear to value strongly the individuality of our own life course. Take our stories of the past away from us and each of us would be forced to live as stereotyped contemporaries, out of time and out of self.

escapes much the richer and wiser. The protagonists of these stories are unassuming children, like the listeners, and their deeply felt fears and concerns match closely the unconscious fears lurking in the hearts of children. In Bettelheim's view, the fairy tale speaks softly and subtly to the child, gently but steadily promoting psychological growth and adaptation. The fairy tale encourages the child to face the world with confidence and hope. Cinderella and Jack live happily ever after. Wicked stepsisters and ogres are punished in the end. Things have a way of working out, even when they look really scary.

As adults, we too may identify strongly with the protagonist of a story, experiencing vicariously what the character experiences and emerging from the narrative encounter happier, better adjusted, more enlightened, or improved in some way. In *When Bad Things Happen to Good People*, Rabbi Harold Kushner (1981) tells many true stories of pain and heartbreak from the lives of people he has known and, in some cases, loved. The book has been a great comfort to many people. Good friends whose baby was stillborn have told me that Kushner's book helped them deal with their grief. In this case, they identified strongly with the author himself, who was motivated to write the book after his own son died at an early age. By hearing a story with which they could relate intimately, my friends worked through an emotionally wrenching period in their own lives. Kushner reports that the stories helped *him*, too. By collecting and considering the tales of grief and suffering he had encountered in his years as a rabbi, Kushner reports, he was able to piece together parts of his own shattered life.

Simply writing or performing a story about oneself can prove to be an experience of healing and growth, as many who have written their own autobiographies will attest. A good autobiography puts life into story form, complete with setting, characters, initiating events, attempts, consequences, reactions, climaxes, denouement, recurrent themes and images, and the self-conscious reconstruction of human time through narrative. One of the first and most famous autobiographies in Western history was written by the Christian Saint Augustine (354–430 A.D.). His *Confessions* is a retrospective self-analysis written to regroup and recover from what he described as a "shattered" and "disordered" state of mind. By composing the story, Augustine was able to construct a unified view of himself and his place in God's creation and to orient to the envisioned future with direction and purpose (Jay, 1984).

Many men and women have tried to do what Augustine did, with varying degrees of success. There are many reasons to write an autobiography, but one commonly expressed is the desire to find some kind of personal integration—to put the pieces together into a meaningful whole. The writer may feel that the time in life has finally come to undertake this kind of synthesizing project. It may seem a natural time to look back. Or the writer may feel a great deal more urgency, like Augustine, looking to the story as a salvation for or solution to an impending crisis in life.

In his brief autobiography entitled *The Facts*, the novelist Philip Roth (1988) writes that he is seeking to "depathologize" his own life, to set things right after years of confusion and trouble. In Roth's case, the process of composing a life story involves distilling from his own complex past the stark truisms—"the facts"—concerning how he came to be a writer. Roth describes this process as a clearing away of the many layers of stories that he has created as a prolific novelist in order to arrive at a core of truth—shredding through the layers of superficial narrative in order to get at a single and simple tale to believe. The task is tricky and perhaps not well advised, as Roth seems to admit at the beginning and the end of the book when he engages in an imaginary conversation with Nathan Zuckerman, who is the fictional hero of a series of Roth's novels. Zuckerman tells Roth that he is a fool to strip away the stories in his fiction, for those are as much a part of Roth as anything else. Zuckerman seems to imply that he, Zuckerman, is more a part of Roth than is Roth himself—than is the Roth, that is, who functions as the central character in *The Facts*. Without me, Zuckerman seems to be saying, you (Roth) are a pretty boring and superficial fellow. "This is what you get in practically any artist without his imagination," Zuckerman says. "Your medium for the really merciless, self-evisceration, your medium for genuine self-confrontation, is me" (pp. 184–185).

Perhaps Roth actually agrees with Zuckerman, at least to a point. How else might we explain his choice of the most clichéd kind of chapter titles you could imagine for an autobiography? He gives his chapters titles like "Joe College," "Girl of My Dreams," and "All in the Family." Is Roth telling us that, when you strip away "the Roth" that he has projected onto his own fictional characters, like Zuckerman, all you are left with is cliché? Is he saying that without our imaginations, our lives reduce to simplistic platitudes and worn-out expressions? Is he saying that "the facts" are not enough? In Roth's case, autobiography turns ironic and self-mocking, as the story-writer comes to doubt the validity of the story he has composed. Yet the whole process seems to be enlightening, as well as entertaining. We feel that we *do* learn something important about Roth that we didn't know before. And we feel that he, too, has discovered something about himself, that he has made progress toward the goal of "de-pathologizing" his own life. Of course, we can never know for sure.

The healing power of story arises as a major theme in certain forms of psychotherapy, wherein the explicit goal of treatment is the depathologizing of life. For instance, some psychoanalysts maintain that the development of a coherent life story is a major goal in therapy. According to this view, psychoanalysis involves the coordination of successive narrations whereby the analyst and the client come to construct more adequate and vitalizing stories about the self (Schafer, 1981). Writes Marcus (1974), "human life is, ideally, a connected and coherent story, with all the details in explanatory place, and with everything (or as close to everything as is practically possible) accounted for, in its proper causal or other sequence." Similarly, "illness amounts at least in part to suffering from an incoherent story or an inadequate narrative account of oneself." The therapist and the client work together to produce a healing narrative of the self (Borden, 1992). Some psychological problems and a great deal of emotional suffering stem from our failures in making sense of our lives through story. Therapists help us rewrite and revise our stories of self (White & Epston, 1990). The process may produce a triumphant transformation, like that in the case of Saint Augustine. Or progress may be slower and less obvious, in therapeutic fits and starts, as Roth cautions in his own explorations in healing the self.

Researchers have explored the extent to which life-storytelling can have positive effects on coping and mental health. Most notably, James Pennebaker (1988, 1989b, 1992, 1997) and his colleagues have conducted a series of studies on the salutary effects of disclosing narrative accounts of personal traumas. Volunteer participants in Pennebaker's studies receive instructions like these:

> Once you are seated in the experimental cubicle and the door is closed, I want you to write continuously about the most upsetting or traumatic experience of your entire life. Don't worry about the grammar, spelling, or sentence structure. In your writing I want you to discuss your deepest thoughts and feelings about the experience. You can write about anything you want, but whatever you choose, it should be something that has affected you very deeply. Ideally, it should be about something you have not talked with others about in detail. It is critical, however, that you let yourself go and touch those deepest emotions and thoughts that you have. I should warn you that many people find this study quite upsetting. Many people cry during the study and feel somewhat sad or depressed during and after it. (Pennebaker, 1989b, p. 215)

Many of the respondents in these studies are college students. Here are some representative sketches:

> A female who has lived in fear for several weeks because of the physical and psychological harassment of a jealous woman who has apparently hired two thugs.

> A male who, in his high school years, was repeatedly beaten by his stepfather. After attempting suicide with his stepfather's gun, the stepfather humiliated the subject by laughing at his failed attempt.

> A female who, in a fit of rage at her father, accused him of marital infidelity in front of her mother. The accusation, which apparently was true and unknown to the mother, led to the separation and divorce of the parents and overwhelming guilt on the part of the daughter.

A female who, at the age of 10, was asked to clean up her room because of her grandmother who was to visit the home that evening. The girl did not do so. That night, the grandmother slipped on one of the girl's toys and broke her hip. The grandmother died a week later during a hip operation.

A man who, at age 9, was calmly told by his father that he was divorcing the boy's mother because their home life had been disrupted ever since the boy had been born. (Pennebaker, 1989b, p. 218)

As many as one quarter of the participants in these studies cry during their disclosures, and many feel depressed for a time after the telling. Yet the respondents tend to rate the experience of disclosing the traumatic event to be especially valuable, and 98% of them say that they would do the experiment again. More important, the narrative act of translating personal trauma into words appears to have long-term health benefits. For example, Pennebaker and Beall (1986) required 46 healthy undergraduates to write about either the most traumatic and stressful experience of their lives or about a trivial assigned topic *for four consecutive days*. Of those assigned to write about traumatic events, one experimental group wrote about the facts surrounding the trauma but not their feelings about the trauma (trauma-factual condition), another about their feelings concerning the trauma but not the facts (trauma-emotion), and a third about both their feelings and the facts concerning the trauma (trauma-combination group). A six-month followup questionnaire revealed that the participants who disclosed information about both the facts and their feelings in the traumatic event had better health during those six subsequent months than did the participants in the other three groups. As Figure 11.1 shows, the trauma-combination group showed the lowest number of visits to the student health center during that period. The authors argued that the opportunity to tell the *full story* of a stressful experience from the past—providing both the facts and one's feelings about the facts—works to enhance one's health.

These findings are consistent with studies showing how personal confession and disclosure of negative events can improve health and minimize unwanted thoughts about traumas. Pennebaker and O'Heeron (1984) surveyed people whose spouses had died in automobile accidents or suicides. They found that individuals who ruminated obsessively about the death of their spouse had more health problems during the year following the death. But those who talked with others about their spouses' deaths reported (1) fewer problems with unwanted ruminations and obsessive thoughts and (2) fewer health problems during the following year. Greenberg and Stone (1992) found a drop in physician visits for students who wrote about deeply traumatic events compared with students who either wrote about mild traumas or those who wrote about superficial topics. Francis and Pennebaker (1992) found that those who wrote about traumas once a week for four consecutive weeks had fewer absentee days and improved liver enzyme function in the two months after writing, compared with controls. Obtaining a series of blood samples on each participant, Pennebaker, Kiecolt-Glaser, and Glaser (1988) found that students who wrote about traumas over four consecutive days showed improved immune-system functioning by the fourth day, compared with those who wrote about trivial events.

Why does disclosure of traumatic events improve health? Pennebaker (1988) argues that the process of actively inhibiting feelings and thoughts about negative events requires excessive physiological work, as in higher heart rate, skin conductance, and

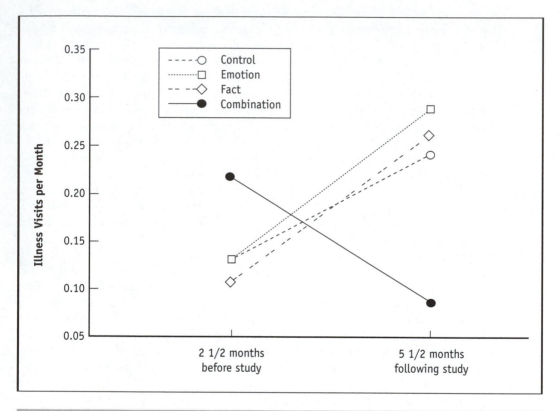

blood pressure. Over the long haul, the effects of physiological arousal accumulate, leading to such stress-related illnesses as infections, ulcers, and so on. Furthermore, the more that a person tries to inhibit thoughts and emotions, the more he or she is likely to think about that which is being inhibited, leading to heightened anxiety and arousal (Wegner, Schneider, Carter, & White, 1987). But confiding and consciously confronting the perceptions and feelings associated with a traumatic event allow for the integration or cognitive reorganization of the event. The narrative disclosure of the event enables the person to "put it behind" him or her, to "close the book" on the problem. This leads to a reduction in physiological arousal, and it negates the need for further obsessing and inhibiting.

But what is it about disclosure itself that makes for the reduction in physiological arousal and obsessive thought? Research by Pennebaker (1992) suggests two important factors: (1) the degree of negative emotion expressed and (2) the extent to which a traumatic event is reconstructed as a *well-formed story*. Employing a computer content coding scheme to analyze accounts of traumatic events, Pennebaker discovered that people whose health improved the most following disclosure used significantly more negative emotion words and fewer positive emotion words compared to other people. In addition, individuals whose health improved evidenced overall higher levels of story organization and increasing degree of acceptance and optimism compared with those who failed to improve. Indeed, those who did not improve evidenced a gradual deterioration in their stories. They started their writing sessions with a clear story that, over time, fell apart. Pennebaker concludes that "both the disclosure of negative emotion and the building of a clear cognitive story are important components in healthy writing" (1992, p. 5). The movement over time toward a well-constructed story, then, is a desired outcome in writing and in some forms of therapy, and it appears to bring with it benefits for health.

FEELING AND STORY: TOMKINS'S SCRIPT THEORY

The central role of story and storytelling in human lives is one defining feature of the broad perspective on personality offered by Silvan Tomkins (1911–1991). A drama student who wrote plays as a college undergraduate, Tomkins came to psychology as a storywriter. It was through dramatic narrative that Tomkins first wrestled with the question that has since driven his life's work: "What do human beings really want?" (Tomkins, 1981, p. 306). In search of an answer, Tomkins entered graduate school in psychology in 1930 but left a year later, disappointed with what he saw as psychology's failure to address adequately the question of motivation, or what people want. He then turned to philosophy to study logic and the theory of value, receiving a Ph.D. Tomkins

eventually returned to psychology to work with Henry Murray at the Harvard Psychological Clinic. Tomkins's early work reflected the influence of Murray, as he published a book on the TAT (Tomkins, 1947) and devised a new projective test called the Tomkins–Horn Picture Arrangement Test (Tomkins & Miner, 1957).

Though Tomkins initially accepted Murray's belief that psychogenic needs were the main factors in human motivation, he soon departed from this view in favor of a theory emphasizing **affect,** or human emotion. As Tomkins tells it, two personal discoveries led directly to his own conviction that affects, not drives (Freud) or needs (Murray), are the primary motivators of human behavior.

The first discovery occurred in the late 1940s when Tomkins was struck by the sudden insight that such affects as excitement, joy, and anger are independent of drives, like hunger and sexuality, but *amplify* drives by providing them

Silvan Tomkins

with motivational power. In Tomkins's view, for instance, the sex drive in and of itself is *not* generally a strong motivator of behavior. Rather, sex moves the person to act in a sexual manner when amplified (strengthened) by the affect of excitement. Tomkins's second discovery occurred when he became a father:

> The second critical discovery occurred when my son was born in 1955 while I was on sabbatical leave. Beginning shortly after his birth, I observed him daily, for hours on end. I was struck with the massiveness of the crying response. It included not only very loud vocalization and facial muscular responses, but also large changes in blood flow to the face and engagement of all the striate musculature of the body. It was a massive total bodily response which, however, seemed to center on the face. Freud had suggested that the birth cry was the prototype of anxiety, but my son didn't seem anxious. What, then, was the facial response? I labelled it distress. Next, I was to observe intense excitement on his face when he labored after the first few months of his life to shape his mouth to try to imitate the speech he heard. He would struggle minutes on end and then give up, apparently exhausted and discouraged. I noted the intensity of the smiling response to his mother and to me, and again I became aware that nothing in psychoanalytic theory (and any other personality theory at that time) paid any attention to the specificity of enjoyment as contrasted with excitement. (Tomkins, 1981, p. 309)

In collaboration with psychologists Carroll Izard and Paul Ekman, Tomkins has articulated a broad theory of human emotion that proposes the existence of some 10 primary affects, each rooted in human biology and evolution (Ekman, 1972; Izard, 1977; Tomkins, 1962, 1963; Tomkins & Izard, 1965). Each affect is linked to characteristic movements of the muscles in the face. Thus, the face may be considered the organ of emotion. Later, Tomkins expanded his theory to encompass the concepts of *scene* and *script*, providing a dramaturgical and narrative approach to personality that is reminiscent of his entry into psychology, more than 70 years ago, as a writer of plays (Carlson, 1981; Tomkins, 1979, 1987).

Affects

When I worked in the steel mills in Gary, Indiana, I made friends with a man called "Tiny." I was a college student working summers; he was about 40 years old, married with three children, and he had never finished the sixth grade. Tiny's dream was to be a coal miner; by contrast, I could think of nothing more gruesome. I hated the steel mills; Tiny didn't mind the work, and he often tried to cheer me up when I was particularly fed up and discouraged. I don't understand why we liked each other when we had so little in common. But I remember that we talked a lot, and I especially remember one conversation we had—I think the original topic was women and marriage—when Tiny cryptically observed, "Emotion is everything." In his own way, Tiny seemed to hit on the central point of human living in Tomkins's theory of personality. As Tomkins puts it:

> The primary function of affect is urgency via analogic and profile amplification to make one care by feeling. . . . Without affect amplification nothing else matters, and with its amplification anything can matter. (1981, p. 322)

According to Tomkins, natural selection has operated on humans to favor the evolution of a highly differentiated and specialized system of emotions. Therefore,

According to Tomkins, the face is the organ of emotion.

the human being is equipped with innate affective responses which bias him to want to remain alive and to resist death, to want sexual experiences, to want to experience novelty and to resist boredom, to want to communicate, to be close to and in contact with others of his species and to resist the experience of head and face lowered in shame. (Tomkins, 1962, p. 27)

Those emotions most often identified as primary by Tomkins include interest/excitement, enjoyment, surprise, distress, anger, disgust, fear/anxiety, sadness, shame, and guilt. The first two are positive emotions; surprise can be positive, negative, or neither: and the last seven are negative emotions. In general, people seek to maximize experiences of positive emotions and minimize experiences of negative ones.

Each of the primary emotions can be distinguished on a number of different levels. First, each *feels* qualitatively different from all the others. For example, the phenomenology of surprise—the sudden increase in arousal in the wake of an unexpected event—is very different from the phenomenology of shame, joy, or sadness. Second, each emotion is innately linked to a specific *facial response*. As Darwin (1872/1965) believed over 100 years ago, human beings have evolved with particular facial expressions for showing particular emotions: enjoyment by the smile; surprise and interest/excitement by raised eyes and a focused, head-forward stance; sadness by a drooping mouth and slackening jaw muscles; disgust by tightened muscles beneath the nose and wrinkling of the nose; anger by clenched and exposed teeth and a flushed complexion; and fear by widened eyes. Each of these facial expressions sends sensory feedback from the face to the brain, and some psychologists believe that this feedback is instrumental in the experience of the emotion itself, especially in infancy. In one sense, then, the experience of joy is the result of the sensory information sent to the brain by the smiling face. In addition, facial expressions send social information to other persons who may observe the individual's smiles, frowns, or sneers.

Particular facial expressions, therefore, are thought to be natural manifestations of primary emotions. Evidence for this proposition comes from many sources. Cross-cultural research suggests that people from very different societies tend to agree on what facial responses "go with" what emotions. For instance, research by Izard (1971, 1977) and Ekman, Friesen, and Ellsworth (1972) showed that when people from 12 different countries were shown photographs selected to represent fundamental emotions, the percentage of agreement was very high. Mexicans, Brazilians, Germans, Japanese, Americans, and members of certain preliterate tribes tend to agree about the meaning of different facial expressions. Even when there is no obvious change in facial expression, the occurrence of certain emotions can be shown by measuring electrical activity in the face and brain. In one study, individuals were asked to imagine pleasant and unpleasant scenes while changes in the electrical muscular impulses in their faces were monitored (Schwartz, Fair, Greenberg, Freedman, & Klerman, 1974). The results indicated that electrical activity in the face matches the muscular movements that have been documented for various emotions. For example, during happy thoughts, the same facial muscles that produce a smile show increased electrical activity even though the facial expression appears blank.

While primary emotions appear to be biologically linked to specific facial expressions, different cultures establish different **display rules** that determine the appropriateness of expressing certain emotions through facial behavior in certain situations (Ekman, 1972). In American society, for example, it is generally considered more appropriate for women than men to cry when experiencing the emotion of sadness. While some societies sanction the full expression of many different affects in a wide variety of situations, other societies are more circumspect and may strongly discourage the public display of strong emotions.

A last way in which different emotions can be distinguished is in terms of their developmental course. As Izard (1978) has asserted, "emotions emerge as they become adaptive in the life of the infant" (p. 390). The cry of the newborn is generally a sign of *distress*, an extremely rudimentary emotion that signals that something is not quite right in the world. The distress cry motivates caregivers to attend to the infant and address the source of distress. The origins of *enjoyment* may reside in the early social smile and face-to-face interaction with the caregiver that is usually displayed by infants by 2 months of age. Out of early joyful interactions develop the caregiver–infant attachment bond and the first love relationship in the baby's life, as we saw in Chapter 2.

Interest/excitement can be traced back to at least the third and fourth months of life, when infants are engaged in what the developmental psychologist Jean Piaget (1952) viewed as attempts to "make interesting events last." The function of interest/ excitement is to focus and maintain attention and to motivate exploratory activity. Interest is activated by novelty and change and serves as the basis for the infant's first self-initiated interactions with the world of objects. *Fear* and *sadness* may appear in the second half of the first year of life, especially in response to novelty, separation, and loss. It is quite common for 8-month-old infants to fear strangers and to cry when separated from their mothers and fathers. Finally, the emergence of *shame* and (later) *guilt* generally awaits the development of self-consciousness in the second year, following the child's consolidation of an initial sense of self-as-object, a sense of "me" (Chapter 10).

Scenes and Scripts

Basic Concepts   While affect is the supreme motivator in life, scenes and scripts are the great organizers. Tomkins views the person as a playwright who fashions his or her own personal drama from the earliest weeks of life. The basic component of the drama is the **scene,** the memory of a specific happening or event in one's life that contains at least one affect and one object of that affect. Each scene is an "organized whole that includes persons, place, time, actions, and feelings" (Carlson, 1981, p. 502). We may each view our own lives, therefore, as a series of scenes, one after the other, extending from birth to the present. But certain kinds of scenes appear again and again, and certain typical groupings or families of scenes can be discerned. **Scripts** enable us to make sense of the relations among various scenes. A script is a set of rules for interpreting, creating, enhancing, or defending against a family of related scenes (Carlson, 1988). Each of us organizes the many scenes in our lives according to our own idiosyncratic scripts.

The *short-term* importance of any particular scene in a person's life is likely to be a function of the quality of the affect in the scene. In thinking back over yesterday's events, therefore, you may recall a particular happening that stands out because of the intense emotion you experienced during it. For instance, the lunchtime volleyball game you played with friends may have elicited strong feelings of joy, an argument with your mother may have brought forward feelings of anger, or the conversation you had with an attractive man or women may have elicited excitement—each of these scenes could conceivably stand out as special or important, for that given day. The *long-term* importance of a scene in the context of a person's entire life drama or narrative is likely to be a function of **psychological magnification,** which is the process of connecting related scenes into a meaningful pattern. To connect scenes into meaningful patterns, we must recognize basic similarities and differences among various scenes. For instance, an argument with your mother may remind you of a similar disagreement you had with a professor. In both cases, say, what began as a friendly exchange deteriorated into shouting over a petty difference of opinion. The two arguments appear to be *analogs* of each other. Psychological magnification often works by constructing such analogs—the detection of similarities in different experiences. When construing analogs in your life, you are likely to get that feeling of "here we go again," replaying the same scenario over and over. According to Tomkins, *negative*-affect scenes are often psychologically magnified through the formation of analogs. Therefore, in making sense of the many scenes of fear or sadness in your life, you are likely to discern the ways in which these scenes are essentially similar.

When, by contrast, you focus on *differences* in organizing various life scenes, you are employing psychological magnification to construct *variants.* You are most likely to do this, argues Tomkins, in the magnification of *positive*-affect scenes. Therefore, in construing the many experiences of joy in your past, you are likely to focus on the ways in which the various scenes differ around a stable core. Consider joyful family gatherings. Last summer's family reunion, Thanksgiving dinner two years ago, and the day your mother brought your baby sister home from the hospital may all stand out in your life narrative as joyful scenes. While the various scenes are similar in some ways, you are likely to magnify them such that differences are accentuated. Therefore, the family reunion may stand out as "special" for the great conversation you had with your uncle who works for the FBI; the highlight of the Thanksgiving dinner may have been your sister's announcement that she and her boyfriend were planning to get married; and the day you saw your baby sister for the first time may stand out for the overwhelming feelings of tenderness and affection you felt.

Types of Scripts   While psychologists have been able to identify a finite number of basic human affects, the number of possible scenes and scripts in human life appears to be much larger. Therefore, no definitive list of scenes and scripts has been developed. However, Tomkins has identified at least two types of scripts that seem especially significant in human life and that help organize in powerful ways people's life narratives. These are commitment scripts and nuclear scripts (Carlson, 1988; Tomkins, 1987).

In a **commitment script,** the person binds him- or herself to a life program or goal that promises the reward of intense positive affect. A commitment script involves a long-term investment in "improving things." The person may have a vision of the ideal life or the ideal society and dedicate his or her life to realizing or accomplishing this vision. According to Tomkins, commitment scripts begin with an intensely positive early scene or series of scenes from childhood. This scene of enjoyment or excitement comes to represent an optimistic ideal of what might be—a Garden of Eden from the past that holds out the hope of a paradise in the future, the pursuit of which becomes one's life task.

A commitment script: Mother Theresa dedicated her life to helping others.

In a commitment script, the person organizes scenes around a clearly defined and undisputed goal (Table 11.1). Therefore, commitment scripts are *not* likely to entail significant conflict between competing goals or troubling ambivalence about any single goal. The person whose life is organized around a strong commitment script strives, instead, to accomplish his or her desired paradise with singleness of purpose and steadfast dedication, much like Jerome Johnson as he pursued his dream to be a police chief. Even in the face of great obstacles and repeated negative-affect experiences, such a person focuses steadily upon the object of commitment, laboring under the conviction that "bad things can be overcome" (Carlson, 1988).

In sharp contrast to commitment scripts are **nuclear scripts,** which are generally marked by ambivalence and confusion about one's life goals. In the terms of Miller and Dollard's conflict theory of Chapter 4, a nuclear script always involves complex approach–avoidance conflicts. The person is irresistibly drawn toward and repelled by particularly conflictual scenes in his or her life narrative. The result is a life narrative that resembles the literary form of tragedy, as we see in such great Greek tragedies as *Oedipus Rex* and the *Oresteia*.

A nuclear script begins with a **nuclear scene,** which is a positive childhood scene that eventually turns bad. As a good scene, it may involve the experience of enjoyment or excitement in the presence of others, especially those others who may provide the person with "stimulation, guidance, mutuality, support, comfort and/or reassurance." The scene turns bad with the appearance of "an intimidation, or a contamination, or a confusion, or any combination of these which jeopardize the good scene" (Tomkins, 1987, p. 199). What begins, therefore, as joyful or exciting turns frightening, disgusting, contemptuous, shameful, or sad. A nuclear script is initially formed as an attempt to reverse the nuclear scene, to turn the bad scene into a good scene again. The attempt is only partially successful, however, as the person ultimately appears fated to repeat the nuclear scene continually through subsequent analog scenes.

Carlson (1981) describes a nuclear scene from the early childhood of one Jane W., a 37-year-old college professor:

TABLE 11.1	*Commitment Scripts* Versus *Nuclear Scripts*	
	TYPE OF SCRIPT	
SCRIPT FEATURE	**COMMITMENT**	**NUCLEAR**
Ratio of positive to negative affect	Positive greater than negative	Negative greater than positive
Affect socialization	Intense, rewarding	Intense, ambivalent
Clarity of ideal scene	Clear, monistic	Confusing, pluralistic
Magnification of scenes via	Variants	Analogs
Sequences	"Bad things can be overcome"	"Good things turn bad"

Source: Adapted from Carlson (1988), p. 111.

> Four-year-old Janie is playing when she hears her mother cry for help. Running into the hall, she finds her mother lying on the floor in a heap of boxes, having fallen from a makeshift ladder to the attic. Mother asks Janie to call her father. Father arrives, helps mother to her feet, and supports her as they walk to the living room with Janie hovering nearby. Janie hears her father say "Sit here, honey" and promptly perches on the designated couch. Father angrily yells, "Get out of here!" and pushes Janie away so that her mother may lie down. Janie retreats in confusion, feeling deeply ashamed. (p. 504)

It turns out that Jane's mother was pregnant at the time of the fall and that this event probably caused her subsequent miscarriage. Further, when Jane's father said, "Sit here, honey," he was probably speaking to her mother, though of course the 4-year-old Janie assumed he was addressing her.

Carlson identifies five key features in this scene: (1) good things turn bad, (2) seduction and betrayal, (3) disorientation in space, (4) affects of shame and anger, and (5) withdrawal and inhibition. Each of these features was replayed in subsequent scenes in Jane's life, attesting to the power of the nuclear scene as the precipitating event in a nuclear script. Evidence for the psychological magnification of this scene through the formation of many analogs is evident in Jane's memories of her past, and in her dreams, fantasies, and interpersonal relationships. For example, she experienced many instances in her adult life in which she felt disoriented in space, in the same way she was disoriented in the nuclear scene when her father pushed her off the couch to make room for her mother. Further, each of her 30 dream reports was characterized by repeated shifts in location. Shame, which was the dominant affect in the original scene, was abundantly evident as a recurrent emotional experience in both dreams and daily life. Inhibition and withdrawal were evident in autobiographical data suggesting that, despite her competence in many realms of life, Jane was often "frozen" at critical moments, especially when a difficult decision was to be made. Jane's inhibition was also evident in her repeated difficulties in mastering realms of physical activity, especially athletics and games.

Carlson suggests that at least two other scenes from Jane's childhood might be considered nuclear scenes, giving birth to nuclear scripts. The point of the analysis of the case of Jane, however, is not to show how any of these scenes actually *caused* subsequent events. Carlson does not contend that Jane is inhibited today *because* of the scene on the couch. Rather, the couch scene is a nuclear scene because it *organizes* the narrative of her life, giving meaning to many different experiences and serving as a template or pattern for other scenes in the story. As dramatists and storytellers of the self, human beings seek to discern a narrative order in their lives so that they may cast the many discordant events of the past into a meaningful and coherent life story. A major undercurrent in Jane's life story is a nuclear script about how good things can lead to disorientation, withdrawal, and shame.

IDENTITY AND THE LIFE STORY

In Chapter 10, I introduced Erik Erikson's concept of *identity*. According to Erikson, beginning in adolescence and young adulthood modern people are faced with the psychosocial challenge of constructing a self that provides their lives with unity, purpose, and meaning. For the first time in the life course, these questions become problematic, and interesting: "Who am I?" "How do I fit into the adult world?" As we address these questions, Erikson maintained, we begin to construct what he called a *configuration*, which includes "constitutional givens, idiosyncratic libidinal needs, significant identifications, effective defenses, successful sublimations, and consistent roles" (Erikson, 1959, p. 116). The identity configuration works to integrate "all identifications with the vicissitudes of the libido, with the aptitudes developed out of endowment, and with the opportunities offered in social roles." The formulation of an identity configuration brings with it "the accrued confidence that the inner sameness and continuity prepared in the past are matched by the sameness and continuity of one's meaning for others" (Erikson, 1963, p. 261). Therefore, the identity configuration serves to *integrate*, or bring into a meaningful pattern, many different things. It brings together skills, values, goals, and roles into a coherent whole. It brings together what the person can and wants to do with what opportunities and constraints for action exist in the social environment. It brings together aspects of the remembered past with the experienced present and the anticipated future.

What might this unique "configuration" of identity look like? In my own theoretical writing, I have argued that the identity configuration of which Erikson speaks should be seen first and foremost as an integrative **life story** that a person begins to construct in late adolescence and young adulthood (McAdams, 1984c, 1985b, 1985c, 1987, 1988b, 1990b, 1993, 1997b). *Identity is a life story*—an internalized and evolving narrative of the self. The story binds together many different aspects of the self to confer upon a life some degree of unity, purpose, and meaning.

It is in adolescence that we first come to recognize that, living in a modern society, our lives *need* some form of purpose and meaning. Unlike children, adolescents have the cognitive ability and the psychosocial motivation to see their lives as evolving narratives that they are able to "work on" over time. Research on cognitive development has demonstrated that not until adolescence have people mastered the cognitive abilities necessary to construct an internalized life story. Habermas and Bluck (in press) argue that adolescents develop a *life story schema*, or stored skeletal version of one's life course, which serves as a superordinate autobiographical knowledge structure. In Piaget's (1970) terms, adolescents are able to think in an abstract, formal-operational manner. The abstract problem of unity and purpose in life now poses itself as a meaningful conundrum. Able to entertain hypothetical realities through formal operational thought and motivated to re-evaluate personal history and to explore new possibilities for the future, we begin to operate as both historians of the past and prophets for the future, seeking to cast our time-driven lives into narratives that work. Our first attempts to do this may seem naïve and fantastical. Examining diaries and personal correspondence of adolescents, Elkind (1982) finds evidence for the construction of *personal fables*—fantastical stories about the self, underscoring the teenager's sense that he or she is unique in the world, destined for great goodness or badness, and forever misunderstood by others. For some adolescents, the personal fable may serve as a "rough first draft" of an evolving identity narrative, a story that will become more realistic and plausible in the years to come. Moving into young adulthood, Hankiss (1981) identifies *ontological strategies* that people adopt to explain how they came to be. For example, in a "dynastic" ontological strategy, a young adult fashions a story about how a very positive past life has now given birth to a very positive current life. By

TABLE 11.2	*Views From Six Different Scholars on the Relation Between Stories and Human Lives*	
SOURCE	**CONCEPT**	**DESCRIPTION**
Northrop Frye, literary scholar (1957)	Mythic archetypes	There exist four fundamental story forms, which reflect four stages of human existence and the four seasons. *Comedy* highlights birth and spring; *romance* depicts the passion and adventure of youth and early adulthood, and the season of summer; *tragedy* suggests deterioration and eventual dying in later adulthood, and the season for autumn; *irony* depicts death and winter.
Lawrence Elsbree, literary scholar (1982)	Generic plots	There exist five basic plots in stories, each reflecting a fundamental human striving: (1) establishing a home; (2) fighting a battle; (3) taking a journey; (4) enduring suffering; and (5) pursuing consummation or completion.
Jean-Paul Sartre, philosopher (1964)	True novels	The essential form of the self is a retrospective story, or "true novel," that creates order out of the chaos of experience. Because contemporary religion and social institutions no longer provide people with sacred myths with which to identify, modern men and women are faced with seeking truth and meaning through creating their own myths about themselves. Ideally, a person's own true novel should reflect a central truth or dilemma about his or her historical epoch.
Alasdair MacIntyre, philosopher (1984)	Moral virtues	The "good" in human life must be understood in the context of narrative. What is good for a single person is what contributes to the completion of his or her life story. What is good for humankind must be derived from an analysis of the features that are common to all life stories.
David Elkind, developmental psychologist (1982)	Personal fable	In early adolescence, a person may construct a fantastical story about the self, underscoring the teenager's sense that he or she is unique in the world, destined for great goodness or badness, and forever misunderstood by others. Elkind sees personal fable as a relatively normal phenomenon that is partly a result of the beginning of formal operational thinking. In terms of McAdams's theory of identity, personal fable may be a "rough draft" of an evolving narrative identity that will mature and become more realistic in later years.
Agnes Hankiss, sociologist (1981)	Ontological strategy	In early adulthood, people attempt to explain how they "came to be" (ontology) by "mythologically rearranging" the past and evaluating the present according to one of four different strategies: (1) dynastic (good past, good present), (2) antithetical (good past, bad present), (3) compensatory (bad past, good present), or (4) self-absolutory (bad past, bad present).

contrast, a "compensatory" strategy involves a story of how a bad past has given birth to a good present, as in the proverbial "rags to riches" life story celebrated by many Americans throughout our nation's history. (See Table 11.2.)

Therefore, we begin to construct self-defining life stories in adolescence and young adulthood, when first confronted with the challenge of identity. But we do not begin our stories from scratch. And we do not quit working on our stories as we move beyond our early adult years. The origins of life stories can be traced back to infancy, and the process of life storymaking continues well into midlife and beyond (Cohler, 1982; McAdams, 1990b, 1993). In infancy and childhood, we are implicitly "gathering material" for the story we will someday compose. When we arrive in adolescence ready to make sense of who we are, we are already bestowed with a wealth of experience that constitutes some of the most important "stuff" out of which our identities will be made. These are the biographical resources for our life stories. There is much that we can do with these resources, many possibilities that we can create. But in identity, as in life, we can never fully transcend our resources.

A person's life story is a *psychosocial construction* (McAdams, 1996a). This means that although the story is constructed by the person whose story it is, the possibilities for story construction—identity formation—are determined by culture. Indeed, there is a sense in which the person co-authors identity with culture. Different kinds of stories make sense in different kinds of cultures. For example, Martin Luther's narrations (Chapter 10) about physical encounters with devils made sense in 16th-century Germany, but they strike the modern ear as quite odd (Erikson, 1958). A member of a rural Indian village may account for his feelings of tranquility this morning as resulting from the "cool and dispassionate" food he ate last night (Shweder & Much, 1987). His story will make sense to his peers in the village, but it will not fit expectations for life-narrative accounts in contemporary Los Angeles. Furthermore, within modern societies like the contemporary United States, different groups are given different narrative opportunities and face different narrative constraints. Especially relevant here are gender, race, and class divisions in modern society (Chapter 4). Feminist author Carolyn Heilbrun (1988) remarks that many women have traditionally "been deprived of the narratives, or the texts, plots, or examples, by which they might assume power over—take control of—their own lives" (p. 17). The historical and contemporary life experiences of many African Americans do not coalesce nicely into the kind of life-narrative forms most valued by the white majority in the United States (Boyd-Franklin, 1989). Life stories, therefore, reflect gender and class divisions and the patterns of economic, political, and cultural power that prevail in society, within which individual lives are embedded (Franz & Stewart, 1994; Rosenwald & Ochberg, 1992).

As psychosocial constructions, life stories are based on empirical facts, but they also go beyond facts. For example, take this fact from my own life: I was born on February 7, 1954. This fact can be documented through my birth certificate. My own life story, therefore, includes this simple fact concerning the date of my birth. Another fact about my birth was that I was a premature infant—weighing 3 pounds and 13 ounces at birth. Now, here is where it gets murky. My father always told me growing up that the doctors said I had a 50/50 chance to live because I was so premature. Looking back on what I have learned about my father over the past 45 years, I now think he made up that "fact." But maybe he didn't. In any case, that conversation with the doctor has always been part of my life story, even though it may never have happened. This is to say that growing up, I always considered myself to be an especially lucky person—the 50/50 coin flip at birth came up heads, and I lived. More importantly, I think that an early knowledge that I might have died has always sensitized me to the possibility of my own death, the death of others whom I love, and the overall fragility of human life. I also believe this knowledge about my past has made me a relatively cautious person, unwilling to take big risks in life—or perhaps I merely rationalize my caution in this way. In recent years, the doctor's conversation has come to play itself out in my growing realization that since I may have been lucky to survive, I need to be very careful that I do something worthwhile with my life, as a kind of payback for getting the lucky break early on. Now, you must realize that I consciously suspect that the conversation with the doctor never took place. But part of my life story has been constructed around the possibility that the conversation did happen. I have imaginatively appropriated certain "facts" and possibilities in my own unique way, to make a story that makes sense to me. Consequently, life stories are not purely factual, but neither are they purely fiction. They lie somewhere in between.

Let us go back to Jerome Johnson, the African-American police chief who had a fateful encounter with the Reverend Martin Luther King, Jr. Did Johnson's meeting with King "really" convince him to stay the course and take the police department promotional exam? How can we ever know? Perhaps Johnson would still have taken the exam had he never met King. Perhaps he would have become police chief anyway. And while I am pretty confident that Jerome Johnson did not completely fabricate the King story, how do we know the conversation occurred exactly as he said it did? Did King really say, "Never stop dreaming the dream"? Does it matter? What does matter is that Johnson sees this event today, as he has reconstructed it, as the most important turning point in his life story. The reconstructed scene is a central element of Jerome Johnson's self-defining narrative. If you are to understand who Jerome Johnson is and how he makes sense of his own life, you must know his account of his brief meeting, sometime in the mid-1960s, with Dr. Martin Luther King, Jr.

Story Themes and Episodes

How might a psychologist obtain information concerning a person's life story? Typically, life-story accounts are obtained through structured interviews or open-ended written questionnaires (McAdams, 1999). Table 11.3 outlines a standard life-story interview that I have employed in my own research. This is the interview protocol that Jerome Johnson followed. In this interview, the participant is first asked to think of his or her life as if it were a book with chapters and to identify each chapter and outline each chapter's contents. Next, the participant describes eight key scenes or episodes that stand out in the story as especially important or self-determining events. These include a high-point event, a low-point event, and a life-story turning point. For each episode, the respondent should describe in detail exactly what happened, who was involved, what he or she was thinking and feeling during the event, and what the event may say about his or her life story overall. In subsequent questions, the participant is asked to describe the main life challenge he or she has faced, important positive and negative characters in the story, the future chapters of the story (including goals and dreams for the future), and an account of his or her fundamental religious, ethical, and political values and how they were formed. At the end of the interview, the participant

TABLE 11.3	A Life Story Interview
1. Life chapters	Participant divides life into its main chapters and provides a plot summary for each.
2. Eight key episodes	For each of eight scenes, participant describes what happened, who was involved, what he or she was thinking and feeling in the scene, and what he or she thinks the scene says about who he or she was, is, or might be. The eight episodes are: a. High point b. Low point c. Turning point d. Earliest memory e. Important childhood episode f. Important adolescent episode g. Important adult episode h. One other important episode
3. Life challenge	Participant identifies and describes the biggest challenge or problem he or she has faced in life, how the challenge developed, and what he or she has done to meet the challenge.
4. Main characters	Participant identifies and describes in detail the one character with the most positive influence in the story and the one with the most negative influence.
5. Future plot	Participant provides an account of where the story is going, what will happen next, what the future chapters will look like, including main goals, dreams, and fears for the future.
6. Personal ideology	A series of questions on fundamental values, religious and political beliefs, and so on, including how those values have developed over time.
7. Life theme	Participant identifies a single integrative theme in the life story.

Source: McAdams (1985b, 1993).

is asked to look back over the story and identify a central theme or message. The interview takes about 2–3 hours to complete. Typically, the interview is tape-recorded and transcribed into a typed copy, which is then subjected to various kinds of analyses.

There are many ways to analyze a life-story account. In recent years, researchers have been especially interested in identifying the central *thematic lines* in life stories. Thematic lines refer to what the characters in the story recurrently want or desire (McAdams, 1985b). In many stories, characters are often trying to get some form of power or love, or both. More generally, thematic lines often reflect what Bakan (1966) has called **agency** and **communion.** As we saw in Chapter 6, Bakan identified agency and communion as two fundamental modalities in all living forms. Agency refers to the individual's efforts to expand, assert, perfect, and protect the self, to separate the self from others, and to master the environment within which the self resides. With respect to personality traits (Chapters 5–6), agency is captured in concepts such as dominance and extraversion and is reflected as well in achievement and power motivation

(Chapter 8). Communion refers to the individual's efforts to merge with other individuals, to join together with others in bonds of love, intimacy, friendship, and community. With respect to traits, communion is captured in concepts such as agreeableness and nurturance, and it is also reflected in intimacy and affiliation motivation. Life stories may be compared and contrasted with respect to the strength and salience of agentic and communal thematic lines. In an agentic life story, characters strive for power, achievement, independence, mastery, and so on. In a life story dominated by communal themes, characters strive for friendship, love, intimacy, community, and so on. Some life stories contain high levels of both agentic and communal themes. And some life stories are low on both agency and communion.

Researchers have coded life stories for agency and communion themes in various ways. My colleagues and I developed and validated a system that breaks down agency and communion into four main subthemes each (McAdams, Hoffman, Mansfield, & Day, 1996). Each of these subthemes can be reliably coded in narrative accounts of key episodes in a life story, such as accounts of life story high points and turning points. Table 11.4 lists the subthemes. For agency, life-story episodes can be reliably coded for subthemes of self-mastery, status/victory, achievement/responsibility, and empowerment. For communion, life-story episodes can be reliably coded for subthemes of friendship/love, dialogue, care/help, and unity/togetherness.

Research suggests that themes of agency and communion in life stories are consistently related to people's motivational tendencies. For example, my colleagues and I have consistently found that people who tell life stories filled with the agency subthemes, like those listed in Table 11.4, tend to score relatively high on TAT achievement and power motivation and tend to list personal strivings concerning being successful and feeling strong (McAdams, 1982b, 1984a; McAdams et al., 1996). People who tell life stories high on communion subthemes tend to score relatively high on TAT intimacy motivation and to list personal strivings concerning establishing warm and close relationships with others. Woike (1995; Woike, Gershkovich, Piorkowski, & Polo, 1999) has conducted a number of studies showing links between agentic and communal themes on the one hand and TAT motives on the other. In asking individuals to describe their most memorable life experiences, Woike has shown that agentic stories line up with power and achievement motivation while communal stories tend to link to the intimacy motive. In addition, Woike has demonstrated that motives (Level 2 in personality) link not only to the content of life stories (Level 3) but also to the cognitive style that the storyteller displays when describing a most memorable experience. People with strong power and/or achievement motivation tend to employ an analytical and differentiated style when describing agentic events, perceiving more differences, separations, and oppositions in their life stories. By contrast, people with strong intimacy motivation, as assessed on the TAT, tend to employ a synthetic and integrated style when describing communal events, detecting similarities, connections, and congruence among different elements in their life stories.

Whereas agency and communion, then, refer to content themes in autobiographical recollections, the concepts of differentiation and integration refer more to the structure or style of the narrative. With respect to structure, life stories vary widely in terms of narrative complexity. Highly complex stories contain many different ideas and plots and articulate many different connections among these elements. By contrast, simpler stories contain fewer plots and develop fewer interconnections among ele-

TABLE 11.4	*Themes of Agency and Communion in Significant Autobiographical Episodes*

Agency

Self-mastery	The protagonist strives to successfully master, control, enlarge, or perfect the self. Through forceful and effective action, the protagonist is able to strengthen the self, to become a larger, wiser, or more powerful agent in the world.
Status/victory	The protagonist attains a heightened status or prestige among peers through receiving a special recognition or winning a contest or competition.
Achievement/ responsibility	The protagonist attains success in the achievement of tasks, jobs, or instrumental goals or in the assumption of important responsibilities.
Empowerment	The protagonist is enlarged, enhanced, empowered, ennobled, built up, or made better through an association with something larger or more powerful than the self.

Communion

Love/friendship	The protagonist experiences an enhancement of erotic love or friendship toward another person.
Dialogue	The protagonist experiences a reciprocal and noninstrumental form of communication or dialogue with another person or group of others.
Caring/help	The protagonist provides care, assistance, nurturance, help, aid, support, or therapy for another, promoting physical, material, social, or emotional welfare or well-being for another person.
Unity/togetherness	The protagonist experiences a sense of oneness, unity, harmony, synchrony, togetherness, belongingness, allegiance, or solidarity with a group of people, a community, or even all of humankind.

Source: McAdams, Hoffman, Mansfield, & Day (1996).

ments. Complex stories are not better or worse than simpler stories; they are just different. For example, contrast the multiple characters and complex subplots contained in a typical novel by Charles Dickens (e.g., *David Copperfield*) or Fyodor Dostoyevsky (e.g., *The Brothers Karamazov*) to the spare elegance of F. Scott Fitzgerald's *The Great Gatsby* or Ernest Hemingway's *The Old Man and the Sea*. All four of these novels are classics; the fact that two of them are structurally more complex than the other two seems irrelevant in determining their overall worth as literary products.

Certain personality variables at Levels 1 (traits) and 2 (characteristic adaptations) may be associated with narrative complexity in life stories. In particular, research suggests that Loevinger's concept of ego development (Chapter 10) is correlated with the complexity of people's life stories. In a study of 50 life stories, I found that adults high in ego development tended to include more different kinds of plots in their stories than did adults low in ego development (McAdams, 1985b). Helson and Roberts (1994) found that midlife women high in ego development were more likely than those scoring low to narrate negative life scenes in such a way as to suggest that they had changed considerably through the diversity. More complex stories may involve greater levels of change in the characters. In a study of how college students narrate their own religious development, my colleagues and I found that students high in ego development (conscientious, or I-4 and above in Loevinger's scheme) were more likely to articulate a story of *transformation and growth*, suggesting that they had gone through significant religious doubts and uncertainties and were developing toward a new and more personalized religious perspective (McAdams, Booth, & Selvik, 1981). By contrast, students relatively low in ego development (mainly in the conformist, or I-3, stage) tended to deny that they had ever gone through a crisis in faith or described a period of questioning in their life that was then abandoned as they returned to their original beliefs. The low-ego development students, therefore, tended to construct a narrative of *stability and consistency*. Furthermore, they tended to accentuate the role of group standards and the beliefs of others, showing the conformist mindset associated with Loevinger's low-middle stages. Below are two verbatim accounts of religious crises. The first example is from a woman high in ego development. The second is from a man in the low-middle range of ego development (Loevinger's conformist, or I-3, stage). What differences do you see between these two accounts?

A college student high (autonomous stage, I-5) in ego development: I think most of the serious questions evolved out of ethical problems—friends aborting fetuses, shady practices at my place of work, etc. Right and wrong were no longer clear—if they ever had been. These single issues were maybe resolved one by one, but greater ones arose. I guess one's appreciation (in the pure sense) of evil increases proportionate to age and experience. [On a trip to Germany] I stood at the ovens of Dachau [the World War II concentration camp] and asked how my Sunday-school class God could have let it happen. The questioning has not yet been resolved, but nor has it been abandoned. I rejoice in the opportunity to rail like Job against my God. (McAdams, 1985b, p. 221)

A college student low (conformist stage, I-3) in ego development: I search for what is real. At college my previous assumptions concerning the Bible, the nature of God, and my personal beliefs and experiences were questioned and, as I perceived it, threatened. The Bible was said to be nonauthoritative, only a book. God was more of a concept and ideal and not a friend. My personal experience of conversion and of sensing God was considered to be a subjective emotional experience. I prayed and prayed and read a variety of books presenting a variety of ways of looking at God. My search was led by a sense inside me that said that Jesus was real, God is alive, and the Bible is his Word. Looking at people's lives was the main reason for *reaccepting my first views*. I looked at people and watched their lives to see who was different in a good sense—who really cared and loved others. Then I looked at what they believed and listened to them. They also confirmed my inner yearnings. The academic look at God lacked life and life-giving potential. It was interesting and logical, but it didn't have what I was looking for in my life. (McAdams, 1985b, pp. 222–223)

Researchers sometimes focus on narrative accounts of one or two key episodes in a person's life rather than the entire life story per se (Thorne, Cutting, & Skaw, 1998). Pillemer (1998) has focused on people's recollections of momentous events in their lives. These personal event memories depict a single scene or moment in life that stands out for its rich sensory imagery and the great detail that the person remembers. Pillemer underscores the importance of four kinds of events that are vividly recalled: (1) *originating* events, marking the beginning of a plot line in the story; (2) *turning points*, marking a significant change from one plot line to another; (3) *anchoring* events, representing the stability or continuity of a given plot line; and (4) *analogous* events, displaying a pattern of activity that is very similar to what can be seen in a family of other events in the life story.

Jefferson Singer (1995; Singer & Salovey, 1993) has coined the term **self-defining memories** to denote recollections of events in one's life that the person believes to have been especially influential in shaping who he or she is. A self-defining memory is "vivid, affectively charged, repetitive, linked to other similar memories, and related to an important unresolved theme or enduring concern in an individual's life" (Singer & Salovey, 1993, p. 13). Moffitt and Singer (1994) collected narrative accounts of self-defining memories and reports of personal strivings or goals (Chapter 8) from college students. They found that students who recalled more self-defining memories relevant to the attainment of their strivings expressed greater levels of positive affect about their memories. In addition, participants who reported a high number of strivings involving avoiding undesirable outcomes also recalled fewer self-defining memories with positive emotional themes. Singer (1997) also documented the role of self-defining memories in the life stories of men addicted to alcohol and drugs. These memories are typically devoid of positive agency and communion themes. Recovery from addiction involves recrafting a life story that affirms agency and communion, argues Singer, and establishes new self-defining memories that sustain hope and commitment.

Story Characters: The Imago

Early experiences likely have a significant impact on the construction of identity. Even before a person reaches adolescence and begins to craft a self-defining life story, he or she is collecting experiences—both good and bad—that may help shape the contours and influence the color of the life story he or she will eventually create. The quality of attachment in the first few years of life, for example, may eventually help to influence the overall *tone* of the story (McAdams, 1993). Secure attachment bonds may leave a legacy of trust and optimism, which may help to color the life story in brighter hues. Insecure attachments may have the reverse effect of reinforcing pessimism and a somber narrative tone. Children collect a wide variety of *images* in peer play, in family life, through the media, in church, in school, and so on, and these images may endure well into adolescence to find their way into the life stories that they will someday create. Many different forces and factors, some within the person (e.g., genetic factors) and some in the person's environment, may help shape identity by providing raw materials for the making of the self. In adolescence, people begin to draw upon the resources at hand to make their own identities. But identities are always made in a psychosocial context, in relationships with others, in the midst of an interpersonal world. Our friends, families, teachers, pastors, and many others influence our identities. Still, identities are made; we author who we are. Therefore, we should not underestimate the power of the individual to shape his or her own destiny, to create a fulfilling life story even when the resources seem less than wonderful, and to create a dismal one even when one seems to be blessed with the best and brightest of possibilities. While nobody can make a silk purse out of a sow's ear, we are all nonetheless active creators and synthesizers in the construction of our own life stories.

By the time we reach the teenage years, therefore, we have already internalized information and experiences that are likely to influence markedly the particular tone, images, and themes that our life story will eventually reveal. In adolescence, it is finally time to begin putting things together into narrative form. The adolescent may begin by consciously and unconsciously working through an *ideological setting* for the life story. An ideological setting is the backdrop of belief and value that situates the story within a particular ethical and religious location. A person's beliefs and values about truth, right versus wrong, God, and other ultimate concerns situate the action of the story in a particular ideological time and place. With the advent of formal-operational thinking, the adolescent may begin to search for answers to abstract philosophical, ethical, political, and religious questions. Indeed, the consolidation of an ideological setting may be the central task of identity formation for many adolescents (McAdams et al., 1981). It is very difficult to construct a meaningful life narrative before this setting of belief and value is firmly established, as we saw, for example, in the biography of Martin Luther (Chapter 10). Once established, however, the ideological setting generally does not change much. Like the geographical and historical settings of most stories, the ideological setting remains in the background, rarely questioned or examined by the person after adolescence and young adulthood and thus fairly resistant to change.

While the adolescent begins to formulate personalized beliefs and values, he or she is also likely to adopt, for the first time in the life course, an historical perspective on the self. Teenagers realize that childhood is now a thing of the past. For the first time in their lives, adolescents have a history. In their minds, they *were* something before, and now they *are* something else. They seek to understand the meaning of what they were in the context of what they are now and what they may become in the future. As a way, then, of gaining perspective on the past, adolescents begin to sort through their memories in order to highlight key events and major turning points in their perceived autobiography—the self-defining memories identified by Singer.

Moving from adolescence into young adulthood, the central task in identity formation becomes the creation and refinement of "main characters" in the life story. All stories have main characters. In a life story, the main character is also the author—the person whose identity the story is. However, this main character may appear in a variety of forms. The various forms may be understood as main characters in their own right—semi-autonomous agents whose actions and interactions define the plot of the story. I call these **imagoes.** An imago is an idealized personification of the self that functions as a main character in the life story (McAdams, 1984c, 1985b, 1985c, 1993). Imagoes are one-dimensional, "stock" characters in the life story, and each integrates a host of different characteristics, roles, and experiences in the person's life. Imagoes are like little "me's" inside of me who act and think in highly personalized ways. The concept of imago resembles the idea of "possible selves" (Markus & Nurius, 1986) or "ideal" and "ought" selves (Higgins, 1987) described in Chapter 9. Imagoes also share conceptual space with certain psychoanalytic ideas such as "internalized objects" (Chapter 3) and inner "states" (Berne, 1964), "voices" (Watkins, 1986), and "personifications" (Sullivan, 1953). A person may see him- or herself as "the good boy (or girl) who never gets into trouble," "the sophisticated and intellectual professor," "the rough-around-the-edges working-class kid from the wrong side of town," "the corporate executive playing out the American dream," "the worldly traveler in search of all that is new and exotic," "the athlete," "the loyal friend," "the sage," "the soldier," "the teacher," "the clown," or "the peacemaker." Each of these capsule self-definitions might qualify as an imago. Each might exist within a particular life story as a carefully crafted part of the self that shows up as a main character in many different parts of the narrative. A person's life story is likely to contain more than one imago. Each of the imagoes lays claim to a particular set of identity resources.

In adulthood, imagoes may incorporate social roles. But imagoes are larger and more internal than social roles. The general features of a given role are defined by the society within which the role is operational. With respect to social roles, then, a mother is a woman who bears and/or raises children, providing care and counsel and endeavoring to promote her children's development in accord with her own values and society's demands. With respect to roles, a federal judge is a man or woman who presides over a courtroom trial, hears legal arguments, makes rulings about the admissibility of evidence, renders judgments in accord with law, and so on. These roles are elaborately scripted by societal norms and expectations. And we are all very familiar with them.

If a role is to become an imago, however, the role must be *internalized and broadened* to function as a personally crafted aspect of the self that is applicable to a wide range of life activities. A person whose life story contains a strong *imago* of "the mother" acts, thinks, feels, and strives as a mother does in a wide variety of ways that go well beyond caring for her own biological or adopted children. She magnifies and personalizes the social role and appropriates it within her own self-defining life story in such a way as to make it a central identity character. Similarly, the woman who develops an imago of "the judge" may be concerned, as a judge would be, about issues of justice and fairness in many different realms of her life, acting and thinking as if she were a judge even in those situations in which, sociologically speaking, she isn't one, as when she is with her family and friends. This kind of judge is not merely enacting social roles. The script is as much her own as it is the one society handed her when she accepted the judicial appointment.

Imagoes may personify aspects of who you believe you are now, who you were, who you might be in the future, who you wish you were, or who you fear you might become. Any or all of these aspects of the self—the actual perceived self, the past self, the future self, the desired self, the undesired self—can be incorporated into the main characters of life stories. Any or all of them can be given a distinctive characterization in narrative such that the resultant imago can come to dominate a particular chapter or personify a particular theme, idea, or value in the story. Any or all of them can serve to consolidate different social roles that one plays and internalize those roles in a self-defining manner.

As main characters in life stories, imagoes provide a narrative mechanism for accommodating the diversity of modern life. In seeking pattern and organization for identity, the person in the early adult years (ages 20–40) may psychologically pull together social roles and other divergent aspects of the self to form integrative imagoes. Central conflicts or dynamics in one's life may be represented and played out as conflicting and interacting imagoes, as main characters in any story act and interact to push forward the plot. While modern life often insists that we be many different things to many different people, that we act in accord with a wide variety of roles (Gergen, 1992; Goffman, 1959), we are able to reduce the multiplicity by organizing our many roles and demands into a smaller and more manageable cast of life-story characters. As a modern adult who must find meaning at home, at work, and in all the other domains in my life, I cannot and do not want to be everything to everybody at every place and time. But I can be some important things in some important ways for some important people, at particular times and in particular places. Furthermore, I can be these things in a way that is unique to me, and in a way that is self-consistent, coherent, meaningful, purposeful, and gratifying. Creating a life story that contains a rich but finite source of characterization—a suitable cast of imagoes—enables me to resolve the problem of simultaneously playing many different roles but still being "myself" (Knowles & Sibicky, 1990).

Imagoes are partly scripted by culture, and they partly reflect the values to which a given culture aspires. The philosopher Alasdair MacIntyre (1984) writes, "*Characters are the masks worn by moral philosophies*" (p. 28). According to MacIntyre, all societies generate their own stock characters that personify those beliefs and standards that the society as a whole or a significant segment of society holds in greatest esteem. The character furnishes people at a given time and in a given place with a cultural and moral ideal, legitimating a particular mode of social existence. For example, Bellah and others (1985) suggest that "the independent citizen" served as a representative moral character type for early-19th-century Americans. Reaching its culmination in the life of Abraham Lincoln, the independent citizen was the self-made, self-sufficient farmer or craftsman of small town America who held strongly to biblical religion and was fiercely devoted to the values of freedom and autonomy. The independent citizen captured the ideological spirit of the times, the moral exemplar of a young and idealistic nation.

The moral character types of which MacIntyre and Bellah speak are general models around which adults can pattern their own lives and articulate their own more personalized characterizations of self. Like moral character types at the societal level, personal imagoes often speak a language of value and belief at the level of individual adult identity. Significant aspects of the adult's ideological setting may be clearly expressed in life-story imagoes. A fundamentalist Christian may develop an imago of "the evangelist," a character devoted to spreading the Christian gospel to all who have yet to accept it. A Christian with a slightly different perspective may create an imago of "the loyal friend," seeing in St. Paul's teachings on love and charity the ideological inspiration for his own life. Outside the realm of religion, imagoes may personify ethical, political, and aesthetic values. A prime function of imagoes in some life stories is to be a mouthpiece or an exemplar for what a person holds to be right and to be true.

How many different kinds of imagoes are there? Because imagoes reflect, in part, a culture's values and possibilities and because people can be especially creative and imaginative in fashioning personifications of the self, there would appear to be a very large number of different kinds of imagoes that might be constructed by adults to serve as main characters in their life stories. In my studies of middle-class American adults, I have generated a taxonomy of general imago forms, into which many particular imagoes may be placed (McAdams, 1993). The taxonomy is presented in Figure 11.2. This classification system is organized along the twin thematic lines of agency and communion. Therefore, Class 1 imagoes are highly powerful and agentic characters such as "the warrior" and "the sage"; Class 3 imagoes are highly loving and communal such as "the friend" and "the caregiver"; Class 2 imagoes combine agency and communion to be both powerful and loving, these include "the healer" and "the teacher"; finally, Class 4 imagoes express little agency or communion, such as "the survivor" and "the escapist." I have also labeled some of these forms (Classes 1 and 3) with names from the mythology of ancient Greece in order to make them easier to remember. (Thus, the warrior is "Ares," and the caregiver is "Demeter.") In addition, the Greek labels draw on a comprehensive and timeless characterization of human diversity, for the deities of Mount Olympus represent projected personifications of what the ancient Greeks believed to be fundamental human qualities and propensities. Each imago category, moreover, should be seen as a type of *character in narrative*, not a type of person. A person's identity is not a single, simple imago. You are not "the sage," no matter how many of the qualities of Zeus your story suggests. You are more complex and multifaceted than any characterization coming from a Greek god, or from any other

---

FIGURE 11.2   *Imago Types*

Imagoes are personified and idealized images of the self that play the roles of main characters in life stories. Imagoes may be classified in terms of their relative emphasis on agency or communion. Some common imago types reflect classic characters in the mythology of ancient Greece.

Class 2: Agency and Communion
The healer
The teacher
The counselor
The humanist
The arbiter

Class 1: Agency
The warrior (Ares)
The traveler (Hermes)
The sage (Zeus)
The maker (Hephaestus)

Class 3: Communion
The lover (Aphrodite)
The caregiver (Demeter)
The friend (Hera)
The ritualist (Hestia)

Class 4: LOW Agency, LOW Communion
The escapist
The survivor

Source: Adapted from McAdams (1985b, 1993).

| TABLE 11.5 | *Motive Scores According to Predominant Imago* | | | |

| | IMAGO CLASS | | | |
	1 (AGENCY)	2 (AGENCY + COMMUNION)	3 (COMMUNION)	4 (LO/LO)
Power motivation	59.3	51.7	47.5	45.6
Intimacy motivation	47.8	53.1	57.9	45.6
N (Women/Men)	11 (9/2)	7 (1/6)	12 (9/3)	20 (11/9)

Power and intimacy motivation are assessed via objective content analysis of imaginative stories written to six standard pictures on the Thematic Apperception Test (TAT). The mean differences among the four groups on power motivation are significant ($F[3,46] = 6.16, p < .01$), with Class 1 imagoes having significantly higher power motivation than Classes 3 and 4 combined ($p < .001$), and Classes 1 and 2 having higher power motivation than Classes 3 and 4 ($p < .01$). The mean differences among the four groups on intimacy motivation are significant ($F[3,46] = 5.31, p < .01$), with Class 3 imagoes having significantly higher intimacy motivation than Classes 1 and 4 combined ($p < .001$). and Classes 2 and 3 imagoes having higher intimacy motivation than 1 and 4 combined ($p < .01$).
$N = 50$ adults between ages of 35 and 50 years.
Source: McAdams (1985b), pp. 192–196.

character type. A person's identity is *the story itself*, not any single character or part of the self in the story.

In a study of 50 men and women between the ages of 35 and 50, my colleagues and I attempted to identify and classify dominant imagoes in our subjects' life stories (McAdams, 1985b). Each of the adults in the study was asked to tell his or her life story. In addition, we administered a number of other personality measures, including the TAT. TAT responses were scored for power motivation and intimacy motivation, as described in Chapter 8. For each participant, we drew on an imago classification scheme similar to the one shown in Figure 11.2 and tried to discern the idealized personification that was most prominent in the story. As Table 11.5 shows, we found that those adults whose life stories displayed a highly agentic and powerful central imago (e.g., the warrior, the sage, the traveler, the maker) scored significantly higher on power motivation than other adults. Similarly, adults constructing life stories with a central communal imago (the lover, the friend, the caregiver, the ritualist) scored high on intimacy motivation. The results suggest an important connection between motivation and identity. People with a substantial need to feel strong and to have impact (high power motivation) construct self-defining life narratives with powerful and agentic protagonists. People with a strong need to feel close to others (high intimacy motivation) compose life stories whose central characters are caregivers, lovers, and loyal friends.

Types of Stories

Since the time of Aristotle, scholars have speculated about the extent to which the world of stories might be reduced to a finite number of types. Aristotle identified four mythic archetypes, or basic story forms: comedy, tragedy, romance, and irony. Some researchers have provided case data to suggest that life stories may contain elements of each of these four mythic archetypes (Crewe, 1997; McAdams, 1985b; K. Murray,

1989). Focusing on the protagonist's developmental movement, Gergen and Gergen (1986) distinguish among stability, progressive, and regressive life narratives. In stability narratives, the main character does not develop or change very much; in progressive narratives, the main character grows and expands over the course of time; in regressive narratives, the main character goes backward or loses developmental ground over the course of the story. Along with many other authors, Gergen and Gergen (1986) identify what Joseph Campbell (1949) labeled as the *myth of the hero* to be a common narrative form for the establishment of identity in Western cultures, especially among men. Appearing in countless tales and stories from a wide range of cultures, the hero myth is a story of separation, initiation, and return. The general form goes like this: "A hero ventures forth from the world of common day into a region of supernatural wonder; fabulous forces are there encountered and decisive victory is won; the hero comes back from this mysterious adventure with the power to bestow boons [gifts, advantages] on his fellow man" (Campbell, 1949, p. 30).

Campbell's hero myth is an especially linear narrative; the protagonist moves forward over time and continues to grow, expand, and progress. Gergen and Gergen (1993) suggest that such a linear structure may work well for mapping the lives of some men but that women's life stories are rather less linear. Instead, women may construct stories with more multiple and contradictory plot lines, with recursive or cyclical movements and ambivalent emotional states. Furthermore, Gergen and Gergen suggest, women's life stories may be more *embodied* than men's, more intimately linked to their understanding of and experiences with their own bodies. Other authors have suggested that the structures of women's stories, as well as those of economically and culturally disadvantaged groups, remain largely a mystery to psychologists, in that these stories have often been silenced or trivialized in patriarchal societies (Heilbrun, 1988; Stewart, 1994).

While some authors have tried to develop general taxonomies of story types, others have worked from the bottom up by identifying patterns they observe in particular studies of, say, "work" stories (Mishler, 1992; Ochberg, 1988) or "parenting" stories (Pratt et al., in press). For example, Modell (1992) identified common themes and narrative strategies in the stories that birth parents tell about why they gave up their children for adoption. Walkover (1992) found that married couples on the edge of parenthood crafted stories about their imagined future in which they romanticized and idealized the children they were about to have, suggesting an implicit (but irrational) belief in the perfectibility of childhood. Linn (1997) identified common narrative types among Israeli soldiers who refused to engage in what they believed to be immoral acts of aggression. Gregg (1996) identified a hybrid narrative form that mixes themes of modernity and traditional Islamic faith among contemporary young Moroccans. In her study of life stories constructed by American adults, Linde (1990) found that many of her participants routinely borrowed stock images and themes from popular psychology to make narrative sense of their own lives. In a study of published autobiographies of ex-criminals, Maruna (1997) identified a common life-narrative form that most of the authors seemed to draw on to explain how they got into crime and how they eventually got out of it. In this standard *reform narrative*, early scenes of passive victimization lead to a delinquent quest and repeated scenes of "bottoming out." The negative cycle is not broken until the protagonist experiences a second chance for agency and/or communion, often through the intervention of a good friend or potential lover.

The final life-story chapters consolidate reform through the protagonist's generative efforts to "give something back" to the world as he endeavors to help other actual and would-be criminals develop their own reform stories.

In an intensive interview study, my colleagues and I compared the life stories of 40 midlife adults who had distinguished themselves for high levels of what Erikson called generativity (Chapter 10) to the stories constructed by 30 less-generative adults, both groups matched for demographic characteristics (McAdams, Diamond, de St. Aubin, & Mansfield, 1997). The 40 highly generative adults were chosen for their generative efforts in paid work or volunteer activities and for their high scores on self-report measures of generativity. The 30 less-generative adults scored low on our generativity scales and evidenced only modest concern for the next generation through their paid work and volunteer activities. The highly generative adults were much more likely than their less-generative peers to formulate life stories that approximated what we termed a *commitment story*, similar to Tomkins's (1987) concept of a commitment script. Table 11.6 summarizes the five main themes of the commitment story: (1) early advantage, (2) suffering of others, (3) ideological steadfastness, (4) redemption sequences, and (5) prosocial goals for the future. Although every person's life story was unique, the highly generative adults, as a whole, showed statistically significantly higher levels of these five themes in their life stories compared with those of the less-generative adults.

Overall, the prototypical commitment story constructed by the highly generative adults in McAdams et al. (1997) was a story in which the protagonist comes to believe early on that he or she has a special advantage or blessing that contrasts markedly to

TABLE 11.6	*The Commitment Story: Five Themes Characterizing Life Stories Constructed by Highly Generative Adults*
1. Early advantage	As a young child, the story's protagonist enjoys a special advantage or blessing that singles him or her out in the family or vis-a-vis peers. From an early age onward, the protagonist feels that he or she is special in a positive way.
2. Suffering of others	Early in the story, the protagonist witnesses the suffering or misfortune of other people and feels sympathy or empathy for them. Objects of the protagonist's concern might include the sick, dying, disabled, mentally ill, economically disadvantaged, or any of a number of other groups or individuals that might require special care or help.
3. Ideological steadfastness	By adolescence, the protagonist has established a clear and coherent belief system that governs his or her life. The belief system, often rooted in religion, remains relatively stable and steadfast over time. Once the belief system is established, the protagonist does *not* experience profound ideological doubt, uncertainty, or crisis.
4. Redemption sequences	Bad or affectively negative life events are immediately followed by good or affectively positive outcomes. The bad scene is redeemed, salvaged, made better by what follows.
5. Prosocial future	In looking to the future chapters of the life story, the protagonist sets goals that aim to benefit society in general or its institutions.

Source: McAdams, Diamond, de St. Aubin, & Mansfield (1997).

the pain and misfortunes suffered by others. From an early age onward, then, the protagonist feels special in a positive way. Maybe I am my mother's favorite child; maybe I am blessed with a special talent; maybe my family was poor, but the people in our neighborhood were especially friendly and they helped one another out, as Jerome Johnson, the black police chief, related in his life story. While I am fortunate, others suffer. Highly generative adults were much more likely than nongenerative adults to recall early experiences in which they witnessed the suffering of others and felt empathy for those other people. Experiencing the world as a place where people need to care for others (because some are blessed and some suffer), the protagonist commits the self, typically in adolescence or even earlier, to living in accord with a set of clear and enduring values and personal beliefs that continue to guide behavior across the course of the story (ideological steadfastness). Moving ahead with the confidence of early blessing and steadfast belief, the protagonist encounters his or her fair share of personal misfortune, disappointment, and even tragedy in life, but these bad events often become transformed or "redeemed" into good outcomes, sometimes because of the protagonist's own efforts and sometimes by chance or external design. Jerome Johnson's chance meeting with Martin Luther King, Jr., is a good example of just such a redemption sequence. Thus, bad things happen, but they often turn good. Looking to the future with an expanded radius of care, the protagonist sets goals that aim to benefit others, especially those of the next generation, and to contribute to the progressive development of society as a whole and of its more worthy institutions.

While our original study of commitment stories focused mainly on white, middle-class adults, a second qualitative study examined the life stories of 35 midlife African-American adults, approximately half of whom scored extremely high on our measures of generativity and half of whom scored extremely low (McAdams, Bowman, Hart, Lewis, & Cole, 2000). The analysis confirmed the differences we observed in the first study. Highly generative African-American adults, like Jerome Johnson, were more likely than less-generative African-American adults to construct commitment stories to make sense of their lives. In addition, the life stories of black adults revealed other themes that were not generally observed among whites. For example, the narrative accounts of the African-American participants, both highly generative and less-generative, were noteworthy for the early emergence of danger and threat in the story, the clear identification of a (bad) antagonist against whom the (good) protagonist struggled, and the powerful and beneficent role of religion and extended kin networks in coping with the dangers and the antagonists that life presents. In both studies with white and black adults, nonetheless, the commitment story appears to be an especially powerful identity format for modern adults who are committed to doing good work for the next generation. This kind of story provides a way of talking about and thinking about one's life that sustains and supports a caring, compassionate, and responsible approach to social life. While doubtlessly many kinds of life stories might be associated with strong generativity, the commitment story would appear to qualify as one story type that, in contemporary American society, may be worth emulating.

One of the most appealing features of the commitment story is the *redemption sequence*. In a redemption sequence, a bad or emotionally negative scene turns suddenly good or emotionally positive. The bad episode is redeemed by the good that follows it. The theme of redemption is found in myths and folklore worldwide, and it is an especially powerful idea in all of the world's major religions (James, 1902/1958; Miller &

C'deBaca, 1994; von Franz, 1980). Redemption sequences capture the hope that experiences of fear, loss, sadness, guilt, and the like can lead to outcomes that affirm joy, excitement, and other positive emotional states. In sharp contrast, a *contamination sequence* is the move in narrative from an emotionally positive or good scene to an emotionally negative or bad outcome. In a contamination sequence, the initial good scene is spoiled, ruined, contaminated, or undermined by what follows it. Contamination sequences suggest that good events cannot be trusted to last, that bad outcomes will inevitably follow even the best moments in life. Therefore, while redemption sequences sustain hope and commitment in narrative, contamination sequences suggest despair, hopelessness, and the endless repetition of a negative past. Redemption and contamination sequences come in many varieties. Table 11.7 provides some condensed examples gleaned from recent life-narrative studies.

We have already seen that redemption sequences in life narratives are related to individual differences in adults' generativity. But do redemption and contamination sequences connect to other aspects of psychological functioning? We might expect, for example, that people who construct life narratives with a preponderance of redemption sequences should also report higher life satisfaction and better overall mental health compared with individuals with fewer redemption sequences. By contrast, we might expect that contamination sequences should be negatively associated with mental well-

---

TABLE 11.7   *Condensed Examples of Redemption and Contamination Sequences*

Redemption Sequences

Father dies → the family becomes emotionally closer
Loneliness of childhood → protagonist becomes a resilient adult
Severe depression → protagonist recovers and feels euphoric
Pain of delivery → birth of a beautiful baby
Divorce → protagonist develops better relationship with her son
Protagonist is fired from job → comes to see himself as a whole person
Drugs, dereliction → protagonist moves to a new place, changes name, gets life organized
A very bad teaching experience → protagonist moves to a new school and experiences success
Severe criticism from a co-worker → protagonist becomes a better employee
Traffic accident → all of a sudden "it became a cool experience"

Contamination Sequences

Marriage is wonderful → spouse says she wants a divorce
Protagonist is proud at graduation → father comments on how fat she looked onstage
Joy at birth of first son → protagonist learns child has a serious disorder
Protagonist marries the man she loves → he starts to have extramarital affairs
Protagonist gets a desired promotion → the new job brings frustrations and hassles
Protagonist builds model airplane, is proud, takes it to school → class bully breaks the plane
Looking forward to class trip → protagonist is horrified by poverty she sees on the trip
New house is a joy → repairs and bills become a nightmare
Sex is great before marriage → after they marry, wife is no longer interested
Playing happily in a park → young protagonist is injured and cannot find parents
Protagonist receives a gift → gift is stolen

Note: The designation of "→" connects the first scene to the outcome and thus means "leads to," "is followed by," or "results in."
Source: Adapted from McAdams and Bowman (in press).

being. To test these hypotheses, my colleagues and I collected life-narrative data and self-report measures of psychological well-being from two different samples of participants (McAdams, Reynolds, Lewis, Patten, & Bowman, in press). The first sample consisted of 74 adults between the ages of 35 and 65 years. In life-story interviews, each adult described eight key life episodes, including a life-story high point, low point, and turning point. The second sample consisted of 125 college students, each of whom completed a lengthy, open-ended questionnaire asking the participant to describe in full 10 key life episodes, again including a life-story high point, low point, and turning point. We coded all the episodes for redemption sequence; however, since the students related very few contamination sequences in their written accounts, we coded for contamination sequences only the scenes described by the adults. We then correlated the redemption and contamination scores with self-report measures of psychological well-being.

Table 11.8 presents some of the results from the adult sample in this study. As you can see, redemption scores in life stories were significantly and positively associated with life satisfaction, self-esteem, and sense of life coherence and negatively associated with self-reported depression. By contrast, contamination sequences were highly and negatively associated with the three indices of well-being and positively associated with depression. The data from the student sample replicated the results for redemption sequences. Overall, then, people who construct life stories in which bad events are redeemed by good outcomes tend to be more satisfied with their lives, report higher self-esteem and life coherence, and show lower levels of depression compared with people who have fewer redemption sequences in their life stories. By contrast, people who construct life stories with relatively more contamination sequences, wherein good events are suddenly spoiled or ruined, tend to be highly depressed and report especially low levels of satisfaction, self-esteem, and life coherence compared with individuals whose life stories show few contamination sequences.

Why do redemption sequences in life stories predict well-being and contamination sequences predict depression? The reasons are at least twofold. First, it is probably true that redemption and contamination sequences reflect objective realities from the past. Therefore, happier people may be happier because they have enjoyed many events in the past in which good outcomes did, indeed, follow bad events. These sequences are reflected in their life stories. However, a second reason surely relates to the selective power of memory and the constructive nature of life narratives.

TABLE 11.8	*Correlations Between Redemption and Contamination Sequences on the One Hand and Self-Report Indices of Well-Being on the Other, in 74 Midlife Adults*	
WELL-BEING	**REDEMPTION**	**CONTAMINATION**
Life satisfaction	.37**	−.40***
Self-esteem	.28*	−.56***
Life coherence	.33**	−.46***
Depression	−.32**	.49***

*$p < .05$; **$p < .01$; ***$p < .001$.
Source: McAdams, Reynolds, Lewis, Patten, & Bowman (in press).

Redemption and contamination sequences reflect implicit *choices* that people make in how they understand and narrate their autobiographical past. Choice is implicated not only in the selection of what particular scene to narrate but also in how to narrate the scene, how to frame its antecedents and consequences, and what conclusions to draw from it. In a redemption sequence, the individual narrates a sequence in which a very bad scene eventually results in some kind of positive outcome. In many instances, there are likely to be multiple outcomes for any particular event in a person's life. Yet the person telling the story in a redemptive manner manages, as Jerome Johnson did repeatedly in his life story, to elaborate on a particularly positive outcome. By contrast, the person who tells a contamination sequence manages to find the negative consequence of a particularly positive scene, and some people may be especially wont to reconstruct their lives in this manner. In both cases, the consequences may have really occurred, but there are likely to have been other consequences as well, some of which the individual has chosen not to narrate.

Therefore, it is likely that individual differences in the ways in which people narrate self-defining memories reflect both differences in the objective past and differences in the styles and manners in which people choose to make narrative sense of life. Furthermore, the individual styles employed are likely to be both the causes and the consequences of different levels of psychosocial adaptation. Thus, depressed and nongenerative people may be especially prone to narrating life in contamination terms, and the tendency to narrate life via contamination sequences may exacerbate depression itself and undermine the person's efforts to make positive contributions to the next generation. Similarly, people who feel relatively satisfied with their lives and feel that they are making important contributions to others may be especially prone to narrating their lives in redemptive terms, which in turn may further enhance their generative efforts and their sense of well-being.

What Is a Good Story?

People are working on their life stories, consciously and unconsciously, throughout most of their adult years. At times the work is fast and furious, as during phases of exploration and moratorium. Periods of major identity change may follow significant life changes, such as getting married or divorced, having one's first child, changing jobs, changing residences, losing one's parents or one's spouse, menopause, or retirement. They may also correspond to symbolic watersheds in the life course, such as hitting one's 40th birthday, the marriage of one's last child, the death of one's parents, retirement, or even getting those first gray hairs. During these periods, adults may call into question some of the assumptions they have lived by. They may recast their life stories to embody new plots and characters and to emphasize different scenes from the past and different expectations for the future. They may set new goals. The sense of the story's ending may change substantially, and as the envisioned ending changes, the entire narrative may become oriented in a very different way. At other times, however, adults experience relative stability in identity. During these more tranquil periods, the story evolves slowly and in a very small way. Adults may refine slightly their imagoes or tinker in minor ways with the sense of an ending. During these periods, major identity change may not seem to occur.

We see, therefore, that it is misleading to characterize the development of the life story in adulthood as either a smooth and continuous affair or a rollercoaster process of repeated change and growth. Rather, the development is both smooth and sudden, tranquil and tumultuous. Times of dramatic change and reformulation may be followed by long periods in which very little storymaking seems to occur. Every life is different in this regard, and every life story follows a unique course of development.

Nonetheless, certain developmental trends in storymaking may be observed as people move into and through midlife. There is a sense in which the development of identity in the midlife years should ideally move in the direction of *increasingly good narrative form* (McAdams, 1993, 1996b). Six standards of good life-story form may be identified: (1) coherence, (2) openness, (3) credibility, (4) differentiation, (5) reconciliation, and (6) generative integration. The prototype of "the good story" in human identity—the life narrative that suggests considerable maturity in the search for unity and purpose in life—is one that receives high marks on these six narrative standards.

Coherence refers to the extent to which a given story makes sense on its own terms. Do the characters do things that make sense in the context of the story? Do the motivations for their behavior make sense in terms of what we know about how human beings generally act? Do events follow events in a causal manner? Do parts of the story contradict other parts? A story that lacks coherence is one that leaves the reader scratching his or her head, wondering why things turned out in such an inexplicable, puzzling way. Some stories, however, are almost too coherent. They hang together so neatly that they seem too consistent to be true. A life story need not make everything fit together in a person's life. We do not need perfect consistency in order to find unity and purpose in life. Indeed, a good life story is one that also shows considerable *openness* to change and tolerance for ambiguity. Such a story propels the person into the future by holding open a number of different alternatives for future action and thought. Life stories need to be flexible and resilient. They need to be able to change, grow, and develop as we ourselves change. Openness is, nonetheless, a difficult criterion to judge in life narrative, for there is always the danger that too much openness reflects lack of commitment and resolve.

A third standard is *credibility*. The good, mature, and adaptive life story cannot be based on gross distortions. Identity is not a fantasy. People create their identities, for sure. But they do not create them out of thin air, as one might a poem or a story of pure fiction. In identity, the good story should be accountable to the facts that can be known or found out. While identity is a creative work of the imagination, it is still grounded in the real world in which we all must live.

The good story is rich in characterization, plot, and theme. The reader is drawn into an intricately textured world in which full-bodied characters develop in intriguing ways over time, and their actions and interactions define compelling plots and subplots, as tension builds to climax and then resolution. In other words, good story tends to be richly *differentiated*. Similarly, a life story should develop in the direction of increasing differentiation. As the adult matures and gathers new experiences, his or her personal myth takes on more and more facets and characterizations. It becomes richer, deeper, and more complex. As differentiation increases, however, the adult may seek *reconciliation* between and among conflicting forces in the story, harmony and resolution amidst the multiplicity of self. The good story raises tough issues and dynamic

When Did Identity Become a Problem?

The problem of identity may be a modern problem, most characteristic of middle-class Westerners living in industrial societies. In more agrarian and traditional societies and at earlier points in history, the problem of finding or creating the self in late adolescence and young adulthood may not have been as crucial. In societies in which sons are expected to grow up to do what their fathers do and daughters expected to follow directly in the footsteps of their mothers, identity is *conferred* upon the young person by a social structure. In such a context, ideology and occupation are received from established authorities, exploration of alternatives is minimal, and commitment to the status quo is a fait accompli.

Even among the intellectuals of Western societies, however, the notion that a person should find or create a unique self may be a relatively recent idea. In his book *Identity: Cultural Change and the Struggle for Self*, psychologist Roy Baumeister (1986) asks at what point in the history of Western civilization identity became a central concern. When did Westerners begin to report that they were experiencing identity "crises" in their own lives?

As Baumeister views it, evidence of identity exploration and crisis may be gleaned from reports of two different kinds of problems in human living. The first is the problem of *continuity over time*. In this case, identity poses itself as a problem when the person begins to wonder or worry about the extent to which he or she is essentially the same kind of person over time: "Am I the same today as I was 3 years ago?" "Will I be the same 10 years from now?" The second is the problem of *differentiation*. In this case, identity confronts the person with the task of determining how he or she is different from other people—others who, on the surface at least, seem quite similar to the self. In Baumeister's view, then, the person in the throes of an identity crisis is preoccupied with how he or she is essentially the same over time and how he or she is essentially different from other people.

Baumeister concludes that identity was not a major problem in Western societies before 1800, although many trends emerged before this time to prepare the way for it to become a problem. Medieval society in Europe operated on the basis of lineage, gender, home, and social class. A person's identity was as-

contradictions. And the good story provides narrative solutions that affirm the harmony and integrity of the self. Reconciliation is one of the most challenging tasks in the making of life stories, especially in midlife and beyond.

The sixth standard for good story in identity is what I call *generative integration*. To understand well this last criterion, we must again remember that a life story is about a human life. It is not simply a story that one might read in *The New Yorker* magazine. It is a mythic rendering of a particular life of a real person living in a particular society at a particular point in history. The life story seeks coherence, credibility, and reconciliation to a greater extent than might some very good stories that are purely fiction. Similarly, the human life exists in a social and ethical context that does not generally signed to him or her according to these external criteria. Even during the medieval era, however, certain strains of individualism emerged, including Christianity's emphasis on individual judgment and on individual participation in the church ritual. The Protestant Reformation split the ideological consensus of Europe and made religious belief a serious identity problem for many educated people. The rise of capitalism opened up economic opportunities and created an upwardly mobile middle class. Many people of the 17th and 18th centuries, therefore, confronted significant choices in their religious beliefs—whether to follow Rome or the Protestants, for instance—and enjoyed the prospect of enhancing one's material well-being in life through entrepreneurial activity in the marketplace. Other developments before 1800 that paved the way for identity's emergence as a central problem in human lives include a general rise in individualistic attitudes, increased desires for privacy, and the growing recognition that one's private self may be quite different from one's public self.

As Europe entered what has been termed the Romantic era in the last decade of the 1700s, the two great institutions of church and state were undergoing major transformation. While the Christian church's power and influence were waning rapidly, Europeans were also questioning the legitimacy of long-established political systems, as happened in the French Revolution. Men and women of the Romantic era substituted creativity, passion, and cultivation of the inner self for Christianity as new models for identity formation. If the self were not determined by God, then its construction was left to the individual. The Romantics also became increasingly dissatisfied with the relationship of the individual to society. This dissatisfaction was expressed as a concern with individual freedom, and it eventually gave birth to various Utopian movements as well as the rise of anarchism in the 19th century. In general, Europeans after 1800 believed that society's consensus about basic truths and ultimate values had been lost. The person was now to fashion a personal ideology as a foundation for identity.

In the 20th century, the concern for identity grew stronger as Westerners witnessed a great proliferation of occupational and ideological choices. In addition, many social critics lamented a growing alienation among

continued on next page

apply, or apply in the same way, to other kinds of stories (Booth, 1988). In mature identity, the adult is able to function as a productive and contributing member of society. He or she is able to take on adult roles in the spheres of work and family. He or she is able and willing to promote, nurture, and guide the next generation, to contribute in some small or large way to the survival, enhancement, or progressive development of the human enterprise. Mature identity in adulthood requires a creative involvement in a social world that is larger and more enduring than the self. It is to that world, as well as to the self, that the story is to be oriented. Ideally, the storymaker's search for unity and purpose in life should benefit both the person fashioning the story and the society within which the story is fashioned.

contemporary adults who, more than ever before, felt cut off from and had lost faith in authoritative institutions (Lasch, 1979; Lifton, 1979; Sartre, 1965). In the Romantic literature of the 19th century, individual heroes struggled valiantly against societal constraints. In much of 20th-century literature, on the other hand, the individual feels overwhelmed, even helpless, and more concerned than ever with finding continuity over time and establishing differentiation vis-à-vis other people.

Who am I? How do I fit into the adult world? In the wake of the industrial revolution, widespread urbanization, the decline of traditional religion, the rise of capitalism, the growing alienation of workers from their work, the demystification of life by science, the discovery of the unconscious, two world wars, and the atom bomb, these two questions appear more vexing today than ever before. As the literary critic Robert Langbaum (1982) puts it, identity may now be "*the* spiritual problem of our time" (p. 352).

LIVES AS TEXTS

Long before there were psychologists, human beings created and told stories about the problems and the possibilities in their lives. Poets, novelists, and film makers have continued to provide insights into life meanings through the stories they create, just as all of us—even as children—seek and find truths about ourselves and each other through making, hearing, and telling stories. In the past 15 years, psychologists seem to have rediscovered the story (McAdams, 1999). A growing number of developmental psychologists are now examining children's astute appreciation for stories and the ways in which they use stories in discourse (e.g., Lucariello, 1990; Mancuso, 1986; Pellegrini & Galda, 1990). Psychologists interested in education have begun to stress the powerful role of stories in teaching and learning, especially in education for values, and in moral development (Tappan, 1990; Tappan & Brown, 1989; Vitz, 1990). Social and personality psychologists now explore the different kinds of narrative *accounts* that adults devise to cope with personal problems and explain puzzling or problematic life events (e.g., Baumeister, Stillwell, & Wotman, 1990; Harvey, Weber, Galvin, Huszti, & Garnick, 1986; Leith & Baumeister, 1998). Lifespan theorists argue for the primacy of narrative in the understanding of adult lives. According to theorists such as Cohler (1982, 1990) and Whitbourne (1985), the adult life course should *not* be viewed as an orderly progression of developmental stages nor as a predictable expression of stable personality traits, but rather as an evolving narrative, situated in culture and history.

Three influential spokespersons for *narrative psychology* are Theodore Sarbin (1986), Donald Polkinghorne (1988), and Jerome Bruner (1986, 1990). Sarbin (1986) argues that the narrative can serve as a **root metaphor** for contemporary psychology. According to Pepper (1942), a root metaphor is a basic analogy for understanding the world. The dominant root metaphor in Western civilization is *mechanism*, the basic analogy of the machine. "The kind of machine employed to provide imagery may be a clock, a dynamo, a computer, an internal combustion engine," or any other mechanism to which the workings of the human mind, human behavior, and human affairs may be compared (Sarbin, 1986, p. 6). Sarbin views the narrative as a liberating metaphor for psychology because narrative reveals part of what is distinctively human about human beings—humans, unlike machines, are by nature storytellers—and it provides for a nuanced understanding of how human lives are situated in social and historical context. Polkinghorne (1988) agrees. He argues that at the heart of the *human sciences*—the sciences concerned with human conduct—is *narrative knowing*:

> Our lives are ceaselessly intertwined with narrative, with the stories that we tell and hear told, with the stories that we dream or imagine or would like to tell. All these stories are reworked in the story of our own lives which we narrate to ourselves in an episodic, sometimes semiconscious, virtually uninterrupted monologue. We live immersed in narrative, recounting and reassessing the meanings of our past actions, anticipating the outcomes of our future projects, situating ourselves at the intersection of several stories not yet completed. We explain our actions in terms of plots, and often no other form of explanation can produce sensible statements. (p. 160)

As we have already seen, Bruner (1986, 1990) suggests that the narrative mode of human thought is especially amenable to the analysis of human intention and action, whereas the paradigmatic mode better addresses the demands for physical cause-and-effect explanations, like those required in the physical sciences. Bruner (1990) also points out that within the human sciences stories are especially useful in providing explanations for events that do not fit socially expectable patterns. He writes, "the function of the story is to find an intentional state that mitigates or at least makes comprehensible a deviation from a canonical cultural pattern" (1990, pp. 49–50). Similarly, Chafe (1990) writes that people devise stories when a particular event or phenomenon is "difficult to account for" (p. 83). If I wake up in the morning, brush my teeth, read the paper, and then get in my car to drive to work, as I do most days, I will not be very motivated to create a story to explain what I did. Nothing really needs to be accounted for, in that my morning routine fits what Bruner calls a "canonical cultural pattern." But if I wake up to find a baby lying in a basket on my doorstep, where the newspaper usually is, then there are stories to be learned and told, for events have transpired in a way that deviates from the expectable pattern. Where did this baby come from? Who abandoned her on my doorstep? What do I do now? As I rush the baby into the house, yell upstairs to my wife, and telephone the police, I am already creating narrations to explain what at the moment seems inexplicable.

If we extend this point to the field of personality psychology *in toto*, then we might suggest that each individual human life is analogous to an event or phenomenon that must be accounted for because each individual life, in one way or another, deviates from what Bruner calls the "canonical cultural pattern." To put it another way, each person is unique. The uniqueness must be explained. It can best be explained through story. As we saw in Chapter 1, personality psychologists who have focused their attention on the uniqueness of the individual have adopted what Allport called the *idiographic* approach to investigation, as with in-depth analyses of single cases. By contrast, those personality psychologists more interested in general laws and patterns across different individuals have traditionally adopted *nomothetic* approaches. How to put these two approaches together has been a perennial problem in personality psychology since the days of Allport.

Hermans's Dialogical Self

One contemporary personality psychologist who believes strongly that idiographic and nomothetic methods can be creatively combined in the study of lives is Hubert Hermans (1976, 1988, 1991, 1992a, 1992b, 1992c, 1996; Hermans & Bonarius, 1991; Hermans, Kempen, & van Loon, 1992). In a flurry of publications, Hermans has described his own narrative approach to understanding the self. It is an approach that draws upon both nomothetic and idiographic perspectives to make sense of how people make sense of themselves, through stories.

Hermans begins with the concept of **valuation.** A valuation is "anything that a person finds to be of importance when thinking about his or her life situation" (Hermans, 1988, p. 792). Valuations can include beloved persons in one's life as well as those whom one dislikes, disturbing dreams, difficult problems, cherished opportunities, memories of particularly important events from the past, plans or goals for the future, and so on. Each valuation is a unit of meaning in the person's life. Each valuation has either a positive, negative, or mixed (ambivalent) emotional quality. Through self-reflection, people organize their valuations into narratives that situate them in time and space.

From a nomothetic standpoint, Hermans suggests that different persons' valuations can be interpreted in terms of two primary motivational systems. Adapting Bakan's (1966) concepts of agency and communion (this chapter), Hermans distinguishes between agentic *S-motives* and communal *O-motives*. S-motives concern *s*elf-strivings for superiority, expansion, power, control, and so on. O-motives are *o*ther-oriented, longing for contact, union, intimacy, and so on, with others. These two motives give direction and organization to the wide variety of valuations in an individual's life story. A second dichotomy for organizing valuations is that between *positive* and *negative* affectivity. Different people may be compared and contrasted, then, with respect to the extent to which their valuation systems exhibit relatively high-to-low levels of S-motives, O-motives, positive affect, and negative affect.

Hermans has developed a *self-confrontation method* for collecting and assessing valuations. It is a method through which the research subject serves as a "co-investigator" rather than purely an object of investigation (Hermans & Bonarius, 1991). In other words, Hermans and his colleagues view the research enterprise as a matter of mutual cooperation between participants and researchers. Data are obtained through dialogue, or conversation, between the researcher and the research participant. The philosophy of this approach assumes that participants themselves are the "experts" when it comes to understanding their own lives. The researcher provides a series of questions to guide the conversation and to obtain a listing of the subject's most important valuations. Some of those questions are presented in Table 11.9.

The self-confrontation method typically yields between 20 and 40 discrete valuations for each participant. In the second phase of the research, the person goes back to each valuation and rates it, on 6-point scales, for each of 16 different emotion terms. Four of the terms refer to S-motives ("self-esteem," "strength," "self-confidence," and "pride"); four refer to O-motives ("caring," "love," "tenderness," and "intimacy"); four refer to positive affect only ("joy," "happiness," enjoyment," and "inner calm"); and

TABLE 11.9	*Questions Used to Elicit Valuations in the Self-Confrontation Method*

Set 1: The Past
—Was there something in your past that has been of major importance or significance for your life and which still plays an important part today?
—Was there, in the past, a person, an experience, or circumstances that greatly influenced your life and still appreciably affects your present existence?
You are free to go back into the past as far as you like.

Set 2: The Present
—Is there in your present life something that is of major importance for, or exerts a great influence on, your existence?
—Is there in your present life a person or circumstance which exerts a significant influence on you?

Set 3: The Future
—Do you foresee something that will be of great importance for, or of major influence on, your future life?
—Do you feel that a certain person or circumstance will exert a great influence on your future life?
—Is there a goal or object that you expect to play an important role in your future life?
You are free to look as far ahead as you wish.

Source: Hermans (1991), p. 222.

four refer to negative affect only ("worry," unhappiness," "despondency," and "disappointment"). For each valuation, the researcher then calculates an S index by summing ratings on the four corresponding S-motive affects and comparable indexes for O (O-motives), P (positive affect), and N (negative affect). Other important indices include the "S minus O" score, to determine whether self or other motive ratings are stronger for a given valuation, and the "P minus N" score to determine the relative strength of positive versus negative affect.

In terms of nomothetic research, Hermans has explored how certain patterns of valuations characterize certain groups of people. For example, Hermans (1992b) identified an interesting group of psychotherapy clients whose valuations manifested "unhappy self-esteem." Whereas a considerable body of research suggests that ratings of happiness and self-esteem are positively correlated, certain people go against the grain, revealing valuations that score high on both S and N. Compared to other psychotherapy clients, these individuals have developed narratives of the self in which especially meaningful events and persons elicit in them a paradoxical mix of self-respect and strength on the one hand and unhappiness on the other. Hermans and van Gilst (1991) identified another group of psychotherapy clients whose valuations resembled the affective ratings made by 10 students of the ancient story of Narcissus (Feature 5.A in this book). When we think of "narcissism" and the story of Narcissus, we usually think of a person who is self-centered—high "S" in Hermans's scheme. However, the pattern of ratings that best captured the meaning of the Narcissus myth was *low* S, *high* O, low P, and high N. Therefore, the psychotherapy clients whose valuations most closely resembled the Narcissus myth seemed to be suffering more from a frustrated longing for union with others, rather than an overabundance of self-striving.

From the idiographic standpoint, Hermans suggests that the examination of valuations is a window into each person's uniquely positioned **dialogical self** (Hermans, Kempen, & van Loon, 1992). Following William James (Chapter 10), Hermans distinguishes between the senses of self as "I" and "Me." The I is the self as author of a life narrative, complete with the valuations that provide life with meaning. The Me is the self as actor in the life narrative, an actor who "moves" throughout the story to assume many different roles. But the I also moves, from one "I position" to another, making for multiple authors, multiple I's, for the same life story. Most views of the self with which we, as Westerners, are familiar are individualistic and rationalistic, viewing the I as a potentially rational and self-contained "thinker" or "knower." In Descartes' famous expression, "I think; therefore, I am." But Hermans rejects this prevailing view in favor of a dialogical self that is *multiple and embedded in dialogue.* As an author of its own life story, the I moves from one "I position" to another, adopting different perspectives from which to understand the self. The different I positions are in dialogue with each other. Hermans, Kempen, and van Loon (1992) write:

> We conceptualize the self in terms of a dynamic multiplicity of relatively autonomous *I* positions in an imaginal landscape. In its most concise form this conception can be formulated as follows. The *I* has the possibility to move, as in a space, from one position to the other in accordance with changes in situation and time. The *I* fluctuates among different and even opposed positions. The *I* has the capacity to imaginatively endow each position with a voice so that dialogical relations between positions can be established. The voices function like interacting characters in a story. Once a character is set in motion in a story, the character takes on a life of its own and thus assumes a certain narrative necessity. Each character has a story to tell about experiences from its own stance. As different voices, these characters exchange information about their respective *Mes* and their worlds, resulting in a complex, narratively structured self. (pp. 28–29)

This is a difficult idea to comprehend at first. We take for granted that the self is singular in some sense, that *I* create *my* life story. We may concede that the story may have many characters (or imagoes), but it is a single *I* who creates them. From Hermans's point of view, however, the I is really a host of storytellers; there is no single perspective for an author, but rather many different positions from which the story is told. Each I position can establish itself as a more-or-less autonomous "voice." Drawing from the Russian literary critic M. M. Bakhtin (1973), Hermans conceives of the self as a *polyphonic novel*—a complex story with many voices. Each voice presents its own unified world, as in the great novels of Fyodor Dostoyevsky wherein different characters develop their own ideologies and world views, which in turn play off against each other:

> In Dostoyevsky's novels there is not one single author, Dostoyevsky himself, but several authors or thinkers (e.g., the characters Raskolnikov, Myshkin, Stavrogin, Ivan Karamazov, and the Grand Inquisitor). Each of these heroes has his own voice ventilating his own view, and each hero is authoritative and independent. A hero is not simply the object of Dostoyevsky's finalizing artistic vision but comes across as the author of its own ideology. According to Bakhtin, there is not a multitude of characters within a unified objective world, illuminated by Dostoyevsky's individual vision, but a plurality of perspectives and worlds: a polyphony of voices. As in a polyphonic composition, the several voices or instruments have different spa-

tial positions and accompany and oppose each other in a dialogical relation. (Hermans, Kempen, & van Loon, 1992, p. 27)

In summary, Hermans offers a provocative theory of the self in which persons provide their lives with meaning by organizing their valuations into life narratives. Rather than seeing the narrative as the product of a single author—a single storymaking "I"— Hermans argues that the I moves in imagination from one authorial position to another, as if it were a single *body* moving over a variegated landscape offering many different scenic views. Certain positions, or viewpoints, become especially important over time, and these are the positions from which the I develops a distinctive voice. Ultimately, a life story is the product of many different authors—many different I positions. The different authors may contradict one another, as different characters in a polyphonic novel offer their own unique and discordant world views. Instead of an individual, rational self, the person is endowed with multiple, storytelling selves, each in dialogue with the others.

Music and Story: Gregg's Approach

Another perspective on narrative that emphasizes the multiplicity of the self is offered by Gary Gregg (1991, 1995). Like Hermans, Gregg argues that the self is expressed through many different voices. For any given person, the different voices may seem to create a confusing cacophony; it may seem that there is little pattern, order, or organization to the different selves a person shows. However, closer examination of individual life stories convinces Gregg that beneath the phenotypic noise of clashing voices lies a genotypic piece of music, complexly patterned and meaningful, expressing endless variations on a small number of themes, like a fugue.

Music is the driving metaphor for Gregg's approach. Life stories reveal a musical structure of the self. The two primary axes of music are harmony (vertical) and melody (horizontal). Harmony is expressed in chords, as the musician plays different notes simultaneously to create an instantaneous blend. Melody is expressed as a sequence of notes, played over time. Harmony and melody are made possible by the structure of scales, such as the familiar diatonic scale of whole and half notes within an octave. (If you are having trouble following this, just sing "do, re, mi, fa, so, la, ti, do" to remind yourself of what a scale is. The range from the first "do" to the second "do" is called an octave.) How each note is heard in a musical piece is determined by the musical structures of the scales employed. For Gregg, personality is like a fugue, a musical form in which several voices play variations on a single theme. Typically, one voice introduces the theme (melody), and others answer it with variations, producing a dialogical form, a kind of musical conversation among the voices. In each voice, the theme can be expressed in a wide variety of ways. One voice may express the theme twice as quickly as another; another voice may change the rhythm of the theme; a third may invert the theme; and so on. Each voice is, therefore, both *the same as* and *different from* every other voice, in that each voice expresses the theme but is likely to express it in a very different way. And so it is in personality, argues Gregg. Among the many different voices of the self, one may discern an underlying "identity-in-difference" (p. 52).

Like Hermans and McAdams, Gregg suggests that the major themes of human identity concern power and love, or what Bakan (1966) calls agency and communion.

People often invest the meanings associated with these themes into concrete images and objects in their worlds. For example, Gregg describes the case of "Sharon," a young woman whose major life themes are captured in the images of "tofu" and "junk food." When Gregg interviewed her in 1979, Sharon was one of two partners who had built a successful business that manufactures and distributes tofu and other health foods in the Midwestern United States. For Sharon, tofu was more than just health food. It rather symbolized *for her* an entire "New Age" ideology celebrating diet, nutrition, exercise, good health, the simple life, and social renewal—a personal ideology that provided her life with a great deal of coherence. As an entrepreneur running a cooperative business, she could be an autonomous, healthy, and effective woman involved in improving the lives of those who worked in her company and those who consumed her products. Tofu also symbolized a number of personal habits and commitments connected with her New Age ideology. In addition to keeping a nondairy vegetarian diet, she studied T'ai Chi, practiced Yoga meditation, attended various self-fulfillment workshops, experimented with herbal medicines, campaigned against nuclear energy, and worked to sustain egalitarian community institutions.

By contrast, junk food symbolizes Sharon's past, growing up in Wisconsin, in a large family with an overweight mother, eating meat, dairy products, candy, and junk food. It was a "warm, cozy, still-in-the-womb type of existence," but it eventually proved too stifling and too indicative of what Sharon now views as an exceptionally unhealthy American lifestyle—eat lots of junk, get fat, have lots of kids, drive lots of cars, keep consuming, get lazier and lazier, die young. Junk food, therefore, symbolizes a way of living—a theme in her identity—that Sharon finds disgusting and wasteful. She never wants to be fat. She believes she is not ready to start a family. Yet, recently, she has felt a craving to have a baby. Pregnancy would make her "fat." The craving frightens her now, for it threatens to undermine the healthy, New Age existence she has created for herself. In a sense, junk food opposes tofu. In another sense, junk food and tofu are the same:

> To come to the theoretical point: Sharon craves love and nurturance in the form of dairylike foods. She differentiates this craving by symbolically differentiating its objects into natural and healthy foods, on the one hand, and chemicalized junk foods, on the other. Tofu and junk food thus stand in an essentially octave relation to each other: tofu is ice cream "raised" an octave, ice cream is tofu "lowered" an octave. The "raised" and "lowered" have moral, existential, and political meanings that are the essentials of "sublimation" and "regression," respectively. That is, tofu and ice cream encode the imperative she emphasizes in outlining her biography: to strive for autonomous self-nurturance against the recurrent beckoning of passive indulgence. They "work" by virtue of their "identity-in-difference." They are identical in some properties (their appearance, texture, and taste similarities make them interchangeable) and in the meanings these properties represent to her (nurturance, safety, and love). But at the same time they possess other properties that are different (origin, manufacturing, packaging, and preparation in particular) and so can represent antithetical meanings (natural versus artificial; healthy versus poisonous; industry versus lethargy). Logically represented: B = A and C = A, yet B ≠ C. The structural ambiguity of these symbols enables Sharon to establish an "octave" craving for nurturance via food into adult and autonomous versus infantile and dependent forms. (Gregg, 1991, p. 89)

What ultimately links and differentiates junk food and tofu, then, is their relation to each other as ends of an "octave." Each is like the "do" on the scale you sang to yourself a moment ago. But *tofu is the higher "do,"* the one an octave up. What makes it higher is its *moral significance*. Tofu connects to a New Age ideology within which Sharon finds a great deal that is good, right, and true. Tofu is the way people *should* live if the world is to be a better, happier, and healthier place. Junk food is lower because it connects to a slothful and wasteful lifestyle; it is bad, wrong, and false, in this sense. And yet there is another sense in which both tofu and junk food are good, in that both connote love and nurturance. Junk food is the easy love of her mother, cozy and warm. Tofu is a New Age kind of adult love, love for one's fellow woman or man, love between equals.

Tofu and junk food receive their moral significance from the culture in which Sharon lives. Her personal meanings for these symbols come ultimately from her experiences growing up in the 1950s and 60s in small-town Wisconsin and coming of age in the 1970s as a student at the University of Wisconsin. At the university, she was exposed to a wide variety of alternative lifestyles, out of which she developed her current New Age viewpoints. An essential point in Gregg's approach to lives is his insistence that personal meanings derive ultimately from social, political, economic, and cultural realities. Following the sociologist Emile Durkheim, Gregg argues that social organization provides general categories of thought to the members of any particular society. Social organizations are not necessarily kind and gentle, and encouraging of healthy development, self-actualization, and the like. Rather, social organizations embody stratification and oppression, as revealed in class, ethnic, and gender inequalities. The life narratives that people create to provide their lives with the "identity-in-difference" that we find in the musical fugue reflect and even reinforce the social order in many cases. Gregg writes:

> I have insisted that a reality exists outside of the narratives: a reality of social/political inequality into which each individual is "thrown" and in which each individual constructs a self as an ideological tool with which to struggle for power and a semblance of personal dignity—typically denying equality and dignity to groups of Others in the process. I have argued that this reality is to be found not only outside the narrative as its efficient cause, but at its core, in the semantic/syntactic kernel that generates it: in [for example] Sharon's spiritual-dietary struggle for "New Age" self-sufficiency . . . (p. 199)

In conclusion, Gregg's approach to the self as both music and text underscores the multiplicity of voices with which the self speaks (or sings). It views the self as an orchestration of voices, each a variation on one of a small number of themes, that are similar to and different from each other by virtue of their formal relations within the music. The voices express a great deal of tension and conflict within the music, as well as peace and resolution. Voices and themes are often symbolized in complexly determined and emotionally charged images or objects, as we see in Sharon's appropriation of the images of tofu and junk food. Voices and themes express both personal and cultural meanings. Personal meanings are typically couched in cultural terms, reflecting the macrosocial order of the world within which the self is made.

The Postmodern Self

The 1980s and 1990s brought a good deal of discussion among some social scientists about the unique problems of making sense of the self in a *postmodern* world (e.g., Davies & Harre, 1990; Denzin, 1989; Gergen, 1992; Holstein & Gubrium, 2000;

Sampson, 1985, 1988, 1989a, 1989b; Shotter & Gergen, 1989). The term **postmodern** is used in many different ways to refer to an assortment of perceived trends in art, architecture, literature, the media, social organization, and human consciousness that seem to have come to the fore in Western thinking since the 1970s. It is difficult to characterize the idea of postmodernity in a few sentences, in part because it means different things in different arenas. At its heart, however, is a skeptical and playfully ironic attitude about grand systems, universal truths, and conventional ways of doing things (Harvey, 1990). In general, the postmodern attitude is to embrace, or at least "deal with," the ambiguity and multiplicity that follow a rejection of all universal claims. In a postmodern world, there ultimately are no large truths. Instead, there are various versions, accounts, narratives, and so on—"texts," all of them—each subjectively construed from a particular point of view. Texts change from one moment to the next. Nothing stays the same. "Postmodernism swims, even wallows, in the fragmentary and the chaotic currents of change as if that is all there is" (Harvey, 1990, p. 44). In general, we may celebrate postmodernity for its openness, tolerance, and dynamism. Yet at the same time, we may find the postmodern refusal to believe in anything for the long run, to count anything as holding intrinsic truth and goodness and value, to be discouraging and even frightening, especially since human beings seem always to have demanded that there be something enduring "to believe in."

The concept of narrative is especially appealing in considering the problems of the postmodern self. Lives are like texts, narratives that continue to be written and rewritten over time. But what are texts? They are nothing but patterns of words, pictures, signs, and other sorts of representations. There is nothing substantially "real" about them; nor is there any sense in which a text can be said to be really "true" or "good." In some ways, postmodernity dovetails with the influential literary movement of the 1970s and 1980s called *deconstructionism* (Derrida, 1972). Among the many claims of deconstructionism is the idea that literary texts have no inherent and stable meanings. Language is indeterminate. Every word is ambiguous in and of itself, and its particular meaning in a particular moment is dependent on its relation to other equally ambiguous words with which it is spoken or written.

If lives are like texts, then lives, too, have no inherent meanings (Denzin, 1989). People may think that they understand who they are, that their lives "stand for something" or "express something true." But they are mistaken, just as readers are mistaken when they think they have found a single meaning in a given novel or short story. The mistakes are to be expected, because "stories and texts are written 'as if' they do have centers. Thus, writers and readers presume and 'read into' texts real authors, real intentions, and real meanings" (Denzin, 1989, p. 45). From the standpoint of deconstructionism, however, these readings are fallacies. A valid deconstructionist reading of a text, by contrast, exposes the many *inconsistencies* and *contradictions* in the text, and even reveals how authors of texts who think they are saying something true, or making a particular point, subtly "turn on themselves," proving themselves wrong in the texts themselves even when they don't realize it! Exhibiting a postmodern theme, a deconstructionist interpretation of a text may be "playfully ironic" in its revelation of texts as merely "language games" (Harre, 1989).

If lives are like texts, people construct selves in and through the sharing of texts in *discourse*. In other words, identities are made through talk, by uttering words and putting forth symbols in a social context. Shotter and Gergen (1989) write, "The primary medium within which identities are created and have their currency is not just linguistic but textual; persons are largely ascribed identities according to the manner of their embedding within a discourse—in their own or in the discourses of others" (p. ix). In a sense, each moment of discourse brings with it a new expression of the self. Over time, expressions are collected and patched together, much like a montage or collage.

The central problem of the postmodern self, then, is that of *unity*. Because all texts are indeterminate, no single life can really mean a single thing, no organizing pattern or identity can be validly discerned in any single human life. In his provocative book, *The Saturated Self*, Kenneth Gergen (1992) makes this point quite forcefully:

> The postmodern condition more generally is marked by a plurality of voices vying for the right to reality—to be accepted as legitimate expressions of the true and the good. As the voices expand in power and presence, all that seemed proper, right-minded, and well understood is subverted. In the postmodern world we become increasingly aware that the objects about which we speak are not so much "in the world" as they are products of perspective. Thus, processes such as emotion and reason cease to be real and significant essences of persons; rather, in the light of pluralism we perceive them to be impostors, the outcomes of our ways of conceptualizing them. Under postmodern conditions, persons exist in a state of continuous construction and reconstruction; it is a world where anything goes that can be negotiated. Each reality of self gives way to a reflexive questioning, irony, and ultimately the playful probing of yet another reality. The center fails to hold. (p. 7)

Drawing on deconstructionism and other postmodern themes, Edward Sampson (1989a, 1989b) has argued that psychology needs to develop a new understanding of the person. Because postmodern life is so indeterminate and because technology and the global economy now link people together from all over the world, it no longer makes sense to think of persons as individuals. Indeed, thinking of persons as individuals has never made sense in many cultures. Geertz (1979) writes: "The Western conception of the person as a bounded, unique, more or less integrated motivational and cognitive universe, a dynamic center of awareness, emotion, judgment, and action, organized into a distinctive whole and set contrastively against other such wholes and against a social and natural background is, however incorrigible it may seem to us, a rather peculiar idea within the context of the world's cultures" (p. 229). The Western view of the person as a self-contained individual reached its zenith in the "modern" period of Western history, suggests Sampson, beginning in the 16th century and running into the 20th.

In Sampson's view, the person is a "location" of intersecting forces and interacting voices situated within a particular social community and linked in the postmodern era to many other communities around the globe. It is difficult to know just how literally to interpret Sampson's argument, however. He surely is not suggesting that biologically distinct organisms are not in fact individual organisms. My body is not your body. Psychologically, however, what I consider to be "my" self—that which is mine, that which I have authored—may not really be mine, Sampson suggests. "Persons become the *guardians of* particular assets, not their owners," Sampson writes (1992a, p. 919). Selves are "constitutive." "Persons are creatures whose very identities are constituted by their social locations" (Sampson, 1992a, p. 918). The stories of self are not inside the person, waiting to be told. Instead, the person seems to reside amidst the stories, which surround and define him or her. The self is as much "out there," in the swirl and confusion of the postmodern world, as it is "in the mind" of "the person."

In conclusion, the postmodern approaches to understanding self are more skeptical than other theories reviewed in this chapter about the extent to which people's lives are integrated and purposeful. Whereas Tomkins's script theory, McAdams's life-story model of identity, Hermans's theory of the dialogical self, and Gregg's music-based approach to life texts all suggest that human lives are endowed with some kind of dynamic structure and internal organization, the postmodern approaches, like Gergen's (1992), tend to emphasize the extent to which lives are contingent and selfhood is fleeting and socially determined. With their emphasis on the determining power of social context and their denial of inner coherence in human lives, postmodern approaches resemble behaviorism (Chapter 4) and the purely "situationist" position in the "person versus situation debate" (Chapter 5). In place of the behaviorist's emphasis on environmental "stimuli" and situational "cues," the postmodern approaches substitute patterns of discourse and the language games that prevail in particular cultural contexts. For both the behaviorists and the postmodernists, what we do and what we say seem almost completely to be determined by factors in the environment.

Nonetheless, the postmodern approaches to selfhood share with the other perspectives in this chapter a strong and abiding belief in the power of human narratives. Human life is storied, conceived in terms of settings, scenes, characters, plots, and themes. Stories are ideally suited to capture how a human actor, endowed with consciousness and motivated by intention, enacts desires and strives for goals over time and in social context (Barresi & Juckes, 1997). Life stories are psychosocial texts that are jointly crafted by the individual him- or herself and the culture within which the individual's life has meaning. Our stories reflect who we are, but they also reflect the world in which we live.

SUMMARY

1. While personality traits provide an initial sketch and characteristic adaptations fill in the details of human individuality, narrative approaches to personality address directly the question of what a life means, in particular what it means to the person who is living it. More than traits, motives, stages, and so on, life stories convey the overall meaning and purpose of a human life. In order to provide a full account of human individuality, therefore, the personality psychologist must examine people's self-defining life narratives.

2. Human beings are storytellers by nature, and stories appear in every known human culture. The narrative mode of human knowing emphasizes the realization of human intention organized in time whereas the paradigmatic mode of human knowing explains natural events in terms of material cause-and-effect relationships. Stories have certain recognizable structures and features, such as settings, characters, and temporally organized action sequences.

3. While stories entertain and inform, they also serve to integrate and heal. One prime psychological function of autobiographical writing is to bind together disparate aspects of a person's life in order to construct a narrative that confers unity and purpose on life.

Many forms of psychotherapy implicitly or explicitly urge the client to re-story his or her life. Research also suggests that narrating personal events can enhance health and well-being. Studies by Pennebaker show that disclosing narrative accounts of personal trauma can facilitate coping with trauma and can help prevent sickness and promote good physical health.

4. Tomkins's script theory of personality puts the role of narratives at the center of human individuality. The theory begins by positing the motivational primacy of discrete human affects, such as joy, excitement, sadness, and anger. Affects energize and direct human behavior, which over time becomes organized into scenes and scripts. Tomkins views the person as a playwright who fashions a self-defining drama by linking affectively charged scenes together into life scripts, a process that he terms psychological magnification. Positive-affect scenes are magnified through variants, as the mind accentuates differences among them as variations on a theme. Negative-affect scenes are magnified through analogs, as the mind accentuates similarities and repetitions among different negative events. Scenes can be organized into many kinds of scripts. Two important scripts identified by Tomkins are commitment scripts, which involve clear ideal scenes and the striving to overcome obstacles, and nuclear scripts, which involve ambivalent and confusing scenes and the repetition of sequences in which good things turn bad.

5. McAdams's narrative approach focuses on Erikson's concept of identity. According to this view, identity is itself a life story that the person begins constructing in late adolescence and young adulthood. As an internalized and evolving narrative of the self, the life story integrates disparate roles and brings together the reconstructed past, perceived present, and anticipated future in order to provide a person with a purposeful identity in modern life. Culture provides the narrative resources for identity, and life stories are strongly shaped by gender, social structure, and the material and ideological givens of a particular society.

6. Research has examined life-story scenes or episodes for the central themes of agency and communion. Studies have shown that self-defining episodes, such as life-story high points and turning points, reflect thematic tendencies that can be predicted from personality variables outside the story itself, such as social motives and ego development. People scoring high on power and achievement motivation, therefore, tend to construct (and remember) life episodes emphasizing agency while people high in intimacy motivation tend to construct (and remember) more communal life episodes. High stages of ego development have been associated with greater levels of complexity and change in accounts of important life-narrative scenes. Life-story episodes and themes are also conveyed through the representations of the story's main characters, or imagoes. Imagoes are personified idealizations of the self that serve as protagonists in the life story and help to plot the multiplicity of selfhood within a more-or-less unifying life narrative.

7. Recent research has sought to delineate different types of life stories. One general type that has been identified in studies of midlife adults is the commitment story, similar to Tomkins's commitment script. In the commitment story, the protagonist (a) enjoys an early family blessing or advantage, (b) is sensitized to the suffering of others at an early age, (c) is guided by a clear and compelling personal ideology that remains relatively stable over time, (d) transforms or redeems bad scenes into good outcomes, and (e) sets goals for the future to benefit society and its institutions. Variations on the commitment life story appear to be relatively common among highly generative midlife adults—that is, adults committed to promoting the well-being of youth and the next generation. For both midlife adults and students, the tendency to construct life stories in which bad events are ultimately redeemed into good outcomes is associated with greater psychological well-being. Over the human lifespan and with maturity, people's life stories should ideally move in the direction of greater coherence, openness, credibility, differentiation, reconciliation, and generative integration.

8. Hermans has developed a narrative theory of the dialogical self. The basic units of life stories are valuations, which may be classified in terms of positive and negative affect and in terms of agentic S-motives and communal O-motives. Valuations are organized into narratives through a dialogical process, or a conversation within the self among different voices. There is no single, overarching storyteller, but rather a collection of voices that produce a polyphonic novel, which is itself the self.

9. Gregg offers another narrative-based approach to understanding human lives which, like that of Hermans, emphasizes multiplicity and the self's involvement in dialogue. The driving metaphor in Gregg's theory, however, is music. Personality is akin to a musical fugue, with different voices expressing different melodies and motifs. Especially noteworthy are examples in life narratives of emotionally charged images that reflect personal tendencies that are both opposite to each other and fundamentally similar, as different musical notes in an octave relation.

10. In recent years, a number of writers have employed the idea of narrative in considering the problems and possibilities of the postmodern self. According to some, the contemporary self is deconstructed into a swirl of fleeting stories and postures, expressed in the ever-changing discourse of contemporary life and in the particular cultural contexts within which selves are constituted. Unlike other approaches reviewed in this chapter, postmodern theories of selfhood are skeptical of any integrative or unifying forces within the person. Nonetheless, these approaches share the view that human lives are storied and that life stories reflect both who the person is and what kind of world the person lives in.

Writing Stories of Lives: Biography and the Life Course

If you met Grope, you would be unimpressed. Picture a short, dark-haired, slightly disheveled young man, enrolled at Harvard College in the 1930s. Aside from his association with a prestigious university, he seems a rather unremarkable undergraduate—quiet, apathetic, uninvolved, and uninspired. By his own account, he is a "small frog in a big puddle," a "pretty nice guy." He is shy, and he speaks softly and rarely. He is a member of no extracurricular clubs or organizations. He dates no women and spends very little time studying. His withdrawal from so many instrumental and interpersonal activities enables him to "devote the maximum amount of time to sleep, relaxation, daydreaming, and playing bridge with a small clique" of buddies (Murray, 1955/1981, p. 544). Though you might call him lazy, there is nothing grossly wrong with Grope: He is not psychotic; he is not a psychopath; he has never committed a crime. We might be surprised to learn, therefore, that in his dreams, fantasies, and through the *story of his own life*, Grope longs to fly.

ICARUS: AN ANCIENT STORY

In the ancient story of Icarus, a young boy fashions wings and flies toward the sun. As he soars higher and higher, the heat from the sun melts the wax in his wings, sending him plummeting to the sea below. The Icarus legend is a story about hot sun and cold sea, about fiery ambition ultimately quenched by watery defeat, about rising and falling. In a profound sense, the story of Icarus is the story of Grope's life. In a famous case study, Henry A. Murray (1955/1981) interpreted the life and the personality of this unassuming college student in terms of an ancient Greek story about a young boy who rises and then falls. According to Murray, Grope revealed a pervasive **Icarus complex.**

Grope was one of a number of students who volunteered to participate as subjects in a series of interviews, tests, and experiments conducted by Murray and his associates at the Harvard Psychological Clinic in the 1930s and 1940s (Murray, 1938). As a subject, Grope wrote a detailed autobiography that laid the groundwork for three subsequent 1-hour interviews. In addition, Grope was administered a series of questionnaires and rating scales and certain open-ended exercises such as the Thematic Apperception Test (TAT) in which a person is asked to create imaginative stories in response to pictures.

Some highlights from Grope's autobiography: Grope was the first of three children born to a college-educated couple. Grope's earliest memory was dumping his supper on the floor in a fit of revenge aimed at his mother. Grope wet his bed and his pants regularly until about the age of 11. By sixth grade, he had established himself as the premier student and athlete in his class. By seventh, he had started his self-described "fall" from supremacy after losing weight, failing to grow even an inch in the course of a year, and suffering repeated colds and bouts of sluggishness. Grope seemed to rebound slightly in high school, as he was elected treasurer of his sophomore class, chosen to serve on the student council and yearbook staff, and applauded as "Biggest Joker" in the senior class upon graduation. Attending Harvard, however, marked another fall into the mediocrity of the small frog in the big puddle. At the time of his first interview, Grope viewed himself as entering a behavioral and emotional limbo: "I am just biding my time and waiting for the day when my 'soul' will *ignite* and this inner *fire* will send me hurtling (two rungs at a time) *up* the ladder of success" (p. 543). Once his soul "ignited" and he began his ascent, Grope would be able to achieve what he saw as the ultimate values in life: "money, power, glory, and fame."

Murray tells us of a few of the stories Grope most liked to tell himself:

> His major recurrent fantasy was one of landing on a desert island in the Pacific with a band of followers, discovering an inexhaustible spring of fresh water and an abundant food supply, and then founding a new civilization with himself as king and lawgiver. He often dreamed and daydreamed of self-propelled flights and of jumping off a high place and floating gracefully and gently to the ground. But he was almost equally hospitable to less extravagant fantasies: he considered becoming a prize fighter, an actor, an army general, a millionaire, an inventor, a psychiatrist, and a teacher. "It would be a lot of fun working with kids, teaching them with a sense of humor, and having them think you are a 'good guy.'" He has imagined himself a famous tap dancer, a singer, and a movie comedian. He is attracted by the stage and has a tentative plan of enrolling in some school of drama. His more immediate intention, however, is to enlist in the Air Corps and become a pilot. Although in his opinion world wars are preventable evils, he expects another one within fifteen years, which will destroy much or most of civilization. The two worst things that might happen to him are (a) to be maimed in the war and (b) to lose his self-confidence. Finally, he writes: "If I could remodel the world to my heart's content, I would establish a sound World Government and would like to be the dictator, a good dictator." He would be "most proud" of having his name "go down in history as a leader, or as an artist, or as a discoverer or inventor." (pp. 542–543)

The story of Icarus was reflected in Grope's images of who he was and who he had been, Grope's fantastical scripts foreshadowing who he might be and what he might do in the future, the critical scenes in Grope's past that stood out as turning points in his own life story, and the ideological underpinnings of the story that celebrated money, fame, and glory as the ultimate life values. Drawing mainly from Grope's autobiography, dreams, fantasies, and narrative responses on the TAT, Murray delineated a number of recurrent themes in Grope's life, summarized in Table 12.1, that converged to form the Icarus complex.

The first theme in the Icarus complex is *urethral erotism*, which means the thematic association of "hot" sexuality and "wet" urination. Images of urethral erotism concern the "cathection of fire, 'burning' ambition, exhibitionism, and voyeurism" (p. 548). Murray points to Grope's reported childhood belief that babies are made by urinating into a woman's rectum, the high incidence of fire imagery in Grope's imagination, a lifelong fascination with fire ("fire is a yellow-orange gas from outer space," Grope proclaimed as a precocious 6-year-old), and the persistent problem of enuresis (bedwetting).

Murray argued that urethral erotism was fused, in the case of Grope, with a second theme of *ascensionism*, or sudden rising. Ascensionism assumed a variety of guises for Grope as he imagined himself riding through the air perched upon the buttocks of his childhood nurse (a significant night dream), shooting through space and landing on the planet Mars, hurtling up the ladder of success, and reaching dizzying heights of prestige and influence. Witness the merger of urethral erotism and ascensionism in

TABLE 12.1   *The Icarus Complex in the Case of Grope*

Urethral Erotism

In short, sex was apperceived in urinary terms. Also he manifested, in high degree, every other concomitant of urethral erotism, as defined by Freud and his followers: cathection of fire, "burning" ambition, exhibitionism, and voyeurism. Remember Grope's bright saying: "Fire is a yellow-orange gas from outer space." Even today he "gets a thrill" by lighting wastepaper in his tin scrap basket and seeing it flare up. There is a high incidence of pertinent fire imagery in his projective protocols. Finally, there is the association of persistent enuresis and urethral erotism (dreams of urination accompanied by ejaculation) which we and others have found in a number of personalities. (p. 548)

Ascensionism

This is the name I have given to the wish to overcome gravity, to stand erect, to grow tall, to dance on tiptoe, to walk on water, to leap or swing in the air, to climb, to rise, to fly, or to float down gradually from on high and land without injury, not to speak of rising from the dead and ascending into heaven. There are also emotional and ideational forms of ascensionism—passionate enthusiasm, rapid elevations of confidence, flights of the imagination, exultation, inflation of spirits, ecstatic mystical up-reachings, poetical and religious—which are likely to be expressed in the imagery of physical ascensionism. (p. 548)

Cynosural Narcissism

This strikes me as a suitable term (more embracing than exhibitionism) to denote a craving for unsolicited attention and admiration, a desire to attract and enchant all eyes, like a star in the firmament. (p. 549)

Falling/Precipitation

"Falling" denotes an undesired or accidental descension of something (usually a human body or the status [reputation] of a person, but it may be feces, urine, or any cathected object). "Precipitation," on the other hand, means a consciously or subconsciously desired calamitous descension: the S allows himself to fall or leaps from a height (precipitative suicide), or he pushes another person over a cliff, throws something down, or purposely urinates or defecates on the floor. (p. 551)

Craving for Immortality

No doubt the narcissistic core in every man yearns for perpetual existence; but of all our subjects Grope is unexampled in giving Everlasting Life ("I might settle for 500 years") as one of his seven wishes for himself. (p. 553)

Depreciation and Enthrallment of Women, Bisexuality

Grope spoke contemptuously of his mother, and cynically of women generally. Love was never a felt experience. But, as his projective protocols made plain, women were nonetheless important, if not indispensable, to him as glorifying agents: a female was (a) someone to be "swept off her feet," to be driven "sex-mad" by the mere sight of him; (b) someone to applaud his exploits; (c) someone of "wide hips" to bear him sons; and (d) someone to mourn his death. As one might expect in such a person, there were abundant evidences of a suffusing feminine component coupled with some degree of homosexuality. This is best illustrated by a story he told in the Tri-Dimensional Test. A king announces he will give half his kingdom to the person who creates the most beautiful thing in the world. The last contestant (hero of the story) comes forward and says, "I have created a replica of myself." Whereupon the king says, "*That* is the most beautiful thing in the world, therefore *you* are the most beautiful thing in the world. Will you be my queen?" The king takes the hero as his male queen and gives his androgynous beauty half his kingdom. (p. 554)

Source: From Murray (1955/1981).

this remarkable story Grope told in response to a TAT picture of a barn surrounded by snow and a winged horse flying across the sky:

An old hermit went out into the woods and built himself a farm. After thirty years of living all by himself on the crops he produced, he got pretty tired of this humdrum existence, so he decided that he wanted to re-enter the competitive world, and try to sell, was planning on selling his crops, planning to build some sort of fortune. So he worked for a few years, couldn't seem to get very large crops, really good crops. They wouldn't grow. What he needed was more fertilizer, but he couldn't afford fertilizer in any quantity, so he was practically at his wit's end, and one night he decided to turn to religion; and as miracles will happen, the very next day Pegasus flew over and fertilized all his plants [assumedly by urinating on them]. Not only that, but the cow in the barn bore him a daughter [impregnated by Pegasus?!—urethral erotism]; something he had always wanted. In the picture here, he is squinting in his happiness; feeling that life has really been rewarding. So the picture is the spirit of happiness. (p. 549)

The third theme of the Icarus complex is *cynosural narcissism*, which denotes a craving for unsolicited attention and admiration. Grope's fantasies about who he might be in the future were populated by heroic images of self as the benevolent dictator, actor, prize fighter, inventor—all superstars acclaimed and venerated by millions. Murray commented on the significance of Grope's drawings for the Draw-A-Family Test in which he drew his own portrait twice the size of his father's and mother's, as well as his narrative response to a blank TAT card upon which he projected the image of a virtually naked, gigantic man surrounded by an adoring crowd. The man is the "most perfect physical specimen in all of Greece . . . a sensation . . . a wonderful box-office draw" (p. 550).

Finally, the fourth theme of *falling/precipitation* is linked to the first three themes in a series of ascension–decension cycles that Murray perceived at a number of different levels. In Grope's early memories, dreams, and TAT responses, as well as in his reconstruction of his own "falls" from prominence in seventh grade and upon entering Harvard, what goes up always comes down, and with a crash. (Indeed, Grope's supper falls crashing to the floor in his earliest memory.) In one grizzly story Grope told in response to a TAT picture, six people eventually die, four by falling into water. The "cold sea" quenched the flaming ambition of both the ancient Icarus and his modern counterpart. The images of fire and water, sun and sea, recall the first theme of urethral erotism.

Why did Henry Murray decide to relate the fantasies and feelings of an unremarkable college undergraduate to the ancient story of Icarus? What is the point of saying that Grope has an Icarus complex? I believe that Murray settled on the Icarus story because only a story could account for so many different aspects of Grope's life as a whole. As we saw in Chapter 11, stories serve to integrate lives. We construct and live according to our own internalized and evolving narratives of self—the integrative life stories that constitute our very identities. In the case of Grope, however, it is Murray, as much as Grope, who is looking to articulate a story. The Icarus legend gives Murray the story he needs to make sense of Grope's life. The Icarus legend provides Murray with an elegant and provocative narrative for making sense of some of Grope's fantasies and dreams, his imaginative responses to TAT pictures, his values and aspirations, his memories of the past, and the current malaise he is experiencing as an undirected college student without an identity. In short, the Icarus complex is *Murray's story about Grope*. In order to convey key aspects of Grope's individuality, Murray finds he must tell a story.

Lament for Icarus

We typically do not (and should not) think of personality psychologists as story-tellers. Like other behavioral scientists, personality psychologists typically work within what we identified in Chapter 11 as the *paradigmatic mode* of knowing (Bruner, 1990). This means that personality psychologists collect reliable and valid data, test hypotheses, perform precise measurements, and attempt to uncover lawful cause-and-effect relations concerning human individuality. Every chapter in this textbook has illustrated different scientific methods and theories employed in paradigmatic personality research. Even psychologists who work with life stories, as we saw in Chapter 11, typically use those stories in a paradigmatic, scientific manner, attempting, for example, to classify, systematize, and measure aspects of life narratives and to use those assessments in a paradigmatic way. Having said this, it is nonetheless also true that certain forms of personality study do involve the psychologist's operating in what Bruner (1990) has called the *narrative mode* of knowing. This does not mean that personality psychologists occasionally write novels and short stories (though there is no law that says they cannot). Instead, I am referring here to psychologically informed efforts to conduct *biographical studies* of individual cases (Elms, 1994). Because stories are so effective in conveying the meaning of a human life in time, personality psychologists sometimes try to account for individual lives by discovering, relating, or constructing integrative interpretive stories. In the case of Grope, Murray relied on the ancient story of Icarus to convey aspects of his individuality that he could not effectively convey in any other way.

In this last chapter in the text, we explore different ways in which personality psychologists employ integrative stories to make sense of human lives. Whereas in Chapter 11 our focus was on the stories that people construct to make sense of their own lives, our focus in the current chapter is on the stories that psychologists employ to make sense of the lives of their research subjects. In a sense, the life stories we considered in Chapter 11 may be seen as *first-person accounts*—the stories people construct to make sense of who they are. In this chapter, we will consider stories as *third-person accounts*—storied interpretations that psychologists construct to make sense of who other people are. These third-person interpretations may indeed draw upon the first-person accounts. For example, in order to develop his Icarus interpretation (third-person), Murray used as data stories that Grope told about his own life (first-person). In describing the uses of stories in personality research, Barresi and Juckes (1997) write: "Researchers use first-person narratives as source material and third-person narratives in describing and interpreting lives because the temporal nature of experience makes it difficult for human beings not to attribute order, direction, and purpose to experience. It is because lives are structured through experience in a storylike manner that their study takes the narrative form" (p. 693).

We begin our exploration by following Murray through his seminal work at the Harvard Psychological Clinic in the 1930s, where he launched what has come to be known as the "personological tradition" in personality psychology. The personological tradition has emphasized biography, myth, narrative, and the intensive investigation of the single case. The role of case studies in personality psychology was as controversial in Murray's day as it is today. We examine the controversy and comment on the appropriate use of case studies in personality psychology. We then consider the related, and also controversial, topic of psychobiography, which usually refers to especially ambitious efforts to interpret the course of an individual's life in terms of broad personality theory. Many personality theories implicitly view aspects of human individuality in narrative terms. For example, Erikson's eight stages of development can be seen as eight "chapters" in a generic narrative of life (McAdams, 1997c). In the current chapter, we explore two theories that explicitly describe the life course in narrative terms—Alfred Adler's individual psychology and Daniel Levinson's theory of adult development. Finally, we reconsider social context and the vagaries of social training in adult lives by touching on the life course perspective as it applies to the stories people tell to make sense of human lives. The life course perspective brings us back to the issue of human agency and individuality, which is why personality psychology exists in the first place.

PERSONOLOGY AND THE STUDY OF LIVES

Murray and the Harvard Psychological Clinic

In 1927 Harvard University hired a little-known physician with a Ph.D. in biochemistry to serve as an assistant to Morton Prince, a prominent psychologist at the Harvard Psychological Clinic. Although the 34-year-old Henry Murray had begun to distinguish himself in medical research, he was virtually untrained in psychology proper, having taken (and not enjoyed) only one undergraduate course in the subject 15 years before.

Born of a wealthy family in New York City in 1893, Murray had traveled and studied widely in his 20s and 30s. He had been unable to find a fulfilling intellectual project for himself until he read, in 1923, Carl Jung's *Psychological Types* and, shortly thereafter, spent a vacation with Jung. Murray later wrote, Jung "provided [me] with an exemplar of genius that settled the question of [my] identity to come" (1967, p. 291). "We talked for hours, sailing down the lake and smoking before the hearth of his Faustian retreat. . . . Within a month a score of bi-horned problems were resolved, and I went off decided on depth psychology" (Murray, 1940, p. 153). At about the same time in Murray's life, a number of other influences appeared to work together to nudge him in the direction of psychology, including his reading of romantic authors such as Dostoyevsky and Melville and his growing professional and personal relationship with Christiana Morgan, who shared Murray's strong interest in human personality (Anderson, 1988; Murray, 1940, 1967; Robinson, 1992). Two years after Murray signed on at the Harvard clinic, Morton Prince died. Murray succeeded him as the director.

Prince had started the clinic as a place where undergraduates might be taught abnormal psychology with the aid of clinical demonstrations (Robinson, 1992; White, 1981). Known for his work on hysteria, multiple personality, and unconscious mental processes, Prince was able to draw upon his own intriguing case accounts to make abnormal psychology vivid for the students. Indeed, he was even able to bring patients into the classroom so that they could display firsthand their often bizarre symptoms and strange abilities. While the method might sound like good pedagogy to us today, the Psychology Department at Harvard was not enthusiastic about Prince's showmanship, and they looked askance upon his enthusiasm for such unscientific-sounding phenomena. Thus, it was agreed that the clinic would be housed in a location far removed from the proper psychology laboratories, lest people get the wrong idea about what respectable psychology was supposed to be about. When Murray moved in to help, Prince's operation was moving along rather nicely. Classes were being taught and experiments were being undertaken in the domains of hypnotism and hysteria. A student at the clinic during this time, Robert White (1981) suggests in retrospect that if Prince had lived longer the clinic might have won some marginal respectability as a center for specialized research into rather peripheral human phenomena. Everything changed, however, when Murray took over:

Henry A. Murray

I was present as a graduate student during the year before and the year after Prince's death, then absent for the next three years in a teaching position. When I returned, it was to a wholly different world. Everyone was talking about needs, variables, and a mysterious process called thematic apperception. Strange people were wandering in and out, neither staff, patients, nor students, but simply personalities undergoing study. The ship had radically changed its course.

When I recovered from my initial confusion I learned that certain important decisions had been made during the time I was away. First, because it was hard to interpret the results of an experiment when one knew nothing else about the subjects, the scheme had been adopted that all experimenters should use the same pool of subjects. Each worker could thus see his or her own findings in light of what the others had discovered. Second, the interpretations could be further enriched if one knew still more about the subjects, so it was decided to study them as individuals by means of interviews and tests. The third decision was the big one. If a lot of different workers were going to use each other's findings, there had to be a common language, a common scheme of variables, adequate to account for what was significant in personality. To accomplish such a purpose it was necessary to decide what really was significant, then work out a taxonomy to bring observation under orderly control. (White, 1981, p. 5)

Murray put the person at the center of inquiry. If the person is the center, then the investigator must become familiar with the person in many different contexts. Each person would be interviewed in depth and subjected to a wide assortment of data-gathering procedures. Different investigators should approach the person from different angles. The investigators should meet regularly to compare notes and synthesize their results on particular persons. Different investigators, therefore, made up what Murray called a *Diagnostic Council.* The diagnostic council entertained and synthesized information on the same person (subject) obtained from many different vantage points. So that different investigators would be able to communicate with one another, Murray devised an elaborate new nomenclature for personality processes. His comprehensive system provides a language for describing personality that remains highly influential today.

During the 1930s Murray headed a remarkable intellectual collaboration at the Harvard Psychological Clinic, bringing together scholars from academic psychology, psychoanalysis, anthropology, biology, and other disciplines to focus on personality study. Among the most noteworthy scholars who passed through the clinic in the years shortly before and after World War II were Robert White (this chapter), Donald MacKinnon, Jerome Frank, Saul Rosenzweig, R. Nevitt Sanford, Samuel Beck, M. Brewster Smith, Erik Erikson (Chapter 10), Daniel Levinson (this chapter), Jerome Bruner (Chapter 11), and Silvan Tomkins (Chapter 11). The clinic became the setting for intensive, interdisciplinary, longitudinal studies of relatively normal college men. The overall aim of the research was to arrive at a complex understanding of the whole person. Murray's enterprise was especially remarkable in light of American psychology's commitment in the 1930s to the most rigorous and reductionistic methods and models of behavioral science. While American psychology glorified laboratory investigations of rats and pigeons, Murray sought to study real people in their natural habitats. While American psychology focused on the elementary laws of simple learning, Murray was fascinated with human motivation, especially as it functioned in complex and unconscious ways. While American psychology was decidedly suspicious of psychoanalysis, Jungian psychology, and anything smacking of nonorthodoxy, Murray invited scholars of all stripes, even some from the humanities, to partake in the heady intellectual discussions and analyses occurring at the clinic.

Murray himself looked to literature and mythology for inspiration in understanding human personality. He developed an abiding passion for the novels and short

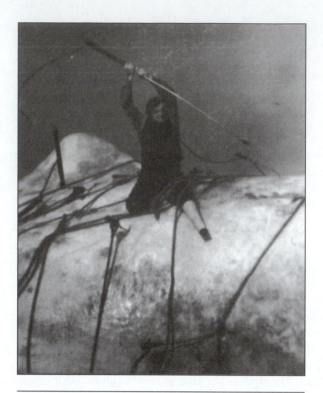

Henry A. Murray was fascinated with the life and work of Herman Melville, author of Moby-Dick. *Here Gregory Peck is Captain Ahab in the movie version of Melville's classic.*

stories of Herman Melville, publishing in 1951 an influential analysis of Melville's *Moby Dick* (Murray 1951a). Drawing on Freud, Murray argues for an id/superego conflict between Captain Ahab and the mighty white whale. For Murray, Ahab represents the Devil and his forces of evil, psychologically transformed into the primitive forces of the id. And Moby Dick himself, the great white sperm whale, is an incarnation of the Protestant God, a mighty superego projected outward.

The early work at the Harvard Psychological Clinic culminated in the publication of *Explorations in Personality* (Murray, 1938). In this landmark volume reporting the results of intensive studies of 50 college men, Murray and his colleagues envisioned a new agenda for what Murray came to call "personology." Murray conceived of personology as an interdisciplinary exploration of the psychology of persons, with particular emphasis on incorporating myth, folklore, biography, and investigations of the human imagination. Whereas psychologists of other persuasions studied discrete processes and functions of the human organism, the personologist was to operate on a more molar and synthetic level, casting his or her empirical eye upon the overall pattern of an individual's unique adaptation to the world. The personologist was to search for recurrent thematic constellations that characterized the individual as a whole. The molar approach to inquiry sacrifices a certain degree of precision and predictive power at the molecular level of particular behaviors and situations to achieve theoretical coherence at the level of the person.

A personological system must begin with a view of the person. What do you see when you see a person? Murray (1940) described what he saw:

> Instead of seeing merely a groomed American in a business suit, travelling to and from his office like a rat in a maze, a predatory ambulating apparatus of reflexes, habits, stereotypes, and slogans, a bundle of consistencies, conformities and allegiances to this or that institution—a robot in other words—I visualize (just as I visualize the activity of his internal organs) a flow of powerful subjective life, conscious and unconscious; a whispering gallery in which voices echo from the distant past; a gulf stream of fantasies with floating memories of past events, currents of contending complexes, plots and counterplots, hopeful intimations and ideals. To a neurologist such perspectives are absurd, archaic, tender-minded; but in truth they are much closer to the actualities of inner life than are his own neat diagrams of reflex arcs and nerve anastomoses. A personality is a full Congress of orators and pressure groups, of children, demagogues, communists, isolationists, war-mongers, mugwumps, grafters, log-rollers, lobbyists, Caesars and Christs, Machiavellis and Judases, Tories and Promethean revolutionists. And a psychologist who does not know this in himself, whose mind is locked against the flux of images and feelings, should be encouraged to make friends, by being psychoanalyzed, with the various members of his household. (pp. 160–161)

There are many metaphors in this passage. Particularly powerful, however, is the metaphor of the personality as a "household" or "congress"—a collection of very different and often competing personages, like various *characters* in a narrative drama. To "know thyself," suggests Murray, is to become acquainted with the characters within oneself, to discern their disparate identities and the ways in which they interact with each other to produce the narrative of life. Thus, in Grope's life story a main character is Icarus. But there are doubtlessly many other characters in Grope's story, given that personality is extraordinarily complex and multifaceted. In the view of Elms (1987), Murray envisioned personality as a "fluid conglomerate" that is "constantly shifting, lacking a single stable core"; "individual combinations of components reign briefly and are then dethroned by new rulers" (pp. 3, 4). In other words, internal characters in the life story interact over time; certain protagonists capture center stage for a while, only to be replaced, eventually, by new heroes.

A key idea in Murray's system is that *human lives are set in time*. The human being is a "time-binding organism," Murray wrote. Not merely a creature of the moment, the person can look beyond immediate stimuli in the environment and immediate urges within to act in accord with one's own view of the past or future. Time is a defining feature of the person. Murray wrote that the "organism consists of an infinitely complex series of temporally related activities extending from birth to death" (1938, p. 39). The life course of the individual should, therefore, be the long unit of analysis for personology. While it is feasible to examine a person's life at a particular moment in time, one must never forget that such a venture represents an arbitrary selection of a part from the whole. One must never forget, therefore, that "the *history* of the organism *is* the organism" (p. 39). But what is a history? And how can an organism be a history? A history is a narrative reconstruction of how the past gave birth to the present, in light of an anticipated future. A history is a consensual interpretation of the past in light of what followed. It is a *story* about how events and changes *led up to* a subsequent state of affairs. Time, story, the person. Human beings are time-binding, story-telling creatures, whose lives themselves are situated in time, as time-binding narratives—past, present, future—to be interpreted by the personologist.

The smallest meaningful unit of time in human behavior is what Murray called the *proceeding*. A proceeding is a single episode of behavior abstracted from the temporal complexity of ongoing life. We may see it as a single instance of interaction between a person and his or her environment, an interaction long enough to initiate and complete "a dynamically significant pattern of behavior" (Murray, 1951b, p. 269). In that people may do more than one thing at a time, it is possible that at any given moment a person may be involved in more than one proceeding. For example, I may be talking to my mother on the phone while I am also flipping through a series of cards in my rolodex, searching for an address of one of my colleagues. I am involved in two proceedings at once. Murray argues that each proceeding is unique, and that a person's own uniqueness is a result in part of the cumulative effect of proceedings over time:

> Every proceeding leaves behind it some trace of its occurrence—a new fact, the germ of an idea, a re-evaluation of something, a more affectionate attachment to some person, a slight improvement of a skill, a renewal of hope, another reason for despondency. Thus, slowly, by scarcely perceptible graduations—though sometimes suddenly by a leap forward or a slide backward—the person changes from day to day. Since his familiar associates also change, it can be said that every time he meets with one of them, both are different. In short, every proceeding is in some respects unique. (Murray & Kluckhohn, 1953, p. 10)

When you take all of the overlapping proceedings during a given period of time you have what Murray called a *durance*. Durances range from short scenes in a person's life (a visit to grandmother's house) to longer periods that may be viewed as "chapters" in one's evolving life story (living with grandmother between the ages of 3 and 5). A 30-year-old stockbroker, for example, may divide his life into four long durances: childhood, college years, early 20s while working at first job and living alone, and last four years while working for a large company and living with his wife. In this case, the transition to a new job and the marriage occurred around the same time in the man's life, marking a transition from the third to the fourth long durance or life chapter. A long durance may also be made up of what Murray called *serials*. A serial is a relatively long and directionally organized series of proceedings involving a particular life domain. Examples of serials are particular friendships, marriages, careers, etc. Each serial, therefore, organizes a sequence of life events having to do with a particular important area of personal investment. Serials may interact, such that the problems in, say, one's marriage may influence how well things go in one's career.

Remember that human beings are time-binding organisms. We act and interact in the present with views of the past and future in mind. As we survey the various serials in our lives, we evaluate our well-being and progress in each with respect to goals and aims for the future. Where is this relationship with my girlfriend going? Should I be taking more political science courses to prepare for law school? Do I need to lose some weight before I take that trip to Florida? We often develop particular programs for given serial domains in order to meet future goals. Murray called these *serial programs*. A serial program is an orderly arrangement of subgoals stretching into the future for months or years such that achievement of the subgoals will assure progress toward some desired end state. Serial programs provide our strivings with direction and purpose. And they often connect up with fundamental psychological needs.

If the directional nature of human lives is to be known, then human behavior must be viewed in terms of proceedings, durances, serials, and serial programs organized in time. As we saw in Chapter 8, Murray argued that psychological needs help to organize human lives in time. Needs interact with environmental press to produce characteristic behavior patterns. Recurrent need—press interactions are called themas. Some lives are so dominated by a characteristic patterning of need, press, and thema that they may be said to exemplify a *unity-thema*. A unity-thema is a well-organized pattern of related needs and press that provides meaning to a large portion of the individual's life. Ultimately derived from infantile experience, a unity-thema may be viewed as the central, organizing motif of a person's life story. Grope's Icarus complex may qualify as one unity thema, though Murray preferred to call it a "complex." A unity-thema links the distant past with the present and anticipated future:

> A *unity-thema* is a compound of interrelated—collaborating or conflicting—dominant needs that are linked to press to which the individual was exposed on one or more particular occasions, gratifying or traumatic, in early childhood. The thema may stand for a primary infantile experience or a subsequent reaction formation to that experience. But, whatever its nature and genesis, it repeats itself in many forms during later life. (Murray, 1938, pp. 604–605).

The Personological Tradition

World War II interrupted the program of research and theorizing at the Harvard Psychological Clinic as many researchers, including Murray himself, became involved in the war effort. Murray directed personality assessment programs for the Office of Strategic Services (OSS) a forerunner to the CIA. In order to choose the right men for sensitive positions in foreign espionage, Murray's staff designed a series of tests and assessment activities measuring a wide variety of abilities, competencies, traits, interests, opinions, and other personal characteristics assumed to predict human performance under oftentimes dangerous conditions. Reported in Murray's and the OSS Assessment Staff's (1948) *Assessment of Men*, the OSS assessment regimen was partly built on the principles of personology that Murray developed at the Harvard Psychological Clinic:

> Assessment was "multiform," which is to say that the "whole person" was scrutinized in numerous and various settings. There were standardized tests of intelligence and mechanical comprehension; personal history forms and interviews; group problem-solving sessions, some of them "leaderless"; various measures of physical strength and endurance; stress tests, debating tests, even an indirect assessment of the candidates' need and tolerance for alcohol. Using a six-point rating scale, the staff rated the candidates on eleven variables (motivation for assignment, energy and zest, practical intelligence, emotional stability, and so on). Brief personality profiles were prepared for a culminating staff meeting at which final recommendations were hammered out. It was the [Harvard Psychological] Clinic in a nutshell, complete with ingenious procedures, an informal social setting, heavy staff involvement, an expanded Diagnostic Council, and a modified version of the concluding biographical narrative. (Robinson, 1992, p. 282)

After the war, Murray's brand of personology continued to stimulate an interdisciplinary tradition of inquiry in the social sciences which is sometimes called *the study of lives*. The most prolific spokesman for this tradition has been Robert White (1948, 1952, 1963, 1972, 1981, 1987). In books such as *The Study of Lives, Lives in Progress*, and *The Enterprise of Living*, White illustrated the value of Murray's program of personology by analyzing and bringing together intensive case studies of normal adults studied over time. Another important contributor to the study of lives was Donald MacKinnon (1962, 1963, 1965), who headed the Institute for Personality Assessment and Research (IPAR) at the University of California, Berkeley, and launched an influential series of studies of especially creative individuals.

Like Murray's original formulations for personology in the 1930s, the study of lives moved against the dominant tides in American academic psychology during the 1950s, 1960s, and 1970s. The study of lives requires a "generalist" approach to psychology whereby the investigator is able to draw from many different domains in order to construct a synthetic portrait of the human life in context. Yet American academic psychology became increasingly specialized after World War II and fewer and fewer psychologists cultivated a generalist perspective. Similarly, personality psychologists focused much of their energy after the war on the development and refinement of particular measures of carefully defined and specific constructs, such as particular personality traits. Psychology departments and research funding agencies tended to favor quantitative, construct-driven research over the more qualitative, person-driven approaches advocated by Murray, White, and other proponents of the study of lives. In the past 20 years, however, a number of trends in personality psychology and adjacent fields have come together to suggest that the study of lives is enjoying something of a renaissance. One small indication of this is the establishment of the Henry A. Murray Research Center for the Study of Lives, at Radcliffe College in 1979. Another is the founding of the Society for Personology in the early 1980s, a small organization dedicated to the principles of Murray's personology.

What are those principles? In organizing a collection of Murray's writings, Edwin Shneidman (1981) sets forth six general propositions that characterize Murray's personological approach and the tradition of studying lives that he and his followers developed.

1. *Personology (as well as the personologist) is shaped by numerous and various forces.* While many approaches to personality try to rule out competing explanations in order to arrive at the simplest and most consistent interpretation of an individual's behavior, Murray tended to welcome alternative formulations, suggesting that lives are shaped by a panoply of conflicting and inconsistent forces and factors. Recall his metaphor of the person as a "congress of orators and pressure groups." More than most other approaches, Murray challenges the psychologist to consider the person from many different standpoints, to consider forces existing in biology, society, culture, and history. This inclusive approach to inquiry is well illustrated in White's (1952, 1966, 1975) scrupulous analyses of the lives of three American adults—Hartley Hale, Joseph Kidd, and Joyce Kingsley. In each of these "lives in progress," White painstakingly documents the influence of biologically based drives and instincts, social motivations, constitutional endowments, learning patterns, psychosexual and psychosocial stages, values and beliefs, family dynamics, social structures, religion, and culture. Furthermore, both Murray and White leave room for the extraordinary influence of random events and luck on the course of human life. In Murray's own life, a chance meeting with a fellow passenger on a ship directed Murray's attention to the writings of Melville, which piqued his curiosity about psychology and ultimately led him to personology. With so many forces to consider, it should not be surprising to learn that lives are difficult to understand and that behavior is sometimes impossible to predict.

2. *Personology is a complex, lifelong, never-ending enterprise.* As we have seen, a cardinal feature of Murray's approach is the emphasis on human lives situated *in time*. The history of the organism is the organism. In the terms of White (1952, 1972), lives are always "in progress"; living is a constantly evolving "enterprise." The personologist is likely to be frustrated in his or her attempts to get a final read on any given life in progress, in that personality continues to be constructed and reconstructed across the lifespan. Any approach that attempts to fix the person in time—say, by focusing too closely on unchanging traits—fails to convey the dynamic quality of lives, in Murray's view.

3. *Personology focuses on the close examination of mental life—conscious and unconscious processes, including creativity.* Here Murray and the study of lives share affinities with psychoanalysis (Chapter 3) and the cognitive movement in psychology (Chapter 9). Like Freud and Jung, Murray wished to explore the deep gulf streams of the human unconscious. But like Kelly, he found human consciousness to be equally worthy of the psychologist's attention. For Murray, human lives are inherently creative, as people partially create themselves amidst the many forces and factors that shape that creation. But certain people are *more* creative than others. Either through the personalities they work to create or via their more tangible creative outpourings, individuals like Herman Melville reveal special gifts for transforming things and ideas into especially novel and useful combinations. In extraordinary creativity, boundaries between the conscious and unconscious are sometimes blurred. In some cases, a creative solution or configuration seems to spring forth spontaneously, like sea water shooting upward from the great whale's spout. One cannot fully control the creative urge. "The psyche is a *region* where creations may or may not flourish," but we cannot make them flourish, nor readily stop them from flourishing should they "wish" to flourish (Murray, 1959/1981, p. 322). One follows one's creative urges, even if this means that, like Melville, one sacrifices happiness and well-being along the way (Murray, 1959/1981; Robinson, 1992).

4. *Personology requires a multidisciplinary approach, as well as special strategies and techniques of investigation.* From the early days of the Harvard Psychological Clinic, through the OSS programs on assessing men, to the present-day interest among personologists in biography and narrative methods of analysis, psychologists who have followed Murray's agenda have tended to distrust the conventional methods of assessing personality dispositions, such as self-report questionnaires and rating scales. They have argued that personality must be examined instead from the standpoints of widely diverse methodologies, especially those that allow the participant to create imaginative responses. Murray's (1938) *Explorations* describes over 20 innovative methods of assessing personality, including the well-known Thematic Apperception Test (TAT), and measures of musical reverie, imaginal productivity, reactions to frustration, memories for failures, and autobiography. White's analyses of lives in progress employ interviews, autobiographical accounts, story responses to the TAT, intelligence tests, personality questionnaires, and many more. Murray suggested that a Diagnostic Council should synthesize the many different kinds of data on a single personality. Multiple researchers, therefore, might arrive at a coherent interpretation of a single case by pouring over a wide assortment of data and then discussing their different points of view.

5. *Personology studies living, historical, fictional, and mythological figures as well as special human "complexes."* As we saw in the case of Grope, Murray was not reluctant to borrow from ancient mythology to shed light on the shadowy workings of a contemporary life in progress. The "Icarus Complex" is one of a number of different portraits, inspired by literature and mythology, that have been composed by personologists in the Murray tradition. Murray (1962) himself described a malignantly narcissistic personality syndrome by detailing "The Personality and Career of Satan." McClelland (1963) delineated a "Harlequin Complex," to suggest that some women have historically held a strange fascination with death—death viewed as a seducer. Drawing inspiration from the character of Ishmael in Melville's *Moby Dick*, Keniston (1963) painted a prophetic personological portrait of youthful alienation in the early 1960s. He wrote of a "prototypically alienated young man, separated partly by his own volition from the people, institutions, and beliefs which sustain most young men at his age in America; rejecting the forms by which most American men and women live; and condemned, like the Biblical Ishmael by his past and like Melville's Ishmael by his own temper, to live on the outskirts of society" (p. 42). For Murray, McClelland, Keniston, and others in this tradition, clues into the meanings of human lives may be found almost anywhere. Some of the richest sources are indeed outside science per se, in the great works of religion, mythology, and literature.

6. *Personology encompasses a wide range of concerns, from specific practical issues to human values and urgent global problems.* Like Freud and Skinner, Murray held strong views on a wide range of issues inside and outside of psychology, and he translated some of those views into print. After World War II, he became increasingly convinced that the survival of humankind in a nuclear age depended on the establishment of a world democratic government and the universal adoption of an enlightened humanistic philosophy to augment impersonal science and replace authoritarian religious systems (Murray, 1960/1981). Although others who have followed in the tradition Murray began have been somewhat less vocal in their pronouncements about social policy, the study of lives has always endeavored to situate personality within the complex social and cultural forces of the day, implicitly examining how human lives are impacted by the social opportunities and constraints produced by national and international events and by social policies.

Murray's humanistic inclinations are also reflected in the metaphors and models for human growth and development that have come out of case research in the study of lives. For example, White (1975) describes five general growth trends in human personality, observable across different case studies of American men and women. In White's view, healthy personality development involves:

1. *The stabilization of ego identity.* Over time, people should develop a clearer and more coherent understanding of who they are and how they fit into the adult world.

2. *The freeing of personal relationships.* Traumatic and conflictual experiences from childhood may exert negative influences on relationships later on, but healthy development involves a freeing of the self from the negativities of the past and the positive engagement of others in mutual, collaborative, intimate interpersonal relationships.

3. *The deepening of interests.* Children and adolescents form short-term and superficial interest in many different areas, but as one moves into adulthood one should begin to focus interests and develop competence in those arenas of living that are deemed central to the self.

4. *The humanizing of values.* The direction of moral development is away from simple, authoritarian, and egocentric perspectives toward greater complexity in moral reasoning and greater tolerance for other points of view.

5. *The expansion of caring.* As people mature, their emotional investments in other people deepen considerably and they cultivate relationships of care and commitment for children, friends, lovers, spouses, and even casual acquaintances and fellow citizens of the world.

Science and the Single Case

Since the time of Murray's *Explorations*, the study of lives has always been controversial because of its unswerving commitment to the psychology of the single case. While many personality psychologists would submit that "the whole person" is ideally the appropriate unit of analysis for personality studies, very few have taken this idea as literally as have Murray, White, and those other advocates of the study of lives who argue for "exploring personality the long way" (White, 1981, p. 3). To explore personality the long way, they maintain, one must focus inquiry on the single human life, examined over time through the **case study.** As we saw in Chapter 1, a case study is a "systematic presentation of information about the life of a single unit" (Runyan, 1982, p. 127). In personality psychology, the single unit is the individual life. But the case-study method has been used profitably, though sparingly, in many branches of psychology, from neurophysiology (Luria, 1972; Sacks, 1985) to social psychology (Festinger, Riecken, & Schachter, 1956; Janis, 1972). Outside of psychology proper, case studies have been extensively employed in anthropology (Agar, 1986), sociology (Becker, 1970; Thomas & Znaniecki, 1927), and political science (Redman, 1973). The "single unit" of analysis in an anthropological case study may be a particular culture or subculture; the sociologist may focus on a specific demographic group or organization; the political scientist may investigate a single political institution or event. In all of these instances, the scientist investigates in depth a single, specific phenomenon within its real-life context, synthesizing many different kinds of data drawn from multiple sources (Yin, 1984).

Going back to Freud, personality psychologists have used case studies in a number of different ways (McAdams & West, 1997). In his famous clinical cases, such as the analysis of Dora (Chapter 3), Freud portrayed the complex workings of psychic conflict and neurosis in the single life. For the most part, Freud's cases served to *exemplify* and showcase his own theory. As we saw in his analysis of Dora, Freud found much in her case to confirm his theoretical views of oral fixations and the Oedipus complex. Allport (1942) criticized Freud and the psychoanalysts for ignoring individuality in their efforts to confirm general theories. By paying closer attention to those aspects of the case that were unusual or even unique. Allport suggested, the psychologist might *discover* new things about personality and develop new theories. Yet another use of case studies is *comparison*. Psychologists can compare different constructs with one another—say, extraversion (Chapter 6) and intimacy motivation (Chapter 8)—by illustrating how they play out in a single case study. Different personality theories can also be compared with respect to their applicability to the single case. For many years now, a common assignment in college classes on personality has been to take two of the grand theories of personality—say, Freud (Chapter 3) and Rogers (Chapter 8)—and compare how they would each approach a particular case study. White's (1952) case studies of lives in progress have been used for this purpose on countless occasions.

Critics of the case study method have argued that such efforts are too subjective and too focused on the idiosyncracies of a single life to be of much scientific use. After all, science is supposed to aim at generating common laws and theories that should apply to many different lives, not just a single case. More specifically, criticism of case studies has focused on five important issues: (1) reliability, (2) internal coherence, (3) interpretive truth, (4) external validity, and (5) the problem of discovery versus justification in the study of lives. Let us consider each of these issues in turn.

First, critics have argued that the analysis of the single case is inherently unreliable. You cannot count on the results obtained, suggest many critics. A different observer of the case data could readily come up with a very different interpretation. The problem is particularly serious in psychoanalytic case studies, like Dora (Chapter 3), because of the many leaps in inference typically involved. Psychologists employing case studies often must analyze complex *qualitative data*—data that are not readily quantified (Kirk & Miller, 1986). The case-study researcher faces the triple task of (1) arriving at a high-level inference or interpretation about a critical aspect of the whole person's functioning by making sense of (2) an overabundance of unwieldy, qualitative data (3) in the absence of explicit rules for quantifying the data. The result, therefore, may be a highly *subjective* interpretation of the case with which another researcher, analyzing the same data in his or her own equally subjective way, may not agree.

The problem of low interjudge reliability in personality research is not limited to case studies, however. Scoring reliability tends to be a problem with qualitative data in general, such as interview conversations, reports of dreams, stories, and other open-ended response formats that are not readily quantified. In principle, a case study need not rely on qualitative data (Runyan, 1982) but can employ a wide range of data-gathering and data-interpreting methods, from the most quantifiable and reliable questionnaires and rating scales to the most qualitative and unreliable dream reports and interviews. Murray advocated a judicious blending of qualitative and quantitative measures, synthesized by a Diagnostic Council. Qualitative data, furthermore, may be translated into quantitative form through rigorous scoring rules and content-analysis systems (Krippendorff, 1980; Yin, 1984). Interviews may be videotaped and later subjected to objective content analysis to increase scoring reliability (Horowitz, 1979). To the extent that specific scoring rules for carefully recorded qualitative data are delineated and objectively employed, interjudge reliability will increase, and the personologist will be better able to count on the results and interpretations that are made. However, quantified scoring of qualitative data usually exacts a price, too. Important information can be lost because it cannot readily be translated into numbers.

A major criterion for judging the adequacy of a case study is the degree to which the psychologist's interpretation makes sense given the facts of the case. Does the analysis hang together? Is it consistent with what is known about the individual being studied? Is it *internally coherent?* A major problem with the criterion of internal coherence in evaluating case studies, however, is that many different explanations of a given case could conceivably be offered, each one equally internally coherent. As Campbell (1975) and others have pointed out, the human mind has an uncanny ability to make internal sense out of just about anything, even if that thing seems senseless at first. Thus, a given psychologist may have little trouble coming up with a coherent explanation for the facts in virtually any case study, after those facts have become known. Campbell warns that social scientists should be aware of these *post hoc* explanations. He adds, however, that there is probably no way to get around them completely. Indeed, Campbell suggests that for certain questions about human behavior and experience, the case study may be "the only route to knowledge—noisy, fallible, and biased though it may be" (1975, p. 179). Therefore, personologists should evaluate carefully and critically their own interpretations of intensive case studies.

The personologist who seeks to formulate an internally coherent interpretation of an individual case usually proceeds according to an implicit **pattern-matching plan** (Bromley, 1986; Campbell, 1975; Runyan, 1982). Approaching the case data openly but with certain theoretical expectations that help orient his or her approach, the personologist looks for a *conceptual pattern* in the data that makes logical and psychological sense—the Icarus pattern, for example. The conceptual pattern that emerges gives rise to theoretical implications, which then function as a minitheory from which predictions can be generated and evaluated by looking at additional data in the case. Ideally, the personologist should function as a devil's advocate for his or her own interpretation, objectively testing the implications of that interpretation against the data of the case. The personologist should, in fact, invite alternative explanations of the same case from other investigators, and the scientific community should be able to evaluate rival interpretations of the same case against each other, in the way a judge or jury evaluates the cases made by opposing lawyers, to determine which one seems to be the best (Bromley, 1986; Campbell, 1975).

What is a *true* interpretation in the study of the single life? While many people would say that truth means correspondence to the objective "facts" of the case, some investigators of human lives argue that, in addition to factual truth, case studies should be evaluated according to standards of *narrative truth* (Habermas, 1971; Schafer, 1981; Spence, 1982). Writes one scholar:

> Narrative truth can be defined as the criterion we use to decide when a certain experience has been captured to our satisfaction; it depends on continuity and closure and the extent to which the fit of the pieces takes on an aesthetic finality. Narrative truth is what we have in mind when we say that such and such is a good story, that a given explanation carries conviction, that *one* solution to a mystery must be true. Once a given construction has acquired narrative truth, it becomes just as real as any other kind of truth. (Spence, 1982, p. 31)

FEATURE 12.A

Studying Famous People in History

In the vast majority of the research studies conducted by psychologists and social scientists, the participants are relatively normal people like you and me. For example, a researcher might wish to study the relation between a particular personality trait—say, conscientiousness (Chapter 6)—and involvement in extracurricular activities in a sample of, say, 100 college students. For research purposes, the assumption is that the "subjects" or participants in the study are essentially interchangeable. Of course, we realize that each person is unique in many ways. But for the nomothetic and statistical purposes of the study, we can treat each individual as if he or she were the same, in order to examine trends or relations in the sample as a whole. But sometimes psychologists study individuals who are chosen because they are indeed so different from everybody else. Sometimes the subjects in the study are Beethoven, Catherine the Great, Elvis Presley, Shakespeare, and the like. These are individuals who have to some degree "made a name for themselves" in history. As research subjects, they stand out from the crowd.

Psychologist Dean Keith Simonton (1976, 1994, in press) has devoted his career to studying what he calls "significant samples." Rather than college undergraduates or middle-aged businesspersons, Simonton recruits the likes of classical composers, Nobel laureates, U.S. presidents, and even famous psychologists as subjects for his studies. Of course, most of these people are dead. But as we saw in Erik Erikson's analysis of Martin Luther (Chapter 10), we can learn much about personality from the study of eminent historical figures. Although we may not be able to interview them or give them standard psychological tests, eminent figures often leave behind diaries, memoirs, creative works, and other artifacts that may prove to be valuable data for the personality psychologist. As we saw in Chapter 8, for example, David Winter was able to analyze the inaugural addresses of U.S. presidents in order to measure achievement, power, and intimacy motivation. In Chapter 3, I described how I studied the novels and autobiographical writings of Yukio Mishima in order to generate a psychoanalytic interpretation of his suicide. Furthermore, the accomplishments (and failures) of eminent individuals are part of the public record, and the evaluation of those accounts

According to this view, the psychologist who seeks the true meaning of the single case must engage in **hermeneutics**—the art and science of interpreting texts (Ricoeur, 1970; Schafer, 1981; Steele, 1982). For centuries, hermeneutics was confined to sacred texts, such as the holy books of Christianity, Judaism, and Islam. In the past 150 years, however, certain social scientists such as Dilthey (1900) and Stern (in Allport, 1968) have brought hermeneutics into psychology and sociology, arguing that human lives and human societies are analogous to holy scriptures that hold within them many meanings. For Dilthey, hermeneutics involves a *dialogue* between investigator and text—be the "text" a holy book or another person—designed to decipher the many

Personological studies of eminent individuals can illuminate interesting patterns of human individuality. Left: Albert Einstein, physicist. Right: Selena, singer.

by historians and other experts can also inform psychological research.

Simonton identifies four different traditions in the study of eminent individuals. The first and oldest is what he calls *historiometric* research. In these studies, researchers extract quantitative and indirect assessments from historical data. An early example is a study called *Early Mental Traits of Three Hundred Geniuses* (Cox, 1926), in which the researcher made estimates of intellectual abilities and personality tendencies based on the archival records for 300 historical figures deemed to be especially intelligent. Historiometric

continued on next page

signs and symbols conveyed by the text. Through this highly subjective dialogue with the text emerge meaning and truth.

Interpreters of texts and single cases, therefore, often aim for narrative truth, argue Schafer and Spence. They evaluate their own interpretations according to the standards of "good story." A good story (1) is internally coherent, (2) makes for a continuous plot line in which early events "cause" or logically lead to later events, (3) embodies closure or a sense of things fitting into a final form, and (4) is aesthetically pleasing (Spence, 1981). Yet, narrative truth is at best but one criterion of a "good" interpretation of a human life. Indeed, the interpretation of the single case can be

FEATURE 12.A *continued*

studies can be used to test hypotheses. For example, Simonton (1989) evaluated the compositions of 172 classical composers for melodic originality and other musical attributes. He found that the musical pieces composed toward the very end of a composer's career tend to be somewhat less original and complex than his or her earlier compositions, but also especially moving and popular. These "swan songs" seem to make a powerful and elegant musical statement. They are the composer's last and culminating work, and as such they prove to be especially memorable and well-received in the long run.

A second tradition of research with significant samples is the *psychometric* approach. In these studies, researchers administer direct measurements, such as surveys and interviews, to eminent individuals while they are still alive. Developing methods pioneered by Henry Murray (1948) in his work during World War II, researchers at the University of California's Institute for Personality As-

sessment and Research (IPAR) conducted psychometric studies of eminent architects, writers, and scientists. In these studies, the researchers identified men and women whose artistic or scientific contributions to their fields were already well-recognized for excellence. The researchers were mainly interested in exploring the development of creativity over the lifespan and the relationship of creative genius to other aspects of personality (e.g., Barron, 1969; Dudek & Hall, 1984).

Psychobiographical research is Simonton's third tradition. As we see later in this chapter, psychobiographical studies were launched by Sigmund Freud's seminal study of Leonardo da Vinci. Psychobiographical studies are radically different from historiometric and psychometric investigations (Elms, 1994). While historiometric and psychometric studies are typically quantitative and nomothetic, psychobiography involves qualitative investigations of the single, idiographic case, studied

profitably compared with the construction of scientific theories, as described in Chapter 1 of this book. Like a theory, an interpretation of a case study consists of a set of propositions designed to explain events. Scientists agree that, in principle, some theories are better than others, though they may disagree as to exactly which ones are better and worse. Scientists judge theories according to the criteria of (1) comprehensiveness, (2) parsimony, (3) coherence, (4) testability, (5) empirical validity, (6) usefulness, and (7) generativity (see Chapter 1). Similarly, in determining the "goodness" (rather than truth) of interpretations of the single case, the best that we can do may be to follow these same criteria. A good interpretation of the single case, therefore, may be one that (1) takes into consideration a comprehensive body of case information, (2) is simple and straightforward, (3) is internally coherent and consistent in the same way, perhaps, that a good story is, (4) provides hypotheses about human behavior that can be tested empirically, (5) is in accord with what empirical studies have documented to be valid, (6) is useful, and (7) generates new ideas.

But even if a personologist formulates an exceptionally illuminating interpretation of a single life in progress, what can the single case tell us about people in general? How can a single case be representative of any sample or population beyond itself?

over time. Furthermore, a psychobiography usually involves the application of a broad theoretical framework, typically a Freudian or psychodynamic approach. Especially popular have been psychobiographies of political figures, such as the numerous analyses of Adolf Hitler, Woodrow Wilson, and Richard M. Nixon.

Finally, the *comparative* tradition shares with psychobiography an emphasis on qualitative and indirect assessments of eminent individuals, but it tends to incorporate multiple cases that are compared and contrasted to one another. An excellent example is Howard Gardner's (1993) *Creating Minds*, in which he examined the lives and works of seven especially creative men and women who lived in the first half of the 20th century. Gardner chose the seven carefully to represent seven different "fields" and seven different and corresponding types of creativity: Sigmund Freud in psychology, Albert Einstein in physics, T. S. Eliot for literature, Pablo Pi-

casso for the visual arts, Igor Stravinsky for music, Martha Graham for dance, and Mahatma Gandhi for creative social leadership. Across the seven cases, Gardner observed interesting commonalities in the development of a creative career, such as the requirement of a 10-year apprenticeship period in which each mastered the conventions of the discipline and the need to downplay interpersonal relationships in order to devote the self unswervingly to creative work. Gardner also illuminated differences among the seven, reflective both of personality variables and of mental and structural differences in the kinds of creative enterprises with which they were involved.

The world's libraries and archives are filled with fascinating data for personological investigations. Studies of eminent individuals can shed light on principles of personality that are common to all of us. And they can illuminate startling differences and unique patterns of individuality as well.

This is the problem of *external validity*, and because of this problem some psychologists dismiss case studies out of hand. They argue that experiments and large-scale correlation studies are more powerful research strategies because they allow the scientists to sample many different subjects drawn from a large population. These approaches also allow the researcher to compare and contrast different individuals, and "comparison is essential to science" (Carlsmith, Ellsworth, & Aronson, 1976, p. 39). The answer to poor external validity in the single case study, according to this view, is to sample many different individuals whose behavior and experience are studied in a more limited fashion, the general assumption being that many individuals together are more representative of a large population than is one.

In response to this criticism of case studies, some psychologists suggest that investigators collect multiple cases that can be compared and contrasted, gradually building up representative samples in given areas of investigation. Bromley (1986) maintains that personologists should eventually attempt to group and classify multiple cases, identifying key features of cases that distinguish them one from the other. In this way, certain exemplary cases could be chosen as prototypes that exhibit several distinguishing features of a given phenomenon. Other cases could then be compared and contrasted to the prototypes to determine the extent to which their features match those exhibited in the "ideal" or "pure" case.

Other proponents of the intensive study of the single case concede that single case studies can never be representative of large populations, but they counter that such cases need not be representative anyway. First of all, very few single experiments or correlation studies in personality psychology can truly claim to obtain fully representative samples. As we saw in Chapter 1, the scientist should strive to obtain the sample most appropriate for the given question to be addressed. The assumption that his or her sample is fully representative of a particularly robust population, however, may be based on the misguided belief that a single empirical study can establish truth once and for all, and for all time (Gergen, 1973).

Second, external validity refers to sampling of not only *subjects* but *situations* and *topics*, too (Brunswik, 1956; Dukes, 1965). Although a case study samples only one subject, it samples many different situations and topic areas in that participant's life. Conversely, an experiment or correlational study that samples many participants probably samples only a few situations and a few areas of human functioning.

Third, generalization from a single case should be assessed in light of the soundness of the given analysis of that case rather than a prior notion about how "typical" a given case is. When a scientist makes a good interpretation of a case, he or she is justified in asserting that the analysis should hold for *comparable cases*, that is, cases of that sort (Mitchell, 1983). In case-study research, then, "the cases themselves come to define the population" (Bromley, 1986, p. 288). Grope, for example, might be an exemplar for the Icarus complex—a unity-theme to which a small number of other lives might also be assimilated. The extent to which Grope is a "prototypical" case against which psychologists could compare others may be determined by analyzing the entire family of cases within that genre.

Whatever one concludes about the external validity of any particular case study, certain general advantages of case studies over other research approaches that employ larger subject samples should be acknowledged. Unlike most other methods, "a case study allows an investigation to retain the holistic and meaningful characteristics of real-life events" (Yin, 1984, p. 14). A good case study may provide insight into a person's experience, clarifying what at first may have seemed incomprehensible; a good case study may effectively portray the person's social and historical milieu; and a good case study may deepen the reader's sympathy and empathy for the individual, while being vivid, evocative, and emotionally compelling to read (Runyan, 1982). (See Table 12.2.)

Finally, in Chapter 1 I made an important distinction between two different ways of doing science. In the *context of discovery*, the scientist derives ideas, builds theories, and comes up with various hypotheses about a given phenomenon. In the *context of justification*, on the other hand, the scientist tests the validity of ideas, theories, and hypotheses that have already been derived. These two approaches to science build on each other as ideas are formulated, tested, and reformulated over time in a given area of scientific investigation. For which of these two contexts, then, is the single case appropriate? Should we derive (discover) theories through cases? Should we test (justify) theories through cases? Should we do neither? Should we do both?

A case study may be utilized to *disprove* a particular hypothesis that asserts that a given phenomenon is always true (Dukes, 1965). For instance, if scientists claim that event B always follows event A, then a single case in which B does not follow A would

TABLE 12.2	*Six Rules for Preparing a Psychological Case Study*

1. The investigator must report truthfully on the person's life and circumstances and must be accurate in matters of detail.

2. The aims and objectives of the case study must be stated explicitly.

3. The case study should include an evaluation of the extent to which the stated aims and objectives have been achieved.

4. If the inquiry deals with material of deep emotional significance for the subject, then it must be carried out by someone trained and equipped to establish and manage a close, fairly long, and possibly difficult personal relationship.

5. The subject must be understood in the context of the specific historical, social, and symbolic world in which he or she lives.

6. The case report should be written in good plain English in a direct and objective way without, however, losing its human interest as a story. This can be done with sympathy and imagination and with due regard for high standards of evidence and argument.

Source: Bromley (1986), pp. 24–25.

disprove the hypothesis. Unfortunately, there are very few such universal claims in personality psychology, and therefore this particular context-of-justification use of the case study is rare.

The prevailing view, then, is that cases are rarely useful in the context of justification, at least with respect to testing general propositions. Especially when it comes to justifying general case-and-effect relationships, case studies are vastly inferior to experiments. As vehicles for discovery, however, case studies may be extremely useful, indeed much more useful than experiments, correlational designs, and any other imaginable mode of investigation. As emphasized in Chapter 1, the context of discovery is a freewheeling realm in scientific inquiry. Ideas, hypotheses, and theories may be discovered in a multitude of ways, and among the most fruitful ways, as far as the personality psychologist is concerned, is the intensive study of the single case. Studies of lives in the tradition of Murray and White are goldmines for the derivation of ideas, hypotheses, and theories, which may then be put to the test via conventional scientific methodologies of justification.

BIOGRAPHY, NARRATIVE, AND LIVES

How do we come to understand fully the life course of a single person? What is the most effective medium through which we may view the single life evolving over time so that we may discover what that whole life is all about? Along with Erik Erikson (Chapter 10), Murray, White, and those personologists dedicated to the "study of lives" suggested that a psychologically informed *biography* is probably the best means for capturing a human life situated in time. Erikson is particularly well known in this regard for his psychobiographies of Martin Luther (1958), Mahatma Gandhi (1969), and George Bernard Shaw (1959).

Yet, most personality psychologists have *not* historically viewed themselves as biographers (Elms, 1988). Despite the intuitively appealing claim that people may be best understood in their biographical contexts, biographical approaches to the person have traditionally occupied a controversial and ambiguous status in personality psychology (Anderson, 1981; Runyan, 1982, 1990). Critics have asserted that biographical methods of investigation, like case studies, are generally too unwieldy and subjective for clear and rigorous scientific study and that biographical examinations of the single case lack reliability and external validity, as discussed above. Biography's defenders counter that these critics hold an overly narrow view of science, that good biographical studies are highly illuminating, and that personologists are essentially shirking their intellectual responsibility to study the whole person if they dismiss biography out of hand. Nonetheless, the past 15 years have witnessed an upsurge of interest in and a growing acceptance of biographical and autobiographical approaches and frameworks among personality psychologists and other social scientists (Bertaux, 1981, McAdams, 1999; McAdams & Ochberg, 1988; Moraitis & Pollack, 1987; Runyan, 1990).

Psychobiography

Before the 20th century, literary biographers rarely employed psychological concepts to interpret the lives of their subjects. During the Roman Empire, Plutarch (A.D. 46–120) wrote the *Lives of the Noble Greeks and Romans*, taking as subjects such famous men as Pericles (the Athenian statesman) and Julius Caesar. Essentially, Plutarch composed moral vignettes from history to illustrate exemplary character traits such as honesty and courage. In the Middle Ages, Christian scholars wrote **hagiographies** to venerate the saints. These biographical accounts of the lives of great Christians were written mainly to glorify God and to teach the reader about faith. Many followed a standard form, culminating in the saint's trial before a court of "unbelievers" and his or her sentencing and execution—mirroring the story of Christ's trial and crucifixion. These religious tales, however, were not penetrating explorations in personality. Instead, they functioned as moral and spiritual lessons.

The hagiographies and art of the early Christian period depicted the saints as a way to teach people about being faithful.

James Boswell (left) and the subject of his classic biography, Samuel Johnson (right).

In the 17th century, biography began to assume a more sophisticated form when biographers such as Izaak Walton, who wrote about the lives of high churchmen, and John Aubrey, who focused on more common folk, began to think of themselves as literary artists (Gittings, 1978). As artists, therefore, they sought to create narratives that were entertaining and artistically satisfying. The most artful and illuminating early biography—indeed, the most famous biography in Western literature—was published by James Boswell in 1791. In *The Life of Samuel Johnson*, Boswell wrote about Dr. Johnson (1709–1784), the prominent English author, critic, and lexicographer who traveled in the elite circles of European intellectual society. In striking contrast to his eminent subject, the younger Boswell was a loud-mouthed gossip and a heavy drinker, initially known more for his womanizing than his literary talents. At the age of 22, Boswell befriended Johnson (then age 54), and for years after they traveled together.

Boswell's study was a flesh-and-blood portrait that explored many facets of Johnson's life, from Johnson's sparkling conversations with the great men of the day to his persistent depression. Though Boswell clearly admired his subject, the central aim of his analysis was not to eulogize. Rather, he sought to explore the many dimensions of Johnson's character so as to illustrate the sweep and grandeur of one particular life. Boswell's biography was one of the first to entertain the problem of the biographer's own relationship to the subject of the study. Indeed, Johnson was something of a father-figure and a best friend for the younger Boswell. Yet their relationship was ambivalent and multilayered. As he moved in his text from one passage to the next, Boswell played the various roles of critic, fan, observer analyst, and participant in relation to Johnson's life.

In 1910, Freud wrote *Leonardo da Vinci and a Memory of his Childhood*, considered to be the first **psychobiography.** Much of Freud's interpretation rested on his analysis of

Leonardo da Vinci's self-portrait from a sketch in his notebooks.

a fantasy from Leonardo's childhood in which, "when I was still in the cradle, a vulture came down to me, opened my mouth with his tail and struck me many times with his tail against my lips" (Freud, 1916/1947, pp. 33–34). In a much-disputed line of reasoning, Freud speculated that this particular fantasy symbolizes themes of homosexuality and infantile dependency. On one level, the vulture's tail is a phallic symbol, suggesting a male homosexual fantasy about fellatio. On another level, the vulture represents mother, an association for which Freud found some indirect evidence in Egyptian mythology. In this case, the tail is the breast, and the fantasy an expression of Leonardo's longing to regress to the secure maternal world of oral dependency.

In order to preserve his mother as the sole love object in his life, Leonardo subsequently turned away from all gross sensual activities and dedicated himself to the life of the mind. The small portion of libido not exhausted in his relentless scientific and artistic work was transformed into an ideal love of boys, for boys offered no viable threat to his consuming love for mother. Thus, homosexuality served to protect his love of mother. During his early adult years, Leonardo's severe sexual inhibition carried over into his creative life, too. Despite his genius, Leonardo repeatedly failed to complete his artistic projects, producing many "unfinished masterpieces" with which he was never thoroughly satisfied. Around the age of 50, however, he was rejuvenated, Freud maintained, by reexperiencing the love of his mother through meeting and eventually painting the woman who has become known as the Mona Lisa.

TABLE 12.3	*Common Criticisms of Psychobiography*
Critical-period fallacy	Some psychobiographers overemphasize the influence of one early "critical period" such as the first year of life or the Oedipal period while neglecting formative influences at later stages.
Eventism	Attempting to explain major trends in a human life solely in terms of one or two key or "traumatic" events is poor practice. While some events are obviously more important than others, the entire life must be viewed as a complex and multiple determined whole.
Inadequate evidence	Some psychobiographical interpretations rest on limited or erroneous evidence. The psychobiographer must synthesize many different kinds of data from multiple sources that converge on a particular interpretation. He or she must check and doublecheck historical and biographical sources.
Neglect of social and historical factors	Too many psychobiographies do not take into careful consideration the complex social and historical context within which the individual's life is or was embedded. A person's life is strongly shaped by culture. The biographer cannot understand the life if he or she does not attempt to understand the culture.
Originology	Many biographers attempt to trace everything about a person to its origins in childhood. Given that the issue of continuity and consistency in personality from childhood to adulthood is a controversial one in personality and development psychology, the biographer runs the risk of placing too much emphasis on childhood events as determinants of adult outcomes.
Overpathologizing	A good psychobiography should not aim to reduce an entire life to a particular psychiatric syndrome or neurotic tendency. A life must be evaluated in terms of both its weaknesses and strengths.
Reconstruction	The psychoanalytically oriented biographer may reconstruct unknown or unsubstantiated childhood events from known adult outcomes. For instance, a biographer may assume that an anally retentive and compulsive adult experienced severe toilet training as a toddler. In the absence of evidence from childhood, these kinds of reconstructions are usually unwarranted.

Sources: Anderson (1981); Elms (1994); Runyan (1982).

Psychobiography may be defined as "the systematic use of psychological (especially personality) theory to transform a life into a coherent and illuminating story" (McAdams, 1988c, p. 2, italics omitted). In psychobiography, the life to be transformed is usually that of a famous, enigmatic, or paradigmatic figure. Most psychobiographies are more comprehensive than Freud's brief sketch of Leonardo. Many psychobiographical studies take the entire life, from birth to death, as their subject of study, aiming to discern, discover, or formulate the central story of the entire life, a story structured according to psychological theory.

In the case of Leonardo, Freud's theory of choice was, of course, psychoanalysis. Yet psychobiography need not employ a strictly psychoanalytic framework (Runyan, 1982). Many psychobiographies have drawn on the theories of Jung, Erikson, and the object-relations approaches to personality (e.g., de St. Aubin, 1998). Psychobiographies have also been written from the theoretical standpoints of social-learning theory

TABLE 12.4	*Nine Guidelines for Extracting Psychobiography Data*
Primacy	That which comes *first*. "The association of 'first' with importance has a long-standing history in folklore and in human customs and mores. Certainly in psychology the idea is upheld in the importance assigned to early experience in the development of personality by both Freud and Adler and countless successors. The first as the 'foundation stone' upon which structures are built is also a common metaphor in language."
Frequency	That which appears *often*. "For the most part, we are tuned to frequency or repetition as increasing signs of certainty and of importance. The kind of importance a frequent message has, however, may be complex in terms of its value for the discovery of dynamic sequence. In many instances, frequency may be an expression of powerful conscious value schemas."
Uniqueness	That which is *singular,* odd. "A powerful example of this occurred in the autobiographical sketch of a paid student volunteer intensively studied in a graduate personality assessment course. The student recalled an incident from his first year in elementary school: At the end of a school day he returned home to find his mother hanging from a rope in her bedroom, a description that he followed only with a statement that he was sent off to a private school shortly afterward. Uniqueness in this instance is signaled not only by the event itself but by the kind of response to the event reported by the subject."
Negation	That which is denied, or turned into its *opposite*. "Imagine, for example, a therapeutic interview in which a dream about the father is mentioned, followed by the statement, 'Let's move on to something else. *It's not* that I think talking about father would drive me crazy, it usually leads to a feeling of helplessness.'"
Emphasis	That which is *underscored* or stressed. The biographer should be aware of that which seems either overemphasized or underemphasized. "Overemphasis can usually be detected when the hearer or reader begins to wonder why so much attention is focused on something considered to be so commonplace. 'I just could not get over the fact that this person, a native of the country, for whom I as a tourist had inquired about directions, took such pains to make sure I understood how to find my way. From that moment on I adored my visit to _____.' would be an example chosen by the criterion of overemphasis for retention in the reduced data pool. Its ultimate transformation

(Mountjoy & Sundberg, 1981), humanistic psychology (Rogers, 1980), existential psychology (Sartre, 1991), McClelland's theory of motives (Winter & Carlson, 1988), and Tomkins's theory of scripts (Carlson, 1988). Furthermore, many contemporary biographies, written by nonpsychologists, draw liberally from personality theory. While some of these use theory naively or inappropriately, others have been celebrated as masterful and illuminating, such as Leon Edel's monumental study of the American author Henry James (Edel, 1985).

Since Freud's *Leonardo,* many psychobiographies have been written, and advances in understanding particular lives have been made (Elms, 1994). Still it is very difficult to write a *good* psychobiography. The best-intentioned psychobiographers face major constraints and obstacles that usually do not confront other kinds of researchers. For instance, the subjects of their studies are often dead and thus cannot be interviewed, tested, or directly observed. The data for the analysis come in a troubling variety of

TABLE 12.4	*Continued*

	might be, unexpected attention (kindness) when in distress → euphoria. This may be an analogue of the expectation that when one is in trouble, no help is expected."
Omission	That which is *missing*. "An illustrative example might be one in which the subject describes a memory of being punished by his mother after she had accused him of hostile behavior toward a sibling. The retelling goes on to include the subject's feelings as a results of the mother's actions but speaks not at all to whether he had in fact treated the other child in the manner suggested. What is omitted is attention to the subject's role in a sequence with a negative outcome which must be investigated for its possible repetitive properties."
Error, or Distortion	That which is a *mistake*. "In written exposition this is sometimes indicated by obvious undetected error by the subject in an otherwise error free or minimally error-prone sample. An example might be the statement, 'I came from a family of tall people, my father is 6'5", my brother is 6'4", my mother is 9'5", and I am the runt at 5'8"'. This not only calls attention to the possible importance of the size dimensions in the life of the subject but highlights (error signaled by incredibility) the overvaluing of mother on whatever dimension the size variable symbolizes, and by contrast the undervaluing of the writer who is described uniquely as a runt. Underlying these pointers there most likely exists a dynamic set of conditioned sequences constituting the subject's view of the family drama."
Isolation	That which is *alone*, or *doesn't fit*. "I remember how we saved a touchdown by our opponents in a high school football game by something we learned from observing their game films. Oh! Did I remember to bank the fire in the fireplace before I left the house to come here? The films showed that the quarterback. . . . "
Incompletion	That which is *not finished*. "'All through college I dated John. It started as a casual friendship, but within a short period of time we found that we enjoyed the same interests and people. By the time we reached senior year we were making plans for a future together. Marriage, while not an immediate prospect, was our ultimate goal. Three years later I married Fred Perkins, whom I had recently met, and moved to Pittsburgh where we have lived ever since.' This illustrates an uncompleted fragment or portion of a descriptive segment about courtship and marriage which in itself has an aura of completion."

Source: Alexander (1988). pp. 269–278.

forms—from unsubstantiated hearsay about the person being studied, to personal correspondence and other writings, to publicly documented facts about the person's life. The most reliable data (such as birthdate or number of siblings) may be the least illuminating. The most intriguing data (such as personal fantasies, reflections, or dreams) may be the least reliable and the most difficult to interpret in an intellectually responsible way. Indeed, one of the problems facing some psychobiographers is the sheer amount of biographical data they face. How does one choose which data to interpret?

Irving Alexander (1988) provides nine helpful guidelines by which the psychobiographer may reduce huge amounts of data to manageable quantities, by identifying which data are worthy of further consideration and which may be tossed aside for the time being. Alexander argues that the data may be evaluated in terms of primacy, frequency, uniqueness, negation, emphasis, omission, error, isolation, and incompletion (Table 12.4). Each may be viewed as a rule for storymaking employed by the biographer

FEATURE 12.B

Why Did Van Gogh Cut Off His Ear?

On the evening of December 23, 1888, Vincent van Gogh, then 35 years old, cut off the lower half of his left ear and took it to a brothel, where he requested to see a prostitute named Rachel. He handed her the ear and asked that she "keep this object carefully."

Van Gogh (1853–1890) is famous today for the many brilliant expressionist masterpieces he painted during his short and very troubled life. The Dutch artist developed a unique style of painting—using rough strokes and bold colors to portray scenes that are often haunting and ominous—a style that even the most untutored art observers immediately recognize. While millions of art lovers have enjoyed his paintings, psychologists and biographers have puzzled over his life. The incident with the ear stands out as the most memorable of all van Gogh's odd behaviors. We can't help but wonder, over and over: Why did van Gogh cut off his ear?

Psychologist William McKinley Runyan (1981, 1982) has surveyed the psychobiographical literature on van Gogh and identified at least 13 different psychological explanations for this bizarre incident in the artist's life. Here are a few of the more interesting ones:

1. He was frustrated by the failure to establish a working and friendly relationship with his fellow artist Paul Gauguin and turned his resultant aggressive feelings toward himself.

2. He felt conflict over his homosexual feelings toward Gauguin. The ear was a phallic symbol (the Dutch slang word for penis, *lul*, resembled the Dutch word for ear, *lel*), and the act was a symbolic self-castration.

3. He was imitating the actions of bullfighters with whom he had been especially impressed in his visits to Arles. In such events, the matador receives the ear of the bull as an award, displays his prize to the crowd, and then gives the ear to the lady of his choice.

4. He was influenced by a number of newspaper reports concerning Jack the Ripper, who mutilated the bodies of prostitutes, sometimes cutting of their ears. Adopting the masochistic over the sadistic approach, van Gogh turned on himself.

5. He was reenacting a scene from the New Testament in which Simon Peter cuts off the ear of Malchus, a servant of the high priest, who had come to seize Christ. Van Gogh had been thinking about this event recently and had tried to paint it.

6. He was experiencing auditory hallucinations and during a psychotic episode cut off his ear to silence the disturbing sounds.

What do we make of these different, competing interpretations? Are they all right, or

who seeks to discern or create the central story of a life. Each gives the biographer a clue about what may be important in narrative. Thus, the guideline of *primacy* suggests that what comes first in stories is especially significant; *uniqueness* suggests that what stands out as odd and intriguing in a story may be of special consequence; *omission* suggests that what seems to be missing in the story may be revealing; *distortion* and *isolation* suggest that when something in the story does not follow logically, the biographer wrong (in one way or another)? Are some better interpretations than others?

Runyan argues that competing psychobiographical interpretations can be reasonably compared and contrasted and evaluated according to clear standards. Different explanations may be judged according to standards such as:

(1) their logical soundness, (2) their comprehensiveness in accounting for a number of puzzling aspects of the events in question, (3) their survival of tests of attempted falsification, such as tests of derived predictions or retrodictions, (4) their consistency with the full range of available relevant evidence, (5) their support from above, or their consistency with more general knowledge about human functioning or about the person in question, and (6) their credibility relative to other explanatory hypotheses. (Runyan, 1982, p. 47)

Runyan maintains that there is room for more than one good explanation for any given biographical event. Indeed, events are highly overdetermined, and influences from many different levels may come to bear in producing a particular behavior in a particular situation.

Carefully weighing the various explanations for van Gogh's behavior, Runyan favors those interpretations that emphasize the role of the artist's brother, Theo. The ear-cutting incident and two later mental breakdowns coincide with Vincent's learning that Theo is to be married, Theo's wedding, and the birth of Theo's first child. Each of these events may have reinforced Vincent's fear that he was losing his brother's care and his financial support. In the past, van Gogh had exhibited masochistic responses to rejection. In 1881, he had visited the parents of Kee Voss, a woman whom he loved. When he learned that Kee had left the house to avoid seeing him, he thrust his hand into the flame of a lamp and vowed to keep it there until she returned. On one level at last, Vincent may have cut off his ear in response to the perceived loss of and rejection by his brother.

But, then, why did he mutilate himself in this way? Why the ear? And why did he give it to this particular prostitute? The Jack-the-Ripper explanation seems farfetched, for there is no evidence that van Gogh was familiar with or impressed by the exploits of this criminal. Runyan also finds little support for explanations emphasizing symbolic castration. Van Gogh had been impressed, however, by the bullfights. And he had pondered over the scene in the Garden of Gethsemane when Peter cut off Malchus's ear. Perhaps these latter two interpretations hold a grain of truth. Perhaps not. Without more definitive evidence from the life of the artist, at least a few plausible but competing interpretations will invariably remain.

should seek to straighten it out; and *incompletion* suggests that when stories do not end properly, the biographer should seek to understand why. The psychobiographer must be sensitive to the clues in the data suggesting how the story of a person's life is to be discovered, created, and told (Edel, 1984; McAdams, 1988c).

While Alexander's nine guidelines may assist the biographer in identifying the important data in a particular life, he or she is still faced with the task of using psychological theory to organize the data into an illuminating and coherent narrative. Psychological theory must be applied with flexibility and grace. Too many psychobiographers force life-history data into rigid theoretical categories, as if to prove that all aspects of a particular life fit perfectly in an existing theoretical scheme. Others apply theory in the most desultory and trite ways, relentlessly dragging a human life, say, through each of Erikson's eight psychosocial stages or Murray's 20 psychogenic needs. Still others fail to understand the single life within its particular social, cultural, and historical matrix, reducing complex behavior and experiences, for instance, to early problems in toilet training or single traumatic events. These kinds of psychobiographies are boring. Worse, they make straightjackets out of theories and caricatures out of lives. In a sophisticated psychobiography, the data and the theory relate to each other as equals, as if they were two speakers in a lively conversation. Each influences and is influenced by the other, and each respects the other's integrity. Therefore, the skilled psychobiographer uses theory in a subtle and nuanced manner, making sense out of what can be made sensible, struggling with complexity and contradiction, knowing when to back off from lofty theories and let the concrete, unique human life speak for itself.

In recent years, scholars of psychological biography have become especially interested in the possibilities and the problems in writing women's lives. Since the time of Boswell and Dr. Johnson, biographers have mainly focused on white men whose political, military, scientific, artistic, athletic, religious, or entrepreneurial achievements have made them famous. Theirs have been the life stories that our society has traditionally valued most, the stories deemed most appropriate for telling. In the last few decades of the 20th century, however, scholars, popular writers, film-makers, and others have begun to turn their attention toward women, people of color, and members of disadvantaged groups in an effort to explore and present those life stories that have traditionally been marginalized and dismissed (Bateson, 1990; Franz & Stewart, 1994; Josselson & Lieblich, 1993; Rosenwald & Ochberg, 1992). Through this process, biographers and psychologists are learning that approaches and frameworks traditionally used to make sense of middle-class white men's lives do not always work well when applied to other people.

Abigail Stewart (1994) argues that writing the stories of women's lives requires a set of strategies that are sometimes difficult to employ. She outlines seven "feminist strategies" that she has found especially useful in her own psychobiographical work.

The first strategy is to keep an eye open for *what's been left out*. Traditional categories such as work and family may not always capture a woman's experience. Certain areas of women's experience, such as close same-sex friendships and the politics of the family, have rarely been explored by biographers, and yet these uncharted domains may be central to understanding a woman's life. Stewart (1994) remarks, "Feminist theory would lead us to expect that the things that will be missing will be things that those who are not women are not likely to be able to know and things that those who have a stake in the status quo are unlikely to want to know" (p. 18). Second, a biographer should always analyze his or her *own role or position as it affects understanding and the research process*. While science may be seen as glorifying objective observation, biographical studies, for men or women, are inherently subjective and dialogical. By virtue of the researcher's gender, social position, and historical experiences, he or she stands in an implicit relationship to the subject of the study. That relationship will surely have an impact on what kind of interpretation the researcher makes.

Third, Stewart urges the biographer to *identify women's agency in the midst of social constraint.* While we are all products of our cultural milieu, some biographers are too quick to explain women's lives completely in terms of social forces and constraints. Such an explanation feeds the stereotype of the woman as passive victim. Yet even under the most oppressive circumstances, human agency is a strong force to be reckoned with. Stewart writes that "within the context of relative powerlessness, women—like all people in a subordinate status—make choices and resist oppression" (p. 21). Fourth, Stewart asserts that the biographer should use *gender as an analytic tool.* Beyond sex roles and stereotypes, the very concept of what it means to be a man or a woman varies across cultures and over historical time. Therefore, "in studying a woman's life we must always inquire into her understanding of gender, as well as the consistencies and inconsistencies between her understandings and those of the people closest to her and in the wider culture affecting her at the time" (p. 24). Relatedly and fifth, the biographer must be sensitive to the precise ways in which *gender defines power relationships and in which power relationships are gendered.* Some feminist theorists emphasize that while gender seems to be related to people's bodies (men and women are anatomically different, by virtue of differences regarding sexuality and reproduction), gender is just as much about social power as it is about sex and reproduction. Characteristics and experiences that have been traditionally associated with being a woman or being a man may sometimes be better understood as the consequences of social power. "Many aspects of women's experience that are 'gendered'—that is, associated with maleness or femaleness—are also experiences of subordination and can be understood better in those terms" (p. 26).

Stewart's sixth strategy is to identify other significant aspects of an *individual's social position* and explore the implications of that position. Stewart points out that many middle-class, white women of the 1960s and 1970s assumed that their experience of the women's liberation movement was identical to that experienced by black women at the time. But they were wrong, many black scholars have since argued. While occupational and social opportunities opened up for white women, black women still faced obstacles connected less to their gender and more to issues of race and class. By failing to take into consideration the profound influences of social class and race/ethnicity on the experience of gender, researchers fail to comprehend the full meanings of women's experience. Finally, Stewart warns researchers to be suspicious of psychological prescriptions that stem ultimately from the experiences of the male elite. In particular, she suggests that biographers of women should *avoid the search for a neatly unified and coherent self or voice.* The idea that people do or should strive to have a perfectly unified and consistent sense of self, grounded in fundamental life principles and coherent ideological stance, may come from observations of privileged men who, to put it simply, have the socioeconomic luxury to have these kinds of selves. Stewart urges researchers to leave open the possibility that women's lives are often more contingent and contextually nuanced than men's. While she does not wish to conclude that such a difference is itself a clear psychological fact, she believes it is most wise to avoid projecting onto women, and onto people of color, a cultural ideal that seems to characterize better the life experiences of middle- and upper-middle-class Euro-American men living in the last half of the 20th century.

In sum, Stewart suggests that if women's life experience is different from men's, the stories that psychologists construct to make sense of women's lives are sure to be different as well. The research strategies she outlines are, fundamentally, strategies for the making and telling of life stories. As psychologists and biographers explore a wider range of human lives, they are sure to find that the kinds of stories they invoke and affirm will multiply and diversify.

Story Beginnings and Endings: Alfred Adler's Theory

Constructing the story of a person's life was a central, though implicit, goal for one of the most well-known and most misunderstood theorists in the history of personality psychology. I am speaking here of Alfred Adler (1870–1937). Long before the study of narrative and life stories became fashionable in psychology and the social sciences, Adler had a keen appreciation for the way in which the human life course may assume the form of a story. Adler is usually lumped together with Freud and the psychoanalysts (Chapter 3) because he was an early follower of Freud. But this grouping is misleading, for Adler's approach to personality, which he labeled **individual psychology**, actually bears little similarity to Freud or the tradition Freud launched. Adler made little use, for example, of the notion of unconscious processes, and he did not see human life as driven by erotic instincts. Furthermore, his theory has little to say about the kind of psychic conflict that is so important to most psychoanalytic approaches. Like Erikson and Murray, Adler presented instead a very eclectic and original theory of the person that reveals an astute understanding of the role of psychosocially constructed narrative in human lives organized in time.

Alfred Adler

Alfred Adler and Individual Psychology Alfred Adler was born in Vienna in 1870 of a middle-class Jewish family. He was a second son, who, throughout his childhood, found himself continually trying to match the high achievements of his older brother. His family constellation included an envious younger brother and three other siblings. Sibling position and rivalry in the family are major themes of Adler's theory of personality development, as he maintained that the second-born child often needed to rebel against authority in order to obtain power vis-a-vis the more conventional first-born. (I discussed this idea briefly in Chapter 1 to illustrate the correlational method in personality research and considered it again in Chapter 7 when we explored birth order as an environmental influence on personality.) Adler received a degree in medicine from the University of Vienna in 1895 and began a private practice shortly thereafter. In 1897, he married Raissa Epstein, an ardent socialist whom he met at a political convention. Though he was not a militant activist, Adler espoused a decidedly socialist political philosophy throughout his life. Unlike Freud,

Jung, and most of the other grand theorists of personality, Adler identified strongly with the working classes, giving many lectures to workers' groups in Europe and the United States in the 1920s and 1930s.

In 1902, Adler met Freud and immediately became active in psychoanalytic circles. He became the first president of the Viennese Psychoanalytic Society in 1910, but he cut his ties with Freud only a year later after a series of bitter disputes. As early as 1908, Adler had taken issue with Freud's insistence that sexuality was at the center of human instinctual life. Adler argued, instead, for a basic motive of aggression, an idea that Freud, ironically, accepted some 12 years later in his reformulation of human motivation to include both life and death instincts. At the time of Adler's proposal, however, such a departure from orthodox psychoanalytic theory was not welcomed. Adler formed his own group under the auspices of individual psychology, and he eventually attracted followers from all over the world. During World War I, Adler served as a physician in the Austrian army, and after the war he established the first child-guidance clinics in Vienna. Foreseeing the imminent Nazi menace, he left Europe in the early 1930s and settled in New York, where he continued his practice as a psychiatrist and his extensive lecturing and writing on individual psychology.

In contrast to Freud and Jung, Adler represents a very straightforward theory of the person. It is premised on a view of humankind that emphasizes conscious thought and the social determinants of personality. Like the social-learning theorists of Chapter 4, Adler suggests that personality is shaped by learning in a social environment. Like the cognitive approaches in Chapter 9, individual psychology argues that people are generally conscious of the reasons for their behavior and are capable of making rational life decisions with regard to conscious life goals and plans. Like the humanistic theories of Rogers and Maslow (Chapter 8), individual psychology paints a relatively optimistic picture of a developing and enhancing human organism, mastering the environment and creating the self over the human life course.

Beginnings: The Earliest Memories   Human beings are fascinated with beginnings. We want to know "how it all started," "where things come from," what the "origins" of a particular event or phenomenon are. We tend to believe that we can understand something fully only when we know its beginnings. Witness our fascination with creation myths, the theory of evolution, and scientists' speculations about the "Big Bang." Indeed, the very first verse of the first chapter of the Bible—the book of Genesis, whose name itself means "beginnings"—reads: "In the beginning God created the heaven and the earth." For Christians and Jews, this verse had traditionally served as the ultimate explanatory utterance.

When it comes to explaining our own lives and the lives of others, furthermore, we are just as strongly drawn to beginnings. From childhood onward, we want to know "where we came from" and what our "roots" might be. In this vein, Adler accorded a great deal of significance to the person's earliest memory. What a person can consciously remember from the earliest years holds clues about that person's present and future identity (Adler, 1927, 1931). In Adler's view, the earliest memory reveals major themes in a person's **style of life,** that is, the person's unique mode of adjustment to life most notably including the person's self-selected goals and means of achieving them. Adler believed that each life was patterned according to a unique style, the central features of which are outlined through early relationships in the person's family.

Although he did not couch his theory in explicitly narrative terms, Adler appeared to view the earliest memory as something like a personal creation myth or scene that implicitly foreshadows and symbolizes the overall tone of the person's subsequent life story. A number of his own examples are illuminating in this regard (Adler, 1927, 1931). Adler describes the case of a man whose first memory was that of being held in his mother's arms, only to be summarily deposited on the ground so that she could pick up his younger brother. His adult life involved persistent fears that others would be preferred to him, including extreme mistrust of his fiancée. Another man whose style of life emphasized fear and discouragement recalled falling out of his baby carriage. A woman who distrusted most people and feared that they would hold her back in her pursuits recalled that her parents prevented her from attending school until her younger sister was old enough to accompany her. And a young man who was being treated for severe attacks of anxiety recalled an early scene in which he sat at a window and watched workmen build a house, while his mother knitted stockings. To Adler, this recollection indicated that the young man was probably pampered as a child and that he preferred to be a spectator who watches things happen rather than a participant who makes things happen. Adler believed that this interpretation was supported by the man's current situation, in that he perennially became anxious whenever he tried to take up a new vocation. In an effective piece of vocational counselling, Adler suggested to this patient that he find an occupation that involves looking and observing. He took Adler's advice and became a successful art dealer.

Although psychologists outside Alderian circles have been slow to investigate the role of early memories in personality, a small flurry of research supports Adler's general insight that such memories illuminate current personality trends and strivings (Kihlstrom & Harackiewicz, 1982). Tying together early memories and Marcia's identity statuses (described in Chapter 10), Orlofsky and Frank (1986) found that college students in identity achievement and moratorium expressed more mature developmental themes in their early memories compared with students in foreclosure and identity diffusion.

Bruhn and Schiffman (1982) analyzed early memories provided by over 200 college students. Each student recalled earliest memories and filled out a questionnaire designed to assess the extent to which the student believed that he or she exerted effective control in the world. The early memories were analyzed from the standpoint of (1) mastery, (2) punishment, and (3) interpersonal difficulties. Bruhn and Schiffman found that those students who felt they had control over their worlds described early memories in which (1) they actively mastered the environment, (2) punishment was contingent on their own behavior, and (3) they caused their own interpersonal difficulties. Those students whose questionnaire responses indicated that they felt little control over their worlds expressed opposite themes. They tended to describe early memories in which (1) they were passive rather than active, (2) punishment was unrelated to their behavior, and (3) they were victims rather than causes of interpersonal difficulties. Some examples of these responses can be seen in Table 12.5. In this study, we see that early memories reveal the beginnings of a general orientation toward life. For those students who believed they could control and master the world, early memories emphasized how they had exerted control in the past. For the other students, however, early memories hint at a very different kind of story: a story premised on the assumption that the world controls them, that they cannot control it.

TABLE 12.5	*Early Memories According to Feelings of Control Over the World*	
CATEGORY OF MEMORY	**EXAMPLE FROM STUDENT HIGH ON CONTROL**	**EXAMPLE FROM STUDENT LOW ON CONTROL**
Achievement mastery	I was playing with my dolls. I was teaching them spelling. Since I couldn't spell, I would write down random combinations of letters and take them to my mother. After many trials and errors I spelled "home"—the first word I ever wrote.	I remember sitting on the floor near my mother's feet and watching her iron. She was ironing a favorite outfit of mine. I remember stroking the skirt once or twice.
Punishment	When I wanted to put ketchup on my potatoes, my father said I would have to eat it even if I didn't like it. I poured a bottle of ketchup on the potatoes and was made to sit there until I ate every bite.	I wanted to prove that I was a "big boy" by going to the store alone. When I got home, my parents punished me for "running away from home."
Interpersonal difficulty	One day a carpenter came to fix the bathroom. I locked him and my mother in the bathroom. Finally after an hour a neighbor let them out.	I was wrestling with an older boy. He pinned me down and sat on me for more than 10 minutes. It hurt like hell.

Note: Feelings of control were assessed through a self-report questionnaire.
Source: Bruhn & Schiffman (1982), pp. 389–390.

Endings: Fictional Finalism   In Adler's earliest theorizing, he argued that a prime motive for human behavior was striving to be aggressive. Later he replaced this motivational idea with a more general **will to power.** Adler believed that human beings want to feel strong and powerful in their interactions with the world and that they seek to avoid experiences in which they feel weak or inferior. Yet many children encounter repeated experiences of weakness and helplessness in the face of physical deficits and anomalies. Adler termed such deficits **organ inferiorities.** While these inferiorities can exert a debilitating effect on personality development, many people compensate for their own perceived inferiorities by working extra hard to strengthen what is weak. For example, a child who stutters may train him- or herself to be an exceptional speaker in adulthood. Or a child who is weak and sickly may undergo rigorous training to become a physical stalwart as an adult, as we saw in the case of Yukio Mishima in Chapter 3.

Adler eventually abandoned his concept of will to power in favor of an even more general motivational tendency termed **striving for superiority.** He described this universal, innate tendency as the "great upward drive" of human behavior and experience:

> I began to see clearly in every psychological phenomenon the striving for superiority. It runs parallel to physical growth and is an intrinsic necessity of life itself. It lies at the root of all solutions to life's problems and is manifested in the way in which we meet these problems. All our functions follow its direction. They strive for conquest, security, increase, either in the

right or in the wrong direction. The impetus from minus to plus never ends. The urge from below to above never ceases. Whatever premises all our philosophers and psychologists dream of—self-preservation, pleasure principle, equalization—all these are but vague representations, attempts to express the great upward drive. (Adler, 1930, p. 398)

We see in this wonderful quotation that Adler meant something quite general and encompassing when he posited a universal striving for superiority. The striving aims toward superiority over the environment as well as perfection, completion, and wholeness. In the context of this general life force, Adler reconceptualized organ inferiority to refer more generally to any feeling of weakness that arises from a sense of incompletion or imperfection in any sphere of life. He also blended with his great upward drive the concept of **social interest,** or the person's innate sense of kinship with all humanity. According to Adler, the well-adjusted person strives for superiority and wholeness in his or her environment while expressing a true love for and communion with other people. An important individual difference in personality, therefore, is the prominence of social interest in the lives of different persons. In an attempt to operationalize this concept for research, Crandall (1980, 1984) developed a short social-interest questionnaire. Supporting Adler's theoretical claims, Crandall found that people with strong social interest score higher on various measures of psychological adjustment and report fewer negative results of stress in their lives, compared with people who are low in social interest.

Though all persons strive for completion and wholeness in their lives, each person strives in a different way and toward a different end. In the motivational terms of Chapter 8, behavior is energized by the great upward drive of superiority but it is given direction and guidance by the person's thoughts about the future. A major theme in Adlerian psychology is that people are more oriented to the subjectively expected and hoped-for future than they are bound to the objective past:

Individual Psychology insists absolutely on the indispensability of finalism for the understanding of all psychological phenomena. Causes, powers, instincts, impulses, and the like cannot serve as explanatory principles. The final goal alone can explain man's behavior. Experiences, traumata, sexual development mechanisms cannot yield an explanation, but the perspective in which these are regarded, the individual way of seeing them, which subordinates all life to the final goal, can do so. (Adler, 1930, p. 400)

According to Adler, persons understand their lives in terms of *final goals*, and they organize their behavior and experience accordingly. Early experiences, traumata, and so on are not in and of themselves the determinants of behavior. Rather, like Erikson, Adler argues that early events are subjectively reorganized in light of the (later) final goals. The final goals envisioned by each person are subjective expectations about what might happen in the future. They are products of the imagination, not empirical or logical facts. Envisioned final goals are fictions, with respect to which we act *as if* they were true. According to Adler, then, human behavior and experience is guided, for better or worse, by **fictional finalism.** What each of us perceives to be the final goal of our lives is a fiction that we create to give our lives direction and purpose. Though some fictions may be impossible to realize, they nonetheless function in our lives as supreme organizers for our strivings and ultimate explanations for our conduct. Adler was quick to point out that a widely unrealistic fictional finalism may be the root cause of a neurotic's misery. Yet, all people create fictions about the future of one sort or another. The most adaptive fictional finalism incorporates realistic expectations into an imaginative narrative about the future, capable of sustaining and stimulating the person's strivings for superiority, wholeness, and completion.

Adler's concept of fictional finalism resembles Murray's "unity thema" and certain aspects of Erikson's "identity." Murray, Erikson, and Adler present us with theories of the person that assume that the individual's life is a patterned psychosocial totality that integrates past, present, and future, with beginnings, middles, and endings. People strive for narrative unity and purpose as their lives evolve over time.

The Seasons of Adult Life

Around the time that Henry Murray was launching the personological tradition in psychology, sociologists and other social scientists became especially interested in collecting *life histories* from many different walks of life in order to expose and explain societal problems such as delinquency and crime (e.g., Shaw, 1930). Sociologist John Dollard (1935) argued that life histories should provide biographical accounts that mirror society and the cultural milieu. The spirit and method of their efforts motivated Charlotte Bühler (1933) and Else Frenkel (1936) to collect and analyze autobiographical accounts written by almost 400 European men and women in the 1930s, representing various nationalities, social classes, and vocations. Whenever possible, the written accounts were supplemented by letters, diaries, and other personal documents produced by the subjects. The content analysis of all the data "revealed rather sharply demarcated phases through which every person passed in the course of his life" (Frenkel, 1936, p. 2). Fifty years ago, Bühler and Frenkel proposed a surprisingly modern and detailed model of adult development complete with five well-articulated stages and numerous references to a kind of "midlife crisis" around the age of 40. More concerned with general principles in all lives than with the uniqueness of any single life, these researchers focused on three dimensions of the adult biography: (1) significant external events (such as economic and political changes, war), (2) internal reactions to these events (such as thoughts, feelings, wishes), and (3) specific accomplishments and creative contributions to life. Here are a few of their more interesting findings:

1. During the first half of life, a person's subjective experience appears strongly influenced by bodily needs and short-term wishes, but the latter half is marked by a preoccupation with internalized duties that one "has set himself, or which have been set for him by society, or which have come from some code of values such as religion or science" (Frenkel, 1936, p. 15). Deviations from this general pattern were observed only in subjects who had been diagnosed by psychiatrists as neurotic.

2. Lives in which the pursuit of sexual gratification takes precedence over work and child rearing suffer "an unquestionable subjective decline in the second half" (p. 20).

3. Experiences of loneliness and daydreaming peak in late adolescence and again in the midforties. The latter period is also occasioned by a transitory reexamination of one's past and, in many cases, a heightened interest in literature.

4. The search for a "meaning in life" begins in late adolescence.

The life-history studies conducted by Bühler and Frenkel in the 1930s presaged narrative studies of adult life stages which became very popular in the 1970s and 80s. In both instances, psychologists collected first-person narrative accounts in order to generate their own third-person narratives about the developmental course of adult life. Bühler and Frenkel began to articulate a general narrative about adult life stages in which the protagonist begins to search for the meaning of his or her life in adolescence (as Erikson was later to suggest) and later experiences a second chapter of self-examination and questioning in the 40s—what we might now call a midlife crisis.

It is now commonplace in American society to talk about adult development in terms of predictable stages, phases, seasons, and the continual evolution of the self. This way of narrating the adult life course is apparent in Erikson (Chapter 10) and Jung (Chapter 3), but it was given an especially strong stimulus in the 1970 and 80s by theorists like Gould (1980), Levinson (1978), and Vaillant (1977), and by popular books such as Gail Sheehy's (1976) *Passages*.

Daniel Levinson (1978, 1981) formulated a detailed and influential model of the "seasons of man's life," based in part on biographical interviews of 40 American men. Levinson and his colleagues interviewed men between the ages of 35 and 45 years who were employed in one of four occupational groups: biology professors, novelists, business executives, and hourly workers in industry. Each man was interviewed 6 to 10 times, each interview lasting between 1 and 2 hours. Participants were asked to tell their life stories, concentrating mainly on the years from adolescence onward. Although the interviewers did not follow a standardized format of questions and answers, they were guided by a number of general considerations for the investigations, such as these:

1. We have to cover various "areas of living" such as family of origin, education, occupation, love relationships, marriage and family of procreation, leisure, bodily health and illness, ethnicity, religion, politics, and relation to self.

2. Within each area, it is essential to trace the sequence over the adult years, being alert to major events, choices, and turning points, as well as to the character of relatively stable periods.

3. We must learn about the "interpretation" of the areas. Occupational and family life, for example, are often closely intertwined.

4. As a series of interviews progresses, the interviewer gets a sense of different "chapters" in the life story: three years in military service; four to five years of relatively transient living; the years of starting a family and getting settled in a new city and job. It is important to comprehend the overall character of life within each of these chapters, as well as the kinds of changes that occurred within it. Here the emphasis is on the patterning among the many areas of living—the forms of integration as well as the contradictions, gaps, and fragments.

5. In the lives of many persons, there are occasional periods, lasting a few months to a few years, that constitute dramatic "high points" or "rock bottom" periods. These times often mark the end of one life phase and the beginning of another. They must be examined from many vantage points.

6. We are interested in the participant's view of his life as a whole, and of the interrelations among various parts and times within it. . . . [The past is] part of the present, and the biographer must so represent it. Likewise, the person's defined plans and more shadowy imaginings of the future shape and are shaped by the present. The future, too, forms a part of the present that the biographer must explore. (Levinson, 1981, pp. 61–62)

The central concept in Levinson's model is the individual **life structure,** which "refers to the patterning or design of the individual life at a given time" (Levinson, 1978, p. 99). One of the more encompassing concepts in personality theory, the individual life structure includes the individual's sociocultural world (class, religion, family, political systems, historical era), his participation in this world (relationships and roles with respect to significant people and institutions in his life), and various "aspects of the self," which may remain stable or may be transformed over time. Levinson views adult development as the evolution of the life structure. From adolescence through middle age, the life structure evolves through periods (seasons) of relative calm and periods of significant transition.

The first period in Levinson's scheme, Early Adult Transition (ages 17–22), roughly corresponds to the late-adolescent and early-adult period in which Erikson (1959) places the psychosocial crisis of identity *versus* role confusion (see Figure 12.1). The young man leaves home for college, the military, first employment, or some other living situation in which he begins to assume financial independence from his parents and achieves greater levels of autonomy. During the next phase, Entering the Adult World (ages 22–28), many young men explore adult roles and responsibilities and make provisional occupational commitments that link them to the wider society. In the late 20s, the man is likely to formulate a *dream* for the future. According to Levinson, the dream may include visions of occupational success and enhanced prestige, the development of a fulfilling family life, the establishment of certain kinds of relationships with friends and peers, and many other hopes and goals for the self, family, and significant others. Another significant aspect of development in the twenties, according to Levinson, is the establishment of a relationship with a *mentor.* The mentor is a man or woman who is usually somewhat older and more experienced than the young adult and therefore well positioned to shepherd the young adult through some of the difficult and challenging periods of the twenties. Mentors would appear to be most valuable and most common in the professional workplace. For example, a graduate student or junior professor heading for a career in college academia may find a mentor in his advisor. Through actions and advice, the adviser can teach the younger man how to make his way in the world of higher education, how to teach effectively, do good research, obtain governmental grants, get along with colleagues, and so on.

Around the age of 30, some men may encounter a significant transition period in which they feel the need to consolidate or rethink their tentative commitments from the 20s. The "Age 30 Transition" is followed by a period of Settling Down (early 30s). During Settling Down, the man is trying to carve a niche in the world and establish a timetable for advancement in his occupation, while simultaneously putting down roots in the sphere of his family. According to Levinson, the man in his early 30s is preoccupied both with "making it" and "building a nest," and he invests himself dearly in issues of order, stability, security, and control. By this time he has often generated a dream for the future, which will serve as a motivating vision of what he would like to accomplish and become.

FIGURE 12.1   *Levinson's Seasons of a Man's Life*

Source: From Levinson (1978), p. 57.

With its emphasis on order and control, the Settling Down period of the 30s is oddly reminiscent of Erikson's second stage of psychosocial development: the toddler's period of autonomy *versus* shame and doubt. Like the toddler, the man in his early 30s seeks to control self and environment as an independent and autonomous agent. For the toddler, the next phase is Oedipal: Freud's universal ontogenetic tragedy of becoming the conquering king and then falling from power, captured in Erikson's third stage of initiative *versus* guilt. Levinson's next phase of the life structure—Becoming One's Own Man, or BOOM—likewise has a certain Oedipal ring to it:

BOOM tends to occur in the middle to late 30s, typically in our sample around 35–39. It represents the high point of early adulthood and the beginning of what lies beyond. A key element in this period is the man's feeling that, no matter what he has accomplished to date, he is not sufficiently his own man. He feels overly dependent upon and constrained by persons or groups who have authority over him or who, for various reasons, exert great influence upon him. The writer comes to recognize that he is unduly intimidated by his publisher or too vulnerable to the evaluation of certain critics. The man who has successfully risen through the managerial ranks with the support and encouragement of his superiors now finds that they control too much and delegate too little, and he impatiently awaits the time when he will have the authority to make his own decisions and to get the enterprise really going. The untenured faculty member imagines that once he had tenure he will be free of all the restraints and demands he's been acquiescing to since graduate school days. (The illusions die hard!) (Levinson, Darrow, Klein, Levinson, & McKee, 1974, pp. 250–251)

BOOM sets the stage for the Midlife Transition. During this period (ages 40–45 years), 80% of the men Levinson interviewed encountered serious doubts concerning the directions of their lives. Taking stock of the various areas of commitment making up their life structures, many came to question the validity and worth of their hitherto most cherished goals and their plans for attaining them. For many, the Midlife Transition represented the bust following BOOM. Marital satisfaction, job performance, and enjoyment of outside pursuits declined. Confusion and despair became common as the sense of having established a home and a niche in the adult world, consolidated during Settling Down, gradually disintegrated, replaced by the nagging apprehension that one's life had been directed by and for the sake of illusions.

The Midlife Transition may be a very painful period in a man's life. Some of the men in Levinson's sample emerged from this period "cynical, estranged, unable to believe in anything" (Levinson, 1978, p. 108). Many others, however, benefited from the searching reevaluation of life structure precipitated by the transition. Those who benefited fashioned new life structures that opened up new opportunities and outlets for fulfillment in family, work, and friendships. Thus, the Midlife Transition may eventuate in a rejuvenated life structure in the second half of life—a restabilization around new plans and goals designed to maximize the individual's potential for fulfillment in many realms of life, especially the realms of intimacy and generativity.

Roberts and Newton (1987) describe four studies examining the life course of women, each of which employed Levinson's approach. Across the four studies, biographies from 39 contemporary women (ranging in age from 31 to 53, most middle-class and employed outside the home) were analyzed for the relevance and meaning of such Levinsonian concepts as (1) the dream, (2) the mentor, (3) the Age 30 Transition, and (4) the Midlife Transition. The authors conclude that these women passed through the same developmental seasons that Levinson sketched out for men. But a number of important differences were also noted. For example, women's dreams tended to be more complex and conflictual than men's, incorporating competing demands and hopes for family life and career success. Second, the women were much less likely than Levinson's men to report the existence of a satisfying mentoring relationship. Third, the women tended to place less emphasis than did Levinson's men on the importance of a Midlife Transition. However, they were more likely than the men to underscore the Age 30 transition as a period of accelerated and often dramatic personality change. This seemed to be especially true for women who by age 30 had not yet married or started a family. Some of these women began to feel a sense of urgency at this time. Soon it might be "too late" to become pregnant and bear children, some worried. Some of the women also began to question seriously the commitments they made in their 20s, and began to formulate a new life structure and a new dream to move them more rewardingly into their 30s. it would appear, therefore, that the Age 30 Transition *in women* could be somewhat analogous to the Midlife Transition *in men*. Both periods are described as having the potential for an urgent reexamination of the life structure because of the feeling that, in some sense or another, "time is running out."

The general idea that the adult life course may be viewed in terms of a sequence of periods or seasons is a controversial one today. Outside of in-depth biographical explorations like Levinson's, researchers have not found a great deal of support for a dramatic Midlife Transition in adult lives. For example, Costa and McCrae (1980a) developed a Midlife Crisis Scale to reflect the stresses of this portion of life identified by Levinson. No age differences were found on this scale in a large sample of men aged 33 to 70. Rossi (1980) and others have argued that the whole concept of an orderly life course in adulthood, complete with a progression of stages or seasons, does not accommodate well the lives of working-class adults and the lives of women. Levinson's stages may be descriptive of the lives of white, upper-middle class, professional men in America who entered midlife in the 1960s and 70s, but they may not generalize well to other samples.

On the other side of the coin, Helson and Wink (1992) found empirical support for some of Levinson's ideas in a longitudinal study of 101 women, followed between their early 40s and early 50s. The researchers document the existence of noteworthy developmental change around the age of 40, akin to a midlife transition, followed by increasing security, confidence, and decisiveness. Mercer, Nichols, and Doyle (1989) report data on women's lives that is both consistent with and different from Levinson's scheme. Overall, women in their study "tended to experience developmental periods at later ages and in sequences that were much more irregular" than those reported by Levinson (p. 180). However, something akin to a Midlife Transition manifested itself around the age of 40. The authors describe the age-40 time as a "Liberating Period" in many women's lives:

> For many women, the age-40 liberating period was the time of formulating a life dream. If they had rushed or were pushed into earlier choices such as marriage or had taken on a foreclosure identity, this was the time they focused on themselves. Earlier, their intense relationships with their husbands and children had had priority.

For many of the women in this study, therefore, the Midlife Transition signaled "A time to be yourself" (Mercer, Nichols, & Doyle, 1989, p. 182).

The Life Course

Like Murray and Adler, Levinson sought to capture the time-binding nature of human life. Using first-person narrative accounts (autobiographical interviews), he constructed a third-person developmental story about how certain men living in the United States in the 1960s and 70s described their own development from late adolescence through midlife. The plot entails periods (chapters) of relative calm (e.g., Settling Down), which eventually give way to periods of transformation and tumult (e.g., the midlife transition). The setting is post–World War II corporate America; the protagonist is the middle-class, well-educated white man; heroes include the mentor and the special woman who inspires the man's progress; the high point is BOOM; the low point is the advent of the midlife transition; the plot moves forward according to the development of the dream; the theme is meeting the challenges of change.

The most interesting plot turn in this story is the midlife transition. In contemporary American society, midlife or middle age is considered to last from roughly age 40 to age 65. Certain biological changes play a role in demarcating this period of life, such as the end of the childbearing years. But for the most part, midlife is *socially* defined, based on the assumptions that most Americans have about the course of human life (Cohler, 1982). Midlife is situated in the temporal course of the human lifespan according to what Neugarten (1968) called the **social clock.** The social clock is a set of expectations about age-appropriate transitions, setting the standards against which individuals evaluate the extent to which their lives are "on time" (Cohler & Boxer, 1984). Graduating from college in one's early 20s, raising a family in one's 20s and 30s, seeing the children leave home in one's 40s, witnessing parents' deaths in one's 50s and 60s, retiring at age 65 or 70—these are a few transitions in the lifespan that, in contemporary middle-class American society, are considered "on time." Many Americans expect to live well into their 70s and 80s. The midlife chunk of time is seen as comprising that period following early adulthood and preceding the retirement years.

As the adult enters midlife, he or she comes to realize that the life course is likely to be about half over and that there is now less time ahead in the future than behind in the past. Such a realization may lead to an increased concern with one's own mortality (Marshall, 1975; Sill, 1980), or what Neugarten and Datan (1972) call the "personalization of death." Experiences of loss become more salient—loss of others through death of parents and friends and through separation from children who have moved away, loss of vitality through changes in athletic and reproductive capacities, and loss of hopes and aspirations through the inevitable disappointments—both on-time and off-time—that accompany adult life (Jacques, 1965; Kernberg, 1980; Levinson, 1981).

Psychologists have observed a number of behavioral and attitudinal trends in midlife that may, on one level or another, be viewed as responses to one's growing, on-time concern about mortality. The middle years may bring an increase in the use of reminiscences in daily life (Livson & Peskin, 1980; Lowenthal, Thurnher, & Chiriboga, 1975), an enhanced appreciation for the internal world of thoughts and feelings, and somewhat less interest in establishing new interpersonal and instrumental engagements (Neugarten, 1979). According to Jung (1961), it is not until midlife that men are finally able to accept and integrate their suppressed femininity (the *anima*) and that women are able to express an inner masculinity (the *animus*), as we saw in Chapter 3. With the end of active parenting at midlife, Gutmann (1987) argues, women are likely to become more instrumental and executive in their approach to life, eschewing the dependent and self-effacing ways of their youth. Midlife men, on the other hand, are more likely to abandon the vigorous and aggressive manner of young adulthood in favor of more passive and contemplative roles.

Jacques (1965) has suggested that midlife may mark significant changes in the adult's efforts to be creative. Jacques examined biographical information and artistic productions for 310 painters, composers, poets, writers, and sculptors "of undoubted greatness or of genius" (p. 502). Included in his list were Mozart, Michelangelo, Bach, Gauguin, Raphael, and Shakespeare. Jacques found that before midlife the artists were more likely to produce masterpieces in a rapid and passionate fashion, as "hot-from-the-fire" productions. Their work tended to be highly optimistic and idealistic, laden

At the age of 29, Spanish painter Francisco José de Goya y Lucientes possessed the idealism and optimism of a romantic.

with themes of pure desire and romance. After the age of about 40, however, the artists appeared to work in a more deliberate fashion, creating more refined and "sculpted" masterpieces. With the increasing concern over mortality at midlife, youthful idealism gave way to a more contemplative pessimism and a "recognition and acceptance that inherent goodness is accompanied by hate and destructive forces within" (Jacques, 1965, p. 505). Creative products speak a more philosophical and sober language during and after midlife—a result, says Jacques, of the artist's own confrontation with the prospect of death.

Though men and women may be at the prime of their lives in their middle years, the social clock suggests that the end of life is closer to the present than is the beginning of life. It is likely, therefore, that midlife men and women should be especially concerned with *endings*. In their 40s and 50s, men and women in contemporary Western societies begin to consider in more detail and with greater urgency the problem of construing appropriate imagined endings for their self-defining life narratives. Even though the literal end of life is likely to be far off in the future, thoughts about endings become more and more salient as people move through their middle-adult years, deeply influencing the stories that people continue to construct to make sense of their lives.

Most lifespan developmental psychologists agree that important changes occur during the midlife years. But they disagree when it comes to saying that such changes occur at a particular time (e.g., the early 40s) and as part of a cleanly demarcated midlife

By age 69, Francisco José de Goya y Lucientes's work had lost the idealism of youth. Instead his paintings depicted the realities of life, such as in The Execution of Madrilenos on the Third of May, 1808 *(1814–1815).*

crisis or transition. Levinson's attempt to write a generic story of men's lives in time has been highly influential, but it is but one kind of story about adult development. The study of human individuality should leave room for more stories. Consequently, theorists and researchers who adopt what has been called a **life course** perspective tend to see more diversity and unpredictability in the interpretive stories social scientists might invoke to account for adult lives over time. Cohler, Hostetler, and Boxer (1998) describe this view:

> The course of development is much less clearly ordered than stage theories would predict and cannot be understood apart from either larger social and historical trends or unique events within particular lives. Certain sequentially negotiated tasks across the adult life course, related to work, intimate partnership, providing for the next generation, and dealing with the finitude of life, appear to be ubiquitous within contemporary society, yet no simple checklist can capture the full range of variation in developmental pathways or the ways in which certain tasks and prescribed social roles are experienced. (p. 266)

A life course perspective on writing stories of lives offers an especially nuanced and situated approach to adult development. In the spirit of Chapter 4 in this textbook, individual lives are viewed in their full social, cultural, and historical contexts, allowing for tremendous variety in developmental pathways that is observed across many different lives, across cultures, and across historical epochs (Bronfenbrenner, 1994; Dannefer, 1984; Elder, 1995). Life stories are shaped by economic conditions, cultural norms, social change, historical events, and chance happenings. At the same time, individuals exert their own agentic influence on the course of development, actively co-constructing their lives in a complex and evolving social context. A life-course perspective, therefore, brings to the fore (1) social time and timing, (2) social roles and relationships, and (3) the role of human agency and individual variability in psychosocial development in the adult years.

Social timing "refers to the incidence, duration, and sequence of roles and to related age expectations and beliefs" concerning the course of human life as understood in a given society or social context (Elder, 1995, p. 14). Thus, the extent to which a given social event or role is "on-time" or "off-time" is of prime importance for social life and individual well-being. Cohler and Boxer (1984) have argued that the experience of positive morale, or life satisfaction, is significantly determined by the sense of being on-time for expectable role transitions or life changes. Adults who move through role changes in a timely manner, line up their own life narratives with the stories that society holds up as the models for good development. Being off-time, therefore, brings with it a special challenge in life storytelling.

Social timing concerns the sequencing and patterning of *social roles*. Roles strongly influence the ways in which developmental tasks are met. For example, MacDermid, Franz, and DeReus (1998) have argued that Erikson's concept of generativity should not be viewed as a stage or chapter in a generic narrative of life but rather as a dynamic arrangement of roles, each carrying its own story line. Generativity is spread out unevenly across work, marital, parental, civic, and religious roles, and the strength or quality of generativity in one role is no predictor of the strength or quality of generativity in another. Within any given life, furthermore, generativity may move around from one role to another, according to the dictates of the social clock, on-time and off-time events, and a host of other factors. Over the adult life course, generativity ebbs and flows and spreads itself across different roles and life domains, sometimes in an unpredictable manner. Furthermore, particular love and family relationships, friendships, and other unpredictable interpersonal bonds strongly impact how generativity plays itself out. Life course theorists speak of *linked lives* (Elder, 1995) and *social convoys* (Kahn & Antonucci, 1981) to underscore the many senses in which individual development is thoroughly interdependent. People's lives and the stories they construct to make sense of them are linked to the lives and stories of those with whom they share significant involvements. Over time, people move through life with a group of family, friends, and colleagues—like a convoy traveling across a storied landscape, from one chapter to the next.

Social timing, social roles, and social relationships shape life stories, but people are not passive recipients of these shaping influences. Adults actively construct their lives within social contexts, as interpretive *agents* who appropriate life experience and make it their own. Indeed, adults often defy social clocks and fly in the face of conventional social norms and roles. They make meaning out of life on their own terms. Most amazingly, everybody does this is a different way.

This is why human individuality is so utterly fascinating. We are all so fundamentally the same, so rooted in human nature and evolution. We are all so thoroughly determined by cultural context, so tightly linked to family, society, history. And yet we are all so completely different, and so self-determining in the stories we tell to convey just how different we are. It is mainly because people are so different from one another, so different in the ways they begin life and the developmental pathways they follow over life's course, that psychologists have bothered to study this thing called "personality." It is because people are so complexly different, so different from one another in so many different ways, that we must think about human individuality in terms of this textbook's multiple levels of dispositional traits, characteristic adaptations, and life stories. You can't reduce these differences to a simple attribution or two; you can't sum it all up in four simple types or five different traits. There is simply too much variability, too much diversity to account for. And this is why, in my view, personality psychology is just about the most interesting thing in the world.

SUMMARY

1. The ancient story of Icarus—the boy who flew so close to the sun that it melted his wings and sent him plummeting to the sea below—provided the theoretical model for a famous case study written by Henry Murray about an unassuming college undergraduate. Combining themes of rising, falling, urethral eroticism, narcissism, and craving for immortality, the Icarus complex was Murray's storied interpretation of the student's life, based in part on the student's stories. Murray's interpretation is an example of psychologists' efforts to construct third-person narratives to interpret person's lives in time, often relying on those individuals' own first-person narrative accounts.

2. In the 1930s, Murray launched the personological traditional in the social sciences, assembling an interdisciplinary team of researchers at the Harvard Psychological Clinic. The personological tradition emphasized biography, myth, narrative, and the intensive exploration of the single case in the study of human lives.

3. A key feature of Murray's personological viewpoint was that human beings are time-binding organisms. The history of the organism is the organism, Murray suggested, which mandated the use of biographical methods of inquiry. In decomposing a life in time, the personologists can begin by focusing on the single proceeding or life episode and work up to durances (strings of overlapping proceedings), serials (long-term sequences within a given life domain), and serial programs (sequences that extend in a goal-directed manner into the future). Lives are given direction by internal needs and environmental press, which interact to form life themas. A self-defining patterning of needs, press, and thema constitutes a unity thema, which is the central, organizing motif of a person's life story.

4. A major figure in the personological tradition was Robert White, who championed the intensive study of the single case. White's case studies illustrate important growth trends in personality over time. With healthy personality development over the adult life course, White argued, five growth trends are revealed: (a) the stabilization of ego identity, (b) the freeing of personal relationships, (c) the deepening of interests, (d) the humanizing of values, and (e) the expansion of caring.

5. Even before the time of Murray, case studies were used to exemplify personality theories, to provide new data for theory development, and to compare the contrast different constructs and theories as they might apply to the single life set in time. Yet case studies have always been controversial. Critics of case study methodology have argued that cases are inherently too subjective, unreliable, and unwieldy to be of good scientific use. In evaluating the appropriateness of case study research, one needs to pay close attention to issues of reliability, internal coherence, interpretive truth, external validity, and the fundamental distinction in science between discovery and justification. A reasoned consideration of the strengths and limitations of case studies suggests a number of appropriate venues in which they can be scientifically valuable, including especially the derivation of new ideas, hypotheses, and theoretical insights.

6. Psychobiography is the systematic use of psychological theory to transform a life into a coherent and illuminating story. Beginning with Freud's famous study of Leonardo da Vinci, psychobiographies have typically employed psychodynamic theories to construct broad theoretical interpretations of the lives of relatively famous people. While many criticisms have been levied against psychobiography, advances in method and theory have been observed in recent years, and scholars have developed informal standards for the evaluation of different psychobiographical efforts. To help organize the voluminous data that a psychological biographer might gather, Alexander has delineated nine guidelines for determining which data might prove most useful for the narrative interpretation. He suggests that the data need to be evaluated with respect to primacy, frequency, uniqueness, negation, emphasis, omission, error, isolation, and incompletion.

7. In the last few decades of the 20th century, biographers turned their attention to the life stories of women, people of color, and members of other traditionally marginalized groups. Stewart has argued that writing a woman's life offers unique challenges for the psychological biographer. She outlines seven feminist strategies for the biographical study of women's lives: (a) pay attention to what has been left out, (b) analyze your own role and position vis-a-vis the subject of study, (c) identify women's agency in the midst of social constraint, (d) use gender as an analytic tool, (e) be aware of how gender defines power relationships, (f) identify other aspects of the subject's social position such as class and ethnicity, and (g) be skeptical of the search for a neatly unified and coherent self or voice.

8. Like Murray and White, Alfred Adler developed a system for personality studies that emphasized the temporal nature of human lives. Adler's theory shows a keen appreciation for the way in which the human life course may assume the form of a story. According to Adler's individual psychology, the earliest memory serves as an origin myth for life, setting the stage for the development of a person's unique style of life. While the earliest memory sets up the story's beginning, the person's fictional finalism, or imagined goals for the future, provides the life story with direction and purpose and orients it toward an envisioned narrative ending. Main themes in the story relate to the agentic striving for superiority and the communal tendency toward social interest.

9. Daniel Levinson and other life-stage theorists have articulated a generic story of adulthood around the metaphor of "seasons of life." Basing his conception on intensive interviews of mainly middle-class, middle-aged American men, Levinson formulated a model of the evolution of a man's life structure from adolescence through middle age. The life structure is the overall design of a man's life. Especially important in the evolution of the structure are the man's articulation of a life dream and the influence of a mentor. An especially dramatic chapter in Levinson's third-person story of adult life is the midlife transition, which typically entails a thoroughgoing re-evaluation of one's life commitments and priorities. While many lifespan researchers agree that important changes in life structure may occur sometime in the midlife years, they disagree on the prevalence of a dramatic and circumscribed midlife crisis. Some efforts have been made to extend Levinson's model to the lives of women, with mixed success.

10. In partial reaction to stage models of adult life, the life course perspective tends to emphasize social timing, social roles and relationships, and the power of human agency and individuality. The life course perspective sees adult development as more historically and culturally determined and socially contingent than is apparent in life-stage theories. According to the life course perspective, life stories are shaped by economic conditions, cultural norms, social change, historical events, and chance happenings. At the same time, individuals exert their own agentic influence on the course of development, co-authoring their lives in a complex and evolving social context. In underscoring human agency and individuality, the life course perspective reminds us of the importance of personality psychology in general and the efforts of personality psychologists to formulate scientifically credible accounts of human individuality.

Glossary

A-babies insecurely attached infants who manifest a good deal of avoidant behavior in the presence of the caregiver. Contrast with *B-babies* and *C-babies*.

absolute continuity the extent to which a personality attribute exists in the same amount over time. Absolute continuity usually refers to group averages on personality characteristics assessed at two or more points in time. Contrast to *differential continuity, ipsative continuity,* and *coherence*.

achievement motivation a recurrent preference or desire for experiences of doing well and being successful; also called the "need for achievement." Individual differences in achievement motivation may be assessed through the TAT.

act frequency Buss and Craik's approach to personality study whereby the researcher views personality dispositions as summary categories containing discrete and representative behavioral acts.

Adult Attachment Interview an interview for adults developed by Mary Main and colleagues and focused on the person's recollections of his or her own childhood attachments to parents. The interview yields four types of attachment: Secure/autonomous, Dismissing, Preoccupied, and Unresolved.

affect a term usually designating emotion.

affiliation motivation a recurrent preference or desire for establishing, maintaining, or restoring positive affective relationships; also called the "need for affiliation." Individual differences in affiliation motivation

may be assessed through the TAT.

agency Bakan's general concept for the tendency to separate self from others, to master, dominate, and control the self and the environment. Contrast with *communion*.

agreeableness one of the Big Five traits, agreeableness encompasses personality descriptors having to do with interpersonal warmth, altruism, affection, empathy, cooperation, and other communal facets of personality.

aggregation the principle in psychological measurement that urges an investigator to collect many different samples of the same behavior across many different situations and/or over time in order to obtain a reliable estimate of personality and behavioral trends.

altruistic personality a personality type characterized by high ratings or scores on dimensions such as sympathy for others, social responsibility, and mature perspective taking.

amygdala a small, almond shaped region in the forebrain linked to the experience of fear and responses to danger. Certain parts of the amygdala are hypothesized to be implicated in the working of the behavioral inhibition system (BIS) and, by extension, individual differences in traits associated with negative affectivity, or neuroticism.

anal-expulsive type according to Freud, one resultant cluster of personality characteristics associated with fixation at the anal stage. These characteristics include disorganization and disorderliness, explosiveness,

and cruelty. Contrast with *anal-retentive type*.

anal-retentive type according to Freud, one resultant cluster of personality characteristics associated with fixation at the anal stage. These characteristics include stubbornness, stinginess, and an overly scheduled and compulsive life style. Contrast with *anal-expulsive type*.

anal stage the second stage of psychosexual development, according to Freud, wherein libidinal expression is concentrated in the anus, manifested in bowel movement, and shaped by toilet training.

analytical psychology Carl Jung's theory of personality.

anima the unconscious archetype of femininity in men (Jung).

animus the unconscious archetype of masculinity in women (Jung).

archetypes Jung's structural elements of the collective unconscious, referring to universal patterns or predispositions that influence how all humans consciously and unconsciously adapt to their world. Common archetypes include "the mother," "the child," "the hero," "the anima," "the animus," and "the shadow."

associationism the doctrine that various objects and ideas that are contiguous in time or space come to be connected, or associated, with each other into meaningful units.

attachment a bond of love formed between two people, especially infant and caregiver, in which various behaviors are organized into an evolutionarily adaptive system designed to ensure close physical proximity of the two.

attachment behaviors in infancy, these include sucking, clinging, following, vocalizing, and smiling.

attachment styles three styles of approaching romantic relationships developed from research on adult romantic love. The three styles parallel Ainsworth's attachment types for infants: secure, avoidant, and resistant (anxious/ambivalent).

attitudes two general orientations to life: extraversion and introversion (Jung).

authoritarian personality a pattern of attitudes and traits suggesting an overly conventional, rigid, aggressive, hostile, and power-oriented kind of person.

autonomy *versus* shame and doubt the second stage in Erikson's scheme of psychosocial development, during which the toddler seeks to establish him- or herself as an independent and competent agent in the environment.

basic anxiety Horney's term for the feeling a child has of being isolated and helpless in a potentially hostile world.

B-babies securely attached infants, who use the caregiver as a secure base from which to explore the world. Contrast with *A-babies* and *C-babies*.

behavioral approach system (BAS) In Gray's trait theory, one of two brain systems dealing with human emotionality. As the biological grounding for the trait "impulsivity," the BAS mediates positive affect and arouses a person to seek rewards. The BAS and impulsivity may be

contrasted to the BIS (behavioral inhibition system) and anxiety.

behavioral inhibition system (BIS) in Gray's trait theory, one of two brain systems dealing with human emotionality. As the biological grounding for the trait "anxiety," the BIS mediates negative affect and motivates a person to inhibit goal-based behavior in order to avoid punishment. The BIS and anxiety may be contrasted to the BAS and impulsivity.

behavior genetics a scientific field, with roots in genetics, biology, psychology, and related fields, that explores the empirical evidence concerning the relative influences of genetic and environmental factors in accounting for variability in human behavior.

behaviorism an intellectual tradition in psychology emphasizing the rigorous and objective study of observable behavior shaped by learning and the environment.

being cognition Maslow's term for perceiving and understanding objects and events in terms of their wholeness.

being values in Maslow's theory, values that promote growth and the enrichment of experience.

belief in the species Erikson's term for the adult's hope for and faith in humankind, enabling him or her to be generative.

Big Five five broad personality traits assumed by some researchers to subsume the entire domain of possible traits. According to one formulation, the Big Five are extraversion–

introversion, neuroticism, openness to experience, conscientiousness, and agreeableness.

bipolar self Kohut's term for the center of personality, made up of the opposite poles of ambitions and goals, which are connected via a tension arc of talents and skills.

California Psychological Inventory (CPI) a popular personality inventory for normal samples providing scores on 20 trait scales.

California Q-sort a standard assessment procedure in which psychologists sort 100 statements about personality into a distribution designed to explain many different facets of a single person.

case study an in-depth investigation of a single individual, sometimes conducted over a substantial period of time.

castration anxiety the Oedipal boy's unconscious fear that his penis will be cut off, symbolizing a loss of power.

causal attributions the perceived causes of events.

C-babies insecurely attached infants who manifest a good deal of resistance and ambivalence in the presence of the caregiver. Contrast with *A-babies* and *B-babies*.

character structure in Hogan's socioanalytic theory, the person's characteristic ways of displaying the self to family members, especially parents. Contrast with *role structure*.

characteristic adaptation a motivational, cognitive, or developmental concern whose meaning comes in part from the particular temporal, situational, or social-role-oriented context within which it is embedded. Characteristic adaptations—such as goals, motives, plans, schemas, and stages—comprise Level 2 of personality. Level 1 is made up of dispositional traits and Level 3 is made up of integrative life stories.

circumplex model of traits a circular arrangement of traits, proposed by Wiggins and others, in which trait terms are organized according to the two independent dimensions of strength (dominance *versus* submissiveness) and warmth (warm *versus* cold).

classical conditioning a form of simple learning whereby an unconditioned stimulus is repeatedly paired with a conditioned stimulus such that the conditioned stimulus, originally not likely to evoke a response, comes to be associated with the unconditioned stimulus so that it eventually does evoke a conditioned response.

client-centered therapy Rogers's brand of psychotherapy, emphasizing empathy, sincerity, warmth, acceptance, role playing, and respect for the dignity of the client.

cognition mental processes associated with the acquisition, organization, and use of knowledge, including attention, perception, thinking, abstraction, problem-solving, learning, memory, and language.

cognitive evaluation theory Deci and Ryan's theory of how rewards interact with intrinsic motivation, based on the assumption that people are self-determining beings.

cognitive niche the particular position that human beings have

evolved to occupy in the evolutionary landscape, whereby their main adaptive advantages center on the computational powers of the human mind. The human mind has evolved to enable human beings to adapt to the many threats and challenges faced in the environment through mental manipulations of situations, innovative strategies for attaining goals, analysis, reasoning, language, and so on.

cognitive/social-learning/ person variables Mischel's characteristic styles or strategies for approaching situations. Mischel lists five types of cognitive/social learning/person variables: competencies, encoding strategies, expectancies, subjective values, and self-regulatory systems and plans.

cognitive styles characteristic and typically preferred modes of processing information, such as field independence–dependence and integrative complexity.

coherence this term can mean many things, but in Chapter 7 I use it to refer to one form of continuity in personality characteristics over time. Coherence is continuity not in a particular behavior or trait but in an underlying phenomenon or structure that coherently links together things, over the course of development, that appear on the surface to be different. Contrast to *absolute continuity, differential continuity,* and *ipsative continuity.*

cohort effect a finding with respect to a particular psychological phenomenon that is a function of the particular historical cohort being studied, rather than, say, due to developmental factors. In cross-sectional stud-

ies, it is difficult to disentangle cohort and developmental effects because different age cohorts are examined at the same time.

collective unconscious Jung's concept for an inherited storehouse of human potential that is a result of the evolution of the species, containing unconscious patterns and images called *archetypes.*

collectivism as a cultural construct, a meaning system emphasizing the priority of the collective or in-group over and against the individual self. Many Asian societies are considered to be relatively collectivists. Contrast to *individualism.*

commitment script one kind of script identified by Tomkins, in which a person binds him- or herself to a life program or goal that promises the reward of intense positive affect.

common trait Allport's term for any trait that can be viewed as a disposition upon which many people differ. From the standpoint of nomothetic research, psychologists often study common traits, comparing and contrasting people's trait scores. Contrast to *personal disposition.*

communion Bakan's general concept for the tendency to merge or unite with others, to surrender the self as part of a larger whole. Contrast with *agency.*

complex in Jung's theory, a clustering of emotionally charged ideas through which the psyche expresses itself.

condensation an aspect of Freud's concept of dream work whereby different latent elements are fused into a single manifest element.

conditioned generalized reinforcers in operant conditioning, reinforcers that acquire their power because of their associations with a large variety of other reinforcers.

conditions of worth in Rogers's theory, the belief that some aspects of one's experience are good or worthy and others are not worthy.

conscientiousness one of the Big Five traits, conscientiousness encompasses personality descriptors denoting self-control, dependability, responsibility, persistence, and an achievement-oriented approach to life.

conservation of energy the 19th-century idea, adopted by Freud in his libido theory, that a system runs on a fixed amount of energy that cannot be created or destroyed.

construct approach to test construction an approach to designing a self-report questionnaire, or indeed any psychological measure, in which the investigator begins with a theory about the construct and then moves back and forth between theory and data to refine the evolving measure and the theory, following well-defined steps of test construction.

construct validity the extent to which a test measures the construct that it is theoretically intended to measure. Construct validity increases as empirical support is garnered for the various propositions contained in the construct's nomological net. Construct validity is the most basic and encompassing form of

validity, and other forms of validity can be seen as derivatives from it.

content validity the degree to which the items of a test cover the entire content domain of a construct and are not confounded with other domains.

context of discovery the process of discovering new ideas and building theories in science. Contrast with *context of justification*.

context of justification the process of testing ideas derived from theory in science. Contrast with *context of discovery*.

continuous reinforcement reinforcement of a particular response after every occurrence. Contrast with *partial reinforcement*.

convergent validity the extent to which different measures of the same construct relate to each other. Contrast with *discriminant validity*.

coping strategies patterns of thought and behavior aimed at relieving anxiety and stress.

correlational design a methodology for research whereby the scientist examines the extent to which variables covary or relate to each other. Contrast with *experimental design*.

countertransference a term used in psychoanalytic therapy to refer to the therapist's tendency to relate to the patient in a way that unconsciously repeats or plays out his or her (the therapist's) own relationships with personally important people. Contrast with *transference*.

criterion-key method of test construction a method of test construction employed with the

MMPI, in which items are chosen solely for their differential endorsement by subjects in different criterion groups.

criterion validity the extent to which a test is associated with external behaviors that it is designed to predict.

cross-sectional study a research design in which different age cohorts are compared to each other at a given point in time. Contrast to *longitudinal study*.

culture a tradition of rules and mores embraced by a particular society of people.

current concern Eric Klinger's concept which refers to the motivational state that a person is in between the time he or she commits to a goal and the time he or she either attains or abandons the goal.

D-babies a recent classification category in attachment research, the D-baby suffers from disorganized or disoriented attachment patterns with the caregiver, appearing dazed and confused in the presence of the attachment object. This pattern is found among some victims of child abuse.

death instincts Freud's concept for a group of instinctual drives assumed to motivate the person toward behavior and experience promoting one's own death and destruction or aggression toward others. Contrast with *Eros* and *life instincts*.

declarative-episodic knowledge knowledge of experiences, thoughts, and actions of other people (person memory) and one's personal autobiographical record (autobiographical memory).

declarative-semantic knowledge abstract and categorical information that the person gleans over time concerning various phenomena.

deduction reasoning from the abstract and general to the concrete and particular. Contrast with *induction*.

defense mechanisms unconscious strategies of the ego (Freud) designed to distort reality in order to lessen anxiety.

deficiency motives in Maslow's theory, those needs based on lacks, absences, and tensions in the organism.

denial a primitive defense mechanism in which the person baldly refuses to acknowledge an anxiety-provoking event.

depressive schemata the overly negativistic frameworks for interpreting reality that depressed people often employ.

developmental elaboration the process through which childhood temperament dimensions may gradually develop into full-fledged personality traits in adulthood. Caspi has identified six mechanism of developmental elaboration: learning processes, environmental elicitation, environmental construal, social and temporal comparisons, environmental selection, and environmental manipulation.

dialectical humanism Fromm's view that the person's behavior is the complex and overdetermined product of internal needs manifesting themselves within the external social arrangements prescribed by a society at a particular moment in history.

dialogical self Hermans's concept of the self as a multiple narrator of experience. The dialogical self is a dynamic multiplicity of relatively autonomous I positions in an imaginal landscape. Each I position develops its own voice, or point of view.

differential continuity the longitudinal consistency of individual differences. Differential continuity assesses the extent to which people maintain their relative positions within a particular distribution with respect to a particular personality characteristic over time. Contrast to *absolute continuity*, *ipsative continuity*, and *coherence*.

difficult babies one of three temperament types identified by Thomas, Chess, and Birch, referring to babies with consistently negative moods, intense emotional reactions, and irregular sleeping and eating cycles. Contrast with *easy babies* and *slow-to-warm-up babies*.

discriminant validity the extent to which different measures of different constructs do *not* relate to each other.

displacement an aspect of Freud's concept of dream work whereby the dreamer unconsciously shifts the emphasis in a dream from an important but threatening source to a trivial but safer one, as when one displaces a powerful emotion from its intended object to a substitute.

display rules societal norms for the expression of different emotions.

dream work Freud's term for the processes utilized unconsciously by the dreamer as he or she creates a manifest dream

from latent unconscious material. Aspects of dream work include condensation, displacement, symbolism, and secondary revision.

easy babies one of three temperament types identified by Thomas, Chess, and Birch, referring to babies with consistently positive mood, low-to-moderate intensity of emotional reactions, and regular sleeping and eating cycles. Contrast with *difficult babies* and *slow-to-warm-up babies*.

ego one of three divisions in Freud's structural model of the mind, serving as the mediator among the id, superego, and external reality, and operating according to the reality principle. According to Lovevinger, a person's overall framework of meaning, the master synthesizing I.

ego control the extent to which a person is able to reign in impulses ranging from extreme undercontrol to overcontrol. One of two basic dimensions of personality in Jack Block's approach to personality typologies. See also *ego resiliency*.

ego integrity *versus* despair the eighth and last stage of psychosocial development in Erikson's scheme, associated with old age and the acceptance or rejection of one's own life as something that was.

ego psychology a modern derivative of Freudian theory emphasizing the adaptive and integrating power of the ego over and against the id and superego.

ego resiliency the capacity to modify one's typical level of ego control—toward either more control or less control of impulses—to adapt to demands of the situation. One of the two basic dimensions of personality in Jack Block's approach to personality typologies. See also *ego control*.

Embedded Figures Test a test of field-independence/field-dependence in which a person attempts to find forms hidden in an embedding field.

emergenesis an emergent property of a configuration of genes. Some personality characteristics may be a product of emergenesis whereby a unique combination of genes produces an effect that would not be produced, in even an attenuated form, by the parts that make up the configuration. See also **nonadditive genetic variance.**

empathy vicarious affective response to others, as when one person feels vicariously what another person feels directly.

empty-nest syndrome the supposed negative results for parents when their children attain adulthood and leave home.

entrepreneurship a collection of behavioral and attitudinal characteristics associated with high achievement motivation, including moderate risk taking, personal responsibility for performance, striving for productivity and innovative change, and careful attention to costs and profits.

environment of evolutionary adaptedness (EEA) the hypothesized world of the Pleistocene epoch during which human beings evolved and human nature was forged. It is believed that humans evolved over a 2–4 million year span as hunters and gatherers living in small, migratory groups.

erogenous zones bodily sites for libidinal expression, including the mouth, anus, and genitals.

Eros Freud's *life instincts*.

expectancy in Rotter's and Mischel's social-learning theories, a subjectively held probability that a particular reinforcement will occur as the outcome of a specific behavior.

experience sampling method method of collecting samples of daily behavior, thought, and affect through the use of electronic pagers and other such devices.

experimental design a methodology for research whereby the scientist manipulates or alters one variable of interest (the independent variable) to observe its effect on another variable of interest (the dependent variable).

explanatory style the characteristic way in which a person attributes cause in explaining social events. A debilitating explanatory style is implicated in depression. Depressed people tend to explain negative events in their lives as due to internal, stable, and global causes.

exploitative type Fromm's characterization of the aggressive and self-centered person, who exploits other people and the environment.

extraversion–introversion a broad personality trait, identified in many theories (including Eysenck's and Jung's), denoting a tendency to be outgoing, sociable, and impulsive on the one hand (extraversion) versus a tendency to be inwardly oriented, withdrawn, and deliberate on the other (introversion).

face validity the extent to which test items seem, in the eyes of the respondent, to measure what they are supposed to measure.

factor analysis a statistical procedure through which various items (as on a self-report questionnaire) are correlated with each other to determine the empirical clustering of the items.

feedback the self-regulation of a system through the repeated accumulation of information concerning the system's deviation from a particular set point or goal.

feedback hierarchy a system in which the output of one feedback loop becomes the reference value for the feedback loop that is subordinate to it.

fictional finalism Adler's concept for an envisioned end or goal with respect to which the person orients his or her strivings. The goal is fictional in that it has not been realized and indeed may likely not be fully realized, but it still serves to energize and direct behavior.

field-independence/field-dependence a general dimension of cognitive style ranging from highly analytical and differentiated processing of information (field-independence) to highly contextual and global processing (field-dependence).

Five Factor Model a conception of personality traits that has become increasingly accepted in recent years indicating that traits can be grouped into five basic categories. See **Big Five.**

fixation   Freud's concept for a problem, resulting from either overindulgence or deprivation, at a particular stage of psychosexual development. Fixations result in the development of particular personality characteristics in adulthood associated with earlier psychosexual stages.

flow   the subjective experience that a person feels when he or she is engaged in an intensely joyful and involving experience, characterized by a focused and ordered state of consciousness and an optimal ratio of skills to challenges.

folk concepts   on the California Psychological Inventory (CPI), the name employed for the various trait scales to denote categories of personality that arise naturally out of human interactions in most, if not all, societies. Examples of the folk-concept scales include "responsibility," "socialization," and "flexibility."

foreclosure   one of Marcia's four identity statuses, referring to the person who has not explored identity options but has rather made commitments to identity goals and outcomes that arose from childhood and remained unquestioned.

formal operations   Piaget's term for abstract, hypothetico-deductive thinking, generally evidenced in adolescence and adulthood.

free association   a procedure used in psychoanalytic therapy in which the patient lets his or her mind wander in response to a stimulus or event and reports all thoughts (associations) aloud to the therapist, spontaneous and uncensored.

frustration-aggression hypothesis   Miller and Dollard's hypothesis that aggressive behavior is a socially molded behavior aimed at injuring another organism as a consequence of the frustration of goal-directed activity.

fully functioning person   in Rogers's theory, the person who has attained maturity and actualization and is therefore consciously aware of the many different facets of his or her life and able to symbolize many seeming inconsistent aspects of experience and integrate them into a coherent whole.

functions   four ways in which persons make sense of reality: thinking, feeling, sensing, and intuiting (Jung).

fundamental attribution error a general tendency for people to overemphasize traits and underemphasize situations in explaining the causes of other people's behavior.

gender schema theory   Bem's theory concerning the ways in which people differ with respect to their tendency to understand their life and the world in gender-related terms.

generation   those people born at the same point in historical time and who thereby develop a shared understanding of the world, common beliefs and aims, and a shared generational style.

generativity *versus* stagnation the seventh stage of psychosocial development in Erikson's scheme, in which the adult seeks to guide the next generation and generate a legacy of the self.

genital stage   Freud's fifth and last stage of psychosexual development, attained at puberty with full sexual maturation.

group socialization theory of development   a theory proposed by Judith Harris which argues that because shared environments have so little impact on personality traits, the main environmental determinants of traits are likely to reside in group processes, especially in children's peer groups.

hagiographies   biographical accounts of the lives of Christian saints written in the Middle Ages to venerate the Christian life.

heritability quotient   a numerical estimate of the proportion of variability in a given characteristic that can be attributed to genetic differences between people.

hermeneutics   the art and science of interpreting texts.

higher-order conditioning the formation of complex associations in classical conditioning through which conditioned stimuli, which have obtained their eliciting power through associations with unconditioned stimuli, come to be associated with other neutral stimuli, which themselves become conditioned stimuli by virtue of the association.

hoarding type   Fromm's characterization of the person who strives to accumulate possessions, power, and love, and to hold on to all that is accumulated.

hostile aggression   aggression explicitly aimed at hurting or injuring the victim. Contrast with *instrumental aggression*.

humanistic psychology   a general orientation in

psychology that rose to prominence in the 1960s, emphasizing the creative, optimistic, and self-actualizing tendencies of human beings.

hysteria a form of psychopathology in which a person suffers from bodily symptoms, such as blindness or paralysis, that have no physical or biological cause.

Icarus complex Murray's concept for a cluster of themes in personality functioning, including urethral erotism, ascensionism, cynosural narcism, falling, craving for immortality, and depreciation and enthrallment of women—all modeled after the ancient Greek story of Icarus.

id one of three main divisions in Freud's structural model of the mind, serving as the home for instinctual impulses of sex and aggression and their unconscious derivative wishes, fantasies, and inclinations.

identification Freud's concept for the unconscious desire to "be" or to "be like" the other person. Contrast with *object choice*.

identity achievement one of Marcia's four identity statuses, referring to the person who has explored various identity options and successfully made commitments to realistic identity goals.

identity diffusion one of Marcia's four identity statuses, referring to the person who has not yet explored identity options and who has not made commitments.

identity status Marcia's concept referring to the extent to which a young person has ex-

plored and made commitments to different identity options, especially in the realms of occupation and ideology. The four statuses are identity achievement, moratorium, foreclosure, and identity diffusion.

identity *versus* role confusion the fifth stage in Erikson's scheme of psychosocial development, during which the adolescent strives to answer the questions "Who am I?" and "How do I fit into the adult world?"

ideological setting in the life-story model of identity, the background of a person's fundamental beliefs and values which provide the life story with a taken-for-granted setting.

idiographic Allport's term for an approach to personality study which focuses on the uniqueness of the individual case. Also called morphogenic. Contrast with *nomothetic*.

I–E Scale a popular self-report measure of locus of control, developed by Rotter.

imago in the life-story model of identity, a personified and idealized image of self that functions as a main character in the life story.

implicit learning one of four related systems in what Kihlstrom calls the "psychological unconscious," implicit learning is the acquisition of knowledge in the absence of any reflective awareness of the knowledge itself.

implicit memory one of four related systems in Kihlstrom's "psychological unconscious," implicit memory is shown when a person's behavior is modified by the apprehension of a past

event, though the event itself is not consciously remembered.

implicit perception one of four related systems in Kihlstrom's "psychological unconscious," implicit perception may be seen when the performance of a task changes as the result of some current event, but the current event is not consciously perceived.

implicit personality theory a person's own theory of human functioning, made up of intuitive knowledge concerning the causes of human behavior, population norms for various attributes of personality, and beliefs about how various personality attributes may relate to each other.

implicit thought one of four related systems in Kihlstrom's "psychological unconscious," implicit thought is problem-solving activity that occurs outside the problem solver's awareness.

imprinting very rapid learning during a particular sensitive period in development whereby the organism forms a lasting preference for a particular stimulus.

inclusive fitness an organism's overall (total, inclusive) ability to maximize the replication of the genes that were operative in its design. Natural selection has designed organism to act in ways that maximize inclusive fitness. In human beings, behavioral systems and mechanisms that work, directly or indirectly, to promote the reproduction of one's own genes (and those same genes one shares with biological relatives) enhance inclusive fitness.

inclusive mode Erikson's concept for the young girl's characteristic approach to the world, involving "teasing, demanding, and grasping" in an attempt to "snare" others.

individual differences characteristics of persons that can be said to differ with respect to amount or degree from one person to the next. Such concepts as personality "traits," "motives," "schemas," and "stages" are typically understood as aspects of individual differences in personality. These may be contrasted to *species-typical characteristics*, which are assumed to be more-or-less universal features of persons, that is, most all members of the human species.

individual psychology a term used to designate the personality theory developed by Alfred Adler.

individuation the full development of the self in Jungian theory, understood as a dynamic, complex, and life-long process whereby the person seeks to synthesize the various opposites in personality in order to become whole (Jung).

individualism as a cultural construct, a meaning system emphasizing the autonomy and independence of the individual over and against the collective. The United States, Canada, Australia, and the democracies of northern and western Europe are considered to be relatively individualist cultures. Contrast to *collectivism*.

induction reasoning from the concrete and the particular to the abstract and general. Contrast with *deduction*.

industry *versus* inferiority the fourth stage in Erikson's scheme of psychosocial development, during which the schoolboy or schoolgirl receives systematic instruction from social institutions and begins to learn how to use the tools and adopt the characteristic roles of society.

initiative *versus* guilt the third stage in Erikson's scheme of psychosocial development, during which the young child experiences the Oedipus complex and becomes increasingly concerned with issues of power and taking initiative.

instinct for Freud, a mental representation of a physical or bodily need. Instincts are the ultimate motivators of behavior, providing the energy whereby action is driven and guided. In modern ethology, instincts are biologically rooted and adaptive motivational tendencies giving rise to particular urges, emotions, and behavioral plans that can be influenced, within limits, by the environment.

instrumental aggression aggression aimed at attaining a nonaggressive goal. Contrast with *hostile aggression*.

instrumental conditioning learning influenced by reinforcement and punishment. See *operant conditioning*.

integrative complexity the extent to which a person sees and interprets events in differentiated and integrated ways.

interactionism the general view that behavior is a function of the interaction of the person and the environment.

internalized objects internal representations of others with whom one has been involved in emotionally charged relationships, as discussed in object-relations theories.

interview a method of collecting data whereby the interviewer asks questions and engages the subject in a conversation with a purpose.

intimacy life task the developmental challenge of young adulthood to establish long-term bonds of warmth, closeness, and love with other people.

intimacy motivation a recurrent preference or desire for experiences of warm, close, and communicative interaction with others. Individual differences in intimacy motivation may be assessed through the TAT.

intimacy status parallel to Marcia's concept of *identity status*, referring to the characteristic quality of a person's interpersonal relationships and commitments at given point in time. At least four statuses have been identified: intimate, preintimate, stereotyped relationships, and isolate.

intimacy *versus* isolation the sixth stage of psychosocial development in Erikson's scheme, in which the young adult seeks to establish long-term affiliations with spouse, co-workers, friends, and so on.

intrinsic motivation motivation from within, rather than from external reinforcers and rewards.

intrusive mode Erikson's concept for the young boy's characteristically phallic and aggressive approach to the world.

ipsative continuity continuity in the configuration of

personality characteristics for a given individual over time. In contrast to *absolute* and *differential continuity* which are typically viewed as characteristics of groups of individuals, ipsative continuity refers solely to consistency for a particular individual.

item analysis a procedure in test construction whereby the investigator determines the relative contribution of each item to the total score on the test.

kin selection one evolutionary principle used to explain altruism, whereby an organism will engage in a helping or even self-sacrificial behavior that promotes the survival or reproductive success of kin.

latency Freud's fourth stage of psychosexual development, associated with elementary-school years, wherein the libido is rarely expressed in an overt manner.

L-data one of three data sources for Cattell, information pertaining to a person's real-life behavior, such as ratings of the person's behavior made by peers or spouse. Contrast to *Q-data* and *T-data*.

lexical hypothesis the idea that the most important individual differences in personality functioning are encoded in language. Many researchers working with the lexical hypothesis have argued for a five-factor model of personality traits.

libido Freud's concept for the sensual energy of sexual or life instincts.

life course the span of human life. The "life course perspective" in psychology today tends to emphasize the influence of social context, history, timing,

social roles, and human agency on the multiple developmental pathways that people follow over time.

life instincts Freud's concept for a group of instincts serving sexual reproduction and survival. Contrast with *death instincts*.

life review the process of taking stock of one's entire life, often evidenced in old age.

life-story model of identity the view that identity may be seen as a dynamic life story integrating a person's reconstructed past, present, and anticipated future into a coherent narrative whole that provides life with unity and purpose.

life story an internalized and evolving narrative of the self that integrates the reconstructed past, perceived present, and anticipated future. Beginning in late adolescence and young adulthood, many persons in modern societies construct life stories to provide their lives with some semblance of unity, purpose, and meaning. Life stories confer upon personality the quality of "identity." Life stories comprise Level 3 of personality. Level 1 is made up of dispositional traits, and Level 2 is made up of characteristic adaptations.

life structure Levinson's concept referring to the overall patterning or design of an individual's life at a given time.

life tasks the problems that individuals explicitly see themselves trying to solve at a particular time in their lives.

locus of control a personality dimension referring to individual differences in the extent to which a person believes that re-

inforcements are contingent on his or her behavior. A person who believes that behavior will lead to predictable reinforcements is said to have an *internal* locus of control; the person who believes that behavior and reinforcements tend to be unrelated—thus, assuming that external forces such as luck, fate, or powerful others determine reinforcement—is said to have an *external* locus of control.

longitudinal study a study in which researchers follow the same group of individuals over time to assess continuity and change in personality characteristics. Contrast to *cross-sectional study*.

macrocontext the most encompassing and distal contexts for behavior, including social class, gender, race, culture, and the historical context.

maintenance system a culture's ecological, economic, and sociopolitical structure and the child-training or socialization practices accepted by the society as good and appropriate. Contrast with *projective system*.

mandala the ancient symbol of unity, representing individuation in Jungian psychology.

marketing type Fromm's characterization of the person who seeks to market him- or herself as a commodity to be bought and sold in the societal and interpersonal marketplace.

mechanistic interactionism the procedure of partitioning the variance in behavior into that accounted for by the person, by the situation, and by the person-situation, interaction. Contrast with *reciprocal interactionism*.

metatrait the trait of having or not having a particular trait, which is conceptually independent of one's score on a trait scale. For a given trait, the behavior of "traited" people (those who "have" the trait) should be more predictable from trait scores than the behavior of "untraited" people (those who do not have the trait).

microcontext the more immediate and short-term environmental contexts for behavior, such as the particular social situation within which a person's behavior is displayed.

midlife crisis a period of profound personal questioning and reformulations reported by some men and women during their late 30s, 40s, or early 50s.

Minnesota Multiphasic Personality Inventory (MMPI) A very widely used personality inventory, containing 550 true-false statements and 10 different clinical scales.

moderator variables a variable that influences the relation of two other variables, such that the two other variables may be strongly related at certain levels of the moderator variable and only weakly related at other levels. In the wake of the situationist critique of the 1970s, some personality psychologists have successfully employed such moderator variables as self-reported "trait relevance" and "inner directedness" to improve the ability of trait scores to predict behavior.

modernity a cultural concept referring to the economic, political, and cultural systems spawned by the Industrial Revolution and related developments in the 19th and 20th centuries.

Modernity ushered in a new way of thinking about the self—the self as a reflexive project that a person works on. Given that the modern self has considerable depth and dynamism, a major psychological challenge for modern people is to integrate the self into a unifying and purposeful whole.

moratorium one of Marcia's four identity statuses, referring to the person who is currently exploring various identity options but has not yet made commitments.

morphogenic see *idiographic*.

motivation a term used to denote the forces and factors, usually viewed as residing within the person, that energize and direct behavior. Common motivational ideas in personality psychology include wants, desires, needs, goals, strivings, projects, and tasks.

motive a term sometimes used synonymously with Murray's *need*. McClelland defines a motive as a recurrent preference or readiness for a particular quality of experience, which energizes, directs, and selects behavior in certain situations.

narcissism a preoccupation with the self, manifested in an apparent excess of self-love, grandiose sense of self-importance, and the need for constant attention and praise.

narrative mode one of two general modes of human thought, according to Jerome Bruner, referring to the human tendency to make sense of experience through stories. Stories are centrally concerned with the vicissitudes of human intention organized

in time. Contrast to *paradigmatic mode*.

natural selection the process whereby those characteristics of organisms that promote survival and reproductive success come to predominate over less-adaptive characteristics in the course of evolution.

need in Murray's theory, a construct which stands for a force in the brain region which organizes perception, apperception, intellection, conation, and action in such a way as to transform in a certain direction an existing unsatisfying situation.

need hierarchy Maslow's ladder of needs, in which physiological needs provide a foundation for the successive emergence and satisfaction of safety needs, belongingness and love needs, esteem needs, and actualizing needs, respectively.

negative identities Erikson's term for representations, often embodied in other people, of everything that a person does *not* want to become.

NEO-PI-R the Neuroticism-Extraversion-Openness Personality Inventory Revised, developed by Costa and McCraw. The NEO-PI-R is a 240-item self-report inventory designed to measure the Big Five traits of neuroticism, extraversion, openness to experience, agreeableness, and conscientiousness. For each of the five traits there are six subscales assessing individual facets of that trait.

neuroticism a broad personality trait, identified primarily with the theory of Eysenck, denoting a tendency to experience chronic anxiety, depression, emotional lability, nervousness, moodiness, hostility, vulnerability, self-consciousness, and hypochondriasis.

nomological network the interlocking system of propositions that constitute the theory of a given construct along with the empirical findings that support or fail to support those propositions.

nomothetic Allport's term for an approach to personality study which seeks to discover general laws for all persons. Contrast with *idiographic*.

nonadditive genetic variance the configural or interactive influence of genes on traits. Nonadditive genetic variance has been invoked to explain why the ratio of trait concordance for MZ twins and DZ twins is sometimes greater than 2.0, as in the case of recent studies on extraversion.

nonshared environment a term referring to the effects on personality characteristics that come from environments that family members do not share. Nonshared environmental effects are environmental influences that operate to make family members different from each other. Contrast with *shared environment*.

nuclear episode in the life-story model of identity, a particular scene that stands out in the story as especially important, often a high point, low point, or turning point in the story.

nuclear scene in Tomkins' script theory, a very good childhood scene that eventually turns very bad.

nuclear script one kind of script identified by Tomkins,

marked by ambivalence and confusion about one's life goals.

object choice Freud's concept for the unconscious desire to "have" the other (another person) in a powerful and sensual way. In object choice, the person seeks to invest his or her libido, or sexual energy, in another. Contrast with *identification*.

object-relations theories a group of theories, owing varying intellectual debts to Freud, which center around the person's emotionally charged relationships with other people and the resultant development of representations of those people in the unconscious realms of the mind.

observational learning learning through observing an event and then imitating what is observed.

Oedipus complex Freud's concept denoting an unconscious struggle of power and sensuality experienced by boys and girls in the phallic stage of psychosexual development. In short, the child unconsciously desires to have the parent of the opposite sex in a powerful and sensual way but ultimately is forced to renounce that desire and settle for an unconscious identification with the same-sex parent.

openness to experience a broad personality trait, assessed by Costa and McCrae among others, designating a cluster of characteristics having to do with how reflective, imaginative, artistic, and refined a person is.

operant conditioning learning influenced by reinforcement and punishment through which

behavior is modified by its consequences. In operant conditioning, freely emitted behaviors will increase when followed by positive consequences (reinforcement) or decrease when followed by negative consequences (punishment).

oral personality type according to Freud, the resultant pattern of personality characteristics associated with fixation at the oral stage. These characteristics cluster around either the *oral-passive* type, who is blithely cheerful and overly dependent, or the *oral-sadistic* type who is cynical, pessimistic, and bitingly sarcastic.

oral stage the first stage of psychosexual development, according to Freud, wherein the libido is expressed mainly through oral activities.

organ inferiorities Adler's concept for deficits and anomalies in the person with respect to which the person strives to compensate.

organismic valuing process in Rogers' theory, the fully functioning person's ability to view events and developments from the standpoint of his or her own growth and maturation.

overdetermination Freud's idea that the manifest content of dreams, symptoms, and certain other forms of behavior and experience are determined or caused by a vast amount of latent material, including unconscious wishes, impulses, and conflicts.

paradigmatic mode (of thought) one of two general modes of human thought, identified by Jerome Bruner, and referring to the human ability to understand reality through tightly reasoned analyses, propositional logic, and cause-and-effect relationships in the physico-chemical world. Contrast to *narrative mode.*

paratelic mode in Apter's reversal theory, the way of being characterized by activity-oriented as opposed to goal-oriented consciousness. See also *telic mode.*

partial reinforcement intermittent reinforcement of a particular response. Contrast with *continuous reinforcement.*

pattern-matching plan a procedure whereby an investigator seeks to find conceptual coherence in a case study according to certain preconceived theoretical assumptions or hypotheses.

peak experiences episodes in one's life filled with joy, excitement, wonder, and so on emphasized as signs of self-actualization in Maslow's humanistic theory.

peak performance performance above and beyond expectations, as in breaking an athletic record or putting on a truly exceptional performance in the arts.

penis envy the Oedipal girl's unconscious disappointment concerning her lack of a penis, symbolizing a lack of power.

perceptual defense the unconscious monitoring of sensory perception by the censoring forces of repression within the person.

personal action units (PACs) the characteristic concerns, strivings, projects, and tasks that organize the motivational life of a person at a particular time in his or her life. PACs are espe-

cially important characteristic adaptations of personality, residing at Level 2 in this book's three-level scheme.

personal construct Kelly's concept of a characteristic way of construing how some things are alike and some things are different from each other.

personal disposition Allport's term for any trait that is especially characteristic of a particular individual. From the standpoint of the idiographic examination of the single case, the psychologist may search for a handful of personal dispositions that express the particular person's uniqueness. Contrast to *common trait.*

personality inventories self-report questionnaires containing many personality-trait scales.

Personality Research Form (PRF) a personality inventory assessing individual differences in 20 of Murray's psychogenic needs.

Personal Orientation Inventory (POI) a self-report measure of dimensions of self-actualization.

personal projects activities with which a person is currently involved that are designed to achieve personal goals.

personal strivings characteristic goals that individuals try to achieve through their daily behavior.

personal work ethic a general interest and satisfaction in performing tasks industriously.

phallic stage the third stage of psychosexual development, according to Freud, wherein the libido is expressed through the genital region. The phallic stage is associated with ages 3–5 years

and centers around the *Oedipus complex.*

phenomenal field Rogers' term for the entire panorama of a person's experience, and subjective apprehension of reality.

pleasure principle the principle whereby the id operates, dictating that the individual seek immediate gratification of instinctual impulses and wishes. Contrast with *reality principle.*

positive reinforcement the presentation of a stimulus which increases the probability of the behavior it follows, commonly viewed as a reward.

possible selves a person's representations of what he or she would like to become, might become, or would be afraid to become.

postmodern referring to a diverse set of trends perceived in Western culture since the 1970s and emphasizing a skeptical and ironically playful attitude toward grand systems, universal truths, and authoritative conventions of virtually every kind.

power motivation a recurrent preference or desire for experiences of having an impact on others and on one's own environment; also called the "need for power." Individual differences in power motivation may be assessed through the TAT.

press in Murray's theory, a term denoting a determinant of behavior in the environment. A press can be seen as a situational opportunity or obstacle to the expression of a need in behavior.

primary process a very loose and irrational form of thinking driven by instinctual demands and associated with Freud's *id.* Contrast with *secondary process.*

private self-consciousness a tendency to introspect about the self.

procedural knowledge various competencies, strategies, and rules that enable the person to form impressions of others, make attributions, encode and retrieve memories, and predict social behaviors.

productive type Fromm's characterization of the most mature personality type, manifested in the person who fulfills his or her inner potential to become a creative worker and lover within a well-defined social identity.

projection a common defense mechanism in which the person attributes unacceptable internal states and qualities to external others.

projective system a culture's art, religion, folklore, and other expressive media. Contrast with *maintenance system.*

proprium Allport's concept for the self, or all aspects of personality that make for inward unity.

psychoanalysis a general term for the approach to psychology pioneered by Freud and others who tend to focus on the unconscious determinants of behavior, intrapsychic conflict, and instinctual drives concerning sexuality and aggression. The term also denotes the process of engaging in psychotherapy from a psychoanalytic standpoint.

psychobiography the systematic use of psychological (especially personality) theory to transform a life into a coherent and illuminating story.

psychological androgyny the combination of masculine and feminine characteristics. A person who is highly androgynous sees him- or herself as possessing traits highly characteristic of both masculine and feminine sex-role stereotypes.

psychological magnification in Tomkins's script theory, the process of connecting related scenes into a meaningful pattern. Positive affect scenes are often magnified through the production of variants, or variations around a stable core. Negative affect scenes are often magnified through the production of analogs, or the detection of similarities in different scenes.

Q-data one of three data sources for Cattell, self-report data on questionnaires, such as self-ratings and scores on self-report personality questionnaires. Contrast to *L-data* and *T-data.*

range of convenience Kelly's concept of the extent to which a given personal construct is likely to guide a person's interpretation of events and the behavior he or she is likely to show.

reality principle the principle whereby the ego operates, pushing the individual toward behavior aimed at coping with conflicting demands, rationally weighing choices, and defending against various threats to the well-being of the person. Contrast with *pleasure principle.*

receptive type Fromm's characterization of the person who fulfills his or her needs by adopting a passive and dependent orientation in life, manifesting traits of cowardice, submissiveness, and sentimentality.

reciprocal altruism one evolutionary principle used to explain altruism, whereby an organism will aid another organism when such behavior is likely to result in reciprocation of the aid by the other organism at a later time.

reciprocal determinism in Bandura's social-learning theory, the idea that behavior is multiply determined by factors in the environment and in the person.

reciprocal interactionism the viewpoint suggesting that behavior, the person, and the environment influence each other through repeated and mutual transactions. Contrast with *mechanistic interactionism.*

reformulated learned-helplessness theory an attributional interpretation of depressive cognition, emphasizing the depressed person's tendency to explain negative events in his or her life as caused by internal, stable, and global factors.

regression in service of the ego the activity of employing primary-process thinking or other regressive strategies and behaviors in order to adapt to one's environment in a unique and highly creative way.

reinforcement value in Rotter's social-learning theory, the subjective attractiveness of a particular reinforcement.

relational schema a cognitive structure representing regularities in patterns of interpersonal relationships. As an important aspects of declarative-semantic knowledge in social intelligence, relational schemas encode important information about what to expect when interacting with certain people and, therefore, serve as cognitive maps in navigating the social world.

reliability   the consistency of a particular measure. Three forms of reliability are test–retest, split-half, and interscorer.

repression   Freud's concept for the process of casting thoughts, memories, feelings, and conflicts out of consciousness, rendering them unremembered.

repressors   as operationalized in recent research, individuals who show low levels of anxiety but high levels of defensiveness. Research suggests that repressors have less access than do other people to negative emotional memories about the self.

reversal theory   Apter's theory of personality and motivation which argues that human experience shifts over time between opposing metamotivational modes, such as the telic and the paratelic modes.

Role Construct Repertory (REP) Test   Kelly's test designed to explore personal constructs in people's lives.

role structure   in Hogan's socioanalytic theory, the person's characteristic ways of displaying self to one's colleagues, friends, peers, and children, and even to society at large.

Romanticism   an intellectual movement in Western civilization (circa 1790–1850) rejecting classical teachings of reason, order, and the common good in favor of the celebration of the vigorous and passionate life of the individual.

root metaphor   a basic analogy for understanding the world. Pepper has identified the following root metaphors: animism, mysticism, formism, mechanism, organicism, and contextualism.

scene   a concept in Tomkins's script theory referring to a specific happening or event in one's life which contains at least one affect and one object of the affect.

schema   an abstract knowledge structure.

script   according to Tomkins, a set of rules for interpreting, creating, enhancing, or defending-against a family of related scenes. According to Abelson, encoded knowledge of stereotypic event sequences.

secondary process   rational cognitive activity associated with the functioning of the ego (Freud). Contrast with *primary process.*

secondary revision   an aspect of Freud's concept of dream work whereby the dreamer unconsciously smooths over the dream's rough spots, fills in gaps, clears up ambiguities, and edits the dream experience into a more-or-less coherent account.

self-actualization   a term from humanistic psychology referring to the fundamental human striving toward fulfilling one's entire potential.

self as I   following James's dichotomy, the self-as-subject, the I as actor and thinker. James believed that the self as I is but a moment in consciousness. Contrast with *self as Me.*

self as Me   following James's dichotomy, the self-as-object, which refers to the self-concept. For James, the self as Me was composed of the material, social, and spiritual selves. Contrast with *self as I.*

self-defining memories   recollections of events in one's life that the person believes to have been especially influential in shaping the self. According to Singer, self-defining memories are vivid, affectively charged, repetitive, linked to other similar memories, and related to an important theme of enduring concern in the person's life story.

self-discrepancy theory   a theory put forth by Higgins focusing on the emotional outcomes of various discrepancies among actual, ideal, and ought selves.

self-efficacy   Bandura's concept referring to a person's belief that he or she can successfully carry out courses of action required to deal with various challenging situations.

self-esteem   a person's subjective, affective evaluation of the self.

self-guides   In Higgins' self-discrepancy theory, self-guides are the ideal selves and ought selves against which the person compares the actual self.

self-monitoring   the extent to which a person tends to modify his or her own behavior in response to shifting situational demands and contingencies.

self-objects   in Kohut's theory, people who are so central to an individual's life that he or she feels that they are part of him or her.

self psychology   a contemporary derivative of psychoanalytic theory, championed by Heinz Kohut, which is concerned with how people find unity and cohesiveness in life.

self-recognition   the ability to recognize the self, especially in a mirror reflection as in studies with babies and toddlers.

self-schema   an abstract knowledge structure about the self.

self-with-other   a person's representation of his or her own characteristics as they are typically displayed in interaction with a particular other person. In Ogilvie and Ashmore's research, self-with-other representations exist in a complex configuration as basic units of the social Me.

sensation seeking   the need for varied, novel, and complex sensations and experiences and the willingness to take physical and social risks for the sake of such experiences, measured on a scale developed by Zuckerman.

separation-individuation Mahler's term for the process of gaining independence from early symbiotic unions with caregivers and establishing a coherent sense of self and of others.

shadow   the unconscious archetype representing a variety of socially unacceptable, even bestial, desires and impulses, inherited by virtue of humankind's evolution from lower forms (Jung).

shared environment   a term referring to the effects on personality characteristics that come from environments that family members have in common. Shared environment effects are environmental influences that operate to make family members alike. Twin and adoption studies suggest that shared environments have very little effect on most personality traits. Contrast to *nonshared environment*.

shyness   a personality trait defined as discomfort and inhibition in the presence of others.

situational prototypes   an abstract set of features about a given class of situations.

situationism   a general point of view, linked to social learning theory and the impact of experimental social psychology, that behavior is best explained and predicted by reference to the situation within which behavior occurs. The person-situation debate of the 1970s and early 1980s pitted situationism against trait perspectives in personality psychology.

Sixteen Personality Factor Questionnaire (16PF)   Cattell's self-report inventory designed to measure individual differences in 16 source traits.

slow-to-warm-up babies   one of three temperament types identified by Thomas, Chess, and Birch, referring to babies with relatively negative moods, low intensity of emotional reactions, and the tendency to withdraw from new events at first but approach them later. Contrast with *easy babies* and *difficult babies*.

social clock   a set of expectations about age-appropriate transitions, setting the standards against which individuals evaluate the extent to which their lives are "on time."

social desirability   a term denoting the person's desire to present a favorable impression in responding to test items.

social ecology   the many different environmental contexts that situate a person's behavior. The social ecology includes the proximal contexts of the immediate situation (microcontexts) as well as the progressively more encompassing and distal contexts of family, community, society, culture, and history.

social intelligence   each person's set of skills, abilities, and knowledge about social situations.

social interest   Adler's concept for the person's innate sense of kinship with all humanity.

social-learning theories   theories such as those proposed by Rotter, Mischel, and Bandura which adopt certain emphases of behaviorism but blend these with a greater emphasis on cognitive variables and social relationships.

social structure   the conditions of society that differentiate people along the lines of power and status. The most common lens through which to view social structure is social class. Research indicates that social class has a profound effect on how people see themselves and the world.

socioanalytic theory Hogan's theory of personality, emphasizing the evolutionary adaptiveness and ritualized social quality of patterns of human behavior.

sociosexuality   the extent to which an individual will (restricted sociosexuality) or will not (unrestricted sociosexuality) insist on closeness and commitment in an interpersonal relationship before engaging in sexual intercourse with the partner. Recent thinking in evolutionary personality psychology suggests that both restricted and unrestricted sociosexuality patterns may have proven adaptive (for both men and women) throughout evolution, in conjunction with various environmental constraints and selection pressures.

source traits   Cattell's 16 basic factors underlying the many different surface traits that might be identified.

species-typical characteristics characteristics of persons that are believed to be nearly universal for the human species. They may be contrasted to *individual differences* in personality, which refer to characteristics ways in which persons can be said to differ from each other.

specification equation   Cattell's approach to behavioral prediction whereby different trait scores for an individual are plugged into an equation and given differential weights according to the extent to which each is deemed to be relevant to the particular situation in which behavior is to occur.

split-half reliability   the extent to which a test's results are consistent across different parts of the test, that is, the extent of internal consistency in the test.

stimulus generalization   the expansion of a conditioned response so that it is evoked in response to a wide variety of stimuli which resemble the conditioned stimulus in some way.

story grammar   the implicit rules by which a story is structured. Most stories include a setting and characters, and action in the story proceeds in a sequence of initiating event, action attempt, consequence of attempt, reaction, and resolution.

Strange Situation   an experimental procedure used to assess individual differences in the quality of caregiver-infant attachment, by subjecting the infant to brief separations from the caregiver and novel events.

striving for superiority Adler's concept for the "great upward drive" of human behavior, leading to perfection, completion, and wholeness.

style of life   Adler's term for a person's unique mode of adjustment to life, most notably including the person's self-selected goals and means of achieving them.

subception   Rogers' term for the detection of an experience before it enters awareness.

superego   one of the three main divisions in Freud's structural model of the mind, serving as a primitive internalized representation of the norms and values of society as acquired through identification with the parents at the resolution of the Oedipus complex.

surface traits   Cattell's term for the many readily observable traits that can be found as clusterings of related behaviors. Underlying the many surface traits are a smaller number of source traits.

symbolism   an aspect of Freud's concept of dream work whereby the dreamer conjures up concrete images and actions that convey hidden but common meanings.

TAT   see *Thematic Apperception Test.*

T-data   One of three data sources for Cattell, observations of behavior under controlled conditions, as in the laboratory. Contrast to *L-data* and *Q-data.*

Telic Dominance Scale   derived from Apter's reversal theory, a self-report scale assessing individual differences in the extent to which the telic and paratelic modes tend to characterize a person's experience over time.

telic mode   in Apter's reversal theory, the way of being characterized by goal directedness and future-time orientation. See also *paratelic mode.*

temperament   individual differences in basic behavioral style assumed to be present at birth in some form and, thus, largely biologically determined.

template matching   an approach to personality study in which the researcher classifies situations according to the personality traits of the person who "fits" the situation in a particular way.

test–retest reliability   the extent to which a test's results are consistent over time.

thema   in Murray's theory, a particular behavioral unit represented as a need/press interaction.

Thematic Apperception Test (TAT)   an assessment procedure, devised by Murray and Morgan, in which the subject writes or tells stories in response to a set of ambiguous picture cues.

theory   a set of interrelated statements proposed to explain certain observations about reality.

topographical model   Freud's model of the mind, which distinguishes among the conscious, preconscious, and unconscious regions. The conscious corresponds to everyday awareness; the preconscious contains the contents of ordinary memory, to which awareness may be directed at any time; and the unconscious contains wishes, feelings, memories, and so on that have been repressed because they threaten the well-being of the conscious self.

trait a general term in personality psychology referring to an individual-difference variable assumed to reflect an underlying, internal, and stable personality disposition. Traits are generally viewed to be linear and bipolar in nature, additive and independent, and suggestive of relatively broad individual differences in social and/or emotional functioning. Dispositional traits comprise Level 1 of personality. Level 2 is made up of characteristic adaptations, and Level 3 is made up of integrative life stories.

transference a term used in psychoanalytic therapy to refer to the patient's tendency to relate to the therapist in a way that unconsciously repeats or plays out his or her relationships with other personally important people. Contrast with *counter-transference*.

triple bookkeeping Erikson's view that the person's life must be comprehended on the three levels of body, ego, and family/society.

trust *versus* mistrust the first stage in Erikson's scheme of psychosocial development, in which the infant seeks to establish a hopeful and trusting relation with the environment.

unconditional positive regard in Rogers' theory, love and acceptance provided in an uncritical and noncontingent manner.

unconscious the state of being outside of awareness. For Freud, the unconscious is a shadowy realm of the mind wherein reside repressed thoughts, feelings, memories, conflicts, and the like.

utilitarianism intellectual movement of the eighteenth and nineteenth centuries, associated with Bentham and Mill, arguing that the general good is defined in terms of the greatest good for the greatest number of people.

valuation in Hermans' theory of the self, anything that a person deems important in his or her life situation. Valuations are units of meaning in the life narrative. Each valuation is either positive, negative, or ambivalent in emotional tone.

Washington University Sentence Completion Test for Ego Development (WUSCTED) Loevinger's standardized assessment device for assessing stages of ego development: impulsive, self-protective, conformist, conformist/conscientious, conscientious, individualistic, autonomous, and integrated.

will to power in Adler's theory, the striving to feel strong and powerful in interactions with the world, later generalized by Adler to become a "striving for superiority."

working model in Bowlby's theory of attachment, a representation of the caregiver built up in the mind of the infant. A working model of the attachment object is an unconscious set of expectations about the caregiver's behavior and one's relation to the caregiver and serves as the earliest template for human love.

References

Abelson, R. (1981). Psychological status of the script concept. *American Psychologist, 36,* 715–729.

Abramson, L.Y., Seligman, M.E.P., & Teasdale, J.P. (1978). Learned helplessness in humans: Critique and reformulation. *Journal of Abnormal Psychology, 87,* 49–74.

Ackerman, S., Zuroff, D., & Moscowitz, D.S. (in press). Generativity in midlife and young adults: Links to agency, communion, and well-being. *International Journal of Aging and Human Development.*

Adams, G.R., Ryan, J.H., Hoffman, J.J., Dobson, W.R., & Nielson, E.C. (1984). Ego identity status, conformity behavior, and personality in later adolescence. *Journal of Personality and Social Psychology, 47,* 1091–1104.

Adler, A. (1927). *The practice and theory of individual psychology.* New York: Harcourt Brace World.

Adler, A. (1930). Individual psychology. In C. Murchison (Ed.), *Psychologies of 1930.* Worcester, MA: Clark University Press.

Adler, A. (1931). *What life should mean to you.* Boston: Little Brown.

Adorno, T.W., Frenkel-Brunswik, E., Levinson, D.J., & Sanford, R.N. (1950). *The authoritarian personality.* New York: Harper & Brothers.

Agar, M.H. (1986). *Speaking of ethnography.* Beverly Hills, CA: Sage.

Ainsworth, M.D.S. (1967). *Infancy in Uganda: Infant care and the growth of love.* Baltimore, MD: Johns Hopkins University Press.

Ainsworth, M.D.S. (1969). Object relations, dependency, and attachment: A theoretical review of the infant-mother relationship. *Child Development, 40,* 969–1025.

Ainsworth, M.D.S. (1989). Attachments beyond infancy. *American Psychologist, 44,* 709–716.

Ainsworth, M.D.S., Blehar, M.C., Waters, E., & Wall, T. (1978). *Patterns of attachment.* Hillsdale, NJ: Lawrence Erlbaum.

Ainsworth, M.D.S., & Bowlby, J. (1991). An ethological approach to personality development. *American Psychologist, 46,* 333–341.

Ainsworth, M.D.S., & Eichberg, C. (1991). Effects on infant-mother attachment of mother's unresolved loss of an attachment figure, or other traumatic experience. In C.M. Parkes, J. Stevenson-Hinde, and P. Marris (Eds.). *Attachment across the life cycle* (pp. 160–183.) London: Tavistock/Routledge.

Akbar, N. (1991). The evolution of human psychology for African Americans. In R.L. Jones (Ed.), *Black psychology* (3rd Ed.) (pp. 99–124). Berkeley, CA: Cobb & Henry.

Alexander, I.E. (1988). Personality, psychological assessment, and psychobiography. *Journal of Personality, 56,* 265–294.

Aldwin, C.M., & Levensen, M.R. (1994). Aging and personality assessment. In P.M. Lawton and J.A. Teresi (Eds.), *Annual review of gerontology and geriatrics* (Vol. 14, pp. 182–209). New York: Springer.

Alker, H.A. (1972). Is personality situationally specific or intrapsychically consistent? *Journal of Personality, 40,* 1–16.

Allick, J., & Realo, A. (1997). Emotional experience and its relation to the Five-factor model in Estonian. *Journal of Personality, 65,* 625–647.

Allport, G.W. (1937). *Personality: A psychological interpretation.* New York: Holt, Rinehart & Winston.

Allport, G.W. (1942). *The use of personal documents in psychological science.* New York: Social Science Research Council.

Allport, G.W. (1950). *The individual and his religion.* New York: Macmillan.

Allport, G.W. (1954). *The nature of prejudice.* Cambridge, MA: Addison-Wesley.

Allport, G.W. (1955). *Becoming: Basic considerations for a psychology of personality.* New Haven, CT: Yale University Press.

Allport, G.W. (1961). *Pattern and growth in personality.* New York: Holt, Rinehart & Winston.

Allport, G.W. (1965). *Letters from Jenny.* New York: Harcourt, Brace & World.

Allport, G.W. (1968). *The person in psychology: Selected Essays.* Boston: Beacon Press.

Allport, G.W., Bruner, J.S., & Jandorf, E.M. (1941). Personality under social catastrophe: Ninety-five life histories of the Nazi revolution. *Character and Personality, 10.* 1–22.

Allport, G.W., & Odbert, H.S. (1936). Trait-names, a psychological study. *Psychological Monographs, 47,* (1, Whole No. 211).

Allport, G.W. & Postmand, L. *The psychology of rumor.* New York: Holt.

Allport, G.W., & Vernon, P.E. (1931). A test for personal values, *Journal of Abnormal and Social Psychology, 26,* 231–248.

Allport, G.W., & Vernon, P.E. (1933). *Studies in expressive movement.* New York: Macmillan.

Altemeyer, B. (1981). *Right-wing authoritarianism.* Winnepeg: University of Manitoba Press.

Altemeyer, B. (1988). *Enemies of freedom: Understanding right-wing authoritarianism.* San Francisco: Jossey-Bass.

Altemeyer, B. (1993). *Authoritarianism in American legislators.* Address at the annual meeting of the International Society of Political Psychology, Cambridge, MA.

Amabile, T.M., DeJong, W., & Lepper, M.R. (1976). Effects of externally imposed deadlines on subsequent intrinsic motivation. *Journal of Personality and Social Psychology, 34,* 92–98.

Amelang, M., & Borkenau, P. (1986). The trait concept: Current theoretical considerations, empirical facts and implications for personality inventory construction. In A. Angleitner and J.S. Wiggins (Eds.), *Personality assessment via questionnaires: Current issues in theory and measurement* (pp. 7–34). New York: Springer-Verlag.

Amsterdam, B.K. (1972). Mirror self-image reactions before age two. *Developmental Psychology, 5,* 297–305.

Anastasi, A. (1976). *Psychological testing* (4th Ed.). New York: Macmillan.

Anderson, J.W. (1981). Psychobiographical methodology: The case of William James. In L. Wheeler (Ed.), *Review of personality and social psychology* (Vol. 2, pp. 245–272). Beverly Hills, CA: Sage.

Anderson, J.W. (1988). Henry A. Murray's early career: A psychobiographical exploration. *Journal of Personality, 56,* 139–171.

Anderson, K.J., & Revelle, W. (1994). Impulsivity and time of day: Is rate of change in arousal a function of impulsivity? *Journal of Personality and Social Psychology, 67,* 334–344.

Anderson, L.R., & Blanchard, P.N. (1982). Sex differences in task and social-emotional behavior. *Basic and Applied Social Psychology, 3,* 109–139.

Anderson, W. (1970). *Theophrastus: The character sketches.* Kent, OH: Kent State University Press.

Andrews, J.D.W. (1967). The achievement motive in two types of organizations. *Journal of Personality and Social Psychology, 6,* 163–168.

Andrews, M. (1991). *Lifetimes of commitment: Aging, politics, psychology.* Cambridge: Cambridge University Press.

Angelou, M. (1970). *I know why the caged bird sings.* New York: Random House.

Angleitner, A., & Ostendorf, F. (1994). Temperament and the big five factors of personality. In C.F. Halverson, Jr., G.A. Kohnstamm, and R.P. Martin (Eds.), *The developing structure of temperament and personality from infancy to adulthood* (pp. 69–90). Hillsdale, NJ: Lawrence Elbaum.

Angleitner, A., Ostendorf, F., & John, O.P. (1990). Toward a taxonomy of personality descriptors in German: A psycholexical study. *European Journal of Personality, 4.*

Anthony, E.J. (1970). The behavior disorders of childhood. In P.H. Mussen (Ed.), *Carmichael's handbook of child psychology,* (Vol. 1, pp. 667–764). New York: John Wiley & Sons.

Applebee, A.N. (1978). *The child's concept of story.* Chicago: University of Chicago Press.

Apter, M.J. (1982). *The experience of motivation: The theory of psychological reversals.* New York: Academic Press.

Apter, M.J. (1989). *Reversal theory: Motivation, emotion, and personality.* London: Routledge.

Archer, J. (1988). The sociobiology of bereavement: A reply to Littlefield and Rushton. *Journal of Personality and Social Psychology, 55,* 272–278.

Ardrey, R. (1970). *The social contract.* New York: Atheneum.

Arend, R., Gove, F.L., & Sroufe, L.A. (1979). Continuity of individual adaptation from infancy to kindergarten: A predictive study of ego-resiliency and curiosity in preschoolers. *Child Development, 50,* 950–959.

Argyle, M., & Little, B.R. (1972). Do personality traits apply to social behavior? *Journal for the Theory of Social Behavior, 2,* 1–35.

Argyle, M., & Lu, L. (1990). Happiness and social skills. *Personality and Individual Differences, 11,* 1255–1262.

Arthur, W., Jr., & Graziano, W.G. (1996). The five-factor

model, conscientiousness, and driving accident involvement. *Journal of Personality, 64,* 593–618.

Asendorpf, J.B., & Wilpers, S. (1998). Personality effects on social relationships. *Journal of Personality and Social Psychology, 74,* 1531–1544.

Ashmore, R.D., & Ogilvie, D.M. (1992). He's such a nice boy . . . when he's with grandma: Gender and evaluation in self-with-other representations. In T.M. Brinthaupt and R.P. Lipka (Eds.), *The self: Definitional and methodological issues* (pp. 236–289). Albany, NY: State University of New York Press.

Atkinson, J.W. (1957). Motivational determinants of risk-taking behavior. *Psychological Review, 64,* 359–372.

Atkinson, J.W. (Ed.). (1958). *Motives in fantasy, action, and society.* Princeton, NJ: D. Van Nostrand.

Atkinson, J.W., & Birth, D. (1978). *An Introduction to motivation* (2nd ed.). New York: D. Van Nostrand.

Atkinson, J.W., Bongort, K., & Price, L.H. (1977). Explorations using computer simulation to comprehend TAT measurement of motivation. *Motivation and Emotion, 1,* 1–27.

Atkinson, J.W., Heyns, R.W., & Veroff, J. (1954). The effect of experimental arousal of the affiliation motive on thematic apperception. *Journal of Abnormal and Social Psychology, 49,* 405–410.

Atkinson, J.W., & Raynor, J.O. (Eds.). (1978). *Motivation and achievement* (2nd Ed.). Washington, DC: Winston.

Atkinson, M., & Violato, C. (1994). Neuroticism and coping with anger: The transituational consistency of coping responses. *Personality and Individual Differences, 17,* 769–782.

Bagby, R.M., Joffe, R.T., Parker, J.D.A., Kalemba, V., & Harkness, K.L. (1995). Major depression and the five-factor model of personality. *Journal of Personality Disorders, 9,* 224–234.

Bailey, J.M., Gaulin, S., Agyei, Y., & Gladue, B.A. (1994). Effects of gender and sexual orientation on evolutionarily relevant aspects of human mating psychology. *Journal of Personality and Social Psychology, 66,* 1081–1093.

Bakan, D. (1966). *The duality of human existence: Isolation and communion in Western man.* Boston: Beacon Press.

Bakan, D. (1971). *Slaughter of the innocents.* Boston: Beacon Press.

Bakhtin, M.M. (1973). *Problems of Dostoyevsky's poetics.* Ann Arbor, MI: Ardis. (Transl. By R.W. Rotsel). (Original work published 1929).

Baldwin, J.M. (1897). *Mental development in the child and the race.* New York: Macmillan.

Baldwin, M.W. (1992). Relational schemas and the processing of social information. *Psychological Bulletin, 112,* 461–484.

Ball, D.W. (1972). The definition of situation: Some theoretical and mythological consequences of taking W.I. Thomas seriously. *Journal for the Theory of Social Behaviour, 2,* 61–82.

Baltes, P.B., & Baltes, M.M. (1990). Psychological perspectives on successful aging: The model of selective optimization with compensation. In P.B. Baltes and M.M. Baltes (Eds.), *Successful aging: Perspectives from the behavioral sciences* (pp. 1–34). Cambridge, England: Cambridge University Press.

Bandura, A. (1965). Influence of models' reinforcement contingencies on the acquisitions of imitative responses. *Journal of Personality and social Psychology, 1,* 589–595.

Bandura, A. (1971). *Social learning theory.* Morristown, NJ: General Learning Press.

Bandura, A. (1977). *Social learning theory* (2nd Ed.). Englewood Cliffs, NJ: Prentice-Hall.

Bandura, A. (1978). The self system in reciprocal determinism. *American Psychologist, 33,* 344–358.

Bandura, A. (1983). Temporal dynamics and decomposition of reciprocal determinism: A reply to Phillips and Orton. *Psychological Review, 90,* 166–170.

Bandura, A. (1988). Perceived self-efficacy: Exercise of control through self-belief. In J.P. Dauwalder, M. Perez, & V. Hobi (Eds.), *Annual series of European research in behavior therapy* (Vol. 2, pp. 27–59). Lisse, the Netherlands: Swets & Zeitlinger.

Bandura, A. (1989). Human agency in social cognitive theory. *American Psychologist, 44,* 1175–1184.

Bandura, A. (1999). Social cognitive theory of personality. In L. Pervin and O. John (Eds.), *Handbook of personality: Theory and research* (2nd Ed., pp. 154–196). New York: Guilford Press.

Bandura, A., Ross, D., & Ross, S.A. (1961). Transmission of aggression through imitation of aggressive models. *Journal of Abnormal and Social Psychology, 63*, 575–582.

Bandura, A., Ross, D., & Ross, S.A. (1963). Imitation of film-mediated aggressive models. *Journal of Abnormal and Social Psychology, 66*, 3–11.

Bandura, A., & Schunk, D.H. (1981). Cultivating competence, self-efficacy, and intrinsic interest through proximal self-motivation. *Journal of Personality and Social Psychology, 41*, 586–598.

Barash, D.P. (1977). *Sociobiology and behavior.* New York: Elsevier.

Barash, D.P. (1979). *The whisperings within: Evolution and the origin of human nature.* New York: Penguin.

Bargh, J.A. (1996). Automaticity in social psychology. In E.T. Higgins and A.W. Kruglanski (Eds.), *Social psychology: Handbook of basic principles* (pp. 169–183). New York: The Guilford Press.

Bargh, J.A. (1997). The automaticity of everyday life. In R.S. Wyer and T.K. Srull (Eds.), *Advances in social cognition* (Vol. 10). Hillsdale, NJ: Erlbaum.

Barnett, P.A., & Gotlib, I.H. (1988). Psychosocial functioning and depression: Distinguishing among antecedent, concomitant, and consequences. *Psychological Bulletin, 104*, 97–126.

Barresi, J., & Juckes, T.J. (1997). Personology and the narrative interpretation of lives. *Journal of Personality, 65*, 693–719.

Barrett, L.F. (1997). The relationships among momentary emotion experiences, personality descriptions, and retrospective ratings of emotion. *Personality and Social Psychology Bulletin, 23*, 1100–1110.

Barrick, M.R., & Mount, M.K. (1991). The Big Five personality dimensions and job performance: A meta-analysis. *Personnel Psychology, 44*, 1–26.

Barrick, M.R., & Mount, M.K. (1993). Autonomy as a moderator of the relationship between the Big Five personality dimensions and job performance. *Journal of Applied Psychology, 78*, 111–118.

Barron, F. (1969). *Creative person and creative process.* New York: Holt, Rinehart & Winston.

Baruch, G.K. (1984). The psychological well-being of women in the middle years. In G.K. Baruch and J. Brooks-Gunn (Eds.), *Women in midlife* (pp. 161–180). New York: Plenum Press.

Baruch, R. (1967). The achievement motive in women: Implications for career development. *Journal of Personality and Social Psychology, 5*, 260–267.

Barry, H.H., Child, I.L., & Bacon, M.K. (1959). Relation of child rearing to subsistence economy. *American Anthropologist, 61*, 51–63.

Bateson, M.C. (1990). *Composing a life.* New York: Plume.

Batson, C.D., Dyck, J.L., Brandt, J.R., Batson, J.G., Powell, A.L., McMaster, M.R., & Griffit, C. (1988). Five studies testing two new egotistic alternatives to the empathy-altruism hypothesis. *Journal of Personality and Social Psychology, 55*, 52–77.

Baumeister, R.F. (1986). *Identity: Cultural change and the struggle for self.* New York: Oxford University Press.

Baumeister, R.F. (1990). Suicide as escape from self. *Psychological Review, 97*, 90–113.

Baumeister, R.F., Dale, K., & Sommer, K.L. (1998). Freudian defense mechanisms and empirical findings in modern social psychology: Reaction formation, projection, displacement, undoing, isolation, sublimation, and denial. *Journal of Personality, 66*, 1081–1124.

Baumeister, R.F., Stillwell, A., & Wotman, S.R. (1990). Victim and perpetrator accounts of interpersonal conflict: Autobiographical narratives about anger. *Journal of Personality and Social Psychology, 59*, 994–1005.

Baumeister, R.F., & Tice, D.M. (1988). Metatraits. *Journal of Personality, 56*, 571–598.

Baumgarten, F. (1933). Die Charaktereigenschaften. [The character traits.] In *Beiträge zur Charakter- und Persönlichkeitsforschung.* (Whole No. 1). Bern: A Francke.

Baumrind, D. (1971). Current patterns of parental authority. *Developmental Psychology Monograph, 4* (1, Pt. 2).

Beck, A.T. (1967). *Depression: Clinical, experimental, and theoretical aspects.* New York: Hoeber.

Beck, A.T. (1976). *Cognitive therapy and the emotional disorders.* New York: International Universities Press.

Becker, E. (1973). *The denial of death*. New York: The Free Press

Becker, G.S. (1976). *The economic approach to human behavior*. Chicago: University of Chicago Press.

Becker, H.S. (1970). *Sociological work*. Chicago: Aldine.

Behrends, R.S., & Blatt, S.J. (1985). Internationalization and psychological development throughout the life cycle. In A.J. Solnit, R.S. Eissler, and P.S. Neubauer (Eds.), *The psychoanalytic study of the child* (Vol. 40, pp. 11–39). New Haven, CT: Yale University Press.

Beit-Hallahmi, B. (1980). Achievement motivation and economic growth: A replication. *Personality and Social Psychology Bulletin*, 6, 210–215.

Bellah, R.N., Madsen, K., Sullivan, W.M., Sandler, A., & Tipton, S.M. (1985). *Habits of the Heart*. Berkeley, CA: University of California Press.

Bellah, R.N., Madsen, R., Sullivan, W.M., Swidler, A., & Tipton, S.M. (1991). *The good society*. New York: Knopf.

Belsky, J. (1996). Parent, infant, and social-contextual antecedents of father-son attachment security. *Developmental Psychology*, 32, 905–913.

Belsky, J., Crnic, K., & Woodworth, S. (1995). Personality and parenting: Exploring the mediating role of transient mood and daily hassles. *Journal of Personality*, 63, 905–929.

Belsky, J., Steinberg, L., & Draper, P. (1991). Childhood experience, interpersonal development, and reproductive strategy: An evolutionary theory of socialization. *Child Development*, 62, 647–670.

Bem, D.J., & Allen, A. (1974). On predicting some of the people some of the time: The search for cross-situational consistencies in behavior. *Psychological Review*, 81, 506–520.

Bem, D.J., & Funder, D.C. (1978). Predicting more of the people more of the time: Assessing the personality of situations. *Psychological Review*, 85, 485–501.

Bem, S.L. (1981). Gender schema theory: A cognitive account of sex typing. *Psychological Review*, 88, 354–364.

Bem, S.L. (1987). Gender schema theory and the romantic tradition. In P. Shaver and C. Hendrick (Eds.), *Sex and gender: Review of personality and social psychology* (Vol. 7, pp. 251–271). Beverly Hills, CA: Sage.

Bendig, A.W. (1963). The relation of temperament traits of social extraversion and emotionality to vocational interests. *Journal of General Psychology*, 69, 311–318.

Berkowitz, J., & Powers, P.C. (1979). Effects of timing and justification of witnesses aggression on the observer's punitiveness. *Journal of Research in Personality*, 13, 71–80.

Berkowitz, L. (1974). Some determinants of impulsive aggression: The role of mediated associations with reinforcements for aggression. *Psychological Review*, 81, 165–176.

Berman, J.S., & Kenny, D.A. (1976). Correlational bias in observer ratings. *Journal of Personality and Social Psychology*, 34, 263–273.

Berne, E. (1964). *Games people play*. New York: Grove.

Bernstein, B.A. (1970). A sociolinguistic approach to socialization: With some reference to educability. In F. Williams (Ed.), *Language and poverty: Perspectives on a theme*. Chicago: Markham.

Berry. J.W. (1976). *Human ecology and cognitive style*. New York: Russell Sage.

Bertaux, D. (Ed.). (1981). *Biography and society: The life history approach in the social sciences*. Beverly Hills, CA: Sage.

Bertenthal, B.I., & Fischer, K.W. (1978). Development of self-recognition in the infant. *Developmental Psychology*, 14, 44–50.

Bertini, M. Pizzamiglio, L., & Wapner, S. (Eds.). (1986). *Field dependence in psychological theory, research, and application*. Hillsdale, NJ: Lawrence Erlbaum.

Bettelheim, B. (1977). *The uses of enchantment: The meaning and importance of fairy tales*. New York: Vintage Books.

Bierhoff, H.W., Klein, R., & Kramp, P. (1991). Evidence for the altruistic personality from data on accident research. *Journal of Personality*, 59, 263–280.

Biernat, M., & Wortman, C.B. (1991). Sharing of home responsibilities between professionally employed women and their husbands. *Journal of Personality and Social Psychology*, 60, 844–860.

Biesanz, J.C., West, S.G., & Graziano, W.G. (1998). Moderators of self-other agreement: Reconsidering temporal stability in personality. *Journal of Personality and Social Psychology*, 75, 467–477.

Binswanger, L. (1963). *Being-in-the-world*. New York: Basic Books.

Bird, S.E., & Dardenne, R.W. (1988). Myth, chronicle, and story: Exploring the narrative qualities of news. In J.W. Carey (Ed.), *Media, myths, and narratives: Television and the press* (pp. 67–86). Newbury Park, CA: Sage Publications.

Birren, J., Kenyon, G., Ruth, J.E., Shroots, J.J.F., & Svendson, J. (1996). (Eds.). *Aging and biography: Explorations in adult development*. New York: Springer.

Blasi, A. (1988). Identity and the development of the self. In D.K. Lapsley and F.C. Power (Eds.), *Self, ego, and identity: Integrative approaches* (pp. 226–242). New York: Springer-Verlag.

Blass, J. (1984). Social psychology and personality: Toward a convergence. *Journal of Personality and Social Psychology, 47*, 1013–1027.

Blehar, M.C., Lieberman, A.F., & Ainsworth, M.D.S. (1977). Early face-to-face interaction and its relationship to later mother—infant attachment. *Child Development, 48*, 182–194.

Block, J. (1961). *The Q-sort method in personality assessment and psychiatric research*. Springfield, IL: Charles C. Thomas.

Block, J. (1965). *The challenge of response sets: Unconfounding meaning, acquiescence, and social desirability in the MMPI*. New York: Appleton-Century-Crofts.

Block, J. (1971). *Lives through time*. Berkeley, CA: Bancroft Books.

Block, J. (1977). Advancing the psychology of personality: Paradigmatic shift or improving the quality of research? In D. Magnusson and N.S. Endler (Eds.), *Personality at the crossroads: Current issues in interactional psychology*. Hillsdale, NJ: Lawrence Erlbaum.

Block, J. (1981). Some enduring and consequential structures of personality. In A.I. Rabin, J. Arnoff, A.M., Barclay, and R.A. Zucker (Eds.), *Further explorations in personality* (pp. 27–43). New York: John Wiley & Sons.

Block J. (1993). Studying personality the long way. In D.C. Funder, R.D. Parke, C. Tomlinson-Keasey, and K. Widaman (Eds.), *Studying lives through time: Personality and development* (pp. 9–41). Washington, D.C.: American Psychological Association Press.

Block, J. (1995). A contrarian view of the five-factor approach to personality description. *Psychological Bulletin, 117*, 187–215.

Block, J., Weiss, D.S., & Thorne, A. (1979). How relevant is a semantic similarity interpretation of personality ratings? *Journal of Personality and Social Psychology, 37*, 1055–1074.

Block, J.H., & Block, J. (1980). The role of ego control and ego resiliency in the organization of behavior. In W.A. Collins (Ed.), *Development of cognition, affect, and social relations* (pp. 39–101). Hillsdale, NJ: Lawrence Erlbaum.

Bloom, A. (1987). *The closing of the American mind: How educa-tion has failed democracy and impoverished the souls of today's students*. New York: Simon & Schuster.

Bloom, A.R. (1971). *Achievement motivation and occupational choice: A study of adolescent girls*. Unpublished doctoral dissertation, Bryn Mawr College.

Blos, P. (1972). The epigenesis of the adult neurosis. In *The psychoanalytic study of the child* (Vol. 27). New York: Quadrangle.

Blos, P. (1979). *The adolescent passage*. New York: International Universities Press.

Bob, S. (1968). *An investigation of the relationship between identity status, cognitive style, and stress*. Unpublished doctoral dissertation, State University of New York at Binghampton.

Bolen, J.S. (1985). *Goddesses in everywoman: A new psychology of women*. New York: Harper & Row.

Bolger, N. (1990). Coping as a personality process: A prospective study. *Journal of Personality and Social Psychology, 59*, 525–537.

Bolger, N., & Schilling, E.A. (1991). Personality and the problems of everyday life: The role of neuroticism in exposure and reactivity to daily stressors. *Journal of Personality, 59*, 355–386.

Bonanno, G.A., Davis, P.J., Singer, J.L., & Schwartz, G.E. (1991). The repressor personality and avoidant information processing: A dichotic listening study. *Journal of Research in Personality, 25*, 386–401.

Booth, W.C. (1988). *The company we keep: An ethics of fiction*. Berkeley, CA: University of California Press.

Borden, W. (1992). Narrative perspectives in psychosocial intervention following adverse life events. *Social Work, 37*(2), 135–141.

Borgatta, E.F. (1964). The structure of personality characteristics. *Behavioral Science, 9,* 8–17.

Bornstein, R.F., & Masling, J.F. (1998). Introduction: The psychoanalytic unconscious. In R.F. Bornstein and J.F. Masling (Eds.), *Empirical perspectives on the psychoanalytic unconscious* (pp. xiii–xxvii). Washington, D.C.: APA Press.

Boswell, T. (1904). *Life of Samuel Johnson L.L. D.* New York: Oxford University Press. (Originally published in 1791).

Bouchard, T.J., Jr., Lykken, D.T., McGue, M., Segal, N.L. & Tellegen, A. (1990). Sources of human psychological differences: The Minnesota Study of Twins Reared Apart. *Science, 250,* 223–228.

Bourne, E. (1977). Can we describe an individual's personality? Agreement on stereotype vs. individual attributes. *Journal of Personality and Social Psychology, 35,* 863–872.

Bourne, E. (1978). The state of research on ego identity: A review and appraisal (Part 1). *Journal of Youth and Adolescence, 7,* 223–255.

Bowers, K.S., & Meichenbaum, D. (Eds.). (1984). *The unconscious reconsidered.* New York: John Wiley & Sons.

Bowlby, J. (1969). *Attachment and loss. Vol. 1: Attachment.* New York: Basic Books.

Bowlby, J. (1973). *Attachment and loss. Vol. 2: Separation.* New York: Basic Books.

Bowlby, J. (1980). *Attachment and loss. Vol. 3: Loss.* New York: Basic Books.

Bowlby, J. (1988). *A secure base.* New York: Basic Books.

Bowman, P.J. (1989). Research perspectives on black men: Role strain and adaptation across the adult life cycle. In R.L. Jones (Ed.), *Black adult development and aging* (pp. 117–150). Berkeley, CA: Cobb & Henry.

Bowman, P.J. (1990). Coping with provider role strain: Adaptive cultural resources among black husband-fathers. *Journal of Black Psychology, 16,* 1–21.

Boxer, S. (1997). How Oedipus is losing his complex. *New York Times,* December 6, pp. A–13, A–15.

Boyatzis, R.E. (1973). Affiliation motivation. In D.C. McClelland and R.S. Steele (Eds.), *Human motivation: A book of readings* (pp. 252–276). Morristown, NJ: General Learning Press.

Boyd-Franklin, N. (1989). *Black families in therapy: A multisystems approach.* New York: Guilford Press.

Bradley, C.L., & Marcia, J.E. (1998). Generativity-stagnation: A five-category model. *Journal of Personality, 66,* 39–64.

Bradstatter, H. (1994). Well-being and motivated person-environment fit: A time-sampling study of emotions. *European Journal of Personality, 8,* 75–94.

Brazelton, T.B., Koslowski, B., & Main, M. (1974). The origins of reciprocity: The early mother–infant interaction. In M. Lewis and L.A. Rosenblum (Eds.), *The effect of the infant on the caregiver.* New York: John Wiley & Sons.

Brebner, J., & Cooper C. (1985). A proposed unified model of extraversion. In J.T. Spence and C.E. Izard (Eds.), *Motivation, emotion, and personality.* Amsterdam: North-Holland.

Breger, L. (1974). *From instinct to identity: The development of personality.* Englewood Cliffs, NJ: Prentice-Hall.

Breslow, R., Kocis, J., & Belkin, B. (1981). Contribution of the depressive perspective to memory function in depression. *American Journal of Psychiatry, 183,* 227–230.

Breuer, J., & Freud, S. (1893–1898). *Studies on hysteria.* In Vol. 2 of J. Strachey (Ed.), *The standard edition of the complete psychological works of Sigmund Freud.* London: Hogarth.

Brewer, M.B., & Caporael, L.R. (1990). Selfish genes versus selfish people: Sociobiology as origin myth. *Motivation and Emotion, 14,* 237–243.

Brewer, W.F., & Lichtenstein, E.H. (1982). Stories are to entertain: A structural-affect theory of stories. *Journal of Pragmatics, 6,* 473–486.

Bridges, L.J., Connell, J.P., & Belsky, J. (1988). Similarities and differences in infant–mother and infant–father interaction in the strange situation: A component process analysis. *Developmental Psychology, 24,* 92–100.

Briggs, S.R. (1989). The optimal level of measurement for personality constructs. In D.M. Buss and N. Cantor (Eds.), *Personality psychology: Recent trends and emerging directions* (pp. 246–260). New York: Springer-Verlag.

Brittain, V. (1933/1970). *Testament of youth*. New York: Wideview Books.

Brody, L. (1999). *Gender, emotion, and the family*. Cambridge, MA: Harvard University Press.

Bromley, D.B. (1977). *Personality description in ordinary language*. Chichester, England: John Wiley & Sons.

Bromley, D.B. (1986). *The case-study method in psychology and related disciplines*. New York: John Wiley & Sons.

Bronfenbrenner, U. (1979). *The ecology of human development*. Cambridge, MA: Harvard University Press.

Bronfenbrenner, U. (1994). Ecological models of human development. In T. Husten and T.N. Postlewaite (Eds.), *International encyclopedia of education* (2nd Ed.). New York: Elsevier Science.

Broughton, J.M. & Zahaykevich, M.K. (1988). Ego and ideology: A critical review of Loevinger's theory. In D.K. Lapsley and F.C. Power (Eds.), *Self, ego, and identity: Integrative approaches* (pp. 179–208). New York: Springer-Verlag.

Brown, K.W., & Moskowitz, D.S. (1998). Dynamic stability of behavior: The rhythms of our interpersonal lives. *Journal of Personality*, 66, 105–134.

Browning, D.S. (1975). *Generative man: Psychoanalytic perspectives*. New York: Dell.

Bruch, M.A., Gorsky, J.M., Collins, T.M., & Berger, P.A. (1989). Shyness and sociability reexamined: A multicomponent analysis. *Journal of Person-*

ality and Social Psychology, 57, 904–915.

Bruhn, A.R. & Schiffman, H. (1982). Invalid assumptions and methodological difficulties in early memory research. *Journal of Personality Assessment*, 46, 265–267.

Bruner, J.S. (1986). *Actual minds, possible worlds*. Cambridge, MA: Harvard University Press.

Bruner, J.S. (1990). *Acts of meaning*. Cambridge, MA: Harvard University Press.

Bruner, J.S., & Tagiuri, R. (1954). The perception of people. In G. Lindzey (Ed.), *Handbook of social psychology* (Vol. 2). Reading, MA: Addison-Wesley.

Brunstein, J.C., Schultheiss, O.C., & Grassmann, R. (1998). Personal goals and emotional well-being: The moderating role of motive dispositions. *Journal of Personality and Social Psychology*, 75, 494–508.

Brunswick, E. (1956). *Perception and the representative design of psychological experiments*. Berkeley, CA: University of California Press.

Brunswik, E. (1957). Scope and aspects of the cognitive problem. In H. Gruber, R. Jessor, and K. Hammond (Eds.), *Cognition: The Colorado Symposium* (pp. 5–31). Cambridge, MA: Harvard University Press.

Buber, M. (1947). *Between man and man*. London: Reoutledge & Kegan Paul.

Buber, J. (1970). *I and Thou*. New York: Charles Scribner's Sons.

Bühler, C. (1933). *Der menschliche lebenslauf als psychologisches problem*. Leipzig: S. Hirzel Verlag.

Bushman, B.J., & Baumeister, R.F. (1998). Threatened egotism, narcissism, self-esteem, and direct and displaced aggression: Does self-love or self-hate lead to violence. *Journal of Personality and Social Psychology*, 75, 219–229.

Burisch, M. (1984). Approaches to personality inventory construction: A comparison of merits. *American Psychologist*, 39, 214–227.

Buss, A.H. (1986). Social rewards and personality. *Journal of Personality and Social Psychology*, 44, 553–563.

Buss, A.H. (1989). Personality as traits. *American Psychologist*, 44, 1378–1388.

Buss, A.H., & Finn, S.E. (1987). Classification of personality traits. *Journal of Personality and Social Psychology*, 52, 432–444.

Buss, A.H., & Plomin, R. (1975). *A temperament theory of personality*. New York: John Wiley & Sons.

Buss, A.H., & Plomin, R. (1984). *Temperament: Early developing personality traits*. Hillsdale, NJ: Lawrence Erlbaum.

Buss, D.M. (1988). The evolution of human intrasexual competition: Tactics of mate attraction. *Journal of Personality and Social Psychology*, 54, 616–628.

Buss, D.M. (1989a). Sex differences in human mater preference: Evolutionary hypotheses tested in 37 cultures. *Brain and Behavior Sciences*, 12, 1–49.

Buss, D.M. (1989b). Conflict between the sexes: Strategic interference and the evocation of anger and upset. *Journal of Personality and Social Psychology*, 56, 735–747.

Buss, D.M. (1990). Toward a biologically informed psychology of personality. *Journal of Personality, 58,* 1–16.

Buss, D.M. (1991a). Evolutionary personality psychology. In M.R. Rosenzweig and L.W. Porter (Eds.), *Annual review of psychology* (pp. 459–491). Palo Alto, CA: Annual Reviews, Inc.

Buss, D.M. (1991b). Conflict in married couples: Personality predictors of anger and upset. *Journal of Personality, 59,* 663–688.

Buss, D.M. (1995). Evolutionary psychology: A new paradigm for psychological science. *Psychological Inquiry, 6,* 1–30.

Buss, D.M. (1997). Evolutionary foundations of personality. In R. Hogan, J. Johnson, and S. Briggs (Eds.), *Handbook of personality psychology* (pp. 317–344). San Diego, CA: Academic Press.

Buss, D.M., & Barnes, M. (1986). Preferences in human mate selection. *Journal of Personality and Social Psychology, 50,* 559–570.

Buss, D.M., & Cantor, N. (1989). Introduction. In D.M. Buss and N. Cantor (Eds.), *Personality psychology: Recent trends and emerging directions* (pp. 1–12). New York: Springer-Verlag.

Buss, D.M., & Craik, K.H. (1983). Act prediction and the conceptual analysis of personality scales: Indices of act density, bipolarity, and extensity. *Journal of Personality and Social Psychology, 45,* 1081–1095.

Buss, D.M., & Craik, K.H. (1984). Acts, dispositions, and personality. In B.A. Maher and W.B. Maher (Eds.), *Progress in experimental personality research* (Vol. 13, pp. 241–301). Orlando, FL: Academic Press.

Buss, D.M., Larsen, R.J., Westen, D., & Semmelroth, J. (1992). Sex differences in jealousy: Evolution, physiology, and psychology. *Psychological Science, 3,* 251–255.

Butler, R.N. (1975). *Why survive? Being old in America.* New York: Harper & Row.

Calder, B.J., & Staw, B.M. (1975). The interaction of intrinsic and extrinsic motivation: Some methodological notes. *Journal of Personality and Social Psychology; 31,* 76–80.

Campbell, A. (1975). The American way of mating: Marriage or children, only maybe. *Psychology Today,* May, 39–42.

Campbell, D.T. (1975). "Degrees of freedom" and the case study. *Comparative Political Studies, 8,* 178–193.

Campbell, D.T., & Fiske, D.W. (1959). Convergent and discriminant validity by the multitrait-multimethod matrix. *Psychological Bulletin, 56,* 81–105.

Campbell, J. (1949). *The hero with a thousand faces.* New York: Bollingen Foundation, Inc.

Campbell, J.B., & Hawley, C.W. (1982). Study habits and Eysenck's theory of introversion-extraversion. *Journal of Research in Personality, 16,* 139–146.

Cantor, N. (1990). From thought to behavior: "Having" and "doing" in the study of personality and cognition. *American Psychologist, 45,* 735–750.

Cantor, N., Acker, M., & Cook-Flannagan, C. (1992). Conflict and preoccupation in the intimacy life task. *Journal of Personality and Social Psychology, 63,* 644–655.

Cantor, N., & Kihlstrom, J.F. (1985). Social intelligence: The cognitive basis of personality. In P. Shaver (Ed.), *Self, situations, and social behavior* (pp. 15–34). Beverly Hills, CA: Sage.

Cantor, N., & Kihlstrom, J.F. (1987). *Personality and social intelligence.* Englewood Cliffs, NJ: Prentice-Hall.

Cantor, N., & Kihlstrom, J.F. (1989). Social intelligence and cognitive assessments of personality. In R.S. Wyer, Jr., and T.K. Srull (Eds.), *Advances in social cognition: Vol. II. Social intelligence and cognitive assessments of personality* (pp. 1–59). Hillsdale, NJ: Lawrence Erlbaum.

Cantor, N., & Mischel, W. (1979). Prototypes in person perception. In L. Berkowitz (Ed.), *Advances in experimental social psychology* (Vol. 12). New York: Academic Press.

Cantor, N., Mischel, W., & Schwartz, J.C. (1982). A prototype analysis of psychological situations. *Cognitive Psychology, 14,* 45–77.

Cantor, N., Norem, J.K., Niedenthal, P.M., Langston, C.A. & Brower, A.M. (1987). Life tasks, self-concept ideals, and cognitive strategies in a life transition. *Journal of Personality and Social Psychology, 53,* 1178–1191.

Cantor, N., & Zirkel, S. (1990). Personality, cognition, and purposive behavior. In L. Pervin (Ed.), *Handbook of personality theory and research* (pp. 135–164). New York: Guilford Press.

Cantor, N.F. (1971). *Western civilization, its genesis and destiny: The modern heritage. From 1500 to the present*. Glenview, IL: Scott, Foresman and Company.

Caporael, L.R. (1997). The evolution of truly social cognition: The core configurations model. *Personality and Social Psychology Review, 1*, 276–298.

Caporael, L.R., & Brewer, M.B. (1995). Hierarchical evolutionary theory: There *is* an alternative, and it's not creationism. *Psychological Inquiry, 6*, 31–34.

Carlo, G., Eisenberg, N., Troyer, D., Switzer, G., & Speer, A.L. (1991). The altruistic personality: In what contexts is it apparent? *Journal of Personality and Social Psychology, 61*, 450–458.

Carlsmith, J.M., Ellsworth, P.C. & Aronson, E. (1976). *Methods of research in social psychology*. Reading, MA: Addison-Wesley.

Carlson, R. (1971). Where is the person in personality research? *Psychological Bulletin, 75*, 203–219.

Carlson, R. (1981). Studies in script theory: I. Adult analogs of a childhood nuclear scene. *Journal of Personality and Social Psychology, 40*, 501–510.

Carlson, R. (1984). What's social about social psychology? Where's the person in personality research? *Journal of Personality and Social Psychology, 47*, 1304–1309.

Carlson, R. (1988). Exemplary lives: The uses of psychobiography for theory development.

Journal of Personality, 56, 105–138.

Carlson V., Cicchetti, D., Barnett, D., & Braunwald, K. (1989), Disorganized/disoriented attachment behaviors in maltreated infants. *Developmental Psychology, 25*, 525–531.

Carment, D.W., Miles, G.D., & Cervin, V.B. (1965). Persuasiveness and persuasability as related to intelligence and extraversion. *British Journal of Social and Clinical Psychology, 4*, 1–7.

Carstensen, L.L. (1995). Evidence for a life-span theory of socioemotional selectivity. *Current Directions in Psychological Science, 4*, 151–155.

Cartwright, L.K., & Wink, P. (1994). Personality change in women physicians from medical student years to mid-40s. *Psychology of Women Quarterly, 18*, 291–308.

Carver, C.S. (1975). Physical aggression as a function of objective self-awareness and attitudes towards punishment. *Journal of Experimental Social Psychology, 11*, 510–519.

Carver, C.L., & White, T.L. (1994). Behavioral inhibition, behavioral activation, and affective responses to impending reward and punishment: The BIS/BAS scales. *Journal of Personality and Social Psychology, 67*, 319–333.

Carver, C.S., & Scheier, M.F. (1981). A control systems approach to behavioral self-regulation. In L. Wheeler (Ed.), *Review of personality and social psychology* (Vol. 2, pp. 107–140). Beverly Hills, CA: Sage.

Carver, C.S. & Scheier, M.F. (1992). *Perspectives on personal-*

ity. 2nd Ed Boston, MA: Allyn & Bacon.

Caspi, A. (1998). Personality development across the life course. In W. Damon (Ed.), *Handbook of child psychology* (5th Ed.). Vol. 3: *Social, emotional, and personality development* (pp. 311–388). New York: John Wiley & Sons.

Caspi, A., Elder, G.H., Jr., & Bem, D.J. (1988). Moving away from the world: Life-course patterns of shy children. *Developmental Psychology, 24*, 824–831.

Caspi, A., & Moffitt, T.E. (1993). When do individual differences matter? A paradoxical theory of personality coherence. *Psychological Inquiry, 4*, 247–271.

Cattell, R.B. (1943). The description of personality: Basic traits resolved into clusters. *Journal of Abnormal and Social Psychology, 38*, 476–506.

Cattell, R.B. (1947). Confirmation and clarification of the primary personality factors. *Psychometrika, 12*, 197–220.

Cattell, R.B. (1950). *Personality: A systematic, theoretical, and factual study*. New York: McGraw-Hill.

Cattell, R.B. (1957). *Personality and motivation structure and measurement*. Yonkers-on-Hudson, NY: World Book.

Cattell, R.B. (1965). *The scientific analysis of personality*. Baltimore, MD: Penguin.

Cattell, R.B. (1990). Advances in Cattellian personality theory. In L.A. Pervin (Ed.), *Handbook of personality theory and research* (pp. 101–110). New York: Guilford Press.

Cervone, D., & Shoda, Y. (1999a). Beyond traits in the

study of personality coherence. *Current Directions in Psychological Science, 8,* 27–32.

Cervone, D., & Shoda, Y. (1999b). Social-cognitive theories and the coherence of personality. In D. Cervone and Y. Shoda (Eds.), *The coherence of personality: Social-cognitive bases of consistency, variability, and organization* (pp. 3–33). New York: Guilford Press.

Chafe, W. (1990). Some things that narratives tell us about the mind. In B.K. Britton and A.D. Pellegrini (Eds.), *Narrative thought and narrative language* (pp. 79–98). Hillsdale, NJ: Lawrence Erlbaum.

Chaikin, A.L., Derlega, V.J., Bayma, B., & Shaw, J. (1975). Neuroticism and disclosure reciprocity. *Journal of Consulting and Clinical Psychology, 43,* 13–19.

Chaplin, W.F. (1991). The next generation of moderator research in personality psychology. *Journal of Personality, 59,* 143–178.

Chaplin, W.F., & Goldberg, L.R. (1984). A failure to replicate the Bem and Allen study of individual differences in cross-situational consistency. *Journal of Personality and Social Psychology, 47,* 1074–1090.

Charme, S.T. (1984). *Meaning and myth in the study of lives: A Sartrean perspective.* Philadelphia: University of Pennsylvania Press.

Chassan, J.D. (1967). *Research designs in clinical psychology and psychiatry.* New York: Appleton-Century-Crofts.

Cheek, J.M. (1982). Aggregation, moderator variables, and the validity of personality tests:

A peer-rating study. *Journal of Personality and Social Psychology, 43,* 1254–1269.

Cheek, J.M., & Buss, A.H. (1981). Shyness and sociability. *Journal of Personality and Social Psychology, 42,* 330–339.

Chodorow, N. (1978). *The reproduction of mothering: Psychoanalysis and the sociology of gender.* Berkeley, CA: University of California Press.

Christie, R., & Lindauer, F. (1963). Personality structure. In *Annual review of psychology* (Vol. 14, pp. 201–230). Palo Alto, CA: Annual Reviews, Inc.

Church, A.T., & Katigbak, M.S. (1989). Internal, external, and self-report structure of personality in a non-Western culture: An investigation of cross-language and cross-cultural generalizability. *Journal of Personality and Social Psychology, 57,* 857–872.

Church, A.T., Reyes, J.A.S., Katigbak, M.S., & Grimm, S.D. (1997). Filipino personality structure and the Big Five model: A lexical approach. *Journal of Personality, 65,* 477–528.

Cialdini, P.B., Schaller, M., Fultz, J., & Beaman, A.L. (1987). Empathy based helping: Is it selflessly or selfishly motivated? *Journal of Personality and Social Psychology, 52,* 749–758.

Clark, L.A., Watson, D., & Mineka, S. (1994). Temperament, personality, and the mood and anxiety disorders. *Journal of Abnormal Psychology, 103,* 103–116.

Clarke-Stewart, K.A. (1989). Infant day care: Maligned or ma-

lignant? *American Psychologist, 44,* 266–273.

Cloninger, C.R. (1987). A systematic method for clinical description and classification of personality variants. *Archives of General Psychiatry, 44,* 573–588.

Cloninger, C.R. (1991). Brain networks underlying personality development. In B.J. Carroll and J.E. Barrett (Eds.), *Psychopathology and the brain* (pp. 183–208). New York: Raven Press.

Cochran, S.D., & Hammen, C.L. (1985). Perceptions of stressful life events and depression: A test of attributional models. *Journal of Personality and Social Psychology, 48,* 1562–1571.

Cohler, B.J. (1982). Personal narrative and the life course. In P. Baltes & O.G. Brim, Jr. (Eds.), *Life span development and behavior* (Vol. 4, pp. 205–241). New York: Academic Press.

Cohler, B.J. (1990). The life-story and the study of resilience and response to adversity. New England Symposium on Narrative Studies, Clark University.

Cohler, B.J., & Boxer, A.M. (1984). Personal adjustment, well-being, and life events. In C.Z. Malatesta and C.E. Izard (Eds.), *Emotion in adult development* (pp. 85–100). Beverly Hills, CA: Sage.

Cohler, B.J., Hostetler, A.J., & Boxer, A. (1998). Generativity, social context, and lived experience: Narratives of gay men in middle adulthood. In D.P. McAdams and E. de St. Aubin (Eds.), *Generativity and adult development: How and why we care for the next generation* (pp.

265–309). Washington, D.C.: APA Press.

Cohn, L.D. (1991). Sex differences in the course of personality development: A meta-analysis. *Psychological Bulletin, 109,* 252–266.

Colby, A., & Damon, W. (1992). *Some do care: Contemporary lives of moral commitment.* New York: The Free Press.

Cole, E.R., & Stewart, A.J. (1996). Meanings of political participation among black and white women: Political identity and social responsibility. *Journal of Personality and Social Psychology, 71,* 130–140.

Cole, J. (1970). Culture: Negro, black, and nigger. *Black Scholar, 1,* 341–350.

Coles, R. (1989). *The call of stories: Teaching and the moral imagination.* Boston: Houghton Mifflin.

Comer, R.J. (1995). *Abnormal psychology* (5th Ed.). New York: W.H. Freeman.

Conger, J.J., & Petersen, A.C. (1984). *Adolescence and youth: Psychological development in a changing world* (3rd ed.). New York: Harper & Row.

Conley, J.J. (1985a). A personality theory of adulthood and aging. In R. Hogan and W.H. Jones (Eds.), *Perspectives in personality* (Vol. 1, pp. 81–116). Greenwich, CT: JAI Press.

Conley, J.J. (1985b). Longitudinal stability of personality traits: A multitrait-multimethod-multioccasion analysis. *Journal of Personality and Social Psychology, 49,* 1266–1282.

Cook, T.D., & Campbell, D.T. (1979). *Quasi-experimentation: Design and analysis issues for field settings.* Chicago: Rand McNally.

Cooper, J., & Scalise, C.J. (1974). Dissonance produced by deviations from life-styles: The interaction of Jungian typology and conformity. *Journal of Personality and Social Psychology, 29,* 566–571.

Cordes, C. (1986). Narrative thought neglected. Interview with Jerome Bruner in the *APA Monitor* (monthly newspaper of the American Psychological Association).

Corr, P.J. (in press). Psychoticism. In A. Kazdin (Ed.), *Encyclopedia of psychology.* Washington, D.C.: APA Press.

Costa, P.T., Jr., & McCrae, R.R. (1978). Objective personality assessments. In M. Storandt, I.C. Siegler, and M.F. Elias (Eds.), *The clinical psychology of aging.* New York: Plenum.

Costa, P.T., Jr., & McCrae, R.R. (1980a). Influence of extraversion and neuroticism on subjective well-being: Happy and unhappy people. *Journal of Personality and Social Psychology, 38,* 668–678.

Costa, P.T., Jr., & McCrae, R.R. (1980b). Somatic complaints in males as a function of age and neuroticism: A longitudinal analysis. *Journal of Behavioral Medicine, 3,* 245–257.

Costa, P.T., Jr., & McCrae, R.R. (1984). Personality as a lifelong determinant of well-being. In C.Z. Malatesta and C.E. Izard (Eds.), *Emotion in adult development* (pp. 141–158). Beverly Hills, CA: Sage.

Costa, P.T., Jr., McCrae, R.R. (1985). *The NEO Personality Inventory.* Odessa, FL: Psychological Assessment Resources.

Costa, P.T., Jr., & McCrae, R.R. (1988a). Personality in adulthood: A six-year longitudinal study of self-reports and spouse ratings on the NEO Personality Inventory. *Journal of Personality and Social Psychology, 54,* 853–863.

Costa, P.T., Jr., & McCrae, R.R. (1988b). From catalog to classification: Murray's needs and the five-factor model. *Journal of Personality and Social Psychology, 55,* 258–265.

Costa, P.T., Jr., & McCrae, R.R. (1992). *The NEO-PI-R:* Professional manual. Odessa, FL: Psychological Assessment Resources.

Costa, P.T., Jr., & McCrae, R.R. (1994). Set like plaster? Evidence for the stability of adult personality. In T.F. Heatherton and J.L. Weinberger (Eds.), *Can personality change?* (pp. 21–40). Washington, D.C.: APA Press.

Costa, P.T., McCrae, R.R. & Arenberg, P. (1980). Enduring dispositions in adult males. *Journal of Personality and Social Psychology, 38,* 793–800.

Costa, P.T., Jr., McCrae, R.R., Zonderman, A.B., Barbano, H.E., Lebowitz, B., & Larson, D.M. (1986). Cross-sectional studies of personality in a national sample: 2. Stability in neuroticism, extraversion, and openness. *Psychology and Aging, 1.* 144–149.

Costa, P.T., Jr., McCrae, R.R., & Zonderman, A.B. (1987). Environmental and dispositional influences on well-being: Longitudinal followup of an American national sample. *British Journal of Psychology, 78,* 299–306.

Cox, C. (1926). *The early mental traits of three hundred geniuses.* Stanford, CA: Stanford University Press.

Cox, W.M., & Klinger, E. (1988). A motivational model of alcohol use. *Journal of Abnormal Psychology, 97,* 168–180.

Coyne, J.C., & Gotlib, I.H. (1983). The role of cognition in depression: A critical appraisal. *Psychological Bulletin, 94,* 472–505.

Craig, J-A., Koestner, R., & Zuroff, D.C. (1994). Implicit and self-attributed intimacy motivation. *Journal of Social and Personal Relationships, 11,* 491–507.

Cramer, P. (1987). The development of defense mechanisms. *Journal of Personality, 55,* 597–614.

Cramer, P. (1991). *The development of defense mechanisms.* New York: Springer-Verlag.

Crandall, J.E. (1980). Adler's concept of social interest: Theory, measurement and implications for adjustment. *Journal of Personality and Social Psychology, 39,* 481–495.

Crandall, J.E. (1984). Social interest as a moderator of life stress. *Journal of Personality and Social Psychology, 47,* 164–174.

Crewe, N.M. (1997). Life stories of people with long-term spinal cord injury. *Rehabilitation Counseling Bulletin, 41,* 26–42.

Crockett, H.J., Jr. (1962). The achievement motive and differential occupational mobility in the United States. *American Sociological Review, 27,* 191–204.

Crockett, W.H. (1965). Cognitive complexity and impression formation. In B.A. Maher (Ed.), *Progress in experimental personality research* (Vol. 1, pp. 47–90). New York: Academic Press.

Cronbach, L.J. (1975). Beyond the two disciplines of scientific psychology. *American Psychologist, 30,* 116–127.

Cronbach, L.J., & Meehl, P.E. (1955). Construct validity in psychological tests. *Psychological Bulletin, 52,* 281–302.

Cross, H., & Allen, J. (1970). Ego identity status, adjustment, and academic achievement. *Journal of Consulting and Clinical Psychology, 34,* 288.

Crowne, D.P., & Marlowe, D. (1960). A new scale of social desirability independent of psychopathology. *Journal of Consulting Psychology, 24,* 349–354.

Crowne, D.P., & Marlowe, D. (1964). *The approval motive: Studies in evaluative dependence.* New York: Wiley.

Csikszentmihalyi, M. (1977). *Beyond boredom and anxiety.* San Francisco: Jossey-Bass.

Csikszentmihalyi, M. (1982). Toward a psychology of optimal experience. In L. Wheeler (Ed.), *Review of personality and social psychology* (Vol. 3, pp. 13–36). Beverly Hills, CA: Sage.

Csikszentmihalyi, M. (1990). *Flow: The psychology of optimal experience.* New York: Harper & Row.

Cunningham, M.R. (1981). Sociobiology as a supplementary paradigm for social psychological research. In L. Wheeler (Ed.), *Review of personality and social psychology* (Vol. 2, pp. 69–106). Beverly Hills, CA: Sage.

Cunningham, M.R. (1985). Measuring the physical in physical attractiveness: Quasi-experiments on the sociobiology of female facial beauty. *Journal of Personality and Social Psychology, 50,* 925–935.

Cunningham, M.R., Barbee, A.P., & Pike, C.L. (1990). What do women want? Facial-metric assessment of multiple motives in the perception of male facial physical attractiveness. *Journal of Personality and Social Psychology, 59,* 61–72.

Cushman, P. (1990). Why the self is empty: Toward a historically situated psychology. *American Psychologist, 45,* 599–611.

Damon, W. (1983). *Social and personality development.* New York: W.W. Norton.

Damon, W., & Hart, D. (1982). The development of self-understanding from infancy through adolescence. *Child Development, 53,* 841–864.

Dannefer, D. (1984). Adult development and social theory: A paradigmatic reappraisal. *American Sociological Review, 49,* 100–116.

Darwin, C. (1859). *On the origin of the species by means of natural selection.* New York: Appleton.

Darwin, C. (1871/1981). *The descent of man, and selection in relation to sex.* Princeton, NJ: Princeton University Press.

Darwin, C. (1872/1965). *The expression of the emotions in man and animals.* Chicago: University of Chicago Press.

Dauber, R.M. (1984). Subliminal psychodynamic activation in depression: On the role of autonomy issues in depressed college women. *Journal of Abnormal Psychology, 93,* 9–18.

Davidson, R.J. (1992). Emotion and affective style: Hemispheric substrates. *Psychological Science, 3,* 39–43.

Davidson, R.J. (1993). Cerebral asymmetry and emotion: Conceptual and methodological conundrums. *Cognition and Emotion, 7,* 115–138.

Davison, R.J., Ekman, P., Saron, C.D., Senulis, J.A., Friesen, W.V. (1990). Approach-withdrawal and cerebral asymmetry: Emotional expression and brain physiology. *Journal of Personality and Social Psychology, 58,* 330–341.

Davidson, R.J., & Tomarken, A.J. (1989). Laterality and emotion: An electrophysiological approach. In F. Boller and J. Grafman (Eds.). *Handbook of neuropsychology* (pp. 419–441). Amsterdam: Elsevier.

Davies, B., & Harre, R. (1990). Positioning: The discursive production of selves. *Journal for the Theory of Social Behavior, 20,* 43–63.

Davis, M. (1986). Pharmacological and anatomical analysis of fear conditioning using the fear-potentiated startle paradigm. *Behavioral Neuroscience, 100,* 814–824.

Davis, P.J. (1987). Repression and the inaccessibility of affective memories. *Journal f Personality and Social Psychology, 53,* 585–593.

Davis, P.J., & Schwartz, G.E. (1987). Repression and the inaccessibility of affective memories. *Journal of Personality and Social Psychology, 52,* 155–162.

Dawkins, R. (1976). *The selfish gene.* New York: Oxford University Press.

Deary, I.J., Ramsay, H., Wilson, J.A., & Raid, M. (1988). Stimulated salivation: Correlations with personality and time of day effects. *Personality and Individual Differences, 9,* 903–909.

De Charms, R., & Moeller, G.H. (1962). Values expressed in American children's readers: 1800–1950. *Journal of Abnormal and Social Psychology, 64,* 136–142.

Deci, E.L. (1971). Effects of externally mediated rewards on intrinsic motivation. *Journal of Personality and Social Psychology, 18,* 105–115.

Deci, E.L. (1975). *Intrinsic motivation.* New York: Plenum.

Deci, E.L., & Ryan, R.M. (1980). The empirical exploration of intrinsic motivational processes. In L. Berkowitz (Ed.), *Advances in experimental social psychology* (Vol. 13, pp. 39–80). New York: Academic Press.

Deci, E.L., & Ryan, R.M. (1985). *Intrinsic motivation and self-determination in human behavior.* New York: Plenum.

Deci, E.L., & Ryan, R.M. (1991). A motivational approach to self: Integration in personality. In R. Diestbier and R.M. Ryan (Eds.), *Nebraska symposium on motivation: 1990* (pp. 237–288). Lincoln, NE: University of Nebraska Press.

Dentan, R.N. (1968). *The Semai: A non-violent people of Malaysia.* New York: Holt, Reinhart & Winston.

Denzin, N.K. (1989). *Interpretive biography.* Newbury Park, CA: Sage.

DePaulo, B.M., Kenny, D.A., Hoover, C., Webb, W., & Oliver, P.V. (1987). Accuracy of person perception: Do people know what kinds of impressions they convey? *Journal of Personality and Social Psychology, 52,* 303–315.

Depue, R.A., Luciana, M., Arbisi, P., Collins, P., & Leon, A. (1994). Dopamine and the structure of personality: Relationship of agonist-induced dopamine activity to positive emotionality. *Journal of Personality and Social Psychology, 67,* 485–498.

DeRaad, B., Mulder, E., Kloosterman, K., & Hofstee, W.K. (1988). Personality-descriptive verbs. *European Journal of Personality, 2,* 81–96.

DeRaad, B., & Szrimak, Z. (1994). The search for the "Big Five" in a non-Indo-European language: The Hungarian trait structure and its relationship to the EPQ and PTS. *European Review of Applied Psychology, 44,* 17–24.

Derrida, J. (1972). *Positions.* Chicago: University of Chicago Press.

Derry, P.A., & Kuiper, N.A. (1981). Schematic processing and self-reference in clinical depression. *Journal of Abnormal Psychology, 90,* 286–297.

de St. Aubin, E. (1996). Personal ideology polarity: Its emotional foundation and its manifestation in individual value systems, religiosity, political orientation, and assumptions concerning human nature. *Journal of Personality and Social Psychology, 71,* 152–165.

de St. Aubin, E. (1998). Truth against the world: A psychobiographical exploration of generativity in the life of Frank Lloyd Wright. In D.P. McAdams and E. de St. Aubin (Eds.), *Generativity and adult development: How and why we care for the next generation* (pp. 391–428). Washington, D.C.: APA Press.

de St. Aubin, E. (in press). Personal ideology: The intersection of personality and religious beliefs. *Journal of Personality.*

de St. Aubin, E., & McAdams, D.P. (1995). The relations of generative concern and generative action to personality traits, satisfaction/happiness with life, and ego development. *Journal of Adult Development, 2,* 99–112.

deWaal, F. (1996). *Good natured: The origins of right and wrong in humans and other animals.* Cambridge, MA: Harvard University Press.

Diamond, J. (1997). *Guns, germs, and steel: The fates of human societies.* New York: Norton.

Dickens, C. (1853/1956). *Bleak house.* Cambridge, MA: The Riverside Press.

Diener, E. (1984). Subjective well-being. *Psychological Bulletin, 95,* 542–575.

Diener, E., Colvin, C.R., Pavot, W.G., & Allman, A. (1991). The psychic costs of intense positive affect. *Journal of Personality and Social Psychology, 61,* 492–503.

Diener, E., Larsen, R.J., & Emmons, R.A. (1984). Person-situated interactions: Choice of situations and congruence response models. *Journal of Personality and Social Psychology, 47,* 580–592.

Diener, E., Sandvik, E., Pavot, W., & Fijita, F. (1992). Extraversion and subjective well-being in a U.S. probability sample. *Journal of Research in Personality, 26,* 205–215.

Digman, J.M. (1989). Five robust trait dimensions: Development, stability, and utility. *Journal of Personality, 57,* 195–214.

Digman, J.M. (1990). Personality structure: Emergence of the five-factor model. In M.R. Rosenzweig and L.W. Porter (Eds.), *Annual review of psychology* (Vol. 41, pp. 417–440). Palo Alto, CA: Annual Reviews, Inc.

Digman, J.M. (1996). A curious history of the Five-Factor model. In J. Wiggins (Ed.), *The five-factor model of personality: Theoretical perspectives* (pp. 1–20). New York: Guilford Press.

Digman, J.M. (1997). Higher-order factors of the Big Five. *Journal of Personality and Social Psychology, 73,* 1246–1256.

Digman, J.M., & Inouye, J. (1986). Further specification of the five robust factors of personality. *Journal of Personality and Social Psychology, 50,* 116–123.

Digman, J.M., & Takemoto-Chock, N.K. (1981). Factors in the natural language of personality: Reanalysis, comparison, and interpretation of six major studies. *Multivariate Behavioral Research, 16,* 149–170.

Dillehay, R.C. (1978). Authoritarianism. In H. London and J.E. Exner (Eds.), *Dimensions of personality* (pp. 85–128). New York: John Wiley & Sons.

Dilthey, W. (1976). The development of hermeneutics. In H.P. Rickman (Ed.), *W. Dilthey: Selected writings.* Cambridge: Cambridge University Press. (Originally published in 1900).

Dixon, T.M., & Baumeister, R.F. (1991). Escaping the self: The moderating effect of self-complexity. *Personality and Social Psychology Bulletin, 17,* 363–368.

Dixon, V.J. (1976). World views and research methodology. In L. King, V.J. Dixon, and W. Nobles (Eds.), *African philosophy: Assumptions and paradigms for research on black persons.* Los Angeles: Fanon Center Publication.

Doherty, W.J., & Baldwin, C. (1985). Shifts and stability in locus of control during the 1970s: Divergence of the sexes. *Journal of Personality and Social Psychology, 48,* 1048–1053.

Doi, L.T. (1962). Amae: A key concept for understanding Japanese personality structure. In R.J. Smith and R.K. Beardsley (Eds.), *Japanese culture: Its development and characteristics* (pp. 132–139). Chicago: Aldine.

Dollard, J. (1935). *Criteria for the life history.* New Haven: Yale University Press.

Dollard, J., Doob, L.W., Miller, N.E., Mowrer, O.H., & Sears, R.R. (1939). *Frustration and aggression.* New Haven, CT: Yale University Press.

Dollard, J., & Miller, N.E. (1950). *Personality and psychotherapy.* New York: McGraw-Hill.

Dollinger, S.J., & Clancy, S.M. (1993). Identity, self, and personality: II. Glimpses through the autophotographic eye. *Journal of Personality and Social Psychology, 64,* 1064–1071.

Dollinger, S.J., & Cramer, P. (1990). Children's defensive responses and emotional upset following a disaster: A projective assessment. *Journal of Personality Assessment, 54,* 116–127.

Dollinger, S.J., & Dollinger, S.M.C. (1997). Individuality and identity exploration: An autophotographic study. *Journal of Research in Personality, 31,* 337–354.

Donley, R.E., & Winter, D.G. (1970). Measuring the motives of public officials at a distance: An exploratory study of American presidents. *Behavioral Science, 15,* 227–236.

Donnerstein, E. (1980). Aggressive erotica and violence toward women. *Journal of Personality and Social Psychology,39,* 269–277.

Donovan, J.M. (1975). Identity status and interpersonal style. *Journal of Youth and Adolescence, 4,* 37–55.

Dostoyevsky, F. (1881/1933). *The brothers Karamazov.* New York: The Heritage Press.

Dostoyevsky, F. (1960). *Notes from underground* and *The grand inquisitor.* New York: Dutton (Transl. By Ralph E. Matlaw). (*Notes from Underground* was written in 1864).

Doty, R.M., Peterson, B.E., & Winter, D.G. (1991). Threat and authoritarianism in the United States, 1978–1987. *Journal of Personality and Social Psychology,61,* 629–640.

Duck, S.W. (1973). *Personal relationships and personal constructs: A study of friendship formation.* London: John Wiley & Sons.

Duck, S.W. (1979). The personal and interpersonal in construct theory: Social and individual aspects of relationships. In P. Stringer and D. Bannister (Eds.), *Constructs of sociality and individuality* (pp. 279–297). London: Academic Press.

Duck, S.W., & Craig, G. (1978). Personality similarity and the development of friendship: A longitudinal study. *British Journal of Social and Clinical Psychology, 17,* 237–242.

Duck, S.W., & Spencer, C. (1972). Personal constructs, and friendship formation. *Journal of Personality and Social Psychology, 23,* 40–45.

Dudek, S.Z., & Hall, W.B. (1984). Some test correlates of high level creativity in architects. *Journal of Personality Assessment, 48,* 351–359.

Duke, M.P. (1986). Personality science: A proposal. *Journal of Personality and Social Psychology, 50,* 382–385.

Dukes, W.F. (1965). $N = 1$. *Psychological Bulletin, 64,* 74–79.

Duncan, L.E., & Agronick, G.S. (1995). The intersection of life stage and social events: Personality and life outcomes. *Journal of Personality and Social Psychology, 69,* 558–568.

Duncan, L.E., Peterson, B.E., & Winter, D.G. (1994). *Authoritarianism and gender roles: Toward a psychological analysis of hegemonic relationships.* Unpublished manuscript, University of Michigan.

Dunn, J., & Plomin, R. (1990). *Separate lives: Why siblings are so different.* New York: Basic Books.

Dweck, C.S. (1996). Capturing the dynamic nature of personality. *Journal of Research in Personality, 30,* 348–362.

Dweck, C.S., Chiu, C., & Hong, Y. (1995). Implicit theories and their role in judgments and reactions: A world from two perspectives. *Psychological Inquiry, 6,* 267–285.

Dworkin, R.H. & Goldfinger, S.H. (1985). Processing bias: Individual differences in the cognition of situations. *Journal of Personality, 53,* 480–501.

Eagly, A.H. (1987). *Sex differences in social behavior: A social role interpretation.* Hillsdale, NJ: Erlbaum.

Eagly, A.H., & Crowley, M. (1986). Gender and helping behavior: A meta-analytic review of the social psychological literature. *Psychological Bulletin, 100,* 283–308.

Eagly, A.H., & Johnson, B.T. (1990). Gender and leadership style: A meta-analysis. *Psychological Bulletin, 108,* 233–256.

Eagly, A.H., & Steffen, V.J. (1986). Gender and aggressive behavior: A meta-analytic review of the social psychological literature. *Psychological Bulletin, 100,* 309–330.

Eagly, A.H., & Wood, W. (1991). Explaining sex differences in social behavior: A meta-analytic perspective. *Personality and Social Psychology Bulletin, 17,* 306–315.

Eagly, A.H., & Wood, W. (1999). The origins of sex differences in human behavior: Evolved mechanisms versus social roles. *American Psychologist, 54,* 408–423.

Eaves, L.J., Eysenck, H.J., & Martin, N.J. (1989). *Genes, culture, and personality.* London: Academic Press.

Edel, L. (1984). *Writing lives: Principia biographica.* New York: W.W. Norton.

Edel, L. (1985). *Henry James: A life.* New York: Harper & Row.

Edwards, A.L. (1957). *The Edwards Personal Preference Schedule.* New York: The Psychological Corporation.

Edwards, C.P., & Whiting, B.B. (1980). Differential socialization of girls and boys in light of cross-cultural research. In C.M. Super and S. Harkness (Eds.), *Anthropological perspectives on child development.* San Francisco: Jossey-Bass.

Egeland, B., & Farber, E.A. (1984). Infant–mother attachment: Factors related to its development and change over time. *Child Development, 57,* 753–771.

Egeland, B., & Sroufe, L.A. (1981). Attachment and early maltreatment. *Child Development, 52,* 44–52.

Einstein, D., & Lanning, K. (1998). Shame, guilt, ego development, and the five-factor model of personality. *Journal of Personality, 66,* 555–582.

Eisenberg, N., & Lennon, R. (1983). Sex differences in empathy and related capacities. *Psychological Bulletin, 94,* 100–131.

Eisenberg, N., & Miller, P.A. (1987). The relation of empathy to prosocial and related behaviors. *Psychological Bulletin, 101,* 91–119.

Eisenberger, R., & Cameron, J. (1996). Detrimental effects of reward: Reality or myth? *American Psychologist, 51,* 1153–1166.

Ekehammer, B. (1974). Interactionism in personality from an historical perspective. *Psychological Bulletin, 81,* 1026–1048.

Ekman, P. (1972). Universal and cultural differences in facial expression of emotion. In J.R. Cole (Ed.), *Nebraska symposium on motivation* (Vol. 26). Lincoln, NE: University of Nebraska Press.

Ekman, P., Friesen, W.V., & Ellsworth, P.C. (1972). *Emotion in the human face: Guidelines for research and an integration of findings.* New York: Pergamon.

Elder, G.H., Jr. (1986). Military times and turning points in men's lives. *Developmental Psychology, 22,* 233–245.

Elder, G.H., Jr. (1995). The life course paradigm: Social change and individual development. In P. Moen, G.H. Elder, Jr., and K. Luscher (Eds.), *Examining lives in context: Perspectives on the ecology of human development* (pp. 101–139). Washington, D.C.: American Psychological Association Press.

Elkind, D. (1981). *Children and adolescents.* (3rd ed.). New York: Oxford University Press.

Elkins, I.J., McGue, M., & Iacono, W. (1997). Genetic and environmental influences on parent-son relationships: Evidence for increasing genetic influence during adolescence. *Developmental Psychology, 33,* 351–363.

Ellenberger, H. (1970). *The discovery of the unconscious.* New York: Basic Books.

Elliot, A.J., Sheldon, K.M., & Church, M.A. (1997). Avoidance personal goals and subjective well-being. *Personality and Social Psychology Bulletin, 23,* 915–927.

Elms, A.C. (1987). The personalities of Henry A. Murray. In R. Hogan and W.H. Jones (Eds.), *Perspectives in personality* (Vol. 2, pp. 1–14). Greenwich, CT: JAI Press.

Elms, A.C. (1988). Freud as Leonardo: Why the first psychobiography went wrong. *Journal of Personality, 56,* 19-40.

Elms, A.C. (1994). *Uncovering lives: The uneasy alliance of biography and psychology.* New York: Oxford University Press.

Elsbree, L. (1982). *The rituals of life: Patterns in narratives.* Port Washington, NY: Kennikat Press.

Emmons, R.A. (1984). Factor analysis and construct validity of the Narcissistic Personality Inventory. *Journal of Personality Assessment, 48,* 291–300.

Emmons, R.A. (1986). Personal strivings: An approach to personality and subjective well-being. *Journal of Personality and Social Psychology, 51,* 1058–1068.

Emmons, R.A. (1987). Narcissism: Theory and measurement. *Journal of Personality and Social Psychology, 52,* 11–17.

Emmons, R.A. (1989). The personal striving approach to personality. In L.A. Pervin (Ed.), *Goal concepts in personality and social psychology* (pp. 87–126). Hillsdale, NJ: Lawrence Erlbaum.

Emmons, R.A. (1992). Abstract versus concrete goals: Personal striving level, physical illness, and psychological well-being. *Journal of Personality and Social Psychology, 62,* 292–300.

Emmons, R.A. (1997). Motives and life goals. In R. Hogan, J. Johnson, and S. Briggs (Eds.), *Handbook of personality psychology* (pp. 485–512). San Diego, CA: Academic Press.

Emmons, R.A. (1999). *The psychology of ultimate concerns: Motivation and spirituality in personality*. New York: Guilford Press.

Emmons, R.A., & Diener, E. (1985). Personality correlates of subjective well-being. *Personality and Social Psychology Bulletin, 11*, 89–97.

Emmons, R.A., & Diener, E. (1986a). Influence of impulsivity and sociability on subjective well-being. *Journal of Personality and Social Psychology, 50*, 1211–1215.

Emmons, R.A., & Diener, E. (1986b). An interactional approach to the study of personality and emotion. *Journal of Personality, 54*, 371–384.

Emmons, R.A., Diener, E., & Larsen, R.J. (1986). Choice and avoidance of everyday situations and affect congruence: Two models of reciprocal interactionism. *Journal of Personality and Social Psychology, 51*, 815–826.

Emmons, R.A., & King, L.A. (1988). Conflict among personal strivings: Immediate and long-term implications for psychological and physical well-being. *Journal of Personality and Social Psychology, 54*, 1040–1048.

Emmons, R.A., & McAdams, D.P. (1991). Personal strivings and motive dispositions: Exploring the links. *Personality and Social Psychology Bulletin, 17*, 648–654.

Endler, N.S. (1983). Interactionism: A personality model, but not yet a theory. In M.M. Page (Ed.), *Personality: Current theory and research* (pp. 155–200). Lincoln, NB: University of Nebraska Press.

Endler, N., & Parker, J. (1990). Multidimensional assessment of coping: A critical review. *Journal of Personality and Social Psychology, 58*, 844–854.

Entwisle, D.R. (1972). To dispel fantasies about fantasy-based measures of achievement motivation. *Psychological Bulletin, 77*, 377–391.

Epsin, O., Stewart, A.J., & Gomez, C.A. (1990). Letters from V: Adolescent personality development in sociohistorical context. *Journal of Personality, 58*, 347–364.

Epstein, S. (1979). The stability of behavior: 1. On predicting most of the people much of the time. *Journal of Personality and Social Psychology, 37*, 1097–1126.

Epstein, S. (1984). The stability of behavior across time and situations. In R.A. Zucker, J. Aronoff, and A.I. Rabin (Eds.), *Personality and the prediction of behavior* (pp. 209–268). New York: Academic Press.

Epstein, S. (1986). Does aggregation produce spuriously high estimates of behavior stability? *Journal of Personality and Social Psychology, 50*, 1199–1210.

Epstein, S. (1994). Integration of the cognitive and psychodynamic unconscious. *American Psychologist, 49*, 709–724.

Epstein, S., & Meier, P. (1989). Constructive thinking: A broad coping variable with specific components. *Journal of Personality and Social Psychology, 57*, 332–350.

Erdelyi, M.H. (1974). A new look at the new look: Perceptual defense and vigilance. *Psychological Review, 81*, 1–25.

Erdelyi, M.H. (1985). *Psychoanalysis: Freud's cognitive psychology*. New York: Freeman.

Erdelyi, M.H., & Goldberg, B. (1979). Let's not sweep repression under the rug: Toward a cognitive psychology of repression. In J.F. Kihlstrom and F.J. Evans (Eds.), *Functional disorders of memory* (pp. 355–402). Hillsdale, NJ: Lawrence Erlbaum.

Erikson, E.H. (1950). *Childhood and society*. New York: Norton.

Erikson, E.H. (1958). *Young man Luther: A study in psychoanalysis and history*. New York: W.W. Norton.

Erikson, E.H. (1959). Identity and the life cycle: Selected paper. *Psychological Issues, 1*(1), 5–165.

Erikson, E.H. (1963). *Childhood and society* (2nd ed.). New York: W.W. Norton.

Erikson, E.H. (1964). *Insight and responsibility*. New York: W.W. Norton.

Erikson, E.H. (1968). *Identity: Youth and crisis*. New York: W.W. Norton.

Erikson, E.H. (1969). *Gandhi's truth: On the origins of militant nonviolence*. New York: W.W. Norton.

Erikson, E.H. (1975). *Life history and the historical moment*. New York: W.W. Norton.

Erikson, E.H. (1978). Reflections on Dr. Borg's life cycle. In E.H. Erikson (Ed.), *Adulthood* (pp. 1–31). New York: W.W. Norton.

Erikson, E.H. (1980). Themes of adulthood in the Freud-Jung correspondence. In N.J. Smelser and E.H. Erikson (Eds.), *Themes of work and love in adulthood* (pp. 43–74). Cambridge, MA: Harvard University Press.

Erikson, E.H. (1982). *The life cycle completed: A review.* New York: W.W. Norton.

Eron, L.D. (1950). A normative study of the Thematic Apperception Test. *Psychological Monographs, 64,* (315).

Eron, L.D. (1982). Parent–child interaction, television, violence, and aggression of children. *American Psychologist, 37,* 197–211.

Eron, L.D. (1987). The development of aggressive behavior from the perspective of a developing behaviorism. *American Psychologist, 42,* 435–442.

Eron, L.D., & Huesmann, L.R. (1984). The relation of prosocial behavior to the development of aggression and psychopathology. *Aggressive Behavior, 10,* 243–253.

Eron, L.D., Huesmann, L.K., Lefkowitz, M.M., & Walder, L.O. (1972). Does television violence cause aggression? *American Psychologist, 27,* 253–263.

Eron, L.D., Laulicht, J.H., Walder, L.O., Farber, I.E., & Spiegel, J.P. (1961). Application of role and learning theories to the study of the development of aggression in children. *Psychological Reports, 9,* 291–334.

Eysenck, H.J. (1952). *The scientific study of personality.* London: Routledge & Kegan Paul.

Eysenck, H.J. (1967). *The biological basis of personality.* Springfield, IL: Thomas.

Eysenck, H.J. (1973). *Eysenck on extraversion.* New York: John Wiley & Sons.

Eysenck, H.J. (1976). *Sex and personality.* London: Open Books.

Eysenck, H.J. (1980). Hans Jurgen Eysenck. In G. Lindzey (Ed.), *A history of psychology in autobiography* (Vol. 7, pp. 153–187). San Francisco: W.H. Freeman.

Eysenck, H.J. (1990). Biological dimensions of personality. In L. Pervin (Ed.), *Handbook of personality theory and research* (pp. 244–276). New York: Guilford Press.

Eysenck, H.J., & Eysenck, M.W. (1985). *Personality and individual differences: A natural science approach.* New York: Plenum Press.

Eysenck, H.J., & Eysenck, S.B.G. (1964). *Manual of the Eysenck Personality Inventory.* London: University of London Press.

Eysenck, H.J., & Wilson, G.D. (1976). *Know your personality.* New York: Penguin.

Eysenck, M.W. (1982). *Attention and arousal: Cognition and performance.* New York: Springer.

Eysenck, S.B.G., Rust, J., & Eysenck, H.J. (1977). Personality and the classification of adult offenders. *British Journal of Criminology, 17,* 169–179.

Fagles, R. (1990). (transl.). Homer's *The Iliad.* New York: Penguin.

Fagot, B.I. (1997). Attachment, parenting, and peer interactions of toddler children. *Developmental Psychology, 33,* 489–499

Fairbairn, W.R.D. (1952). *Psychoanalytic studies of the personality: The object relation theory of personality.* London: Routledge & Kegan Paul.

Falbo, T. (1997). To rebel or not to rebel? Is this the birth order question? *Contemporary Psychology, 42,* 938–939.

Feather, N.T. (1961). The relationship of persistence at a task to expectation of success and achievement-related motives. *Journal of Abnormal and Social Psychology, 63,* 552–561.

Feather, N.T. (1984). Masculinity, femininity, psychological androgyny, and the structure of values. *Journal of Personality and Social Psychology, 47,* 604–620.

Feeney, J.A., & Noller, P. (1990). Attachment style as a predictor of adult romantic relationships. *Journal of Personality and Social Psychology, 58,* 281–291.

Fehr, B., Baldwin, M., Collins, L., Patterson, S, & Benditt, R. (1999). Anger in close relationships: An interpersonal script analysis. *Personality and Social Psychology Bulletin, 25,* 299–312.

Feinstein, D., & Krippner, S. (1988). *Personal mythology: The psychology of your evolving self.* Los Angeles: Jeremy P. Tarcher.

Fenigstein, A., Scheier, M.F., & Buss, A.H. (1957). Public and private selfconsciousness: Assessment and theory. *Journal of Consulting and Clinical Psychology, 43,* 522–527.

Feshbach, N.D., & Feshbach, S. (1969). The relationship between empathy and aggression in two age groups. *Developmental Psychology, 1,* 102–107.

Feshbach, S. (1974). The development and regulation of aggression: Some research gaps and a proposed cognitive approach. In W.W. Hartup and J. De Wit (Eds.), *Determinants and origins of aggressive behavior.* The Hague: Morton.

Festinger, L. (1957). *A theory of cognitive dissonance.* Standford, CA: Stanford University Press.

Festinger, L., Riecken, H. & Schachter, J. (1956). *When prophecy fails.* Minneapolis, MN: University of Minnesota Press.

Fingarette, H. (1969). *Self-deception.* London: Routledge & Kegan Paul.

Finn, S.E. (1986). Stability of personality self-ratings over 30 years: Evidence for an age/cohort interaction. *Journal of Personality and Social Psychology, 50,* 813–818.

Fiske, D.W. (1949). Consistency of the factorial structures of personality ratings from different sources. *Journal of Abnormal and Social Psychology, 44,* 329–344.

Fiske, D. W. (1974). The limits of the conventional science of personality. *Journal of Personality, 42,* 1–11.

Fiske, S.T., & Taylor, S.E. (1984). *Social cognition.* Reading, MA: Addison-Wesley.

Floderus-Myrhed, B., Pedersen, N., & Rasmuson, I. (1980). Assessment of heritability for personality, based on a short form of the Eysenck Personality Inventory: A study of 12,898 twin pairs. *Behavior Genetics, 10,* 153–162.

Fodor, E.M. (1984). The power motive and reactivity to power stresses. *Journal of Personality and Social Psychology, 47,* 853–859.

Fodor, E.M. (1985). The power motive, group conflict, and physiological arousal. *Journal of Personality and Social Psychology, 49,* 1408–1415.

Fodor, E.M., & Smith, T. (1982). The power motive as an influence on group decision making. *Journal of Personality and Social Psychology, 42,* 178–185.

Fodor, J. (1983). *The modularity of mind.* Cambridge, MA: MIT Press.

Folkman, S., & Lazarus. R.J. (1980). An analysis of coping in a middle-aged community sample. *Journal of Health and Social Behavior, 21,* 219–239.

Folkman, S., & Lazarus, R.J. (1985). If it changes it must be a process: Study of emotion and coping during three stages of college examination. *Journal of Personality and Social Psychology, 48,* 150–170.

Folkman, S., Lazarus, R.S., Fruen, R.J., & DeLongis, A. (1986). Appraisal, coping, health status, and psychological symptoms. *Journal of Personality and Social Psychology, 50,* 571–579.

Fonagy, P., Steele, H., & Steele, M. (1991). Maternal representations of attachment during pregnancy predict the organization of infant–mother attachment at one year of age. *Child Development, 62,* 891–905.

Forer, L.K. (1977). Bibliography of birth order literature in the '70's. *Journal of Individual Psychology, 33,* 122–141.

Forgas, J.P. (1978). Social episodes and social structure in an academic setting: The social environment of an intact group. *Journal of Experimental Social Psychology, 14,* 434–448.

Forgas, J.P. (1983). Episode cognition and personality: A multidimensional analysis. *Journal of Personality, 51,* 34–48.

Foster, E.M. (1910). *Howards end.* Hammondsworth, Middlesex: Penguin.

Forster, E.M. (1954). *Aspects of the novel.* San Diego, CA: Harcourt Brace Jovanovich.

Fowler, J.W. (1981). *Stages of faith: The psychology of human development and the quest for meaning.* New York: Harper & Row.

Fox, N.A., & Davidson, R.J. (1986). Taste-elicited changes in facial signs of emotion and asymmetry of brain electrical activity in human newborns. *Neuropsychologia, 24,* 417–422.

Fox, N.A., Kimmerly, N.L., & Schafer, W.D. (1991). Attachment to mother/attachment to father: A meta-analysis. *Child Development, 62,* 210–225.

Francis, M.E., & Pennebaker, J.W. (1992). Putting stress into words: The impact of writing on physiological, absentee, and self-reported emotional well-being measures. *American Journal of Health Promotion, 6,* 280–287.

Frank, B.M., & Noble, J.P. (1985). Field independence-dependence and cognitive restructuring. *Journal of Personality and Social Psychology, 47,* 1129–1135.

Frank, S., & Quinlain, D. (1976). Ego developmental aspects of female delinquency. *Journal of Abnormal Psychology, 85,* 505–510.

Franz, C., & Stewart, A. (1994). (Eds.). *Women creating lives: Identities, resilience, and resistance.* Boulder, CO: Westview Press.

Frauman, D.C., Lynn, S.J., Hardaway, R., & Molteni, A. (1984). Effect of subliminal symbiotic activation on hypnotic rapport and susceptibility. *Journal of Abnormal Psychology, 93*, 481–483.

Frenkel, E. (1936). Studies in biographical psychology. *Character and Personality, 5*, 1–35.

Freud, A. (1946). *The ego and the mechanism of defense.* New York: International Universities Press.

Freud, S. (1898/1962). Sexuality in the aetiology of the neuroses. In Vol. 3 of *The standard edition.* London: Hogarth.

Freud, S. (1900/1953). *The interpretation of dreams.* In Vols. 4 and 5 of *The standard edition.* London: Hogarth.

Freud, S. (1901/1960). *The psychopathology of everyday life.* In Vol. 6 of *The standard edition.* London: Hogarth.

Freud, S. (1905/1953). Three essays on the theory of sexuality. In Vol. 7 of *The standard edition.* London: Hogarth.

Freud, S. (1905/1960). Jokes and their relation to the unconscious. In Vol. 8 of *The standard edition.* London: Hogarth.

Freud, S. (1905/1963). *Dora: An analysis of a case of hysteria.* (With an Introduction by P. Rieff). New York: Macmillan.

Freud, S. (1909/1955). Analysis of a phobia in a five-year-old boy. In Vol. 10 of *The standard edition.* London: Hogarth.

Freud, S. (1909/1963). Notes upon a case of obsessional neurosis. In S. Freud, *Three case histories* (pp. 15–102). New York: Collier Books.

Freud, S. (1910/1957). *Five lectures on psychoanalysis.* In Vol. 11 of *The standard edition.* London: Hogarth.

Freud, S. (1910/1957). Leonardo da Vinci and a memory of his childhood. In Vol. 11 of *The standard edition.* London: Hogarth.

Freud, S. (1913/1958). *Totem and taboo.* In Vol. 13 of *The standard edition.* London: Hogarth.

Freud, S. (1914/1957). On narcissism: An introduction. In Vol. 14 of *The standard edition.* London: Hogarth.

Freud, S. (1915/1957). Repression. In Vol. 14 of *The standard edition.* London: Hogarth.

Freud, S. (1916/1947). *Leonardo da Vinci: A study in psychosexuality.* New York: Vintage Books. (Trans. By A.A. Brill).

Freud, S. (1916/1961). *Introductory lectures on psychoanalysis.* In Vols. 15 and 16 of *The standard edition.* London: Hogarth.

Freud, S. (1917/1957). Mourning and melancholia. In Vol. 14 of *The standard edition.* London: Hogarth.

Freud, S. (1920/1955). *Beyond the pleasure principle.* In Vol. 18 of *The standard edition.* London: Hogarth.

Freud, S. (1921/1955). Group psychology and the analysis of the ego. In Vol. 18 of *The standard edition.* London: Hogarth.

Freud, S. (1923/1961). *The ego and the id.* in Vol. 19 of *The standard edition.* London: Hogarth.

Freud, S. (1927/1961). *The future of an illusion.* In Vol. 22 of *The standard edition.* London: Hogarth.

Freud, S. (1930/1961). *Civilization and its discontents.* In Vol. 21 of *The standard edition.* London: Hogarth.

Freud, S. (1933/1964). *New introductory lectures.* In Vol. 21 of *The standard edition.* London: Hogarth.

Freud, S. (1924). *A general introduction to psychoanalysis.* New York: Permabooks (Boni & Liveright Edition).

Freud, S. (1954). *The origins of psychoanalysis: Letters to Wilhelm Fliess, drafts and notes, 1897–1902.* M. Bonaparte, A Freud, and E. Kris (Eds.). New York: Basic Books.

Friedman, H.S., Tucker, J.S., Schwartz, J.E., Tomlinson-Keasy, C., Martin, L.R., Wingard, D.L., & Criqui, M.H. (1995). Psychosocial and behavioral predictors of longevity: The aging and death of the "Termites." *American Psychologist, 50*, 69–78.

Friedman, H.S., Tucker, J.S., Tomlinson-Keasy, C., Schwartz, J.E., Wingard, D.L., & Criqui, M.H. (1993). Does childhood personality predict longevity? *Journal of Personality and Social Psychology, 65*, 176–185.

Friedman, L. (1999). *Identity's architect: A biography of Erik H. Erikson.* New York: Pantheon.

Friedrich-Cofer, L., & Houston, A.C. (1986). Television violence and aggression: The debate continues. *Psychological Bulletin, 100*, 364–371.

Fromm, E. (1941). *Escape from freedom.* New York: Farrar & Rinehart.

Fromm, E. (1947). *Man for himself.* Greenwich, CT: Fawcett.

Fromm, E. (1955). *The sane society.* Greenwich, CT: Fawcett.

Fromm, E. (1962). *Sigmund Freud's mission: An analysis of his personality and influence*. New York: Simon & Schuster.

Fromm, E. (1973). *The anatomy of human destructiveness*. New York: Holt, Rinehart and Winston.

Frye, N. (1957). *Anatomy of criticism*. Princeton, NJ: Princeton University Press.

Fujita, F., Diener, E., & Sandvik, E. (1991). Gender differences in negative affect and well-being: The case for emotional intensity. *Journal of Personality and Social Psychology, 61*, 427–434.

Funder, D.C. (1989). Accuracy in personality judgments and the dancing bear. In D. Buss and N. Cantor (Eds.), *Personality psychology: Current issues and emerging directions* (pp. 210–223). New York: Springer.

Funder, D.C. (1993). Judgments of personality and personality itself. In K.M. Craik, R.T. Hogan, and R.N. Wolfe (Eds.), *Fifty years of personality psychology* (pp. 207–214). New York: Plenum Press.

Funder, D.C. (1995). On the accuracy of personality judgment: A realistic approach. *Psychological Review, 102*, 652–670.

Funder, D.C., & Block, J. (1989). The role of ego-control, ego-resiliency, and IQ in delay of gratification in adolescence. *Journal of Personality and Social Psychology, 57*, 1041–1050.

Funder, D.C., & Colvin, C.R. (1988). Friends and strangers: Acquaintanceship, agreement, and the accuracy of personality judgment. *Journal of Personality and Social Psychology, 55*, 149–158.

Funder, D.C., & Dobroth, K.M. (1987). Differences between traits: Properties associated with interjudge agreement. *Journal of Personality and Social Psychology, 52*, 409–418.

Funder, D.C., & Colvin, C.R. (1991). Explorations in behavioral consistency: Properties of persons, situations, and behaviors. *Journal of Personality and Social Psychology, 60*, 773–794.

Funder, D.C., & Ozer, D.J. (1983). Behavior as a function of the situation. *Journal of Personality and Social Psychology, 44*, 107–112.

Furnham, A. (1992). *Personality at work: The role of individual differences in the workplace*. London: Routledge.

Gaertner, S.L., & Dovidio, J.F. (1977). The subtlety of white racism, arousal, and helping behavior. *Journal of Personality and Social Psychology, 35*, 691–707.

Galton, F. (1994). Measurement of character. *Fortnightly Review, 36*, 179–185.

Gangestad, S.W. (1989). The evolutionary history of genetic variation: An emerging issue in the behavioral genetic study of personality. In D.M. Buss and N. Cantor (Eds.), *Personality psychology: Recent trends and emerging directions* (pp. 320–332). New York: Springer-Verlag.

Gangestad, S.W., & Simpson, J.A. (1990). Toward an evolutionary history of female sociosexual variation. *Journal of Personality, 58*, 69–96.

Gangestad, S.W., Simpson, J.A., DiGeronimo, K., & Biek, M. (1992). Differential accuracy in person perception across traits: Examination of a functional hypothesis. *Journal of Personality and Social Psychology, 62*, 688–698.

Gardner, R.W. (1951). Impulsivity as indicated by Rorschach test factors. *Journal of Consulting Psychology, 15*, 464–468.

Gardner, H. (1993). *Creating minds*. New York: Basic Books.

Garnett, A.C. (1928). *Instinct and personality*. New York: Dodd, Mead & Company.

Garnett, J.C.M. (1919). General ability, cleverness, and purpose. *British Journal of Psychology, 9*, 345–366.

Gatchel, R.J., & Mears, F.G. (1982). *Personality: Theory assessment, and research*. New York: St. Martin's Press.

Gay, P. (1984). *The bourgeois experience: Victoria to Freud*. Volume 1. *The education of the senses*. New York: Oxford University Press.

Gay. P. (1986). *The bourgeois experience: Victoria to Freud*, Volume 2. *The tender passion*. New York: Oxford University Press.

Geen, R.A. (1984). Preferred stimulation levels in introverts and extraverts: Effects on arousal and performance. *Journal of Personality and Social Psychology, 46*, 1303–1312.

Geen, R.G. (1997). Psychophysiological approaches to personality. In R. Hogan, J.A. Johnson, and S. Briggs (Eds.), *Handbook of personality psychology* (pp. 387–414). San Diego, CA: Academic Press.

Geen, R.A., & Thomas, S.L. (1986). The mediated effects of media violence on behavior. *Journal of Social Issues, 42* (3), 7–28.

Geertz, C. (1973). *The interpretation of cultures*. New York: Basic Books.

Geertz, C. (1979). From the native's point of view: On the nature of anthropological understanding. In P. Rabinow and W.M. Sullivan (Eds.), *Interpretive social science* (pp. 225–241). Berkeley, CA: University of California Press.

George, C., Kaplan, N., & Main, M. (1985). An adult attachment interview: Interview protocol. Unpublished manuscript, University of California at Berkeley.

Gergen, K.J. (1973). Social psychology as history. *Journal of Personality and Social Psychology, 20*, 209–320.

Gergen, K.J. (1982). *Toward transformation in social knowledge.* New York: Springer-Verlag.

Gergen, K.J. (1992). *The saturated self: Dilemmas of identity in contemporary life.* New York: Basic Books.

Gergen, K.J., & Gergen, M.M. (1986). Narrative form and the construction of psychological science. In T.R. Sarbin (Ed.), *Narrative psychology* (pp. 22–44). New York: Praeger.

Gergen, M.M., & Gergen, K.J. (1993). Narratives of the gendered body in popular autobiography. In R. Josselson and A. Lieblich (Eds.), *The narrative study of lives* (Vol. 1, pp. 191–218). Thousand Oaks, CA: Sage.

Ghiselli, E.E. (1956). Differentiation of individuals in terms of their predictability. *Journal of Applied Psychology, 40*, 374–377.

Giddens, A. (1991). *Modernity and self-identity: Self and society in the late modern age.* Stanford, CA: Stanford University Press.

Giese, H., & Schmidt, S. (1968). *Student sexualität.* Hamburg: Rowohlt.

Gilligan, C.A. (1982). *In a different voice: Psychological theory and women's development.* Cambridge, MA: Harvard University Press.

Gittings, R. (1978). *The nature of biography.* Seattle, WA: University of Washington Press.

Glaser, B.G., & Strauss, A.L. (1967). *The discovery of grounded theory.* Chicago: Aldine.

Goffman, E. (1959). *The presentation of self in everyday life.* Garden City, NY: Doubleday.

Goffman, E. (1961). *Asylums: Essays on the social situation of mental patients and other inmates.* Chicago: Aldine.

Gold, S.N. (1980). Relations between level of ego development and adjustment patterns in adolescents. *Journal of Personality Assessment, 44*, 630–638.

Goldberg, L.R. (1981). Language and individual differences: The search for universals, in personality lexicons. In L. Wheeler (Ed.), *Review of personality and social psychology* (Vol. 2, pp. 141–166). Beverly Hills, CA: Sage.

Goldberg, L.R. (1990). An alternative "description of personality": The Big-Five factor structure. *Journal of Personality and Social Psychology, 59*, 1216–1229.

Goldberg, L.R. (1993). The structure of phenotypic personality traits. *American Psychologist, 48*, 26–34.

Golding, W. (1962). *Lord of the Flies.* New York: Coward-McCann.

Goleman, D. (1985). *Vital lies, simple truths: The psychology of self-deception.* New York: Simon & Schuster.

Gong-Guy, E., & Hammen, C.L. (1980). Causal perceptions of stressful live events in depressed and nondepressed outpatients. *Journal of Abnormal Psychology, 89*, 662–669.

Goodenough, D.R. (1978). Field dependence. In H. London and J.E. Exner (Eds.), *Dimensions of personality* (pp. 165–216). New York: John Wiley & Sons.

Goosens, F.A. (1987). Maternal employment and day care: Effects on attachment. In L.W.C. Tavecchio and M.H. van Ijzendoorn (Eds.), *Attachment in social networks* (pp. 135–183). Amsterdam: Elsevier.

Gough, H.G. (1957). *California Psychological Inventory: Manual.* Palo Alto, CA: Consulting Psychologists Press.

Gough, H.G. (1960). Theory and measurement of socialization. *Journal of Consulting Psychology, 24*, 23–30.

Gough, H.G. (1987). *California Psychological Inventory: Administrator's guide.* Palo Alto, CA: Consulting Psychologists Press.

Gough, H.G. (1995). Career assessment and the California Psychological Inventory. *Journal of Career Assessment, 3*, 101–122.

Gough, H.G., & Bradley, P. (1992). Delinquent and criminal behavior as assessed by the revised California Psychological Inventory. *Journal of Clinical Psychology, 48*, 298–308.

Gould, R.L. (1980). Transformations during early and middle adult years. In N.J. Smelser and E.H. Erikson (Eds.), *Themes of work and love in adulthood* (pp. 213–237). Cambridge, MA: Harvard University Press.

Gray, J.A. (1982). *The neuropsychology of anxiety: An enquiry into the functions of the septo-hippocampal system.* New York: Oxford University Press.

Gray, J.A. (1987). Perspectives on anxiety and impulsivity: A commentary. *Journal of Research in Personality, 21,* 493–509.

Graziano, W.G., & Eisenberg, N. (1997). Agreeableness: A dimension of personality. In R. Hogan, J.A. Johnson, and S. Briggs (Eds.), *Handbook of personality psychology* (pp. 795–824). San Diego, CA: Academic Press.

Graziano, W.G., Feldesman, A.B., & Rahe, D.F. (1985). Extraversion, social cognition, and the salience of aversiveness in social encounters. *Journal of Personality and Social Psychology, 49,* 971–980.

Graziano, W.G., Jensen-Campbell, L.A., & Sullivan-Logan, G.M. (1998). Temperament, activity, and expectations for later personality development. *Journal of Personality and Social Psychology, 74,* 1266–1277.

Graziano, W.G., & Ward, D. (1992). Probing the Big Five in adolescence: Personality and adjustment during a developmental transition. *Journal of Personality, 60,* 425–439.

Green, R.C. (1981). Behavioral and physiological reactions to observed violence: Effects of prior exposure to aggressive stimuli. *Journal of Personality and Social Psychology, 40,* 868–875.

Greenberg, M.A., & Stone, A.A. (1992). Writing about disclosed versus undisclosed traumas: Immediate and long-term effects on mood and health.

Journal of Personality and Social Psychology, 63, 75–84.

Greene, L.R. (1973). *Effects of field independence, physical proximity, and evaluative feedback on affective reactions and compliance in a dyadic interaction.* Unpublished doctoral dissertation, Yale University.

Gregg, G.S. (1991). *Self-representation: Life narrative studies in identity and ideology.* New York: Greenwood Press.

Gregg. G. (1995). Multiple identities and the integration of personality. *Journal of Personality, 63,* 617–641.

Gregg. G. (1996). Themes of authority in life-histories of young Moroccans. In S. Miller and R. Bourgia (Eds.), *Representations of power in Morocco.* Cambridge, MA: Harvard University Press.

Grossman, K.E., & Grossman, K. (1991). Attachment quality as an organizer of emotional and behavioral responses in a longitudinal perspective. In C.M. Parkes, J. Stevenson-Hinde, and P. Marris (Eds.), *Attachment across the life cycle* (pp. 93–114). London: Tavistock/Routledge.

Groth-Marnat, G. (1984). *Handbook of psychological assessment.* New York: Van Nostrand Reinhold.

Guilford, J.P., & Guilford, R.B. (1939). Personality factors D, R, T, and A. *Journal of Abnormal and Social Psychology, 34,* 21–36.

Guilford, J.P., (1959). *Personality.* New York: McGraw-Hill.

Guilford, J.P., & Zimmerman, W.S. (1949). *The Guilford-Zimmerman temperament survey.* Beverly Hills, CA: Sheridan Supply Company.

Gunter, B., & Furnham, A. (1986). Sex and personality differences in recall of violent and non-violent shows from three presentation modalities. *Personality and Individual Differences, 6,* 829–838.

Gurtman, M.B. (1991). Evaluating the interpersonalness of personality scales. *Personality and Social Psychology Bulletin, 17,* 670–677.

Gurtman, M.B. (1992). Construct validity of interpersonal personality measures: The interpersonal circumplex as a nomological net. *Journal of Personality and Social Psychology, 63,* 105–118.

Gutmann, D. (1987). *Reclaimed powers: Toward a new psychology of men and women in later life.* New York: Basic Books.

Habermas, J. (1971). *Knowledge and human interests.* Boston: Beacon.

Habermas, T., & Bluck, S. (in press). Getting a life: The emergence of the life story in adolescence. *Psychological Bulletin.*

Hale, H.D., & Goldberg, L.R. (1967). Comparative validity of different strategies of constructing personality inventory scales. *Psychological Bulletin, 67,* 231–248.

Hall, C.S. (1953). *The meaning of dreams.* New York: Harper & Row.

Hall, J.A., & Taylor, M.C. (1985). Psychological androgyny and the masculinity–femininity interactions. *Journal of Personality and Social Psychology, 49,* 429–435.

Hall, J.A. (1984). *Nonverbal sex differences: Communication accuracy and expressive style.* Baltimore, MD: John Hopkins University Press.

Hall, M.H. (1968). A conversation with Abraham H. Maslow. *Psychology Today, 2*(92), 35–37, 54–57.

Hallaq,. J.H. (1977). Scaling and factor analyzing peak experiences. *Journal of Clinical Psychology, 33*, 77–82.

Hamilton, W.D. (1964). The genetical evolution of social behaviour. *Journal of Theoretical Biology, 7*, 1–52.

Hammen, C., & Cochran, S. (1981). Cognitive correlates of life stress and depression in college students. *Journal of Abnormal Psychology, 90*, 23–27.

Hampson, S.E. (1988). *The construction of personality* (2nd Ed.). London: Routledge.

Hampson, S.E., John, O.P., & Goldberg, L.R. (1986). Category breadth and hierarchical structure in personality: Studies of asymmetries in judgments of trait implications. *Journal of Personality and Social Psychology, 51*, 37–54.

Hankiss, A. (1981). On the mythological rearranging of one's life history. In D. Bertaux (Ed.), *Biography and society: The life history approach in the social sciences* (pp. 203–209. Beverly Hills, CA: Sage.

Hansen, R.D., & Hansen, C.H. (1988). Repression of emotionally tagged memories: The architecture of less complex emotions. *Journal of Personality and Social Psychology, 55*, 811–818.

Hanson, N.R. (1972). *Patterns of discovery: An inquiry into the conceptual foundations of science.* Cambridge: Cambridge University Press.

Harkins, S.G., & Geen, R.G. (1975). Discriminability and criterion differences between extraverts and introverts during vigilance. *Journal of Research in Personality, 9*, 335–340.

Harmon-Jones, E., & Allen, J.J.B. (1998). Anger and frontal brain activity: EEG asymmetry consistent with approach motivation despite negative affective valence. *Journal of Personality and Social Psychology, 74*, 1310–1316.

Harre, R. (1989). Language games and the texts of identity. In J. Shotter and K.J. Gergen (Eds.), *Texts of identity* (pp. 20–35). London: Sage.

Harre, R. (1998). *The singular self: An introduction to the psychology of personhood.* London: Sage.

Harre, R., & Gillett, G. (1994). *The discursive mind.* London: Sage.

Harris, J.R. (1995). Where is the child's environment? A group socialization theory of development. *Psychological Bulletin, 102*, 458–489.

Hart, D. (1988). The adolescent self-concept in social context. In D.K. Lapsley and F.C. Power (Eds.), *Self, ego, and identity: Integrative approaches* (pp. 71–90). New York: Springer-Verlag.

Hart, H.M., McAdams, D.P., & Hirsch, B.J. (in press). Generativity and social involvements among African-American and Anglo-American adults. *Personality and Social Psychology Bulletin.*

Harter, S. (1983). Development perspectives on the self-system. In P.H. Mussen (Ed.), *Handbook of child psychology (4th ed.):*

Vol. 4. Socialization, personality, and social development (pp. 275–386). New York: John Wiley & Sons.

Hartmann, H. (1939). *Ego psychology and the problem of adaptation.* New York: International Universities Press.

Hartshorne, H., & May, M.A. (1928). *Studies in the nature of character.* Vol. 1. *Studies in deceit.* New York: Macmillan.

Hartup, W.W. (1974). Aggression in childhood: Developmental perspectives. *American Psychologist, 29*, 336–341.

Harvey, D. (1990). *The condition of postmodernity: An enquiry into the origins of cultural change.* Cambridge: Basil Blackwell.

Harvey, J.H., Weber, A.L., Galvin, K.S., Huszti, H.C., & Garnick, N.N. (1986). Attribution in the termination of close relationships: A special focus on the account. In R. Gilmour and S. Duck (Eds.), *The emerging field of personal relationships* (pp. 189–201). Hillsdale, NJ: Lawrence Erlbaum.

Hassan, M.K., & Sarkar, S.N. (1975). Attitudes toward caste system as related to certain personality and sociological factors. *Indian Journal of Psychology, 50*, 313–319.

Hastie, R., Park, B., & Weber, R. (1984). Social memory. In R. Wyer and T.K. Srull (Eds.), *Handbook of social cognition* (Vol. 2). Hillsdale, NJ: Lawrence Erlbaum.

Hauser, S.T. (1976). Loevinger's model and measure of ego development: A critical review. *Psychological Bulletin, 80*, 928–955.

Hazan, C., & Shaver, P. (1987). Romantic love conceptualized as an attachment process. *Journal of Personality and Social Psychology, 52,* 511–524.

Hazan, C., & Shaver, P. (1990). Love and work: An attachment-theoretical perspective. *Journal of Personality and Social Psychology, 59,* 270–280.

Hazen, N.L., & Durrett, M.E. (1982). Relationship of security of attachment to exploration and cognitive mapping abilities in 2-year-olds. *Development Psychology, 18,* 751–759.

Heatherton, T.F., & Weinberger, J.L. (1994). (Eds.). *Can personality change?* Washington, D.C.: APA Press.

Heckhausen, H. (1967). *The anatomy of achievement motivation.* New York: Academic Press.

Heilbrun, C.G. (1988). *Writing a woman's life.* New York: Norton.

Helson, R. (1967). Personality characteristics and developmental history of creative college women. *Genetic Psychology Monographs, 76,* 205–256.

Helson, R., Klohnen, E.C. (1998). Affective coloring of personality from young adulthood to midlife. *Personality and Social Psychology Bulletin, 24,* 241–252.

Helson, R., & Moane, G. (1987). Personality change in women from college to midlife. *Journal of Personality and Social Psychology, 53,* 176–186.

Helson, R., & Roberts, B.W. (1994). Ego development and personality change in adulthood. *Journal of Personality and Social Psychology, 66,* 911–920.

Helson, R., & Stewart, A.J. (1994). Personality change in

adulthood. In T.F. Heatherton and J.L. Weinberer (Eds.), *Can personality change?* (pp. 201–225). Washington, D.C.: APA Press.

Helson, R., & Wink, P. (1992). Personality change in women from early 40s to the early 50s. *Psychology and Aging, 7,* 46–55.

Hermans, H.J.M. (1976). *Value areas and their development: Theory and method of self-confrontation.* Amsterdam: Swets & Zeitlinger.

Hermans, H.J.M. (1988). On the integration of nomothetic and idiographic research methods in the study of personal meaning. *Journal of Personality, 56,* 785–812.

Hermans, H.J.M. (1991). The person as co-investigator in self-research: Valuation theory. *European Journal of Personality, 5,* 217–234.

Hermans, H.J.M. (1992a). The narrative approach in personality psychology. Sixth Conference of the European Association for Personality Psychology, Groningen, the Netherlands.

Hermans, H.J.M. (1992b). Unhappy self-esteem: A meaningful exception to the rule. *Journal of Psychology, 126,* 555–570.

Hermans, H.J.M. (1992c). Telling and retelling one's self-narrative: A contextual approach to life-span development. *Human Development, 35,* 361–375.

Hermans, H.J.M. (1996). Voicing the self: From information processing to dialogical interchange. *Psychological Bulletin, 119,* 31–50.

Hermans, H.J.M., & Bonarius, H. (1991). The person as co-investigator in personality research. *European Journal of Personality, 5,* 199–216.

Hermans, H.J.M., & Hermans-Jansen, E. (1995). *Self-narratives: The construction of meaning in psychotherapy.* New York: Guilford Press.

Hermans, H.J.M., Kempen, H.J.G., & van Loon, R.J.P. (1992). The dialogical self: Beyond individualism and rationalism. *American Psychologist, 47,* 23–33.

Hermans, H.J.M., & van Gilst, W. (1991). Self-narrative and collective myth: An analysis of the Narcissus story. *Canadian Journal of Behavioural Science, 23,* 423–440.

Herrnstein, R.J., & Boring, E.G. (1965). (Eds.). *A sourcebook in the history of psychology.* Cambridge, MA: Harvard University Press.

Hess, R.D., & Shipman, V.C. (1965). Early experience and the socialization of cognitive modes in children. *Child Development, 34,* 869–886.

Hewitt, J.K. (1984). Normal components of personality variation. *Journal of Personality and Social Psychology, 47,* 671–675.

Higgins, E.T. (1987). Self-discrepancy: A theory relating self and affect. *Psychological Review, 94,* 319–340.

Higgins, E.T. (1997). Beyond pleasure and pain. *American Psychologist, 52,* 1280–1300.

Higgins, E.T. (1999). Persons and situations: Unique explanatory principles or variability in general principles? In D. Cervone and Y. Shoda (Eds.), *The coherence of personality: So-*

cial-cognitive bases of consistency, variability, and organization (pp. 61–93). New York: Guilford Press.

Hill, G.J. (1980). An unwillingness to act: Behavioral appropriateness, situational constraint, and self-efficacy in shyness. *Journal of Personality, 57*, 872–890.

Hill, T., & Lewicki, P. (1991). The unconscious. In V.J. Derlega, B.A. Winstead, and W.H. Jones (Eds.), *Personality: Contemporary theory and research* (pp. 207–229). Chicago: Nelson-Hall.

Hillman, J. (1979). *The dream and the underworld.* New York: Harper & Row.

Himsel, A.J., Hart, H.M., Diamond, A., & McAdams, D.P. (1997). Personality characteristics of highly generative adults as assessed in Q-Sort ratings of life stories. *Journal of Adult Development, 4*, 149–161.

Hoffman, M.L. (1981). Is altruism part of human nature? *Journal of Personality and Social Psychology, 40*, 121–137.

Hofstee, W.K.B., deRaad, B., & Goldberg, L.R. (1992). Integration of the Big Five and the circumplex approaches to trait structure. *Journal of Personality and Social Psychology, 63*, 146–163.

Hogan, R. (1976). *Personality theory: The personological tradition.* Englewood Cliffs, NJ: Prentice-Hall.

Hogan, R. (1982). A socioanalytic theory of personality. In M. Page (Ed.), *Nebraska symposium on motivation* (pp. 55–89). Lincoln, NE: University of Nebraska Press.

Hogan, R. (1986). *Hogan Personality Inventory manual.* Minneapolis, MN: National Computer Systems.

Hogan, R. (1987). Personality psychology: Back to basics. In J. Aronoff, A.I. Rabin, and R.A. Zucker (Eds.), *The emergence of personality* (pp. 79–104). New York: Springer.

Hogan, R., DeSoto, C.B., & Solano, C. (1977). Traits, tests, and personality research. *American Psychologist, 32*, 255–264.

Hogan, R., Jones, W.H., & Cheek, J.M. (1985). Socioanalytic theory: An alternative to armadillo psychology. In B.R. Schlenker (Ed.), *The self and social life* (pp. 175–198). New York: McGraw-hill.

Hogan, J., & Ones, D.S. (1997). Conscientiousness and integrity at work. In R. Hogan, J.A. Johnson, and S. Briggs (Eds.), *Handbook of personality psychology* (pp. 849–870). San Diego, CA: Academic Press.

Hogan, R., Hogan, J., & Roberts, B.W. (1996). Personality measurement and employment decisions. *American Psychologist, 51*, 469–477.

Hogan, R., Johnson, J., & Briggs, S. (1997). (Eds.). *Handbook of personality psychology.* San Diego, CA: Academic Press.

Holland, D. (1997). Selves as cultured: As told by an anthropologist who lacks a soul. In R.D. Ashmore and L. Jussim (Eds.), *Self and identity: Fundamental issues* (pp. 160–190). New York: Oxford University Press.

Holland, J.L. (1996). Exploring careers with a typology: What we have learned and some new directions. *American Psychologist, 51*, 397–406.

Holstein, J.A., & Gubrium, J.F. (2000). *The self we live by: Narrative identity in a postmodern world.* New York: Oxford University Press.

Holmes, D.S. (1967). Pupillary response, conditioning and personality. *Journal of Personality and Social Psychology, 5*, 98–103.

Holmes, D.S. (1974). Investigations of repression: Differential recall of material experimentally or naturally associated with ego threat. *Psychological Bulletin, 81*, 632–653.

Holmes, D.S. (1978). Projection as a defense mechanism. *Psychological Bulletin, 85*, 677–688.

Holt, R.R. (1962). Individuality and generalization in the psychology of personality: An evaluation. *Journal of Personality, 30*, 377–402.

Holt, R.R. (1978). *Methods in clinical psychology. Vol. 1: Projective assessment.* New York: Plenum.

Holt, R.R. (1980). Loevinger's measure of ego development: Reliability and national norms for male and female short forms. *Journal of Personality and Social Psychology, 39*, 909–920.

Hoppe, C. (1972). *Ego development and conformity behavior.* Unpublished doctoral dissertation, Washington University in St. Louis.

Horney, K. (1939). *New ways in psychoanalysis.* New York: Norton.

Horney, K. (1945). *Our inner conflicts.* New York: Norton.

Horney, K. (1980). *The adolescent diaries of Karen Horney.* New York: Basic Books.

Horowitz, M.J. (1979). *States of mind: Analysis of change in psychotherapy*. New York: Plenum.

Houts, A.C., Cook, T.D., & Shadish, W.R., Jr. (1986). The person-situation debate: A critical multiplist perspective. *Journal of Personality, 54*, 52–105.

Howard, G.S. (1989). *A tale of two stories: Excursions into a narrative psychology*. Notre Dame, IN: University of Notre Dame Press.

Howard, G.S. (1991). Culture tales: A narrative approach to thinking, crosscultural psychology, and psychotherapy. *American Psychologist, 46*, 187–197.

Howard, A., & Bray, D. (1988). *Managerial lives in transition: Advancing age and changing times*. New York: Guilford Press.

Howarth, E., & Eysenck, H.J. (1968). Extraversion, arousal, and paired-associate recall. *Journal of Experimental Research in Personality, 3*, 114–116.

Huesmann, L.R., & Malamuth, N.M. (1986). Media violence and antisocial behavior. *Journal of Social Issues, 42*(3), 1–6.

Hull, C. (1943). *Principles of behavior*. New York: Appleton-Century-Crofts.

Hy, L.X., & Loevinger, J. (1996). *Measuring ego development* (2nd Ed.). Mahwah, NJ: Erlbaum.

Hyland, M.E. (1988). Motivational control theory: An integrative framework. *Journal of Personality and Social Psychology, 55*, 642–651.

Ibrahim, Y.M. (1997). Locked in the grip of attack and reprisal, Algeria votes. *New York Times*, October 24, A1, A7.

Ickes, W., Snyder, M., & Garcia, S. (1997). Personality influences on the choice of situations. In R. Hogan, J.A. Johnson, and S. Briggs (Eds.), *Handbook of personality psychology* (pp. 165–195). San Diego, CA: Academic Press.

Ingelhart, R. (1990). *Cultural shift in advanced industrial societies*. Princeton, NJ: Princeton University Press.

Ingram, R.E. (1984). Toward an information-processing analysis of depression. *Cognitive Therapy and Research, 8*, 443–478.

Ingram, R.E., Smith, T.W., & Brehm, S.S. (1983). Depression and information processing: Self-schemata and the encoding of self-referent information. *Journal of Personality and Social Psychology, 45*, 412–420.

Inhelder, B., & Piaget, J. (1958). *The growth of logical thinking from childhood to adolescence*. New York: Basic Books.

Inkeles, A. (1960). Industrial man: The relation of status to experience, perception, and value. *American Journal of Sociology, 66*, 1–31.

Inkeles, A., & Smith, D. (1974). *Becoming modern: Individual change in six developing countries*. Cambridge, MA: Harvard University Press.

Isabella, R.A., Belsky, J., & von Eye, A. (1989). Origins of infant–mother attachment: An examination of interactional synchrony during the infant's first year. *Developmental Psychology, 25*, 12–21.

Izard, C.E. (1971). *The face of emotion*. New York: Appleton-Century-Crofts.

Izard, C.E. (1977). *Human emotions*. New York: Plenum.

Izard, C.E. (1978). On the ontogenesis of emotions and emotion—cognition relationships in infancy. In M. Lewis and L.A. Rosenblum (Eds.), *The development of affect* (pp. 389–413). New York: Plenum.

Izzett, R.R. (1971). Authoritarianism and attitudes toward the Vietnam war as reflected in behavioral and self-report measures. *Journal of Personality and Social Psychology, 17*, 145–148.

Jackson, D.N. (1971). The dynamics of structured personality tasks. *Psychological Review, 78*, 229–248.

Jackson, D.N. (1974). *The Personality Research Form*. Port Huron, MI: Research Psychologists Press.

Jackson, D.N., & Messick, S. (1958). Content and style in personality assessment. *Psychological Bulletin, 55*, 243–252.

Jackson, D.N., & Paunonen, S.V. (1980). Personality structure and assessment. In M.R. Rosenzweig and L.W. Porter (Eds.), *Annual review of psychology: 31* (pp. 503–552). Palo Alto, CA: Annual Reviews, Inc.

Jacques, E. (1965). Death and the midlife crisis. *International Journal of Psychoanalysis, 46*, 502–514.

James, W. (1892/1963). *Psychology*. Greenwich, CT: Fawcett.

James, W. (1902/1958). *The varieties of religious experience*. New York: New American Library of World Literature.

Jang, K.L., Livesley, W.J., & Vernon, P.A. (1996). Heritability of the Big Five personality dimensions: A twin study. *Journal of Personality, 64*, 577–591.

Jang, K.L., McCrae, R.R., Angleitner, A., Riemann, R., &

Livesley, W.J. (1998). Heritability of facet-level traits in a cross-cultural twin sample: Support for a hierarchical model of personality. *Journal of Personality and Social Psychology, 74*, 1556–1565.

Janix, I.L. (1972). *Victims of group think.* Boston: Houghton Miflin.

Janoff-Bulman, R., & Brickman, P. (1980). Expectations and what people learn from failure. In N.T. Feather (Ed.), *Expectancy, incentive, and failure.* Hillesdale, NJ: Lawrence Erlbaum.

Jay. P. (1984). *Being in the text: Self-representation from Wordworth to Roland Barthes.* Ithaca, NY: Cornell University Press.

Jemmott, J.B., III. (1987). Social motives and susceptibility to disease: Stalking individual differences in health risks. *Journal of Personality, 55*, 267–298.

Jenkins, S.R. (1987). Need for achievement and women's careers over 14 years: Evidence for occupational structure effects. *Journal of Personality and Social Psychology, 53*, 922–932.

Jenkins, S.R. (1994). Need for power and women's careers over 14 years: Structural power, job satisfaction, and motive change. *Journal of Personality and Social Psychology, 66*, 155–165.

Jensen-Campbell, L.A., Grabiano, W.G., & West, S.G. (1995). Dominance, prosocial orientation, and female preferences: Do nice guys really finish last? *Journal of Personality and Social Psychology, 68*, 427–440.

John, O.P. (1989). Toward a taxonomy of personality descrip-

tors. In D.M. Buss and N. Cantor (Eds.), *Personality psychology: Recent trends and emerging directions* (pp. 261–271). New York: Springer-Verlag.

John, O.P. (1990). The "Big Five" factor taxonomy: Dimensions of personality in the natural language and in questionnaires. In L. Pervin (Ed.), *Handbook of personality theory and research* (pp. 66–100). New York: Guilford Press.

John, O.P., Pals, J.L., & Westenberg, P.M. (1998). Personality prototypes and ego development: Conceptual similarities and relations in adult women. *Journal of Personality and Social Psychology, 74*, 1093–1108.

Johnson, J.A. (1997). Units of analysis for the description and explanation of personality. In R. Hogan, J.A. Johnson, and S. Briggs (Eds.), *Handbook of personality psychology* (pp. 73–93). San Diego, CA: Academic Press.

Johnson, J.E., Petzel, T.P., Hartney, L.M., & Morgan, L.M. (1983). Recall and importance ratings of completed and uncompleted tasks as a function of depression. *Cognitive Therapy and Research, 7*, 51–56.

Johnson, R.N. (1972). *Aggression in man and animals.* Philadelphia: W.B. Saunders.

Jones, A., & Crandall, R. (1986). Validation of a short index of self-actualization. *Personality and Social Psychology Bulletin, 12*, 63–73.

Jones, E. (1961). *The life and work of Sigmund Freud.* New York: Basic Books.

Jones, E.E., Kanouse, D.E., Kelley, H.H., Nisbett, R.E., Valins, S., & Weiner, B. (1971).

Attribution: Perceiving the causes of behavior. Morristown, NJ: General Learning Press.

Jones, E.E., & Nisbett, R.E. (1972). The actor and the observer: Divergent perceptions of the causes of behavior. In E.E. Jones, D.E. Kanouse, H.H. Kelley, R.E. Nisbett, S. Valins, and B. Weiner (Eds.), *Attribution: Perceiving the causes of behavior* (pp. 79–94). Morristown, NJ: General Learning Press.

Jones, J.M. (1983). The concept of race in social psychology: From color to culture. In L. Wheeler and P. Shaver (Eds.), *Review of personality and social psychology* (Vol. 4, pp. 117–150). Beverly Hills, CA: Sage.

Jones, W.H., Briggs, S.R., & Smith, T.G. (1986). Shyness: Conceptualizatoin and measurement. *Journal of Personality and Social Psychology, 51*, 629–639.

Jones, W.H., Couch, L., & Scott, S. (1997). Trust and betrayal: The psychology of getting along and getting ahead. In R. Hogan, J. Johnson, and S. Briggs (Eds.), *Handbook of personality psychology* (pp. 465–482). San Diego, CA: Academic Press.

Jones, W.H., & Russel, D. (1982). The social reticence scale: An objective measure of shyness. *Journal of Personality Assessment, 46*, 629–631.

Jordan, D. (1971). *Parental antecedents and personality characteristics of ego identity statuses.* Unpublished doctoral dissertation, State University of New York at Binghampton.

Josselson, R.L. (1973). Psychodynamic aspects of identity formation in college women. *Journal of Youth and Adolescence, 2,* 3–52.

Josselson, R.L. (1988). The embedded self: I and Thou revisited. In D.K. Lapsley and F.C. Power (Eds.), *Self, ego, and identity: Integrative approaches* (pp. 91–106). New York: Springer-Verlag.

Josselson, R. (1995). Narrative and psychological understanding. *Psychiatry, 58,* 330–343.

Josselson, R. (1996). *Revising herself: The story of women's identity from college to midlife.* New York: Oxford University Press.

Josselson, R., & Lieblich, A. (1993). (Eds.). *The narrative study of lives* (Vol. 1). Thousand Oaks, CA: Sage.

Judson, H.F. (1980). The rage to know. *Atlantic Monthly.*

Jung, C.G. (1913/1971). A contribution to the study of psychological types. In H. Read, M. Fundham, G. Adler, and W. McGuire (Eds.), *The collected works of C.G. Jung* (Vol. 6, pp. 499–509). Princeton, NJ: Princeton University Press.

Jung, C.G. (1923/1971). *Psychological types.* In H. Read and others (Eds.), *The collected works of C.G. Jung* (Vol. 6, pp. 1–495). Princeton, NJ: Princeton University Press.

Jung, C.G. (1936/1969). *The archetypes and the collective unconscious.* In Vol. 9 of *The collected works of C.G. Jung.* Princeton, NJ: Princeton University Press.

Jung, C.G. (1936/1971). Psychological typology. In H. Read and others (Eds.), *The collected works of C.G. Jung* (Vol. 6, pp. 542–555. Princeton, NJ: Princeton University Press.

Jung, C.G. (1961). *Memories, dreams, reflections.* New York: Vintage.

Jung, C.G., von Franz, M.-L., Henderson, J.L., Jacobi, J., & Jaffe, A. (1964). *Man and his symbols.* Garden City, NY: Doubleday.

Justice, M.T. (1969). *Field dependency, intimacy of topic and interpersonal distance.* Unpublished doctoral dissertation, University of Florida.

Kagan, J. (1984). *The nature of the child.* New York: Basic Books.

Kagan, J. (1989). Temperamental Contributions to Social behavior. *American Psychologist, 44,* 668–674.

Kagan, J. (1994). *Galen's prophecy.* New York: Basic Books.

Kagan, J. (2000). Temperament. In A. Kazdin (Ed.), *Encyclopedia of psychology.* New York: Oxford University Press.

Kahn, S., Zimmerman, G., Csikszentmihalyi, M., & Getzels, J.W. (1985). Relations between identity in young adulthood and intimacy at midlife. *Journal of Personality and Social Psychology, 49,*1316–1322.

Kahn, R., & Antonucci, T. (1981). Convoys of social support: A life-course approach. In S. Kiesler, J. Morgan, and V. Oppenheimer (Eds.), *Aging: Social change* (pp. 383–405. New York: Academic Press.

Kahneman, D., & Tversky, A. (1984). Choices, values, and frames. *American Psychologist, 39,* 341–350.

Kashima, Y., Yumaguchi, S., Kim, U., Choi, S-C., Gelfand, M.J., & Yuki, M. (1995). Culture, gender, and self: A perspective from individualism-collectivism research. *Journal of Personality and Social Psychology, 69,* 925–937.

Kasser, T., & Ryan, R.M. (1996). Further examining the American dream: Differential correlates of intrinsic and extrinsic goals. *Personality and Social Psychology Bulletin, 22,* 280–287.

Kelley, H.H., & Michela, J.L. (1980). Attribution theory and research. In M.R. Rosenzweig and L.W. Porter (Eds.), *Annual review of psychology* (Vol. 31, pp. 457–502). Palo Alto, CA: Annual Reviews, Inc.

Kelly, E.L., & Conley, J.J. (1987). Personality and compatibility: A prospective analysis of marital stability and marital satisfaction. *Journal of Personality and Social Psychology, 52,* 27–40.

Kelly, G. (1955). *The psychology of personal constructs.* New York: W.W. Norton.

Keniston, K. (1963). Inburn: An American Ishmael. In R.W. White (Ed.), *The study of lives* (pp. 40–70). New York: Holt, Rinehart & Winston.

Kenrick, D.T. (1989). A biosocial perspective on mates and traits: Reuniting personality and social psychology. In D.M. Buss and N. Cantor (Eds.), *Personality psychology: Recent trends and emerging directions* (pp. 308–319). New York: Springer-Verlag.

Kenrick, D.T., & Funder, D.C. (1988). Profiting from controversy: Lessons from the person-situation debate. *American Psychologist, 43,* 23–34.

Kenrick, D.T., Keefe, R.C., Bryan, A., Barr, A., & Brown, S. (1995). Age preferences and mate choice among homosexuals and heterosexuals: A case for modular psychological mechanisms. *Journal of Personality and Social Psychology, 69,* 1166–1172.

Kenrick, D.T., Montello, D.R. & McFarlane, S. (1985). Personality: Social learning, social cognition, or sociobiology? In R. Hogan and W.H. Jones (Eds.), *Perspectives in personality* (Vol. 1, pp. 201–234). Greenwich, CT: JAI Press.

Kenrick, D.T., & Stringfield, D.O. (1980). Personality traits and the eye of the beholder: Crossing some traditional philosophical boundaries in the search for consistency in all the people. *Psychological Review, 87,* 88–104.

Kernberg, O. (1980). *International world and external reality.* New York: Jason Aronson.

Keyes, C.L.M., & Ryff, C.D. (1998). Generativity in adult lives: Social structural contours and quality of life consequences. In D.P. McAdams and E. de St. Aubin (Eds.), *Generativity and adult development: How and why we care for the next generation* (pp. 227–263). Washington, D.C.: APA Press.

Kiesler, D.J. (1982). The 1982 interpersonal circle: A taxonomy of complementarity in human transactions. *Psychological Review, 90,* 185–214.

Kihlstrom, J.F. (1981). On personality and memory. In N. Cantor and J.F. Kihlstrom (Eds.), *Personality, cognition, and social interaction* (pp. 123–179). Hillsdale, NJ: Lawrence Erlbaum.

Kihlstrom, J.F. (1984). Conscious, subconscious, unconscious: A cognitive perspective. In K.S. Bowers and D. Meichenbaum (Eds.), *The unconscious reconsidered* (pp. 149–211).

Kihlstrom, J.F. (1990). The psychological unconscious. In L. Pervin (Ed.), *Handbook of personality theory and research* (pp. 445–464). New York: Guilford Press.

Kihlstrom, J.F., & Harackiewicz, J.M. (1982). The earliest recollection: A new survey. *Journal of Personality, 50,* 134–148.

Kihlstrom, J.F., & Hastie, R. (1997). Mental representations of persons and personality. In R. Hogan, J. Johnson, and S. Briggs (Ed.), *Handbook of personality psychology* (pp. 711–735). San Diego, CA: Academic Press.

King, L.A. (1995). Wishes, motives, goals, and personal memories: Relation of measures of human motivation. *Journal of Personality, 63,* 985–1007.

Kirk, J., & Miller, M.L. (1986). *Reliability and validity in qualitative research.* Beverly Hills, CA: Sage.

Klages, L. (1926/1932). *The science of character.* London: George Allen & Unwin.

Klavetter, R.E., & Mogar, R.E. (1967). Peak experiences: Investigation of their relationship to psychedelic therapy and self-actualization. *Journal of Humanistic Psychology, 7,* 171–177.

Klinger, E. (1966). Fantasy need achievement as a motivational construct. *Psychological Bulletin, 66,* 291–308.

Klinger, E. (1977). *Meaning and void.* Minneapolis, MN: University of Minnesota Press.

Klinger, E. (1987). Current concerns and disengagement from incentives. In F. Halisch and J. Kuhl (Eds.), *Motivation, intention, and volition* (pp. 337–347). Berlin: Springer-Verlag.

Klinger, E., Barta, S.G., & Maxeiner, M.E. (1981). Current concerns: Assessing therapeutically relevant motivation. In P.C. Kendall and S. Hollon (Eds.), *Assessment strategies for cognitive-behavioral interventions* (pp. 161–195). New York: Academic Press.

Kluckhohn, C., & Murray, H.A. (1953). Personality formation: The determinants. In C. Kluckhohn, H.A. Murray, and D.M. Schneider (Eds.), *Personality in nature, society, and culture* (pp. 53–67). New York: Alfred A. Knopf.

Knowles, E.S., & Sibicky, M.E. (1990). Continuity and diversity in the stream of selves: Metaphorical resolutions of William James's one-in-many-selves paradox. *Personality and Social Psychology Bulletin, 16,* 676–687.

Kobak, R.R., & Hazan, C. (1991). Attachment in marriage: Effects of security and accuracy of working models. *Journal of Personality and Social Psychology, 60,* 861–869.

Kock, S.W. (1965). *Management and motivation.* Unpublished doctoral dissertation, Swedish School of Economics.

Koenig, H.G. (in press). (Ed.). *Handbook of religion and mental health.* San Diego, CA: Academic Press.

Koestner, R., Bernieri, F., & Zuckerman, M. (1989). Trait-specific versus person-specific moderators of cross-situational consistency. *Journal of Personality*, *57*, 1–16.

Koestner, R., & McClelland, D.C. (1990). Perspectives on competence motivation. In L. Pervin (Ed.), *Handbook of personality: Theory and research* (pp. 527–548). New York: Guilford Press.

Koestner, R., Weinberger, J., & McClelland, D.C. (1991). Task-intrinsic and social-extrinsic sources of arousal for motives assessed in fantasy and self-report. *Journal of Personality*, *59*, 57–82.

Koestner, R., Zuckerman, M., & Koestner, J. (1987). Praise, involvement, and intrinsic motivation. *Journal of Personality and Social Psychology*, *53*, 383–390.

Kohlberg, L. (1969). Stage and sequence: The cognitive-developmental approach to socialization. In D.A. Goslin (Ed.), *Handbook of socialization theory and research* (pp. 347–480). Skokie, IL: Rand McNally.

Kohlberg, L. (1981). *The philosophy of moral development: Moral stages and the idea of justice* (Vol. 1). *Essays on moral development*. New York: Harper & Row.

Kohn, M.L. (1969). *Class and conformity: A study in values*. Homewood, IL: Dorsey Press.

Kohn, M.L., Naoi, A., Schoenbach, C., Schooler, C., & Slomczynski, K.M. (1990). Position in the class structure and psychological functioning in the United States, Japan, and polan. *American Journal of Sociology*, *95*, 964–1008.

Kohn, M.L., & Schooler, C. (1969). Class, occupation, and orientation. *American Sociological Review*, *34*, 659–678.

Kohn, M.L., & Schooler, C. (1973). Occupational experience and psychological functioning: An assessment of reciprocal effects. *American Sociological Review*, *38*, 97–118.

Kohnstamm, G.A., Halverson, C.F., Jr., Mervielde, I., & Havill, V.L. (1998). *Parental descriptions of child personality: Developmental antecedents of the Big Five?* Mahweh, NJ: Lawrence Erlbaum.

Kohut, H. (1971). *The analysis of the self*. New York: International Universities Press.

Kohut, H. (1977). *The restoration of the self*. New York: International Universities Press.

Kohut, H. (1984). *How does analysis cure?* Chicago: University of Chicago Press.

Konner, M. (1983). *The tangled wing: Biological constraints on the human spirit*. New York: Harper & Row.

Kotre, J. (1984). *Outliving the self: Generativity and the interpretatin of lives*. Baltimore, MD: Johns Hopkins University Press.

Kotre, J. (1999). *Making it count: How to generate a legacy that gives meaning to your life*. New York: The Free Press.

Krahe, B. (1992). *Personality and social psychology: Toward a synthesis*. London: Sage.

Krebs, D.L. (1975). Empathy and altrusim. *Journal of Personality and Social Psychology*, *32*, 1124–1146.

Kretschmer, E. (1921). *Korperbau und charakter*. Berlin: Springer.

Krippendorff, K. (1980). *Content analysis: An introductin to its methodology*. Beverly Hill, CA: Sage.

Kruglanski, A.W. (1989). The psychology of being "right": The problem of accuracy in social perception and cognition. *Psychological Bulletin*, *106*, 395–409.

Kunce, J.T., & Anderson, W.P. (1984). Perspectives on uses of the MMPI in nonpsychiatric settings. In P. McReynolds and G.J. Chelune (Eds.), *Advances in psychological assessment* (Vol. 6, pp. 41–76). San Francisco: Jossey-Bass.

Kushner, H. (1981). *When bad things happen to good people*. New York: Avon.

Labov, W. (1972). *Language in the inner city*. Philadelphia: University of Pennsylvania Press.

Lachman, M.E. (1986). Locus of control in aging research: A case for multi-dimensional and domain-specific assessment. *Psychology and Aging*, *1*, 34–40.

Lachman, R., Lachman, J.L., & Butterfield, E.C. (1979). *Cognitive psychology and human information processing*. Hillsdale, NJ: Lawrence Erlbaum.

LaFreniere, P.J., & Sroufe, L.A. (1985). Profiles of peer competence in the preschool: Interrelations between measures, influence of social ecology, and relation to attachment history. *Developmental Psychology*, *21*, 56–69.

Lamb, M.E. (1976). *The role of the father in child development*. New York: John Wiley & Sons.

Lando, H.A., & Donnerstein, E.I. (1978). The effects of a model's success or failure on subsequent aggressive behavior. *Journal of Research in Personality*, *12*, 225–234.

Langbaum, R. (1982). *The mysteries of identity: A theme in modern literature.* Chicago: University of Chicago Press.

Lapsley, D.K., & Power, F.C. (Eds.). (1988). *Self, ego, and identity: Integrative approaches.* New York: Springer-Verlag.

Lapsley, D.K., & Rice, K. (1988). The "new look" at the imaginary audience and personal fable: Toward a general model of adolescent ego development. In D.K. Lapsley and F.C. Power (Eds.), *Self, ego, and identity: Integrative approaches* (pp. 109–129). New York: Springer-Verlag.

Larsen, R.J., & Diener, E. (1987). Affect intensity as an individual difference characteristic: A review. *Journal of Research in Personality, 21,* 1–39.

Larsen, R.J., & Kasimatis, M. (1991). Day-to-day symptoms: Individual differences in the occurrence, duration, and emotional concomitants of minor daily illness. *Journal of Personality, 59,* 387–423.

Lasch, C. (1979). *The culture of narcissism: American life in an age of diminishing expectations.* New York: W.W. Norton.

Leary, T. (1957). *Interpersonal diagnosis of personality.* New York: Ronald Press.

LeDoux, J. (1996). *The emotional brain: The mysterious underpinnings of emotional life.* New York: Touchstone Books.

Leith, K.P., & Baumeister, R.F. (1998). Empathy, shame, guilt, and narratives of interpersonal conflicts: Guilt-prone people are better at perspective taking. *Journal of Personality, 66,* 1–37.

Lee, L., & Snarey, J. (1988). The relationship between ego and moral development: A theoretical review and empirical analysis. In D.K. Lapsley and F.C. Power (Eds.), *Self, ego, and identity: integrative approaches* (pp. 151–178). New York: Springer-Verlag.

Lefcourt, H.M., Martin, R.A., Fick, C.M., & Salch, W.E. (1985). Locus of control for affiliation and behavior in social interactions. *Journal of Personality and Social Psychology, 48,* 577–759.

Lepper, M.R., & Greene, D. (1978). *The hidden costs of reward: New perspectives on the psychology of human motivation.* New York: Halsted.

Lepper, M.R., Greene, D. & Nisbett, R.E. (1973). Undermining children's intrinsic interest with extrinsic rewards: A test of the "overjustification" hypothesis. *Journal of Personality and Social Psychology, 28,* 129–137.

Levine, L.E., & Hoffman, M.L. (1975). Empathy and cooperation in 4-year-olds. *Developmental Psychology, 11,* 533–534.

LeVine, R.A. (1982). *Culture, behavior, and personality.* (2nd ed.). New York: Aldine.

Levinson, D.J. (1978). *The seasons of a man's life.* New York: Alfred A. Knopf.

Levinson, D.J. (1981). Explorations in biography: Evolution of the individual life structure in adulthood. In A.I. Rabin, J. Aronoff, A.M. Barclay, and R.A. Zucker (Eds.). *Further explorations in personality* (pp. 44–79). New York: John Wiley & Sons.

Levinson, D.J., Darrow, C.M., Klein, E.B., Levinson, M.H., & McKee, B. (1974). The psychosocial development of men in early adulthood and the mid-life transition. In D. Ricks, A. Thomas, and M. Roff (Eds.), *Life history research in psychopathology* (Vol. 3). Minneapolis, MN: University of Minnesota Press.

Levy, K.N., Blatt, S.J., & Shaver, P.R. (1998). Attachment styles and parental representations. *Journal of Personality and Social Psychology, 74,* 407–419.

Lewicki, P. (1984). Self-schemata and social information processing. *Journal of Personality and Social Psychology, 47,* 1177–1190.

Lewicki, P. (1986). *Nonconscious social information processing.* New York: Academic Press.

Lewin, K. (1935). *A dynamic theory of personality.* New York: McGraw-Hill.

Lewis, H.B. (1971). *Shame and guilt in neurosis.* New York: International Universities Press.

Lewis, H.B. (1985). Depression vs. paranoia: Why are there sex differences in mental illness? *Journal of Personality, 53,* 150–178.

Lewis, M. (1990). Self-knowledge and social development in early life. In L. Pervin (Ed.), *Handbook of personality theory and research* (pp. 277–300). New York: Guilford Press.

Lewis, M., & Brooks-Gunn, J. (1979). *Social cognition and the acquisition of self.* New York: Plenum.

Liebert, R.M., & Baron, R.A. (1972). Short-term effects of televised aggression on children's aggressive behavior. In J.P. Murray, E.A. Rubinstein, and G.A. Comstock (Eds.), *Television and social behavior: II.*

Television and social learning. Washington, DC: U.S. Government Printing Office.

Liebert, R.M., & Spiegler, M.D. (1978). *Personality: Strategies and issues.* (3rd ed.). Homewood, IL: Dorsey Press.

Lifton, R.J. (1979). *The broken connection: On death and the continuity of life.* New York: Simon & Schuster.

Linde, C. (1990). *Life-stories: The creation of coherence.* Palo Alto, CA: Institute for Research on Learning Monograph No. IRL90–0001.

Lindzey, G. (1952). Thematic Apperception Test: Interpretive assumptions and related empirical evidence. *Psychological Bulletin, 49,* 1–25.

Lindzey, G. (1959). On the classification of projective techniques. *Psychological Bulletin, 56,* 158–168.

Lindzey, G. (1961). *Projective techniques and cross-cultural research.* New York: Appleton-Century-Crofts.

Linn, R. (1997). Solders' narratives of selective moral resistance: A separate position or the connected self? In A. Lieblich and R. Josselson (Eds.), *The narrative study of lives* (Vol. 5, pp. 94–112). Thousand Oaks, CA: Sage.

Linville, P.W. (1987). Self-complexity as a cognitive buffer against stress-related illness and depression. *Journal of Personality and Social Psychology, 52,* 663–676.

Lishman, W.A. (1972). Selective factors in memory. Part I: Age, sex, and personality attributes. *Psychological Medicine, 2,* 121–138.

Little, B.R. (1989). Personal projects analysis: Trivial pursuits, magnificent obsessions, and the search for coherence. In D.M. Buss and N. Cantor (Eds.), *Personality psychology: Recent trends and emerging directions* (pp. 15–31). New York: Springer-Verlag.

Little, B.R. (1998). Personal project pursuit: Dimensions and dynamics of personal meaning. In P.T.P. Wong and P.S. Fry (Eds.), *The human quest for meaning: Handbook for research and clinical applications* (pp. 193–212). Mahwah, NJ: Lawrence Erlbaum.

Little, B.R. (1999). Personality and motivation: Personal action and the conative evolution. In L.A. Pervin and O. John (Eds.), *Handbook of personality: Theory and research* (2nd ed., pp. 501–524). New York: Guilford Press.

Little, B.R., Lecci, L., & Watkinson, R. (1992). Personality and personal projects: Linking Big Five and PAC units of analysis. *Journal of Personality, 60,* 501–525.

Littlefield, C.H., & Rushton, J.P. (1986). When a child dies: The sociobiology of bereavement. *Journal of Personality and Social Psychology, 51,* 797–802.

Littlefield, C.H., & Rushton, J.P. (1988). Levels of explanation in sociobiology and psychology: A rejoinder to Archer. *Journal of Personality and Social Psychology, 56,* 625–628.

Livson, N., & Peskin, H. (1980). Perspectives on adolescence from longitudinal research. In J. Adelson (Ed.), *Handbook of adolescent psychology* (pp. 47–98). New York: John Wiley & Sons.

Lloyd, G.G., & Lishman. W.A. (1975). Effect of depression on the speed of recall of pleasant and unpleasant experiences. *Psychological Medicine, 5,* 173–180.

Locke, J. (1690). *An essay concerning human understanding.* Excerpted in R.J. Herrnstein and E. G. Boring (Eds.). (1965). *A source book in the history of psychology* (pp. 584–586). Cambridge, MA: Harvard University Press.

Loehlin, J.C. (1989). Partitioning environmental and genetic contributions to behavioral develoment. *American Psychologist, 44,* 1285–1292.

Loehlin, J.C. (1992). *Genes and environment in personality development.* Newbury Park, CA: Sage.

Loehlin, J.C., McCrae, R.R., & Costa, P.T., Jr. (1998). Heritabilities of common and measure-specific components of the Big Five personality factors. *Journal of Research in Personality, 32,* 431–453.

Loehlin, J.C., & Nichols. R.C. (1976). *Heredity, environment, and personality: A study of 850 sets of twins.* Austin, TX: Texas University Press.

Loehlin, J.C., Willerman, L., & Horn, J.M. (1987). Personality resemblance in adoptive families: A 10-year followup. *Journal of Personality and Social Psychology, 53,* 961–969.

Loevinger, J. (1957). Objective tests as instruments of psychological theory. *Psychological Reports, 3,* 635–694.

Loevinger, J. (1969). Theories of ego development. In L. Breger (Ed.), *Clinincal-cognitive psychology: Models and integrations.* Englewood Cliffs, NJ: Prentice-Hall.

Loevinger, J. (1976). *Ego development*. San Francisco: Jossey-Bass.

Loevinger, J. (1979). Construct validity of the sentence-completion test of ego development. *Applied Psychological Measurement, 3*, 281–311.

Loevinger, J. (1983). On ego development and the structure of personality. *Developmental Review, 3*, 339–350.

Loevinger, J. (1984). On the self and predicting behavior. In R.A. Zucker, J. Aronoff, and A.I. Rabin (Eds.), *Personality and the prediction of behavior* (pp. 43–68). New York: Academic Press.

Loevinger, J. (1987). *Paradigms of personality*. New York: W.H. Freeman.

Loevinger, J. (1992). Has psychology lost its conscience? Henry Murray Award Address, American Psychological Association, Washington, DC.

Loevinger, J., Cohn, L.D., Bonneville, L.P., Redmore, C., Streich, D.D., & Sargent, M. (1985). Ego development in college. *Journal of Personality and Social Psychology, 48*, 947–962.

Loevinger, J., & Wessler, R. (1970). *Measuring ego development 1. Construction and use of a sentence-completion test*. San Francisco: Jossey-Bass.

Loevinger, J., Wessler, R., & Redmore, C. (1970). *Measuring ego development 2. Scoring manual for women and girls*. San Francisco: Jossey-Bass.

Lohr, J.M., & Staats, W.W. (1973). Attitude conditioning in Sino-Tibetan languages. *Journal of Personality and Social Psychology, 26*, 196–200.

Lorenz, K. (1969). *On aggression*. New York: Harcourt, Brace & World.

Lowenthal, M.F., Thurnher, M., Chiriboga, D., & Associates. (1975). *Four stages of life: A comparative study of men and women facing transitions*. San Francisco, CA: Jossey-Bass.

Lucariello, J. (1990). Canonicality and consciousness in child narrative. In B.K. Britton and A.D. Pellegrini (Eds.), *Narrative thought and narrative language* (pp. 131–150). Hillsdale, NJ: Lawrence Erlbaum.

Luria, A.R. (1972). *The man with a shattered world*. New York: Basic Books. (Transl. By L. Solotaroff).

Lundy, A. (1985). The reliability of the Thematic Apperception Test. *Journal of Personality Assessment, 49*, 141–145.

Lütkenhaus, P., Grossmann, K.E., & Grossmann, K. (1985). Infant-mother attachment at twelve months and style of interaction with stranger at the age of three years. *Child Development, 56*, 1538–1542.

Lykken, D.T., McGue, M., Tellegen, A., & Bouchard, Jr., T.J. (1992). Emergenesis: Genetic traits that may not run in families. *American Psychologist, 47*, 1565–1577.

Lykken, D., & Tellegen, A. (1996). Happiness is a stochastic phenomenon. *Psychological Science, 7*, 186–189.

Lyons-Ruth, K. (1996). Attachment relationships among children with aggressive behavior problems: The role of disorganzied early attachment patterns. *Journal of Consulting and Clinical Psychology, 64*, 64–73.

Lyons-Ruth, K., Connell, D.B., Zoll, D., & Stahl, J. (1987). Infants at social risk: Relations among infant maltreatment, maternal behavior, and infant attachment behavior. *Developmental Psychology, 23*, 223–232.

Maccoby, E.E. (1991). Different reproductive strategies in males and females. *Child Development, 62*, 676–681.

Maccoby, E.E., & Jacklin, C.N. (1974). *The psychology of sex differences*. Stanford, CA: Stanford University Press.

Maccoby, E.E., & Martin, J.A. (1983). Socialization in the context of the family: Parent–child interaction. In P.H. Mussen (Ed.), *Handbook of child psychology*, (4th ed.), Vol. 4 (pp. 1–102).

MacDermid, S.M., Franz, C.E., & DeReus, L.A. (1998). Generativity: At the crossroads of social roles and personality. In D.P. McAdams and E. de St. Aubin (Eds.), *Generativity and adult development: How and why we care for the next generation* (pp. 181–226). Washington, D.C.: APA Press.

MacIntyrre. A. (1984). *After virtue*. Notre Dame, IN: University of Notre Dame Press.

Mackenzie-Mohr, D., & Zanna, M.P. (1990). Treating women as sexual objects: Look to the (gender schematic) male who has viewed pornography. *Personality and Social Psychology Bulletin, 16*, 296–308.

MacKinnon, D.W. (1962). The nature and nurture of creative talent. *American Psychologist, 17*, 484–495.

MacKinnon, D.W. (1963). Creativity and images of the self. In R.W. White (Ed.), *The study of lives* (pp. 250–279). New York: Prentice-Hall.

MacKinnon, D.W. (1965). Personality and the realization of creative potential. *American Psychologist, 20,* 273–281.

MacLean, P.D. (1949). Psychosomatic disease and the "visceral brain": Recent developments bearing on the Papez theory of emotion. *Psychosomatic Medicine, 11,* 338–353.

Maddi, S.R. (1980). *Personality theories: A comparative analysis* (4th ed.). Homewood, IL: The Dorsey Press.

Maddi, S.R. (1984). Personology for the 1980s. in R.A. Zucker, J. Aronoff, and A.I. Rabin (Eds.), *Personality and the prediction of behavior* (pp. 7–41). New York: Academic Press.

Maddi, S.R., Kobasa, S.C., & Hoover, M. (1979). An alienation test. *Journal of Humanistic Psychology, 19*(4), 73–76.

Magnus, K., Diener, E., Fujita, F., & Pavot, W. (1993). Extraversion and neuroticism as predictors of object life events: A longitudinal analysis. *Journal of Personality and Social Psychology, 65,* 1046–1053.

Maher, B. (1969). (Ed.). *Clinical psychology and personality: The selected papers of George Kelly.* New York: John Wiley & Sons.

Mahler, M.S. (1968). *On human symbiosis and the vicissitudes of individuation: Infantile psychosis.* New York: International Universities.

Mahler, M.S., Pine, F., & Bergman, A. (1975). *The psychological birth of the human infant,* New York: Basic Books.

Main, M. (1981). Avoidance in the service of attachment: A working paper. In K. Immelmann, G. Barlow, L. Petrinovich, and M. Main (Eds.), *Behavioral development: The Bielefeld interdisciplinary project.* New York: Cambridge University Press.

Main, M. (1983). Exploration, play, and cognitive functioning related to mother–infant attachment. *Infant Behavior and Development, 6,* 167–174.

Main, M. (1991). Metacognitive knowledge, metacognitive monitoring, and singular (coherent) vs. multiple (incoherent) model of attachment. In C.M. Parkes, J. Stevenson-Hinde, and P. Marris (Eds.), *Attachment across the life cycle* (pp. 127–159). London: Tavistock/Routledge.

Main, M., & Cassidy, J. (1988). Categories of response to reunion with the parent at age 6: Predictable from infant attachment classifications and stable over a 1-month period. *Developmental Psychology, 24,* 415–426.

Main, M., Kaplan, N., & Cassidy, J. (1985). Security in infancy, childhood, and adulthood: A move to the level of representation. *Monographs of the Society for Research in Child Development, 50,* (1 & 2), 66–104.

Main, M., & Weston, D. (1981). Security of attachment to mother and father: Related to conflict behavior and the readiness to establish new relationships. *Child Development, 52,* 932–940.

Malamuth, N.M., & Briere, J. (1986). Sexual violence in the media: Indirect effects on aggression against women. *Journal of Social Issues, 42*(3), 75–92.

Mancuso, J.C. (1986). The acquisition and use of narrative grammar structure. In T.R. Sarbin (Ed.), *Narrative psychology: The storied nature of human conduct* (pp. 91–110). New York: Praeger.

Mandel, N.M., & Shrauger, J.S. (1980). The effects of self-evaluation statements on heterosocial approach in shy and nonshy males. *Cognitive Therapy and Research, 4,* 369–381.

Mandler, J.M. (1984). *Stories, scripts, and scenes: Aspects of schema theory.* Hillsdale, NJ: Lawrence Erlbaum.

Mannheim, K. (1952). The problem of generations. In *Essays on the sociology of knowledge.* New York: Oxford University Press. (Originally published in 1928.).

Manning, M.M., & Wright, T.L. (1983). Self-efficacy expectancies and the persistence of pain control in childbirth. *Journal of Personality and Social Psychology, 45,* 421–431.

Marcia, J.E. (1966). Development and validation of ego identity status. *Journal of Personality and Social Psychology, 3,* 551–558.

Marcia, J.E. (1967). Ego identity status: Relationships to change in self-esteem, "general maladjustment," and authoritarianism. *Journal of Personality, 35,* 119–133.

Marcia, J.E. (1980). Identity in adolescence. In J. Adelson (Ed.), *Handbook of adolescent psychology* (pp. 159–187). New York: John Wiley & Sons.

Marcia. J.E., & Friedman, M.L. (1970). Ego identity status in college women. *Journal of Personality, 38,* 249–263.

Marcia, J.E., Waterman, A.S., Matteson, D.R., Archer, S.L., & Orlofsky, J.L. (1993). *Ego identity: A handbook for psychosocial research.* New York: Springer-Verlag.

Markus, H. (1977). Self-schemata and processing information about the self. *Journal of Personality and Social Psychology, 35,* 63–78.

Markus, H. (1983). Self-knowledge: An expanded view. *Journal of Personality, 51,* 543–565.

Markus, H.R., & Kitayama, S. (1991). Culture and the self: Implications for cognition, emotion, and motivation. *Psychological Review, 98,* 224–253.

Markus, H.R., Kitayama, S., & Heiman, R.J. (1998). Culture and "basic" psychological principles. In E.T. Higgins and A.W. Kruglanski (Eds.), *Social psychology: Handbook of basic principles* (pp. 857–913). New York: Guilford Press.

Markus, H., & Nurius, P. (1986). Possible selves. *American Psychologist, 41,* 954–969.

Markus, H., & Sentis, K. (1982). The self in social information processing. In J. Suls (Ed.), *Psychological perspectives on the self* (Vol. 1, pp. 41–70). Hillsdale, NJ: Lawrence Erlbaum.

Markus, H., & Smith, J. (1981). The influence of self-schema on the perception of others. In N. Cantor and J.F. Kihlstrom (Eds.), *Personality, cognition, and social interaction* (pp. 233–262). Hillsdale, NJ: Lawrence Erlbaum.

Markus, H.R., & Wurf, E. (1987). The dynamic self-concept: A social psychological perspective. In M.R. Rosenzweig and L.W. Porter (Eds.), *Annual review of psychology* (Vol. 38, pp. 299–337). Palo Alto, CA: Annual Reviews, Inc.

Marshall, V. (1975). Age and awareness of finitude in developmental gerontology. *Omega, 6,* 113–129.

Martin, J.A. (1981). A longitudinal study of the consequence of early mother-infant interaction: A microanalytic approach. *Monographs of the Society for Research in Child Development, 46,* (3, Serial No. 190).

Maruna, S. (1997). Going straight: Desistance from crime and life narratives of reform. In R. Josselson and A. Lieblich (Eds.), *The narrative study of lives* (Vol. 5, pp. 59–93). Thousand Oaks, CA: Sage.

Maslow, A.H. (1954). *Motivation and personality.* New York: Harper & Row.

Maslow, A.H. (1968). *Toward a psychology of being* (2nd ed.). New York: D. Van Nostrand.

Matarazzo, J.D. (1965). The interview. In B. Wolman (Ed.), *Handbook of clinical psychology.* New York: McGraw-Hill.

Matas, L., Arend, R., & Sroufe, L.A. (1978). Continuity of adaptation in the second year: The relationship between quality of attachment and later competence. *Child Development, 49,* 547–556.

Matthews, G. (1992). Extraversion. In A.P. Smith and D.P. Jones (Eds.), *Handbook of human performance: Vol. 3. State and trait.* London: Academic Press.

Matthews, G., Coyle, K., & Craig, A. (1990). Multiple factors of cognitive failure and their relationships with stress vulnerability. *Journal of Psychopathology and Behavioral Assessment, 12,* 49–64.

Matthews, G., & Deary, I. (1998). *Personality traits.* Cambridge, England: Cambridge University Press.

Matthews, G., Dorn, L., & Glendon, A.I. (1991). Personality correlates of driver stress. *Personality and Individual Differences, 12,* 535–549.

Matthews, G., Jones, D.M., & Chamberlain, A.G. (1989). Interactive effects of extraversion and arousal on attention task performance: Multiple resources or encoding processes? *Journal of Personality and Social Psychology, 56,* 629–639.

Matthews, G., Jones, D.M., & Chamberlain, A.G. (1992). Predictors of individual differences in mail coding skills, and their variation with ability level. *Journal of Applied Psychology, 77,* 406–418.

Mayo, P.R. (1990). A further study of the personality-congruent recall effect. *Personality and Individual Differences, 10,* 247–252.

McAdams, D.P. (1980). A thematic coding system for the intimacy motive. *Journal of Research in Personality, 14,* 413—432.

McAdams, D.P. (1982a). Intimacy motivation. In A.J. Stewart (Ed.), *Motivation and Society* (pp. 133–171). San Francisco: Jossey-Bass.

McAdams, D.P. (1982b). Experiences of intimacy and power: Relationships between social motives and autobiographical memory. *Journal of Personality and Social Psychology, 42,* 292–302.

McAdams, D.P. (1984a). Human motives and personal relationships. In V. Derlega (Ed.), *Communication, intimacy, and close relationships* (pp. 41–70). New York: Academic Press.

McAdams, D.P. (1984b). Scoring manual for the intimacy motive. *Psychological Documents, 14,* No. 2613, p. 7.

McAdams, D.P. (1984c). Love, power, and images of the self. In C.Z. Malatesta and C.E. Izard (Eds.), *Emotion in adult development* (pp. 159–174). Beverly Hills, CA: Sage.

McAdams, D.P. (1985a). Fantasy and reality in the death of Yukio Mishima. *Biography: An Interdisciplinary Quarterly, 8,* 292–317.

McAdams, D.P. (1985b). *Power, intimacy, and the life story: Personological inquiries into identity.* New York: The Guilford Press.

McAdams, D.P. (1985c). The "imago": A key narrative component of identity. In P. Shaver (Ed.), *Review of personality and social psychology* (Vol. 6, pp. 115–141). Beverly Hills, CA: Sage.

McAdams, D.P. (1987). A life-story model of identity. In R. Hogan and W.H. Jones (Eds.), *Perspectives in personality* (Vol. 2, pp. 15–50). Greenwich, CT: JAI Press.

McAdams, D.P. (1988a). Personal needs and personal relationships. IN S.W. Duck (Ed.), *Handbook of personal relationships* (pp. 7–22). London: John Wiley & Sons.

McAdams, D.P. (1988b). Self and story. In A.J. Stewart, J.M. Healy, and D.J. Ozer (Eds.), *Perspectives in personality: Approaches to understanding lives.* London: Jessica Kingsley.

McAdams, D.P. (1988c). Biography, narrative, and lives: An introduction. *Journal of Personality, 56,* 1–18.

McAdams, D.P. (1989). *Intimacy: The need to be close.* New York: Doubleday.

McAdams, D.P. (1990a). *The person: An introduction to personality psychology.* San Diego, CA: Harcourt Brace Jovanovich.

McAdams, D.P. (1990b). Unity and purpose in human lives: The emergence of identity as a life story. In A.I. Rabin, R.A. Zucker, R.A. Emmons, and S. Frank (Eds.), *Studying persons and lives* (pp. 148–200). New York: Springer.

McAdams, D.P. (1992). The five factor model in personality: A critical appraisal. *Journal of Personality, 60,* 329–361.

McAdams, D.P. (1992a). How the I and the Me come to be: Attachment vs. intimacy. Invited address, Sixth International Conference of the Society for the Study of Personal Relationships, Orono, Maine.

McAdams, D.P. (1992b). The five-factor model in personality: A critical appraisal. *Journal of Personality, 60,* 329–361.

McAdams, D.P. (1993). *The stories we live by: Personal myths and the making of the self.* New York: William Morrow.

McAdams, D.P. (1994a). Image, theme, and character in the life story of Karen Horney. In C. Franz and A.J. Stewart (Eds.),

Women creating lives: Identities, resilience, and resistance (pp. 151–171). Boulder, CO: Westview Press.

McAdams, D.P. (1994b). *The person: An introduction to personality psychology* (2nd Ed.). Fort Worth, TX: Harcourt Brace.

McAdams, D.P. (1994c). Can personality change? Levels of stability and growth in personality across the life span. In T.F. Heatherton and J.L. Weinberger (Eds.), *Can personality change?* (pp. 229–314). Washington, D.C.: APA Press.

McAdams, D.P. (1995). What do we know when we know a person? *Journal of Personality, 63,* 365–396.

McAdams, D.P. (1996a). Personality, modernity, and the storied self: A contemporary framework for studying persons. *Psychological Inquiry, 7,* 295–321.

McAdams, D.P. (1996b). Narrating the self in adulthood. In J. Birren, G. Kenyon, J.E. Ruth, J.J.F. Shroots, and J. Svendson (Eds.), *Aging and biography: Explorations in adult development* (pp. 131–148). New York: Springer.

McAdams, D.P. (1997a). A conceptual history of personality psychology. In R. Hogan, J. Johnson, and S. Briggs (Eds.), *Handbook of personality psychology* (pp. 3–39). San Diego, CA: Academic Press.

McAdams, D.P. (1997b). The case for unity in the (post)modern self: A modest proposal. In R. Ashmore and L. Jussim (Eds.), *Self and identity: Fundamental issues* (pp. 46–78). New York: Oxford University Press.

McAdams, D.P. (1997c). The three voices of Erik Erikson. *Contemporary Psychology*, *42*, 575–578.

McAdams, D.P. (1999). Personal narratives and the life story. In L. Pervin and O. John (Eds.), *Handbook of personality: Theory and research* (2nd Ed., pp. 478–500). New York: Guilford Press.

McAdams, D.P., Booth, L., & Selvik, R. (1981). Religious identity among students at a private college: Social motives, ego stage, and development. *Merrill-Palmer Quarterly*, *27*, 219–239.

McAdams, D.P., & Bowman, P.J. (in press). Narrating life's turning points: Redemption and contamination. In D.P. McAdams, R. Josselson, and A. Lieblich (Eds.), *Life transitions and turning points: The narrative study of lives*. Washington, D.C.: APA Press.

McAdams, D.P., Bowman, P.J., Lewis, M., Hart, H.M., & Cole, E. (in press). Generativity and the construction of life stories among African-American adults: A qualitative study.

McAdams, D.P., & Bryant, F. (1987). Intimacy motivation and subjective mental health in a nationwide sample. *Journal of Personality*, *55*, 395–413.

McAdams, D.P., & Constantian, C.A. (1983). Intimacy and affiliation motives in daily living: An experience sampling analysis. *Journal of Personality and Social Psychology*, *45*, 851–861.

McAdams, D.P., Diamond, A., de St. Aubin, E., & Mansfield, E. (1997). Stories of commitment: The psychosocial construction of generative lives.

Journal of Personality and Social Psychology, *72*, 678–694.

McAdams, D.P., & de St. Aubin, E. (1992). A theory of generativity and its assessment through self-report, behavioral acts, and narrative themes in autobiography. *Journal of Personality and Social Psychology*, *62*, 1003–1015.

McAdams, D.P., de St. Aubin, E., & Logan, R.L. (1993). Generativity among young, midlife, and older adults. *Psychology and Aging*, *8*, 221–230.

McAdams, D.P., Healy, S., & Krause, S. (1984). Social motives and patterns of friendship. *Journal of Personality and Social Psychology*, *47*, 828–838.

McAdams, D.P., Hart, H.M., & Maruna, S. (1998). The anatomy of generativity. In D.P. McAdams and E. de St. Aubin (Eds.), *Generativity and adult development: How and why we care for the next generation* (pp. 7–43). Washington, D.C.: APA Press.

McAdams, D.P., Hoffman, B.J., Mansfield, E.D., & Day, R. (1996). Themes of agency and communion in significant autobiographical scenes. *Journal of Personality*, *64*, 339–377.

McAdams, D.P., Jackson, R.J., & Kirshnit, C. (1984). Looking, laughing, and smiling in dyads as a function of intimacy motivation and reciprocity. *Journal of Personality*, *52*, 261–273.

McAdams, D.P., Lensky, D.B., Daple, S.A., & Allen, J. (1988). Depression and the organization of autobiographical memory. *Journal of Social and Clinical Psychology*, *7*, 332–349.

McAdams, D.P., Lester, R., Brand, P., McNamara, W., &

Lensky, D.B. (1988). Sex and the TAT: Are women more intimate than men? Do men fear intimacy? *Journal of Personality Assessment*, *52*, 397–409.

McAdams, D.P., & Losoff, M. (1984). Friendship motivation in fourth and sixth graders: A thematic analysis. *Journal of Social and Personal Relationships*, *1*, 11–27.

McAdams, D.P., & Ochberg, R.L. (Eds.). (1988). *Psychobiography and life narratives*. Durham, NC: Duke University Press.

McAdams, D.P., & Powers, J. (1981). Themes of intimacy in behavior and thought. *Journal of Personality and Social Psychology*, *40*, 573–587.

McAdams, D.P., Reynolds, J., Lewis, M., Patten, A.H., & Bowman, P.J. (in press). When bad things turn good and good things turn bad: Sequences of redemption and contamination in life narrative and their relation to psychosocial adaptation in midlife adults and in students. *Personality and Social Psychology Bulletin*.

McAdams, D.P., Rothman, S., & Lichter, S.R. (1982). Motivational profiles: A study of former political radicals and politically moderate adults. *Personality and Social Psychology Bulletin*, *8*, 593–603.

McAdams, D.P., Ruetzel, K., & Foley, J.M. (1986). Complexity and generativity at mid-life: Relations among social motives, ego development, and adults' plans for the future. *Journal of Personality and Social Psychology*, *50*, 800–807.

McAdams, D.P., & Vaillant, G.E. (1982). Intimacy motivation and psychosocial adjustment: A longitudinal study. *Journal of Personality Assessment, 46*, 586–593.

McAdams, D.P., & West, S. (1997). Introduction: Personality psychology and the case study. *Journal of Personality, 65*, 757–783.

McClelland, D.C. (1951). *Personality*. New York: Holt, Rinehart & Winston.

McClelland, D.C. (1961). *The achieving society*. New York: D. Van Nostrand.

McClelland, D.C. (1963). The Harlequin complex. In R.W. White (Ed.), *The study of lives* (pp. 94–119). New York: Holt, Rinehart & Winston.

McClelland, D.C. (1965). *N* achievement and entrepreneurship: A longitudinal study. *Journal of Personality and Social Psychology, 1*, 389–392.

McClelland, D.C. (1975). *Power: The inner experience*. New York: Irvington.

McClelland, D.C. (1979). Inhibited power motivation and high blood pressure in men. *Journal of Abnormal Psychology, 88*, 182–190.

McClelland, D.C. (1980). Motive dispositions: The merits of operant and respondent measures. In L. Wheeler (Ed.), *Review of personality and social psychology* (Vol. 1, pp. 10–41). Beverly Hills, CA: Sage.

McClelland, D.C. (1981). Is personality consistent? In A.I. Rabin, J. Aronoff, A.M. Barclay, & R.A. Zucker (Eds.), *Further explorations in personality* (pp. 87–113). New York: John Wiley & Sons.

McClelland, D.C. (1985). *Human motivation*. Glenview, IL: Scott, Foresman.

McClelland, D.C., Alexander, C., & Marks, E. (1982). The need for power, stress, immune function, and illness among male prisoners. *Journal of Abnormal Psychology, 91*, 61–70.

McClelland, D.C., Atkinson, J.W., Clark, R.A., & Lowell, E.L. (1953). *The achievement motive*. New York: Appleton-Century-Crofts.

McClelland, D.C., & Boyatzis, R.E. (1982). The leadership motive pattern and long term success in management. *Journal of Applied Psychology, 67*, 737–743.

McClelland, D.C., & Burnham, D.H. (1976). Power is the great motivator. *Harvard Business Review*, March-April, 100–110, 159–166.

McClelland, D.C., Davidson, R.J., Floor, E., & Saron, C. (1980). Stressed power motivation, sympathetic activation, immune function, and illness. *Journal of Human Stress, 6*, (2), 11–19.

McClelland, D.C., Davis, W.N., Kalin, R., & Wanner, E. (1972). *The drinking man: Alcohol and human motivation*. New York: The Free Press.

McClelland, D.C., & Franz, C.E. (1992). Motivational and other sources of work accomplishments in midlife: A longitudinal study. *Journal of Personality, 60*, 679–707.

McClelland, D.C., & Jemmott, J.B., III (1980). Power motivation, stress, and physical illness. *Journal of Human Stress, 6*(4), 6–15.

McClelland, D.C., Koestner, R., & Weinberger, J. (1989). How do self-attributed and implicit motives differ? *Psychological Review, 96*, 690–702.

McClelland, D.C., Ross, G., & Patel, V. (1985). The effect of an academic examination on salivary norepinephrine and immunoglobulin levels. *Journal of Human Stress, 11*(2), 52–59.

McClelland, D.C. & Steele, R.S. (1972). *Motivation workshops*. New York: General Learning Press.

McCrae, R.R., & Costa, P.T., Jr. (1980). Openness to experience and ego level in Loevinger's Sentence Completion Test: Dispositional contributions to developmental models of personality. *Journal of Personality and Social Psychology, 39*, 1179–1190.

McCrae, R.R., & Costa, P.T., Jr. (1984). Personality is transcontextual: A reply to Veroff. *Personality and Social Psychology Bulletin, 10*, 175–179.

McCrae, R.R., & Costa, P.T., Jr. (1985a). Updating Norman's "adequate taxonomy": Intelligence and personality dimensions in natural language and in questionnaires. *Journal of Personality and Social Psychology, 49*, 710–721.

McCrae, R.R., & Costa, P.T. Jr. (1985b). Openness to experience. In R. Hogan and W.H. Jones (Ed.), *Perspectives in personality* (Vol. 1, pp. 145–172).

McCrae, R.R., & Costa, P.T., Jr. (1986). Personality, coping, and coping effectiveness in an adult sample. *Journal of Personality, 54*, 385–405.

McCrae, R.R., & Costa, P.T., Jr. (1987). Validation of the five-factor model of personality across instruments and observers. *Journal of Personality and Social Psychology, 52,* 81–90.

McCrae, R.R., & Costa, P.T., Jr. (1989). The structure of interpersonal traits: Wiggins' circumplex and the five-factor model. *Journal of Personality and Social Psychology, 56,* 586–595.

McCrae, R.R., & Costa, P.T., Jr. (1990). *Personality in adulthood.* New York: Guilford Press.

McCrae, R.R., & Costa, P.T., Jr. (1991). Adding *Liebe und Arbeit:* The full five-factor model and well-being. *Personality and Social Psychology Bulletin, 17,* 227–232.

McCrae, R.R., & Costa, P.T., Jr. (1995). Trait explanations in personality psychology. *European Journal of Personality, 9,* 231–252.

McCrae, R.R., & Costa, P.T., Jr. (1996). Toward a new generation of personality theories: Theoretical contexts for the five-factor model. In J. Wiggins (Ed.), *The five-factor model of personality: Theoretical perspectives* (pp. 51–87). New York: Guilford Press.

McCrae, R.R., & Costa, P.T., Jr. (1997a). Conceptions and correlates of openness to experience. In R. Hogan, J. Johnson, and S. Briggs (Eds.), *Handbook of personality psychology* (pp. 825–847). San Diego, CA: Academic Press.

McCrae, R.R., & Costa, P.T., Jr. (1997b). Personality trait structure as a human universal. *American Psychologist, 52,* 509–516.

McCrae, R.R., Costa, P.T., Jr., de Lima, M.P., Simoes, A., Osten-

dorf, F., Angleitner, A., Marusic, I., Bratko, D., Caprara, G.V., Barbaranelli, C., Chae, J-H., & Piedmont, R.L. (in press). Age differences in personality across the adult lifespan: Parallels in five cultures. *Developmental Psychology.*

McCrae, R.R., & John, O.P. (1992). An introduction to the five-factor model and its applications. *Journal of Personality, 60,* 175–215.

McDougall, W. (1908). *Social psychology.* London: Methuen.

McDowall, J. (1984). Recall of pleasant and unpleasant words in depressed subjects. *Journal of Abnormal Psychology, 93,* 401–407.

McFarland, S.G., Ageyev, V.S., & Abalakina-Papp, M.A. (1992). Authoritarianism in the former Soviet Union. *Journal of Personality and Social Psychology, 63,* 1004–1010.

McGinnies, E. (1949). Emotionality and perceptual defense. *Psychological Review, 56,* 244–251.

McGue, M., Bacon, S., & Lykken, D.T. (1993). Personality stability and change in early adulthood: A behavioral genetic analysis. *Developmental Psychology, 29,* 96–109.

McKenna, F.P. (1984). Measures of field dependence: Cognitive style or cognitive ability? *Journal of Personality and Social Psychology, 47,* 593–603.

Mead, G.H. (1934). *Mind, self, and society.* Chicago: University of Chicago Press.

Meehl, P.E. (1954). *Clinical versus statistical prediction: A theoretical analysis and a review of the evidence.* Minneapolis, MN: University of Minnesota Press.

Meloen, J.D., Hagendoorn, L., Raaijmakers, Q., & Visser, L. (1988). Authoritarianism and the revival of political racism: Reassessments in the Netherlands of the reliability and validity of the concept of authoritarianism by Adorno et al. *Political Psychology, 9,* 413–429.

Mercer, R.T., Nichols, E.G., & Doyle, G.C. (1989). *Transitions in a woman's life: Major life events in developmental context.* New York: Springer.

Meyer, G.J., & Shack, J.R. (1989). Structural convergence of mood and personality: Evidence for old and new directions. *Journal of Personality and Social Psychology, 57,* 691–706.

Mikulincer, M. (1995). Attachment style and the mental representation of the self. *Journal of Personality and Social Psychology, 69,* 1203–1215.

Mikulincer, M. (1997). Adult attachment style and information processing: Individual differences in curiosity and cognitive closure. *Journal of Personality and Social Psychology, 72,* 1217–1230.

Mikulincer, M., Florian, V., & Weller, A. (1993). Attachment styles, coping strategies, and posttraumatic psychological distress: The impact of the Gulf War in Israel. *Journal of Personality and Social Psychology, 64,* 817–826.

Mikulincer, M., & Nachson, O. (1991). Attachment styles and patterns of self-disclosure. *Journal of Personality and Social Psychology, 61,* 321–331.

Mikulincer, M., & Orbach, I. (1995). Attachment styles and repressive defensiveness: The accessibility and architecture of affective memories. *Journal of Personality and Social Psychology, 68,* 917–925.

Miles, D.R., & Carey, G. (1997). Genetic and environmental architecture of human aggression. *Journal of Personality and Social Psychology, 72,* 207–217.

Miller, G.A., Galanter, E., & Pribram, K.H. (1960). *Plans and the structure of behavior.* New York: Holt, Rinehart & Winston.

Miller, J.G. (1984). Culture and the development of everyday social explanation. *Journal of Personality and Social Psychology, 46,* 961–978.

Miller, N.E., & Dollard, J. (1941). *Social learning and imitation.* New Haven, CT: Yale University Press.

Miller, P.C., Lefcourt, H.M., Holmes, J.G., Ware, E.E., & Saleh, W.E. (1986). Marital locus of control and marital problem solving. *Journal of Personality and Social Psychology, 51,* 161–169.

Miller, W.R., & C'deBaca, J. (1994). Quantum change: Toward a psychology of transformation. In T.H. Heatherton and J.L. Weinberger (Eds.), *Can personality change?* (pp. 253–280). Washington, D.C.: APA Press.

Mills, C.W. (1959). *The sociological imagination.* New York: Oxford University Press.

Millon, T. (1973). (Ed.). *Theories of psychopathology and personality* (2nd ed.). Philadelphia: W.B. Saunders.

Mink, L.O. (1978). Narrative form as a cognitive instrument. In R.H. Canary and H. Kozicki (Eds.), *Literary form and histori-* *cal understanding* (pp. 129–149). Madison, WI: University of Wisconsin Press.

Minuchin, S. (1974). *Families and family therapy.* Cambridge, MA: Harvard University Press.

Mischel, W. (1961). Delay of gratification, need for achievement, and acquiescence in another culture. *Journal of Abnormal and Social Psychology, 62,* 543–552.

Mischel, W. (1968). *Personality and assessment.* New York: John Wiley & Sons.

Mischel, W. (1973). Toward a cognitive social learning reconceptualization of personality. *Psychological Review, 80,* 252–283.

Mischel, W. (1977). On the future of personality measurement. *American Psychologist, 32,* 246–254.

Mischel, W. (1979). On the interface of cognition and personality: Beyond the person-situation debate. *American Psychologist, 34,* 740–754.

Mischel, W. (1983). Delay of gratification as process and as person variable in development. In D. Magnusson and V.P. Allen (Eds.), *Interactions in human development* (pp. 149–165). New York: Academic Press.

Mischel, W. (1999). Personality coherence and dispositions in a cognitive-affective personality system (CAPS) approach. In D. Cervone and Y. Shoda (Eds.), *The coherence of personality: Social-cognitive bases of consistency, variability, and organization* (pp. 61–93). *New York: Guilford Press.*

Mischel, W., & Gilligan, C. (1964). Delay of gratification, motivation for the prohibited gratification, and response to temptation. *Journal of Abnormal and Social Psychology, 69,* 411–417.

Mischel, W., & Peake, P.K. (1982). Beyond déjà vu in the search for cross-situational consistency. *Psychological Review, 89,* 730–755.

Mischel, W., & Shoda, Y. (1995). A cognitive-affective system theory of personality: Reconceptualizing situations, dispositions, dynamics, and invariance in personality structure. *Psychological Review, 102,* 246–268.

Mischel, W., & Shoda, Y. (1998). Reconciling processing dynamics and personality dispositions. In J.T. Spence, J.M. Darley, and D.J. Foss (Eds.), *Annual review of psychology* (pp. 229–258). Palo Alto, CA: Annual Reviews, Inc.

Mishima, Y. (1958). *Confessions of a mask.* New York: New Directions Books.

Mishima, Y. (1970). *Sun and steel.* New York: Grove Press.

Mishler, E. (1992). Work, identity, and narrative: An artist-craftsman's story. In G.C. Rosenwald and R.L. Ochberg (Eds.), *Storied lives: The cultural politics of self-understanding* (pp. 21–40). New Haven, CT: Yale University Press.

Mitchell, J.C. (1983). Case and situation analysis. *The Sociological Review, 31,* 187–211.

Modell, J. (1992). How do you introduce yourself as a childless mother? Birthparent interpretations of parenthood. In G.C. Rosenwald and R.L. Ochberg (Eds.), *Storied lives: The cultural politics of self-understanding* (pp.

76–94). New Haven, CT: Yale University Press.

Moen, P., Elder, G.H., Jr., & Luscher, K. (Eds.). (1995). *Examining lives in context: Perspectives on the ecology of human development.* Washington, D.C.: American Psychological Association Press.

Moffitt, K.H., & Singer, J.A. (1994). Continuity in the life story: Self-defining memories, affect, and approach/avoidance personal strivings. *Journal of Personality, 62,* 21–43.

Monte, C.F. (1995). *Beneath the mask: An introduction to theories of personality* (5th Ed.). Fort Worth, TX: Harcourt Brace.

Moos, R.H. (1973). Conceptualizations of human environments. *American Psychologist, 28,* 652–665.

Moos, R.H. (1974). Systems for the assessment and classifications of human environments: An overview. In R.H. Moos and P.M. Insel (Eds.), *Issues in social ecology* (pp. 5–28). Palo Alto, CA: National Press Books.

Moos, R.H. (1976). *The human context: Environmental determinants of behavior.* New York: John Wiley & Sons.

Moraitis, G., & Pollack, G.H. (Eds.). (1987). *Psychoanalytic studies of biography.* Madison, CT: International Universities Press.

Morris, D. (1967). *The naked ape.* New York: McGraw-Hill.

Mortimer, J.T., Finch, M.D., & Kumka, D. (1982). Persistence and change in development: The multidimensional self-concept. In P.B. Baltes and O.G. Brim, Jr. (Eds.), *Life span development and behavior (Vol. 4, pp. 264–315). New York: Academic Press.*

Moskowitz, D.S. (1982). Coherence and cross-situational generality in personality: A new analysis of old problems. *Journal of Personality and Social Psychology, 43,* 754–768.

Moskowitz, D.S. (1990). Convergence of self-reports and independent observers: Dominance and friendliness. *Journal of Personality and Social Psychology, 58,* 1096–1106.

Mountjoy, P.J., & Sundberg, M.L. (1981). Ben Franklin the protobehaviorist I: Self-management of behavior. *The Psychological Record, 31,* 13–24.

Mroczek, D.K., & Kolarz, C.M. (1998). The effect of age on positive and negative affect: A developmental perspective on happiness. *Journal of Personality and Social Psychology, 75,* 1333–1349.

Mroczek, D.K., & Spiro, A. (in press). Modelling intraindividual change in personality: Findings from the Normative Aging Study.

Mumford, M., Stokes, G.S., & Owens, W.A. (1990). *Patterns of life history: The ecology of human individuality.* Hillsdale, NJ: Lawrence Erlbaum.

Murray, H.A. (1938). *Explorations in personality.* New York: Oxford University Press.

Murray, H.A. (1940). What should psychologists do about psychoanalysis? *Journal of Abnormal and Social Psychology, 35,* 150–175.

Murray, H.A. (1943). *The Thematic Apperception Test: Manual.* Cambridge, MA: Harvard University Press.

Murray, H.A. (1949). Introduction. In H. Melville, *Pierre, or the ambiguities* (pp. xiii–ciii). New York: Farar Straus.

Murray, H.A. (1951b). Some basic psychological assumptions and conceptions. *Dialectica, 5,* 266–292.

Murray, H.A. (1955/1981). American Icarus. In E.S. Shneidman (Ed.), *Endeavors in psychology: Selections from the personology of Henry A. Murray* (pp. 535–556). New York: Harper & Row.

Murray, H.A. (1959). Preparations for the scaffold of a comprehensive system. In S. Koch (Ed.), *Psychology: A study of a science.* New York: McGraw-Hill.

Murray, H.A. (1959/1981). Vicissitudes of creativity. In E.S. Schneidman (Ed.), *Endeavors in psychology: Selections from the personology of Henry A. Murray* (pp. 312–330). New York: Random House.

Murray, H.A. (1960/1981). Two versions of man. In E. Shneidman (Ed.), *Endeavors in psychology: Selections from the personology of Henry A. Murray* (pp. 581–604). New York: Harper & Row.

Murray, H.A. (1962). The personality and career of Satan. *Journal of Social Issues, 28,* 36–54.

Murray, H.A. (1966). Bartleby and I. In H.P. Vincent (Ed.), *Bartleby the scrivener* (pp. 3–24). Ohio: Kent State University Press.

Murray, H.A. (1967). The case of Murr. In E.G. Boring and G. Lindzey (Eds.), *A history of psychology in autobiography* (Vol. 5, pp. 285–310). New York: Appleton-Century-Crofts.

Murray, H.A. (1967). Dead to the world: Or the passions of Herman Melville. In E.J. Shneidman (Ed.), *Essays in self-destruction*. New York: Science House.

Murray, H.A., & Kluckhohn, C. (1953). Outline of a conception of personality. In C. Kluckhohn, H.A. Murray, and D. Schneider (Eds.), *Personality in nature, society, and culture* (2nd ed.) (pp. 3–52). New York: Knopf.

Murray, H.A. with staff. (1948). *Assessment of men*. New York: Rinehart & Co.

Murray, H.A. (1951a). *In nomine diaboli. New England Quarterly*, 24, 435–452.

Murray, K. (1989). The construction of identity in the narratives of romance and comedy. In J. Shotter and K.J. Gergen (Eds.), *Texts of identity* (pp. 176–205). London: Sage.

Muslin, H., & Gill, M. (1978). Transference in the Dora case. *Journal of the American Psychoanalytic Association*, 26, 311–328.

Myers, D.G., & Diener, E. (1995). Who is happy? *Psychological Science*, 6, 10–19.

Myers, L.B., & Brewin, C.R. (1994). Recall of early experience and the repressive coping style. *Journal of Abnormal Psychology*, 103, 288–292.

Nakagawa, K. (1991). *Explorations into the correlates of public school reform and parental involvement*. Unpublished doctoral dissertation, Human Development and Social Policy, Northwestern University, Evanston, IL.

Narayanan, L., Mensa, S., & Levine, E.L. (1995). Personality structure: A culture-specific examination of the five-factor model. *Journal of Personality Assessment*, 64, 51–62.

Nasby, W. (1985). Private self-consciousness, articulation of the self-schema, and the recognition memory of trait adjectives. *Journal of Personality and Social Psychology*, 49, 704–709.

Nasby, W., & Read, N. (1997). The life voyage of a solo circumnavigator: Integrating theoretical and methodological perspectives. Introduction. *Journal of Personality*.

Nathan, J. (1974). *Mishima: A biography*. Boston: Litle, Brown.

National Institute of Mental Health. (1982). *Television and behavior: Ten years of scientific progress and implications for the eighties* (Vol. 1). Washington, DC: U.S. Department of Health and Human Services.

Neisser, U. (1976). *Cognition and reality: Principles and implications of cognitive psychology*. San Francisco, CA: W.H. Freeman.

Nemiah, J.C. (1984). The unconscious and psychopathology. In K.J. Bowers and D. Meichenbaum (Eds.), *The unconscious reconsidered* (pp. 49–87). New York: John Wiley & Sons.

Neugarten, B.L. (Ed.). (1968). *Middle age and aging*. Chicago: University of Chicago Press.

Neugarten, B.L. (1979). Time, age, and the life cycle. *American Journal of Psychiatry*, 136, 887–894.

Neugarten, B.L., & Datan, N. (1974). The middle years. In S. Arieti (Ed.), *American handbook of psychiatry* (Vol. 1). New York: Basic Books.

Nichols, S.L., & Newman, J.P. (1986). Effects of punishment on response latency in extraverts. *Journal of Personality*

and Social Psychology, 50, 624–630.

Nikula, R., Klinger, E., & Larson-Gutman, M.K. (1993). Current concerns and electrodermal reactivity: Responses to words and thoughts. *Journal of Research in Personality*, 61, 63–84.

Niitamo, P. (1999). *"Surface" and "depth" in human personality: Relations between explicit and implicit motives*. Helsinki: Finnish Institute of Occupational Health.

Nisbett, R.E., & Ross, L.D. (1980). *Human inference: Strategies and shortcomings of social judgment*. Englewood Cliffs, NJ: Prentice Hall.

Noam, G. (1998). Solving the ego development-mental health riddle. In P.M. Westenberg, A. Blasi, and L.D. Cohn (Eds.), *Personality development: Theoretical, empirical, and clinical investigations of Loevinger's conception of ego development* (pp. 271–295). Mahwah, NJ: Erlbaum.

Nolen-Hoeksema, S., Girgus, J.S., & Seligman, M.E.P. (1986). Learned helplessness in children: A longitudinal study of depression, achievement, and explanatory style. *Journal of Personality and Social Psychology*, 51, 435–442.

Norem, J.K. (1989). Cognitive strategies as personality: Effectiveness, specificity, flexibility, and change. In D.M. Buss and N. Cantor (Eds.), *Personality psychology: Recent trends and emerging directions* (pp. 45–60). New York: Springer-Verlag.

Norem, J.K. & Cantor, N. (1986). Defensive pessimism: Harnessing anxiety as motivation. *Journal of Personality and Social Psychology, 51,* 1208–1217.

Norman, R.M.G., & Watson, L.D. (1976). Extraversion and reactions to cognitive inconsistency. *Journal of Research in Personality, 10,* 446–456.

Norman, W.T. (1963). Toward an adequate taxonomy of personality attributes: Replicated factor structure in peer nomination personality ratings. *Journal of Abnormal and Social Psychology, 66,* 574–583.

Norman, W.T. (1967). *2800 personality trait descriptors: Normative operating characteristics for a university population.* Ann Arbor, MI: University of Michigan, Department of Psychology.

Novacek, J., & Lazarus, R.S. (1990). The structure of personal commitments. *Journal of Personality, 58,* 693–715.

Noy. P. (1979). Form creation in art: An ego-psychological approach to creativity. *Psychoanalytic Quarterly, 48,* 229–257.

Nucci, L. (1981). Conceptions of personal issues: A domain distinct from moral or societal concepts. *Child Development, 52,* 114–121.

O'Brien, R., & Dukore, B.F. (1969) *Tragedy: Ten major plays* (Sophocles' *Oedipus Rex.*) New York: Bantom Books.

Ochberg, R.L. (1988). Life stories and the psychosocial construction of careers. *Journal of Personality, 56,* 173–204.

Ochse, R., & Plug, C. (1986). Cross-cultural investigations of the validity of Erikson's theory of personality development. *Journal of Personality and Social Psychology, 50,* 1240–1252.

Ogilvie, D.M. (1987). The undesired self: A neglected variable in personality research. *Journal of Personality and Social Psychology, 52,* 379–385.

Ogilvie, D.M., & Ashmore, R.D. (1991). Self-with-other representation as unit of analysis in self-concept research. In R.A. Curtis (Ed.), *The relational self: Theoretical convergences in psychoanalysis and social psychology* (pp. 282–314). New York: Guilford Press.

Ogilvie, D.M., Fleming, C.J., & Pennell, G.E. (1998). Self-with-Other representations. In D.F. Barone, M. Hersen, and V.B. Van Hasselt (Eds.), *Advanced personality* (pp. 353–376). New York: Plenum Press.

Oliner, S.P., & Oliner, P.M. (1988). *The altruistic personality: Rescuers of Jews in Nazi Europe.* New York: The Free Press.

Ones, D.S., Viswesvaran, C., & Schmidt, F.L. (1993). Comprehensive meta-analysis of integrity test validation: Findings and implications for personnel selection and theories of job performance. *Journal of Applied Psychology, 78,* 679–703.

Orlofsky, J.L. (1978). Identity formation, achievements, and fear of success in college men and women. *Journal of Youth and Adolescence, 7,* 49–62.

Orlofsky, J.L., & Frank, M. (1986). Personality structure as viewed through early memories and identity status in college men and women. *Journal of Personality and Social Psychology, 50,* 580–586.

Orlofsky, J.L., Marcia, J.E., & Lesser, I.M. (1973). Ego identity status and the intimacy ver-

sus isolation crisis of young adulthood. *Journal of Personality and Social Psychology, 27,* 211–219.

Ormel, J., & Wohlfarth, T. (1991). How neuroticism, long-term difficulties, and life situation changes influence psychological distress: A longitudinal model. *Journal of Personality and Social Psychology, 60,* 744–755.

Osborne, J. (1961). *Luther.* New York: Criterion Books.

Oshman, H., & Manosevitz, M. (1974). The impact of the identity crisis on the adjustment of late adolescent males. *Journal of Youth and Adolescence, 3,* 107–216.

Ozer, D.J. (1986). *Consistency in personality: A methodological framework.* New York: Springer-Verlag.

Ozer, D.J., & Gjerde, P.F. (1989). Patterns of personality consistency and change from childhood thorugh adolescence. *Journal of Personality, 57,* 483–507.

Ozer, E.M., & Bandura, A. (1990). Mechanisms governing empowering effects: A self-efficacy analysis. *Journal of Personality and Social Psychology, 58,* 472–486.

Pachter, M. (Ed.). (1979). *Telling lives: The biographer's art.* Washington, DC: New Republic Books.

Pals, J.L., & John, O.P. (1998). How are dimensions of adult personality related to ego development? An application of the typological approach. In P.M. Westenberg, A. Blasi, and L. Cohn (Eds.), *Personality development: Theoretical, empirical, and clinical investigations of Jane*

Loevinger's conception of ego development (pp. 113–132). Hillsdale, NJ: Erlbaum.

Palys, T.S., & Little, B.R. (1983). Perceived life satisfaction and the organization of personal project systems. *Journal of Personality and Social Psychology, 44,* 1221–1230.

Parke, R.D., & Walters, R.H. (1967). Some factors influencing the efficacy of punishment training for inducing response inhibitions. *Monographs of the Society for Research in Child Development, 32,* (1, Serial No. 109).

Parker, C.R., Bolling, M.Y., & Kohlenberg, R.J. (1998). Operant theory of personality. In D.F. Barone, M. Hersen, and V.B. Van Hasselt (Eds.), *Advanced personality* (pp. 155–171). New York: Plenum.

Passini, F.T., & Norman, W.T. (1966). A universal conception of personality structure? *Journal of Personality and Social Psychology, 4,* 44–49.

Patterson, C.M., Kosson, D.J., & Newman, J.P. (1987). Reaction to punishment, reflectivity, and passive avoidance learning in extraverts. *Journal of Personality and Social Psychology, 52,* 565–575.

Paulhus, D.L., & Martin, C.L. (1987). The structure of personality capabilities. *Journal of Personality and Social Psychology, 52,* 354–365.

Paulhus, D.L., Fridhandler, B., & Hayes, S. (1997). Psychological defense: Contemporary theory and research. In R. Hogan, J. Johnson, and S. Briggs (Eds.), *Handbook of personality psychology* (pp. 543–579). San Diego, CA: Academic Press.

Paunonen, S.V. (1998). Hierarchical organization of personality and prediction of behavior. *Journal of Personality and Social Psychology, 74,* 538–556.

Paunonen, S.V., Jackson, D.N., & Keinonen, M. (1990). The structured nonverbal assessment of personality. *Journal of Personality, 58,* 481–502.

Paunonen, S.V., Jackson, D.N., Trzebinski, J., & Fosterling, F. (1992). Personality structure across cultures: A multimethod evaluation. *Journal of Personality and Social Psychology, 62,* 447–456.

Paykel, E.S., Emms, E.M., Fletcher, J., & Rassaby, E.S. (1980). Life events and social support in puerperal depression. *British Journal of Psychiatry, 136,* 339–346.

Pearce-McCall, D., & Newman, J.P. (1986). Expectation of success following noncontingent punishment in introverts and extraverts. *Journal of Personality and Social Psychology, 50,* 439–446.

Pearson, C.S. (1986). *The hero within: Sex archetypes we live by.* New York: Harper & Row.

Pederson, D.R., Moran, G., Sitko, C., Campbell, K., Ghesquire, K., & Acton, H. (1990). Maternal sensitivity and the security of infant-mother attachment: A Q-sort study. *Child Development, 61,* 1974–1983.

Pekala, R.J., Wenger, C.F., & Levine, R.L. (1985). Individual differences in phenomenological experience: States of consciousness as a function of absorption. *Journal of Personality and Social Psychology, 48,* 125–132.

Pellegrini, A.D., & Galda, L. (1990). The joint construction of stories by preschool children and an experimenter. In B.K. Britten and A.D. Pellegrini (Eds.), *Narrative thought and narrative language* (pp. 113–130). Hillsdale, NJ: Lawrence Erlbaum.

Pennebaker, J.W. (1988). Confiding traumatic experiences and health. In S. Fisher and J. Reason (Eds.), *Handbook of life stress, cognition, and health* (pp. 669–682). New York: Wiley.

Pennebaker, J.W. (1989a). Stream of consciousness and stress: Levels of thinking. In J.S. Uleman and J.A. Bargh (Eds.), *Unintended thought* (pp. 327–349). New York: Guilford Press.

Pennebaker, J.W. (1989b). Confession, inhibition, and disease. In L. Berkowitz (Ed.), *Advances in experimental social psychology* (Vol. 22, pp. 211–244). New York: Academic Press.

Pennebaker, J.W. (1992). Putting stress into words: Health, linguistic, and therapeutic implications. Paper presented at the American Psychological Association Convention, Washington, DC.

Pennebaker, J.W. (1997). Writing about emotional experiences as a therapeutic process. *Psychological Science, 8,* 162–166.

Pennebaker, J.W., & Beall, S.K. (1986). Confronting a traumatic event: Toward an understanding of inhibition and disease. *Journal of Abnormal Psychology, 95,* 274–281.

Pennebaker, J.W., Kiecolt-Glaser, J.K., & Glaser, R. (1988). Disclosure of traumas and immune function: Health implications for psychotherapy. *Journal of Consulting and Clinical Psychology, 56,* 239–245.

Pennebaker, J.W., & O'Heeron, R.C. (1984). Confiding in others and illness rate among spouses of suicide and accidental death victims. *Journal of Abnormal Psychology, 93,* 473–476.

Pepper, S. (1942). *World hypotheses.* Berkeley, CA: University of California Press.

Perry, W.C. (1970). *Forms of intellectual and ethical development in the college years.* New York: Holt, Rinehart & Winston.

Pervin, L.A. (1989). (Ed.). *Goal concepts in personality and social psychology.* Hillsdale, NJ: Lawrence Erlbaum.

Pervin. L. (1990). (Ed.). *Handbook of personality theory and research.* New York: Guilford Press.

Pervin, L. (1996). *The science of personality.* New York: Wiley.

Peterson, B.E., Doty, R.M., & Winter, D.G. (1993). Authoritarianism and attitudes toward contemporary social issues. *Personality and Social Psychology Bulletin, 19,* 174–184.

Peterson, B.E., & Klohnen, E.C. (1995). Realization of generativity in two samples of women at midlife. *Psychology and Aging, 10,* 20–29.

Peterson, B.E., & Stewart, A.J. (1990). Using personal and fictional documents to assess psychosocial development: The case study of Vera Brittain's generativity. *Psychology and Aging, 5,* 400–411.

Peterson, C., Luborsky, L., & Seligman, M.E.P. (1983). Attributions and depressive mood shifts: A case study using the symptom–context method. *Journal of Abnormal Psychology, 92,* 96–103.

Peterson, B.E., Smirles, K.A., & Wentworth, P.A. (1997). Generativity and authoritarianism: Implications for personality, political involvement, and parenting. *Journal of Personality and Social Psychology, 72,* 1202–1216.

Peterson, B.E., & Stewart, A.J. (1996). Antecedents and contexts of generativity motivation at midlife. *Psychology and Aging, 11,* 21–33.

Peterson, C., & Seligman, M.E.P. (1984). Causal explanations as a risk factor for depression: Theory and evidence. *Psychological Review, 91,* 347–374.

Peterson, C., Seligman, M.E.P., & Vaillant, G.E. (1988). Pessimistic explanatory style is a risk factor for physical illness: A thirty-five year longitudinal study. *Journal of Personality and Social Psychology, 55,* 23–27.

Peterson, C., Seligman, M.E.P., Yurko, K.H., Martin, L.R., & Friedman, H.S. (1998). Catastrophizing and untimely death. *Psychological Science, 9,* 127–130.

Peterson, C., Villanova, P., & Raps, C.S. (1985). Depression and attributions: Factors responsible for inconsistent results in the published literature. *Journal of Abnormal Psychology, 94,* 165–168.

Pettigrew, T.F. (1997). Personality and social structure: Social psychological contributions. In R. Hogan, J. Johnson, and S. Briggs (Eds.), *Handbook of personality psychology* (pp. 417–438). San Diego, CA: Academic Press.

Petty, R.E., & Cacioppo, J.T. (1981). *Attitudes and persuasion: Classical and contemporary approaches.* Dubuque, IA: Wm. C. Brown.

Phares, E.J. (1957). Expectancy changes in skill and chance situations. *Journal of Abnormal and Social Psychology, 54,* 339–342.

Phares, E.J. (1978). Locus of control. In H. London and J.E. Exner, Jr. (Eds.), *Dimensions of personality* (pp. 263–304). New York: John Wiley & Sons.

Phares, E.J. (1984). *Introduction to personality.* Glenview, IL: Scott, Foresman and Company.

Phares, E.J. (1988). *Introduction to personality* (2nd ed.). Glenview, IL: Scott, Foresman and Company.

Piaget, J. (1952). *The origins of intelligence in children.* New York: International Universities Press.

Piaget, J. (1965). *The moral judgment of the child.* New York: The Free Press.

Piaget, J. (1970). *Genetic epistemology.* New York: Columbia University Press.

Pilkonis, P.A. (1977). The behavioral consequences of shyness. *Journal of Personality, 45,* 596–611.

Pillemer, D.B. (1998). *Momentous events, vivid memories.* Cambridge, MA: Harvard University Press.

Pinker, S. (1997). *How the mind works.* New York: Norton.

Plomin, R., & Bergman, C.S. (1991). The nature of nurture: Genetic influences on "environmental" measures. *Behavioral and Brain Sciences, 14,* 373–386.

Plomin, R., Chipuer, H.M., & Loehlin, J.C. (1990). Behavioral genetics and personality. In L. Pervin (Ed.), *Handbook of personality theory and research* (pp. 225–243). New York: Guilford Press.

Plomin, R., DeFries, J.C., & McClearn, G.E. (1980). *Behavior genetics: A primer.* San Francisco: Freeman.

Plomin, R., Lichtenstein, P., Pederson, N.L., McClearn, G.E., & Nesselroade, J.R. (1990). Genetic influence on life events during the last half of the life span. *Psychology and Aging, 5,* 25–30.

Podd, M.H. (1972). Ego identity status and morality: The relationships between two developmental constructs. *Developmental Psychology, 6,* 497–507.

Polkinghorne, D. (1988). *Narrative knowing and the human sciences.* Albany, NY: State University of New York: Press.

Popper, K. (1959). *The logic of scientific discovery.* New York: Basic Books.

Porter, C.A., & Suedfeld, P. (1981). Integrative complexity in the correspondence of literary figures: Effects of personal and societal stress. *Journal of Personality and Social Psychology, 40,* 321–330.

Postman, L., Bruner, J.S., & McGinnies, E. (1948). Personal values as selective factors in perception. *Journal of Abnormal and Social Psychology, 32,* 142–154.

Powers, W.T. (1973). Feedback: Beyond behavorism. *Science, 179,* 351–356.

Pratt, M., Danso, H.A., Arnold, M.L., & Norris, J. (in press). Adults' generativity and the socialization of adolescents: Relations to mothers' and fathers' parenting styles, beliefs, practices, and goals.

Privette, G. (1983). Peak experience, peak performance, and flow: A comparative analysis of positive human experiences. *Journal of Personality and Social Psychology, 45,* 1361–1368.

Privette, G., & Landsman, T. (1983). Factor analysis of peak performance: The full use of potential. *Journal of Personality and Social Psychology, 44,* 195–200.

Proust, M. (1923/1934). *Remembrance of things past.* New York: Random House.

Quinn, S. (1988). *A mind of her own: The life of Karen Horney* (with a Foreword by Leon Edel). Reading, MA: Addison-Wesley.

Radke-Yarrow, M., Zahn-Waxler, C., & Chapman, M. (1983). Children's prosocial dispositions and behavior. In P.H. Mussen (Ed.), *Handbook of child psychology.* (4th ed.) Vol. 4: *Socialization, personality and social development* (pp. 469–546). New York: John Wiley & Sons.

Raskin, R.N., & Hall, C.J. (1979). A narcissistic personality inventory. *Psychological Reports, 45,* 590.

Raskin, R.N., & Hall, C.J. (1981). The Narcissistic Personality Inventory: Alternate form reliability and further evidence of construct validity. *Journal of Personality Assessment, 45,* 159–162.

Raskin, R.N., & Shaw, R. (1988). Narcissism and the use of personal pronouns. *Journal of Personality, 56,* 393–404.

Redman, E. (1973). *The dance of legislation.* New York: Simon & Schuster.

Redmore, C., Loevinger, J., & Tamashiro, R. (1978). *Measuring ego development: Scoring manual for men and boys.* Unpublished manuscript.

Redmore, C., & Waldman, K. (1975). Reliability of a sentence completion measure of ego development. *Journal of Personality Assessment, 39,* 236–243.

Reichenbach, H. (1938). *Experience and prediction.* Chicago, IL: University of Chicago Press.

Rescorla, R.A. (1987). A Pavlovian analysis of goal-directed behavior. *American Psychologist, 42,* 119–129.

Rescorla, R.A. (1988). Pavlovian conditioning: It's not what you think it is. *American Psychologist, 43,* 151–160.

Reuman, D.A., Alwin, D.F., & Veroff, J. (1984). Assessing the validity of the achievement motive in the presence of random measurement error. *Journal of Personality and Social Psychology, 47,* 1347–1362.

Revelle, W. (1995). Personality processes. In L.W. Porter and M.R. Rosenzweig (Eds.), *Annual review of psychology* (Vol. 46, pp. 295–328). Palo Alto, CA: Annual Reviews, Inc.

Rhodewalt, F., & Morf, C.C. (1995). Self and interpersonal correlates of the Narcissistic Personality Inventory: A review and new findings. *Journal of Research in Personality, 29,* 1–23.

Rhodewalt, F., & Morf, C.C. (1998). On self-aggrandizement and anger: A temporal analysis of narcissism and affective reactions to success and failure. *Journal of Personality and Social Psychology*, *74*, 672–685.

Ricoeur, P. (1970). *Freud and philosophy: An essay on interpretation*. New Haven, CT: Yale University Press.

Ricoeur, P. (1984). *Time and narrative* (Vol. 1). Chicago: University of Chicago Press. (Translated by Kathleen McGlaughlin and David Pellauer.).

Riemann, R., Angleitner, A., & Strelau, J. (1997). Genetic and environmental influences on personality: A study of twins reared together using self-and peer-repor (NEO-FFI scales. *Journal of Personality*, *65*, 449–475.

Rizzo, R., & Vinacke, E. (1975). Self-actualization and the meaning of critical experiences. *Journal of Humanistic Psychology*, *15*, 19–30.

Roberson, L. (1989). Development and validation of the Work Concerns Inventory: A measure of employee's work goals. *Organizational Behavior and Human Decision Processes*, *44*, 345–367.

Roberts, B.W. (1994). *A longitudinal study of the reciprocal relation between women's personality and occupational experience*. Unpublished doctoral dissertation, University of California, Berkeley.

Roberts, B.W., & Friend-DelVecchio, W. (in press). Consistency of personality traits across the life course: A quantitative review of longitudinal studies. *Psychological Bulletin*.

Roberts, J.E., Gotlib, I.H., & Kassel, J.D. (1996). Adult at-

tachment security and symptoms of depression: The mediating role of dysfunctional attitudes and low self-esteem. *Journal of Personality and Social Psychology*, *70*, 310–320.

Roberts, P., & Newton, P.M. (1987). Levinsonian studies of women's adult development. *Psychology and Aging*, *2*, 154–163.

Robins, C.J. (1988). Attributions and depression: Why is the literature so inconsistent? *Journal of Personality and Social Psychology*, *54*, 880–889.

Robinson, D.N. (1981). *An intellectual history of psychology*. New York: Macmillan.

Robinson, F.G. (1992). *Love's story told: A life of Henry A. Murray*. Cambridge, MA: Harvard University Press.

Robinson, J.A. (1976). Sampling autobiographical memory. *Cognitive Psychology*, *8*, 578–595.

Roche, S.M., & McConkey, K.M. (1990). Absorption: Nature, assessment, and correlates. *Journal of Personality and Social Psychology*, *59*, 91–101.

Roedinger, H.L. (1990). Implicit memory: Retention without remembering. *American Psychologist*, *45*, 1043–1056.

Rogers, C.R. (1942). *Counseling and psychotherapy: Newer concepts in practice*. Boston: Houghton.

Rogers, C.R. (1951). *Client-centered therapy*. Boston: Houghton-Mifflin.

Rogers, C.R. (1959). A theory of therapy, personality, and interpersonal relationships, as developed in the client-centered framework. In S. Koch (Ed.), *Psychology: A Study of a Science* (Vol. 3). New York: McGraw-Hill.

Rogers, C.R. (1980). Ellen West and loneliness. In C.R. Rogers, *A way of being*. Boston: Houghton-Mifflin.

Rokeach, M. (1973). *The nature of human values*. New York: The Free Press.

Romer, D., Gruder, C.L., & Lizzadro, T. (1986). A person-situation approach to altruistic behavior. *Journal of Personality and Social Psychology*, *51*, 1001–1012.

Rootes, M.D., Moras, K., & Gordon, R. (1980). Ego development and sociometrically evaluated maturity: An investigation of the validity of the Washington University Sentence-Completion Test of Ego Development. *Journal of Personality Assessment*, *44*, 613–620.

Rorer, L.G. (1991). Some myths of science in psychology. In D. Cicchetti and W. Grove (Eds.), *Thinking clearly about psychology: Essays in honor of Paul E. Meehl* (pp. 61–87). Minneapolis, MN: University of Minnesota Press.

Rosch, E. (1975). Cognitive reference points. *Cognitive Psychology*, *1*, 532–543.

Rosenberg, S. (1976). New approaches to the analysis of personal constructs in person perception. In A.W. Landfield (Ed.), *Nebraska symposium motivation* (Vol. 23). Lincoln, NE: University of Nebraska Press.

Rosenwald, G.C. (1968). The Thematic Apperception Test (TAT). In A.I. Rabin (Ed.). *Projective techniques in personality assessment* (pp. 172–221). New York: Springer.

Rosenwald, G.C., & Ochberg, R.L. (Eds.). (1992). *Storied lives: The cultural politics of self-under-*

standing. New Haven, CT: Yale University Press.

Ross, L.D. (1977). The intuitive psychologist and his shortcomings: Distortions in the attribution process. In L. Berkowitz (Ed.), *Advances in Experimental Social Psychology* (Vol. 10). New York: Academic Press.

Rossi, A.S. (1980). Life-span theories and women's lives. *Signs, 6*(1), 4–32.

Rosznafszky, J. (1981). The relationship of level of ego development to Q-sort personality ratings. *Journal of Personality and Social Psychology, 41,* 99–120.

Roth, P. (1988). *The facts: A novelist's autobiography.* London: Penguin.

Rothbart, M.K. (1986). Longitudinal observation of infant temperament. *Developmental Psychology, 22,* 356–365.

Rotter, J.B. (1954). *Social learning and clinical psychology.* Englewood Cliffs, NJ: Prentice-Hall.

Rotter, J.B. (1966). Generalized expectancies for internal versus external control of reinforcement. *Psychological Monographs, 80,* (1, Whole No. 609).

Rotter, J.B. (1972). *Applications of a social learning theory of personality.* New York: Holt.

Rotter, J.B. (1975). Some problems and misconceptions related to the construct of internal versus external reinforcement. *Journal of Consulting and Clinical Psychology, 43,* 56–67.

Rouse, J. (1978). *The completed gesture: Myth, character, and educatin.* New Jersey: Skyline Books.

Rowe, D.C. (1997). Genetics, temperament, and personality. In R. Hogan, J. Johnson, and S. Briggs (Eds.), *Handbook of personality psychology* (pp. 367–386). San Diego, CA: Academic Press.

Rowe, D.C. (1999). Heredity. In V.J. Derlega, B.A. Winstead, and W.H. Jones (Eds.), *Personality: Contemporary theory and research* (2nd Ed.) (pp. 66–100). Chicago: Nelson-Hall.

Royko, M. (1986). Modified Cub rule says bet the Mets. *Chicago Tribune,* October 17.

Ruehlman, L.S., West, S.G., & Pashahow, R.J. (1985). Depression and evaluative schemata. *Journal of Personality, 53,* 46–92.

Ruehlman, L.S., & Wolchik, S.A. (1988). Personal goals and interpersonal support and hindrance as factors in psychological distress and well-being. *Journal of Personality and Social Psychology, 55,* 293–301.

Runyan, W.M. (1981). Why did Van Gogh cut off his ear? The problem of alternative explanations in psychobiography. *Journal of Personality and Social Psychology, 40,* 1070–1077.

Runyan, W.M. (1982). *Life histories and psychobiography: Explorations in theory and method.* New York: Oxford University Press.

Runyan, W.M. (1990). Individual lives and the structure of personality psychology. In A.I. Rabin, R.A. Zucker, R.A. Emmons, and Frank (Eds), *Studying persons and lives* (pp. 10–40). New York: Springer.

Rushton, J.P. (1980). *Altruism, socialization, and society.* Englewood Cliffs, NJ: Prentice-Hall.

Rushton, J.P., Brainerd, C.J., & Presley, M. (1983). Behavioral development and construct validity: The principle of aggregation. *Psychological Bulletin, 94,* 18–38.

Rushton, J.P., Fulker, D.W., Neale, M.C., Nias, D.K., & Eysenck, H.J. (1986). Altruism and aggression: The heritability of individual differences. *Journal of Personality and Social Psychology, 50,* 1192–1198.

Russell, B. (1945). *A history of Western philosophy.* New York: Simon & Schuster.

Rutter, D.R., Morley, I.E., & Graham, J.C. (1972). Visual interaction in a group of introverts and extraverts. *European Journal of Social Psychology, 2,* 371–384.

Rutter, M. (1987). Temperament, personality, and personality disorder. *British Journal of Psychiatry, 150,* 443–458.

Ryan, R.M. (1991). The nature of the self in autonomy and relatedness. In J. Strauss and G.R. Goethals (Eds.), *The self: Interdisciplinary approaches* (pp. 208–238). New York: Springer-Verlag.

Ryan, R.M. (1995). Psychological needs and the facilitation of integrative processes. *Journal of Personality, 63,* 397–427.

Ryff, C.D., & Heincke, S.G. (1983). Subjective organization of personality in adulthood and aging. *Journal of Personality and Social Psychology, 44,* 807–816.

Sackheim, H.A. (1983). Self-deception, self-esteem, and depression: The adaptive value of lying to oneself. In J. Masling (Ed.), *Empirical studies of psychoanalytical theories* (Vol. 1. pp.

101–158). New York: The Analytic Press.

Sacks, O. (1985). *The man who mistook his wife for a hat, and other clinical tales*. New York: Summit Books.

Sales, S.M. (1973). Threat as a factor in authoritarianism: An analysis of archival data. *Journal of Personality and Social Psychology, 28*, 44–57.

Sampson, E.E. (1962). Birth order, need achievement, and conformity. *Journal of Abnormal and Social Psychology, 64*, 155–159.

Sampson, E.E. (1985). The decentralization of identity: Toward a revised concept of personal and social order. *American Psychologist, 40*, 1203–1211.

Sampson, E.E. (1988). The debate on individualism: Indigenous psychologies of the individual and their role in personal and societal functioning. *American Psychologist, 43*, 15–22.

Sampson, E.E. (1989a). The challenge of social change for psychology: Globalization and psychology's theory of the person. *American Psychologist, 44*, 914–921.

Sampson, E.E. (1989b). The deconstruction of the self. In J. Shotter and K.J. Gergen (Eds.), *Texts of identity* (pp. 1–19). London: Sage.

Sander, L.W. (1975). Infant and caretaking environment: Investigation and conceptualization of adaptive behavior in a system of increasing complexity. In J. Anthony (Ed.), *Explorations in child psychiatry* (pp. 129–165). New York: Plenum.

Sanderson, C.A., & Cantor, N. (1997). Creating satisfaction in steady dating relationships: The role of personal goals and situational affordances. *Journal of Personality and Social Psychology, 73*, 1424–1433.

Sarbin, T.R. (1986). The narrative as a root metaphor for psychology. In T.R. Sarbin (Ed.), *Narrative psychology: The storied nature of human conduct* (pp. 3–21). New York: Praeger.

Sarte, J.-P. (1965). *Essays in existentialism*. Secaucus, NJ: The Citadel Press.

Sartre, J.-P. (1981). *The family idiot: Gustave Flaubert, 1821–1857* (Vol. 1). Chicago: University of Chicago Press (Transl. By C. Cosman.).

Saucier, G., & Goldberg, L.R. (1996). The language of personality: Lexical perspectives on the five-factor model. In J.S. Wiggins (Ed.), *The five-factor model of personality: Theoretical perspectives* (pp. 21–50). New York: Guilford Press.

Sawyer, J. (1966). Measurement and prediction, clinical *and* statistical. *Psychological Bulletin, 66*, 178–200.

Scarr, S. (1997). Why child care has little impact on most children's development. *New Direction in Psychological Science, 6*, 143–148.

Scarr, J., Webber, P.L., Weinberg, R.A., & Wittig, M.A. (1981). Personality resemblance among adolescents and their parents in biologically related and adoptive families. *Journal of Personality and Social Psychology, 40*, 885–898.

Scarr, S., & Grajek, S. (1982). Similarities and differences among siblings. In M.E. Lamb and B. Sutton-Smith (Eds.), *Sibling relationships: Their na-*ture and significance across the lifespan* (pp. 357–382). Hillsdale, NJ: Lawrence Erlbaum.

Scarr, S., & McCartney, K. (1983). How people make their own environments: A theory of genotype → environment effects. *Child Development, 54*, 424–435.

Schacter, D.L. (1992). Understanding implict memory: A cognitive neuroscience approach. *American Psychologist, 47*, 559–569.

Schafer, R. (1968). *Aspects of internalization*. New York: International Universities Press.

Schafer, R. (1981). Narration in the psychoanalytic dialogue. In W.J.J. Mitchell (Ed.), *On narrative* (pp. 25–49). Chicago: University of Chicago Press.

Schank, R.C., & Abelson, R.P. (1977). *Scripts, plans, goals, and understanding*. Hillsdale, NJ: Lawrence Erlbaum.

Scheibe, K.E. (1985). Historical perspectives on the presented self. In B.R. Schlenker (Ed.), *The self and social life* (pp. 33–64). New York: McGraw-Hill.

Scheier, M.F., & Carver, C.J. (1981). Private and public aspects of self. In L. Wheeler (Ed.), *Review of personality and social psychology* (Vol. 2, pp. 189–216). Beverly Hills, CA: Sage.

Schenkel, S., & Marcia, J.E. (1972). Attitudes toward premarital intercouse in determining ego identity status in college women. *Journal of Personality, 40*, 472–482.

Schooler, C. (1972). Birth order effects: Not here, not now! *Psychological Bulletin, 78*, 161–175.

Schroder, H.M., Driver, M.J., & Streufert, S. (1967). *Human information processing.* New York: Holt, Rinehart & Winston.

Schuerger, J.M., Zarrella, K.L., & Hotz, A.S. (1989). Factors that influence the temporal stability of personality by questionnaire. *Journal of Personality and Social Psychology, 56,* 777–783.

Schultheiss, O.C., & Brunstein, J.C. (1999). Goal imagery: Bridging the gap between implicit motives and explicit goals. *Journal of Personality, 67,* 1–37.

Schutte, N.S., Kenrick, D.T., & Sadalla, E.K. (1985). The search for predictable settings: Situational prototypes, constraint, and behavioral variation. *Journal of Personality and Social Psychology, 49,* 121–128.

Schwartz, G.E. (1990). Psychobiology of repression and health: A systems approach. In J.L. Singer (Ed.), *Repression and dissociation: Implications for personality theory, psychopathology, and health* (pp. 405–434). Chicago: University of Chicago Press.

Schwartz, G.E., Fair, P.L., Greenberg, P.S., Freedman, M., & Klerman, J.L. (1974). Facial electromyography in the assessment of emotion. *Psychophysiology, 11,* 237.

Scott-Stokes, H. (1974). *The life and death of Yukio Mishima.* New York: Farrar, Straus & Giroux.

Seligman, M.E.P. (1975). *Helplessness: On depression, development, and death.* San Francisco: W.H. Freeman.

Seligman, M.E.P., & Maier, S.F. (1967). Failure to escape traumatic shock. *Journal of Experimental Psychology, 74,* 1–9.

Seligman, M.E.P., Nolen-Hoeksema, S., Thornton, N., & Thornton, K.M. (1990). Explanatory styles as a mechanism of disappointing athletic performance. *Psychological Science, 1,* 143–146.

Seligman, M.E.P., & Schulman, P. (1986). Explanatory style as a predictor of productivity and quitting among life insurance sales agents. *Journal of Personality and Social Psychology, 50,* 832–838.

Selman, R.L. (1980). *The growth of interpersonal understanding.* New York: Academic Press.

Semmer, N., & Frese, M. (1985). Action theory in clinical psychology. In M. Frese and J. Sabini (Eds.), *Goal directed behavior: the concept of action in psychology* (pp. 503–549). Hillsdale, NJ: Lawrence Erlbaum.

Shaver, P.R., & Brennan, K.A. (1992). Attachment styles and the "Big Five" personality traits: Their connections with each other and with romantic relationship outcomes. *Personality and Social Psychology Bulletin, 18,* 536–545.

Shaver, P., & Rubenstein, C. (1980). Childhood attachment experience and adult loneliness. In L. Wheeler (Ed.), *Review of personality and social psychology* (Vol. 1, pp. 42–73). Beverly Hills, CA: Sage.

Shaw, C. (1930). *The jackroller: A delinquent boy's own story.* Chicago: Univrsity of Chicago Press.

Sheehy, G. (1976). *Passages: Predictable crises of adult life.* New York: E.P. Dutton.

Sheldon, K.M., & Elliot, A.J. (1999). Goal striving, need satisfaction, and longitudinal well-being: The self-concordance model. *Journal of Personality and Social Psychology, 76,* 482–497.

Sheldon, K.M., & Kasser, T. (1995). Coherence and congruence: Two aspects of personality integration. *Journal of Personality and Social Psychology, 68,* 531–543.

Sheldon, K.M., & Kasser, T. (1998). Pursuing personal goals: Skills enable progress, but not all progress is beneficial. *Personality and Social Psychology Bulletin, 24,* 1319–1331.

Sheldon, W.H. (1940). *The varieties of human physique: An introduction to constitutional psychology.* New York: Harper.

Shelton, B.A. (1992). *Women, men and time: Gender differences in paid work, housework, and leisure.* New York: Greenwood Press.

Shneidman, E.S. (1981). (Ed.). *Endeavors in psychology: Selections from the personology of Henry A. Murray.* New York: Harper & Row.

Shoda, Y. (1999). Behavioral expressions of a personality system: Generation and perception of behavioral signatures. In D. Cervone and Y. Shoda (Eds.), *Personality coherence: Social-cognitive bases of consistency, variability, and organization* (pp. 155–181). New York: Guilford Press.

Shostrom, E. (1965). An inventory for the measurement of self-actualization. *Educational and Psychological Measurement, 24,* 207–218.

Shostrom, E. (1966). *Manual for the Personal Orientation Inventory (POI): An inventory for the measurement of self-actualization.* San Diego, CA: Educational and Industrial Testing Service.

Shotter, J. (1970). Men, and man-makers: George Kelly and the psychology of personal constructs. In D. Bannister (Ed.), *Perspectives in personal construct theory.* New York: Academic Press.

Shotter, J., & Gergen, K.J. (1989). Preface and Introduction. In J. Shotter and K.J. Gergen (Eds.), *Texts of identity* (pp. ix–xi). London: Sage.

Shweder, R.A. (1975). How relevant is an individual difference theory of personality? *Journal of Personality, 43,* 455–484.

Shweder, R.A., & D'Andrade, R.G. (1979). Accurate reflection or systematic distortion? A reply to Block, Weiss, and Thorne. *Journal of Personality and Social Psychology, 37,* 1075–1084.

Shweder, R.A., & Sullivan, M.A. (1993). Cultural psychology: Who needs it? *Annual Review of Psychology, 44,* 497–523.

Shweder, R.A., & Much, N.C. (1987). Determinants of meaning: Discourse and moral socialization. In W.M. Kurtines and J.L. Gerwirtz (Eds.), *Moral development through social interaction* (pp. 197–244). New York: Wiley.

Sill, J. (1980). Disengagement reconsidered: Awareness of finitude. *Gerontologist, 20,* 457–462.

Silverman, L.H., & Fishel, A.K. (1981). The Oedipus complex: Studies in adult male behavior. In L. Wheeler (Ed.), *Review of personality and social psychology* (Vol. 2, pp. 43–67). Beverly Hills, CA: Sage.

Silverstein, L.B. (1991). Transforming the debate about child care and maternal employment. *American Psychologist, 46,* 1025–1032.

Simonton, D.K. (1976). Biographical determinants of achieved eminence: A multivariate approach to the Cox data. *Journal of Personality and Social Psychology, 33,* 218–226.

Simonton, D.K. (1986). Presidential personality: Biographical use of the Gough Adjective Check List. *Journal of Personality and Social Psychology, 51,* 149–160.

Simonton, D.K. (1989). The swan-song phenomenon: Last-works effects for 172 classical composers. *Psychology and Aging, 4,* 42–47.

Simonton, D.K. (1994). *Greatness: Who makes history and why.* New York: Guilford Press.

Simonton, D.K. (in press). Significant samples: The psychological study of eminent individuals. *Psychological Assessment.*

Simpson, J.A. (1990). Influence of attachment styles on romantic relationships. *Journal of Personality and Social Psychology, 59,* 971–980.

Simpson, J.A. (in press). Attachment theory in a modern evolutionary perspective. In J. Cassidy and P.R. Shaver (Eds.), *Handbook of attachment theory and research.* New York: Guilford Press.

Simpson, J.A., & Gangestad, S.W. (1991). Individual differences in sociosexuality: Evidence for convergent and discriminant validity. *Journal of Personality and Social Psychology, 60,* 870–883.

Simpson, J.A., & Gangestad, S.W. (1992). Sociosexuality and romantic partner choice. *Journal of Personality, 60,* 31–51.

Simpson, J.A., Gangestad, S.W., & Biek, M. (1993). Personality and nonverbal social behavior: An ethological perspective on relationship initiation. *Journal of Experimental Social Psychology, 29,* 434–461.

Simpson, J.A., Rholes, W.S., & Neligan, J.S. (1992). Support seeking and support giving within couples in an anxiety-provoking situation: The role of attachment styles. *Journal of Personality and Social Psychology, 62,* 434–446.

Simpson, J.A., Rholes, W.S., & Phillips, D. (1996). Conflict in close relationships: An attachment perspective. *Journal of Personality and Social Psychology, 71,* 899–914.

Singer, J.L. (1984). *The human personality.* San Diego, CA: Harcourt Brace Jovanovich.

Singer, J.L. (1987). Private experience and public action: The study of ongoing conscious thought. In J. Aronoff, A.I. Rabin, and R.A. Zucker (Eds.), *The emergence of personality* (pp. 105–146). New York: Springer.

Singer, J.A. (1995). Seeing one's self: Locating narrative memory in a framework of personality. *Journal of Personality, 63,* 429–457.

Singer, J.A. (1997). *Message in a bottle: Stories of men and addiction.* New York: The Free Press.

Singer, J.A., & Salovey, P. (1993). *The remembered self: Emotion and memory in personality.* New York: The Free Press.

Singh, S. (1978). Achievement motivation and entrepreneurial success: A follow-up study. *Journal of Research in Personality, 12,* 500–503.

Singh, I.L. (1989). Personality correlates and perceptual detectability of locomotive drivers. *Personality and Individual Differences, 10,* 1049–1054.

Skinner, B.F. (1938). *Behavior of organisms.* New York: Appleton-Century-Crofts.

Skinner, B.F. (1948/1962). *Walden two.* New York: Macmillan.

Skinner, B.F. (1966). Operant behavior. In W.K. Honig (Ed.), *Operant behavior: Areas of research and application* (pp. 12–32). New York: Appleton-Century-Crofts.

Skinner, B.F. (1971). *Beyond freedom and dignity.* New York: Alfred A. Knopf.

Skinner, B.F. (1979). *The shaping of a behaviorist.* New York: Alfred A. Knopf.

Skinner, B.F. (1987). *Upon further reflection.* Englewood Cliffs, NJ: Prentice-Hall.

Slade, A. (1987). Quality of attachment and early symbolic play. *Developmental Psychology, 23,* 78–85.

Slavin, M.O. (1972). *The theme of feminine evil: The image of women in male fantasy and its effects on attitudes and behavior.* Unpublished doctoral dissertation. Harvard University.

Slife, B.D., & Rychlak, J.F. (1982). Role of affective assessment in modelling aggressive behavior. *Journal of Personality and Social Psychology, 43,* 861–868.

Smith, G.M. (1967). Usefulness of peer ratings of personality in educational research. *Educational and Psychological Measurement, 27,* 967–984.

Smith, K.D., Keating, J.P., & Stotland, E. (1989). Altruism reconsidered: The effect of denying feedback on a victim's status to empathic witnesses. *Journal of Personality and Social Psychology, 57,* 641–650.

Smith, R.J. (1985). The concept and measurement of social psychopathy. *Journal of Research in Personality, 19,* 219–231.

Snarey, J. (1993). *How fathers care for the next generation: A four-decade study.* Cambridge, MA: Harvard University Press.

Sneed, C.D., McCrae, R.R., & Funder, D.C. (1997). Lay conceptions of the Five-factor model and its indicators. *Personality and Social Psychology Bulletin, 24,* 115–126.

Snowdon, C.T. (1983). Ethology, comparative psychology, and animal behavior. In M.R. Rosenzweig and L.W. Porter (Eds.), *Annual review of psychology* (Vol. 34, pp. 63–94). Palo Alto, CA: Annual Reviews, Inc.

Snyder, M. (1974). The self-monitoring of expressive behavior. *Journal of Personality and Social Psychology, 30,* 526–537.

Snyder, M. (1979). Self-monitoring processes. In L. Berkowitz (Ed.), *Advances in experimental social psychology* (Vol. 12). New York: Academic Press.

Snyder, M. (1983). The influence of individuals on situations: Implications for understanding the links between personality and social behavior. *Journal of Personality, 51,* 497–516.

Snyder, M., & Gangestad, S. (1986). On the nature of self-monitoring: Matters of assessment, matters of validity. *Journal of Personality and Social Psychology, 51,* 125–139.

Sobotka, S.S., Davidson, R.J., & Senulis, J.A. (1992). Anterior brain electrical asymmetries in response to reward and punishment. *Electroencephalography and Clinical Neurophysiology, 83,* 236–247.

Spangler, W.D. (1992). Validity of questionnaire and TAT measures of need for achievement: Two meta-analyses. *Psychological Bulletin, 112,* 140–154.

Spence, D.P. (1982). *Narrative truth and historical truth: Meaning and interpretation in psychoanalysis.* New York: Norton.

Spence, J.T. (1985). Gender identity and its implications for concepts of masculinity and femininity. In T.B. Sonderegger (Ed.), *Nebraska symposium on motivation.* Lincoln, NE: University of Nebraska Press.

Spieker, S.J., & Booth, C.L. (1988). Maternal antecedents of attachment quality. In J. Belsky and T. Nezworksi (Eds.), *Clinical implications of attachment* (pp. 95–135). Hillsdale, NJ: Lawrence Erlbaum.

Spoto, D. (1983). *The darker side of genius: The life of Alfred Hitchcock.* New York: Ballatine.

Sprecher, S., Sullivan, Q., & Hatfield, E. (1994). Mate selection preferences: Gender differences examined in a national sample. *Journal of Personality and Social Psychology, 66,* 1074–1080.

Sroufe, L.A. (1983). Infant-caregiver attachment and patterns of adaptation in the preschool: The roots of maladaption and competence. In M. Perlmutter (Ed.), *Minnesota symposium on child psychology* (Vol. 16, pp. 41–83). Minneapolis, MN: University of Minnesota Press.

Sroufe, L.A. (1985). Attachment classification from the perspective of infant–caregiver relationships and infant temperament. *Child Development, 56*, 1–14.

Sroufe, L.A. (1988). The role of infant–caregiver attachment in development. In J. Belsky and T. Nezworksi (Eds.), *Clinical implications of attachment* (pp. 18–38). Hillsdale: NJ: Lawrence Erlbaum.

Sroufe, L.A. & Waters, E. (1977). Attachment as an organizational construct. *Child Development, 48*, 1184–1199.

Steele, R.S. (1977). Power motivation, activation, and inspirational speeches. *Journal of Personality, 45*, 53–64.

Steele, R.S. (1982). *Freud and Jung: Conflicts of interpretation.* London: Routledge & Kegan Paul.

Steinberg, L., Darling, N.E., & Fletcher, A.C. (1995). Authoritative parenting and adolescent adjustment: An ecological journey. In P. Moen, G.H. Elder, Jr., & K. Luscher (Eds.), *Examining lives in context: Perspectives on the ecology of human development* (pp. 423–466). Washington, D.C.: American Psychological Association Press.

Stelmack, R.M. (1990). Biological bases of extraversion: Psychophysiological evidence. *Journal of Personality, 58*, 293–311.

Stelmack, R.M., & Stalikas, A. (1991). Galen and the humour theory of temperament. *Personality and Individual Differences, 16*, 543–560.

Stern, D.N. (1985). *The interpersonal world of the infant: A view from psychoanalysis and developmental psychology.* New York: Basic Books.

Sternberg, R.J., & Grigorenko, E.L. (1997). Are cognitive styles still in style? *American Psychologist, 52*, 700–712.

Steuer, F.B., Applefield, J.M., & Smith, R. (1971). Televised aggression and the interpersonal aggression of preschool children. *Journal of Experimental Child Psychology, 11*, 442–447.

Steven, P.J. (1976). *C.G. Jung: The haunted prophet.* New York: Braziller.

Stevens, A. (1983). *Archetypes.* New York: Quill.

Stewart, A.J. (1975). *Longitudinal prediction from personality to life outcomes among college educated women.* Unpublished doctoral dissertation, Harvard University.

Stwart, A.J. (1982). The course of individual adaptation to life changes. *Journal of Personality and Social Psychology, 42*, 1100–1113.

Stewart, A.J. (1994). Toward a feminist strategy for studying women's lives. In C. Franz and A.J. Stewart (Eds.), *Women creating lives: Identities, resilience, resistance* (pp. 11–35). Boulder, CO: Westview Press.

Stewart, A.J., & Chester, N.L. (1982). Sex differences in human social motives. In A.J.

Stewart (Ed.), *Motivation and society* (pp. 172–218). San Francisco, CA: Jossey-Bass.

Stewart, A.J., Franz, C., & Layton, L. (1988). The changing self: Using personal documents to study lives. *Journal of Personality, 56*, 41–74.

Stewart, A.J., & Healy, J.M., Jr. (1985). Personality and adaptation to change. In R. Hogan and W.H. Jones (Eds.), *Perspectives in personality* (Vol. 1, pp. 117–144). Greenwich, CT: JAI Press.

Stewart, A.J., & Healy, M.J., Jr. (1989). Linking individual development and social changes. *American Psychologist, 44*, 30–42.

Stewart, A.J., & Ostrove, J.M. (1998). Women's personality in middle age: Gender, history, and midcourse corrections. *American Psychologist, 53*, 1185–1194.

Stewart, A.J., & Rubin, Z. (1976). Power motivation in the dating couple. *Journal of Personality and Social Psychology, 34*, 305–309.

Stewart, A.J., Sokol, M., Healy, J.M., Jr., & Chester, N.L. (1986). Longitudinal studies of psychological consequences of life changes in children and adults. *Journal of Personality and Social Psychology, 50*, 143–151.

Stewart, A.J., Sokol, M., Healy, J.M., Jr., Chester, N.L., & Weinstock-Savoy, D. (1982). Adaptation to life changes in children and adults: Cross-sectional studies. *Journal of Personality and Social Psychology, 43*, 1270–1281.

Stewart, A.J., & Vandewater, E.A. (1993). Career and family clocks in a transitional cohort: The

Radcliffe class of 1964. In K. Hulbert and D. Schuster (Eds.), *Women's lives through time: Educated American women of the twentieth century* (pp. 235–258). San Francisco: Jossey-Bass.

Stewart, A.J., & Vandewater, E.A. (1998). The course of generativity. In D.P. McAdams and E. de St. Aubin (Eds.), *Generativity and adulthood: How and why we care for the next generation* (pp. 75–100). Washington, D.C.: APA Press.

Stier, D.S., & Hall, J.A. (1984). Gender differences in touch: An empirical and theoretical review. *Journal of Personality and Social Psychology, 47,* 440–459.

Stokes, J.P. (1985). The relation of social network and individual difference variables to loneliness. *Journal of Personality and Social Psychology, 48,* 981–990.

Stokes, J.P., & McKirnan, D.J. (1989). Affect and the social environment: The role of social support in depression and anxiety. In P.C. Kendall and D. Watson (Eds.), *Anxiety and depression: Distinctions and overlapping features.* New York: Academic Press.

Suedfeld, P. (1985). APA Presidential addresses: The relation of integrative complexity to historical, professional, and personal factors. *Journal of Personality and Social Psychology, 49,* 1643–1651.

Suedfeld, P. (in press). Cognitive styles. In A. Kazdin (Ed.), *Encyclopedia of psychology.* Washington, D.C.: APA Press.

Suedfeld, P., & Piedrahita, L.E. (1984). Intimations of mortality: Integrative simplification as a precursor of death. *Journal of Personality and Social Psychology, 47,* 848–852.

Sullivan, H.S. (1953). *The interpersonal theory of psychiatry.* New York: W.W. Norton.

Sulloway, F.J. (1972). Family constellations, sibling rivalry, and scientific revolutions. Unpublished manuscript.

Sulloway, F.J. (1979). *Freud: Biologist of the mind.* New York: Basic Books.

Sulloway, F.J. (1996). *Born to rebel: Birth order, family dynamics, and creative lives.* New York: Pantheon.

Surtees, P.G., & Wainwright, N.W.J. (1996). Fragile states of mind: Neuroticism, vulnerability and the long-term outcome of depression. *British Journal of Psychiatry, 169,* 338–347.

Sutton, S.K., & Davidson, R.J. (1997). Prefrontal brain asymmetry: A biological substrate of the behavioral approach and behavioral inhibition systems. *Psychological Science, 8,* 204–210.

Tappan, M. (1990). Hermeneutics and moral development: Implementing narrative representation of moral experience. *Developmental Review, 10,* 239–265.

Tappan, M., & Brown, L. (1989). Stories told and lessons learned: Toward a narrative approach to moral development and moral education. *Harvard Educational Review, 59,* 182–205.

Taylor, C. (1989). *Sources of the self: The making of the modern identity.* Cambridge, MA: Harvard University Press.

Taylor, J. (1953). A personality scale of manifest anxiety. *Journal of Abnormal and Social Psychology, 48,* 285–290.

Taylor, M.C., & Hall, J.A. (1982). Psychological androgyny: Theories, methods, and conclusions. *Psychological Bulletin, 92,* 347–366.

Tekiner, A.C. (1980). Need achievement and international differences in income growth: 1950–1960. *Economic Development and Cultural Change,* 293–320.

Tellegen, A. (1982). *Brief manual for the Differential Personality Questionnaire.* Unpublished manuscript, University of Minnesota.

Tellegen, A. (1985). Structures of mood and personality and their relevance to assessing anxiety, with an emphasis on self-report. In A.H. Tuma and J.D. Masser (Eds.), *Anxiety and the anxiety disorders* (pp. 681–716). Hillsdale, NJ: Lawrence Erlbaum.

Tellegen, A., & Atkinson, G. (1974). Openness to absorbing and self-altering experiences ("absorption"), a trait related to hypnotic susceptibility. *Journal of Abnormal Psychology, 83,* 268–277.

Tellegen, A., Lykken, D.J., Bouchard, T.J., Jr., Wilcox, K.J., Segal, N.L., & Rich, S. (1988). Personality similarity in twins reared apart and together. *Journal of Personality and Social Psychology, 54,* 1031–1039.

Tesch, S.A., & Whitbourne, S.K. (1982). Intimacy and identity status in young adults. *Journal of Personality and Social Psychology, 43,* 1041–1051.

Teti, D.M., Gelfand, D.M., Messinger, D.S., & Isabella, R. (1995). Maternal depression and the quality of early attachment: An examination of infants, preschoolers, and their mothers. *Developmental Psychology, 31,* 364–376.

Tetlock, P.E. (1981a). Pre- to post-election shifts in presidential rhetoric: Impression management or cognitive adjustment? *Journal of Personality and Social Psychology, 41,* 207–212.

Tetlock, P.E. (1981b). Personality and isolationism: Content analysis of senatorial speeches. *Journal of Personality and Social Psychology, 41,* 737–743.

Tetlock, P.E. (1984). Cognitive style and political belief systems in the British House of Commons. *Journal of Personality and Social Psychology, 46,* 365–375.

Tetlock, P.E., Armor, D., & Peterson, R.S. (1994). The slavery debate in antebellum America: Cognitive style, value conflict, and the limits of compromise. *Journal of Personality and Social Psychology, 66,* 115–126.

Tetlock, P.E., Bernzweig, J., & Gallant, J.L. (1985). Supreme Court decision making: Cognitive style as a predictor of ideological consistency of voting. *Journal of Personality and Social Psychology, 48,* 1227–1239.

Tetlock, P.E., Hannum, K., & Micheletti, P. (1984). Stability and change in the complexity of senatorial rhetoric: Testing the cognitive versus rhetorical style hypotheses. *Journal of Personality and Social Psychology, 46,* 979–990.

Tetlock, P.E., Peterson, R.S., & Berry, J.M. (1993). Flattering and unflattering personality portraits of integratively simple and complex managers. *Journal of Personality and Social Psychology, 64,* 500–511.

Thayer, R.E. (1989). *The biopsychology of mood and arousal.* Oxford: Oxford University Press.

Thomas, A., & Chess, S. (1977). *Temperament and development.* New York: Bruner/Mazel.

Thomas, A., Chess, S., & Birch, H.G. (1970). The origin of personality. *Scientific American, 223,* 102–109.

Thomas, W.I., & Znaniecki, F. (1927). *The Polish Peasant in Europe and America.* New York: Alfred A. Knopf.

Thompson, C. (1942). Cultural pressures in the psychology of women. *Psychiatry, 5,* 311–339.

Thorne, A. (1989). Conditional patterns, transference, and the coherence of personality across time. in D.M. Buss and N. Cantor (Eds.), *Personality psychology: Recent trends and emerging directions* (pp. 149–159). New York: Springer-Verlag.

Thorne, A., Cutting, L., & Skaw, D. (1998). Young adults' relationship memories and the life story: Examples or essential landmarks? *Narrative Inquiry, 8,* 1–32.

Thorndike, R.L. (1959). Review of the California Psychological Inventory. In O.K. Buros (Ed.), *Fifth mental measurements yearbook.* Highland Park, NJ: Gryphon Press.

Thurstone, L.L. (1934). The vectors of mind. *Psychological Review, 41,* 1–32.

Tice, D.M. (1980). Metratraits: Interitem variance as personality assessment. In D.M. Buss and N. Cantor (Eds.), *Personality psychology: Recent trends and emerging directions* (pp. 194–200). New York: Springer-Verlag.

Tidwell, M-C.O., Reis, H.T., & Shaver, P.R. (1996). Attachment, attractiveness, and social interaction: A dairy study. *Journal of Personality and Social Psychology, 71,* 729–745.

Toder, N., & Marcia, J.E. (1973). Ego identity status and response to conformity pressure in college women. *Journal of Personality and Social Psychology, 26,* 287–294.

Tolman, E.C. (1948). Cognitive maps in rats and men. *Psychological Review, 55,* 189–208.

Tomkins, S.S. (1947). *The Thematic Apperception Test.* New York: Grune & Stratton.

Tomkins, S.S. (1962). *Affect, imagery, consciousness* (Vol. 1). New York: Springer.

Tomkins, S.S. (1963). *Affect, imagery, consciousness* (Vol. 2). New York: Springer.

Tomkins, S.S. (1979). Script theory. In H.E. Howe, Jr., and R.A. Dienstbier (Eds.), *Nebraska symposium on motivation* (Vol. 26, pp. 201–236). Lincoln, NE: University of Nebraska Press.

Tomkins, S.S. (1981). The quest for primary motives: Biography and autobiography of an idea. *Journal of Personality and Social Psychology, 41,* 306–329.

Tomkins, S.S. (1987). Script theory. In J. Aronoff, A.I. Rabin, and R.A. Zucker (Eds.), *The emergence of personality* (pp. 147–216). New York: Springer.

Tomkins, S.S., & Izard, C.E. (1965). *Affects, cognition, and personality.* New York: Springer.

Tomkins, S.S., & Miner, J.R. (1957). *The Tomkins—Horn picture arrangement test.* New York: Springer.

Tooby, J., & Cosmides, L. (1990). On the universality of human nature and the uniquesness of the individual: The role of genetics and adaptation. *Journal of Personality, 58,* 17–67.

Tooby, J., & Cosmides, L. (1990). On the universality of human nature and the uniqueness of the individual. *Journal of Personality, 58,* 17–67.

Tooby, J., & Cosmides, L. (1992). The psychological foundations of culture. In J.H. Barkow, L. Cosmides, and J. Tooby (Eds.), *The adapted mind: Evolutionary psychology and the generation of culture* (pp. 19–136). New York: Oxford University Press.

Trabasso, T., Secco, T., & Van Den Broek, P. (1984). Causal cohesion and story coherence. In H. Mandl, N.L. Stein, and T. Trabsso (Eds.), *Learning and comprehension of text.* Hillsdale, NJ: Lawrence Erlbaum.

Trapnell, P.D. (1994). Openness versus intellect: A lexical left turn. *European Journal of Personality, 8,* 273–290.

Trapnell, P.D., & Wiggins, J.S. (1990). Extension of the Interpersonal Adjective Scales to include the Big Five dimensions of personality. *Journal of Personality and Social Psychology, 59,* 781–790.

Triandis, H.C. (1997). Cross-cultural perspectives on personality. In R. Hogan, J. Johnson, and S. Briggs (Eds.), *Handbook of personality psychology* (pp. 439–464). San Diego, CA: Academic Press.

Triandis, H.C., & Gelfand, M.J. (1998). Converging measurement of horizontal and vertical individualism and collectivism. *Journal of Personality and Social Psychology, 74,* 118–128.

Trivers, R.L. (1971). The evolution of reciprocal altruism. *Quarterly Review of Biology, 46,* 35–57.

Tulving, E. (1972). Episodic and semantic memory. In B. Tulving and W. Donaldson (Eds.), *Organization and memory.* New York: Academic Press.

Tupes, E.C., & Christal, R.E. (1958). *Stability of personality trait rating factors obtained under diverse conditions.* (USAF ASD Technical Note, No. 58–61.) Lackland Air Force Base, TX: U.S. Air Force.

Tupes, E.C., & Christal, R.C. (1961). *Recurrent personality factors based on trait ratings.* (Tech. Rep. No. ASD-TR-61-97). Lackland Air Force Base, TX: U.S. Air Force.

Tupes, E.C., & Kaplan, M.N. (1961). *Relationships between personality traits, physical proficiency, nd cadet effectiveness reports of Air Force Academy Cadets.* (USAF AFD Technical Report, No. 61–48.) Lackland Air Force Base, TX: U.S. Air Force.

Turner, P.J. (1991). Relations between attachment, gender, and behavior with peers in preschool. *Child Development, 62,* 1475–1488.

Uleman, J.S. (1966). *A new TAT measure of the need for power.* Unpublished doctoral dissertation, Harvard University.

Underwood, B., & Moore, B.J. (1981). Sources of behavioral consistency. *Journal of Personal-ity and Social Psychology, 40,* 780–785.

Vaillant, G.E. (1971). Theoretical hierachy of adaptive ego mechanisms. *Archives of General Psychiatry, 24,* 107–118.

Vaillant, G.E. (1977). *Adaptation to life.* Boston: Little, Brown.

Vaillant, G.E., & Drake, R.E. (1985). Maturity of ego defense in relation to DSM III Axis II personality disorder. *Archives of General Psychiatry, 42,* 597–601.

Vaillant, G.E., & Milofsky, E. (1980). The natural history of male psychological health: IX. Empirical evidence for Erikson's model of the life cycle. *American Journal of Psychiatry, 137,* 1349–1359.

Vallacher, R.R., & Wegner, D.M. (1987). What do people think they're doing? Action identificaiton and human behavior. *Psychological Review, 94,* 3–15.

Van de Water, D., & McAdams, D.P. (1989). Generativity and Erikson's "belief in the species." *Journal of Research in Personality, 23,* 435–449.

vanlJzendoorn, M.H., & Bakermans-Kranenburg, M.J. (1996). Attachment representations in mothers, fathers, adolescents, and clinical groups: A meta-analytic search for normative data. *Journal of Consulting and Clinical Psychology, 64,* 8–21.

Veroff, J. (1957). Development and validation of a projective measure of power motivation. *Journal of Abnormal and Social Psychology, 54,* 1–8.

Veroff, J. (1982). Assertive motivation: Achievement versus power. In A.J. Stewart (Ed.), *Motivation and society* (pp.

99–132). San Francisco: Jossey-Bass.

Veroff, J. (1983). Contextual determinants of personality. *Personality and Social Psychology Bulletin, 9*, 331–343.

Veroff, J., Douvan, E., & Kulka, R. (1981). *The inner American.* New York: Basic Books.

Veroff, J., & Feld, S.C. (1970). *Marriage and work in America.* New York: Van Nostrand Reinhold.

Vitz, P.C. (1990). The use of stories in moral development: New psychological reasons for an old education method. *American Psychologist, 45*, 709–720.

von Franz, M. (1980). *The psychological meaning of redemption motifs in fairy tales.* Toronto: Inner City Books.

Wainer, H.A., & Rubin, I.M. (1969). Motivation of research and development entrepreneurs. *Journal of Applied Psychology, 53*, 178–184.

Walkover, B.C. (1992). The family as an overwrought object of desire. In G.C. Rosenwald and R.L. Ochberg (Eds.), *Storied lives: The cultural politics of self-understanding* (pp. 178–191). New Haven, CT: Yale University Press.

Waller, N.G., & Shaver, P.R. (1994). The importance of nongenetic influences on romantic love styles: A twin-family study. *Psychological Science, 5*, 268–274.

Wallston, K.A., & Wallston, B.S. (1981). Health locus of control scales. In H.M. Lefcourt (Ed.), *Research with the locus of control construct: Assessment methods* (Vol. 1, pp. 189–243). New York: Academic Press.

Walster, E.H., & Walster, G.W. (1978). *A new look at love.* Reading, MA: Addison-Wesley.

Washburn, S.L., & Lancaster, C.J. (1973). The evolution of hunting. In C.L. Brace and J. Motress (Eds.), Man in evolutionary perspective. New York: John Wiley & Sons.

Waterman, A.S. (1982). Identity development from adolescence to adulthood: An extension of theory and a review of research. *Developmental Psychology, 18*, 341–358.

Watkins, M. (1986). *Invisible guests: The development of imaginal dialogues.* Hillsdale, NJ: Analytic Press.

Watson, D., & Clark, L.A. (1984). Negative affectivity: The disposition to experience aversive emotional states. *Psychological Bulletin, 96*, 465–490.

Watson, D., & Clark, L.A. (1992). Affects separable and inseparable: On the hierarchical arrangement of the negative affects. *Journal of Personality and Social Psychology, 62*, 489–505.

Watson, D., & Clark, L.A. (1997). Extraversion and its positive emotional core. In R. Hogan, J. Johnson, and S. Briggs (Eds.), *Handbook of personality psychology* (pp. 767–793). San Diego, CA: Academic Press.

Watson, D., Clark, L.A., McIntyre, C.W., & Hamaker, S. (1992). Affect, personality, and social activity. *Journal of Personality and Social Psychology, 63*, 1011–1025.

Watson, D., & Tellegen, A. (1985). Toward a consensual structure of mood. *Psychological Bulletin, 98*, 219–235.

Watson, D., & Walker, L.M. (1996). The long-term stability and predictive validity of trait measures of affect. *Journal of Personality and Social Psychology, 70*, 567–577.

Watson, J.B. (1913). Psychology as the behaviorist views it. *Psychological Review, 20*, 158–177.

Watson, J.B. (1924). *Behaviorism.* Chicago: University of Chicago Press.

Watson, J.B., & Raynor, R. (1920). Conditional emotional reactions. *Journal of Experimental Psychology, 3*, 1–14.

Watson, P.J., Grisham, S.O., Trotter, M.V., & Biderman, M.D. (1984). Narcissism and empathy: Validity evidence for the Narcissistic Personality Inventory. *Journal of Personality Assessment, 48*, 301–305.

Webb, E. (1915). Character and intelligence. *British Journal of Psychology Monographs, 1*(3), 1–99.

Wegner, D.M., Schneider, D.J., Carter, S.R., & White, T.L. (1987). Paradoxical effects of thought suppression. *Journal of Personality and Social Psychology, 53*, 5–13.

Weinberger, D.A. (1990). The construct validity of the repressive coping style. In J.L. Singer (Ed.), *Repression and dissociation: Implications for personality theory, psychopathology, and health* (pp. 337–386). Chicago: University of Chicago Press.

Weinberger, D.A., Schwartz, G.E., & Davidson, R.J. (1979). Low-anxious, high-anxious, and repressive coping styles: Psychometric patterns and behavioral and physiological responses to stress. *Journal of Abnormal Psychology, 88*, 369–380.

Weiner, B. (1979). A theory of motivation for some classroom experiences. *Journal of Educational Psychology, 71,* 3–25.

Weiner, B. (1980). *Human motivation.* New York: Holt, Rinehart & Winston.

Weiner, B. (1990). Attribution in personality psychology. In L. Pervin (Ed.), *Handbook of personality theory and research* (pp. 465–485). New York: Guilford Press.

Weiner, B. (1992). *Human motivation: Metaphors, theory, and research.* Newbury Park, CA: Sage.

Weisen, A. (1965). *Differential reinforcing effects of onset and offset of stimulation on the operant behavior of normals, neurotics, and psychopaths.* Unpublished doctoral dissertation, University of Florida.

Werner, H. (1957). The concept of development from a comparative and an organismic point of view. In D. Harris (Ed.), *The concept of development.* Minneapolis, MN: University of Minnesota Press.

West, K.Y., Widiger, T.A., & Costa, P.T., Jr. (1993). *The placement of cognitive and perceptual abberations within the five-factor model of personality.* Unpublished manuscript. University of Kentucky, Lexington, KY.

West, S.G. (1983). Personality and prediction: An introduction. *Journal of Personality, 51,* 275–285.

Westen, D. (1990). Psychoanalytic approaches to personality. In L. Pervin (Ed.), *Handbook of personality theory and research* (pp. 21–65). New York: Guilford Press.

Westen, D. (1995). A clinical-empirical model of personality: Life after the Mischelian ice age and the NEO-lithic era. *Journal of Personality, 63,* 495–524.

Westen, D. (1998). Unconscious thought, feeling, and motivation: The end of a century-long debate. In R.F. Bornstein and J.F. Masling (Eds.), *Empirical perspectives on the psychoanalytic unconscious* (pp. 1–43). Washington, D.C.: APA Press.

Westenberg, P.M., Blasi, A., & Cohn, L.D. (Eds.). (1998). *Personality development: Theoretical, empirical, and clinical investigations of Loevinger's conception of ego development.* Mahwood, NJ: Erlbaum.

Whitbourne, S.K. (1985). The psychological construction of the life span. In J.E. Birren and K.W. Schaie (Eds.), *Handbook of the psychology of aging* (2nd ed.) (pp. 594–618). New York: Van Nostrand Reinhold.

Whitbourne, S.K. (1986). Openness to experience, identity flexibility, and life changes in adults. *Journal of Personality and Social Psychology, 50,* 163–168.

Whitbourne, S.K., Zuschlag, M.K., Elliot, L.B., & Waterman, A.S. (1992). Psychological development in adulthood: A 22-year sequential study. *Journal of Personality and Social Psychology, 63,* 260–271.

White, J.L., & Parham, T.A. (1990). *The psychology of blacks: An African-American perspective.* Englewood Cliffs, NJ: Prentice-Hall.

White, M., & Epston, D. (1990). *Narrative means to therapeutic ends.* New York: Norton.

White, R.W. (1948). *The abnormal personality.* New York: Ronald Press.

White, R.W. (1952). *Lives in progress* (1st ed.). New York: Holt, Rinehart & Winston.

White, R.W. (1959). Motivation reconsidered: The concept of competence. *Psychological Review, 66,* 297–333.

White, R.W. (1960). Competence and the psyschosexual stages of development. In M.R. Jones (Ed.), *Nebraska symposium on motivation* (Vol. 8). Lincoln, NE: Universtiy of Nebraska Press.

White, R.W. (1963). Sense of interpersonal competence: Two case studies and some reflections on origins. In R.W. White (Ed.), *The study of lives* (pp. 72–93). New York: Prentice-Hall.

White, R.W. (1963). (Ed.). *The study of lives: Essays on personality in honor of Henry A. Murray.* New York: Prentice-Hall.

White, R.W. (1966). *Lives in progress* (2nd ed.). New York: Holt, Rinehart & Winston.

White, R.W. (1972). *The enterprise of living: A view of personal growth.* New York: Holt, Rinehart & Winston.

White, R.W. (1975). *Lives in progress* (3rd ed.). New York: Holt, Rinehart & Winston.

White, R.W. (1981). Exploring personality the long way: The study of lives. In A.I. Rabin, J. Aronoff, A.M. Barclay, and R.A. Zucker (Eds.), *Further explorations in personality* (pp. 3–19. New York: John Wiley & Sons.

White, R.W. (1987). *Seeking the shape of personality: A memoir.*

Marlborough, NH: The Homstead Press.

Whiting, B.B., & Whiting, J.W.M. (1975). *Children of six cultures*. Cambridge, MA: Harvard University Press.

Whiting, J.W.M., & Child, I.L. (1953). *Child training and personality: A cross-cultural study*. New Haven, CT: Yale University Press.

Wicklund, R.A., & Duvall, J. (1971). Opinion change and performance facilitation as a result of objective self-awareness. *Journal of Experimental Social Psychology, 7*, 319–342.

Wiebe, D.J., & Smith, T.W. (1997). Personality and health: Progress and problems in psychosomatics. In R. Hogan, J.A. Johnson, and S. Briggs (Eds.), *Handbook of personality psychology* (pp. 891–918). San Diego, CA: Academic Press.

Wiedenfeld, S.A., O'Leary, A., Bandura, A., Brown, S., Levine, S., & Raska, K. (1990). Impact of perceived self-efficacy in coping with stressors on components of the immune system. *Journal of Personality and Social Psychology, 59*, 1082–1094.

Wiggins, J.S. (1973). *Personality and prediction: Principles of personality assessment*. Reading, MA: Addison-Wesley.

Wiggins, J.S. (1979). A psychological taxonomy of trait-descriptive terms: The interpersonal domain. *Journal of Personality and Social Psychology, 37*, 395–412.

Wiggins, J.S. (1982). Circumplex models of interpersonal behavior in clinical psychology. In P.C. Kendall and J.N. Butcher (Eds.), *Handbook of research methods in clinical psychology* (pp. 183–221). New York: Wiley.

Wiggins, J.S. (1992). Have model, will travel. *Journal of Personality, 60*, 527–532.

Wiggins, J.S. (1996). (Ed.). *The five-factor model of personality: Theoretical perspectives*. New York: Guilford Press.

Wiggins, J.S., & Broughton, R. (1985). The interpersonal circle: A structural model for the integration of personality research. In R. Hogan & W.H. Jones (Eds.), *Perspectives in personality* (Vol. 1, pp. 1–47). Greenwich, CT: JAI Press.

Wiggins, J.S., & Trapnell, P.D. (1996). A dyadic-interactional perspective on the five-factor model. In J.S. Wiggins (Ed.), *The five-factor model of personality: Theoretical perspectives* (pp. 88–162). New York: Guilford Press.

Wiggins, J.S., & Trapnell, P.D. (1997). Personality structure: The return of the Big Five. In R. Hogan, J. Johnson, and S. Briggs (Eds.), *Handbook of personality psychology* (pp. 737–766). San Diego, CA: Academic Press.

Wilson, E.O. (1978). *On human nature*. Cambridge, MA: Harvard University Press.

Wilson, G.D. (1978). Introversion-extroversion. In H. London and J.E. Exner, Jr. (Eds.), *Dimensions of personality* (pp. 217–261). New York: John Wiley & Sons.

Wilson, G.D., & Nias, D.K.B. (1975). Sexual types. *New Behavior, 2*, 330–332.

Wink P. (1991). Two faces of narcissism. *Journal of Personality and Social Psychology, 61*, 590–597.

Wink, P. (1992a). Three types of narcissism in women from college to midlife. *Journal of Personality, 60*, 7–30.

Wink. P. (1992b). Three narcissism scales for the California Q-set. *Journal of Personality Assessment, 58*, 51–66.

Wink, P. (1996). Transition from the early 40s to the early 50s in self-directed women. *Journal of Personality, 64*, 49–69.

Wink, P., & Helson, R. (1993). Personality change in women and their partners. *Journal of Personality and Social Psychology, 65*, 597–605.

Winnicott, D.W. (1965). *The naturational processes and the facilitating environment*. New York: International Universities Press.

Winter, D.G. (1973). *The power motive*. New York: The Free Press.

Winter, D.G. (1987). Leader appeal, leader performance, and the motive profiles of leaders and followers: A study of American Presidents and elections. *Journal of Personality and Social Psychology, 52*, 196–202.

Winter, D.G. (1996). *Personality: Analysis and interpretation of lives*. New York: McGraw-Hill.

Winter, D.G., & Barenbaum, N.B. (1999). History of modern personality theory and research. In L.A. Pervin and O. John (Eds.), *Handbook of personality: Theory and research* (2nd Ed., pp. 3–27). New York: Guilford Press.

Winter, D.G., & Carlson, L.A. (1988). Using motive scores in the psychobiographical study of an individual: The case of Richard Nixon. *Journal of Personality, 56*, 75–103.

Winter, D.G., John, O.P., Stewart, A.J., Klohnen, E.C., & Duncan, L.E. (1998). Traits and motives: Toward an integration of two traditions in personality research. *Psychological Review, 105,* 230–250.

Winter, D.G., McClelland, D.C., & Stewart, A.J. (1981). A new case for the liberal arts: Assessing institutional goals and student development. San Francisco, CA: Jossey-Bass.

Winter, D.G., & Stewart, A.J. (1977). Power motive reliability as a function of retest instructions. *Journal of Consulting and Clinical Psychology, 45,* 436–440.

Winter, D.G., & Stewart, A.J. (1978). The power motive. In H. London and J.E. Exner (Eds.), *Dimensions of personality* (pp. 391–447). New York: John Wiley & Sons.

Witkin, H.A. (1949). Perception of body position and of the position of the visual field. *Psychological Monographs. 63,* (7 Whole No. 302).

Witkin, H.A. (1950). Individual differences in ease of perception of embedded figures. *Journal of Personality, 19,* 1–15.

Witkin, H.A., & Berry, J. (1975). Psychological differentiation in cross-cultural perspective. *Journal of Cross-Cultural Psychology, 6,* 4–87.

Witkin, H.A., Goodenough, D.R., & Oltmann, P.K. (1979). Psychological differentiation: Current status. *Journal of Personality and Social Psychology, 37,* 1127–1145.

Woike, B.A. (1995). Most-memorable experiences: Evidence for a link between implicit and explicit motives and social cognitive processes in everyday life. *Journal of Personality and Social Psychology, 68,* 1081–1091.

Woike, B.A., Gershkovich, I., Piorkowski, R., & Polo, M. (1999). The role of motives in the content and structure of autobiographical memory. *Journal of Personality and Social Psychology, 76,* 600–612.

Wolf, E.S. (1982). Comments on Heinz Kohut's conceptualization of a bipolar self. In B. Lee (Ed.), *Psychosocial theories of the self* (pp. 23–42). New York: Plenum.

Wolfenstein, M., & Trull, T.J. (1997). Depression and openness to experience. *Journal of Personality Assessment, 69,* 614–632.

Wolpe, J. (1973). *The practice of behavioral therapy* (2nd ed.) New York: Pergamon Press.

Wright, J.C., & Mishel, W. (1987). A conditional approach to dispositional constructs: The local predictability of social behavior. *Journal of Personality, 53,* 1159–1177.

Wright, R. (1994). *The moral animal.* New York: Pantheon.

Wymer, W.E., & Penner, L.A. (1985). Moderator variables and different types of predictability: Do you have a match? *Journal of Personality and Social Psychology, 49,* 1002–1015.

Wynne-Edwards, V.C. (1963/1978). Intergroup selection in the evolution of social systems. In T.H. Clutton-Brock and P.H. Harvey (Eds.), *Readings in sociobiology* (pp. 10–19). San Francisco, CA: Freeman.

Yik, M.S.M., & Bond, M.H. (1993). Exploring the dimensions of Chinese person perception with indigenous and imported constructs: Creating a culturally balanced scale. *International Journal of Psychology, 28,* 75–95.

Yin, R.K. (1984). *Case study research: Design and methods.* Beverly Hills, CA: Sage.

Yoda, S., Mishel, W., & Wright, J.C. (1994). Intraindividual stability in the organization and patterning of behavior: Incorporating psychological situations into the idiographic analysis of personality. *Journal of Personality and Social Psychology, 67,* 674–687.

York, K.L., & John, O.P. (1992). The four faces of Eve: A typological analysis of women's personality at midlife. *Journal of Personality and Social Psychology, 63,* 494–508.

Zajonc, R.B. (1976). Family configuration and intelligence: Variations in scholastic aptitude scores parallel trends in family size and the spacing of children. *Science, 192* (4236), 227–236.

Zeldow, P.B., & Daughterty, S.R. (1991). Personality profile and specialty choices of students from two medical school classes. *Academic Medicine, 66,* 283–287.

Zeldow, P.B., & Bennett, E. (1997). Stability of a Q-sort model of optimal mental health. *Journal of Personality Assessment, 69,* 314–323.

Zeldow, P.B., Daugherty, S.R., & McAdams, D.P. (1988). Intimacy, power, and psychological well-being in medical students.

The Journal of Nervous and Mental Disease, 176, 182–187.

Zimbardo, P.G. (1977). *Shyness: What is is, what to do about it.* Reading, MA: Addison-Wesley.

Zimbardo, P.G., & Leippe, M.R. (1991). *The psychology of attitude change and social influence.* New York: McGraw-Hill.

Zubin, J., Eron, L.D., & Schumer, F. (1965). *An experimental approach to projective techniques.* New York: John Wiley.

Zuckerman, M. (1978). Sensation seeking. In H. London and J.E. Exner (Eds.), *Dimensions of personality* (pp. 487–560). New York: John Wiley & Sons.

Zuckerman, M. (1979). *Sensation seeking: Beyond the optimal level of arousal.* Hillsdale, NJ: Lawrence Erlbaum.

Zuckerman, M. (1991). *Psychobiology of personality.* Cambridge, England: Cambridge University Press.

Zuckerman, M. (1994). An alternative five factor model for personality. In C.F. Halverson, G.A. Kohnstamm, and R.P. Martin (Eds.), *The developing structure of temperament and personality from infancy to adulthood* (pp. 53–68). Hillsdale, NJ: Erlbaum.

Zuckerman, M. (1995). Good and bad humours: Biochemical bases of personality and its disorders. *Psychological Science, 6,* 325–332.

Zuckerman, M. (1998). Psychobiological theories of personality. In D.F. Barone, M. Hersen, and V.B. Van Hasselt (Eds.), *Advanced personality* (pp. 123–154). New York: Plenum.

Zuckerman, M., Bernieri, F., Koestner, R., & Rosenthal, R. (1989). To predict some of the people some of the time: In search of moderators. *Journal of Personality and Social Psychology, 57,* 279–298.

Zuckerman, M., Miyake, K., Koestner, R., Baldwin, C.H., & Osborne, J.W. (1991). Uniqueness as a moderator of self-peer agreement. *Personality and Social Psychology Bulletin, 17,* 385–391.

Zukav, G. (1979). *The dancing Wu Li masters: An overview of the new physics.* New York: William Morrow & Company.

Zuroff, D.C. (1986). Was Gordon Allport a trait theorist? *Journal of Personality and Social Psychology, 51,* 993–1000.

Copyrights and Acknowledgments

Figure 9.4, p. 533. "Self-Guides and Negative Emotion," based on E. T. Higgins, "Self-discrepancy: A theory relating self and affect." *Psychological Review, 94,* © 1987, pp. 319-340.

Figure 9.5, p. 536. "Sarah's Self-With-Other Representations," based on D. M. Ogilvie and R. D. Ashmore © 1991. "Self-with-other representation as a unit of analysis in self-concept research. In R. A. Curtis (Ed.), *The Relational Self: Theoretical Convergences in Psychoanalysis and Social Psychology.* © 1991 (pp. 282-314). Guilford Publications, Inc. New York. Reprinted by permission.

Figure 9.6, p. 545. "A Simple Self-Regulation System," based on Charles S. Carver & Michael F. Scheir, *Perspectives on Personality.* Copyright © 1988 by Allyn and Bacon. Boston, MA. Reprinted by permission, p. 476.

Figure 9.7, p. 547. "Self-Focus and the Link Between Behavior and Values," based on Charles S. Carver & Michael F. Scheir, *Perspectives on Personality.* Copyright © 1988 by Allyn and Bacon. Boston, MA. Reprinted by permission, p. 480.

Figure 9.8, p. 548. "A Three-Tiered Hierarchy of Feedback Systems," based on Charles S. Carver & Michael F. Scheir, *Perspectives on Personality.* Copyright © 1988 by Allyn and Bacon. Boston, MA. Reprinted by permission, p. 482.

Figure 11.1, p. 634. "Self-Disclosure Stories and Health," based on APA, J. W. Pennebaker & S. K. Beall, "Confronting a traumatic event: Toward an understanding of inhibition and disease." *Journal of Abnormal Psychology, 95.* © 1986, pp. 274-281.

TEXT AND TABLES

Table 1.2, p. 13. "Questionnaire Measuring Extraversion," from G. Wilson, Introversion/extraversion. In H. London & J. E. Exner, *Dimensions of Personality,* (pp. 217-261). 1978, p. 219.

Table 1.4, p. 19. "An Excerpt from Karen Horney's Adolescent Diaries," from *The Adolescent Diaries of Karen Horney* by Karen Horney. Copyright © 1980 by Basic Books, Inc. Reprinted by permission of Basic Books, a member of Perseus Books, L.L.C.

Table 2.1, p. 65. "Average Levels of Upset Elicitors in Male and Female Partners," from American Psychological Association, D. Buss, Conflict between the sexes: Strategic interference and the evocation of anger and upset, *JPSP, 56.* © 1989, pp. 735-747.

Chapter 2, p. 79. Lines from The Iliad by Homer, translated by Robert Fagles, copyright © 1990 by Robert Fagles. Introduction and Notes copyright © 1990 by Bernard Knox. Used by permission of Viking Penguin, a division of Penguin Putnam Inc.

Table 2.7, p. 107. "Attachment Styles," from C. Hazan & P. Shaver (1987) Romantic love conceptualized as an attachment process. *JPSP, 59,* p. 515. Used by permission of Cindy Hazan.

Chapter 3, p. 144. Lines from *Oedipus Rex* by Sophocles. Bantam Books in R. O'Brien & B. F. Dukore, *Tragedy: Ten Major Plays (Sophocles' Oedipus Rex).* © 1969, p. 21.

Chapter 4, pp. 188, 189. Reprinted with the permission of Macmillan Publishing Company from *Walden Two* by B. F. Skinner. Copyright © 1948, 1976 by B. F. Skinner, pp. 240, 241.

Table 4.5, p. 233. Key Differences Between Independent and Interdependent Construals of Self, from H. Markus & S. Kitayama (1991). Culture and the self: Implications for cognition, emotion, and motivation. *Psychological Review, 98,* p. 230. Used by permission of Hazel Markus.

Table 5.3, p. 262. "The Fifteen Source Traits of Personality Assessed by the 16PF," from G. Matthews & I. J. Deary, (1998) *Personality traits.* New York: Cambridge University Press, p. 22. Reprinted with the permission of Cambridge University Press.

Table 5.6, p. 277. "Scales on the California Psychological Inventory," modified and reproduced by special permission of the Publisher, Consulting Psychologists Press, Inc., Palo Also, CA 94303 from *California Psychological Inventory* by Harrison G. Gough, Ph.D. Copyright 1987 Consulting Psychologists Press, Inc., pp. 6-7. All rights reserved. Further reproduction is prohibited without the Publisher's written consent.

Chapter 5, p. 281. In M. Royko, "Modified Cub Rule Says Bet on the Mets," *Chicago Tribune,* Oct. 17, 1986.

Table 5.8, p. 291. "Coefficients of Generalizability Dominance and Dependency Behaviors of Preschool Children," from American Psychological Association, for D. S. Moskowitz, Coherence and cross-

Name Index

Subject Index